CONTEMPORARY THEORIES
ABOUT THE FAMILY

CONTEMPORARY THEORIES ABOUT THE FAMILY

Research-Based Theories

VOLUME I

Edited by

Wesley R. Burr

Reuben Hill

F. Ivan Nye

Ira L. Reiss

THE FREE PRESS

A Division of Macmillan Publishing Co., Inc.

NEW YORK

Collier Macmillan Publishers

LONDON

The Free Press
A Division of Macmillan Publishing Co., Inc.
866 Third Avenue, New York, N.Y. 10022

Collier Macmillan Canada, Ltd.

Library of Congress Catalog Card Number: 77-81430

Printed in the United States of America

printing number

1 2 3 4 5 6 7 8 9 10

Library of Congress Cataloging in Publication Data

Main entry under title:

Contemporary theories about the family.

 Bibliography: p.
 Includes index.
 1. Family. I. Burr, Wesley R.
HQ728.C618 301.42   77-81430
ISBN 0-02-904940-7 (v.1.)

CONTENTS

SECTION FOUR: THE FAMILY AND PROBLEMS

ACKNOWLEDGMENTS

Since this volume was over five years in preparation and involved the active participation of colleagues in 49 different universities, there are many individuals and organizations who have made valuable contributions. We are particularly indebted to the 38 theorists who authored or coauthored chapters as they worked at a difficult task, and many of them had meager resources and tight deadlines. Future years will determine the value of their contributions, but we suspect it will be monumental. The authors are identified at the beginning of the chapter they wrote. Since the royalties from this volume will be assigned to a professional association, the only rewards these authors will receive from their work will be those intangible ones that come from working effectively at a challenging task.

A number of individuals provided advice and suggestions while this project was being designed, and the final product is much better for their participation. Those involved in the Theory Construction Workshops of the National Council on Family Relations in 1972 and 1973 were very useful. David Klein, Joan Aldous, Carlfred Broderick, Darwin Thomas, Boyd Rollins, Brent Miller, Jay Schvaneveldt, and Steven Bahr were also consultants in one or more of the planning meetings, and their contributions were invaluable.

Appreciation is also expressed to the following individuals who critically reviewed the manuscript for one or more of the chapters in this volume. Their suggestions were of inestimable value to the authors in completing their assignments, and the reviewers received no monetary compensation for their efforts.

Vern L. Bengtson, University of Southern California
K. Dean Black, Brigham Young University
Marbaret Bubolz, Michigan State University
Larry Bumpass, University of Wisconsin
Kenneth Cannon, Brigham Young University
John Carlson, University of Idaho
Bruce Chadwick, Brigham Young University
Edward Z. Dager, University of Maryland
J. Ross Eshleman, Wayne State University
Paul Glasser, University of Michigan
W. Ross Greenleaf, University of West Virginia
Carl Harter, Tulane University
Mary Hicks, Florida State University
Kenneth Kammeyer, University of Maryland
Denise Kandel, Columbia University
Susan Klein, University of Colorado
Alan Kerckhoff, Duke University
Raymond King, University of Sydney

Virginia Ktsanas, Tulane University
Phillip Kunz, Brigham Young University
Lyle Larson, University of Alberta
George Levinger, University of Massachusetts
Roger Libby, Syracuse buniversity
Eugene Mead, Brigham Young University
Sherod Miller, University of Minnesota Hospital
Jeylan Mortimer, University of Minnesota
J. Joel Moss, Brigham Young University
David Olson, University of Minnesota
E. Jane Oyer, Michigan State University
Leonard Pearlin, National Institute of Mental Health
David Reiss, George Washington University Medical School
Brent Roper, Texas Tech University
Constantina Safilios-Rothschild, Wayne State University
Jay D. Schvaneveldt, Utah State University

Lynn Scoresby, Brigham Young University
Barbara Settles, University of Delaware
Thomas Smith, University of South Carolina
Graham Spanier, Pennsylvania State University
Suzanne K. Steinmetz, University of Delaware
Darwin L. Thomas, Brigham Young University

Kay Troost, Boston College
James Walters, University of Georgia
Stephen Wieting, University of Iowa
Melvin Wilkinson, University of Northern Iowa
Karen Bartz, University of Missouri–Kansas City

Several organizations provided the resources that were needed to complete this volume. Those organizations that assisted in the preparation of specific chapters are mentioned at the beginning of the chapters. Several organizations, however, provided assistance for the total project, and without these resources the project could not have been completed. The Committee on Problems of the Discipline in the American Sociological Association provided a grant in 1974 to assist in the planning of the project. The Family Research Institute at Brigham Young University repeatedly came to the aid of the project when other resources were not available. It provided substantial operating funds for tasks such as duplicating pages, mailing, and telephone calls in addition to underwriting part of the time of the senior editor when other expected resources were not available. The Department of Child Development and Family Relations at Brigham Young University provided a half-time research grant and secretarial services during 1974–1975, and the Family Studies Program at BYU provided the funds for two graduate assistants during the summer of 1976. Margaret Rae Jensen and Terry Baker were the assistants, and appreciation is expressed to them. The Center for Family Life Studies at Arizona State University provided time and funds for editorial tasks in 1976–1977. We wish also to thank Charles E. Smith of The Free Press. He was helpful, cooperative, and accommodating in facilitating the publication of this complex volume.

ABOUT THE EDITORS

Wesley R. Burr is professor of child development and family relationships and professor of sociology at Brigham Young University. His previous activities in theory construction include a four-year project that resulted in several papers and a monograph, *Theory Construction and the Sociology of the Family* (1973). He has also published papers that deal with the methodology of theory construction, and his work on the methodology of theory application has resulted in several papers and a volume titled *Successful Marriage* (1976).

Reuben Hill is Regents' Professor of family sociology at the University of Minnesota. He has directed projects that have dealt with inventorying, codifying, testing, and evaluating theories. He directed a large-scale study of changing patterns of family decision-making and planning that resulted in the monograph, *Family Development in Three Generations* (1970). After that project he directed a six-year research and theory building program in family problem-solving. He was the first recipient of the Ernest W. Burgess Award for continuous and meritorious contributions to the family field, and was a co-organizer of the NCFR Theory Construction Workshops.

F. Ivan Nye is professor of sociology at Florida State University. He has been involved in theory construction in widely different areas such as deviance, age at marriage, marriage stability, maternal employment, and has written a book and papers on strategies of theory development. His latest book is *Role Structure and Analysis of the Family* (1976). He has been president of the National Council on Family Relations and was co-organizer of its Theory Construction Workshop.

Ira L. Reiss is professor of sociology at the University of Minnesota. His systematic development of theories of sexual permissiveness has progressed through several cycles of stating the theory, gathering data to test parts of it, and then using the data as a basis for subsequent improvements in the theory. Monographs appearing in this series include *Premarital Sexual Standards in America* (1960) and *The Social Context of Premarital Sexual Permissiveness* (1967). In recent years he has also focused his theoretical interests on the development and testing of a theory of extramarital sexual relationships. He is a member of the honorary Sociological Research Association and has been president of the Midwest Sociological Society.

LIST OF CONTRIBUTORS

Bert N. Adams
Department of Sociology
University of Wisconsin
Madison, Wisconsin

Joan Aldous
Department of Sociology
University of Notre Dame
Notre Dame, Indiana

Stephen J. Bahr
Department of Child Development and
    Family Relationships
Brigham Young University
Provo, Utah

Vern Bengtson
Department of Sociology
University of Southern California
Los Angeles, California

Carlfred B. Broderick
Department of Sociology
University of Southern California
Los Angeles, California

John E. Carlson
Department of Sociology
University of Idaho
Moscow, Idaho

Betty E. Cogswell
Department of Family Medicine
School of Medicine
University of North Carolina
Chapel Hill, North Carolina

Viktor Gecas
Department of Sociology
Washington State University
Pullman, Washington

Richard Gelles
Department of Sociology
University of Rhode Island
Kingston, Rhode Island

Anne C. Greif
Department of Psychology
University of Massachusetts
Amherst, Massachusetts

Donald A. Hansen
School of Education
University of California
Berkeley, California

Mary W. Hicks
Department of Sociology
Florida State University
Tallahassee, Florida

Marilyn Ihinger
Department of Sociology
Washington State University
Pullman, Washington

Vicky A. Johnson
Moral Education Project
Pacific School of Religion
Berkeley, California

David M. Klein
Department of Sociology
University of Notre Dame
Notre Dame, Indiana

Gary R. Lee
Department of Sociology
Washington State University
Pullman, Washington

Robert A. Lewis
Center for Family Studies
Arizona State University
Tempe, Arizona

Brent C. Miller
Department of Child and Family Studies
University of Tennessee
Knoxville, Tennessee

Jane Nugent
Department of Psychology
University of Massachusetts
Amherst, Massachusetts

Marie W. Osmond
Department of Sociology
Florida State University
Tallahassee, Florida

Luther B. Otto
The Center for the Study of Youth
   Development
Boys Town, Nebraska

Harvey Pulliam-Krager
Department of Sociology
University of Southern California
Los Angeles, California

E. M. Rallings
Department of Sociology and
Anthropology
University of North Carolina
Greensboro, North Carolina

Harold L. Raush
Department of Psychology
University of Massachusetts
Amherst, Massachusetts

Boyd C. Rollins
Department of Child Development and

Family Relationships
Brigham Young University
Provo, Utah

John Scanzoni
Department of Child Development and
   Family Relations and Department of Sociology/
   Anthropology
University of North Carolina
Greensboro, North Carolina

Jay D. Schvaneveldt
Department of Family and Child
   Development
Utah State University
Logan, Utah

Graham B. Spanier
College of Human Development
Pennsylvania State University
University Park, Pennsylvania

Suzanne K. Steinmetz
Department of Individual and Family Studies
University of Delaware
Newark, Delaware

Murray A. Straus
Department of Sociology
University of New Hampshire
Durham, New Hampshire

Marvin B. Sussman
Department of Medical Social Sciences
Bowman Gray School of Medicine
Wake Forest University
Winston-Salem, North Carolina

Darwin L. Thomas
Family Research Institute
Brigham Young University
Provo, Utah

Lillian Troll
Department of Psychology
Rutgers University
New Brunswick, New Jersey

Robert F. Winch
Department of Sociology
Northwestern University
Evanston, Illinois

I

INTRODUCTION

1

INTRODUCTION

The Editors

The scientific method is a tedious and gradual process in which the cycle of creating, revising, testing, and then reformulating theories is repeated many times. This volume is a part of this process as it is an attempt to pull together in one place and evaluate the most recent reformulations of a large number of theories about family phenomena. The many who have been involved in the preparation of this volume hope that this compilation will improve the quality of theories about the family and stimulate additional research and theory construction. They also believe that since this volume is part of a cycle, it should be viewed as a working publication that is designed to be revised and modified rather than canonized or accepted as ultimate truth. Without exception the authors of the chapters view their work as setting the stage for future developments rather than as summarizing an area where all of the scientific work has been completed.

This introductory chapter is an attempt to place this volume in a historical and developmental context and explain why and how it was prepared. The first section reviews the history of theory building in the family area, and the next section describes the procedures that were used in preparing this volume. The third section explains some of the similarities and differences in the chapters that follow, and concludes briefly with predictions of future directions the theory-building movement may take.

A HISTORY OF THEORY BUILDING ABOUT FAMILIES

Harold Christensen (1964) has divided the history of family thought into four stages, each with its own dominant orientations:

Preresearch (prior to 1850), drawing on a rich family lore of traditional beliefs and proverbs, poetic fantasies and insights, and philosophic speculations
Social Darwinism, (1850–1900), producing a body of scholarly literature of grand theory concerned with the social evolution of marriage and family forms in broad historical and institutional perspective
Emerging science (1900–1905), tempering the speculations about family and society of the historical past with empirical data about the range and variety of contemporary family patterns and focusing on more narrowly defined problems
Systematic theory building (1950 to the present), a period of self-conscious stocktaking and perspective taking, resulting in the recognition of the trivial and noncumulative quality of much family research; identification of competing conceptual frameworks for family study; inventorying of propositions and their codification into partial theories; and developing strategies for building and formalizing theories about family phenomena

We note that Christensen saw very little systematic theory building underway before 1950. This historical note provides, accordingly, more details about the developments in family theory since midcentury.

Grand Theory Building

Christensen dates the first attempts to generalize about families across time and societies to the Social Darwinism period when scholars were concerned about the social origins and development of the family. The search was for "universals," the writers asserting that all forms of family life have a common sequence of development, with observed variations really just representing different stages of development. It was not too big a step to assert that families everywhere performed similar functions to meet what are universal needs. If a society did not have an institution like the family, it would have to invent one to survive.

Some of the grand-scale propositions generated by

these pioneer macrotheorists and their successors are still found in textbooks about the family today:

1. There has been no stage in the social history of mankind where marriage has not existed (Westermark).

2. The family is the microcosm of society; indeed families are the smallest societies capable of spontaneous endurance (Comte).

3. For a civilization to survive, it must foster a strong family system (Zimmerman).

4. Because the family is essential to societal persistence, all societies have developed protective devices to ensure *its* continuity: the prohibition of incest, provisions for the orderly distribution of sexual property, the principle of legitimacy of children, and the cultural regulation of jealousy and conflict (Murdock).

5. Families everywhere are in transition from a consanguinity orientation to a conjugal orientation (Goode).

6. As societies have industrialized, patriarchal patterns have been displaced by equalitarian patterns of authority in families, and functions have been lost to other institutions (Ogburn).

The generalizations produced by these macrotheorists have been largely *unresearchable* to date and have therefore been subject more to debate than to resolution by scientific procedures. (Serious work by family historians and comparative family sociologists on these issues reappeared in the late 1960s and is now a thriving industry.)

Building Theories from Everyday Family Life

Let us now turn to Christensen's empirically oriented scholars of the emerging-science period, whose work has left a much stronger imprint on contemporary theory construction. They took the *contemporary family group* as their focus and sought to understand it through empirical studies of everyday family life. To focus upon the *family as a group* required new microconcepts and methods for collecting and analyzing the new data which the theorists of the earlier evolutionary and institutionalist focus did not possess. LePlay in France in the nineteenth century anticipated this latter-day emphasis. His was essentially an *empirically based* descriptive *stance*. He is credited with the first use of the survey method and the family budget technique for describing families, which was later followed in studies of poverty at the turn of the century by Booth and Rowntree in England and by pioneer social work researchers in the United States.

The motivation among these early empiricists in England and the United States was to understand the problematic aspects of the family of their times. Problems of interpersonal relations in the family pressed for public attention. In 1908 the problems of the family were salient enough, Calhoun (1919) tells us, that the annual meeting

of the American Sociological Society was devoted entirely to them. The empirical tradition of the *survey* researchers was factual, descriptive, and not given to overgeneralizations. Their questions, in contrast to those of the institutionalists, were eminently researchable: Under what conditions did families live and function? How were poverty and level of living related to family size and composition?

Farber (1964) credits Ernest W. Burgess for *speeding the shift* from the institutional-historical focus, which dominated the study of the family in the universities in the first decades of the twentieth century, to the emphasis upon the family group. Burgess (1926) coined the phrase "the family as a unity of interacting personalities." In terms of influence upon the theoretical emphases of succeeding generations of graduate students in family sociology, Burgess appears unique, since most of the major investigators who received their training in the family prior to World War II studied or worked with Burgess at some time in their career. His work on marital prediction with Leonard S. Cottrell and Paul Wallin precipitated dozens of studies, not only of husband-wife relations but of parent-child relations and of crises in family relations.

The social scientists focusing upon the problems of the contemporary family group, in contrast to their predecessors the institutionalists, found little utility in debating the universality of family functions. Far from hypothesizing that forms of family organization persisted because they were efficient in *meeting* universal needs, Farber (1964) reminds us that theorists of this tradition were searching for the factors which account for the *persistence of problems* in family life and, by implication, the inefficiencies of family organization. The Burgess influence, furthermore, converted the problematic focus and the descriptive stance of the survey period into a search for explanations and hypothesis testing. Burgess reasoned that if the problems of the family were to be solved, diagnosis leading to explanation and experimental validation was needed.

Theory, for this early-twentieth century group of researchers, was constructed inductively from empirical regularities rather than deductively from assumptions about the nature of man and society, as grand theory had been built. From the observed relations between variables in family behavior, the procedure became one of framing hypotheses (usually two variable hypotheses), testing them, and then building multivariate models of explanation. The payoff of this knowledge-building enterprise is only being realized, however, in the present period—namely, the constructing of partial theories which would encompass and account for the several component hypotheses of earlier studies.

In summary, two quite different *approaches* developed for orientating theory in the period 1850 to 1950. The first sought universals and knowledge for its own sake and spun grand theory that transcended social time and space.

This has usually been called the comparative and historical study of the family as an institution. The second concern has been practical, to understand and perhaps improve contemporary family living, using the knowledge acquired to provide a basis for changes in community policy affecting families. Oriented to serving immediate personal and community ends, the second approach has focused on the pragmatic study of the family as a group, and its generalizations have been accordingly provincially limited to the families studied. Farber (1964) states that the institutional approach looked to the development of a theory based upon "simplicity" and "complete explanation," assuming *strict determinism*. The family-as-group approach sought *utility of explanation* and assumed possible manipulation of variables in programs of social intervention. The tendency is for social scientists to vacillate between these approaches in their research and theory construction, which may account for the eclecticism of much contemporary family theory.

Critiques of Family Research and Theory at Midcentury

At midcentury the knowledge-building enterprise of family research was worldwide and growing rapidly, publications amounting to about 15,000 from 1900 to 1964 and running to over 700 books and articles annually (about 87 percent in English and 13 percent in 25 other languages; see Aldous and Hill, 1967: 7). The American emphasis on microstudies of contemporary issues of mate selection, marriage and divorce, sex and fertility, family interaction, and family transactions with community and kinship networks dominated the total product, with less than 15 percent of the writing concerned with the macro issues of family and society (Aldous and Hill, 1967). The Minnesota Inventory of Marriage and Family Research content-analyzed a 15 percent sample of the U.S. output and all of the family researches in 14 countries of Europe and Asia for a UNESCO report concerning the 12 years after World War II, 1945–1956 (Hill, 1958). The analysts reported an upswing in methodological sophistication, including increasing attention to representative sampling and use of probability statistics in analysis of data, but the relevance of the studies to any body of theory was hard to deduce. To be sure, the findings were increasingly accretive, explicitly identifying hypotheses to be tested from one or more previous studies (about 50 percent in the U.S. were hypothesis-testing studies compared to 17 percent in European studies). There was no attempt to go beyond verification to link propositions together into more complex propositions or to integrate these further into partial theories. Nor was there any evidence of relating empirical generalizations from family research to similar phenomena in other primary groups. The 1958 UNESCO report concluded that the worldwide family research enterprise was quantitatively productive, showing methodological sophistication, but had as yet shown little evidence of generating theories which could be used in the planning and execution of future research activities (Hill, 1958).

One distinguished critic (Cottrell, 1948), in the lead article of the *American Sociological Review,* saw American family research as disjunctive, not adding up to significant new knowledge, showing little evidence of imagination in the formulation of creative hypotheses, and recommended that the Social Science Research Council make a major investment in orienting research on the family for "a concerted and persistent attack on what we can agree are significant problems." Komarovsky and Waller (1945), writing for the *American Journal of Sociology* semicentennial issue, reviewed 50 years of family studies more sympathetically but saw scholars still shackled by taboos that constrained them in the problems they could study and in the adequacy of the analysis they gave to their data. They decried the presentation of findings in the form of correlations without a search for the explanations behind the correlations, reminding readers that "the facts can't speak for themselves." They were, in effect, anticipating a theory construction principle advanced much later by Hage (1972) of providing theoretical rationales for all two-variable propositions.

Theory Issues within General Sociology Affecting Family Scholars

It may be enlightening to examine the issues being debated with respect to theory in general sociology at midcentury, when family scholars are alleged to have first begun attending to the theoretical relevance of their enterprise. The domination of sociology by the University of Chicago pragmatists whose researches on the concrete problems of families, neighborhoods, and cities gave a distinctive problem-solving orientation to general sociology was dramatically challenged in the 1940s in the attempt by Talcott Parsons to formulate a general theory of society under the general rubric of "functionalism." For more than a decade Parsons' elaborations of his overarching "theory of society" in more than a dozen books and articles preempted any rival discourse about the sociological enterprise. Not a theory by any reasonably rigorous definition of theory, but a most comprehensive conceptual framework (Hill and Hansen, 1960), Parsons' construction furnishes what Kaplan has termed an "explanatory shell" for a wide range of social phenomena. Parsons' "theory" was so broad, abstract, and general that there was little possibility of alternative formulations. It provided the most conceptually precise taxonomy to date for distinguishing among social phenomena and between social and other phenomena, rendering obsolete and partial all earlier theoretical systems.

Mark Krain (1971), from whom we have borrowed liberally here, notes that the reaction to Parsons' grand theory of society was not so much to offer serious rival formulations as it was to reject global theorizing altogether as sociologists earlier in the century had rejected social philosophy—as too abstract and general to provide guidelines for intellectual programs. Theories which explained everything usually proved capable of explaining nothing. In the thousands of pages of Parsonsian prose scholars found few decisive statements for which empirical tests could be designed. Indeed, in almost four decades since its initial statement, no clear line of research had stemmed from this body of theory.

The call for a moratorium on grand theorizing, however, came neither from survey research–oriented empiricists nor from their rivals, the qualitatively oriented symbolic interactionists from the Middle West, but from Harvard-trained Robert Merton, a theorist of impeccable credentials at Columbia University, writing a commissioned paper on the status of sociological theory for the special semicentennial-anniversary issue of the *American Journal of Sociology* (May 1945). Instead of supporting "theory in the large," which Merton felt to be often sterile though "suggestive" and "splendored," he called for a switch in emphasis to "special theories applicable to limited range of data." These special theories were to be grouped and ultimately consolidated into a more encompassing general scheme. Merton was arguing for a program of inductive theory building in three phases:

Phase 1. Select a limited range of phenomena.
Phase 2. Derive theories about these phenomena from empirical generalizations.
Phase 3. Derive a theory which consolidates these theories, such that the consolidating theory serves as a "reducing theory."

Merton's call was quickly echoed by other sociologists who now saw the sociological researches in which they were engaged in a different light. Much of their inductive generalizing was now being legitimized as *theory production*. Sociological researchers who heretofore had been peripheral to the formulation of theories were, in Merton's recasting, in the thick of the "real" theory business. As Krain (1971) puts it, "every researcher was now involved with his limited range of phenomena and was trying to derive theories about it." Whatever theory "really" was, the important theorizing was no longer the monopoly of philosophically oriented theorists. The important theorizing was now the legitimate domain of those who were also doing the important researching.

Family researchers were most responsive to the call for "theories of the middle range," since their own enterprise was producing empirical findings that begged theoretical attention. Here was legitimization for codifying their substance-bound explanations into theories about family phenomena.

Inventorying and Codifying the Products of the Family Research Enterprise

The first serious attempts at readying the family literature for inductive theory building involved a series of perspective-taking activities by family scholars in the late 1950s and early 1960s in the form of, first, critiques of the accomplishments and deficits of family research; second, inventorying of publications about family phenomena and production of classified key words in context-type bibliographies (Aldous and Hill, 1967; Aldous and Dahl, 1974; Olson and Dahl, 1975) and trend reports (Hill, 1958); and third, inventorying for research-grounded propositions (Hill, Katz, and Simpson, 1956).

Within the decade of the sixties, Mogey (1971) reports, more than 80 critiques assessing family research and theory had been written in the U.S. and abroad. He found high consensus in his survey of more than 40 countries about methods of sampling, methods of data collection, data processing, and data analysis appropriate for family research but little consensus about the utility of any of the extant conceptual frameworks for family study outside the United States. Reference in research articles to an explicit conceptual vocabulary from which hypotheses might have been drawn for verification was the exception rather than the rule outside the U.S.

A major critique of family theory prepared for the American Sociological Association's benchmark publication *Sociology Today* (1959) by William J. Goode noted that more research investigations had been reported on family phenomena than any other sociological domain but few of these sought to advance theories about the family. With the exception of Durkheim and Malinowski no theorist of first rank had dealt with the sociology of the family systematically. Goode's impressions were that the family was incorrectly perceived as accommodating rather than determinant among social institutions and was therefore not likely to explain total societal systems. He saw the empirical base adequate at this point to make theoretical contributions at three levels of analysis: type I, deductions from general sociological theory to explain family behaviors; type II, inductions from specific findings about family phenomena abstracted into theoretical statements of utility to general sociological theory; and type III, theories about family phenomena treating the family as a closed system. Goode sees type III theory building as the direction in which the major efforts of American family sociologists have been mistakingly directed. In an effort to rectify this deficit Goode and his associates at Columbia University have been engaged for a number of years in making an inventory of thousands of propositions about marriage and family from research investigations, essays, and anthropological field studies which has recently been published, *Social Systems and Family Patterns: A Propositional Inventory* (1971). In the hopes of encouraging a wide use by others of this inventory Goode has demonstrated in a series of articles how higher-order theory can be induced from mining the cross-cultural propositions about romantic love and social structure (1959b), illegitimacy and social structure (1960), and family mobility and personality structure (1963).

Even more ambitious as an order-creating enterprise has been the work of Reuben Hill and associates at the University of North Carolina, 1953–1957, and subsequently at the University of Minnesota, 1957–1973, known as the Minnesota Inventory of Marriage and Family Research, whose objectives sound as if they might have been inspired by Merton's plea for theory building through codification:

1. The identification of the empirical foci which have been investigated by marriage and family researchers.
2. The classification and summarization of the research findings among these foci.
3. The identification of the competing frames of reference which have been used as theoretical approaches by marriage and family researchers.
4. The isolation of the major conceptual apparatus of each of the frameworks that are identified.
5. The theoretical organization, where possible, of research findings into a set of interrelated hypotheses and propositions.

An early product of the Minnesota Inventory was a demonstration by Katz and Hill of a codification procedure for theory building drawn from the domain of mate selection research, "Residential Propinquity and Mate Selection: A Review of Theory, Method and Fact," *Marriage and Family Living* (1958). The codifiers examined over 20 pieces of research on residential propinquity published over a 30-year period and chose 14 of these to illustrate the evolution of improved methods for measuring the phenomenon and the increasing sophistication of explanatory theories. Beginning with the original and most primitive statement by Bossard, that the more propinquitous the residences, the more likely people would be to marry, the codifiers noted refinements in method and in phrasing of explanatory theory in each of the subsequent studies cited. A chain of propositions termed "norm-interaction theory" was finally generated which appeared to be more encompassing than any of its three predecessors (residential propinquity, norm segregation, and intervening opportunities) in accounting for "who marries whom." The Hill-Katz procedures have subsequently served well for several other research domains codified by colleagues utilizing the Minnesota Inventory. Since the Hill-Katz procedures are to be compared later in this chapter with procedures developed a decade later by Nye and associates and by Burr, we summarize the Hill-Katz procedures here:

1. Begin with an inventory of determinants of a given dependent variable yielding a series of ordinary propositions, and rephrase these propositions in formal language.
2. Arrange these propositions chronologically and look for the most primitive explanations as the point of departure.
3. Examine both the conceptualization advances and the issues of measurement as well as the increased complexity of the propositions over the period covered by the inventory.
4. Note and name partial theories, if any, generated by researchers opening up new dimensions over the period inventoried.
5. Draw on more general, context-free theory to construct a more encompassing theory than the last partial theory in the series tapped by the inventory.
6. Place the final formulation either in a taxonomy or in an accounting-for-variance model.

A second product of the Minnesota Inventory, the identification of conceptual frameworks for family study, is credited by Broderick in his lead article in *A Decade of Family Research* (1971) with having "more than any other influence . . . shaped the field of family theory in the decade of the sixties."

The several frameworks for family study have been inferred from the content analysis of hundreds of American publications going back in time to 1920. Substantial progress has occurred in the identifying of current conceptual frameworks. The initial work of Hill, Katz, and Simpson (1957) in naming seven frameworks and their users was followed by a much more detailed specification by Hill and Hansen (1960) in which the chief conceptual properties and the basic underlying assumptions of five frameworks were provided in taxonomic tables. Three categories of concepts were specified in these tables: type of behavior treated, social space in which it occurred, and the dimension of social time. The frameworks delineated were the institutional, the structure-function, the symbolic interactional, the situational, and the family developmental.

In making the requirement that, to be included, a framework must possess concepts for the description of the family, either as group or as institution, Hill and Hansen added no new frameworks to the Hill-Katz-Simpson list and dropped two (learning theory and consumption economics). This initial work has stimulated dozens of theory assessment articles in Asia and Europe as well as in America and has since been followed by the production of four framework-oriented chapters in Christensen's already classic *Handbook on Marriage and the Family* (1964) which provided the intellectual history of each of these five frameworks, the chief researches utilizing the approach, and the generalizations which have flowed from these researches.

The most recent effort at extending the identification and specification of conceptual frameworks for family study is the book-length work of Ivan Nye and associates (1966). Nye's group built on the Hill-Hansen treatise to specify further the underlying assumptions, the value positions of those using the frameworks, and the contributions and limitations of the framework for research, theory, and practice. Broderick's article "Beyond the Five Conceptual Frameworks: A Decade of Development in Family Theory" (1971) makes a persuasive case based on infrequency of use during the decade of the sixties for dropping both the situational and institutional frameworks and adding the systems theory framework to the lexicon of conceptual vocabularies in active use. Broderick also notes the heuristic contributions of three "theories" that family scholars are currently utilizing to illuminate intrafamily relationships, namely balance, theory, game theory, and exchange theory (see Broderick, 1971: 7–9).

Nye's Explorations of Axiomatic Procedures

The interest in theory construction among family scholars was initially kindled by the validation to the enterprise given by Merton (1945), but the tempo was even more explicitly stimulated by Zetterberg's second edition of *On Theory and Verification in Sociology* (1963). The book not only provided a further rationale for theory building but also offered guidance for undertaking axiomatic theory construction. Ivan Nye and his associates at Washington State University were the first family scholars to undertake a demonstration of the utility of the Zetterberg procedures of axiomatic theory building for three research domains—early marriage (Bartz and Nye, 1970), family size (Nye, Carlson, and Garrett, 1970), and family stability (Nye, White, and Frideres, in Blalock, *Theory Construction,* 1969: 38–39). Their procedures in these three demonstrations parallel those of Hill and Katz at points but employ a distinctive sequence:

1. An inventory of determinants of a given dependent variable from the research literature is undertaken, yielding a long series of ordinary propositions (67 in the family stability theory piece) phrased in formal language.

2. After completion of the inventory of determinants, attention is given to the degree of support for each and to issues of compatibility of supporting studies in nominal definition of concepts and in their operational indicators.

3. Creation of a limited number of theoretical propositions of higher informative values by noting commonalities follows.

4. These more encompassing theoretical propositions are combined, where fruitful, to derive new propositions using the principle of transitivity.

5. One or more general theories are examined to justify rewriting the theoretical propositions at an even higher level of generality.

6. The final result is placed in a heuristic flow chart to demonstrate visually and formally the product of the several retroductions as a quasi-path diagram of interrelated variables.

Impacts of Burr's Pioneering Work

Too recently published to assess its full impact on the family-theory-building enterprise is the trailblazing book-length publication reporting a program of theory building for several domains of the family by Wesley Burr, *Theory Construction and the Sociology of the Family* (1973). Challenged by the Minnesota Inventory, on which he worked as a graduate student in the 1960s, but convinced that the building and repair of family theories required a more informed and more deductive set of procedures than had yet been developed, Burr innovated his own strategy of theory construction. For ideas and methods he drew selectively on the philosophy of science literature and on the several manuals of theory construction and metatheoretical writing which emerged in the wake of Zetterberg's repeatedly revised treatise—namely, the writings of Nagel (1961), Homans (1964), Stinchcombe (1968), Dubin (1969), and Blalock (1969). He quotes from Blalock (1969, p. 27) to indicate the central task:

> The careful reworking of verbal theories is the most challenging task confronting us. The major portion of this enterprise will undoubtedly consist of clarifying concepts, eliminating or consolidating variables, translating existing verbal theories into common languages, searching the literature for propositions and looking for implicit assumptions connecting the major propositions in important theoretical books.

Burr's theory-building book was brought to term at Brigham Young University. His procedures differ significantly in many respects from those reported above by Hill and Katz and by Nye and associates at Washington State. Burr's is a theory-repairing program using both deductive and inductive procedures, borrowing theories from contiguous disciplines, and drawing from general theories to deduce family phenomena. Burr's procedures follow:

1. Begin with a conceptual clarification of the major dependent variable to be explained or the major determinant variable whose consequences are to be assessed.

2. Review theories pertaining to the phenomenon of interest that might be rendered context free.

3. Formulate a limited number of general context-free propositions in formal language.

4. For each of these propositions deduce the context-specific propositions that would follow by subsumption at lower orders of abstraction.

5. From the research literature scan for the empiri-

cal support, if any, for the deduced propositions, including the direction and shape of the relationships.

6. Incorporate all of these propositions into an accounting model format with higher-order propositions displayed at the periphery and derived propositions with their variegated connections in the body proper.

From the illustrations of the three strategies by Hill and Katz, Nye and associates, and Burr, we find Burr's the most open-ended and most subject to revision and extension. Nye and associates' axiomatic strategy and Hill and associates' codification of theory development strategy tend to be more bounded by their original inventoried propositions, and the theorists using them know when they have finished their task. Burr's products are frankly recognized as unfinished and are offered for criticism with the implied challenge to readers to seek to improve on them.

Debates about Strategies for Theory Systemization

From the foregoing discussion of procedures developed after Zetterberg for theory building and repair, it may not be apparent that some debating was underway about the payoffs and limitation of contemporary theory-building strategies. Hill (1966) noted in his Burgess Award address, "Contemporary Developments in Family Theory," that the choice of a well-developed conceptual framework for the theory-building task provided the theorist with a head start, since the interrelations and interdefinitions of concepts could often be linked to the family phenomenon to be explained to suggest partial theories within a well-defined taxonomy of concepts. He proposed extracting from the framework those interrelated concepts in propositional form most closely linked causally to the variable to be explained to produce a theoretic paradigm or model.

It was the challenging article by Joan Aldous (1970), however, which really precipitated the debate about strategies among family scholars. She offered a range of five strategies for developing family theory: axiomatic theory, factor theory, grounded theory, borrowed theory, and conceptual frameworks strategies. The response within the profession to her critical comments included two spirited counterthrusts from Ivan Nye (1970) and Jetse Sprey (1970) and an equally spirited rejoinder from Aldous (1970). Well after the dust had settled, Hill (1971) offered his own list of five strategies with an assessment of their likely payoffs and limitations in a position paper for a first invitational meeting he and Ivan Nye convened at Estes Park of theory sponsors, to be known as Friends of Family Theory Development. Hill's five strategies and examples are listed and illustrated below:

Strategy I. Search for and assessment of *general nonsubstantive theories* (with respect to personality, group associations, and social cultural systems).

Example: Modern systems theory and some of its predecessors (exchange, information, communication); see Reuben Hill, "Modern Systems Theory and the Family: A Confrontation," *Social Science Information* (1971)

Strategy II. Search for and Codification of *Partial Theories,* and *Principles* about the Family Phenomenon.

Examples: Farber's permanent availability theory; Goode's role-bargaining and role strain theory; Waller's courtship bargaining and summatory process theories; Hill's family crisis theory; Litwak's theory of linkages; Winch-Kerkhoff filter and complementary needs theory; Hill-Katz, normative interaction theory; Bott's conjugal roles and social network theory; Turner's identity conflict theory; several family development theories, including Pineo's disenchantment theory and Cumming's disengagement theory; family communication theories, including Jackson's double-bind theory and Bernstein's linguistic modes.

Strategy III. Search for theories and models developed in other contexts translatable to the family (drawing on the intellectual capital of other disciplines to generate family theory).

Examples: Heider-Cartright-Festinger balance and dissonance theory (Davis, in Berger et al.); Newcomb's A-B-X theory; Thibaut-Kelly and Homans exchange theories; Bartos concession-making and negotiation theory (Berger et al.); Becker's occupational commitment theory; Bales et al., status characteristics and power–prestige order theory (Berger et al.), and Gouldner's reciprocity theory (*ASR,* 25, April 1960); Berscheid and Walters, equity theory; Gamson and Caplow, coalition theory.

Strategy IV. *Codification* of *research propositions* from empirical research into *higher-order partial* theories (drawing from Goode's Propositional Inventory and the Minnesota Inventory of Marriage and Family Research, 1900–1970).

Examples: Note differences in procedures implied in the work of Hill-Katz, residential propinquity, and mate selection, or Glaser and Strauss in their grounded theory generation and integration, or Nye and associates' use of the axiomatic format, or Wesley Burr's theory reworking and assessment.

Strategy V.   *Conceptual integration and taxonomy building* (creation and defining of new concepts, interdefining of interrelated concepts as research about them imporves).

Examples: Essays by Scanzoni reconceptualizing family disorganization, by Edwards and by Richer clarifying family behavior as social exchange, by Sprey and by Bernard introducing social conflict and game theory concepts to family frameworks; the exercise in interdefinition of the concepts of action, interaction, position, norms, and structure by Ann Blalock; the essay of Hill and Rodgers building on Bates, Deutscher, and Farber in interdefining the components of family career and of role sequence, positional career, and position-role complex.

The debate over which should be the preferred strategies for future family theory development may be less important than the discovery of the range and mix of stragegies already being employed by family scholars. Burr's preference in his theory-reworking strategy is for a mix of strategies. To that end he has created a typology of theory- building strategies in which the major types divide between inductive and deductive strategies (Burr, 1973, pp. 277–84).

There is clearly work enough to be done to bring some order to the mass of research findings in the several domains of family study to encourage scholars to use whatever strategy or combination of strategies seems indicated by the phenomena to be explained and to do so wherever their talents may be most profitably used. There is work at several levels of abstraction, intellectually demanding enough for everyone interested in family theory:

At the level of concept clarification and definitions in preparation for developing interdefinitions to improve the classificatory systems available

Or in inventorying bivariate and multivariate propositions leading to proposition chains

Or in inventorying partial theories already formulated and axiomatizing them

Or in borrowing theories developed in other settings and adapting them for explaining family phenomena

Indeed, there are large payoffs for all such intellectual activities awaiting family scholars. A survey by Mogey (1971) in the early 1970s shows active theory-building activity sometimes linked to ongoing research projects but often separately organized in every major region of North America and in parts of Europe and Asia, espe-

cially Japan. We can affirm Harold Christensen's predictions with which we began this historical note, that the period 1950 to the present has been an era of systematic theory building.

With this backdrop we turn to the description of the present collaborative effort in theory reviewing and construction. It too has a history and has developed an identity which justifies interpretation in the pages which follow.

PROCEDURES USED IN THIS PROJECT

There are several reasons that the procedures used in this project should be described in some detail. One reason is that the methodology of theory building in the social sciences is still much more of an art than a systematic set of procedures. There have been a few volumes (Zetterberg, 1965; Stinchcombe, 1968; Blalock, 1969; Mullins, 1971; Reynolds, 1971; Gibbs, 1972; and Hage, 1972) that have begun the process of developing and explicating the methods of theory building, but these are pioneering efforts rather than definitive works. A documentation of the unforeseen events that were encountered in this project and the many choices that have been encountered may help in the development of this methodology. A second reason is that revealing some of the complexities and difficulties that were encountered in the six years between the beginning of this project and the publication of the first volume will help readers better understand the constraints that limited what could be done.

The idea of developing a multiuniversity project that would summarize and evaluate the current status of theories about the family initially occurred to the editors of this project in the summer of 1972. It seemed like a sufficiently promising idea that they presented a brief proposal at the Theory Construction Workshop of the National Council on Family Relations in October of that year to get the reaction and suggestions of colleagues. The response of the participants in the workshop was sufficiently enthusiastic that it was decided that the four should explore further the feasibility and desirability of the project. During the ensuing year and a half they met several times to discuss plans for the project, and they consulted with a large number of colleagues about how such a project could be structured. In these deliberations they first tried to determine which of several alternatives would probably move theory in the family field forward with the greatest speed and efficiency.

Several different strategies were considered such as developing a series of monographs that would each deal with a relatively narrow theoretical issue, organizing several committees to work at different theory-building tasks, organizing a special issue of a journal devoted to theoretical papers, and rejecting any type of coordinated effort in favor of encouraging individuals to give theory their attention. Eventually it was decided that the most useful and timely contribution would be a project involving several committed scholars from different universities. The goals would be to identify, extend, and evaluate theories in one large publication.

A more detailed proposal was then prepared for the 1973 NCFR Theory Construction Workshop in Toronto. It was the consensus of participants in the workshop that the project was timely and appropriate, but to be manageable the goals should be scaled down. For example, the objective of creating a "Comprehensive Statement of Family Theory" appeared too pretentious for the first undertaking of this genre. It would not be realistic to try to be comprehensive, but it did seem feasible to try to summarize and evaluate a large number of contemporary theories. The name of the project was therefore changed to "Contemporary Theories about the Family." It was also agreed that the project could not include *all theories* about the family.

The editors were charged with the task of developing a set of criteria for selecting which theoretical areas should be included and which excluded. After considerable deliberation, a benchmark type of volume was envisioned that would focus on areas where prior theoretical work had been done, excluding the many areas where little systematic codification had occurred. Eventually, the following criteria were selected:

1. The phenomena to be explained should have maximum scope and generality (that is, be more conceptually encompassing than historical events, with minimum time and space limitations).

2. There should be multiple explanatory theories generated by prior theorizing about the phenomena requiring formalization and integration.

3. There should be an acceptable scale of empirical research about the phenomena to verify or disprove component propositions in the competing theories.

4. There seemed to be some likelihood that the phenomena themselves might be interdependent, leading to integration of the chief explanatory theories.

5. Theoretical areas should highlight a *family concept* as either determinant or consequent variables. (For example, socialization theories where the independent variables are family processes would be included but socialization theories dealing with nonfamilial explanations would not.)

Using these criteria, the editorial committee and several other colleagues met in a two-day session at Brigham Young University in Jaunary 1974. The goals of this session were to pare down to manageable proportions a list of theoretical areas in which research and some theorizing had been done and make additional decisions about the structure of the project. The colleagues who met with the editors in those sessions were Stephen Bahr,

Boyd Rollins, Jay Schvaneveldt, and Darwin Thomas. These sessions resulted in a manageable list of 24 topical domains that didn't overlap seriously yet seemed to comply with most of the criteria of theoretical development espoused by the editors.

A fairly lengthy prospectus was written after this conference to describe how the project would be structured, what the goals and procedures would be, which 24 theoretical areas would be included, what the eventual publication would be like, and what the projected timetable would be for completing the project. This prospectus was then circulated to 95 colleagues who had previously indicated they would be interested in collaborating in the project—depending on how the project was eventually structured. The colleagues were asked to scan the suggested theory domains and indicate if they had an interest in one or more of these domains and would devote time to participate during the 1974–75 academic year as either leader of or member of a task force to develop the domain. They were asked if they had any suggestions about modifying the way the field had been divided into theory domains. They were told that the editorial committee was hoping to meet in April of 1974 to begin making decisions about which individuals should be commissioned to assess the theories for the various areas.

In April the editorial committee met with several other colleagues, Joan Aldous, David Klein, and Brent Miller, in a two-day session at the University of Minnesota. Three major tasks were accomplished then. First, the division of the field into substantive areas was changed slightly as a result of the feedback from colleagues. Second, taking into account the expression of interest and commitment of colleagues, the editorial committee made some decisions about which scholars would be asked to take the leadership in developing specific theoretical areas. Third, after considerable discussion of the anticipated consequences of several proposed strategies, it was decided that the project would move ahead best if the theory construction were to be undertaken in two separate phases. Phase I would be a systematization, formalization, extension, clarification, and evaluation of theory in the 24 substantive areas, and the majority of the work for this phase would be done during the 1974–75 academic year, it was hoped. The papers that would result from phase I would be published in the first of a two-volume series.

The second phase was to begin in the summer of 1975, and it would have two parts. One part would be to have several scholars each write a chapter that would integrate ideas in Volume I with a particular theoretical orientation (Hage, 1972, ch. 8). The theoretical orientations that seemed at that time to be among the most promising were exchange theory, role theory–symbolic interaction, systems theory, conflict theory, and phenomenological theory. The second part of phase II was to have other scholars pursue what Merton (1968:69–72; also see Burr,

1973:283–84) refers to as codification procedures with the chapters in Volume I to try to induce more general formulations than had been achieved by the writers working within the 24 separate domains.

The editors and their consultants believed that this two-phase strategy would have several advantages. It would integrate the more context-domain-specific theories in the 24 areas with the more widely used general theories in the field (Broderick, 1971), and it would make the project more comprehensive, while still manageable. In addition, there are many who believe that the family area has been somewhat isolated from the mainstream theoretical developments in the basic disciplines that inform the family field, and this systematic integration would deliberately tie them together.

The editors realized at this time that the project would be sufficiently complex that some division of labor would be necessary in the editorial committee. After some discussion it was decided that Wesley Burr would assume the executive role and be responsible for coordinating the various parts of the project. It was also decided that the entire editorial committee would be involved in all major decisions and that the editors would divide the chapters so each editor would provide a critical reaction to several chapters.

Negotiations were undertaken in the summer of 1974 with prospective collaborators for the work in each of the 24 substantive areas. A meeting was then held with all of the "survivors" of these negotiations at the time of the annual meetings of the American Sociological Association in Montreal in August. In this session the editors and authors discussed the procedures and conventions for the project. These included the reconstructed language of propositions and the use of symbols and heuristic diagrams to further objectify the products of the theory-building process. A similar session was held at the National Council on Family Relations meeting in St. Louis in October. Decisions were also made then about whether to include or exclude additional chapters that had been suggested to the editorial committee. Several suggestions were accepted, but 15 topics were not because they did not seem to meet enough of the criteria for inclusion. The majority of the excluded chapters seemed to be promising areas, but they were domains where scholars were initially developing a theory rather than areas where there had been both prior theoretical work and empirical research.

One of several dilemmas faced by the editors became very crucial at this stage of the project. It was important to have some common groundrules about how to go about the process of systematizing theory and how to prepare a manuscript so the several chapters would appear as a reasonably coordinated product rather than as a series of unconnected theoretical essays. This was doubly important because a second group of scholars would be using the 24 manuscripts to integrate the domain-specific

theories and more general theoretical orientations. Controlling the method, content, or style of the individuals working in the 24 areas might, however, reduce their creativity, and it might be that different strategies would be appropriate for different domains. The editors deliberated for some time about what types of formalizing conventions would be desirable, and again advice was sought from the authors and other colleagues. Eventually it was decided that some of the chapters might be exempted from the conventions if the authors made a strong case but that adhering to the formalizing conventions would be desirable for the project as a whole. The following conventions were eventually identified and circulated to the authors during 1974.

1. First, the 24 sections selected are areas in which there has been the best development of existing research and theory. That is, the project is organized toward examining areas that are already developed empirically and theoretically. It is not a project of speculative thinking in an area in which there has been no theory and research.

2. The project is aimed at more than just a clarification of terms and a more explicit statement of propositions. There should be a comparison of the existing theories in the area with some evaluation and judgment on the part of the writer or writers. That is, there should be some evaluation of level of proof that goes beyond what is found in existing literature; and an attempt perhaps to integrate theories in this area with other theories. In short, there is ample room for creative theorizing, providing it is adequately labeled as to the level of proof and it involves integrating previously clarified theoretical propositions.

3. Next, we think it should be stressed that part of each paper should include an attempt to diagrammatically present the theoretical state of that field. This can be done several places during the course of the chapter, as well as summarized at the end of the chapter. One value of the diagram is that it forces the writer to clarify thinking. The diagram need not be a path analysis type of causal diagram, but any causal diagram relating variables in a heuristic fashion. The important thing is that some causal diagram presenting the theoretical state of the subfield should be presented so that future researchers can pick what part of the theoretical model they wish to pursue or can further reason through the implications of the diagram for other propositions. Ira Reiss and Brent Miller have developed some conventions for causal diagrams. (These conventions are presented in full in Chapter 2.) Authors should, however, feel free to use other systems if they wish as long as the system communicates clearly and is not contradictory to the Reiss-Miller conventions.

4. We think that it is important for each of us to make a clear distinction between several styles or methods of presenting ideas that have been traditionally used in the field and the style we think should be used in this project. We are all familiar with the method of reviewing research that is usually used in research proposals, where the

presentation is organized around previous studies or research projects and the goal is to identify the contributions of each project. We are also familiar with historically oriented presentations such as a decade review, where the goal is to chronicle the advances made over a period of time. Both of these strategies of presenting theoretical or research ideas are very different from the strategy we think will be most useful in this project. The strategy that seems the most useful here is to organize the presentation and analysis around theoretical ideas rather than studies, authors, or evolutionary patterns. Such a strategy will result in an explication of the basis for the theoretical ideas, an evaluation of the evidence for or against them, an analysis of conceptual controversies and similarity or dissimilarity with other theories as well as a pointing up of new areas where additional work will probably be maximally efficient.

5. The point of each chapter is not to examine how various theoretical orientations or conceptual frameworks (structure-function, symbolic interaction, developmental, systems, exchange, etc.) can be used to illuminate a substantive domain. If past theorizing and research have focused on one or more such perspectives, this ought to be pointed out, but we should maximize our attempts to locate competing as well as complementary theories and researches about the central phenomenon. Part of the creative work will be to indicate how complementary work can be integrated and to juxtapose competing theories and findings so that scientific decisions can be made among alternatives.

6. A concern for methodological rigor and testability should be paramount throughout the work of contributors. This has several implications. First, it requires that we take a critical stance toward the work of others that we review and incorporate. Are the theoretical assertions testable? Are the empirical findings appropriate or optimal given the theory to be tested? Second, our own assertions (whether borrowed or paraphrased from the work of others or created for the chapter) should preferably meet reasonable standards of testability. This means that all concepts and propositions should be stated as clearly and unambiguously as possible. It means that operationalization techniques should be proposed (how might variables best be measured, and what methods of data collection might be fruitful?) wherever feasible. It also means that we could indicate what types of evidence would refute the assertions being made by the theorist being reviewed. Also, where theories are deductively complex (incorporating two or more levels of abstractness and/or generality), the most concrete level is the most directly testable and the logical links from abstract concepts and propositions to concrete ones should be spelled out in sufficient detail that readers can follow and evaluate the line of reasoning for themselves. If theories are causally complex (incorporating a dense web of multivariate antecedents, intervening variables, and/or con-

sequences, with or without feedback), some procedure for testing the theory all at once or in a sequence of steps could be proposed. The editorial committee does not subscribe to the rather extreme position that the theorist is obligated to include exhaustive information about how to test the theoretical product, but we do believe that considerable attention should be given in your assessment to the testability of theories. When it is feasible, theorists can provide a service by specifying details about how theories can be empirically tested.

Later in the project another convention was identified. It was that a "punctuated" style of stating the propositions would be used. This procedure is to indent propositions to set them off from the other text and to number them whenever possible. The numbers should also be used as reference cues in the heuristic diagrams.

Why have we not moved further in this venture to formalize theories where feasible into the linguistic symbols and formula of mathematics? Some of the theories about the family can be easily translated into a mathematical language, and it is likely that many of them will probably be mathematized a decade from now. The editors and authors decided to use a verbal rather than a mathematical language in this volume, but it is likely that some of the theories in a revised edition will be mathematized. The rationale for avoiding mathematical language here was twofold. First, we agreed with Blalock (1969:27–28) that the first task that faces the discipline is the careful reworking and formalizing of verbal theories, and when considerable improvement is made in our theories it will then be an easy task to transform them into a mathematical language. This volume is an attempt to work at the prior task of improving verbal theories. The second factor that seemed to justify a decision to avoid mathematization here was that many individuals in the field, including some of the authors and editors, do notave the training to use mathematical languages. It may be that this too will be different a decade from now, but it is a reality for the present.

The final group of 22 theoretical domains that are included in this volume is slightly different from the initial group of 24 that was envisioned in 1974. The chapters on problem solving and socialization were each divided and recombined several times before a final structure was decided, and in several cases two chapters were collapsed into one. Two initial chapters had to be dropped. Originally there was to be a chapter on sex roles and one on family development theories, but the essential resources of willing authors, time, student assistance, and secretarial help could not be acquired for them. Several other chapters were added during this period when it became evident that there was sufficient prior work and individuals could acquire the resources they would need to complete them. The focus of several of the chapters also changed as the teams of scholars worked with the theoretical ideas. In most of the situations where changes appeared in the focus, the authors and editors gradually realized that the scope of the chapter that was originally envisioned was too broad and inclusive to be manageable, and the authors restricted their concerns to a more limited range of issues.

During the 1974–75 academic year, about 50 scholars from 25 different universities were actively involved in phase I. Their task was to clarify, rework, extend, and evaluate the theoretical issues in the 24 substantive areas. This was not a time for seeking new empirical data to test the theoretical ideas so much as a period for assessing and reworking the body of extant generalizations to advance the theory as far as possible—given current conceptual sophistication and existing empirical data. The initial deadline for completion of the first drafts of work was May 1975.

Beginning in the summer of 1975, those manuscripts that were ready were critically read by two or more outside reviewers. These readers made valuable suggestions for revision, and each group of scholars was given until November 1975 to make those revisions that seemed desirable to bring their manuscript into shape for publication. At least those dates were the deadlines toward which the teams directed their efforts.

A variety of circumstances began to create delays in the project during 1975. Some of the teams were not able to complete the first draft of their manuscript at the designated time. The reasons for these delays included new professional duties such as becoming a chairperson or dean, unforeseen work in revising other manuscripts, moving, leaves of absence, health problems, difficulties in establishing communication and working relations between members of a team, difficulties in communicating when on leave in Europe, inability to secure resources such as time or secretarial assistance, and underestimating the difficulty and the amount of work involved in the preparation of a theoretical manuscript. The result was that the first drafts of several chapters were not completed until 1976.

Another dilemma that the editors and authors had to deal with was deciding when to close the project and send the manuscript in hand to be published. Some of the chapters were completed on the initial schedule and were ready for publication at that time. Some of the authors, however, encountered unforeseen problems that prevented their manuscripts from being completed on time. This meant that the "on time" manuscripts had to wait, and in some cases become somewhat dated, while the others were being finished. This dilemma was further complicated by the fact that some of the chapters were extremely difficult to write and needed to go through the process of review and rewriting several times. At some point a decision had to be made that the project needed to go to press without all of the manuscripts that had been commissioned. Several chapters seemed marginal to the authors, editors, and reviewers. They were clearly an improvement over what had been done before for their particular domain, but they needed further revision. A revision, however, would take several additional months, and the costs of making the other chapters outdated by further delaying the publication date were mounting. The decision that seemed the most reasonable was to include several of the chapters in the form that they appear in this volume even though the editors and authors recognized that it would have been preferable to undergo further revisions. This explanation is offered, not as a "cop-out," but because it is part of the reality of cooperative professional projects. Discussing the pros and cons of various alternatives will probably improve our methodology and clarify editorial policies for future collaborative projects.

The completion of the manuscripts for Volume II has been delayed because the manuscripts for that volume could not be begun until the manuscripts for Volume I had been virtually completed. Initially the editors and authors thought that those working with Volume II could use the "draft" versions of the manuscripts for Volume I. It became apparent, however, that this would not be feasible, and the second phase of the project had to be delayed until the finished manuscripts were in hand. Some work was begun on Volume II in 1975–76, but the first drafts of the manuscripts for Volume II could not be completed until early 1977. At the time Volume I went to press, it was hoped that Volume II would be published by early 1979.

A PROLOGUE

The editors believe that the process of theory construction is a long-term activity that is still in its early stages with respect to family phenomena, and they want to do what they can to motivate others to become involved in the process of further improving these theories. Some preliminary comments about the following chapters may help accomplish that.

The areas that are dealt with in this volume vary in the amount of prior empirical and theoretical work. One result of this variability is that some of the chapters have theory that is more advanced, clearer, more precise, more testable, and more fully corroborated than others. The goal of each of the authors was to improve, summarize, and evaluate the theory in his or her area, but some authors have had more to work with than others. One implication is that each chapter should be read and assessed against its own baseline of development. It is premature to expect a uniformly high quality of conceptual or theoretical work across all domains. This, of course, also has implications for future work. In some of the areas the greatest future need is for conceptual clarification. In others it is devising designs for empirical research to test what may have hitherto seemed to be untestable theory. In still others it is theoretical speculation about the effects of additional contingency variables that might round out the theory.

Readers should also expect to find some differences in the style of presentation of the material in the various chapters. One reason is that the individuals writing the chapters differ in their disciplines, training, and perspectives. The theory teams included sociologists, home economists, psychologists, and experts in child development. Another reason for the differences in style is that there is considerable ambiguity in methodological procedures and enough dissonance in metatheoretical perspectives that some of the authors differ in the appraoches they prefer.

Another reason for the diversity in style of the various chapters arises from the way the project was structured. The editors and authors agreed that the best procedure would be to give a fairly free rein to the teams to work up their area recognizing that reviewers and editors could later feed back suggestions leading to a more uniform style. The editors and authors agreed on several parameters, but the editors granted considerable leeway within which teams could operate. Even in retrospect this seems the best strategy. There is a trade-off of losing some similarity of style and interchapter continuity, but given the diversity of the subject matter and of the individuals writing, the advantages were more creativity, higher morale among the teams, and a respect for professionally defensible differences. The editors believe that such differences in style as are found in the volume will not interfere with readers getting at the basic conceptual, theoretical, and empirical issues that are addressed. Hopefully, readers will look beyond the stylistic differences and the differences in the sophistication of the content of the various chapters to learn and then rework, build, expand, and further test the theories that have been given shape and visibility by this common enterprise.

The editors and a number of colleagues with whom they interact have given some thought to what will happen after the publication of these two volumes. They, of course, do not have a crystal ball, but several hopes and tentative plans can be identified. One hope is that those who are responsible for charting the editorial policies of journals in the field will respond to several needs that have been created by theoretical developments. The crux of these needs is that the field is gradually becoming more mature as a science and the type of articles published in journals in recent years and at present are more suited to the past than to the present and future. As the concepts and theory in a field become more clear and formal, it becomes increasingly useful to publish short articles that test parts of a theory. All of the more mature sciences have moved to a style of publishing where brief reports are the most widely used medium, and it is now appropriate that this be done in the family sciences. There is also an increasing need for more journal space to be devoted to conceptual and theoretical articles that do not report empirical findings. These articles can focus on a variety of theoretical issues such as conceptual clarification, integration of divergent theories, analyses of when and how theoretical ideas can be borrowed from other areas, and the systematic reworking of theoretical ideas in the light of new conceptual, empirical, or theoretical improvements.

Another hope is that the theoretical essays in these volumes and other publications will stimulate a large amount of empirical research that will test these models. If this is done and a large number of conceptual and theoretical papers appear, it may be desirable to publish a revised edition of Volume I in another decade or so. At that time it is likely that theoretical work in a number of domains not treated in this volume will have progressed far enough that they ought to be included. The meetings sponsored by professional organizations such as the National Council on Family Relations and the family section of the American Sociological Association will be good places to discuss these possibilities in the early 1980s.

REFERENCES

ALDOUS, J.
1970   "Strategies for developing family theory." *Journal of Marriage and the Family* 32:250–57.

ALDOUS, J. AND N. DAHL
1974   *International Bibliography of Research in Marriage and the Family*, vol. 2, 1965–1972. Minneapolis: University of Minnesota Press.

ALDOUS, J. AND R. HILL
1967   *International Bibliography of Research in Marriage and the Family, 1900–1964*. Minneapolis: University of Minnesota Press.

BARTZ, K. W. AND F. I. NYE
1970   "Early marriage: a propositional formulation." *Journal of Marriage and the Family* 32:258–68.

BERGER, J., M. ZELDITCH, AND B. ANDERSON (EDS.)
1966/   *Sociological Theories in Progress*. Boston: Houghton
1972   Mifflin, vols. 1 and 2.

BLALOCK, A.
1954   "A conceptual scheme for analyzing families as small groups." Unpublished M.A. thesis, University of North Carolina.

BLALOCK, H. M., JR.
1969   *Theory Construction*. Englewood Cliffs, N.J.: Prentice-Hall.

BRODERICK, C. B. (ED.)
1971   *A Decade of Family Research and Action, 1960–69*. Minneapolis: National Council on Family Relations.

BURGESS, E. W.
1926   "The family as a unity of interacting personalities." *Family* 7:3–9.

BURR, W. R.
1973   *Theory Construction and the Sociology of the Family*. New York: Wiley.

CALHOUN, A. W.
1919   *Social History of the American Family*, 3 vols. Cleveland: The Arthur H. Clark Company. New York: Barnes and Noble, Inc., 1945.

CHRISTENSEN, H. T.
1964 "Development of the family field of study." In H. T. Christensen (ed.), *Handbook of Marriage and the Family*. Chicago: Rand McNally.

COTTRELL, L.
1948 "The present status and future orientation of research on the family." *American Sociological Review* 13:123–33.

DUBIN, R.
1969 *Theory Building*. New York: Free Press.

EDWARDS, J. N.
1969 "Familial behavior as social exchange." *Journal of Marriage and the Family* 31:518–26.

FARBER, B.
1964 *The Family: Organization and Interaction*. San Francisco: Chandler.

GIBBS, J.
1972 *Sociological Theory Construction*. Hinsdale, Ill.: Dryden Press.

GOODE, W. J.
1959a "Horizons in family theory." In R. K. Merton, et al. (eds.), *Sociology Today*. New York: Basic Books.
1959b "The theoretical importance of love." *American Sociological Review* 24:38–47.
1960 "Illegitimacy in the Caribbean social structure." *American Sociological Review* 25:21–30.

GOODE, W. J.
1963 *Family and Mobility*. New York: Institute of Life Insurance.

GOODE, W. J., E. H. HOPKINS, AND H. M. MCCLURE
1971 *Social Systems and Family Patterns: A Propositional Inventory*. Indianapolis: Bobbs-Merrill.

HAGE, J.
1972 *Techniques and Problems of Theory Construction in Sociology*. New York: Wiley-Interscience.

HILL, REUBEN
1958 "Sociology of marriage and family behavior, 1945–1956: A trend report and bibliography." *Current Sociology* 7:1–98.
1966 "Contemporary developments in family theory." *Journal of Marriage and the Family* 28:10–25.
1971a "Payoffs and limitations of contemporary strategies for family theory systematization." Paper presented at NCFR Meetings in Estes Park, Colorado, August.
1971b "Modern systems theory and the family: A confrontation." *Social Science Information* 10:7–26.

HILL, R., A. M. KATZ, AND R. L. SIMPSON
1957 "An inventory of research in marriage and family behavior: A statement of objectives and progress." *Marriage and Family Living* 19:89–92.

HILL, R. AND D. A. HANSEN
1960 "The identification of conceptual frameworks utilized in family study." *Marriage and Family Living* 22:299–311.

HOMANS, G. C.
1958 "Social behavior as exchange." *American Journal of Sociology* 63:597–606.
1964 "Bringing men back in." *American Sociological Review* 29:809–18.

KATZ, A. AND R. HILL
1958 "Residential propinquity and marital selection." *Marriage and Family Living* 20:27–35

KOMAROVSKY, M. AND W. WALLER
1945 "Studies of the family." *American Journal of Sociology* 50:443–51.

KRAIN, M.
1971 "A philosophical perspective on some unrecognized and divergent aspects in the theory construction movement in sociology." Unpublished manuscript, University of Minnesota, January.

MERTON, R. K.
1945 "Sociological theory." *American Journal of Sociology* 50:462–73.
1968 *Social Theory and Social Structure*. New York: Free Press.

MOGEY, J.
1971 "Sociology of marriage and family behavior, 1957–1968." *Current Sociology* 17:5–364.

MULLINS, N. C.
1971 *The Art of Theory: Construction and Use*. New York: Harper and Row.

NAGEL, E.
1961 *The Structure of Science*. New York: Harcourt, Brace and World.

NYE, F. I.
1970 "Comments on Aldous' strategies for developing family theory." *Journal of Marriage and the Family* 32:338–39.

NYE, F. I. AND F. BERARDO
1966 *Emerging Conceptual Frameworks in Family Analysis*. New York: Macmillan.

NYE, F. I., J. CARLSON, AND G. GARRETT
1970 "Family Size, Interaction, Affect, and Stress." *Journal of Marriage and the Family* 32:216–26.

OLSON, D. AND N. DAHL
1975 *Inventory of Marriage and Family Literature, 1973 and 1974*, vol. 3. St. Paul: Family Social Science, University of Minnesota.

REISS, I. L.
1976 *Family Systems in America*, Appendix 4. New York: Holt, Rinehart & Winston.

REYNOLDS, P. D.
1971 *A Primer in Theory Construction*. Indianapolis: Bobbs-Merrill.

SPREY, J.
1970 "On Aldous' 'strategies for developing family theory.'" *Journal of Marriage and the Family* 32:496–97.

STINCHCOMBE, A. L.
1968 *Constructing Social Theories*. New York: Harcourt, Brace and World.

ZETTERBERG, H. L.
1963 *On Theory and Verification in Sociology*, second ed. Totawa, N.J.: Bedminster Press.
1965 *On Theory and Verification in Sociology*, third ed. Totawa, N.J.: Bedminister Press.

2

METATHEORY AND DIAGRAMMING CONVENTIONS

The Editors

Since this book is about theory and that term has several different meanings in the scientific community, it seems useful to describe how the word "theory" is used in this volume. This is done in the first part of this chapter. The second part then discusses several additional metatheoretical issues, and the final part identifies most of the diagramming conventions that emerged in the project.

THE BASIC PARTS OF THEORY

"Theory" as used in this volume, can be briefly defined as a set of logically interrelated *propositional* statements that identify how variables are covariationally related to each other. Propositional statements are abstract and are attempts to state universalistic laws rather than to describe either particularistic laws or particularistic events. There is always a hierarchial arrangement of propositions in a theory because some of the propositions are relatively general and they can be used to encompass and/or explain more specific propositions or hypotheses. The more that characteristics of the co-variational relationships such as their direction, shape, strength, and time lag can be identified, the more sophisticated and informative the theory. Propositional statements contain clear scientific concepts, and hence a theory always has an implicit or explicit conceptual framework. Theories also always make assumptions about many phenomena, and usually some of these assumptions are identified when a theory is presented.

This brief description of theory will be sufficient for some, but many who use this volume will want a more detailed explanation of the many technical terms and complex ideas in the preceding paragraph. Therefore the following pages discuss in some detail what the various components of theory are and how they are interrelated.

Concepts

Concepts are probably the most basic part of theory in the scientific method, and they are terms or words that symbolize or stand for some aspect of reality. Some examples of concepts are social norm, occupational prestige, family, and marriage. Some concepts are *primary* terms and others are *derived* concepts. Primary terms are those that are commonly understood in the scientific community but extremely difficult to define. They can be illustrated with examples, and there is considerable consensus about what they mean, but it is difficult to develop dictionarylike definitions for them. Derived concepts are those scientific terms that can be defined using primary concepts, other scientific concepts, or nonscientific terms.

The term "concept" is also used several other ways in the English language, and there is one particular way that some educators use "concept" that tends to be confused with the way "concept" is used in scientific theories. Educators frequently use the term "concept" to refer to very complex ideas that are described with a fairly elaborate sentence or paragraph. For example, a unit in a marriage course might try to teach the idea or "concept" that when couples are emotionally upset, they can frequently be more effective in solving a problem and have fewer problems later if they deal with their emotional feelings before they attempt to cope with the problem itself. The term "concept" is used this way so much that it can hardly be argued that such use is inappropriate. However, it is imperative that this use not be confused with the definition of "concept" when used as a component of scientific theories. In theories a concept is not a complex idea, but is one single term or couplet of terms. Those of us who interact in scientific and educational circles need to be alert to these two uses of the term if we are to be understood.

Stinchcombe (1968:38–40) has persuasively argued that concepts are not static ideas in the social sciences. Rather, as new developments are made, concepts are revised, redefined, and in some cases discarded. This creates some frustration for scientists because they must continually assess and check out the "meaning" of concepts whenever they use them. At the present stage of the social sciences, however, this evolutionary nature of scientific concepts seems to be inescapable.

Since concepts are symbols in the minds of social scientists, it is extremely important that the meaning of a symbol be clear enough that it is unambiguous and that it can be communicated from one scientist to another. There are four different properties that can help clarify these meanings if scientists use them properly. One is the *label,* or name, of a concept. Labels should be brief and easily remembered, and should be fairly descriptive of the phenomenon they stand for. Ideally, each lable should only refer to one phenomenon and each phenomenon of concern to science should only have one label. At the present time, however, the situation is less than ideal. There are many different labels for some concepts, and the same label is sometimes used for more than one phenomenon. Two other things that can help clarify the meaning of concepts are theoretical and operational definitions. Theoretical definitions (Hage, 1972:62–66) are "dictionary-type" definitions that use other words to define what a concept means. There are several other terms that also have been used to refer to theoretical definitions. Guilford (1954) and Straus (1964) call them rational definitions. Kerlinger (1964:33) calls them constitutive definitions, and others call them nominal definitions. Operational definitions are generated when we use a measuring strategy such as a questionnaire, instrument, or scale to define a concept. An operational definition of IQ, for example, is that IQ is what intelligence tests measure. Hage (1972:66–67) has persuasively argued that it is wise to provide both theoretical and operational definitions whenever possible because they each have a unique contribution. Having both increases our chances of having unambiguous concepts.

Since most concepts in the social sciences occur as a part of a larger "conceptual framework," knowing which framework a concept originated in and how it is inter-defined with other concepts in that framework can also help clarify the meaning of a concept. A conceptual framework refers to a large group of interrelated concepts that are developed in a school of thought or theoretical orientation. Sometimes conceptual frameworks reflect fairly unique assumptions, and an awareness of these assumptions can help clarify the meaning of concepts.

Variables

Those concepts that vary along an identifiable dimension are called *variables,* and those that do not have an identifiable dimensionality are *nonvariables* (Hage, 1972, ch.1).

The following list illustrates several common variables and nonvariables. Some of the nonvariables in this list are categories within a variable. Middle-class, for example, is a category within the variable of socioeconomic status. Other nonvariables are generic terms that are involved

with many variables. The term "family," for example, could encompass dozens of variables.

Nonvariables	*Variables*
Middle-class	Socioeconomic status
Family	Size of family
Divorce rate	Divorced
Premarital sexual permissiveness	Premarital sex
Marital happiness	Happy
Severity of a crisis	Crisis

In scientific theories it is occasionally useful to distinguish between variables that are causes and effects, and there are several terms that are used. One set of terms is used to refer to causes as *independent* variables and effects as *dependent* variables. Another set is used to refer to causes as *antecedent* variables and effects as *consequent* variables.

There are several different ways that properties can vary. One way is that they can be nominal, ordinal, interval, or ratio scales. When a factor varies in a nominal manner, terms are used to identify the categories or values it has. Some examples of nominal variables are gender (male and female), urbanity (urban and rural), type of solidarity (organic and mechanical), and marital status (married, single, divorced, widowed, etc.). The categories in ordinal variables have an order to them, but the distance between the categories may not be equal. Some examples of ordinal variables are marital happiness, attraction, parental support, and aggressiveness. Interval variables are ordinal variables that have equal intervals between the categories or values, and ratio variables are interval variables that have an absolute zero.

Relationships between Variables

Relationships are patterns of covariation between variables. They exist whenever variation in one variable tends to be systematically accompanied by variation in another. There are several different types of assertions that can be made about relationships, and five of these are:

1. Assertions that a relationship exists. These are declarative statements that assert that one variable is covariationally related to another variable. These statements assert that the concomitant variation tends to be a universal phenomenon rather than a historical accident or unique event.

2. Assertions about the direction of a relationship. These are declarative statements about whether a relationship is positive or negative (inverse).

3. Assertions about the shape of relationship. These are declarative statements about whether a relationship is linear or curvilinear. When a realtionship is curvilinear, the more precisely the shape or function can be described, the better.

4. Assertions about time lag. These are assertions about how much time elapses between the variation in the independent variable and the dependent variable. Very few of this type of assertions are made in contemporary theories about the family.

5. Assertions about causality. These are statements that identify whether causation is thought to exist or not. If there is no reason to assert causality, they state that covariation exists but that nothing is speculated or known about causation. Some scholars such as Dubin (1969) and Gibbs (1972) think that causal assertions should be omitted from theories, while others such as Nagel (1961) and Blalock (1969) think they are valuable.

Propositions

Propositions can be defined in a general way as declarative statements that assert, or at least attempt to assert, a truth. They are different from concepts because concepts are terms that symbolize some aspect of reality and propositions are declarative sentences that assert something about the relationships among these terms. This general statement about propositions needs to be refined, however, because there are some important differences in the way the term "proposition" is used. One difference is that there has been a tendency in some recent sociological literature to use the term in a slightly more restricted way than has been customary in the philosophy-of-science literature. Philosophers such as Braithwaite (1953) view propositions as statements about the characteristics of a concept, predictions, assertions that a relationship exists, and so on. Sociologists such as Homans (1964:811), Zetterberg (1965:64), and Blalock (1969:2), however, prefer to restrict the meaning of the term "proposition" to those statements that identify relationships between variables.

Obviously, it would be irrational to use all of these definitions of the term "proposition" here, and a choice must be made among the competing definitions. Since there seems to be value in differentiating between the different types of declarative statements that are used in theorizing, the definition selected here is that propositions are statements that identify relationships between variables.

When propositions are restrictively viewed as statements that relate variables, it is necessary to use different labels to refer to several other types of declarative statements that are used in theorizing. One convention that is extensively used in the methodological literature is to use the term "definition" (Zetterberg, 1965, ch. 3) to refer to those declarative statements that define concepts. Another widely used convention is the use of the term "prediction" (Simon, 1969:435; Dubin, 1969:170–71; Gibb, 1972) or "estimation" (Blalock, 1969:3) to refer to those statements that make predictions about the values that specific variables will assume in various circumstances. Authors in this project were encouraged to use the terms "definition" and "prediction" to refer to these two types of declarative statements.

It would be convenient if this set of terms were the only ones that had to be defined to communicate what propositions are and what they are not. Unfortunately, however, there is ambiguity in the literature on whether propositions are different from or synonymous with hypotheses, theorems, axioms, postulates, etc. For example, the term "hypothesis" is used by some writers such as Braithwaite (1953) as a synonym for the term "proposition," whereas others such as Zetterberg (1965:101) view hypotheses as *one* type of proposition. Others, including Marx (1963, ch. 1), use "hypothesis" in lieu of "proposition." This variability in the way these terms are used illustrates that at the present time the only way to be positive of what these definitions mean is to find out how the contributors have used them in each context.

The Logical Relationship between Propositions

The components of theory that have been discussed in the last several sections are all necessary components for making up a theory, but there is one additional component that is absolutely essential. It would be possible to have a large conceptual framework and to have a larger number of propositions spelling out the relationships among concepts, but if this additional component is not present, there is as yet no theory. What we lack is *explanation* for the relationships—the rationale, if you will, without which the concepts and propositions which link the concepts are scientifically useless. This component is the logical relationship between propositions that provides explanation or understanding. It involves using one or more propositions and other identifiable conditions as a basis for explaining why other propositions are true. Braithwaite explains this logical process in the following manner:

> The propositions in a deductive system may be considered as being arranged in an order of levels, the hypotheses at the highest level being those which occur only as premises in the system, and those at the lowest level being those which occur as conclusions in the system, and those at intermediate levels being those which occur as conclusions of deductions to higher level hypotheses and which serve as premises for deductions to lower level hypotheses [1953:12].

Some theories have several different levels of generality where there are highly abstract, inclusive propositions that can be deduced from the most general ones or from the intermediately general ones. At the simplest level, a theory would have several propositions from which testable hypotheses could be deduced. In these simple theories the logical relationship that provides the explanation is between the hypotheses and the slightly more general propositions or generalizations. If an area or domain has no generalizations that are more abstract, inclusive, or general than the testable hypotheses, there is no theory, as that term is used here and in the scientific community generally.

This analysis of how the logical relationship between propositions provides explanation would be inadequate unless this particular type of explanation were contrasted with a second type of explanation that also exists in most scientific theory. The type of explanation that has just been identified is acquired by deducing either relatively specific propositions or empirically observable hypotheses from other propositions that serve as premises. This is generally known as *deductive explanation* (Braithwaite, 1953; Nagel, 1961), and it explains why the relationships exist in the more specific propositions. It is important to realize that this type of explanation does not explain everything. For example, it does not explain why some propositions are more useful than others or why a given dependent variable varies at a certain time. It merely explains why there is a relationship between certain variables.

The other type of explanation that exists in most scientific theories is labeled *causal explanation* by Braithwaite (1953, ch. 10). It explains that the reason variation occurs in a dependent variable is that there is variation in a certain independent variable. In other words, causal explanation is explanation of *why there is variation* in a particular variable, and deductive explanation is explanation of *why there is a relationship between* certain variables. Causal explanation occurs within a proposition, and deductive explanation occurs by deducing between propositions that have different levels of generality. Causal explanation is involved in chain sequences, where X influences Y and Y influences Z, because variation in X is indirectly the cause of variations in Z.

The use of inductive, deductive, and transitive logical processes is valuable for other reasons in addition to the fact that they provide explanations of why relationships in specific propositions exist. One additional reason is that they permit deducing propositions that have not been known before. Thus deduction from highly general theoretical propositions is a useful tool in helping to extend scientific theories. In addition, the use of highly general propositions and more specific deductions is a parsimonious way of summarizing knowledge. Hence the use of multiple levels of generality is not only informing in that it provides explanations of more specific phenomena, but it extends and is an efficient way of summarizing knowledge. Higher levels of generality can also be arrived at *inductively*, that is, by proceeding from the specific findings to a more general level. One can then deduce from this general level new specific propositions. Thus, induction and deduction are interrelated processes.

Ceteris Paribus

Ceteris paribus is Latin for "other things being equal," and it is an indispensable part of theorizing. It would be impossible to take into account all of the circumstances and conditions that influence the relationships studied in the social sciences. Because of this, whenever a proposition is asserted, there is an assumption that all other variables are invariant or held constant. As Marshall says:

> We reduce to inaction all other forces by the phrase "other things being equal," we do not suppose that they are inert, but for the time we ignore their activity. This scientific device is a great deal older than science; it is the method by which, consciously or unconsciously. sensible men have dealt from time immemorial with every difficult problem of ordinary life [1961:xiv].

In Sum

The basic ingredients that have been identified— variables, propositions, and relationships, generating explanation by logically deducing and inducing, assuming the principle of *ceteris paribus*—are the basic components of scientific theory. Homans has summarized the essential nature of these components in a statement on the nature of theory:

> One may define properties and categories, and one still has no theory. One may state that there are relations between the properties, and one still has no theory. One may state that a change in one property will produce a definite change in another property, and one still has no theory. Not until one has properties, and propositions stating the relations between them, and the propositions from a deductive system—not until one has all three does one have a theory. [1964:812].

Theorizing is a mental process. It is the process of scientists acquiring explanations about why certain variations occur and why they do not. It is not merely a matter of finding empirical relationships that happen to occur in the real world, but rather of learning the circumstances under which variation in variables brings about variation in other variables in a way that acquires multiple levels of generality. It is usually not appropriate to label one isolated simple proposition a theory. One proposition may provide causal explanation, and, in doing so, it is the beginning of a theory. In order, however, to have an explanation that can be dignified with the title of theory, there should usually be a group of interrelated propositions with multiple levels of generality.

It should also be noted that theory is useful for more than just understanding. It can be used for predicting when variation will occur in a certain explanation. However, it is possible to predict and to predict very accurately and not have a theory. As Dubin (1968:10) and others have pointed out, it is also possible to have extensive theoretical understanding and not be able to predict well at all. Theoretical development should facilitate at least some types of prediction, but it is erroneous to conclude that because theory exists, it will then be possible to predict efficiently, or that it is prediction rather than explanation that is the end of science. Prediction may occur or it may not occur when theory exists, and both are goals of science.

SEVERAL RELEVANT METATHEORETICAL ISSUES

Other Useful Types of Scholarship

One of the additional metatheoretical issues that should be discussed in this chapter is the relationship between the view of theory taken in this volume and several closely related types of scholarship. This is important because these different types of scholarship are frequently confused in the modern scientific community. One closely related type of scholarship is descriptive research. This is where data are gathered about one or more variables to determine what the trends or distributions are in a social group or to determine how the various variables tend to be interrelated in that social group. Examples of this type of research are polls, census reports, vital statistics, and the various ways of breaking these data down by social class, religion, age, and so on. This type of scientific activity is useful in many ways, but it is not theory. Occasionally those doing descriptive research will use a body of theory to guide them in their research, and occasionally descriptive data can be used to test some of the ideas in a theory, but descriptive research is different from theory or theory building.

A second type of scholarship that is different from theory building is more difficult to identify and contrast because there is no single or widely shared label for it. It has been called different things such as social analysis, social system analysis, role analysis, and interpretive analysis. The goal of this type of scholarship is to develop a number of scientific concepts or constructs and methods of analysis that can be used to analyze various phenomena. The goal of the analysis is to increase understanding of the phenomenon that is analyzed. In the version of this type of scholarship that is advocated by Wilson (1970) and some other symbolic interactionists the goal is to use social psychological concepts to describe and analyze human interaction. A majority of the writings of Parsons (1951–53) focuses on different phenomena and uses different concepts, but it is social system analysis or role analysis (Komarovsky, 1973) rather than theory as the term "theory" is used in this volume. Much of what is done with general systems theory (Buckley, 1967) is also systems analysis rather than systems theory.

Much of the systems literature is called theory, but when the term "theory" is used to describe that literature, it is a different use of the term than the one employed here. The key difference is that the definition used here seeks to identify "law-like" covariational propositions that can be used to explain and predict, and the analytic approach consists of analytic interpretations and commentaries on specific phenomena. Some current scholars believe that "social analysis" is a useful prelude to theory in that it helps create concepts and provides considerable data that can be used to test theoretical propositions. There are those who have reservations about our approach to theory. For example, Bolton (1963) and Blumer (1956) argue that the view of theory taken in this volume is a dead-end street and should be abandoned. The view taken here is that these two types of scholarship complement each other, and it would be premature to abandon either of them. The approach taken in this volume has considerable promise in providing useful and valuable knowledge, but there are many issues and concerns that cannot be included. The analytic approach is able to deal with a wider array of issues and concerns. It is more flexible, and it may have an immense practical value. It also has a richness to it that cannot be matched in the view of theory taken here. The view taken here, like that of the physical sciences, focuses on a very restricted range of issues. It is valuable, but it is only one way rather than *the* way to do science.

Theory and Path Analysis

Path analysis is becoming an increasingly popular strategy for data analysis, and it is a very useful tool in theory construction. It also uses a diagramming technique that is similar to the causal models that are often used to summarize theoretical ideas. This has led some scholars to believe that path models are the same thing as theoretical models, and this error needs to be avoided because there are important differences between theoretical models and path diagrams.

The crux of the difference between path analysis and theory is the difference between the two words "variance" and "variation." "Variance" is a statistical term that refers to how much deviation there is from the mean in a distribution of scores. The goal of path analysis is to determine what proportion of the variance in a dependent variable is covariance with certain independent variables or groups of independent variables. This statistical manipulation is useful in theory construction because it is one strategy for determining whether predictions from a theory occur in the real world.

Variation is a very different concept from variance. Variation refers to the changes that occur in variables. If, for example, a married couple were to change the amount they interact intimately with friends in a social network, this is variation in a variable. Bott's (1957) theory suggests that this change would probably have an influence on other aspects of their relationship such as the amount of their role segregation. If Bott's theoretical idea is true, variation in one variable would create variation in another variable. "Variance" is a technical statistical term that refers to how much scores in a sample deviate from the mean of the scores.

This difference between variance and variation is important because theory has ideas about *variation*, not *variance*. A theory is a set of ideas that are more abstract than particular populations or samples or the particular variance they may have when social scientists happen to study them. Theoretical ideas are also always hypothetical in that they specify that *if* certain things occur, *then* other things will occur. If changes or variation were to occur in a particular variable, or if certain combinations of events were to happen, then certain variation in other variables or events would tend to happen. Empirical studies about patterns of covariance are absolutely essential in the process of corroborating or refuting theoretical ideas, but those processes, techniques, or products of empirical studies should not be viewed as theory themselves. They should be viewed as research about theories or, as Zetterberg has labeled them, verification research (1965). Path models and many other statistical techniques are valuable in making inferences about the truth or falsity of theoretical ideas, but they are not the ideas themselves. Thus the point being made here is that path models, and other statistical calculations or diagrams for that matter, are not theory because theory consists of hypothetical, abstract ideas about the effects of variation of variables on other variables.

Interaction of Variables

Most of the theoretical propositions that are currently stated in the social sciences are sufficiently simple that little or nothing is known about the circumstances under which they operate. Thus most of them can be stated only as assertions that variation in a certain variable influences another variable—when all other variables remain invariant. Increasingly, however, theorists and the researchers that test theories are paying more attention to how variables interact in influencing each other, and this is increasing the quality and potential value of theories. The theoretical models in the following chapters deal with several different types of interaction, so it seems useful to briefly describe them.

One form of interaction is when a third variable influences something about the relationship between an independent and dependent variable. Lazarsfeld (1955:122) and Zetterberg (1965:71) refer to propositions that employ these third variables as contingent propositions. The contingent factors can influence the direction, shape, amount of time involved, strength, or amount of influence in a relationship. The following section discusses this type of interaction as well as other types of causal rela-

tions and should help orient the reader to the chapters that follow.

These various forms of interaction in theoretical models are not the same thing as "interaction effects" in statistical tests that deal with analysis of variance. Interactions that are identified in a theoretical model are always hypothetical statements that assert what is expected to happen. Interaction effects in statistical tests are estimates from particular samples, and they only take into account the variation that happens to occur in a sample in a particular historical and cultural setting. Thus interaction effects in statistical tests can be used to make inferences about the interaction of variables in theoretical models, but the interaction effects are limited by measurement errors, sampling bias, distortions of distributions, and the fact that often the observed variation only occurs in part of the potential range of variation, as well as all of the other sources of error.

DIAGRAMMING THEORETICAL PROPOSITIONS*

The general intention of this section of this chapter is to facilitate the transition from natural language to diagrammatic representations of theory. In particular we wish to clarify the meaning of the conventions we use. Natural language is more expressive and perhaps more easily understood than formalized modes, but it can also be bulky and imprecise. When understood, diagrammatic representations have the advantages of being both more concise and precise.

Occasionally variables are said to be related to each other without specifying the nature of their relationship. Usually, however, relationships are further explicated in some way. In two broad categories, relationships between variables can be considered covariational or causal. Covariation (also correlation or association) means that variables simply vary together, whereas causation means that changes in one variable "cause" changes in another variable. We developed the ideas here using a causal vocabulary. However, causal terminology is complicated because frequently used terms imply different degrees of causality: to say "X determines Y" or "Y is a function of X" suggests that X is necessary and sufficient to cause Y; "X causes Y," while still sounding sufficient, leaves open the possibility that Q is also sufficient to cause Y; "X influences Y" or "X effects Y" is milder causal language which communicates that X is *a* cause of Y rather than *the* cause. Because the terms "influence" and "effect" in normal language best express causal relation-

This section was initially written by Ira L. Reiss and Brent C. Miller in 1973 and published as Appendix 4 in Reiss (1976). It was then circulated to the authors in this project to increase the consistency in diagrams, and it is included here to help readers understand some of the diagrams in the following chapters. Reiss and Miller express appreciation to Boyd C. Rollins and David Klein for their suggestions.

Figure 2.1. *Causation:* X influences Y in a negative direction; an increase in X contributes to a decrease in Y.

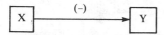

ships in social science, where single-variable determinism is rare or nonexistent, we have used these terms in presenting our propositions.

Relationships can be further refined by specifying the direction of changes that occur in one variable for given changes in the other. Thus relationships (both causal and covariational) can be classified as positive (or direct) when both variables increase or decrease, and negative (or inverse) when one variable increases while the other decreases. In causal terminology it is proper to say "X influences Y in a negative direction" or "X inversely influences Y." We have diagrammatically represented causal relationships by using a line with an arrowhead between variables; the arrowhead indicates the direction of influence.

Variables often form chains, and those in intermediate positions are referred to as *intervening variables*. The direction of a relationship between variables at the beginning and end of a three-variable chain might be derived from their separate relations with the intervening variable between them. However, to justify these transitive derivations (or transductions), the bivariate correlations need to be very high (Costner and Leik, 1964).

Occasionally a contingency variable seems to influence the *relationship* between X and Y rather than influencing either of these variables directly. This is represented by a directed line from the contingency variable bisecting the relationship line. A contingency variable specifies conditions under which the relationship between X and Y is altered, and is often thought of as an interacting variable. For diagramming purposes, we suggest the following codes to clarify these relationships:

Code for Symbolizing Interaction

SYMBOL	MEANING
↑	as the interacting variable *increases*
↓	as the interacting variable *decreases*
S	strengthens the relationship
↑ S	as the interacting variable increases, the relationship becomes stronger
↓ S	as the interacting variable decreases, the relationship becomes stronger

Figure 2.2. *Intervening Variable (I):* X positively influences I, I negatively influences Z, and X negatively influences Z through I (by multiplicative sign rule).

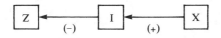

In our diagrams we draw a circle around these symbols (e.g., S) to set them off from the other arrows and notations. An example of how a contingency variable is diagrammed is given below.

Figure 2.3. *Contingency Relationship:* C influences the strength of the relationship between X and Y. Increases in C strengthen the direct relationship between X and Y, and decreases in C decrease the strength of the X and Y relationship. For example, as motivation (C) increases, the relationship between intelligence (X) and academic achievement (Y) becomes stronger.

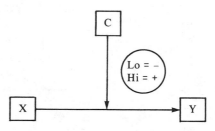

Some authors illustrate interaction by use of a plus or minus sign on the interacting line instead of our symbol of an arrow and an S. However, there are difficulties with that practice, for the plus or minus sign is used in all diagrams to indicate a positive or negative relationship between two variables. In the situation of interaction that same sign would refer to an effect on a *relationship* and not on a single variable. Also, the effect in interaction is to strengthen or weaken a relationship and not to just show a positive or negative relationship. Thus the plus or minus sign, if used in interaction situations, would be used differently. Giving more than one meaning to the exact same symbol can add confusion, and that is why we introduced our method of representing interaction.

There is one other type of contingency relation that can also be described with symbols. This is when the direction of the basic two-variable relationship is altered so that under one category of the interacting variable (e.g., low institutional support) the basic relationship will be negative and under the other category of the interacting variable (e.g., high institutional support) the basic relationship will be positive. An example of this is given below.

Figure 2.4. *Contingency Relationship:* C influences the direction of the relationship between X and Y; when C is low, the relationship between X and Y is inverse, and when C is high, the relationship between X and Y is positive.

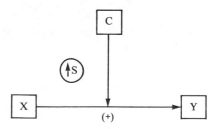

If the interacting variable produced such a reverse set of relations we would illustrate it by:

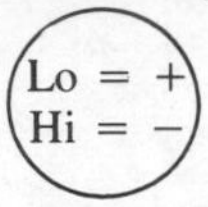

$$Lo = +$$
$$Hi = -$$

Several basic forms of curvilinear relationships can also be expressed symbolically. Eight curvilinear shapes are given below, along with the notation appropriate for each.

Figure 2.5.

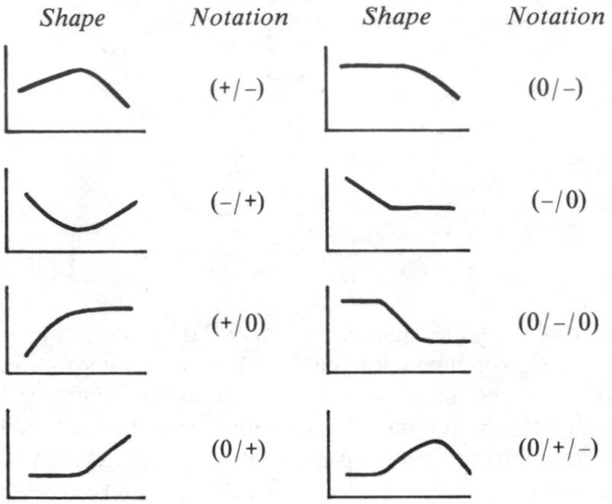

Shape	Notation	Shape	Notation
	(+/−)		(0/−)
	(−/+)		(−/0)
	(+/0)		(0/−/0)
	(0/+)		(0/+/−)

Finally, one may diagram deductive relations by use of a dotted line as below.

Figure 2.6.

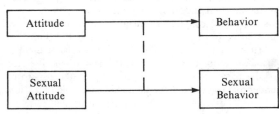

REFERENCES

BLALOCK, H.M., JR.
1969   *Theory Construction.* Englewood Cliffs, N.J.: Prentice-Hall.
BLUMER, H.
1956   "Sociological analysis and the variable." *American Sociological Review* 21:683–90.
BOLTON, C. D.
1963   "Is sociology a behavior science?" *Pacific Sociological Review* 6:3–9.

BRAITHWAITE, R. B.
1953   *Scientific Explanation.* Cambridge: At the University Press.
BUCKLEY, W.
1967   *Sociology and Modern Systems Theory.* Englewood Cliffs, N.J.: Prentice-Hall.
DUBIN, R.
1969   *Theory Building.* New York: Free Press.
GIBBS, J. P.
1972   *Sociological Theory Construction.* Hinsdale, Ill.: The Dryden Press.
GUILFORD, J. P.
1954   *Psychometric Methods,* second ed. New York: McGraw-Hill.
HAGE, J.
1972   *Techniques and Problems of Theory Construction in Sociology.* New York: Wiley-Interscience.
HOMANS, G.C.
1964   "Bringing men back in." *American Sociological Review* 29:809–19.
KERLINGER, F. N.
1964   *Foundations of Behavioral Research.* New York: Holt, Rinehart, and Winston.
KOMAROVSKY, M.
1973   "Some problems in role analysis." *American Sociological Review* 6:649–62.
LAZARSFELD, P.F.
1955   "Interpretation of statistical relations as a research operation." In P. F. Lazarsfeld and M. Rosenberg (eds.), *The Language of Social Research.* New York: Free Press.
MARSHALL, A.
1961   *Principles of Economics,* ninth ed. New York: Macmillan.
MARX, M. H.
1963   *Theories in Contemporary Psychology.* New York: Macmillan.
NAGEL, E.
1961   *The Structure of Science.* New York: Harcourt, Brace and World.
PARSONS, T.
1951   *The Social System.* New York: Free Press.
PARSONS, T., R. F. BALES, AND E. A. SHILS
1963   *Working Papers in the Theory of Action.* New York: Free Press.
REISS, I. L.
1976   *Family Systems in America,* 2nd ed. New York: Holt, Rinehart & Winston.
SIMON, J. L.
1969   *Basic Research Methods in Social Science.* New York: Random House.
STINCHCOMBE, A. L.
1968   *Construction Social Theories.* New York: Harcourt, Brace and World.
STRAUS, M.
1964   "Measuring families." in H. T. Christensen (ed.), *Handbook of Marriage and the Family.* Chicago: Rand McNally.
WILSON, T. P.
1970   "Conceptions of interaction and forms of sociological explanation." *American Sociological Review* 35:697–707.
ZETTERBERG, H. L.
1965   *On Theory and Verification in Sociology,* third ed. Totawa, N.J.: Bedminster Press.

II

FAMILY AND CHANGE

3

EFFECTS OF SOCIAL NETWORKS ON THE FAMILY

Gary R. Lee

INTRODUCTION

Many different aspects of family behavior are related, in either a causal or a systemic sense, to the roles played by family members in external groups or social structures. The social contexts within which families are embedded are of the utmost importance in explaining family phenomena. Family behavior cannot be fully explained or understood from a "closed system" perspective; much family behavior may emanate from transactions between families (or their members) and other social groups, organizations, or institutions (see Rodgers 1973:42).

In this chapter we shall focus our attention on certain aspects of the exchanges between the family and its social environment. Our sphere of inquiry will be limited in two general ways. First, our concern is with social *networks* rather than all extrafamilial structures or systems. The concept of social network is difficult to define in a manner that is both precise and useful; I intend to employ the concept in a rather broad sense. A social network is defined here as a collection of individuals among whom there are varying numbers of direct sociometric connections, but where each individual stands in a direct social relationship to at least one other network member. A network is thus not the same as a group, but under this definition a group would be one kind of network.[1] A social group would be, in common sociological parlance, the epitome of a "close-knit" network (Bott 1971:59), because each member of the group knows and interacts with each other member of the group. At the opposite extreme of the continuum of network "connectedness" are networks whose members have in common only their relationship to some single "ego"; they are otherwise socially unrelated to one another. Such a situation might

occur in the case of the occupational contacts of a traveling salesman. None of his customers may know any of his other customers, but they may be collectively defined as a social network because they are related to the salesman. This type of network is termed "loose-knit" (Bott 1971:59). For our purposes here, it is reasonable to include collectivities such as voluntary associations within the definition of social network. However, it would serve no purpose to extend the definition to include more abstract entities such as the occupational structure. This is partly because other chapters in this volume will be devoted to these topics, and partly because theories developed to account for the effects of social networks on the family are somewhat distinct from those which deal with the effects of such phenomena as occupational role performance.

Second, we are interested in effects *on* the family, not *of* the family. Social scientists have traditionally regarded the family as a passive agent in social processes, responding to influences from other systems but rarely exerting influence in return.[2] Thus our narrowed focus has a long tradition in the history of sociological theory. However, this tradition does not happen to be our justification here. It is undoubtedly the case that the individual's performance of family roles and relationships with other family members has many consequences in terms of participation in extrafamily systems. But, as family sociologists contributing to a volume on theories about the family, we are constrained by the academic division of labor to discover and explain sources of variance in family behavior.

These two restrictions taken in combination interact to produce a third, which defines our focus most specifically. Although the theoretical and empirical literature on the antecedents of participation by families and family members in social networks is quite extensive, that issue is peripheral to the central concerns of this chapter. We will not deal with the determinants of differential rates of participation in the various types of social networks, but rather with the effects of such participation on the family

NOTE: Grateful appreciation is extended to those who reviewed earlier drafts of this chapter, including Wesley R. Burr, Edward F. Dager, Reuben Hill, and R. J. A. King, for their invaluable comments. Their efforts have immensely improved the chapter. I alone am responsible for the inadequacies it undoubtedly still contains.

and its members. This means, for example, that we will treat extent of interaction with kin as an independent rather than a dependent variable, and concentrate upon those of its correlates which are presumed or demonstrated to be consequences (for the family) of such kinship involvement.

Now that we have discoursed at some length upon those topics which we will not cover, it is perhaps appropriate to specify what the objects of our inquiry actually are. The substance of this chapter is determined in part by the statement of our topic in abstract terms ("the effects of social networks on the family") and in part by the more specific content of previous research which may be categorized under this heading. We will, as noted above, take aspects of participation in social networks as our independent variables, and treat selected family phenomena as dependent upon them.

This chapter is organized according to classes of family variables which may, in part, be consequences of social network factors. There are two major categories here. First, social networks appear to have certain theoretically specified effects upon the marital relationship. These include effects upon mate selection and the formation of marriages, conjugal role organization, the distribution of decision-making authority, and marital adjustment. Second, we will discuss the effects of social networks on the family proper, i.e., the residential unit which includes the married couple and children. There are two primary subcategories of effects on the family proper: effects on migration and housing, and effects on the economic stability of independent families.

Before embarking upon our discussion of the substantive issues involved in this analysis, we are obligated to insert and emphasize a qualification on the terminology we have been employing thus far. We have been speaking of the *effects* of social networks on the family, implying that the *causes* of some family behaviors are to be found in the realm of social networks. If taken literally, this statement is clearly false (or at least not demonstrably true). Almost all the evidence we will review in this chapter is correlational. That is, previous research has provided us with estimates of the extent to which social network variables coincide or covary with family variables, but rarely with any documentation of cause-effect or antecedent-consequent relationships among these variables. Therefore causal assertions are not technically justified by the data.

However, we shall continue in many cases to employ causal terminology, for two reasons. First, the theoretical statements which will be reviewed or developed in the course of this analysis are, by and large, attempts to make sense of correlational data in terms of causal relationships. Causal theories are never "proven," but are more or less credible according to the quality of evidence and the logical properties of the arguments advanced. The reader will have to judge the adequacy of the logic in specific instances, but the mandate of this chapter is to deal with the effects of social networks on the family. If any given correlation between social network and family variables might be better explained by treating the family variables as independent rather than dependent, then this correlation would be grist for someone else's mill. Second, for a variety of reasons, causal terminology facilitates communication. We use these terms in everyday language; to insert the appropriate substitute phrasings or technical qualifications at all relevant points in the analysis would produce an even more cumbersome manuscript. Therefore we ask the reader's indulgence in refraining from too literal interpretations of some of the cause-effect statements which follow.

SOCIAL NETWORKS AND THE CONJUGAL RELATIONSHIP

Mate Selection and Marital Timing

One defining characteristic of conjugal family systems is that parental influence in the mate selection process is relatively minimal (Goode, 1964). Stephens (1963: 199) has shown that the institutionalization of "arranged marriage" is positively correlated with the prevalence of both extended families and unilineal kin groups. The explanation for this association may reside in differences in the structural location of marriage within the various types of family systems (see Goode, 1964:39; Winch, 1971:37–39; Udry, 1974:135–137). In conjugal family systems with neolocal residence, marriage constitutes the formation of a new family which has an identity independent of the spouses' respective families of orientation. But in extended family systems, marriage is a means of recruiting new adult members to existing families. The decision as to whom to recruit is thus a familial rather than a personal decision, is based on the perceived best interests of the family as a whole, and is consequently made by those empowered to make such important family decisions, the family elders. Furthermore, the extended family in a preindustrial society is likely to control a great proportion of resources. Since these resources are allocated according to kinship and family membership, kin networks have the clout to make their collective mate selection decisions with some authority, and individuals are highly motivated to conform with these decisions, since their livelihoods depend largely on their good standing in the kin group.

Two recent studies, by Fox (1975) in Turkey and by Lobodzinska (1975) in Poland, lend credibility to this position. Lobodzinska observes a trend in Poland away from arranged marriages based on status and economic criteria, in the direction of autonomous mate selection based on romantic attraction; she also notes that this trend seems to be proceeding more rapidly in urban areas, due in part to the influence of industrialization (1975:57). Fox, on a random sample of married people in Ankara, Turkey, found autonomous mate selection to be positively correlated with length of urban residence and education. Both of these authors interpret their results in terms of "modernization" and the declining influence of traditional norms. But there is some value value in specification of the components of the modernization process which are effective in this regard, even if it is somewhat speculative. We know (Goode, 1963, among many others) that urbanization and, especially, industrialization operate to decrease family structural complexity and the functional importance of kinship, particularly in the economic sphere. Thus the increased frequency of autonomous mate selection may be due, at least in part, to the declining structural complexity of family and kin groups. This is summarized in Propositions 1 and 2:

1. Family structural complexity is positively related to kin network control over mate selection.
2. The presence of unilineal kin groups is positively related to kin network control over mate selection.

This implies that societies with conjugal family systems are characterized by "free" or autonomous choice of spouse (Reiss, 1971:187–89). But, as Goode (1959) pointed out in his classic work on "the theoretical importance of love," mate choice is nowhere completely free. Constraints on the mate selection behavior of young adults are always imposed to some extent by the kinship network, even though these constraints may be unintentional. The location of the family residence influences the composition of childhood and adolescent peer groups, which structure the "pool of eligibles" from which the spouse is eventually chosen. The demonstrated efficacy of propinquity in mate selection (Katz and Hill, 1958) means that parents, by their choice of residence, structure the set of marital choices their children will have. Since neighborhoods tend to be homogeneous in terms of socioeconomic, ethnic, and sometimes religious characteristics, propinquity is a major antecedent of homogamy in mate choice. The "family of orientation," one part of the kinship network, plays a central role in this process.

But the individual's parental family may also influence mate selection in more overt ways. It has long been observed that parents often involve themselves in the courtship and mate selection activities of their children, by giving advice, encouraging or discouraging certain associations, and occasionally attempting to exercise veto power over the child's decisions. Such involvement is particularly common on the part of mothers with regard to their daughters' choice of spouse (Bates, 1942). Burgess and Wallin (1953) found a strong positive relationship between approval of girls' choices of husbands by their parents and the consummation of engagement in marriage. Bruce (1974) discovered considerable variation in the extent to which mothers encourage marriage-oriented behavior on the part of daughters, some of which is attributable to the mother's employment status.

For theoretical purposes, documentation of the existence of such parental influence over mate selection is of much less interest than an analysis of the conditions according to which it varies. We have already pointed out that the mother-daughter relationship is the arena of most such influence. Goode (1959; 1964:83–86) argues that upper-class families are both more motivated and better equipped to control the mate selection of their offspring than other social strata. According to his reasoning, the upper classes have the greatest personal stake in the status quo, and they wish to preserve their privileged status. The completely unchecked operation of romantic attraction as a basis for mate selection would result in many marriages between children of the upper classes and children from lower strata, resulting in a dilution of inherited wealth and providing some members of lower classes with opportunities to move into positions of wealth and power through marriage. Since the number of such positions is perceived as finite, this constitutes a threat to the continued well-being of the upper classes. Links of affinity (marriage) between upper-class families also allow for the further consolidation of family resources and the maintenance of the "symbolic estate" (Gordon and Noll, 1975). Upper-class families therefore have more to lose by unrestrained mate choice based on romantic love (after all, any vertical mobility by members of this class is by definition downward), and take steps to ensure that their children marry homogamously in terms of social class and related characteristics.[3]

The upper classes are also better equipped than members of other strata to control the behavior of their offspring in terms of many dimensions, including, but not limited to, mate selection. They have the resources to send their children to "exclusive" private schools and colleges which are patronized primarily by other members of the same class. They can afford to live in neighborhoods which are de facto segregated according to socioeconomic status by virtue of the expense of housing in these neighborhoods. And they can provide their children with many material advantages not available to members of other classes, which might be withdrawn or diminished if the child's choice of spouse were to conflict with parental desires. Thus upper-class parents are in a stronger position than other parents to restrict their child's field of eligibles, and also to exercise veto power over disapproved matches. Baltzell (1964: 251) found that upper-class parents often encouraged their children to marry cousins, in order to preserve the child's share and maintain the family wealth intact. Rosen and Bell (1966) found, in their study of mate selection in the upper class, that parents did in fact take many precautions against too frequent and too close associations between their own children and the children of families from other class levels. They also concluded that, contrary to much popular folklore and mythology, upper-class children rarely resist this sort of parental interference. This is summarized in Proposition 3:

3. Socioeconomic status is positively related to the influence of kin in mate selection.

Ties to families of orientation may also inhibit marriage among lower socioeconomic strata, although such occurrences are probably more common in societies with extended family systems. Humphreys (1965, 1966) reports that among the rural Irish, characterized by the "stem family" form of organization where only one son inherits the family farm and remains on the land, aging fathers would not decide which son was to get the farm or turn over control to that son until the father was ready to retire. Prior to this point, all sons were defined as "boys" and were unable to marry. This produced an extremely high average age at marriage for men (Humphreys, 1965:244–247). Furthermore, Humphreys reports (1966:21) that many of the sons who did inherit the farms did not marry until their mothers died. The sons often expressed reluctance to risk disturbing their mothers (particularly if the mother had been widowed) by introducing a new, unrelated female into the household. Judith Blake, in her study of Jamaican family structure and fertility, found that among poorer families parents often "procrastinated" in arranging marriages for their daughters, because they expected any prospective son-in-law to be irresponsible and unreliable. Thus their daughter's marriage would mean that they might lose her as a source of both economic and emotional aid, without a corresponding increase in assistance from the new member of the family (Blake, 1961:137).

Other factors also operate to delay or prevent marriages among the lower classes, which emanate from social network involvements and which pertain especially to males. Rosenberg and Bensman (1968), studying Ap-

palachian migrants to Chicago, found that membership in a "gang" versus nonmembership was associated with later age at marriage. Presumably emotional involvements with females and marriages which might result from such involvements threaten the solidarity of the male peer group. Thus the members of the group discourage the development of affectional heterosexual relationships. Komarovsky (1967:28–32) reports that the male peer group in the working class continues to exert pressure on men long after their marriage to participate more in the "clique" and less in marital and family roles; this is a topic we will discuss more intensively in the section on conjugal role organization below. But for the moment it appears reasonable to hypothesize that, for lower- and working-class men, the stronger the peer group ties, the greater the peer network's control over the timing of marriage and thus the higher the age at marriage.[4] In support of this hypothesis, Miller (1963) found that the members of one gang who wished to marry in spite of gang pressure to remain single managed to "inadvertently" neglect the use of contraceptives in sexual relations. Then, when the girl became pregnant, they had a justification for marriage which was acceptable to the gang. From these results, we may infer Proposition 4:

4. In the lower socioeconomic strata, the strength of network ties is positively related to age at marriage.

The propositions relating mate selection to social network variables are summarized in Figure 3.1.[5]
This diagram says essentially that the influence of the kin network over mate selection is greatest where the network controls significant resources. Furthermore, strong network ties appear to delay age at marriage in the lower socioeconomic strata.

Conjugal Role Organization

One of the pioneering studies of the effects of social networks on the family was the work of Elizabeth Bott

Figure 3.1.   Social Networks and Mate Selection

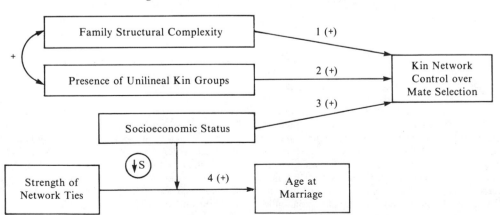

(1971), who was among the first to propose that the characteristics of the social networks in which a married couple was involved might influence the couple's internal division of labor and marital companionship. Specifically, she argued, on the basis of an intensive study of 20 young families living in London, that

> The degree of segregation in the role-relationship of husband and wife varies directly with the connectedness of the family's social network [1971:60].

In categorical terms, this hypothesis translates into a statement that "close-knit" social networks are associated with segregated conjugal role relationships, and "loose-knit" social networks coincide with "joint" role relations. Before proceeding to review the research this hypothesis has spawned, it is essential to clarify the definitions of the relevant variables.

The nature of conjugal role organization is determined, in this terminology, by two dimensions: the extent to which husbands and wives perform household and other tasks interchangeably, and the extent to which the leisure-time activities of the spouses are pursued as a couple rather than as separate individuals. Couples who are high on task interchangeability and on companionship in leisure are said to be characterized by a *joint* conjugal role relationship. Couples who evince a more rigidly defined sex-specific division of labor and who pursue leisured activities separately have *segregated* conjugal role relationships. Oppong (1971) and others (Platt, 1969) have pointed out that perhaps these categories should be disaggregated, in the sense that it is logically possible for couples to have a joint relationship with respect to household task performance but behave in segregated fashion in the pursuit of leisure, or vice versa. The extent to which these two dimensions of role organization are correlated is at present unknown, and it is probably the case that the issues involved could be clarified by investigations of segregation in instrumental and expressive roles as discrete variables. However, it does appear that these variables are positively correlated, and most previous research has assumed that generalizations about one type of organization are applicable to the other. With certain exceptions which will be duly noted, we will continue under this assumption.

The independent variable in Bott's analysis involves the "connectedness" of the social networks in which the spouses are embedded. It is not clear from Bott's description of the concept whether she is speaking of the networks which husbands and wives share in common, or whether she is refering to husbands' networks as distinct from wives' networks. However, the latter interpretation is implied at several points, and is most consistent with the logic of her causal analysis. The "connectedness" of a social network is given by the extent to which the members of ego's networks are also members of one another's networks—that is, the extent to which the members of ego's network know and interact with each other *independently of ego*. An individual whose friends are also friends among themselves possesses a "close-knit network," whereas one whose friends are strangers to one another is involved in a "loose-knit network."

According to the hypothesis, the greater the network connectedness, the greater the conjugal role segregation. Bott's hypothetical explanation for this association again has two related, but somewhat distinct, components. First, the members of close-knit networks exert pressure upon one another to conform to sex-specific behavior norms, and to the norms of the group which they constitute. Since close-knit networks usually exist in situations where the married couple live in the same neighborhood in which they grew up, or at least lived for some time prior to marriage (Bott, 1971:92), these networks existed for each spouse before the marriage was formed. The behaviors characteristic of network members, and the norms and expectations arising from and governing their relationships with one another, did not initially take account of members' spouses. Thus, in Bott's terms,

> If both husband and wife come to marriage with such close knit networks, and if conditions are such that the previous pattern of relationship is continued, then the marriage will be superimposed on these pre-existing relationships, and both spouses will continue to be drawn into activities with people outside their own elementary family (family of procreation) [1971:60].

The normative pressures exerted by these networks will presumably continue to favor sex-segregated roles and activities. On the other hand, spouses without such networks will not experience organized network or group pressure to continue the performance of roles which do not take account of their marriages.

Second, the existence of viable social networks outside of the marriage means that each spouse has access to nonmarital sources for the satisfaction of certain needs. The need for companionship comes immediately to mind; people with strong friendship groups need to depend less upon their spouses for companionship in leisure. Furthermore, Bott argues, a more rigid segregation of task-oriented roles within the marriage will be possible because the networks provide potential sources of help in accomplishing tasks. The social networks of wives are particularly likely to consist of female kin— mothers, sisters, etc. (Komarovsky, 1967). The exchange of aid in household tasks, babysitting, and similar chores is likely among these relatives if they are available to one another, as is the case within a close-knit social network. Consequently the wife places fewer demands upon her husband for help with household tasks. Couples without such networks, however, are left to their own devices for the satisfaction of both instrumental and expressive needs. In the absence of alternative sources of support they become companions as well as spouses, and must assist one another in the accomplishment of their marital and family obligations. Sex segregation in both task accomplishment and leisure activity breaks down, because the networks which facilitate such segregation do not exist.

Bott's research, because of the small sample size and the post hoc nature of the explanations developed, was highly exploratory in nature. Her conclusions are clearly offered as hypotheses rather than empirical generalizations. These hypotheses have stimulated quite a few studies dealing with the effects of network connectedness and the determinants of conjugal role organization. We are still awaiting conclusive results. However, many suggestions have emerged from these studies regarding refinements of the theory and certain limitations upon its applicability.

Four studies were done in the United States in the 1960s, two of which found support for Bott's hypothesis and two of which did not. In the first of these (Udry and Hall, 1965), network connectedness was measured by the extent to which the four best friends of each parent of 43 college students knew and interacted with one another. Conjugal role segregation was found to be unrelated to the connectedness of the wife's social network, and related to husband's network connectedness in curvilinear fashion such that role segregation was highest for those with intermediate network connectedness. Udry and Hall interpret these results as failing to support Bott's hypothesis, pointing out that in their study the antecedents of low conjugal role segregation were high education and outside employment on the part of the wife, rather than any specific features of social networks. They also note, however, that their sample consists of middle-class rather than working-class couples (the working classes were overrepresented in Bott's sample), and that the couples in their sample were older than those studied by Bott. Udry and Hall suggest that Bott's hypothesis may be more appropriate for younger, working-class couples.

Aldous and Straus (1966) measured network connectedness for a sample of 391 married women by asking how many of the respondent's eight best friends knew one another. Under controls for socioeconomic status and residence[6] they found no relationship between network connectedness and task differentiation in marriage, again failing to support Bott's hypothesis. They suggest that the theory may apply only to differences between social networks which are extremely close- or loose-knit, but that finer gradations of network connectedness have no effect upon conjugal role organization.

Joel Nelson (1966) studied the relationship between participation in friendship networks and "family orientation" among a sample of working-class wives. Network connectedness (or the existence of "cliques," in Nelson's terminology), was measured according to whether the respondent saw her four best friends most often separately or together. Nelson found that wives participating in cliques are less likely than others to conceive of marriage in companionate terms, and thus place less attitudinal emphasis on companionship in marriage. In accord with Bott's reasoning, he theorizes that such women have their needs for companionship more effectively satisfied outside of marriage, and thus place fewer demands for companionship on their husbands.

From these three studies, it appears that the theory should be refined such that the conceptualization of the dependent variable differentiates between segregation in task-oriented roles and segregation in leisure pursuits (companionship), as Oppong (1971) suggested. The two studies which take task differentiation as the dependent variable (Udry and Hall, 1965; Aldous and Straus, 1966) find no relationship with network connectedness, but the one (Nelson, 1966) dealing with companionship finds the predicted association. However, the fact that Nelson dealt with normative orientations toward marital companionship rather than with companionate behavior must be considered as a limitation on the applicability of his study to Bott's hypothesis. There is also an alternative explanation of his findings to which we will turn shortly.

In the fourth relevant American study, Robert Blood (1969a) examined the effects of proximity to and interaction with relatives on marital role organization. On data from the Detroit Area Study, he found a curvilinear association between these variables and several measures of marital solidarity. For example, he found that the relationship between frequency of interaction with kin and wives' marital satisfaction is positive up to the point of seeing kin once a week, but those who visited with kin more frequently evinced a marked drop in marital satisfaction scores. He speculates about the causes of this pattern in terms consistent with Bott's logic:

> One clue to the cause of this declining satisfaction was a corresponding decline in the frequency with which wives told their troubles to their husbands after a bad day. Presumably the more deeply involved these people were with their relatives, the more apt they were to rely on their relatives instead of on their spouses. If kin dependencies were sufficiently strong, there was very little chance for marital dependencies to grow [1972:208].

These results appear to support Bott's hypothesis of an inverse relationship between close-knit networks and joint conjugal role performance, at least in terms of mutuality and communication in the marital relationship. However, it is not clear that interaction with relatives is indicative of close-knit social networks. Furthermore, it is possible that the relationship observed by Blood might be susceptible to an interpretation in terms of social class. We know that members of the lower and working classes are more likely to live near relatives after marriage (Adams, 1968a), and that these classes place relatively less emphasis on mutuality in marriage (Rainwater, 1964:462–63; Komarovsky, 1967). Thus it is not clear that Blood's findings support Bott's hypothesis; while they are not inconsistent with it, neither do they provide unambiguous support.

Christopher Turner (1967), building on Bott's research, tested her hypothesis on a sample of 115 married couples from a small rural community in England. Turner contended that neither the study by Udry and Hall (1965) nor that by Aldous and Straus (1966), the two which failed to support Bott, constituted an adequate test of the hypothesis, for two reasons. First, Turner interprets Bott as referring to the collective networks of married couples, not those of individual spouses;[7] both of the above-mentioned American studies used individual networks. Second, he argues that in determining the extent of network connectedness, one must take the objective size of the network into account rather than predefine the network as consisting of either the four (Udry and Hall) or eight (Aldous and Straus) best friends. In Turner's interpretation,

> Bott defined the "interconnectedness" of each social network in terms of the extent to which households other than focal households are linked directly by regular interaction between members [1967:122].

Accordingly, he first determined the number of households in each couple's social network, and then defined a "loose-knit network" as one in which fewer than one-third of the nonfocal households were characterized by regular interaction (once per fortnight or more), and close-knit networks as those where more than two-thirds of the nonfocal households were engaged in regular interaction. Role segregation was measured in terms of leisure activity, domestic tasks, and child rearing, with role organization characterized as joint or segregated in each area. Couples were defined as intermediate on role segregation unless they were rated as either joint or segregated in all three areas.

In general, the hypothesis that conjugal role segregation is positively associated with extent of network connectedness was supported by Turner's data. Segregated conjugal roles were much more common among couples with close-knit networks. Also in conformity with Bott, Turner found that close-knit networks (and therefore segregated conjugal roles) were more common among lifelong residents of the community than among immigrants. Neither variable was related to education, contrary to the findings of Udry and Hall.

There are several possible explanations for the differences between Turner's results and those of the other studies. First, Turner may be correct in his contention that the variable of social network connectedness was improperly operationalized in the earlier studies. Turner himself aggregated the social networks of husband and wife to produce a household network. However, this explanation for the negative results of the earlier studies appears unlikely, since Turner reports that an analysis of the *individual* networks of 32 couples with close-knit same-sex networks showed that those couples evinced a high degree of conjugal role segregation. Second, it is possible that there are differences in the causal processes operating

in the United States and Britain, since two British studies support the hypothesis and two American studies do not. However, no one has as yet offered an explanation for why different processes should be operative in these two societies, and in any case we have no broadly representative sample of either society in any of the relevant studies.

Third, it may be that none of the existing conceptualizations or measures of the independent variable (social network connectedness) are quite adequate. Harris (1969: 173) argues that "nothing follows from the interconnectedness of the networks of the spouses taken singly or together." He contends (1969:165–75) that both Bott's and Turner's data may be explained just as well or better by substituting the variable "involvement in mono-sex groups" for the variable "interconnectedness of social networks." A social network consisting either of individuals or couples, which could be characterized as close-knit, is probably a highly solidary and cohesive group from the point of view of any one of its members. Thus it seems quite possible that the close-knit networks observed by Bott and Turner contain within them two internally integrated but sex-segregated peer groups. These groups provide their members with emotional support, companionship, and help in the accomplishment of instrumental tasks, leading to segregated marital roles. They would also exert normative pressure upon their members to participate in group rather than in marital activities, and to conform to normative expectations regarding appropriate sex role behavior. In fact, such groups are most likely to exist where the norms specify rigid distinctions between sex roles.

In the absence of such peer group involvement, Bott's logic would lead correctly to the expectation that married couples would evince joint marital roles. But according to Harris, the causal variable in this system is the extent to which each spouse is integrated into an extrafamilial peer group, not the extent to which the married couple's friends and/or relatives constitute a close-knit social network. As Harris points out (1969:173), it is difficult to understand why, if both spouses participate in a shared, close-knit network, this should not lead in part to joint rather than segregated marital role performance, at least in terms of the companionship and leisure activities the couple shares with other network members.

Both Udry and Hall (1965) and Aldous and Straus (1966) asked whether their respondents saw a defined number (defined by the researcher) of their best friends separately or together, or whether these friends knew one another. These measurement procedures would not necessarily indicate how strongly the individual is integrated into a monosex group. Therefore, if Harris is correct, we would not expect to find an association between network connectedness and marital role segregation, and in fact no such relationship was observed in these studies. Turner, however, checked for an association between role segregation and both network interconnectedness and involvement in monosex groups, and found a stronger association with the latter. Harris argues that, since close-knit networks and highly integrated same-sex groups are probably not independent,

> we should expect to find an irregular relationship between network interconnectedness and role segregation, but a strong relationship between membership of monosex networks and marital role segregation. This is exactly what [Turner] found [Harris, 1969:174–75].

The logic of both Harris and Turner was applied to an empirical analysis of the relationship between conjugal roles and social networks in Japan by Howard Wimberley (1973). Although his sample was small (40 couples) and nonrandom, and although neither network connectedness nor participation in monosex groups were measured in precise quantitative terms, his results lend qualified support to Harris's position. Whereas the modal category in Turner's English data was that of close-knit networks coinciding with segregated conjugal roles (supporting Bott's hypothesis), Wimberley found a loose-knit–segregated mode, and no evidence of support for the hypothesis of a direct relationship between marital role segregation and close-knit social networks. Part of the explanation, Wimberley believes, may lie in the differing normative systems of England and Japan. Japanese men are expected to have strong ties with male peers, particularly co-workers, and are also expected to leave housework to their wives (see Vogel, 1963).

However, he also reads his data as supportive of Harris's argument regarding the causal efficacy of monosex peer group participation. Although this variable is not measured, Wimberley argues that such peer group participation is characteristic of Japanese men (Vogel, 1963, 1970), and that this may account for the complete absence of joint conjugal role relationships in his Japanese sample.

Further support for this position comes from a study in Israel by Ginsberg (1975). She compared two neighborhoods in Tel Aviv, one of which was highly integrated internally (she terms this neighborhood "close-knit," following Bott) and one of which was low on internal integration ("loose-knit"). Her dependent variable was the extent to which spouses engaged in leisure activities jointly rather than separately. She found, as predicted, that joint marital relations were markedly more common in the loose-knit neighborhood; this was partly, but not entirely, due to a positive association between education and joint role performance, and higher average educational levels in the loose-knit neighborhood.

However, the negative association between neighborhood integration and joint marital roles emerged only among males. Females, if they engaged in leisure activities at all, did so only with their husbands; thus there was no variance on marital role organization for women. Furthermore, Ginsberg found that the neighborhood differences in conjugal role organization

were not attributable to the localization of male friendship networks. Ginsberg concludes that the more segregated marital roles in the close-knit network are due primarily to the existence of norms favoring male participation in same-sex peer groups in this neighborhood. Thus her results seem more in accord with Harris's logic than with Bott's.

Both Harris and Wimberley argue that the context of cultural norms regarding marital roles is important for this issue, and that different results from England, the United States, and Japan may reflect differential normative systems. It may be, for example, that participation in a monosex group serves to maximize normative pressure toward marital role segregation only where the norms in fact specify the desirability and value of rigorous sex role distinctions. But the second part of the causal process, the ability of integrated peer groups to satisfy emotional and instrumental needs of individuals indpependently of the members' marriages, should operate under any normative system. We would expect, then, that the relationship between conjugal role segregation and involvement in same-sex peer groups should be stronger under conditions of normative approval of sex role segregation but should also occur under other normative conditions. There is some indirect evidence in support of this position.

Kerckhoff (1972), summarizing the results of previous research (Rainwater, 1965; Kerckhoff and Bean, 1970), concludes that joint marital relationships are more common among the middle classes in industrialized societies. According to many sources (Bernard, 1964; Rainwater, 1964; Komarovsky, 1967) mutuality and companionship in marriage are valued more highly by the middle than the working classes. Thus we might expect that extensive participation in and integration into same-sex peer groups would be less likely to produce segregated role relationships in middle-class marriages, leading to a higher frequency of joint relationships. This argument corresponds with two facets of the results of the Udry and Hall (1965) study: no association between network connectedness and conjugal role segregation on a middle-class sample, and a positive association between joint role performance and wife's education.

Another study by Kerckhoff (1965) indicates a correspondence between segregated conjugal roles and "extended familism" on the normative level, but not in behavior. He also found that people espousing joing marital norms were oriented more toward the nuclear family and less toward the extended, but again there was no carryover of these norms to behavior. The absence of a behavioral effect is attributed by Kerckhoff to occupational constraints on the extent to which individuals are capable of actualizing their preferences. While the correlations on the normative level support Blood's (1969a) argument, those concerning behavior do not. And once again, neither proximity of relatives nor endorsement of extended-family norms is clearly related to close-knit social networks.

From this review it appears that Bott's hypothesis regarding a direct relationship between network connectedness and conjugal role segregation has received less empirical support than Harris's modification, which substitutes involvement in monosex groups for network connectedness. Harris's hypothesis appears to serve equally well in the explanation of data often thought to constitute support for Bott. Furthermore, several studies offer stronger support for the explanation involving peer group membership than for network connectedness (Turner, 1967; Wimberley, 1973); the variables involved in Harris's explanation are also easier to conceptualize and operationalize.

Therefore, we suggest the following propositions as worthy of further investigation in this area of inquiry:

5. The integration of individual spouses into monosex groups influences conjugal role segregation, and this is a positive relationship.

6. The positive relationship between conjugal role segregation and integration into monosex groups is stronger under conditions of normative approval of sex role segregation.

7. The positive relationship between conjugal role segregation and integration into monosex groups is stronger on lower socioeconomic levels than higher levels.

These propositions are represented in diagrammatic form in Figure 3.2.

This model predicts a positive association between the integration of each spouse into same-sex groups (which may consist of friends, relatives, or both) and conjugal role segregation. The predicted relationship should be stronger under normative conditions which specify the desirability of rigid sex distinctions in behavior, and in the lower socioeconomic strata. (These two interacting variables are clearly not independent; sex roles are more rigidly defined in the lower classes.) In addition, it appears likely that each of the two interacting variables

has a separate impact on conjugal role organization, as specified in the diagram, over and above the contribution they make to the effect of peer group integration.

Conjugal Power

The balance of power in marriage has been of particular interest to social scientists since the publication of Blood and Wolfe's (1960) study of Detroit wives, which focused in part on the determination of decision-making authority in the marriage.[8] In this volume they explicated the "resource theory" of conjugal power, which, in brief, says that

> the power to make decisions stems primarily from the resources which the individual can provide to meet the needs of his marriage partner and to upgrade his decision-making skill [1960:44].

These resources are derived, in their conceptualization, from positions, roles, and achievements by spouses in extrafamilial structures. One such structure, in which participation serves to increase conjugal power according to the theory, is the voluntary association or formal organization.

Blood and Wolfe found (1960:38–40) that conjugal power was related positively to comparative organizational memberships. The husband who belonged to a greater number of organizations than his wife had comparatively greater marital decision-making authority than the husband whose wife had more memberships. Furthermore, they contend that in this case church participation may be classified as a special case of organizational participation for theoretical purposes; a similar (in fact, slightly stronger) relationship was found between conjugal power and comparative church attendance, with the spouse who attended services more frequently having correspondingly higher scores on the conjugal power index. Lupri (1969:143) found that the positive relationship between conjugal power and comparative church

Figure 3.2.   Social Networks and Conjugal Role Organization

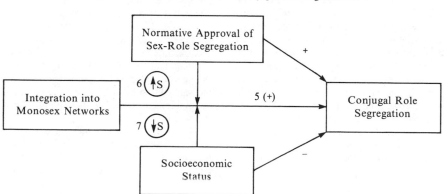

attendance also obtained for a West German sample. While it is clear from these data that conjugal decision-making authority and participation in extrafamily organizations are positively correlated, it is not clear what sort of interpretation should be attached to this correlation. Blood and Wolfe themselves offer two. First, in conformity with resource theory, they note that participation in organizations outside the family may foster the acquisition of knowledge and interpersonal skills which enhance the individual's decision-making abilities. In this interpretation, organizational participation is clearly employed as a resource base, which has the effect of increasing marital authority. However, the second interpretation points out that the relationship between conjugal power and organizational participation may be, at least in part, spurious:

> Moreover, a person who has enough initiative to be active in the community seems also more likely to participate in family decision-making [1960:38].

In this version, organizational participation is employed as a consequence of an activity dimension of personal life style, which is also antecedent to participation in decision making, but the cause of which is undetermined.

While these two explanations probably both have merit, and while it is not necessary to distinguish between them if the theoretical focus of interest is conjugal power, future research on the effects of social networks might be oriented toward the determination of the extent to which the correlation between organizational participation and conjugal power represents a causal relationship, versus the extent to which these two variables are simultaneously consequences of some third factor or factors.

Komarovsky (1967:228–29) provides some evidence to the effect that the wife may increase her power in the family by participating in external organizations such as the PTA. Although her evidence is illustrative rather than quantitative, Komarovsky argues that lower rates of male dominance among higher-status blue-collar couples than lower-status couples may be attributable to a complex process involving both education and organizational participation. She points out that more educated blue-collar husbands (those with high school education) have more equalitarian marital norms. They therefore allow or encourage their wives to participate more in organizations and other extrafamilial relationships. As a consequence of such participation, the wife acquires skills and knowledge by virtue of which she is defined as an "expert" in areas related to her external participation, and she is accordingly allocated more decision-making authority in these areas. Conversely, among couples with less education, "the husband has wider contacts in the community than his wife" (1967:228), and his power is increased accordingly. Those contacts, however, involve his job and informal group relations rather than organizational memberships.

The less-educated husband may not belong to more organizations than does his wife (the rate of participation is identical for the two), but he is more mobile, and his experience on the job, in the labor union, and in the tavern lead his wife to feel, as one woman said, that "he is in the middle of it" [1967:229].

Thus differential community involvement may explain the inverse correlation between education and husband's power for blue-collar couples.

Komarovsky also reports (1967:229) that she did not observe the positive correlation between comparative church attendance and conjugal power found by Blood and Wolfe (1960:39). In her sample, she found that wives were more likely to belong to and attend church than husbands, but she judges the impact of this on conjugal power to be negligible. She suggests that the relationship found by Blood and Wolfe may not characterize the working class. Although the Blood and Wolfe sample covered a very large portion of the socioeconomic spectrum, they did not control for class in their analysis of the relationship in question. Therefore Komarovsky's interpretation is plausible.

The relationship between marital power and organizational participation is complicated by the fact that organizational participation is distributed differentially across the socioeconomic structure. Membership in voluntary associations is a predominantly middle-class phenomenon, with membership rates much higher than in the working and lower classes. Suttles (1971) has suggested, however, that for lower-class male slum-dwellers, the male peer group of "neighborhood gang" serves many of the same functions which are served by formal organizations in the middle class. On the basis of this information, Robert Blood argues that

> it seems likely that lower-class men gain resources relevant to their power position within the home from participating in gangs on the street corner or in the neighborhood tavern or pool room [1972:539].

This speculation is in conformity with Blood and Wolfe's (1960) resource theory of family power and Heer's (1963) subsequent interpretation. Participation in these peer groups may constitute a source of emotional rewards alternative to the marital relationship, thus decreasing reliance on the marriage in that regard. This permits a certain independence from the spouse, as we argued in the section on conjugal role organization. Exchange theory (Thibaut and Kelley, 1959; Blau, 1964) would lead us to predict that independence from the spouse with respect to the satisfaction of needs such as emotional support and companionship would be positively related to power in the marriage.

Thus voluntary associations and neighborhood gangs may both serve as social networks with respect to the determination of conjugal power, but in different ways and for different segments of the population. Participation in voluntary associations increases the power of the spouse with the highest participation rate by means of maximizing that spouse's status in the community and increasing his or her "expert knowledge" and decision-making skills. While not restricted to the middle class, this is primarily a middle-class phenomenon, since rates of voluntary association participation are much less in the lower and working classes. In the latter social strata, participation in informal neighborhood groups has the same consequence (increasing marital power), but for a different reason: it reduces dependence on the spouse for the satisfaction of emotional and companionship needs. Thus participation in social networks is positively related to marital power, but the specific manifestations of this relationship vary according to social class.

These relationships are roughly summarized in the following proposition:

    8. Conjugal decision-making authority is positively related to participation in extrafamily networks and associations.
        a. In the lower strata, the primary avenue of such participation is the informal neighborhood, friendship, or kinship network.
        b. In the middle strata, the primary avenue of such participation is the voluntary association.

The examples of power emanating from informal network memberships given above related specifically to males. This is not to say, however, that the same process does not apply to females; we suspect it does. In fact, in the working classes it appears that women are much more likely to have "confidants" outside of marriage than are men (Komarovsky, 1967:208, 215). There has been little systematic research on the extent to which intimate relationships among women result in increments of marital power. However, Rogers (1975), in an ethnographic study of a French peasant village, shows how participation in informal neighborhood and community networks may serve to increase the power of the participating spouse. In this village most of the men worked in urban factories to which they commuted daily. The women remained at home. However, the males' factory jobs carried quite low levels of compensation, and the bulk of the food was produced by the horticultural and pastoral activities of the women. This, in accord with resource theory, resulted in considerable decision-making influence for wives at the behavioral level, although both sexes contributed to the perpetuation of what Rogers calls the "myth of male dominance." A further source of power for the wives, however, resided in the fact of the daily absence of males from the community. The women could and did associate with one another during the day, and took advantage of these opportunities to exchange opinions and solidify their collective stance on community issues. Thus women presented a united front to men on matters of importance to the group. The men had no

comparable opportunity to organize because of their occupational dispersion. Thus the women, by virtue of their unity, actually possessed the greatest share of decision-making authority.

We also know that kin networks can be an important resource in marital bargaining. Bell (1962) found that in marriages characterized by conflict and dissension spouses aligned their respective relatives on their own side of the argument.[9] And Komarovsky points out (1967:208) that in her sample of working-class couples 63 percent of all "confidants" named by the wives were either their mothers or sisters. The potential for the use of relatives as power resources is obviously present. And, although Komarovsky presents no quantitative data on the subject, it is apparent that the members of this sample are aware of this potential and actualize it with some frequency. For example, some wives report a certain hesitancy to discuss marital problems with their mothers, because the mothers would "take their side" and, perhaps, aggravate the conflict (Komarovsky, 1967:212). Later, in the chapter on marital power, Komarovsky alludes directly (but by illustration) to the use of kin in the bargaining situation:

> The parental family constitutes a second line of defense for the wife if her husband fails her. One wife reported that had she had a home to which to return, she would have left her husband during the first year of marriage. In similar circumstances another wife did return to her parental home, and this forced her husband to come back on her terms [1967:231].

She then goes on to report that one possible source of the greater marital power wielded by more educated wives (high school graduates) may lie in the fact that a higher proportion of them than of the less educated had close relationships with their mothers, and this might serve to reduce their dependence on husbands.

The reports on kinship relations in British working-class samples (Townsend, 1957; Young and Willmott, 1957) are replete with examples of ramifications of kin relationships for marital power. As in virtually all American data, the strongest and most viable kin ties are between mothers and their married daughters. Since the working classes generally, in both the United States and Britain, are characterized by relatively low rates of geographic mobility (Adams, 1968a:23–26), it is very often the case that working-class mothers and their married daughters live in relative proximity to one another. This augments their opportunities to form coalitions with one another, and specifically increases the daughter's opportunities to enlist her mother's aid in marital disputes. Therefore, working-class wives are more likely to be involved in kinship interaction, especially with their mothers, and more likely to employ the kin network as a power resource.

Farber (1966) provides indirect evidence for a positive relationship between asymmetry in kinship relationships and asymmetry in the marital balance of power, with the power imbalance favoring the spouse whose kinship network predominates. In a study of the causes of emotional disturbances in children, Farber argues (1966:71–72) that greater interaction and solidarity with the kindred of one spouse than the kindred of the other places the spouse whose kin group is favored in a correspondingly favorable power position. He then notes that, according to many previous studies, there is a marked tendency for the parents of emotionally disturbed children to evince unilateral rather than equalitarian power structures. It follows, therefore, that kin relationships should exhibit greater asymmetry in families with emotionally disturbed children than those with normal children. This hypothesis is supported on a small sample (16 families). Although Farber has no data on the conjugal power structure per se, his study lends support to the proposition that participation in the kinship network increases the spouse's marital power.

From these data it appears fairly certain that participation in social networks results in greater marital power for the spouse who is the more active participant. Available studies indicate that this proposition is applicable to all social classes and both sexes, but the specific manifestation of the indicated process varies across these conditions. For the middle class, the most viable social network in this regard is the voluntary association. For lower- and working-class men, a neighborhood same-sex peer group is the social network which is most likely to be employed as a power resource; for their wives, it is the kinship network which is most relevant.

Figure 3.3 graphically represents the relationships in proposition eight. The diagram highlights the different processes which are hypothesized to operate in various class levels. The basic proposition, however, should not be obscured: participation in extrafamily social networks results in greater conjugal power for the spouse whose rate of participation is higher.

Marital Solidarity[10]

Social scientists and laymen alike have recognized for some time that relationships between spouses and extrafamilial groups can have serious implications for the marital relationship in terms of the adjustment of the spouses to one another. In-laws particularly are often cited as sources of difficulty, but kin networks can also be supportive of the marriage. Furthermore, participation by spouses in networks of friends, neighbors, and coworkers, in addition to kin, may have important ramifications for qualities of the marriage.

In more than 60 percent of the world's societies, cultural prescriptions for the relationship between a man and his wife's mother specify some kind of mutual avoidance (Schlein, 1962). This is, perhaps, direct rec-

ognition of the potential for conflict inherent in this relationship, conflict which might carry over into the marriage itself. Stephens (1963:88) points out that, cross-culturally, "the classic avoidance relationship is between a man and his mother-in-law," and that "avoidance implies 'formality,' a restriction on intimacy and spontaneous expression of emotion" (1963:87). Perhaps intimacy between a man and his wife's mother constitutes a threat to the intimacy of the marital relationship.

However, in spite of the prevalence of avoidance relationship between men and their mothers-in-law, and in spite of the fact that most "mother-in-law jokes" in our society involve men, research established quite a while ago that most in-law problems are women's problems (Duvall, 1954). The most sensitive in-law relationship, and the one most likely to produce marital conflict, seems to be the relationship between a woman and her husband's mother.[11] This is, very probably, because most kinship relations fall within the female's domain of concern in our society (Adams, 1968a, 1970).

Sweetser (1963) hypothesized that the greater proximity to and interaction with the wife's parental family commonly observed in Western societies might be due to greater potential for conflict between the wife and her mother-in-law than between any other pair of in-laws. This, she argues, is because the wife is both a stranger to her husband's family and a successor to her husband's mother in the role of caring for the son-husband. She tested several hypotheses, consistent with this theory, to the effect that avoidance taboos between in-laws should exist when the in-marrying spouse is a successor to power in the lineage into which he marries. The hypotheses were strongly supported on a cross-cultural sample of 18 societies.

Difficulties with in-laws in general, and particularly those which lead to marital tension, decline as age and length of marriage increase (Blood and Wolfe, 1960: 247–48). The time when the marital relationship is most vulnerable to conflict stemming from in-law relationships is early in the marriage; this is particularly true when the young couple is living with one or the other set of parents, especially the husband's (Sweetser, 1966). In a study of broken Catholic marriages, Thomas (1956:264) found that conflict between the young couple and their parents was the greatest single cause of dissolution during the first year of marriage. It is clear, then, that inharmonious relationships with the families of orientation of each spouse may have important consequences for marital stability.[12]

But there is more involved in this issue than the degree to which relationships between spouses and their parents are harmonious. Ackerman (1963) demonstrated the importance of kin networks for marital stability, attempting to reconcile anthropological and sociological theory on the determinants of divorce. From the anthropologists (Gluckman, 1950, 1955; Fallers 1957; Fortes, 1959) he drew the observation that divorce rates are lowest where spouses share common group memberships and where the disposition of children (their affiliation with a lineage) is threatened by divorce. From sociological theory he drew the hypothesis that homogamy is positively related to marital stability (Burgess and Cottrell, 1939; Goode, 1956; Zimmerman, 1956; for a more recent review of this literature, see Udry 1974:240–58). Ackerman speculated that the cause of these relationships may reside in the extent to which they represent "conjunctive" as opposed to "disjunctive" affiliations of the spouses with extramarital networks. Homogamous marriage, for example, may produce situations in which both spouses are affiliated with the same sets of nonfamily members. This would in turn result in similarity of the normative systems and value sets to which the spouses are exposed, and in concerted pressure to conform to these group norms and values. These normative pressures would favor marital stability, whereas the potentially different normative sets experienced by spouses with disjunctive affiliations might encourage instability.

Ackerman tested hypotheses derived from this proposition on a sample of 62 societies, drawn primarily from ethnographic reports contained in the Human Relations Area Files. In societies with some form of unilineal descent system (either patrilineal or matrilineal), he argued, the existence of the levirate may be taken as an indication of conjunctive spousal affiliations. This practice provides for the continued membership of the wife in her husband's kinship network even after his death, by ensuring that she will become the spouse of some other member of his kin group. The woman is therefore severed by marriage from her own kin group and irrevocably incorporated into that of her husband, so that competing attachments from her own lineage are minimized. Di-

vorce rates should therefore be lower in unilineal societies which practice the levirate than in those which do not. This hypothesis was strongly supported by the data.

For societies with bilateral kinship systems a different set of indicators of the extent to which spousal affiliations are conjunctive is necessary. Ackerman contended that in bilateral societies where community and consanguine exogamy are practiced, divorce rates should be relatively high, since spouses come from different communities or different kinship networks or both. On the other hand, the conjunctive affiliations produced by endogamous mate selection practices, where both spouses come from the same community and/or kin group, should result in greater group pressure for stability. Again, the data on bilateral societies strongly supported the hypotheses. Divorce rates were in fact higher where marriages were exogamous according to either community or consanguine kin group, and highest of all when both types of exogamy existed simultaneously. For both unilineal and bilateral societies, exceptions to the hypothesized correlations were explained by extensions of the same basic logic.

On the basis of Ackerman's study, we may conclude that marital stability is positively related to the extent to which the social networks of spouses are conjunctive or overlapping. There is considerable evidence from the United States to the effect that this hypothesis also holds for individuals within this society. Zimmerman found that the more traits families have in common with close friends, the lower the probability of divorce (1956:111). The homogeneity between married couples and their friends could also indicate homogeneity between spouses, and thus similarity or overlap in social networks; spouses with very divergent characteristics would be likely to have different kinds of friends and associates, and their friendship networks would therefore be more diverse.

Figure 3.3. Social Networks and Conjugal Power

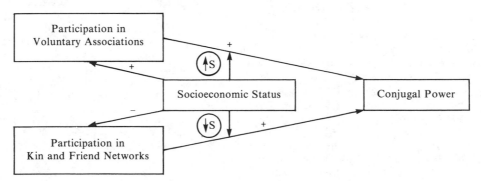

Whyte (1957) found that a tightly knit neighborhood, in which couples knew and interacted with one another on a regular basis, promoted marital solidarity through the normative pressures stemming from joint involvement of husband and wife with their common friends and neighbors. The divorce rate among this group, Whyte estimates, was lower than it might otherwise have been because of the group pressure for stability.

Komarovsky (1967), in her study of working-class couples, noted that joint social life was quite uncommon in this stratum as compared with others. However, when it did occur, the simultaneous participation of husband and wife in a friendship network of married couples served, in her judgment, to promote marital solidarity in a variety of ways. The group of couples to which a given couple belongs has a stake in the continued existence of the marriage, unlike the same-sex cliques which are much more common at this socioeconomic level, because the existence of the group depends on the continued existence of component couples. In Komarovsky's terms,

> The male clique can survive only if it defends itself against the claims of the wives. But a "bunch" or a "crowd" composed of couples acquires a stake in enforcing marital solidarity. Its social activities require that both husband and wife be present and that centrifugal interests be curbed [1967:43].

Komarovsky argues that the "crowd" exerts pressure on husbands and wives to conform to normative definitions of sex and spouse roles (this is in concert with Ackerman's position, of course), and that it provides an avenue by which spouses can observe other marriages and judge their own in a more appropriate context. This serves to minimize resentments against spouses which arise from "the common frustrations of marriage," as spouses see that other couples experience the same problems, and thus that their own husbands or wives are not uniquely rotten. The crowd may also promote communication between husband and wife, by allowing the spouses to express themselves under the cover of the crowd and in a nonintimate context, permitting both direct and indirect exchanges between spouses which might not occur within the dyad alone (Komarovsky, 1967:43–44).

But perhaps most important, by participating as a couple in a collectivity of couples, the married pair comes to be identified as a set by significant others, and each individual is encouraged to adopt and maintain a conception of self which focuses around the spousal role. In Komarovsky's terms,

> The couple with a joint social life has the experience of being treated as a unit, and this tends to heighten their sense of interdependence [1967:319].

This may be particularly true in the working classes, where the norms do not uniformly encourage joint husband-wife social participation as a normal aspect of marital companionship. Komarovsky's observation also reinforces Harris's point regarding Bott's hypothesis that

close-knit networks lead to segregated marital roles, which we cited above: "when both spouses share the same group membership outside marriage it is hard to see why this should not lead to *joint* activities on the part of the spouses" (Harris, 1969:173; see also Fallding, 1961:342).

It also appears that joint conjugal role organization is itself positively related to marital adjustment, stability, and similar variables (Rainwater, 1965, 1966; Orthner, 1975). The relationship between joint spousal participation in leisure pursuits and marital satisfaction was investigated by Orthner (1975), who found a positive association.[13] He also found that participation in leisure activities which are clearly individual in nature is negatively related to marital satisfaction. To the extent that conjugal role organization is attributable to the characteristics of social networks (see above), these same network characteristics are indirect determinants of marital satisfaction.

Ackerman's hypothesis that conjunctive affiliations promote marital stability may also explain, in part, the inverse correlation between socioeconomic status and divorce. It has been fairly well established that lower- and working-class marriages are characterized by greater frequencies of disjunctive spousal affiliations that are middle-class marriages (Rainwater and Handel, 1964; Scanzoni, 1965; Komarovsky, 1967; and many others). Therefore, perhaps some of the socioeconomic variance in divorce is attributable to class differences in patterns of spousal affiliations along the conjunction-disjunction dimension (see also Benson, 1971:306–07).

Farber's (1966) study of the differences between families of emotionally disturbed and normal children may also be interpretable within this framework. As reported earlier, he found that families of disturbed children were characterized by asymmetrical kinship relations, with much stronger orientations to one parent's kin group than the other. Families with normal children, on the other hand, exhibited relatively symmetrical kin relationships. Farber interprets these findings by saying that equalitarian kinship relations are associated with equalitarian intrafamily relations, which in turn indicate efficient family functioning and a relatively stable and, perhaps, satisfying marital relationship. Symmetrical patterns of interaction with kin probably indicate that both spouses are affiliated with both sides of the family and thus have conjunctive affiliations at least with respect to kinship. This would promote marital solidarity and thus, by extension, effective socialization techniques and harmonious parent-child as well as husband-wife relationships.

A later study by Charles Mindel (1972) tests hypotheses drawn more or less directly from Ackerman (1963) on the correlates of imbalance in affective links with the husband's and wife's families of orientation. On a sample of 82 American middle-class marriages, each couple was characterized as bilateral, patrilateral, or matrilateral according to the relative strength of affective relationships with each spouse's family. Mindel hypothesized, first, that unilateral affiliations should be more common among couples where the spouses were from different regions of the country, and also in interreligious marriages. These hypotheses were supported. He then argued that couples with unilateral affectional bonds (either matrilateral or patrilateral) would have attitude sets more favorable to divorce, as indexed by a scale measuring favorability, or lack thereof, toward a series of 18 possible grounds for divorce. This hypothesis follows, although indirectly, from Ackerman's logic on the effects of disjunctive spousal affiliations.

Mindel found virtually no association between kinship asymmetry and attitudes toward divorce for the wives in his study. For husbands, however, he found that those with bilateral kinship orientations were least favorable, in conformity with the hypothesis, and those oriented primarily toward their wives' families were most favorable. Those with patrilateral orientations were, in general, intermediate. Mindel speculates (1972:262–63) that there is little variability among American women in attitudes toward divorce, in part because of the strength of the mother-daughter bond. Even a woman who is involved in stronger affectional relations with her husband's family than her own could count on support from her family in the event of divorce. The husband in a matrilaterally oriented couple may be favorable to divorce because he is in a relatively weak power position in the family: his wife and her relatives could form a coalition against him in the event of marital disagreements. He would thus be more open to divorce as a potential "escape hatch" from an untenable situation.

This study provides support, albeit indirect and partial, for Ackerman's hypothesis that disjunctive affiliations lead to divorce. In conjunction with observations such as Scanzoni's (1965) that spouses may retreat into their own kin groups in attempts to resolve or avoid marital conflicts, these results indicate that qualities of kinship relationships probably influence both the willingness and the ability of spouses to resort to divorce as an ultimate solution to marital tension.

Ackerman's proposition that conjunctive spousal affiliations promote marital stability and disjunctive affiliations make for instability has proven useful in a variety of ways. It helps to explain cross-cultural variation in divorce rates as well as to predict both stability and adjustment for individual marriages, and can also be employed with equal effectiveness in attempts to understand the influences of both friendship and kinship networks on marital relations. It is important to point out that Ackerman's conceptual dimensionalization of affiliations bears certain similarities to Bott's distinction between close-knit and loose-knit social networks but is nonetheless distinct from it. Whereas Bott distinguishes between network types according to the extent of acquaintance

and/or interaction between members of ego's social network other than ego, Ackerman directs our attention toward the extent to which the spouses are simultaneously participating in, or influenced by, the same social network. Our previous discussion of Bott's hypothesis regarding the effects of social networks on conjugal role organization may now be enlightened by Ackerman's concept of affiliations. As Harris (1969), Wimberley (1973), and others suggest, the operative variable with respect to the determination of conjugal role organization may be involvement in monosex groups rather than the extent to which social networks are "close-knit" or "loose-knit." If one or both spouses are highly integrated into monosex groups, this would by definition constitute disjunctive spousal affiliations. Thus it appears likely that disjunctive affiliations may be antecedent to conjugal role organization as well as marital satisfaction or adjustment. This also implies the positive correlation between joint conjugal role organization and marital adjustment noted above (Rainwater, 1965, 1966; Orthner, 1975).

While the extent to which the nonfamily affiliations of spouses overlap is important in the determination of many marital phenomena, other characteristics of social networks and participation in them also influence marital adjustment. The study by Joel Nelson (1966) cited above was designed to test a hypothesis derived explicitly from Bott's (1971) research. Nelson pursued Bott's reasoning that a close-knit social network constitutes a source of emotional gratification and satisfaction of needs for companionship which is an alternative to the marital relationship in these respects. He therefore hypothesized that wives who participate in a highly "connected" social network are more satisfied with the degree to which their husbands understand their problems and feelings than those without such network resources, not necessarily because their husbands are in fact more understanding, but because the existence of the close-knit network ("clique") minimizes dependence on the husband for emotional support.

Nelson measured the extent of network connectedness by asking whether the respondents (American working-class wives) saw their four best friends most often separately or together. Those who typically saw their friends together were characterized as belonging to "cliques." He found that the hypothesized relationship was contingent upon the type of marital norms espoused by the wife, specifically whether she expected high levels of companionship from her marriage, or whether she subscribed to a "traditional" (noncompanionate) marital ideology. He found that satisfaction with husband's understanding was highest under either one of two conditions. First, wives with traditional norms were most satisfied when they were members of cliques; second, wives with companionate norms expressed higher levels of satisfaction when their contacts with friends were individualistic.

These findings imply that where marriage is regarded

as a companionate relationship, a highly integrated same-sex peer group may compete with the marital relationship as a source of emotional satisfaction. The marriage may be more rewarding if the spouses participate in particularistic relationships with friends and avoid the possible entanglements of friendship groups. On the other hand, spouses with companionate marital norms may choose to seek out integrated same-sex friendship groups or not to, depending on whether their expectations for marital companionship and understanding are being realized. Again, measuring social networks in terms of this ''connectedness'' may be covering up or confounding the variable of integration into same-sex peer groups. A woman who reports that she sees her four best friends most frequently together has, at least, four good friends. The woman who sees them separately may actually be reporting that her circle of friends is very limited, or that she sees her friends infrequently. The causal variable may thus be intergration into monosex networks rather than the connectedness of these networks per se. But since ''traditional'' or noncompanionate marital norms are relatively more common in the working class than the middle class, Nelson's findings may explain in part the apparently greater applicability of hypotheses derived from Bott's theory to the working class.

One of the most intensive studies of the effects of kinship relations on marriage emanated from the Detroit Area Study (Blood, 1969a). Blood points out that, since both marital and kinship relations are primary or expressive in nature, there is considerable potential for conflict between them in any given family network. Although he found that financial aid from parents (usually the husband's) is positively related to wives' marital satisfaction and to spousal communication and inversely related to marital role segregation, he also discovered that certain aspects of kinship solidarity had negative impacts upon qualities of the marriage. For his Detroit-area housewives, the number of kin residing in their immediate neighborhood was inversely related to his indices of marital satisfaction and directly related to marital role segregation. However, this pattern might be caused by class differences in geographic mobility. Working-class people are less likely to move in pursuit of a career, and therefore more likely to live near their kin (Adams, 1968a:22–26, 53–44). We also know from a variety of sources that the working classes are characterized by relatively higher levels of marital role segregation and lower levels of marital satisfaction.

While social class has not been ruled out as a possible explanation for these findings, Blood (1969a) provides other evidence to the effect that extensive and intensive kin contact may be disruptive of marital relations. He hypothesized that kinship interaction in moderate amounts might be supportive of the spousal relationship, but that very high frequencies of kin contact might compete and interfere with the expressive qualities of the marriage. He found, in fact, a curvilinear relationship between kinship interaction and his several measures of marital satisfaction, with the peak of marital satisfaction occurring at intermediate levels of kin contact. That is, up to the inflection point (seeing relatives once a week), the correlation between kin contact and marital satisfaction was positive; beyond that point, the association was negative (see also Blood, 1969b:256–69; and Blood, 1972:194–95, 208–14).

It seems reasonable to hazard a generalization, at this point, that both kinship and friendship networks may be sources of marital conflict, or may constitute alternative sources of emotional gratifications for spouses who are not receiving these gratifications from marriage. Thus extensive involvement in these networks may be positively related to marital tension. However, the evidence reviewed leads us to suspect that the point at which such contact becomes ''excessive'' may vary according to social class and according to the normative system that governs both marital interaction and network involvement. In the working classes, the norms place relatively less emphasis on the companionate aspects of marriage; therefore friendship networks and, particularly, kinship networks are viable alternatives as sources of companionship, and do not appear to impact negatively on the marriage unless the members of the network (for instance, the wife's mother or other confidant) are overtly hostile to the spouse who is not a member of that network. On the other hand, in the middle classes husbands and wives are more likely to participate in the same shared networks, especially friendship networks. The norms specify both joint network participation and the value of marriage for companionship. This joint network participation is likely to positively reinforce marital solidarity. It also appears that the degree to which the individual spouse or couple is integrated into the network may prove to be a more useful independent variable, in these kinds of analyses, than the extent to which the network itself is ''close-knit'' or connected.

The following propositions are an attempt to summarize what is known about the relationships between marital solidarity and variables relevant to social networks:

9. Joint conjugal role organization is positively related to marital solidarity.

10. The ''conjunctiveness'' of spousal affiliations is positively related to marital solidarity.

11. Adjustment to affinal kin is positively related to marital solidarity.

12. The relationship between interaction with kin and marital solidarity is curvilinear, with marital solidarity attaining its highest values at an intermediate point on the continuum of interaction with kin.

We should point out that the variables in these propositions are couched in rather abstract terms, in order that the propositions may imply a number of more specific hypotheses. Proposition 9, for example, implies that the relationship between integration into monosex groups and marital solidarity is negative, and Proposition 10 that the symmetry of contact with kin is also positively correlated with solidarity. In addition, for reasons already specified, we expect the correlations implied by Proposition 9 and 10 to be of greater magnitude in the higher socioeconomic strata. These relationships and several other relationships that are implicit in the earlier discussion are summarized in diagrammatic form in Figure 3.4.[14]

SOCIAL NETWORKS AND FAMILY VARIABLES

We have discussed, to this point, some of the ways in which social networks affect aspects of the marital relationship. There are also indications that social networks may have some important influences on more strictly familial behaviors. These include effects on migration

and housing and on mutual aid among the component families of kinship networks. We will deal with these areas of inquiry sequentially.

Migration and Housing

According to recent census figures (U.S. Bureau of the Census, 1970, 1972), in 1970 only about one household in seven contained members other than nuclear-family members (parents and dependent children), and in 1972 more than 98 percent of all married couples had their own households. Joint living arrangements, including two or more nuclear families, are obviously very uncommon in the United States (see also Winch, 1974). But these statistical generalizations cover up some important variations in living arrangements according to stage of the family life cycle. Schorr (1962) estimated that between 10 and 20 percent of all newly married couples in the United States start off married life living with one or the other set of parents, usually the wife's. Glick (1957) also noted that

Figure 3.4. Social Networks and Marital Solidarity

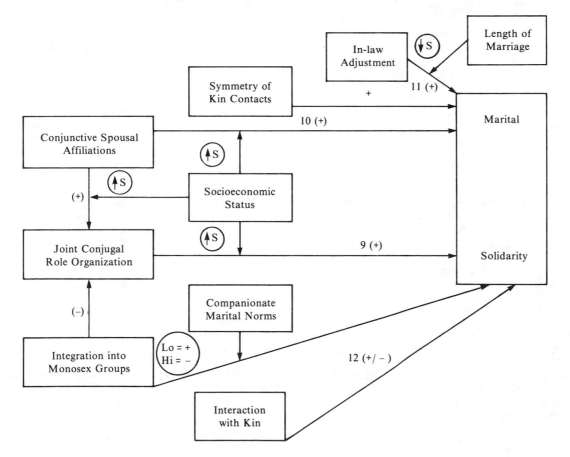

young couples are likely to move in with the wife's parents in case of financial or other emergency. Furthermore, according to Shanas et al. (1968:300–01), the proportion of people 65 and older who live with children or other relatives besides (or in addition to) their spouses is surprisingly high. For her United States sample, percentages living in the households of relatives, including children and others, ranged from a low of 15 percent for married white-collar women to a high of 57 percent for unmarried working-class women.

According to Shanas's data and others, residential "doubling up" of the generations is more common among the working than the middle class. This class difference may be usefully viewed as a manifestation or special case of differences between the classes in patterns of intergenerational aid, which we will discuss in more detail below. Mutual aid between generations in the working class, though, is more likely than in the middle classes to focus on the exchange of services; aid in the middle class is more often direct financial assistance, and also frequently includes the exchange of major gifts such as furniture, appliances, or money for a down payment on a residence for younger couples. The working classes, with generally less disposable income, more often assist older parents or married children by offering to share the residence they have than by providing financing for a separate residence for the other generation. This practice is facilitated by the generally lower geographic dispersion of the generations in the working class (Adams, 1968a).

Glick (1957) found that matrilateral ties predominate in the sharing of housing; mothers move in with daughters rather than sons about 55 percent of the time. This finding has been replicated in a great many studies (see Schorr, 1960; Sweetser, 1963, 1964; Adams, 1968b), many of which are summarized by Sweetser (1966). Sweetser, as noted earlier, has argued (1963) that one cause for this may be the greater potential for conflict between mothers-in-law and daughters-in-law than in other in-law relationships. She points out that in industrial societies such as the United States there is continuity in the roles of women across generations because their roles generally involve household and family tasks. In an industrial economic system the continuity of the males' occupational roles is restricted. The daughter-in-law is therefore a "successor" to her mother-in-law in a direct sense, involving the care of the son-husband as well as household responsibilities. She is also, from the mother-in-law's point of view, a relative stranger. Intergenerational tension and conflict are therefore more likely when families sharing a household are connected by kinship linkages involving males, and this may account for the greater proportion of mother-daughter ties in joint households.

The greater possibility of intergenerational tension when multiple generations share a residence has been noted in many studies (Komarovsky, 1967; Willmott and Young, 1960). In support of Sweetser's argument, Rosser and Harris (1965:151) found that elderly parents were more likely to live with married daughters than married sons, and also that the tensions and strains which emanated from this arrangement were less if the married child was a daughter. Adams (1968b) also notes another factor which mitigates the stress caused by joint living arrangements: people are quite conscious of the increased possibility of strain involved, and consider the potential for conflict carefully before entering into these situations. Those who feel that living with parents or married children would not work out usually don't do it. Thus there is a self-selection factor involved which probably minimizes conflict.[15]

Most people are in fact ideologically opposed to sharing a household with relatives in our society (Morgan, 1962); older people are even more opposed to such arrangements than younger couples. But where feasible, people do prefer to live *near* relatives, especially parents and children. Kinship ties have frequently been noted as having important effects on migrating patterns of families. Blumberg and Bell (1959) found that the location of kin was an influential factor in determining the destination of rural-to-urban migrants. Of the 133 black female migrants to Philadelphia they interviewed, 86 percent mentioned that they came to Philadelphia because relatives and/or friends were already there. The early British kinship studies (Townsend, 1957; Willmott and Young, 1960) also point to the importance of kin in determining residential location, in that young married couples tend to remain in their parents' neighborhood whenever possible. An American study by Brown et al. (1963) reports that migrants to urban centers are attracted to areas already populated by relatives and also by former neighbors. Such networks provide help in finding employment and housing, and aid immigrating families in overcoming crises such as temporary unemployment following the move (see also Hendrix, 1976).

Most studies of kinship and residence have found that matrilateral ties predominate in the determination of residential area, with newly married couples tending to live nearer the wife's parents than the husband's, and with married daughters being more likely to live near parents than are married sons (Mogey, 1956; Young and Willmott, 1957; Rogers and Leichter, 1964; Sweetser 1964, 1966).[16] Aged parents are more likely to live with or near daughters than sons (Young and Geertz, 1961; Shanas et al., 1968). In their study of three-generation families, all generations of which resided in or near the Minneapolis–St. Paul metropolitan area, Aldous and Hill (1965; Hill et al., 1970) found more than twice as many families linked exclusively by ties through females (36 percent) as families linked by male ties only (17 percent).

On the basis of studies such as these, Troll (1971:266) concludes that related nuclear families strongly prefer to live near (although not with) one another. However, several studies have found that strong ties with kin and/or friends in the community do not appear to impede residential mobility (Rossi, 1955; Leslie and Richardson, 1961; Berardo, 1966, 1967). Berardo (1967) particularly found that strong attachment to the kin network did not reduce willingness to move in pursuit of occupational advancement. These discrepancies may perhaps be explained by differential effects of class and ethnic status, or of area of residence.

Hendrix (1976) compared lifelong residents of a small town in the Ozarks with former residents of the same town who had emigrated; he further divided the emigrants into those who moved to other small towns and those who moved to metropolitan areas. He found that frequency of interaction with kin is positively related to commitment to residential stability among "home-towners" and "small-towners," but negatively related among urban immigrants. He also found that the "connectedness" of the respondent's network of acquaintances (that is, the extent to which the friendship network is close-knit) has a positive effect on commitment to residential stability in all three groups, and concludes that as a network progressively takes on the characteristics of a social group, it exerts greater and more concerted pressure for stability, in terms of permanence of residence as well as a number of other variables. The differences between the results of Hendrix and Berardo may thus be due to the different residential characteristics of their respondents, as well as to measurement differences.

Adams (1968a) pursues the question of class differences in residence patterns most intensively. He finds that the dispersion of kin is greater for individuals from white-collar than from blue-collar backgrounds (1968a:25), and that blue-collar respondents are more likely to live near their parents. His explanation for these differences (1968a:23–24) involves variation in the relative emphasis given to family and occupational roles between the classes, and the lower rates of geographic mobility required of people in working-class occupations. In his terms,

> since industrial working classes can find semi- or unskilled work in one modern city about as well as in another, their migration tends to be related most directly to social group, especially kin, relations. Satisfactory relations make movement unlikely; unsatisfactory relations at times result in movement for the sake of escape, not because of greater opportunity elsewhere.... The modern middle or white-collar class, on the other hand, tend to move primarily in response to career demands with less direct concern for the location of kin [1968a:23–24].

In fact, the bulk of the data indicating the importance of kin networks in determining migration, or lack thereof, comes from working-class samples. In the middle class, career concerns and the location of job opportunities are more important than kinship concerns in determining residence. This does not mean, however, that the middle classes feel less concern, affection, or obligation toward kin; Adams presents a multitude of data to show that this is not the case. It means, rather, that the normative systems of the two classes are different, with proximity to kin being paramount in the determination of residence for the working classes, and occupational opportunity taking priority in the middle classes. This coincides with the observation of Leslie and Richardson (1961) that the major cause of geographic mobility is upward social mobility.

Winch (1974) investigated differences in familism between major religious categories, and interprets his results in terms of ethnic differences. In a sample from the Chicago area, he found that Jews were least isolated geographically from extended kin and Protestants were most isolated, with Catholics intermediate. He hypothesized that this difference might be attributed to the higher frequency of entrepreneurial occupations among Jews, and thus lower rates of migration. However, differences between Jews and Christians in isolation from kin remained under controls for migration. He concluded, therefore, that Jews are less migratory because they are more familistic, not vice versa. According to Winch,

> Migration appears to account for the differences in familism among categories of Christians but not for the differences between Christians and Jews. Here the cause may be found in the long history of persecution and segregation of the Jews and a firmly learned conviction as to the protective value of kinsmen [Winch 1974:160; see also Winch, Greer, and Blumberg, 1967; and Winch and Greer, 1968].

Other ethnic minorities may also exhibit the pattern of residing with or near kin to a greater extent than does the general population (see Barnett, 1960, for an example of Chinese migrants to the United States). Adams has concluded, on the basis of his own review of relevant research, that

> minority status tends to result in residential compounding, and in strong kin ties for the sake of mutual aid and survival in a hostile environment [Adams, 1970:587; see also Adams, 1968c].

Our conclusion, then, is that the location of kin may exert a strong influence on a family's choice of residential area or decision to move, but that this influence is probably specific to certain segments of the population, particularly the working classes and ethnic minorities. In the middle classes, career opportunities are far more important. Furthermore, where residence is affected by the location of kin, there is a notable matrilocal bias even in our nominally neolocal residence system. This matrilocal tendency extends to the sharing of a single residence as well as to proximity if residences are separate. The sharing of a residence by members of two related nuclear families is a form of mutual aid, a service which is also more common in the working class.

In addition to the importance of kin for migration in

certain socioeconomic and ethnic categories, both kinship and friendship networks may facilitate adjustment to the new environment for the emigrant. However, the effects of these networks are not uniformly positive. We have already mentioned that kin and friends often assist the immigrant family in finding employment and housing (Brown et al., 1963). Schwarzweller and Seggar (1967), analyzing this same data set, found that under certain conditions involvement with kin in the destination area was positively related to personal stability and inversely related to psychological tensions. But in an earlier publication Schwarzweller (1964) reported that for the rural-to-urban migrants interaction with parents was inversely related to satisfaction with the community and directly related to anomie. Thus he feels that the kinship network might be inhibiting social integration in certain respects. However, he found no relationship between interaction with parents and either community involvement or occupational achievement. This substantiates the results of a previous study by Omari (1956), who found that kin do indeed extend aid to migrating families, but that such aid is not associated with either socioeconomic or community adjustment.

In a recent study of migration among Indians who were forced out of Uganda, Adams (1974) found that economic factors were more important than the location of kin in determining destination of migration, although the latter still had some effect. He also found that the association varied according to sex. For men, the importance of kin was positively related to feelings of "ability to cope" but negatively related to a sense of security. For women, these correlations were reversed.

Hendrix (1976), in his study of Ozark out-migrants, found no relationship between interaction with kin and feelings of isolation among either rural or urban migrants. He did find, though, that interaction with acquaintances is negatively related to feelings of isolation for migrants; this was not true of network connectedness, however. Given the diversity of results from these studies, perhaps the safest conclusion is that interaction with kin has no demonstrated effect on the adjustment of migrants, but integration into a network of friends and acquaintances increases the probability of successful adaptation. On the basis of this research, the following propositions concerning the effects of social networks on family migration and housing seem appropriate:

13. The residential location of kin is positively related to the destination of migration; this relationship is particularly strong in the lower and working socioeconomic strata and among minority groups.

14. The frequency of interaction with kin is positively related to residential stability; this relationship is particularly strong among minorities and rural residents.

15. The connectedness of the friendship network is positively related to residential stability.

16. The frequency of interaction with friends is positively related to psychological adjustment to migration; and this relationship is particularly strong among urban residents.

17. Sharing a residence with nonnuclear kin is positively related to intergenerational conflict; this relationship is stronger when the consanguine kin ties between household members are patrilateral.

These relationships are summarized in Figure 3.5, and the absence of relationships between certain variables is at least as significant theoretically as the presence of other relationships. For example, the cumulative evidence does not warrant the inclusion of a direct effect of interaction with kin on adjustment to migration (see also Hendrix, 1976). However, further research on more broadly representative samples is clearly required for the formation of any firm conclusions.

Mutual Aid

One of the distinguishing features of the "isolated nuclear family," according to Parsons (1943), is the economic independence of related nuclear families from one another. Gibson points out that in many important respects this characterization of the American family is quite correct:

> Parsons posits the isolated nuclear family because it is the normal household unit where neither household arrangements nor source of income bears any specific relation to either family of orientation, and because its social status and economic support depend on the husband's occupation which is held independently of any particularistic relation to kinsmen. Very little of the literature that claims to have disproved Parsons has even addressed itself to these points, let alone challenged them. [1972:14].

We suspect that few contemporary sociologists would disagree with the contention that the primary source of economic support for nuclear families, in industrialized societies, is something other than the network of extended kin. But this point is not at issue here. The research of Sussman and others (see Sussman, 1965, for a summary) has documented the existence of substantial amounts of mutual aid between related nuclear families. Such aid, when it occurs, clearly constitutes an effect of kin networks upon the family unit. We therefore grant the point that, in our society at least, the nuclear family may be characterized as a primarily independent economic unit; but we also maintain that the *extent* of economic interdependence between related families is a variable of more than descriptive interest. The questions we will address in this section involve the sources of variance in both the quantity and types of mutual aid that flows between related family units.

Just how important are kin as actual or potential sources of economic assistance? In the early 1950s, Sussman (1953) found that almost 80 percent of the people in his

Figure 3.5. Social Networks and Migration

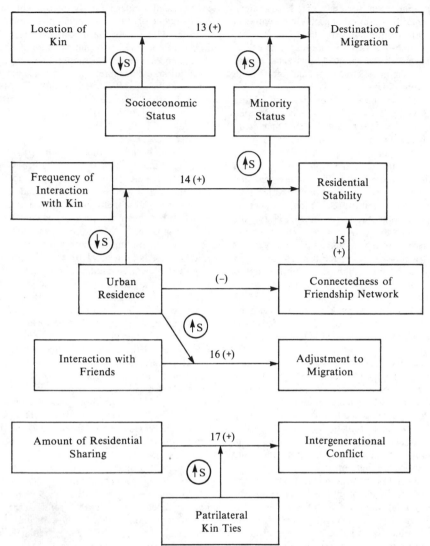

sample with married children were giving help, in the form of either financial assistance or services, to these children. On the other hand, Gibson (1972:20–22) reports that 49 percent of his 705 respondents receive no services from kin. What accounts for this discrepancy?

One possibility is the difference in time between these two surveys. However, it seems unlikely that mutual aid between kin should have declined so drastically in less than two decades. Another possibility is that Sussman asked about services *given,* whereas Gibson asked about services *received;* a "social desirability" factor may be operating to inflate reports of gifts and deflate reports of

receipts. Furthermore, a closer look at the items employed by Gibson (1972:20) to measure mutual aid indicates that, for at least two reasons, low frequencies of aid might be expected. He asked whether respondents received services of the following kinds from kin *on a regular basis:* cooking or housework, shopping, help in finding employment, help in finding a home, looking after children, financial loans, and gifts of goods or clothing. On this list, receipt of the first five kinds of aid would seem to depend heavily on geographic proximity; and loans of money could be highly significant to a family but still not be forthcoming on a regular basis. Litwak's

(1960a, 1960b) conception of the "modified extended family" in modern industrial societies includes the stipulation that the normal functioning of such kin networks is not contingent upon geographic proximity. The fact that slightly more than one-half of Gibson's respondents did receive one or more of these varieties of assistance from kin regularly perhaps indicates the continued significance of mutual aid among kin.

Recent studies of the importance of kin in providing assistance during crises are relevant here because they have compared assistance from kin to assistance from other possible sources. Drabek and Boggs (1968), in their study of 3,700 victims of flooding in the Denver area, found that kin were the preferred source of aid for a majority of victims. Croog et al. (1972) discovered that relatives, especially parents and siblings, were most likely to be rated "very helpful" by middle-aged men who had experienced their first heart attacks. Neighbors were most likely to provide help in terms of essential services—there is, of course, a built-in proximity factor working here—but relatives were the primary source of financial assistance and, in combination with friends, of moral support. Rosow (1967), in his study of elderly residents of Cleveland, found that nonkin were relied upon for help in illness only when kin were unavailable. Both Rosow and Croog et al. conclude that neighbors and friends are supplements to, rather than replacements for, relatives as sources of aid. And Drabek et al. (1975) document the extensive support and assistance provided by kin to victims of a Topeka tornado; they also provide some empirical indications that certain kinds of kinship ties may be strengthened by such experiences.

Litwak and Szelenyi (1969) studied the extent to which housewives in Detroit and Hungary would rely on different kinds of primary groups (neighbors, friends, and kin) for help in emergencies of varying immediacy and duration. They found that neighbors, due to the advantage of proximity, would be asked much more often than kin to assist in day-to-day problems of relatively short duration (a one-day illness, minding the children for an hour), but in case of more extensive problems such as recovery from surgery relatives would be called upon by a substantial majority. This was particularly true for those respondents who had relatives living in the same city, which, for both samples, constituted more than 80 percent of the respondents. These findings indicate that the kin network does perform a substantial service for its members on occasion of serious medical disability or other long-term crisis, and also that geographic separation does not necessarily render the kin network ineffective in the provision of such services (see also Litwak, 1960b, on the latter point). However, for short-term problems, the neighborhood and friendship networks are important sources of assistance.

Over 15 years ago Litwak (1960a, 1960b) contended that American families could best be characterized as "modified extended" rather than "isolated nuclear." A primary difference between these two ideal types is that the isolated nuclear family is thought to be entirely independent of kin in an economic sense, whereas the families which comprise modified extended systems are linked to one another through a web of economic interdependence. Since, in a money economy, major assets are liquid rather than real property, mutual aid and assistance can be extended over considerable distances in the form of gifts, loans, etc., so economic interdependence is not necessarily diminished by geographic separation (Litwak, 1960b).

There are, however, some interesting social class variations which indicate that the concept of the "modified extended family," whose network of mutual aid is unimpaired by distance, may be more applicable to the middle than the working class (see Troll, 1971:270). This does not mean, though, that working-class nuclear families are isolated, but rather that their exchanges are more dependent on proximity. Many investigators have discovered that whereas mutual aid between related families in the middle class is more likely to take the form of money or other valuable gifts or loans, aid in the working class most often takes the form of services (Schorr, 1960; Sussman and Burchinal, 1962; Adams, 1964, 1968a, 1970; Komarovsky, 1967; Troll, 1971). The exchange of services, particularly those offered on a day-to-day basis, is of course dependent on some degree of geographic propinquity. But, as we have already mentioned, related working-class families are more likely than middle-class families to live near one another; there is, in fact, a considerably greater frequency of joint or extended households in the working class (Adams, 1964, 1968a; Shanas, 1967; Shanas et al., 1968). The working classes are in general less well off financially, and therefore have fewer financial resources to expend on gifts and loans to relatives. But their typically closer residences permit significantly greater exchanges of services. Therefore, the frequent generalization that mutual aid is more likely to flow between related middle-class families than between related working-class families needs some qualification. The monetary value of exchanges in the middle classes may in fact be greater, particularly since the value of service such as babysitting, help in home repairs or transportation, or sharing of a residence is not easily quantifiable. But the objective value of these services to working-class families, who might otherwise have to pay for them, may be considerable.

There also appear to be class-linked differences in the direction, as well as the kind, of aid exchanged between related families. It has been fairly well documented that mutual aid flows primarily between parents and children, with aid between siblings being much less common (see Sussman, 1965, and Adams, 1970, for reviews). But there is some disagreement as to the directional balance of aid between aging parents and adult children—that is, which generation gives the most and which generation primarily receives. At least two factors seem to be relevant to the determination of direction: social class and the specific generational location of each family in the network. Sussman (1959) found that the majority of interfamily mutual aid flowed down the generational ladder, from parents to children. However, subsequent research has indicated that this generalization may be a more accurate characterization of the middle class than the working class. Shanas (1967; Shanas et al., 1968), on her data from the three-nation study, found that aging middle-class parents gave more help to their children than they received, but in the working class the opposite was true. This makes sense in light of differential patterns of earning power over the life cycle between the classes. White-collar or middle-class workers often begin their careers at salaries which differ little from wages available to skilled and semiskilled blue-collar workers, but experience more rapid and extensive increases in earnings as their careers progress. Therefore, in the 10 years or so immediately preceding retirement middle-class families are likely to have considerably higher income than working-class families. This enables them (1) to make more assets available to their married children, who are likely to be in the expanding-family or child-rearing stage where family living expenses are highest; and (2) to make more adequate provision for their own financial security in the retirement years, thus reducing their potential dependence upon their children. Older blue-collar workers, whose earnings, retirement pensions, and investments are usually lower, are financially less able to assist children and more in need of assistance from them. This observation is buttressed by the speculation of Shanas et al. (1968) that aging middle-class parents are less likely than aging working-class parents to share a residence with their children or other relatives simply because they are better able to afford their own homes or apartments.

Adams's study of young families in Greensboro, North Carolina, partially corroborates Shanas's findings. In his sample, though, his young adult respondents who were not occupationally mobile (those whose occupations or husbands' occupations fell into the same general category as their fathers' occupations) were more likely to receive aid from their parents than to give aid to them. This was true for both occupational strata (white-collar and blue-collar), for both sexes, and for both tangible aid and services (Adams, 1968a:75). However, this is probably interpretable in terms of the age range of Adams's sample. All of his respondents had been married (for the first time) for 20 years or less; the median age was 34.5 years for males and 32.3 years for females (Adams, 1968a:9). This means that the parents of these people were probably, for the most part, in their late fifties or early sixties; even the blue-collar parents would not be likely to be members of a primarily dependent age category.

Adams also introduced the factor of generational occupational mobility into his analysis. He found that, where

the child's status was lower than that of his parents, the flow of aid from parent to child was accentuated, but that when the child's status was higher, the exchange was more balanced, and even slightly reversed for males on the "tangibles" dimension (Adams 1968a:57). This pattern would probably have emerged more clearly in these data had Adams studied an older population, whose parents would also have been older, and who consequently would exhibit greater class differences in economic independence.

Comparing Adams's results with those of Hill et al. (1970) from their three-generation study provides considerable insight into the effects of relative age on the direction of intergenerational aid. This study, of course, dealt with three-generational-family linkages, consisting of a grandparent generation, a parent generation, and a married-child generation. About two-thirds of the grandparent generation were between 71 and 80 years of age, with the parent generation focused around the 46–to–55 age bracket. Over 80 percent of the married children were between 21 and 30 (Hill et al., 1970:29). The parent and married-child generations in Hill's study corresponds roughly to the parents and respondents, respectively, in Adams's sample in terms of stage of the family life cycle, although Adams's subjects are slightly older on the average. Hill's grandparent generation, though, provides a third baseline for estimating the directional flow of mutual aid.

Hill et al. found (1970:59–80) that most assistance exchanged between the generations in this sample was given by the intermediate or parent generation, and flowed in both directions. Both the grandparent and the married-child generations received more than they gave. Aid to the grandparent generation was disproportionately in the form of help in illness and household management, in addition to emotional support. The married children provided some of these services to their grandparents. The children, in turn, received aid primarily in the areas of child care (obviously not relevant to the parents and grandparents) and direct financial assistance. The members of the intermediate generation, then, were instrumental in providing both tangible materials and services to their parents and their children. Presumably, as they age and their children mature and start families of their own, the current married children will become the major kin-based source of assistance for other families in the network, and their parents will become receivers rather than givers of aid. Hill and his associates apply the term "patron" to the parent generation, and characterize the status of the grandparents as "dependent." The married children most closely approximate equality between giving and receiving, although they still receive more than they give, and are thus termed "reciprocators" (Hill et al., 1970:79).

On the basis of this evidence, we hypothesize that the extent of balance or reciprocity in mutual aid between vertically related families varies over the life cycle in curvilinear fashion, with most frequent giving occurring in late middle age, and most frequent receiving during the retirement years, increasing with advancing age. A secondary peak in the receiving curve, slightly lower than that during old age, would occur in the young adult years when children are small. We would also hypothesize that if only tangible or material goods are considered, the curve would be flatter for the working class than the middle class but would nonetheless be observed in both strata. On the other hand, if only the exchange of services (including sharing a residence) is considered, the relationship would be more clear-cut among the working class due to greater spatial proximity. (Hill's data obviously do not pertain to this point, since geographic propinquity of the generations was a prerequisite for selection into his sample.)

In addition to class- and age-related differences, certain kinds of sex links between families seem more conducive than others to the exchange of aid. Specifically, most reviewers agree that aid is more likely to flow between families related through females than between those related through males (Sussman, 1965; Adams, 1970; Troll, 1971). As noted above, Sweetser (1963, 1966) has made this observation and attempted to explain it in terms of the greater possibilities for conflict between women and their mothers-in-law than is the case with other kinds of intergenerational relationships. Shanas's data provide rather strong support for this argument; she reports (Shanas et al., 1968:171–74) that older people are more likely to live with daughters than with sons. Rosow (1967) also found that daughters provided more help to older people than sons did (see also Troll, 1971).

This matrilateral bias in the extension of aid clearly needs some qualification, however, particularly in light of Adams's data (1964; 1968a). In conformity with the studies previously cited, he found that a higher percentage of young adult women than men (64 percent versus 53 percent) had received aid from parents during the previous two years. However, 43 percent of the males had given aid to parents during the same time period, as opposed to 37 percent of the females. Adams interprets this in terms of differential independence training of the sexes: "The young married male has been taught greater independence from his family than has the young married female" (1968a:58; see also Komarovsky, 1950, and Bronfenbrenner, 1961). While the differences are small, they do show that the exchange of aid between related families is not at all restricted to matrilateral ties. Adams goes on to point out some theoretically significant differences in the types of aid exchanged between patrilineally and matrilineally related families:

> Much of the aid given by the males is either in direct finances, i.e., cash or loan, or involves helping the parents in their home. The aid received by females is largely baby-sitting or child care help from her mother, or maybe in the form of sizable gifts. The wife's parents are ordinarily careful not to

offer direct sums of money, in order not to unsurp the young son-in-law's position as family provider [1968a:58].

Others have commented that services are in fact more likely to be exchanged among women (Rosser and Harris, 1965; Townsend, 1957; Willmott and Young, 1960), but that financial aid to young married couples is most likely to come from the husband's parents (Blood, 1969b). This seems to be interpretable in the context of Adams's remark on the husband's normatively defined role as the principal family provider: cash loans from the wife's parents might be perceived as a negative reflection on the husband's ability to support his family, whereas resources provided by his own parents would be more consistent with his provider role.

On the basis of Adams's data and others, it seems reasonable to hypothesize that the exchange of services between parents and their married children is somewhat more likely to involve the wife's parents than the husband's, whereas direct financial assistance more often comes from the husband's side of the family. However, this should not necessarily be extrapolated to the situation where the parents are elderly and the children middle-aged; middle-aged couples have not been shown to be more likely to support one or the other set of aging parents financially.

In conclusion, while we would not dispute the contention that the typical American conjugal family is largely responsible for its own economic fortunes, there are important kinds and amounts of assistance exchanged between related families. This does not mean that conjugal families involved in kin-based mutual aid networks are mutually dependent in an economic sense, but only that economic *interdependence* should not be overlooked. Adams (1964), Udry (1974), and many others point out that family independence is a value in modern society, and that the larger amounts of financial aid often extended to young middle-class couples by parents are frequently "disguised" as gifts to maintain the sense of independence. But it is also apparent that aid from kin makes important contributions to the stability and functional effectiveness of many American families (see Hill et al., 1970:59–80), particularly as long as the appearance of dependence is avoided. Blood (1969a) discovered, for example, that the correlation between wives' marital satisfaction and the extent of aid received from relatives is positive.

On the basis of the studies we have reviewed, the following propositions relating social networks to interfamily aid and assistance are suggested: They are also diagrammed in Figure 3.6.

18. Socioeconomic status is positively related to financial aid between related nuclear families but negatively related to the exchange of services; this is due, in part, to the typically greater proximity of the generations in the lower and working strata.

19. In case of crisis, the duration of the crisis is

Figure 3.6. Social Networks and Assistance from Kin and Neighbors

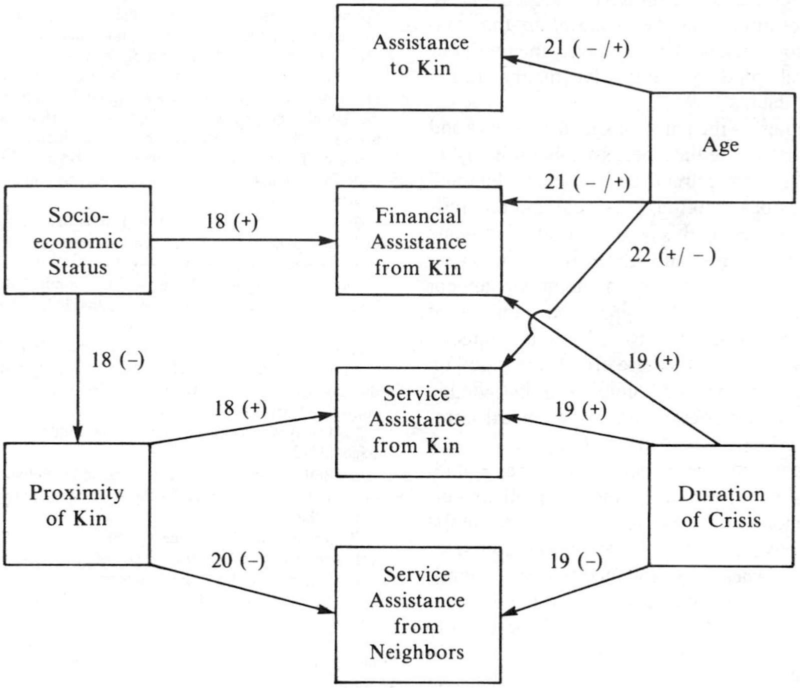

positively related to aid from kin but negatively related to aid from neighbors.

20. The availability (proximity) of kin is negatively related to aid from neighbors in the form of services.

21. The relationship between age and receipt of aid from kin is curvilinear, with the greatest receipt of aid occurring in early adulthood and, particularly, old age.

22. The relationship between age and provision of aid to kin is curvilinear, with the greatest provision of aid occurring in middle age and the least in old age.

We would expect the relationships in Propositions 21 and 22 to be stronger for the middle and upper strata in the case of financial aid, and stronger for the working and lower strata if services alone are considered. There also appear to be differences between patrilateral and matrilateral kin ties in the types and directions, if not the amounts, of aid exchanged. However, these differences do not appear to be of sufficient magnitude to warrant extensive theoretical concern at the moment.

Mutual aid between related families, particularly parents and their married children, is quite common in a variety of forms and is, at least in moderation, a widely accepted feature of intergenerational relations. Arguments about its pervasiveness, or conversely the "isolation" of the nuclear family in terms of the "functionality" of the kin network, are much less useful

theoretically than the study of the patterns and regularities which characterize interfamily exchanges.

CONCLUSION

This review of the effects of social networks on the family has been, at best, partial. We certainly cannot claim to have covered all of the relevant topics, nor have we analyzed exhaustively all those which were included. This chapter is obviously a rather primitive beginning of a very complex, but important process.

It seems to me, at this point, that the major problem facing researchers interested in developing explanatory theory in this area involves the nature of the variables implicated by the social network concept. (Perhaps I have spuriously created a part of this problem by my own selection strategy.) We have not yet ascertained whether, for example, conjugal role organization is responsive to variation in network connectedness or to variation in simple network membership, nor have we determined how to most effectively conceptualize the network phenomenon itself (that is, does our theory point to the networks of spouses as individuals or as married couples?). I am not saying here that we need more research; we always need it, but I'm not saying it. I am

saying that we need more *theory*. We need to step back
and take a careful look at the cumulative evidence that we
have, and then determine the implications of that evidence for explanatory theory. Then and only then will our
subsequent research produce cumulative theory, rather
than accumulated data.

With specific regard to the study of social networks and
the family, the most immediate necessity is probably to
organize and synthesize coherent sets of independent and
dependent variables based on the empirical and theoretical knowledge we possess at this point. The involvements
of family members, singly and collectively, in social
networks consisting of kin, friends, and neighbors appear
to have important effects on the types and qualities of
family behaviors and relationships. If our attempts to
discern, document, and explain these effects are based on
systematic theory and on the cumulative knowledge
generated by previous research, progress toward complete explanation will be much more efficient.

A final point that must be made, or rather reiterated,
relates to the causal terminology and symbolism employed in this chapter. It is important to recognize that the
vast majority of causal statements made in the course of
this chapter are *presumed,* not documented. In general,
we lack data of the quality necessary for the documentation of causal assertions. We have, by and large, only
correlational evidence, which we attempt to interpret in
ways consistent with our theoretical and commonsensical
notions of the order of things. One of the more prevalent
of these notions is that family phenomena are primarily
dependent upon nonfamily events, rather than vice versa,
and I have employed this logic in the analyses which
comprise this chapter. However, as I have argued previously (Lee, 1974), this orientation may be a result more
of culturally induced biases than of solid and defensible
theoretical principles. Since our objective here involved
the explanation of family behaviors, the interpretation of
correlations between family and nonfamily variables
which employs the family variables as dependent may be
justified in terms of that objective; but it is not necessary
justifiable within the more complete context of the logic
of social inquiry. An investigator interested in the determinants of social network participation might quite reasonably reverse the order of many of our causal assertions.

Scientific study of the patterns of interrelationships
between family and nonfamily systems is really just
beginning. I hope this chapter will contribute to a good
start in this area of inquiry; the definitive work, quite
obviously, lies many years in the future.

NOTES

1. I am differing here from Elizabeth Bott, one of the pioneers in social
network research. She stipulates that social networks differ from groups in
that ''in network formation... only some, not all, of the component
individuals have social relationships with one another'' (Bott, 1971:58).
For present purposes I wish to consider groups, in which all members are
(by definition) socially related to one another, as one form of network.
This is not to say that Bott is wrong, although I do think that her definition
is slightly inconsistent with her subsequent use of the concept. Rather,
given our current objectives, it would not be useful to exclude groups from
the domain of the network concept (see also Hendrix, 1976). For a concise
review of the many different meanings which have been attached to the
concept of social network, see Bott (1971:319–23).

2. For summaries of this position, see Nye and Berardo (1973:624–26)
and Lee (1974:523).

3. Leichter and Mitchell (1967) show that strong kinship ties result in
increased pressure for homogamy according to religion.

4. This should not be interpreted to mean that since gang membership
is more common at the lower socioeconomic levels, age at marriage is
inversely related to socioeconomic status. In fact the opposite is true, since
higher-status people are subject to pressures involving continued education and the pursuit of job security which delay marriage beyond ages
typical in the lower strata. However, the pressures do not seem to emanate
directly from social network participation, and are consequently not
considered here.

5. The symbols employed in this and future diagrams are explained on
pages 22–24.

6. Both of these variables were related to network connectedness, with
close-knit networks more frequent among rural respondents and high-
status urban residents.

7. It is not clear to me that Turner is correct in this matter. However, I
will argue below that network connectedness is not actually the causal
variable here, and thus that the debate over whether connectedness should
be measured on individual or couple networks is of little consequence.

8. Conceptual and measurement problems in research on conjugal
power are especially complex, and we do not have the space to sensitize
the reader to them here. These issues, however, are of extreme importance. For detailed discussions of differing concepts and measures, and
the outcomes they produce, see Safilios-Rothschild (1970, 1972), Gillespie (1971), Bahr (1972), Olson and Rabunsky (1972), Sprey (1972), Turk
and Bell (1972), and Cromwell and Wieting (1975).

9. Relatives themselves may of course cause marital conflict. This,
however, is a separate topic, to be investigated in somewhat greater detail
below.

10. The term ''marital solidarity'' is intended here to encompass at
least three conceptually distinct variables: marital satisfaction, adjustment, and stability. These variables are not at all perfectly correlated;
however, their intercorrelations are undoubtedly positive (see Hicks and
Platt, 1970). Furthermore, as far as I can determine, we have no evidence
that they behave differently with respect to their associations with social
network variables. My guess is that at this point we are justified in
combining them under one rubric for purposes of this review. However,
the use of the generic solidarity variable here should not be taken as a claim
that all three component variables actually do behave in identical fashion,
but rather as an admission that we don't know enough yet to specify their
differences.

11. For contrary findings, see Switzer (1966). For supporting evidence, see Landis and Landis (1968:330–33) and Rogers and Leichter
(1964:216).

12. It is also clear that relations with affinal kin are heavily mediated by
the marriage itself. Divorce results in a substantial reduction in or total
elimination of contact between an individual and his or her ex-spouse's
relatives. Contact between the children of divorced couples and the kin of
each spouse is contingent upon the degree of contact between the children
and each parent. See Spicer and Hampe (1975) and Anspach (1976).

13. Orthner clearly distinguished between *joint* spousal activities,
which involve interaction between spouses, and *parallel* activities, which
require simultaneous participation but little interaction. Although both
categories of leisure pursuits evinced positive correlations with marital
satisfaction, the relationship was markedly stronger for joint activities.
Thus the causal process must involve more than simply spending time with
the spouse. Orthner also discovered considerable variation in the mag-

nitude of these relationships according to length of marriage; however, since this appears to be beyond the bounds of our topic here, the reader is referred to Orthner for the specifics.

14. The symbol ''Lo = +, Hi = −'' means, in this case, that the relationship between integration into same-sex peer groups and marital solidarity is positive when marital norms are relatively noncompanionate, and negative when these norms specify a high value on marital companionship.

15. A complete discussion of the sources of tension in intergenerational relations is beyond the scope of this chapter.

16. For an exception to this, probably caused by relatively unusual situational factors, see Adams (1968a).

REFERENCES

ACKERMAN, C.
1963 ''Affiliations: Structural determination of differential divorce rates.'' *American Journal of Sociology* 69:13–20.

ADAMS, B. N.
1964 ''Structural factors affecting parental aid to married children.'' *Journal of Marriage and the Family* 26:327–31.
1968a *Kinship in an Urban Setting.* Chicago: Markham.
1968b ''The middle-class adult and his widowed or still-married mother.'' *Social Problems* 16:50–59.
1968c ''Kinship systems and adaptation to modernization.'' *Studies in Comparative International Development* 4:47–60.
1970 ''Isolation, function, and beyond: American kinship in the 1960s.'' *Journal of Marriage and the Family* 32:575–97.
1974 ''The kin network and the adjustment of the Ugandan Asians.'' *Journal of Marriage and the Family* 36:190–95.

ALDOUS, J. AND R. HILL
1965 ''Social cohesion, lineage type, and intergenerational transmission.'' *Social Forces* 43:471–82.

ALDOUS, J. AND M. A. STRAUS
1966 ''Social networks and conjugal roles: A test of Bott's hypothesis.'' *Social Forces* 44:576–80.

ANSPACH, D. F.
1976 ''Kinship and divorce.'' *Journal of Marriage and the Family* 38: 323–30.

BAHR, H.
1972 ''Comment on ''The study of family power structure: A review 1960–1969.''' *Journal of Marriage and the Family* 34:239–43.

BALTZELL, E. D.
1964 *The Protestant Establishment: Aristocracy and Caste in America.* New York: Random House.

BARNETT, M. L.
1960 ''Kinship as a factor affecting Cantonese economic adaptation in the United States.'' *Human Organization* 19:40–46.

BATES, A.
1942 ''Parental roles in courtship.'' *Social Forces* 20:483–86.

BELL, N. W.
1962 ''Extended family relations of disturbed and well families.'' *Family Process* 1:175–93.

BENSON, L.
1971 *The Family Bond.* New York: Random House.

BERARDO, F. M.
1966 ''Kinship interaction and migrant adaptation in an aerospace-related community.'' *Journal of Marriage and the Family* 28:296–304.
1967 ''Kinship interaction and communications among space-age migrants.'' *Journal of Marriage and the Family* 29:541–54.

BERNARD, J.
1964 ''The adjustments of married mates.'' In H. T. Christensen

(ed.), *Handbook of Marriage and the Family.* Chicago: Rand McNally.

BLAKE, J.
1961 *Family Structure in Jamaica: The Social Context of Reproduction.* New York: Free Press.

BLAU, P.
1964 *Exchange and Power in Social Life.* New York: Wiley.

BLOOD, R. O., JR.
1969a ''Kinship interaction and marital solidarity.'' *Merrill-Palmer Quarterly* 15:171–84.
1969b *Marriage,* second ed. New York: Free Press.
1972 *The Family.* New York: Free Press.

BLOOD, R. O., JR. AND D. M. WOLFE
1960 *Husbands and Wives: The Dynamics of Married Living.* New York: Free Press.

BLUMBERG, L. AND R. R. BELL
1959 ''Urban migration and kinship ties.'' *Social Problems* 6:328–33.

BOTT, E.
1971 *Family and Social Network,* second ed. New York: Free Press.

BRONFENBRENNER, U.
1961 ''The changing American child—a speculative analysis.'' *Journal of Social Issues* 17:6–18.

BROWN, J. S., H. K. SCHWARZWELLER, AND J. J. MAGALAM
1963 ''Kentucky mountain migration and the stem family: An American variation on a theme by LePlay.'' *Rural Sociology* 28:48–69.

BRUCE, J. A.
1974 ''The role of mothers in the social placement of daughters: Marriage or work?'' *Journal of Marriage and the Family* 36:492–497.

BURGESS, E. W. AND L. S. COTTRELL
1939 *Predicting Success or Failure in Marriage.* New York: Prentice-Hall.

BURGESS, E. W. AND P. WALLIN
1953 *Engagement and Marriage.* Chicago: Lippincott.

CROMWELL, R. E. AND S. G. WIETING
1975 ''Multidimensionality of conjugal decision making indices: Comparative analyses of five samples.'' *Journal of Comparative Family Studies* 6:139–52.

CROOG, S. H., A. LIPSON, AND S. LEVINE
1972 ''Help patterns in severe illness: The roles of kin network, non-family resources, and institutions.'' *Journal of Marriage and the Family* 34:32–41.

DRABEK, T. E. AND K. S. BOGGS
1968 ''Families in disaster: Relations and relatives.'' *Journal of Marriage and the Family* 30:443–51.

DRABEK, T. E., W. H. KEY, P. E. ERICKSON, AND J. L. CROWE
1975 ''The impact of disaster on kin relationships.'' *Journal of Marriage and the Family* 37:481–94.

DUVALL, E. M.
1954 *In-Laws: Pro and Con.* New York: Association Press.

FALLDING, H.
1961 ''The family and the idea of a cardinal role.'' *Human Relations* 14:329–51.

FALLERS, L.
1957 ''Some determinants of marriage stability in Bugosa: A reformulation of Gluckman's hypotheses.'' *Africa* 27:106–23.

FARBER, B.
1966 ''Kinship laterality and the emotionally disturbed child.'' In B. Farber (ed.), *Kinship and Family Organization.* New York: Wiley.

FORTES, M.
1957 ''Descent, filiation, and affinity: A rejoinder to Dr. Leach, Part I.'' *Man* 59:193–97.

Fox, G. L.
1975   "Love match and arranged marriage in a modernizing nation: Mate selection in Ankara, Turkey." *Journal of Marriage and the Family* 37:180–93.

Gibson, G.
1972   "Kin family network: Overheralded structure in past conceptualizations of family functioning." *Journal of Marriage and the Family* 34:13–23.

Gillespie, D. L.
1971   "Who has the power? The marital struggle." *Journal of Marriage and the Family* 33:445–58.

Ginsberg, Y.
1975   "Joint leisure activities and social networks in two neighborhoods in Tel Aviv," *Journal of Marriage and the Family* 37:668–76.

Glick, P.
1957   *American Families*. New York: Wiley.

Gluckman, M.
1950   "Kinship and marriage among the Lozi of Northern Rhodesia and the Zulu of Natal." In A. R. Radcliffe-Brown and D. Forde (eds.), *African Systems of Kinship and Marriage*. London: Oxford University Press.
1955   "Estrangement in the African Family." In Max Gluckman, *Custom and Conflict in Africa*. Oxford: Basil Blackwell.

Goode, W. J.
1956   *After Divorce*. New York: Free Press.
1959   "The theoretical importance of love." *American Sociological Review* 24:38–47.
1963   *World Revolution and Family Patterns*. New York: Free Press.
1964   *The Family*. Englewood Cliffs, N.J.: Prentice-Hall.

Gordon, M. and C. E. Noll
1975   "Social class and interaction with kin and friends." *Journal of Comparative Family Studies* 6:239–48.

Harris, C. C.
1969   *The Family: An Introduction*. New York: Praeger.

Heer, D. M.
1963   "The measurement and basis of family power: An overview." *Journal of Marriage and the Family* 25:133–39.

Hendrix, L.
1976   "Kinship, social networks, and integration among Ozark residents and out-migrants." *Journal of Marriage and the Family* 38:97–104.

Hicks, M. W. and M. Platt
1970   "Marital happiness and stability: A review of research in the sixties." *Journal of Marriage and the Family* 32:553–74.

Hill, R., with N. Foote, J. Aldous, R. Carlson, and R. Macdonald
1970   *Family Development in Three Generations*. Cambridge, Mass.: Schenkman.

Humphreys, A. J.
1965   "The family in Ireland." In M. F. Nimkoff (ed.), *Comparative Family Systems*. Boston: Houghton Mifflin.
1966   *The New Dubliners: Urbanization and the Irish Family*. New York: Fordham University Press.

Katz, A. and R. Hill
1958   "Residential propinquity and mate selection," *Marriage and Family Living* 20:27–35.

Kerckhoff, A. C.
1965   "Nuclear and extended family relationships: A normative and behavioral analysis." In E. Shanas and G. F. Streib (eds.), *Social Structure and the Family: Generational Relations*. Englewood Cliffs, N.J.: Prentice-Hall.
1966   "Norm-value clusters and the 'strain toward consistency' among older married couples." In I. H. Simpson and J. C.

McKinney (eds.), *Social Aspects of Aging*. Durham, N.C.: Duke University Press.
1972   "The structure of the conjugal relationship in industrial societies." In M. B. Sussman and B. E. Cogswell (eds.), *Cross-National Family Research*. Leiden, Netherlands: E. J. Brill.

Kerckhoff, A. C. and F. D. Bean
1970   "Social status and interpersonal patterns among married couples." *Social Forces* 49:264–71.

Komarovsky, M.
1950   "Functional analysis of sex roles." *American Sociological Review* 15:508–16.
1967   *Blue-Collar Marriage*. New York: Vintage Books.

Landis, J. T. and M. G. Landis
1968   *Building a Successful Marriage,* fifth ed. Englewood Cliffs, N.J.: Prentice-Hall.

Lee, G. R.
1974   "Marriage and anomie: A causal argument." *Journal of Marriage and the Family* 36:523–32.

Leichter, H. J. and W. E. Mitchell
1967   *Kinship and Casework*. New York: Russell Sage Foundation.

Leslie, G. R. and A. H. Richardson
1961   "Life cycle, career pattern, and the decision to move." *American Sociological Review* 26:894–902.

Litwak, E.
1960a   "Occupational mobility and extended family cohesion." *American Sociological Review* 25:9–21.
1960b   "Geographical mobility and extended family cohesion." *American Sociological Review* 25:385–94.

Litwak, E. and I. Szelenyi
1969   "Primary group structures and their functions: Kin, neighbors, and friends." *American Sociological Review* 34:465–81.

Lobodzinska, B.
1975   "Love as a factor in marital decisions in contemporary Poland." *Journal of Comparative Family Studies* 6:56–73.

Lupri, E.
1969   "Contemporary authority patterns in the West German family: A study in cross-national validation." *Journal of Marriage and the Family* 31:134–44.

Miller, W. B.
1963   "The corner gang boys get married," *Trans-action* 1:10–12.

Mindel, C. H.
1972   "Kinship affiliation: Structure and process in divorce." *Journal of Comparative Family Studies* 3:254–64.

Mogey, J.
1956   *Family and Neighborhood*. London: Oxford University Press.

Morgan, J. N., M. H. David, W. J. Cohen, and H. E. Brazer
1962   *Income and Welfare in the United States*. New York: McGraw-Hill.

Nelson, Joel I.
1966   "Clique contacts and family orientations." *American Sociological Review* 31:663–72.

Nye, F. I. and F. M. Berardo
1973   *The Family: Its Structure and Interaction*. New York: Macmillan.

Olson, D. H. and C. Robunsky
1972   "Validity of four measures of family power." *Journal of Marriage and the Family* 34:224–34.

Omari, T. P.
1956   "Factors associated with urban adjustment of rural Southern migrants." *Social Forces* 35:47–53.

Oppong, C.
1971   "'Joint' conjugal roles and 'extended' families: A preliminary note on a mode of classifying conjugal family relationships." *Journal of Comparative Family Studies* 2:178–87.

ORTHNER, D. K.
1975   "Leisure activity patterns and marital satisfaction over the marital career." *Journal of Marriage and the Family* 37:91–102.

PARSONS, T.
1943   "The kinship system of the contemporary United States." *American Anthropologist* 45:22–38.

PLATT, J.
1969   "Some problems in measuring jointness of conjugal-role relationships." *Sociology* 3:287–98.

RAINWATER, L.
1964   "Marital sexuality in four cultures of poverty." *Journal of Marriage and the Family* 26:457–66.
1965   *Family Design.* Chicago: Aldine.
1966   "Some aspects of lower class sexual behavior." *Journal of Social Issues* 22:96–108.

RAINWATER, L. AND G. HANDEL
1964   "Changing family roles in the working class." In A. B. Shostak and W. Gombert (eds.), *Blue-Collar World.* Englewood Cliffs, N.J.: Prentice-Hall.

REISS, I. L.
1971   *The Family System in America.* New York: Holt, Rinehart and Winston.

RODGERS, R. H.
1973   *Family Interaction and Transaction.* Englewood Cliffs, N.J.: Prentice-Hall.

ROGERS, C. L., AND H. J. LEICHTER
1964   "Laterality and conflict in kinship ties." In W. J. Goode (ed.), *Readings on the Family and Society.* Englewood Cliffs, N.J.: Prentice-Hall.

ROGERS, S. C.
1975   "Female forms of power and the myth of male dominance: A model of female/male interaction in peasant society." *American Ethnologist* 2:727–56.

ROSEN, L. AND R. R. BELL
1966   "Mate selection in the upper class." *Sociological Quarterly* 7: 157–66.

ROSENBERG, B. AND J. BENSMAN
1968   "Sexual patterns in three ethnic subcultures of an American underclass." *Annals of the AAPSS* 376:61–75.

ROSOW, I.
1967   *Social Integration of the Aged.* New York: Free Press.

ROSSER, C. AND C. HARRIS
1965   *The Family and Social Change: A Study of Family and Kinship in a South Wales Town.* London: Routledge and Kegan Paul.

ROSSI, P. H.
1955   *Why Families Move.* New York: Free Press.

SAFILIOS-ROTHSCHILD, C.
1970   "The study of family power structure: A review 1960–1969." *Journal of Marriage and the Family* 32:539–52.
1972   "Answer to Stephen J. Bahr's 'Comment on the study of family power structure: A review 1960–1969.'" *Journal of Marriage and the Family* 34: 245–46.

SCANZONI, J.
1965   "A reinquiry into marital disorganization." *Journal of Marriage and the Family* 27:483–89.

SCHLEIN, J.
1962   "Mothers-in-law: A problem in kinship terminology." *ETC* 19:161–71.

SCHORR, A. L.
1960   *Filial Responsibility in the Modern American Family.* Washington, D.C.: U.S. Department of Health, Education, and Welfare.
1962   "Current practices of filial responsibility." In R. F. Winch, R. McGinnis, and H. R. Burringer (eds.), *Selected Studies in Marriage and the Family.* New York: Holt, Rinehart and Winston.

SCHWARZWELLER, H. K.
1964   "Parental family ties and social integration of rural to urban migrants." *Journal of Marriage and the Family* 26:410–16.

SCHWARZWELLER, H. K. AND J. F. SEGGAR
1967   "Kinship involvement: A factor in the adjustment of rural migrants." *Journal of Marriage and the Family* 29:662–71.

SHANAS, E.
1967   "Family help patterns and social class in three countries." *Journal of Marriage and the Family* 29:257–66.

SHANAS, E., P. TOWNSEND, J. STEHOUWER, AND H. FRIIS
1968   *Old People in Three Industrial Societies.* New York: Atherton.

SPICER, J. W. AND G. D. Hampe
1975   "Kinship interaction after divorce." *Journal of Marriage and the Family* 37:113–19.

SPREY, J.
1972   "Family power structure: A critical comment." *Journal of Marriage and the Family* 34:235–38.

STEPHENS, W. N.
1963   *The Family in Cross-Cultural Perspective.* New York: Holt, Rinehart and Winston.

SUSSMAN, M. B.
1953   "The help pattern of the middle class family." *American Sociological Review* 18:22–28.
1959   "The isolated nuclear family: Fact or fiction." *Social Problems* 6:333–40.
1965   "Relationships of adult children with their parents in the United States." In E. Shanas and G. F. Streib (eds.), *Social Structure and the Family: Generational Relations.* Englewood Cliffs, N.J.: Prentice-Hall.

SUSSMAN, M. B. AND L. BURCHINAL
1962   "Kin family network: Unheralded structure in current conceptualizations of family functioning." *Marriage and Family Living* 24:231–40.

SUTTLES, G. D.
1971   "Vigilante peer groups and the defended neighborhood." In G. D. Suttles, *Cultural and Structural Issues in the Study of Territoriality.* Chicago: University of Chicago Press.

SWEETSER, D. A.
1963   "Asymmetry in intergenerational family relationships." *Social Forces* 41:346–52.
1964   "Urbanization and the patrilineal transmission of farms in Finland," *Acta Sociologica* 7:215–24.
1966   "The effect of industrialization on intergenerational solidarity." *Rural Sociology* 31:156–70.

SWITZER, A. L.
1966   "Some factors related to in-law difficulty and conflict." Purdue University: Unpublished M.S. thesis.

THIBAUT, J. W. AND H. H. KELLEY
1959   *The Social Psychology of Groups.* New York: Wiley.

THOMAS, J. L.
1956   *The American Catholic Family.* Englewood Cliffs, N.J.: Prentice-Hall.

TOWNSEND, P.
1957   *The Family Life of Old People: An Inquiry in East London.* London: Routledge and Kegan Paul.

TROLL, L. E.
1971   "The family of later life: A decade review." *Journal of Marriage and the Family* 33:263–90.

TURK, J. L. AND N. W. BELL
1972   "Measuring power in families." *Journal of Marriage and the Family* 34:215–23.

TURNER, C.
1967   "Conjugal roles and social networks: A re-examination of an hypothesis." *Human Relations* 20:121–30.

UDRY, J. R.
  1974   *The Social Context of Marriage,* third ed. Philadelphia: Lippincott.

UDRY, J. R. AND M. HALL
  1965   "Marital role segregation and social networks in middle-class middle-aged couples." *Journal of Marriage and the Family* 27:392–95.

U. S. BUREAU OF THE CENSUS
  1970   1970 Census of the Population: General Population Characteristics: United States Summary. PC (1)-B1. Washington, D.C.: U. S. Government Printing Office.

  1972   Current Population Reports: Population Characteristics. Series P-20, No. 237.

VOGEL, E.
  1963   *Japan's New Middle Class.* Berkeley: University of California Press.

  1970   "Beyond salary: Mamachi revisited." *The Japan Interpreter* 6:105–13.

WHYTE, W. H., JR.
  1957   *The Organization Man.* Garden City, N.Y.: Doubleday Anchor.

WILLMOTT, P. AND M. YOUNG
  1960   *Family and Class in a London Suburb.* London: Routledge and Kegan Paul.

WIMBERLY, H.
  1973   "Conjugal-role organization and social networks in Japan and England." *Journal of Marriage and the Family* 35:125–31.

WINCH, R. F.
  1971   *The Modern Family,* third ed. New York: Holt, Rinehart and Winston.

  1974   "Some observations on extended familism in the United States." In R. F. Winch and G. Spanier (eds.), *Selected Studies in Marriage and the Family,* fourth ed. New York: Holt, Rinehart, and Winston.

WINCH, R. F. AND S. GREER
  1968   "Urbanism, ethnicity, and extended familism." *Journal of Marriage and the Family* 30:40–45.

WINCH, R. F., S. GREER, AND R. L. BLUMBERG
  1967   "Ethnicity and extended familism in an upper-middle-class suburb." *American Sociological Review* 32:265–72.

YOUNG, M. AND H. GEERTZ
  1961   "Old age in London and San Francisco: Some families compared." *British Journal of Sociology* 12:124–41.

YOUNG, M. AND P. WILLMOTT
  1957   *Family and Kinship in East London.* New York: Free Press.

ZIMMERMAN, C.
  1956   "The present crisis." In C. Zimmerman and L. F. Cervantes (eds.), *Marriage and the Family.* Chicago: Henry Regnery.

4

HETEROSEXUAL PERMISSIVENESS: A THEORETICAL ANALYSIS

Ira L. Reiss and Brent C. Miller

PART ONE

INTRODUCTION

The purpose of this work is to clarify and extend theory in the area of heterosexual permissiveness, with particular emphasis on premarital permissiveness. We focus upon Reiss's work, since it has explicit theoretical propositions and has been frequently tested.

In Part One we present and clarify Reiss's (1967) original propositions and review the relevant evidence, most of which is recent. We then reformulate the propositions, paying close attention to nominal and operational definitions of the concepts and noting how they are thought to vary. Part One thoroughly documents that theories are never finished, but we support the point of view that they can be refined and improved.

In Part Two we integrate the propositions which were clarified in Part One and discuss new implications. We also attempt to link the theory of premarital sexual permissiveness we have developed with theoretical explanations advanced by others. Finally, extensions of the theory of premarital sexual permissiveness into the areas of marital and extramarital sexual permissiveness are suggested.

In summary, our intention is to clarify and refine extant theoretical statements, reformulate them in the light of recent evidence, and integrate and extend them into new

areas. It should be clear at the outset that we are building upon existing theory, and thus our focus will not be upon all key aspects of premarital sexual relationships, but rather upon those aspects that have been most developed in existing research and theory. Thus we shall here focus upon premarital sexual permissiveness, which is the attitudinal side of premarital sexual relationships. We shall later relate this to premarital sexual behavior, but our focus shall remain in part on the area of attitudes, since that has been most thoroughly developed. This is not a judgment of the relative worth of attitudes and behavior. On that issue we feel sure that both are vital to any complete theory of premarital sexuality and neither is sufficient alone.

While the coauthors have worked together on this chapter, it should be noted that Brent Miller is the primary author of Part One and Ira Reiss of Part Two.

A DESCRIPTIVE PRESENTATION OF REISS'S PREVIOUS WORK

It is our purpose in this section to critically review the propositions formulated in *The Social Context of Premarital Sexual Permissiveness* (Reiss, 1967).* This work is chosen because it is generally recognized as the major theoretical work on premarital sexual permissiveness; however, other work will be related to it in the course of our examination. In Reiss's book, findings were reported from analyses of sex data from student samples and a national probability sample of adults. There appeared to be seven areas of related findings, and each of these seven clusters was summarized with a proposition or statement which specified major concepts and their relationships.

NOTE: This chapter is a revised version of Ira L. Reiss and Brent C. Miller, "A Theoretical Analysis of Heterosexual Permissiveness," University of Minnesota Family Study Center, Technical Bulletin #2, August 1974, 113 pages. Special thanks are extended to the following individuals who read part or all of earlier drafts of this paper: Al Banwart; Wesley Burr; Reuben Hill; Steve Jorgensen; David Klein; Boyd Rollins; Gary Sponaugle, and Robert Walsh. Our appreciation also to Graham Spanier and Roger Libby, who read a later draft of this chapter and gave us the benefit of their comments.

*Unless otherwise indicated, all pagination references to Reiss's work will refer to this book.

Although initially guided by hypotheses, the final propositions were thus largely generated from data; the value of this "grounded" approach has been reasserted by Glaser and Strauss (1967). In his book Reiss attempted to create a summarizing theoretical statement of premarital sexual permissiveness that captured the seven propositions which subsumed most of the findings. Reiss's theoretical effort has stimulated many retests and some theoretical analysis (Burr, 1973).

Propositions are conspicuous theoretical statements, and as such they should be expected to carefully relate concepts so that the nature of these relationships is precise and unambiguous. Since a theory is best understood by decomposing it—reducing it to its concepts and their interrelationships—each of the quoted original propositions will be followed by a specification of the concepts and relational connectives used. This will clarify what the proposition asserted, and will make visible any redundancies, gaps, or inconsistencies. Figure 4.2 will be employed to summarize the information in each proposition. (If the reader is not familiar with the conventions used in these diagrams, a quick reading of Chapter 2 on diagramming theoretical propositions will be most helpful.) We will examine each proposition in order, first to clarify it and then again to reformulate it, as needed.

Reiss's Proposition One: The lower the traditional level of sexual permissiveness in a group, the greater the likelihood that social forces will alter individual levels of sexual permissiveness [51].

This proposition contains three concepts: the traditional level of sexual permissiveness in a group, social forces, and individual sexual permissiveness. The relational connective between social forces and individual permissiveness, the term "alter," asserts causality. "The traditional level of sexual permissiveness in a group is a concept developed to explain observed race and gender differences in permissiveness; it was found that blacks were more permissive than whites, and males were more permissive than females. Accordingly, "the traditional level of permissiveness in a group" is a more general variable which ranged continuously from group traditions of low to high permissiveness. A tradition of permissiveness refers to shared permissive attitudes or beliefs which have existed in a group for at least two generations or more. The "social forces" examined in connection with this proposition were frequency of church attendance, romantic love beliefs, and number of times in love. Unfortunately, the term "social forces" is not a quantitative variable; that is, it does not vary from low to high, and it is also vague. These problems will be dealt with in the reformulation section.

The individual level of sexual permissiveness is the dependent variable in Proposition One; it is clearly a continuous variable ranging from low to high individual permissiveness. The concept of premarital sexual permis-

siveness refers to the degree of acceptance of various levels of physical intimacy in premarital heterosexual relationships (Reiss, 1964:189). This important dependent variable was operationalized using the Guttman scales developed by Reiss (1964) for this purpose. The scale is presented in Exhibit 1. Reiss (ch. 2) discusses a shorter version of the scale. The kissing questions can be eliminated for most groups today. Also one can change the term "full sexual relations" to "sexual intercourse." Finally one can personalize the scale further by having the question refer to "me" instead of "male" or "female." For a college age group one could simply use questions 10, 11, and 12. Once a Guttman scale is established, one need not continue to use all questions. Work on such alterations in the use of the scale is being done by Robert Walsh of Illinois State University. The interested reader can pursue some of the recent methodological discussion here in Delamater (1974) and Hampe and Ruppel (1974) as well as in Reiss (1967). Although the term "social forces" is too general, the intended relationships of the variables in this proposition are quite clear. They can be diagrammatically represented showing a causal relationship between social forces and individual permissiveness, with the traditional level of permissiveness in a group interacting with and inversely influencing this relationship. Because social forces could positively or inversely influence permissiveness, depending on the specific measure used (e.g., number of times in love and church attendance influence permissiveness in opposite directions), a single sign will not be attached to this bivariate relationship at this point. A revised statement of this proposition will be presented in the final section of Part One.

Figure 4.1 shows that the *traditional* level of premarital sexual permissiveness specifies conditions that affect the relationship between social forces and individual premarital sexual permissiveness. The reader should locate this proposition in Figure 4.2. All other propositions will be presented in this summary diagram. The symbol ↓S indicates that the specification is such that the lower ↓ the traditional level of PSP in a group, the stronger S the relationship is between social forces and individual premarital sexual permissiveness. For example, the relationship would be expected to be stronger in groups of whites than in groups of blacks. The place of Proposition One in terms of the total set of propositions can be seen in Figure 4.2. We will return to this proposition after we briefly clarify and diagram the remaining propositions.

Reiss's Proposition Two: The stronger the amount of general liberality in a group, the greater the likelihood that social forces will maintain high levels of sexual permissiveness [73].

In this proposition there are also three concepts. The concept of the amount of general liberality in a group was *indicated by a composite* of factors, but since this variable

Exhibit 1.   Reiss Male and Female Premarital Sexual Permissiveness Scales

First decide whether you agree or disagree with the view expressed. Then circle the degree of your agreement or disagreement with the views expressed in each question. We are not interested in your tolerance of other people's beliefs. Please answer these questions on the basis of how YOU feel toward the views expressed. Your name will never be connected with these answers. Please be as honest as you can. Thank you.

We use the words below to mean just what they do to most people but some may need definitions:

Love means the emotional state which is more intense than strong affection and which you would define as love.

Strong affection means affection which is stronger than physical attraction, average fondness, or "liking"—but less strong than love.

Petting means sexually stimulating behavior more intimate than kissing and simple hugging, but not including full sexual relations.

MALE STANDARDS (Both Men and Women Check This Section)

1. I believe that kissing is acceptable for the male before marriage when he is engaged to be married.

   Agree: 1) Strong,   2) Medium,   3) Slight
   Disagree: 1) Strong,   2) Medium,   3) Slight
2. I believe that kissing is acceptable for the male before marriage when he is in love. (The same six-way choice found in Question 1 follows every question)
3. I believe that kissing is acceptable for the male before marriage when he feels strong affection for his partner.
4. I believe that kissing is acceptable for the male before marriage even if he does not feel particularly affectionate toward his partner.
5. I believe that petting is acceptable for the male before marriage when he is engaged to be married.
6. I believe that petting is acceptable for the male before marriage when he is in love.
7. I believe that petting is acceptable for the male before marriage when he feels strong affection for his partner.
8. I believe that petting is acceptable for the male before marriage even if he does not feel particularly affectionate toward his partner.
9. I believe that full sexual relations are acceptable for the male before marriage when he is engaged to be married.
10. I believe that full sexual relations are acceptable for the male before marriage when he is in love.
11. I believe that full sexual relations are acceptable for the male before marriage when he feels strong affection for his partner.
12. I believe that full sexual relations are acceptable for the male before marriage even if he does not feel particularly affectionate toward his partner.

FEMALE STANDARDS (Both Men and Women Check This Section)

1. I believe that kissing is acceptable for the female before marriage when she is engaged to be married.
2. I believe that kissing is acceptable for the female before marriage when she is in love.
3. I believe that kissing is acceptable for the female before marriage when she feels strong affection for her partner.
4. I believe that kissing is acceptable for the female before marriage even if she does not feel particularly affectionate toward her partner.
5. I believe that petting is acceptable for the female before marriage when she is engaged to be married.
6. I believe that petting is acceptable for the female before marriage when she is in love.
7. I believe that petting is acceptable for the female before marriage when she feels strong affection for her partner.
8. I believe that petting is acceptable for the female before marriage even if she does not feel particularly affectionate toward her partner.
9. I believe that full sexual relations are acceptable for the female before marriage when she is engaged to be married.
10. I believe that full sexual relations are acceptable for the female before marriage when she is in love.
11. I believe that full sexual relations are acceptable for the female before marriage when she feels strong affection for her partner.
12. I believe that full sexual relations are acceptable for the female before marriage even if she does not feel particularly affectionate toward her partner.

SOURCE: Reiss 1967:211–14. For groups that are not very young or conservative one may wish to use only the higher permissive questions. For details on shorter versions see Reiss (1967, ch.2).

was not anticipated in the research there were no good, direct measures of it. It can be considered to be a continuous variable ranging from low to high group liberality. What was actually measured was the general liberality of a social setting; the liberality of individual attitudes was not assessed directly. We have discussed the term "social forces" in connection with Proposition One. The meaning and measurement of "sexual permissiveness" are

Figure 4.1.

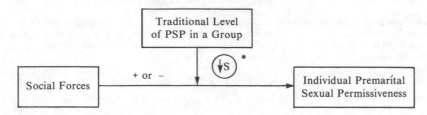

*See the conventions in the Appendix for full explanations of these and all other symbols.

clear and are the same in all propositions as in Proposition One (see Exhibit 1); it refers to the conditions of acceptance of premarital sexual behaviors as measured by the Guttman scale (the meaning and measurement of "permissiveness" will not be elaborated hereafter as they remain constant). The relation term "maintain" in Proposition Two is not as clear as it might be, and thus the term "promote" would be a better choice.

The proposition asserts that the greater the amount of general liberality in a group, the greater the likelihood that social forces will *promote* individual premarital sexual permissiveness. Here "general liberality" specifies the conditions which alter the relation of social forces to premarital sexual permissiveness. This is represented in Figure 4.2.

Reiss's Proposition Three: To the extent that individual ties to the marital and family institutions differ, individuals will tend to display a different type of sensitivity of permissiveness to social forces [89].

While this proposition also contains three concepts, the terms for two of these are similar to those in Propositions One and Two; only the term "ties to the marital and family institutions" is entirely new. However, the social forces concept, with the exception of "number of times in love," here refers to something different from what it did in Propositions One and Two. Proposition Three summarizes findings which relate various dating characteristics to permissiveness. Using the umbrella term "social forces" again gives little indication of what specifically is being related to permissiveness. Actually, it was found that dating characteristics affected individual permissiveness differently for males and females, and this was attributed to differential "ties to the marital and family institutions." It would seem that these "ties" could vary continuously from being quite strong to relatively weak.

Ties to marriage and the family could be assessed within and across genders by developing a scale that would ask individuals about their commitment to the institutions of marriage and the family. As it is stated, the proposition does not specify the different types of sen-

sitivity to expect when ties to marital and family institutions differ. There are no relational connectives between the concepts in Proposition Three, but they are assumed to be causal. Diagrammatically this proposition could only be represented without signs, simply asserting that the relationship between social forces and permissiveness is influenced by ties to marital and family institutions but not specifying the nature of these relationships. We will clarify and elaborate upon this proposition after the others have been presented. The reader can view this proposition in Figure 4.2.

Reiss's Proposition Four: The higher the overall level of permissiveness in a group, the greater the extent of equalitarianism within the abstinence and double-standard classifications [103].

This proposition breaks out of the set of the first three propositions which relate social forces to individual permissiveness. It summarizes a finding that was confined to part of the sample (those in two particular categories of a typology of premarital sexual standards, hence the limiting scope conditions, "within the abstinence and double-standard classifications." Also, only two concepts are related, both of which can be thought of as continuous variables. The operationalizations of "permissiveness in a group" included three dichotomous variables representing populations which the scale had shown to differ on permissiveness; these were gender (males more permissive than females); race (blacks more permissive than whites); and church attenders (low attenders more permissive than high attenders). Equalitarianism is the extent to which one approved of the same sexual activities for both sexes; i.e., acceptance of exactly the same level of sexual permissiveness for both sexes in high equalitarianism. It was found that within the double standard and abstinence classifications, individuals who were more equalitarian tended to be members of more permissive groups or populations (males, blacks, non-church attenders). Although the "the higher . . . the greater" format might mean either covariation or causality, the latter was intended in this case. Basically, the

Figure 4.2. Summary Diagram of Reiss's 1967 Propositions

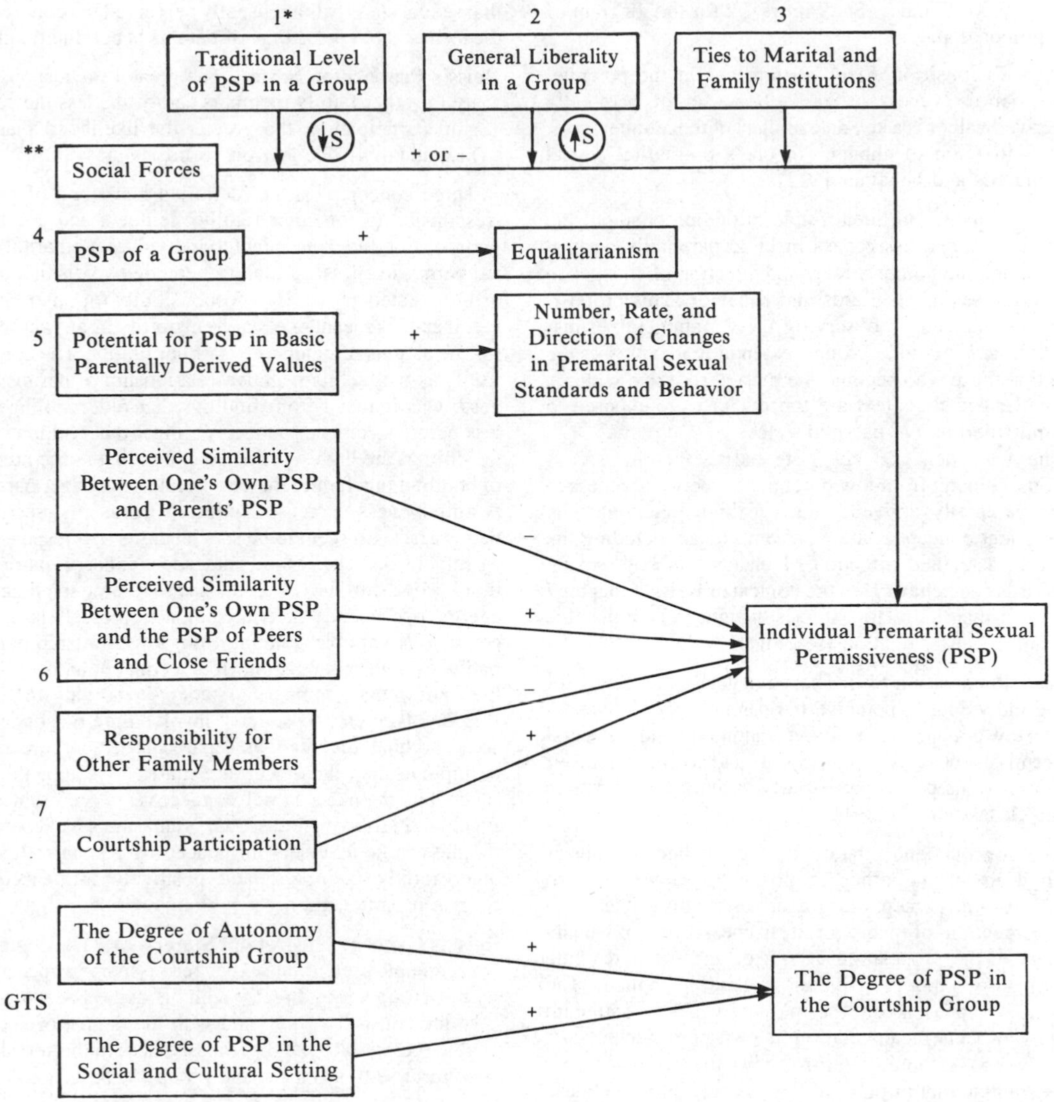

*The numbers identify the proposition being illustrated.

**As presented initially, social forces could influence permissiveness in either positive or negative directions, depending on the specific operationalization used.

proposition asserts that within abstinence and double-standard classifications, the permissiveness of one's membership groups influences the individual's equalitarianism in a positive direction. The proposition applies to abstinence and double standards because these are the two standards within which equalitarianism has

considerable room to vary. For example, in the abstinence category one may accept abstinence from coitus but feel only males have the right to pet and females can only kiss, while others feel both male and female can pet. Further, within the double-standard category one may accept the double standard and feel females can have intercourse when in love but males can copulate anytime. Such a position is more equalitarian than one which always rules out coitus for females. See Figure 4.2 for the diagram of this proposition.

Reiss's Proposition Five: Differences in the potential for permissiveness in one's basic set of parentally derived values is a key determinant of the number, rate, and direction of changes in one's premarital sexual standards and behavior [122].

Two concepts are identifiable in this proposition: the potential for permissiveness in basic parentally derived values, and the number, rate, and direction of changes in premarital sexual standards and behavior. This proposition was induced by observing the variation in permissiveness *within* similar groups; essentially it expresses the idea that those who become the most permissive within a particular social context are those who were exposed to the most permissive parental values.

The antecedent concept (potential) is viewed as continuous, ranging from low potential for permissiveness in basic parentally derived values to high potential. The consequent concept contains several ideas including the number, rate, and direction of changes in both sexual standards and behavior. In the context of Reiss's chapter 7 it is clear that the relationship is thought to be a positive one and a causal relation (see Figure 4.2).

Reiss's Proposition Six: There is a general tendency for the individual to perceive his parents' permissiveness as a low point on a permissive continuum and his peers' permissiveness as a high point, and to place himself closer to his peers, particularly to those he regards as his close friends [139].

The concepts and relationships stated here are not as explicit as in the other propositions. However, two concepts—the perception of parental permissiveness and the perception of peer permissiveness—are obviously present in the proposition as stated, and the perceiving person's own permissiveness is clearly implied. The placing of oneself on the permissiveness continuum closest to peers means that one's own permissiveness is perceived to be more *similar to* or *like* the permissiveness of peers than that of parents. To meaningfully link these concepts to the dependent variable of premarital sexual permissiveness (PSP) requires their reformulation from just the perceptions of parental and peer permissiveness to perceptions of *similarity* between individual and parental and peer permissiveness. Actually, this is what the original proposition was intended to represent. The survey questionnaire assessed perceived similarity between individual permissiveness and that of parents, peers, and close friends. The findings indicated that the amount of similarity to parental standards inversely influences individual permissiveness. Conversely, the amount of similarity to peer standards influences individual permissive-

ness in a positive direction. These relationships are depicted in Figure 4.2, although the descriptive information that sexual standards are usually perceived to be more like the standards of peers than of parents is not diagrammed.

Reiss's Proposition Seven: The greater the responsibility for other family members and/or the less the courtship participation, the greater the likelihood that the individual will be low on permissiveness [156].

Three concepts can be identified here, two of which (responsibility for other family members and courtship participation) are antecedent to individual premarital sexual permissiveness. Actually, there are two distinct propositions stated above. By "responsibility for other family members" is meant one's accountability or answerability for the actions of others in his or her family. The concept itself, as well as its negative relationship to permissiveness, was induced from findings that older siblings are less permissive than younger siblings, that children with no siblings are highly permissive, and that as the number of children in a family increases and as they age, parental permissiveness decreases (inferred from cross-sectional data). These all seem to be special cases of a responsibility dimension. The second antecedent concept, participation in courtship, is a concept used to refer to the time and energy one spends in courtship activities. It is also a continuous variable, ranging from low courtship participation to high participation. It is a concept induced from the finding that, comparing students who vary in courtship involvement, those most involved are most permissive and that divorced or separated persons are more permissive than those who are married. Again, the unstated but intended causal connective is represented in Figure 4.2, showing individual premarital sexual permissiveness to be inversely influenced by responsibility for other family members, and positively influenced by courtship participation.

Reiss's General Theoretical Statement: The degree of acceptable premarital sexual permissiveness in a courtship group varies directly with the degree of autonomy of the courtship group and with the degree of acceptable premarital sexual permissiveness in the social and cultural setting outside the group [167].

After the seven basic propositions were presented in the 1967 book, another chapter was written to summarize the propositions and unite them in a general theory. The theoretical statement above is the culmination of that effort. Given the early stage of research and theory in sexual permissiveness, it was too much to expect a fully developed theory with the interrelations all spelled out; consequently, the logical relationships of the seven propositions to this general statement were not developed. This will be examined further on in this chapter.

The dependent variable in the general theoretical statement is the degree of acceptable premarital sexual permissiveness in a courtship *group,* which "varies directly with" its autonomy and the degree of acceptance of permissiveness in the social and cultural setting outside the group. Both the permissiveness in the social and cultural setting and the courtship group's autonomy are considered to be antecedents to group permissiveness. Although the relational connective used was covariational, causality was intended. Both causal influences are represented in Figure 4.2, where the original propositions are all summarized diagrammatically. It should be noted that Propositions Four and Five and the general theoretical statement (GTS) have dependent variables which are different from individual premarital sexual permissiveness. Also, remember that Proposition Six did not initially identify a relationship between variables, but this was inferred. The value of diagramming is in part precisely this pressure toward clarification and explicit statements of relationships.

ASSESSING RESEARCH ON THE SPECIFIC PROPOSITIONS

Here it should be reiterated that the propositions were formulated to account for patterns in Reiss's data. The findings from which the propositions just reviewed were generated were based on several samples (Reiss, 1967, ch.1). Briefly, there were five student samples included which were chosen to represent the high school or college from which they were drawn. A national sample of 1,500 adults chosen (by the National Opinion Research Center) to be representative of the United States was also included. A sixth, nonrepresentative student sample was later added but only for special checks (Reiss, 1967, ch.7). The analyses were primarily cross-tabulations or contingency table analyses (Lazarsfeld, 1955), with special attention paid to higher than first-order relationships.

Taking Reiss's 1967 empirical findings as a base, this section is devoted to a consideration of the relevant evidence collected by others. Zetterberg (1965) contended that while taxonomies would summarize and inspire descriptive studies, theories composed of interrelated propositions would inspire verificational studies. A number of studies with the stated purpose of testing the initial propositions have appeared in the literature, while numerous other investigators have used the permissiveness scales or referred extensively to the 1967 work while developing the justification for their own hypotheses. In addition, there are researches which do not intend to test Reiss's work but which provide relevant evidence for evaluating whether or not his theoretical explanations fit observations other than his own.

In this section each proposition will again be considered sequentially, and key research that bears on that proposition will be presented. Propositions One, Two, Six, and Seven have each been tested several times.

Propositions Three, Four, and Five have received very little explicit attention, and it seems that this may be at least partly because they were less clearly stated. In evaluating each piece of research we will indicate the nature and size of the sample, and how the concepts were operationalized. The meaning of each cluster of studies pertaining to a proposition will be summarized before considering the evidence for the next proposition.

Reiss's Proposition One: The lower the traditional level of sexual permissiveness in a group, the greater the likelihood that social forces will alter individual levels of sexual permissiveness [51].

Heltsley and Broderick (1969) were probably the first to explicitly test any of Reiss's propositions. Choosing religiosity as the social force of interest, they changed the first proposition to read:

The lower the level of premarital sexual permissiveness in a group, the greater the likelihood that religiosity would alter the level of sexual permissiveness [144].

They interpreted Proposition One to say that groups can be considered traditionally more or less permissive, and the influence of religiosity on permissiveness is either reinforced or counteracted by the traditional permissiveness of the group. They used Reiss's permissiveness scale and Bardis's religion scale with a sample of 1,435 college students who were largely single, female, white, Protestant, middle-class southerners. When black and white racial groups were used to operationalize high and low traditions of permissiveness respectively, their hypothesis following Reiss's Proposition One was supported; religiosity and permissiveness were negatively related for whites but not for blacks. However, when using a male-female comparison to operationalize high and low traditions of permissiveness, the data did not show the predicted difference; for both genders the negative relationship between religiosity and permissiveness was equally strong and significant. Heltsley and Broderick admitted that their "more permissive" groups were not as permissive as those in Reiss's samples, and they also cautioned that the Bardis religion scale may measure something different than is reflected by church attendance. They concluded that a simpler proposition might be

that when sexual abstinence is emphasized by a church, religiosity will be related to sexual permissiveness; but when it is not stressed, the two will be unrelated [1969:443].

Reiss (1969) responded to the Heltsley-Broderick article in part by pointing out the inadequacy of their sample. In particular he noted that any retest should be conducted on a sample with a wide range of variation in the contextual variable (the traditional level of sexual permissiveness). It was pointed out that this retest sample was 85 percent white, 90 percent highly religious, and drawn from family relations classes which usually do not attract representative males or blacks. Reiss also stressed that the first proposition was based on several related findings, and not just the relationship of religiosity to permissiveness; the relationship between the other social forces (number of times in love, romantic love beliefs) and permissiveness was also affected by the traditional levels of permissiveness. In short, Reiss felt that their retest was not conclusive.

By using a probability sample (N = 383) and a different instrument to measure religiosity, Ruppel (1970) attempted to clear up some of the questions remaining after the Heltsley-Broderick retest of Proposition One. He employed Faulkner and DeJong's 5-D Scale of Religiosity, Reiss's scale to measure permissiveness, and the following measures of the tradition of permissiveness: gender (male and female); academic class (senior and freshman); father's social class (blue collar and white collar); and three types of religious affiliation (liberal, moderate, and conservative). The zero-order relationship between religiosity and permissiveness was found to be negative, as expected. Proposition One predicts that social factors (like religiosity) will have more effect on the permissiveness of individuals who are members of groups which are traditionally less permissive, for example, females compared with males. However, when controlling for the contingency variables, Ruppel found no difference in the relationship of religiosity to permissiveness between males and females or the other groups thought to have different traditions of permissiveness. The results on gender differences coincide with those of Heltsley and Broderick and fail to support Proposition One. Ruppel pointed out the multidimensionality of the religiosity measure he used, which he felt was superior to tapping only a single component like church attendance. All five dimensions of the 5-D religiosity scale correlate negatively with permissiveness, but the ritual dimension (church attendance) relationship is of only moderate strength.

The first proposition might still be defended in spite of Ruppel's study by pointing out the homogeneity of his sample. While it was a probability sample, there was no information given about its racial composition, and presumably there was not much racial variability. It should also be noted that comparing seniors and freshmen and different social classes does not get at what was meant by *traditions* of permissiveness. In Reiss's own and the Heltsley-Broderick study, Proposition One was supported when blacks and whites were compared as representatives of different traditions of permissiveness. However, it still remains that the gender dichotomy did not support the proposition in either the Heltsley-Broderick or Ruppel retests.

Staples (1971) studied 429 college students from two universities in Florida and one in California. The sample was about equally divided by gender and race (blacks and whites). Religiosity was considered to be reflected by church attendance, and permissiveness was assessed with Reiss's scale. In accordance with Proposition One, Staples found religiosity inversely related to permissiveness for whties but not for blacks; similarly, the relationship was stronger for females than males, but only in the white racial group. Another social force, romantic love beliefs, was found to be unrelated to permissiveness. However, testing the relationship to permissiveness of still another social force, Staples found that the number of times in love was positively associated with permissiveness among white females, less strongly among white males, and not at all among blacks. These results generally support Proposition One.

Harrison et al. (1969) found that both blacks (N = 49) and whites (N = 83) in their Mississippi high school sample were more permissive than Reiss's Virginia high school sample had been. Using Reiss's Guttman scale to measure permissiveness, they found that 70 percent of white males and 16 percent of white females accepted full sex relations before marriage; among blacks, 74 percent of the males and 64 percent of the females approved of premarital coitus. The basic relationship, that religiosity inversely influences permissiveness, was found, but contrary to the first proposition (and the Reiss, Heltsley-Broderick, and Staples data), this relationship was *not* stronger for whites than blacks. In this sample religious involvement (operationalized as religious membership, attendance, and leadership positions) decreased permissiveness for *both* races. However, in accordance with Proposition One, the number of times a student had gone steady positively influenced permissiveness for whites but not for blacks. This is an example, in line with Proposition One, of a different "social force" (the number of times one has gone steady, instead of religiosity) having a greater influence on members of groups which are traditionally less permissive.

Libby's (1974) dissertation focused explicitly on Reiss's Propositions Six and Seven, but also included data relevant to Proposition One. In his sample of 421 undergraduate college students, he found a strong inverse relationship between frequency of church attendance and individual permissiveness, and the strength of this relationship was virtually the same for males and females. In other words, gender differences in traditions of permissiveness appeared to have no effect on the relation of church attendance and individual premarital sexual permissiveness.

Clayton (1969) reviewed a number of articles and concluded that religiosity "exerts a restraining influence" on premarital sex values and behavior. He noted that three operationalizations of religiosity have often been used: (1) church attendance, (2) denominational affiliation, and (3) the importance one attaches to religion. He asserted that there are problems with these operationalizations in that they do not tap ideological commitment. Using a Likert-type scale to assess religiosity in a sample of 887 Florida undergraduates, he hypothesized that the ideologically more orthodox would be less likely to engage in premarital intercourse than the ideologically less orthodox. Clayton noted that for any individual both religiosity and sexual behavior can fluctuate during one's lifetime; since he was measuring current religiosity, he also limited the measure of sexual behavior to coitus within the preceding year. He found rates of premarital coitus of 42 percent for the males and 22 percent for females. It was found that religious orthodoxy does negatively influence premarital coitus generally, but not for members of fraternities and sororities. For "Greeks" in his sample, orthodoxy did not operate to restrain premarital sex. Thus if Greeks and non-Greeks are considered to be groups with permissiveness traditions which are respectively high and low, then Reiss's Proposition One is supported. However, this interpretation hardly seems justified, since among females the nonsorority girls were actually more permissive than sorority members.

In summary, there are a number of studies which report a strong inverse relationship between religiosity and premarital sexual permissiveness (see Hunter, 1971, and Vandiver, 1972) and a very few which consider other social forces such as the number of times in love, romantic love beliefs, etc. However, only a few of these studies actually compare groups with different traditions of permissiveness, and this is essential to the meaning of Reiss's first proposition. The Heltsley-Broderick, Ruppel, Staples, Harrison et al., and Libby studies are clearly important in evaluating Proposition One against research, but their findings often disagree with each other, and certainly none of them are decisive. Looking at Table 4.1 we see that at times a social force which significantly

influences permissiveness differently by race and sex groups in one study fails to do so in another. The samples of some of these studies can be criticized for not having adequate variation, particularly among males and blacks. The Harrison sample included more permissive subjects, but it was quite small. In a national sample of 4,600 girls between the ages of 15 and 19, Zelnik and Kantner (1972, 1974) reported racial differences in permissiveness which are in line with Proposition One, namely that premarital sexual behavior of black girls was less dramatically affected by religiosity than was the premarital sexual behavior of white girls. These recent data add support from a national sample and are thus important. However, it should be noted that this study was dealing with behavior and not attitudes.

It appears that the predicted racial comparison holds up quite well. However, how should one decide on the validity of Proposition One if some social forces show the predicted relationships while others do not? That the vagueness of the social forces concept makes Proposition One problematic should be evident. Using a term as general as "social forces" makes a theoretical statement difficult to falsify because it has such a wide array of possible meanings. By now it should be clear that we will delimit the meaning of "social forces" in our reformulation.

Another kind of evidence, which could be called trend research, might also be taken into account in evaluating the first proposition. Reiss (1967:53) has suggested that:

Proposition One implies a strong tendency toward long-range, unidirectional change. Once a group becomes highly permissive and stays that way long enough to become traditionally so, then it becomes quite difficult for social forces to reduce that permissiveness. On the other hand a group with a tradition of low permissiveness can be altered either way. Since such a

Table 4.1. Key Studies* Pertaining to Reiss's Proposition One

AUTHOR AND YEAR	SOCIAL FORCE MEASURE	EXPECTED DIFFERENCE OBSERVED IN CONTRASTING TRADITIONS OF PSP	
		Gender	*Race*
Heltsley-Broderick (1969)	Bardis religion scale	no	yes
Ruppel (1970)	Faulkner and DeJong's 5-D scale of religiosity	no	
Staples (1971)	Church attendance	yes (whites only)	yes
	Number of times in love	yes	yes
Harrison et al. (1969)	Composite of church membership, attendance, leadership		no
	Number of times gone steady		yes
Libby (1974)	Church attendance	no (whites only)	yes
Zelnik and Kantner (1974)	Church attendance		yes

*All of these studies except the last used Reiss's scale to measure premarital sexual permissiveness.

group is already low on permissiveness, there is little room to move down, and there is a good chance of increasing the traditional level of permissiveness. The implications are that often it should be possible to find in history a long-range trend in any society toward increased permissiveness.

One might interpret any long-range unidirectional increase in sexual permissiveness as support for Proposition One. However, it would seem to support Proposition One more clearly if we could discover that there has been little increase over time in the permissiveness of groups which have traditions of high permissiveness, but relatively much greater increases in the groups with low traditions of permissiveness. Given our operational definitions of traditions of permissiveness, i.e., that they have existed for at least two generations (e.g., males and females having high and low traditions respectively), there are several recent trend reports which are relevant.

Robinson, King, Dudley, and Clune (1968) assessed both premarital sexual attitudes and premarital sexual behavior of 244 college students (129 male, 175 female) at the University of Georgia, using questions that Kinsey (1948) used about 20 years earlier. As Kinsey had found, males had much more sex experience than females, but there were no major changes over time observed in rates of actual petting or coital experience. Robinson et al. found rates of premarital coitus for males and females respectively at 65.1 percent and 28.7 percent in their sample. Attitudinally, both males and females still maintained the double standard. While the authors concluded that sex behavior has remained stable over time, they interpreted their data to show an attitudinal trend away from community and religious concern with sexual behavior, toward a person locus of sexual morality. Essentially, they asserted that sex behavior had not changed, but that attitudes had changed toward more open personal sex codes and away from the Judeo-Christian ''sinful'' connotation. The reader will recall that our focus in this chapter is upon sexual attitude even though behavior is closely related to such attitudes (Reiss, 1967, ch. 7).

In 1968 Christensen and Gregg (1970) used the same instrument they had used in 1958 to replicate their earlier study of the sex norms and behavior of university students in Denmark, Indiana, and Utah. The three cultures which comprised the sample thus ranged on a continuum from most to least permissive respectively. In each culture it was found that while sex attitudes concerning premarital intercourse had liberalized considerably during the 1958–68 decade (especially among females), actual coital behavior had increased more slowly (for American males, not at all). Tying back to Proposition One, the salient point is that the greatest increases in permissiveness were found among females, the gender with the lower tradition of permissiveness.

Bell and Chaskes (1970) replicated a coed sexual behavior study done in 1958. The two studies were conducted at the same university using the same instru-

ment on closely matched female samples of sizes 250 and 205. The general hypothesis was that significant changes have been occurring in the premarital sexual experience of college coeds since the mid-1960s. The trend between 1958 and 1968 is reflected in these figures: for dating, steady, and engagement relationships respectively, the percent of coeds having premarital coitus increased from 10 to 23 percent, 15 to 28 percent, and 31 to 39 percent. The 1968 coeds were more likely to have had intercourse, and the relative importance of engagement as a precondition seemed to be diminishing. There were no comparative data for males. These authors then reported a dramatic increase in female permissiveness. This also fits Reiss's predictions.

Robinson, King, and Balswick (1972), whose mid-1960s permissiveness data revealed no change since the Kinsey reports, compared data gathered in 1968 to see if there had been a more recent sexual behavior and attitude change among college students. Their results coincide closely with Bell and Chaskes (1970), showing a dramatic increase in rates of premarital coitus and petting, and liberalization of attitudes among females. Among males, premarital coitus had not changed, petting behavior had fluctuated only slightly, and there was even a hint that attitudinally males may be becoming more conservative, possibly in reaction to female sexual liberalization. In summary, the two studies by Robinson and colleagues (1968, 1972) and those by Christensen and Gregg (1970) and Bell and Chaskes (1970) all indicate that the permissiveness of the traditionally less permissive gender (female) is increasing much more rapidly than it is among males, and this fits with Proposition One.

The most wide-ranging statement about recent trends of premarital sexual permissiveness is an overview article by Cannon and Long (1971) which reviews previous research. In their introduction they make this summarizing statement:

> The evidence is that a substantial increase has taken place in the proportion of girls who indicate they have had premarital coitus. Studies comparing similar groups utilizing the same questionnaires show a substantial increase in female approval of premarital coitus and experience therewith [36].

Looking back to the turn of the century and considering sexual behavior since then, they noted that Ehrmann (1964) suggested that premarital coitus increased substantially for both men and women, but particularly for women. After citing a large number of studies conducted in the decade of the 1960s, they reported that there has been a definite recent shift toward increased permissiveness:

> Apparently, there is not a single major study that has been made in the late sixties that has found premarital coital rates that were the level of those found in the late 1950's and early 1960's [40].

Taking these trend reports all together, two general conclusions seem to be justified:

    1. In the United States premarital sexual behavior (and approval of the same) has increased significantly since the turn of the century among both sexes.

    2. Relatively speaking, the increase in female sexual behavior and sexual permissiveness has been much greater than that of males, particularly in the recent decade.

These two conclusions seem to be what the first proposition implies. The trend literature reviewed does seem to support an implication of Proposition One, namely, that over an extended period permissiveness will increase more in groups which have been traditionally less permissive. It would be interesting and meaningful for evaluating Proposition One if we also had trend data on racial differences in permissiveness. The prediction would be that permissiveness should have increased more among whites than among blacks. Changes in the illegitimacy rates for whites and blacks since 1960 would support this prediction (U.S. Department of Health, Education and Welfare, 1975). Also the recent 1976 study by Zelnik and Kantner when compared to their 1971 study shows a much larger increase in sexual behavior by white females as compared to black females (Zelnik and Kantner, 1977).

Reiss's Proposition Two: The stronger the amount of general liberality in a group, the greater the likelihood that social forces will maintain high levels of sexual permissiveness [73].

In the fourth chapter of *The Social Context of Premarital Sexual Permissiveness* findings were reported relating social class to permissiveness, and at the end of that chapter, Proposition Two was formulated, which included the concepts of general liberality, social *forces,* and individual permissiveness. Several subsequent research studies have tested the relationship between social class and permissiveness as it is influenced by either individual liberality or a generally liberal setting. Although the social class–permissiveness relationship was not all that was originally intended in Proposition Two, the social class evidence will be reviewed here.

Vandiver (1972) used Reiss's premissiveness scale to study 300 college students at Sourthern Illinois University. Since his primary emphasis was on reference groups, his work is most applicable to Proposition Six. However, he also examined the relationship between five separate dimensions of "general ideology" and permissiveness. Unfortunately, he did not usually report how the relationship between social class and permissiveness was influenced by ideology; instead he emphasized the bivariate relationships between these ideological variables and permissiveness. It is relevant to Proposition Two, though, that he reports tolerance (of drugs, youth culture, etc.), as

a component of general ideology, to be a very useful predictor of permissiveness *regardless* of social class. Vandiver's finding that "tolerance" is strongly related to premarital sexual permissiveness seems to fit the "liberality" idea in Proposition Two. Vandiver's dissertation will be referred to more extensively as evidence relevant to Proposition Six.

In an explicit retest of Proposition Two, Maranell, Dodder, and Mitchell (1970:85) pointed out that Reiss had classified persons as generally liberal if they were from liberal settings or cultural backgrounds, whereas "being a liberal or conservative person and being in a liberal or conservative setting are somewhat independent characteristics." Therefore, they measured the contingency variable, each individual's liberalism-conservatism, with idealism, academic orientation, authoritarianism, and religious fundamentalism scales, while retaining Reiss's permissiveness scale for the dependent variable. The independent variable, social class, was operationalized as father's occupation. The sample of sociology students (N = 437; 39 percent male and 61 percent female) was quite homogeneous with regard to social class. As Reiss found, there was no relationship between social class and permissiveness at the zero order, but contrary to Reiss's data, this did not change with the introduction of liberalism as an interacting variable. Rather than advancing their findings over Reiss's, the authors offered the caveat that their homogenous sample might restrict the range of variation in the variables and thus obscure their relationships. This study supported the empirical generalizations that (1) there is no zero-order relationship between social class and permissiveness, and (2) males are much more permissive than females. It can be noted that both the Vandiver and Maranell, *et al.* studies operationalized the liberality variable by measuring individual attitudes, whereas Reiss compared liberal settings, seeking to show a contextual effect of the social system.

Middendorp, Brinkman, and Koomen (1970) conducted a test of Reiss's Proposition Two which was unique in several ways. The authors were all located in the Netherlands, and they used previously collected Netherlands data to provide a secondary analysis of Reiss's second proposition. The 1,704 subjects varied in age from 17 to 70, and thus differed widely from the younger subjects of other samples except Reiss's national adult sample. The concept "general liberality" was operationalized as the degree of acceptance of six items reflecting unconventional marriage and family norms. Premarital sexual permissiveness was measured by responses to three items (not from the Reiss scale), and social class was a composite of education, occupation, and income. Reiss's data showed a positive relationship between social class and permissiveness among liberals, and a negative relationship between social class and permissiveness among conservatives. However, dichotomizing the sample into liberals and conservatives, these researchers still found no relationship between social class and permissiveness. Not finding the realtionship predicted by Proposition Two, the Netherlands authors searched for other important independent variables. They found that religious affiliation (Roman Catholic, Dutch Reformed, Reformed, and no religion) and age (17 to 35, young; 36 to 70, old) explained much more variation in permissiveness than other factors.

Reiss (1970) criticized the Middendorp et al. study because of (1) the inadequate measurement of the dependent and control variables, (2) its misinterpretation and confusion of Propositions One and Two, and (3) its announcement of religion and age as some primary determinants of permissiveness without sufficient reference to earlier studies which had found the same thing. Proposition Two was basically not supported, but the comparability of the Middendorp et al. study to Reiss (1967) is highly questionable. The importance of age and religion and the absence of a relationship between social class and permissiveness were reasserted.

Staples's (1971) research was cited earlier in connection with Proposition One. He also tested the relationship between social class and permissiveness while controlling for the level of liberality. He found that ther was "no significant relationship between social class and permissiveness in either a liberal or conservative setting" (1971:47). This did not fit with Reiss's findings.

Hunter's (1971) study of students attending an ex-

tremely conservative and very homogeneous church college also tested the relationship between social class and permissiveness while controlling for sociopolitical attitudes, but the tendency he observed was not significant. Again, in this sample the variability in most variables was very low, and this was probably especially true for liberality. Hunter noted that his total sample was very conservative, and so he was actually comparing two groups, both of whom were probably below average on liberalism.

Further evidence for the absence of any relationship between social class and premarital sexual permissiveness comes from a national sample of adults studied in 1970 by the Institute for Sex Research under grant by the National Institute of Mental Health to Albert Klassen and Eugene Levitt (1972, and Levitt and Klassen, 1974). These data also show no significant class differences in sexual permissiveness, which is in agreement with what Reiss had reported in 1967. Further, there were in this 1970 sample sharp differences in permissiveness within social classes which appear to be related to liberality in nonsexual spheres (Reiss, 1973), and this is in accordance with Proposition Two. It is worth stressing here that this finding comes from a representative national sample. For a recent national study partially related to Proposition Two see Bayer (1977). Bayer gives only partial support to this proposition.

In summary, as can be seen in Table 4.2, almost all studies agree that there is no consistent zero-order rela-

Table 4.2. Key Studies Pertaining to Reiss's Proposition Two

AUTHOR AND YEAR	SOCIAL FORCE MEASUREMENT	LIBERALITY MEASUREMENT	RESULTS
Maranell et al. (1970)	Father's occupation	Individual attitudes; composite of idealism, academic orientation, authoritarianism, and religious fundamentalism	No relationship between SES and PSP regardless of level of liberality
*Middendorp et al. (1970)	Composite of education, occupation, and income	Individual attitudes; six items reflecting unconventional marriage and family norms	No relationship between SES and PSP regardless of level of liberality
Hunter (1971)	Hollingshead's Index of Social Position	Individual attitudes; social-political	Nonsignificant tendency in opposite direction
Staples (1971)	Hodge et al. occupational scale (applied to students' fathers)	Kerlinger's social attitudes scale	No relationship between SES and PSP regardless of level of liberality
Vandiver (1972)	Social class not measured	Individual attitudes; tolerance of drugs, youth culture, etc.	Strong bivariate relationship between general attitude of liberality and PSP
*Klassen and Levitt (1972)	Father's occupation	Church attendance	No relationship between SES and PSP and found the predicted relationship when church attendance was controlled
*Bayer (1977)	Parental income and education	Political liberalism	Weak relation between SES and PSP. Relation alters as predicted only when using mother's education to measure SES

*Did not use Reiss's scale to measure permissiveness.

tionship between social class and premarital sexual permissiveness, even when the former is operationalized in a variety of ways. (See also the national college study by Simon, Berger, and Gagnon, 1972). Banwart (1973), summarizing the literature about the lack of a relationship between social class and the acceptance of premarital intercourse, notes that the manner in which social class has been measured has made virtually no difference. He also points out that Reiss's permissiveness scales have been widely accepted as valid instruments. For further discussion of Kinsey's findings, see Reiss (1967, ch.4).

The variable in Proposition Two which has been the most problematic is liberality. (See Reiss, 1967:61–62, for a definition of liberality.) It had not been planned to use this variable in Reiss's initial research, and so it was not measured as an attitude or characteristic in the survey schedules; instead, it was asserted that liberal "settings" strengthen the relation of social forces to permissiveness. More careful measures, attitudinal measures at least, of liberality have subsequently been used, but usually with samples from only one university. The evidence is very inconclusive because six of the studies cited used attitudinal measure of liberality, whereas Proposition Two was based on a contextual influence. It would be most helpful to know which of the many kinds of liberality influence the relationship between social class and permissiveness. Vandiver's (1972) study was the only study reviewed showing a strong relationship between attitude liberality (tolerance) and premarital sexual permissiveness. Reiss (1967) had also reported a positive relationship between liberality and permissiveness. The contextual influence of a liberal setting appears to have been largely unexamined since Reiss's work in 1967. It must also be reiterated that Propositon Two related social *forces* to permissiveness, with contextual liberality as the contingency variable. In essence, the effects on permissiveness of many factors besides social class were theorized to differ depending on the level of liberality; but these implications have gone almost unexamined because of the attention given to the interesting social class relationship. Reiss believes that this lack of an inverse relationship between social class and permissiveness is largely due to a twentieth-century increase in premarital sexual permissiveness in the upper one-third of the social class hierarchy (Reiss, 1967, ch. 4). In fact we may today be in a situation wherein the upper one third of our social classes are the most permissive segment. This seems to be the situation today in countries like Sweden (Reiss, 1978).

Reiss's Proposition Three: To the extent that individual ties to the marital and family institutions differ, individuals will tend to display a different type of sensitivity of permissiveness to social forces [89].

There have been no explicit tests of this proposition that we are aware of. It appears that an ambiguously stated proposition does not stimulate additional research as readily as clearer ones. Reiss (76) wrote that Proposition Three

> basically asserted that the different courtship roles of males and females in American society made them sensitive to different social factors or to the same social factors in different ways.

Many checks on male-female differences such as in the role of affection have been made; but the tying up of such findings with differences in the priority of marriage roles has not been done. Since no researcher has attempted to fully test this proposition to our knowledge, we will not present any evidence which appears to be relevant to it until after it has been reformulated in the final section of Part One.

Reiss's Proposition Four: The higher the overall level of permissiveness in a group, the greater the extent of equalitarianism within the abstinence and double-standard classifications [103].

This is another of the original propositions in which other investigators have shown little interest. Perhaps it is because this proposition is limited to abstinence and double-standard individuals that subsequent research has been very rare. Part of the reason might be that equalitarianism is stated as the dependent variable. Whatever the reasons, there is only one piece of research that we are aware of which has the stated purpose of testing Proposition Four.

Hunter's (1971) study has already been referred to. The midwestern college from which this sample was drawn does not allow drinking, smoking, dancing, or card playing, so it is not surprising that his first set of hypotheses, suggesting that his students would show less variability and be less permissive than other college students, was supported. He also found the students in his sample to be even less permissive than adults generally when compared with Reiss's adult sample. Given the conservative nature of Hunter's sample (there were many double-standard and abstinence adherents), he was in a position to check Proposition Four. Contrary to the proposition, he found that among abstinence adherents, equalitarianism was lower for males (the more permissive group) than females (the less permissive group). Hunter (1971:93) concluded that his findings opposed Reiss's as follows:

> As far as Proposition Four is concerned, then, we must disagree with Reiss. Equalitarianism seems to be accompanied by low permissiveness in the religious subculture of the church related college.

Proposition Four applies only to double-standard and abstinence adherents, and equalitarianism (rather than individual permissiveness) is the dependent variable. Obviously, there is little evidence either disconfirming or confirming Proposition Four, and it appears to be much in need of further refinement and testing. It would be well to use two different groups with distinctively different permissiveness levels to test this proposition.

Reiss's Proposition Five: Differences in the potential for permissiveness in one's basic set of parentally derived values is a key determinant of the number rate and direction of changes in one's premarital sexual standards and behavior [122].

Again, we can find no intentional tests of this proposition. The justification for Proposition Five is that as early as age 10 males and females accept different standards of sexual permissiveness, and even within gender groups, especially females, there is considerable variation in what standard (kissing, petting, coitus) is personally accepted (Reiss, 1967, ch. 7). Different amounts of guilt experienced among holders of the same standard were considered to be a reflection of differences in basic values. In Reiss's (1967) Iowa College Sample it was also observed that some individuals moved much faster than others from less to more permissive sexual standards. All of these findings were indications that while other factors might appear to more directly influence permissiveness as one matures, often accepting more permissive personal standards is the actualization of a potential for permissiveness in one's basic parentally derived values. Hopefully, the reformulation in the final section of Part One will make this proposition clearer and more easily tested.

Reiss's Proposition Six: There is a general tendency for the individual to perceive his parents' permissiveness as a low point on a permissive continuum and his peers' permissiveness as a high point, and to place himself closer to his peers, particularly to those he regards as his close friends [139].

It almost seems too obvious to say that parents serve as a primary reference group from birth through early childhood, but that from childhood on, peers become increasingly important until by late adolescence the peer group typically exerts a very significant influence over the individual. Testing this notion, Bowerman and Kinch (1959) found that while peer orientation increases from fourth through tenth grades, family orientation decreases. They noted, though, that it is important to differentiate between different measures of "orientation" (e.g., desire to associate with vs. acceptance of values). Still, their basic finding is that as reference groups in these intermediate school years, peers increase in importance, and the family orientation decreases. Newcomb (1958) found that as college students moved from freshman to senior year, the college community became an increasingly important reference group for their political attitudes. We hasten to add that parents do not become *unimportant* in influencing the attitudes of their older children; we are only pointing out that the relative

influence of peers appears to increase. The relative influence of a group also may well depend on what issues are involved (see Brittain, 1959, and Miller, 1973).

A number of researches directly bearing on Proposition Six will not be reported. The first two studies follow Reiss's earlier work quite closely; they are concerned with comparing perceptions of parental and peer permissiveness on a continuum, and with respondents' judgments of the closeness or *similarity* between what they perceive their own, their peers', and their parents' permissiveness to be. This information is largely descriptive. The studies reviewed after the first two focus more explicitly on the effects of perceived parental and peer permissiveness on one's own sexual permissiveness. These studies examine relationships between perceptions of reference group permissiveness and the perceiver's own permissiveness and assert causal or covariational relationships.

Glass (1972) studied reference group orientations of 280 high school–age church youth leaders to determine how they compared their own sexual standards to those of their parents, peers, and close friends. Using Reiss's typology of standards (1960:251), he found that males would permit more sexual intimacy than females and that most of the church youth leaders viewed themselves in the "petting with affection" category. The reference group information of interest is that "own standards" were considered most *similar to* close friends' (93.6 percent), next most similar to peers' (84.3 percent), and least to parents' (73.2 percent). It does appear, then, that these high school youth felt their standards to be more similar to those of their friends and peers than to those of their parents. Note that this information is purely descriptive but that it seems similar to Proposition Six as it was originally stated.

Raschke (1972) studied the relationship between religiosity and several types of sexual permissiveness using a homogeneous availability sample of 264 introductory sociology students. It is relevant to Proposition Six that his analyses also included the respondents' perceptions of *similarity* between their own premarital sexual permissiveness attitudes (measured by Reiss's scale) and those of their parents, ministers, and friends. In line with Reiss's findings and Proposition Six, one's own attitudes were perceived to be much closer to those of friends than to those of parents or ministers. Parents and ministers were perceived to have more restrictive attitudes toward permissiveness than were peers. In summary, both the Glass (1972) and Raschke (1972) studies provide support for Reiss's descriptive assertion that student sexual standards are perceived to be closer to peers' standards than parents' standards.

Expecting to find a relationship between parent permissiveness and child permissiveness, Walsh (1970) actually measured permissiveness in two generations within the same families; but surprisingly, he found no relationship between parents' reports of their own permissiveness and children's reports of permissiveness. Examining this further, Walsh discovered that what really affected a child's permissiveness was his *perception* of his parents' permissiveness; that is, children formulate their own basic values based on what they think or perceive their parents' standards or values to be, and not necessarily on what they actually are. After finding strong evidence that college students *mis*perceived their parents' actual permissiveness, but noting the strong relationship between *perceived* parental standards and students' standards, Walsh (1970:121) wrote, "We then conclude that the perception of reality is the key variable in the study of students permissiveness." In addition, as Reiss (1967) had reported, perceptions of mothers' permissiveness were much more strongly related to student permissiveness than were perceptions of fathers' permissiveness; however, perceptions of close friends' permissiveness were a better predictor of the students' own permissiveness than either of the parental perceptions.

The next two studies to be discussed differ from the previous ones in that they report relationships between perceived reference group permissiveness and individuals' sexual *behavior*. Kaats and Davis (1970) studied self-reported rates of premarital coitus, but included questions asking the respondents to judge the attitudes of salient reference groups toward premarital intercourse. Among females, close friends were perceived as least disapproving and grandparents and parents most disapproving of premarital coitus (although all reference groups were perceived to disapprove, none to approve). Among males, close friends and fraternity brothers were perceived to *approve* premarital coitus, whereas it was perceived that grandparents and parents, especially mothers, would most disapprove. Nonvirginal females in the sample, when compared with virgins, felt siginificantly less disapproval of premarital intercourse from close friends, fathers, brothers, and clergymen. Similarly, nonvirginal males perceived less disapproval from fathers and clergymen than did male virgins. In other words, respondents who had premarital coital experience perceived less disapproval of this behavior from their reference groups than did virgin respondents. (See also Perlman, 1974.)

Mirande (1968) hypothesized that the sexual behavior of an indivudual would be influenced by his peer reference group, irrespective of the direction of influence. His data showed rates of female premarital coitus at a midwestern college that were quite similar to those observed by Robinson et al. (1968); in the sample of 93 undergraduates, 63 percent of the males and 23 percent of the females reported that they had experienced premarital intercourse. His subsequent analyses were based on the respondent's perceived peer group expectations. Respondents who had not engaged in coitus perceived their peer reference groups as disapproving intercourse with any-

one; those who had experienced coitus generally perceived their peer groups as approving of premarital intercourse. In either case the behavior of the respondent was generally consistent with the perceived expectations of peers. Also, the conformity of sex behavior to peer expectations tended to increase from freshman to senior year; in other words, consistency between behavior and perceived reference group attitudes increased with year in school. Conformity to peer expectations was also greater for females than males and for Greek-affiliated respondents than non-Greeks. In summary, both the Kaats and Davis and the Mirande researches reported a positive relationship between the sexual behavior of individuals and the perceived permissiveness of their reference groups. However, both studies used sexual behavior and not sexual attitudes as the dependent variable. This is important to note despite the evidence of a strong association of premarital sex behavior with premarital sexual attitudes (Reiss, 1967 ch. 7).

Some additional support for the importance of reference groups comes from Zelnik and Kantner's (1972) national sample of 15- to 19-year-old females. They found that nonvirginal females had significantly higher likelihood of having nonvirginal friends. Further, the nonvirgins were less likely to confide in their parents. Simon, Berger, and Gagnon (1972) also reported that in their national college sample nonvirgins were less likely to be intimate with their parents.

Like the first two studies reviewed under Proposition Six, the following three studies asked respondents to judge how similar their own sexual standards were to those of their parents and peers. In addition, the following studies also examined the relative strength of the bivariate relationships between (1) perceived similarity to parents' standards and the individuals's premarital sexual permissiveness, and (2) the perceived similarity to peers' standards and individual sexual permissiveness.

Studying college undergraduates (N = 678) at the University of Tennessee, Lanning (1970) found that perceived *similarity* to parental sexual standards was inversely associated with individual sexual permissiveness. Further, he found that the inverse relationship was stronger for perceived similarity to mothers than fathers; perceived similarity to the mother's standards was more strongly related to one's own permissiveness than was perceived similarity to the father's standards. This is what Reiss (1967) and Walsh (1970) also found.

Vandiver (1972) asked his random sample of 300 students at Southern Illinois University to compare their own views on sexual behavior with the views of their parents and close friends. He then constructed a score of perceived permissiveness of parents and close friends by using the direction and amount of differences from the respondent's own permissiveness score. Parents and close friends were thus categorized as being either high or low on permissiveness. He found that (1) there was a strong positive relationship between close friends' perceived sexual standards and the individual's sexual standards (the former accounted for 48 percent of the variance in the latter), and (2) there was a moderate positive relationship between perceived parental and sexual standards and the individual's sexual standards (the former accounted for 15 percent of the variance in the latter). From his regression analyses Vandiver felt confident enough to conclude that close friends' sexual standards were much more closely related to the individual's sexual standards than were the parents' sexual standards.

Libby (1974) and Vandiver (1972) asked similar questions and both used regression analyses, but their findings disagreed. However, Libby did utilize path analysis and did use Reiss's exact questions in his research. In Libby's final path-analytic models for each gender, perceived similarity to mothers' standards was more predictive of male and female premarital sexual permissiveness than was any other antecedent. Closeness to peers' and close friends' standards was only moderately predictive of individual permissiveness among males, and not at all among females. This was so despite the fact that the respondents' permissiveness was closer to that of peers than of parents.

There are at least two interesting possibilities to explain why Libby found closeness to mother's standards to be most predictive of individual sexual permissiveness but Vandiver found closeness to friends' standards to be more important. First, Vandiver (1972:78) scaled perceived permissiveness scores for parents and peers from the questions asking about similarity, while Libby used the comparisons of similarity directly as his independent variables. Second, Vandiver grouped perceptions of parents together; that is, mothers and fathers were not differentiated in his study. Reiss (1967), Lanning (1970),

Kaats and Davis (1970), Walsh (1970), and Libby (1974) all agreed that the perceived permissiveness of mother, or perceived closeness to her standard, is a much more slaient variable than the same measures for father or a combined parental indicator.

Using Table 4.3 as a summarizing device, we can see that the data do support the descriptive statement that parents and peers are perceived to be at different ends of a permissiveness continuum, with parents perceived to be least and peers most permissive. The Glass (1972) and Raschke (1972) studies both provide evidence that one's own standard of permissiveness is perceived as more similar to the sexual standards of peers and close friends than to those of parents. Again, this is descriptive. However, a subtle consideration is that this statement exists within time constraints. From the Newcomb (1958) and the Bowerman and Kinch (1959) studies, it is evident that reference orientations to peers and parents shift over time; while peer orientation increases, parental orientation decreases as one matures. Similarly, Mirande (1968) showed that sex *behavior* becomes more consistent with reference group standards as students move through college. At the college age individuals usually perceive their own permissiveness to be more like their peers' permissiveness than like their parents' permissiveness. Walsh, Ferrell, and Tolone (1976) report panel data showing a shift during college from parent to peer reference groups. Parents are usually perceived to be less permissive than peers; and consequently, as Lanning (1970) and Libby (1974) found, perceived similarity to parental permissiveness is inversely related, while perceived similarity to peer permissiveness is positively related to college students' permissiveness. There is support for these two propositions, and they are in line with the way we clarified Proposition Six earlier in this chapter. Libby's

Table 4.3. Key Studies Pertaining to Reiss's Proposition Six

Glass (1972)	High school students perceived their sexual standards to be most similar to those of close friends, then to those of peers, then to those of parents.
Raschke (1972)	College students perceived their own sexual standards to be more similar to those of peers than to those of parents.
Walsh (1976)	No relationship was found between independent parent and college student reports of permissiveness; however, the *perceived* permissiveness of close friends, mother, and father (in order of strength) were directly related to individual permissiveness.
Kaats and Davis (1970)	There was a positive relationship observed between perceived reference group permissiveness and the extent of college student sexual behavior.
Mirande (1968)	There was a positive relationship observed between perceived reference group permissiveness and the extent of college student sexual behavior.
Lanning (1970)	There was a strong inverse relationship observed between the perceived *similarity* to mother's standard and college student sexual permissiveness; there was a weaker inverse relationship between perceived similarity to father's standard and college student sexual permissiveness.
Vandiver (1972)	There was a strong positive relationship found between the perceived permissiveness of close friends and one's own permissiveness; there was a moderate positive relationship between the perceived permissiveness of parents and one's own permissiveness.
Libby (1974)	Among college students there was a strong inverse relationship between perceived *similarity* to mother's standard and individual sexual permissiveness. For males only, there was a moderate positive relationship between perceived similarity to peers' standards, and also between close friends' standards, and individual premarital sexual permissiveness.

data would indicate that perceived similarity to mothers' standards is a stronger predictor of student permissiveness than is perceived similarity to peers' permissiveness.

Not concerned in their analyses with perceptions of similarity, Mirande (1968), Kaats and Davis (1970), Walsh (1970), and Vandiver (1972) all found that perceived permissiveness of various reference groups influences one's own sexual permissiveness regardless of whether these reference groups' permissiveness is perceived to be high or low. The perceived attitudes of parents, grandparents, peers, fraternity brothers, sorority sisters, close friends, clergymen, etc., have all been studied, and the higher any reference group's permissiveness is perceived to be, the higher student permissiveness is. The two reference groups most often studied have been parents and peers, since these two reference groups appear to have the greatest influence on a respondent's own permissiveness. There is substantial evidence that one's own permissiveness is positively influenced by the perceived permissiveness of both parents and peers. Among college-age subjects, perceived permissiveness of peers, especially of close friends, appears to have an important effect; but Libby's work (1974) points to the great importance of perceived maternal permissiveness too. One can feel close to peers' permissiveness but still be strongly influenced by perception of parental permissiveness.

Although it has been very confusing in the literature, there are actually four major antecedent variables being related to individual permissiveness:

1. Perceived parental permissiveness
2. Perceived peer permissiveness
3. Perceived *similarity* between one's own permissiveness and the permissiveness of parents
4. Perceived *similarity* between one's own permissiveness and the permissiveness of peers

To help distinguish between these variables, note that the relationships between individual premarital sexual permissiveness and 1 and 2 above are both positive; the relationship between 3 above and individual permissiveness is negative, and the relationship between 4 above and individual permissiveness is usually positive.

Reiss's Proposition Seven: The greater the responsibility for other family members and/or the less the courtship participation, the greater the likelihood that the individual will be low on permissiveness [156].

Reiss found that older siblings who were responsible for younger brothers and sisters were less permissive than only children who did not have such responsibility. Analogously, parents of children closer to teenage were less permissive than parents with younger children. In a similar way those divorced but without children were more permissive than those divorced with children. All of these findings seemed to be special cases where responsibility for other family members, appeared to decrease

individual permissiveness. What have other investigators found that is relevant to this proposition?

Lanning (1970), studying parental role convergence and its effect on children's permissiveness in a sample of 600 University of Tennessee undergraduates, found that as the number of siblings increased, so did permissiveness. He interpreted this positive relationship between number of siblings and student permissiveness to be due to less influential parental socialization of children (i.e., number of siblings is inversely related to parental influence in socialization, which is inversely related to individual permissiveness). He used the Reiss permissiveness scale, and his cutting point on the number of siblings was between only child and one or more siblings.

The number of siblings in the Bell and Chaskes (1970) study of 205 coeds failed to distinguish between the respondents' different reported rates of coitus. However, in this article we are not told how the number of siblings was broken down, and the Reiss scale was not used. It should also be noted that Reiss assumed birth order was an important factor for it determined responsibility for other siblings.

The Kaats and Davis (1970) trend study of college students (319 females, 239 males) at the University of Colorado included some questions which might have an indirect bearing on this proposition. The first part of Proposition Seven predicts that increases in the responsibility for other family members will decrease permissiveness. The Kaats and Davis data indicate that brothers and especially sisters would be encouraged by their siblings *not* to participate in premarital intercourse; respondents were more restrictive regarding premarital intercourse for their own brothers and sisters than for themselves. These findings might be loosely interpreted as suggestive support for the seventh proposition. However, it should not be considered equally with the kind of direct support that an analysis would provide if the actual permissiveness of respondents had been differentiated by the number of brothers and sisters they had, or whether they were the oldest or youngest child.

Harris and Howard (1968) studied the relationship of birth order and responsibility in a sample of 1,200 male and female high school and university students in Chicago. They found that the first-born children of each sex (in comparison with later-borns) tend to internalize more strongly the injunctions and expectations of parents and have a stronger sense of serious moral responsibility. They noted that parental control was stricter with first children than with second children, a finding that coincides with the notion of greater internalization of parental indoctrinations by first children. The older subjects in comparison to the younger subjects had a higher responsibility orientation. While there was no measurement of permissiveness, this study is somewhat related to Reiss's Proposition Seven: first-born children, because of their greater internalization of responsibility injunctions, and older children because of their greater responsibility toward younger siblings, would be expected to be less permissive than later-born children. This was observed to be the case in Reiss's data. As noted previously, Lanning's (1970) data and interpretation disagree by suggesting that *only* children are more effectively socialized and less permissive. Libby & Whitehurst (1973) attempted to operationalize responsibility for other family members among college students with a short Likert-type scale. However, this scale score, reflecting responsibility around the house and for siblings, was not significantly related to premarital sexual permissiveness. They also used sibling ordinal position of the respondent, and this too was unrelated to permissiveness.

In summary, responsibility for other family members is a concept which applies to both unmarried individuals, whose responsibility for siblings is of interest, and married individuals, whose responsibility for their children inversely influences their permissiveness. However, as Table 4.4 shows, almost all studies have been conducted with younger, unmarried subjects. The relevant evidence we have deals only with responsibility for siblings, and here the evidence is not conclusive. Perhaps it has not been clear enough that the important contrasting positions of sibling responsibility are oldest as opposed to only children. Regarding adult permissiveness, Reiss observed a positive linear relationship between parents' permissiveness and the age of their children. Studies are needed which more carefully measure sibling responsibility *and* which use older subjects who have responsibility for children. In that way the appropriateness of the term ''responsibility for other family members'' and its relationship to premarital sexual permissiveness can be judged.

The second part of Proposition Seven related courtship participation to individual permissiveness. Reiss found that the amount of participation in courtship positively influenced individual premarital sexual permissiveness. Divorce and separated statuses, as against married and widowed statuses, were considered to reflect courtship participation. While this is probably true on the aggregate level, it seems somewhat hazardous to explain differences in permissiveness between divorced, widowed, and married individuals on the basis of their courtship participation without some more direct measure of their actual involvement. Again, this is the aggregation question; just as aggregates from generally liberal settings tend to have liberal attitudes, divorced or separated aggregates might have relatively high courtship participation; but more direct measures of participation in courtship would seem to be desirable in order to test this proposition.

The evidence from several investigations seems to support the notion that the more time, energy, and activity individuals expend in courtship pursuits, the more permissive they become. Bell and Chaskes (1970) found that girls who began dating at age 14 or earlier had higher rates of coitus than those who began dating when they were 15 or older. The authors interpreted high rates of premarital coitus among those who began dating early to be due to the fact that they had been dating longer and probably had more opportunity. This seems compatible with our idea of courtship participation. However, in Reiss's (1967) analysis, age at first date was not an important explanatory variable. His three white female samples showed nonsignificant tendencies in opposing directions between the age at first dating and permissiveness. In Reiss's study this is one relationship which was stronger for males than females; white males showed a curvilinear relationship, with those who started dating at 12 or younger and those who started at 16 or older being the most permissive. Ehrmann (1959) also found the relationship to be stronger for males than females.

The Kaats and Davis (1970) study previously referred to also collected data which appear to support the positive relationship between courtship participation and permissiveness. They found that the more attractive coeds had more friends of the opposite sex, dated more often, had been in love more often, and also had more petting experience. The authors concluded that their data appear to support their hypothesis that girls who were rated high on physical attractiveness at least had increased opportunities for premarital coitus. Basically, they argued that physically attractive girls are confronted with more pressures and opportunities to engage in premarital sex. The part of their study that is clearly applicable to Proposition Seven is that highest dating frequency (participation in courtship) was characteristic of the most attractive girls, who also had the most petting experience and engaged in sex with more partners. They did not, however, find that the most attractive girls had the most premarital coitus overall.

Libby (1974) found courtship participation (as measured by current courtship status) to be significantly related to permissiveness when bivariate analysis was used, but only for females. The closer one was to engagement, the more permissive she was likely to be. In the multivariate analysis, courtship participation was not strongly enough related to permissiveness to be retained in the path model. More recently Lewis and Burr (1975) found a relationship between commitment in courtship and permissiveness which held for both males and females. The lower part of Table 4.4 summarizes the evidence pertaining to this aspect of Proposition Seven, and it does appear that participation in courtship positively influences premarital sexual permissiveness. The frequency of dating seems to be an especially appropriate indicator of courtship participation, and the age at which dating starts seems to fit the concept less well. Other operationalizations, like the number of times one has been in love or whether the individual goes steady, seem to be infused with the component of affection, and this needs to

Table 4.4. Key Studies Pertaining to Reiss's Proposition Seven

AUTHOR AND YEAR	FAMILY RESPONSIBILITY MEASURE	RESULTS
Harris and Howard (1968)	Ordinal position	Suggests that ordinal position might be a way to operationalize responsibility; first-born of each sex has more strongly internalized responsibility
Bell and Chaskes (1970)	Number of siblings	No relation between number of siblings and rates of premarital coitus
Kaats and Davis (1970)	Brothers and sisters (especially the latter) would be encouraged not to have premarital coitus	Suggestive in support of Proposition Seven
Lanning (1970)	Number of siblings; ordinal position	Only children least permissive (contradicts Harris and Howard); positive relationship between number of siblings and premarital sexual permissiveness; reverse of Proposition Seven
Libby and Whitehurst (1973)	Four-item summated scale assessing responsibility for siblings and household tasks	No relationship between family responsibility and premarital sexual permissiveness

AUTHOR AND YEAR	MEASURE OF COURTSHIP PARTICIPATION	RESULTS
Ehrmann (1959)	Age at first date	Negative relationship; consistent
Bell and Chaskes (1970)	Age at first date	Negative relationship; consistent
Kaats and Davis (1970)	Number of dates	Positive relationship; consistent
Libby (1974)	Courtship status	Positive relationship for females only; consistent*
Lewis and Burr (1975)	Courtship status	Positive relationship for both sexes; consistent

*This held only at the bivariate level.

be controlled for here. The relationship between permissiveness and affection in dating will be considered in the reformulation of Proposition Three.

Reiss's General Theoretical Statement: The degree of acceptable premarital sexual permissiveness in a courtship group varies directly with the degree of autonomy of the courtship group and with the degree of acceptable premarital sexual permissiveness in the social and cultural setting outside the group [167].

It is very hard to evaluate the evidence for this proposition. Courtship groups having different levels of autonomy and imbedded in subcultures with differing levels of acceptance of premarital sexual permissiveness would have to be compared. Obviously, this is a vast undertaking. There is one reputable group of researchers who have studied premarital sexual behavior and attitudes in three different cultures (Christensen, 1960, 1966, 1969; Christensen and Carpenter, 1962a, 1962b). Christensen and Gregg (1970:617) reported data collected in the

> highly restrictive Mormon culture in the Intermountain region of western United States; moderately restrictive Midwestern culture in central United States; and highly permissive Danish culture which is a part of Scandinavia.

The attitudes and sex behavior of the three different samples range from least to most permissive in accord with their respective social and cultural setting. Besides this general idea, that premarital sexual permissiveness in a courtship group is influenced by its acceptance in other

institutional settings, the general theoretical statement indicated that the autonomy of the courtship group influences its permissiveness. The importance of autonomy will be further expanded in the following sections as there has been little writing or research about this important factor.

REWORKING EACH OF THE PROPOSITIONS

This final section of Part One is primarily an example of what Burr (1973) called a "reworking" strategy; it is an attempt to utilize recent theory construction methodological improvements to increase the clarity, testability, and communicability of earlier theoretical statements. In this section each proposition will again be considered in sequence. First, the term used to express each concept will be examined and refined when necessary. Second, nominal and operational definitions will be explicitly provided for each concept. Third, each proposition will be restated, roughly following the format suggested by Burr (1973). At the end of Part One, all of the reformulated propositions will be collected in a summary diagram, Figure 4.3.

Reiss's Proposition One: The lower the traditional level of sexual permissiveness in a group, the greater the likelihood that social forces will alter individual levels of sexual permissiveness [51].

Two of the concepts in Proposition One (See Figure 4.1)—the traditional level of permissiveness in a group and premarital sexual permissiveness—are cast at an appropriate level of generality and are meaningfully abstract. Since these two concepts deal with group and individual attributes respectively, it might be helpful to have both labels reflect their "unit terms" as Gibbs (1972) advises. The suggested terms are "the traditional level of premarital sexual permissiveness norms in the community" and "individual premarital sexual permissiveness."

As has been noted, the concept "social forces," besides not being a quantitative variable, is too general—it simply includes too much. One concept, which Reiss now proposes to use in the reformulation in place of social forces is "sexual orientation." Most of the explicit tests of Proposition One have used church attendance or some other measure of religiosity to tap the independent variable (Heltsley and Broderick, 1969; Ruppel, 1970; and Libby, 1974). However, we suggest that religiosity is useful primarily because it is an indicator of one's basic sexual orientation, since those high on religiosity are very likely to accept what are considered to be the traditional religious values toward sex, namely, that premarital sex leads to negative consequences like disease, pregnancy, guilt, and social condemnation. Therefore, we are asserting that the reward-cost balance in one's orientation toward premarital sex in general is one of the "social forces" that influences premarital sexual permissiveness. We might think of those who generally stress the *rewards* of premarital sex (such as physical pleasure and psychic satisfaction) as having highly favorable orientations to sex, and those who stress the *risks* or *costs* of premarital sex as having low or unfavorable orientations to sex.

Reward-cost balance of one's sexual orientation = the degree to which individuals view premarital heterosexual permissiveness as leading to physically and psychologically satisfying consequences, as opposed to viewing premarital sex as having undesirable consequences.
Indicators:
  a. Questions assessing the specific risks and rewards associated with premarital coitus. For example, "Premarital coitus is an activity in which consequences such as guilt are likely to occur" versus "Premarital coitus is very likely to involve psychological as well as physical rewards."
  b. Ask, "How likely do you think it is for premarital sexual intercourse to result in (1) venereal disease, (2) pregnancy, (3) social condemnation, (4) physical satisfaction, (5) psychological satisfaction, (6) guilt feelings, (7) better marital sexual adjustment, (8) weakening of future marriage?" (See Reiss, 1960, for an examination of these eight consequences of premarital sexual permissiveness.)

We would predict that those with more favorable sex orientations will also be higher on acceptance of premarital sexual permissiveness. In accord with Proposition One it would also follow that the relation would be stronger in communities which have traditions of low permissiveness.

In addition to the sexual orientation concept described above, another concept which is more specific than social forces, and which we will also use in its place, is "love orientation." Reiss now proposes this because initially several of the "social forces" were love-related. Briefly, the concept of love orientation refers to the nature of one's outlook on love, that is, whether one is oriented to stressing the rewards and benefits rather than the risks and costs of love experiences. We propose that the more favorable one's love orientation is, the more premaritally permissive one will be. In addition, this relationship will be stronger in communities which have traditions of low permissiveness. The definitions of these variables are given below, followed by the statement of the four propositions reformulated from the original Proposition One (see also Figure 4.3).

Reward-cost balance of one's love orientation = the degree to which individuals view love as having positive consequences and perceive rewards rather than perceiving costs resulting from being in love.
Indicators: Ask, "How likely do you think it is for love to result in (1) psychological damage, (2) a broadened social perspective, (3) the achievement of valued goals, (4) making life meaningful, and (5) economic costs?"
The traditional level of premarital sexual permissiveness in a community = the degree to which the community in which one resides has a history of accepting premarital sexual permissiveness which goes back at least two generations. (One can delimit this concept to apply to only a part of a community.)
Indicators:
  a. Rates of premarital intercourse or of sexual attitudes in the community which go back in time far enough to establish the degree to which such a tradition exists.
  b. In our society males are high on this variable compared to females, and blacks are high compared to whites.
Individual premarital sexual permissiveness = the degree of acceptance of various levels of physical intimacy in premarital heterosexual relationships.
Indicators: Reiss's scales of premarital sexual permissiveness.
The reformulated Proposition One now reads:
Proposition 1a. One's sexual orientation influences in a positive direction one's premarital sexual permissiveness.
Proposition 1b. The traditional level of premarital

sexual permissiveness in the community influences in a negative direction the strength of the relation of one's sexual orientation to one's premarital sexual permissiveness.

Proposition 1c. One's love orientation influences in a positive direction one's premarital sexual permissiveness.

Proposition 1d. The traditional level of premarital sexual permissiveness in the community influences in a negative direction the strength of the relation of one's love orientation to one's premarital sexual permissiveness.

For a presentation of these propositions in diagram form, see the relevant parts of Figure 4.3.

Reiss's Proposition Two: The stronger the amount of general liberality in a group, the greater the likelihood that social forces will maintain high levels of sexual permissiveness [73].

Although others (Maranell et al., 1970; Vandiver, 1972; Banwart, 1973; Miller, 1973) have tended to see the *individual's* attitudinal liberality as the important variable in this proposition, the original formulation intended to describe a *contextual* effect (see Figure 4.2).

In the original research, the control by indicators of liberality on the relationship between social class and permissiveness gave rise to Proposition Two. To make this proposition clearer, Reiss has suggested the concept of "current institutional support for premarital sexual permissiveness in the community." We are suggesting that this concept influences the relationship between individual sexual and love orientations (social forces) and individual permissiveness. General liberality was a fuzzy concept, and we are offering this new concept which incorporates much of the previous meaning of liberality without its confusion. The higher the support for sexual permissiveness in the setting where one resides, the greater the effect of variables which promote permissiveness and the less the effect of variables which inhibit permissiveness. Definitions of individual sex and love orientations and individual permissiveness have already been provided and will not be repeated here, but the new concept of community support for premarital sexual permissiveness is defined below and combined with the other new concepts in the revised Proposition Two.

Institutional support for premarital sexual permissiveness in one's community = the degree to which the major institutions where one lives accept alternative sexual views and practices and have laws which permit sexual freedom of choice.

Indicators: Questions might be asked about the community's customs regarding the showing of X-rated movies, censorship of books and magazines, policies of the school boards which condemn or support premaritally pregnant girls, and views of

religious organizations (The reader should note that the "traditional" level of premarital sexual permissiveness refers to attitudes specifically on premarital sex permissiveness and to attitudes that have prevailed for two or more generations. The institutional support concept refers to *current* customs and to customs that relate to premarital sexual permissiveness but are *not* direct measures of PSP.)

Proposition 2a. The degree of institutional support for premarital sexual permissiveness in one's community influences in a positive direction the strength of the relation of sexual orientation to individual premarital sexual permissiveness.

Proposition 2b. The degree of institutional support for premarital sexual permissiveness in one's community influences in a positive direction the strength of the relation of love orientation to individual premarital sexual permissiveness.

See Figure 4.3 for a diagrammatic presentation of these reformulated propositions.

Reiss's Proposition Three: To the extent that individual ties to the marital and family institutions differ, individuals will tend to display a different type of sensitivity of permissiveness to social forces [89].

In this proposition, one of the important concepts related to permissiveness was obscured by the term "social forces," but we have already introduced "sexual and love orientations" to take its place. We will use only love orientations in this proposition. One of the generalizations that stands out in Reiss's work as well as in Ehrmann's (1959), is that when females are emotionally involved in an affectionate relationship, their permissiveness increases markedly. Similarly, Walsh (1970) found that girls who had entered into love-related dating experiences were much more permissive than those who had not, and Kaats and Davis (1970), who studied only females, found the same to be true. These findings all have some relevance to the independent variable we have termed the "reward-cost balance of one's love orientation." We are assuming a close positive relationship between love orientation and love experiences. This needs to be empirically tested. In sum, favorableness of love orientation is thought to positively influence individual permissiveness, but particularly so among females. This is so because of the ties of females to the family. It is believed that the stronger one's ties to marriage and family institutions—or, to substitute a more descriptive set of terms, the higher the priority of marriage and family roles—the stronger will be the relationship between love orientations and individual permissiveness. The definition of this contingency variable and the proposition which connects it with previously clarified concepts is stated below.

Priority of marriage and family roles = the degree to

which marriage and family roles (e.g., wife-mother or husband-father) are viewed to be personally important, primary, lifetime activities.
Indicators:
  a. Asking attitudinal questions directly; e.g., "In comparison with occupational or other roles, how important to you is becoming a mother/father?"
  b. Asking respondents to rank roles by their priority to them, e.g., spousal, parental, occupational, student, etc.
  c. In American society, gender (females greater than males).
  Proposition 3. The priority of one's marriage and family roles influences in a positive direction the relationship between love orientation and individual premarital sexual permissiveness (see Figure 4.3.)

Reiss's Proposition Four: The higher the overall level of permissiveness in a group, the greater the extent of equalitarianism within the abstinence and double-standard classifications [103].

There is no explicit causal linkage in the proposition stated above, but elsewhere Reiss noted that group permissiveness is viewed as a "key determinant" (99) and "causes" (103) equalitarianism. The overall level of permissiveness in a group and equalitarianism are quite straightforward concepts, given that a group is defined as an aggregate of individuals who share or have similar attitudes or values. The slight label changes we suggest are "premarital sexual permissiveness of one's reference groups" and "individual equalitarianism."

Premarital sexual permissiveness of one's reference groups = the degree to which physical intimacies are considered acceptable prior to marriage by groups with which one identifies.
Indicators:
  a. Reiss's scales of premarital sexual permissiveness administered for the particular reference group rather than the individual.
  b. Church attendance (groups of low church attenders have high permissiveness, and vice versa).
  c. Race (groups of blacks have high permissiveness when compared with groups of white individuals).
  d. Gender (males have high permissiveness as compared with females).
Individual equalitarianism = the extent to which one approves of males and females engaging in the same premarital sexual behaviors.
Indicators:
  a. Comparison of a respondent's scale types for male and female referents on Reiss's Guttman scales of premarital sexual permissiveness.

  b. Ask the following question: "Men should be allowed more freedom than women in sexual behavior before marriage. How do you feel about this attitude?" (Reiss, 1967:188)

Reiss (1967) found that within the abstinence and double-standard classifications, individuals who were members of more permissive groups or aggregates (blacks, males, and low church attenders) tended to also be more equalitarian. The interpretation of this finding was that the context of permissiveness that the group possesses can affect individual equalitarianism by raising female permissiveness.

It had really not been intended that the fourth proposition would have a dependent variable (equalitarianism) which differed from the major dependent variable of premarital sexual permissiveness. In fact, the context of Reiss's ch. 6 (1967) implies that equalitarianism in sexual norms produces a high level of sexual permissiveness. Combining this intended linkage with the original proposition results in the two propositions stated below and diagrammed in Figure 4.3.

  Proposition 4a. Among abstinence and double-standard adherents, the level of premarital sexual permissiveness of reference groups influences in a positive direction the amount of individual equalitarianism.
  Proposition 4b. The amount of individual equalitarianism influences in a positive direction the level of individual premarital sexual permissiveness.

Reiss's Proposition Five: Differences in the potential for permissiveness in one's basic set of parentally derived values is a key determinant of the number, rate, and direction of changes in one's premarital sexual standards and behavior [122].

Both the antecedent and consequent concepts in this original proposition are in need of being reformulated. The proposition meant essentially that certain nonsexual values of parents relevant to pleasures, comfort, eating, risk taking, and such would be related to the premarital sexual permissiveness of their children. However, it is likely that as Walsh (1970) discovered, the effects of parents on their children's permissiveness are much more strongly reflected by what the children *perceive* their parents' values to be than by what the parents report their own values to be. Therefore, the antecedent concept we are suggesting here is labeled "the perceived parental acceptance of nonsexual pleasures." The original consequent concept—"the number, rate, and direction of changes in one's premarital sexual standards and behavior"—was different from premarital sexual permissiveness as measured by the Guttman scales. Since the dependent variable in the original Proposition Five is actually a cluster of concepts and the dependent variable of major interest is individual premarital sexual permissiveness, the former is dropped and the latter takes its place in the reformulation.

> The perceived parental approval of nonsexual pleasures = the degree to which children perceive their parents to accept and encourage such things as risk taking and pleasure in general.
>
> Indicators: Ask children to rate the degree of their parents' approval of nonsexual pleasures, such as personal comfort, rewards of eating, avoidance of all pain, risk taking, and emphasis on immediate rather than deferred gratification.
>
> *Proposition 5.* The degree to which one's parents are perceived to approve of nonsexual pleasures influences in a positive direction the level of individual premarital sexual permissiveness (see Figure 4.3).

Reiss's Proposition Six: There is a general tendency for the individual to perceive his parent's permissiveness as a low point on a permissive continuum and his peers' permissiveness as a high point, and to place himself closer to his peers, particularly to those he regards as his close friends [139].

As was noted before, the proposition as stated above is only descriptive, and the relationships are not explicit. Figure 4.2 shows the intended dependent and independent variables. It will be remembered from the literature reviewed in the preceding section that there have been four key concepts in this area related to individual premarital sexual permissiveness: (1) perceived parental premarital sexual permissiveness; (2) perceived peer premarital sexual permissiveness; (3) perceived *similarity* between one's own permissiveness and the permissiveness of parents; and (4) perceived *similarity* between one's own permissiveness and the permissiveness of peers and close friends. The relationships between individual premarital sexual permissiveness and (1), (2), and (4) above are all positive, whereas the relationship between (3) above and individual premarital sexual permissiveness is negative. All four of these predictor variables are important; and one of the authors (Miller, 1973) previously emphasized the first two, asserting that the higher the perceived parental and/or peer permissiveness, the higher the individual's permissiveness. However, the original formulations were based on the idea that perceived *similarity to peers'* permissiveness was positively related to individual permissiveness, but perceived *similarity to parents'* permissiveness was inversely related to individual permissiveness. The terms to be used for these concepts are the same as those previously refined and shown in Figure 4.2. The concepts are defined and combined in propositions below.

Perceived similarity between one's own PSP and

parental PSP = the degree to which individuals view their own premarital sexual permissiveness as similar to the permissiveness of their own parents.
Indicators:
> a. Ask, "How do you feel your premarital sexual standards compare with your mother's standards about premarital sex?" with a range of four to six similarity categories.
>
> b. Use the five-item short form of Reiss's scale (1967:35), changing the referent "I believe" to "my mother believes," and then assess the similarity of the individual's and his/her mother's permissiveness.

Perceived similarity between one's own PSP and peer-friend PSP = the degree to which individuals view their own premarital sexual permissiveness as like the permissiveness of their peers-friends.
> a. Ask, "How do you feel your premarital sexual standards compare with the standards of others your own age?" and/or "How do you feel your premarital sex standards compare with the standards of your close friends?"
>
> b. Use the five-item short form of Reiss's scale (1967:35), changing the referent "I believe" to "my peers believe," "my close friends believe," and then assess the similarity of the individual's and his peers' or close friends' permissiveness.
>
> *Proposition 6a.* The amount of similarity perceived between one's own premarital sexual permissiveness and parents' permissiveness influences in a negative direction individual premarital sexual permissiveness.
>
> *Proposition 6b.* The amount of similarity perceived between one's own premarital sexual permissiveness and peers' permissiveness influences in a positive direction individual premarital sexual permissiveness.

There is a contingency variable which affects the strength of the relationships asserted in Propositions 6a and 6b, and that is the importance to the individual of the particular reference group. If parents are very important to an individual, then the inverse relationship between their standards and individual permissiveness is likely to be quite strong. Likewise, the positive relationship between similarity to peer standards of permissiveness and individual permissiveness (Proposition 6b) will be especially strong for those to whom peers are a very important reference group. In situations of parental and peer cross-pressures on the individual the value of the contingency variable (because it regulates the influence of a reference group) will help predict the probable value of the dependent variable. The contingency variable of the importance of the reference group is almost self-explanatory, but it will be defined and then related in Propositions 6c and 6d below (see also Figure 4.3).

The importance of the reference group to the individual = the degree to which the reference group is felt to be significant to the individual in forming and maintaining his/her own values and attitudes.

Proposition 6c. The importance of the parental reference group to the individual influences in a positive direction the strength of the relationship between similarity to parental standards and individual premarital sexual permissiveness.

Proposition 6d. The importance of the peer reference group to the individual influences in a positive direction the strength of the relationship between similarity to peer standards of permissiveness and individual premarital sexual permissiveness.

Reiss's Proposition Seven: The greater the responsibility for other family members and/or the less the courtship participation, the greater likelihood that the individual will be low on permissiveness [156].

The original labels for the two independent variables in this proposition are clear enough to be retained. However, a specific value of a variable should not be indicated in a proposition (e.g., *low* permissiveness in this case) unless there is information only about that specific value or there is some reason to believe that the relationship does not hold at other values. Therefore, in restating the proposition, we use again the term "individual premarital sexual permissiveness" as a variable rather than as specifying a single value.

Responsibility for other family members = the degree to which one is accountable or answerable for the behavior of others in his/her nuclear family.

Indicators:

a. Among siblings, responsibility differences are inferred when only children are contrasted with oldest children who have younger brothers and sisters. Alternatively, specific tasks and family "responsibilities" might be assessed by direct inquiries.

b. Among married individuals, responsibility differences are most evident between those with and without children, and between parents with children in the salient age of courtship participation and those with preteenagers.

Courtship participation = the degree to which one is actively involved and expends time and energy in courtship activities, that is, heterosexual dyadic interaction.

Indicators:

a. Frequency of dating.

b. The amount of time one spends in formal or informal dating as compared to the time spent at work, school and other activities.

c. Divorced and separated (high) versus married and widowed (low) statuses.

Proposition 7a. The amount of responsibility for other family members inversely influences the level of individual premarital sexual permissiveness.

Proposition 7b. The amount of courtship participation influences in a positive direction the level of individual premarital sexual permissiveness.

Reiss's General Theoretical Statement: The degree of acceptable premarital sexual permissiveness in a courtship group varies directly with the degree of autonomy of the courtship group and with the degree of acceptable premarital sexual permissiveness in the social and cultural setting outside the group [167].

In this original proposition as stated above the dependent variable is the premarital sexual permissiveness of a courtship *group,* whereas *individual* permissiveness has been the focus of most of the earlier propositions. This inconsistency is resolved by substituting the dependent variable which has been of major interest throughout this work, namely, the concept of individual premarital sexual permissiveness. It appears defensible to assert that individual permissiveness is influenced by the autonomy of the courtship group one belongs to or is a part of. This variable will be referred to as the degree of "perceived autonomy of one's courtship group." We use "perceived autonomy" because we feel the perception is more important than objective measures and also to keep this variable distinct from other variables like "institutional support for PSP in one's community." We expect that the greater the courtship group's perceived autonomy, the greater the individual permissiveness.

The other antecedent in the general theoretical statement—the degree of premarital sexual permissiveness in the social and cultural setting—implies an even broader contextual effect. In the interest of parsimony and because of similarity in meaning, we will use the new concept described in Proposition Two (institutional support for premarital sexual permissiveness in one's community) in place of the degree of permissiveness in the social and cultural setting. The concept refers to the extent to which social institutions, as reflected in civil laws and policies of educational and religious institutions, support premarital sex. This variable was defined in conjunction with Proposition Two, so only the autonomy concept is nominally and operationally defined below, but then both are related in Propositions 8a and 8b (see Figure 4.3).

Perceived autonomy of one's courtship group = the degree to which one perceives that oneself and the group of friends one usually dates with are allowed freedom from adult constraints or supervision.

Indicators: Ask questions like the following. (Possible answers might be in an always-usually-sometimes-never range.)

a. "Do you believe that most of your close friends

are told by parents how late they may stay out on dates?''

b. ''Do you believe that most of your close friends are free to choose whom they date?''

c. ''Do you believe your dating activities are free from constraints by other adults?''

Proposition 8a. The degree of perceived autonomy of one's courtship group influences in a positive direction the level of individual premarital sexual permissiveness.

Proposition 8b. The degree of institutional support for premarital sexual permissiveness in one's community influences in a positive direction the level of individual premarital sexual permissiveness.

This completes our reworking of the premarital sexual permissiveness propositions first put forward in 1967. Our reformulation is summarized in Figure 4.3, which can be informatively compared with Figure 4.2. Note particularly that all propositions in Figure 4.3 are ultimately related to the single dependent variable, whereas Figure 4.2, which reflects more closely the original 1967 propositions, shows some of them with dependent variables other than individual premarital sexual permissiveness.

It is hoped that our strategy of descriptively presenting the initial propositions, reviewing the evidence for them, and reformulating them will serve to increase their clarity and testability. To this end we have attempted throughout to break the more complex propostions down into their component concepts, and have provided both rational and operational definitions for the concepts we used. In addition we have been careful to specify the nature of each relationship we asserted. We will next turn our attention to more fully integrating the several propositions, elaborating them, and suggesting bridges and extensions into the areas of marital and extramarital sexual permissiveness.

PART TWO

INTEGRATING AND ELABORATING THE PROPOSITIONS

Introduction

Part One of this chapter clarified, operationalized, and discussed the research evidence for each of the original propositions. This is an important set of precedures in any theory-building program. Nevertheless there is a crucial task that must now be performed, and that is to interrelate the refined propositions. After all, it is just such integration of propositions that constitutes a theory. Separate propositions that relate to a common dependent variable are valuable, but their value increases immensely if they can be interrelated in a theoretically meaningful fashion. It is to this task that we turn in this part of the chapter. Propositions will be formulated here in their final form in relation to premarital sexual permissiveness. Only a few new varibales will be introduced, and they will be briefly operationalized. *The reader can depend on Part One for key definitions and operationalizations and for much of the empirical evidence.*

The independent variables can be related to each other and to the dependent variable in literally hundreds of possible ways. Theoretical orientation is the key way to choose the important interrelations from among all the logically possible relationships. One of the basic concepts that integrated the propositions when they were first put forth in 1967 was the notion of autonomy of one's dyadic heterosexual interaction—in short, how free from external controls was the individual in his relationships with the opposite sex. Originally we referred to the autonomy of one's courtship group. However, this was a less direct way of referring to the individual's own autonomy; therefore, we here refer to the individual's own perceived autonomy as a more direct measure of what we are interested in. The characteristic of autonomy is in a general way a key factor and one that is seemingly related to many of the other variables. When the propositions were originally formulated, little elaboration of these intcrrelations was put forth. Let us now further explain the centrality of this concept of autonomy and then proceed to lay out the integration of all propositions.

Centrality of Autonomy

In an open courtship society like our own, there is a great deal of autonomy that is normatively allowed in dyadic heterosexual interactions. That is, young people are given considerable freedom in choosing whom they date and where they go. Also, cars and apartments afford them privacy to do what they wish. In most societies the older peers inform the younger ones about the pleasures of heterosexual relationships. This has been particularly true for males in the Western world; but females too are informed, if not by older females, then by the males they are going with. Young people seek the freedom to pursue these sexual and other interpersonal rewards. The courtship group generally promotes the right to opportunities for premarital sexual relationships. The family, on the other hand, has a vested interest in avoiding problems of pregnancy and venereal disease involving their adolescent children, and is accordingly relatively low on support for premarital sexual permissiveness. Those sexual acts viewed to be least threatening to the family are most accepted (see Davis, 1966, for a development of this idea). For example, intercourse involving engaged couples is the most acceptable form of premarital coitus.

Figure 4.3. Summary Diagram of the Reformulated Reiss Propositions

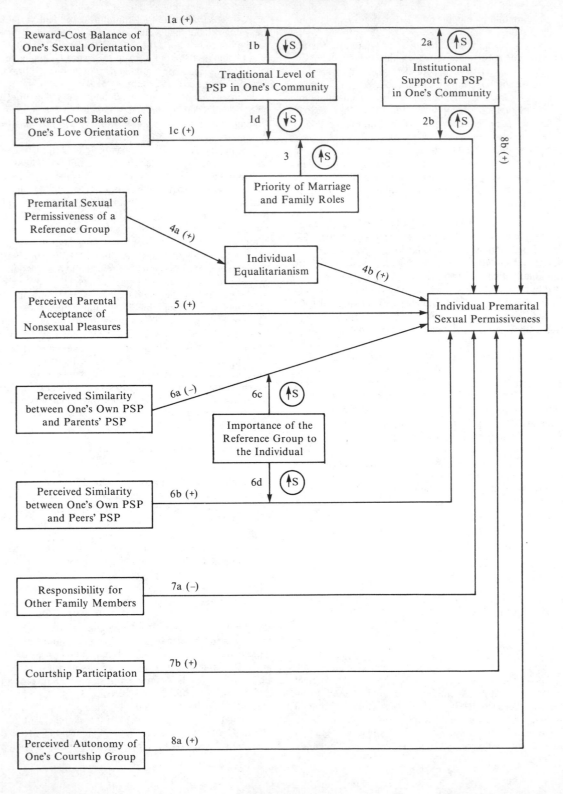

Reiss's 1967 data indicated that when one looks at people *of the same age,* those who are married and have teenage children are the most restrictive concerning premarital sexuality (Reiss, 1967, ch 9.). Thus there is presumptive evidence for assuming a general tension between a courtship subculture which furthers a high emphasis on the *rewards* of sexuality and a family subculture which stresses the *costs* of sexuality. Our measure of sexual orientation is designed to bring out exactly this type of difference in evaluation of costs and rewards.

It follows from the above that if youth culture stresses the rewards of sexuality, then to the extent that young people are free from the constraints of the family and other adult-type institutions, they will be able to develop their emphasis on sexuality. The physical and psychic pleasures connected to human sexuality are rewards basically to the participants and not to their parents, and this fact helps explain further the difference in orientation of the courtship and family groups. Thus the autonomy of young people is assumed to be a key variable in determining how sexually permissive one will be.

A glance at Figure 4.4 will show the reader how many other variables act either as causes of *perceived* autonomy levels or as effects of perceived autonomy levels. It should be noted that in variable 6 in Figure 4.4 we use the phrase "dyadic heterosexual interaction" instead of the term "courtship" because this permits us to generalize to marital and extramarital sexuality in the final section of this chapter. Not every variable is related to autonomy, but it is clear from Figure 4.4 that autonomy is the most central of all the variables, there being eight causal lines connected to it. The specific causal connections and importance of this variable will become more apparent as we go through the interrelations of our propositions. The four variables which precede perceived autonomy (variables 1, 2, 3 and 4) can also be viewed as affecting the objective amount of autonomy allowed to young people and not just the perception of autonomy that young people feel. *Thus even without variable 6 (perceived autonomy) the centrality of autonomy would be clear in this theory.* Because of the centrality of this variable we have chosen to name the theory presented in Figure 4.4 the "Autonomy Theory of Premarital Sexual Permissiveness."

In the discussion of each proposition that follows, the reader should be aware that we are abiding very much by the principle of parsimony. Specifically, we are minimizing the number of interrelationships we assert and keeping only those that seem central to the importance of autonomy and that seem most in line with the evidence available at this time. One way to simplify is to drop direct relationships to the dependent variable if indirect relations are indicated and if no basic evidence or reasoning strongly supports the direct relationship. This can be seen in Figure 4.4. With so many variables present it is important not to overwhelm the potential researcher but rather to try to excite curiosity so he or she will commence research on some aspect of the total causal model. There is need for elaboration on all of the subsets of variables. For example, one could take just variables 11, 12, and 14 and develop them into a subtheory and in doing so add new variables and qualify existing ones. We are here only laying down the general outlines of a broad theory, and by no means is this a finished work. We feel certain that many of the interrelations will have to be altered but a start must be made.

One way in which economy was accomplished was to limit many of the variables to either an attitude of the individual or a shared orientation of the individual's reference groups or institutions. Now, of course, one may want to look precisely at the relationship of the attitude of an individual (on, say, variable 5, "Sexual Orientation," or variable 6, "Autonomy") to the shared attitudes or experience of those in his reference group on the same variable. The obvious relationships that could have been hypothesized were resisted, due to lack of empirical evidence and in order again to be parsimonious and to be able to present a manageable overview of the area. As intensive work is undertaken by others on particular segments of our causal design, it will be necessary to break up the overall causal design by levels of analysis as well as substantively and then at a later time put it back together again. In this way each segment may be more fully developed and tested.

The independent variables are ordered into four columns in Figure 4.4. The order is based on the length of time the variable has exerted influence over the individual. Thus column 1 (furthest to the left of the diagram) contains both traditional norms and current institutional influences that are assumed present throughout the formative years of the individual; the second column contains parental influences on the individual as he or she ages; the third column includes more recent attitudes and structural positions of the individual; and the fourth column includes the most recent influences in activity, perception, and orientation. There are many other ways of ordering these independent variables; but it was felt that this "length of influence" approach would lend itself to causal clarification, and thus it was adopted. All the influences are pictured as asymmetrical or one-way causal influences. This too was done for simplicity's sake, but it surely does not rule out the development of nonrecursive models as the theory is further elaborated.

Propositions Derived from Reiss's Original Proposition One

The original first proposition was elaborated upon in the first part of this chapter. The restatement here can be seen in Figure 4.4. The positive relationship between "Sexual Orientation" (variable 5) and individual premarital sexual permissiveness is presented toward the top of the diagram. We have marked this line with the number 1

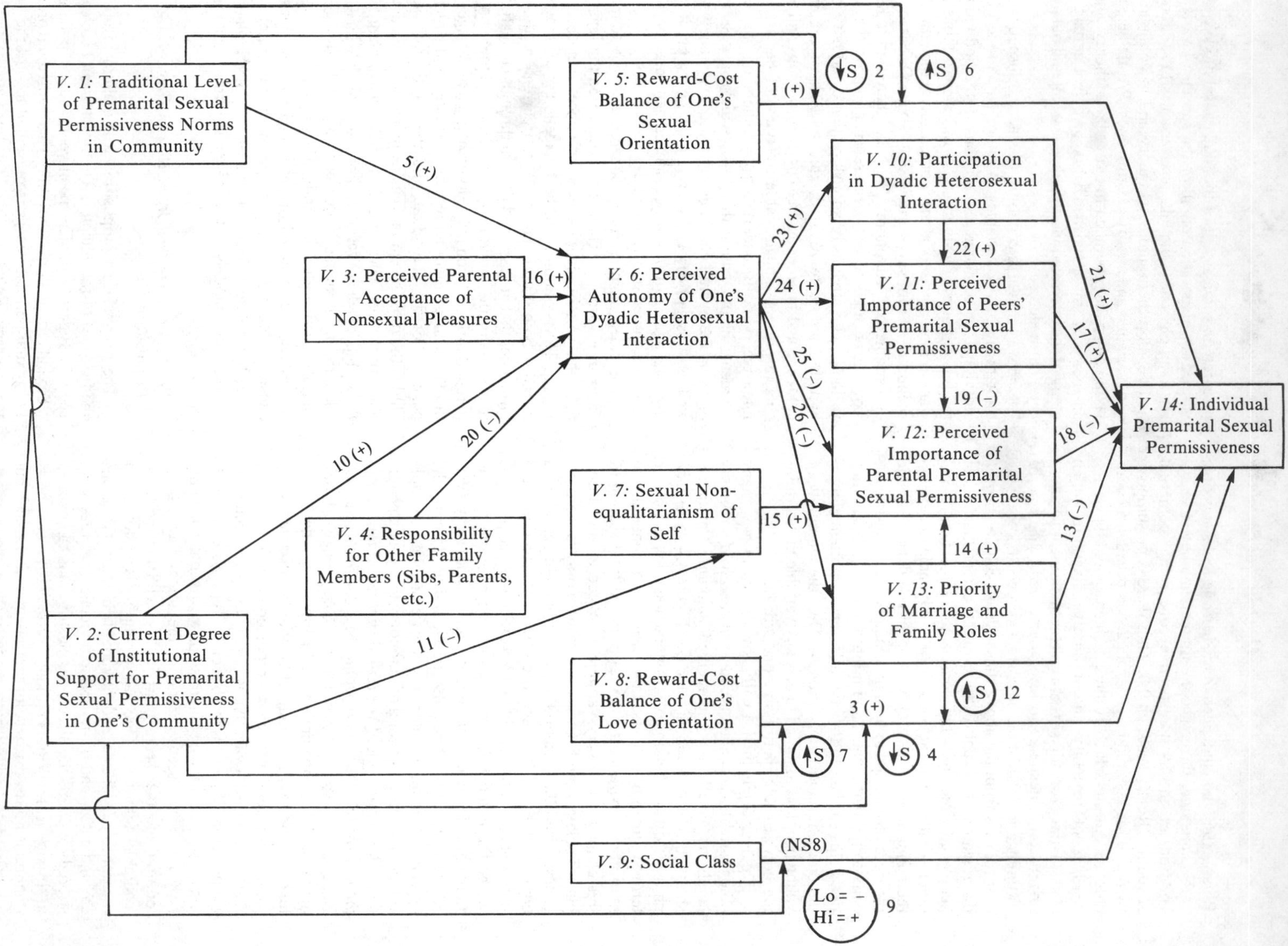

Figure 4.4. Autonomy Theory of Premarital Sexual Permissiveness

to signify that the relationship shown by the line represents Proposition 1 and with a plus sign to show it is in a positive direction. *Proposition 1* reads:

    1. The reward-cost balance of one's sexual orientation influences in a positive direction one's premarital sexual permissiveness.

Proposition 2 was also derived from the original first proposition of Reiss and refers to the interaction of variable 1 ("Traditional Level of Premarital Sexual Permissiveness") with the relationship posited in Proposition 1 (between sexual orientation and individual premarital sexual permissiveness). *Proposition 2* states that:

    2. The traditional level of premarital sexual permissiveness norms in a community influences in a negative direction the strength of the relation of one's sexual orientation to one's premarital sexual permissiveness.

It will be recalled that love orientation and sexual orientation were the two variables that we developed to operationalize the vague term "social forces." *Proposition 3* states that:

    3. The reward-cost balance of one's love orientation influences in a positive direction one's premarital sexual permissiveness.

Proposition 4 shows the interaction effect of variable 1, this time on the positive relationship between variable 8 ("Love Orientation") and the dependent variable. *Proposition 4* is:

    4. The traditional level of premarital sexual permissiveness norms in a community influences in a negative direction the strength of the relation of one's love orientation to one's premarital sexual permissiveness.

These four propositions represent the original Proposition One as put forth by Reiss (1967). The reasoning and evidence have been discussed in Part One. We have added one additional relationship stemming from variable 1 by showing the positive relationship between variable 1 and variable 6 ("Autonomy"). The assertion here is *Proposition 5*, which states:

    5. The traditional level of premarital sexual permissiveness norms in a community influences in a positive direction the amount of perceived autonomy in one's dyadic heterosexual interaction.

The reasoning underlying this additional proposition is that in communities that have had traditionally high levels of premarital sexual permissiveness, there will be available the means of achieving the allowed sexual relationships; that would involve the acceptance of high levels of individual autonomy for young people, and this would in turn result in the perception of high autonomy. Otherwise one would have traditional acceptance but lack the means of allowing for the acting out of the accepted values.

There is only tenuous evidence to support this proposition. For example, the traditional acceptance of premarital sexual permissiveness is higher for males than for females; and it is also true that males have generally greater autonomy than do females in terms of freedom from adult supervision and restrictions, particularly during courtship ages. Finally, males do seem to also perceive that they have high autonomy. What is needed is improvement in operationalization of "traditional level of premarital sexual permissiveness" and additional tests of this on specific groups. Nevertheless, there is presumptive evidence for this proposition that makes it important to assert and thus help ensure that it will receive an early test. "Perceived autonomy" refers to feelings of a lack of external constraint and could be measured by a Guttman-type scale asking for feelings of autonomy from various external sources. Please note that this proposition 5 is *not* derived from the original proposition 1 but rather is a result of our attempt to interrelate variables.

Propositions Derived from Reiss's Original Proposition Two

As discussed in Part One, there were some changes made in this proposition. First, the same change in operationalization was made for social forces; i.e., variables 5 and 8 ("Sexual Orientation" and "Love Orientation") were substituted for the term "social forces." General liberality was also found difficult to use as a unidimensional concept, and variable 2, "Current Degree of Institutional Support for Premarital Sexual Permissiveness in One's Community," was substituted for it. This variable incorporates the notion of community institutions and pinpoints them in terms of the premarital sexual permissiveness dimension. A community high on support for premarital sexual permissiveness in its educational, political, and religious institutions would be one that most would call "liberal" also, so the "liberality" dimension is not lost. Reiss did find that those individuals who were high on his measures of liberality were also high on his measures of premarital sexual permissiveness (Reiss, 1967, ch. 4). Such individual characteristics should influence community characteristics accordingly.

Looking at Figure 4.4 we see that variable 2 interacts with the relation of variable 5 and the dependent variable and also with the relation of variable 8 and the dependent variable. These interactions form *Propositions 6 and 7*, which are:

    6. The degree of institutional support for premarital sexual permissiveness in one's community influences in a positive direction the strength of the relation of one's sexual orientation to one's premarital sexual permissiveness.

    7. The degree of institutional support for the pre-

marital sexual permissiveness in one's community influences in a positive direction the strength of the relation of one's love orientation to one's premarital sexual permissiveness.

These relations are basic to the original formulation of this proposition by Reiss and were discussed in Part One.

In addition we have indicated other important causal effects of variable 2. The startling finding that social class was not related in the national or the student samples to the dependent variable is presented at the bottom of Figure 4.4 as *Proposition 8*. We include this null proposition because it has significant relationships in interaction with other variables. This proposition states:

8. Social class is not significantly related to one's premarital sexual permissiveness.

Relatedly, Figure 4.4 shows that variable 2 ("Institutional Support for Premarital Sexual Permissiveness") interacts with the nonsignificant relationship of social class to the dependent variable in such a way that those low on variable 2 will display a negative relation of social class and the dependent variable and those high on variable 2 will display a positive relationship of social class and our dependent variable. (Of course, it is the combination of these two categories of the control variable that produces the nonsignificant zero-order relationship in Proposition 8.) Thus *Proposition 9* asserts:

9. The degree of institutional support for premarital sexual permissiveness in one's community influences the nonsignificant relationship between one's social class and one's premarital sexual permissiveness so that those from a community with a low degree of institutional support for premarital sexual permissiveness will display a negative relationship and those from a community with a high degree of support for premarital sexual permissiveness will display a positive relationship of social class and one's premarital sexual permissiveness.

Definition and Indicators: Social class refers to the position one occupies in a prestige and power hierarchy in a society. Social class was measured by Reiss in several ways, but the preferred method was Duncan's Socio-Economic Index, which combines occupation, education, and income measures (A. J. Reiss, 1960).

This specification of Proposition 9 has not been fully tested, but the reasoning underlying the proposition is in line with leadership studies and asserts that the upper classes endorse the values of the group more than does the average member (Gibb, 1969). Thus in a group where the community supports high permissiveness, so will the upper classes; and in a group where the community institutions are low on permissiveness, then the upper classes will lead in endorsing these norms. No specific test of this explanation has ever been carried out; and thus

although general evidence of leadership groups does fit, this surely is only a weakly supported proposition in terms of causal explication. The original empirical finding appeared not only in Reiss's 1963 national samples but also in Albert Klassen and Eugene Levitt's 1970 national sample. However, the measures used for variable 2 are not fully adequate in those studies, and future testing is sorely needed on these exciting propositions.

In Proposition 10 we assert that variable 2 influences in a positive direction the level of perceived autonomy incorporated in variable 6. *Proposition 10* states that:

10. The degree of institutional support for premarital sexual permissiveness in one's community influences in a positive direction the degree of perceived autonomy in one's dyadic heterosexual interaction.

The reasoning behind this is analogous to that discussed above for Proposition 5. If the current institutional support for premarital sexual permissiveness is high, one would expect that such support would lead to the allowance of high autonomy and the resultant perception of high autonomy by the individual in his/her heterosexual interactions. Such a community would be more acceptant of the outcomes of sexual encounters. Empirical evidence for this proposition is not yet available.

Finally, variable 2 has further been elaborated to form Proposition 11, which asserts that variable 2 influences in a negative direction variable 7, "Sexual Nonequalitarianism." ("Sexual Nonequalitarianism will be explained further on in this section.) *Proposition 11* states:

11. The degree of institutional support for premarital sexual permissiveness in one's community influences in a negative direction the degree of sexual nonequalitarianism of oneself.

This too is largely untested except for some indirect support (Reiss, 1967, ch. 6), but is based on the reasoning that a community which is more likely to accept premarital sexual permissiveness is a more highly permissive community and that such a community will promote female permissiveness (for male permissiveness is already high) and will thereby achieve higher levels of equalitarianism. Some relevant evidence here was discussed in Part One and consists of data such as that from Christensen's studies (1966, 1969) which indicates that recent changes in premarital sexual permissiveness have been more common in female than in male groups and that in countries like Denmark there is more equality in views between the sexes than in countries like the United States. Testing on subgroups in our own country would be one way to more fully examine the workings of this proposition.

A final comment on the changes made in the original second proposition is that direct connections to the dependent variable are altered to include indirect relationships as well; variable 2 now impacts on the dependent variable indirectly via variables 5, 6, 7, 8, and 9. This type of change will be apparent throughout Figure 4.4. When one interrelates propositions, one inevitably alters in many ways the direct connection to the dependent variable that may have been present in the original bivariate propositions. This situation increases the number of untested relationships but also points directly toward which precise relationships need to be examined. Here, as elsewhere these interrelationships are offered only tentatively as a first step in the long-term process of scientific clarification and testing.

Propositions Derived from Reiss's Original Proposition Three

Proposition Three originally also used the vague term "social forces." For purposes of this proposition, one of the two new substitute variables used in the above propositions were utilized here, namely, "Love Orientation" (variable 8). Proposition Three related love orientation to the dependent variable of individual premarital sexual permissiveness. Proposition 12 points out how variable 13, "Priority of Marriage and Family Roles," interacts with that relationship and incorporates a major part of the original proposition. This interaction is described in *Proposition 12,* which states:

12. The priority of marriage and family roles influences in a positive direction the strength of the relationship between one's love orientation and individual premarital sexual permissiveness.

Reasoning and evidence for this were discussed in Part One of this chapter.

Further interrelations are posited involving "Priority of Marriage and Family Roles" (variable 13). *Proposition 13* states:

13. The priority of marriage and family roles influences in a negative direction individual premarital sexual permissiveness.

The reasoning underlying this proposition asserts that a high priority on marriage and family roles implies identification with low permissive sexual values. This fits with our basic theoretical orientation of the family and courtship groups as being fundamentally different on sexual values. The most direct support of such an assertion comes from comparison of males and females in our society. All such studies reveal that females are lower on individual premarital sexual permissiveness and that they do place higher priority on marriage and family roles. A more precise test would involve comparing individuals of the same sex who have different priorities and seeing if their individual sexual permissiveness differs as predicted.

One final additional interrelationship ties variable 13 to variable 12. This is *Proposition 14,* which states:

14. The priority of marriage and family roles influences in a positive direction the perceived importance of parental premarital sexual permissiveness.

The reasoning here contends that those who place higher priority on marriage and family roles will, because of this emphasis, be more likely to feel that their parents' views on sex are important in helping form their own views on sexuality. There is general evidence showing females giving higher priority to marriage and family roles and also being more likely to hold low permissive sexual values, as their parents do. However, this is not direct evidence on felt importance of parental views on sex. The only direct evidence for this proposition comes from the research of Robert Walsh (1970) and is supportive. Walsh's sample was a freshman class at Illinois State University.

Proposition Derived from Reiss's Original Proposition Four

The present conception of this original proposition is in part embodied in Proposition 11, stated above, which relates variable 2 ("Current Institutional Support for Premarital Sexual Permissiveness in One's Community") to variable 7 ("Sexual ·Nonequalitarianism of Self"). The original independent variable was simply the premarital sexual permissiveness of a reference group. We have equated that variable with variable 2. It seems reasonable to assume that a community in which there is high support for premarital sexual permissiveness in all the major social institutions will be a community that will have generally high acceptance of premarital sexual permissiveness in its reference groups. By making this assumption we eliminate the need for an additional variable, simplify our causal diagram, and, we hope, lose little in substantive meaning.

It should be clear that we are of necessity speaking of nonequalitarianism within only those standards that allow for nonequalitarianism, namely, the abstinence standard which can allow males to pet and females only to kiss and the double standard which can allow males various degrees of greater access to premarital coitus than females are allowed. The other two major standards are "permissiveness with affection" and "permissiveness without affection" and are basically equalitarian. (For a statement of these four standards, see Reiss, 1960.) In order to best indicate that we are referring only to those standards that can embody inequality (abstinence and double standard), we have labeled this variable sexual *non*equalitarianism instead of sexual equalitarianism.

This nonequalitarianism variable was related to the dependent variable in Part One of this chapter. Here we have given it an indirect route to the dependent variable by asserting *Proposition 15* as follows:

15. Sexual nonequalitarianism of self influences in

a positive direction the perceived importance of parental premarital sexual permissiveness.

The reasoning here assumes that youth culture in general is more equalitarian than adult culture and thus to the extent that a courtship group holds nonequalitarian sexual standards, they will perceive the nonequalitarian views of their parents as similar and thus as more important. The general idea here is that nonequalitarianism is produced by the basic institutions in one's community. Only indirect evidence is available here. Generally, we have data showing that lower permissive groups in Reiss's sample were more nonequalitarian (Reiss, 1967, ch. 6). We also found that adults in general are lower on sexual permissiveness. However, we have few data on perceived importance of parental premarital sexual permissiveness. Robert Walsh's (1976) study at Illinois State University. did show parents to be a more important reference group for those low as opposed to those high on premarital sexual permissiveness. This is relevant evidence and supports Proposition 15.

Proposition Derived from Reiss's Original Proposition Five

In Part One this proposition was refined to refer to the variable of Perceived Parental Acceptance of Nonsexual Pleasures (variable three) and this variable was related to the dependent variable. In Figure 4.4 we have related this independent variable to autonomy and then through autonomy to the dependent variable. *Proposition 16* asserts:

16. Perceived parental acceptance of nonsexual pleasures influences in a positive direction the perceived autonomy of one's dyadic heterosexual interaction.

The reasoning behind this proposition is that if one's parents accept pleasure as important, then as soon as the child learns that sex is a source of pleasure, he or she will want the freedom to pursue that pleasure and parents high on nonsexual pleasures will view autonomy as a necessary right to pursue pleasures. Thus the perception of autonomy should be high in this case. No data exist which are directly relevant to this proposition.

Propositions Derived from Reiss's Original Proposition Six

This proposition, in its refined form in Part One, involved two key independent variables, 11 and 12, as seen in Figure 4.4. The hypothesized relationship is rather straightforward. *Proposition 17* asserts that:

17. The perceived importance of peers' premarital sexual permissiveness influences in a positive direction the individual's premarital sexual permissiveness.

In Part One we discussed variables measuring "perceived similarity to peers" and "perceived permissiveness of peers" as well as "felt importance of peers' permissiveness."We have chosen here to be parsimonious and use only the "felt importance" variable. We believe that this variable reflects the "perceived similarity" variable and has the advantage of informing us on the importance of peers' views. The "importance" dimension should reflect the likelihood of peers affecting one's own attitudes.

The reasoning underlying Proposition 17 is that peers are a high permissive group as compared to most other community groups, certainly as compared to parents. Thus those who feel they are most influenced by peers will be peer-oriented in a way that promotes high permissiveness for themselves. We do have evidence (Reiss, 1967; Walsh, 1976) that shows that those who feel close to their peers' sexual permissiveness are more permissive than those who feel close to parental levels of sexual permissiveness. That brings us to our next proposition. *Proposition 18* states:

18. The perceived importance of parental premarital sexual permissiveness influences in a negative direction one's own premarital sexual permissiveness.

The reasoning and evidence for this are analogous to what was mentioned in connection with Proposition 17 above.

Variables 11 and 12 are asserted to be interrelated in *Proposition 19:*

19. The perceived importance of peers' premarital sexual permissiveness influences in a negative direction the perceived importance of parental premarital sexual permissiveness.

If one feels that peers are important for one's sexual values, then we assume that one will feel that parents are not so important for these values. The basis for this was put forth earlier when we stated that parental and peer permissiveness are at odds with each other. The reason the reverse relationship of these two variables is not asserted is that it is felt that peer influence increases in the sexual area in time and so those influenced by parental values may, in adolescent years, find that they shift to being more influenced by peer values. Relevant evidence was reviewed in Part One. Some evidence is available from Reiss (1967, ch. 8), where it was found that those close to peers were indeed more permissive than those who felt their standards were closer to parents. Further, if one felt close to peers' permissiveness, one was less likely to feel close to parental permissiveness. However, this is not the best test, and more appropriate research is needed.

Propositions Derived from Reiss's Original Proposition Seven

The two key independent variables involved in this proposition are variables four and ten in Figure 4.4. Variable four, Responsibility for Other Family Members, is interrelated by linking it with variable six, Autonomy. Thus *Proposition 20* states:

> 20. Responsibility for other family members influences in a negative direction the perceived autonomy of one's dyadic heterosexual interaction.

The reasoning here centers on the expectation that if a person is, for example, responsible for his/her siblings' care, then that person will be more likely to be inculcated with parental values in sex as well as other areas because of the close work connection with his/her parents. The tieup with parents produced by responsibility for other family members not only affects one's values in a conservative direction, but it is assumed that it also restricts the time and energy that one will have for dyadic heterosexual interaction and restricts the extent of perceived autonomy. Thus in these ways family responsibility restricts one's autonomy. Evidence on this was discussed in Part One. Reiss (1967, ch. 9) did find that family responsibility correlated with lower premarital sexual permissiveness. But no check was made as to whether this occurred due to lowered perceived autonomy of one's dyadic heterosexual interaction.

Variable 10 is our basic measure of courtship participation. We have given it the more general title "Participation in Dyadic Heterosexual Interaction" because we want to apply it to marital and extramarital relations in the final section of this chapter. *Proposition 21* is basically the same as the reformulated part of the original 1967 Proposition Seven.

> 21. Participation in dyadic heterosexual interaction influences in a positive direction the individual's premarital sexual permissiveness.

The reasoning here is that it is by the sexual opportunities that occur in courtship that one increases the sexual behavior and pleasure involved and thereby gains encouragement to increase his premarital sexual permissiveness. Evidence supporting this was presented by Reiss (1967, ch. 9) and has been discussed in Part One. Further testing and detailing of this is, of course, still needed to determine effects of different types of dating and of the quality versus the quantity of dating. We would expect experience in love to strengthen Proposition 21 for females. One may search for this by using variable 8 as a control on this proposition (Reiss, 1967, ch. 5).

One other relationship of variable 10 is put forth as *Proposition 22:*

> 22. Participation in dyadic heterosexual interaction influences in a positive direction the perceived importance of peers' premarital sexual permissiveness.

The reasoning here is that the more one participates in courtship, the more likely one is to be influenced by peers' sexual attitudes. This is so because one will then be interacting more with peers as one dates and such peers have similar interests in supporting an autonomous court-

ship system. Such similarity of objectives will bind peers together and make them subject to each other's values. Also parental values, being more restrictive, will increasingly seem inappropriate as one becomes more permissive in accord with Proposition 21. Evidence for this proposition is not present in any direct form, but Ehrmann (1959) did report a positive relation between dating frequency and likelihood of premarital coitus for females. Kaats and Davis (1970) also report positive correlations of dating frequencies with physical attractiveness and with some types of sexual experience. But such data are only indirectly relevant.

Propositions Derived from Reiss's General Theory

The general theory stressed the importance of two variables. One has been operationalized as variable 2, "Current Institutional Support for Premarital Sexual Permissiveness in One's Community." This variable we have already integrated into the overall schema. The second key variable was perceived autonomy, and this has been made one of the dominant variables in Figure 4.4. There are four relations in which perceived autonomy acts as the independent variable in a two-variable relationship. Those will now be presented as Propositions 23, 24, 25, and 26. First, *Proposition 23:*

> 23. Perceived autonomy of one's dyadic heterosexual interaction influences in a positive direction one's participation in dyadic heterosexual interaction.

The reasoning here is that as one perceives an increase in freedom in courtship, one will be more likely to participate in such courtship behavior. This is so because perceived autonomy motivates one to act on that perception and the youth culture emphasizes the value of exercising this perceived freedom. There is little direct evidence on this proposition except reports (Broderick, 1966) indicating that heterosexual interaction is a gradual, stepwise development that can be seen as part of youth culture socialization.

Proposition 24 is:

> 24. Perceived autonomy of one's dyadic heterosexual interaction influences in a positive direction the perceived importance of peers' premarital sexual permissiveness.

The reasoning here is that the more one feels free in courtship, the more one will relate to peers and be influenced by their sexual values. Perceived freedom from outside constraints seems important in order to establish the importance of the peer world. Evidence of a direct sort is lacking for this proposition, but the youth culture literature gives impressionistic support to the idea (Gottlieb and Ramsey, 1964; Douvan and Adelson, 1966).

Proposition 25 is:

> 25. Perceived autonomy of one's dyadic heterosex-

ual interaction influences in a negative direction the perceived importance of parental premarital sexual permissiveness.

The reasoning here is similar to that of Proposition 24 and involves viewing the parental and peer world as competitors with different sexual values. There is evidence that such differences in values exist (Reiss, 1967), but there is no direct evidence of the precise working of this proposition.

Proposition 26 is:

26. Perceived autonomy of one's dyadic heterosexual interaction influences in a negative direction the priority of marriage and family roles.

The reasoning here is in support of Proposition 20, which asserted that responsibility for other family members lowered perceived autonomy. In short it is assumed that perceived autonomy from the ties of one's family and community will leave one much more influenced by the ties of one's peers, and that peers will not put as high a priority on marriage and family roles. This is so since such things are not of high priority for young people because courtship and sexual activity are emphasized as good in themselves. Some evidence on this was discussed in Part One.

Summary of the Autonomy Theory of Premarital Sexual Permissiveness

At this point we should emphasize that this is clearly only an initial attempt to formulate an interrelated theory composed of 26 propositions derived from Reiss's work and from our recent theorizing. Many of the propositions are only weakly supported by empirical evidence. The advantage of taking this step is that we incorporate the best evidence and what we feel are the most productive propositions into one single theory. We also have focused the theory on autonomy as the central concept and thus have afforded an integration beyond just the mechanical tying together of propositions. This advance should afford a target for future researchers and theoreticians. Surely the theory is unfinished, and many of the individual propositions can be elaborated upon and even related to other propositions not present in the theory. Also, feedback relationships are quite plausible at places; but for simplicity's sake we have not inserted them. In short, we stress the tentativeness of this formulation but also stress the value it has for encouraging further theorizing.

RELATING THE AUTONOMY THEORY TO CHRISTENSEN'S PROPOSITIONS

Few other researchers have put forth explicit propositions in the areas of premarital sexuality. The most

systematic source for such propositions, other than Reiss's work, is the work of Harold Christensen. Four of the propositions Christensen presented in 1969 are suitable for use in this paper. We will go over these propositions and relate them to our autonomy theory. The reader is referred to Figure 4.5 for a diagrammatic statement of these propositions. Christensen refers to his propositions as forming a "Theory of Relative Consequences." The basic ideas of this notion are borne out most in what will be explained below as Proposition 30. In any case, his propositions are compatible with ours; and together they present a more complete view of the causal landscape of premarital sexual permissiveness. Burr (1973) did make some initial statements concerning relationships of a few of Reiss's and Christensen's propositions, but our analysis goes much further.

First, it is necessary to tie together at a common point our set of propositions and Christensen's set of propositions. It seems that the best point to do this is at our dependent variable, individual premarital sexual permissiveness. Thus we posit *Proposition 27:*

27. One's premarital sexual permissiveness influences in a positive direction the premarital sexual permissiveness norms in one's community.

The dependent variable here differs from our variable 1 in that it is current norms and variable 1 refers to traditional norms. The reasoning supporting this proposition assumes that as more individuals in a community come to share private attitudes, there will develop a public normative structure (a "social fact" in Durkheim's terms) to support these shared private attitudes. It is assumed that norms do not develop full-blown, and that it is from such steady growth of individual attitudes and the gradual awareness of similarity that norms develop and stabilize. This is precisely what we feel has happened in the area of premarital sexuality during the twentieth century (Reiss, 1960, 1973). Evidence on this process of norm development is indirect at best. We do have difficulty because so often the presence of shared attitudes is taken as the index of the presence of norms. It will be most worthwhile if this proposition encourages people to look more carefully into this area and into ways of measuring these concepts. We are not positing a feedback relation in Proposition 27, but in our discussion below of Proposition 32 a notion of this sort will be introduced.

The four propositions of Christensen relate to variable 15, "Premarital Sexual Permissiveness Norms in a Community." One proposition that Christensen asserts relates permissiveness norms to premarital sexual behavior in a community. Basically this *Proposition 28* asserts:

28. Premarital sexual permissiveness norms in a community influence in a positive direction premarital sexual behavior in that community.

The concept of premarital sexual behavior could be oper-

Figure 4.5.   Christensen Propositions on Premarital Sexual Permissiveness

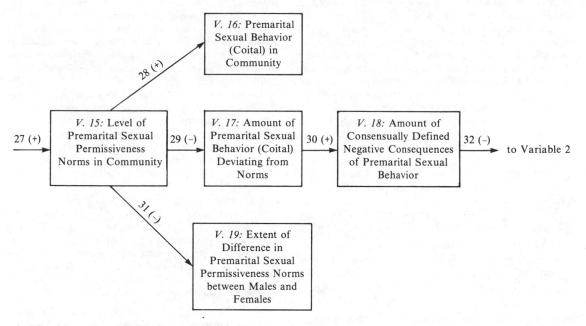

ationalized in terms of kissing, petting, and coital relationships; but we focus here on coitus. The reasoning behind the proposition is that attitudinal acceptance promotes behavior in line with those attitudes. There is a good deal of evidence available in Reiss (1967, ch. 7) which supports the connection of premarital attitudes and behavior. Christensen presents evidence from his research on students in Denmark, Indiana, and Utah. He found a high correlation between sexual attitudes and behavior and reported that the Danish students were highest on both permissive attitudes and behavior and Utah students lowest on both. Of course, one can here enter into the debate over whether the behavior came first and influenced the attitude. This is another point where our rule of parsimony will prevail and we will not enter into this debate. However, we should mention that other related attitudes and behaviors are contained in the 13 independent variables in Figure 4.4, and thus the precise relation of attitudes and behavior in toto is certain to be a very complex matter.

Premarital sexual permissiveness norms in a community are also viewed by Christensen as affecting the amount of premarital sexual behavior which deviates from those norms. *Proposition 29* puts the relation as follows:

> 29. The level of premarital sexual permissiveness norms in a community influences in a negative direction the amount of premarital sexual behavior deviating from such norms.

The evidence for this comes from Christensen's 1958

study of three subcultures, mentioned above. He did find that there was the greatest amount of difference between norms and behavior in the Utah culture (the lowest permissive culture) and the least amount of such difference in the Danish culture (the one highest on permissiveness). It is interesting to note that what difference there was in the Danish culture between sexual attitudes and behavior was in the direction of *less* behavior than the attitudes accepted; whereas in the Utah culture the large difference was in having *more* behavior than the attitudes accepted. The reasoning here would include the view that the opportunities for sexual behavior in our type of courtship are great and they can, in restrictive subcultures, lead to behavior that goes beyond acceptance levels.

The "Amount of Premarital Sexual Behavior Deviating from Norms" (variable 17) is also related to the amount of negative consequences of premarital sexual behavior, and this is put forth as *Proposition 30*:

> 30. The amount of premarital sexual behavior deviating from norms influences in a positive direction the amount of consensually defined negative consequences of such premarital sexual behavior.

Negative consequences here were those consensually defined by a group and were measured by Christensen in terms of likelihood of divorce, guilt feelings, pressure to have coitus, and rushing the wedding when pregnant. The reasoning is that when the coital act is accepted, such "negative" consequences are less likely to happen because such consequences are a direct result of feeling that the coital act is not accepted. Danish culture had the least increase of such consequences when norms were violated and Mormon Utah the most. This is the major proposition of Christensen's theory, as we see it. It points out the relativity of the consequences of premarital coitus. Reiss asserted this type of relationship in his 1960 book (191–94), but Christensen's data are the best empirical confirmation of it that is available. It is a particularly important point for those who are interested in moral judgments or in trying to decide what is best for themselves. Reiss (1967, ch. 7) also presented evidence showing that guilt was directly related to the gap between sexual attitudes and behavior. However, Reiss found a considerable amount of guilt (although the least) even for those whose attitudes and behavior were in line with each other. This is surely a most promising area to research for those with a social psychological interest.

The last of the Christensen propositions relates variable 15 to variable 19 (see Figure 4.5). This is *Proposition 31:*

31. The level of premarital sexual permissiveness of norms in a community influences in a negative direction the extent of differences in premarital sexual permissiveness norms between males and females.

The reasoning here is that in high permissive communities females have increased their permissiveness close to that of males and in low permissive communities it is the females who are more restrictive than the males. In short, it is because of the double standard in low permissive communities that males and females differ in the permissiveness of their sexual norms. Males are almost universally high in permissiveness, and that makes similarity to females possible only in high permissive cultures. Christensen's three-culture study does support this proposition as does Reiss (1967, ch. 2). Proposition Eleven, discussed above, can be compared here, but it refers to "self" and not to "normative" orientations.

Summary on Relating Christensen's Propositions to Reiss's

Definitions and Indicators. The definition and operationalization of Christensen's concepts are rather straightforward and noncomplex.

In variable 15 we would operationalize the level of premarital sexual permissiveness norms in the community by use of the Reiss Guttman scale. One would measure the average level of acceptance in a particular community. One could further inquire whether individuals felt the pressure of community norms in this area and if so what the norms were thought to be in terms of the range of the Reiss scale.

Variable 16 would simply be measured by asking the same sample of individuals questions concerning the occurrence of premarital intercourse during the same period of time they held a particular premarital sexual permissiveness norm.

Variable 17 would be a discrepancy measure comparing the answers to variable 15 with those for variable 16.

Variable 18 would be operationalized by asking a representative sample of a community to name the consequences of premarital coitus and the amount of them which one viewed as negative. An average score could be composed from the answers to such questions to form a consensual opinion.

Finally, *variable 19* would simply compare male and female responses to the Reiss scale for a particular community. An alternative method would be to see what differences there were in conception of community norms (using the Reiss scale) when the reference was to one sex or the other. The reader is referred to Christensen's writings for further elaboration of the possible ways of measuring his key variables.

Christensen's propositions are a valuable addition because they connect individual sexual attitudes to community norms and relate those norms to other important aspects of sexuality. The autonomy notion remains central, for it is the key variable in producing the current sexual norms that tie in with all four of Christensen's propositions. The overall tieup of these new and old propositions can be seen in *Proposition 32:*

32. The amount of consensually defined negative consequences of premarital sexual behavior influences in a negative direction the institutional support for premarital sexual permissiveness in a community.

The reasoning here is that as negative consequences increase (define "negative" to include whatever the majority of the community dislikes, e.g., venereal disease and premarital pregnancy), the community will be less likely to have a favorable attitude toward premarital sexuality as expressed through its major institutional frameworks. Little direct evidence of such changes is available. This is considered an important proposition to assert because it does tie up the variables at the beginning of Figure 4.4 and the end of Figure 4.5 and thereby proposes some interesting interrelationships.

GENERALIZING FROM PREMARITAL TO MARITAL AND EXTRAMARITAL SEXUALITY

It is believed that there is a compelling amount of face validity to support the generalizability of the autonomy theory of premarital sexual permissiveness to marital and extramarital sexual permissiveness. In short, what we have just formulated above does, with very little alteration, apply to the explanation of two other forms of heterosexuality, namely, marital and extramarital sexuality. The major thrust of this chapter concerns premarital sexuality, and thus we shall not go into very great detail here on marital and extramarital sexuality. The discussion here should be taken as a preliminary statement aimed at encouraging future work.

Exhibit 2. Reiss Marital Sexual Permissiveness Scale

Please indicate the degree of agreement you have with the following items concerning sex practices for husbands and wives. We are not interested in what you would "tolerate", "forgive", or "understand." Answer in terms of what you *personally* would find acceptable.

1. It is acceptable for a husband and wife to have intercourse if they are willing to accept the possibility of pregnancy occurring.

<blockquote>
Strongly agree   Slightly disagree
Moderately agree   Moderately disagree
Slightly agree   Strongly disagree
(These choices follow each question)
</blockquote>

2. It is acceptable for the husband and wife to have intercourse even when the motivation is primarily pleasure.
3. It is acceptable for a husband and wife to have intercourse when in the position where the husband is on top.
4. It is acceptable for a husband and wife to have intercourse in other positions in addition to the husband on top.
5. It is acceptable for the wife to make oral love to her husband (that is, mouth-penis contact).
6. It is acceptable for the husband to make oral love to his wife (that is, mouth-vagina contact).
7. It is acceptable to use the anal area as part of one's marital lovemaking.
8. Anything that the married couple agree upon as sexual practice is acceptable.

SOURCE: Composed in 1971 by Ira L. Reiss (tested and found to fit Guttman scaling criteria by Vernon J. Raschke, "Religiosity and Sexual Permissiveness," Ph.D. thesis, University of Minnesota, 1972). See discussion in Reiss (1976, ch. 15). The scale order of questions 2, 4, 5, 6, 7, and 8 was 2, 4, 8, 5, 6, 7. Questions 1 and 3 were not tested as worded above.

Perhaps a good way to open this discussion is to simply point out how some of the independent variables in Figures 4.4 and 4.5 would be altered if they applied to all three types of heterosexual permissiveness. Figure 4.6 is a representation of precisely this. (See Appendix A of this chapter for a full statement of all propositions in Figure 4.6.) One obvious change is that all references to premarital sexual permissiveness would be altered to refer to heterosexual permissiveness, except in Propositions 12 and 13, where specific ties are asserted to only premarital sexual permissiveness. There are two new permissiveness variables, and they are marital and extramarital permissiveness.

Definitions and Indicators. Marital sexual permissiveness would be operationalized by referring to the variety of sexual acts accepted by the married couple (going from coital to oral and to anal sex acts) for use in marital sexual relations. This marital sexual permissiveness measure is presumed to also fit a Guttman scale pattern (for an example of such a scale see Exhibit 2). Extramarital sexuality would be operationalized also by a Guttman-type scale asserting the conditions under which such sexual relations outside the marriage are permitted, such as conditions like the unhappiness of the marriage, the separation of the spouse due to travel, and the amount of affection involved in the extramarital relationship (for an example of such a scale see Exhibit 3).

The key variable of "Perceived Autonomy of One's Dyadic Heterosexual Interaction" (variable 6) as applied to marital and extramarital sexuality would simply refer to the extent to which religious orientations, kinship ties, and such are perceived as restricting one's heterosexual interaction with one's mate (marital) and/or with other people of the opposite sex (extramarital). In short, how

Exhibit 3. Reiss Extramarital Permissiveness Scale*

1. I believe that sexual intercourse with someone other than one's mate is acceptable for someone of my sex if they have strong affection for this extramarital partner and they are unhappily married.
2. I believe that sexual intercourse with someone other than one's mate is acceptable for someone of my sex if they have little affection for this extramartial partner and they are unhappily married.
3. I believe that sexual intercourse with someone other than one's mate is acceptable for someone of my sex if they have strong affection for this extramarital partner and they are happily married.
4. I believe that sexual intercourse with someone other than one's mate is acceptable for someone of my sex if they have little affection for this extramarital partner and they are happily married.

*The same questions with only the words "erotic kissing" or "petting" substituted for "sexual intercourse" can be added, making a total of 12 questions. The entire 12 questions can be asked a second time for "someone of the opposite sex" instead of for "someone of my sex" in order to discern equalitarianism and can also be changed to refer to "my mate." Sponaugle's (1975) administration of the above version of this scale (to measure general normative acceptance) on 117 married people in Minneapolis found the rank order from most acceptable to least acceptable to be the order of the above four questions. One can also reword the questions and personalize them by substituting "me" for the words "someone of my sex." (See discussion in Reiss, 1976, ch. 16.)

Figure 4.6.   Autonomy Theory of Heterosexual Permissiveness

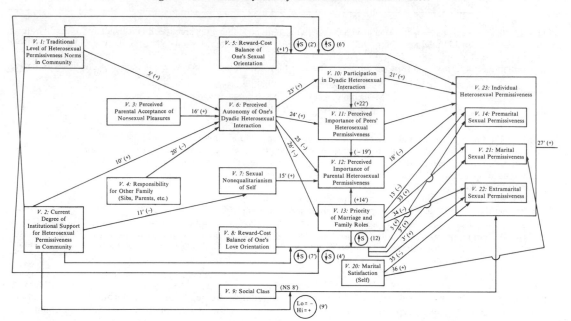

free from external constraint do the married individuals perceive themselves to be to do what they want with their mate and/or with others?

The parental variables, such as variable 3, may be less powerfully related because of the greater passage of time since such parental contact and influence, but we assert it will still be relevant. Variable 4 is concerned with responsibility for other family members, and this can be assumed to mean siblings and parents and should also perhaps be weaker but still in operation for married people.

The sexual and love orientation variables would of course be separately measured for each of the three types of sexuality. One would relate the premarital measures of sexual and love orientation to premarital permissiveness, the marital measures to marital permissiveness, and the extramarital measures to extramarital permissivenss. However, it is assumed that the direction of the relationship remains unaltered in these three cases; and thus no new propositions are required. One could explore the interrelationship among the three propositions that relate each of these three independent variables to one type of permissiveness, but this exploration would take us into a very complex area that is virtually unexplored, and in the interest of parsimony we leave this task to others. In the early stages of theory building one cannot develop all possible interrelationships.

Variable 10, "Participation in Dyadic Heterosexual Interaction," would simply refer to all opportunities for

interaction with members of the opposite sex (not just one's mate) and would include various settings on and off the job and in and out of one's community. In this way a measure of heterosexual interaction for each of the three types of heterosexuality could be compared. The term "heterosexual" here would simply mean that both sexes are involved in these situations and does not necessarily refer to sexual behavior.

A few causal ties of variables need to be altered when generalizing from premarital sexual permissiveness to marital and extramarital sexual permissiveness. For example, "Priority of Marriage and Family Roles" (variable 13) is hypothesized to interact only with the relation of premarital love orientation and premarital sexual permissiveness. Nevertheless, the basic relationship of love orientation to all three types of sexual permissiveness was assumed to be a positive one. Thus Figure 4.6 shows this basic relationship (Proposition 3) to hold by three separate causal lines, with the premarital line being the only one that the priority of family roles interacts with. The use of separate causal lines for each type of permissiveness is needed if only one type involves interaction or differs in other ways. It is interesting to note how infrequently such differences appear in Figure 4.6.

Variable 13, "Priority of Marriage and Family Roles," requires further elaboration. The relationship of this variable to marital sexual permissiveness is positive and thus different than the relation in Proposition 13 and also different from that postulated for extramarital sexual

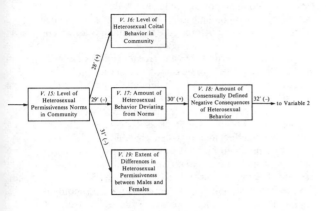

permissiveness. Thus new *Propositions 33* and *34* are needed:

33. Priority of marriage and family roles influences in a positive direction marital sexual permissiveness.
34. Priority of marriage and family roles influences in a negative direction extramarital sexual permissiveness.

In both of these propositions it is assumed that if one places a high priority on marriage and family roles, one will be more cautious about risking damage to those roles through extramarital sex and will focus sexual experimentation within the marriage.

Both of the above propositions lack strong empirical support. Virtually no evidence exists for Proposition 33, and inconclusive evidence exists for Proposition 34. J. Edwards's 1973 article contains an excellent summary of evidence and propositions on extramarital sexual permissiveness. Libby and Whitehurst (1973) also have a summary in their ch. 7. Reiss comments on these questions (Reiss, 1976, ch. 15 & 16) at some length. The reasoning supporting these propositions is rather straightforward and based on the influence of marriage and the family on sexuality. It is popular reasoning, but only future research will settle the validity of this type of reasoning. It seems likely that researchers will have to consider the type of extramarital relationship and thereby further specify Proposition 34. Extramarital relationships that occur with the consent of both husband and wife may well make a

difference in this proposition, but such consensual extramarital sex is not the dominant form today.

One new independent variable needs to be added to make the autonomy theory fit all three types of heterosexuality. It is significant that only one such variable is needed. The variable is number 20, "Marital Satisfaction."

Definition and Indicators. Marital satisfaction is the degree to which personally defined rewards from a marital relationship exceed personally defined costs. We would operationalize this with the measures used by Bradburn (1969:275, 297) which incorporate both rewards and tensions in the marital interaction and thereby secure a balance score. The literature on extramarital sexual permissiveness indicates support for the view that marital satisfaction influences in a negative direction extramarital sexual permissiveness (Edwards, 1973; Sponaugle, 1977; Gilmartin, 1976; Whitehurst, 1969; Johnson, 1970). Bell et al. (1975) support this with behavioral data. But other authors argue that there is no such relation (Libby and Whitehurst, 1973). We accept the studies showing the negative relation as more valid, for such studies are more common and just as well done. Thus we put forth *Proposition 35:*

35. Marital satisfaction influences in a negative direction extramarital sexual permissiveness.

However, here too we need to specify the type of marriage and the type of extramarital relationship (Reiss, 1973, 1976). In relation to marital sexual permissiveness, Kinsey et al. (1953) and Burgess and Wallin (1953) would support the view that marital satisfaction influences in a positive direction marital sexual permissiveness at least in terms of coital orgasms. There are data supporting the relation of marital closeness to sexual satisfaction in Hunt (1974), Clark and Wallin (1965) and Rainwater (1966). Accordingly we assert *Proposition 36:*

36. Marital satisfaction influences in a positive direction marital sexual permissiveness.

The reasoning here is rather obvious. In a generally satisfying relation, one is more willing to experiment with new forms of sexual satisfaction, for one feels comfortable enough to take whatever risks are involved and to do whatever self-revelation is required.

The above indicates that by adding just four new propositions and just one new independent variable, we have produced an autonomy theory of all three types of *Heterosexual permissiveness.* The potential importance of the theory is increased by this wider substantive scope. The original dependent variable, premarital sexual permissiveness, was expanded to include marital sexual permissiveness and extramarital sexual permissiveness as separate variables and also to include a global variable comprising these three, called heterosexual permissiveness. Although we have cited many of the key studies relevant to marital and extramarital sexuality, we have not described these studies to the same extent as we did the premarital sex studies. This was so because the paper focuses on premarital sex and is already quite lengthy. For more details see Reiss (1976, chs. 15 and 16).

In Figure 4.6, when an arrow stops at the border of heterosexual permissiveness, the measure of the antecedent variable affects all three subvariables in the same direction. When there is a differential effect postulated, the arrows go separately to each of the three subvariables. This can mean a change in direction (e.g., Propositions 13, 33, 34) or an interaction effect that does not apply to all three types of permissiveness (e.g., Propositions 3 and 12).

Summary and Conclusions

Heterosexual permissiveness and behavior in the Western world have both apparently been on an upward trend since the late 1960s (Reiss, 1973). This is a particularly interesting time, then, to do research on a theory of heterosexuality such as that presented above. We can test notions of change quite easily on the current cultural scene. It may well become necessary to specify theories of heterosexuality by the social context in terms of change and the direction of change that is occurring in that society.

On an individual level, there appears to also be a constant element of change that operates regardless of the social context. By this we mean that there is an upward trend in individual heterosexual permissiveness that operates within each individual's lifetime (Reiss, 1973). For example, from age 10 to age 20 there is a constant increase in individual levels of premarital sexual permissiveness (Reiss, 1967, ch. 7; Zelnik and Kantner, 1972; Sorensen, 1973). We would speculate that during at least the first 10 years of marriage there is a constant increase in sexual experimentation despite the lack of any increase in coital frequency. However, little evidence exists on this particular point.

Kinsey's data on college-educated males showed a tendency for extramarital coitus to begin to increase after about 10 years of marriage (Kinsey, 1948). Working-class males started much earlier and were declining by the time college-educated males were increasing their extramarital coitus rates. There are no comparable data on females, and even the male data need to be tested on more recent samples. Nevertheless, it appears that the particular age and place in the marital system an individual is in are key variables to consider in any theoretical analysis.

Another factor of considerable importance that should be borne in mind by anyone testing this theoretical schema is the role of the double standard. For example, variable 2, "Institutional Support for Heterosexuality," will no doubt vary with regard to males and females. Laws punish female prostitutes more than their customers; juries tend to accept male revenge for extramarital sex more than similar action by females; sex education in the schools and in religious organizations tends to stress the male as the sexual inititiator. All of this is a reflection of the general proposition that the gender which is in economic and political power will be the gender given greater sexual rights. In good measure that is because the gender in power enacts and enforces the laws and the customs of the community.

Variable 13 ("Priority of Marriage and Family Roles") in our theory is likely to be quite different for males and females because each sex is brought up differently in this regard, and this has a crucial effect on their sexuality. Males take a more casual, pleasure-centered view of sex because they do not have to be as concerned with how sexuality will affect their marriage chances. Thus in many ways one needs to be alert to the action of the double standard even in a society such as ours with its increasing degree of equalitarianism (Reiss, 1976, ch. 5).

One final comment on our key concept of autonomy is that what we mean by it is self-rule. Often the measures of autonomy indicate separation from religious, family, or community controls. These same measures can be taken as indices of anomie or alienation, and thus we suggest that researchers add indices of the degree to which one is favorably oriented to this freedom from constraint (autonomy) as opposed to the degree to which one feels turned off, hostile, or excluded by this freedom (alienation). Development of this theory will require precise handling of this key concept of autonomy. Many of our variables embody this autonomy concept, and thus clarity is quite important here.

Our basic aim is to develop causal understanding of the ways in which heterosexual permissiveness is altered. Thus we are not wedded to the approach that stresses only variables that explain the most variance. We want to explain variance, but our first concern is with theoretical understanding of this area of human behavior (see Burr, 1973, ch. 14). These two goals are not always identical. If a proposition has great theoretical potential, one may well hesitate to discard it without further testings on different samples even if parts of it explain only small amounts of variance.

The theory presented covers the major areas that seem important, but any of the variables can be expanded upon and new relations and new variables introduced. Many parts of the theory are supported by evidence cited in Part One or in Part Two, while other propositions are not so clearly supported. In short, more research is needed on all the propositions. One could proceed by testing the reformulated propositions in Figure 4.3 and then proceed to test the integrated propositions in Figure 4.6. One might also reorder some variables in Figure 4.6. We expect individuals will tackle different parts of this causal puzzle, although some few may want to try their hand at testing or expanding the total theoretical design. Robert Walsh at Illinois State University in 1974 undertook such an overall testing of the design in Figure 4.4. His findings are still being analyzed, but initial reports indicate there will indeed be alternations needed (Walsh, 1977). This is as we would expect, since theorizing is always a tentative endeavor. Reiss is currently starting on a research project that will test some of the propositions here plus others that bear on the area of extramarital sexuality.

Finally, we should note that there is a vast amount of sexual behavior such as autoerotic or homosexual behavior that we have not considered in this chapter. It is imperative that such areas be researched and eventually be theoretically tied to the heterosexual theories (see Reiss, 1976, ch. 12). Some work is being done now on such interrelationships (Levitt and Klassen, 1974).

It is also very important to stress again that we have focused in this chapter on Reiss's theoretical work since it is the most developed in the field, but there are other approaches that need to be worked upon and joined to it. We hope in presenting the autonomy theory to add incentive toward future theory and research in this fruitful area of human sexuality. We do not expect that these 36 propositions will all hold up. Rather, we hope that their presentation will start the testing and development of an integrated theory of human sexuality.

APPENDIX A:

STATEMENT OF PROPOSITIONS IN FIGURE 4.6, "AUTONOMY THEORY OF HETEROSEXUAL PERMISSIVENESS"

1'. The reward-cost balance of one's sexual orientation influences in a positive direction one's heterosexual permissiveness.

2'. The traditional level of heterosexual permissiveness norms in a community influences in a negative direction the strength of the relation of one's sexual orientation to one's heterosexual permissiveness.

3'. The reward-cost balance of one's love orientation influences in a positive direction one's heterosexual permissiveness.

4'. The traditional level of heterosexual permissiveness norms in a community influences in a negative direction the strength of the relation of one's love orientation to heterosexual permissiveness.

5'. The traditional level of heterosexual permissiveness norms in a community influences in a positive direction the amount of perceived autonomy in one's dyadic heterosexual interaction.

6'. The degree of institutional support for heterosexual

permissiveness in one's community influences in a positive direction the strength of the relation of one's sexual orientation to one's heterosexual permissiveness.

7'. The degree of institutional support for heterosexual permissiveness in one's community influences in a positive direction the strength of the relation of one's love orientation to one's heterosexual permissiveness.

8'. Social class is not significantly related to one's heterosexual permissiveness.

9'. The degree of institutional support for the heterosexual permissiveness in one's community influences the nonsignificant relationship between one's social class and one's heterosexual permissiveness so that those from a community with a low degree of institutional support for heterosexual permissiveness will display a negative relationship and those from a community with a high degree of support for heterosexual permissiveness will display a positive relationship of social class and one's heterosexual permissiveness.

10'. The degree of institutional support for heterosexual permissiveness in one's community influences in a positive direction the degree of perceived autonomy in one's dyadic heterosexual interaction.

11'. The degree of institutional support for heterosexual permissiveness in one's community influences in a negative direction the degree of sexual nonequalitarianism of oneself.

12. The priority of marriage and family roles influences in a positive direction the strength of the relationship between one's love orientation and individual premarital sexual permissiveness.

13. The priority of marriage and family roles influences in a negative direction individual premarital sexual permissiveness.

14'. The priority of marriage and family roles influences in a positive direction the perceived importance of parental heterosexual permissiveness.

15'. Sexual non-equalitarianism of self influences in a positive direction the perceived importance of parental heterosexual permissiveness.

16. Perceived parental acceptance of non-sexual pleasure influences in a positive direction the perceived autonomy of one's dyadic heterosexual interaction.

17'. The perceived importance of peers' heterosexual permissiveness influences in a positive direction the individual's heterosexual permissiveness.

18'. The perceived importance of parental heterosexual permissiveness influences in a negative direction one's own heterosexual permissiveness.

19'. The perceived importance of peers' heterosexual permissiveness influences in a negative direction the perceived importance of parental heterosexual permissiveness.

NOTE: Prime sign (') next to the proposition number indicates that the original reference in the variable to "premarital sexual permissiveness" has been changed to "heterosexual permissiveness."

20′. Responsibility for other family members influences in a negative direction the perceived autonomy of one's dyadic heterosexual interaction.

21′. Participation in dyadic heterosexual interaction influences in a positive direction the individual's heterosexual permissiveness.

22′. Participation in dyadic heterosexual interaction influences in a positive direction the perceived importance of peers' heterosexual permissiveness.

23′. Perceived autonomy of one's dyadic heterosexual interaction influences in a positive direction one's participation in dyadic heterosexual interaction.

24′. Perceived autonomy of one's dyadic heterosexual interaction influences in a positive direction the perceived importance of peers' heterosexual permissiveness.

25′. Perceived autonomy of one's dyadic heterosexual interaction influences in a negative direction the perceived importance of parental heterosexual permissiveness.

26′. Perceived autonomy of one's dyadic heterosexual interaction influences in a negative direction the priority of marriage and family roles.

27′. One's heterosexual permissiveness influences in a positive direction the heterosexual permissiveness norms in one's community.

28′. Heterosexual permissiveness norms in a community influences in a positive direction heterosexual (coital) behavior in that community.

29′. The level of heterosexual permissiveness norms in a community influences in a negative direction the amount of heterosexual (coital) behavior deviating from such norms.

30′. The amount of heterosexual coital behavior deviating from norms influences in a positive direction the amount of consensually defined negative consequences of such heterosexual behavior.

31′. The level of heterosexual permissiveness of norms in a community influences in a negative direction the extent of differences in heterosexual permissiveness norms between males and females.

32′. The amount of consensually defined negative consequences of heterosexual behavior influences in a negative direction the institutional support for heterosexual permissiveness in a community.

33′. Priority of marriage and family roles influences in a positive direction marital sexual permissiveness.

34. Priority of marriage and family roles influences in a negative direction extramarital sexual permissiveness.

35. Marital satisfaction influences in a negative direction extramarital sexual permissiveness.

36. Marital satisfaction influences in a positive direction marital sexual permissiveness.

REFERENCES

BANWART, A. L.
1973   "Social class and the acceptance of premarital intercourse in the United States: A literature test of a proposition." Unpublished manuscript. Department of Sociology, University of Minnesota.

BAYER, ALAN E.
1977   "Sexual Permissiveness and Correlates as Determined through interaction analyses." *Journal of Marriage and the Family* 39:29–40.

BELL, R. AND J. B. CHASKES
1970   "Premarital sexual experience among coeds, 1958 and 1968." *Journal of Marriage and the Family* 32:81–84.

BELL, R. R., S. TURNER, AND L. ROSEN
1975   "A multivariate analysis of female extramarital coitus." *Journal of Marriage and the Family* 36:375–84.

BOWERMAN, C. E. AND J. W. KINCH
1959   "Changes in family and peer orientation of children between the fourth and tenth grades." *Social Forces* 37:206–11.

BRADBURN, N.
1969   *The Structure of Psychological Well-Being*. Chicago: Aldine.

BRITTAIN, C. V.
1959   "Parents and peers as competing influences in adolescence." Unpublished Doctoral Dissertation, University of Chicago.

BRODERICK, C. B.
1966   "Socio-sexual development in suburban community." *Journal of Sex Research* 2:1–24.

BURGESS, E. W. AND P. WALLIN
1953   *Engagement and Marriage*. Chicago: J. B. Lippincott.

BURR, W. R.
1973   *Theory Construction and the Sociology of the Family*. New York: Wiley.

CANNON, K. AND R. LONG
1971   "Premarital sexual behavior in the sixties." *Journal of Marriage and the Family* 33:36–49.

CHRISTENSEN, H. T.
1960   "Cultural relativism and premarital sex norms." *American Sociological Review* 25:31–39.
1966   "Scandinavian and American sex norms: Some comparisons, with sociological implications." *The Journal of Social Issues* 22:60–75.
1969   "Normative theory derived from cross-cultural family research." *Journal of Marriage and the Family* 31:209–22.

CHRISTENSEN, H. T. AND G. R. CARPENTER
1962a   "Timing patterns in the development of sexual intimacy." *Marriage and Family Living* 24:30–35.
1962b   "Value-behavior discrepancies regarding premarital coitus in three western cultures." *American Sociological Review* 27:66–74.

CHRISTENSEN, H. T. AND C. F. GREGG
1970   "Changing sex norms in America and Scandinavia." *Journal of Marriage and the Family* 32:616–27.

CLARK, A. L. AND P. WALLIN
1965   "Women's sexual responsiveness and the duration and quality of their marriages." *American Journal of Sociology* 21:187–96.

CLAYTON, R.
1969   "Religious orthodoxy in premarital sex." *Social Forces* 47:469–74.

COSTNER, H. L. AND R. K. LEIK
1964   "Deductions from 'axiomatic theory'." *American Sociological Review* 29:819–35.

CUBER, J. F. AND P. HARROFF
1965   *The Significant Americans*. New York: Appleton-Century-Crofts.

DAVIS, K.
1966   "Sexual behavior." In R. K. Merton and R. A. Nisbet (eds.), *Contemporary Social Problems*. New York: Harcourt, Brace, Jovanovitch.

DELAMATER, J. D.
1974   "Methodological issues in the study of premarital sexuality." *Sociological Methods and Research* 3:31-61.

DOUVAN, E. AND J. ADELSON
1966   *The Adolescent Experience*. New York: Wiley.

EDWARDS, J. N.
1973   "Extramarital involvement: Fact and theory." *Journal of Sex Research* 9:210-24.

EHRMANN, W.
1959   *Premarital Dating Behavior*. New York: Henry Holt.
1964   "Marital and nonmarital sexual behavior." In H. T. Christensen (ed.), *Handbook of Marriage and the Family*. Chicago: Rand McNally.

GIBB, C. A.
1969   "Leadership." In G. Lindzey and E. Aronson (eds.), *Handbook of Social Psychology,* second ed. Reading, Mass: Addison-Wesley.

GIBBS, J. P.
1972   *Sociological Theory Construction*. Hinsdale, Ill.: Dreyden Press.

GILMARTIN, B.
1976   "Co-marital sex." Unpublished Doctoral Dissertation, University of Iowa.

GLASER, B. G. AND A. L. STRAUSS
1967   *The Discovery of Grounded Theory: Strategies for Qualitative Research*. Chicago: Aldine.

GLASS, J. C.
1972   "Premarital sexual standards among church youth leaders: An exploratory study." *Journal for the Scientific Study of Religion* 11:361-67.

GOTTLIEB, D. AND C. RAMSEY
1964   *The American Adolescent*. Homewood, Ill.: Dorsey Press.

HAGE, J.
1973   *Techniques and Problems of Theory Construction in Sociology*. New York: Wiley-Interscience.

HAMPE, G. D. AND H. J. RUPPEL, JR.
1974   "Measurement of premarital sexual permissiveness: Comparison of two Guttman scales." *Journal of Marriage and the Family* 36:451-63.

HARRIS, I. D. AND K. I. HOWARD
1968   "Birth order and responsibility." *Journal of Marriage and the Family* 30:427-32.

HARRISON, D. E., W. H. BENNETT, AND G. GLOBETTI
1969   "Attitudes of rural youth toward premarital sexual permissiveness." *Journal of Marriage and the Family* 31:783-87.

HELTSLEY, M. AND C. BRODERICK
1969   "Religiosity and premarital sexual permissiveness: Re-examination of Reiss' traditional proposition." *Journal of Marriage and the Family* 31:441-43.

HUNT, M.
1974   *Sexual Behavior in the 1970's*. Chicago: Playboy Press.

HUNTER, T. L.
1971   "Premarital sexual standards in a religiously conservative college." Doctoral Dissertation, University of Georgia.

JOHNSON, R. E.
1970   "Some correlates of extramarital coitus." *Journal of Marriage and the Family* 32:449-57.

KAATS, G. R. AND K. E. DAVIS
1970   "The dynamics of sexual behavior in college students." *Journal of Marriage and the Family* 32:390-99.

KINSEY, A. C. ET AL.
1948   *Sexual Behavior in the Human Male*. Philadelphia: W. B. Saunders.
1953   *Sexual Behavior in the Human Female*. Philadelphia: W. B. Saunders.

KLASSEN, A. AND E. LEVVITT
1972   National Sex Survey, Personal Correspondence.

LANNING, A. B., III.
1970   "Parental role structure and sexual permissiveness of offspring." Doctoral Dissertation, University of Tennessee.

LAZARSFELD, P. F.
1955   "Interpretation of statistical relations as a research Operation." in P. F. Lazarsfeld and M. Rosenberg (eds.), *The Language of Social Research*. New York: Free Press.

LEVITT, E. AND A. KLASSEN
1974   "Public attitudes toward homosexuality." *Journal of Homosexuality* 1:29-43.

LEWIS, R. A. AND W. R. BURR
1975   "Premarital coitus and commitment among college students." *Archives of Sexual Behavior* 4:73-79.

LIBBY, R. W.
1974   "A multivariate test of reference group and role correlates of Reiss' premarital permissiveness theory." Unpublished Ph.D. Dissertation, Washington State University.

LIBBY, R. W. AND C. C. NASS
1971   "Parental views on teenage sexual behavior." *Journal of Sex Research* 7:226-36.

LIBBY, R. W. AND R. WHITEHURST
1973   *Renovating Marriage*. San Ramon, Calif.: Consensus Publications.

MARANELL, G. M., R. A. DODDER, AND D. F. MITCHELL
1970   "Social class and premarital sexual permissiveness: A subsequent test." *Journal of Marriage and the Family* 32:85-88.

MIDDENDORP, C. P., W. BRINKMAN, AND W. KOOMEN
1970   "Determinants of premarital sexual permissiveness: A secondary analysis." *Journal of Marriage and the Family* 32:368-73.

MILLER, B. C.
1973   "The relative influence of parents and peers considered developmentally." Unpublished paper, University of Minnesota.
1974   "Assessing and reworking Ira Reiss' theory of premarital sexual permissiveness." Paper presented at the National Council on Family Relations Preconference Theory Workshop, Toronto, Ontario.

MIRANDE, A.
1968   "Reference group theory in adolescent sexual behavior." *Journal of Marriage and the Family* 30:572-77.

NEWCOMB, T.
1958   "Attitude development as a function of reference groups: The Bennington study." In E. E. Maccoby, T. M. Newcomb, and E. L. Hartley (eds.), *Readings in Social Psychology*. New York: Holt, Rinehart and Winston.

PERLMAN, D.
1974   "Self esteem and sexual permissiveness." *Journal of Marriage and the Family* 36:470-74.

RAINWATER, L.
1966   "Some aspects of lower class sexual behavior." *Journal of Social Issues* 22:96-108.

RASCHKE, V. J.
1972   "Religiosity and sexual permissiveness." Doctoral Dissertation, University of Minnesota.

REISS, A. J., JR.
1960   *Occupation and Social Status*. New York: Free Press.

REISS, I. L.
1960 *Premarital Sexual Standards in America.* New York: Free Press.
1964 "The scaling of premarital sexual permissiveness." *Journal of Marriage and the Family* 26:188–98.
1967 *The Social Context of Premarital Sexual Permissiveness.* New York: Holt, Rinehart and Winston.
1969 "Response to the Heltsley and Broderick re-test of Reiss' proposition one." *Journal of Marriage and the Family* 31:444–45.
1970 "Comments on Middendorp's 'The determinants of premarital sexual permissiveness'." *Journal of Marriage and the Family* 32:379–80.
1973 "Heterosexual relationships: Inside and outside of marriage." Morristown, N.J.: Module for General Learning Press.
1976 *Family Systems in America,* second ed. New York: Holt-Dryden.
1978 "Sexual customs and gender roles in Sweden and America: An analysis and interpretation." In H. Lopata (ed.), *Research in the Interweave of Social Roles: Women and Men.* Greenwich, Conn.: Jai Press.

REISS, I. L. AND B. C. MILLER
1974 "A theoretical analysis of heterosexual permissiveness." University of Minnesota Family Study Center, Technical Bulletin # 2, 113 pp.

REISS, I. L., A. BANWART, AND H. FOREMAN
1975 "Premarital contraceptive usage: A study and some theoretical explanations." *Journal of Marriage and the Family* 37:619–30.

ROBINSON, I. E., K. KING, C. J. DUDLEY, AND F. J. CLUNE
1968 "Changes in sexual behavior and attitudes of college students." *Family Coordinator* 17:119–23.

ROBINSON, I. E., K. KING, AND J. O. BALSWICK
1972 "The premarital sexual revolution among college females." *Family Coordinator* 22:189–94.

RUPPEL, H.
1970 "Religiosity and premarital sexual permissiveness: A response to the Reiss-Heltsley and Broderick debate." *Journal of Marriage and the Family* 32: 647–55.

SIMON, W., A. BERGER, AND J. GAGNON
1972 "Beyond anxiety and fantasy." *Journal of Youth and Adolescence* 1:203–22.

SORENSEN, R.
1973 *Adolescent Sexuality in Contemporary U.S.A.* New York: World Publishers.

SPONAUGLE, G. C.
1977 "Extramarital Sexual Relations." Paper presented at the Midwest Sociological Society, Minneapolis.

STAPLES, R. E.
1971 "A study of the influence of liberal-conservative attitudes on the premarital sexual standards of different racial, sex-role and social class groupings." Doctoral Dissertation, University of Minnesota.

U.S. DEPARTMENT OF HEALTH, EDUCATION AND WELFARE
1975 *Monthly Vital Statistics Report,* vol. 23, #11. Washington, D.C.: Government Printing Office.

VANDIVER, R. D.
1972 "Sources and interrelation of premarital sexual standards and general liberality conservatism." Doctoral dissertation, Southern Illinois University.

WALSH, R. H.
1970 "A survey of parents and their own children's sexual attitudes." Doctoral dissertation, University of Iowa.

WALSH, R. H., M. ZEY-FERRELL, AND W. TOLONE
1976 "Selection of reference group, perceived reference group permissiveness, and personal permissiveness attitudes and behavior: A study of two consecutive panels (1967–71; 1970–74)." *Journal of Marriage and the Family* 495–507.
1977 "Reiss' Proposition One: A test and comparison of the 1967 original and the 1975 reformulation." Paper presented at the American Sociological Association Annual Meeting, Chicago.

WHITEHURST, R.
1969 "Extramarital sex: Alienation or extension of normal behavior." In G. Neuberk (ed.), *Extramarital Relations.* Englewood Cliffs, N.J.: Prentice-Hall.

ZELNIK, M. AND J. F. KANTNER
1972 "Sexuality, contraception and pregnancy among young unwed females in the United States." In the United States Commission on Population Growth and the American Future, *Demographic and Social Aspects of Population Growth,* vol. 1. Washington, D.C.: Government Printing Office.
1974 Personal communicatiommunication to the authors.
1977 "Sexual and contraceptive experience of young unmarried women in the U.S., 1976 and 1971." *Family Planning Perspectives* 9:55–711

ZETTERBERG, H. L.
1965 *On Theory and Verification in Sociology.* New York: Bedminster Press.

5

ANTECEDENTS AND CONSEQUENCES OF MARITAL TIMING

Luther B. Otto

Of the many forms of human interaction studied by social scientists, marriage is one of the most important for the individuals and the society of which they are a part. The union is expected to be intimate and durable. But that it is governed only by individual and dyadic decisions—concerning, for example, whom to marry and when to marry—would be an overstatement; for marriage is a social institution that has evolved out of social needs. Societies employ a variety of mechanisms for regulating pre- and postmarital behavior which interact in complex ways with individual predispositions and decisions with the result that there is both between and within society variability in marital behavior.

This Chapter focuses on intrasocietal variability in marital timing. It is based primarily, though not exclusively, on studies conducted in the United States, where data have been most systematically recorded and the theoretical and empirical literature is most abundant. Unlike previous efforts bent upon explaining cross-cultural differences, long-term trends, or subgroup deviations, our effort will be to develop a conceptual framework and theoretical model within which the antecedents and consequences of variations in marital timing may be examined. Family sociologists and demographers have contributed most to the marital timing literature. That literature has been systematically culled and integrated first into a conceptual scheme, then into a model specifying the interrelationships of concepts. We proceed inductively following Merton's (1957:89) mandate quoted with approbation by Wallace (1969:x):

> It is only when . . . concepts are interrelated in the form of a scheme that a theory begins to emerge. Concepts, then,

constitute the definitions (or prescriptions) of what is to be observed; they are the variables between which empirical relations are to be sought.

Before proceeding, the reader is alerted to three important caveats. The first concerns the uneven quality of the evidence marshaled in support of specific propositions. The literature cited is exceptionally diffuse. It spans nearly a century, 1883–1977 (see Bell, 1883). Sample size and representation vary from national probability samples to unspecified groups contributing to clinical and experiential observations. Sophistication in data analysis encompasses mathematical modeling of cohort experience, at one extreme, and head counts, at the other. The technical competence of the authors ranges from that of the skilled research reporter to that of the journalist and popularizer. Moreover, most of the literature is purely descriptive, neither analytic nor theoretical. It represents an association of indicators. Although it has been impossible to properly qualify all of the literature cited, some critical judgment is exercised by emphasizing the quality material while acknowledging the other. Nonetheless, the reader is forewarned that for other review purposes, more critical evaluation of specific research findings may be warranted.

Second, this review does not incorporate the literature on mathematical models of the process of entry into first marriage of a cohort's members as they age (e.g., Hernes, 1972; Hastings, 1973). This literature suggests that social pressure to marry intensifies with incremental increases in the percent of a cohort already married until the majority is married, whereafter social pressure and marriageability decline with age. Stochastic models contribute little to understanding the interactive and decision-making processes culminating in either normative age at marriage or in deviations from the norm. In our judgment the stochastic models presuppose an oversimplified passive view of the nature of man in portraying him simply as a victim of probability formulas operating totally beyond his control. In contrast, the implicit view of man governing the

NOTE: Grateful acknowledgment is made of the library research assistance provided by Julie C. Wolfe. Vaughn R. A. Call's critical comments at various stages of the manuscript preparation and his evaluation of an earlier draft were especially helpful, as were suggestions from F. Ivan Nye, Jay D. Schvaneveldt, and J. Joel Moss. Financial support during preparation of the early stage of the manuscript was provided by The Grant Foundation, Inc.

present synthesis and most of the literature is that man is an actor and reactor, a participant and decision maker, however constraining may be the social parameters within which he functions as an individual.

Finally, this chapter focuses on *marital timing*, whereas most of the literature concerns *early marriage*. Bartz and Nye (1970) have noted that early marriage has been defined in about as many ways as there are researchers who have employed the concept. The preoccupation with early marriage so evident in past theory and research reflects the humanistic and applied orientation of practitioners who, on the one hand, have tried to explain the sustained trend of declining age at marriage that characterized the first half of the twentieth century and, on the other hand, have wanted to curb the alleged detrimental consequences attending precocious marriages. The two issues—one explaining population trends, the other explaining deviations from the mean—are sometimes blurred in their common focus on early marriage. Moreover, the preoccupation with early marriage, however defined, has been accompanied by a general neglect of normative and late marriages. From a theoretical perspective, however, normative marriage and late marriage are also of interest and also in need of explanation, which is reflected in our preference for discussing antecedents and consequences of marital timing or age at first marriage. Thus a conceptual distinction must be observed. The task undertaken is an exercise in theory construction concerning the antecedents and consequences of marital timing, though much of the empiri-

cal literature focuses on early marriage, variously defined.

We proceed by outlining a heuristic model of the marital timing complex. Although the causes and effects are not unrelated, each is comprised of conceptually distinct processes operating over different stages in the life course which are related by virtue of the common intervening variable, age at first marriage. First treated as a dependent variable, itself in need of explanation, marital timing is then examined as an independent variable or determinant of subsequent occurrences and as an intervening variable or mechanism by which temporally earlier influences affect what follows first marriage. The chapter concludes with an evaluation of the current state of knowledge regarding variations in marital timing and outlines directions for further theory and research.

I. ANTECEDENTS OF MARITAL TIMING

The plethora of variables that have been causally related to age at first marriage in the United States is illustrated in Landis and Kidd's (1956) study of 286 high school principals in California who reported on what they believed influenced student marriage rates. Determinants most often cited included lax parental care (discipline, supervision, poor home conditions) and the military draft with accompanying uncertainty about plans for the future, after which some 20 other presumed causes at various levels of abstraction are identified, including "glorifica-

Figure 5.1.

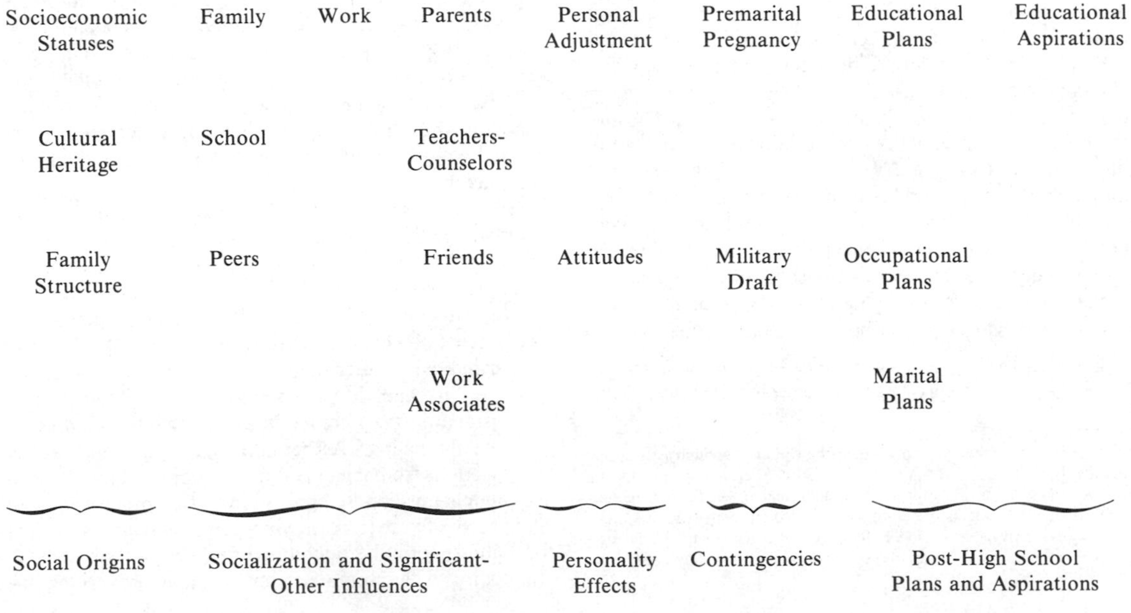

Socioeconomic Statuses	Family	Work	Parents	Personal Adjustment	Premarital Pregnancy	Educational Plans	Educational Aspirations
Cultural Heritage	School		Teachers-Counselors				
Family Structure	Peers		Friends	Attitudes	Military Draft	Occupational Plans	
			Work Associates			Marital Plans	

Social Origins	Socialization and Significant-Other Influences		Personality Effects	Contingencies	Post-High School Plans and Aspirations

tion of marriage," "fad," "prosperity and youth employment," "mass media emphasis on sex," "lack of success in school," and the like. The complete listing variously attributes causation to social structural variables, personality traits, economic conditions, significant-other influences, changing norms, and a variety of situational factors. What the cataloguing lacks, however, as does the literature more generally, is a meaningful conceptual scheme and specification of processes within which the accumulated literature, theoretical and empirical, can be meaningfully integrated and interpreted. We take as our initial task that of identifying the social influences which obtain at birth and those factors which sequentially affect marital timing. As an exercise in theory construction the task is to develop an appropriate conceptual scheme and to specify the mechanisms, if any, by which antecedents affect marital timing. These preliminary remarks suggest that the life course is an appropriate framework within which to examine the relationship between concepts associated with the causes and consequences of marital timing.

A processual model of the life course effects bearing on marital timing is displayed in Figure 5.1. Explicitly, Figure 5.1 is not a measurement model, but an outline of the major concepts that have been associated with age at first marriage and a summary statement, however rudimentary, of how they temporally relate to marital timing. The processes incorporate four conceptually discrete effects—social structural, social psychological, psychological, and certain contingencies—which are the

major classes of variables most often employed by theoreticians and researchers in explaining the phenomenon. The components undoubtedly have a mixture of unique and overlapping effects whose decomposition is essential to an understanding of the mechanisms operating in the life course processes. Therefore, standard conventions drawn from the literature on interpreting causal theories in sociology (e.g., Finney, 1972; Alwin and Hauser, 1975) are followed in discussing the models presented. A *total effect* (sometimes called simply an effect) is that portion of a total association or zero-order correlation between two variables in a causal model which is not due to common antecedents, to correlations between their causes, or to unanalyzed correlations among predetermined variables. Total effects indicate the amount of change in a dependent variable contributed by a specified change in the independent variable. Total effects consist of a direct and indirect component. An *indirect effect* is that component of the total effect of an independent variable which is mediated by linkages intervening between the independent and dependent variables. To say that a variable affects another indirectly is to say that there is a mechanism by which the former affects the latter. An indirect effect reveals the proportion of the total effect that is mediated by intervening variables. A *direct effect* is that portion of the total effect which remains after the indirect effects have been taken into account. To say that an independent variable affects a dependent variable directly is to indicate that there are no linkages or mechanisms by which the effect is mediated. Following

Marital Timing	Marital Role Enactment	Fertility Patterns	Educational Attainment	Occupational Attainment	Income	Marital Stability
	Spouse Employment					

Marital Timing	Marriage Inputs	Socioeconomic Attainments	Marital Outcome

these conventions, *explanation* consists of a theoretical accounting for the mechanisms by which the (total) effects of antecedents are mediated to the dependent variable. Operationally, the adequacy of an explanation can be assessed by the proportion of the total effect that is explained by the mechanisms specified.

The processual model specifies that post-high school plans are key mechanisms in the sequence of life course processes that affect marital timing. The planning stage occurs about the time of high school graduation when the individual is released from the adolescent student role and is given comparative freedom to choose to go to work, continue his/her education, or marry—or some combination of the three. Several influences bear upon that decision. The individual assesses his/her own past performance; significant others provide models and communicate expectations based upon their observations of the youth's attributes and past performance; and certain contingencies may impose upon the plans. A variety of socialization outcomes provide the basis for the significant-other influences and individual predispositions. Socialization experiences and the significant-other influences, the presence or absence of specific contingencies, and the individual's predispositions are affected by his/her social origins. Thus the multiple stages are linkages which mediate the effect of social origins and/or contribute independently to the variability in marital timing. Though the concepts appear in the order of the processes represented, the arrangement is not intended to foreclose the possibility of causal relationships among the concepts within each column. The referent of each concept is the experience of the individual as he/she passes through that stage of the life course.

Although the processual model (Figures 5.1) could be operationalized, given an appropriate design, no single piece of research has provided estimates for the theoretical processes it embodies. It is possible, however, to interpret past theory and research in the context of this general framework, identifying specific propositions, evaluating the research evidence that has been generated, and citing relationships that are imprecisely specified and/or untested empirically. The figure provides a general analytic framework for summarizing the present state of theory and research and a basis for outlining further theoretical and empirical activity.

Social Origin Effects

The background influences specified in the first column of Figure 5.1 are social conditions established at birth. Speculation on the determinants of these conditions is beyond the purview of the present effort. We take them as givens. By accident of birth an individual is injected into a social milieu governed by his family's position in the social structure, the cultural heritage of its members,

and the structural characteristics of his family of origin. There are several theoretical propositions and empirical regularities associating these social structural antecedents with marital timing.

The concept most often associated with age at first marriage is social class or socioeconomic status variously operationalized in terms of parental positions in the social hierarchy. That low social position is positively associated with earlier marriages for both males and females was an early hypothesis that has been documented empirically (Notestein, 1931; Havighurst, 1962; Burchinal, 1965; Elder, 1972). Similarly, Bayer (1969) and Burchinal and Chancellor (1963) establish that higher socioeconomic status is positively related to later ages at marriage. The research is not altogether convincing, however, because of the variety and crudeness of the class and status indicators employed (Otto, 1975), Moreover, with few exceptions most studies assume that the relationship is linear and fail to examine the functional form of the relationships between indicators of specific status dimensions and marital timing.

Research employing alternative conceptions of socioeconomic status (e.g., education, occupational prestige, and income) is not wholly consistent in its findings. Burchinal (1959e), for example, reports that lower levels of parental education are positively associated with earlier marriages of children, but the finding is not supported by either DeLissovoy and Hitchcock (1965) or by Moss and Gingles (1959). Burchinal (1959e) reports that on an alternative status indicator, occupational prestige, low status is also positively associated with early marriage. But DeLissovoy and Hitchcock (1965) find no difference in the occupational attainments of the parents of early married students and controls. The relationship between parental income or wealth and age at marriage is also ambiguous. Moss and Gingles (1959) report that a son or daughter's perceived parental financial ability to support a college education is not related to marital timing. However, DeLissovoy and Hitchcock (1965) report that children of working mothers marry earlier. Therefore on the somewhat tenuous assumption that mothers who work do so at least in part out of economic necessity, there appears to be some support for the hypothesized positive relationship between family income and age at marriage. On balance, one is led to believe that there is a very modest relationship between socioeconomic status and marital timing. Bayer (1969) reports that socioeconomic status and aptitude together account for 2 percent of the variability in marital timing for males and 4 percent for females. Call and Otto (1977) account for 3 percent of the variability in marital timing for males with family socioeconomic statuses. But whether the relationships are linear, whether social status interacts with such other variables as residency (Moss and Gingles, 1959), and whether alternative indicators of socioeconomic status are unidimensional with respect to marital timing are issues that have been raised but not widely studied.

Theorists and researchers have long recognized that cultural heritage is an important determinant of marital age norms (Duncan, 1934). Six diverse dimensions of cultural heritage are proposed. The first is religion. Studies have consistently shown that among females membership in the Roman Catholic Church is associated with later age at marriage (Smith, 1971; Burchinal and Chancellor, 1963; Elder and Rockwell, 1977) and that membership in Protestant denominations is associated with earlier marriage. Differences by denominational affiliation probably occur for at least three reasons: the later age at marriage for Catholics may reflect vestiges of norms from European countries from which American Catholics came; the Roman Catholic doctrinal position against mixed marriages may have the effect of relegating the membership to a minority position within the population with a restricted field of eligibles; and, finally, believing that marriage is a sacrament may prompt Roman Catholics to value marriage more highly and to make more elaborate and time-consuming preparations. There is, then, some suggestion that the effect of denominational affiliation is transmitted indirectly to marital timing by way of socialization into norms, values, and beliefs that are likely to be associated with the home. There is also some possibility that the effect is mediated via heterosexual experiences. Thus Heiss (1960) reports that Jewish courters go steady without entertaining serious marital intentions, a less common practice among Roman Catholics and Protestants. Studies have shown that extent of religious involvement, regardless of denominational affiliation, is positively associated with marital timing for both males and females (Burchinal and Chancellor, 1963). Both interreligious marriages (Burchinal and Chancellor, 1963) and lack of religious affiliation (Havighurst, 1962; Painter, 1967) are associated with earlier marriage. Finally, Lowrie (1965) introduces the possibility that the effect of religious involvement on marital timing may be indirect inasmuch as the amount of religious instruction is inversely related to the probability of premarital pregnancy, which affects marital timing. In summary, an association between religious affiliation and extent of religious involvement with marital timing has been established, but additional theoretical specification is required in understanding the mechanism(s) by which the effect occurs. Inasmuch as denominational affiliation and socioeconomic status are closely associated in contemporary United States society, there remain the additional theoretical and empirical issues of whether the effects of religion on marital timing exist when controlling for socioeconomic status (see Elder and Rockwell, 1977).

The second component of the cultural heritage construct is regional variation, particularly the long-recognized and continuing pattern of relatively late marriage in the northeastern states (Rele, 1965a, 1965b). It is possible that geographic variation operates as a proxy for religion (the New England states have strong Roman Catholic populations) or for age (the western states, e.g., California, have younger populations). Whether there is a contextual geographic effect net of these components requires further attention.

A third element in the cultural heritage construct is the prevailing legal requirement regarding age at marriage, parental consent, and/or mandatory school enrollment. Rosenwaike (1967) hypothesizes and demonstrates that states permitting lower legal ages at marriage without requiring parental approval (e.g., Maryland) have lower modal ages at marriage than do states with higher age requirements (e.g., Pennsylvania and Virginia). Migratory marriages may slightly increase the contrast. The age falsification phenomenon appears to have generated as much interest as the legal age variability issue, however. Thus Gover and Jones (1964) demonstrate that parental consent laws do not result in later marriages for females willing to falsify their age, which suggests an interaction effect with personality variables. Apropos of considering the effect of parental consent regulations over time is Womble's (1966) investigation of the rate of age falsification from 1913 to 1963. Womble determined that the rate of falsification is relatively constant from decade to decade for both sexes until the late 50s, when a marked increase in falsifications occurs for both sexes. This trend research suggests that the interaction with personality hypothesis may not be valid, unless one were to assume that the 50s were populated with personality types willing to falsify their age. Though ambiguous concerning the effect of legal regulations regarding age of marriage without parental consent, the age falsification literature does suggest that to some undetermined extent the average ages at marriage reported, particularly for precocious unions, are overestimated and that the *de facto* ages at marriage may be somewhat lower than either state or national reports suggest.

The fourth dimension of the cultural heritage influence is indicated by rural versus urban residency. Duncan (1934) reports that the bulk of all marriages occur from two to three years earlier in rural areas than in urban areas. The general relationship between rural residency and low age at marriage was more recently replicated by DeLissovoy and Hitchcock (1965) and is reflected in census data, which also reveals, however, that the rural-urban difference has diminished over time. Thus Eshleman (1974) notes that by 1960 rural-urban differences in age at marriage had largely disappeared. That the relationship may be confounded with such factors as sex and socioeconomic status was noted early. Notestein (1931), for example, analyzed the 1910 census data and reports that women of urban populations generally marry later than those of rural populations, but that women from the three lowest urban classes marry earlier than those of the highest rural class. Whether the Notestein finding demonstrates an interaction between socioeconomic status, sex, and rural residency or whether residency is but a contextual effect that disappears in the face of more refined indicators of socioeconomic status has not been addressed theoretically or explored empirically.

As a fifth dimension of cultural heritage we specify the respondent's sex. As a sixth dimension we note his/her race. That marital timing and the processes affecting marital timing differ by sex and race is widely documented (e.g., Rele, 1965a, 1965b), and the two indicators constitute the primary demographic controls employed in measurement models. Specifying these individual characteristics as dimensions of the cultural heritage concept emphasizes the social reality that different normative structures govern individuals depending upon their sex and race.

In summary, proceeding inductively we propose a multidimensional concept, cultural heritage, as an abstract synthesis of several factors alleged to be associated with marital timing. The concept indicates that different patterns of normative expectations bear upon the individual depending upon his location in the social categories embodied in each dimension. Relationships between several indicators of the categories and marital timing are reported.

The model specifies that family structural characteristics further contribute to explaining variability in age at first marriage. Whether the individual is raised in an intact or broken family has received theoretical and research attention. Inselberg (1961) and Havighurst (1962) hypothesize that with one or both parents absent, age at marriage is lower. Their evidence supports the hypothesis for both males and females. However, Burchinal (1959e) reports no difference in marital timing for females from disrupted homes. Similarly, DeLissovoy and Hitchcock (1965) find no difference between age at marriage for prospective brides and grooms from intact families and age at marriage for those from families broken by divorce, separation, or a deceased parent. Thus the evidence is equivocal. DeLissovoy and Hitchcock (1965) also report that family size is inversely related to age at marriage. With increased number of siblings, marital age decreases. Finally, the authors report that if the mother works, children marry earlier. The evidence is inconsistent concerning the effect of parental happiness on daughter's age at marriage. Inselberg (1961) found that parental happiness was unrelated to daughter's age at first marriage, but Lowrie (1965) reports that the lower the reported happiness of a female's parents, the lower the age at first marriage of the daughter. Elder (1972) reports that strained relationships with father were characteristic of girls marrying both early and late, a curvilinear relationship.

Birth order effects on marital timing have also been examined. Commins (1932) suggests that first-borns marry as much as two years earlier. Murdock and others have applied Schacter's work on birth order and affiliation in anxiety-provoking situations to age-at-marriage research. In two experiments Murdock (1966; Murdock and Smith, 1969) reports that mean age at marriage for first-born males is lower than that of later-borns, but that there is no difference among females. However, when asked to indicate the best marriage age, the mean suggested by first-born females is lower than that for later-borns. Prothro and Diab (1968), however, find no significant difference in the average age at marriage between first-borns and later-borns among either males or females. Thus a birth order effect has been hypothesized, but the evidence is inconclusive.

Family stability, family size, birth order, whether mother works, intraparental affect, and parent-child relations have been related to marital timing, but it is doubtful that these exhaust the catalogue of relevant family characteristics that bear upon individual decisions concerning marital timing. Unexamined, for example, is the effect of power and authority patterns—concepts closely associated with whether the mother works and family size. Similarly, the kind of work performed by the parent(s) (as opposed to occupational prestige) has been related to children's beliefs and attitudes (Pearlin and Kohn, 1966) and may influence an adolescent's approach to marital planning and timing. Although the family is an identifiable unit apart from the socioeconomic and cultural forces that influence the individual, additional effort is required to further isolate the dimensions of family structure that influence marital timing.

We have isolated three social origin concepts associated with marital timing: socioeconomic status, cultural heritage, and family structural characteristics. Further theoretical attention must be given not only to the question of the complementarity of the diverse dimensions of such omnibus concepts as cultural heritage but also to the issue of whether the concepts are discrete. Thus, for example, rural residency, a dimension of cultural heritage, is closely associated with occupational prestige, a socioeconomic status dimension. The possibility of conceptual overlap must be examined. A further challenge is to specify the mechanisms by which social structural conditions affect marital timing. Thus, for example, there is ample evidence that educational aspirations vary by sex (Haller et al., 1973) and the sex-typing literature is redundant with documentation for differential socialization patterns and significant-other encouragement by sex (Rossi, 1965). Given these linkages (and there may be others), the proposition is that the relationship between sex and marital timing occurs indirectly: significant others take into account the individual's sex in defining appropriate expectations which influence the individual's educational aspirations which, in turn, are known to be associated with marital timing. The indirect effect patterns operating within the model are specified as sequential stages of the model and are discussed below.

Socialization and Significant-Other Influences

A fundamental postulate of role "theory" is that an individual's attitudes and behaviors are affected by the role or role set that he/she occupies in the social system (Newcomb, 1950; Parsons, 1951). One or both of two processes are presumed to operate. First, a change in roles almost invariably involves a change in reference group, which Kemper (1968:32) defines as "a group, collectivity, or person which the actor takes into account . . . in the course of selecting a behavior from among a set of alternatives, or in making a judgment about a problematic issue." Reference groups socialize the individual attitudinally and behaviorally. Their mode of functioning— whether normative and comparative (Kelley, 1968) or comparative and audience (Kemper, 1968)—varies. For example, the influence of parents, teachers, and work associates is generally regarded as normative, while that of peers may be thought to be comparative. New reference groups socialize the individual into new orientations, new perceptions, and new vested interests which produce new attitudes affecting behavior. Second, changes in roles require new behaviors that the role occupant must display if he/she is to enact the new roles. If we assume that people need to have attitudes that are consistent with their behaviors, then required behavioral changes will affect attitudes (Bem, 1970). Although the reference group explanation and the self-consistency principle postulate somewhat different mechanisms, both predict that role changes will be accompanied by changes in attitude and behavior.

We interpret the effects of socialization on marital timing in terms of a succession of major roles that are imposed upon and/or are assumed by the individual. In each role the individual is essentially cast as a learner. He is taught by reference groups which act as socialization agents. The processual model (Figure 5.1) provides that an individual's social origins dictate reference group emphases in four conceptually discrete socialization domains through which the individual passes in the early stages of the life course, namely, family, school, peer group, and work. These are the primary contexts of social learning, although such other sources of influence as voluntary associations (e.g., Sunday school and Scouts) and mass media (e.g., television, films, magazines, and newspapers) undoubtedly also operate. Unfortunately, there is comparatively little reliable theory and research on these effects, although the impact of television-viewing habits on children and adults is receiving increased attention (Goranson, 1970).

Completion of high school is the normative prescription in contemporary U.S. society; but as the individual approaches graduation, he/she enters a stage in the life course governed increasingly by individual plans and decisions. Following Bayer (1969), therefore, we argue that whatever influences an individual's post-high school plans and decisions, however tentative these may be, is of crucial importance in determining marital timing. Socialization experiences and outcomes affect an individual's post-high school plans indirectly and directly. Indirectly, socialization effects are mediated by significant other influences. Shibutani (1961:339) defines significant others as those persons who are of crucial importance for the construction and reinforcement of one's self-conception. The principal significant others (corresponding to the major socialization domains) are parents, teachers, best friends, and work associates, respectively. Significant others evaluate an individual's past performance and communicate expectations that they hold for him/her (Woelfel and Haller, 1971; Otto and Haller, 1978). They thereby function as important mechanisms by which socialization experiences and outcomes are transmitted to marital timing. It is argued elsewhere (e.g., Sewell et al., 1969) that significant others influence the respondent's behavior by way of influencing post-high school educational plans, a pattern that might also obtain in the present model. It is also likely that significant others directly influence post-high school occupational and marital plans, whether, for example, the respondent should take a job, pursue an education, get married, or do some combination of the three. Socialization experiences also affect post-high school plans directly in that the individual reflects upon his/her own past performance and the evaluations and expectations of significant others. Thus post-high school plans are affected by both a social interaction component and a cognitive motivational component.

The first three socialization domains—family, school, and peer group—contribute both unique and overlapping effects whose decomposition poses profound theoretical and empirical problems (Figure 5.2). Concurrent specification of the three is not to deny that each has its greatest influence at a different point in the life course, but it underscores the complexity of the interrelationships that bear upon the individual and the fact that all three have continuing contact with the individual over a period of years. The interrelationships of school and peer group effects are particularly complex because the school provides the peer group for most children (McCandless, 1968:810). Work experience effects appear later inasmuch as early employment normally represents leaving the educational track after mandatory age–related enrollment requirements have been satisfied.

At the risk of oversimplification we concentrate on the unique effects of each socialization experience while acknowledging the complex interactions between family, school, and peer influences that continue to escape the grasp of theorists and researchers. The effect of the family

Figure 5.2. Partial Elaboration of the Direct and Indirect Effect Patterns of Socialization and Significant-Other Influences on Post-High School Plans

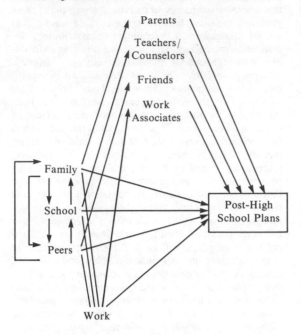

is strongest and least challenged during the preschool years. The primary significant others who evaluate the individual's family role performances are mother and father. Family roles are not clearly defined for the adolescent. Indeed, the literature generally suffers for lack of theory and research on adolescent roles. Parents, however, expect their children to display evidence of normal development in areas that bear upon post-high school plans and decisions: cognitive ability, use of language, interpersonal skills, and psychosexual development (Witkin, 1968; Jenkins, 1968; Weinstein, 1968; Simon and Gagnon, 1968; see also Clausen, 1968, and Kerckhoff, 1972). More specific expectations are differentiated by sex (Sears et al., 1957; Bronfenbrenner, 1961; Mussen, 1968). Males are expected to manifest an understanding of the adult provider role and to increasingly provide evidence of an ability to secure gainful employment. Traditionally, females have been expected to learn domestic skills associated with housekeeping and child supervision, a complementary role to the provider. Increasingly females also may be expected to demonstrate their self-sufficiency.

Socialization emphases and processes differ between families by social origins and especially by socioeconomic status. Thus, for example, whether the expectation is that a young male will learn the provider role by academic preparation for a career or by going to work at an early age differs by family socioeconomic status. Of particular relevance to explaining marital timing are socioeconomic correlates of child-rearing practices (Bronfenbrenner, 1958), the development of conceptual ability and communication skills (McCarthy, 1954; Hess and Shipman, 1965), content of the self-image (Gurin et al., 1960), the values of self-direction and conformity (Kohn, 1969; see also Hyman, 1966), and achievement motivation (Rosen, 1959). The kind of parent-child relationships that are associated with socioeconomic statuses— Whether love-oriented or power-assertive, whether explanatory or expressive—and parental values are likely to result in variations on these outcomes. Outcomes favorable to continuing on a post-high school educational track are generally associated with middle and higher levels of family socioeconomic statuses, which translates into direct social origin effects on family role expectations and performance. (In the interest of simplifying the graphic presentation in Figure 5.2 and subsequent figures, effect patterns are selectively, not fully displayed.) Although family socialization efforts may be relatively unstructured and the specific criteria by which parents assess a youth's developments may be ill defined, parents progressively formulate overall evaluations of their children's role performances (family, school, and peer group), which influences their definition of appropriate career expectations and governs their encouragement of the youth. Also, the youth directly reflects upon his own performance and the significant-other feedback in formulating his post-high school plans. Thus the effect of social origins on marital timing is explained in part by family socialization patterns. Background socioeconomic statuses, family structure, and cultural heritage influence family role performance expectations for adolescents. The youth's role performance is evaluated by parents, whose definition of appropriate career expectations and encouragement affects the adolescent's post-high school plans on independent evaluations of his/her past performance.

In addition to general parental influences that may bear upon an individual's post-high school plans—e.g., whether one has developed the necessary skills for attending college—there is evidence that parents have a modeling influence on their children with respect to what the child believes is an optimal age for marriage. Burchinal (1959a) reports that the earlier a female's mother married, the earlier the female marries; and Rose (1955) reports that the age at which a male desires to marry is correlated with the age at which his father married. Rose also reports that there is a positive relationship between the age at which parents wish they had married and the age at which their children eventually marry. Family socialization includes communicating information about appropriate ages at which to marry.

As a youth matures the school increasingly assumes importance as an agency of socialization, and teachers and counselors, together with parents, become the significant others who evaluate school performance and provide career counseling. It has been argued that the classroom reflects the basic democratic values of our society (Parsons, 1959) in that there is no formal differentiation by sex, race, or socioeconomic status. It has been noted that the only formal prerequisites to admission are related to age and a broad definition of normal ability. Nonetheless, family socialization has an important effect on school socialization experiences (Figure 5.2) inasmuch as variation in family socialization experiences affects the individual's readiness and preschool ability to assume the student role. Thus it has been argued that children from lower socioeconomic statuses are disadvantaged because the majority of teachers represent values and behaviors characteristic of higher socioeconomic statuses (Becker, 1952; Carlson, 1961). Others (Jensen, 1968; Stendler, 1951) have noted that children from lower socioeconomic statuses are comparatively disadvantaged in their levels of basic skill development and because of a general parental disregard for school work; therefore, they are likely to suffer early discouragement. Moreover, it has been argued that teacher expectations influence student performance levels, and that their expectations vary by the student's family socioeconomic status. The so-called "pygmalion effect" (Rosenthal and Jacobson, 1968) also governs expectations by sex (Doubrovsky, 1971) and race (Kerckhoff, 1972:138–52). In summary, the criticism is that the educational system operates as a mechanism for perpetuating social inequality rather than as a remedial instrument for assuring equality of opportunity. The explanation is that both the individual and his/her significant others—teachers-counselors and parents—reflect upon school performance in formulating and encouraging appropriate career expectations, which affect marital timing through the direct and indirect effect patterns outlined above. If the student does not perform adequately on school-related criteria, continuation in the formal educational track is progressively discouraged if not denied.

The two school performance dimensions that have received most empirical attention are academic achievement and extracurricular activities. A widely documented empirical regularity is that academic ability and performance in high school are in part a function of background socioeconomic statuses (Jensen, 1972; Sewell and Hauser, 1975; see Lavin, 1965, for a literature review). Closely associated is research reported by Rainwater (1965) demonstrating differences in cognitive functioning by socioeconomic statuses. Individuals from lower socioeconomic statuses think less abstractly, less in terms of causal relationships, and less in terms of internal control. Therefore, the implications of marriage may not be as fully understood among the lower socioeconomic statuses, which may result in precocious marriages.

A positive relationship between academic ability and age at first marriage has been demonstrated (Burchinal, 1965; Bayer, 1969; Elder, 1972). Similarly, Burchinal (1960), Havighurst (1962), and Painter (1967) found that the early-married had reached a "dead end" academically. Otto and Call (1976), controlling on socioeconomic background statuses for males, report significant effects on marital timing for both mental ability, measured with the Cattell IPAT Test of G: Culture Free, Scale 3A, and academic performance, as indicated by GPA. In their structural equations model they estimate that 40 percent of the effect of father's occupation and 51 percent of the effect of mother's education on marital timing is mediated by academic performance, which provides strong support for incorporating the concept as an intervening mechanism in the life course process affecting marital timing.

Participation in extracurricular activities provides a second basis for recognition in secondary schools (Coleman, 1961; Spady, 1971). Academic achievement is not a prerequisite for membership in the leading crowd. As a result, a student has alternative ways of achieving recognition by teachers and fellow students. One is to establish himself on academic criteria. The other is to establish himself on social criteria, e.g., athletics. While the two are not necessarily mutually exclusive and schools may differ in the values espoused by the students themselves, the possibility of "making it" by alternative routes reflects a tracking structure that has implications for post-high school plans. The student who performs on academic criteria is rewarded within the school system, and opportunities for further academic achievement are open to him. For the less successful academic performers, school rewards are less evident, and nonacademic options become more salient.

There is limited evidence that a relationship exists between marital timing and the extracurricular performance dimension. Martinson (1959) notes that early-married males had slightly higher rates of participation in extracurricular activities; Heiss (1960) reports a curvilinear relationship between participation in extracurricular activities and courtship progress; and Painter (1967) indicates that college women who married early belonged to fewer clubs. Noting that participation in extracurricular activities has a salutary effect on subsequent socioeconomic attainments (Otto, 1975, 1976a, 1976b), Otto and Call (1976) reason that involvement in extracurricular activities may provide an alternative source of rewards within the educational system and, therefore, delay formal opting out of the educational track into marriage, at least until high school is completed. To date that proposition has not been tested.

Our model specifies reciprocal effects not only between family and school but also with peer groups. Eisenstadt (1956) reasons that in complex societies, where familial and occupational role requirements are dissimilar and the manner of relating in adult social situations is greatly different from that experienced in family life, peer groups form to ease the transition from the ascriptive and particularistic relations of the family to the universalistic relations of the extended world governed by achievement criteria. Peer groups provide temporary support for a young person's current dispositions and values and encourage greater spontaneity in expressive activity (Eisenstadt, 1956:166). Campbell (1968:839) has summarized the norms and values governing the youth culture as follows:

> Having a good time is important, particularly social activities in company with the opposite sex; there is a strong hedonistic quality. On the male side, extreme emphasis is given to athletics, and this is a measure of valued masculinity, as sexual attractiveness is a measure of valued femininity for females. Explicit acceptance of adult-sponsored interests, expectations, and discipline is negatively valued. Common human elements are emphasized among associates, such as, that a person is valued humanistically for his general demeanor and attractiveness rather than instrumentally for performance as a competent specialist. Glamour and excitement are sought, and the luxuriant waste of time is virtuous.

The complementarity and conflict between family, school, and adolescent values represented by the feedback relationships in Figure 5.2 have been discussed elsewhere at length (e.g., Coleman, 1961). Whether adolescent values are subvertive or substitutive of adult values is not at issue. Indeed, the general conclusion is that the adolescent's orientation toward parental influence does not necessarily diminish during adolescence (Campbell, 1968:831). But the model does provide for the independent reinforcement of fellow adolescents as a source of approval and disapproval and molder of behavior. Peer criteria are represented as a third socialization influence which affects individual plans directly and indirectly via the modeling influence of peer significant others, namely best friends.

No area of peer group activity has been researched more enthusiastically than have the patterns and intensities of heterosexual involvements. Heterosexual experiences are associated with background socioeconomic statuses, on the one hand, and with age at marriage, on the other. Thus the concept is a likely mechanism by which the effects of social origins are transmitted to marital timing. There is some evidence that heterosexual experiences are also related to religion in that Heiss (1960) reports that Jewish courters go steady without serious marital intentions, a less common practice among Roman Catholics and Protestants. Bayer (1968) reports an inverse relationship between socioeconomic status and both age at first date and courtship duration. One of the best-documented relationships is that within social classes the earlier dating is initiated, the earlier males and females marry (Moss and Gingles, 1959; Burchinal, 1959e; Bayer, 1968). Bayer (1968) also notes that early dating is associated with later marriage in the higher social strata,

which suggests an interaction between early dating and socioeconomic status. Other indicators of heterosexual experiences associated with early marriage for females are going steady at an early age (Burchinal, 1959e; Moss and Gingles, 1959; Inselberg, 1961); having only one suitor (Moss and Gingles, 1959) or a number of steady boyfriends (Burchinal, 1959e); being in love with a number of steadies (Burchinal, 1959e); frequency of dates (Burchinal, 1959e); dating males five years older or more (Moss and Gingles; 1959); early engagement (Moss and Gingles, 1959); and early involvement at all levels of sexual experimentation (Broderick and Fowler, 1961; Chilman, 1966; Elder, 1972). Broderick and Fowler (1961) provide a more detailed causal ordering in suggesting that increased cross-sex interaction at early ages leads to greater romantic attachment, earlier sexual experimentation, and an increase in earlier marriage rates. Elder (1972) provides evidence that the effect of lower socioeconomic status on age at marriage is largely mediated by heterosexual involvement. Thus heterosexual experiences have been shown to vary by socioeconomic background statuses, on the one hand, and to influence timing of first marriage, on the other.

The significant others who provide expectations and reinforcement contingencies in heterosexual involvements are best friends of the opposite sex (Otto, 1977). Same-sex best friends are a second set of significant others whose modeling influence on earlier career plans has also been investigated. For example, a positive relationship between best friends' educational plans and individual educational plans has been documented (Sewell and Hauser, 1975; Otto and Haller, 1978). With respect to marital timing, Burchinal (1959e) reports that females who married early had more close friends that were married than did a nonmarried control group. Same- and opposite-sex significant others influence the individual's post-high school plans by modeling and sanctioning attitudes and behaviors evaluated on peer performance criteria (Otto, 1977; Otto and Alwin, 1977). Thus Burchinal (1960), for example, discusses a "band-wagon effect" on early marriage. The direct effect of peer group experiences on post-high school plans (Figure 5.2) indicates that the individual also evaluates his/her own performance on peer group criteria in formulating career and marital plans.

School and peer group influences interact in complex ways. Indeed, the participation-in-extracurricular-activities effects and peer group influences are probably indiscernible insofar as both reinforce nonacademic interests. While education is valued at some status levels, others value nonscholastic interests and pursue rewards that satisfy their predispositions. The important point is that two tracks become increasingly apparent as an adolescent matures, one emphasizing scholastic criteria and the other emphasizing the nonacademic. The track which an individual follows will have an important bearing on his post-high school plans. In an early study Lieberman (1950) demonstrated that individuals placed in new occupational positions develop attitudes congruent with the expectations associated with the role. If an adolescent leaves the academic track and enters the labor force, his/her attitudes and behaviors increasingly reflect the accompanying economic independence and associated attitudes of work colleagues.

Bartz and Nye (1970:267; see also Landis and Kidd, 1956:130) suggest the possibility that early, well-paid employment of the male may further facilitate early marriage, although the proposition has not been researched. Apropos are correlates with such economically related indicators as occupational fringe benefits including health and hospitalization plans (Burchinal, 1960; Tarver, 1961). Further, Burchinal (1960) has established a positive association between early marriage and the possible employment of wives or the fact that a prospective bride is working. These may be interpreted as proxy indicators for the couple's level of economic security. However, with respect to the general relationship of socioeconomic status to age at marriage, Bogue (1969:642) concludes that "it has been found almost universally that persons standing high in the socioeconomic scale marry at a later age than persons in other socioeconomic strata." Similarly, with respect to the occupational status of prospective grooms, Burchinal and Chancellor (1963) observe that the lower the occupational status of males, the earlier they marry. Assuming that higher socioeconomic status is related to higher income and better fringe benefits, these predictions conflict with Bartz and Nye hypothesis. The conflict may possibly be resolved by noting that neither occupational status nor socioeconomic status is necessarily a proxy measure for income (Duncan, 1961). Indeed, education, occupation, and income typically correlate between .4 and .6, which suggests that no more than 36 percent and as little as 16 percent of the variance between any two status dimensions is common (Blau and Duncan, 1967). Therefore, one would not necessarily expect alternative statuses to operate unidimensionally with respect to any specific dependent variable (Otto, 1975). A second possible resolution of the discrepancy is that the relationship between income and age at marriage may be curvilinear. Lower-income individuals may marry earlier for normative reasons, whereas the relatively high-income individuals may marry earlier because they have the economic security to do so. This possibility underscores the importance of using class and status indicators appropriate to the theoretical propositions being tested and of avoiding employing surrogate and composite indicators which conceal rather than reveal specific relationships.

In conclusion, we have specified that an individual sequentially passes through four socialization domains. Each has an independent influence on the processes affecting marital timing even as each interacts in complex ways with preceding socialization agencies in influencing the dependent variable. The effect patterns are both direct and indirect. Directly, socialization experiences and outcomes affect the cognitive-motivational component of post-high school plans, which, we argue, are an important influence on individual behavior. Indirectly, the socialization outcomes are evaluated by significant others who, in turn, influence the plans of the respondent by communicating expectations and giving encouragement.

Conceptualization of the role performance expectations in the four socialization domains is sorely underdeveloped. Nye and Berardo (1973:375), for example, note that "the conceptualization of children's roles has failed to emerge as an explicit formulation." Little attention has been given to adolescent family roles; school performance studies have been largely limited to measurement of mental ability and academic performance; the study of peer group performance has been largely limited to descriptive studies of heterosexual involvement; and the impact of early labor force experience is largely unexamined. A fundamental presupposition of the social sciences is that attitudes and behaviors are learned in social interaction, and we have emphasized the role of reference groups as agents of socialization. Significant others progressively make evaluations and communicate post-high school expectations to the youth. The individual takes these into account, together with his own evaluation of his past performance, in making his post-high school educational, occupational, and marital plans. Before considering the effect patterns of post-high school plans on marital timing, the pattern of antecedents is further complicated by incorporating the influences of personality effects and specific early career contingencies.

Personality and Contingency Effects

The search for explaining variation in marital timing inevitably leads to a consideration of personality effects. One major class of variables that affects personality development is the system of social interactions out of which the individual emerges (Smelser and Smelser, 1970:14). Our heuristic model emphasizes the distinctly social determinants in specifying personality characteristics as intervening variables following socialization experiences and significant other influences. Although personality is formed early in the life course and is presumed to be rather stable over time, the specification provides for the bearing of personality characteristics on age of marriage at about the time when post-high school plans are beginning to develop. Emphasizing the social antecedents should not obscure the facts that social situations always implicate both social and psychological variables and that complicated feedback relationships may operate between the two analytic levels. In developing the explanatory model, however, we find it necessary to ignore these complications for present purposes of

Figure 5.3. Outline of the Major Effect Patterns by Which Socialization, Significant Others, Personality, and Career Contingencies Affect Post-High School Plans

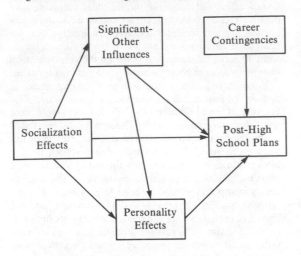

analytic simplicity and to invite more complex specifications after the basic effect patterns and processes among the major concepts are better understood.

Research generally indicates a rather modest social origin effect on personality (e.g., Sewell and Haller, 1956; Sewell, 1961). Elder (1972), however, reports that the relationship between family deprivation and early marriage is largely mediated by adjustment, which supports the specification of personality variables as an intervening mechanism in the life course processes influencing marital timing. But most of the literature is more simplistic than Elder's (1972) specification. Typically, correlates between personality variables and marital timing are reported (i.e., direct effects) without regard for specifying the timing of personality effects in the life course process. The general finding regarding emotional maturity among both males and females is that the lower the emotional adjustment of the individual, the lower the age at first marriage (Moss and Gingles, 1959; Havighurst, 1962). Martinson (1959) reports that ego deficiency is associated with early marriage, holding constant (by matched sample) age, nationality, intelligence, father's occupation, community of residence, and high school attended. Martinson (1955) and Havighurst (1962) also report that low social adjustment is related to early marriage. Moss and Gingles (1959), however, find no differences associated with social adjustment.

In examining the relationship of personality variables to the possibility of contracting marriage, the literature is more equivocal. For example, Duvall and Hill (1945) propose that although an emotionally mature personality is the best dowry one can bring to marriage, marriage has its greatest appeal to the immature and the not-so-well-

adjusted. Landis (1955), however, speculates that the more poorly equipped emotionally are those who remain single. It is possible that over a more complete range on an adjustment continuum the relationship between age at marriage and adjustment may be nonlinear. Perhaps the maladjusted rush toward early marriage; but if they are unsuccessful in contracting an early marriage, they may be at a competitive disadvantage within their cohort at normative age of marriage. Murstein (1967), for example, demonstrates that neuroticism is associated with difficulty in attracting a spouse, which would presumably delay if not deny marriage. Murstein (1967) also reports that the mental health of the male is more critical for the courtship progress than is that of the female, which suggests an interaction effect between mental health and sex.

Siegel (1963) argues that premarital pregnancy is the mechanism by which social and psychological immaturity affects age at marriage, a specification we adopt in the present model (see Figure 5.3). The Siegel hypothesis is a more precise theoretical statement inasmuch as it specifies not only that adjustment affects marital timing but also that the effect is indirectly transmitted via the mechanism of premarital pregnancy. This specification differs from the direct effects hypothesized by Martinson, Havighurst, and Moss and Gingles. Though different, the two specifications are not necessarily inconsistent if the reader will regard the hypothesis of indirect effects as a refinement of the earlier specification.

Early marriage has also been associated with several attitudes that develop in the socialization process and in interaction with significant others, particularly one's peers. Most prominent among them is what Burchinal (1960) and others label escapism, a belief that occupying an alternative role, e.g., being married and recognized as an adult, is preferable to some present role, e.g., being an adolescent or child. Burchinal and Chancellor (1958), for example, speculate that marriage removes the fringe-area status of adolescents. Several studies have concentrated on perceived deprivations and dissatisfactions among adolescents. Moss and Gingles (1959) report that among females, dissatisfaction with parental relations is associated with early marriage; Martinson (1955, 1959) links poor home adjustment with early marriage; Inselberg (1961) finds an association between disagreement with parents and early marriage; and Elder (1972) reports that early-married females felt estranged from their parents and perceived a detached and disinterested attitude by their parents.

An idealized image of marriage has also been associated with early marriage. An idealized image of marriage differs from the escapism thesis in that it emphasizes the advantages of the marital role rather then the deprivations of the adolescent role. From an exchange theory perspective, whether the theoretical focus is on the presumed "costs" associated with the adolescent role or the "rewards" presumed to be associated with the marital role, the comparison favors the marital role. Moss and Gingles (1959) report that with females, high levels of anticipated satisfaction in marriage are related to early marriage. Similarly, Herrman (1965) and Burchinal (1959b, 1959d) found that optimistic expectations and attitudes regarding marriage were associated with early marriage for females.

In summary, we specify personality characteristics as a third set of intervening variables in the life course processes affecting marital timing. The key dimension—variously labeled emotional maturity, ego deficiency, psychological immaturity, and the like—appears to be indicated by personal adjustment, though some attention has also been given to social adjustment. In addition, certain attitudes, notably those exalting the marital state and/or demeaning the adolescent role, are also associated with marital timing. Although the literature generally specifies direct personality effects on marital timing, there is evidence that the effects may occur indirectly via premarital pregnancy.

Premarital pregnancy is one of two career contingencies for which provision is made in our model (Figure 5.3), the other being the military draft. These effects are temporally specified at the time they are most likely to strongly and directly affect post-high school plans and behaviors. Premarital pregnancy is unquestionably the contingency that has generated the most attention by theorists and researchers. Lowrie (1965) demonstrates relationships between premarital pregnancy and several antecedents: low levels of parental education, little religious instruction, no engagement or an engagement of short duration, and an unhappy home life. Burchinal (1959e), Christensen and Rubenstein (1956), and Siegel (1963) found differences in personality traits and attitudes between females who were premaritally pregnant and those who were not. Thus the antecedents of premarital pregnancy include social structural considerations, socialization effects, and personality characteristics, all of which are specified in Figure 5.1. The relationship between premarital pregnancy and marital timing is well documented for females (Landis and Landis, 1958; Moss and Gingles, 1959; Burchinal, 1959c, 1960; Inselberg, 1961; Lowrie, 1965). However, in their analysis of male data, Otto and Call (1976) report that taking premarital pregnancy into account—premarital pregnancy operationalized as a first birth occurring within seven months prior to marriage—did not have a statistically significant effect on marital timing controlling on socioeconomic statuses, mental ability and academic performance, significant-other influences, and aspirations. In our general explanatory model we provide for an effect of premarital pregnancy by way of its effect on educational, occupational, and marital plans.

A final contingency is the military draft. It is not argued that whether or not a military draft is operational during adolescence is a consequence of background and socialization effects and, therefore, serves as an intervening mechanism in the life cycle process (although there is criticism that compulsory military service programs, when operational, have drawn recruits discriminately on the basis of socioeconomic and academic performance criteria.) It is argued, however, that the presence or absence of the military draft impinges on post-high school plans, having a direct effect upon them (Burchinal, 1960).

Post-High School Plans and Level of Educational Aspirations

We specify that post-high school plans are the key mechanism in mediating the influence of social origins, socialization effects, significant-other influences, personality characteristics, and career contingencies on marital timing. As an individual approaches completion of high school, he/she enters a period in the life course wherein behavior is more self-determined and outcomes increasingly reflect conscious decisions that are made. The three major dimensions of post-high school plans are educational, occupational, and marital. How an individual will align these planning dimensions largely reflects a tracking effect that begins with the inculcation of values associated with social origins and becomes most apparent in secondary school experiences and outcomes. Specifically, those who achieve on academic criteria are rewarded in the educational system and are encouraged to pursue a college career. The nonperformers receive less educational encouragement from their significant others and, independently comparing their scholastic achievements with those of their peers, focus on other career dimensions, namely occupation and/or marriage. High school students who opt out of the educational track into early employment largely foreclose on the possibility of an educational career, as does that very small percentage who marry prior to completing high school.

Following high school an individual must choose, however tentatively, between continuing an education, going to work, marrying, or some combination of the three. The decision gives direction and charts a tentative course through an otherwise unstructured period of life. The three planning dimensions—educational, occupational, and marital—undoubtedly interact in complex ways (see Figure 5.4). Thus an individual weighs his marital and occupational prospects in making his educational plans, weighs marital and educational plans in making occupational choices, and weighs educational plans and occupational prospects in considering marital possibilities. The decision concerning which track(s) an individual will pursue is normally operationalized during the last months of high school or very shortly after graduation—often within three months with the individual's enrollment in college and/or taking a first full-time

Figure 5.4. Elaboration of the direct and Indirect Effect Patterns of Post-High School Plans and Educational Aspirations on Marital Timing

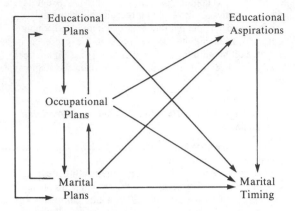

job and/or marrying. However tentative, once an immediate direction is set, inevitable consequences follow (Rossi, 1965). The tracking effect, now internalized by the individual, becomes more pronounced. New reference groups and significant others emerge who affect and reinforce individual attitudes and behaviors as post-high school plans are enacted. If successful, those pursuing an educational track will realize that new opportunities await them within academia. Those pursuing an occupational track may see opportunity for advancement and economic security. Alternatively, they may derive sufficient social and psychological rewards from early employment to aspire to nothing more prestigious. Those orienting their lives around marriage will have to assure themselves of a financial base, which has implications for further educational pursuits over the short term and, given the functional relationship between education and occupational prestige, has implications for occupational attainment over the long term. Post-high school pursuits are tentative in that educational, occupational, even marital plans may be changed early without apparent handicap; but after as little as a few months have elapsed, the effects of tracking—especially with respect to pursuing further education—increasingly foreclose the options open to an individual. Having enacted initial educational, occupational, and marital plans, time is of the essence in consciously altering life course plans. As an individual's plans are formulated, enacted, and adjusted, so one might expect his life course to be affected.

Evidence for the effect of marital plans on marital timing is presented by Bayer (1969:558), who concluded that "the best means to predict at what age a person will marry is to ask him." Unfortunately, there is precious little additional empirical evidence that bears upon the effect of post-high school plans on marital timing.

There is evidence with respect to the effect of level of

educational aspirations on achievement. (By "plans" we refer to the direction of an individual's orientation. By "level of aspirations" we refer to the extent to which one intends to pursue the planning dimension.) The literature shows consistently that for both males and females, lower levels of educational aspirations are associated with lower age at first marriage (Moss and Gingles, 1959; Burchinal, 1960; Havighurst, 1962; DeLissovoy and Hitchcock, 1965). Similarly, Bayer's (1969) analysis reveals that higher levels of educational aspirations are associated with later marriage plans. This stage of the heuristic model provides that level of educational aspirations intervenes between post-high school plans and marital timing in the following ways (Figure 5.4): Plans to marry directly affect marital timing but also exert an effect through two indirect effect patterns. The first occurs through the complex feedback patterns of marital plans with educational and occupational plans discussed above. The second is more straightforward: plans to marry are likely to attenuate an individual's level of educational aspirations, which, in turn, are positively related to marital timing. Plans to pursue post-high school occupational and/or educational interests affect marital timing directly and, through the double pattern of indirect effects, via educational aspirations.

With broad strokes of the theoretical brush we have outlined basic processes which affect marital timing. Post-high school plans figure prominently in the model as a key intervening variable. They are the result of a tracking effect which, although beginning in the social matrix at time of birth, becomes most apparent in the secondary educational system. By the time of graduation from high school one's plans dictate his life course pursuits. They reinforce the tracking effect. They put the individual on a course which, though tentative and not necessarily irrevocable, structures the patterns of interaction and reinforcement which constitute the social milieu in which the individual operates and bears upon the individual's marital timing directly and indirectly via its influence on educational aspirations.

The following section outlines the consequences of marital timing. Thereafter we review the current state of theory and research on the antecedents and consequences of marital timing and outline directions for further study.

II. CONSEQUENCES OF MARITAL TIMING

Marital timing has been causally associated with a variety of life course consequences. The most important concern fertility patterns, continuing education, labor force participation, occupational attainment, income adequacy, and marital stability. An additional concept, marital role enactment, will also be usefully employed in the discussion. These provide the conceptual apparatus for extensions of the model within which the literature on the effects of marital timing is integrated. This section of the heuristic model is displayed in more detail in Figure 5.5. As with earlier figures, the model is generalized to apply to both sexes, and the effect patterns are selectively displayed.

Labor Force Participation and Fertility Patterns

Marital timing is associated with several dimensions of fertility: the probability of parenthood, timing of first birth, child spacing, and parity (number of children). Demographers have been interested in marital timing as a causal antecedent of fertility, and the statistical relationship between the constructs is well documented in both the inter- and intrasocietal literature. Veevers (1971), for example, presents data from Canada which show that the probability of achieving motherhood is associated with marital timing. Teenage brides had a 94.8 percent chance of ever becoming mothers; brides in their early 30s had a 71.6 percent chance; and brides in their late 30s had about a 50 percent chance of motherhood. The corresponding probabilities for a rural sample are that teenage brides have a 97.1 percent chance of achieving motherhood; brides marrying in their early 30s have an 85.6 percent chance; and brides marrying in their late 30s have a 76.2 percent chance. The fact that the probabilities of achieving parenthood change by age may admit to a physiological explanation, but the fact that the probabilities are consistently higher for rural females than for nonrural females indicates that differences by age are in part normatively prescribed.

Jain (1969) indicates that women who marry before their sixteenth birthday take longest to conceive. The delay reduces with increasing age at marriage, then remains relatively stable for women who marry between

ages 21 and 25, after which there is a further decline in the marriage-to-conception interval. Notestein (1931) and Christensen (1963) report a positive relationship between early marriage and early childbirth. The bivariate association is undoubtedly inflated due to the high proportion of early marriages involving premarital pregnancy (i.e., the relationship is partially spurious). The duration of pregnancy intervals following pregnancy losses or live births increases with advancing age, which suggests that child spacing is also affected by marital timing (Jain, 1969). The consistent finding concerning the association between age at marriage and parity is that the two are positively related (Schorr, 1966). Kiser and Frank (1967) report that age at marriage and race interact with respect to fertility— that delays in first birth due to college attendance have more impact on the fertility of nonwhite than of white married women. The heuristic model also provides for a direct effect of educational aspirations on fertility patterns: the higher the educational aspirations, the fewer the number of children, the later the first is born, and the longer the interval between pregnancies—though these propositions have not been empirically examined. The effect of educational aspirations on fertility patterns is also expected to be indirect via marital timing.

Our model provides for two intervening mechanisms that explain the effect of marital timing on fertility patterns and subsequent concepts (see Figure 5.5). For brevity of presentation, discussion focuses primarily on processes affecting the female, though selected examples of how the model may be interpreted relative to the male are also provided. The first explanatory concept is marital role enactment. The second is whether the spouse works. Especially the latter takes into account the fact that following marriage the interactive effects of one's spouse have an important bearing on individual outcomes.

Marital role enactment refers to the manner in which an individual perceives, defines, and carries out his/her domestic roles. A wife may be primarily oriented to being a mother and housekeeper or pursuing a career of her own. It has been traditionally assumed that the husband will occupy the provider role, though enactment of the provider role may be delayed due to schooling. The antecedents of marital role enactment have not been widely researched, and there is little theory to inform our specification other than the plausible assumption that a husband's and wife's definition of their respective marital roles is learned in their socialization experiences. We specify that level of educational aspirations also has an effect on marital role enactment: the higher the level of wife's educational aspirations, the higher the probability that she has a career–marital role orientation; and the higher the level of husband's educational aspirations, the higher the probability that he delays enactment of the provider role due to his educational pursuits.

The effect of marital timing on fertility patterns occurs primarily by way of the wife enacting (and the husband

Figure 5.5. Elaboration of the Direct and Indirect Effect Patterns by Which Marital Timing Affects Marital Role Enactment, Fertility Patterns, and Whether Spouse is Employed

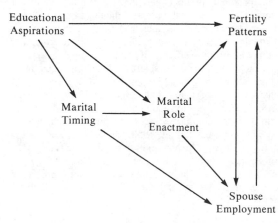

imposing or supporting) a mother-housekeeper or domestic marital role orientation. Hence the effect of marital timing on female fertility patterns is indirect. To press the illustration further, a career definition of the female's marital role is likely to produce different effect patterns (see Figure 5.5). A career definition is likely to delay timing of first birth and reduce the number of children born. It will directly affect whether the wife works and indirectly affect whether she works via her fertility patterns. Given that a wife's labor force participation affects her fertility patterns, marital role enactment also affects fertility patterns indirectly. Therefore, the relationship between fertility patterns and wife's participation in the labor force is reciprocally specified.

The model also provides for a direct effect of marital timing on whether the wife works. The later the female marries, the more likely it is that she will be gainfully employed. Manpower studies (Rele, 1965b; Sobol, 1973) have emphasized that early marriage results in a significant labor force loss to the nation. Single women have substantially higher labor force participation rates than their married counterparts, and those who marry earlier have comparatively much lower participation rates, especially during the first five years of marriage. Explanations for the attenuating effect emphasize the role of marital timing both as a mediating variable in a long-term process and as an independent influence. Rossi (1965), for example, argues persuasively that age at marriage and marital role enactment operate as intervening variables in suppressing the effects of female career aspirations on attainments:

> There is not enough time in late adolescence for young women to evolve a value system of their own and a sense of direction toward an individual goal, for they are committing themselves prematurely to marriage and adapting to the goals of their husbands at the expense of their own emotional and intellectual growth [1965:476].

A consistent finding in research on married professional women is that they view their careers as secondary to their family obligations and see their own careers as secondary to their husbands' (Hubback, 1957; Lopate, 1968; Sommerkorn, 1966). Other literature has emphasized the tension arising from attempts to combine the domestic and career marital role orientation (Coser and Rokoff, 1971). Ginzberg (1966), however, emphasizes the luxury of choice the two roles afford: depending upon the female's point of view, marriage either enables or forces a woman to ignore a career of her own. Whether focusing on the implied tensions or choice, the definition of the marital role enacted by the wife is a key mechanism by which the effects of her marital timing are mediated to her labor force participation.

It is instructive to briefly consider the effect patterns influencing female fertility and whether wife works in the case where the husband does not enact the provider role as necessity may dictate in the case of illness or injury or choice may dictate in the case of the male pursuing an education. In this circumstance the female may be forced to work (a direct effect of husband's marital role enactment on whether the wife works). Given that the wife works, her fertility patterns are likely to be directly affected. However, whether or not she has children, their ages, spacing, and number will also affect the probability of her working even when the husband does not enact the provider role. Thus, again, the relationship between whether spouse works (wife) and fertility patterns is reciprocal.

The complexity of these interrelationships is presupposed in examining the effects of marital timing on educational and occupational attainments, income adequacy, and marital stability.

Education, Occupation, Income and Marital Stability

In Figure 5.6 we extend the model to examine the effect of marital timing on levels of educational attainment, occupational attainment, income, and marital stability. Although education has usually been treated as the independent variable when associated with age at marriage, there is a literature which examines the direct effect of marital timing on an individual's continuing education, particularly that of females. The general finding is that marriage attenuates the level of educational attainment, terminating schooling at about the time of marriage. The earlier the marriage, the earlier formal schooling is discontinued. Burchinal (1965), for example, reports that estimates of school dropout rates for married females (high school) range from about half to over 90 percent and from about 35 to 45 percent for married males. Moreover, few married students who drop out ever reenter school (Burchinal, 1960; Havighurst, 1962; DeLissovoy and Hitchcock, 1965).

Numerous studies have tried to determine why the relationship exists between marital timing and educational attainment, and the major themes can be outlined. Elder (1972) notes that marital timing is an intervening variable and acts as a suppressor effect in mediating an otherwise positive effect of IQ on educational attainment. Others have stressed social structural effects—that public schools have historically been oriented to serve the unmarried and unemployed adolescent and have frequently discouraged if not forbidden attendance to such nonconformists as the married and the pregnant (Burchinal, 1960; Cavan and Beling, 1958; Landis and Kidd, 1956). Early marriage deprives an individual of the full benefits of formal schooling; and the earlier the marriage, the earlier the deprivation. These deprivations are represented as direct marital timing effects in the heuristic model.

Figure 5.6. Partial Elaboration of the Direct and Indirect Effect Patterns of Marital Timing on Socioeconomic Attainments and Marital Stability

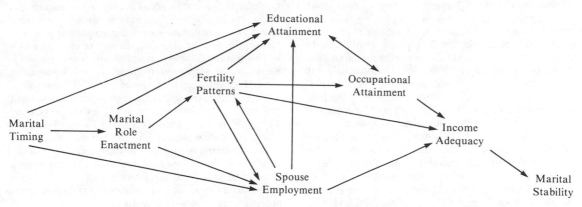

The negative attitude of many teachers toward married-student public school attendance is indicated in a 1960 poll conducted by the National Education Association, in which 55 percent of the teachers polled believed that married girls should be excluded from school and 47 percent stated that married boys should be excluded (Atkyns, 1968). Andersen (1965) studied Minnesota high school policies regarding married students and reports that in half, pregnant females were required to withdraw from school, that in 43 percent school policies prohibited pregnant females from participation in extracurricular activities, and that in 9 percent married students were perceived as performing at a lower academic level than singles. The fact that married students are perceived by teachers as being poorer academic performers raises the possibility that marrieds may be the victims of biased teacher evaluations which effectively discriminate against them. Studies of college academic performance, however, generally reveal no differences between marrieds and unmarrieds with respect to performance (Jensen and Clarke, 1958; Cohen et al., 1963; Medalia, 1962). Indeed, Schroeder (1963) and Feldman (1973) report that among male college students marriage is associated with higher academic performance.

We propose that the effect of marital timing on level of educational attainment operates not only directly but also through a complex pattern of indirect effects (see Figure 5.6). Consider the case of females. Marital role enactment—whether reflecting a domestic or career orientation—is a linkage by which the effects are mediated. Wives who define their primary marital role as mother and housekeeper are less likely to achieve high levels of education. Those who are career-oriented are likely to reach higher educational attainment levels. The case of males pursuing an education is obvious. Males enacting the provider role normally opt out of the educa-

tional track, which attenuates their eventual educational attainment levels. However, those who delay enactment of the provider role to pursue an education will likely achieve higher levels of educational attainment.

There is evidence that even among female college undergraduates high proportions appear to have internalized a social definition of the female's "place" and opt for what Philip Slater (1970) has called the "Spockian Challenge," the belief that child rearing is the most important aspiration and task for any woman. In a national sample (Cross, 1968), 55 percent of college women stated that they expect their lifelong satisfactions to come from marriage and family, and only 18 percent said they expect their major satisfactions to come from a career of their own. In a study of 1,400 female high school seniors (Turner, 1964), 4 percent opted for a career of their own, 48 percent chose a career as a homemaker, and another 48 percent preferred to try to combine the two. These studies document the primacy of the domestic marital role definition among females, which we specify as having a direct negative effect on female educational attainments.

Feldman (1973) notes that marriage may assist male academic careers at the graduate level. The positive effect of marital timing for males may be largely indirect via wife's labor force participation, which reduces the probability of early parenthood, on the one hand, and generates resources to assure husband's continued schooling, on the other hand. The indirect effect patterns for females are likely to differ, however, with the result that level of education is attenuated. Given that marriage imposes domestic obligations that conflict with career interests and that females tend to resolve the tension by opting for the domestic definition of their marital role, marital role enactment is a key concept in mediating the effect of marital timing on educational attainment (Painter, 1967). The earlier the marriage, the earlier the presumed role conflict is likely to be resolved by sacrificing educational pursuits. Moreover, given that marital timing is associated with fertility patterns—timing of first child, child spacing, and number of children—there is also likely to be an indirect effect of marital timing on educational achievement via fertility patterns. Further, in the event that her working provides resources for the husband to pursue his education, it is unlikely that a wife will complicate her domestic and occupational roles yet further by also pursuing her own education. Therefore, wife's participation in the labor force will be negatively associated with her own educational attainment.

There are conditions, however, under which marital timing may facilitate a wife's educational attainment. For example, if early parenthood does not follow an early marriage, the negative effect of fertility patterns on educational attainment will not exist and the conflict between the mother-housekeeper definition of the marital role and the career definition may be minimized with the result that a wife is free to pursue her own educational interests—indeed, a working spouse (husband) may generate the resources for doing so. Feldman (1973) notes that females who choose an education and sacrifice marriage are freed to pursue a career-primary model and tend to become "the most committed and active graduate students." We submit that females who marry but choose to forgo raising a family not only may largely escape the detrimental effects of early marriage on educational attainment but may even benefit by marrying early.

In summary, we propose that the complexities introduced by marriage for both male and female educational attainments are much more involved than previous theory would indicate. In addition to direct effects, our model provides several indirect effect patterns by which marital timing may influence educational attainment. We have given examples. The reader is invited to speculate on the net results of other effect combinations mediated by marital role enactment, spouse's labor force participation, and fertility patterns.

The direct and indirect effect patterns affecting educational attainment also bear upon occupational attainment inasmuch as educational attainment is a principal predictor of occupational attainment (Rele, 1965b; Blau and Duncan, 1967; Sobol, 1973; Sewell and Hauser, 1975). In the case of females, Nye and Berardo (1973) note that the labor market demand is for females with appropriate educational credentials. To the extent that marital timing interferes with developing marketable educational credentials, level of educational attainment is a key mechanism whereby the effects of marital timing are mediated to level of occupational attainment. This relationship obtains in the case of both males and females. Similarly, fertility patterns affect the occupational attainment of females. The presence or anticipated arrival of a child or children interferes with employer demands and, at least during the early years of marriage and child

rearing, requires successful accommodation if not resolution of the competing domestic and career roles. As with marital role tensions involved in pursuing an educational career, conflicting role demands involving occupations tend to be resolved by sacrificing employment opportunities. In the case of males, the role of education as a mechanism for the selection and distribution of individuals within the social system (Sorokin, 1927) and as an agent of socialization for inculcating work-related values and norms (Parsons, 1959) has been much discussed and researched (Blau and Duncan, 1967; Sewell and Hauser, 1975) and is a plausible mechanism for mediating the effect of marital timing on occupational attainment. Fertility patterns form a second intervening mechanism insofar as timing of first birth, child spacing, and number of children may force the provider to favor short-term economically rewarding occupations over opportunities holding more long-term promise.

The functional relationship between education, occupation, and income has been noted by others (Blau and Duncan, 1967; Sewell and Hauser, 1975). Level of educational attainment affects level of occupational attainment, which, in turn, affects income. There is also bivariate evidence that marital timing affects income. Burchinal (1965) reports that young marriages are typically established and maintained on a very meager financial basis and that parents must generally "help out" (Burchinal, 1959a). In his longitudinal study of 73 women, Elder (1972) finds that early marriage is accompanied by economic deprivation. Glick and Landau (1950) report that for husbands married less than five years, income is directly related to median age at marriage. Our model provides for a more complicated pattern of indirect effects, however. We specify that wife's labor force participation, which is affected by marital timing both directly and through the series of indirect effect patterns previously outlined, has a direct influence on family income adequacy (i.e., the amount of income relative to the number of family members). Inasmuch as income adequacy is a function of family size, fertility patterns will also affect the family economy and constitute a second major linkage whereby the effects of marital timing are mediated to family income adequacy. The full complexity of the effect patterns is undoubtedly even more involved, as Lowrie (1965) suggests in noting that premaritally pregnant wives, who tend to marry early, are least likely to work after marriage and to assist the family financially.

Following Cutright (1971), we specify marital stability at the end of the causal chain, assigning the immediate cause to income although other predictors are specified. No correlate is better documented than the positive relationship between marital timing and marital stability, whether the latter is defined as marital maladjustment (Burgess and Cottrell, 1939; Monahan, 1953; Burchinal, 1959e; Moss and Gingles, 1959), instability (Glick,

1970), disruption (Bumpass and Sweet, 1970), strain (Uhlemberg, 1972), perceived dissatisfaction (Burchinal, 1965), or divorce (Glick and Norton, 1971; Palmer, 1971). Monahan (1953) reports that divorce rates among young marrieds are between two and four times greater than among persons married in their 20s. However, the relationship does not appear to be linear. Several authors report that the relationship holds up to 30 years of age (Burchinal, 1959c; Christensen and Meissner, 1953; Monahan, 1953). Bumpass and Sweet (1970) report that women who marry before age 20 have substantially higher rates of marital disruption than women who marry older. England and Kunz (1975), however, report no atypical divorce rates for teenage wives.

Although the descriptive relationship between age at marriage and marital discord is not debated, there are various explanations for the relationship. The classic studies of Terman (1938), Burgess and Cottrell (1939), and Burgess and Wallin (1953) all suggest that personality and background factors affect marriage. Similarly, Eshleman (1965) emphasizes the personality characteristic of individuals. The "Glick effect" (Glick, 1957), that increased marital instability is associated with dropping out of high school and college, is essentially an argument that the relationship reflects spurious associations with a psychological attribute acquired earlier in life. Others have emphasized that the source of discord is related to depressed socioeconomic attainments (Burchinal, 1959c), number of children, timing of births (Gordon, 1968), race, and rural versus urban residency (Glick, 1970; Glick and Norton, 1971; Bernard, 1966; Bauman, 1967; Udry, 1967; Gordon, 1968). These explanations suggest that marital timing effects are not direct, but are mediated by a complex interaction of intervening processes. Alternatively, marital timing may function as a mediator of other causes of marital instability. Thus the relationship between marital timing and marital instability may be an essentially spurious association due to parental dissatisfactions accompanying precocious marriages, social and economic handicaps (Monahan, 1953; Herrman, 1965), premarital pregnancy or the female's attitude toward the pregnancy condition (Christensen and Rubenstein, 1956), courtship histories including length of acquaintance and engagement (Christensen and Rubenstein, 1956), personality characteristics (Glick, 1957) and the rapid onset of parental responsibilities (Herrman, 1965). Monahan (1953), in fact, concluded, "Of itself, age at marriage does not appear to be a major point of difficulty in family life." The conclusion underscores the need for precise theoretical specification of presumed relationships.

In summary, marital timing operates, not simply, but in interaction with other life course processes that affect marital stability. For simplicity of presentation we have not unduly complicated Figure 5.6 by displaying the many direct effect patterns that presumably obtain. In our judgment the immediate need is to specify the indirect effect patterns through which earlier causal effects are presumed to operate on marital stability. Marital timing may serve as an intervening mechanism in mediating the effects of earlier antecedents (e.g., socialization into marital roles) on marital stability; and marital timing may have a direct effect on marital stability; or, as we suggest, the effect of marital timing on marital stability is teansmitted through a complex series of indirect effect patterns that have not yet been specified by theorists or estimated by researchers. The complexities of the relationships require greater analytic sensitivity and more precise theoretical specification than past bivariate theory and research have demonstrated. These and related issues are considered in greater detail in the following section, which evaluates the present state of knowledge regarding the antecedents and consequences of marital timing and outlines direction for further theory and research.

III. DISCUSSION AND CONCLUSIONS

We have elaborated a model of the life course processes that attend marital timing. The specifications identify a succession of influences that bear upon an individual's age at marriage or are affected by it. At birth an individual is injected into a social matrix composing an opportunity and reward structure that has an important influence on his/her early career plans and behaviors. Those influences are mediated by a network of linkages which successively incorporate the independent effects of socialization experiences and outcomes, significant other evaluations and encouragment, personality dispositions, certain contingencies, post-high school plans, and educational aspirations. The key mechanism that mediates the effect of earlier antecedents on marital timing is post-high school plans. How the individual aligns his educational, occupational, and marital opportunities and interests has a direct effect on his marital timing and an indirect effect by way of their influence on his/her educational aspirations. The model further specifies complex effect networks whereby marital role definition, whether spouse works, and fertility patterns mediate the effect of marital timing on socioeconomic attainments, i.e., levels of educational and occupational attainment and income adequacy. Marital stability is specified as the final consequence in the causal chain. Based on the accumulated literature, the model organizes propositions and findings into a general analytic framework which, in this concluding section, provides a basis for evaluating the present state of knowledge regarding the antecedents and consequences of marital timing and for formulating directions for future theoretical and empirical endeavor.

The model is heuristic. It represents an initial effort. As a first approximation it invites and requires further conceptual refinement. As the concepts are refined, the specifications of theoretical relationships must also be altered. Indeed, a mature understanding of the marital timing complex will require that theoreticians and researchers also grapple with isolating age, period, and cohort effects. The critical reader will note that some components of the model are tightly specified, whereas the specification of other components is crude and loose. An example of the former is the specification of complex effect patterns whereby marital timing affects socioeconomic attainments (see Figures 5.5 and 5.6). An example of the latter is the labeling of socialization domains (see Figures 5.1 and 5.2) which affect marital timing. The contrast in refinement of concepts reflects the current state of the literature. Some issues have received considerable theoretical and empirical attention with the result that key concepts are well developed and refined. Other parts of the model draw upon literature that is conceptually underdeveloped, and the research has been more limited and less rigorous. Because much of the literature suffers from lack of conceptual development and refinement, in the aggregate it is more aptly characterized as a set of unrelated reports on associations of indicators than a coherent body of theory and research. Too often measurement has been substituted for definition with little regard for either the abstract concepts that are, presumably, being indicated or the cumulative nature of the findings. The result is that there exists an abundance of reported relationships with marital timing, most of them bivariate, but little understanding of the meaning and substantive significance of the relationships. The challenge, therefore, is to proceed both inductively and deductively. Inductively the opportunity is to construct concepts that embrace previously observed associations between empirical indicators. Deductively the need is not only to generate and refine new concepts but also to specify the conditions of relationship between them. Some initial conceptual spadework has been accomplished; but further conceptual development and refinement must continue to occupy a high priority on the theoretician's agenda.

Our presentation draws a distinction between *explanation* and *prediction*. Indeed, the emphasis has been on specifying processes—i.e., disaggregating associations into total effects, indirect effects, and direct effects—with only passing attention given to proportions of variation accounted for (R^2). This interpretive strategy represents a conscious departure from approaches to theory construction which concentrate only on direct effects, equate direct with total effects, ignore indirect effects, and emphasize accounting for increased variation in dependent variables. Although prediction is a legitimate goal of the scientific enterprise, of itself it does not satisfy the quest for understanding or exhaust the potential of theory for explaining social phenomena. Our approach to social scientific analysis seeks not only to establish theoretical and empirical relationships but also to elaborate on the

relationships in order to interpret them. Although we have employed rhetoric commonly associated with interpreting causal theories estimated by structural equation models, the reader will recognize that the analytic strategy is identical to that variously referred to as "the Lazarsfeld method," "the Columbia school," "the interpretation method," or "the elaboration model." (The fact that the latter was developed primarily through use of contingency tables whereas the former was developed in conjunction with analysis of structural equations is purely of scientific analysis or theory construction.) Both procedures require not only a statement of relationship but explicit theoretical specification of whether a variable operates as an independent, intervening, or dependent variable, inasmuch as different configurations of the three (or more) posit different theoretical relationships.

The primary logic and theoretical utility of the analytic paradigm implicit in both procedures are illustrated in the following three variable prototypical models. In the first two (Figures 5.7a and 5.7b) the relationship between variable B and C is partially spurious. It is explained by a common antecedent, variable A. When the common antecedent is introduced, the original relationship between B and C is reduced or neutralized whether the relationship is represented as correlation (Figure 5.7a) or causation (Figure 5.7b). In the second model (Figure 5.7b) an effort is made to explain, i.e., interpret, the relationship between variables A and C by means of the mediating influence of the intervening variable B. In the rhetoric of structural equation analysis, the question is what proportion of the total effect of A on C is mediated by B. That proportion mediated by B is indirect. The remaining component of the total effect is direct. Given the nomenclature of the elaboration method, variable B "interprets" the relationship of A and C. The third model (Figure 5.7c) differs from Figure 5.7b in that variable B is specified as an antecedent rather than an intervening variable. Figures 5.7b and 5.7c do not represent the same explanation for the antecedents of C; neither is either equivalent to the bivariate proposition that A affects C

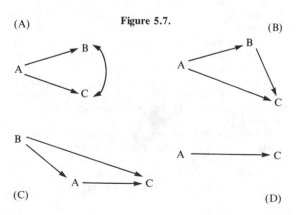

(A)   **Figure 5.7.**   (B)

(C)   (D)

(Figure 5.7d) or, for that matter, to the notion that B and C are concurrently influenced by A (Figure 5.7a). While it is possible (though improbable) that in a given application the affect of A on C would be constant across estimates for all four theoretical models, it is imperative that two fundamental distinctions be observed:

1. Figures 5.7a, 5.7b, 5.7c, and 5.7d are *not* equivalent theoretical specifications.
2. Figures 5.7a, 5.7b, and 5.7c are preferable theoretical specifications because they indicate the conditions and processes by which A affects C, which are not specified in Figure 5.7d.

In summary, we submit that the logic of scientific inquiry requires the identification of empirical relationships and the specification of the conditions under which the relationships obtain. The goal is not limited to prediction, but encompasses explanation of the processes by which effects occur. Whether the theoretician feels more comfortable with the rhetoric of the elaboration model (Rosenberg, 1968) or that of structural equation models (Alwin and Hauser, 1975) is not at issue. What is at issue is whether the goal of theory construction is perceived as limited to specifying relationships and accounting for variation in dependent variables, or whether it includes explaining the processes by which relationships occur. Our understanding of the nature and utility of theory is consistent with the latter view, and we commend it to those who would further develop understanding of the antecedents and consequences of marital timing.

The deficiencies in past theory and research extend beyond the need for further conceptual development, refinement, and systematic elaboration of theoretical relationships, but include related issues of sampling, measurement, and data analysis. The first issue related to sampling is a clear requirement for more representative samples. The recurring question is, to what populations do the theories and empirical findings apply? Closely related is a second requirement, the need for more research on males. The processes that affect males undoubtedly differ from those that affect females, but little comparative research has been done. Third, the literature is seriously deficient in longitudinal studies of marital timing. Adequate discussion of the logic of causation far exceeds the coverage of this chapter, but we note that a primary criterion for establishing causation is that cause must temporally precede effect. Although longitudinal designs and data sets will not resolve all problems of establishing sequences of complicated social phenomena, the preference for longitudinal over cross-sectional designs for life course analysis is obvious.

Analysis of life course processes—which incorporate indicators of social structural, social psychological, psychological, and contingency effects—pose extraordinarily complex measurement problems. In operationalizing concepts, the challenge is to arrive at valid indicators of the theoretical concepts. Inasmuch as the relationship between concepts and indicators is contingent and loose rather than fixed and exact (Duncan, 1975:130), future estimates of theoretical models must be more sensitive to problems of measurement error (unreliability), which fix an upper limit to validity. Strictly speaking, all observations are fallible, no matter how refined the measurement and how careful the procedures employed. The problem of measurement error is one of degree. It may be that in a particular model the errors of measurement are uniformly negligible, in which case the assumption that the measurements are error-free may be warranted. More likely, however, the indicators are "dirty" measures of the theoretical concepts (reflecting random and/or systematic deviations from the "true" variable) and the errors are too large to ignore. The effect of measurement error (unreliability) in estimating relationships has been discussed at length by others. Suffice it to say that in the case of single equation models the effect is to attenuate the size of the coefficients (Heise, 1969; Blalock, Wells, and Carter, 1970). In models encompassing an interplay of processes, however the problem can be greatly exacerbated, as Bohrnstedt and Carter (1971) have demonstrated. It is especially complicated in theoretical specifications which incorporate variables with differential or even unknown reliability, as may occur in explanations incorporating the effects of demographic variables, which are normally highly reliable, and social psychological variables, which are comparatively less reliable. The effect of measurement error on such complex models, of which life course models of the marital timing complex are an example, may be unpredictable. Estimates may be severely distorted, and substantive interpretations may be meaningless. Under such circumstances researchers are well advised to accommodate their theoretical specifications and statistical procedures to the realities of measurement errors (see, for example, the symposium edited by Goldberger and Duncan, 1973). Although it is impossible to measure variables without error, a mature science "properly manages its errors, controlling their magnitudes and correctly calculating their implications for substantive conclusions" (Duncan, 1975:114).

In 1969 Bayer illustrated path analysis with a model employing age at marriage as the dependent variable. Bayer was critical of earlier studies of age at marriage:

> most have employed cross-tabular analyses and only one or two independent variables. As a consequence, the results of these several studies are not additive. That is, the independent variables from the various studies are often intercorrelated to such an extent that if statistical control were introduced for one of the variables, the influence of the other variables on the criterion (age at marriage) would be substantially diminished. . . . [1969:557].

Bayer went on to extol the virtues of more advanced analytic techniques and to demonstrate their application to family phenomena. Since 1969 significant additional advances have been made with respect to analytic strategies and techniques, but the "marked divergence in the analytical mode(s)" between family sociology and other more developed areas of the discipline noted by Bayer continues, as does the result: "family research can still be largely characterized as based on small samples and descriptive or bivariate analysis" (Bayer, 1969:551). Advanced data analysis techniques—including multiple contingency tables, structural equation models, the use of multiple indicators, and unobserved variables— constitute methodological advances that require a degree of theoretical specificity that the literature does not exemplify. The immediate need is to specify theoretical formulas with sufficient precision that the most powerful analytic procedures available may be employed in estimating proposed relationships. This chapter is an attempt to provide theoretical frameworks for considering marital timing in the life cycle process, for which appropriate modes of analysis are available. It is hoped that the heuristic models will capture the critical imagination of theorists and researchers alike.

REFERENCES

ALWIN, D. F. AND R. M. HAUSER
1975   "The decomposition of effects in path analysis." *American Sociological Review* 40:37–47.

ANDERSON, W. J. AND S. M. LATTS
1965   "High school marriages and school policies in Minnesota." *Journal of Marriage and the Family* 27:266–70.

ATKYNS, G. C.
1968   "Trends in the retention of married and pregnant students in American public schools." *Sociology of Education:* 57–65.

BARTZ, K. W. AND F. I. NYE
1970   "Early marriage: A propositional formulation." *Journal of Marriage and the Family* 32:258–68.

BAUMAN, K. E.
1967   "The relationship between age at first marriage, school dropout, and marital instability: An analysis of the Glick effect." *Journal of Marriage and the Family* 29:672–80.

BAYER, A. E.
1968   "Early dating and early marriage." *Journal of Marriage and the Family* 30:628–32.
1969   "Life plans and marriage age: An application of path analysis." *Journal of Marriage and the Family* 31:551–58.

BECKER, H. S.
1969   "Social-class variations in the teacher-pupil relationship." In B. C. Rosen, H. J. Crockett, and C. Z. Nunn (eds.), *Achievement in American Society.* Cambridge, Mass.: Schenkman.

BELL, A. G.
1883   "Upon the formation of a deaf variety of the human race." *Memoirs of the National Academy Science* 2:179–262.

BEM, D. J.
1970   *Beliefs, Attitudes, and Human Affairs.* Belmont, Calif.: Brooks/ Cole.

BERNARD, J.
1966   "Marital stability and patterns of status variables." *Journal of Marriage and the Family* 28:421–39.

BLALOCK, H. M., C. S. WELLS, AND L. F. CARTER
1970   "Statistical estimation with random measurement error." In E. F. Borgatta (ed.), *Sociological Methodology 1970.* San Francisco: Jossey-Bass.

BLAU, P. M. AND O. D. DUNCAN
1967   *The American Occupational Structure.* New York: Wiley.

BOGUE, D. J.
1969   *Principles of Demography.* New York: Wiley.

BOHRNSTEDT, G. W., AND T. M. CARTER
1971   "Robustness in regression analysis." In E. F. Borgatta (ed.), *Sociological Methodology 1970.* San Francisco: Jossey-Bass.

BRODERICK, C. G. AND S. E. FOWLER
1961   "New patterns of relationships between the sexes among preadolescents." *Marriage and Family Living* 23:27–30.

BRONFENBRENNER, URIE
1958   "Socialization and social class through time and space." In E. Maccoby, T. M. Newcomb, and E. L. Hartley (eds.), *Readings in Social Psychology,* third ed. New York: Henry Holt.
1961   "The changing American child: A speculative analysis." *Merrill-Palmer Quarterly* 7:73–84.

BUMPASS, L. L. AND J. A. SWEET
1970   "Differentials in marital instability: 1970." *American Sociological Review* 37:754–66.

BURGESS, E. W. AND L. S. COTTRELL, JR.
1953   *Engagement and Marriage.* Philadelphia: Lippincott.

BURCHINAL, L.
1959a   "Does early dating lead to school-age marriage?" *Iowa Farm Science* 13:11–12.
1959b   "How successful are school-age marriages?" *Iowa Farm Science* 13: 7–10.
1959c   "Comparison of factors related to adjustment in pregnancy-provoked and nonpregnancy-provoked youthful marriages." *Midwest Sociologist* 21:92–96.
1959d   "Study of patterns of cross religious marriage and divorce in Iowa." Reported at the American Sociological Association meeting, September. Unpublished paper.
        "Adolescent role deprivation and high school age marriages." *Marriage and Family Living* 21:378–84.
1960   "Research on young marriage: Implications for family life education." *The Family Coordinator* 9:6–24.
1965   "Trends and prospects for young marriages in the United States." *Journal of Marriage and the Family:* 243–54.

BURCHINAL, L. G. AND L. CHANCELLOR
1958   "What about school-age marriages." *Iowa Farm Science* 12:12–14.
1963   "Social status, religious affiliation, and age at marriage." *Journal of Marriage and the Family* 25:219–21.

BURGESS, E. W. AND L. S. COTTRELL, JR.
1939   *Predicting Success or Failure in Marriage.* New York: Prentice-Hall.

BURGESS, E. W. AND P. WALLIN
1944   "Personal appearance and neuroticism as related to age at marriage." *Human Biology* 16:15–22.

CALL, V. R. A. AND L. B. OTTO
1977   "Age at marriage as a mobility contingency: Esitmates for the Nye-Berardo model." *Journal of Marriage and the Family* 39:67–79.

CAMPBELL, E. Q.
1968   "Adolescent socialization." In D. A. Goslin (ed.), *Handbook of Socialization Theory and Research.* Chicago: Rand McNally.

CARLSON, R. O.
1961   "Variation and myth in social status of teachers." *Journal of Educational Sociology* 35:104–18.

CAVIN, R. S. AND G. BELING
1958 "A study of high school marriages." *Marriage and Family Living* 20:293–95.

CHILMAN, C. S.
1966 "Dating, courtship, and engagement behavior of married compared to single undergraduates with an analysis of early-marrying and late-marrying students." *The Family Life Coordinator* 15:112–18.

CHRISTENSEN, H. T.
1963 "Child spacing analysis via record linkage: New data plus a summing up from earlier reports." *Marriage and Family Living* 25:272–80.

CHRISTENSEN, H. T. AND H. H. MEISSNER
1953 "Studies in child-spacing: III—Premarital pregnancy as a factor in divorce." *American Sociological Review* 18:641–44.

CHRISTENSEN, H. T. AND B. B. RUBENSTEIN
1956 "Premarital pregnancy and divorce: A follow-up study by the interview method." *Marriage and Family Living* 18:114–23.

CLAUSEN, J. A.
1968 *Socialization and Society.* Boston: Little, Brown.

COHEN, D. B., F. J. KING, AND W. NELSON
1963 "Academic achievement of college students before and after marriage." *Marriage and Family Living* 25:98–99.

COLEMAN, JAMES S.
1961 *The Adolescent Society.* New York: Free Press.

COMMINS, W. D.
1932 "The marriage age of oldest sons." *Journal of Social Psychology* 3:487–90.

COSER, R. L. AND G. ROKOFF
1971 "Women in the occupational world: Social disruption and conflict." *Social Problems* 18:535–54.

CROSS, P. A.
1968 "College women: A research description." Paper presented at 1968 annual meeting of National Association of Women Deans and Counselors. Mimeographed.

CUTRIGHT, P.
1971 "Income and family events: Marital stability." *Journal of Marriage and the Family* 33:291–306.

DELISSOVOY, V. AND M. E. HITCHCOCK
1965 "High school marriages in Pennsylvania." *Journal of Marriage and the Family* 27:263–65.

DOUBROUSKY, C. P.
1971 "Report on sex bias in the public schools." New York: National Organization for Women, 1971.

DUNCAN, O. D.
1934 "The factor of age in marriage." *American Journal of Sociology* 39:469–82.
1961 "A socioeconomic index for all occupations." In A. J. Reiss, Jr. et al., *Occupations and Social Status.* New York: Free Press.
1975 *Introduction to Structural Equation Models.* New York: Academic Press.

DUVALL, E. AND R. HILL
1945 *When You Marry.* Boston: D. C. Heath.

EISENSTADT, S. N.
1956 *From Generation to Generation.* New York: Free Press.

ELDER, G. H., JR.
1972 "Role orientations, marital age, and life patterns in adulthood." *Merrill-Palmer Quarterly* 18:3–24.

ELDER, G. AND R. C. ROCKWELL
1977 "Marital timing in women's life patterns." *Journal of Family History* 1:34–53.

ENGLAND, J. L. AND P. R. KUNZ
1975 "The application of age-specific rate to divorce." *Journal of*

Marriage and the Family 37:40–48.

ESHLEMAN, J. R.
1965 "Mental health and marital integration in young marriages." *Journal of Marriage and the Family:* 255–62.
1974 *The Family: An Introduction.* Boston: Allyn and Bacon.

FELDMAN, S. D.
1973 "Impediment or stimulant? Marital status and graduate education." *American Journal of Sociology* 78:982–94.

FINNEY, J. M.
1972 "Indirect effects in path analysis." *Sociological Methods and Research* 1:175–86.

GINZBERG, E.
1966 *Life Styles of Educated Women.* New York and London: Columbia University Press.

GLICK, P. C.
1957 *American Families.* New York: U. S. Bureau of Census.
1970 "Marriage and marital stability among blacks." *Milbank Memorial Fund Quarterly* 48:99–116.

GLICK, P. C. AND E. LANDAU
1950 "Age as a factor in marriage." *American Sociological Review* 15: 519–29.

GLICK, P. C. AND A. J. NORTON
1971 "Frequency, duration, and probability of marriage and divorce." *Journal of Marriage and the Family* 33:307–17.

GOLDBERGER, A. S. AND O. D. DUNCAN
1973 *Structural Equation Models in the Social Sciences.* New York: Seminar Press.

GORANSON, R. E.
1970 "Media violence and aggressive behavior: A review of experimental research." In Leonard Berkowitz, *Advances in Experimental Social Psychology,* vol. 5. New York: Academic Press.

GORDON, M. S.
1968 "Introduction: Women in the labor force." *Industrial Relations* 7:187–92.

GOVER, D. A. AND D. G. JONES
1964 "Requirement of parental consent: A deterrent to marriage?" *Journal of Marriage and the Family* 26:205–206.

GURIN, G., J. VEROFF, AND S. FELD
1960 *Americans View Their Mental Health: A Nationwide Interview Survey.* New York: Basic Books.

HALLER, A. O., L. B. OTTO, R. F. MEIER, AND G. W. OHLENDORF
1973 "Level of occupational aspiration: An empirical analysis." *American Sociological Review* 39:113–21.

HASTINGS, D. W. AND J. G. ROBINSON
1973 "A re-examination of Hernes model on the process of entry into first marriage for United States women, cohorts 1891–1945." *American Sociological Review* 38:138–42.

HAVIGHURST, R. J.
1962 *Growing Up in River City.* New York: Wiley.

HEISE, D. R.
1969 "Problems in path analysis and causal inference." In Edgar F. Borgatta (ed.), *Sociological Methodology 1970.* San Francisco: Jossey-Bass.

HEISS, J. S.
1960 "Variations in courtship progress among high school students." *Marriage and Family Living* 22:165–70.

HERNES, G.
1972 "The process of entry into first marriage." *American Sociological Review* 37:173–82.

HESS, R. D. AND V. C. SHIPMAN
1965 "Early experience and the socialization of cognitive modes in children." *Child Development* 36:869–86.

HERRMANN, R. O.
1965 "Expectations and attitudes as a source of financial problems

in teen-age marriages." *Journal of Marriage and the Family* 27:89–91.

HUBBACK, J.
1957   *Wives Who Went to College*. London: Heinemann.

HYMAN, H. H.
1966   "The value systems of different classes." In R. Bendix and S. M. Lipset (eds.), *Class Status and Power,* second ed. New York: Free Press.

INSELBERG, M. R.
1961   "Social and psychological factors associated with high school marriage." *Journal of Home Economics* 53:766–72.

JAIN, A. K.
1969   "Fecundability and its relation to age in a sample of Taiwanese women." *Population Studies* 23:69–86.

JENKINS, J. J.
1968   "The acquisition of language." In D. A. Goslin (ed.), *Handbook of Socialization Theory and Research*. Chicago: Rand McNally.

JENSEN, A. R.
1968   "Social class and verbal learning." In M. Deutsch, I. Katz, and A. R. Jensen (eds.), *Social Class, Race, and Psychological Development*. New York: Holt, Rinehart and Winston.

JENSEN, A. R.
1972   *Genetics and Education*. New York: Harper and Row.

JENSEN, V. H. AND M. H. CLARKE
1958   "Married and unmarried college students: Achievement, ability, and personality." *Personnel Guidance Journal* 37: 123–25.

KELLEY, H. H.
1968   "Two functions of reference groups." In H. H. Hyman and E. Singer (eds.), *Readings in Reference Group Theory and Research*. New York: Free Press.

KEMPER, T. D.
1968   "Reference groups, socialization and achievement." *American Sociological Review* 33:31–45.

KENKEL, W. F.
1973   *The Family in Perspective*. New York: Appleton-Century-Crofts.

KERCKHOFF, A. C.
1972   *Socialization and Social Class*. Englewood Cliffs, N. J.: Prentice-Hall.

KISER, C. V. AND M. E. FRANK
1967   "Factors associated with the low fertility of non-white women of college attainment." *Milbank Memorial Fund Quarterly* 45:427–49.

KOHN, M. L.
1969   *Class and Conformity*. Homewood, Ill.: Dorsey Press.

LANDIS, P. H.
1955   *Making the Most of Marriage*. New York: Appleton-Century-Crofts.

LANDIS, J. T. AND K. C. KIDD
1956   "Attitudes and policies concerning marriages among high school students." *Journal of Marriage and the Family* 18:128–36.

LANDIS, J. T. AND M. G. LANDIS
1958   *Building a Successful Marriage,* third ed. Englewood Cliffs, N. J.: Prentice-Hall.

LAVIN, D. E.
1965   *The Prediction of Academic Performance*. New York: Russell Sage Foundation.

LIEBERMAN, SEYMOUR
1970   "The effects of changes in roles on the attitudes of role occupants." In Neil J. Smelser (ed.), *Personality and Social Systems,* second ed. New York: Wiley.

LOPATE, C.
1968   *Women in Medicine*. Baltimore: Johns Hopkins University Press.

LOWRIE, S. H.
1965   "Early marriage: Premarital pregnancy and associated factors." *Journal of Marriage and the Family* 27:48–56.

MARTINSON, F. M.
1955   "Ego deficiency as a factor in marriage." *American Sociological Review* 20: 161–164.
1959   "Ego deficiency as a factor in marriage: A male sample." *Marriage and Family Living* 21:48–52.

McCANDLESS, B. R.
1968   "Childhood socialization." In D. A. Goslin (ed.), *Handbook of Socialization Theory and Research*. Chicago: Rand McNally.

McCARTHY, D.
1954   "Language development in children." In L. Carmichael (ed.), *Manual of Child Psychology*. New York: Wiley.

MEDALIA, N. Z.
1962   "Marriage and adjustment: In college and out." *Personnel Guidance Journal* 40:454–550.

MERTON, R. K.
1957   *Social Theory and Social Research,* revised ed. New York: Free Press.

MOMENI, D. A.
1972   "The difficulties of changing the age at marriage in Iran." *Journal of Marriage and the Family* 34:545–51.

MONAHAN, T. P.
1952   "How stable are remarriages?" *American Journal of Sociology* 58:280–88.
1953   "Does age at marriage matter in divorce?" *Social Forces* 32:81–87.

MOSS, J. J. AND R. GINGLES
1959   "The relationship of personality to the incidence of early marriage." *Marriage and Family Living* 21:373–77.

MURDOCK, P. H.
1966   "Birth order and age at marriage." *British Journal of Social and Clinical Psychology* 5:24–29.

MURDOCK, P. H. AND G. F. SMITH
1969   "Birth order and affiliation." *British Journal of Social and Clinical Psychology* 8:235–45.

MURSTEIN, B. I.
1967   "The relationship of mental health to marital choice and courtship progress." *Journal of Marriage and the Family* 29:447–51.

MUSSEN, P. H.
1968   "Early sex-role development." In D. A. Goslin (ed.), *Handbook of Socialization Theory and Research*. Chicago: Rand McNally.

NEWCOMB, T. M.
1950   *Social Psychology*. New York: Dryden Press.

NOTESTEIN, F. W.
1931   "Differential age at marriage according to social class." *American Journal of Sociology* 37:22–48.

NYE, F. I. AND F. M. BERARDO
1973   *The Family*. New York: Macmillan.

OTTO, L. B.
1975a   "Class and status in family research." *Journal of Marriage and the Family* 38: 315–32.
1975b   "Extracurricular activities in the educational attainment process." *Rural Sociology* 40:162–76.
1976a   "Social integration and the status attainment process." *American Journal of Sociology* 81:1360–83.
1976b   "Extracurricular activities and aspirations in the status

attainment process." *Rural Sociology* 41:162–76.

1977 "Girl friends as significant-others: Their influence on young men's career aspirations and achievements." *Sociometry* 40:287–93.

OTTO, L. B. AND D. F. ALWIN
1977 "Athletics, aspirations, and attainments." *Sociology of Education* 42:102–113.

OTTO, L. B. AND V. R. A. CALL
1976 "Social policy implications of marital timing research on males." Paper presented at the annual meetings of the American Sociological Association, New York.

OTTO, L. B. AND A. O. HALLER
1978 "A social psychological view of the status attainment process: A comparison of estimates." Social Forces. Forthcoming.

PAINTER, E. G.
1967 "Significant variables as predictors of early college marriage." *National Association of Women Deans and Counselors Journal* 30:111–14.

PALMER, S. E.
1971 "Reasons for marriage breakdown: A case study in southwestern Ontario (Canada)." *Journal of Comparative Family Studies* 2:251–62.

PARSONS, T.
1951 *The Social System.* New York: Free Press.
1959 "The school class as a social system: Some of its functions in American society." *Harvard Educational Review* 29:297–318.

PEARLIN, L. I. AND M. L. KOHN
1966 "Social class, occupation, and parental values: A cross national study." *American Sociological Review* 31:466–79.

PROTHRO, E. T. AND L. N. DIAB
1968 "Birth order and age at marriage in the Arab Levant." *Psychological Reports* 23:1236–38.

RAINWATER, L.
1965 *Family Design, Marital Sexuality, Family Size and Contraception.* Chicago: Aldine.

RELE, J. R.
1965a "Trends and differentials in the American age at marriage." *Milbank Memorial Fund Quarterly* 43:219–34.
1965b "Some correlates of the age at marriage in the United States." *Eugenics Quarterly* 12:1–6.

ROSE, A. M.
1955 "Parental models for youth." *Sociology and Social Research* 40: 3–9.

ROSEN, B. C.
1959 "Race, ethnicity, and the achievement syndrome." *American Sociological Review* 24:47–60.

ROSENBERG, M.
1968 *The Logic of Survey Analysis.* New York: Basic Books.

ROSENTHAL, R. AND L. JACOBSON
1968 *Pygmalion in the Classroom.* New York: Holt, Rinehart and Winston.

ROSENWAIKE, I.
1967 "Parental consent ages as a factor in state variation in bride's age at marriage." *Journal of Marriage and the Family* 29:452–55.

ROSSI, A. S.
1965 "Women in science: Why so few?" *Science* 148:1196–1202.

SCHORR, A.
1966 *Poor Kids.* New York: Basic Books

SCHROEDER, R.
1963 "Academic achievement of the male college students." *Marriage and Family Living* 25:420–23.

SEARS, R. R. MACCOBY, E. E., AND LEVIN, J.

1957 *Patterns of Child Rearing.* New York: Harper and Row.

SEWELL, W. H.
1961 "Social class and childhood personality." *Sociometry* 24:340–56.

SEWELL, W. H. AND A. O. HALLER
1956 "Social status and personality adjustment of the child." *Sociometry* 19:114–25.

SEWELL, W., A. O. HALLER, AND A. PORTES
1969 "The educational and early occupational attainment process." *American Sociological Review* 34:82–92.

SEWELL, W. H. AND R. M. HAUSER
1975 *Education, Occupation and Earnings: Achievement in the Early Career.* New York: Academic Press.

SHIBUTANI, T.
1961 *Society and Personality.* Englewood Cliffs, N. J.: Prentice-Hall.

SIEGEL, E.
1963 "Medical problems of the teen-age mother." *Marriage and Family Living* 25:488–91.

SIMON, W. AND J. H. GAGNON
1968 "On psychosexual development." In D. A. Goslin (ed.), *Handbook of Socialization Theory and Research.* Chicago: Rand McNally.

SLATER, P.
1970 *The Pursuit of Loneliness.* Boston: Beacon.

SMELSER, N. J. AND W. T. SMELSER
1970 *Personality and Social Systems.* New York: Wiley.

SMITH, P. C.
1971 "Philippine regional and provincial differentials in marriage and family building: 1960." *Philippine Sociological Review* 19:159–181.

SOBOL, M. G.
1973 "A dynamic analysis of labor force participation of married women of childbearing age." *Journal of Human Resources* 8:497–505.

SOMMERKORN, I.
1966 "On the position of women in the university teaching profession in England." Ph.D. dissertation, University of London.

SOROKIN, P.
1927 *Social Mobility.* New York: Harper.

SPADY, W. G.
1971 "Status, achievement, and motivation in the American high school." *School Review* 79:379–403.

STENDLER, C. B.
1951 "Social class differences in parental attitudes towards school at grade 1 level." *Child Development* 22:37–46.

TARVER, J. D.
1951 "Age and duration of marriages of divorced couples." *Sociology and Social Research* 36:102–106.

TERMAN, L. M.
1938 *Psychological Factors in Marital Happiness.* New York: McGraw-Hill.

TURNER, R. H.
1964 "Some aspects of women's ambition." *American Journal of Sociology* 70:271–85.

UDRY, J. R.
1967 "Marital instability by race and income based on 1960 census data." *American Journal of Sociology* 72:673–74.

UHLENBERG, P.
1972 "Marital instability among Mexican Americans: Following the patterns of Blacks." *Social Problems* 20:49–56.

VEEVERS, J. E.
1971 "Childlessness and age at first marriage." *Social Biology* 18:

292–95.

WALLACE, W. L.
1969   *Sociological Theory*. Chicago: Aldine.

WEINSTEIN, E. A.
1968   "The development of interpersonal competence." In D. A. Goslin (ed.), *Handbook of Socialization Theory and Research*. Chicago: Rand McNally.

WITKIN, H. A.
1968   "Social influences in the development of cognitive style." In D. A. Goslin (ed.), *Handbook of Socialization Theory and Research*. Chicago: Rand McNally.

WOELFEL, J. AND A. O. HALLER
1971   "Significant others, the self-reflexive act and the attitude formation process." *American Sociological Review* 36:74–87.

WOMBLE, D. L.
1966   "Trends in falsification of age at marriage in Ohio." *Journal of Marriage and the Family* 28:54–56.

6

GENERATIONS IN THE FAMILY

Lillian Troll and Vern Bengtson
with the assistance of Dianne McFarland

Relations between generations in the family are a common theme in drama, from classical Greek theater to today's television serials. In contemporary social and behavioral science, intergenerational processes are central to theory of both individual development and societal change. Unfortunately, knowledge and understanding of these processes are among the more undeveloped areas of family research—despite increasing numbers of empirical studies.

The purpose of this chapter is to evaluate existing findings about generations from the perspective of the family and, where possible, to derive propositions that summarize consistent results. Frequently the results are noncumulative, often they are contradictory; but their explication should lead to more direct research.

Two general issues are involved in family studies regarding generations. One concerns socialization, specifically the transmission of characteristics across generations. The second focuses on interpersonal relationships among family members of different generations. The first section of this chapter examines conceptual and methodological issues which must undergird adequate evaluation of research findings; for example, the interplay between the system or process of generations in the family and other generational systems or processes. Six overarching research questions can be summarized from the literature, as well as six methodological problems faced by researchers attempting to answer these questions. The second section reviews findings on generational transmission—similarities or contrasts between parents and children. It examines relevant issues in the light of the growing body of empirical data and draws tentative summary propositions at varying levels of specificity.

The third section focuses on the interaction dynamics of cross-generational relationships, reviewing substantive areas parallel to those in the second section.

I. CONCEPTUAL AND METHODOLOGICAL ISSUES

During the 1960s the theme of generational cleavage dominated both popular and academic literature. Less than a decade later, however, most of these "generation gap" analyses appear conceptually simplistic and methodologically naive. Moreover, few of these discussions deal with specific intrafamily comparisons as such. The concern over generational cleavage has been useful, however, in that it highlighted the many problems in concepts and research design.

Surveys of the literature have noted a tendency to confound different concepts of generations (Troll, 1970; Bengtson, 1970; Bengtson, Furlong, and Laufer, 1974; Bengtson and Cutler, 1976; Cutler, 1976). Many analyses recognize three structural generational units: the individual, the family, and the larger society. Some also attend to the effects of variations in time span between different generational units and to variations in historical periods and cultural styles or *Zeitgeist* (Braungart, 1974).

As conceived here, the generational process within the family simultaneously exerts an influence upon and is influenced by, the generational process in individual development throughout the course of life as well as by the succession of age cohorts in the larger society. Development of each individual in the family lineage as well as changes in the society to which the family belongs, are both intricately related to cross-generational relationships within the family.

Thus three generational processes or systems are relevant to family research and theory: generations of family lineage, generations as developmental levels, and genera-

NOTE: The authors wish to acknowledge the contribution to bibliographic research made by Mitchell Deutsch. Professors Reuben Hill, Denise Kandel, Alan Acock, Roberta Siegel, and especially Neal Cutler are to be thanked for helpful comments on the first draft.

tions as age strata (or cohorts) in the social system. These are delineated below.

Generations of Family Lineage

From the point of view of the family, the focal generational system is the ascendant-descendant chain of grandparent-parent-child. The first family generation is commonly considered the oldest one currently alive, although it may be meaningful in some contexts to include those now-dead parents and grandparents who have an influence upon family members still living. An esteemed grandfather could be a model for his descendants for 100 years and more, and most parents leave a legacy to their children which lasts at least so long as the children survive (Troll, 1972; Sussman, Cates, and Smith, 1971).

Family generation rank or lineage position is independent of chronological age. A second-generation member may be anywhere from two seconds to 72 years old, depending in part on the longevity of that family (Jarvik, 1975). Furthermore, lineage positions can be different along maternal and paternal lines. One could be second generation on the maternal side and first generation on the paternal side; influenced by three generations of ancestors on one side and only one on the other. Not only do women now tend to live longer than men, but they have usually married younger, have married men who are older than they, and have become a parent at a younger age. Thus, women, relative to men, can have a doubled impact upon new generations. They are likely to be more involved than men in child rearing, and there are likely to be more generations of them around.

Time between generations—which affects the number of coexistent generations—is related to such biological factors as age of sexual maturity and to such social factors as age of marriage, or social maturity. There have been secular trends for both earlier age of sexual maturity (Tanner, 1961) and age of marriage, at least until very recently. Fertility is also a factor. The number of children per set of parents and the distance between these children are important. For example, if the time span between the oldest and youngest child in one lineage generation is 30 years and many children are spread over those 30 years, the distinction between lineage generations itself can be blurred, and solidarity among siblings attenuated. Two or three children born within four years might heighten sibling ties, perhaps at the expense of parent-child bonds.

Generations as Developmental Levels

In the course of their life span, individuals move through a developmental progression that can be heuristically divided into segments or stages. These segments are sometimes informally referred to as "generations." For example, adolescence has been termed a different generation from childhood, youth from adolescence, adulthood from youth, and old age from adulthood. The ontogenetic

developmental system is linked more directly to chronological age than is the family system, though still far from synchronous with it (Troll, 1975).

Any consideration of generations in the family must take into account the developmental or ontogenetic status of the people in each lineage position (Riley, Foner, Hess, and Toby, 1969). A parent's influence on a child of 10—or reciprocally that child's influence on its parent— is different if the parent is a young adult or middle-aged (Nydegger, 1973). Adolescents interact differently with their parents from the way they did when they were young children and the way they are going to when they are adults. Grandparents who are youthful, vigorous, and involved in the world have a different impact on their families than if they are feeble and withdrawn. The effect can go both ways; belonging to the oldest living generation in a five-generation family, knowing that one is next in line to die, or looking down at many steps of descendants could make a person feel, think, and act very "old." Another person the same age or even in the same physical condition whose first child has just gotten married could feel much younger. From the perspective of the youngest generation, having a long line of living grandparents and great-grandparents could have a profound effect on one's relations with and feelings toward one's parents.

Generations as Age Strata or Cohorts in Society

The third process of generations has its base neither in the family nor in the individual, but rather in wider social systems (Riley, Johnson, and Foner, 1972). It cuts across developmental and family statuses, simultaneously influencing both. Such an age and culture-homogenous group includes all people born at the same time who have been raised under comparable historical and cultural circumstances and were thus subject to similar socialization. Members of such an age cohort may share many attitudes and values, perceive themselves as belonging together, and be recognized as belonging together by others. This is the kind of generation implied by the terms "youth culture," "the establishment," and "the aged." The particular age cohort to which a grandparent, a parent, or a grandchild belongs conceivably affects all their relationships. Parents who grew up in the Depression probably treat their children differently from those who grew up after World War II, even if they are dealing with children the same age and have many other characteristics in common.

Mannheim (1952) makes a distinction between *lifelong* and *temporary* age groups. In the former, membership is maintained throughout life. Even though the members get older, they continue to belong to the group into which they were born. This kind of cohort usually has a historical derivation (Braungart, 1974). We can speak of the generation of those born at the turn of the century, or of the Depression generation. Pinder (1926) emphasizes the "noncontemporaneity of the contemporaneous." All people living at the same time do not necessarily share the same history. Critical events have impacted them at different points in their life and thus affected them differently. Americans born at the beginning of the century, today's grandparents or great-grandparents, were adolescents at the time of World War I, for example. That war was a different kind of experience for them than it was for their parents. Experiencing the war as adolescents affected many of their future relationships and attitudes and made them a different group of people from those before and after them.

Mannheim suggests that the function of the temporary age group, on the other hand, whose membership lasts only for a limited period of the life span, seems to be largely that of easing a transition from one period of life to another that is very different. Such age groups seem to emerge at times of developmental crises, particularly during the transition from youth to adulthood. Once adult status is reached, they may dissolve and their former members merge with all other adults. According to Eisenstadt (1956), such youth groups arise in societies with sharp differences between the kind of interpersonal associations customary in children's early life in the family and those prevailing in the wider social system in which they must function after maturity. Because relationships within a youth group are intermediary between those in family and society, they bridge the gap. This interpretation of youth groups had much salience in discussions of the "generation gap," to be reviewed below. It has been argued that a parallel case may be arising among older people in our society (Rose, 1962; Bengtson and Cutler, 1976). As greater numbers of individuals live to older ages and as compulsory retirement policies induce many commonalities among those in the 60s, such shared experience could induce a meaningful "senior citizen" cohort unity.

Structure and Process

Each of these three generational systems can be seen from either a static or a dynamic perspective. From a static or cross-sectional view they reflect a series of hierarchical or sequential positions. The family lineage system could thus be characterized as a ladder with grandparents at the top and grandchildren at the bottom. The individual developmental system could be described as a sequence of stages from infancy to senescence, and the age cohort system could be described in terms of age strata in society (Riley, Johnson, and Foner, 1972). From a dynamic perspective, each of these systems can be perceived as a process. Family members are continuously changing; over time, the grandparents die and are replaced by their descendants, who thereby assume different kinds of relationships with other family members. The members themselves change, partly in response to interaction with each other, partly as a consequence of

maturational and social changes. And historical processes can alter the character of any or all coexistent generations (Mannheim, 1952).

For example, on the basis of modal cultural characteristics or *Zeitgeist* (Mannheim, 1952), a series of current age groups might be distinguished. There is a cohort born shortly before the turn of the century that started out life in a spirit of expanding economy where conventional "Protestant ethic" virtues such as thrift, industry, respect, and and obedience might be rewarded (Neugarten, 1968). Then there are those who came of age during the economic depression of the thirties who might be less optimistic and value material gains more. Those who grew up in the shadow of the atom bomb, the present child-rearing generation, could, as Margaret Mead (1970) asserts, have found both the present and the future precarious and have turned to radical political action, become alienated, or resorted to violence, depending in part on family background and personality. Finally, a new upcoming youth group, marked by cynicism consequent on the Watergate scandals and a resultant neofundamentalism, could resemble in some ways their grandparents or great-grandparents more than their own parents. To illustrate the effects of historical periods on age cohorts, consider the interactions between a father and son in which the father's attitudes were formed during the Depression and the son's in facing the possibility of world atomic destruction.

The German and French sociologists who studied generations at the beginning of the century (Mannheim, 1952) were impressed with the evidence for a 30-year unit to mark distance between generations, both in the family and in society. Their review of history showed significant changes every 30 years, and this corresponded roughly to the number of years between the births of parent and child at that time. Today, however, accelerating social change and altering communicative styles may have made it strategic to consider an ever-shortening unit. Twenty years seems better than thirty, both for social change and distance between family generations. In some respects, a new age group seems to emerge every four or five years.

The "Generation Gap"

Most generational analysis in the late 1960s dealt with the issue of the "generation gap" in a simplistic fashion. Not only did analysts usually fail to distinguish between different generational processes or systems, but they also did not distinguish among what characteristics might or might not be transmitted. Was the generational cleavage primarily in values, in styles and fashions, or in behavior? Was it a feeling of estrangement, conflict, or difficulty in communication rather than a difference in values or personality?

In general, most generational theorists reviewed by Mannheim and more recently by Bengston, Furlong, and Laufer (1974) focused on political and value shifts evident among contemporary age groups, and some of these theorists assumed that differences would necessarily be accompanied by conflict. Mannheim himself considered conflict between age groups usual but not inevitable. Davis (1940), however, thought that conflict is unavoidable, especially in present technological societies. Universals such as the basic developmental stage difference between parent and child and a decreasing rate of socialization with the coming of maturity (so that youth changes more rapidly than later adulthood) would result in intrinsic differences between parents and children in physiological, sociological, and psychological planes of behavior; these differences would inevitably lead to conflict. The degree of conflict could depend upon four variables: the rate of social change, the complexity of the social structure, the degree of integration of the culture, and the veolocity of movement within the culture.

Bengtson (1970) identified three positions that characterized scholars writing in the 1960s about generational differences. He termed these the "great gap," the "nothing really new," and the "selective continuity" position.

Great Gap

One of the most eloquent exponents of the "great gap" orientation is Friedenberg (1959, 1965, 1969), who noted, "Young people aren't rebelling against their parents; they're abandoning them." He saw a "real and serious conflict of interest" between generations rather than mutual misunderstanding, with youth a discriminated minority and parents the discriminating majority. Freudians have long asserted that sons must rebel against their father in order to achieve the power and independence essential to adult masculinity. Bettelheim (1965) saw this rebellion assuming truly divisive proportions in modern-day life. He believed that parents who once would have been able to balance their child's rebellion so as to achieve eventual harmony as co-adults no longer have the resources necessary either for playing an important role in socializing their children or for coping with the world. According to Bettelheim, their children must take over and turn the world in a new direction. In fact he, like Margaret Mead (1970) and others (e.g., Slater, 1970) suggested that in the face of rapid social change, generational discontinuity is adaptive because old responses become inappropriate to radically new situations.

Nothing Really New

The opposite position emphasizes continuities across generations. It points to within-family similarities in basic political attitudes (e.g., Troll, Neugarten, and Kraines, 1969; Thomas, 1971; Westby and Braungart, 1966), to the importance of parents compared with peers as reference persons for adolescents (Kandel and Lesser, 1972), and to closeness of communication between parents and children of all ages (Troll, 1971). Adelson (1970) suggested that we have translated the basic ideological differences which exist in our deeply divided society into

generational conflict and differences—that the "generation gap" is just a projection of other social contrasts.

Selective Continuity

An intermediate position is presented by researchers such as Hill, Foote, Aldous, Carlson, and Macdonald (1970), who, in their impressive study of consumership and life style of three-generation lineages of couples, found that some characteristics tend to be continuous over generations, in certain kinds of families, and others not. For some, this position means that most conflicts between generations are over secondary issues and that substantial continuity and solidarity prevail. While the rapid pace of social change encourages new ways of expressing old values, it is largely old values that are expressed. Some writers who originally concluded that change was overwhelming or that really nothing had changed have since moved over to this more balanced viewpoint. Some make a distinction between central or core values and peripheral values (Keniston, 1968; Hess and Torney, 1967; Jennings and Niemi, 1968; Tedin, 1974; Angres, 1975). In a 1965 study of student activists (Troll et al., 1969), a variable called "dedication to causes" showed the highest parent-child correlations—around .50. However, the parents may have been dedicated to "modernizing" practices of the Catholic Church or eliminating reading problems by adapting a phonetic method of teaching, and their children to promoting interracial housing or opposing the war in Vietnam. The *modus vivendi* of the parents may have been committee meetings and public speaking, and of their children marches and "sit-ins," but for both generations the core value of dedicating one's life to righting wrongs and improving the world seemed to be the same. Dedication to causes persisted as a "family theme" (cf. Hess and Handel, 1959), though the particular wrongs to be righted and the particular means of trying to do so were different with each new lineage generation.

Methodological Problems in Generational Analysis

At least six general methodological problems beset existing empirical data on generations in the family and make it hazardous to draw firm conclusions from them.

Measurement at One Point in Time Only

Generational studies suffer from the same problems as research in life-span development; we must rely primarily on cross-sectional data when we need cross-sequential, time-sequential, or at least longitudinal (Schaie, 1965, 1973). Where present cross-sectional data show low parent-child correlations for high school or college students and their middle-aged parents, we might find much higher congruence if we could study these dyads again 20 years later or compare a comparable group of high school students and their parents 20 years from now. So far, the only longitudinal reports of lineage-generational comparisons are those of Angres (1975) from the Chicago

Youth and Social Change Project; Clausen (1974) from the Berkeley longitudinal files; and Jennings and Niemi (1975) from a seven-year follow-up of a national sample of high school seniors and their parents.

Equilibration across Families

In evaluating parent-child resemblances, the centrality of values or other characteristics measured should be taken into account. If there is such a thing as a "family theme" (Hess and Handel, 1959) and children resemble their parents more in salient or core characteristics than in peripheral dimensions, then the first step in any transmission research should be to ascertain the individual value hierarchies of the parents. Ultimately, we should need to evaluate each family individually, as Hess and Handel (1959) did, because to some extent each has a unique culture. In current empirical literature perhaps only Tedin (1974) can be said to have approached this criterion, although Thomas (1971), in that he chose his sample on the basis of parents' own political activity, was moving in this direction. (We are presuming that extreme political activity reflects core political values and that family themes are described better by the parents than the children.)

Thomas and Stankiewicz (1974) have followed the general typology of "core" and "peripheral" values utilized by Rokeach (1960, 1968) and referred to by Douvan and Adelson (1966). Unfortunately, this procedure confronts further problems. Judging values from overt behavior has long been known to be risky, if not invalid. Parents who consider themselves very radical and receive high scores on self-reports of radical ideology may never have shown any overt signs of such ideology. They may never have mounted a soap box, never marched in a demonstration, never even voted anything but a straight Democratic ticket. Yet their activist children may be carrying out the beliefs that form their basic political orientation. In fact, they often seem to know they are carrying out the same beliefs and conclude that their parents have "sold out" (Keniston, 1965; Flacks, 1967). A few investigators have made preliminary steps toward weighting transmission for centrality of values. Some have asked all respondents to rank-order a list of goals or values (e.g., Furstenberg, 1967; Flacks, 1967; Goldsmid, 1972; Bengtson, 1975; and Angres, 1975). Tedin (1974) used the dimension of issue salience as an independent or intervening variable systematically.

Most of the studies reviewed here have chosen a more indirect course toward considering centrality of value. They have assumed that certain categories of attitudes or values would be salient throughout our culture, that there would be universality in salience. Thus political transmission has received most attention (Jennings and Niemi, 1968, 1974, 1975; Cutler, 1976). Because it is assumed to be salient in most citizens' ideology, and because it is relatively easy to elicit responses—easier than eliciting responses on sexual orientations or money—about

three-quarters of family transmission research deals with political party preference and political beliefs. This approach was of course reinforced by the heightened concern during the 1960s, particularly in the media and on college campuses, over the possibility of a coming generational revolution. Unfortunately for our present purposes, which are focused on the family, many of these studies ignored individual parent-child comparisons and focused instead upon aggregate or group comparisons, in which the responses of all the parents were pooled and compared with the pooled responses of their children, even when the samples had been selected by family membership.

Statistical Analysis

The majority of studies on generations in the family have utilized either inappropriate, nonrigorous, or naive analytic procedures. Correlation coefficients are probably the most appropriate measure of pair correspondence (Connell, 1972). However, correlations cannot indicate causal direction—who influences whom (Lerner and Spanier, 1978). Transmission is not necessarily all from parent to child. Similar values and beliefs could be the result of the child influencing the parent as much as the other way around (Angres, 1975) or of both parent and child being exposed to the same milieu (Bandura, 1969). For more precise determination of direction of influence or of relative influence of societal, family, or developmental processes, some form of multiple regression analysis might be better. Only a few investigations in this area have utilized any kind of sophisticated procedures, however (e.g., Bengtson, 1975; Thomas, 1972; Troll et al., 1969; Tedin, 1974).

A further problem is that covariation does not necessarily reflect agreement or similarity (Acock and Bengtson, 1976). Parents and children may exhibit high covariation (correlation) but low absolute agreement.

Elements Compared

As pointed out by Connell (1972), most of the comparisons are of aggregates of grouped members of each generation rather than of lineages (parents with their own children). He points out that we must distinguish between pair and group correspondences. Pair (or lineage) correspondence refers to measures of lineage similarities (intrafamily) and is usually represented in terms of a correlation coefficient. Tedin (1974) further distinguishes between relative pair correspondence and absolute pair correspondence. The former, measured by the correlation coefficient, assesses the congruence in relative position in the separate distributions. Thus, a high correlation would mean that the most conservative fathers, for example, would have the most conservative sons. However, the son's generation might be, as a whole, much less (or more) conservative than the father's generation. Absolute pair correspondence is the extent to which the scale scores of the sons are exactly the same as the scale scores of their fathers. This correspondence is usually measured by percentage agreement. A measure of group correspondence is used to compare cohorts as aggregates, parents as a group with children as a group. Group correspondence can be reported by giving each cohort's percentage agreement on the variable measured or by the mean agreement scores of each cohort; and cohort differences can be represented by means of a t-test or analysis of variance (Bengtson and Acock, 1977).

However, as Connell (1972) points out, the distinctions between the types of intergenerational correspondence have often been blurred in actual practice. One particular difficulty is that several early studies reported group correspondence in terms of correlation coefficients. In addition to the correlation being a poor statistic for group correspondence, group data presented in this manner are easily misconstrued as measures of pair correspondence (Bengtson, 1975; Acock and Bengtson, 1976).

Sampling

Problems in the area include poor sampling methods, low response rates, and reliance on only one parent (often the father) in estimating parental influences. These problems are prevalent in the early studies of parent-child political congruence reported in Hyman's (1959) comprehensive review of the early political socialization research. Connell (1972) argues that the samples of many of these early studies, which depended on children for obtaining their parent's responses, were likely to have been biased (Duffy, 1941; Stagner, 1936; Hirschberg and Gilliland, 1942; Weltman and Remmers, 1946; Fisher 1948; and Himmelhoch, 1950). It is possible that those children who were able to get their parents to fill out the questionnaire might have had a closer relationship with their parents than those who could not and thus were more likely to share more of their parents' opinions. Indirect evidence of this was reported by Kirkpatrick (1936), who found that students who were under pressure to elicit their parent's cooperation had double the parental response rates of students who were not under such pressure; the pair correspondence in the pressured group was lower. Such sampling bias is particularly noteworthy because the response rates of these early studies is low. Connell (1972) computed approximate rates of 42 percent for Duffy (1941), 17 percent for Weltman and Remmers (1946), 40 percent for Himmelhoch (1950), and "relatively few" for Fisher (1948). Some of these early reports did not even provide information from which response rates could be computed. Finally, it has been demonstrated that mothers' versus fathers' opinions lead to quite different levels of prediction of youth's attitudes (Acock and Bengtson, 1976).

Reliability and Validity of Measures

Most data on parent-child similarity consist of either self-descriptions, descriptions by others, or behavioral ratings. Self-descriptions are susceptible to response biases which may artificially inflate or diminish congruence scores. If the same person rates both self and other, rater contamination is particularly likely. Questionnaire techniques, which tend to focus on self-descriptions, may give little information about actual behavior or attitudes of the other, as is demonstrated by Bengtson and Acock (1977) in parent-child comparisons. In addition questionnaires are subject to problems of response set, item ambiguity, measurement unreliability, and social desirability of response. Behavioral ratings (seldom found in the generational literature) are similarly subject to problems of reliability and validity, of response bias. For a discussion of these and similar problems in examining parent-child agreement or levels of prediction see Acock and Bengtson (1976); in studying "identification," see Bandura (1969) and Troll (1967).

In the light of these grave methodological handicaps, it is clear that we must observe extreme caution in considering most of the generational literature. The following two sections will, therefore, be limited to citing those studies which are based on research designs that appear both appropriate and sound. In view of the intense interest in the whole subject of the "generation gap" and generational transmission, it is indeed surprising that relatively few studies can meet these criteria, even marginally.

Major Questions in Generational Analysis

Six major questions run through the generational literature. These are listed briefly here; they will be treated in more detail in the following two parts of the chapter.

1. What (if indeed anything) is transmitted across family generations? Is it a general orientation to life, or is it particular values, attitudes, or personality characteristics?

2. What is the effect of historical events or societal changes upon family transmission and interpersonal bonds?

3. Is there a gender difference in either transmission or attachment? Are mothers closer and more influential than fathers, and daughters closer to and more like their parents than sons?

4. What is the relative influence of parents, as compared with friends or age peers, in the socialization of orientations and behaviors?

5. What is the effect of family emotional climate or quality of interrelationships among family members on transmission or consensus?

6. What is the effect of ontogenetic developmental processes upon transmission and interpersonal bonds?

II. TRANSMISSION

The empirical data on intergenerational transmission in the family will be discussed in terms of the six questions raised in the literature and listed in the preceding introduction. Evidence regarding each question will be evaluated, and a theoretical proposition then formulated if the evidence justifies it.

The topic of intergenerational transmission focuses upon the degree of similarities—or differences—between parents and children and, to a lesser extent, between grandparents and grandchildren. To what extent do people in different generations of the same family replicate each other? Do their differences indicate different developmental statuses, their coming of age at different times, or the differential influence of sociohistorical trends?

At the extreme of family transmission—the "no gap" position—children would be expected to differ from their parents only because of ontogenetic developmental state. To be adolescent is to be different from an older adult, but when youths in turn become middle-aged or old, they will then presumably resemble their parents and grandparents at these equivalent times of life. Relevant to this position is the concept of the "generational stake" (Bengtson and Kuypers, 1971). The perspective of middle-aged parents on the coming generation is in part a product of their developmental position. The effort and commitment they have invested in raising their children and their present diminished influence on them, as well as the shortening of their own future, make it important|that|the |next generation "carry on." Their children, on the other hand, looking forward to a whole life ahead and needing to express their uniqueness at least with respect to their parents, view their parents' goals from a different perspective. They want to establish their own identity.

Because of the methodological flaws in most of the earlier—and some recent— studies in this area, two kinds of investigations will be largely ignored in the present discussion. The first consists of group instead of pair comparisons, where data from each generation are aggregated and comparisons between generations are based on group means. The second kind of study ignored here is that in which one generation provides the information about the other or others—where there is no examination of different generations directly. Unfortunately, these two criteria eliminate a large proportion of the research on generational transmission. For example, Hyman (1959), reviewing the early literature, did not critically evaluate the methodology of studies available to him, and most of the correlations he reports are probably inflated. But since his book influenced subsequent theorizing on the subject of political socialization, he may have encouraged overestimation of the effect of parents on the formation of their children's political values and attitudes.

Question 1. What Is Transmitted?

Which of the three possible positions on the "generation gap" described in the previous section—"great gap," "nothing really new," or "selective continuity"—is consistent with accumulated research findings? Further, if these findings point to selective continuity, can we say what kind of characteristics are more likely to be transmitted than others?

Politics

POLITICAL PARTY AFFILIATION. All five of the studies investigating parent-child similarity in political party preference that met our criteria for inclusion found substantial cross-generational continuity, though all used different statistical analyses. In a study of Illinois high school students and their parents (Levin, 1961), party preference of parents accounted for 68 percent of the variance in party choice of children. In a national probability sample of high school students and their parents (Jennings and Niemi, 1968), the correlation was .59 (see Table 6.1). Two other studies of high school students and parents (Blumenfield, 1964; Tedin, 1974) report a correlation of contingency of .54 and a product-moment correlation of .48, respectively. The data of Dodge and Uyeki (1962) are based on college students; they found much more agreement for Republican than for Democratic families: 68 percent versus 32 percent. Note that this investigation was conducted in 1956, a period of Republican victory. Also note that the younger generation in all these studies is on the brink of adulthood but not yet full adults. These points will be treated further below. It is surprising that in the voluminous literature of political socialization, only four studies contain data which actually asked the parents themselves what their party choice was.

GENERAL POLITICAL ORIENTATION. As Thomas (1974) points out, there are different ways to distinguish between general value orientations and particular attitudes. He cites two ways: that of Easton (1965), based on political concepts, and that of Rokeach (1960, 1968), based on psychological orientations. Several general political orientations have been studied: liberalism, political cynicism, and egalitarianism; Bengtson's (1975) statistically derived "humanitarianism-materialism" and "collectivism-individualism"; and "dedication to causes" (Troll et al., 1969). As can be seen in Table 6.1, there is mixed support for a hypothesis of transmission in general political orientation.

Overall, parent-child congruence on liberalism (Angres, 1975; Thomas and Stankiewicz, 1974), egalitarianism (Angres, 1974, but only for activists in Time 1), "dedication to causes" (Troll, et al., 1969), and "collectivism-individualism" (Bengtson, 1975) is most consistent with the assumption of moderate transmission of orientations, although "humanitarianism" (Troll et al., 1969) and "political participation obligation" (Thomas & Stankiewicz, 1974) are consistent with a hypothesis of moderate transmission. Furthermore, Thomas (1971) reports that children of liberal parents are significantly more likely to have taken part in radical causes (11 out of 30 families); while none of the children

Table 6.1. Parent-Child Agreement on Politics

VARIABLE	STUDY	PARENT-CHILD	MOTHER-DAUGHTER	MOTHER-SON	FATHER-DAUGHTER	FATHER-SON
		Affiliation				
Party identification	Jennings & Langton[a]		.45	.36	.37	.20
	Blumenfeld[b]	.54				
	Jennings & Niami[a]	.59				
	Tedin[a]	.48				
		General Political Orientation				
Liberalism	Angres					
	Activists T1	.40[c]*				
	T2	.27[d]				
	Nonactivists T1	.63[c]*				
	T2	.26[d]				
	Thomas & Stankiewicz[a]		.26	.42*	.29*	.29*
	Acock & Bengtson 1976[h]	.40				
Conservative patriotism	Thomas & Stankiewicz[a]		.36*	.26	.02	.15
Economic conservatism	Thomas & Stankiewicz[a]		−.03	.01	.19	.36*
Egalitarianism	Angres					
	Activists T1	.41[c]*				
	T2	.15[d]				
	Nonactivists T1	.29[c]				
	T2	.16[d]				
	Linder & Nahemow[j]	31%				
Humanitarianism	Troll et al.[a]		.16	.32*	.31*	.49*
	Troll & Smith[a]		.20[f]*			
Materialism	Troll et al.[a]		.18	.25	−.02	.34*
Humanitarianism-materialism	Bengtson 1975	9% variance[e] 5% variance[f]				
Political participation obligation	Thomas & Stankiewicz[a]		.35*	.29*	.30*	.01
Dedication to causes	Troll et al.[a]		.46*	.54*	.41*	.50*
Collectivism-individualism	Bengtson 1975	15% variance[e] 29% variance[f]				
Political cynicism	Jennings & Niemi[a]	.12				
		Political Attitudes and Opinions				
Approval of Russia	Helfant[a]			.28*		.18*
Friendliness in international relations				.11		.27*
Approval of war				.16*		.05
Federal government's role in integrating schools	Jennings & Niemi[g]	.34				
Prayers allowed in school		.29				
Allowing legally elected Communist to take office		.13				
Allowing speakers against religion in school		.05				
Racial integration		.34				
Average of political attitudes	Jennings & Niemi[g]	.24	.22		.22	.20
Machiavellian tactics	Friedman et al.[a]			.16		.25*
Machiavellian cynicism				.15		.04
New Left philosophy				.22*		.18
Revolutionary tactics				.08		.04

continued

Table 6.1. Continued

VARIABLE	STUDY	PARENT-CHILD	MOTHER-DAUGHTER	MOTHER-SON	FATHER-DAUGHTER	FATHER-SON
Ecological awareness	Thomas & Stankiewicz[a]		−.04	.30*	.40*	−.02
Side with workers in strikes	Thomas 1971		88%	88%	86%	77%
Government-owned dams			76%	75%	71%	62%
Expanded Medicare			76%	88%	71%	85%
Socialized medicine			65%	81%	86%	85%
Bombing North Vietnam			76%	69%	71%	69%
House Unamerican Activities Committee			82%	81%	86%	62%
U.S. in UN			82%	69%	78%	85%
Ronald Reagan			94%	75%	93%	77%
Aid to India			70%	75%	64%	69%
Martin Luther King			82%	69%	64%	77%
Civil rights protest	Thomas 1971		76%	81%	86%	62%
Student protests			80%	69%	71%	62%
Limiting role of military	Linder & Nahemow	25%[b] 42%[c]				
Blacks' attitudes toward whites and whites' toward blacks		58% .41				
Attitude toward war	Newcomb & Svehla[a]		.46*	.44*	.44*	.40*
Attitude toward communism			.51*	.61*	.62*	.40*
Law and order	Acock & Bengtson 1976[h]	.35				
Status quo		.29				
Racial integration	Tedin[a]	.32				
China policy		.27				
Marijuana laws		.40				
Specific Attitudes and Life Style Characteristics						
Age-grade consciousness	Thomas & Stankiewicz[a]		.26	.22	.25	−.06
Aging	Kalish & Johnson[a]		.14[e] .20[f,i]			
Old people			.23[e] .40[f]			
Death attitude			.23[b] .40[f]			
Marijuana use	Kandel[g]	.10[j] .12[k]				
	Linder & Nahemow[j]	32%				

*Significant at .05 level or better.

[a] Product-moment correlation.
[b] Coefficient of contingency.
[c] Mother-college student.
[d] Mother-child; reinterviewed seven years later.
[e] G1-G2 dyad (grandparent-parent).
[f] G2-G3 dyad (parent-college-age child).
[g] Tau beta correlation.
[h] Multiple correlation.
[i] Three-generation continuity.
[j] Mother's alcohol use.
[k] Father's alcohol use.

of liberal parents had taken part in right-wing causes. Only five out of thirty children of conservative parents, on the other hand, took part in conservative causes—but none took part in liberal activities, either.

On the other hand, Bengtson (1975) found that the family did not contribute significantly to the factor of "humanitarianism-materialism," which *a priori* seems like a general orientation. It will be noticed in Table 6.1

that the findings of both Troll et al., (1969) and Thomas & Stankiewicz (1973) are also deviating on this variable. Fathers and sons are similar, but not other dyadic combinations. Sex differences will be discussed more fully later. It is notable that "political cynicism," though it would appear to be in the same domain as "dedication to causes," shows no parent-child agreement in the Jennings and Niemi 1968 study.

POLITICAL OPINIONS AND ATTITUDES. Some of the data presented in Table 6.1 show parent-child agreement on specific political attitudes to be about the same as that on general orientations.

Proposition 1a. Parents and children are substantially similar in party affiliation, and to a lesser extent general political orientation. On some specific attitudes and opinions there appears high similarity: on others, independence.

Religion

RELIGIOUS DENOMINATION. Parent-child agreement on religious affiliation is consistently high—at least 70 percent (74 percent for Jennings and Niemi, 1966; 68 percent to 79 percent for Hill et al., 1970; and 72 percent for Acock & Bengtson, 1975). Sixty-four percent of Hill's sample showed three-generation continuity. Thus there seems to be even less generational change in religious than in political affiliation.

GENERAL RELIGIOUS ORIENTATION. As can be seen in Table 6.2, generational congruence in general religious orientation is substantial in most investigations, though it is lower than for denominational affiliation. The two exceptions to this trend are the Thomas and Stankiewicz (1974) findings on "belief in the Bible" and Angres's (1975) on "conventional moralism."

SPECIFIC RELIGIOUS ATTITUDES AND BEHAVIORS. While Linder and Nahemow (1970) found relatively low family continuity in religious behavior, Acock and Bengtson (1976) report generally high levels of parent-child similarity on frequency of church attendance, self-rated religiosity, and traditional religious beliefs.

Proposition 1b. Continuity in denominational affiliation is particularly high across generations in the family. Similarity in general religious orientation and in specific attitudes or practices is lower but still impressive compared to other characteristics.

Sex Roles and Sexual Behavior

Almost all investigators agree that there has been a notable generational shift in sex role affiliation or restrictiveness and in orientation and attitudes toward sex role behavior (Bengtson and Starr, 1975). However, not only have there been very few intrafamily comparisons, but these have been mostly confined to general orientations (see Table 6.3). From these data, generational shifts within the family seem to parallel those in the larger society. The negative correlation on "femininity" found by Parkman (1965) is relevant. Acock and Bengtson (1976) report low parent-child correspondence on sexual permissiveness. The only exception seems to be Angres's finding of a correlation of .57 between mothers and their nonactivist young adult children. Perhaps traditional people are slower to move away from older norms (see discussion of the "forerunner effect" below).

Work and Achievement

In the face of an occupationally upwardly mobile society over the past century, the fact that Hill et al. (1970) found some three-generational continuity in husband's occupation (47 percent over three generations), particularly for fathers and sons, is notable (see Table 6.4). One might expect to find greater similarity in orientation toward achievement (need) than in actual educational or occupational attainment, since the latter are contingent upon economic opportunity. As Hill et al. (1970:322) state, "Under conditions of rapid economic and social change, each generational cohort encounters . . . a unique set of historical constraints and incentives." The Hill study did not measure achievement orientation or motivation as such. Those studies that did look at interest, plans, or motivation (Kandel and Lesser, 1972; Troll et al., 1969; Switzer, 1974) report parent-child agreement in these characteristics (see Table 6.4). In fact, the only deviating results are those of Thomas and Stankiewicz (1974) and of Angres (1975). Because their populations are more "avant-garde," they may be picking up the beginnings of a new historical shift away from the "Protestant ethic." This possible "forerunner effect" will be discussed further below.

Life Style Characteristics

Most of the findings listed in Table 6.5 show little family similarity. There are some interesting exceptions: neighborhood type, order of life values, cognitive style, and consumership style. The effect of intervening variables is notable. When Clausen's (1974) data on "order of life values" are differentiated by social class or perceptoion of closeness to parents, family resemblances emerge for higher social class and for dyads felt to be "close." Similarly, satisfaction with consumership pattern in Hill's (1970) data makes a striking difference in continuity of consumership patterns. Families with high satisfaction show high continuity, and vice versa. However, "low consumership (low plans fulfilled and few actions preplanned) is more likely to persist over three generations than any other consumership pattern. . . . High consumership is, nevertheless, more likely to be continuous than noncontinuous since thirty-four of fifty-nine (58 percent) of high consumership families were continuous over two or more generations" (232). It seems that the poor stay poor unless they become dissatisfied with their lot—which does not necessarily happen. So far as cognitive style is concerned, since it has long been known that parent-child correlations are high for intelligence test scores, it should not be surprising that the way intelligence is expressed also tends to be consistent across generations.

Proposition 1: There is substantial but selective intergenerational continuity within the family. Parent-

Table 6.2. Family Similarity in Religion

VARIABLE	STUDY	PARENT-CHILD	MOTHER-DAUGHTER	MOTHER-SON	FATHER-DAUGHTER	FATHER-SON
		Religious Affiliation				
	Jennings and Niemi	74%				
	Aldous & Hill[a]	64%				
	Acock & Bengtson 1975[b]	.46				
		Orientation				
Religiosity						
Traditional beliefs	Acock & Bengtson[b]	.32*	.53*	.42*	.13	.39*
	Acock & Bengtson 1975[b]	.54*	.57*	.65*	.37*	.41*
	Braun & Bengtson					
	Kalish & Johnson					
	G1-G2[c]		.46*			
	G2-G3		.70*			
Belief in God	Thomas & Stankiewicz[c]		.47*	.08	.29*	.12
Belief in Bible	Troll et al.[c]		-.04	.19	.05	-.13
Conventional moralism	Friedman et al.[c]		.40*	.58*	.43*	.55*
	Angres[c]					
	Activists T1	.18				
	T2	.30				
	Nonactivists T1	.33				
	T2	.20				
	Troll & Smith[c]					
	G1-G2	.36*		.32*		.31*
	G2-G3	.41*				
Attitude toward church	Newcomb & Svehla		.71*	.57*	.64*	.59*
		Attitudes or Behaviors				
Frequency of church attendance	Acock[b]	.55*				
Religious behaviors	Linder & Nahemow[a]	40%				
	Acock & Bengtson 1976[e]	.67				
Interpretation of Bible	Jennings & Niemi[b]	.30				
Allowing prayers in school	Jennings & Niemi[b,d]	.29				
Allowing speakers against organized religion in school	Jennings & Niemi[b,d]	.05				

*Significant at .05 level or better.
aThree-generational continuity.
bTau beta correlation.
cProduct-moment correlations.
dThese attitudes may also fall into the realm of politics and thus are also included in Table 6-1.
eMultiple correlation (mother-father-child).

Table 6.3. Parent-Child Agreement on Sex Roles and Sexual Behavior

VARIABLE	STUDY	PARENT-CHILD	MALE LINEAGE	FEMALE LINEAGE	
Conventional sex roles	Angres T2[a]				
Activists		.31			
Nonactivists		.57*			
	Aldous & Hill	23%	31%	25%	
Role task specialization		34%	29%	38%	

		Mother-Daughter	Mother-Son	Father-Daughter	Father-Son
Sex role stereotyping	Thomas & Stankiewicz[a]	.24	−.08	.13	.27
	Troll et al.[a]	.02	.18	.03	−.09
Sexual permissiveness	Thomas & Stankiewicz[a]	.22	−.25	−.05	.23
	Acock & Bengtson 1976[c]	.28			
Sanctity of marriage	Linder & Nahemow	22%			
Gough Femininity Scale	Parkman[a]	−.36*	−.21	.06	.11
Franck Drawing Completion Test		.12	−.07	.05	.08

		Father Liberal, Mother Conservative		Mother Liberal, Father Conservative	
		Percentage of Students Liberal			
Sanctity of marriage	Fengler & Wood	43%		55%	
Sexual norms and boundaries	Fengler & Wood	42%		80%	

*Significant at .05 level or better.
[a]Product-moment correlation.
[b]Three-generational continuity.
[c]Multiple correlation (mother-father-child).

Table 6.4. Parent-Child Agreement on Work Ethic and Achievement

VARIABLE	STUDY	PARENT-CHILD	MOTHER-DAUGHTER	MOTHER-SON	FATHER-DAUGHTER	FATHER-SON
Work ethic	Angres[c] T2					
activists		.20				
nonactivists		.07				
	Acock & Bengtson 1976[d]	.30				
Mobility orientation	Furstenberg[b]	.24				
Perceive parental goals		.48				
Don't perceive parental goals		−.18				
	Kerckhoff & Huff					
Twelfth grade				.69		.67
Ninth grade				.65		.61
Husband's occupation	Hill[a,b]	25%				47%
Husband's education		12%				20%
Achievement need	Troll et al.[c]		.30	.27*	.39*	.45*
	Thomas & Stankiewicz[c]		−.01	.02	−.09	.01
Level of achievement motivation	Switzer[c] G1-G2		.26*			
	G2-G3		.42*			
Work achievement	Thomas & Stankiewicz[c]		−.18	.06	.15	−.22
Work security			−.01	.36*	.37*	.14
Competence	Troll & Smith[c] G1-G2		.13			
	G2-G3		.30*			
Women's education	Troll & Smith[c] G1-G2		.28			
	G2-G3		.46*			
Educational plans	Kandel & Lesser[a]					
U. S.		.50				
Denmark		.48				
Achievement level	Hill[b]	80%				
Occupational interests	Grotevant (1976)		.25	.19	.12	.04

*Significant at .05 level.
[a]Tau beta correlation.
[b]Three-generational continuity.
[c]Product-moment correlation.
[d]Multiple correlation (mother-father-child).

child similarity is most noticeable in religious and political areas, least in sex roles and life style characteristics.

Question 2. What is the effect of societal processes upon lineage transmission?

This question focuses on the interface among two generational processes—the effects of generations outside the family, in society at large, upon generations within the family. Some recent writers (e.g., Connell, 1972; Thomas, 1974: Bengtson, 1975; Jennings and Niemi, 1975) conclude that similarities between parents and children are more likely the result of their joint exposure to what goes on around them than the result of specific within-family socialization.

In considering this question, three kinds of societal generation processes could be differentiated: a period effect, a cohort effect, and a "generational unit" effect. To illustrate a period effect, Cutler and Bengtson (1975) point out that "trends in alienation can be attributed to the societal events which comprise social and political history" (140) and that these effects reflect changes in the population as a whole, changes which cannot be attributed to identifiable age, region, sex, education, or income groups. Mannheim (1952) related social change to cohort effects. Because there is a "continuous emergence of new participants in the cultural process" (293), one "comes to live within a specific, individually acquired, framework of useable past experience, so that every new experience has its form and its place largely marked out for it in advance" (296). He further pointed out that "members of any one generation can only participate in a temporally limited section of the historical process" (296). It is because each new cohort comes afresh upon the social scene and can see it with new perspective that new variations of old themes can occur.

Mannheim also mentioned the independent effect of the "generational unit." Not all people born at the same time share the same socialization or perceive historical events in the same way. "Only where contemporaries are in a position to participate as an integrated group in certain common experiences can we rightly speak of community of location of a generation" (298). No single characterization of youth in the 1960s would be completely descriptive of all members of that cohort. Rather, a range of styles can be discerned, including activists, revivalists, communalists, and "freaks" (Laufer and Bengtson, 1974). While all of these youth may be considered members of the same generational cohort, they are clearly not of the same generational unit. Such other social structural variables as social class, race, and geographic location would be expected to influence "generational unit" membership.

Bengtson and Cutler (1976) argue that all three of these generation-in-society processes interact with each other (as well as with generation-in-the-family processes) to influence values, attitudes, and behaviors. The effects of period and cohort are apparent in Tables 6.6 and 6.7. In Table 6.6, cohorts A through E, born at different times and thus of different ages in 1968 when alienated feelings permeated our country, show corresponding different levels of susceptibility to the alienated mood (period effect). However, all the cohorts are more alienated in 1968 than at other times (period effect). Similarly, both people in their 20s and in their 60s were more in favor of Federal medical aid in 1960 than they were in 1952 and 1968 (period effect), although the older cohort (E) endorsed the idea better than younger ones in each of these years (cohort effect).

Politics

Riesman (1950) states that "political attitudes and preferences are substantially influenced by the particular historical era in which a person comes of age." Similarly, Hyman (1959) concludes that a generation tends to become affiliated with the political party in power during the period of its socialization. Are they right?

Parent-child congruence in political party affiliation (see discussion above under Question 1 and Table 6.1) shows fluctuations over the 20 years in which studies have been done. These fluctuations seem to be synchronized with fluctuations in the political climate of the country. From the 1950s to the 1970s, the voting majority shifted from Democrat to Republican to Democrat to Republican, loosely corresponding to a left-right-left-right alternation. In times of Republican, or conservative victory, conservative parents were more likely to have children who were in political agreement with them. In times of Democratic victory, it was the children of the Democrats who were more likely to vote like their parents. During the late 1950s, when Republicans were on top, Levin (1961) found that 95 percent of the children of Republicans voted Republican and only 75 percent of the children of Democrats voted Democrat. Dodge and Uyeki (1962), who also collected their data in the mid-1950s, found that 96 percent of Republicans' children voted Republican and 51 percent of Democrats' children voted Democrat. The converse obtained in the more liberal 1960s. Jennings and Langton (1968) found 68 percent of Republican offspring Republican and 85 percent of Democratic offspring Democratic. Thomas (1971) reports that in 1965, the college-age children of politically active liberal parents were somewhat more congruent with them than were the children of conservative parents. The left-wing college students investigated by the University of Chicago Youth and Social Change Project in 1965 (Goldsmid, 1972) were as a group, more in political agreement with their liberal parents than were the less active, more conservative students with their more conservative parents.

The same data—those presented above and those in Table 6.1—show that the influence of generations in

Table 6.5. Parent-Child Similarity in Life Style Characteristics

VARIABLE	STUDY	PARENT-CHILD	MOTHER-DAUGHTER	MOTHER-SON	FATHER-DAUGHTER	FATHER-SON
Machiavellianism	Thomas & Stankiewicz[a]		.01	.28	.30*	.14
Anomie			.07	.03	-.06	.26
Purpose in life			.20	-.04	.10	-.02
Neighborhood grade	Hill et al.	38%[b]* 47%[c]**				
Order of life values	Clausen[d]					
Classes 1, 2			.60	.80	.81	.78
Class 3			.60	.70	.55	.67
Class 4, 5			.70	.55	.42	.29
Practicality	Troll et al.[a]		.17	.25*	.22	.15
Aestheticism	Troll et al.[a]		.26*	.18	.28*	.25
	Troll & Smith[a]		.09[g]			
			.12[g]			
			.39[g]			
People orientation	Troll et al.[a]		.20[c]			
Self-realization	Jennings & Niemi[e]	.17				
Localism-cosmopolitanism			.14	.21	-.17	.10
Family and child-rearing values	Hill et al.	17%[b] 37%[c]				
Consumership style	Hill et al.[f]					
Low planning & failure		60%				
High planning & success		20%				
Cognitive style	Troll et al.[a]		.14	.37*	-.01	.23
	Troll & Smith[a]					
Objectivity			.45[b]*			
			.28*			
Differentiation			.42[b]*			
			.12[b]*			
Categorization			.38[b]*			
			.50[b]*			
Bernreuter Neuroticism Scale	Hoffeditz[a]		.27*	.01	.23*	.06
	Sward & Friedman[a]					
Sample of Jews			.31*	.16	.24	.29
Sample of Gentiles			.11	.27	.05	.31
Self-sufficiency scale	Hoffeditz[a]		.17	.05	.09	.20
Dominance scale			.28*	.02	.20	.19
Realistic	Grotevant[a]		.43*	.31*	-.02	.03
Investigative			.39*	.21	.10	.13
Artistic			.24*	.22	.36*	.15
Social			.06	-.21	.14	.31*
Enterprising			.05	.14	.13	.34*
Conventional			.26*	.16	.08	.29*
Satisfaction with consumership	Hill et al.[f]					
High		92%				
Low		8%				

Child's Perception of Relationship with Parents

Clausen	Close	Not Close	Close	Not Close	Close	Not Close	Close	Not Close
Sympathetic	.52*	.19	-.35	.21	.33	-.07	.29	.20
Overcontrolled	.22	.18	-.12	.13	.22	.09	.03	-.42
Calm, relaxed	.24	.12	-.48	.30	.24	.03	.71*	-.25
Irritable, overreactive	-.15	-.17	-.36	.27	.36	.01	.63	.15
Warm	.11	.15	-.20	.17	.19	.19	.46	.16
Fearful	.47*	-.39	-.11	-.16	-.16	.17	-.12	-.30
Brittle ego	.47*	-.02	-.15	-.21	-.03	-.25	.38	.05
Distrustful	.38	.24	-.31	-.19	.09	.44*	.54	-.36
Cheerful	.45	.04	.47*	-.08	.16	.25	.24	-.12
Power-oriented	.21	-.14	-.16	-.21	.06	.20	.67*	.23
Socially poised	.54*	-.31	-.16	.45	-.01	.20	.51	.24
Expressed hostile feelings directly	.25	.16	-.09	.67*	.49*	.49*	-.12	.16

Table 6.6. Cohort Analysis of Political Alienation 1952–1968 (Percent Giving Alienated Response)[a]

AGE GROUP	COHORT LABEL	1952	1960	1968
21–28	A	31	10	31
29–36	B	28	26	34
37–44	C	25	25	37
45–52	D	29	29	40
53–60	E	35	27	49
61–68		40	32	54
69+		41	37	53
TOTAL		31	27	41

[a]Percentage agreeing with the statement "People like me don't have any say about what the government does." Adapted from Cutler and Bengtson (1974, table 1, 169).

society, while clear, is not absolute. In Republican years, not all the children of Democrats vote Republican. In fact, a majority still keep to the party affiliation of their parents. Jennings and Langton (1968), for example, found that 57 percent of their mother–father–high school child triads all favored the same party, and only 17 percent had agreeing parents and a deviating child.

Proposition 2a: So far as politics is concerned, social climate can be said to have an intervening or tempering effect upon family transmission rather than an overriding influence (see Jennings and Niemi, 1975).

Religion

Since the early 1960s there has been a historical shift in this country away from organized religion (Bengtson and Starr, 1975). Middle-aged parents as a group show wide differences in religiosity from their college-age children as a group (Yankelovich, 1970, 1972; Payne, Summers, and Stewart, 1973; Weinstock and Lerner, 1972; Armstrong and Sotzin, 1974; Weiting, 1975; Acock and Bengtson, 1975). What do lineage data show?

As noted earlier with reference to Question 1 and presented in Table 6.2, family continuity in religious beliefs and practices, while substantial, is not as great as in denominational affiliation. The younger generation mostly adheres to the religious identity of its parents and grandparents but gives the actual working out of practices new meanings and new structure (Jennings and Niemi, 1968; Linder and Nahemow, 1970; Kalish and Johnson, 1972; Braun and Bengtson, 1972; Acock and Bengtson, 1975).

As seen in Table 6.2, family continuity in denominational affiliation is impressive (Jennings and Niemi, 1968; Hill et al., 1970; Acock and Bengtson, 1975). The

Table 6.7. Attitudes Toward Federal Governmental Medical Aid Programs[a] (Percent in Favor)

AGE GROUP	1956[b]	1960	1964	1968	1972
21–24	70	77	67	67	
25–28		69	62	56	56
Change		−1	−15	−12	−11
61–64	69	84	64	72	
65–68		85	73	76	69
Change		+16	−11	+12	−4
Total sample	70	77	65	67	61
Change		+7	−12	+2	−6

[a]SOURCE: Bengtson and Cutler (1976). Data were made available by the Inter-University Consortium for Political and Social Research, through the USC Political and Social Data Laboratory.

[b]The questions read, for 1956 and 1960: "The government ought to help people get doctors and hospital care at low cost." For 1964 and 1968: "Some people say the government in Washington ought to help people get doctors and hospital care at low cost; others say the government should not get into this. Have you been interested enough in this to favor one side or the other?" For 1972: "There is much concern about the rapid rise in medical and hospital costs. Some feel there should be a government insurance plan which would cover all medical expenses. Others feel that medical expenses should be paid by individuals through private insurance like the Blue Cross. Which side do you favor?"

same is true for lineage continuity in the related general orientation of conventional moralism, where Troll et al. (1969), Troll and Smith (1972), and Friedman et al. (1972) found both dyadic and three-generational family similarity, even though aggregate data (pooled parents versus pooled children) show cohort shifts.

Proposition 2b: Cohort changes may not override lineage transmission in religious identification but they do seem to modify religious expression.

Sex Roles and Sexual Behavior

A marked shift toward liberalization of both sex roles and sexual behavior has taken place in this country since the middle 1960s. Both acceptance of premarital sex in general and admission of having engaged in it have increased significantly. Actual experience with premarital sex increased from 10 percent in 1958 to 23 percent in 1968 in a dating relationship, and from 31 percent to 39 percent in an engagement (Bell and Chaskes, 1970). Over this same period, premarital sex had remained at about 50 percent for male undergraduates but had increased from about 10 percent to 34 percent for female (Christensen and Gregg, 1970). Attitudes of acceptance increased even more rapidly than did practices. In the Bell and Chaskes study, those Temple University coeds who thought they had "gone too far" decreased from 65 percent in 1958 to 36 percent 10 years later. A Purdue Public Opinion Survey of high school students in 1952 found that 56 percent of high school boys and 67 percent of high schools girls "would not consider them good friends any more" if their friends did not follow morals and rules for behavior of unmarried people; in 1965 the proportions had dropped to 22 percent for boys and 38 percent for girls (Christenson and Gregg, 1970). Comparisons between aggregates of parents and of youth show wide differences (Yankelovich, 1972; Freeman, 1972; Walsh, 1970; Steininger and Lesser, 1974; Armstrong and Sotzin, 1974).

Changes between 1969 and 1973 suggest a period effect as noticeable as a cohort effect. What do the lineage data show?

We have few data on lineage comparisons of sexual norms, but those which we do have point to greater lineage differences than in either politics or religion (see Table 6.3). This is true for sexual permissiveness (Thomas and Stankiewicz, 1974) and sex role stereotyping (Aldous and Hill, 1965; Troll et al., 1969; Angres, 1975; and Thomas and Stankiewicz, 1974) Angres's findings could be interpreted as suggesting that the influence of the larger society can override that of parents, but more so for those children who themselves are most influenced by (or most likely to influence) social trends. The political activists were as ready to espouse a liberal view of sex role equality and, to a lesser extent, sexual permissiveness as they were to espouse a liberal political view. They would thus tend to differ more from their parents than the nonactivists.

Proposition 2c: There seems to be greater overriding of lineage effects by cohort and period effects in sex role ideology and sexual behavior than in either politics or religion. However, some family continuity is still apparent, partly because all generations in the family are being influenced by period affects and partly because the most liberal children, tend to come from the most liberal parents.

Work and Achievement

The cohort of the mid-1960s (or at least the college youth unit of that cohort) adopted a different orientation not only toward politics and sex roles and sexual permissiveness but also toward work (Flacks, 1968; Bengtson and Starr, 1975). Flacks observed that "the dissatisfaction of socially advantaged youth with conventional career opportunities is a significant social trend, the most important single indicator of restlessness among sectors of the youth population." While only a small portion of that cohort actually turned its back upon jobs as such, most of the cohort had a different orientation toward such jobs. Over three-fourths of the students surveyed by Yankelovich (1970) in 1969 said that "commitment to a meaningful career is a very important part of a person's life." However, they no longer believed in inevitable rewards for hard work (only 39 percent said they did in Yankelovich's (1972) 1971 survey) and were more concerned with personal fulfillment and social service than with financial rewards. In 1969, only 56 percent of college youth agreed that "hard work will always pay off," as opposed to 76 percent of their parents, 79 percent of noncollege youth, and 85 percent of parents of noncollege youth (Yankelovich, 1972). The youth observed by Flacks in 1965 were still, seven years later, looking for personal fulfillment in their work. Angres (1975) noted significant aggregate generational differences in work attitudes in 1972. However, this change in work attitudes did not seem to affect achievement motivations. The youth in their late twenties still wanted to do well, although doing well was defined differently. How do within-family comparisons look?

Hill's (1970) data on three-generational families who all—even the youngest couples—predate the cohort shift described above, point sharply to the strong influence of sociohistorical conditions in providing differential climates for achievement. Upgrading in education and income (of the husbands) over the three generations was allied to greater opportunities. Even so, relative consumership achievement level shows 80 percent continuity over three generations (Table 6.4).

The aggregate generational differences in work ethic attitudes reported by Angres are duplicated in lineage generational differences; mother-child correlations are not significant. Thomas and Stankiewicz (1974) found similar lacks of agreement between parents and college-age children on work achievement values (Table 6.4). But Acock and Bengtson (1976) found mothers' scores on the Work Ethic to be highly predictive of youths' orientations—and much more so than the fathers' scores. An interesting sex difference emerges between lineage similarities of men (Hill et al., 1970) and of women (Troll and Smith, 1972). This will be discussed further with reference to the next question about gender differences.

So far as achievement orientation and achievement motivation are concerned, we see more continuity than we do for work ethic (Table 6.4). The children studied by Furstenberg (1967) tended to duplicate their parents' desires for status mobility ($r = .48$) if they perceived these goals correctly ($r = -.18$ when the children did not understand their parents' views). Two studies of high school students (Kerkhoff and Huff, 1974; Kandel and Lesser, 1972) show substantial correlations between youth and their parents' achievement goals. The

achievement need of the college students who were interviewed seven years later by Angres correlated significantly in achievement need with their parents (Troll et al., 1969). And so do the three-generation women's lineages in Troll's later Detroit sample (Switzer, 1974).

Proposition 2d. Period and cohort influences may override family influence in work orientation and belief in conventional work ethic more than they do in general achievement orientation. While high-achievement-motivated parents still tend to have high-achievement-motivated children, the areas in which achievement is sought varies.

A Special Look at Forerunners

Earlier in the discussion of Question 2, reference was made to generational units. It is possible to consider "forerunners" as a kind of generational unit. Mannheim (1952) remarks that the "nucleus of attitudes particular to a new generation is first evolved and practiced by older people who are isolated in their own generation (forerunners)" (308) and Adelson (1970) makes a similar point. In a somewhat speculative vein, we suggest that there is a relationship between "forerunners," defined in terms of societal cohorts, and lineage transmission. The following three-step process could occur. (See Bengtson and Black, 1973 for a similar formulation based on systems theory and focusing on generational cohorts instead of on the family.)

STEP 1. A new age cohort of forerunners, on coming of age developmentally, turns to new and vigorous ways of expressing the general political orientation (a dedication to causes, say) it has gotten from its family. If this is in tune with basic political processes going on in the country, it can start a swing in a new direction. In its first move toward this new direction, the forerunners inevitably decrease their congruence with both their parents and their age mates who come from different kinds of families (and perhaps should not truly be called peers).

STEP 2. If this new ideology has appeal for peers and parents of the forerunners, both these groups are influenced to shift toward it. This shift increases the congruence again between parents and children in the forerunner families. At the same time, it decreases the congruence between the second wave of youth which join the forerunners and its parents.

STEP 3. If this new ideology is really in tune with the times, the parents of the second wave of youth are in turn influenced by their children, and their family congruence increases again. In effect, each lineage generation plays both a mediator and a recipient role. This multiple-generation effect would then become manifest in political change that surfaces in the country as a whole.

Proposition 2: Social and historical forces—cohort or period effects—serve as moderator variables in family lineage transmission. Transmission is enhanced where social forces encourage particular values or behavior. It is reduced in areas where social forces discourage them, as where particular characteristics become "keynotes" of a new rising generational unit.

Question 3. Are there gender differences in transmission?

Several not so congruent assumptions pervade the socialization and family transmission literature. The first is that fathers have more influence on the ideology of their children than mothers. Second, mothers affect noncognitive belief areas more than fathers. Third, same-sex lineages are more alike than cross-sex lineages. Fourth, daughters are more susceptible to parental influence than sons. Obviously, sex role stereotypes of the powerful father and the warm, close mother, of the adventurous son and compliant daughter, are at the bottom of these assumptions. Freud (1963) and Parsons (1968) are the underlying theorists. Let us look at these assumptions in the light of available empirical data.

Politics

Jennings and Langton (1969) counter the prevailing view that the father is the dominant influence in shaping his child's political orientations with the fact that most mothers have closer ties with their children than do fathers. Therefore, they postulate that the mother is the primary influence. In a study of political party affiliation of high school students and their parents, Jennings and Langton did indeed find that the students were slightly more likely to share their mother's affiliation than their father's (Table 6.1). This is particularly pronounced in families where parents do not agree on party affiliation—even though such disagreement occurred in only 26 percent of the sample. As shown in Table 6.1, Democratic mothers were most likely to have Democratic children. Remember, this was a period of rising Democratic power (see discussion under Question 2). However, even during a Democratic tide, Republican mothers rallied 45 percent of their children to their side (Democratic mothers only rallied 6 percent more). Fengler and Wood's (1973) findings on college students' liberalism are similar. While the majority of the University of Wisconsin students they surveyed were liberal at the time of the study, more of those whose mothers were also liberal were liberal themselves than those whose fathers were also liberal. Earlier, Helfant (1952) had reported that in two out of three specific political attitudes, children were more in agreement with their mothers than with their fathers. Similar conclusions concerning the greater impact of mothers' influence are noted by Acock and Bengtson (1976).

Aside from the above studies of parental influence,

most investigations in the political area show no evidence for gender difference, either of parent, of same-sex lineage, or of child. Table 6.1 presents the negative findings from the investigations of Troll et al. (1969), Thomas (1971b), Friedman et al. (1972), Jennings and Niemi (1968), Jennings and Langton (1969), and Thomas and Stankiewicz (1973). There is no consistent pattern of dyadic correlation differences by sex.

Proposition 3a: Political party affiliation, which shows more evidence of family transmission that other aspects of political orientation, also shows more evidence of gender effects. Mothers have greater effect on their children than fathers if the two are split in their voting. No other findings about political transmission support a hypothesis of gender differences.

Religion

It has long been held that socialization of religion is the domain of the mother, and it is in this area that most writers, following Hill and his colleagues (1970), see gender effects. What do other data show?

Four independent investigations are consistent with Hill's generalization (Braun and Bengtson, 1972; Fengler and Wood, 1973; Thomas and Stankiewicz, 1973; and Hill et al., 1970). In Table 6.2 it can be seen that in these studies, agreement between mothers and children tends to be higher than that between fathers and children. Continuity along three-generational female lineages and even predominantly female (at least two generations) lineages is greater than male and predominantly male lineages. Only one finding would be consistent with the more-susceptible-daughter hypotheses, that of Thomas and Stankiewicz (1974) on "belief in God."

Conventional or traditional moralism might be considered a type of religious orientation. Niether Troll et al. (1969) nor Friedman et al. (1972) found any differences in conventional moralism among four possible dyadic combinations (mother-daughter, mother-son, father-daughter, or father-son). Similar absence of gender influence on general religious orientation and on specific beliefs is found in the four studies which present relevant data (Aldous and Hill, 1965; Troll et al., 1969; Braun and Bengtson, 1972; and Thomas and Stankiewicz, 1974). However, Acock and Bengtson (1976) found that fathers had considerably more influence than mothers on religious practices. See Table 6.2.

Proposition 3b. While there seems to be greater female continuity in denominational affiliation, there is no support for a conclusion of particular female influence in religious values, attitudes, or behaviors.

Sex Roles and Sexual Behavior

If, in popular belief, politics and jobs are the domains of the man and religion of the woman, transmission of sex roles are held to be same-sex-linked. Fathers are supposed to socialize sons and mothers daughters to proper male and female behavior. What do the data show?

Aldous and Hill (1965) found that three-generation female and "predominantly female" lineages show more agreement on "role-task specialization" than male and predominantly male lineages. The difference is between 38 percent agreement in female line and 29 percent in the male line. Whether this difference is statistically significant is not clear. More impressive evidence for maternal influence can be found in Fengler and Wood's (1973) data (see Table 6.3), particularly related to sexual norms and boundaries. Where the mother is liberal and the father conservative, 80 percent of their children are also liberal. Where the father is liberal and the mother conservative, on the other hand, only 42 percent of their children are liberal.

Proposition 3c. As can be seen from Table 6.3, most gender differences in sex roles and sexual behavior are not significant. Exceptions are the greater maternal influence reported by Aldous and Hill, and Fengler and Wood. There is no evidence for greater daughter susceptibility to parental influence.

Work and Achievement

The extensive research literature on achievement motivation and attitude toward jobs has been notably sex-determined. Early socialization patterns can be related to later need for achievement motivation in boys and men, but not in girls and women (Troll, 1975). This is not hard to understand, since the world of jobs has until very recently been considered the domain of men. In view of this bivalence, one would predict that if there were generational continuity in this area, it would obtain for men and not for women.

The three-generational investigation of Hill et al. (1970) supports this prediction, finding that continuity is greater in husband's occupation, and in educational level in male lineages (Table 6.4). They provide no figures for wife's occupation and education, incidentally.

Most other studies that have looked at work and achievement have either been focused on college students—a different kind of sample—or upon women and children. None of these found sex differences (Table 6.4), either for job attitudes, achievement motivation, or achievement level (Troll et al., 1969; Thomas and Stankiewicz, 1974; Kerkhoff and Huff, 1974). Kandel and Lesser (1972), in fact, report greater mother-daughter than mother-son consensus on educational goals. Mothers' attitudes were much more influential than father's in predicting Work Ethic orientations of their children in one study (Acock and Bengtson, 1976).

Proposition 3d: While there may be marked sex differences in most populations with reference to work

and achievement values, these appear to be subject to period effects from changing societal attitudes toward women in the labor force. Mothers are generally as influential as fathers, daughters as affected as sons, in the socialization of orientations to work and achievement.

Life Style Characteristics

Two alternate socialization hypotheses apply here: (1) that both male and female children would be like their mother because she is the primary socializing agent; (2) that each sex would look to a same-sexed model regardless of amount of contact (see Kohlberg, 1966). The more sex roles are expected to be differentiated, the more one would expect sex linkage in personality transmission.

As can be seen in Table 6.5, there are no consistent sex differences either in maternal versus paternal influence, same- versus opposite-sex lineage, or son versus daughter effects. The data in this area are, of course, both scanty and preliminary (Troll et al., 1969; Thomas and Stankiewicz, 1974; Kandel and Lesser, 1972; Clauson, 1974). However, so far as present data show, there is no gender effect in transmission of life style characteristics.

Proposition 3: At the present time, we cannot conclude that gender effects are important in transmission. While some studies support the common assumption that fathers are more influential than mothers, other studies do not. Sex of child does not appear to be a relevant variable in parent-child similarity.

Question 4. How does family influence compare with that of peers or friends?

According to the traditional view of socialization, family influence is predominant in early childhood, gradually giving way to the influence of school and peers until, by adolescence, the peer group is more powerful than the family (see McCandless, 1969; Campbell, 1969; Coleman, 1961). Sibling influence is usually disregarded. For example, Campbell says that the casual relationships which exist among age mates, as compared with the intense, intimate relationships of family or close friends, help to prepare for the casual relationships of business and community interactions. Kandel and Lesser (1972) highlight the distinction between Danish and American styles of peer interaction among high school students. Danish adolescents tend to engage in intimate, responsible relationships with their parents and a few friends. American youth, on the other hand, are tuned into a generalized peer reference group with whose members they have more diffuse than intimate relations. They are close to their parents, mainly to their mothers. Beyond adolescence, distinctions between family and peers can be even more confusing. For example, is a spouse a friend or family? And what about siblings? Given such conceptual problems, it is not surprising that there are practically no generational data in this area aside from those of Kandel and Lesser (1972) and Kandel (1974), and those only for adolescents and their parents. Are parents more influential in transmission than peers or friends?

Concordance between both Danish and American high school students and their mothers on educational plans—ways to get ahead in life and life goals—was higher than that between the students and their best school friend (Kandel and Lesser, 1972; see Table 6.4). It should be noted that all correlations are high, both with parents and with friends. The investigators suggest that youth do not choose friends to stand in opposition to parents, but are even likely to select as friends those who are the children of their parents' friends.

Aside from the concordance in life plans cited above, the level of agreement between Danish and American youth is no higher with their parents than with their friends. Kandel and Lesser (1972) report only the average correlations for 32 value questions which, as can be seen in Table 6.5, are at zero level with both parents and friends. In a later study, Kandel (1974) examined the relative influence of parents and freinds on adolescent marijuana use. While parents' use of alcohol had virtually no relation to their children's use of marijuana, friends' use of marijuana correlated (tau beta = .48) with their own use of marijuana.

It would obviously be presumptuous to generalize from so few data, beyond saying that parents may be more influential in some areas of socialization and peers or friends in others. At this point, there seems little support for McCandless's (1969) statement that the "peer group may have more influence on the style of expression, the family on the content of expression." (809). Perhaps it is only in "Generation Keynote" issues like the use of marijuana that peers' influence predominates.

Proposition 4: Friends or peers may serve as a moderating influence on family transmission in some areas, such as sexual behavior or use of marijuana, which are particularly salient issues for their cohort. However, parental influences seem strong in achievement, work, and educational orientations. Moreover, in general, peer and parent influences appear complementary rather than oppositional.

Question 5. What is the effect of intrafamily relationships upon generational similarities?

The quality of family interrelationships varies widely. Some families are tightly knit, with strong boundaries keeping members in and nonmembers out. Some dyadic relationships are close and affect as such are treated in section biii below. At this point, we are limiting the discussion to the effect of closeness and affect upon family similarities. Are variations in the quality of family relationships related to lineage transmission? Does closeness lead to greater similarity? Such questions have been asked since the time of Davis (1940) and before. However, partly because the dimensions are so diverse, the accumulated (though surprisingly meager) data are not easy to integrate or interpret.

Politics

Three studies support the hypothesis that the quality of family relationships might influence political transmission (see Table 6.1). One is that of Jennings and Langton (1968), who looked at families in which parents differed in party affiliation. In these families, the high school students were more likely to choose the same party as their mother if they felt closer to her than to their father (51 percent as compared with 26 percent). Another is that of Troll et al. (1969), who found that "family power balance" contributed significantly (in a multiple stepwise regression analysis) to parent-child similarity—but only in "dedication to causes."

Tedin (1974) presented the most systematic investigation of the family factors that might influence political attitude transmission. He looked at three family variables: perceptual accuracy by the high school seniors of their parents' attitudes, salience of the political position to the parents; and "attractiveness" of the parents to the child. He concluded that "the influence of parents on the party identification and public policy attitudes of their children . . .at any point in time, will be highly dependent on the distribution of issue salience and perceptual accuracy for the particular attitude object in question." (1952). While "attractivenss" of parents to children was a less powerful variable, it did have moderately strong effects on party identification and two attitudes, though not on attitude to marijuana laws, and it may explain enough additional variance to warrant consideration.

In contrast to these three studies, most of the other empirical data show remarkable independence between quality of family relationships and parent-child similarity in politics (Jennings and Niemi, 1968; Troll et al., 1969; Thomas, 1971b; Thomas and Stankiewicz, 1973; Angres, 1975; Acock and Bengtson, 1976). The intervening variables studied include parental power styles (Jennings and Niemi, 1968); parent-child closeness (Jennings and Niemi, 1968; Angres, 1975) or affectual solidarity (Acock and Bengtson, 1976); family expression of affect (Troll et al., 1969); parents' approval of each other (Troll et al., 1969); intrafamily conflict (Troll et al., 1969; Thomas, 1971b; Thomas and Stankiewicz, 1974); family integration or solidarity (Troll et al., 1969; Thomas and Stankiewicz, 1974); permissiveness (Thomas, 1971b; Thomas and Stankiewicz, 1974); warmth (Thomas, 1971b; Thomas and Stankiewicz 1974); parental understanding (Thomas and Stankiewicz, 1974); quality of communication (Thomas and Stankiewicz, 1974); frequency of communication (Thomas and Stankiewicz, 1974); and maternal satisfaction with child (Angres, 1975). All of these variables—based on data from both children and parents—have little effect on parent-child similarity in politics.

Religion

Acock and Bengtson (1976) report that associational solidarity (activities shared by parent and child) is significantly related to congruence in church membership and church attendance. Affectual solidarity is related to congruence in religiosity. Troll et al. (1969) found "family integration" related to conventional moralism; and in Angres's (1975) follow-up of the same sample, she found mother-child "bondedness" related to moralism.

Most of the other findings for religion are similar to those for politics; no relation between family closeness variables and lineage continuity (Angres, 1975; Troll et al. 1969; Jennings and Niemi, 1968; Thomas and Stankiewicz, 1974; Acock and Bengtson, 1976).

Work and Achievement

Both in the 1965 round of interviewing with college students and their parents (Troll, 1967) and in the 1972 follow-up seven years later (Angres, 1975), none of the family relationship variables examined had any influence on parent-child similarity in achievement motivation.

Life Style Characteristics

There is somewhat more support for a connection between family quality and similarity in life style than there is in the other areas. Both Furstenberg (1967) and Clausen (1974) show that family climate affects children's and adolescents' agreement with their parents. In Furstenberg's study, the quality of interaction, the use of parents as reference persons, low interaction with peers, and minimal family conflict were all positively related to consensus on social mobility goals. An inspection of Clausen's data in Table 6.5 shows that there are noticeably higher correlations when the relationship is considered "close," at least in same-sex dyads.

There is also some contrary evidence. Kandel and Lesser (1972) found that none of the maternal relationship variables had any influence on mother-child concordance in educational goals. The variables they investigated included maternal authority, extent of explanations for decisions, child's feelings of closeness to mother, reliance on her for advice, adolescent peer orientation, and respect for mother's opinions. Angres (1975) also found no relation between mother-and-child bondedness and consensus on goals of life.

Overall it is the minimal influence of family interrelationships as such upon transmission of life-style characteristics that is most general. Consensus seems to be relatively independent of quality of family behavior and practices. Lack of consensus does not seem to interfere with the strength of parent-child bonds. The only exception may be in some personality areas. "Family themes" or salience of particular issues, as well as how much children are "tuned in" to their parents—an indirect measure of relationships—could be more important.

Proposition 5: Qualitative aspects of family relationships (such as "closeness") do not seem to affect lineage transmission.

Question 6. What is the effect of developmental (ontogenetic) levels upon family transmission?

Up to now, the bulk of the writing on generations has focused on comparisons of youth and middle age, on the emergence of new cohorts, or on the individual's transition into adulthood. Yet many theoretical questions arise from a consideration of change over the course of life. The behavior of parents at any given moment comes not only from their lineage and social position but also from their position along their own life course. One of the earlier findings from the Berkeley longitudinal studies was the lack of constancy in maternal and child behaviors (Bayley, 1964), even during the early part of the child's life. Bengtson and Black (1973) point out that in any intergenerational relationship the actors in each generation are dynamically acting out their own developmental agenda. Further, "the gap between young and old sometimes represents differences in maturational level and life stage responsibilities. Thus, in many instances, the differences between parents and their children are temporary phenomena rooted in developmental process" (140).

The possibly temporary nature of parent-child differences may be most clearly illustrated in adolescent child–parent pairs. Basic similarities might be obscured by adolescents' needs to "try on" attitudes and behaviors different from those of their parents as part of their "search for identity." It is possible that when they pass into a more stable developmental period their values and attitudes may more closely resemble those of their parents, particularly if cohort changes do not override lineage transmission.

Several writers (e.g., Goslin, 1969; Bengtson and Black, 1973; Angres, 1975; Lerner, 1977) point out that socialization is not always from parent to child, but also from child to parent. Also, both generations learn together from their location within the same social structure under the impact of historical or period effects. Greater similarity between older adults and their parents than between adolescents and their parents (or vice versa) may represent either developmental effects, lineage effects, cohort effects, or period effects. The two older generations could be at more stable points in their life—unless the oldest generation is in a terminal decline. Differential expectations and responsibilities could produce different values, attitudes, or personality characteristics. These differences may intertwine with cohort effects; the middle generation could express its separateness from its parents in the area of religion, and the younger generation in the area of life style or politics. Or particular historical circumstances could have induced one kind of change in the growing up of the middle generation and another kind in the growing up of the 1960s youth.

Since sophisticated cross-sequential or time-sequential designs are not yet available in generational research, developmental effects on lineage transmission must be estimated from comparisons of different lineage dyads or triads: of grandparents with their children, and those children with the grandchildren. There have been few investigations of three-generation family lineages (Hill et al., Bengtson and his colleagues, Fengler and Wood, Troll's Detroit study, and Kalish and Johnson). The only longitudinal data available on lineage transmission are those of Angres (1975), Clausen (1974), and Jennings and Niemi (1975).

Two questions are involved here. First, do adolescents or college-age youth differ from their parents more than adults differ from their parents? Second, are parents more like their children than grandparents like their grandchildren? These questions will be discussed in terms of the content areas delineated previously.

Politics

Arranging the generational studies by the age of the younger or youngest generation suggests that parent-child agreement in the area of politics decreases steadily from childhood through young adulthood (Jennings and Niemi, 1975). It is, of course, impossible with present data to separate cohort or period effects from developmental effects. The only pre-adolescent data available are indirect. For example, Hess and Torney (1967) studied family similarity, but among siblings, not cross-generationally, and Radke-Yarrow et al. (1952) used only parents' reports. Thus their findings of strong family similarities are not directly relevant. Most studies of high school students (Douvan and Adelson, 1966; Jennings and Niemi, 1968; Jennings and Langton, 1969; Remmers and Weltman, 1947; Levin, 1961; Blumenfeld, 1964; Tedin, 1974; and Helfant, 1952) show agreement on political party preference but less agreement on attitudes (see Table 6.1). College-age youth show even less consensus with their parents (Goldsmid, 1972; Troll et al., 1969; Troll and Smith, 1972; and Friedman et al., 1972). Agreement in these data varies with "forerunner" status and political climate, as well as with specificity of measure. Thus, in Angres's (1975) follow-up of the Chicago student activist sample, the young adults seem to be in less agreement with their mothers on political issues than they had been seven years earlier. This diminishing similarity, may even continue into later life. Middle-aged children (Kalish and Johnson, 1972; Bengtson, 1975) show less

congruence with their parents than with their children. An exception is the greater congruence for collectivism versus individualism (Bengtson, 1975) in the middle age-old age dyad. Supporting evidence for increasing differentiation comes from grandparent-grandchild agreement (Kalish and Johnson, 1972), which is lower than either parent-child dyad (grandparent-parent or parent-grandchild).

Religion

Much less research has been done in lineage continuity in religion than in politics, and most of that since 1960. While Hill et al. (1970) found relatively little developmental effect in religious affiliation (remember the high level of three-generational continuity), Kalish and Johnson (1972), Troll and Smith (1972), and Braun and Bengtson (1972) all found more agreement on religious belief between young adults and their parents than between middle-aged adults and theirs (see Table 6.2). Similarly, Angres found that consensus on moralism decreased over seven years. Grandparents and their grandchildren are in less agreement than parents and children of any age.

Sex Roles and Sexual Behavior

Because of an overriding period or historical effect journalistically titled "the sexual revolution" (Bengtson and Starr, 1975), developmental effects are impossible to determine. Aggregate data from surveys (Yankelovich, 1970) show sharp generational differences, but Angres's (1975) interviews with middle-aged mothers found that 60 percent said they had been influenced by their daughters' behavior. Against a background of low three-generational continuity (Aldous and Hill, 1965), there appears to be more agreement between youth and their parents than between the two older generations (Fengler and Wood, 9172). Possible developmental effects are suggested by the data of Reiss (1968); while 44 percent of single adults surveyed approved of premarital sexual intercourse, only 23 percent of married adults and only 13 percent of adults whose children were teenage or older approved of this behavior. Angres's (1975) findings further support the three-step "forerunner" effect as proposed above under Question 2. It was the mothers of activists who were most open to the influence of youth. When asked under what circumstances they would consider premarital intercourse for college women, the modal response of the young women was "if there was some emotion," but of their mothers, "if there was deep emotional involvement." We might predict that a new sample of college students (nonforerunners) and their mothers investigated five years from now would move toward increased congruence again.

Work and Achievement

The available data suggest greater similarity in work

and achievement orientations and behavior between the two younger generations than between the two older. However, in line with our earlier discussion, these may represent period instead of developmental effects (Bengtson and Starr, 1975; Hill et al., 1970). Changed attitudes toward work and sex seem to characterize the "youth revolt" of the 1960s when generational means are compared, but Kandel and Lesser (1972) report that parental influence does not seem to decrease during adolescence, either for Danish or American youth. In Troll's three-generation Detroit study (Switzer, 1974), the general level of achievement motivation correlated .42 between young adults and their parents but only .26 between the middle and oldest generations. Finally, Hill et al. (1970) report greater congruence between the oldest and middle family generations for "middle-level achievers" and between the middle and youngest generations for "low-level achievers," but no difference among generational dyads for "high-level achievers." Grandparents and grandchildren are less congruent than contiguous generational dyads.

Life Style Characteristics

Troll and Smith's (1972) findings could probably be considered representative of developmental effects in this diffuse and heterogeneous area. In some characteristics there is greater divergence between grandparents and their children than between the middle generation and their children. In other characteristics, the opposite is true. The older dyad (grandparents and their children) is more congruent in objectivity, differentiation, and people orientation; the younger dyad in categorization, competence, and educational level. There were possible developmental differences in conventional moralism, humanitarianism, and aestheticism. Hill et al. (1970) report larger shifts in child-rearing values between the two older generations than the two younger ones, as do Miller and Schvaneveldt (1977) for fertility-related attitudes of Mormon women. Kalish and Johnson (1972) found more agreement between the two younger generations on attitudes toward students and old people, and no difference in other dimensions. Bengtson (1975) found no dyadic difference in humanism versus materialism, but close agreement between the youngest and middle generation on collectivism versus individualism (see Table 6.5). In general, contiguous generations appear to be more similar than are alternating generations.

Conclusion

When Bengtson and Kuypers (1971) suggested the term "generational stake" to describe the differences in perception of a generational gap on the part of youth and their parents, they were referring to different perspectives one has at different parts of one's own individual and family life course. Youth appears eager to express uniqueness and independence and thus tend to exaggerate the difference between themselves and their parents, even with middle-aged people in general. The middle-aged, about to relinguish some of the authority and responsibility for the actions of their maturing children, are anxious that these children not abandon the values which guided them—the parents—in their child-rearing labors. The oldest generation "senses their finitude and fears loss of their own significance" (Bengtson, Olander, and Haddad, 1976). These different perspectives may reflect cohort or aggregate differences more than within-lineage differences and perception of difference more than actual difference.

Proposition 6: The effect of variation in individual lifespan developmental levels (aging or maturation) upon lineage transmission is neither general nor obvious. It is a prime example of "selective continuity" and cannot at present be separated out from period effects.

III. RELATIONSHIPS

A variety of labels have been used to conceptualize family interrelationships. Most of these deal with the separate concepts of closeness and affect. For example, "solidarity" between generations has been conceptualized in terms of associations, affect, and consensus (Bengtson et al., 1976). Consensus has been treated in the preceding section of this chapter as "transmission." Thus the focus in section III is upon the first two aspects, association and affect, which in turn concern such topics as "attachment," conflict, interaction, and communication.

Unfortunately, data on this subject are even more inadequate than they are for intergenerational transmission. To begin with, there are fewer studies, and these suffer from many of the same methodological problems. They tend to rely on reports of only one family member. They are almost all self-report rather than observational or experimental. They are restricted in age, focusing on either middle-aged parents and their high school or college-age children or on aged parents and their middle-aged children. Until recently, we were faced with a gap of about 30 years of the life span unexplored we are just now beginning to get some reports of interaction between parents and their infant and preschool children (e.g., Halverson and Waldrop, 1970; Cherry and Lewis, 1976; Lewis and Freedle, 1973; Moss, 1967).

Research approaches are generally stereotyped and narrow; few look beyond social expectations and surface behavior to more complex variables. In an area most needy of creative design and measurement—that of long-standing affective bonds between clinically normal people—little application of clinical expertise or theory has been evident. Where clinical approaches have been used, they have too often followed a dogmatic rather than an empirical perspective, as, for example, the body of studies dealing with "schizophrenic" or "problem" families (see review by Riskin and Faunce, 1972).

Concepts and operationalized measures differ so widely that it is dangerous to generalize. Sampling also makes it difficult to generalize, particularly since many studies focus on institutionalized old people or families with mentally ill members. Empirical analyses, with a few exceptions (Kandel and Lesser, 1972; Adams, 1968; Andersson, 1973; Troll et al., 1969; Troll, 1975; Angres, 1975; and Bengtson and his colleagues, 1969-1976) are often primitive. Finally, the dimensions we are interested in, family closeness and affect, have been treated mostly as independent or intervening variables (e.g., Clausen's use of "closeness" as an intervening variable for measuring family similarity), rather than as dependent variables. The data on the relation between perceived similarity to perceived closeness, treated above in Question 5, are among the few exceptions.

Question 7. Are there variations in parent-child attachment through the life course?

A commonly held belief among family theorists is that a child's development is accompanied by a progressive severing of bonds with family members. Some writers believe that this must occur, that parents must "let go" and children must "achieve independence" or both they and society will suffer. By late adolescence, the break with the family should be completed; families of orientation should give way to families of procreation. Adults should be devoted to their new families, free of interference from the old. Yet we are faced with a growing body of data on adult kinship interactions that suggest that such a picture may be simplistic and misleading. In fact, it is the amazing lifelong persistence of some parent-child bonds in the face of geographic separation, socioeconomic differences, and even value conflict which we must explain (cf. Gewirtz, 1972; Troll, 1971; Troll and Smith, 1976; Kalish, 1976).

Granted that there are variations in closeness and amount of affect between parents and their very young children, what can we say about the extent of such "attachments" at later points of the life course? Four kinds of evidence are available: data on residential propinquity, patterns of interaction, helping behaviors, and self-reports of feelings.

Residential Propinquity

Since the norm in our society is that children reside in their parents' home until they are past adolescence (defined as the high school years at this point), only information about post-high school families is relevant here. Assumptions that more families today are split apart by geographic separations have not been substantiated by most survey data (Adams, 1968; Sussman and Burchinal, 1962; Kerkhoff, 1965; Reiss, 1962). In a review of the literature on the family of later life, Troll (1971) reports that young adults as well as their parents and grandparents want to live near each other, though not in the same quarters. This seems to be particularly true after the young are married, and even more true after they have children. As Litwak (1960) pointed out, extended family ties are not broken by migration in the service of better economic opportunities. In fact, he concludes, it is the support of the family back home that enables trial explorations into new territory, and where yonder fields *are* greener, the "family scouts" are followed by other kin. In middle-class careers, where executives and professionals are transferred or look for promotion to other parts of the country, ties are maintained in other ways than by living nearby and frequent visiting. In many cases, eventual return of the younger generation or migration of the older tends to reunite the separated generations. While late adolescents and young adults may live far from parents, this kind of separation may be temporary. The studies cited above and many others (Berardo, 1967; Britton et al., 1961; Bultema, 1969; Gibson, 1969; Hawkinson, 1965; Rosenberg, 1970; Schorr, 1960; Shanas, 1961; Shanas et al, 1968; and Winch and Greer, 1968) show that old people, whenever possible, live in their own homes but near their children. Moreover, moving in with children is resorted to only where there is not enough money to live alone, where health is so poor that self-care is impossible, or—to a lesser extent—where a spouse has died. Even so, one-third of all people over 65 who have living children do live with one of them. Such joint households, though, are usually two-generation, not three-generation. It is usually postparental couples and their very old parents who live together after the younger generation is out of the house.

Interaction

Interaction, control, and communication may also follow a life course pattern. They are presumably all highest in early childhood, gradually diminishing through the school years and then increasing again as young adults form their own "families of procreation." The findings of Bayley (1964) and of Hill et al. (1970) are consistent with such a hypothesis. According to Hill's data, in fact, it is the middle-aged generation that has the most interaction, combining contacts with both parents and children (and probably also grandchildren). In fact, the authors call this generation the "lineage bridge." Since the data on control do not go beyond adolescence, we can only speculate whether the amount of continued control, at least of daughters, exists during the adult years as a concomitant of continued contact.

Parents and adult children see each other often or keep in touch by telephone, letter writing, and intermittent lengthy visits (Adams, 1968; Aldous, 1965; Bengtson, 1975b; Berardo, 1967; Britton et al., 1961; Bultema, 1969; Gibson, 1969; Shanas et al., 1968; Sussman, 1965; see review by Troll, 1971). In the three generations of couples studied by Hill et al. (1970), 70 percent of the married young adults saw their parents weekly and 10 percent saw their grandparents weekly. Forty percent of *their* parents (the middle generation) saw their parents weekly, and 70 percent saw their children weekly. Variation by socioeconomic mobility and by social class did not diminish the effect of massive cross-generational contact. In a similar vein, Angres (1975) found contact frequent among the families she studied, even though there was variation in the number of areas open for communication and the number of activities shared. These latter differences were related to differences in reported affection.

Helping

Most parents and children continue to help each other throughout life. The peak of giving help is probably in middle age and of receiving help in childhood and late old age. Aid may be in the form of services, such as babysitting, shopping housecleaning, or in money or gifts. In some families, the flow of support seems to be stronger down the generation line than up. Like the reversal in living arrangements, which only occurs where old parents who are poor or disabled give up their independence to move in with their children, a shift from parental giving to children to children giving to parents may occur only when parents can no longer give (see Gibson, 1969; Hawkinson, 1965; Hill et al., 1970; Kerckhoff, 1965; Schorr, 1960; Shanas et al., 1968; Streib, 1965; Sussman, 1965; Sussman and Burchinal, 1962; and Winch and Greer, 1968). The amount of help exchanged does not seem to be closely related either to residential nearness or to frequency of visiting. When parents and children live farther apart (more frequent with middle-class and not so old parents), they are more likely to exchange money and serviceable gifts like appliances and cars (see review in Troll, 1971). Unfortunately, most of the information in this area relies upon reports from only one family member. A notable exception is the research of Hill and his associates (1970), who conclude that "in mutual aid as well as in visiting patterns and sharing in common activities the three generations are linked together in a symbiotic network of multiple services and transfers" (66). All three generations in Hill's Minneapolis study said they preferred to get help from family members over other sources. Hill et al., (1970) draw two propositions concerning intergenerational helping patterns. These relate to kinds of help sought and to dependency status. The oldest generation looks to the younger ones for help with problems of illness and household management; it is in a relatively dependent status, receiving more than giving. The middle generation looks for emotional gratification and is in a patron status, giving more than receiving. The youngest adult generation looks for help with problems of child care and economic assistance and is in a reciprocal status, high in both giving and receiving.

In spite of widespread beliefs that old people are isolated from—or even deserted by—their families, almost all surveys find that the oldest generation is an integral and active part of the family structure (Hill et al., 1970; Martin and Bengtson, 1971; review in Troll, 1971).

Affect or Sentiment

Many writers assume that closeness is synonymous with positive affect or sentiment and estrangement with negative affect or sentiment. In the present chapter, we are assuming another perspective: that where affect runs high, it is rarely only positive or negative (Troll and Smith, 1976; Bengtson et al., 1976; Lowenthal et al., 1975). Where love is to be found, hate can also be prevalent. Bengtson et al. (1976) data show high correlations between positive and negative affect, particularly in youth, and similar findings have been reported by Lowenthal et al. (1975). There are analogous data for husband-wife relationships (Feldman, 1964).

Most of the data are self-reports and thus even more likely to be biased by perceptions of the reporters than those relating to residence or visiting. Therefore, unfortunately, the major information about developmental differences in sentiment or affect toward family members has to be treated as tentative.

The youngest subjects for whom parent-child feelings have been reported are high school students. Just as it is rare to find a young child not attached to his or her parents (Ainsworth, 1972)—and vice versa, presumably—so does it seem to be rare to find a high school student who does not report feeling close to his or her parents. In comparisons of Danish and American adolescents (Kandel and Lesser, 1972), only 11 percent of American high school students and 13 percent of Danish did not feel close to their mothers, while 13 percent of Americans and 14 percent of Danes did not feel close to their fathers. Over a third of both groups said they enjoyed doing many things with their parents and wanted to be like them in many ways. Andersson (1973) found that only one-quarter of Swedish youth stated that they did not have warm feelings for their parents. Several other studies of high school students indicate that parent-child relationships are usually perceived as satisfying (Larson and Myerhoff, 1965; Douvan and Adelson, 1966; Lubell, 1968; and Bengtson, 1969).

In support of the "generational stake" hypothesis (Bengtson and Kuypers, 1971) described earlier in this chapter, middle-aged parents consistently overestimated the degree of closeness, understanding, and communication compared to the responses of their college-age children. Mothers expressed more concern for their children's welfare than their children expressed for their mothers' welfare (Angres, 1975). Nonetheless, Hill et al. (1970) report that their youngest adult generation was the strongest endorser of kinship obligations and contact, while the oldest generation was the weakest endorser of these values. Studies of college students (Freeman, 1972; Bengtson and Black, 1973b) show that they and their parents may think there is a generation gap in society as a whole but they rarely perceive there is one in their own family. This is as true of student radicals as it is of more general samples (Angres, 1975).

Lowenthal et al. (1975) state that most of the middle-aged parents in their San Francisco sample felt good about their children. About half had only positive things to say about them, and only about 10 percent of the middle-aged and almost none of those in the 60s had any strong negative comments. "The remaining descriptions can most accurately be described as 'mixed indulgent,' recognizing frailties or irritating ideosyncracies—often viewed as temporary—but stressing the overall likeableness of the child" (41). However, they also included problems of tidiness, lackadaisical attitudes toward studies, difficulties in communication, and troublesome personality traits. Differences in goals and values played a lesser role than anticipated, being mentioned no more often than any of the other problem areas.

For older ages, Bengtson and Black (1973b), who examined trust, understanding, fairness, respect, and affection, found that high levels of regard were reported by both old parents and their middle-aged children. On the other hand, the old parents reported higher levels of sentiment, while their children reported higher levels of giving help. Bengtson and Cutler (1976) suggest that this is another instance of the "generational stake." It seems that parents remain important to their children throughout the life of the children. When adults of all ages were asked to describe a person, they tended spontaneously to refer to their parents more frequently than to any other person (Troll, 1972). The oldest members of the sample, in their 70s and 80s, were still using parents as reference persons.

Bengtson and Black (1973b) found a developmental trend in perception of family solidarity among four age groups of adolescents and young adults; the older groups perceived greater affectual solidarity than did the younger, who were perhaps still trying to achieve independence from parents and thus minimized their ties to them. The older youth, having achieved job and marriage, could feel freer to recognize their feelings of closeness—or to once more feel close to them. This finding was replicated by Angres (1975). She found that when the younger generation had been in college, they had reported more differences with their mothers than the mothers themselves did. These overt conflicts had tended to center on apparently superficial concerns such as style of dress or hair length rather than apparently major issues like political and social values. These "superficial" con-

cerns, incidentally, are the ones that adolescents say they would refer to peers rather than to parents (Brittain, 1963; Larsen, 1972). (Can it be that this is a displacement of anger into areas where it can be handled without disrupting family relations?) However, Angres noted that seven years later the reports of differences between the two generations were no longer discrepant. Newlyweds surveyed by Feldman (1964) had reported that their relations with their parents had improved since they left home. On the other hand, a San Francisco sample of newlyweds (Lowenthal et al., 1975) showed some rejection of their parents.

Grandparents

So far, extremely little attention has been paid to grandparent-grandchild relations. This relationship too may be affected by the "generational stakes" relevant to each of the partners (cf. Hill et al., 1970 cited above). Under recently prevailing conditions of early marriage and childbirth, people most commonly become grandparents in their forties. Not only are they likely to be middle-aged rather than old and to perceive themselves as youthful, but they are also likely to be working. Of five different styles of grandparenting found by Neugarten and Weinstein (1974)—formal, fun seekers, surrogate parents, reservoirs of family wisdom, and distant figures—young grandparents are mostly fun seekers and distant figures. They see grandparenting as a recreational activity, or they are benevolent but infrequent visitors who emerge from the shadows on holidays and ritual occasions. In fact, grandparents interviewed by Cumming and Henry (1961) did not feel particularly close to their grandchildren. They were "glad to see them come and glad to see them go." Gilford and Black (1972) found that geographic separation, which was not an important variable in the adult relationship between parents and children who had once lived together, is important in the grandparent-grandchild relationship. But the effect of separation is not simple. Grandparents' feelings toward their grandchildren have a direct effect on the feelings of the grandchildren when they have the opportunity for frequent interpersonal interaction. But when they live far apart, their relationship is contingent upon the intervening parent-child dyadic bonds. In other words, where grandparents are close to their own children, they are likely to be important to their grandchildren even if they do not see each other very often.

On the whole, the "valued grandparent" is an earned and acquired status, involving personal qualities not automatically ascribed to the role. Family solidarity is built up from parent-child dyadic bonds—or personal dyadic bonds where contact is possible. Also, feelings about grandchildren seem to change as a function of the changes in the developing grandchildren. Clark (1969) found that grandparents liked their grandchildren better when they were small. As the children got older, they were less interested in their grandparents, and this feeling was then reciprocated. When Boyd (1969) studied 45 four-generation upper-middle-class and working-class families, she found age, sex, and class differences in grandparental relationships. As Gilford and Black (1972) found later, Boyd reports that there is a stronger tie with grandparents when they live nearby, particularly for the middle and upper classes. Visiting each other is highly important for the second and third generations of the upper and middle classes and the first and second generations of the working class. Love and affection are stressed only by great-grandparents in the upper and middle classes. In fact, love and understanding are reported to be wanted by all generations of the middle class, but not reported at all by the working class. In another small sample, Kahana and Kahana (1970) found that children of different ages emphasize different aspects of the grandparent-grandchild relationship. They also found that maternal grandmothers and paternal grandfathers show closeness and warmth toward their grandchildren, view them as if they were their own children, and approve of their upbringing. In contrast, maternal grandfathers and paternal grandmothers express negative attitudes.

Aging family members do not feel as "left out" of the family as some observers would contend. Brown (1960) reports that the majority of elderly subjects in his sample did not feel neglected by their children, and Martin, Bengtson, and Acock (1974) report that men over 57 might feel alienated from political and economic institutions in the social structure but not from their families. On the other hand, observational data from one study (Scott, 1962) suggest that grandparents are singularly unimportant to the interactions between parents and an adolescent child.

Proposition 7: Parent-child "attachments" are perceived as exceptionally strong interpersonal bonds throughout the life course. Where variations in perceived level of affect appear, they seem related to the ontogenetic status of the younger-generation member, or to the "generation stake" effect.

Question 8. Does gender of parent or child influence either closeness or affect?

Does it make a difference whether parents are relating to sons or to daughters, or whether children are relating to fathers or to mothers? The psychoanalytic school has long maintained that this is so (cf. Freud, 1963). It has also struck many investigators in the field of kinship interaction that families seem to be linked through females (Troll, 1971).

Accumulating observations suggest that gender differences in parent-child interactions appear at the very beginning of life (Walters and Stinnett, 1971; Maccoby and Jacklin, 1974). For example, boys are allowed to ask

for more comforting and get more praise, particularly if they are first-born (Walters & Stinnett). Mothers of two-year-old girls asked them more questions, used longer statements when talking with them, and repeated their own statements more often than did mothers of two-year-old boys (Cherry and Lewis, 1976). Loving or hating a child is more persistent over the child's life than permissiveness or controlling (Bayley, 1964), but mothers show even greater consistency in how much affect they report for their sons than their daughters. They show less consistency in how much they control their sons than in how much they control their daughters. That is, mothers' control over daughters does not decrease with age as much as their control over sons. Fathers, on the other hand, tend to exercise more control over sons than over daughters (Straus, 1967). Cross-national differences in control over adolescents were found by Kandel and Lesser (1972). In the United States, the giving of orders and the disciplining tended to be the tasks of mothers more than fathers; in Denmark, both parents seem to share control.

Most families around the world seem to be linked through women (Adams, 1968; Kahana et al., 1973; Bengtson et al., 1976; Troll, 1971). Ties between mother and daughter are closer than those between mother and son, or between father and either daughter or son (Bott, 1957; Adams, 1968; Blenkner, 1965; Gans, 1962; Hagestad, 1974; Reiss, 1962; Townsend, 1957; Young and Goertz, 1961; Young and Willmott, 1964). Daughters have also been found to be affectionately closer to both parents than are sons (Andersson, 1973; Gray and Smith, 1960; Sweetser, 1963; Komarovsky, 1964). In the San-Francisco study of Lowenthal et al. (1975) adolescents and young adults as well as the older women reported closer ties to their mother than to any other family member, although other parts of the sample were not so consistent. Mothers report more affectionate feelings for their young adult daughters than for their young adult sons (Angres, 1975). In fact, over the seven years of the Chicago study, mothers' attachment to daughters increased relative to that of sons. According to Hill et al. (1970), cohesiveness in same-sex three-generation lineages is greater than in mixed-sex lineages, and this is particularly true for the female lineages.

In his North Carolina sample, Adams (1968) found that daughters' affections for their father were related to their father's occupational position; they appreciated their father more if he had higher status. The more successful sons appreciated their mother more. While most of the San Francisco respondents (Lowenthal et al., 1975) said they had closer ties to their mothers and daughters, the older men accorded preferred position to their oldest sons, suggesting an emergent concern for succession reminiscent of the concept of "generational stake" proposed by Bengtson and Kuypers (1971). On the other hand, while they evaluated their mother in terms of her nurturance, caring, and understanding, they were more likely to evaluate their father in terms of his moods and other personality characteristics.

Proposition 8: Gender differences are apparent in research on cross-generational family relationships. Parents feel differently about daughters and sons; and daughters and sons relate differently to mothers and fathers. In general, females have stronger kinship ties and more affection is reported for female family members than for males.

Question 9. Does consensus influence closeness or affect?

Do parents and children—or grandparents and grandchildren—feel closer to each other or like each other better if they hold the same values or see the world through similar eyes? Apparently not. Just as in Question 5 above, the quality of family interrelationships did not seem to affect value consensus, the converse also seems to hold. None of the studies in this area have found significant correlation between similarities among family members and any of the dimensions of family closeness or affect (Adams, 1968; Angres, 1975; Bengtson, 1969; Jennings and Niemi, 1968; Kandel and Lesser, 1972; Thomas, 1971a). Whether or not family members see eye to eye, they continue to live near each other, visit and help each other, and like or feel obligated to each other.

There are two possible exceptions to this conclusion. First, when it is perceived congruence that is measured, rather than actual comparisons of responses of both questions, the younger generation's perception of value differences does seem to be associated with reporting of less family closeness (Andersson, 1973; Kandel and Lesser, 1972; Angres, 1975). Second, it seems possible that extreme socialization differences or social discontinuity resulting in marked changes in attitudes and values may also induce feelings of estrangement between generations (Davis, 1940; Campisi, 1948; Gans, 1962; Senior, 1957). This has been noted particularly for immigrant families and seen most in the relations between middle-aged children and their old parents. Clark (1969) points out that in many cases, the model of old age that the immigrant learned in his youth is regarded as strange by his Americanized offspring, even leading in extreme cases to the parent's being institutionalized.

Proposition 9: In the absence of extreme social discontinuity, value congruence does not seem to be related to degree of parent-child attachments. Ties tend to remain close even where there is little consensus.

Question 10. How do family relationships compare with those between friends or peers?

Question 4 of this chapter deals with the relative influence of parents and peers on transmission. At this point, we are interested in the relative quality or quantity of relationships. From later childhood on, are individuals more likely to turn to friends or members of their own age cohort for meaningful interactions than to lineage members—parents or grandparents, children or grandchildren?

In his review of childhood socialization literature, McCandless (1969) concludes that "peer group supplies important confirmation-disconfirmation of self-judgments of competence and self-esteem, although the foundation of these is probably more influenced by the family." (809). In the United States, it is the same-sex peer group that is important. Further, peers are more important for lower-class than for middle- class children.

Campbell (1969) states that there are "two conditions that we regard as beyond dispute: (1) Adolescence is a period of increasing freedom from the influence of parents, including both association and evaluation; peers are correspondingly more important; and (2) Ours *is* an age-graded society, and from this condition flow reasonably coherent behaviors and values among adolescents that permit reference to youth culture and adolescent society" (827).

According to Eisenstadt (1956), societies like ours which are regulated by values which differ from those of the family make it necessary for individuals who are nearing the transition from childhood familial roles to adult societal roles to establish more extensive social relations outside the family. In fact, says Coleman (1961), because the youth group emphasizes the difference between youth and parental values, adolescents are exposed to constant conflict. Thus they live "more and more in a society of (their) own; [they] find the family a less and less satisfying psychological home" (312).

As Campbell (1969) points out, "arguments over whether there are or are not adolescent societies and youth cultures easily become as sterile as the older heredity and environment controversy," and besides this is not the issue here. He does point to the tremendous amount of time that adolescents spend with each other, and to the interpersonal salience they hold for each other. But whether such association and salience attest to loss of association and salience for parents is not clearly demonstrated. When Coleman (1961) asked adolescents, "Which one of these things would be hardest for you to take: your parents' disapproval, your teacher's disapproval, or breaking with your friend," 53 percent selected parents as against 43 percent who selected friends. Coleman himself interpreted this balance as a sign of transitional status, of leaving family behind and moving over to friends. Campbell, however, concludes that adolescent peer group loyalties do not threaten the emotional bond between adolescent and family. Andersson (1973) found that it was those Swedish youth who had very low self-esteem who were most likely to see friends set off against parents, and this finding was replicated in the United States by Condry and Simon (1974), who found that highly peer-oriented children were likely to come from families having a climate of "passive neglect." As Kandel and Lesser (1972) note, "in critical areas, interactions with peers support, express, and specify for the peer context the values of parents and other adults" (168). In both Denmark and the United States, parents were turned to for help in solving problems and peers were turned to for companionship. While the subjective peer orientation of youth is related to the directiveness of the family (adolescents in democratic families more often prefer their parents' company over that of their friends), adolescents' actual peer interaction patterns are not related to family relationship patterns.

The data—equally scarce—that we have for adults suggest that there are qualitative differences between parent-child relationships and friendships in maturity. As noted earlier in this chapter, adults turn to family for help in times of trouble more than they do to friends (Hill et al., 1970: Troll, 1971). Adult respondents in Greensboro, North Carolina (Adams, 1968) say they feel intimate with their parents, have "positive regard" for them, and above all feel obligated and dutiful to them. They are more likely to share their attitudes, interests and recreational activities with friends. Relations with parents persist, however, while those with friends are vulnerable to mobility or other kinds of changes. Some of this difference may be a function of different developmental patterns of attraction and attachment.

In the beginning of any relationship, attraction seems to be high but attachment low. Novelty creates interest, but bonds are not yet cemented. A breakup in such a relationship would cause only temporary distress, and substitutions of loved objects would be relatively easy—"there are many more fish in the sea." In the course of repeated interaction, however, novelty is gone and attraction reduced, but attachment may have become very strong. A breakup at this time may never be overcome. Support for such a proposal comes from a variety of disparate data: studies of marital satisfaction over time (Pineo, 1961; Feldman, 1964; Adams, 1968), of experimentally organized groups (Taylor, 1968), and of qualitative difference in relationships with parents, siblings, and friends (Adams, 1968). Friendships are likely to be of shorter association and thus more interesting, but it is parents—who may be less interesting—who remain important even when one moves away or up the social ladder (Troll and Smith, 1976).

Among older people, relationships with both family and friends tend to be of long duration. Some older people maintain close ties with both (Lopata, 1977), and where they do, intimate relationships may be the strongest survival mechanism possible (Lowenthal and Haven, 1968). Retired teachers surveyed by Candy (1976) found no difficulty in listing five close friends, all of whom they had known for many years. However, other investigators find that the older years are characterized more by disengagement *into* the family (Troll, 1971), though this may

be a cohort effect, influenced by the large numbers of old women of today whose relationships were traditionally restricted to family members (Lopata, 1977).

Proposition 10: Relationships with friends or peers are more likely to be complementary rather than in opposition to relationships with family members of other generations. Age peers or friends are not substitutes for family lineage relations.

IV. CONCLUSIONS

Family transmission and relations between generations are central issues in theory concerning both individual development and societal change or stability. Within the past decade there has been a resurgence of empirical interest in these topics, as indicated by many of the 160 references cited in this chapter. Yet, as we have repeatedly acknowledged, systematic theory in this area of family studies remains undeveloped, and consistent generalizations concerning any of the six major substantive questions posed at the beginning of this chapter remain tentative.

In large part the reason that intergenerational transmission and relationships present difficulties in theory building can be traced to methodological problems in available studies. We need longitudinal as well as cross-sequential research that would distinguish between short-term period-related effects and more enduring conditions. We need replication of findings and more observational or ethnographic studies. We need to examine the effects of various structural variables on the parent-child bond. Above all, we need more systematic attention given to theory building: designing studies built on previous propositions, and specifying linkages among three, four, or five variables in a manner all too rare in existing reports. Considering the number of studies which have been published, it is surprising how few consistent generalizations we can make about generations within the family.

In this chapter, however, some propositions have been suggested which are supported by available research and which should be of use in future research and theory building. Two in particular stand out. First, it is noteworthy that so many studies support the high degree of attachment or cohesion reported by both parents and children. Despite differentials in maturational levels, geographic propinquity, gender, and socioeconomic mobility, as well as possibly confounding effects of cultural change and peer interaction, *parent-child solidarity appears to consistently represent an important interpersonal bond in contemporary American culture*. This appears true at all stages of the life course, and among individuals from varying locations in the social structure.

Second, it is of interest that *high levels of intergenerational cohesion do not necessarily reflect high levels of similarity* in general orientations or specific opinions.

This generalization must of course continue to be tested in empirical work specifying arenas of similarity (transmission) as well as various aspects of parent-child cohesion. But if this proposition remains substantiated, its implications for theory are significant.

Psychoanalytic theory, learning theory, balance theory, and symbolic interactionist theory appear to have one common assumption in their application to family socialization: that the stronger (closer, more attractive) the bond to the parent, the more similar is the behavior or orientation of the offspring to that of the parent. This assumption can now be considered unwarranted. Similarly, many theoretical statements concerning social change assume a generational base rooted in the desire of emergent generations to be independent of existing social institutions (embodied by their parents). Many of the data reviewed here suggest such an explanation to be, at best, simplistic; at worst, distorting of actual parent-child similarities.

Any implications for broader social and developmental theory emerging from the material reviewed in this chapter must be most tentative, since theory development in intergenerational relations is primitive and the data base at present questionable. We have suggested that research on generations in the family must be informed by more careful attention to the interplay between the various concepts of generation as well as to methodological issues. In addition more concern must be given to explicit and systematic theory development. Only then can we confidently generalize about the roles of family transmission and interaction in either individual development or social change.

REFERENCES

ACOCK, A. C. AND V. L. BENGTSON
1975   "Intergenerational transmission of religious behavior and beliefs." Paper presented at the Pacific Sociological Association Annual Meeting, Victoria, B. C.

ACOCK, A. C. AND V. L. BENGTSON
1976   "On the relative influence of mothers or fathers: A covariance analysis of political and religious socialization." Paper presented at the American Sociological Association Annual Meeting, New York.

ADAMS, B.
1968   *Kinship in an Urban Setting*. Chicago: Markham.

ADELSON, J.
1970   "What generation gap?" *New York Times Magazine*, January 18: 10–11, 34–36, 45–46.

AINSWORTH, M.
1972   "Attachment and dependency: A comparison." In J. Gewirtz (ed.), *Attachment and Dependency*. Washington, D.C.: Winston.

ALDOUS, J.
1965   "The consequences of intergenerational continuity." *Journal of Marriage and the Family* 27:462–68.

ALDOUS, J. AND R. HILL
1965   "Social cohesion, lineage type, and intergenerational transmission." *Social Forces* 43:471–82.

ANDERSSON, B.
1973   "The generation gap: Imagination or reality?" Paper presented to the biennial meeting of the International Society for the Study of Behavioral Development. Institute of Education, Göteborg, Sweden.

ANGRES, S.
1975   "Intergenerational relations and value congruence between young adults and their mothers." Unpublished Ph.D. dissertation, University of Chicago.

ARMSTRONG, B. AND M. SOTZIN
1974   "Intergenerational comparison of attitudes toward basic life concepts." *Journal of Psychology* 87:293–304.

BANDURA, A.
1969   "Social-learning theory of identificatory processes." In D. A. Goslin (ed.), *Handbook of Socialization Theory and Research*. Chicago: Rand McNally.

BAYLEY, N.
1964   "Consistency of maternal and child behaviors in the Berkeley growth study." *Vita Humana* 7:73–95.

BELL, R. R. AND J. B. CHASKES
1970   "Premarital sexual experience among coeds, 1958 and 1968." *Journal of Marriage and the Family* 32:81–84.

BENGTSON, V. L.
1969   "The 'generation gap': Differences by generation and by sex in the perception of parent-child relations." Paper presented at Annual Meeting of Pacific Sociological Association, Seattle, Wash.

1970   "The generation gap: A review and typology of social-psychological perspectives." *Youth and Society* 2:7–32.

1971   "Inter-age differences in perceptions of the generation gap." *The Gerontologist*, part 2, 85–89.

1975a   "Generation and family effects in value socialization." *American Sociological Review* 40:358–71.

1975b   Perceptions of intergenerational solidarity: Attitudes of elderly parents and middle-aged children." Proceedings of the Tenth International Congress of Gerontology, Jerusalem, Israel, 1:106–110.

BENGTSON, V. L. AND A. C. ACOCK
1977   "Attribution within the family: Actual vs. perceived similarity among parents and youth." Paper presented at the Annual Meeting of the American Sociological Association, Chicago.

BENGTSON, V. L. AND K. D. BLACK
1973a   "Intergenerational relations and continuities in socialization." In P. Baltes and W. Schaie (eds.), *Life-Span Developmental Psychology: Personality and Socialization*. New York: Academic Press.

1973b   "Solidarity between parents and children: Four perspectives on theory development." Paper presented at the Theory Development Workshop, National Council on Family Relations Annual Meeting, Toronto, Canada, October 16.

BENGTSON, V. L. AND N. CUTLER
1976   " Generations and intergenerational relations: Perspectives on age groups and social change." In R. Binstock and E. Shanas (eds.), *Handbook of Aging and the Social Sciences*. New York: Van Nostrand.

BENGTSON, V. L., M. J. FURLONG, AND R. S. LAUFER
1974   "Time, aging, and the continuity of social structures: Themes and issues in generational analysis." *Journal of Social Issues*. 30:6–11.

BENGTSON, V. L. AND J. A. KUYPERS
1971   "Generational differences and the developmental stake." *Aging and Human Development* 2:249–60.

BENGTSON, V. L. AND M. C. LOVEJOY
1971   "Values, personality, and social structure: An intergenerational analysis." *American Behavioral Scientist* 16:880–911.

BENGTSON, V. L., E. OLANDER, AND E. HADDAD

1976 "The 'generation gap' and aging family members: Toward a conceptual model." In J. F. Gubrium (ed.), *Time, Roles, and Self in Old Age*. New York: Human Sciences Press.

BENGTSON, V. L. AND J. M. STARR
1975 "Contrast and consensus: A generational analysis of youth in the 1970s." in Havighurst, R. J. (ed.), *Youth. The Seventy-Fourth Yearbook of the National Society for the Study of Education*, part 1. Chicago: University of Chicago Press.

BERARDO, F.
1967 "Kinship interaction and communications among space-age migrants." *Journal of Marriage and the Family* 29:541–54.

BETTELHEIM, B.
1965 "The problem of generations." In E. Erikson (ed.), *The Challenge of Youth*. New York: Anchor Press.

BLENKNER, M.
1965 "Social work and family relationships in later life with some thoughts on filial maturity." In E. Shanas and G. Streib (eds.), *Social Structure and the Family: Generational Relationships*. Englewood Cliffs, N.J.: Prentice-Hall.

BLUMENFELD, W. S.
1964 "Note on the relationship of political preference between generations within a household." *Psychological Reports* 15:976.

BOTT, E.
1957 *Family and Social Network*. London: Tavistock.

BOYD, R. R.
1969 "The valued grandparent: A changing social role." In W. Donahue et al. (eds.), *Living in the Multigeneration Family*. Ann Arbor: Institute of Gerontology.

BRAUN, P. AND V. Bengtson
1972 "Religious behavior in three generations: Cohort lineage effects." Paper presented at the Gerontological Society meetings, San Juan, P. R.

BRAUNGART, R. G.
1974 "A sociology of generations and student politics: A comparison of the Functionalist and generational unit models." *Journal of Social Issues* 30:31–54.

BRITTAIN, V.
1963 "Adolescent choices and parent-peer cross-pressures." *American Sociological Review* 28:385–91.

BRITTON, J., W. MATHER, AND K. LANSING
1961 "Expectations for older persons in a rural community: Living arrangements and family relationships." *Journal of Gerontology* 16:156–62.

BROWN, P. G.
1960 "Family structure and social isolation of older persons." *Journal of Gerontology* 15:170–74.

BULTEMA, G.
1969 "Rural-urban differences in the familial interaction of aged." *Rural Sociology* 34:5–15.

CAMPBELL, E. Q.
1969 "Adolescent socialization." In D. A. Goslin (ed.), *Handbook of Socialization Theory and Research*. Chicago: Rand McNally.

CAMPISI, P.
1948 "Ethnic family patterns: The Italian family in the United States." *American Journal of Sociology* 53:443–49.

CANDY, S.
1976 "An exploration of the development of the functions of friendship in women." Unpublished master's thesis, Wayne State University.

CHERRY, L. AND M. LEWIS
1976 "Mothers and two-year-olds: A study of sex-differentiated aspects of verbal interaction." *Developmental Psychology* 12:278–82.

CHRISTENSEN, T. AND F. GREGG

1970 "Changing sex norms in America and Scandinavia." *Journal of Marriage and the Family* 31:612–27.

CLARK, M.
1969 "Cultural values and dependency in later life." In R. Kalish (ed.), *The Dependencies of Old People*. Ann Arbor: Institute for Gerontology.

CLAUSEN, J.
1974 "Value transmission and personality resemblance in two generations." Paper presented at American Sociological Association meeting, Montreal.

COLEMAN, J. S.
1961 *The Adolescent Society*. New York: Free Press.

CONDRY, J. AND M. Simon
1974 "Characteristics of peer and adult oriented children." *Journal of Marriage and the Family* 36:543–54.

CONNELL, R. W.
1972 "Political socialization in the American family." *Public Opinion Quarterly* 36:323–33.

CUMMING, E. AND W. HENRY
1961 *Growing Old*. New York: Basic Books.

DAVIS, K.
1940 "The sociology of parent-youth conflict." *American Sociological Review* 5:523–35.

DODGE, R. W. AND E. S. UYEKI
1962 "Political affiliation and imagery across two related generations." *Midwest Journal of Political Science* 6:266–76.

DOUVAN, E. AND J. ADELSON
1966 *The Adolescent Experience*. New York: Wiley.

DUFFY, E.
1941 "Attitudes of parents and daughters toward war and toward the treatment of criminals." *Psychological Record* 4:366–72.

EISENSTADT, S. N.
1956 *From Generation to Generation*. New York: Free Press.

ERIKSON, E. H.
1959 "Identity and the life cycle: Selected papers." *Psychological Issues*, Monograph No. 1.

FELDMAN, H.
1964 "Development of the husband-wife relationship." Preliminary report, Cornell studies of marital development: Study in the transition to parenthood. Ithaca, N.Y.: Cornell University.

FENGLER, A. P. AND V. WOOD
1972 "The generation gap: An analysis of attitudes on contemporary issues." *The Gerontologist* 12:124–28.
1973 "Continuity between the generations: Differential influence of mothers and fathers." *Youth and Society* 4:359–72.

FISHER, S. C.
1948 *Relationships in Attitudes, Opinions, and Values among Family Members*. Berkeley: University of California Press, 1948.

FLACKS, R.
1967 "The liberated generation: An exploration of the roots of student protest." *Journal of Social Issues* 23:52–75.

FREEMAN, H.
1972 "The generation gap: Attitudes of students and of their parents." *Journal of Counseling Psychology* 19:441–47.

FREUD, S.
1963 "On narcissism: An introduction (1914). In S. Freud, *General Psychological Theory* (edited by Philip Rieff). New York: Collier Books.

FRIEDENBERG, E.
1959 *The Vanishing Adolescent*. Boston: Beacon Press.
1965 *Coming of Age in America*. New York: Random House.
1969 "Current patterns of a generation conflict." *Journal of Social Issues* 25:21–38.

FRIEDMAN, L. N., A. R. GOLD, AND R. CHRISTIE
1972   "Dissecting the generation gap: Intergenerational and in-trafamilial similarities and differences." *Public Opinion Quarterly* 36:334–46.

FURSTENBERG, F., JR.
1967   "Transmission of attitudes in the family." Unpublished doctoral dissertation, Columbia University.

GANS, H. J.
1962   *The Urban Villagers: Group and Class Life of Italian-Americans*. New York: Free Press.

GEWIRTZ, J. L. (ED.)
1972   *Attachment and Dependency*. Washington, D. C.: Winston. Distributed by Halstead Press Div., John Wiley and Sons, N. Y.

GIBSON, G.
1969a   "Kin family network: Overheralded structure in past concep-tualizations of family functioning." *Journal of Marriage and the Family* 34:13–23.
1969b   "Kinship interaction and conjugal role relations." Paper presented at Ohio Valley Society and Midwest Sociological Society Joint meeting, Indianapolis.

GILFORD, R. AND D. BLACK
1972   "The grandchild-grandparent dyad: ritual or relationship." Paper presented at Gerontological Society, San Juan, P. R.

GOLDSMID, P.
1972   "Intergenerational similarity in political attitudes: The ef-fects of parent-child relations and exposure to politics." Unpublished doctoral dissertation, University of Chicago.

GOSLIN, D. A.
1969   *Handbook of Socialization Theory and Research*. Chicago: Rand McNally.

GRAY, R. AND T. C. SMITH
1960   "Effect of employment on sex differences in attitudes toward the parental family." *Marriage and Family Living*, 22:36–38.

HAGESTAD, G.
1974   Personal communication.

HALVERSON, C. AND M. WALDROP
1970   "Maternal behavior toward own and other pre-school chil-dren: The problem of 'Ownness'." *Child Development* 41:839–45.

HAWKINSON, W.
1965   "Wish expectancy and practice in the interaction of genera-tions." In A. Rose and W. Peterson (eds.), *Older People and Their Social World*. Philadelphia: F. A. Davis.

HELFANT, K.
1952   "Parents' attitudes vs. adolescent hostility in the determina-tion of adolescents' sociopolitical attitudes." *Psychological Monographs: General and Applied*.

HESS, R. AND G. HANDEL
1959   *Family Worlds*. Chicago: University of Chicago.

HESS, R. D. AND J. V. TORNEY
1967   *The Development of Political Attitudes among Children*. Chicago: Aldine.

HILL, R., N. FOOTE, J. ALDOUS, R. CARLSON, AND R. MacDONALD
1970   *Family Development in Three Generations*. Cambridge, Mass.: Schenkman.

HIMMELHOCK, J.
1950   "Tolerance and personality needs." *American Sociological Review* 15:79–88.

HIRSCHBERG, G. AND A. GILLILAND
1942   "Parent-child relationships in attitudes." *Journal of Abnor-mal and Social Psychology* 37:125–30.

HYMAN, H. H.

1959   *Political Socialization*. New York: Free Press.

JARVIK, L.
1975   "Thoughts on the psychobiology of aging." *American Psy-chologist* 30:576-83.

JENNINGS, M. AND K. LANGTON
1969   "Mothers versus fathers: The formation of political orienta-tions among young Americans." *Journal of Politics* 31:329–58.

JENNINGS, M. AND R. NIEMI
1968   "The transmission of political values from parent to child." *American Political Science Review* 42:169–84.
1974   *The Political Character of Adolescents*. Princeton, N.J.: Princeton University Press.
1975   "Continuity and change in political orientations: A longitud-inal study of two generations." *American Political Science Review* 69:1316–35.

KAHANA, B. AND E. KAHANA
1970   "Grandparenthood from the perspective of the developing grandchild." *Developmental Psychology* 1: 98–105.

KAHANA, B., R. PEREZ, A. TAGORE, AND E. KAHANA
1973   "Cross-cultural perspectives in inter-generational rela-tions." Paper presented at the American Psychological As-sociation, Montreal.

KALISH, R. AND A. JOHNSON
1972   "Value similarities and differences in three generations of women." *Journal of Marriage and the Family* 34:49–54.

KALISH, R. AND F. W. KNUDSEN
1976   "Attachment vs. disengagement: A life span conceptualiza-tion." *Human Development* 19:171–81.

KANDEL, D.
1974   "Inter- and intragenerational influences on adolescent marijuana use." *Journal of Social Issues* 30:107–35.

KANDEL, D, AND G. LESSER
1972   *Youth in Two Worlds*. San Francisco: Jossey-Bass.

KENISTON, K.
1965   *The Uncommitted*. New York: Harcourt, Brace and World.
1968   *Young Radicals: Notes on Committed Youth*. New York: Harcourt, Brace and World.

KERCKHOFF, A. C.
1965   "Nuclear and extended family relationships: Normative and behavioral analysis." In E. Shanas and G. Streib (eds.), *Social Structure and the Family*. Englewood Cliffs, N. J.: Prentice-Hall.

KERCKHOFF, A. C. AND P. HUFF
1974   "Parental influence on educational goals." *Sociometry* 37:307–27.

KIRKPATRICK, C.
1936   "A comparison of generations in regard to attitudes toward feminism." *Journal of Genetic Psychology* 49:343–61.

KOHLBERG, L.
1966   "A cognitive-developmental analysis of children's sex role concepts and attitudes." In E. Maccoby (ed.), *The Develop-ment of Sex Differences*. Stanford, Calif. Stanford Univer-sity.

KOMAROVSKY, M.
1964   *Blue-Collar Marriage*. New York: Random House.

LARSON, L. E.
1972   "The influence of parents and peers during adolescence: The situation hypothesis revisited." *Journal of Marriage and the Family* 34:67–76.

LARSON, W. R. AND B. MYERHOFF
1965   "Primary and formal family organization and adolescent socialization." *Sociology and Social Research* 50:63–71.

LAUFER, R. AND V. L. BENGTSON

1974 "Generations, aging, and social stratification: On the development of generational units." *Journal of Social Issues* 30:181–205.

LERNER, R. M.
1975 "Showdown at the generation gap: Attitudes of adolescents and their parents toward contemporary issues." In H. D. Thornberg (ed.), *Contemporary Adolescence: Readings*. Belmont, Calif.: Wadsworth.

1978 "Nature, nurture, and dynamic interactionism." *Human Development* 21, forthcoming.

LERNER, R. M. AND J. R. KNAPP
1975 "Actual and perceived intrafamilial attitudes of late adolescents and their parents." *Journal of Youth and Adolescence* 4:17–36.

LERNER, R. M. AND G. B. SPANIER (ED.)
1978 *Child Influences on Marital and Family Interaction: A Life-Span Perspective*. New York: Academic Press.

LEVIN, M. L.
1961 "Political climates and political socialization." *Public Opinion Quarterly* 25:596–606.

LEWIS, M. AND R. FREEDLE
1973 "Mother-infant dyad: The cradle of meaning." In P. Piner, L. Krames, and T. Alloway (eds.), *Communication and Affect Language and Thoughts*. New York: Academic Press.

LINDER, C. AND N. NAHEMOW
1970 "Continuity of attitudes in three-generation families." Paper presented at the Gerontological Society Meeting, Toronto.

LITWAK, E.
1960a "Occupational mobility and extended family cohesion." *American Sociological Review* 25:9–21.

1960b "Geographic mobility and extended family cohesion." *American Sociological Review* 25:385–94.

LOPATA, H.
1977 "Friendships among widows." In L. Troll, J. Israel, and K. Israel (eds.), *The Older Woman*. Englewood Cliffs, N. J.: Prentice-Hall.

LOWENTHAL, M. F. AND C. HAVEN
1968 "Interaction and adaptation: Intimacy as a critical variable." *American Sociological Review* 33:20–30.

LOWENTHAL, M. F., M. THURNHER, AND D. CHIRIBOGA
1975 *Four Stages of Life*. San Francisco: Jossey-Bass.

LUBELL, S.
1968 "That generation gap." *The Public Interest* 13:52–60.

MACCOBY, E. AND C. JACKLIN
1974 *The Psychology of Sex Differences*. Stanford, Calif.: Stanford University Press.

MACCOBY, E. E., R. E. MATHEWS, AND A. S. MORTON
1954 "Youth and political change." *Public Opinion Quarterly* 18: 23–39.

MANNHEIM, K.
1952 "The problem of generations." In K. Mannheim, *Essays on the Sociology of Knowledge*. London: Routledge and Keagan (originally published in 1923).

MARTIN, W. C. AND V. L. BENGTSON
1971 "Alienation of the aged: Its nature and correlates." Paper presented at the meetings of the Gerontological Society, Houston, Texas.

MARTIN, W. C., V. L. BENGTSON, AND A. C. ACOCK
1974 "Alienation and age: A context-specific approach." *Social Forces* 53:266–74.

MAXWELL, P., R. CONNOR, AND J. WALTER
1961 "Family member perception of parent role performance." *Merrill- Palmer Quarterly* 7:31–37.

MCCANDLESS, B. R.

1969 "Childhood socialization." In D. A. Goslin (ed.), *Handbook of Socialization Theory and Research*. Chicago: Rand Mc-Nally.

MEAD, M.
1970 *Culture and Commitment: A Study of the Generation Gap*. New York: Basic Books.

MILLER, B. C. AND J. D. SCHVANEVELDT
1977 "Fertility-related attitudes of Mormon women across three generations." In P. R. Kuntz (ed.), *The Mormon Family*. Provo, Utah: Brigham Young University.

MOSS, H.
1967 "Sex, age, and state as determinants of mother-infant interaction." *Merrill-Palmer Quarterly* 13:19–36.

NIEMI, R. G.
1974 *How Family Members Perceive Each Other: Political and Social Attitudes in Two Generations*. New Haven: Yale University.

NEUGARTEN, B.
1968 *Middle Age and Aging*. Chicago: University of Chicago.

NEUGARTEN, B. AND WEINSTEIN, K. K.
1974 "The changing American grandparent." *Journal of Marriage and the Family* 26:199–204.

NEWCOMB, T. AND G. SVEHLA
1937 "Intrafamily relationships in attitude." *Sociometry* 1: 180–205.

NYDEGGER, C. N.
1973 "Late and early fathers." Paper presented at the Annual Meeting of the Gerontological Society, Miami Beach.

PARKMAN, M.
1965 "Identity, role, and family functioning." Unpublished Ph.D. dissertation, University of Chicago.

PARSONS, T.
1968 "The stability of the American family system." In N. W. Bell and E. F. Vogel, (eds.), *A Modern Introduction to the Family*. New York: Free Press.

PAYNE, S., D. SUMMERS, AND T. STEWART
1973 "Value differences across three generations." *Sociometry* 36: 20–30.

PINDER, A.
1926 *Kunstegeschichte nach Generationen, Zwischen Philosophie und Kunst*. Johann Volkelt zum 100. Lehrsemester dargebracht.

PINEO, P.
1961 "Disenchantment in the later years of marriage." *Marriage and Family Living*. 2:3–11.

RADKE-YARROW, M., H. G. TRAGER, AND J. MILLER
1952 "The role of parents in the development of childrens' ethnic attitudes." *Child Development* 23:13–53.

REISS, I. L.
1968 "How and why America's sex standards are changing." *Transaction* 5:26–32.

REISS, P. J.
1962 "Extended kinship system: Correlates of and attitudes on frequency of interaction." *Marriage and Family Living* 24:333–39.

REMMERS, H. H. AND N. WELTMAN
1947 "Attitude interrelationships of youth, their parents, and teachers." *Journal of Social Psychology* 26:61–68.

RIESMAN, D.
1950 *The Lonely Crowd*. New Haven: Yale University Press.

RILEY, M. A., A. FONER, B. HESS, AND M. TOBY
1969 "Socialization for the middle and later years." In D. A. Goslin (ed.), *Handbook of Socialization Theory and Research*. Chicago: Rand McNally.

RILEY, M. W., M. JOHNSON, A. FONER, AND ASSOCIATES.
1972   *Aging and Society*, vol. 3:1 *A Sociology of Age Stratification.* New York: Russell Sage Foundation.

RISKIN, J. AND E. E. FAUNCE
1972   "An evaluation review of family interaction research." *Family Process* 11:365–455.

ROBINS, A. J.
1962   "Family relations of the aging in three-generation households." In C. Tibbitts and W. Donahue (eds.), *Aging in Today's Society.* Englewood Cliffs, N.J.: Prentice-Hall.

ROKEACH, M.
1960   *The Open and Closed Mind: Investigations into the Nature of Belief Systems and Personality Systems.* New York: Basic Books.
1968   *Beliefs, Attitudes, and Values: A Theory of Organization and Change.* San Francisco: Jossey-Bass.

ROSE, A. M.
1962   "The subculture of the aging: A topic for sociological research." *The Gerontologist* 2:123–27.

ROSENBERG, G.
1970   *The Worker Grows Old.* San Francisco: Jossey-Bass.

SCHAIE, K. W.
1965   "A general model for the study of developmental problems." *Psychological Bulletin* 64:92–107.
1973   "Developmental processes and aging." In Eisdorfer, C. and P. B. Baltes (eds.), *The Psychology of Adult Development and Aging.* Washington, D. C.: American Psychological Association.

SCHORR, A.
1960   *Filial Responsibility in the Modern American Family.* Washington, D. C.: Social Security Administration, Department of Health, Education, and Welfare.

SCOTT, F. G.
1962   "Family group structure and patterns of social interaction." *American Journal of Sociology* 68:214–28.

SENIOR, C.
1957   "Research on the Puerto Rican family in the United States." *Marriage and Family Living* 19:32–37.

SHANAS, E.
1961   "Living arrangements of older people in the United States." *The Gerontologist* 1:27–29.

SHANAS, E., P. TOWNSEND, D. WEDDERBURN, H. FRIIS, P. MILHOJ, AND J. STEHOUWER
1968   *Older People in Three Industrial Societies.* New York: Atherton Press.

SLATER, P.
1970   *The Pursuit of Loneliness.* Boston: Beacon Press.

SPANIER, G. B.
1976a   "Perceived parental sexual conservatism, religiosity, and premarital sexual behavior." *Sociological Focus* 9:285–298.
1976b   "Formal and informal sex education as determinants of premarital sexual behavior." *Archives of Sexual Behavior* 5:39–67.

STAGNER, R.
1936   "Fascist attitudes: Their determining conditions." *Journal of Social Psychology* 7:447–48.

STRAUS, M. A.
1967   "The influence of sex of children and social class on instrumental and expressive family roles in a laboratory setting." *Sociology and Social Research* 52:7–21.

STREIB, G. F.
1965   "Intergenerational relations: Perspectives of the two generations on the older parent." *Journal of Marriage and the Family* 27:469–76.

SUSSMAN, M.
1965   "Relationships of adult children with their parents in the

United States." In E. Shanas and G. Streib (eds.), *Social Structure and the Family: Generational Relations.* Englewood Cliffs, N. J.: Prentice-Hall.

SUSSMAN, M. B. AND L. BURCHINAL
1962   "Kin family network: Unheralded structure in current conceptualizations of family functioning." *Marriage and Family Living* 24:231–40.

SUSSMAN, M., J. CATES, AND D. SMITH
1970   *The Family and Inheritance.* New York: Russell Sage Foundation.

SWEETSER, D. A.
1963   "A symmetry in intergenerational family relationships." *Social Forces* 41:346–52.

SWITZER, K. A.
1974   "Achievement motivation in women: A three generational study." Unpublished master's thesis, Wayne State University.

TANNER, J. M.
1961   *Education and Physical Growth.* London: University of London Press.

TAYLOR, D. A.
1968   "Some aspects of the development of interpersonal relations: Social penetration process." *Journal of Social Psychology* 75:79–98.

TEDIN, K. L.
1974   "The influence of parents on the political attitudes of adolescents." *American Political Science Review* 68:1579–92.

THOMAS, L. E.
1971a   "Family correlates of student political activism." *Developmental Psychology* 4:206–14.
1971b   "Political attitude congruence between politically active parents and college-age children." *Journal of Marriage and the Family* 32:375–86.
1974   "Generational discontinuity in beliefs: An exploration of the generation gap." *Journal of Social Issues* 30:1–21.

THOMAS, L. E. AND J. F. STANKIEWICZ
1973   "Correspondence between related generations on a range of attitudes and values: An attempt to map the domain." Paper presented at the meeting of the American Psychological Association, Montreal.
1974   "Family correlates of parent-child attitude congruence: Is it time to throw in the towel?" *Psychological Reports* 34:10–38.

TOWNSEND, P.
1957   *The Family Life of Old People.* London: Routledge and Kegan.

TROLL, L. E.
1967   "Personality similarities between college students and their parents." Unpublished doctoral dissertation, University of Chicago.
1970   "Issues in the study of generations." *Aging and Human Development* 1:199–218.
1971   "The family of later life: A decade review." In C. Broderick (ed.), *A Decade of Family Research and Action.* Minneapolis, Minn.: National Council on Family Relations.
1972   "Salience of family members in three generations." Paper presented at the meeting of the American Psychological Association, Honolulu, Hawaii.
1975   *Early and Middle Adulthood.* Monterey, Calif.: Brooks/Cole.

TROLL, L. E., B. L. NEUGARTEN, AND R. J. KRAINES
1969   "Similarities in values and other personality characteristics in college students and their parents." *Merrill-Palmer Quarterly* 15:323–36.

TROLL, L. AND J. SMITH
1972   "Three-generation lineage changes in cognitive style and value traits." Paper presented at Gerontological Society

meeting, San Juan, P. R.

1976   "Attachment through the life span: Some questions about dyadic bonds among adults." *Human Development* 19:156–70.

WALSH, H.
1970   "The generation gap in sexual beliefs." Paper presented at the American Sociological Association, Washington, D. C.

WALTERS, J. AND N. STINNETT
1971   "Parent-child relationships: A decade review of research." In C. Broderick (ed.), *A Decade of Family Research and Action*. Minneapolis, Minn.: National Council on Family Relations.

WEINSTOCK, A. AND R. M. LERNER
1972   "Attitudes of late adolescents and their parents toward contemporary issues." *Psychological Reports* 30:239–44.

WELTMAN, N. AND H. H. REMMERS
1946   "Pupils, parents and teachers attitudes: Similarities and differences." *Studies in Higher Education* 56:72–84.

WESTBY, D. L. AND R. G. BRAUNGART
1966   "Class and politics in the family backgrounds of student political activists." *American Sociological Review* 31:690–92.

WIETING, S. G.
1975   "An examination of intergenerational patterns of religious belief and practice." *Sociological Analysis* 36:137–49.

WINCH, R. F. AND S. A. GREER
1968   "Urbanism, ethnicity, and extended families." *Marriage and Family Living* 30:40–45.

YANKELOVICH, D.
1970   "Generations apart: A study of the generation gap." A survey conducted for CBS News.
1972   *The Changing Values on campus*. New York: Simon and Schuster.

YOUNG, M. AND H. GEERTZ
1961   "Old age in London and San Francisco." *British Journal of Sociology* 12:124–41.

YOUNG, M. AND P. WILLMOTT
1964   *Family and Kinship in East London*. Baltimore: Penguin Books.

7

TOWARD A MODEL OF FAMILIAL ORGANIZATION
Robert F. Winch

INTRODUCTION

The major thrust of this chapter is to propose a theoretical approach to account for variation from one society to another in the structure, functions and influence of the social form we call the family—how it turns out to be large and multifunctional in some settings and small and minimally functional in others. We shall also be looking for those engines of social change that convert the family from one size to another and from one level of functionality to another. After outlining the theory, data from the Ethnographic Atlas will be presented to test it.

An orderly way to begin theorizing about a phenomenon is with a definition, but a definition implies the preexistence of a theory that points to relevant features of the phenomenon under study. To get a picture of as seamless a phenomenon as the family, it helps to begin with structure and function (Winch, 1971, table 1.1). Let us begin with the notion of a social system as a social group with two or more differentiated social positions and a social structure as a social system viewed as a network of social roles and positions. When the family is viewed as a social structure, it carries the additional element that the relations between those roles and positions be familistically defined, i.e., in terms of blood, marriage, or adoption.

Elsewhere (Winch, 1971, ch. 1) I have proposed that there are five basic tasks a society must carry out in order to survive and that corresponding to each of these five basic societal functions we may conceive of an analytic category we call a basic societal structure. These are the economy, the polity, the school, the church, and the family. The basic societal function I have proposed that the family universally carries out is that of the replacement, through sexual reproduction and adoption, of dying and emigrating members. As corollaries of its basic societal function the family has the derived functions of parentifying—nurturing and controlling the young—and position conferring; as corollary of its structure—a primary group—it has the derived function of emotional gratification.

Having developed the concepts of structure and function in relation to the family, we may now return to the questions of defining the family. We may define the family structurally as two or more interacting persons related to each other by means of differentiated familial positions such as husband and wife, parent and offspring, uncle and nephew, etc. We may define the family functionally as a pair of individuals carrying out the family's basic societal function—reproduction. Or, since the defining of terms can be viewed as an arbitrary matter, we might extend the functional definition to include social groupings carrying out what had been designated as the family's derived functions: parentifying, position conferring, and/or providing emotional gratification. It seems evident that we should agree in regarding as a family any social group that complies with our structural and our several functional criteria. Some of the more interesting cases arise, however, and may be interpreted as signs of social change, in social groups that satisfy one or another but not all of the criteria. Thus a social grouping that conforms structurally but not functionally might be viewed as a potentially dying familial form. One that conforms functionally but not structurally might be seen as *in statu nascendi*. The contemporary American scene has made us aware of social groups lacking our structural criteria but sharing a common residence and fulfilling one or more of our functional indicators.

By this point in the discussion it should be evident that familial forms may vary considerably in structure and in function. By structural variation is meant the number and designation of the familial positions involved in a familial pattern. By functional variation reference is made to the

NOTE: This chapter is based, in part, on work and theories originally done with Rae Lesser Blumberg, Scott Greer, and Margaret T. Gordon. The present interpretations are, however, mine alone. For a fuller explication of the theory see Winch (1977).

EDITORS' NOTE: Special thanks are due to Gay C. Kitson who kindly agreed to see this chapter through the press after the death of our colleague Robert Winch.

manner and degree to which the functions enumerated above are fulfilled by familial systems.

Two of the more obvious ways in which structure varies are size—that is, number of positions involved—and the nature of the relationships. Thus there are small and large familial systems and those wherein relationships are traced through the male line or through the female line or in some more complex manner.

Functional variation is quite familiar to students of the family. Some familial systems, as that of traditional China, have been multifunctional, so that families were almost little societies, tending toward economic and political self-sufficiency, training their children, and worshipping ancestors. Other familial forms, such as that of some Israeli kibbutzim, have fulfilled only the reproductive function and thus have seemed to some sociologists to be so minimally functional as not to qualify as families.

We have seen that the family in one society may differ from that in another with respect to structure and function. Forms of the family may vary also with respect to influence. By influence I mean the degree to which membership in a familial system controls the totality of a person's activities and attitudes. Later in this chapter I shall argue that a family's influence over its members varies according to its structure and functioning.

We shall look upon the mode of making a living as the most important source of influence on the familial system and upon changes in the technology of subsistence as the most important source of change in the familial system. Although we shall be looking to the economy as the prime determinant, we shall also be alert to influences from other basic societal structures—most notably the polity—as well. Such an approach entitles us to think of the theory as basically ecological-materialist, and since we are interested in change, also as evolutionary. Perhaps it is advisable to add a disavowal of any belief in linear evolution in the sense that all societies must go through some specific sequence of stages. We may look upon the theory as structural and functional in the sense that we use these terms to identify relevant features of the social system whose variation we seek to explain, viz., the family. The sociology we shall employ, then, may be summarized in the somewhat awkward phrase structural-functional-materialist-evolutionary. The study of the influence of the family involves us in social psychology, and in the present chapter we shall pursue this topic only far enough to indicate how our social psychology of the family articulates with our sociology in order to emphasize the point that the theory being proposed has micro- as well as macrosociological implications.

BACKGROUND OF THE PROBLEM

Although efforts to relate the organization of familial systems to other aspects of their societies can be traced back for a century or two (Millar, 1771; Bachofen, 1861; Engels, 1884; Westermarck, 1891), it is works that have appeared since the turn of the century that merit our most serious consideration. Some of these formulations had to do with conditions under which the familial system is small or large, descent is bilineal or unilineal, and, if the latter, whether traced through the male or female line, and whether a newly married couple sets up residence near the kin of the groom, of the bride, or elsewhere.

Lowie (1920:148, 150) wrote that under the simplest conditions of subsistence— hunting and gathering—the familial system tended to be small and bilineal. A larger and unilineal system appeared, he said, "only when horticultural or pastoral activities have partly or wholly superseded the chase as the basis of economic maintenance." He added that the residence of the nuptial couple with kin and the transmission of property rights were important conditions favoring the establishment of unilineal descent.

A similar hypothesis relating complexity of the familial system to that of the subsistence system was offered by Forde (1947), but this writer went on to propose that when societies develop centralized political authority, that condition became unfavorable for large unilineal kinship groups. Thus Forde proposed that there was a curvilinear relationship between societal complexity and familial complexity, with maximum familial complexity appearing at some intermediate point between the very simple type of society and that which involves highly developed political systems.

A somewhat clearer statement of the curvilinear relationship was proposed by Fortes (1953). Among the very simple societies he believed that the lack of durable property hindered development of large familial systems, but that "in the middle range of relatively homogeneous, precapitalistic economies in which there is some degree of technological sophistication . . . value is attached to rights in durable property," and the large unilineal descent group was likely to appear (1953:24). At still higher levels of societal complexity Fortes thought that the introduction of money and the development of occupational differentiation would contribute to the breakdown of large families and foster small familial systems. Thus we see that Lowie, Forde, and Fortes all proposed a curvilinear relationship between societal complexity and familial complexity.

Although the quantitative analysis of ethnographic materials had been going on since the turn of the century (Nieboer, 1900; Steinmetz, 1930; Hobhouse, Wheeler, and Ginsberg, 1915), none of the foregoing writers attempted to support his hypothesis in such a manner. A leader in this type of undertaking has been G. P. Murdock. In 1949 Murdock published a study based on codes derived from ethnographies of 250 preindustrial societies and concluded that type of descent group was uncorrelated with societal complexity. Since unilineal descent groups are associated with large familial systems and bilineal descent groups with small families, Murdock's conclusion was interpreted as finding no correlation between the complexity of society and that of the family.

Subsequently (1957) Murdock published a set of codes on 565 preindustrial societies in the form of a set of punch cards. To this conveniently packaged bank of ethnographic data Murdock gave the name World Ethnographic Sample (WES). Basing their analysis on the WES, Nimkoff and Middleton (1960) explored the degree of association between the subsistence pattern of societies and their types of familial systems. By subsistence pattern is meant such activities as hunting and gathering, fishing, animal husbandry, and agriculture. These authors dichotomized societies into those that had what they called independent (or small) and those having extended (or large) familial systems. They were independent "if they did not normally include more than one nuclear or polygamous family . . . and . . . if the head of the family of procreation is not subject to the authority of any of his relatives or economically dependent upon them" (215). They found that hunting and gathering societies, i.e., those with simpler types of subsistence, tended to have independent (small) familial systems. The prevailing pattern among societies at more complex levels of subsistence was extended familism. They concluded, moreover, that four factors appeared to be conducive to the presence of large familial systems: abundance and stability of the food supply, the family working together as a unit of labor, the mode of subsistence permitting the society to be sedentary, and the presence of familially owned property, especially land.

Murdock continued work on his data bank by coding additional variables and doing so for an increasing number of societies. Furthermore he took advantage of the developing technology in the storage and analysis of data, especially the use of the computer. In 1967 he published a summary article on 862 societies. Subsequently the data he has offered the scholarly public through the pages of *Ethnology* have also become available on computer tape and have been extended to about 1,200 societies. Osmond (1969) recoded Murdock's variable of familial organization into "limited" and "general" types (meaning small and large, respectively), and she found that the "limited" (or small) form of familial organization seemed to be associated with relatively high societal complexity.

Goode (1963) investigated the same topic with a quite different set of data. He was interested in the traditional familial forms of India, China, Japan, the Arab world, Sub-Saharan Africa, and the West. In all of these settings he noted that there was an ongoing process of industrialization and urbanization to which he applied the term "world revolution." Goode concluded that whatever the traditional form of the family may have been, there was a convergence as the "world revolution" ran its course toward a conjugal family system, the main characteristics of which are:

1. The extended family pattern becomes rare, and corporate kin structures disappear.

2. Free choice of spouse, based on love, is possible, and an independent household is set up.

3. Dowry and brideprice disappear.

4. Marriages between kin become less common.

5. Authority of parent over the child, and of husband over wife, diminishes.

6. Equality between the sexes is greater; the legal system moves toward equality of inheritance among all children.

In 1968 Winch and Blumberg noted that the studies by Nimkoff and Middleton on the one hand and by Goode on the other offered, or at least seemed to offer, mutually contradictory conclusions—the former reporting the correlation between societal complexity and familial complexity to be positive and the latter asserting it to be negative. In an effort to reconcile these seemingly contradictory views Winch and Blumberg proposed that the range of societal complexity of the Nimkoff-Middleton study embraced relatively simple preindustrial societies whereas the range studied by Goode involved societies of greater complexity. Accordingly, Winch and Blumberg proposed that the two sets of findings might be reconciled by a curvilinear relationship between societal complexity and familial complexity. Subsequently these same authors published a study (Blumberg and Winch, 1972) embracing societies from the hunting and gathering stage through such developed nation-states as Israel and Japan and demonstrated that a point of inflection could indeed be found whereby the greatest proportion of large familial systems occurred among societies having sedentary intensive agriculture but without irrigation.

In another group of studies, Winch and associates (Winch, Greer, and Blumberg, 1967; Winch and Greer, 1968) in an upper-middle-class suburb of Chicago and a statewide sample of Wisconsin found parallels to the Nimkoff-Middleton findings with respect to variables associated with large familial systems. The most obvious of these findings was that in all studies migration was associated with smaller families. A parallel with the family-as-a-unit-of-labor finding of Nimkoff and Middleton is that in the suburban study it was found that the size of the familial system tended to be large in families in which the father had ever been associated in a family business.

The ways in which descent systems are organized also vary across types of societies. The simplest mode of subsistence is gathering and hunting. In 1936 Steward wrote about the familial organization of hunting and gathering families. Such bands, he said, consisted of several nuclear families grouped together for economic and political purposes. That is, they provided "subsistence insurance" for each other and formed a defensive alliance. He stated that because subsistence and defense were the important activities, there was reason to organize such groups around a core of resident males. Consequently he concluded that such bands tend to be patrilineal and patrilocal. (Actually, of the 179 gathering and hunting societies on the Northwestern version of the tape of the Ethnographic Atlas, 134, or 75 percent, are not unilineal. Of the 45 that are unilineal, 35, or 78 percent, are patrilineal. Thus 78 percent of the unilineal and 20 percent of all the gathering and hunting societies in the Ethnographic Atlas turn out to be patrilineal.)

Schneider (1961:5–16) has distinguished between patrilineal and matrilineal descent groups on the ground that in the former both authority and descent run through the male line whereas in the latter authority runs through the male line but descent runs through the female line. Another difference to which he refers is that esteem goes to the gender through which lineality is traced and that this has bearing upon the status the society accords men and women. (There is of course a considerable correlation between lineality and residence. The correlation is a bit lower in matrilineal societies, but two-thirds of those in the Ethnographic Atlas are either matrilocal or uxorilocal.) Where the society is patrilineal and patrilocal, the bride arrives as a stranger and tends to be seen chiefly as an agent of procreation. In the converse situation the in-marrying male may also be valued chiefly for his procreative contribution, although Gough (1971) doubts there is any society in which man has only the procreative role.

Lowie (1920) has proposed that the nature of work in a society may be a basic determinant of the way the descent system is organized. For example, if a society's major form of subsistence derives from horticulture, which tends to be women's work, the tendency would be for the familial system to show matrilineal descent. He thought this especially likely if tools and land were handed down through the female line. (Again, the Ethnographic Atlas provides corrective information in that a slight majority of the horticultural societies are unilineal but even in horticulture settings the proportion of patrilineal societies is greater than the matrilineal. However, the proportion of matrilineal societies is higher among horticultural societies than among societies with other bases of subsistence.) There is some evidence among contemporary nation-states that where there is a tradition that a young man should follow in his father's occupation, the family of procreation of that young man tends to show more solidarity with his, than with his wife's, parental family. Where no such occupational expectation prevails, in contemporary nations there are reports that the greater solidarity tends to be on the distaff side. (On Finland, see Sweetser, 1966; with respect to Japan, see Koyama, 1965.)

To the foregoing Gough (1961:577) adds that factors favoring a unilineal descent group include scarcity of land and the heritability of valuable immovable property

(buildings, trees, etc.), and a mode of organization whereby the leaders of the descent group control distribution to its members of the fruits of production. Conversely she found that the rise of a market system, access to jobs, and the opportunity to acquire personal property were factors leading to disintegration of the descent group. It is clear, on the other hand, that a market economy does not necessarily toll the knell of a large familial system, since it may provide a ready means for some members to support the family at a distance and also since the family may organize itself as a business (Hammel, 1972; Benedict, 1968). Wealth and the availability of land have been associated with large familial systems in China, Japan, Middle Europe, and North America. (Goody, 1973; Berkner, 1973; Greven, 1970.) Inheritance has been found to be related both to familial organization and lineality in a study of a peasant community: impartible and patrilineal inheritance tends to be associated with patrilocal residence and stem families; patrilineal, partible inheritance tends to be associated with patrilocal residence and joint families; but bilineal inheritance tended to go with nuclear familial systems (Goldschmidt and Kunkel, 1971). The stem family, moreover, has been found by Parish and Schwartz (1972) to be associated with reduced fertility in nineteenth-century France.

A fitting summary of the findings and views in the foregoing literature is reflected in a formulation by Lenski and Lenski to the effect that "subsistence technology is the most powerful single variable influencing the social and cultural characteristics of societies . . . " (1974:110).

THE MODEL

I shall begin the presentation of the explanatory model by talking about the subsistence environment. We think of the subsistence environment as embracing technological, ecological, and economic variables. To us this term refers to the physical environment plus the technology available to exploit it and the mode of social organization employed in its exploitation.

We conceptualize subsistence environment as consisting of four components that influence societies or subsocietal categories largely through the Nimkoff-Middleton factors mentioned above. The four components are:

1. Level of subsistence technology
2. Environmental constraints and potentialities (including the pressure of population on resources)
3. Nature of work and division of labor (both societally and familially, and including unit of labor and mode of compensation)
4. Surplus, capital, and the fruits of production

These four components are represented in boxes A, B, C and D respectively of Figure 7.1. It appears that these four elements comprising subsistence environment may vary greatly in importance from one situation to another. Accordingly, the reliability and abundance of subsistence for any given group may be profoundly influenced by any one or combination of these components.

It may be recalled that Blumberg and I (1972) showed that the probability a society would have a large familial system was a nonmonotonic function of the level of subsistence technology—relatively low at the extreme values of gathering-hunting societies and complex industrial societies but high at the intermediate value of intensive agriculture without irrigation. By reference to Figure 7.1 it can be seen that we do not view the relationship between subsistence technology and familial organization as direct; i.e., there is no 1–9 arrow. Rather, when we consider collectively the four boxes we have labeled subsistence environment, we see that the only arrows from boxes A, B, C, and D to familial organization, box J, come from box C, nature of work and division of labor, and box D, surplus and the social relations of production. Although the literature and our theorizing lead us to the

view that subsistence environment is the major source of general social change and thereby the prime determinant of familial organization, it is also our view that the influence of subsistence environment on the family probably works through a number of aspects of societies which, thereby, become intervening variables.

Probably some reason could be found to draw an arrow in either direction between any pair of boxes in Figure 7.1. The arrows shown represent our view as to the prevailing direction of influence. We have a lively awareness that there may be numerous feedbacks. Where arrows are absent, moreover, it is our view that direct influence between boxes is of lower magnitude than where arrows are present. It should be emphasized that this is a very tentative model and that we hope to improve upon it. The boxes represent ideas that have been developed in the literature and that have been derived from our own research.

In the discussion to follow there will be some explanation of each box and of the arrows issuing from it. Since each arrow represents a bivariate relationship, moreover,

Figure 7.1.   Tentative Model of Determinants of Familial Organization

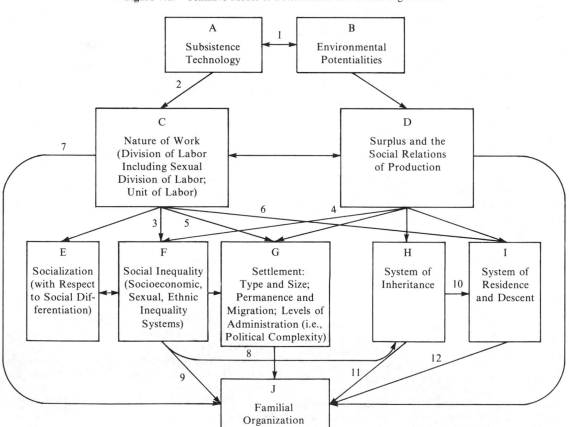

we shall seek in the Ethnographic Atlas for data to check the arrows shown. Table 7.1 shows the boxes of Figure 7.1 and the relevant data available in the Ethnographic Atlas. It can be seen that boxes A, C, F, G, H, I, and J all have indicators, with boxes C, F, G, H, and I having two or more indicators. (See Winch, 1977, for a detailed discussion of these indicators.) On the other hand, boxes B, D, and E have no indicators in the Ethnographic Atlas. We believe that all of the arrows identified in Figure 7.1 are important, but at the present stage of development of the model we have only developed formal statements of the propositions for those arrows that have numbers and can only bring data to bear on those relationships where there are indicators for the relevant variables. It should also be noted that the indicators come in three types of scale (nominal, ordinal, interval), and hence it is not always possible to state the hypotheses in the positive-negative manner appropriate to a bivariate distribution with interval scales.

Subsistence Technology

Modes of subsistence (box A) are affected by the nature of the environment (box B). Desert dwellers do not make their living by fishing. But also the technology can affect the environment, as in the contrast between the lush irrigated fields of Israel and the parched deserts of adjoining countries.

"Environmental potentialities" refers to an environment's resources and the possibility of developing and exploiting these resources—water, mineral, plants, trees, soil, etc. It also refers to population and the pressure exerted by population on resources. The arrow between box A and box B is interactive. This means that the presence of various resources provides a stimulus for the development of means of exploiting them, but also technology can make possible the presence of hitherto unrecognized resources. Thus the presence of water in one part of an area, the remainder of which is arid, may suggest the development of a technology for irrigation. The theoretical proposition that summarizes these ideas can be stated as follows, but we have no data in the Ethnographic Atlas on environmental potentialities and hence are unable to make any empirical demonstration concerning this proposition:

Proposition 1. Modes of subsistence influence and are influenced by the nature of the environment.

Table 7.1. Categories of Analysis Proposed in Figure 7.1 and Relevant Indexes in Ethnographic Atlas

BOX NUMBER IN FIGURE 7.1	DESCRIPTION	INDEX IN ETHNOGRAPHIC ATLAS
A	Mode of subsistence (including technology)	Subsistence technology with following categories: hunting, gathering, herding, fishing, incipient agriculture, extensive agriculture, intensive agriculture, and intensive agriculture with irrigation
B	Environmental potentialities	None
C	Nature of work (including occupational differentiation and unit of labor)	For 11 economic activities (metal working, weaving, leather working, etc.) the EA indicates whether the occupational specialty exists. For each society we have constructed an index of *occupational complexity* by counting the number of "yeses." In addition, indexes of economic activities register gender specializations. From these measures of sexual division of labor we have constructed an index of *gender differentiation*.
D	Surplus and social relations of production	None
E	Socialization with respect to subsistence activities and social differentiation	None
F	Social inequality (socio-economic, sexual, ethnic)	Three indexes register degree of stratification with respect to absence or presence and, if present, degree of development of (a) *caste,* (b) *slavery,* and (c) *social classes.* There is no index for sexual or ethnic *inequality.*
G	Settlement: type and size; permanence and migration; political complexity	One index, (a) *type of settlement,* reflects nomadism-sedentarism and also compactness of settlement. Another, (b) *size of settlement,* shows size and also presence of cities. A third, (c) *political complexity,* shows number of levels of jurisdictional hierarchy beyond the local community.
H	System of inheritance	One index (a) registers mode of *inheritance of real property,* and another (b) *inheritance of movable property.*
I	System of residence and of descent	(a) Index of residence of the *nuptial couple.* Also we have combined indexes of patrilineal, matrilineal, and cognatic kin groups into (b) an index of *descent.*
J	Familial system	(a) The variables involving composition of dwelling units and type of marriage have been developed into an interval scale of *complexity* of *familial structure.* The scale runs from 2 (a mother-child family) to 13 (a joint polygynous family). See Winch, 1977, appendix C.
	(b) Functionality	(b) None
	(c) Influence	(c) None

The arrow from box A to box C implies that the way in which a society derives its major form of subsistence determines the way in which a society will organize its important work. Gathering tends usually to be done by women and does allow women to work while caring for small dependent children. Plow agriculture involves the use of draft animals, and this is usually men's work. Some tasks such as gathering are simple and can be conducted by solitary workers. Other tasks, such as irrigated agriculture, require extensive organization. This general idea can be stated as a theoretical proposition, and then several bodies of data can be identified that partially test it.

Proposition 2. Modes of subsistence influence the nature of work.

We have constructed a scale of subsistence technology that is a composite of two measures of the mode of subsistence: (a) subsistence economy and (b) type and intensity of agriculture. Subsistence economy consists of the following categories: gathering, hunting, fishing, herding, and agriculture. The second component, type and intensity of agriculture, provides a coding scheme that divides agricultural societies into various levels of intensity (shifting, semi-intensive, intensive on permanent fields) and specifies the presence or absence of irrigation. In complex societies we might employ such categories as small entrepreneurs, unskilled day laborers, etc.

As Table 7.1 indicates, the Ethnographic Atlas provides two indicators for box C. The first indicator pertains to the gender-linked division of labor (called here gender differentiation). It provides three categories: one in which males dominate with respect to the major subsistence activity, one in which females dominate, and a third in which the dominance of a gender is not determinable. What might our theory lead us to predict about the correlation between mode of subsistence and gender differentiation? Here it is difficult to distinguish between the intimations our theory might imply and the correlations that are already established in the literature. Gathering and horticulture have been widely reported as wom-

en's work; plow agriculture, herding, and hunting (especially of large game), as men's occupations.

Since we are dealing with one scale that seems clearly nominal—gender differentiation—and one that is ordinal at most—subsistence technology, which we have previously regarded as a measure of societal complexity, it does not seem in order to predict the nature of the relationship between the two indicators with respect to such mathematical function as a positive or negative linear regression, a quadratic function, etc. Rather, it is of interest to see just how the previously reported associations now appear when examined with such a large sample of societies (N = 898).

From Table 7.2 it can be seen that approximately 44 percent of the societies have modes of subsistence in which males are dominant and about 31 percent in which females are dominant (or of those societies in which one gender or the other prevails, about 58 percent show it is the male). It can be seen that there is a discernible correlation between mode of subsistence and the dominance of gender, with females prevailing heavily in gathering and to some extent horticulture societies. On the other hand, hunting, fishing, and herding are heavily masculine activities. With respect to the other categories the issue is less clear-cut. A coefficient of contingency of .58 ($\bar{C}$ = .71) reveals that the association is quite high.[1]

The other indicator for box C consists of a scale indicating the number of occupational specialties in each society. The Ethnographic Atlas provides information on whether any of five modes of subsistence (gathering, hunting, fishing, animal husbandry, agriculture) or six economic activities (metal working, leather working, pottery, weaving, boat building, house construction) are organized as a craft or industrial specialty in each society. Our indicator consists simply of the number of such specialties reported for each society. Inasmuch as number of occupational specialties and subsistence technology can both be regarded as indicators of societal complexity, it may be expected that they will show a positive correlation.

If one were to be statistically brash and treat subsis-

Table 7.2. Percent of Societies Whose Major Form of Subsistence Is Contributed by Males or by Females or Is Not Determinable, by Mode of Subsistence

Gender Differentiation	SUBSISTENCE TECHNOLOGY								
	Gather-ing	Hunt-ing	Fish-ing	Herd-ing	Incipient Agriculture	Extensive Agriculture	Intensive Agriculture	Irrigation Agriculture	Total
Males Dominant	1	100	90	66	20	22	46	56	44
Indeterminate	13	0	9	34	26	35	35	30	25
Females Dominant	86	0	1	0	54	43	19	14	31
Number of Societies	85	82	104	53	81	295	119	79	898

C = .5781; P < .0001
$\bar{C}$ = .7081
G = .0425

Table 7.3. **Percent of Societies Having Specified Number of Ocupational Specialties, by Category of Subsistence Technology**

NUMBER OF OCCUPATIONAL SPECIALTIES	SUBSISTENCE TECHNOLOGY								
	Gathering	*Hunting*	*Fishing*	*Herding*	*Incipient Agriculture*	*Extensive Agriculture*	*Intensive Agriculture*	*Irrigation Agriculture*	*Total*
7 or More							2	1	
6								1	
5						4		6	1
4			3			1	6	4	2
3			5		1	3	11	7	4
2		1	1	9		4	15	18	6
1			10	55	8	48	35	42	29
None	100	99	90	28	91	44	27	21	58
Number of Societies	96	83	115	58	85	308	136	83	964

$\underline{C} = .2946; P < .0001$
$\bar{C} = .3227$
$G = .1216$

tence technology as an interval scale (assigning the values 1, 2, etc., to gathering, hunting, etc.), the result would give $r = .455$ and the linear regression would be $Y = -.462 + .231X$. This gives the nonsensical result that gatherers ($X = 1$) have a degree of occupational specialization of -0.231. Hunters ($X = 2$) would come out with zero occupational specialization. Societies with intensive irrigated agriculture (the highest value on the scale: $X = 7$) would average a level of specialization of 1.15 occupational specialties. It is probably more meaningful to examine the cells of Table 7.3 and to discover that societies whose major modes of subsistence are gathering, hunting, and incipient agriculture tend to have no specialty; pastoral societies and those with extensive agriculture tend to have a single occupational specialty; and the two types of intensive agriculture—with and without irrigation—average two such specialties. The coefficient of contingency of .58 ($\bar{C} = .62$) again indicates that the degree of association is relatively high.

It is our view that nature of work is one of the most critical of the variables intervening between the A and B boxes and familial organization. What we have in mind is a general hypothesis that the nature of work may tend to foster the strength of the family (family enterprise, such as "mom-and-pop" stores) and create a demand for large families (the Rothschilds) or it may seek workers as detached individuals (traveling salesmen) and thereby weaken the organization of the family (for more on this point, see Winch and Kitson, 1977). Unfortunately our indicators for box C do not shed light on the type of relationship being discussed here.

Surplus

Another intervening variable of potentially great significance is represented by box D, surplus and the social relations of production. Among the considerations in-

volved here are the increment of production over what is required for mere subsistence, whether that increment is put into consumers' goods or into capital formation, or what proportion into each, who determines this question, who gets the consumers' goods, who controls the capital, etc. It is our hypothesis that the organization of the family is strengthened to the degree that the family—rather than any other social system or any individual—owns capital and to the degree that the family is the organization through which the fruits of production are distributed. Unfortunately the Ethnographic Atlas contains no indicator relevant to this box. It is our hope in future work to be able to produce an indicator or two for this purpose. For the present, therefore, we are unable to explore empirically the interactive arrow between boxes C and D or the arrows issuing from box D.

Effects of Intervening Variables

Box E, socialization (with respect to social differentiation), includes such ideas as training for occupational specialties, for sex roles, for class ideologies, etc. Again, unfortunately, the Ethnographic Atlas has no relevant indicator, and hence the arrows coming into and out of box E cannot be tested here.

It is our view that both the nature of work and the social relations of production have impact upon and create the system of social inequality within a society. More formally:

Proposition 3. The nature of work in a society influences the nature of the social inequality in that society.

Proposition 4. The surplus and the social relations of production in a society influence the amount of the social inequality in that society.

The data of the Ethnographic Atlas permit us to explore Proposition 3. Social inequality is represented in the

Family and Change

Ethnographic Atlas by indicators of caste, slavery, and social classes. It will be recalled that box C has two indicators, gender differentiation and number of occupations. We are not aware of any line of reasoning that would lead to the prediction of a relationship between gender differentiation and any of the indicators of social inequality (although we might expect some correlation if we had an indicator of gender-linked inequality). On the other hand, we should expect that the greater the number of occupations and hence the more complex the economy (at least among preindustrial societies), the greater would be the social inequality.

As we cross-tabulate gender differentiation with caste, we can see that among those societies in which males are predominant in subsistence as well as those in which dominance is indeterminate, about 17 percent have some form of caste system, whereas among those societies wherein females dominate in the subsistence of activity, only about 6 percent have some form of caste. (See Table 7.4.) The nonsignificant contingency coefficient of .18 ($\bar{C}$ = .22), however, indicates that this relationship is not very strong. With respect to slavery, a roughly similar picture obtains but with an even weaker coefficient. (See Table 7.5.) There is more slavery in male-dominant than in female-dominant societies, and the largest proportion of non-slavery societies is associated with the indeterminate category. The coefficient is even lower than before, .13 ($\bar{C}$ = .16). With respect to social class the picture is again similar—a greater stratification with male dominance and a relatively weak level of association. (See Table 7.6.)

It will be recalled that our second indicator for box C is designated number of occupations. This indicator is cross-tabulated with the indicators for box F, caste, slavery, and social classes. The results show evidence of greater inequality where the number of occupations is relatively high; the C's with caste, slavery, and social classes are .51, .42, and .56 respectively ($\bar{C}$ = .59, .49,

and .62 respectively). Since number of occupations may be construed as an interval scale, there is justification for examining the gamma coefficients between number of occupations and the three measures of social inequality. In the same order as before, they are .46, .44, and .53 respectively. Thus there is substantial evidence of an appreciable correlation, monotonic in nature, between number of occupations and social inequality.

Figure 7.1 shows an arrow from box C to box G. This idea can be explicated in a theoretical proposition as follows:

Proposition 5. The nature of work in a society influences the settlement patterns in that society.

With respect to settlement patterns, the Ethnographic Atlas offers three indicators: type of settlement, which refers to permanence versus nomadism; size of settlement; and political complexity.[2] There are some modes of subsistence and hence types of work that call for mobility of settlement—herding and slash-and-burn agriculture—and others that call for both permanence of settlement and considerable political organization—irrigated agriculture. Our indicators for box C, however, are inadequate for registering the kind of variation just noted. It is not clear that gender differentiation should have any correlation with indicators of settlement; since number of occupations is an indicator of societal complexity, it might be expected to correlate positively with size and permanence of settlement and high level of political complexity.

With gender differentiation as the indicator for box C, the measures of association with indicators of box G are quite low and, indeed, nonsignificant in the case of political complexity. With the number of occupations as the indicator for box C, however, the measures of association are from moderate to impressive and indicate that the relationship is monotonic: C = .43, .62, and .59 for type of settlement, size of settlement, and political complex-

Table 7.4. Percent of Societies Whose Major Subsistence Is Provided by Males, Provided by Females or Is Indeterminate, by Category of Caste

CASTE	GENDER DIFFERENTIATION			
	Males Dominant	*Females Dominant*	*Indeterminate*	*Total*
Absent or Insignificant	82	83	94	86
One or More Despised Occupational Groups	12	12	2	9
Ethnic Stratification	2	2	3	2
Complex Caste Stratification	4	3	1	3
Number of Societies	372	211	270	853

C = .1836: P > .05
$\bar{C}$ = .2250
G = .3113

Table 7.5. **Percent of Societies Whose Major Subsistence Is Provided by Males, Provided by Females or Is Indeterminate, by Category of Slavery**

SLAVERY	GENDER DIFFERENTIATION			
	Males Dominant	*Females Dominant*	*Indeterminate*	*Total*
Absent or Nearly Absent	51	55	53	53
Incipient or Nonhereditary	14	12	15	14
Reported, Type Not Identified	10	17	16	13
Hereditary and Socially	25	16	16	20
Number of Societies	367	200	271	838

C = .1321; .05 > P > .02
C̄ = .1618
G = −.0645

ity, respectively (C=.46, .66, and .66 respectively; G =.43, .67, and .76 respectively).

Next we consider the proposition that relates boxes C and I. It is:

Proposition 6. The nature of work in a society influences the system of residence and descent in that society.

Table 7.1 reveals that the Ethnographic Atlas has two indicators for residence and descent, one pertaining to the location of the residence of the nuptial couple and the other having to do with descent. As before, the correlations of these with gender differentiation are low (C = .27 and .22 respectively; C̄ = .34 and .27), whereas those with number of occupations are higher (C = .42 and .39 respectively; C̄ = .44 and .43 respectively) and tend to support a conclusion of a monotonic relationship.

Our model also contains an arrow leading directly from box C to box J. This theoretical idea is:

Proposition 7. The nature of work in a society influences the familial organization.

Table 7.1 reveals that the indicator for familial organization reflects the number of differentiated positions in the familial structure. The degree of association between gender differentiation and familial structure is not impressive. There appears to be a slight tendency for male dominance in subsistence activities to go with larger-sized familial systems, but a contingency coefficient of .23 (C̄ = .28) is not persuasive. A similarly low degree of association exists between number of occupations and familial structure (C = .29; C̄ = .32), and the evidence is that their relationship is not monotonic (G = .12).

Table 7.6. **Percent of Societies Whose Major Subsistence Is Provided by Males, Provided by Females, or Is Indeterminate, by Category of Social Classes**

SOCIAL CLASSES	GENDER DIFFERENTIATION			
	Males Dominant	*Females Dominant*	*Indeterminate*	*Total*
Absent among Freemen	46	43	57	49
Distinctions Based on Wealth	21	23	16	20
Elite Based on Control of Resources	2	3	2	2
Dual (Hereditary Aristocracy)	19	22	24	21
Complex (Social Classes)	11	9	1	7
Number of Societies	374	210	267	851

C = .1949; P < .0001
C̄ = .2378
G = .1278

Having noted that neither box D nor box E has any indicator, we pass along to box F, social inequality, with its indicators of caste, slavery, and social classes. Our model suggests there is an arrow between boxes F and H, and the theoretical proposition that explicates this relationship is:

Proposition 8. The amount of social inequality in a social influences the system of inheritance.

The Ethnographic Atlas has two indicators of box H, one pertaining to the inheritance of real property and the other to the inheritance of movable property. The correlations between the two indicators of inheritance are very high (C = .88; C̄ = .95; G = .70). With respect to the 5→7 hypothesis, the highest value of C and C̄ pertains to the correlation between slavery and the inheritance of movable property wherein it appears that the categories of "no property rights or inheritance rules" and "equal inheritance to children of both sexes" go with the absence of slavery. (See Table 7.7.)

Another arrow out of box F leads to box J. We have noted Engels's interpretation that industrialization gave rise to both social inequality and small families. It is of some interest, then, to see whether in the absence of industrialization high social inequality is associated with small families. Theoretically, a proposition identifying this relationship is:

Proposition 9. The amount of social inequality influences familial organization, and this is an inverse relationship.

We find that such association as appears in the data goes in the opposite direction. The strongest relationship between any indicator of social inequality and that of familial organization is with slavery (C = .40; C̄ = .47; G = .29). Roughly speaking, there is a tendency for societies having larger familial structures, especially with 10 to 13 differentiated positions in the familial system, to have slavery.

Another idea in the model deals with the relationship between inheritance patterns and patterns of nuptial residence and descent. Where there is inheritance through the male or female line, we might expect that fact to be reflected in patterns of residence and descent. This reasoning provides a basis for asserting that:

Proposition 10. The system of inheritance in a society influences the system of residence and descent in that society.

Both indicators of inheritance (box H) correlate highly with the two indicators of box I. Thus, as can be seen in Table 7.8, patrilineal inheritance goes with patrilocal residence.

The model also shows arrows from boxes H and I to box J, familial organization. We reason that the mode of subsistence and related considerations (boxes A, B, C, and D) will determine what there is to inherit and the most efficient means of transmitting the inheritance. For example, Lowie (1920) has noted that when the soil is tilled with a hoe, it is usually women's work. Consistent with this, he pointed out, was a pattern of inheritance whereby tools were handed down from mother to daugh-

Table 7.7. Percent of Societies by Type of Slavery and by Type of Inheritance of Movable Property

INHERITANCE OF MOVABLE PROPERTY	TYPE OF SLAVERY				
	Absent or Nearly Absent	*Incipient or Nonhereditary*	*Reported, Type Not Identified*	*Hereditary and Socially Significant*	*Total*
No Property Rights or Inheritance Rules	32	10	2	2	16
Matrilineal (Sister's Sons)	2	7	8	9	5
Other Matrilineal Heirs (e.g., Younger Brothers)	2	11	16	11	8
Own Children, Daughters Less	2	2	8	19	7
Own Children, Equally to Both Sexes	17	6	4	8	11
Other Patrilineal Heirs (e.g., Younger Brothers)	4	15	21	10	10
Patrilineal (Sons)	42	49	41	44	43
Number of Societies	348	97	164	177	786

C=.4966; P < .0001
C̄=.5734
G=.1379

Table 7.8.   Percent of Societies by Type of Inheritance of Real Property and by Type of Nuptial Residence

TYPE OF INHERITANCE

	No Property Rights or Inheritance Rules	Matrilineal (Sister's Sons)	Other Matrilineal Heirs	Own Children, Less to Daughters	Own Children, Both Sexes Equally	Other Patrilineal Heirs	Patrilineal Heirs (Sons)	Total
Patrilocal	25	4	15	82	7	91	80	55
Virilocal (without Localized Unilineal Kin Groups)	33	14	14	13	24	6	14	19
Ambilocal, Bilocal, or Utrolocal (Optionally with or near Either set of Parents)	17			3	22	1	2	7
Ambilocal with Option between Patrilocal (or Virilocal) and Avunculocal	3	7	9		24		1	1
Neolocal	3	7	20	3	4		2	4
Matrilocal		18	38			2	1	3
Avunculocal (with or near Maternal Uncle)	1	39						4
Uxorilocal (without Matrilocal or Matrilineal Kin Groups)	19	4			19			6
Ambilocal with Option between Uxorilocal and Avunculocal		7	4					1
Number of Societies	198	28	55	39	54	90	321	785

C = .7151; P < .0001
C̄ = .7724
G = −.5625

173

ter as well as a matrilineal descent system. It would seem that patterns of inheritance can influence patterns of descent and can reinforce patterns of nuptial residence. It is clear that some patterns of inheritance are associated with certain familial patterns, e.g., impartible patrilineal inheritance with the stem family. For a number of other patterns of inheritance, however, the familial patterns are less evident. Accordingly, we feel that there is insufficient theory to make a detailed prediction on the nature of the relationship between boxes H and I on the one hand and box J on the other, but there is sufficient evidence to assert the following proposition:

Proposition 11. The system of residence and descent in a society influences the familial organization in that society.

The indicator for box J, familial structure, correlates more highly with inheritance than with any other indicators (C = .44 and .46 for real and movable property respectively; C = .49 and .50 respectively). In general the larger familial systems go with patrilocal residence, as do patrilineal descent systems. (See Table 7.9.)

MULTIVARIATE ANALYSIS

The model in Figure 7.1 contains 10 boxes. Table 7.1 reveals that we were able to locate in or to create from the codes of the Ethnographic Atlas 14 indicators pertaining to those boxes. Of these we may regard one as a measure of our dependent variable: familial organization. We may think of the other 13 as predictors for independent variables. Then we are left with the question as to what is the most appropriate mode of multivariate analysis for our problem.[3]

Where all indicators are interval scales and where all relationships are linear or at least monotonic, there is a good argument for using regression analysis. In our problem, however, we had already demonstrated that some of our predictors were related monotonically and others nonmonotonically to the dependent variable (Blumberg and Winch, 1972). We had discovered, moreover, that this mixture of relationships also obtained among the set of predictors. Such a state of affairs militated against the use of both regression analysis and path analysis.

In view of the complicated state of affairs resulting from a mixture of nominal, ordinal, and interval scales related to each other in monotonic and nonmonotonic ways, it seemed advisable to make use of a multivariate technique whose assumptions would not be subverted by these complications and whose results would not be rendered correspondingly uninterpretable. Such a technique is the automatic interaction detector (AID) (Sonquist, Baker, and Morgan, 1973).

The AID requires that the dependent variable be in either dichotomized or interval-scale form. The AID program causes the computer to calculate the mean of the dependent variable for each category of each predictor. Within each predictor the computer then arranges the categories in the descending order of means. The next step is that the computer examines the k categories of the first predictor for the purpose of determining between which pair of categories the distribution of that predictor might be dichotomized so as to maximize the ratio of the between sum of squares to the total sum of squares (or the squared correlation ratio). After making the same determination over all predictors, AID locates the cutting point in that predictor which yields the maximum BSS/TSS ratio and at that point breaks the original sample into two subsamples. The computer continues breaking such subsamples down into successively smaller subsamples until certain limiting conditions are reached. At this stage it is possible to review the operation of successive dichotomizations and to determine which predictors have been involved, how much of the original variance of the dependent variable can be accounted for by this procedure, and the proportion of the "explained" variance attributable to each predictor. (For a fuller discussion of the AID, see Winch, 1977, appendix D.)

When we presented the results of such an analysis at an annual meeting of the American Sociological Association, Professor Bernard Farber pointed out that some of the predictors seemed to be part of the familial system, or, in other words, that some of our predictors seemed to be a part of what they were employed to explain. He referred specifically to the indicators in boxes H and I. It was our feeling that Professor Farber's criticism merited serious consideration. Whether he was right or wrong, it did seem reasonable to regard boxes H and I as of a logically posterior order in relation to boxes A–G. Accordingly, it seemed feasible to make use of another feature of the AID: the two-stage analysis. The procedure for this is that the predictors are divided into two groups, one group constituting the predictors for stage 1 and the other for stage 2. The predictors for stage 1 and the dependent variable are run through an AID in the way outlined above. At the conclusion of the analysis each observation is expressed as a deviation in the units of the dependent variable from the mean of its terminal group. These deviations are spoken of as residuals, and they constitute the input for a second analysis in which the predictors of the second stage are employed. We made use of this feature, and Table 7.10 sets forth the results.

There are two features of Table 7.10 that call for explanation: the number of societies and the pair of columns headed N≥15 and N<15 (see Table 7.10). It is a feature of the original AID program that unless each case has a value on each variable, the case is eliminated. Where interval scales are employed, it is customary in such matters to instruct the computer to substitute the mean value for a missing value. In our case, however,

Table 7.9. Percent of Societies by Type of Nuptial Residence and Size of Familial Structure

NUMBER OF POSITIONS IN FAMILIAL STRUCTURE	PATRI-LOCAL	VIRI-LOCAL	AMBI-LOCAL, BILOCAL, OR UTRO-LOCAL	AMBI-LOCAL: PATRI- OR AVUNCU-LOCAL	NEO-LOCAL	MATRI-LOCAL	AVUNCU-LOCAL	UXORI-LOCAL	AMBI-LOCAL: UXORI- OR AVUNCU-LOCAL	TOTAL
2 or 3	18	31	51	9	77	18	29	49	40	28
4 or 5	34	18	12	18	19	12	39	7	40	26
6 or 7	11	23	20		5	22	4	8		14
8 or 9	4	7	10	27		35	4	17		7
10 or 11	16	14	4	27		10	18	10	20	13
12 or 13	18	7	4	18		4	6	8		12
Number of Societies	568	234	81	11	43	51	49	83	5	1125

$C = .4629$; $P < .0001$
$\bar{C} = .5071$
$G = .2009$

many of the scales were nominal. An alternate strategy would have been to create for each variable an additional category of "no information." The consequence, however, would have been a substantial reduction in proportion of explained variance. Accordingly, we followed the original routine. The result was that we lost over 70 percent of our original sample of 1,170 societies. We have analyzed the remaining sample with respect to the criterion of regional distribution and have concluded that the bias from this great loss of cases was not very great (Winch, 1977). There is a bias, of course, favoring well-reported societies.

Since the AID is a search procedure, the logic of tests of significance does not apply. The question of the stability of results is, therefore, a problem that the AID does not illuminate. Because of this state of affairs we sought to get some indication as to which were the more stable results by noting the contributions to explained variance when the resulting subgroups might be small. For this purpose we employed an arbitrary criterion whereby we regarded a dichotomy in which both subgroups contained at least 15 societies as yielding relatively stable results; we reasoned where one or both subgroups resulting from a split contained 14 or fewer societies, the results might well be less statistically stable. This is the basis for the two columns bearing the corresponding headings in Table 7.10.

From Table 7.10 it can be seen that predictors of the first stage explained 37 percent of the variance, with 28 percent coming from "stable" splits and 9 percent from relatively "unstable" splits. It may also be observed that box F contributed the largest proportion of explained variance, with slavery being the single most important predictor. Box G, settlement, is the second most important, with type of settlement its most important contributor.

The second stage contributed a total of 11 percent of the explained variance, with 7 percent coming from "stable" splits and 4 percent from "unstable" ones. Inheritance, box H, seems to have been more important than residence and descent, box I. We may note also that 35 percent of the variance was explained on the basis of "stable" splits in both stages, 13 percent was explained by "unstable" splits, with a total explained variance of slightly over 48 percent.

Early in this chapter we indicated that the major dimensions postulated for the familial systems were structure, function, and influence. Almost all of our subsequent consideration has been devoted to an effort to explain variations in size of familial structure. The reason for our concentration on this one dimension is that it is the most researchable of the three, especially when the research is based upon the secondary analysis of ethnographic data. As indicated in our discussion of the defining criteria of the familial system, however, we do regard function to be as important as structure. It is our plan, moreover, to

Table 7.10. "Explained" Variance of Familial Structure, Scaled Intervally, by Concepts Shown in Figure 7.1 and Indicators from Table 7.1; Based on Two-Stage Analysis by Means of AID, by Size of Smaller Group Resulting from Split

BOX CONCEPT AND INDICATOR	N ≥ 15	N < 15	TOTAL
First Stage			
A Mode of Subsistence	.0347		.0347
Subsistence technology	(.0347)		(.0347)
C Nature of Work	.0427	.0172	.0599
Number of occupations	(.0135)	(.0172)	(.0307)
Gender differentiation	(.0292)		(.0292)
F Social Inequality	.1386	.0192	.1578
Caste		(.0192)	(.0192)
Slavery	(.1180)		(.1180)
Social classes	(.0206)		(.0206)
G Settlement	.0680	.0512	.1192
Type	(.0560)		(.0560)
Size	(.0120)	(.0130)	(.0250)
Political complexity		(.0382)	(.0382)
Totals for First Stage	.2840	.0876	.3716
Second Stage			
H Inheritance	.0372	.0374	.0746
Real property	(.0372)		(.0372)
Movable property		(.0374)	(.0374)
I Residence and Descent	.0322	.0070	.0392
Mode of marriage	(.0089)	(.0070)	(.0159)
Nuptial residence	(.0233)		(.0233)
Descent			
Totals for Second Stage	.0694	.0444	.1138
Totals for Both Stages	.3534	.1320	.4854

construct some codes of ethnographic data with the objective of making familial function a dependent variable for subsequent multivariate analysis. As of now, unfortunately, we are unable to make any report upon this line of our work.

When I talked about influence, I said that in my view this aspect of the total enterprise lay in the realm of social psychology rather than in the sociology of the family. However, because the theory presented above has micro- as well as macrosociological implications for examining the structure and functioning of the family, I shall indicate the direction the social psychological theorizing takes but not go into it in great detail (see Winch, 1977, for a fuller discussion).

From the standpoint of a neophyte the positions of any social system may be regarded as occupied by models. In no social system is this more evident than in the family wherein the neophytes—offspring—look upon their elders as persons of knowledge and skill and models whose behavior is to be simulated.

Although, as the conflict sociologists correctly observe, not all members of every social system reap rewards from the way in which the system functions, still it makes good theoretical sense to argue that many are rewarded. Such a belief is a premise in the social psychology of groups of Thibaut and Kelley (1959), and this is a premise to which I subscribe. Participation in or withdrawal from a social system—such as the family—is based on the rewards derived from or anticipated in the system and an evaluation of the rewards available in alternative social systems. Where families are large and multi-functional or their resources are otherwise seen to be rewarding for the participant, the influence of the family is likely to be great. In such a situation, members are induced to remain in and work for the familial system. An implication of this premise is that the particular rewards that a system generates and the particular individuals whom it rewards and what those rewards may be are all empirical problems. By bringing together the concept of model with that of reward one can see how the social system that generates both of these can be postulated as being in a position of potential influence. (See Figure 7.2.)

In a published study we have concluded that a familial system with more rather than fewer appropriate models influences its members more, and one with greater rather than fewer resources influences its members more. Thus we have argued theoretically and demonstrated empirically that influence is a result of structure and function, although the nature of our demonstration certainly does not exclude the possibility that there are other sources of influence as well (Winch and Gordon, 1974).[4]

CONCLUSION

We have seen that a number of writers have asserted the existence of relationships between variables of familial organization and variables pertaining to properties of other aspects of societal systems, especially those pertaining to the economy and the division of labor. Our quantitative analysis has produced evidence supporting the conclusion that there is a tendency for familial organization (indicated by complexity of family structure) to vary with these other societal variables. Our analysis has not enabled us to make any assertion about cause and effect. Our data are cross-sectional, and hence do not permit inferences as to the direction of the flow of causation. In phrasing our theory, however, we have betrayed a disposition to place causal primacy in the materialist-ecological cluster of considerations and to interpret the familial system as more epiphenomenal than otherwise. Goode appears to believe that, at times at least, the opposite is true (1963). In his analysis of the data on India, for example, he concludes that changes in the family were occurring before industrialization took place. What brought the changes in the familial system? His answer seems to be "ideology." But what can this mean? That the ideas were brought in by the British and adopted by the Indians? Such an argument does not sound greatly persuasive. In a panel study that is longitudinal but of rather

Figure 7.2.   Identification (Influence) Stated as an Outcome of Structure and Function

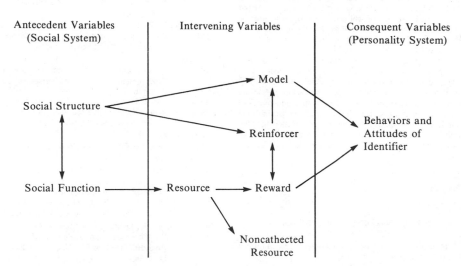

NOTE: Three previous versions of this paradigm have been published, the first being in Winch (1962:147). The present version differs from that in the addition of the reinforcer. The second version appeared in Winch (1970:581). Unfortunately that figure as well as the text generally contained errors, and that presentation should be regarded only as containing a rough statement of the author's intention. The third was in Winch and Gordon (1974:26).

short duration Morgan and associates (1974) conclude that the family is an adaptive system. Ethnographic evidence seems to lead to somewhat the same conclusion (Stack, 1974). Tentatively, then, this is where the present author believes the data are pointing.

Finally we have theorized that Figure 7.1 implies Figure 7.2, i.e., that variation in the influence of the family can be at least partially explained by variation in its structure and functioning.

NOTES

1. As is widely known, the coefficient of contingency has the property that its maximum value varies with the number of rows and columns in a table of contingency. For a 2 x 2 table the upper limit is not 1.0, but .707; for a 5 x 5 table the upper limit is .894. To render the coefficients of contingency comparable without regard to size or shape of the table of contingency, we follow Cramer (1946:282) and norm each coefficient by multiplying it by $°k/k–1$ where k is the number of rows or columns, whichever is smaller. C denotes the original contingency coefficient; C̃ is the corresponding normed value.

2. It should be noted that the reason for combining, under the rubric of settlement, the political dimension with two ecological indicators of habitat stems from the nature of the codes developed by Murdock in the Ethnographic Atlas. There, political complexity is measured from the standpoint of the local community, utilizing as the indicator number of jurisdictional levels beyond the local settlement. Analytically and conceptually we recognize that the political dimension's antecedents and consequences are not isomorphic with those of the two habitat components of box G. But because of Murdock's way of measuring the political dimension in the Ethnographic Atlas and to minimize the number of boxes in an already overcomplex figure, we have lumped the political and size-sedentarism indicators under a single box number.

3. After developing Table 7.1 but before running the multivariate analysis being explained above, we concluded that there was another code in the Ethnographic Atlas that was relevant to our model. This pertains to mode of marriage, the categories of which refer to payment, gift, or exchange made at the time of a marriage contract. This seemed relevant to box I. With the inclusion of mode of marriage we increased the number of predictors from 13 to 14.

4. This line of theorizing also raises a question as to the wisdom and morality of such measures as some municipalities in our country have enacted of holding parents responsible for acts of vandalism committed by their offspring. It makes sense to hold parents responsible only to the extent that they have the means to exert influence over their offspring. The results of this analysis suggest that the degree to which parents have the means to exert influence covaries with the structure and functioning of the family. Not nearly enough is known to resolve this issue, but we believe we now see how to go about trying to get some answers.

REFERENCES

BACHOFEN, J. J.
1861 *Das Mutterrecht*. Stuttgart: Krais and Hoffman.

BENEDICT, B.
1968 "Family firms and economic development." *Southwestern Journal of Anthropology* 24:1–19.

BERKNER, L. K.
1973 "Recent research on the history of the family in Western Europe." *Journal of Marriage and the Family* 35:395–405.

BLUMBERG, R. L. AND R. F. WINCH
1972 "Societal complexity and familial complexity: Evidence for the curvilinear hypothesis." *American Journal of Sociology* 77:898–920; see also 78:1522.

CRAMER, H.
1946 *Mathematical Methods of Statistics*. Princeton, N.J.: Princeton University.

ENGELS, F.
1972 *The Origin of the Family; Private Property and the State:*
(1884) *In the Light of the Researches of Lewis H. Morgan.* Introduction and Notes by E. B. Leacock. New York: International.

FORDE, D.
1947 "The anthropological approach in social science." *The Advancement of Science* 4:213–24.

FORTES, M.
1953 "The structure of unilineal descent groups." *American Anthropologist* 55:17–41.

GOLDSCHMIDT, W. AND E. J. KUNKEL
1971 "The structure of the peasant family." *American Anthropologist* 73:1058–76.

GOODE, W. J.
1963 *World Revolution and Family Patterns*. New York: Free Press.

GOODY, J.
1973 "Strategies of heirship." *Comparative Studies in Society and History* 15:3–20.

GOUGH, E. K.
1961 "Variation in residence." In D. M. Schneider and E. K. Gough (eds.), *Matrilineal Kinship*. Berkeley, Calif.: University of California.

1971 "The origin of the family." *Journal of Marriage and the Family* 33:760–71.

GREVEN, P. J., JR.
1970 *Four Generations: Population, Land, and Family in Colonial Andover, Massachusetts*. Ithaca, N.Y.: Cornell University Press.

HAMMELL, E. A.
1972 "The zadruga as process." In P. Laslett (ed.), *Household and Family in Past Time*. Cambridge: At the University Press.

HOBHOUSE, L. T., G. C. WHEELER, AND M. GINSBERG
1915 *The Material Culture and Social Institutions of the Simpler Peoples*. London: Chapman and Hall.

KOYAMA, T.
1965 "A rural-urban comparison of kinship relations in Japan." Paper presented at the Ninth International Seminar on Family Research, Tokyo.

LENSKI, G. AND J. LENSKI
1974 *Human Societies: An Introduction to Macrosociology*, second ed. New York: McGraw-Hill.

LOWIE, R. H.
1920 *Primitive Society*. New York: Boni and Liveright.

MILLAR, J.
1771 *The Origin of the Distinction of Ranks*. London: John Murray. The third edition (1779) is reprinted in W. G. Lehman, *John Millar of Glasgow, 1735–1801: His Life and Thought and His Contributions to Sociological Analysis*. Cambridge: At the University Press, 1960, pp. 165–322.

MORGAN, J. N., K. DICKINSON, J. BENUS, AND G. DUNCAN
1974 *Five Thousand Families: Patterns of Economic Progress*. An Analysis of the First Five Years of the Panel Study of Income Dynamics, vol. 1. Ann Arbor, Mich.: Institute for Social Research.

MURDOCK, G. P.
1949 *Social Structure*. New York: Macmillan.
1957 "World ethnographic sample." *American Anthropologist* 59: 664–87.

1967 "Ethnographic atlas: A summary." *Ethnology* 6:109–236.

NIEBOER, H. J.
1900 *Slavery as an Industrial System: Ethnological Researcher.* The Hague: Nijhoff.

NIMKOFF, M. F. AND R. MIDDLETON
1960 "Types of family and types of economy." *American Journal of Sociology* 66:215–25.

OSMOND, M. W.
1969 "A cross-cultural analysis of family organization." *Journal of Marriage and the Family* 31:302–10.

PARISH, W. L., JR., AND M. SCHWARTZ
1972 "Household complexity in nineteenth century France." *American Sociological Review* 37:154–173.

SCHNEIDER, D. M.
1961 "Introduction: The distinctive features of matrilineal descent groups." In D. M. Schneider and E. K. Gough (eds.), *Matrilineal Kinship.* Berkeley, Calif.: University of California.

SONQUIST, J. A., E. L. BAKER, AND J. N. MORGAN
1973 *Searching for Structure: An Approach to Analysis of Substantial Bodies of Micro-Data and Documentation for a Computer Program* (revised edition). Ann Arbor, Mich.: Institute for Social Research.

STACK, C. B.
1974 *All Our Kin: Strategies for Survival in a Black Community.* New York: Harper and Row.

STEINMETZ, S. R.
1930 *Classification des Types Sociaux et Catalogue des Peuples: Gesammelte kleinere Schriften zur Ethnologie und Soziologie,* vol 2. Groningen: P. Noordhoff.

STEWARD, J. H.
1936 "The economic and social basis of primitive bands." In R. H. Lowie (ed.), *Essays in Anthropology: Presented to A. L. Kroeber.* Berkeley, Calif.: University of California.

SWEETSER, D. A.
1966 "The effect of industrialization on intergenerational solidarity." *Rural Sociology* 31:156–70.

THIBAUT, J. W. AND H. H. KELLEY
1959 *The Social Psychology of Groups.* New York: Wiley.

WESTERMARCK, E. A.
1891 *The History of Human Marriage.* London: Macmillan.

WINCH, R. F.
1962 *Identification and Its Familial Determinants.* Indianapolis: Bobbs-Merrill.
1970 "Determinants of interpersonal influence in the late adolescent male: Theory and design of research." In R. Hill and R. König·(eds.), *Families in East and West: Socialization Process and Kinship Ties.* Paris: Mouton.
1971 *The Modern Family,* third ed. New York: Holt, Rinehart and Winston.

WINCH, R. F., AND R. L. BLUMBERG
1968 "Societal complexity and familial organization." In R. F. Winch and L. W. Goodman (eds.), *Selected Studies in Marriage and the Family,* third ed. New York: Holt, Rinehart and Winston.

WINCH, R. F. AND M. T. GORDON
1974 *Familial Structure and Function as Influence.* Lexington, Mass.: Lexington Books.

WINCH, R. F. AND S. A. GREER
1968 "Urbanism, ethnicity, and extended familism." *Journal of Marriage and the Family* 30:40–45.

WINCH, R. F., S. GREER, AND R. L. BLUMBERG
1967 "Ethnicity and extended familism in an upper-middle-class suburb." *American Sociological Review* 32:265–272.

WINCH, R. F. AND G. C. KITSON
1977 "Types of American families: An unsatisfactory classification." In R. F. Winch with the collaboration of R. L. Blumberg, M.-P. García, M. T. Gordon, and G. C. Kitson, *Familial Organization: A Quest for Determinants.* New York: Free Press.

8

FAMILY AND FERTILITY: THE EFFECTS OF HETEROGENEOUS EXPERIENCE

Betty E. Cogswell and Marvin B. Sussman

INTRODUCTION

Over the past two decades, concern about the world's population explosion has been an impetus for a plethora of studies on fertility. Despite a sizable body of work, one is severely limited in utilizing existing knowledge in constructing family theories of fertility. Only a small portion of fertility studies are formulated within family theory, measure family properties, or designate family as the unit of analysis. Sociologists certainly have joined the ranks of fertility investigators as have demographers, biostatisticians, epidemiologists, economists, psychologists, political scientists, and anthropologists; but only a small proportion of this cadre of investigators study families. Within family sociology, fertility is only one of many important concerns and tends to be peripheral or at best a secondary concern of most investigators. To date, family studies of fertility are neither sufficient in number to develop inductively a general family theory nor sufficient in number to have heuristic impact on deductive studies. In addition, fertility studies in most instances have been atheoretical. Discrete findings are presented with little theoretical consolidation of these bits of information.

Both the increase in the number of fertility studies and their atheoretical nature are well summarized by Hill (1968) and by Freedman (1962, 1975). In 1968 Hill classified 494 items in an international bibliography comprising work published between 1955 and 1968. In introducing the bibliography, Hill (1968) observes that the trend in the quantity of publications is upward. From 1962 to 1968 there were 125 percent more publications than in the previous seven years. Hill reports:

> The period 1962–68 sees a markedly higher development in field experiments, studies of incentives, and evaluative-type researches, as well as a much greater concern with methodological issues of measurement and model building. There are, moreover, many more publications devoted to inventory and codification and to the identification of new research needed [1968:974].

These early publications made only minor contributions to the development of a theory of fertility.

In 1961, Freedman prepared an annotated bibliography on fertility which included 636 items. In 1975, he completed a book which contained a total of 2,087 references published between 1961 and 1972. By 1975 Freedman found a substantial body of work on fertility and an even greater need for theoretical development:

> As a result of the new research, we know more in the absolute sense relative to our improved perception of the total system to be investigated. The reproductive processes and the social causes and consequences are more complicated than we had imagined. Detailed empirical work has made increasingly suspect some of the historical generalizations of an earlier day. Simplistic statements of the modern "demographic transition" for Europe simply do not fit the emerging body of historical data. The diversity of the historical record may require several different theories for different circumstances or a revised general theory quite different from that which has been accepted for many years.
>
> The trend in fertility research has been to break apart relationships and analyze the component elements in the complex fertility model. While such analysis is undoubtedly useful, because it has produced new and more precise measurements of analytical relationships, we still do not have working models that enable us to put the specific elements back together in such a way as to reconstruct the dynamics of population as a whole [1975:1–2].

NOTE: Work on this paper was supported in part by Grand AID/csd–3325, 73–10, from the Agency for International Development. The authors wish to express their appreciation to Kristin Loken, Brooke McCauley, Glenn Knight, Dona Davis, George Hong, Merida Mercado, Linda Redman, Ann Tickamyer, Martha Daniel, Stella Schwartz, Rosemarie Hester, and Sharon Pigott for their assistance in the preparation of this chapter.

A further problem in using the available body of research to develop family theory is that most reports are based on aggregate data with very little information on the interrelationships of variables and on social interaction within family groups. One, however, would expect a family theory of fertility to deal with interrelationships of family rather than individual characteristics and properties, and deal as well with social interactions and processes that occur within families. Perhaps this high proportion of aggregate data studies has been a matter of expediency which stemmed from public and national concern over the problem of population growth.

Population growth and control are matters of public policy, related to the economic growth, social development, and survival of nations. Government officials, therefore, are constantly seeking data to formulate and to support their policies. The collection of vital statistics has been a basic first step, and analysis of these data has traditionally been the job of the demographer. Census bureaus and demographic units related to planning and health ministries in nations throughout the world are one of the basic organizational structures for fertility research. In addition, many investigators based in universities have been encouraged to engage in demographic studies through the lure of government funding. Thus aggregate data on individuals and households constitute the vast majority of our current information on fertility.

Although tremendous difficulties have been encountered in obtaining valid census and vital registration data—particularly in developing countries—these data have been relatively easy to obtain compared to data describing and measuring decisions within families to have children or the consequences of having children for families. As a result, the fertility research market has been captured initially by those who do aggregate data analysis, whether they are demographers, sociologists, economists, statisticians, or epidemiologists.

Knowledge, attitude, and practice (KAP) studies have been undertaken in most developing countries experiencing high fertility. Even though these studies deal with social psychological variables, they are still cast within an aggregate data framework producing descriptions of patterns for large populations of individuals—such as the number of children desired or contracepting behavior. Variations in these patterns among families and the reasons these patterns occur cannot be fully explained by these data.

With the exception of some macro studies on *family as an institution,* most family investigators are concerned with micro levels of analysis using concepts such as family structure, interactions, and roles to explain phenomena such as mate selection, decision making, power, socialization of children, and changes in the life cycle. Unfortunately, family group phenomena are difficult to infer from individual and household aggregate data.[1] In addition, aggregate data give us little insight into

processes occurring within families. For example, from one of the earliest studies on family and fertility, it is concluded that increased communication between husband and wife is related to the use of contraception and, subsequently, to lower fertility (Hill et al., 1959). But we know little about the qualitative nature of this relationship and the family process of deciding to use contraceptives. In order to document processes, longitudinal rather than cross-sectional data are necessary.

Data collected from individuals also tend to exclude information on family group influence on fertility behavior. Such data usually focus on individual properties such as attitudes, education, or size of family of origin, rather than on family group properties, such as degree of extendedness, permeability or impermeability of family boundaries, or group aspirations. Thus in addition, our building blocks for development of theories of family and fertility are hampered by the small number of studies which deal with group rather than individual properties. A further problem is that theoretical formulations concerned with the entire family group or system are only beginning to emerge (Cogswell, 1976; Hill, 1974; Sussman, 1968).

As family sociologists, we certainly believe that family theory can make a major contribution to the study of fertility behavior; but if explanation and prediction are the goals, we must also recognize that other disciplines have much to contribute. From our perspective, fertility decisions—or often more accurately, fertility nondecisions[2] —occur within the family group. Families, however, live within larger social contexts which greatly influence their daily lives. Thus family theory cannot be developed in isolation, but must take into account phenomena of larger social contexts which influence the phenomena of family life.

In this chapter we posit that low fertility is associated with populations who plan and are more purposive about the course of their lives. Further, we posit that fertility planners have had greater heterogeneous life experiences than nonplanners. Families who live within isolated socially homogeneous groups, with the exception of nomads, tend to have the highest fertility rates and the largest completed family sizes. Families who have socially diverse contacts and experiences tend to have lower fertility rates and smaller completed family sizes.

To facilitate explanation of the influence of the heterogeneous-homogeneous continuum on fertility, a heuristic model is suggested. Variables differing in level of abstraction and universality in relation to fertility are presented, but not all possible variables are included. Those which have been used in research or are the consequences of research and which demonstrate high association or possible cause in fertility decisions and outcomes are included. As with all working models, repeated research using proposed variables will establish those which have the most explanatory power and which can be used in establishing theories of family and fertility.

A HEURISTIC MODEL OF FERTILITY

The model consists of *societal* characteristics specified as contexts and variables; *family* characteristics categorized as contexts, variables, and interpersonal processes; *fertility outcomes* consisting of societal and familial; *intermediate* variables consisting of the Davis and Blake (1956) model of factors affecting intercourse, conception, and gestation; *unanticipated events;* and a *heterogeneity-homogeneity* continuum introduced as an organizing and bridging concept.

Society

Social context refers to all types of social grouping within which families and individuals live and associate with others. Some social contexts are territorial with identifiable geographic boundaries within which families reside. These territories may range in size from continents to nations to cities to villages or neighborhoods. Territories such as nations, states, and cities influence the lives of families through legal and governmental systems. Others such as continents exert influence through their peoples' identification as members of a group such as Africans or Latin Americans. Neighborhoods, although less precisely geographically bounded, influence residents through association with each other and group identity.

The second major type of social context is associational and includes formal and informal organizations, social networks, and primary groups. Boundaries of these social contexts are defined by membership and association and are often unrelated to families' place of residence. Formal organizations such as schools, churches, corporations, and political parties are legitimized by legal charter and are often highly bureaucratic. Informal organizations such as voluntary associations, some clubs, and some political pressure groups and large extended kin groups such as *beraderis*[3] in Pakistan are identified by member participation in the group activities and tend to be more informally and less bureaucratically structured. Social networks are based on serial contact among individual members rather than group phenomenon. Members of a network may never come together as a group but members tend to have some common characteristics or interests and tend to know about each other through relayed information. Primary groups are defined as those that have frequent face-to-face contact and are comprised of a small number of members such as cliques, gangs, and informal clubs. Families are primary groups and serve as important social contexts for their members, but in this paper are treated separately for emphasis.

Figure 8.1.   A Heuristic Model of Fertility

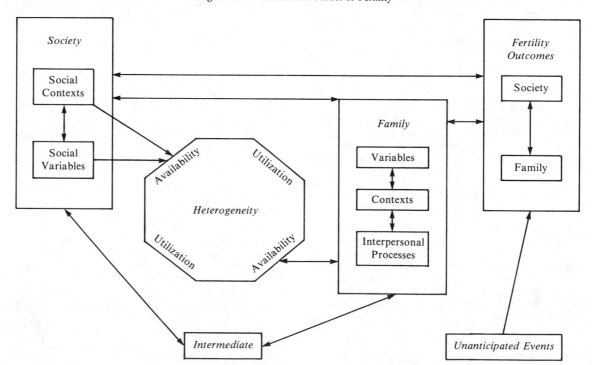

Individuals and families are situated within a social context either by ascribed characteristics that are consequences of birth into a particular family, class, caste, ethnic group, or culture, or by voluntary or involuntary participation with contextually defined groups. Both territorial and associational social contexts influence and set limits upon family behavior and thereby affect fertility outcome.

Social variables are aggregate descriptions of states of being, conditions or properties of families, and may be organized as categorical or continuous variables or attributes (Burr, 1973). Our use of these variables is twofold. First, each variable provides at some level of abstraction and generalization an explanation of the relationship between a given societal parameter and fertility outcomes. Second, each of these social variables separately or in different combinations determines placement in or accessibility to social contexts. Social variables also influence the degree and level of heterogeneous exposure and experience of individuals and the forms and interactions of family systems. Since these social variables define appropriate fertility options, they establish constraints as well as supports for family behavior.

These variables may be dichotomous attributes that are a characteristic which is either present or absent, such as certain laws, policies, or programs in a society. They may be categorical, such as religion, caste, and ethnic group; or they may be continuous variables, such as percent female labor force participation, degree of level of modernity and education, and rates of mortality or fertility.

Family

Family characteristics are conditions, properties, and processes of family units. We have selected variables which appear to be most significantly related to levels of fertility, family size, family planning, child spacing, and contraceptive practice. Also, we have deliberately left the definition of "family" to the reader. For example, the family may be perceived as a legal family, created by the act of marriage, sanctioned by the community and the state. It may be an "everyday family" with members who are legally related by blood or marriage but including others who are not but are considered by its members as such, or it may be a union without legal marriage.

Family variables, contexts, and interpersonal processes are the three subelements of family characteristics in this model. Variables include the socioeconomic status of the family; stage in the life cycle; value orientations; social competence; and norms. Contexts are numbers and types of families in boundaried social and physical space; variations in these contexts have been described as varied family forms (Sussman; 1971). "Interpersonal processes" refers to the kind and quality of interaction of family members, particularly that of the marital dyad; the

division of labor in regard to household tasks and parenting; marital communication, its extensity and quality; and the decision-making process, especially when it involves issues of the family's life style and lifeways. Family size is one such issue.

Fertility Outcomes

Outcome variables are of two types, societal and familial. "Societal" refers to the level of fertility in a society in general or in different subgroups within a particular society. "Familial" outcomes refer to desired and completed family size, child spacing, use and success of family planning and contraception practices. These last-mentioned factors, which are determinants of fertility levels in a society, are properties largely of family systems.

Intermediate

Variables identified as being interstitial between societal and family variables, and fertility outcomes, were labeled "intermediate" by Davis and Blake (1956) and used by Freedman (1975) in developing a model for the sociological analysis of fertility. These intermediate variables include factors affecting exposure to intercourse and conception and those influencing gestation and successful parturition (Freedman, 1975: 13–44). All societies establish norms on permissible sexual behavior and intercourse and exert some control over the use or nonuse of contraceptives by monitoring the dissemination and utilization of contraceptive knowledge and devices. Societies also differ in fetal mortality—often the consequence of health standards and medical care—with subsequent effect on gestation and successful parturition.

Societal and familial social contexts and variables "regulate" the intermediate variables of intercourse, conception, gestation, and parturition, which in turn influence fertility behavior. A society will establish norms for age and circumstance for entry into sexual unions. Some societies provide for permanent or quasi-permanent celibacy for men and women. Families also may provide incentives or disincentives by withholding or granting approval, resources, and status for individual members to enter into a sexual union.

Fecundity, the capacity for bearing children, is affected by both voluntary and involuntary causes. Nonfecundity may be a consequence of sterilization, medical treatment, disease, or other intervening processes. The level of fecundity, as well as the usage or nonusage of contraceptives and the level of fetal mortality, either voluntary or nonvoluntary, influences the level of fertility.

The family, because of its genetic and biological history, its value systems, and its influence over members via the socialization process, defines the conditions for intercourse and conception practices, and has a very specific influence upon gestation and successful parturition. This occurs within a larger framework of constraints or supports provided by the social contexts within which individuals interact. To a large extent, the family *mediates* territorial and associational normative demands and pressures regarding the reproductive process and *determines* what is appropriate participation in this process by its individual members.

Unanticipated (Cataclysmic) Variables

Social stability or rates of change are sometimes beyond a society's control. This may not be completely accurate, since any society may be able to prevent war or a revolution and can even prevent some epidemics, given appropriate interventions. Societies, however, are not able to control natural disasters, such as earthquakes or tidal waves. These infrequent cataclysmic events can radically alter societal and family contexts and change fertility practices of a society over a short period of time. A war or repeated wars may "control" fertility in the short run. But in some instances there may be a baby boom such as occurred in the United States in the post-World War II period, one which lasted almost 15 years (Masnick and McFalls, 1976).

Heterogeneity-Homogeneity

The concept of heterogeneity-homogeneity is formulated as a continuum, and is congruous with analysis of family properties and processes, of larger social contexts, and of societal correlates of fertility.

In this chapter we are using heterogeneity to refer to diversity, variation, and multiformity of social systems and social phenomena.

Family

At the individual or family level, heterogeneity refers to exposure to and experience with people, ideas, knowledge, organizational systems, cultures, values, and life styles which are different from those experienced in the past. These new experiences often provide options for new and different ways of viewing and living one's own life. Heterogeneous exposure is a bombardment of varied messages and situations which catalyze individuals and families to take stock of their usual patterns of response and behavior. Such exposures present new ways of performing current life tasks, and suggest taking on new or additional roles, activities, and behavior. Heterogeneous experience may or may not follow exposure. If a behavioral option is available and the individual or family is favorably impressed by the experience, it may be selected for pursuit. At the family level of analysis, these differences among and between people are directly observable in social interaction.

The exact nature of the influence of heterogeneity on behavior change and lower fertility is a matter for empirical investigation. Currently we do not know the degree of influence different types of heterogeneous experiences exert on behavior, nor do we know the optimal timing of these experiences in the life course of individuals and families in order to effect behavioral change. Further study is also necessary to determine the differential impact of similar experiences on individuals and groups who differ in their social and cultural characteristics. Some events which we hypothesize to have great potential to promote behavioral change include contact with people who differ from oneself as to religion, ethnicity, education, social class, modernization, and family type.

Social Contexts

At the analytic level of social contexts, heterogeneity is exposure and experience in formal and informal, territorial and associational organizations. The actual form the exposure and experience take is related to the characteristics of the social context. For large social contexts such as nations or regions, descriptions of heterogeneous exposure and experience tend to be global and are based on assumptions of imputed rather than measured behaviors. In smaller social contexts, such as neighborhoods, villages, schools, factories, churches, and social networks, the degree of heterogeneity-homogeneity could be directly observed and measured.

Opportunities for degrees of heterogeneous exposure and experience in different social contexts are dependent on both the diversity of characteristics of individuals and families comprising each context and the degree of permeability of the boundaries enclosing each context. The types and numbers of social contexts available may be viewed as the potential each family has for heterogeneity. Those contexts in which families participate are a measure of their heterogeneous experience. Obviously a social context as vast as a nation, region, or city has far too many smaller contexts within its boundaries for any individual or family to participate in more than a very small portion. Identification of the number and types of contexts, however, is useful in delineating potentials for family choice.

Social Variables

In interpreting statistical interaction, the varying degrees of heterogeneity associated with different correlates of fertility must be inferred from aggregate data. The unit of study may be a nation, a group of nations, or particular strata, groups, or social categories within a specified geographic area. From most of the familiar correlates of fertility (female labor force participation, level of literacy and education, percent urban population, level of modernization, degree of social mobility, frequency of rural-urban migration, legal systems which do not preclude minority participation in society) one can infer that heterogeneous exposure has occurred among those families where these social variables are manifest as family properties.

It appears that families experiencing heterogeneous contact are more worldly and seem to make more rational choices, one being the decision to control their fertility. Having heterogeneous contacts provides the means for obtaining perspectives which include greater reliance upon self-decisions than upon traditional group norms. Families in heterogeneous social groups or networks have the opportunity to evaluate alternatives and options available within the overall framework of societal constraints imposed by legal systems and cultural values and norms. The notion is that these families have greater awareness and freedom of choice than those who live in more isolated or homogeneous contexts.

In summary, phenomena and analytic concepts at all levels of analysis can be scrutinized for the degree of heterogeneous exposure of the individuals and families being studied and for the number and type of heterogeneous settings which are potentially available to individuals and families. In discussing the degree of heterogeneity, it is illogical and unrealistic to talk about a continuum from 100 percent homogeneity to 100 percent heterogeneity. No completely heterogeneous or homogeneous social phenomenon or context exists. Furthermore, we anticipate that there is a minimum threshold of heterogeneity necessary to change behavior, and also a point on the continuum beyond which increased heterogeneity has no further effect on planning behavior. At an even higher level, heterogeneity may constitute an overload of experience with which families and individuals are unable to cope.

Illustration of the Heuristic Model

To illustrate how the model operates, let us use *level of modernity*. Modernity can be scaled—however imperfectly—and therefore is considered to be a continuous societal variable. Although there are multiple operational definitions of modernity in the literature, for the sake of simplicity, we will define the level of modernity as the degree of complexity in social organizations and

Figure 8.2. Heterogeneity and Fertility

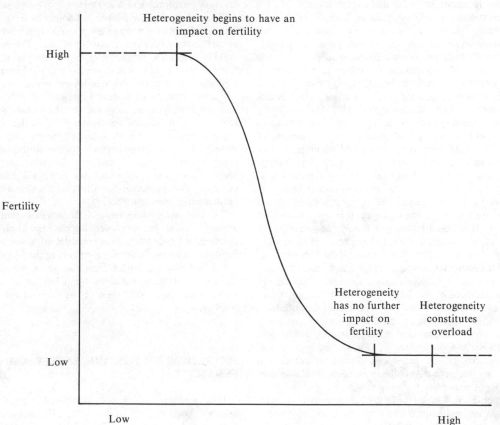

occupational specialization found in a particular society. Modernity is characterized by highly differentiated structures and functions found largely in mass societies, in which urbanization is extensive and bueaucratization relatively high. Bureaucracies provide the formal social contexts for individuals. A high level of modernity is indicated also by a large variety of occupations with needs for skilled workers to fill critical jobs. Such needs may force abandonment of the traditional pattern of allocating work. More and more socially disadvantaged persons, such as women, may be educated and placed in competitive jobs.

Determinants or correlates of modernity are social variables such as labor force participation (LFP), mortality rates, economic status, and national growth aspirations. Also, level of modernity is a variable which can be correlated with increase in number and variety of social contexts. Participation in varieties of social contexts by increasing number of people in a society suggests the reciprocal influence between social contexts and social variables. The number of occupations and organizations created to employ such a diffentiated working population in turn provides varied and increased opportunities for heterogeneous exposure and experience.

Opportunities for heterogeneous interaction are not universally shared by a society's populace, since modernity levels vary among subgroups in the population. A high standard of living based on adequate income and use of health, educational and other social contexts is not uniformly available to or enjoyed by minorities, or socially disadvantaged subgroups. The indication is that social and economic circumstances vis-à-vis the family level of modernity prior to the beginning of the reproductive period have a powerful influence on the outcome of the childbearing process (Masnick and McFalls, 1976). This is expressed in the model as the reciprocal linkage among intermediate and societal and familial parameters.

Differentiation of societal institutions and organizations is likely to catalyze the development of varied family forms and increased sex role change within families. Traditional patterns of family relationships are likely to be modified as a consequence of increasing demands of such complex organizational entities as schools, businesses, social agencies, and industrial corporations. Societal modernization also opens opportunity for social mobility of large numbers of its populace. Response to these demands and opportunities depends on the families' capabilities to monitor heterogeneous exposure or experience or their willingness, motivation, and competence to adopt and handle new normative demands. In the model, family variables and contexts are viewed as having reciprocal relationships with available heterogeneous exposure and experience.

To achieve social mobility—often synonymous with success—and to handle the circumstances and contingencies involving mobility shifts requires not only families' development of competence to reduce the stress endemic to social changes, but also families' willingness to realign individual and family priorities. One such priority is the number of children one should have in relation to achieving desired mobility objectives, and another is the way a decision on the timing and spacing of having children is made. In this sense mobility opportunities within a society present a number of options and the need for choice which families make after considering and weighing resources and opportunities.

Increased female labor force participation, a concomitant of modernization, often results in a ''dual work family.'' Working wives/mothers have a potential impact on family variables, such as values and norms and interrelationships expressed in the division of labor related to household tasks and parenting, decision making, and marital communication. The reciprocal relationships of these three family dimensions—context, variable, and interrelationships—are indicated in the model.

Outcomes such as actual birth and number and spacing of children are mediated by families because of their control over frequency of sexual intercourse, use of contraceptives, and delay of marriage or childbirth. Marital decisions about fertility are correlated with families' levels of modernity and with their mobility aspirations, as well as with their available economic and social resources. Fertility outcomes are a consequence of family contexts, variables, and interrelationships. The birth of a child in dual work families may require couples to recontract on household task allocations or to modify mobility aspirations of one or both marital partners.

Family fertility outcomes aggregate to produce the societal fertility level. Societal social contexts and variables have reciprocal relationships with the level of societal fertility, and both of these nexi are indicated on the model. Unanticipated events, such as earthquakes and other natural disasters, and people-made cataclysms, such as wars and epidemics, may depress fertility temporarily. For particular families such calamities may permanently constrain fertility.

The discussion of the model indicates that components are not isolated, but are closely interrelated. Each one, in combination with others, has potential influence to affect fertility outcomes. In the development of the propositions which follow, we will indicate some of the possible influences of these variables upon one another, their interconnections, and their clustering effects upon fertility.

HETEROGENEITY-HOMOGENEITY AND FERTILITY

Heterogeneity-homogeneity is offered as a dimension relevant both the societal and family influences on fertility and as a measure which could be empirically ascertained for all societal and family contexts and variables.

Proposition 1.1: Heterogeneity is inversely related to fertility.

To serve as a meaningful organizing concept for existing fertility research, the association of heterogeneity with fertility must be discussed in terms of level of analysis. In previous discussion we identified three levels of investigation pertinent to development of a family theory of fertility: (1) societal correlates of fertility; (2) social contexts other than family; and (3) family contexts, variables, and processes. These three foci for analysis will be discussed separately, but an attempt will be made to show interrelationships between and among the levels.

Societal Correlates

Proposition 1.2: Societal correlates of low fertility are properties of families who have had heterogeneous exposure and experience. Societal correlates of high fertility are properties of families who have had homogeneous exposure and experience.

From the extreme cases of high and low fertility, it can be quickly inferred that this outcome is associated with the degree of heterogeneous exposure. Worldwide, families who fall into categories of variables associated with high fertility rates and large completed family sizes are those who experience comparative social isolation. For example, rural residents, where agriculture is nonmechanized, tend to have higher fertility rates than rural residents where agriculture is modernized (Timur, 1971). Urban residents tend to have lower fertility rates than rural residents, but urban residents in nonindustrialized cities have higher fertility rates than those in industrialized cities (Rosen and Simmons, 1971).

It is not difficult to hypothesize greater potential for families to have greater heterogeneous exposure as we move from the high-fertility to the low-fertility end of the continuum (see Figure 8.3). Even when families live in large urban, industrialized centers, it is not difficult to infer from other correlates of fertility that those families with socially isolating properties have higher fertility rates than those in the same city with properties which ensure higher degrees of heterogeneous exposure. For example, Blacks living in urban ghettos (homogeneous) in the United States tend to have higher rates of fertility than others in the urban setting. On the other hand, Blacks who are upwardly mobile and move out of the ghettos (heterogeneous exposure) have lower fertility rates than whites of the *same* socioeconomic level.

Figure 8.3.

High Fertility Low Heterogeneity		Low Fertility High Heterogeneity	
Rural Nonmechanized	Rural Mechanized	Urban Nonindustrial	Urban Industrial

Social Contexts

Proposition 1.3: Social contexts vary in available heterogeneous exposure and experience. Families who are members of social contexts with high heterogeneity have lower fertility. Families who are members of social contexts with low heterogeneity (homogeneous situations) have high fertility.

Social contexts refer to all geographic types of social groupings (such as nations, regions, cities, and villages) and to associational groupings that may be composed of individuals from a variety of geographic locations (formal and informal organizations, informal groups, social networks, and primary groups). These groupings—both geographic and associational—are the social contexts within which role behaviors, family processes, and other social interaction processes occur.

Social contexts serve as a basis for two types of analysis of heterogeneity-homogeneity: (1) *Availability*. Social contexts are the loci for heterogeneous exposure and experience and thus the sites of availability of options which may or may not be utilized by families. (2) *Utilization*. Social contexts are the loci for the families' social interaction and thus the sites of actual heterogeneous exposure and experience.

Availability of heterogeneous experience has two discrete effects. First, there is potential for families and individuals to have heterogeneous exposure, an initial step in the process whereby individuals become aware of behavioral and role options which may be combined into new life styles. Exposure to heterogeneous experience through social contact, education, and mass media can enlarge the individual's potential for perceiving and handling behavioral variations and can lead to awareness of new options as well as knowledge of how these options may be achieved.

Families' realizations that there are behavioral alternatives different from those which they have experienced in the past does not imply that they will automatically discard customary and traditional behavior. They must decide if the new observed form is an improvement over the old, and do the risks of changing behavior justify the gains? A risk-gain-loss evaluation is initiated. The choice of new options depends on a complex set of conditions and circumstances, group values and identities, individual and family characteristics. These set the stage for the particular evaluation of the available options. In summary, heterogeneous exposure first results in awareness of behavioral alternatives and then in knowledge of how these alternatives may be achieved.

The second potential effect of heterogeneous contexts is that more life options are available for families and individuals. There is a greater number of available alternatives from which to choose: occupations, marriage partners, religions, and life styles. There are also greater behavioral alternatives for each role, each having a number of socially recognized and validated alternatives.

For example, in the United States today a woman may play the female role as liberated or traditional; parents may be authoritarian or permissive; partners may opt for a traditional or an open marriage. Further, as societies become more complex, occupational specialization may take place and options for different kinds of work increase markedly. These varied ways of making a living enable increased utilization of the individual's latent capabilities and competencies which have accompanying carryover effects from jobs to other life sectors. In addition, families at particular socioeconomic levels take on congruous life styles. Options available to families at different levels of the social structure make family size a critical issue. Regulated fertility is an option more often taken by families who are socially mobile rather than by those who are stationary, and more often by families who are highly educated and occupationally well placed than by those of lower social status. In mobile and highly educated families fertility control is practiced as a means to achieve other available options. Heterogeneity with its access to a variety of life choices provides greater potential throughout family and individual life cycles. The consequences are continuous exposure to new ideas, facts, ideologies, theories, and modified life styles. To render social contexts analytically powerful in explaining rates of fertility, it is necessary that contexts be described by at least two properties—composition and boundaries.

Composition of Social Contexts

All types of social groupings could be rated on degree of heterogeneity-homogeneity of composition, and the higher the degree of heterogeneity, the greater the potential for coming into contact with persons different from oneself. Contact with these differing individuals is hypothesized to be associated with lower fertility.

Proposition 1.4: The diversity of composition (people represented) of social contexts is inversely related to fertility.

To illustrate this proposition, one might take a large social context—nations. Nations with highly diversified composition provide more opportunities for exposure to heterogeneity and more available options and alternatives for behavior than nations of less diverse composition. Although we have not developed rating scales for heterogeneity of social composition, it is not difficult to point out gross differences. For example, a nation such as the U.S. or Israel is far more diversified in social composition than Saudi Arabia or Brazil.

To mention but a few of the differences, the United States and Israel have been populated by migrants from many countries and cultures, have a wide diversity of occupations which has increased with industrialization, have a wide variety of human service institutions which provide experience with different types of people and different organizational systems, have a larger number of

social classes with less dramatic breaks between classes, and have universal education which yields exposure to a diversity of ideas. In contrast, Saudi Arabia and Brazil are composed of people from fewer nations and cultural heritages; have fewer types of occupations, have fewer and less developed human service institutions; tend to be made up predominantly of two social classes—upper and lower—with a small, newly emerging middle class; and have higher rates of illiteracy. Countries such as the United States and Israel have a higher degree of heterogeneous composition than countries such as Saudi Arabia and Brazil.

Heterogeneous composition provides greater potential for citizens to encounter people different from themselves, who have different perspectives on life and different ways of handling life events. It also provides greater potentiality to assume roles and behaviors different from one's past life or from that of one's parents.

In much the same way, one could rate smaller social groupings on degree of heterogeneous-homogeneous composition. In the U.S., a county political party will in all likelihood have a more diverse composition than a country club in the same county, or a social network of stamp collectors may have greater diversity than a social network of Greek immigrants.

Boundaries

Diversity of composition of social contexts has less effect on lowering fertility if each social context has impermeable boundaries.

Proposition 1.5: The permeability of boundaries of social contexts is inversely related to fertility.

Social contexts, including the family, have both entry and exit boundaries which may vary in permeability. Freedom to exit will vary within different territorial and associational groupings and may be heavily influenced by social characteristics of individuals and by subcultural group norms. For example, in developing countries, some neighborhoods in large industrial cities are composed primarily of migrant villagers. In these neighborhoods exit boundaries may be permeable for male adults but impermeable for females and children. On the other hand, entry boundaries refer to the freedom with which outsiders enter the group. In the United States there was a time when some labor unions were essentially closed to all new members except for those who were kin of existing members. Private clubs often have exclusive membership. Until recently many occupations and professional schools in the United States were essentially closed to women and Blacks (Cogswell, 1976).

Family potential for exposure to the diversity available within each social contexts is limited by its position in the structure of society or in other social groups. Probably no social contexts exist which allow universal access to all options. Within a nation or a city, access may be limited by caste, social class, ethnic origin, age and sex; by one's social, psychological, physical, and personality attributes; and by social identity labels which carry either positive or negative connotations within one's society, i.e., college graduate, opinion leader, female, retired person, disabled person, drug addict, convicted criminal. Many families are denied access to options available in their society by constraints of law, culture, norms, and social sanctions.

Based on individuals' and families' constellations of attributes, each one has different degrees of access to particular groups and options and may experience different degrees of cost for the pursuit of the same option. In other words, the potential for particular families and individuals to have heterogeneous exposure and experience is strongly influenced by the permeability-impermeability of group boundaries.

To return to our illustration of nations, India has a diversified composition, yet boundaries around different social groups and castes have a low degree of permeability, which prevents free association among peoples of different backgrounds. The presence of diversity of composition is necessary but not sufficient to yield heterogeneous exposure and experience—people may live in close proximity to one another yet find that closed entry and exit boundaries encourage contact with persons of one's homogeneous group and discourage contact with those who are different. In the United States residential zoning has led to Black neighborhoods. In India, Moslems and Hindus may live side by side in cities or villages, yet social contact with each other is restricted.

Family

In this chapter we have singled out the family as the social context of major concern. As mentioned in the introduction, the ultimate decisions or nondecisions concerning fertility are made within the family group. Families, however, are greatly influenced by other individuals and families who are encountered in nonfamilial social contexts.

Proposition 1.6: The greater the permeability of family entry and exit boundaries for all family members, the greater the heterogeneous contact and experience, and the lower the fertility.

Families may vary considerably on the permeability of group boundaries. A geographically isolated, self-sufficient farm family would have minimal exposure to others merely by virtue of absence of opportunity. A family living in a city, however, could have impermeable boundaries by virtue of group choice. As in the larger social contexts, the permeability of family entry and exit boundaries may vary by sex and age. Children may remain in the home and adults exit frequently. Entry boundaries may be open to other children but not to adults

or open to females but not to males. Traditionally in all societies women have experienced less permeable exit boundaries than men. The effects of women's liberation, however, have been to increase the permeability of family boundaries for women, so that in increasing numbers they are leaving the home for work, for political participation, and for leisure activities.

Proposition 1.7: Families and individuals who shift from a familiar to an unfamiliar social context have greater heterogeneous contact and lower subsequent fertility.

Voluntary or involuntary shifts from one life setting to another lead to heterogeneous exposure with potential consequential change in existing values and behaviors. Voluntary job changes involving movement from one type of work to another; migration from rural to urban areas, forced migration to another country because of repression, and graduating from school or college to the working world are all examples of shifts to unfamiliar contexts which provide different exposure and experience, and new options for families and individuals.

As families and individuals move through various stages of life, a break in continuity may occur, resulting in heterogeneous exposure even for individuals whose life experience up to that point has been primarily homogeneous. A rural family may migrate to the city. Reaching the age of employability may encourage exit from a homogeneous social context if jobs are available in other locations. Failure to succeed in a new setting may result in a return home with concomitant problems of readjustment and a potential conflict between heterogeneous and homogeneous values and practices. On the other hand, success in the new setting may lead to further opportunities, social mobility, and marriage to someone different from one's family of origin.

Moving from a familiar to an unfamiliar social context requires considerable expenditure of energy and time to adapt to the new demands and expectations of the situation. In some instances economic and social survival depend upon effective accommodation and, in some situations, assimilation. Such expenditures of effort are influenced by the support or rejection received from individuals in the unfamiliar social contexts and the availability of friends and kin who preceded the family's move to the new setting.

Family efforts may extend beyond mere adoption to active seeking and utilization of available resources and options for better jobs, education, income, and life styles. The availability of opportunities like these nourishes establishment of family priorities and decisions regarding childbearing and family size and spacing. Energy expenditure and other costs of parenting are part of priority formation.

The timing of such transitions over the reproductive period of the life cycle affects fertility. The earlier in the reproductive period the transition occurs, the greater the probability that the shift will function as a fertility depressant. The explanation for this is that the demands of the new situation described previously can result in maximal energy and time for adapting and manipulating available resources and options and leave little immediate residual energy or time to take on parenting roles. Families who move after children have been born have fewer energy resources for adapting and manipulating and have established a child-centered life style difficult to modify.

Proposition 1.8: Participation in multiple and varied social contexts prior to and during the reproductive period leads to increased heterogeneous exposure and to lower fertility.

There is wide variation among individuals and families in the number of different social contexts in which they participate at a given time during their lives. In modern societies persons lead lives in multiple life sectors which may include social contexts which are very different from each other. In remote villages in developing countries life is seldom sectorized. One works, plays, and marries within the village group. Place of residence and place of work are often the same, and the locus for other life activities is within the village group, severely limiting opportunities to associate with persons different from oneself. In modern societies, place of work is almost always different from place of residence. There are also many available sports and leisure activities, service and political organizations, clubs, and social networks. Human service systems—which include schools, hospitals and clinics, child care facilities, employment agencies—are diversified and require contact with different types of people and organizational structures.

Opportunities to associate with people different from oneself are expanded. Utilization of these opportunities, however, is another matter. Even within cities that include both large numbers and varieties of social contexts, one finds wide variation among families and individuals in seeking out and utilizing these potential opportunities.

THE RELATION OF SOCIETAL VARIABLES TO FAMILY FERTILITY

In focusing on family analysis, we are concerned with the expression of societal-level variables in individual and group behavior. Family members bring into social interactions their orientations and perspectives, which reflect societal influences. A considerable number of works on fertility substantiate this interrelationship (Cogswell and Sussman, 1974; Collver, 1968; Freedman, 1959, 1962; Freedman et al., 1959; Goldberg, 1960; Hill et al., 1959; Hoffman and Wyatt, 1965; Kiser, 1962; Rainwa-

ter, 1965; Stycos and Weller, 1967; Weller, 1968, 1971; Westoff, 1961; Whelpton and Kiser, 1950).

In analyses of these interrelated societal and family variables, our posture is that the nexus between these two types of variables results in reciprocal influences. For example, family processes are obviously influenced by societal policies and legislation regarding equal rights, affirmative action, and nondiscrimination. These are translated into behaviors by family members which change the traditional dynamic. Although families are less organized than other interest groups, on occasion they can sidestep or even influence societal mandates and policies. Marriage contracts between two people may be written to guarantee rights not given by law and establish new role expectations (Sussman and Cogswell, 1976). Grass-roots movements, such as food boycotts, protest groups formed to object to zoning ordinances, distribution of sex information and/or contraceptives to adolescents, or protestations for or against abortion, often achieve societal change or modification.

Reciprocal influences between society and families do not necessarily mean that societal variables cannot be viewed as determinants of behaviors. Obviously they have varying influences depending upon the size of the population subscribing to them and the circumstances and situations under which they are implemented. The impact of societal variables on families is also effected by families' screening processes which determine whether particular societal variables will be influential on their behavior. Determination of the influence of societal variables on families by societal factors is often derived from inferences by investigators rather than by empirical observation of families.

Improved statistical procedures and tests enable the handling and control of multiple variables—an analytic breakthrough—in establishing their explanatory power. These advances in variable manipulation, however, do not explain the more dynamic and often idiosyncratic factors in making a fertility decision in keeping with or contrary to societal expectations. More refined analysis of family phenomena is necessary to interpret the discrete influences of societal correlates of fertility.

Setting limits and conditions of societal analysis is the task in the remaining portion of this section. To illustrate we have selected the macro variables of gainful employment of women, social mobility, and socioeconomic status (SES), and will analyze these variables in terms of their influence upon family behavior and fertility outcomes.

Female Labor Force Participation (LFP)

Women who work throughout their adult lives as well as those who have worked some have higher heterogeneous exposure than women who have never worked and remain in the home. Not only does entering the work world place these women in organizational contexts different from that of the family, but this activity also leads them to contact with individuals who are often different from themselves. Places of work, as other social contexts, vary by degree of heterogeneity of composition.

We would anticipate that highly heterogeneous places of work would have more impact on reduced fertility than those with lower degrees of heterogeneity. One would expect greater differences (heterogeneity) to be represented among workers in a large factory or bank than among those in a small neighborhood business. In addition, places of work reflect differences in permeability of boundaries around different types of workers in the total enterprise. In some factories, assembly line workers may seldom if ever come into contact with management. In other factories, one may find a more democratic ethos whereby workers on all levels come into contact with each other at recreational facilities shared by all. Depending upon the composition and boundaries within the work place, women in the labor force have different opportunities for heterogeneous exposure.

Obviously, contact among workers occurs at place of work. In addition, however, persons encountered here often become friends and may become part of one's nonwork groups or networks. Individuals may be asked to join others for leisure activities or to join clubs, political parties, or voluntary associations. In turn, joining new groups and social networks leads to meeting other people who may be different from oneself. Working, thereby, may have a rippling effect on increasing the number of new acquaintances. Thus all women who work or have ever worked have experienced greater heterogeneous contact than women who have never worked. Specific jobs and places of work, however, have wide variations in their potential for heterogeneous exposure and experience. If the amount of heterogeneity could be determined for each job and place of work, we would expect this to be an influential intervening variable between female labor force participation and fertility.

Proposition 2.1: There is an inverse relationship between rate of female labor force participation and the fertility rate.

General reviews usually support the proposition that the greater the female labor force participation, the lower the fertility at the societal level (Germain, 1974; Loewenthal and David, 1972; Piepmeier and Adkins, 1973). This inverse relationship holds true primarily for the developed or Western societies (Fortney, 1971; Reed and Udry, 1973; Ridley, 1959; Waite and Stolzenberg, 1976). There is also some support for this proposition in undeveloped countries (Bindary et al., 1973; Davidson, 1973; Gendell et al., 1970; Minkler, 1970; Weller 1968). However, beyond this general societal level statement, the data

become more conflicting, especially when statistical controls for other socioeconomic and familial variables are added.

A number of factors have been identified in different studies which are associated with the inverse relationship between labor force participation and fertility. To list a few, Bindary et al. (1973) working in Egypt, Jaffe and Azumi (1960) working in Puerto Rico, and Goldstein (1972) in Thailand have found that the inverse relationship holds only in urban areas. Federici (1968) in Italy found the relationship held only in nonagricultural areas. Tarver et al. (1970) found that the proportionate number of employed females decreases and fertility increases as the distance from an urban center increases.

Female employment in agriculture is almost always associated with high fertility (Federici, 1968; Goldstein, 1972). In rural areas the work done within the household can be compatible with high fertility. However, where the household is not the primary economic unit, women are forced to make trade-offs between economic and family activities, which may result in lower fertility for those who choose extra-familial alternatives (Kasarda, 1971).

Delayed marriage and low marital fertility were found in communities with high rates of female employment (Collver, 1968). Also, although the study is based on a small sample of university families and does not permit one to generalize to other populations, Fortney (1971) found that women in traditionally male occupations will have higher fertility than other working women although they will be better planners and have fewer unwanted births.

Proposition 2.2: Modernization is positively related to female labor force participation.

Kasarda's study (1971), using data from 50 countries and four time periods, hypothesizes that urbanization and industrialization have a positive effect on female labor force participation and this in turn indirectly depresses fertility. He finds no direct effects of such variables on fertility when female labor force participation is controlled. It may be inferred that urban residence and modern agricultural methods will also have a similar positive relationship with female labor force participation and a concomitant decrease in fertility. However, the variance remains to be explained, and further specification of contingent variables affecting this relationship is required.

Proposition 2.3: Relationships between Black female labor force participation and rates of fertility are unclear and findings are conflicting.

Conflicting findings exist on the relationship of Black female labor force participation and fertility. Generally, Blacks are supposed to have a higher fertility than whites (Campbell, 1965; Kiser and Frank, 1967; Marshall and

Sinnott, 1971). Presser (1971) found that the higher fertility among Black women when compared to white women remained even when occupational status is controlled. But Reed and Udry (1973) and Terry (1975) state that higher Black fertility disappears when other controlling variables (e.g., age, education, fecundity, residence, and length of marriage) are introduced. Further, Terry (1975) notes that the social characteristics which influence the work-fertility relationship are different for Blacks and whites. The occupational status of employed Black mothers is significant for the work-fertility relationship; Black women employed in low status occupations have higher fertility than Black women in professional and other relatively high occupational status.

Although the relationship of employment and fertility for Black women is unclear, educational attainment has more impact in lowering fertility among Black than among white women. Separate investigations conclude that Black high school graduates (Goldscheider and Uhlenberg, 1969) and Black college graduates (Goldscheider and Uhlenberg, 1969; Presser, 1971; and Kiser and Frank, 1967) have lower fertility than their white counterparts. Sly's (1970) data indicated that at all educational levels, in all regions (except the South) white women have higher fertility than nonwhite women. Given a history of minority group status and concommitant disadvantaged opportunities of their parents, Black high school and college graduates are likely to have experienced a greater degree of heterogeneity than whites with comparable educational attainments.

Proposition 2.4: There is an inverse relationship between female educational level and fertility.

Proposition 2.5: There is a positive relationship between female educational level and female labor force participation.

Ridley (1969) questions that women's employment exacts a declining fertility; however, she finds educational differences highly influential. Using United States fertility trend data, Ridley found that since 1940 labor force participation per se is unlikely to act as a major depressant on fertility and that education is a stronger inverse correlate of fertility.

In some less developed countries an inverse work-fertility relationship emerges only in the high-education group (Morcors, 1974; Minkler, 1970), with urbanization (Goldstein, 1972), or with residence in an industrialized city (Rosen and Simmons, 1971). In the United States the work-fertility relationship disappears for high- and low-education groups (Fortney, 1971). Several studies (Gendell et al., 1970; Minkler, 1970; Speare et al., 1973) report education to be more important than work in predicting fertility, and others (Stycos and Weller, 1967) disagree. Goldstein (1972) suggests that labor force participation and education work jointly to affect fertility. Kasarda (1971), Krotki (1972), and Waite and Stolzen-berg (1976) report the effects of education on fertility to be dependent upon the intervening effects of labor force participation. Stycos and Weller (1967) found the inverse relationship to hold only in urban areas. Because the results from various studies report conflicting results, further research is needed to clarify the interrelationships of female labor force participation, education, and fertility.

Generally, it is suggested that when employment is opened to women and it then becomes more attractive because of higher salaries and/or jobs of greater prestige, female labor force participation increases and fertility declines (Chessler, 1970; Oppenheimer, 1973; Piepmeier and Adkins, 1973; Preston, 1972).

Proposition 2.6: In developed countries there is an inverse relationship between length of employment and fertility. For developing countries the relationship between length of employment and fertility is nonexistent.

In developing countries there is no relationship between length of work experience and fertility (Fong, 1975), but an inverse relationship is found in developed countries (Ridley, 1959; Terry, 1975; Waite and Stolzenberg, 1976). Rosen and Simmons (1971) report that in Brazil women who had worked in the past but ceased to work had fertility rates as low as those women who had worked continuously. Rosen and Simmons's finding suggests that if women work for even short periods of time, this employment period provides sufficient heterogeneous experience to reduce fertility.

Proposition 2.7: Employment outside the home is associated with low fertility and work within the home with high fertility.

Work performed at home (i.e. cottage industries) is associated with higher fertility (Kasarda, 1971). Alternately, the greater the incompatibility between mother and worker roles, the lower the fertility rate (Weller, 1968). This relationship is reported to be influenced by availability of birth control methods and place of residence by Stycos and Weller (1967), and by increasing age of youngest child by Darian (1975). No differences were found between part- and full-time female workers (Reed and Udry, 1973), which again suggests the notion that only limited rather than sustained heterogeneous contact in a particular life sector is necessary to reduce fertility. Generally, women who work plan births better (Darian, 1975; Fortney, 1971), whatever their fertility.

Proposition 2.8: Socioeconomic status is inversely related to female labor force participation.

Sweet (1973) reports that the more inadequate the family income, the more likely the woman is to work. Krotki (1972) suggests an inadequate financial situation can also lead to delayed age at marriage, which may lead to lower fertility. At lower income levels, women who do work have lower fertility regardless of race in the United States (Reed and Udry, 1973). At higher SES, women in both less developed countries and in the United States tend to work less and there is no consistent relationship with fertility (Stycos, 1965; Rosenberg, 1973). Stycos (1965) indicates that as socioeconomic status decreases, the inverse relationship between work and fertility is strengthened. At all SES levels women with lower fertility (no children to two children) are more likely to be working (Stycos, 1965).

Social Mobility and Fertility

Heterogeneous exposure and experience are a consequence of social mobility. In this section we examine an often stated hypothesis which correlates upward mobility with lowered fertility. Values which emphasize the wise use of time and the need to strive, to control the environment, and to work tirelessly are inevitably tied to the mobility syndrome. The expenditure of energy required to fulfill the goal and dream of the modern person, and to achieve success and rewards, may dampen whatever desire there is to have any or a large number of children.

Proposition 2.9: Planned or actual upward social mobility is inversely related to fertility.

While many researchers have documented a relationship between upward social mobility and lower fertility (Goldscheider and Uhlenberg, 1969; Powers, 1966), the exact nature of the relationship has yet to be established and delineated. Results of studies to date have been conflicting, possibly because exact values of mobility as a variable are difficult to operationalize. Tien (1966) discovered that the inverse relationship between fertility and mobility found in earlier studies may no longer exist, due to socioeconomic and demographic changes since the turn of the century. He did, however, find that mobile couples have longer intervals between the date of marriage and the first birth.

Dumont (1890, in Eversley, 1959) was one of the first to suggest that men will limit their children in relation to their prospects in life. He hypothesized that childbearing handicaps social "capillarity" (*l'arrivisme*). This was defined as the upward movement of individuals from the lower class, a tendency to push upward as high and as rapidly as possible (P. Leroy-Beaulieu, 1913, in Eversley, 1959). Eversley (1959) suggests a democratic political organization may also increase capillarity. Hawthorn (1968) suggests that capillarity may decline as one rises in a social structure and posits a J-shaped-curve distribution with the lower middle class at the bottom of the curve. Perrucci (1968) and Rosen (1971) question whether the relationship proposed by Hawthorn applies to modern urban industrial societies.

Rosen (1971) found in Brazil that indeed upward mobility does vary by industrial and nonindustrial cities as well as by rural-urban areas. Eighty-one percent of the subjects from an industrial city reported upward mobility, as compared with only 37 percent in the nonindustrial cities, and virtually no mobility was reported in rural areas. Rosen stated:

> Industrialization tells us much about the nature of economic organization, the diversity of occupation and the openness of the opportunity structure in a particular community. It provides a varied occupational structure through which the individual can move [1971:146].

Tien (1966) found that for both mobile and nonmobile couples fertility was differentiated by the wife's desire to work. Therefore, it may be the wife's desire to work, and potentially her mobility, which is more critical in determining a couple's fertility.

Although fertility varies inversely with SES, the relationship with mobility is somewhat more complex. Mobility is probably greatest in the upper lower and lower middle classes (Rosen, 1971). This idea relates to the J-shaped capillarity curve mentioned earlier.

Inconsistency in status characteristics could be defined as potential for mobility among the lower classes. Powers (1966) found that fertility increased as status inconsistency increased for mothers in the high range of SES, but fertility decreased as status inconsistencies increased for mothers in lower SES range. Therefore, we may expect to find different consistency patterns operating, such as higher relative salaries for women in lower SES categories. Also, education may affect fertility more than other SES components only up to some minimum level of attainment achieved by most persons in the top half of the range. On the other hand, Perrucci (1968:281) reported that "with continued exposure to higher education, there appeared to be rather pronounced deferral behavior regarding marriage and, especially, childbearing."

Status inconsistency of mothers and fertility vary by race in the United States. Powers (1966) describes two different patterns. Blacks tend to have lowest fertility when they are of middle SES, lower even than Blacks or whites of higher SES.

> Among white mothers, the number of children per thousand increases with inconsistency of status components, whereas among non-white mothers those with status types in between complete consistency and complete inconsistency have the fewest children per thousand, and those with completely consistent status scores have the most children [1966:478].

Two studies report a direct relationship between mobility orientation, level of striving, and early adoption and frequent use of contraceptives (Bauman and Udry, 1972; Kar, 1971). High achievement motivation is found to be closely associated with upward mobility and low need achievement with downward mobility (Rosen, 1971). Freedman and Coombs (1966), using an index of aspirations, found that while the index was not highly correlated with (current) income, there was an inverse association with family size expectations, suggesting that types of quantity-quality trade-off existed for these families.

Social Status and Fertility

Among fertility studies a variety of operational definitions are used for social status. Studies carried out in industrialized nations sometimes use the combination of educaiton, occupation, and income. This measure is used less frequently in developing countries. Other measures using single variables of income, education, occupation, or type of residence are introduced. Level of education permits one to infer the amount of heterogeneity experienced, but the other measures permit little insight into the relationship of heterogeneity and fertility. In the following section on family variables, it becomes apparent that social status is often less influential on fertility than family process variables.

Proposition 2.10: There is an inverse relationship between social status and fertility.

Recent data indicate an inverse relationship between social status and fertility (Goldberg, 1960; Loewenthal and David, 1972) except in rural or agricultural areas. When social status is measured by occupation, education, and income, this inverse relationship between status and fertility is supported for the U.S. by Ritchey and Stokes (1971), Bacon and Mason (1972), and Kupinsky (1971), who report that the relationship is strengthened by women labor force participation. Many studies also report U- or J-shaped inverse or insignificant relationships (Bernhardt, 1971; Bradshaw, 1971; Safilios-Rothschild, 1965).

Westoff and Ryder (1970) found the effect of near poverty—husband's annual earnings under $4,000— decreases the probability of using contraceptives among whites and Blacks in all residential categories. Many studies report a positive relationship between husband's or family's income and both fertility and use of contraceptives (Freedman et al., 1959; Kunz, 1965; Loewenthal and David, 1972).

Education of both husband and wife is inversely related to fertility (Grabill and Davidson, 1968; Loewenthal and David, 1972), although in the U.S. the magnitude of this inverse relationship decreases after the year 1960 (Mitra, 1966). In the United States educational level is also strongly associated with increased and more efficient use of contraceptives (Hawthorn, 1970; Loewenthal and David, 1972) and with longer birth intervals (Grabill and Davidson, 1968).

Increased occupational status for women (Federici, 1968) and their husbands (Dinkel, 1952) seems to depress fertility and increase use of contraceptives except where employment is agricultural (Goldstein, 1972). Occupa-

tional status of husband is also related to fertility among whites in the United States by Grabill and Davidson (1968), by the U.S. Bureau of the Census (1971) but only among Blacks, and for Great Britain by Chou and Brown (1968). The cumulative childbearing for women whose husbands are employed as white-collar workers is considerably lower than for women whose husbands are blue-collar or farm workers (Grabill and Davidson, 1968).

In developing countries, the results are more ambiguous. Higher status is associated with greater use of contraceptives in Chile (Hall, 1971) and lower fertility in Ghana (Caldwell, 1969). However, Thorat and Fliegel (1968) found contraceptive use to be greater among lower-caste Hindus in Bangladesh. In Brazil, Rosen and Simmons (1971) found that family size in industrial cities was small in all social strata, while in the nonindustrial cities family size was inversely related to social status.

Relationships between social status and fertility may not always hold for less developed countries for the following possible reasons:

1. High fertility norms (Loewenthal and David, 1972)
2. Less Westernized education (Mueller, 1971)
3. Higher infant mortality (Omran, 1971)
4. Economic value of children (Fawcett, 1970; Arnold et al., vol. 1, 1975).

Having used these three societal variables—female labor force participation, social mobility, and social status—as illustrations of societal influences which affect families, we now turn to a discussion of family variables.

FAMILY CHARACTERISTICS AND FERTILITY

In this section family variables, contexts, and interpersonal relationships are presented in propositions and each one is related to a fertility outcome variable. The family is a definable social system whose members are linked with their own subculture and function within a definable social and physical space. Because of age differences of its members and the care children require, adult members have considerable control and influence over its young.

The family is a basic decision-making unit. While its members are guided and sometimes controlled by societal mandates, the family has latent authority and manifest influence over its members. The family sifts messages, demands, and knowledge received from larger social contexts and helps its members develop responses to the normative requirements of society's institutions and organizations.

Families vary widely in resources, capabilities, competencies, motivations, and knowledge needed to be effective caretakers of their members, socializers of their children, and effective decision makers. In this section some of these differences are examined with specific reference to differences in heterogeneity. The first is concerned with the kin network, which can be viewed as a social or family context depending on the functionality of the kin structure.

Proposition 3.1: Autonomy from kinship network in decision making by couples is related negatively to fertility (Matras, 1973).

Autonomy is not to be viewed as synonymous with the lack of closeness to family units of the kin network (Adams, 1968; Sussman, 1970). Rather, it connotes a couple unit which has its own economic resources and some social competence to manage these, and thus be less dependent on kin. With the couples' acquisition of such resources and social competences the decision to have children becomes the province of the dyad rather than of the larger family or kin network.

Proposition 3.2: Equality of women with men in couple decision making is inversely related to fertility.

In most cultures the "decision" to have a child is not a decision at all, and is seldom discussed by the couple. Societal and kin expectations are that after marriage children will be born. As women, through increasing heterogeneous exposure and experience, enter the labor force and receive education and training comparable to that received by men, the trend toward greater equality within marriage accelerates. Husband's and wife's concerns are treated more equally. Wives have more to say in matters concerning themselves, and fertility decisions become a priority issue (Liu et al., 1970; Piepmeier and Adkins, 1973; Rosen and Simmons, 1971).

Proposition 3.3: There is a positive correlation between the degree of interpersonal communication between husband and wife and the use of contraceptives.

Researchers who report this relationship include Hill et al. (1959), Hill et al. (1968), Liu et al. (1970), Mukherjee (1975b), Rosario (1970), and Rosen and Simmons (1971). Liu (1972) and Hutchison (1971) also reach similar conclusions, but their data are not statistically significant. Michel (1970) found that the earlier in a marriage husbands communicated with their wives, the more likely the couple was to use contraceptives. These communication variables are more predictive of effective use of birth control than socioeconomic status (SES) (DeWinter, 1971; Piepmeier and Adkins, 1973). However, SES modifies the communication–birth control nexus. Rainwater (1971) and Stokes (1973) report that couples in higher SES categories have a higher frequency of communication and more effective use of birth control than couples in the lower SES categories. Hill et al. (1959) note that there are fewer resources for effective communication among lower SES couples.

Marital communication may be a U-shaped curve in relation to family size. As families increase in size,

husband-wife communication also increases. Misra (1967) reports that communication among lower SES Black couples increased (as did the use of birth control) after the fourth child was born.

Proposition 3.4: The more segregated the role relationship of husband/wife the less effective the use of contraceptives.

This proposition is akin to Proposition 3.2 on equality in dyadic relationships. It appears to be class-linked as reported by various researchers (Liu et al., 1970; Rainwater, 1965, 1971; Stokes, 1973; Stokes and Dudley, 1972). With increasing numbers of women entering the labor force from all social classes and with the influence of the mass media and the women's movement, there is a push to share household tasks and child care. Dyadic role segregation, although still prevalent, may become less class-linked in the near future as family exit boundaries become more permeable for women and their activities outside the home require as much time and effort as those of men.

In summarizing findings of the authors above, we can report that conjugal role segregation is found most commonly in the lower class, with intermediate degrees of segregation in the upper lower and lower middle classes. Joint role organization is found more often in the upper middle class.

In an effort to link modern and less segregated role relationships to industrialization, Rosen and Simmons (1971) found industrialization closely related to joint or modern role relationships and subsequently lower fertility. Urbanization, while it was predictive of joint role relationships, was less related to lower fertility. Education was found predictive of joint relationships and lower fertility.

When education is controlled, there is little difference in husband-wife roles between the races in the United States (Presser, 1971). However, it appears that the wife and mother role pattern is quite different for Black women than for white women. Being married is less of a prerequisite for motherhood for Black women. This is reflected in the relatively high rate of premarital conceptions, the lower propensity to marry prior to the birth of such children, and the higher rates of marital instability among Black as compared to white women.

Proposition 3.5: The extendedness of family structure is related to fertility, but the direction of the relationship is unclear.

Although family sociologists and other fertility investigators have often assumed that family structure (extended, joint, nuclear) is related to fertility with nuclear families having the lowest fertility, data have not supported this assumption. Joint or extended families have been characterized by high fertility when compared to nuclear ones by Khatri (1970); but other studies indicate conflicting results or no relationship between nuclear versus joint or extended family structure (Bacon and Mason, 1972; Stoeckel and Choudhury, 1969). Poffenberger (1968), however, did find that the extended structure tended to inhibit husband-wife communication and that such inhibition was correlated generally with high fertility. Poffenberger (1968) and Matras (1973) suggest that very often a family is placed by investigators in the nuclear category when it has only moved a short distance from extended relatives who still influence the couple's decision making. Matras hypothesizes a lower fertility only for those nuclear couples who have become independent decision makers.

It appears that fertility rates can be explained better by family processes than by structure. A nuclear family, defined as such because it is living in a household physically separated from other kin, may be dependent for its survival upon those same kin. The lack of independence carries over into many other life sector activities, including fertility decisions. On the other hand, if a joint family so organizes its role system and relationships as to permit independent decision by nuclear dyads in certain areas such as consumption, mate selection, procreation, and parenting, there is a high probability that the joint family system will experience lowered fertility.

Proposition 3.6: Parity is inversely related to age at first regular intercourse, at first union and at first mate exposure (Masnick and McFalls, 1976).

Low-parity women tend to practice contraception much earlier than high parity women after entering a union. These low-parity women also delay entering into a marriage or cohabitation longer than high-parity women after beginning regular intercourse. The longer the delay before regular intercourse, the greater the prospect for childlessness (Masnick and McFalls, 1976). These correlations between intermediate and outcome variables of the model are mediated by family and social variables. The age to begin sexual activities or to marry and the appropriateness of contraceptive use are societal concerns. Social variables establish the parameters for acceptable behaviors. How individuals eventually behave in these matters is determined by family variables, contexts, and interpersonal relationships. The legacies of social experience and of educational and economic resources—those usually transmitted by the family—are properties of individuals by the beginning of the reproductive period and are determinants of such fertility-related behaviors.

Proposition 3.7: Sudden changes in social contexts for families increase the probability of fertility reduction.

Proposition 3.8: Social context changes increase heterogeneous exposure.

Proposition 3.9: Increased heterogeneous exposure effects changes in perceptions, values, motivations, and life style priorities.

Research on migrants adapting to urban ways of life is the major source of data on these propositions. Rosen (1971, 1973) suggests that migration to an industrialized setting may cause psychological changes in the individual family members which eventually decrease fertility. The industrial city has made it possible for some migrants to experience success. The results of success are increased sense of efficacy, new values, and different perceptions of how the world is organized. When these changes in personal orientation and perspective occur, the family— at first the target of change— becomes its active agent.

According to Rosen (1971, 1973), an industrial city affects migrants in the following ways:

1. Overall, it improves the migrants' standard of living.
2. It increases the quality and quantity of resources available to them.
3. It provides experiences which enhance their sense of efficacy.
4. It alters their perception of the kind of world in which their children will grow up.
5. It fosters new values appropriate to industrial life.

The effects of these changed social conditions and psychological states are new patterns of interactions within migrant families.

Emphasis on achievement and independence in lowering fertility is least noticeable in the rural groups, becomes more apparent among recent migrants, and declines in the group with the longest period of residence in the city. Limited support has been found for relationships of such psychological factors as positiveness and achievement motivation with lower fertility (Hutchison, 1971; Rosen, 1971, 1973) among urban migrants regardless of social class.

Changing psychological states are related to heterogeneous exposure and the manner in which individuals handle the wealth of information now available. Migrants to cities in third world countries often maintain their ties with family and friendship networks of their villages. These ties create difficulties in taking on and holding to new psychological states when one is as marginal as the migrant Indian worker (Poffenberger, 1967).

New concepts and motivations acquired by the individual may not be as significant as the kinds of child-rearing practice that have molded his personality. When an individual carries new concepts back into the extended family system and finds that they come into serious conflict with the established family concepts, the degree of dissonance that results may be determined by the degree of guilt the person feels in rejecting parental values. Where a feeling of guilt or shame is strong, dissonance reduction is most easily obtained by minimizing new goals and conforming to more traditional expectations.

Despite these anxieties, ambivalences, and associated guilt experienced by individuals in transit between an essentially rural-traditional and an urban-modern way of life, there are decided shifts in such psychological states as self-concept and fatalism. Stycos (1964) reports on the importance of God and fate in the determination of human events including fertility in the developing countries. Increased belief in and use of science, new technologies, and visible proof of material achievements support a more existentialist philosophy of belief in self and in one's ability to control his life course. Self-control of life events requires skills to cope with change and to manage the demands of beaucracies. The carryover to fertility control is apparent. Such individuals are planners and are more likely to use a rational approach to childbearing and to weigh the costs, benefits, and risks in relation to the number and spacing of children.

Proposition 3.10: Individuals with economic, social, and educational resources who form unions have greater prospects for controlling fertility than persons with none or minimal resources (Matras, 1973; Masnick and McFalls, 1976).

Proposition 3.11: Marriage matchmaking is correlated with high fertility, while self-selection of mates is correlated with low fertility (Matras, 1973).

Proposition 3.12: Size of cohort for mate selection is related to fertility. The larger the cohort, the lower the fertility.

Proposition 3.13: The freedom to select a mate under controlled (matchmaking or parental guidance) or non-controlled conditions is negatively related to fertility.

Couples who do not have sufficient resources to be independent and to explore options and priorities show greater reliance on more traditional beliefs and ways. In joint or extended families couples can explore the possibilities of controlling their fertility when they have sufficient resources to "carry their own weight" and manage their community and social relations independently of the sponsorship or mediation of parents or other relatives (Matras, 1973).

The mate selection process can be conceptualized along a continuum with the polar ends being family control of selection of marriage partners and autonomous decision making. As one moves from the polar ends of this continuum toward the middle, it becomes easy to ascertain the conditions favoring high or low fertility. If a joint or extended family is "permissive" in the timing of marriage and choice of a mate, one can expect it to be similarly "freed up" in other areas, permitting its children some degree of autonomy and independence. While in Western society we have the myth of independence and autonomy in mate selection, there may be large numbers of couples who lack resources to assert independence and autonomy. In those instances where assets are controlled

by parents who are wealthier than the couple, the dyad's freedom of choice may be severely limited.

The larger the size of the cohort for mate selection, the greater is the likelihood of controlled fertility. Larger cohort size means numbers of individuals and, even more important, eligibles who do not belong to the same kinship or other ascriptive grouping (Matras, 1973). Such a large and diversified cohort provides increased opportunities for heterogeneous exposure and experience—including ideas on family-planning options.

Proposition 3.13 is similar to Proposition 3.11 but treats freedom (autonomy and independence) in mate selection specifically in propositional form. Oriental Jewish couples married in Israel under a less traditional matchmaking regime exhibit increasing tendencies toward fertility control and lower birth rates than similar couples in their countries of origin (Matras, 1973). Arab couples residing in Israel and marrying under their rigidly traditional matchmaking regimes retain very high fertility (Matras, 1973). Israeli Arabs are Moslems and as a result have not assimilated into the national culture. They also comprise a tightly bounded minority group (homogeneous) and do not utilize the options of the larger society.

Class and caste also establish norms for mate selection and fertility expectations. Poffenberger (1967) reports that in India the social standing of the extended family within caste is intricately related to the marriage arrangement pattern. Since family status is achieved through marriage, it is important to have a number of children through whom this status can be maintained.

Proposition 3.14: The degree of marital privacy is positively related to contraceptive practice.

Couples who live in crowded conditions or in communal-type housing characterized by openness find it difficult to use or discuss use of contraceptives in privacy or without interference by parents. Also, it is almost impossible to have sexual relations in a leisurely manner. The Poffenbergers' description of the lack of privacy of rural dwellers and city workers is a prototype of the situation in many third world countries (Poffenberger and Poffenberger, 1965). They report:

> The reasons behind the lack of use of contraceptives in India are many and varied. Both in the cities and in the villages, the crowded conditions of living are difficult to imagine for one who has not seen them. The number of people who must share one room makes privacy almost impossible. Sexual intercourse may be hurried—or, in the case of village people, it may take place in the fields instead of in the home. Private lavatory facilities are usually absent and water has to be carried in pots or vessels on the wife's head. Bathing takes place outside the house in the public view.... The relationship of the husband and wife tends to be formal and the wife may find great difficulty in talking with him about such things as family planning and contraceptives. In the joint family, the mother-in-law to a large extent determines the action of the wife. Since the mother-in-law would probably know of any

use of contraceptives, it would not be possible to use them without her approval [1965:342–43].

Proposition 3.15: Individuals in unions who view large numbers of children more as benefits than as costs have higher fertility than those persons who view children as costs.

Existing data support this proposition, which is derived from an economic theory commonly referred to as the new household economics (Leibenstein, 1974; Masnick and McFalls, 1976; Sawhill, 1977). The more children are valued in marriage, the less contraceptives are used (Tobin, 1975). An often cited reason for a family not having additional children is their perception that the costs are too high (Arnold and Fawcett, 1975; Arnold et al, 1975; Bulatao, 1975).

Costs are not limited to economic costs, but include emotional and opportunity (restrictions on alternative activities) costs (Arnold et al., 1975). Urban residents are more likely than their rural counterparts to cite emotional satisfaction as the principal value of children. Rural populations are more likely to value children for their work capacity, for help during old age, and for continuity of the family name (Arnold et al., 1975).

Urban women value children more for the companionship and emotional attachments and the supports which they provide (Arnold et al., 1975). Consequently, if one or two children do meet these needs, controlled fertility is likely. This depends, of course, on the family dynamics, especially the level of equality found in the dyadic relationship. Men are more concerned with the economic costs than the help or emotional support they may receive, need satisfaction currently or in the future, or economic help in old age. Men place more value on continuity of the family name and attain feelings of pride by living vicariously through a child's accomplishments.

Proposition 3.16: Children in early birth orders who meet parents' sex preferences serve as a fertility depressor for higher-order births.

Parents have definite perceptions of what is an appropriate distribution of boys and girls in a family (Arnold et al., 1975). Boys are desired for continuity of the bloodline over generational time and for their potential economic contribution to the farm or family enterprise. Girls are prized for the psychological gift they provide and as mother's helpers, the traditional sex-typed role. Obtaining the desired sex preference in early birth orders may be a fertility depressor. This relationship appears in effect in Hawaii, the U.S., Japan, the Philippines, Korea, Thailand, and Taiwan.

CONCLUSION

In this chapter we have presented a heuristic fertility model consisting of societal and family contexts, variables, and processes; intermediate variables; unanticipated situations; the concept of heterogeneity; and societal and family fertility outcomes. Heterogeneity-homogeneity is suggested as a bridging and organizing concept for integrating societal with family concepts. We have attempted to demonstrate the use of family system analysis to explain the variance of fertility decisions derived from the aggregate analysis. Societal parameters provide the baseline data for establishing the contingencies affecting fertility decisions. Homogeneity-heterogeneity can be used as an interpretive concept linking together societal and family theoretical constructs.

Using the model as a guide, we have posited a number of propositions which explain family-planning behavior in relation to events, conditions, states, problems, and interpersonal processes of families. Wherever possible, we have attempted to cluster propositions around core interrelated variables, which may be viewed as partial theories of family fertility. We recognize that such theory formulation is only a beginning; we have tapped the visible portion of the iceberg, but much more needs to be probed and new propositions formulated for empirical testing.

NOTES

1. The majority of surveys on fertility have collected data only from women, although some family sociologists have collected data from both husbands and wives (Hill et al., 1959; Liu et al., 1970; Mitchell, 1972; Poti, Chakraborti, and Malaker, 1962; Rainwater, 1965; Yaukey, 1967; Yaukey, Roberts, and Griffiths, 1965). In a table on desired family size, Mauldin (1965) lists 47 KAP studies. In 36 studies data were collected only from the female, 9 only from males, and in 2 from both males and females. The authors, together with a Pakistani colleague, Jahangir Khan, have an ongoing study of family structure, family dynamics, and fertility in Sind Province in Pakistan, in which both husband and wife are interviewed. The study is designed to measure family group properties such as degree of family extendedness, degree of heterogeneous exposure, and locus of decision making.

2. Although there is some evidence of fertility planning throughout history, it is our general impression that in populations without easy access to contraception or abortion and even in populations where contraceptives and abortions are available a large proportion of conceptions and deliveries are more often a result of nondecisions than of actual decisions. A primary thrust of our discussion in this chapter is that the question of "to conceive or not to conceive" or "to abort or not to abort" is associated with populations who plan and are more purposive about the course of their lives.

3. A *beraderis* is a large endogamous bilateral kin network (consequineal and affinal) without clearly defined boundaries, which operates to socialize children and is characterized by reciprocal exchanges among its component primary group units.

REFERENCES

ADAMS, B. N.
    1968   *Kinship in an Urban Setting*. Chicago: Markham.
ARNOLD, F., R. A. BULATAO, C. BURIPAKDI, B. S. CHUNG, J. T.
FAWCETT, T. IRITANI, S. J. LEE, AND W. TONG-SHIEN
    1975   *The Value of Children: A Cross National Study, vol. 1.*

Honolulu: East-West Population Institute.

ARNOLD, F. AND J. T. FAWCETT
1975   *The Value of Children: A Cross National Study,* vol. 1. Honolulu: East-West Population Institute.

BACON, T. J. AND K. O. MASON
1972   *Turkish Fertility: A Review of Social and Economic Correlates.* Research Triangle Park, N.C.: Center for Population Research and Services, Research Triangle Institute.

BAUMAN, K. E. AND J. R. UDRY
1972   "Powerlessness and regularity of contraception in an urban Negro male sample: A research note." *Journal of Marriage and the Family* 34:112–14.

BERNHARDT, E.
1972   "Trends and variations in Swedish fertility." University of Pennsylvania Doctoral Dissertation.

BINDARY, A., C. BAXTER, AND T. H. HOLLINGSWORTH
1973   "Urban-rural differences in the relationship between women's employment and fertility: A preliminary study." *Journal of Biosocial Science* 5:159–67.

BRADSHAW, B.S.
1971   "Some aspects of the fertility of Mexican Americans." Unpublished manuscript prepared for Commission on Population Growth and Nation's Future.

BULATAO, R.
1975   *The Value of Children: A Cross National Study,* vol. 2. Honolulu: East-West Population Institute.

BURR, W. R.
1973   *Theory Construction and the Sociology of the Family.* New York: Wiley.

CALDWELL, J. C.
1969   "Some factors affecting fertility in Ghana." Mimeographed.

CAMPBELL, A. A.
1965   "Fertility and family planning among non-white married Couples in the United States." *Eugenics Quarterly* 12:124–131.

CHESSLER, D.
1970   "Contraception and female job-choice and career prospects." *Annals of the New York Academy of Sciences* 175:915–17.

CHOU, R. AND S. BROWN
1968   "A comparison of the size of families of Roman Catholics and non-Catholics in Great Britain," *Population Studies* 22:51–60.

COGSWELL, B. E.
1976   "Conceptual model of family as a group: Family response to disability." In G. L. Albrecht (ed.), *The Sociology of Physical Disability.* Pittsburgh: University of Pittsburgh.

COGSWELL, B. E. AND M. B. SUSSMAN
1974   "Changing roles of women, family dynamics and fertility." In H. Y. Tien and F. D. Bean (eds.), *Comparative Family and Fertility Research.* Leiden: E. J. Brill.

COLLVER, O. A.
1968   "Women's work participation and fertility in metropolitan areas." *Demography* 5:55–60.

DARIAN, J.C.
1975   "Convenience of work and the job constraint of children." *Demography* 12:245–58.

DAVIDSON, M.
1973   "A comparative study of fertility in Mexico City and Caracas." *Social Biology* 20:460–72.

DAVIS, K. AND J. BLAKE
1956   "Social structure and fertility: An analytic framework." *Economic Development and Cultural Change* 4:211–35.

DEWINTER, A. M. T.
1971   "Family interaction, family planning and fertility in the city of Durazno, Uruguay." University of Wisconsin Doctoral Dissertation.

DINKEL, R. M.
1952   "Occupation and fertility in the United States." *American Sociological Review* 17:178–83.

DUMONT, A.
1890   "Dépopulation et civilisation." Etude démographique, Paris.

EVERSLEY, D. E. C.
1959   *Social Theories of Fertility and the Malthusian Debate.* Oxford: Clarendon Press.

FAWCETT, J. T.
1970   *Psychology and Population.* New York: Population Council.

FEDERICI, N.
1968   "The influence of women's employment on fertility." In E. Szabady (ed.), *World Views of Population Problems.* Budapest: Akademiai Kiado.

FONG, M. S.
1975   "Some social and economic determinants of the work of married women in the fertile ages in West Malaysia." Population Association of America Annual Meeting, New York, Collected Papers 4:148–64.

FORTNEY, J. A.
1971   "Role preference and fertility: An exploration of motivation for childbearing." Duke University Doctoral Dissertation.

FREEDMAN, R.
1959   "Family planning in the white population of the United States." New York: Milbank Memorial Fund.
1961/   "The sociology of human fertility: A trend report and bib-
1962   liography," *Current Sociology* 10/11:35–121.
1962   "Family planning: A review of major trends and issues." In V. C. Kiser (ed.), *Research in Family Planning.* Princeton: Princeton University.
1975   *The Sociology of Human Fertility: An Annotated Bibliography.* New York: Halsted Press.

FREEDMAN, R. AND L. COOMBS
1966   "Economic considerations in family growth decisions." *Population Studies* 20:197–222.

FREEDMAN, R., P. K. WHELPTON, AND A. A. CAMPBELL
1959   *Family Planning, Sterility and Population Growth.* New York: McGraw-Hill.

GENDELL, M., M. N. MARAVIGLIA AND P. C. KREITNER
1970   "Fertility and economic activity of women in Guatemala City, 1964." *Demography* 7:273–86.

GERMAIN, A.
1974   "The status and roles of women as factors in fertility behavior: A policy analysis." Population Association of America Annual Meeting, New York, *Collected Papers* 5:1–34.

GOLDBERG, D.
1959   "The fertility of two generation urbanities." *Population Studies* 12:214–22.
1960   "Another look at the Indianapolis fertility data." *Milbank Memorial Fund Quarterly* 38:23–26.

GOLDSCHEIDER, C. AND P. UHLENBERG
1969   "Minority group status and fertility." *American Journal of Sociology* 74:361–72.

GOLDSTEIN, S.
1972   "The influence of labor force participation and education on fertility in Thailand." *Population Studies* 26:419–36.

GRABILL, W. H. AND M. DAVIDSON
1968   "Recent trends in childspacing among American women." *Demography* 5:212–26.

HALL, M.
1971   "Family planning in Santiago, Chile: The male viewpoint." *Studies in Family Planning* 2:143–48.

HAWTHORN, G.
  1968   "Explaining human fertility." *Sociology* 2:65–78.
  1970   *The Sociology of Fertility.* London: Collier-Macmillan.

HILL, R.
  1968   "A classified international bibliography of family planning
              research, 1955–1968," *Demography* 5:973–1001.
  1974   "Modern systems theory and the family: A confrontation."
              In M. B. Sussman (ed.), *Sourcebook on Marriage and the
              Family.* Boston: Houghton Mifflin.

HILL, R., K. BACK, AND J. M. STYCOS
  1068   "Intra-family communication and fertility planning in Puerto
              Rico." In J. Heiss (ed.), *Family Roles and Interaction.*
              Chicago: Rand McNally.

HILL R., J. M. STYCOS, AND K. W. BACK
  1959   *The Family and Population Control: A Puerto Rican Experi-
              ment in Social Change.* Chapel Hill, N.C.: University of
              North Carolina.

HOFFMAN, L. W. AND F. WYATT
  1965   "Social change and motivations for having larger families:
              Some theoretical considerations." *Merrill-Palmer Quarterly*
              6:235–44.

HUTCHISON, I. W.
  1971   "Marital interaction, power, and fertility control in a tran-
              sitional society: The case of the Philippines." Paper pre-
              sented to the 34th Annual Meeting of the Southern Sociologi-
              cal Society, Miami Beach, Florida.

JAFFE, A. J. AND K. AZUMI
  1960   "The birth rate and cottage industries in underdeveloped
              countries." *Economic Development and Cultural Change*
              9:52–63.

KAR, S. B.
  1971   "Individual aspirations as related to early and late acceptance of
              contraception." *Journal of Social Psychology* 83:235–45.

KASARDA, J. D.
  1971   "Economic structure and fertility: A comparative analysis."
              Demography 8:307–17.

KHATRI, A. A.
  1970   "The Indian Family: An empirically derived analysis of
              shifts in size and types." Paper presented at the Seventh
              World Congress of Sociology, Varna, Bulgaria.

KISER, C. V.
  1962   "The Indianapolis study of social and psychological factors
              affecting fertility." In C. V. Kiser (ed.), *Research in Family
              Planning.* Princeton: Princeton University Press.

KISER, C. V. AND M. E. FRANK
  1967   "Factors associated with the lower fertility of non-white
              women of college attainment." *Milbank Memorial Fund
              Quarterly* XVI:427–47.

KROTKI, K.
  1972   "Low male wage and high female education as tools of social
              engineering for the population problem." In J. Husain (ed.),
              Population Analysis and Studies. Bombay: Somaiya.

KUNZ, P. R.
  1965   "The relation of income and fertility." *Journal of Marriage
              and the Family* 27:509–13.

KUPINSKY, S.
  1971   "Non-familial activity and socio-economic differentials in
              fertility," *Demography* 8:353–67.

LEIBENSTEIN, H.
  1974   "An interpretation of the economic theory of fertility: Prom-
              ising path or blind alley?" *Journal of Economic Literature*
              7:467–79.

LEROY-BEAULIEU, P.
  1913   La question de la population. Paris: F. Alcan.

LIU, W. T.
  1972   "Conjugal interaction and fertility behavior: Some concep-

tual methodological and theoretical issues in comparative
family and fertility research." In H. Yuan Tien and Frank D.
Bean (eds.), *Comparative Family and Fertility Research,*
Leiden: E. J. Brill.

LIU, W. T., A. RUBEL, AND V. PATO
  1970   *The Cebu Family Health Project.* South Bend, Ind.: Univer-
              sity of Notre Dame Press.

LOEWENTHAL, N. H. AND A. S. DAVID
  1972   "Social and economic correlates of family fertility: An
              updated survey of the evidence." Research Triangle Park,
              N.C.: Center for Population Research Triangle Institute.

MARSHALL, H. AND J. SINNOTT
  1971   "Urban structure and the black/white fertility differential:
              Examination of the 'assimilationist' model." *Social Science
              Quarterly* 52:588– 601.

MASNICK, G. S. AND J. A. McFALLS, JR.
  1976   "A new perspective on the twentieth century American
              fertility swing," *Journal of Family History* 1:217–44.

MATRAS, J.
  1973   "On changing matchmaking, marriage, and fertility in Israel:
              Some findings, problems, and hypotheses." *American Jour-
              nal of Sociology* 79:364–88.

MAULDIN W. P.
  1965   "Fertility studies: Knowledge, attitude, and practice."
              Studies in Family Planning 7:1–10.

MICHEL, A.
  1970   "Prediction of a theoretical model in family planning sociol-
              ogy." Paper presented at the Seventh World Congress of
              Sociology, Varna, Bulgaria.

MINKLER, M.
  1970   "Fertility and female labor force participation in India: A
              survey of workers in Old Delhi area." *Journal of Family
              Welfare* 17:31–43.

MISRA, B. D.
  1967   "Correlates of males' attitudes toward family planning." In
              D. Bogue (ed.), *Sociological Contributions to Family Plan-
              ning Research.* Chicago: Community and Family Center.

MITCHELL, R. E.
  1972   "Husband-wife relations and family planning practices in
              Urban Hong Kong," *Journal of Marriage and the Family* 34:
              139–46.

MITRA, J.
  1966   "Education and fertility in the United States." *Eugenics
              Quarterly* 13:214–22.

MORCORS, W.
  1974   "Employment of women and fertility, a field study in El-
              Waily District." *Egyptian Population and Family Planning
              Review* 7:21–30.

MUELLER, E.
  1971   "Agricultural change and fertility change: The case of
              Taiwan." Unpublished manuscript.

MUKHERJEE, B. N.
  1975b   "The role of husband-wife communication in family plan-
              ning." *Journal of Marriage and the Family* 37:655–67.

OMRAN, ABDEL
  1971   *The Health Theme in Family Planning.* Chapel Hill, N.C.:
              Carolina Population Center, University of North Carolina.

OPPENHEIMER, V. K.
  1973   "Demographic influence on female employment and the
              status of women." *American Journal of Sociology* 78:946–
              61.

PERRUCCI, C. C.
  1968   "Mobility, marriage and child-spacing among college
              graduates." *Journal of Marriage and the Family* 30:273–83.

PIEPMEIER, K. B. AND T. S. ADKINS

1973   "The status of women and fertility." *Journal of Biosocial Science* 5:507–20.

POFFENBERGER, T.
1967   "Interpersonal relationships of village families relayed to the problems of family planning: A progress report." Unpublished manuscript. Baroda, India: University of Baroda.
1968   "Husband-wife communication and motivational aspects of population control in an Indian village." New Delhi, India:Central Family Planning Institute.

POFFENBERGER, T. AND S. B. POFFENBERGER
1965   "A comparison of factors influencing choice of vasectomy in India and the United States." *Indian Journal of Social Work* 25:339–51.

POTI, S. J., B. CHAKRABORTI AND C. R. MALAKER
1962   "Reliability of data relating to contraceptive practices." In C. V. Kiser (ed.), *Research in Family Planning.* Princeton: Princeton University.

POWERS, M. G.
1966   "Socio-economic status and the fertility of married women." *Sociology and Social Research* 50:472–92.

PRESSER, H. B.
1971   "The timing of the first birth, female roles, and black fertility." *Milbank Memorial Fund Quarterly* 49:329–61.

PRESTON, S. H.
1972   "Female employment policy and fertility." Commission on Population Growth and the American Future. Research Reports Volume 6: *Aspects of Population Growth Policy.* Washington, D.C.: Government Printing Office.

RAINWATER, L.
1965   *Family Design: Marital Sexuality, Family Size, and Contraception.* Chicago: Aldine.
1971   "Marital sexuality in four 'cultures of poverty'." In D.S. Marshall and R. C. Suggs (eds.), *Human Sexual Behavior.* New York: Basic Books.

REED, F. W. AND J. R. UDRY
1973   "Female work, fertility and contraceptive use in a biracial sample." *Journal of Marriage and the Family* 35:597–602.

RIDLEY, J. C.
1959   "Number of children expected in relation to non-familial activities of the wife." *Milbank Memorial Fund Quarterly* 37:277–96.
1969   "The changing position of American women: Education, labor force participation and fertility." Paper presented at the Family in Transition Roundtable Conference, National Institute of Health. Washington, D.C.: U.S. Government Printing Office.

RITCHEY, P. N. AND C. S. STOKES
1971   "Residence background, socio-economic status, and fertility," *Demography* 8:369–77.

ROSARIO, F. Z.
1970   "Husband-wife interaction and family planning acceptance: A survey of the literature." East-West Population Institute Working Paper # 3. Honolulu: East-West Center.

ROSEN B. C.
1971   "Industrialization, personality, and social mobility in Brazil." *Human Organization* 30:137–48.
1973   "Social change, migration, and family interaction in Brazil." *American Sociological Review* 38:198–212.

ROSEN, B. C. AND A. B. SIMMONS
1971   "Industrialization, family and fertility: A structural psychological analysis of the Brazilian case." *Demography* 8:49–69.

ROSENBERG, H. M.
1973   "Fertility strategies as intervening determinants of wives' labor force status." Paper presented at Population Association of American Meeting, New Orleans, Louisiana.

SAWHILL, I. V.
1977   "Economic perspectives on the family." *Daedalus* 106:115–25.

SAFILIOS-ROTHSCHILD, C.
1965   "Some aspects of fertility in urban Greece." *United Nations World Population Conference, Belgrade, Yugoslavia,* 381–84. Vol. 2. New York: United Nations.

SLY, D.
1970   "Minority group status and fertility: An extension of Goldscheider and Uhlenberg." *American Journal of Sociology* 76:443–59.

SPEARE, A., M. C. SPEARE, AND H. LIN
1973   "Urbanization, non-familial work, education and fertility in Taiwan." *Population Studies* 27:323–34.

STOECKEL, J. AND M. A. CHOUDHURY
1969   "Differential fertility in a rural area of East Pakistan." *Milbank Memorial Fund Quarterly* 47:189–98.

STOKES, C. S.
1973   "Family structure and socio-economic differentials in fertility." *Population Studies* 27:295–304.

STOKES, C. S. AND C. J. DUDLEY
1972   "Family planning and conjugal roles: Some further evidence." *Social Science and Medicine* 6:157–61.

STYCOS, J. M.
1964   "Haitian attitudes toward family size." *Human Organization* 23: 42–47.
1965   "Female employment and fertility in Lima, Peru." *Milbank Memorial Fund Quarterly* 43:42–54.

STYCOS, J. M. AND R. H. WELLER
1967   "Female working roles and fertility." *Demography* 4:210–17.

SUSSMAN, M. B.
1968   "Adaptive, directive and integrative behavior of today's family." *Family Process* 7:239–50.
1971   "Family systems in the 1970's: Analysis policies and programs," *Annals of the American Academy of Political and Social Science* 396:40–56.

SUSSMAN, M. B., J. N. CATES, AND D. T. SMITH
1970   *The Family and Inheritance.* New York: Russell Sage Foundation.

SUSSMAN, M. B. AND B. E. COGSWELL
1976   *Personal Marriage Contract Study.* Report in progress.

SWEET, J.
1973   *Women in the Labor Force.* New York: Seminar Press.

TARVER, J. D., C. CYRUS, K. KISER, C. LEE, AND R. MORAN
1970   "Urban influence on the fertility and employment patterns of women living in homogeneous areas." *Journal of Marriage and the Family* 32:237–41.

TERRY, G. B.
1975   "Rival explanations in the work-fertility relationship." *Population Studies* 29:191–205.

THORAT, S. S. AND F. C. FLIEGEL
1968   "Some aspects of adoption of health and family planning practices in India," *Behavioral Sciences and Community Development* 2:1–13.

TIEN, H. Y.
1966   "Mobility, non-familial activity and fertility: Some findings and observations." Paper presented at the Meeting of the Population Association of America, New York.

TIMUR, SERIM
1971   "Socio-economic determinants of differential fertility in Turkey." Ankara: Hacettepe University Institute of Population Studies Paper presented at the Second European Population Conference, Strasbourg, France.

TOBIN, P.
  1975   "Perceived contribution of children to marriage and its effect
              on family planning behavior." *Social Biology* 22:75–85.
U.S. BUREAU OF THE CENSUS
  1971   "Previous and prospective fertility: 1967." *Parent Popula-
              tion Reports* Series P/20, no. 211. Washington: U.S. Gov-
              ernment Printing Office.
WAITE, L. J. AND R. M. STOLZENBERG
  1976   "Intended childbearing and labor force participation of
              young women: Insights from non-recursive models." *Ameri-
              can Sociological Review* 41:235–51.
WELLER, R. H.
  1968   "The employment of wives: Role incompatibility and
              fertility." *Milbank Memorial Fund Quarterly* 46:507–26.
  1971   "The impact of employment upon fertility." In A Michel
              (ed.), *Family Issues of Employed Women in Europe and
              America*. Leiden: E. J. Brill.
WESTOFF, C. F.
  1961   *Family Growth in Metropolitan America*. Princeton: Prince-
              ton University.

WESTOFF, C. F. AND N. B. RYDER
  1970   "Contraceptive practice among urban Blacks in the United
              States, 1965." *Milbank Memorial Fund Quarterly* 48:215–
              33.
WHELPTON, P. K. AND C. V. KISER
  1950   "Fertility planning and fertility rates by socio-economic
              status." In P. K. Whelpton and C. V. Kiser (eds.), *Social and
              Psychological Factors Affecting Fertility*. New York: Mil-
              bank Memorial Fund.
YAUKEY, D.
  1967   "Couple concurrence and empathy on birth control motiva-
              tion in Dacca, East Pakistan," *American Sociological Re-
              view* 32:716–26.
YAUKEY, D., B. J. ROBERTS, AND W. GRIFFITHS
  1965   "Husbands' vs. wives' responses to a fertility survey."
              Population Studies 19:29–43.

9

WIFE-MOTHER EMPLOYMENT, FAMILY, AND SOCIETY

E. M. Rallings and F. Ivan Nye

Most women through the ages have been employed in economic production. However, in many societies such production was carried out entirely or mostly within the home where a wife or mother could be involved in production and at the same time supervise small children. Also, intermittently she could engage in housekeeping tasks as required, then return to production without much loss of time.

With the development of factories away from the home (Abbott, 1910), single women in large numbers took factory employment (as did children); but married women did not become a major part of the American labor force until after World War I. Actually, much family production such as making clothing, canning, baking, laundering, gardening, and a host of other tasks remained in the home. Also, most women from their early 20s to late 40s had large numbers of children, including young ones. "A woman's place is in the home" remained largely unchallenged until World War II, when women's labor was urgently needed in factories. However, childless married women entered paid employment in increasing numbers between World War I and World War II (Nye, 1974c).

The employment outside the home of women with minor children increased during and following World War II and has continued to increase until in 1974 it included on any given day more than half of the women with children six to seventeen but none younger than six, and one-third of those with one or more children below the age of six. This generated some role conflict for mothers in that they might be needed at home in child care, child socialization, or housekeeper roles while their responsibilities as employees required their presence elsewhere. Even if there were no preschool children at home and provision could be made for before- and after-school care, role conflict might still be present in the

mother having too many duties to perform or in the belief that she must personally be available to her children at all times rather than entrust them to substitute care givers. Among some psychologically oriented professionals, questions of whether the personality characteristics needed in the occupational world would serve well in child- and home-oriented roles (Lundberg and Farnham, 1947) were also generated.

Role conflict and at least the possibility of conflicting personality needs generated a broad series of socially oriented questions concerning effects of mothers' working on the stability of marriage and the family, on the children, and on the health and well-being of the mother. These questions were probably even more urgent because the existence of employed mothers as a growing proportion of all mothers raised questions concerning the position of married women who decided against taking employment.

These social problem-oriented questions largely dominated the research of the 1950s and the first half of the 1960s. However, as more and more research generally failed to provide support to the alarmists, some attention shifted to more theoretically oriented issues, such as maternal employment's effects on the parent as a model or the development of personality characteristics in female children relevant to success in professional and executive positions (Hoffman, 1974a).

The other basic question has been the motivations and characteristics of married women who take employment contrasted with those who do not take it or who do not remain in it. These have centered primarily on the training and abilities of the woman and on the extensiveness of competing child care, socialization, and housekeeper roles.

THE CONCEPT EMPLOYMENT

In male employment, employment has usually taken a dichotomous form: if one was employed, he worked 40

NOTE: The authors express appreciation for the thoughtful critiques of Barbara H. Settles and John E. Carlson. A number of their suggestions have been incorporated into this chapter.

hours weekly with anything in excess of that considered overtime. Unless he was a student or retired, it would be thought unusual if he worked fewer than 40 hours weekly. However, the same dichotomy is much less useful for dealing with maternal employment. Many mothers work part of a work week, and many are employed only part of the year. And regardless of how many hours they are in paid employment, almost all retain major responsibilities for housekeeping tasks and most younger ones for child care and socialization as well. Perhaps partly for the latter reason, for women there are two major categories of part-time paid employment: less than full time during the week and less than 50 weeks during the year. Only about 40 percent of women are employed as much as 35 hours weekly and 50 weeks yearly (U.S. Bureau of the Census, 1973). Thus part-time employment is an important phenomenon. Unfortunately, because of the social problem orientation of most of the research to date, relatively little research has focused on part-time employment. It was felt that if there were any detrimental effects on children, women, or interpersonal relations in the family, they would be related to full-time rather than part-time employment. What was not anticipated was the finding that the relationship between numbers of hours employed and some dependent variables is curvilinear. These curvilinear relationships will be reported in this chapter, of course, but much more could be said now if that relationship had been anticipated instead of emerging fortuitously from some of the larger studies.

Because this body of research was mostly social problem–oriented, its dependent variables were dictated by social concern rather than by interest in theory testing or theory development; and the findings have emerged as relationships between maternal employment and the welfare of family members. Researchers, with varying degrees of care and sophistication, tried to control possible spurious correlations by holding other relevant characteristics of individuals constant. What has emerged is a large number of nonrelationships; e.g., maternal employment is not related to school achievement of children. For the findings of a significant relationship, the theorizing had to be of an ad hoc nature, since the analysis was not inspired by theory testing.

To fit this large body of empirical work into the purposes of the present volume, causality has been suggested wherever it seems reasonable to do so; e.g., maternal employment ''positively influences'' or ''negatively influences'' whatever ''outcome'' is involved. This is done as much to stimulate a reaction from the reader as anything else; that is, if the reader doubts the causal influence, he or she may be stimulated to provide an additional test of the relationship.

Our analysis commences with the societal changes which led to an increased demand for the labor of married women, with or without children, and the characteristics and personal situations which permitted and motivated part of these women to take employment. These propositions are diagrammed in Figures 9.1 and 9.2. Then in stage II, taking employment status as the independent variable, we relate it first to its effects on women who are wives and/or mothers. The propositions from this literature are shown in Figure 9.3. The same analysis follows for effects on husbands, diagrammed in Figure 9.4. The propositions relating maternal employment to children and relevant parent-child relationships are reviewed, reformulated, and diagrammed in Figure 9.5. Finally, as we started with the impact of the society on the employment of wives and mothers, we conclude with their impact on the community and the society (Figure 9.6). In the concluding section we shall suggest why the adverse effects feared by many professional and lay persons have not occurred and will place the phenomenon in a more general theoretical perspective.

STAGE I. EMPLOYMENT AS THE DEPENDENT VARIABLE

There are two classes of independent variables which have a significant bearing on whether or not women take paid employment: those which operate at the macro level, e.g., the level of societal facilitation of women's employment, and those which operate at the micro level, e.g., individual motivations, and adequacy of one's personal situation and level of personal training and abilities. The macrolevel variables will be presented first, as independent variables affecting the dependent variable, level of employment of women outside the home. These propositions are logical or reasonable deductions. The specific empirical research needed to prove them has not been done and, because of their macrolevel scope, may not be possible. We present them as reasonable and probable deductions from the limited facts available.

Employment of women away from the home preempts a major part of the time and energy of women and to some extent that of the man and children, who may share more of the household tasks she might otherwise perform. It preempts time which might otherwise be invested in leisure, self- development, and informal visiting. If a society places a comparatively high value on goods and services and if such goods and services are important for prestige and security as well as direct utility, then more women should be employed. There is some evidence that societies vary on the above values. Therefore, it is proposed that:

1. The level of value placed by society on goods and services, as compared to leisure and visiting, positively influences the proportion of women in employment.

The demand for women workers in a society is directly linked to the movement of women into the labor force. In the United States low birth rates during the depression years, combined with a rapid expansion of the economy after World War II, made for a strong demand for women workers (Nye, 1974c). Of course, changing economic conditions result in the fluctuation of this demand.

Certain occupations—teaching, nursing, and secretarial—have been staffed primarily by women. Following World War II, there was a major increase in the demand for personnel in such occupations—occupations in which a preference for women employees had developed. (For a detailed discussion of this, see Oppenheimer, 1970.) Thus, despite some effect from the broadening of opportunities for women in new jobs or in occupations previously closed to them, the principal link between women's employment and labor market demand can be stated:

2. The level of labor market demand in occupations customarily staffed by women influences the proportion of women employed in a positive direction.

Proposition 2 reflects the relationship in the past. The present concerted effort to bring women into occupations formerly staffed entirely or predominantly by men will alter it, but how much and how rapidly cannot be accurately predicted. This same effort is bringing more men into occupations traditionally dominated by women.

The traditional definition of the place of women as being in the home, caring for it and for the small children and engaged in home production and processing, evolved from a milieu characterized by a relatively undifferentiated economy. The mother typically produced food (gardening) and clothing (weaving, sewing, and repair) and performed basic processing such as canning food, baking, and preparing food for cooking. Increased differentiation in the economy means that some tasks become the responsibility of specialized plants and personnel. Many of women's former tasks are performed by specialists, which also means that more income is required to pay for these services. Therefore:

3. The level of specialization of the economy positively influences the proportion of women who are gainfully employed.

If the mother is to take employment away from the home, some kind of substitute child care is frequently necessary. Traditionally, the care of the aged and infirm and of the crippled has been considered part of her responsibility also. Some of this care is supplied by her husband, older children, or other relatives; but if she is to take employment away from the home, some must also be provided by the society or contracted for by her. While institutional day care tends to develop with the market for it in a society, its professional level and the basis of its availability differ; e.g., the mother may have to pay for it entirely, or part of its cost may be born by the society or community. The same is true of the care of the aged or crippled. If a society has subsidized such substitute care

(as in the Soviet Union, in contemporary China, or in the Israeli kibbutz), paid employment is expedited and this proposition may be stated:

4. The level of subsidization of substitute care for dependent persons positively influences the proportion of women in paid employment.

It should be noted, in passing, that such heavy initial subsidization is characteristic of societies which embrace an ideology of equal employment of women and which also feel a pressing need for women's services in factories, fields, offices, and schools.[1]

The quality as well as the cost of substitute care is of concern to families also. The facilitating effect on women's employment of substitute care viewed as equal to family care is considered later as a micro variable.

Even when employed, women still bear the major responsibility for household tasks such as purchasing and preparing food for the family, doing the laundry, cleaning the house, and so on. All societal events which make the accomplishment of these tasks easier or more expeditious have an impact on women's employment. Labor-saving devices in the home, more restaurants, the availability of prepared foods, and housecleaning services are such events. Therefore, it can be stated:

5. The availability of labor-saving devices in the home and other substitutes for the labor of housewives positively influences the proportion of women in paid employment.

Finally, the societal norm with regard to the employment of women must be examined. At once it is apparent that there are several norms having to do with the different categories of women workers. Abbott (1910) documented that the paid employment of single women and those women who have had to assume the provider role has been accepted by society for a long time. Increasingly in this century, however, wives and mothers who were not primary breadwinners have moved into the labor market (U.S. Bureau of Labor Statistics, 1971). Did a societal norm approving such employment exist prior to this behavioral shift, or did the behavior itself result in a new societal norm? It seems apparent that in some societies (e.g., modern Communist societies and the Israeli kibbutz) prescriptions encouraging women's full employment as workers preceded the establishment of the economy in which most women did take employment. Therefore the proposition can be stated:

6. The level of societal approval of women's employment positively influences the proportion of women in paid employment.

Although the level of employment has been considered the dependent variable in this section, it is equally probable that the level of employment has a feedback effect on the macro variables. Undoubtedly, there are also interactive effects between the macro variables. An intuitive effort to suggest some of these effects has been made (indicated by the lines connecting the independent variables in Figure 9.1).

Microlevel Variables Affecting Levels of Employment

We turn now to a consideration of two sets of micro variables: those which involve the personal characteristics of women, e.g., health, abilities, motivations, and competing household responsibilities; and those which involve situational factors in the social environment, e.g., level of the family income. No attempt will be made to examine the effect of personality variables as mo-

tivational factors in women's employment. The reason for this decision is succinctly stated by Hoffman:

> Because of the paucity of data, it is premature to say whether or not personality traits differentiate working from nonworking women within specific groups [1974b:52].

Too, since in excess of 50 percent of the population is involved, it seems unreasonable to expect employed and not employed wives and mothers to differ greatly in this respect.

In the discussion which follows, it should be pointed out that a woman's employability will be assessed differently by the prospective employer, the woman herself, and her reference groups–significant others.[2]

Figure 9.1.   Predicting Women's Employment—Macro Analysis

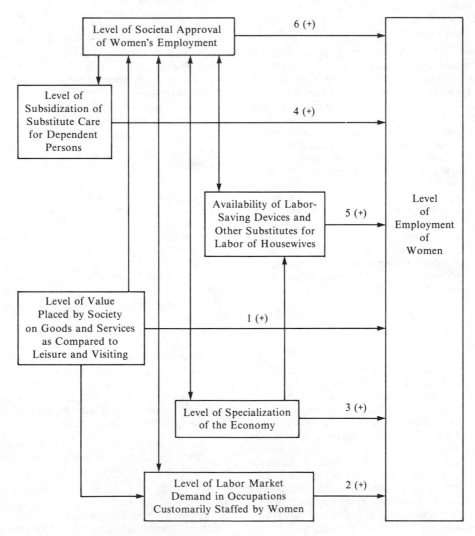

Employers are interested in hiring healthy persons for obvious reasons. Women are likely to think twice about taking a job unless they feel "up to it" physically (Parnes et al., 1975). Out of concern for the woman, reference groups–significant others tend to discourage the employment of their kith and kin if they have subpar health. It is apparent that in some cases great economic need may negate the personal and significant–other concerns over a woman working when not in good health. Also, poor health may be hidden from the prospective employer. The differential health requirements of various positions, the number of hours worked, and perhaps other significant factors indicate there is no absolute, universal health requirement for employed women.

The empirical findings on this point are that employed women are healthier than nonemployed women (Nye, 1974a:208–09). There is some question as to whether this results from a selective process, as the above discussion would suggest, or from the salutary effect of the work itself, or from some other variable or combination of variables. The former seems most likely, so this proposition can be stated:

7. Women's state of health positively influences the likelihood of their employment.

Although it appears that poor health discourages paid employment, there is no reason to think that the relationship is linear. Whether women with exceptionally good health are more likely to be employed than those with average health is still an open question.

Reflecting the attitudes of society, reference groups, and significant others to a degree, women form their own estimates of the rewards and costs of working. We have termed these rewards psychic satisfaction. These satisfactions range from feelings of achievement, competence, and contribution (Hoffman, 1974b) to simply relief over escaping the physically tiring and emotionally draining task of rearing children. Even though the money earned is important in women's assessment of the value of employment, we note here the nonmonetary rewards for working. Counterbalanced against the rewards are the costs: guilt over the neglect of a woman's children and/or her husband, less discretionary time, and so on. Women's evaluation of previous work experience as fulfilling or not enters into their estimate of satisfactions and their final decision, as does their assessment of their roles as housewives and mothers. Their career commitment may also be a factor (Parnes et al., 1975). The proposition showing this relationship can be stated as follows:

8. Women's degree of expected psychic satisfaction from working positively influences the likelihood of their employment.

Education creates competencies valued by employers, providing more job opportunities, more stimulating work, and better pay. Therefore, it can be stated:

9. As women's education level increases, the positive relationship in Proposition 8 is strengthened.

Continuing the examination of the consequences of education on level of employment, there is strong evidence that as the education level increases, so does the likelihood of employment. (See Bowen and Finegan, 1969:116, for an example of these data.) Very confidently, then, it can be stated:

10. Women's level of education positively influences the proportion of women employed.

A unique relationship has been found for black women. They were about as likely to be employed if they had no education as if they had a high school diploma. Also, black women with a four-year degree or graduate training were found in the labor force in the highest proportion of any female group (Bowen and Finegan, 1969:116). Therefore, it can be stated:

11. For black women, the relationship between education and employment is curvilinear, with the likelihood of employment increasing with education beyond the high school level.

Employers, whether hiring men or women, prefer experienced workers. In some instances a lack of experience may be an absolute barrier to employment. The woman's assessment of previous work experience as positive will be a facilitating factor to employment, and her assessment of previous work experience as negative will be a barrier to employment. Reference groups–significant others will find negative attitudes toward employment challenged by obviously successful work experience. It can be stated, then:

12. The amount of previous successful work experience positively influences the likelihood of women's employment.

Demographic data show that women in the age groups of 20–24 and 35–54 are most likely to be employed. From age 55 to age 64 a sizable decline in women's employment occurs (U.S. Bureau of Labor Statistics, 1971). The high employment rate in the younger age group has been linked with the completion of education and nonmarriage. (Never- married women are expected to work unless they are wealthy, provide personal care for a relative or relatives, or are physically or mentally handicapped). The married women in the younger age group are likely to be childless and/or to have an income they consider inadequate. It must be remembered, however, that the shape of the curve relating age to proportion employed is quite different for women who have children in their care than for those who are childless. For those with no children, there is no decline between the ages of 24 and 35.

The high employment in the older group has been

linked with lessened responsibilities for children and, in recent years, women's desires for self-fulfillment. Then, too, prospective employers may react positively to the expectation that older women will not have to drop out of work due to pregnancy or miss work because of sick children. Also, reference groups and significant others are more willing for women of this age to go to work, feeling that their duty to their children has been discharged.

The drop in employment after 55 is seen as related to failing health, a diminution of financial need, and perhaps other factors:

Therefore, with minimum legal age requirements as a relatively stable base, it can be confidently stated:

13. Women's age, as related to the stage in the family life cycle, influences the likelihood of their employment; this is a curvilinear relationship.

As already indicated, the level of economic support available to women has an important effect upon whether or not they seek employment. Using husband's income alone as the measure of economic support, demographic data show an inverse relationship between economic support and women's employment (U.S. Bureau of Labor Statistics, 1971). The picture is incomplete, however, until income from all sources is considered. Therefore, for this chapter the independent variable dealing with economic support is conceptualized as "level of family income" and includes income from all sources which is available to the family. This definition provides for the inclusion of women in all the commonly delineated marital statuses where the husband's income may be unimportant or not a factor at all.

According to data collected by Bowen and Finegan (1969:133–34) the addition of "other income" (than from the woman) increments to the husband's income has the same effect on women's employment as increases in the husband's income, i.e., a continuous decline in the employment of women with increases in income other than the husband's. This is true for all women with children under 18 but not for women without minor children. With no contradictory evidence, it is possible then to state with confidence:

14. Among women with minor children there is a negative relationship between family income, other than a woman's own, and maternal employment.

Where children are involved, the number of dependent children becomes the controlling factor. The evidence is quite clear that married women with no children are more likely to be employed than are women with children and that the proportion of women employed declines with the number of children. This relationship holds for white and black families at all income levels (Sweet, 1970). It seems a logical extrapolation to broaden this to include depen-

dent parents or relatives or, indeed, husbands. Therefore it is stated:

15. The number of dependent persons in the family negatively influences the likelihood of women's employment.

A contingent variable affecting the relationship stated in Proposition 15 is the availability of adequate substitute care for dependent persons, children or otherwise. In some cases, the lack of substitute care of any kind may be an absolute barrier to women's employment. In other cases, extreme economic need or great dissatisfaction with domestic roles may result in the rationalization of substitute care as being adequate. ("Adequate" means as good as would be provided by mother.) The greater availability of members of the extended family in the black than in the white segment of the population and the higher percentage of black women working provides some support for the relationship between adequate, available substitute care for dependents and women's employability. Also, the recent proliferation of day care centers for children and homes for the aged has occurred concomitantly with the increase in women's employment. The cost of the substitute care is always a pragmatic concern, with a differential impact by level of family income. Therefore, the following propositions may be stated:

16. The adequacy of available substitute care for dependent persons in the family positively influences the likelihood of women's employment.

17. The cost to women of substitute care for dependent persons in the family negatively influences the likelihood of women's employment.

Although the contingency affect of the attitudes of significant others and reference groups on other variables influencing the level of employment seems very pervasive, we will limit ourselves to an examination of the direct influence of these variables on the level of women's employment.

Ethnic groups, community groups, religious groups, and others serve as reference groups. These groups may reflect the general societal attitude—ranging from strong disapproval to strong approval of women's employment. By providing an evaluative standard for women with regard to employment, reference groups affect women's ultimate decision to work or not to work (Erskine, 1971).

Significant others also are influential in motivating women to work or not to work. It is in the intimate, face-to-face association with significant others that women receive encouragement or discouragement which enters into their decision (Parnes et al., 1975).

A proposition can be stated which details these similar relationships. It is:

18. The degree of approval of women's reference

groups and significant others positively influences the likelihood they will be employed.

It seems apparent that the obverse is true also; i.e., the proportion of women in employment positively influences the evaluations of reference groups and significant others.

The relationships stated in the numbered propositions are presented in Figure 9.2. Also, an effort is made to suggest probable linkages between the independent variables by lines and directional arrows.

STAGE II. EMPLOYMENT AS THE INDEPENDENT VARIABLE

The dependent variable of stage I, level of employment of women, becomes the independent variable of stage II as we examine the consequences of women's employment. Level of employment is considered as a continuous variable, which equates with Burr's (1973:236) "amount of time wife-mother spends in economic activity."

Since the truly significant data in any consideration of human activities are the subjective assessments of the meaning of that activity to the persons involved, we will alternately consider the effects of women's employment on the woman herself, the husband-father, and the children. Finally, we will attempt to explicate the effect of women's employment on the community and the society.

Effects on the Wife-Mother

Since the consequences of employment for women may be important intervening variables in explicating the effects of women's employment on husbands-fathers, children, the community, and society, it seems appropriate to begin by considering the effects of employment on the physical, psychological, and social well-being of the wife-mother.

In considering the effect of the state of women's health on level of employment in stage I, it was pointed out that employed women, on the average, are physically healthier than women who are not employed. It has been suggested that this is due to the selective recruitment of healthier women and the tendency of women with poor health to leave employment. A closer look at this phenomenon is indicated.

Some of the factors which would seem to have a positive effect on the physical health of working women are that they are (1) more likely to be covered by health insurance and/or feel freer to spend money for health care; (2) more likely to be exposed to educational programs dealing with preventive health measures; (3) more likely to be concerned about their appearance, hence less likely to be obese, due to social contacts at work and work-

related events; (4) less likely to have health problems related to childbearing since they have fewer children.

Some factors which would seem to have a negative effect on the physical health of working women are (1) the physical demands of the job itself, which may cause or aggravate health problems, e.g., back trouble; (2) exposure to unhealthy working conditions, e.g., polluted air; (3) the greater likelihood of accidental injury; (4) the physical demands of playing multiple roles.

The positive and negative factors operative in the area of women's physical health are fairly well balanced, giving us little basis for claiming that work itself is the reason employed women are healthier than women who are not employed. The research, although considerable in extent, provides no solid basis for believing that paid employment does or does not improve health. It seems, then, that to better understand the impact of employment on women's health, neither the physical nor the psychological aspects should be neglected.

Several studies (Kligler, 1954; Feld, 1963; Kaley, 1971; Birnbaum, 1971; White, 1972) have explored the relationship between maternal employment and women's psychological health, most commonly focusing on the guilt and anxiety engendered by employment. The overall findings seem to indicate that although these two outcomes are not limited to employed mothers, they experienced them disproportionately. Birnbaum (1971:190) found that nonemployed mothers' anxiety-guilt levels were more similar to those of employed mothers if their level of education was high and/or they had high aspirations for their children.

Although the findings from research most often link guilt and anxiety, it seems probable that there are two dimensions involved and that something would be gained, empirically and theoretically, by separating the two. Anxiety is a broad-gauged concept which denotes the feelings of inadequacy, in terms of society's expectations, over performing the multiple roles involved in being a working wife-mother. This is similar to what Goode (1960) has labeled role strain. Guilt, on the other hand, results from engaging in behavior which the woman sees as contrary to her internalized values, e.g., neglect of child(ren). A woman may be anxious about her ability to handle her particular set of roles and yet not feel guilty at all about leaving her child(ren) to enter the labor force. Guilt seems more likely to be present when young children or other dependents who are subpar physically or mentally are left in questionable substitute care situations. A key contingent variable seems to be the level of approval of employment by significant others.

After consideration of the research, two provisional propositions are stated:

19. The level of employment positively influences employed mothers' level of anxiety.

Figure 9.2.   Predicting Women's Employment—Micro Analysis

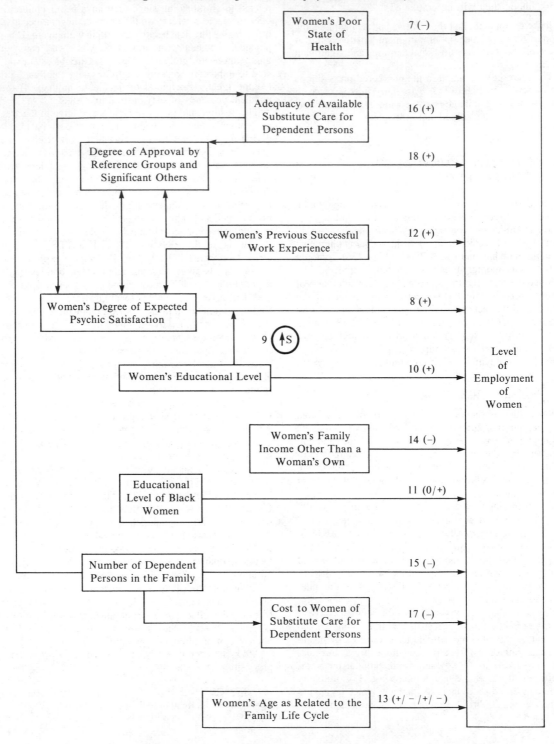

20. The level of employment positively influences employed mothers' level of guilt.

However, it is not clear that the relationship is linear; e.g., part-time employment may not have this consequence.

At a more global level, what is the relationship—if any—between employment and the women's self-concept? Hacker (1971) found that working wives were confident of their interest and attractiveness as persons but felt less secure and successful in playing wife-mother roles.

Feld reported that white employed mothers' feelings about themselves as individuals were more positive than negative. The specific areas tapped were "lack of uniqueness of self," "lack of self-acceptance," "shortcomings in the self," "lack of strong points in the self," (1963:334). However, Feld also found that employed mothers felt inadequate in particular role situations, e.g., as mothers. Nye resolves this apparent contradiction by suggesting

> that employed mothers tend toward higher self-esteem as individuals, but in situations involving conflict between the roles of employee and domestic roles, they often feel inadequate [1963:386].

Those feelings of inadequacy were alluded to above in the rationale for Propositions 19 and 20. Now, somewhat intuitively, and with the direction of causality not firmly established, it can be stated:

21. The level of employment and employed mothers' self-concept are positively related.

Continuing at the global level, is there something about working outside the home which has a deleterious effect on the mental health of women? Considering definitional difficulties and the sparseness of data (Feld, 1963; Sharp, 1960), nothing definitive can be said at this time about the relationship between women's employment and mental illness.

Another global variable attracting some research interest is the effect of maternal employment on the mother's satisfaction with life. A number of studies (Gass, 1959; Nye, 1963c; Feld, 1963; Birnbaum, 1971) have explored this relationship. Despite some disagreements, the weight of the evidence seems to be that employed mothers are better satisfied than are nonemployed mothers while the children are present in the home. The relationship is reversed in the posparental period. For the former group, the higher the mother's educational level, the more likely the feelings of satisfaction will favor employed mothers. Also, despite the fact that full-time employed mothers were better satisfied with their *jobs* than were housewives, part-time employed mothers had a significantly higher *general* level of satisfaction than did either nonemployed mothers or mothers who were employed full time. It can be stated, then:

22. The level of employment is related to mothers' general level of satisfaction with life; the relationship is curvilinear.

Some related but more specific findings from research conducted by Nye (1958) and Birnbaum (1971) make possible the following tentative proposition:

23. The level of employment positively influences mothers' enjoyment of activities and relationships with their children.

Moving from satisfaction with life in general, the effect of employment on the marital satisfaction of the wife-mother is examined. Findings are complex and occasionally contradictory (Locke and Mackeprang, 1949; Gianopulos and Mitchell, 1957; Feld, 1963; Axelson, 1963; Gover, 1963; Powell, 1963; Nye, 1963b; Orden and Bradburn, 1969; Feldman and Feldman, 1973). Nye reviews changes over time and concludes that there has been a change—that in the 1950s, and perhaps the early 1960s, full-time employment contributed, if only slightly, to more conflict and tensions and less marital happiness. But by the 1970s this effect had disappeared, at least in the middle class (Nye, 1974b:205–06). With social class as a contingency, it can be stated:

24. In the lower class, employment is negatively related to the marital satisfaction of the wife-mother.

Orden and Bradburn (1969) suggest that part-time employment may be the way for women to achieve optimum adjustment in marriage, and Nye (1963a) found that part-time employed mothers averaged higher on happiness than either mothers who were employed full time or mothers who were .not employed. Somewhat provisionally, then:

25. The relationship between employment and marital satisfaction for the wife- mother is curvilinear, with the highest level for the part-time-employed.

We don't know why part-time-employed wives average higher in marital as well as general satisfaction. However, several authors maintain that after children are in school, household roles constitute a part-time occupation. Adding another part-time position increases the productive contributions of the wife without crowding her day, as is frequently the case if she adds full-time employment to housework and child care. Also, she can usually avoid direct conflicts between her responsibilities in the housekeeper, child care, and employee roles.

A subject of early and continuing interest is the effect of employment on "power" in the conjugal relationship. In addition to conceptualization problems, and perhaps related to them, the empirical findings have often conflicted. For example, Heer (1963) and Middleton and Putney (1960) found a relationship between employment and what they termed power. In contrast, Blood and Hamblin (1958) and Hoffman (1961) found none.

In this chapter, power is defined as the potential ability

of the husband or wife to influence the other's behavior. In the literature, decision making is almost always used as an indicator of power. Since division of labor and power are so closely related, the two will be examined together.

In addition to the studies mentioned above, a number of others are relevant to this formulation (Hoffman, 1963c; Glueck and Glueck, 1957; Kligler, 1954; Blood, 1963; Bahr, 1972; Scanzoni, 1970; Aldous, 1969). In general, the findings from these research efforts suggest that employment results in greater power for the wife-mother in financial matters. However, there are many contingent variables operating, e.g., size of family and socioeconomic class. Bahr (1974) analyzes the operation of these two variables as follows: Women with large families gain less power through employment than women with small families, presumably because the cost of the mother's leaving the home for employment is greater in a large family. Employment provides a greater gain in power to lower-class women than to middle-class women. (No reason is given for the latter relationship. Possibly it is because the monetary contribution of the lower-class women is more needed.)

Furthermore, it should be noted that the employed mothers' gain in power is "primarily in 'external' decisions regarding finances and the provider role" (Bahr, 1974: 180).

With regard to task behavior, there is general consistency among the studies in reporting that the wife-mother's household labor decreases when she enters the labor market. Again two key contingent variables seem to be operative. If there are adolescent children in the home, the wife-mother's household labor decreases more than if there were none. Also, the greater the wife-mother's commitment to her job, the greater the decrease in her household labor (Bahr, 1972). Therefore, the following two propositions emerge:

26. Employment positively affects the power of the wife-mother in financial matters.

27. Employment negatively affects the amount of household labor performed by the wife-mother.

Another effect of maternal employment is what Burr (1973:240) calls "disengagement" and defines as the degree to which a person fully occupies a social role. This variable seems to be what Hoffman (1961) terms withdrawal from a social role and what Peterson (1961) conceptualizes as the degree of involvement in a social role. Since we have already dealt with household tasks per se, our concern now is with the effect of employment on women's degree of involvement in the interactive aspects of the wife-mother roles. That is, what effect does women's employment have on companionship with their husbands, and what effect does it have on the amount of time spent in the supervision and socialization of their child(ren)? With regard to the former, there is a dearth of empirical evidence. With regard to the latter, however, Hoffman (1961) found that as women's participation in employment increased, their participation in maternal roles decreased. Also, Nye (1963a) found that when women added the provider role, it decreased their involvement in child supervision. Therefore, it can be stated:

28. The level of employment reduces the quantity of women's involvement in domestic roles.

Hoffman (1961) suggested that an important contingent variable in determining how the woman apportions her time between the roles she plays is the woman's attitude toward her work, i.e., whether or not she likes her work. Presumably, if she likes her work, she would be more likely to spend more time at work and in work-related activities and less time in her domestic roles. It seems logical that this could be extended to women engaged in voluntary (nonpaid) work and also to wives in their interactions with their husbands.

Very little research has been attempted to ferret out the effect of employment on the social activities of the mother, i.e., in sharing activities with persons both inside and outside the family. Studies by Nye (1963d) and Sharp (1963) suggest the following propositions:

29. The level of employment negatively affects the involvement of mothers in leadership positions in voluntary community organizations.

30. The level of employment negatively affects the involvement of mothers in non-family-oriented recreation.

Both of the above propositions may simply reflect a pragmatic adjustment to the performance of multiple roles, and the latter proposition may reflect the positive value assigned to family-oriented recreation as opposed to non-family-oriented recreation. It may also reflect the fact that much of a woman's peer-oriented recreation occurs during the day when the husband is at work and the children are in school. Paid employment usually preempts this part of the day, requiring a reduction in such activities. Likewise formal entertaining of other couples or families requires major amounts of time and advanced planning, while family recreation can be more readily fitted into a crowded schedule.

In summary, the main outcomes of women's employment which have attracted sustained research are related to the psychological health of the woman, her role behavior, and her satisfaction with life, her marriage, and her children. Key contingent variables are the woman's social class, the attitudes of reference groups–significant others toward her employment, her liking for and commitment to her work, the stage in the family life cycle, and the size of the family. These relationships are delineated in Figure 9.3.

Figure 9.3. Effects of Employment on the Wife-Mother

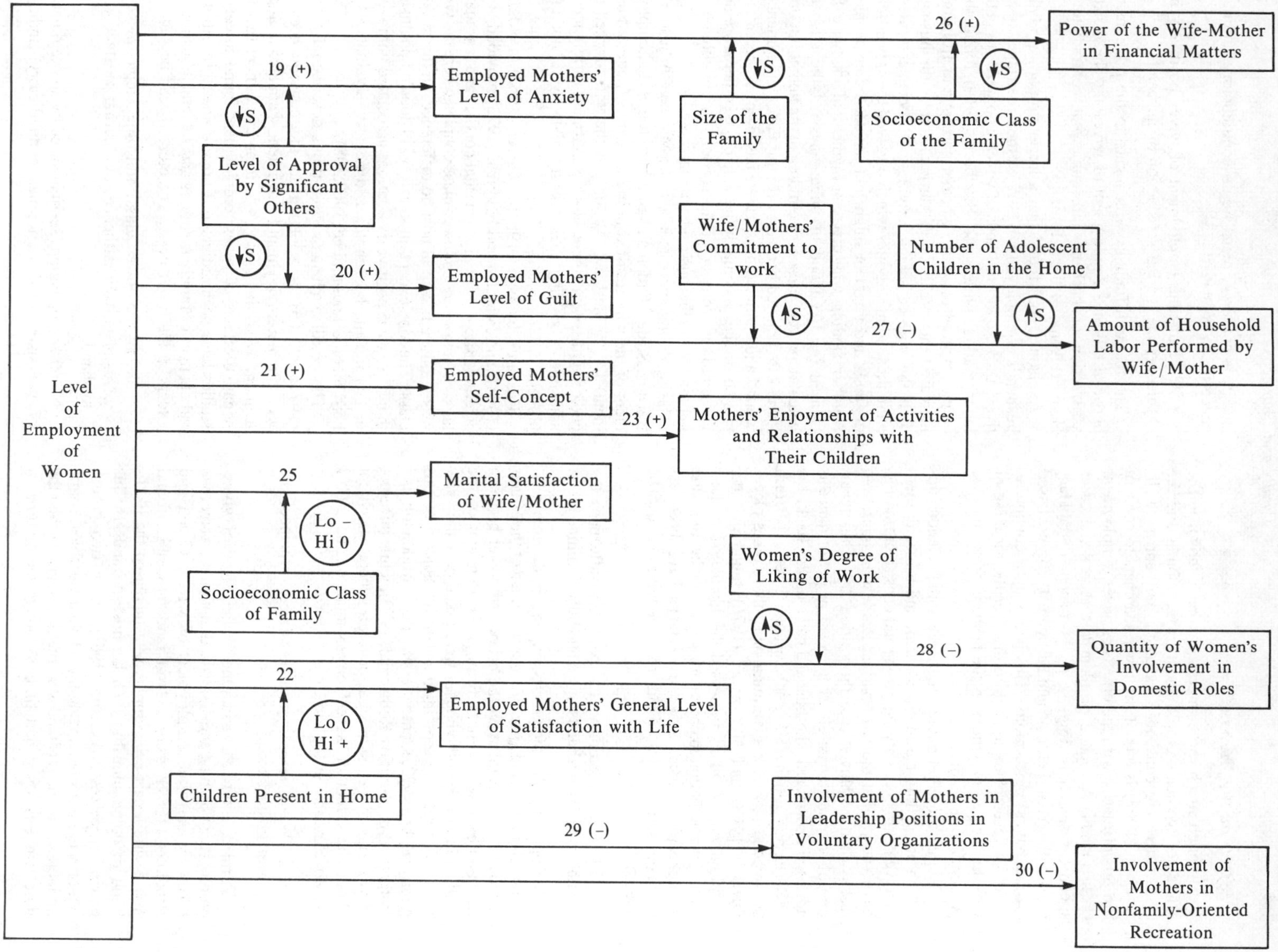

213

Effects on the Husband

Although much more interest has been shown in the effects of women's employment on the mother and the child, there are consequences for the husband as well. Axelson (1963) is one of the few researchers to concern himself primarily with the effects of wives' employment on husbands. A related problem is that in some cases specific research findings, e.g., husbands' dissatisfactions with wives (Feldman and Feldman, 1973), are based on the wives' perceptions. This points up a continuing need for researchers to seek to discover the meaning of wife-mother employment to the husband from his own perception of reality.

Despite these problems, there are some relationships which are solidly based on research, and it is with them that we begin our analysis. Strong and consistent findings have shown that the wife participates less in household tasks when employed (see Proposition 28). This means one of several things: either the level of performance is adjusted downward, the husband takes up the slack, the children perform the tasks, or someone is hired to perform the needed tasks, or a combination of these takes place. Dizard (1968) and Nye et al. (1976) found that the employment of wives increased the likelihood of husbands' participation in child care, child socialization, and housekeeping tasks. Since these tasks have been associated with the traditional roles of wives, it can be stated:

31. Wives' employment positively influences the enactment by husbands of traditionally feminine roles.

Recognizing the reciprocity implied in the role relationships of husband and wife, our statement of the effects of wives' employment on the balance of power between husband and wife results from an examination of the studies in which both spouses were asked how they saw the power relationships in their family. Studies of this genre (Bahr, 1972; Centers et al., 1971; Middleton and Putney, 1960; Safilios-Rothschild, 1970), while differing in findings by decision area, permit a general statement about the effect of wives' employment on the global power structure in the family as follows:

32. Wives' employment negatively influences the power of husbands.

Turning next to a consideration of the effects of wives' employment on husbands' satisfaction with marriage, we focus on part-time employment of wives. Orden and Bradburn (1969), using a large random sample, found that a wife's part-time employment increased the likelihood of companionship with her husband and also his marital happiness. Axelson (1963), using two groups which were not matched on the relevant variables, found an increase in the husband's marital satisfaction when the wife was employed part time. Although the number of studies is not large, there are no contradictory findings, hence it can be stated:

33. Part-time employment of wives positively influences the marital satisfaction of husbands.

The research findings with regard to the relationship between full-time employment of wives and the marital satisfaction of husbands are somewhat contradictory. Here are some of these findings:

Axelson (1963) found that a larger proportion of the husbands of employed wives rated their marriages negatively than did the husbands of wives who were not in the labor market. Orden and Bradburn (1969) found that employment of the wife, whether part time or full time, increased the likelihood of participation by the husband with the wife in social activities. ("Social activities" were those joint activities which involved the expenditure of funds and might or might not include other people.) Another finding was that employment of the wife increased the likelihood of unhappiness of the husband when there were preschool children in the home, but only if the wife enjoyed her work. (In this case "enjoyment of work" and "unhappiness" were based on self-report.) A related finding was that if the wife enjoyed her work and the children were in grade school, the likelihood of happiness for the husband was increased.

Using their composite index, the Marriage Adjustment Balance Scale,[3] Orden and Bradburn found that employment of the wife resulted in higher scores (better adjustment) for the husband, but only if the wife worked by choice. Otherwise, there was a significant difference in adjustment favoring men whose wives were not employed.

Research by Nye (1963b), Gover (1963), Feldman (1965), and Feldman and Feldman (1973) provided considerable support for more marital conflict and less marital satisfaction among lower-class couples where the wife was employed, with almost no differences in the middle class. The lone exception to this was Blood's conclusion that there were positive evaluations associated with work in low-income households and negative evaluations in high-income households (1963:308).

The possible changes over time, described by Nye (1974b:203–06) as applying to the consequences of wife-mother employment for women, seem also to apply to men. What this amounts to is an assessment that the negative effects of wives' employment found in earlier studies have been mitigated if not eliminated by attitudinal changes of family members and societal adjustments, except in the lower class. Therefore, it can be stated:

34. In the lower class, full-time employment of wives negatively influences the marital satisfaction of husbands.

No other propositions seem justified by an examination of the sparse and sometimes contradictory findings.

However, it is possible to identify a number of salient contingent variables on the basis of their effects on wives' marital satisfaction. They are (1) the stage in the family life cycle (specifically the age of the children who are present in the home); (2) the wife-mother's freedom to work or not to work (the economic aspects of working are at issue here); (3) whether or not the wife-mother enjoys working (psychic satisfaction is the focus, but women who work primarily for economic reasons, who enjoy it, are not excluded); (4) whether or not the husband approves the wife-mother's employment (a variable conceptualized earlier in this chapter as ''approval of significant others'' taps the same dimension).

Figure 9.4 depicts graphically the relationships stated earlier in this section. However, the contingent variables do not appear because their effects are entirely speculative at this time. The effects of part-time employment of the wife-mother warrants further attention as there are indications that this level of employment may have significant positive overtones for men and women alike. One of the chapter reviewers (Barbara Settles) has suggested that the addition of the wife's part-time earnings is important in advancing family income from a marginal to a secure basis. At the same time it is no threat to the husband and creates only minimal conflicts with her other roles and activities. The findings to date have been fragmentary and have occurred as by-products of studies in which full-time employment was the focus of interest. Needed are studies which focus specifically on this phenomenon.

Perhaps the principal contribution of this section is not in presenting conclusions, but in pointing to a dearth of information concerning the effects on one member of the family—the husband.

Effects on the Child

Students of the family and the general public alike have evidenced much interest in and concern about the consequences of maternal employment for the child. The results have generally failed to show much effect, but are not entirely conclusive because, as Hoffman (1974a: 126–28) states, the typical study considers only the employment status of the mother as related to a specific characteristic of a child. Many possible intervening variables are either not recognized or not fully controlled. Of course, this is true for the other sections of this chapter as well. Hoffman (1974a:128ff.) has tried to systematize these findings by offering several hypotheses concerning the relationship of maternal employment to the child.

There have been more studies of this relationship than of any other outcome of maternal employment. The principal reason for the lack of theoretical emphasis in this research has been that the intent was centered on a social problem—possible damage to children—rather than on theory testing or theory extension per se. Given that objective, the many studies were reasonably successful in establishing that maternal employment into the decade of the 1970s was not generally damaging to children, although it undoubtedly was in some cases, just as it was beneficial in others. However, this social problem focus was less productive for theory testing or extension, the principal objective of the present enterprise.

Attitudes and Beliefs about Sex Roles

We focus first on the research studies which have implications for the attitudes and beliefs of children about sex roles. A series of these studies are summarized as follows:

I.   Maternal employment increases the likelihood that the child of a working mother will:
  (1) see the division of household tasks to be more egalitarian (Hoffman, 1963a; Finkelman, 1966).
  (2) see maternal employment as nonthreatening to the marital relationship (King, McIntyre, and Axelson, 1968).
  (3) express a higher estimate of his/her own sex (Vogel et al., 1970).
  (4) favor social equality for women (Meier, 1972).
II. (a) Maternal employment increases the likelihood that the son of a lower-class working mother will:
    (1) be less likely to name father as the person

Figure 9.4.   Effects of Wives' Employment on Husbands

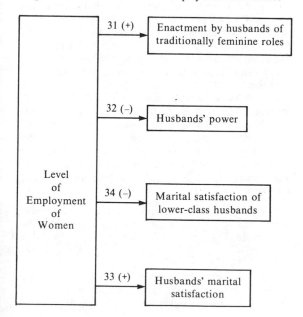

he most admires (Douvan, 1963; Propper, 1972).

(2) be more likely to indicate disapproval of
father (McCord, McCord, and Thurber,
1963).

(3) be more likely to evaluate father lower
(Kappel and Lambert, as cited by
Hoffman, 1974a:133).

(b) Maternal employment increases the likelihood that the son of a middle-class working
mother will:

(1) see his father as a more nurturant figure
(Vogel et al., 1970).

(2) see his father as warm and expressive
(Vogel et al., 1970).

III.   Maternal employment increases the likelihood
that the daughter of a working mother will:

(1) see women as less restricted to the home and
more active in the outside world (Hartley,
1960).

(2) be employed as an adolescent (Douvan,
1963; Roy, 1963).

(3) score low on an index of traditional feminity
(Douvan, 1963).

(4) see women as competent and effective
(Vogel et al., 1970).

(5) name mother as the parent she most resembles and the one she would most want to be
like (Baruch, 1972).

(6) name mother as the person she most admires
(Douvan, 1963).

(7) want to work when she is a mother (Hartley,
1960; Banducci, 1967; Below, 1969; Peterson, 1958; Smith, 1969; Almquist and Angrist, 1971; Zissis, 1964; Astin, 1969;
Birnbaum, 1971).

Despite some sex differences, which might be expected
when the topic under consideration is sex roles, three
propositions can be stated which apply to both sexes.
They are:

35. The level of maternal employment positively
affects the child's approval of egalitarianism in the
family.

36. The level of maternal employment positively
affects the child's approval of maternal employment.

37. The level of maternal employment positively
affects the child's evaluation of female competence.

The research also indicates that maternal employment
results in a more negative evaluation of the father by
lower-class sons but not by middle-class sons. The findings are consistent relevant to this point, but the causal
relationships are not obvious. Lower-class mothers are
more likely to have to work for chronic economic reasons,
whereas the income earned by middle-class mothers may
be seen as an increment which allows luxuries. Therefore,
the lower-class father is seen as inadequate, while this is
not true of the middle-class father. Tentatively, then, it
can be stated:

38. Maternal employment negatively influences
lower-class sons' evaluation of their fathers.

Independence, Conformity, and Household Responsibilities

One of the dependent variables of traditional interest
has been the level of independence or maturity evidenced
by the children of working mothers. Available research
does not permit a conclusion about sons. However,
Douvan's (1963) and Hoffman's (1963a) findings provide support for the greater independence of the daughters
of working mothers, hence it can be stated:

39. Maternal employment positively influences the
independence level of daughters.

In some related research, Yarrow et al. (1962) found
limited support for the idea that working mothers—as a
reality response—imposed more conformity on their
children than those who did not work. And indeed,
Hoffman (1963a) found that employed mothers who liked
working used less severe discipline and indicated less
hostility in the discipline situation than did nonworking
mothers.

The identification by Hoffman (1974a:128–29) of
"role model" as an intervening variable aids in understanding the relationships indicated in Propositions 35 to
39 (see Figure 9.5). Beyond this, however, several things
should be noted. First, the working-mother aspect of the
role model is only one part of the composite model
presented to the child by the mother. Second, the ultimate
outcome is dependent upon the interactive effect of the
role models presented by the mother *and* the father.
Third, the role model is probably influential in areas other
than those directly related to sex roles, e.g., delinquent
behavior.

A number of studies (Douvan, 1963; Roy 1963;
Johnson, 1969; Walker, 1970; Propper, 1972) found that
the children of working mothers assumed more household
responsibilities, i.e., did more household chores. The
only exceptions were the younger children of mothers
with a high level of education who enjoyed their work.
While there are some situational exceptions, it can be
stated:

40. The level of maternal employment positively
influences the number of household tasks performed by
the child.

Social Adjustment

It was reported earlier (Propositions 19 and 20) that
employment results in feeling of guilt and anxiety on the
part of employed mothers about the inadequacy of

mothering. This "emotional state of the mother" (another of the intervening variables identified by Hoffman, 1974a) is of concern because of the possible negative effects on the child. The degree of mother's liking for her work seems to be an important intervening variable also, as a study by Hoffman (1963b) indicates. She found that mothers who liked to work overcompensated by being very permissive and sympathetic with their children, to the detriment of the child's social adjustment and intellectual performance. In contrast, the mothers who didn't like to work seemed to disengage from their children in a pattern of neglect which also had negative effects, but not the same ones. For example, the children were more assertive and hostile toward their peers.

Douvan (1963), in a study of adolescent children in intact families, found that the children with adjustment problems were those of full-time working mothers in the lower class. On the other hand, Woods (1972), in a study of lower-class mothers most of whom were employed, found that the children of full-time workers were the best adjusted.

What is clearly needed in dealing with the variable "social adjustment" is a concerted effort to overcome conceptual ambiguity. One suggestion in this regard is to differentiate between adjustment in the family, i.e., with parents and siblings, and adjustment outside the family, i.e., with peers, teachers, and so on. Also needed is carefully planned research to determine if causal linkages between maternal employment and social adjustment exist. With limited evidence available, we turn now to what could be called an extreme type of social maladjustment—juvenile delinquency.

Several studies (Glueck and Glueck, 1957; Brown, 1970; and Riege, 1972) found no relationship between maternal employment and delinquency. Others (Gold, 1961; Nye, 1958) found a relationship only in the middle class. A number of researchers have either suggested or found a tie between delinquency and inadequate maternal supervision (Glueck and Glueck, 1957; McCord and McCord, 1959). However, the relationship is quite tenuous, and it is apparent that other variables are involved, e.g., stability of the family, quality of the substitute child care, and perhaps regularity of mother's employment. In light of the research findings to date, it is stated:

41. The level of maternal employment positively affects the middle-class child's level of delinquency.

Although the evidence seems sufficient and the temporal sequence clear, i.e., class position precedes delinquent behavior, a compelling rationale for a causal linkage is not at hand. We do know that lower-class employed mothers are less permissive and more demanding of adolescents than are lower-class nonemployed mothers, but this is not true of middle-class mothers. It may be that the added responsibilities demanded of children of lower-class working mothers and the greater direction

provided for them compensates for lack of direct supervision while the mother is at her job, whereas middle-class working mothers supervise less and do not compensate in other ways. Thus there is a small but identifiable difference between middle-class children of employed and nonemployed mothers in delinquent behavior.

Some notice should be taken of the idea that maternal employment adversely affects the development of a child's personality. Nye et al. (1963) found that the separation occasioned by the mother's employment did not have an adverse effect on the personality functioning of the child. Likewise, extensive mother-substitute care of babies and small children in the kibbutzim and in Communist societies has not been associated with negative effects on personality. Although it is probably risky to attempt to rank the many variables which affect the personaltiy of the child, in this context several mediating variables stand out: the extent of the mother's absence, the quality of interaction she provides when present, and the quality of substitute care.

After reviewing the literature in this area, Burr concluded that no relationship exists between the amount of time the wife-mother works and the personality maladjustment of her children (1973:237). One of the reviewers of this chapter, Barbara Settles, stated her conclusions a little more forcefully.

> I have had a standing bet with my students over the past ten years that I would pay off, first $10 and now $50, if they could discover any study with some controls which found damage to children related to maternal employment. As eager as my students are to prove me wrong and earn a little money, I have never had to pay off.

In summary, despite a persistent concern over the effects of maternal employment on the child, we can find little evidence of appreciable effects, positive or negative. Our conclusions are presented graphically in Figure 9.5.

In the future, it seems that researchers and theoreticians alike would do well to focus on the interactive effects of the joint socialization efforts of the mother *and* the father on the child when the mother is employed, social class differences, and the self-concept of the child. Hoffman (1974a:134) dealt with the child's self-concept to a degree, but it seems to merit much closer scrutiny as an intervening variable (see Wylie, 1974).

Effects on the Community and Society

"Community" is used here to mean those associations outside the family and includes reference groups, membership groups and other organizations. Because communities and the society reciprocally influence each other, it seems logical to consider the two together. In the discussion that follows, the effects of women's employment may be more directly related to the community or to the society, depending on the consequences under con-

Figure 9.5.   Effects of Maternal Employment on the Child

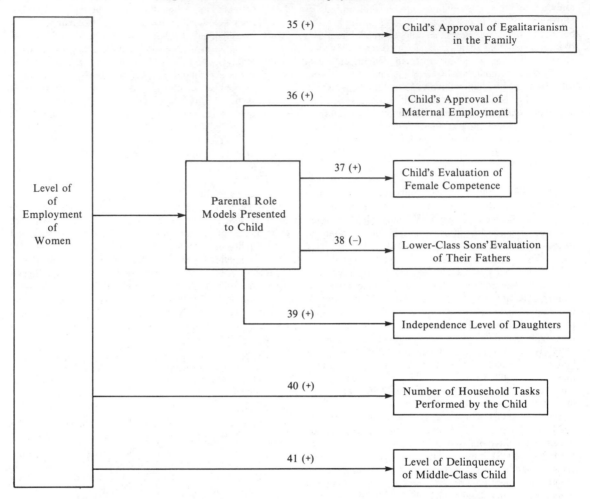

siteration. In returning to this macro level of analysis, the support of extensive, empirical evidence available in the preceding sections is not presently available. *At the macro level, the propositions are based mainly on inference and should not be considered empirically established.*

One of the consequences of women's employment is the need for substitute care facilities for dependent persons, whether children or adult relatives. That need is expressed at the community level through engaging the services of care givers and thus providing employment for many women. At the societal level, this need for substitute care is expressed through pressure on legislative bodies to provide money for care facilities, or to change zoning laws to accommodate such facilities, or to increase payments for dependent persons so they can live in circumstances where the working woman is freed from

responsibility for their personal care, and so on (see Roby, 1973). It can be stated, then:

42. The level of women's employment positively affects the availability of substitute care facilities for dependent persons.

Inasmuch as most working women are employed at some distance from home, transportation needs are increased. In the community this may take the form of car pooling or demands for the expansion of public forms of transportation. While many families with nonworking wives have two or more automobiles, the need is more pressing if the wife is employed (see Parnes et al., 1975:18). From a societal standpoint, women's employment shows up in greater demand for automobiles, concern over adequate gasoline supplies, interest in mass transit systems, and so on. In propositional form, this relationship is:

43. The level of women's employment positively affects the demand for public and private transportation.

The employment of women has caused an increased participation by women in college and graduate education, the obvious connection between level of education and salary not being lost on women who are working or planning to work (or on their husbands and/or parents). In the community this means that the woman, mother or grandmother, who enters school, for the first time or for retraining, is not an anomaly. Part of the enrollment pressure of recent years in higher education—especially professional schools— has come from women. Their competition with men for limited slots in professional schools produces societal controversy over who has the greater right to education, as well as debate over priorities in the expenditure of funds for higher education. Therefore, it can be stated:

44. The level of women's employment positively influences the participation of women in higher education.

By virtue of spending at least an eight-hour day at work (if employed full time), an employed woman has less discretionary time. That she tends to cut down on non-family- oriented recreation, such as golf and entertaining, as well as socializing among friends and neighbors, was pointed out earlier (Proposition 30).

Examining the effects of two salaries in many families as a result of the wife-mother being employed, we see an increase in the level of living. Fueled by omnipresent advertising and conspicuous consumption (or ownership) at the community level, there is great emphasis on an approved package of desired possessions, varying somewhat by socioeconomic level. At the societal level, dual salaries have helped accelerate our economic growth and are currently an important factor in the matrix of variables which will determine the nation's economic future. In propositional form, then:

45. The level of women's employment positively influences families' level of living.

When women work, they have less time to perform household tasks. That this results in a lowering of standards of cleanliness has been suggested, but the evidence suggests otherwise (see Myrdal and Klein, 1956). A degree of task relief is provided by husbands and children (Propositions 31 and 40) and by the extensive use of labor-saving devices. The proliferation of businesses which provide service to housekeepers, being concomitant with the increase in women's employment, suggests a relationship, but the direction is not apparent (see "Stage I" section of this chapter). The effects of increased

female employment, then, are largely felt at the societal level through the law of supply and demand. An extension of this is that the community effects undoubtedly involve a diminishment in the rewards which accrue to the women who are very skilled in homemaking activities. It can be stated, therefore:

46. The level of women's employment positively influences the availability of services to housewives.

In this day of concern over population pressures, great interest has been shown in the consequences of women's employment on fertility. It has been established that the number and age of children affect women's employment. However, the complexity of this phenomenon argues against a simplistic conclusion. Burr (1973:268) identifies a dozen independent variables which affect fertility. Women's employment interacts with many of them, e.g., the amount of contraception used. Societal conditions and norms relating to the size of family and the reasons for having children, mediated through the community and family, are of prime importance. These conditions and norms currently favor low fertility, and technological advances in contraceptives have made the attainment of these goals socially desirable and possible. Also, recent attitude studies (Lozoff, 1972; Hoffman and Hoffman, 1973) are beginning to disclose sizable proportions of couples planning no children. The plan to have no children is related to the presence of plans for the wife to be employed. Hence Proposition 47 seems to follow:

47. Women's employment negatively affects the level of fertility in a society.

As Nye (1974c) has pointed out, an expanding economy and a favorable population distribution were important factors in the increasing movement of women into the labor force. Women employees have been needed, and the general societal reaction, spurred on by the women's rights movement, has been to approve women's employment. The supply of women workers at the professional level has not kept pace with the demand. (This seems to be changing—see Parrish, 1974). What will happen, in the event of an oversupply of women workers who are competing with men for scarce jobs? This may lead to a shorter work week for everyone, and other societal adjustments.

What effect does women's employment have on family stability, specifically the divorce rate? A very high proportion of divorced women work. This could mean that employed women are more likely to be divorced, or it could mean that divorced women, lacking adequate financial support, take employment because of the divorce. An earlier effort (Nye, 1963b) to ascertain which of these explanations is more nearly correct, by looking at the employment of remarried women (where presumably the pressure on the woman to earn money was relieved), resulted in nonsignificant differences. It is probable that women's employment interacts with a host of macro and micro variables to bring about the current high rate of marriage dissolution. However, since causation cannot be specified, no proposition concerning divorce seems warranted.

PERSPECTIVE FROM GENERAL THEORY

So Little Effect on Family Members

While a number of propositions based on analytic relationships have emerged from the research on wife-mother employment, many readers will have been surprised that the effects have been so limited. Perhaps the first question to be asked is, have the changes been so great as they appeared? Although a majority of women with minor children are in the labor force *at some time* during the year, only about two-fifths of these are employed a full work week the year around (U.S. Bureau of the Census, 1973). Therefore, the proportion of mothers who are employed full time for a year is not much in excess of 20 percent, and the majority of these are women with no preschool children. This has meant (we think) that those women who were motivated and who had less pressing child care and housekeeper tasks were able to

move into full-time employment. Those women with younger and/or large families, with poorer child care alternatives, or other situations less favorable to employment remained full-time housekeepers and care givers so could only take part-time employment which was less competitive with those responsibilities. Also, since some 20 percent of employed women enter or leave the labor force each year, women are reacting to temporary stress situations which may increase their home-centered responsibilities, returning to work when such responsibilities again become less (U.S. Department of Labor, 1971). The results, we suspect, might have been different if *all* wives and mothers had decided to take full-time employment regardless of their familial situations and child care alternatives.

More Options Are Available

Even so, the fact that even one mother in five could take and hold full-time employment without typically negative consequences for herself and family is theoretically interesting. It suggests that women, men, and children can adapt successfully to a very wide range of situations in the family context. Women have, perhaps, been "overservicing" their husbands, their children, and themselves. Not that this is necessarily bad—they and their families may

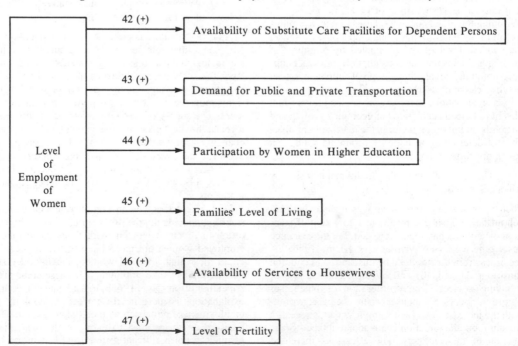

Figure 9.6.   Effects of Women's Employment on the Community and the Society

enjoy these heavy expenditures of mature women's time—it is only that it is hardly necessary, and other options are clearly open. If more evidence were necessary, it is readily available in the Soviet Union and in contemporary China, where women have provided much of the human labor to rebuild the society while providing for the essential needs of themselves and their children in the family.

General Theoretical Perspective

While general theory was more often absent than present in the past, it can be utilized to interpret and organize some of the findings. For that purpose, we employ some of the principal concepts which have been associated with social exchange theories (Thibaut and Kelley, 1959; Ekeh, 1974). Burns (1973) has shown how these concepts can be applied to primary groups. The key concepts are *rewards, costs, profit, comparison level,* and *comparison level for alternatives* (Thibaut and Kelley, 1959).

First, this theoretical perspective will be applied to suggest why larger proportions of some categories of women enter and remain in the labor force. Single women (age constant) have the highest participation, followed by married women with no children, women with school-age children only, women with preschool children, and, finally, those with small babies. The rewards of employment to these categories of women probably vary little (although a larger proportion of single women hold higher-level positions), but the costs vary greatly. The larger the housekeeping, child care, and child socialization responsibilities, the greater the costs to the woman of being employed. That is, she is likely to encounter more role conflicts, likely to work under more pressure in discharging such extensive responsibilities, and more likely to be the recipient of negative sanctions from reference groups. The very different proportion of women in these categories entering the labor force is probably due to differences in costs rather than rewards.

On one variable, however, rewards vary greatly, namely education (and training). It is estimated that women with college degrees earn an average of two and a half times the amount earned by those with no more than an eighth grade education (Bowen and Finegan, 1969). It is intriguing that the relative proportions of employed women in the labor force vary by education level at about the same rate. Of those with no more than eight years of education, 23 percent were employed, compared with 71 percent of those with college degrees. It may be that the costs of the poorly educated women were a little higher, too, since they average more children and fewer household conveniences; but the principal differences are in rewards.

Two populations show less simple reward-cost profit outcomes than the above. More black women are employed than white, and more women with husbands earning low incomes than those with high incomes. In both of these categories rewards, both economic and psychic, are less for the low-income and black women, and costs in terms of other responsibilities are higher. Here the "comparison level for alternatives" is a useful and even necessary concept. The alternative for many black women and low-income white women is chronic poverty as a result of being inadequately supported either by a husband or by welfare. Even though earnings are relatively small and substitute care givers may be less satisfactory, still the added income increment allows the family to survive and to have basic necessities, whereas these might not have been possible otherwise. We suggest that the value of a dollar increase in income is much greater if the base income is $5,000 than if it is $15,000. Taken in conjunction with the previous findings, the employment of women with advanced education married to men with low incomes should be especially high. No one has determined whether this is true.

Smaller proportions of widows, divorcees, and women permanently living apart from husbands are in the labor force than single women; but a much higher proportion of each than of women living with a husband is found in the labor force (Nye, 1974c:5). Single women have the highest incomes and the most secure positions with the most autonomy and/or authority (all assumed to be rewards); and since few have children or male cohabitors, they experience minimum costs due to role conflicts. Futhermore, their alternatives are poor, since no one else wants to support a single woman. Many widows, divorcees, and women separated from husbands have minor children. Their rewards are lower than those of single women because, on the average, they have less education and continuity in employment than single women, so their incomes are lower and psychic rewards less. They have higher costs than single women if they have minor children living with them, because of role conflicts and the need to secure substitute care givers. If they have minor children, their alternatives to employment are better than for single women because they are likely to be eligible for Social Security payments or insurance (widows), welfare and child support from the father of their children (divorcees and those living apart). Compared to married women with minor children, their costs of being employed are lower because of no duties to a husband; but in most instances their alternatives are poorer than those of the married women, since they have no one specifically obligated to support them. Overall, single women have the highest profits from employment because of the highest rewards, lowest costs, and poorest alternatives. Married women have the lowest profits because of relatively low rewards, relatively high costs, and relatively good alternatives. Widows and divorced and separated women are intermediate because of relatively low rewards, intermediate costs, and intermediate alternatives.

With regard to rate of employment, single women vary little by age beyond the period in which many are in school; married women vary greatly because of the number and age of children. The highest rate is for young wives who have not yet had their first child. The rate drops to its lowest point when preschool children are present, increases when only school-age children are present, and increases again when no minor children remain at home; finally after age 55, it again declines. Economically and psychologically, preschool children typically represent the highest cost of being employed, school-age children less, and no minor children even less. The alternative to employment is unattractive to the young married woman. The initial income of the husband is relatively low, while the couple needs to acquire a home, furniture, and other expensive things. This woman's education and training are greater than those of the woman who thinks of entering the labor market after her children are all adults. For the older woman, capital assets have largely been acquired, so that a given amount of income beyond that of a husband has less value. Neither profits nor alternatives vary much for the single woman until after 55, when some are eligible to retire and others have disabilities which affect both their rewards and costs. However, for married women costs vary with the age and number of children and the attractiveness of alternatives because of the changes in the income of husbands and the accumulation of assets.

Black-white contrasts in female employment offer somewhat greater challenges to the present theoretical approach. Married black women are more likely than married white women to be in the labor force, even when income of the husband and number of children are held constant. But the reverse is true of women with no husband present—a large proportion of white women are in gainful employment (U.S. Department of Labor, 9171). Marital dissolutions occur in a larger proportion of black than white marriages, and black women are lower in marital satisfaction. Therefore, it seems probably that black women should find comparatively more social, psychic, and security rewards in employment.

Black women with children not living with husbands are less likely to be employed than are white women in that status. White mothers living alone obtain more rewards from employment because they average higher wages and are more likely to be employed in white-collar occupations. Formerly married black mothers are likely to experience higher costs in role conflicts and in obtaining substitute care because of larger families and less income with which to hire care. The alternative to employment is usually welfare. Since the average income of black women is lower in a larger proportion of cases, welfare will actually provide more net income than employment. Also, it is believed that welfare is more socially acceptable in the black than in the white community, and therefore the costs of accepting it are less.

Theoretical Issues at the Macro Level

This theoretical approach has, to date, had little application to the macro level of society; but some issues can be raised from this perspective. American society is beginning to offer considerable support for the employment of women and some (much less) for the employment of women with minor children. Recent Federal legislation has forbidden discrimination in employment because of sex, and recent administrative edicts and court actions have brought pressure to bear on employers to hire women. Also, various government programs have provided training and child care for mothers who are heads of households so that they can take gainful employment. There is nothing very subtle about the latter development. Costs to society can be cut by investing money to enable solo parents to become self-supporting. We made the point in the introduction to this chapter that the labor of women, especially well-trained women, was badly needed by industry, service establishments, and government. Without the labor of women (including mothers), the society would collapse. Therefore, female employment rewards society in major and even crucial dimensions.

With a high and increasing divorce rate, the gainful employment of married women reduces another set of personal and societal costs. If minor children are involved, divorce typically increases the economic costs of the couple. It is necessary to support two residences, two sets of utilities, two sets of insurance premiums, sometimes an additional automobile, and two sets of meals, clothing, laundering, and the like. Recreational needs change and become much more costly. Many families are experiencing financial strains prior to divorce; most others have no financial surplus. Following a divorce, there must either be a major increase in income or a drastic reduction in level of living. If the divorcée holds a good-paying position, financial strains will be much less than if she has to seek training or take an unskilled job. It is much less likely that she and the children will become dependent on welfare and more likely that the financial burden on the father will be sufficiently manageable that he can help support his children and still be able to consider remarriage. The employment of married women does not increase the rewards of divorce, but it reduces the cost to the individuals and to society, allowing couples to dissolve high-cost, low-reward marriages without forgoing their personal futures or heavily burdening society.

The Impact of Ideology

Since approximately 1970, a number of organizations often collectively identified as the women's movement have undertaken campaigns to bring more women into paid employment and to equalize the proportion of men and women in positions of power and influence. Seen in conjunction with earlier legislation forbidding discrimination in employment and administrative and court actions promoting equal participation of women in professional, administrative, and skilled blue-collar occupations, this movement appears to have had considerable influence in the decision of more women to train for and enter high-level occupations in business, the professions, and government.

Many actions have been taken to reward advanced training by providing admission to restricted programs and by providing stipends to support advanced training. These have both lowered costs and increased rewards for advanced training and placement of women. At the same time, the assumptions that women's lives are and should be focused on the home and children have been challenged by this ideology. Support has been offered to women who do not marry, and to those who choose not to have children and to pursue a career equal or superior to that of their husbands. Such reduction in costs and increase in rewards should lead to more women pursuing advanced careers and/or emphasizing careers as much or more than family. At the same time, the women's movement has provided a rationale for husbands who wish to accept a supportive rather than a principal economic role in the family, or even to become "house husbands" focusing their lives on the home and community. This could lower the cost to husbands of taking primary responsibility for roles traditionally assigned to women. This brief discourse is not, of course, an examination of the rewards and costs of segregated versus identical sex roles. Such an examination would require a chapter by itself. However, it does indicate a reduction in costs and an increase in rewards for couples who choose for the wife a major occupational career.

Accelerated Divorce Trends

The divorce rate has been increasing since about 1962 and more rapidly since 1968. In several states there are more than 50 divorces to 100 marriages. If this trend continues, the norm that marriage is for life will be displaced by the expectation that marriage probably will not last a lifetime. This will encourage women to become fully self-supporting and parents to emphasize the career training of daughters more strongly than in the past. Women will presumably become more interested in full-time employment and in staying employed permanently in order to maximize the rewards of economic security and provide for their own retirement. We have already noted this pattern in black families—one which seems to place a high value on economic security from one's own employment.

In these last pages we have tried to show that some of the key concepts in so-called "exchange theory" can bring some order from disparate facts and relationships involved in the gainful employment of wives and mothers. It should be clear that we are dealing selectively with the concepts sometimes employed in those theories. We are *not* concerned with individuals bargaining with each other in dyads or triads, but with the more general phenomenon of individuals choosing courses of action they anticipate will increase their rewards, reduce their costs, or both and involved in choosing one course of action over relevant alternative courses of action in order to maximize their profits or goodness of outcomes.

We regard this selective, yet broader, application of these concepts to family and family-related behavior as a relatively early theoretical development—one which should gain in comprehensiveness, clarity of concepts, and systematization as additional theoretical development is undertaken.

RETROSPECT AND PROSPECT

As noted initially, the research of the 1950s and 1960s concerning wives and mothers in the provider role was undertaken primarily with social objectives in view— to determine whether consequences deemed detrimental were associated with this development. Those decades of research served that purpose reasonably well in answering the question in the negative; i.e., families with employed wives and/or mothers do not differ greatly in socially valued behaviors from those in which women limit themselves to more traditional role definitions. Where differences are found, these sometimes are favorable (in terms of societal values) to employed wives and mothers, other times unfavorable. Theory played no great part in these researches, although good use was made of some sociological and psychological concepts.

Although theory played a small part in generating this research, we have shown, in the final section of this chapter, that theory can be profitably employed to organize and explain many of the findings.

Looking ahead, it seems likely that research will focus on families in which there is a lifetime commitment of the wife and/or mother to a career; those in which the wife's job and income are equal to those of the husband; those in which the wife is the principal provider; and those in which the husband takes the primary household role or in which he shares equally with the wife. Past research has hardly touched these populations or addressed the structure and relationships in these families. With a growing theoretical sophistication in the behavioral sciences, it seems likely that future research will be guided by theory to a much greater extent than has been true in the past. We can see that the theory developed by Thibaut and Kelley (1959), recently elaborated by Burns (1973) and placed in broad historical perspective by Ekeh (1974), has major potential for guiding and interpreting research in these areas of social life which relate family to occupation and to other societal structures and interaction.

NOTES

1. Considerable international literature could have been used to illuminate the propositions in the consideration of women's employment at the macro level. However, space limitations dictate its omission.

2. A reference group is defined as a group of people whose standards are perceived by any given individual as particularly relevant to use as a basis for evaluating important aspects of her/his life. The individual may be a member of the group or not. A significant other is defined as a person who plays a more influential part in a given individual's self-concept than do mere acquaintances.

3. The Marriage Adjustment Balance Scale is a composite index which balances the tensions in a marriage against the sociability and companionship indexes. Orden and Bradburn (1968) claim it is a good overall indication of happiness in marriage.

REFERENCES

ABBOTT, E.
1910   *Women in Industry.* New York: Appleton-Century-Crofts.

ALDOUS, J.
1969   "Wives' employment status and lower-class men as husband-fathers: Support for the Moynihan thesis." *Journal of Marriage and the Family* 31:469–76.

ALMQUIST, E. M. AND S. S. ANGRIST
1971   "Role model influences on college women's career aspirations." *Merrill-Palmer Quarterly* 17:263–69.

ASTIN, H. S.
1969   *The Woman Doctorate in America.* New York: Russell Sage Foundation.

AXELSON, L. J.
1963   "The marital adjustment and marital role definitions of husbands of working and non-working wives." *Marriage and Family Living* 25:189–95.

BAHR, S. J.
1972   "A methodological study of conjugal power: A replication and extension of Blood and Wolfe." Unpublished doctoral dissertation, Washington State University.

1974   "Effects on power and division of labor in the family." In L. W. Hoffman and F. I. Nye (eds.), *Working Mothers.* San Francisco: Jossey-Bass.

BANDUCCI, R.
1967   "The effect of mothers' employment on the achievement, aspirations, and expectations of the child." *Personnel Guidance Journal* 46:263–67.

BARUCH, G. K.
1972   "Maternal influences upon college women's attitudes toward women and work." *Development Psychology* 6:32–37.

BELOW, H. I.
1969   "Life styles and roles of women as perceived by high school girls." Unpublished doctoral dissertation, Indiana University.

BERGQUIST, V. A.
1974   "Women's participation in labor organizations." *Monthly Labor Review* (Oct.):3–9.

BIRNBAUM, J. A.
1971   "Life patterns, personality style and self-esteem in gifted family oriented and career committed women." Unpublished doctoral dissertation, University of Michigan.

BLOOD, R. O., JR.
1963   "The husband-wife relationship." In F. I. Nye and L. W. Hoffman (eds.), *The Employed Mother in America.* Chicago: Rand McNally.

BLOOD, R. O., JR. AND R. L. HAMBLIN
1958   "The effect of the wife's employment on the family power structure." *Social Forces* 36:347–52.

BOWEN, W. G. AND T. A. FINEGAN
1969   *The Economics of Labor Force Participation.* Princeton: Jersey: Princeton University.

BROWN, S. W.
1970   "A comparative study of maternal employment and nonemployment." Unpublished doctoral dissertation, Mississippi State University.

BURNS, T. A.
1973   "A structural theory of social exchange." *Acta Sociologia,* 16: 188–208.

BURR, W. R.
1973   *Theory Construction and the Sociology of the Family.* New York: Wiley-Interscience.

CENTERS, R., B. H. RAVEN, AND A. RODRIGUES
1971   "Conjugal power structure: A re-examination." *American Sociological Review* 36:264–78.

DIZARD, J.
1968   *Social Change in the Family.* Chicago: University of Chicago.

DOUVAN, E.
1963   "Employment and the adolescent." In F. I. Nye and L. W. Hoffman (eds.), *The Employed Mother in America.* Chicago: Rand McNally.

EKEH, P. P.
1974   *Social Exchange Theory: The Two Traditions.* Cambridge, Mass.: Harvard University.

ERSKINE, H.
1971   "The polls: Women's role." *Public Opinion Quarterly* 35:282–84.

FELD, S.
1963   "Feelings of adjustment." In F. I. Nye and L. W. Hoffman (eds.), *The Employed Mother in America.* Chicago: Rand McNally.

FELDMAN, H.
1965   "Development of the husband-wife relationship." A research report of the National Institute of Mental Health (mimeographed). Ithaca, New York: Department of Human Development and Family Studies, Cornell University.

FELDMAN, H. AND M. FELDMAN
1973   "The relationship between the family and occupational functioning in a sample of rural women" (mimeographed). Ithaca, New York: Department of Human Development and Family Studies, Cornell University.

FINKELMAN, J. J.
1966   "Maternal employment, family relationships and parental role perception." Unpublished doctoral dissertation, Yeshiva University, Israel.

GASS, G. Z.
1959   "Counseling implications of woman's changing role." *Personnel and Guidance Journal* 37:482–87.

GIANOPULOS, A. AND H. E. MITCHELL
1957   "Marital disagreement in working wife marriage as a function of the husband's attitude toward wife's employment." *Marriage and Family Living* 19: 373–78.

GLUECK, S. AND E. GLUECK
1957   "Working mothers and delinquency." *Mental Hygiene* 41:327–52.

GOLD, M.
1963   *Status Forces in Delinquent Boys.* Ann Arbor, Mich.: Institute for Social Research.

GOODE, W. J.
1960   "A theory of role strain." *American Sociological Review* 25: 488–96.

GOVER, D. O.
1963   "Socio-economic differential in the relationship between marital adjustment and wife's employment status." *Marriage and Family Living* 25:452–58.

HACKER, H. M.
1971   "The feminine protest of the working wife." *Indian Journal of Social Work* 31:401–406.

HARTLEY, R. E.
1960   "Children's concepts of male and female roles." *Merrill-Palmer Quarterly* 6:83–91.

HEER, D. M.
1963   "Dominance and the working wife." In F. I. Nye and L. W. Hoffman (eds.), *The Employed Mother in America.* Chicago: Rand McNally.

HOFFMAN, L. W.
1961   "Effects of the employment of mothers on parental power relations and the division of household tasks." *Marriage and Family Living* 22:27–35.

HOFFMAN, L. W.
1963a   "Effects on children: Summary and discussion." In F. I. Nye and L. W. Hoffman (eds.), *The Employed Mother in America.* Chicago: Rand McNally.
1963b   "Mother's enjoyment of work and effects on the child." In F. Ivan Nye and Lois W. Hoffman (eds.), *The Employed Mother in America.* Chigaco: Rand McNally.
1963c   "Parental power relations and the division of household tasks." In F. I. Nye and L. W. Hoffman (eds.), *The Employed Mother in America.* Chicago: Rand McNally.
1974a   "Effects on child." In L. W. Hoffman and F. I. Nye (eds.), *Working Mothers.* San Francisco: Jossey-Bass.
1974b   "Psychological factors." In L. W. Hoffman and F. I. Nye (eds.), *Working Mothers.* San Francisco: Jossey-Bass.

HOFFMAN, L. W. AND M. L. HOFFMAN
1973   "The value of children to parents." In J. T. Fawcett (ed.), *Psychological Perspectives on Population.* New York: Basic Books.

HOFFMAN, L. W. AND F. I. NYE
1974   "Concluding remarks." In Lois W. Hoffman and F. I. Nye (eds.), *Working Mothers.* San Francisco: Jossey-Bass.

JOHNSON, C. L.
1969   "Leadership patterns in working and nonworking mother middle-class families." Unpublished doctoral dissertation, University of Kansas.

KALEY, M. M.
1971   "Attitudes toward the dual role of the married professional woman." *American Psychologist* 26(3):301–306.

KING, K., J. McINTYRE, AND L. J. AXELSON
1968   "Adolescent views of maternal employment as a threat to the marital relationship." *Journal of Marriage and the Family* 30(4):633–637.

KLIGLER, D. H.
1954   "The effects of the employment of married women on husband and wife roles." Unpublished doctoral dissertation, Yale University.

LOCKE, H. J. AND M. MACKEPRANG
1949   "Marital adjustment and the employed wife." *American Journal of Sociology* 18:536–38.

LOZOFF, M. M.
1972   "Changing life styles and role perceptions of men and women students." Paper presented at conference sponsored by Radcliffe Institute, Cambridge, Mass.

LUNDBERG, F. AND M. FARNHAM
1947   *Modern Women: The Lost Sex.* New York: Harper and Row.

McCORD, J., W. McCORD AND E. THURBER
1963   "Effects of maternal employment on lower-class boys." *Journal of Abnormal and Social Psychology* 67:177–82.

MEIER, H. C.
1972   "Mother-centeredness and college youths' attitudes toward social equality for women: Some empirical findings." *Journal of Marriage and the Family* 34:115–21.

MIDDELTON, R. AND S. W. PUTNEY
1960   "Dominance in decisions in the family: Race and class differences." *American Journal of Sociology* 65:605–609.

MYRDAL, A. AND V. KLEIN
1956   *Women's Two Roles: Home and work.* London: Routledge and Kegan Paul.

NYE, F. I.
1952   "Adolescent-parent adjustment: Age, sex, sibling number, broken home, and employed mothers as variables." *Marriage and Family Living* 14:327–32.
1958   *Family Relationships and Delinquent Behavior.* New York: Wiley.
1959   "Employment status of mothers and adjustment of adolescent children." *Marriage and Family Living* 21:240–44.
1963a   "Adjustment of the mother." In F. I. Nye and L. W. Hoffman (eds.), *The Employed Mother in America.* Chicago: Rand McNally.
1963b   "Marital interaction." In F. I. Nye and L. W. Hoffman (eds.), *The Employed Mother in America.* Chicago: Rand McNally.
1963c   "Personal satisfactions." In F. I. Nye and L. W. Hoffman (eds.), *The Employed Mother in America.* Chicago: Rand McNally.
1963d   "Recreation and the community." In F. I. Nye and L. W. Hoffman (eds.), *The Employed Mother in America.* Chicago: Rand McNally.
1974a   "Effects on the mother." In L. W. Hoffman and F. I. Nye (eds.), *Working Mothers.* San Francisco: Josey-Bass.
1974b   "Husband-wife relationship." In L. W. Hoffman and F. I. Nye (eds.), *Working Mothers.* San Francisco: Jossey-Bass.
1974c   "Sociocultural context." In L. W. Hoffman and F. I. Nye (eds.), *Working Mothers.* San Francisco: Jossey-Bass.
1976   *Role Structure and Analysis of the Family.* Beverly Hills, Calif.: Sage Publications.

NYE, F. I., J. B. PERRY, JR., AND R. H. OGLES
1963   "Anxiety and anti-social behavior in preschool children." In F. I. Nye and L. W. Hoffman (eds.), *The Employed Mother in America.* Chicago: Rand McNally.

OPPENHEIMER, V. C.
1970   *The Female Labor Force in the United States.* Population Monograph Series, No. 5. Berkeley, Calif.: University of California.

ORDEN, S. R. AND N. M. BRADBURN
1968   "Dimensions of marriage happiness." *American Journal of Sociology* 73:715–31.
1969   "Working wives and marriage happiness." *American Journal of Sociology* 74:392–407.

PARNES, H. S., C. L. JUSENIUS, F. BLAU, C. NESTEL, R. SHORTLIDGE, JR., AND S. SANDELL
1975   *Dual Careers: A Longitudinal Analysis of the Labor Market Experience of Women,* vol. 4. Columbus: Ohio State University.

PARRISH, J. B.
1974   "Women in professional training." *Monthly Labor Review* 97: 40–43.

PETERSON, E. T.
   1958   "The impact of maternal employment on the mother-daughter relationship and on the daughter's role orientation." Unpublished doctoral dissertation, University of Michigan.
   1961   "The impact of maternal employment on the mother relationship." *Marriage and Family Living* 23:353–61.

POWELL, K. S.
   1963   "Family variables." In F. I. Nye and L. W. Hoffman (eds.), *The Employed Mother in America.* Chicago: Rand McNally.

PROPPER, A. M.
   1972   "The relationship of maternal employment to adolescent roles, activities and parental relationships." *Journal of Marriage and the Family* 34:417–21.

RIEGE, M. G.
   1972   "Parental affection and juvenile delinquency in girls." *British Journal of Criminology* 12:55–73.

ROBY, P. (ED.)
   1973   *Child Care—Who Cares?* New York: Basic Books.

ROY P.
   1963   "Adolescent roles: Rural-urban differentials." In F. I. Nye and L. W. Hoffman (eds.), *The Employed Mother in America.* Chicago: Rand McNally.

SAFILIOS-ROTHSCHILD, C.
   1970   "The influence of the wife's degree of work commitment upon some aspects of family organization and dynamics." *Journal of Marriage and the Family* 30:681–91.

SCANZONI, J. H.
   1970   *Opportunity and the Family.* New York: Free Press.

SHARP, L. J.
   1960   "Employment status of mothers and some aspects of mental illness." *American Sociological Reveiw* 25:714–17.
   1963   "Maternal mental health." In F. I. Nye and L. W. Hoffman (eds.), *The Employed Mother in America.* Chicago: Rand McNally.

SMITH, H. C.
   1969   "An investigation of the attitudes of adolescent girls toward combining marriage, motherhood and a career." Unpublished doctoral dissertation, Columbia University.

SWEET, J. A.
   1970   "Family composition and labor force activity of American wives." *Demography* 7:195–209.

THIBAUT, J. W. AND H. H. KELLEY
   1959   *The Social Psychology of Groups.* New York: Wiley.

U. S. BUREAU OF THE CENSUS
   1973   Employment Status and Work Experience. Washington, D. C.: U. S. Government Printing Office.

U. S. BUREAU OF LABOR STATISTICS
   1971   *Special Labor Report No. 13.* Washington, D. C.: U. S. Government Printing Office.

U. S. DEPARTMENT OF LABOR
   1971   *Working Women and Their Family Responsibilities: United States Experience,* 1–40. Washington, D. C.: U. S. Government Printing Office.

VOGEL, S. R., I. K. BROVERMAN, D. M. BROVERMAN, F. E. CLARKSON, AND P. S. ROSENKRANTZ
   1970   "Maternal employment and perception of sex roles among college students." *Developmental Psychology* 3:384–91.

WALKER, K. E.
   1970   "How much help for working mothers? The children's role." *Human Ecology Forum* 1:13–15.

WHITE, L. C.
   1972   "Maternal employment and anxiety over mother role." *Louisiana State University Journal of Sociology,* Spring.

WOODS, M. B.
   1972   "The unsupervised child of the working mother." *Developmental Psychology* 6:14–25.

WYLIE, R. C.
   1974   *The Self-Concept.* Lincoln, Neb.: University of Nebraska.

YARROW, M. R., P. SCOTT, L. DE LEEUW, AND C. HEINIG
   1962   "Child-rearing in families of working and nonworking mothers." *Sociometry* 25:122–40.

ZISSIS, C.
   1964   "A study of the life planning of 550 freshman women at Purdue University." *Journal of the National Association of Women Deans and Counselors* 28: 153–59.

10

MEN'S WORK AND MEN'S FAMILIES

Joan Aldous, Marie W. Osmond, and Mary W. Hicks

The focus of this chapter is on propositions relating men's participation in two critical areas: family and occupation. We use Hall's broad definition of occupation in our analysis. He defines an occupation as a "social role performed by adult members of society that directly and/or indirectly yields social and financial consequences and that constitutes a major focus in the life of an adult" (1975:6). In relating men's occupations to their family roles, space limitations as well as our own current thinking restrict us to nuclear families. These are units in which during some period in their existence a man and a woman in a socially recognized union and playing spousal and parental roles have shared a common residence with offspring, whether their own or adopted. The effects of work and family influences are intertwined, and as we show, it is sometimes difficult to disentangle the causal order.

We are personally and intellectually aware that increasing numbers of women also perform occupational and family roles and that this dual participation has repercussions on men's work as well as on family interaction. Our assignment, however, is to concentrate on men, leaving a consideration of the literature on women's family and occupational participation to another time. But occasionally in the following discussion we will necessarily point to the interplay of women's and men's occupational involvement on our dependent variables.

The propositions presented here represent a codification of a portion of the existing literature, although they

do not meet the strict theory criteria enunciated by philosophers of science (cf. Nagel 1961; Braithwaite, 1953). We have defined our charge as making sense out of the scattered pieces of existing research so as to enable the reader to determine where the critical issues lie. We also hope to imbue the reader with some of our own conviction that this topic is worthy of further investigations.

At times, we attempt to develop clusters of related propositions, "minitheories" if you will, to which we have given titles to provide easy recognition for the reader. Where conceptual clarification appears necessary for the understanding of our propositions, we also offer an explication of concepts. In addition, we indicate the degree of empirical support for the propositions as well as critical issues where research is lacking. Although the propositions summarize our thinking, our concern for the reader's understanding leads us to present our rationale in discussion form.

The chapter is divided into five main sections. The initial two sections are concerned primarily with structural variables. The first section contains an analysis of men's family background as related to their occupational placement. The following section incorporates a series of propositions relating men's occupations to various family events. There is a change in perspective in the next two sections to largely social psychological propositions. These propositions attempt to explicate some of the family processes resulting in the relationships discussed in the first two sections. The third section considers how men's occupations affect their treatment of sons as reflected in the latter's educational and occupational aspirations. The fourth section looks at marital interaction as influenced by men's work. The final section attempts to distinguish certain overriding themes emerging in the chapter and to suggest new research directions. With this description of our chapter's focus, organization, and aids to readers completed, we now begin the presentation of our substantive material.

NOTE: Much of the work on this chapter was done while Aldous was Visiting Professor at the Sociological Research Institute, University of Leuven, Belgium, 1975–1976. She would like to thank her colleague there, Professor Wilfried Dumon, for the assistance he provided throughout the year. The critiques of F. Ivan Nye, Leonard Pearlin, Reuben Hill and Brent Roper on a prior manuscript draft made the chapter more readable as well as more cogent. We are grateful to Fred Duplain for his technical assistance.

FAMILY STRUCTURE AND MEN'S OCCUPATIONS

The family's influence on males' occupational placement is analyzed on two levels: the macro and the micro. On a macro theoretical level, we review the structure-function and conflict arguments as to the nature and degree of family influence on youth's occupational attainment. On a micro level, we explicate a basic model of males' socioeconomic careers. The socioeconomic career model allows us to examine both the process by which the family of orientation influences: (1) the son's initial and subsequent occupational rank; and (2) the occupational "career contingencies" which arise when the son establishes his own family of procreation.[1]

Before embarking on our major topics, it is necessary to review the bases for three assumptions concerning occupations that underlie our discussion of males' work and the family. The first assumption is that occupations are a major means of locating the individual within the social system. Blau and Duncan (1967:vii) assert, "In the absence of hereditary castes or feudal estates, class differences come to rest primarily on occupational positions and the economic advantages and powers associated with them." Caplow (1954:30) notes that occupational identification has displaced other status-fixing attributes. Hall (1975:240) concludes that "occupation has become the most reliable indicator for placement in the stratification system *and* that occupation is indicative of and closely related to other indicators, such as education or income, that might be used" (emphasis his).

The second assumption is that there is considerable agreement in American society as to how occupations are ranked. The similarity of rankings of occupational prestige scores across societies (Hodge, Treiman, and Rossi, 1966) and across age groups (Simmons and Rosenberg, 1971) offers empirical evidence to support this assumption. There continues to be considerable speculation as to *why* occupational rankings are so highly stable (cf. Caplow, 1954). In line with our subsequent theorizing is Marsh's conclusion that the reason for similarities in prestige of occupations across societies "is that a given occupation has highly similar requirements for recruitment (educational level), role functioning (authority, power) and similar relative rewards (income) across societies" (1971:222).

These two assumptions constitute the major rationale for our focus on occupation (over other attributes) as a stable indicator of socioeconomic status. The third assumption links the first two assumptions to our topic of men's occupations and the family. Much of the extant literature assumes, both implicitly and explicitly, that the occupational position of the husband-father is the primary or even the sole determinant of a *family's* status in American society (cf. Warner, Meeker, and Eels, 1949; Parsons, 1942, 1943, 1953, 1955; Lipset and Bendix, 1952; Barber, 1957; Lenski, 1966; Blau and Duncan, 1967). The extent to which wife-mother's occupation plays a role in social placement of the family has only recently been addressed. Evidence at this time supports the assumption that males' occupations are the *primary* influence on family status.

Rossi et al. (1974), for example, asked 146 white adults (a "modified area probability sample" of households in the city of Baltimore) to rate "vignettes" of households whose adult members varied systematically in their occupational and educational attainment. In the raters' opinion, husbands' *occupational* accomplishment counted roughly one and a half times that of wives. Felson and Knoke (1974), with data from the 628 men and 536 women in the 1972 General Social Survey conducted by the National Opinion Research Center, also conclude:

> Very little support is found in this analysis for an independent status model in which female labor force participation provides women with an independent claim to social status. Nor are husbands inclined to use their wives' educational or occupational achievements to bolster their own class images [159].[2]

In sum, a cumulation of empirical studies indicates that, in industrialized societies, the occupation of the husband-father correlates highly with the placement of his family in the stratification structure. By "stratification structure" we mean the ranking hierarchy according to which each person is socially placed. Those who take a functional stance argue that, in modern societies, this hierarchy is relatively loose (cf. Parsons, 1953; 122), i.e., that family social placement varies on the basis of the male's performance or achievement (primarily in the occupational world). At the other extreme, those who view stratification from a conflict perspective assert that social placement is highly correlated with family influence or power. In the following section we examine evidence with regard to each of these approaches.

Social Placement Theories

Functionalist Theory

The role of the family in transmitting status position to offspring has been viewed traditionally from a functionalist perspective. Goode (1959b:42) includes "status placement" as one of the four functions of the family, with placement serving to link the structures of stratification, kinship, and mate choice in every society. Status, according to Davis (1950:97), is ascribed to the infant on the basis of his socializing agents, usually his parents. "Such arbitrary connection of the child with persons who already have a status in the social structure immediately gives the infant membership in the society and a specific place in the system of statuses." Scott (1972) suggests that one reason why families are employed for the task of status placement through ascription is that "the family has the child first, therefore, has the longest time to train him for statuses requiring lengthy association." Otto (1975:324), likewise, points out that "statuses are rooted in family experience."

The functionalist theory of stratification presented by Parsons (1940) and Davis and Moore (1945) predicates a "broad correlation between direct evaluation of occupational roles, income derived from those roles, and status of the families of the incumbents as collectivities in the scale of stratification" (Parsons, 1953:120). The social class position of the child is, therefore, ascriptively determined by the link between the father's work role and the father's family role (Parsons, 1951).

Both Parsons (1951) and Goode (1959b) recognize that because of this linkage, the family, and particularly the upper-status family, is a "conservative" force in the social system.

> It is strictly inconceivable that most of the men highly placed in the occupational sphere, should fail to share what their incomes can buy with their families and that they should not share their prestige. . . . Thus, as long as there is a solidary kinship unit . . . there is an inherent limit to the development, not only of absolutely equalitarian societies, but even of complete equality of opportunity [Parsons, 1951: 160–61].

However, although the family is seen as the basic area of status ascription, functionalists also have made the "liberal" assumption that the American occupational system, because of its emphasis on universalism and achievement, counters the family's conservative social placement function. Robin Williams (1970:562) provides a classic functionalist explanation:

> In American society the relatively slight emphasis on kinship as a criterion of class position militates against family continuity—and thereby is functional for a mobile open-class system stressing personal achievement as a primary criterion. In this aspect, the "weakness" so often deplored in the American kinship institutions is integrative with the cultural principles of upward social mobility through individual occupational achievement. This is another way of saying that a kinship system with strong intergenerational continuity would be incompatible with the fluidity of social classes that has been one of the remarkable features of America in the past.

Thus the functionalist explanation of stratification does not include the family as an important influence on distribution of rewards (statuses). Rather than family background, this distribution is explained in terms of functional importance of positions and scarcity of personnel (Davis and Moore, 1945). Those occupational statuses that are most essential for the maintenance of the system must receive sufficient reward so that less essential occupations will not compete successfully for personnel. At the same time, people who are most qualified, by virtue of talent and training, must be motivated to fill the more essential occupational positions and to perform adequately in them. In sum, distribution of status is a function of system needs and occupational performance. The influence of family background on occupational status of offspring is weak because "talent" is dispersed throughout the society and "training" occurs through an open educational system.

From the above we can state the functionalist proposition with regard to social placement as follows: *There is a relatively weak association between family background factors and the occupational achievement of men in American society.*

It is difficult to assign precise meaning to the term "relatively weak association," particularly since such stratification theory is couched in nonnumerical terms. Let us see, however, if the available studies can supply quantitative information that appears consonant with such a description. Evidence concerning the functionalist proposition can be gathered primarily from studies of intergenerational occupational mobility. Here we are faced with a complexity of measurement techniques which are not strictly comparable. (The interested reader should refer to Caplow, 1954:59–99; Hall, 1975:266–86; Tully, Jackson, and Curtis, 1970.) The findings, however, appear contrary to the functionalist proposition.

In a classic study of mobility over two time periods before World War II, Rogoff (1953) used data on the occupations of grooms and their fathers as recorded on marriage license applications in Marion County, Indiana. She developed social mobility ratios which measure the extent to which mobility from one occupation to another surpasses or falls short of "chance." In both time periods sons were more likely to enter their father's occupation than any other single occupation. Blau and Duncan (1967) employed this same measure in analyzing a national sample of men's mobility from first job to their 1962 occupation and concluded that occupational inheritance in all cases is greater than expected on the assumption of independence between father's and son's occupation.

A question of great interest to family sociologists has to do with whether the occupational rank of sons today depends more on occupational rank of origin than at some previous time. Tully, Jackson, and Curtis (1970:195) in a replication of Rogoff's study with 1966 and 1968 data report a slight increase in dependence since 1940. They find however, "an increase in upward mobility may be accompanied by a decrease in openness as indexed by the level of dependence of son's on father's occupation" (198). Blau and Duncan (1967:435) also comment on this paradox:

> The apparent contradiction may well be a result of the fact that the amount of mobility, even when presumably standardized, is not the same thing as the degree to which son's status depends on father's. The exceptionally large amount of occupational mobility in the United States, a result of the structural changes that have occurred with rapid industrialization, has inclined people to ignore the degree to which *social origins*

influence occupational achievements here as well as in other societies [emphasis ours].

Blau and Duncan conclude that correlations between fathers' and sons' occupational scores do not reveal a superiority of American opportunity. Comparing their Occupational Changes in a Generation (OCG) data for the United States with Svalastoga's (1965) regression analysis of data on father-son occupational inheritance from nine European nations, they find an *identical* correlation of r = .4. As Hall (1975:270) puts it, "Blau and Duncan's findings indicate that there is a high rate of occupational inheritance and that what movement there is tends to be into adjacent occupational status categories." We cite these findings as evidence against the "weak association" stated in the functionalist proposition.

Given that the family plays a major part in social placement, there still may be occupational variations in its influence. Rogoff (1953:447) reported that occupations which are either highest (professional or semiprofessional) or lowest (unskilled manual, farming, services) in the rewards which they offer were highly selective in nature. "They recruited their personnel disproportionately from some ranks to the exclusion of others." However, the occupations in the middle of the hierarchy (clerical, skilled, semiskilled) showed an even distribution of mobility throughout the population, irrespective of social origins. Blau and Duncan (1967:177) also found that the highest white-collar occupations and the lowest blue-collar occupations exhibited less variation in social origin than intermediately ranked occupations. They found that it is the intermediate-level white-collar and higher-level blue-collar occupations that supply a disproportionate amount of manpower to the occupational system. The occupations at the top have expanded while those at the bottom have contracted. This, in essence, is a major factor in the continued presence of upward mobility between generations in America.

The evidence reported above leads us to modify the functionalist proposition. It appears that only in the middle ranks of the occupational status hierarchy is there a weak association between family background (i.e., father's occupational status) and son's occupational achievement. The proposition for which we find empirical support is as follows:

1.1. Family background influences son's occupational destination, but this relationship is conditioned by the rank of fathers in the occupational status hierarchy. When these ranks are either high or low, the occupational statuses of fathers are highly and positively associated with the occupational attainment of sons. When these ranks are at intermediate levels, the association is greatly reduced.

Conflict Theory

An explanation of why we find "inheritance" of status in families ranked low or high in the status hierarchy is offered by conflict theory. Those who take a conflict approach to stratification argue that talent and training have a greater influence on the distribution of rewards (statuses) than does functional importance (of the occupation) to the system. Further, they note that training-talent avenues can be controlled as a sort of property right in certain groups (i.e., families or classes). Thus, from a conflict perspective, the stratification system takes the form that it does, and occupations are given certain statuses, because of the control of elite groups over the social structure (see Lenski, 1966, and Grandjean, 1974, for discussions of this issue).

In essence, conflict theorists view social placement as a function of family power. Although they may agree with the functionalists that "performance" is associated with occupational position, they qualify this by asserting that it is the chance to perform that is at stake here (cf. Buckley, 1958). This "chance to perform" is highly related to educational attainment.

Functionalists argue that as societies industrialize, a transfer of status inheritance mechanisms from the family to the educational system leads to a change from ascriptive to achievement criteria for social placement (cf. Parsons, 1951; Moore, 1965; Levy, 1966; Smelser and Lipset, 1966). Conflict theorists, on the other hand, contend that the power that goes along with family status "spills over" to control the quality and quantity of education that families can obtain for their offspring and thereby the kind of occupations sons are able to "achieve" (cf. Jencks and Riesman, 1968; Rogers, 1969; Jencks et al., 1972; Boudon, 1974). Thus we examine evidence with regard to the following proposition:

1.2. The influence of family background status on males' occupational achievement is mediated through (rather than conditioned by) educational opportunity.

Where functionalists see the identity of status between parents and children as a mechanism to get parents to do the arduous job of child rearing, Kemper (1974) sees parents under this arrangement as being free to use their resources for their own and not someone else's children (Park and Burgess, 1969, also come to this conclusion). Higher occupational status in our society confers power primarily through command of higher income (Lenski, 1966). Families use this income to pass on their advantages through providing their children access to higher levels of education, education in which the "quality" of the institution varies directly with its expense.

With respect to Proposition 1.2, the copious literature on the influence of socioeconomic status and ability on entrance into college has demonstrated that, even when the effects of student ability are controlled, there are systematic differentials among status groups in access to higher education (cf. Rogoff, 1953; Sewell and Shah, 1967; Folger et al., 1970). Morgan et al. (1962:369), with a cross-sectional, national sample of the noninstitutional population in the United States, conclude that their analysis "supports the hypothesis of transmission of characteristics from one generation to the next and reveals a powerful impact of background factors on educational achievement." Their study showed that plans for children to contribute to their own support during college varied inversely with father's income. Availability of low-cost community and state colleges, so that children could live at home, was the most important factor for the middle and lower income groups in determining the realization of college plans for their children (Morgan et al., 1962:411–14).

In a recent study bearing on the findings of Morgan et al., Karabel and Astin (1975) report on a survey that is unique in offering representative data on the national system of higher education including measures of socioeconomic status, academic ability, college selectivity, and affluence. Karabel and Astin (390) found that working one's way through an elite college is exceedingly rare, and that living at home is negatively correlated with college status. Other of their results revealed the following: students from low SES backgrounds are much more likely to attend a college with low admission standards, while students from high SES backgrounds more often attend a highly selective institution; SES of students is still related to college prestige even when academic ability of students is held constant; and the use of standard admissions criteria in differentiated public systems of higher education helps ensure that the highest subsidies generally go to those students from relatively wealthy families.[3] Karabel and Astin conclude:

> As our findings demonstrate, in a society where status is transmitted primarily through education, the present structure of college ranking is biased in favor of the privileged; by enabling their children to attend elite institutions, this arrangement helps them preserve their position. Social origins influence college prestige which, in turn, affects adult status [397].

In sum, the evidence examined appears to offer little research support for the functionalist argument that educational opportunity conditions the association between family background and son's occupational achievement in American society. On the contrary, there appears to be considerable credibility in the conflict theorists' claim that students are allocated to education programs which (at least roughly) reflect both their family background and an occupational destination commensurate with this background.

Socioeconomic Career Models

Having examined functionalist and conflict explanations of the family's influence on males' occupational *placement,* we attempt next to explicate a basic model of family influence on males' occupational *careers.* First, on a micro level of analysis, we elaborate on a model in which fathers' characteristics influence a number of intervening variables that relate to sons' education and initial occupational achievement. Second, we discuss how these variables, in turn, affect certain outcome variables of sons' occupation and income. In the last part of this section, we examine marriage and birth events in the sons' life cycles that may be affected by, or vary concomitantly with, adult occupations and incomes and subsequently affect their own sons' educational and occupational choices.

Initial Occupational Achievement

Our first problem is one of trying to identify the specific family background characteristics which represent favorable or unfavorable conditions for sons' occupational achievements and the factors which mediate these conditions. Following Blau and Duncan's (1967:170) basic theoretical model, we conceive of three major stages in a males' early socioeconomic life cycle or career: family, formal education, and occupation. Blau and Duncan's model is diagrammed as follows:

Figure 10.1.

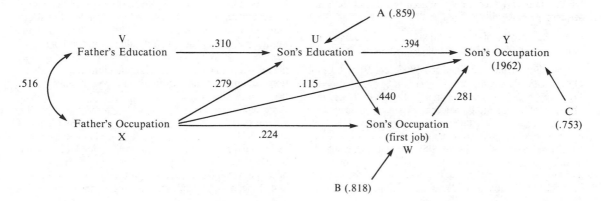

These results are based on the analysis of data derived from the March, 1962, national survey of the Bureau of the Census, "Occupational Changes in a Generation" (OCG). The numbers entered in the diagram, with the exception of r_{XV}, are path coefficients among the variables when they are arranged in the time order indicated. The time order assumptions are that family background characteristics precede son's educational attainment, son's educational attainment precedes son's first job, and son's occupation in 1962 follows son's first job.[4]

This path analysis, conducted on Blau and Duncan's OCG data, can be taken as supporting the following proposition:

2.1. Fathers' education and occupational status both directly and indirectly, through educational attainment of sons, affect sons' occupations in first job and sons' future occupational achievement.[5]

Son's education has the largest path to son's first job as well as to his later occupation in 1962. However, some direct effects of father's occupation are present not only on son's first job but to a lesser degree on son's later occupation. Father's education, on the other hand, appears to have only indirect effects on son's early and subsequent occupational achievement via son's education. Blau and Duncan (1967:201) thus conclude that the degree of perpetuation of family position which occurs is mediated in large part by education. While the model explains only about 25 percent of the variance, Blau and Duncan (175) emphasize that this is no guide whatever to the *validity* of the causal interpretation.

Additional measures of family background structure that were incorporated in the initial Blau and Duncan model are summarized below. We do not intend to be exhaustive in our coverage of the literature on these topics. Our aim is to point out the major variables of theoretical interest and to illustrate the empirical work that incorporates these. These variables are assumed to affect sons' occupational achievement indirectly through their influence on educational attainment. The social psychological dynamics of this process are explicated in the second section of this chapter. The additional family background variables are introduced in each of the subsequent propositions.

2.2. Family size is related to sons' educational attainment, and this is an inverse relationship.

Data from Blau and Duncan (1967, ch. 9) and from Duncan, Featherman, and Duncan (1968: ch. 5) support Proposition 2.2. It appears that family size affects the chances of occupational success of sons primarily because it affects their education. There is a direct path of number of siblings on sons' education ($\gamma = -.29$) and on sons' 1962 occupations ($\gamma = -.05$). A number of research studies suggest that certain variables of a "parental support/encouragement" nature intervene, in the model, between family size and educational attainment (cf. Bossard and Boll, 1956; Nye, Carlson, and Garrett, 1970; Scheck and Emerick, 1976).

2.3. Sibling position is related to sons' educational attainment. This relationship is conditioned by family size: in large families, youngest sons have greater advantages; in small families, oldest sons have greater advantages.

Blau and Duncan (1967:313–16) report that number of siblings and sibling position interact in their effects on sons' adult achievements. Note in this connection that we found support for Proposition 2.2 which stated that the larger the family, the less the son's educational achievement. The negative influence of a large family, however, is apparently ameliorated for youngest sons (the adverse holding true for oldest sons in large families). Blau and Duncan theorize that these differences reflect the role relations among siblings in the family. They suggest that older sons assume responsibilities and are asked to make sacrifices for younger ones.[6] This is particularly true, Blau and Duncan conclude, in large families because parental resources are more likely to need supplementation and the number of siblings an older son might be expected to help is greater.

2.4. A favorable intellectual environment in the family is related to sons' educational attainment, and this is a positive relationship.

While obviously significant for a son's educational achievement, the intellectual environment or educational "climate" in the home is difficult to operationalize. Blau and Duncan (1967:316–28) used the education of a man's eldest brother as a crude indication of the extent to which a family promotes achievement. The positive correlation between brother's and own education, when the background factors were controlled, was conditioned by family size. A well-educated eldest brother improves the educational attainments of his siblings more in small families than in large ones. Their interpretation is that a favorable educational climate in the family affects the educational attainments of sons, at least in part, because it induces the parents and/or the sons to take advantage of any potential resources available for educational achievement. They conclude that if the educational climate is not favorable, it makes little difference if the family can or cannot afford education for sons. We speculate that we may simply be seeing evidence again of the influence of eldest brother's education on son's educational attainment, i.e., of the interaction of sibling position and family size.

Further evidence on this point is offered by a "confluence model," which posits that the intellectual level of children declines with increased family size (Zajonc, 1976). These researchers represent "intellectual environment" in the family as a function of the average absolute intellectual level within the family. As do Blau and Duncan, they emphasize that their operationalization is an oversimplification of a complex process which likely includes amount of time each family member spends with the child, sibling interaction, etc. The "confluence model" predicts that effects of sibling position (or birth order) are mediated entirely by the *age spacing* between siblings. Hence, with large enough time gaps between siblings, the negative effects of birth order can be nullified and even reversed.[7]

The "confluence model" fills a gap in our knowledge about the relationship between family size and educational attainment of sons by showing how *intellectual level* of children may be affected by size and spacing. Thus, for example, we have a more plausible explanation for Blau and Duncan's finding that youngest children in large families appear to have a greater advantage in educational attainment. Zajonc and Markus's (1975) model would predict that these children enter a very mature (i.e., "rich") intellectual environment. Conversely, the oldest child in a small family (indicated to have a greater educational advantage by Blau and Duncan) avoids the "only" child disadvantage of very small families.

Sociologists have frequently suggested that a man who grows up in a home lacking one or both parents is handicapped in his career as compared with the man whose parents' marriage remained intact until he reached adolescence. The following proposition expresses this belief:

2.5. Having both parents present is related to higher educational and occupational achievement by sons; while having one or none present is related to lower achievement.

Whether family stability causes or is caused by socioeconomic background factors is a research question in itself. Family instability whether due to death, separation, or divorce may deplete family resources available to the son, which, in effect, lowers the status of his socioeconomic background. Conversely, low family status may cause greater family instability (Blau and Duncan, 1967:332).

Blau and Duncan (1967:331–37) report that the effect on son's occupational achievement of both parents being present is almost wholly transmitted via education. The educational handicap, which in itself is slight (none of the effects approaches two years of school differences), is reflected in poorer than average occupational achievement of sons. Blau and Duncan consider various types of family—father only, mother only, other parental substitutes, etc.—and find that even with socioeconomic status controlled (i.e., father's education and occupation), any type of broken home handicaps a son in regard to his educational attainment.

Zajonc (1976:23–31) addresses this question and finds evidence that differences in intellectual performance between children from fatherless homes and from intact homes are greater the longer the father's absence and the

younger the child when loss of the parent occurred. Moreover, he posits that deficits in the intellectual test performance of fatherless children are not due simply to possible drops in income from fathers' absence because these deficits are also found when comparisons are made within a single socioeconomic stratum. Zajonc explains these findings in terms of the "confluence model" discussed above. It follows directly from this model that a one-parent home constitutes an inferior "intellectual environment" and should result in intellectual deficits, and that early loss of a parent should be associated with greater deficits than a loss occurring when the child is older and thus has had longer exposure to a two-parent intellectual environment.

2.6. Black racial identity is related to lower educational and occupational achievement by sons.

The disadvantages blacks suffer on the way to occupational achievement are too well known to need documentation. We assess here only the extent to which family background can account for racial differences in son's occupational achievement.

With regard to educational attainment, Treiman and Terrell (1975), utilizing Blau and Duncan's OCG data for males, report that for blacks this depends exclusively on parent's education. Where father's occupational status has a significant direct effect on son's educational attainment for whites, no relationship is observed for blacks.

Further elaboration is offered by Scanzoni's (1971) intensive study of 400 intact, black families (above under class). Scanzoni found that father's education has the most direct influence (as compared to father's occupation or mother's education) on actual "resource-provision" for son's education. According to the Scanzoni study, both mothers (74 percent) and fathers (65 percent) encouraged children to go to college.[8] In general, however, the black males in Scanzoni's sample perceived their mothers, more than their fathers, as being a help in education and in "getting ahead" (68–78).

A number of researchers have pointed out that educational attainment is not the same route to social mobility for blacks as it is for whites (cf. Siegel, 1965; Willie, 1974; Masters, 1975; Staples, 1976).[9] The relative income gap between blacks and whites actually increases with education. Staples's (1976:190) explanation is that higher-status jobs (potentially available to highly educated blacks) are more likely to require certain friendship and family ties than lower-paying positions. In terms of these requisites, blacks are disadvantaged. Moreover, blacks with limited education do not achieve the occupational statuses of their white counterparts. Willie (1969) points out that while 50 percent of whites with eight or fewer years of formal education have jobs as service workers or laborers, approximately 80 percent of black workers with this level of education find work only in these kinds of jobs.

Black males' occupational *mobility* is little affected by

their family backgrounds, Duncan, Featherman, and Duncan (1968:69–76) conclude, from their analyses of intergenerational occupational mobility, that for any given level of father's occupation, a black male is less likely to move into a high-status occupation than is a white male with the same level of origin.[10] There appear to be two distinct patterns of intergenerational mobility for the races: (1) from low origins *white* males tend to move up to higher-status occupations; given high origins, they tend to remain at this high level; (2) from low origins *black* males tend to remain at low occupational levels, while those few with higher origins tend to fall to lower-status levels. "The typical destination of Negroes, *regardless of level of origin,* is the lower category of manual jobs" (69, emphasis theirs).[11]

Further, when these researchers included race as one of five background variables in their basic occupational achievement model, they found that only about one-fourth of the income gap between black and white males can be attributed to the three *family* characteristics in the model of father's education and occupation and family size.[12] In sum, the major effect on occupational attainment of black males appears to be occupational discrimination. This effect is not inherited so much as shared with their families of origin as evidenced by the independent effect of race on occupational achievement and mobility.

Subsequent Occupational Outcomes

There is debate in the sociological literature regarding the extent to which family background factors, particularly father's occupational status, influence son's occupation and income after his initial entry into the labor market (cf. Cutright, 1970: 630–31). Recent research by Kelley (1973), however, has clarified this picture significantly. Utilizing a sample of 715 couples selected from Featherman's longitudinal Princeton Fertility Study data, Kelley shows that these influences vary over the son's life cycle. Early in the life cycle, father's income affects son's occupational status by way of investment in his education and other training which "pays off" in son's later occupational status. Kelley, much like Cutright (1970), concludes that family background factors have little to no direct effect on son's income. However, they do have indirect effects. Furthermore, while these indirect effects of family background are fairly negligible early in the son's work career, they become increasingly important as the son's career advances through later life cycle stages. Kelley explains that this is because father's income operates through son's education and first occupation and that the latter have strong effects on income only after a man's career is well underway. The foregoing provides an empirical basis for the following propositions:

2.7. Fathers' education and occupation influence sons' subsequent income levels indirectly through their influence on sons' occupational attainment.

2.8. The influence of fathers' education and occu-

pation is more pronounced at the middle of the sons' life cycle than at earlier stages.

A plausible rationale for the "sleeper" effect of fathers' income on sons' income level in the middle period of sons' life cycles lies in the differential occupational careers that men experience. Not only is the probability of advancement greater for men at higher-status occupational levels, but the "top" or "peak" of their career line is reached later by white-collar workers than by blue-collar workers (Oppenheimer, 1974). Assuming that occupational rank involves commensurate income levels, this difference in career lines suggests that males with lower-status jobs reach their peak income levels sooner than males with higher-status jobs reach theirs.[13] Moreover, peak income levels for blue-collar jobs generally are lower than those for white-collar jobs. In sum, during the early stages of a man's career his occupation can be changing and his occupational attainment, measured at one point during this time, may appear unrelated to his family background. It is at the point where sons have had enough time to advance to the career "peak" for which they are "qualified" that we can observe the strongest relationship between fathers' and sons' social placement.

It is also at this career point when the family background effects on son's income are the most pronounced that the occupational achievement of this son who is now a father is most important for *his* own son's occupational achievement. This is the time of the so-called "life cycle squeeze" phenomenon, when a man's earnings may not be sufficient to meet his children's educational needs (Wilensky, 1963). At the time when one or more children reach college age, for example, fathers with lower-status occupations are less able to provide the resources necessary for sons to pursue higher education (and so to attain advantageous occupational placement) than are fathers with higher-status occupations. The number and ages of a man's children would mediate (increase or decrease) the severity and duration of the "squeeze" on his earnings from educational investments in his sons' occupational achievements. Thus the intergenerational impact of the father's occupational achievement on his son's income (via the son's education and occupation) is juxtaposed with the educational and subsequent occupational and income opportunities the son will be able to provide his own children.

From the rationale supplied above, we derive the following proposition.

2.9. For males (husbands-fathers) with higher-status occupations, peak income and peak resource demands from the family are synchronous. For males with lower-status occupations, this is not the case.

Recent data presented by Oppenheimer (1974) offer empirical support for Proposition 2.9. Based on 1960 census data on earning patterns by age, Oppenheimer finds that only among men in relatively high-status professional, managerial, and sales occupations do median earnings peak at the same time as do family income demands or needs. Among blue-collar workers, and many medium-level and low-level white-collar workers as well, median earnings are highest at comparatively younger ages (35.44 years of age versus 45 or over for the higher-status categories). At the time when family "costs" are greatest, therefore, blue-collar males display earning patterns which have already leveled off or have actually declined. Thus Oppenheimer concludes that for husband-fathers in lower-status occupations, the "life-cycle squeeze" must be a common experience.[14]

Career Contingencies: Life Cycle Variables

We have reviewed, in the previous sections, findings which are pertinent to the impact of son's *family of orientation* on son's occupational achievement and social placement. At this point we turn to an examination of evidence relating events in the son's *family of procreation* to son's occupations, incomes, and thus his family's social placement. Various "life cycle" events, such as those described here, are often termed "career contingencies" because of the problematic nature of time order in their association with males' occupations and incomes (Blau and Duncan, 1967:337; Duncan, Featherman, and Duncan, 1968, ch. 9). Directions of influence (or of causality) are difficult to assess. Additionally, we hasten to point out that interaction effects of one or more contingency variables are likely to alter the shape of the proposed relationship between any "independent" and "dependent" variables which we review.

In sum, research on the "life cycle" variables is generally inadequate for assessing whether relationships with males' occupations are coterminous, symmetrical, or causal. Unless a cohort of males is studied longitudinally, none of these variables can be unequivocally ordered with respect to occupation and income. While much of the work reviewed does incorporate analytic procedures where assumptions as to the nature of the associations are required (i.e., dependent and independent variables, no concomitant or reciprocal causation, etc.), we must remain aware of possible rival paradigms.

TIMING OF FIRST MARRIAGE. The major portion of the literature on "mate selection" disregards the possible association of males' occupations and timing of their first marriages.[15] This may be because there is little variation in the United States with regard to age at marriage. Sixty percent of all first marriages occur within a four- or five-year period, and 75 percent of them occur within three or four years on either side of age 21 (Mogey, 1965).

To anticipate that occupation and/or education would have substantial effects on mate selection and timing of marriage is counter to the romantic love ethos that pervades our courtship system. However, if we can assume some degree of rationality in the process, it does appear logical that a modicum of "resources"—e.g., potential family aid or son's own educational attainment, occupational credentials, and income—is needed to leave home and start one's own marriage and family. On the basis of this rationale we examine evidence with regard to the following proposition:

2.10. A male's socioeconomic resources are related to the timing of his entry to marriage, and this is a curvilinear relationship; i.e., at both the lowest and the highest extremes of such resources there is delayed entry into marriage.

Using family background, occupation, and income as three such resources, let us consider first, *family background*.[16] There is substantial evidence that the median age at first marriage is older for men at higher socioeconomic status levels (Glick, 1957; Burchinal, 1965). In essence, this difference appears to reflect extended education, delayed economic independence, and parental pressure on sons to achieve occupational credentials before marriage. At the opposite extreme of the status continuum, although females marry younger than the average, males again are somewhat older than average at first marriage (Tietze, 1955; Bell, 1975:54–55). For this group at the lower end of the continuum, we speculate that lack of occupation or low income produces delay in marriage. Others have argued that the lower-socioeconomic-status male "resists marriage" longer than his higher-status counterparts (Bell, 1975:55).

Turning to men's *occupational status*, Carter and Glick (1970:94, table 4.10), on the basis of 1960 census data, showed that professionals, managers, and rural workers all had a median age at first marriage over 25 years of age. This was also true of laborers. Carter and Glick explain the rough curvilinear trend by suggesting that men in occupations requiring the acquisition of more financial resources or the pursuit of specialized training tend to delay their first marriage as do those with insufficient income. Thus male income could explain the later marriage of males in both the high and the low occupational ranks: males aiming for professional statuses delay their job entry and thus their earning power until their late 20s; males in low-status occupations derive insufficient income to start a new household until they have had considerable work experience.

With regard to *income*, the third resource listed above, Cutright (1970) poses a strong argument that male income has the most direct association with time of marriage. Using 1966 census data, Cutright finds evidence that it is empirically more appropriate to place measures of marital status *after* income in the basic socioeconomic career model than it is to use educational or occupational status to *predict* entry to marriage.

First, taking "percent single" as the indicator of entry to marriage, Cutright shows that the direct effect of earnings on percent single, when education, occupation, and earnings are considered simultaneously, is a strong negative: as earnings increase, the percent single decreases. Second, examining the marriage rate for men—the average rate of first marriages during 1958 and 1959 per 1,000 never-married men—he presents overall evidence that within age groups the marriage rate increases as male income increases.

Cutright's descriptive evidence is indeed persuasive but cannot, without further research, be taken as conclusive. On the one hand, as documented earlier, occupational status and income are highly intercorrelated. The more widely used occupational status indices are based upon both occupation per se and median income associated with the occupations. Moreover, some part of the relationship of income and marriage rates, as Cutright also acknowledges, is possibly a spurious consequence of a positive effect of marriage on income. As Rainwater (1971) emphasizes, the family serves as a basic source for the motivation to work for the stable working-class male. The "central role" for the male is that of provider for his family. Thus marriage may have its strongest impact on increasing male income at the earlier stages in the life cycle. We return to this topic in our discussion of timing of first child and fertility. It is in combination with these family events that the impact of variation in age at marriage on the husband's occupational success is strongly accentuated.

MARITAL STABILITY. In the section above we asked how various socioeconomic resources influenced a male's entry into marriage. Here we are concerned with the association between marital stability and males' occupational achievement. "Marital stability" is operationalized as marital intactness versus marital dissolution. Traditionally, in the sociological literature, material intactness has been viewed as dependent upon the husband's occupational success (cf. Hollingshead, 1950; Goode, 1951). Thus we examine evidence with regard to the following proposition:

> 2.11. The husband's occupational achievement influences his marital stability, and this is a positive relationship.

Udry (1966:208), on the basis of 1960 census data, concluded that there is lowest marital stability (i.e., more separation or divorce) among men in the lowest-status occupations. He found that this relationship between low-status occupation and marital dissolution is particularly strong for men in personal service and domestic service occupations. Moreover, according to Udry, this relationship is the same for nonwhite males as for white males, except that the nonwhite rates of marital dissolution are more than double the white rates.[17]

Cutright (1971b) has posited two possible models to explain the impact of males' incomes on marital stability (again operationalized as intactness versus dissolution). In both of these models the independent variable is income and the final dependent variable is marital stability. Family level of consumption and family assets are first-order intervening variables, followed by marital satisfaction. In the "role satisfaction" model, Cutright shows a strong direct impact of marital satisfaction on stability plus a direct effect of consumption level and no direct effect of assets. In the "constraint" model, however, the indicator of marital satisfaction is not so strongly related to marital stability, and assets are shown to have an important direct effect on stability. These models, of course, deserve further investigation.

There is also a need for family sociologists to acquire more evidence with regard to the claim that marriage increases males' occupational achievement, i.e., that marital stability may act as an independent variable in Proposition 2.11. Blau and Duncan (1967:338–40), for example, analyzed marital status (currently married to first wife; currently remarried; currently separated, divorced, or widowed) as a contingency variable intervening between a male's first and subsequent occupational statuses. Figure 10.2 illustrates how marital status (and other contingency variables such as fertility, etc.) is incorporated into the socioeconomic career model. The code for the model is as follows: V is father's education; X is father's occupational status; U is son's education; W is son's occupational status in his first job; M is son's marital status in 1962; and Y is son's occupational status in 1962. The dashed lines indicate that associations with marital status cannot be quantified with path coefficients, since marital status is not a metric variable.

Blau and Duncan found significant gross and net effects of marital status on subsequent occupational status, independent of the other measured determinants in the model. In terms of gross effects the only clearly favorable category of marital status is first marriage, wife present. The net effects, however, suggests a favorable influence of remarriage and widowhood as well.[18] Farley and Hermalin (1971), utilizing 1960 census data, examined black-white differences in the association of marital status and "life chances," measured as differential levels of education, occupation, and income. They too concluded

Figure 10.2.

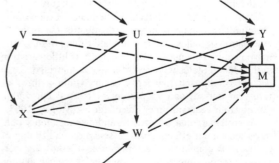

that, for both white and black, currently married men have higher scores on the life chances indicators than do men in other marital statuses.

The evidence above is presented primarily to raise the issue of possible reciprocal causation between these variables. Based on descriptive data, however, it does not resolve the issue of direction of causation. Perhaps lack of occupational achievement is a prelude to marital dissolution; on the other hand, marital dissolution may disrupt or disorganize an occupational career. Only a longitudinal study that follows men throughout (or at a number of points in) their marital-occupational careers will provide the data needed to answer this question.

TIMING OF FIRST BIRTH. The timing of births after marriage, as associated with males' occupations, was brought to the attention of family sociologists by Christensen's research using record linkage (cf. Christensen and Bowden, 1953; Christensen, 1963) In his Utah County study of marriage license applications and birth records for 1,670 couples between the years 1905 and 1931, he found a substantial correlation between the occupation of the husband and length of time before the child was born. Professional occupations were associated with the greatest mean number of days (582), and unskilled occupations with the least mean number of days (376.8).

Interest in the pattern of child spacing as an occupational career contingency has been stimulated by findings reported by Freedman and Coombs (1966). From a longitudinal study of a sample of white couples in Detroit, initially contacted in 1962, Freedman and Coombs concluded, "Whether measured by current income or by the accumulation of several types of assets, a couple's economic position is substantially better the longer the interval to the first birth or the last birth" (647).

From this reasoning, we state the following proposition:

2.12. The time interval between a male's marriage and the birth of his first child is related to his occupational achievement. This is a positive relationship: the longer the time interval, the greater the occupational achievement.

Further evidence on the nature of this association is offered by Duncan, Featherman, and Duncan (1968: 265–73) using a subsample of the OCG data restricted to white males 25 to 44 years of age, employed, married to initial spouse, and whose wives had borne at least one child.[19] Analyses revealed that short intervals between marriage and first birth are unfavorable for occupational success. Moreover, very long intervals are apparently also unfavorable, with the optimum interval being in the neighborhood of three years. Thus the association appears somewhat curvilinear. Also of interest, with reference to Christensen and Bowden's (1953) and Cutright's (1971b) works, Duncan, Featherman, and Duncan

(1968:268–69) found no particular suggestion in their data that premarital pregnancy of spouse affords a special handicap to husband's occupational achievement, apart from that pertaining merely to a very short interval of time.

There is an obvious question of whether Proposition 2.12 is conditioned by age at marriage. Is it more likely to hold for those who marry young than for those who marry at an age at or above the mean? Duncan, Featherman, and Duncan (1968:270) report that age at marriage shows no association with length of interval from marriage to first birth. Other researchers, however, who have further specified these variables indicate some support for a conditional relationship. Morgan for example, views the association between age at marriage and timing of first child as an index of both the planning horizons of the family and its ability to accumulate assets. As Morgan (1962: 379–80) states, "The birth of a child shortly after an early marriage limits the wife's ability to work and imposes a burden on the husband's income." Freedman and Coombs (1966) found low-income males who marry at later ages have longer spacing between children than those marrying earlier; at higher income levels, late marriage is associated with much shorter child spacing. They conclude that "those who have children very quickly after marriage find themselves under great economic pressure, particularly if they married at an early age.... They are more likely than others to become discouraged at an early point and to lose interest more quickly than others in the competition for economic success" (648).

In sum, there is no simple association between timing of children and occupational success. The assumptions of rational behavior and equivalent effects of extraneous variables are not the only problems with regard to generalizations on this subject. There is the unresolved question of reciprocal causation. As with fertility, discussed below, there exists the likelihood of a "vicious cycle" for lower-status families. Timing of birth events influences their occupational achievement, but their socioeconomic background and lower initial occupational status also appear associated with early marriage and short intervals to first child. The question of why this occurs demands further structural as well as social psychologically based research.

MARITAL FERTILITY. The negative association between occupational status and number of children is one of the more widely documented findings in the family literature. In a previous section we discussed the disadvantages of large family size for son's educational achievement. Here we present evidence concerning such a proposition, and possible conditioning effects on the associations of occupation, income, and fertility, as well as information on the effect of male's occupational mobility on fertility.

First we state the association in propositional form:

2.13. Size of family (i.e., number of children) influences a male's occupational achievement, and this is a negative relationship.

Cutright (1971a), using census data, takes husband-wife income as the independent variable and reports a "moderate" negative relationship with number of children. According to Cutright (168), "no direct effect of occupational prestige, independent of education and income" on number of children is indicated. With "per member consumption" as the final dependent variable in the model, he shows a strong positive effect of income and a strong negative effect of number of children on the consumption variable.

Duncan, Featherman, and Duncan (1968:255–65) analyze a path model in which husband's income is the final dependent variable rather than the independent variable as with Cutright. Background variables include husband's occupation, husband's education, husband's first job, wife's education, and wife's father's occupation. Two intervening variables are number of children and husband's subsequent to first job, 1962 occupational status. They conclude, somewhat in accordance with Cutright, that there is only a slight effect of fertility on occupational achievement, and this effect is negative. In contrast to Cutright, however, they report a small positive net effect of fertility on income for six age groups through age 51. Duncan, Featherman, and Duncan (264) suggest that a man with many children is highly motivated to seek and retain such employment as will yield the greatest total income. He may be forced to do this in a manner that sacrifices his occupational prestige for the income available by multiple jobholding.[20]

A number of studies have revealed no differences among men in various occupations with regard to family size preferences (cf. Freedman and Sharp, 1959; Westoff et al., 1961). Thus it is commonly acknowledged that a number of contingency variables must influence the association in proposition 2.13. Several examples of these are listed below:

1. Contraceptive knowledge and utilization (Rainwater, 1965; Reed and Udry, 1973)
2. Rurality (Goldberg, 1959)
3. Race and rurality (Lee and Lee, 1959)
4. Race and educational attainment (Goldscheider and Uhlenberg, 1969)
5. Family size at the particular point in the life cycle (Coombs, 1974; Simon, 1975)
6. Family size of the family of orientation (McAllister et al., 1974)
7. "Relative" income (Heberle, 1942; Kunz, 1965; Bahr, Chadwick, and Strauss, 1975)
8. Lifetime or "potential" income (Bean and Wood, 1974).

These sources offer a fund of information for future researchers who wish to investigate the association of family structure and male's occupational and socioeconomic status.

OCCUPATIONAL MOBILITY AND FERTILITY. There is an inherent plausibility to the argument that males whose occupational statuses exhibit upward mobility would attempt to restrict the size of their families. Space precludes any extensive discussion of the so-called "mobility hypothesis" of differential fertility. This has been publicized sufficiently, however, to warrant a summary statement of current research on the topic. Our primary purpose is to bring to the attention of family sociologists an area in which refined theorizing and research design are obviously needed.

The rationale behind the theorizing that relates social mobility to decreased fertility has been stated succinctly by Westoff (1956:404). He argues that the "ideal-type" couple either in the process of vertical mobility or geared toward its anticipation displays such characteristics as rationality of behavior, competitiveness, careerism, etc.—in short, a pervasive success orientation and all that is implied by it.

A general statement of the proposition is as follows:

2.14. Occupational mobility is directly related to degree of fertility planning and inversely related to the size of the planned family.

There are, of course, both subjective and objective dimensions implied in this proposition. As Blau and Duncan (1967:370) point out, it may not be the actual experience of occupational promotion or demotion that produces fertility differentials, but rather the mere aspiration or desire for mobility. In its objective form, however, the proposition has not received conclusive empirical support (cf. Berent, 1952).

The greatest amount of information on the subject, thus far, is afforded by Blau and Duncan's (1967, ch. 11) intensive study of 6,000 couples drawn from the OCG data. They conclude that the influence of mobility itself on fertility is greatly overshadowed by that of a number of related factors. White-collar status and origin, for example, depress birth rates more than does mobility per se. Among their findings are the following: (1) wives of both upwardly and downwardly mobile men in terms of occupation within the nonfarm sector, have slightly lower mean fertility than wives of men remaining in the same occupational position; (2) the classic pattern of "inverted birth rates" prevails significantly only among couples with farm backgrounds and among women marrying at early ages; (3) the pattern is greater among males who experience a high degree as opposed to a minimum amount of occupational mobility.

Blau and Duncan's (1967:399) theoretical explanation for these findings centers on "the hypothesis that both fertility itself and class differences in it are reduced by the *Gesellschaft* character that distinguishes modern urbanized society in general and its white-collar component in particular.'' They see the slightly lower fertility of mobile couples as a manifestation of the weakening of supportive bonds of social integration that results from a pronounced change in socioeconomic status. ''In short, disruptions of social integration depress fertility, just as they promote suicide'' (417).

In the final section of this chapter the subject of occupational mobility will recur as we examine occupational success and conjugal solidarity.

MEN'S OCCUPATIONS AND PARENT-CHILD RELATIONS: INTRAFAMILIAL DYNAMICS

With this section we leave our structural analysis of men's work and men's families. We are now trying to tease out those propositions from the research literature that spell out the process through which men's occupations influence their sons' occupational choice. The problem of identifying these propositions, composed of social psychological variables, is in no sense a simple one. They have been shown to depend on a number of interconnected, contingent variables. Correlational data provide the basis for causal analysis with all the attendant problems of possible misinterpretation of the data.

The specific variables of concern in this section are the following: parental values, socialization practices and aspirations, achievement, ambition, and motivation. By ''parental values'' we mean those standards that parents would like to see incorporated in their children's behavior. The concepts ''aspirations,'' ''achievement,'' and ''ambition'' are used interchangeably to denote the desire to get ahead or to succeed. Some researchers have used more specific definitions, but, in general, the terms ''getting ahead'' and ''success'' include the meanings utilized in the research we reviewed.

Research data, in spite of the complexity of the findings, permit some tentative theoretical formulation about intrafamilial processes related to fathers' occupations. Proposition 2.1 and the evidence that supported it indicate that males' work experience significantly influences the son's occupational choice or choices. The obvious question is how this influence is exerted. One kind of answer has been that occupation determines the male's basic life

values and these determine how he will treat his child. These socialization practices influence the child's personality development and educational and occupational aspirations. A model illustrating this sequence of events would look like Figure 10.3.

One proposition is as follows:

3.1. The husband-father's occupational experience influences parental values.

There is a considerable body of evidence, which has been accumulating for some time, that supports this proposition. Kohn's nationwide survey (1969) provided evidence that the autonomy-related dimensions of a man's work influence his child-rearing values. Kohn's contention was that the characteristics of the job, to which men devote so much of their time and energy, generate differences in parental values and influence what they think will be important for their children to know in order to get along in the world:

> Members of different social classes by virtue of enjoying (or suffering) different conditions of life come to see the world differently—to develop different conceptions of reality, different aspirations and hopes and fears, different conceptions of the desirable [471].

Three key aspects of occupations were identified by Kohn as critical: (1) the closeness of supervision to which a man is subjected; (2) whether he works with things, with people, or with ideas; and (3) the degree of self-reliance his job requires. Typical middle-class jobs require initiative, independent judgment, and the ability to deal with people. In contrast, working-class occupations generally require conformity and obedience. Parents of each social class value those characteristics which seem most suitable for their children's lives. Self-direction and obedience are the critical value orientations for the middle class and for the working class, respectively.

In a national survey conducted by the National Opinion Research Center in spring and summer of 1964, Kohn and Schooler (1969) confirmed and extended the earlier conclusion of Kohn (1959) and Pearlin and Kohn (1966). They found that the higher the father's class position, the more he valued characteristics in children indicative of self-direction, and the less he valued characteristics indicative of conformity.

Figure 10.3.

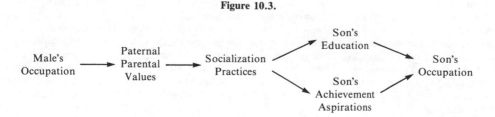

Wright and Wright (1976) used data from the 1973 NORC General Social Survey to examine Kohn's theme. They found that social class remains the primary determinant of self-direction values. The analysis of the data, however, suggests that a fully developed model of self-direction values will have to be expanded beyond social class alone and that relatively more emphasis should be placed on education than occupation.

In an analysis of data from several hundred male participants in the 1962–1967 Michigan Student Study, Mortimer (1976) examined social class and occupationally related differences in family relationships and differences in the impact of family relationships on the vocational socialization process. The findings are consistent with Kohn's contention that self-direction in work is a source of parental values influencing fathers' relationships with children.

Miller and Swanson (1958), on the basis of their study in Detroit, reported that the entrepreneurial versus bureaucratic nature of middle class father's work setting is significantly related to a number of maternal child-rearing values and practices. The findings of Franklin and Scott (1970), however, do not support the Miller and Swanson thesis that families classed as entrepreneurial tend to emphasize self-control for their children, or that families classified as bureaucratic value obedience for theirs. Their data suggest that occupation, education, and income are more significant variables to use to explain variations in parental values.

From this evidence we may formulate the following proposition:

3.2. The more self-control men exercise in their occupations, the more they will value self-direction in their children.

To continue our chain of reasoning, we now need to show that these paternal values do affect sons' occupational choices, Mortimer (1974), using small-space analysis to investigate the relationships between fathers' occupations and male college students' career choice, did find that distinctive characteristics of the fathers' occupations are related to sons' occupational choices. The three occupational characteristics she investigated were (1) extent of work autonomy, (2) rewards of the occupation, and (3) functions of the work activities.

Findings were drawn from a secondary analysis of survey data from a longitudinal study of University of Michigan students. Questionnaire data were obtained from all men in two classes of freshmen entering the liberal arts college in 1962 and 1963, and from a sample of 650 men selected from this freshman population after they had graduated from college. The data revealed a strong tendency for sons to choose their fathers' occupations. When they did not, there was some indication that they still sought the rewards and occupational experiences obtained by their fathers. Although we lack comparable data on sons who do not attend college, we have now given some explanation of the internal family processes whereby the father-son occupational continuity, emphasized in our macro analysis, occurs (see Proposition 2.1). It is these family processes that play an important part, as we have seen, in the maintenance of our existing stratification system.

Sons appear to aspire to higher occupations than their fathers. This is shown by Empey's study (1956) of the occupational aspirations of a probability sample of approximately one-tenth of all male seniors who were in the public high schools in the state of Washington during the spring semester of 1954 and Turner's (1962) data on occupational aspirations of male high school seniors in selected schools in the Los Angeles area. Son's expectations, as opposed to their aspirations, are more limited by their backgrounds. Stephenson (1957), for example, obtained data on father's occupation and respondent's occupational plans and aspirations from some 1,000 ninth-grade students in four "semi-industrial, medium-sized communities in New Jersey" (205). The findings reflected the cultural emphasis upon high aspirations, but expectations were more sharply differentiated by position in the social system. Expectations are made in accordance with the individual's perception of his opportunity and general life chances.

From research indicating that social class is an important factor in determining levels of aspiration and achievement (Jencks et al., 1972; Sewell and Shah, 1968; Cutright, 1970) it can be inferred that value transmission is an important component of occupational heritability. The educational and occupational values held by parents, the father in particular, are transmitted to the son. The parents can influence this value transmission, and the son's occupational choice, in many different ways.

Few research studies provide any helpful analyses of specific ways in which intrafamilial factors associated with occupational status operate in the transmission of educational and occupational values. Aberle and Naegele (1952), in their seminal research on middle-class fathers, found evidence that these fathers were orientated toward their sons as future occupants of middle-class occupational roles, for which certain behaviors were of great importance. The investigators pointed to the relationship between the father's occupational role, his future expectations for his son, and his evaluation of the son's behavior; the father desired for his son college training and a middle-class occupation. His goal in rearing his son was to inculcate those educational and occupational values which would permit the son to penetrate the middle-class occupational hierarchy. Other data support these findings, but the family-linked variables which facilitate this value transmission have received little attention.

Although present research data do not permit the formulation of a specific value transmission theory, relevant propositions can be drawn from what is available. There is substantial research evidence to support the thesis that fathers attempt to transmit their occupational and educational values to their sons, and that there are class differences in the attainment values of adolescents (Jencks, et al., 1972; Cutright, 1970; Kerckhoff, 1974). Some of the class differences in achievement values may be accounted for by the fact that the higher the social class position of the parents, the more likely they are to be aware of the educational and occupational opportunities available for their children, and the more likely they will be to expose their children to them. Data on occupational heritability do not directly support this, since the most likely occupational destination for all sons is the occupation of their fathers; that is, sons are not likely to be in a social class different from their fathers (Werts, 1966; Cutright, 1968; Mortimer, 1974). While the data suggest a limited range of occupations for all class levels, they also suggest that middle-class children do acquire the values and skill necessary to attain a middle-class occupation, while lower-class children do not acquire the values and skill necessary for upward mobility. Thus it would seem that lower-class boys do not learn the requisite skills to move into a different status occupation, while middle-class boys do learn these skills but tend to stay at the same level as their fathers.

Two internal class-related family processes may contribute to this phenomenon. Class difference in spousal participation is a well-established research finding (Komarovsky, 1962; Rainwater, 1965). The division of labor in lower-class families assigns the child-rearing responsibility to the mother, so that if attainment and education are encouraged, it is the mother's function. At the same time, since career commitment is stereotypically more masculine than feminine, the son will not have as strong an occupational role model when the mother has the primary role in socialization. Moreover, the father's withdrawal from family participation means that the mother becomes a more important figure of identification at the lower levels of society and the father a more important one at the upper levels.

A consistent research finding is that the son's identification with the father is a critical antecedent for occupational interest development (Werts, 1968; Crites, 1962). It might therefore be hypothesized that positive identification with the father becomes the mechanism which leads to intergenerational occupational value transmission and which also accounts for some of the class-related differences in values.[21] The following propositions reflect this:

3.3a. Positive identification with the father leads to higher occupational aspirations and achievements.

3.3b. The higher the social class position, the more likely is positive identification with the father.

Parents in the lower status (reward) levels have less resources available for the process of socialization. It might be assumed that positive identification with the father would occur more frequently in middle-class sons because of the greater rewards at the father's disposal. The greater the father's rewards to the son, the greater the likelihood of identification. Mortimer's (1976) data show variations in father-son relationships by social class. The findings indicate that

the *combination* of a prestigious paternal role model and a close father-son relationship engenders the most effective transmission of vocational values and the clearest impacts on sons' occupational decisions [253].

She suggests that identification with the father is an important intervening variable in the transmission of value's and closeness, and warmth in the father-son relationship was seen as mediating identification.

Parental encouragement also has emerged as a critical link in understanding the dynamics of value transmission (Rehberg and Westly, 1967; Bordua, 1960; Kahl, 1965; Sewell and Shah, 1968). It is assumed that parents in the middle classes encourage their sons more since they are inclined to be oriented toward them as future occupants of a middle-class occupation. Parental encouragement as an internal family process remains largely undefined, although it usually is measured in terms of intensity, i.e., how often parents encourage their children to "get ahead" or "succeed." On the basis of the very limited data, it is possible to formulate the following propositions:

3.4. The higher the social class position, the more intense is parental encouragement.

3.5. The more intense the parental encouragement, the higher the level of education and occupational aspirations.

Most researchers have found that higher socioeconomic status correlates with more parental encouragement. Rehberg and Westly (1967) found that of four predictor variables—father's education, father's occupation, parental encouragement, and family size—parental encouragement made the largest contribution to the explained variance in adolescent educational expectations ($R = .50$). Twenty-five percent of the variance in college plans for males was explained by parental encouragement, according to Sewell and Shah's (1968) data.

As noted above, a number of research studies suggested that certain variables of a "parental support–encouragement" nature intervene between family size and educational attainment (Bossard and Boll, 1956; Nye, Carlson, and Garrett, 1970; Scheck and Emerick, 1976).

Bossard and Boll (1956) suggest that parents of large families do not have enough time to be supportive. Nye, Carlson, and Garrett (1970), with a sample of 1,984 mothers and 600 high school students, report that family size is negatively related to adolescents' perceptions of positive parental affect, and in particular that large families tend to decrease control of boys. Scheck and Emerick (1976), with a sample of 552 white male ninth graders, likewise find an inverse relationship between family size and three measures of male adolescents' perceptions of early child-rearing behavior: parental support, constraint, and consistency. According to their analyses, the effects of socioeconomic status (father's occupational status) and family size upon the three child-rearing dimensions are independent and additive. Scheck and Emerick further report that as family size increases, fathers are perceived by sons to be less consistent in their discipline and to disagree more with their spouses on expectations of the son. This finding supports Nye, Carlson, and Garrett's conclusion that large families may be more stressful for fathers. Scheck and Emerick hypothesize that as family size increases, fathers respond by becoming less involved and hence less consistent in discipline and expectations.

Thus the propositions in this third section have sketched the interaction whereby men's occupational experience becomes "translated" into their sons' educational aspirations and occupational choices. They indicate how occupations shape men's child-rearing values as well as sons' identification with fathers, via social class. The ability of men to transmit occupational aspirations and to encourage their achievement through the requisite educational training is thereby affected.

MEN'S OCCUPATIONS AND MARITAL RELATIONS: INTRAFAMILIAL DYNAMICS

In this section our focus is largely on the way men's work affects the marital relation and, so far as possible, how marital interaction influences men's occupational performance. Documentation is sketchy, not only because the review is not exhaustive but because of the large research lacunae in this area waiting to be filled. For this reason documentation is also often dated and based on convenience samples with a white-collar occupational bias. Correlational data provide the basis for causal analyses with all the resulting dangers of misinterpretation of the data. As a result of these weaknesses, the documentation provides primarily an indication of whether the posited relations are worthy of further investigation instead of offering convincing empirical tests of them. With this warning to the reader, let us see what propositions we can develop from the literature.

Role Differentiation Theory

Role differentiation theory is not really a theory as we are using the term, since it does not constitute a set of interrelated propositions. Its rationale, however, is directly related to men's work and men's marriages. The role differentiation proposition stems from the early thinking of Talcott Parsons (1949). Parsons saw conjugal role differentiation as critical to marital stability in industrial societies. The conjugal differentiation concept had to do with couples' division of labor for family task accomplishment. The concept appeared to be a dichotomous rather than a continuous variable. It was either present in the couple in the form as Parsons defined it or absent. Marital stability, the continued existence of the couple relation, was also a dichotomous variable, being either present or absent in individual couples. It was operationalized on a societal basis in divorce rate variations.

Conjugal role differentiation in Parsons' view involved exchanges between the family and occupational system by means of the adult male's performing occupational roles. For his work he received family subsistence resources. Women utilized these resources to care for the physical and emotional well-being of family members.[22]

Such a division of labor, Parsons (1949:195) argued, formed the foundation for marital stability in the open marriage systems of industrial societies. If wives performed occupational roles, they would be in direct competition with husbands for occupational status. Husbands and wives might also be in occupations discrepant enough that their social status placement would not be the same.

The proposition we can derive from this argument is the following:

4.1. Marital role differentiation with the husbands performing the occupational role and wives the family caretaker roles is positively related to marital stability.

At the time Parsons wrote, divorce rates supported his position. Married women's employment outside the home, the operational indicator that marital role differentiation on a Parsonian basis was breaking down, was more common among the "lower range of occupational and income status" (Parsons, 1949:194) than among the "structurally critical middle classes" (Parsons, 1949:193). And it was in these lower ranges that divorce rates were the highest.

Recent trends, however, do not support the proposition. Using nonfarm, white subsamples from the Public Use Samples of the 1960 and 1970 U.S. Censuses, Oppenheimer (1975) classified employed wives into relatively homogeneous pay and occupational groups. Although the employment rates of these wives of men 18 to 64 years old in all occupational groups had gone up over the decade of the sixties, the greatest increase was among the wives of the highest professionals and managers (Oppenheimer, 1975:9–10). (They still, however, have the lowest divorce rates.) These data, therefore, indicate that conjugal role differentiation as posited by Parsons is diminishing.

Parsons might make the rejoinder that divorce rates are going up along with married women's employment, a result that one would predict from the role differentiation proposition. The inverse relation between men's occupational status, defined in terms of income and educational requirements, and divorce rates, indeed, has lessened in recent years, but it continues to exist (Glick 1957:19). Occupational role differentials between wives of middle white-collar occupational groups and wives of manual and service workers no longer exist. The quality of these data testing Proposition 4.1 are good enough that we can fairly confidently reject it.

Oppenheimer (1975:28–32) counters Parsons' structural argument for the necessity of an occupation holder-homemaker type of conjugal role differentiation with an equally plausible structural explanation of why it is not necessary for marital stability. Spouses are rarely in direct occupational competition. Their occupations are often different, or if of the same type are practiced in different settings. Outsiders' knowledge of incomes which would encourage harmful comparisons is limited, and the concentration of women in largely women's jobs also discourages such comparisons. As a result, the decline in role differentiation as Parsons defines it does not necessarily represent a threat to conjugal solidarity. Moreover, the higher divorce rate of couples in lower occupational levels may be due less to wives' employment, as Parsons argues, than to the husband's inability to perform the provider role.

Oppenheimer (1975:28) notes along with Parsons that marital conflict might well eventuate from status competition. This could occur if both spouses were in the same or similar career occupations. With their geographic mobility, increasing responsibilities, and heavy ego and time investments, such occupations conflict with family demands even if direct spousal occupational competition is absent. Although most men and women have jobs and not careers, she also notes (32) the potential threat to conjugal solidarity when women's earnings equal or exceed those of their husbands. It is the societal norm that the husband be the major provider that accounts for the relation. From this reasoning we can develop the following proposition:

4.2. The degree of similarity in career occupation held by husbands and wives is negatively related to marital stability.

We are defining career occupations as those occupations requiring a period of systematic training in an institution of higher education, and where there is a gradation of positions in the occupation with increased responsibilities, power, and remuneration accruing to the person who moves from one level to the next.

Research of Glenn and Keir (1971) in which they looked at the divorce rates of couples both of whom were sociologists, can supply some indication of whether the proposition is worth further investigation. Questionnaire responses from a small, random sample of male members of the American Sociological Association showed di-

vorce rates were higher in couples where both spouses were sociologists. Direct competition between husbands and wives was not necessarily the cause, however, since rates were higher when wives had been sociology majors regardless of the level of the degree. There were no data on wives' employment, but those with advanced degrees would be more apt to be practicing their professions and so in competition with their husbands. The results of this study are intriguing enough to encourage a definitive test of Proposition 4.2. It would be well to use samples of professionals or managers without social science training. Such training can confound the posited relation, since married social scientists regardless of competing careers may be unduly critical of all institutions, including marriage. At present, we would have to say that the proposition falls in the "interesting but not tested" category.

Success Constraint Theory

To this point in our consideration of men's occupations and marital relations, we have had little to say about marital dynamics. We were involved in Parsonian arguments in which women's employment rates and divorce rates served as operational indicators of role differentiation and marital stability, respectively. Now, however, we turn our attention to what exchange theory has to say about the subject. This theory is specifically concerned with interaction, and as a consequence, conjugal satisfaction in terms of spouses' reports on the quality of the relations for the fulfillment of their desires (Burr, 1973:42) becomes the dependent variable. Propositions drawn from exchange theory postulate that the greater success the male experiences in the occupational system, the greater the marital satisfaction he and his wife will experience. This line of reasoning, based on Scanzoni's (1970:19–20) work, follows:

1. The more positive is the husband's performance of his economic duties, the more positively the wife defines her economic rights in terms of style of life and income as being met.
2. The more (1) is true, the more positively she performs her household tasks, and the more positively the husband defines his household rights as being fulfilled.
3. The more positively the wife views her husband as meeting her economic rights, the more positively she will perform her expressive duties.
4. The more (3) is true, the more positively the husband sees his expressive rights as being met, and the more he performs his expressive duties.
5. a. The more (4) is true, the more the wife views her expressive rights as being met.
   b. The more (5a) is true, the more the wife tries to perform her expressive duties.
6. "The more each spouse defines his expressive

and instrumental rights as being met," the more likely each is to feel gratified with each other and "with the system or situation in which they find themselves."

    7. a. The more (6) is true, the more the husband tries to continue performance of his economic duties.

      b. "The more (6) is true, the more the shared feelings of solidarity and cohesion, and the greater the motivation to maintain the system, and the greater the stability of the system."

Scanzoni operationally defined men's economic duties, the indication of their "objective" integration into the "economic opportunity system," in three ways, namely (1) occupational prestige as measured by the Duncan Socio-Economic Index, (2) occupational income, and (3) education (Scanzoni, 1970:29). Men's success is defined as their degree of accomplishments in these areas. Success is seen as multidimensional so that separate analyses are made for these continuous variables, each of which ranges from high to low.

The wives' expressive duties he defined as "positive affiliativeness" (Scanzoni, 1970:30). He does not specifically operationalize this concept, but his discussion suggests that he is defining it in multidimensional terms as the wives' attempts at empathy, companionship, and love and affection giving. These variables seemingly range from high to low on a continuum. Scanzoni used a multistage cluster sample of Indianapolis, Indiana, census tracts with a social class spread according to median income of resident families to test his propositions. His data came from interviews with 497 wives and 419 husbands but not, alas, from couples (Scanzoni, 1970:24).

Although his data were cross-sectional, so that the exchange process is not explicated, Scanzoni concluded that his propositions were supported. The more successful his husbands were as defined in terms of occupational prestige and income, as well as education, the more satisfied were his respondents with their marriages as defined in terms of companionship, mutual understanding, love, and physical affection. If we substitute the label "occupational system" for economic opportunity system, which seems legitimate given his operationalization of integration indicators, his conclusion could be summarized as follows:

    5.1. The more successful the husband is in the occupational system, the greater will be the couple's marital satisfaction, and this is a positive relation (cf. Scanzoni, 1970:23).

We have chosen to label our contrasting perspective "success constraint theory." Too much success in the occupational system, we would argue, limits the man's family participation. His wife must play father as well as mother roles, but without the emotional support her husband is too busy to give (cf. Boss, 1974). Role differentiation along Parsonian lines goes up, and marital satisfaction goes down. To oversimplify, the man who is an occupational success is a marital failure.

In contrast, too little success in the occupational system sets in motion the reverse of the process Scanzoni describes. The husband's poor performance in the occupational system leads to lack of rewards from the wife in terms of affection giving and household maintenance. The man is discouraged from participating in the family, and marital satisfaction declines. We, accordingly, would prefer the following proposition to one that posits a positive relation between occupational integration and marital satisfaction:

    5.2. There is a curvilinear relation between husbands' success in the occupational system and couple marital satisfaction, with less marital satisfaction at the high and low extremes of occupational success.

Let us first look at the relationship between measures of occupational success and marital satisfaction. Relations between occupational prestige or income and couple companionship in Scanzoni's data occasionally increased to a threshold and then leveled off or declined slightly at the higher levels instead of showing a positive relation. This decline was true of husbands' incomes as divided into quartiles and wives' view of companionship. Among husbands, there was also a slight decline in companionship ratings in the next to highest income level (Scanzoni, 1970:215, table 3.1). The same trend occurred in the relation between husbands' occupational prestige and wives' evaluation of marital empathy (Scanzoni, 1970:221, table 4.1).[23]

Blood and Wolfe (1960:168, table 79) in their 1955 interview of a representative sample of Detroit wives also found wives' satisfaction with companionship to be somewhat less when husbands were in professional and managerial occupations as compared with when they were in sales and clerical occupations.[24] With one exception, relations between the occupational measures and the marital measures showed a positive linear trend in the lower occupational prestige levels in the various relationships. (Wives had the same scores on companionship whether their husbands were in high or low blue-collar occupations.)

A more complete picture of the constraints that success places on marriage can be derived from Dizard's report (1968) of the third follow-up of the Burgess-Wallin sample of 1,000 middle-class predominantly white couples contacted first in 1939. Of the 400 married couples who completed questionnaires in 1955–60, all husbands had white-collar jobs, and half were either professionals or managers (Dizard, 1968:59). With this longitudinal study it is possible to control for the effect on marriage of its duration. The findings from the Scanzoni and the Blood and Wolfe studies referred to above might be due to the toll of time on marital satisfaction. Thus couples where the men have succeeded occupationally would generally be older, and marriage duration rather than husbands' occupational performance could explain the findings of lesser marital satisfaction.

The Dizard data, however, do not support the exchange theory propositions. Using the relative increase in salary from the early to the later years of marriage as the measure of occupational success, he found that couples where the husbands had the greatest increase in income from the early to the middle years of marriage showed the greatest decline rather than increase in marital satisfaction as the exchange propositions would suggest. The following propositions based on the Dizard data suggest the process whereby husbands' occupational success affects marriages negatively:

5.3. Occupational success is positively related to husbands' family power.

5.4. There is a curvilinear relation between husbands' power and their performance of family responsibilities, with them performing fewer at the low and high extremes of power.

5.5. The number of family responsibilities husbands perform is negatively related to the family responsibilities wives will have to perform.

5.6. The number of family responsibilities wives have to perform is negatively related to the extent of couple consensus on values.

5.7. The extent of couple consensus on family values is positively related to their conjugal solidarity.

In these propositions power is defined as the ability to make or to modify group choices (Turk, 1975:82). It is a continuous variable ranging from low to high power. Family responsibilities are those caretaker tasks within the home that enable the family to function. This is a multidimensional variable like power, and is usually seen as a "continuous" variable ranging from high to low in terms of task performance. In later discussions we use the term "family participation" to refer to the fulfillment of family responsibilities. Consensus on family values is the concept referring to agreement on the standards of desirability used to govern family members' behaviors.

Note that we have come full circle from the role differentiation theory. It predicted more conjugal solidarity, operationalized as absence of divorce, when marital roles were segregated. Here, our propositions predict that occupational success institutes marital processes leading to role differentiation with less rather than more conjugal solidarity operationalized in terms of quality of the relation as the outcome.

The process appears to begin with a "power spillover" from occupational success to family participation. Blood and Wolfe, for example, found that the greater the occupational success whether operationalized as occupation type—professional and business occupations—(1960:31,

table 6) or income (1960:31, table 7), the greater the influence the wife reported the husband had on eight household decisions, their operationalization of family power.

The husbands' occupational success demands time. The job is also of intrinsic interest—job satisfaction is higher in the professions and managerial occupations (Kahn, 1974)—and time spent on an occupation garners men more social prestige than does time spent in the family. As a result, successful men use their family power to avoid family responsibilities. Blood and Wolfe (1960), for example, discovered that women were responsible for more household tasks as husbands' income went up (60, table 18). This was also true of couples where husbands had experienced upward social mobility in terms of occupational prestige (60, table 19). But as the successful man's concerns center on the occupation and his wife's on the family, couple agreement on family matters decreases and their marital happiness goes down. Husband and wife experience a conflict in values, with his success on the job demanding competitiveness and ruthlessness and hers in the family demanding cooperativeness and love (Dizard, 1968:57).[25]

But Proposition 5.2, based on success constraint theory, and Proposition 5.1, based on exchange theory, posit that occupational failure as well as success operates to decrease marital happiness. Let us look at men in the lower-prestige jobs of the occupational range. For men in low-paying laboring and service occupations, there is also a "power spillover" to their family roles from the earnings they provide. When unemployment or wage cuts threaten these funds, the beneficent spiral of interaction described by Scanzoni (1970:19–20) reverses. Failing in their provider role, husbands lose power in the family, as several of the depression studies showed. Elder (1974:88), for example, using data from 84 boys and 83 girls collected during the depression years of the 1930s for the Oakland Growth Study, found children were more prone to see their mothers as deciding "major issues" affecting their families when families were in poverty and fathers were unemployed. With this loss of power the man loses his legitimization for performing other family responsibilities. Thus a representative sample of 204 employed men in blue-collar occupations in Minneapolis, Minnesota, showed that the lower the income, the less power the man exercised in making household decisions and the fewer household and child care tasks he performed (Aldous, 1970: 109, table 1).

There do not appear to be data on how blue-collar husbands' withdrawal from performance of family responsibilities is related to conjugal value consensus. Komarovsky's interview study (1962:290–92) of 58 blue-collar marriages indicated that husband's failures in the provider role lessened marital interdependencies and disrupted marital communication. Marital satisfaction was low. These data are some of the best we have for determining the dynamics of blue-collar men's occupational achievement and the quality of their marriages. They are inadequate, however, to delineate the process through which occupational failure affects marital satisfaction at lower occupational levels of income and prestige.

The blue-collar man's withdrawal from family participation may also stem, ironically enough from his attempts to be successful in the provider role as well as from his failures. This is the case with workers with unconventional work schedules. Mott et al. (1965) did a questionnaire study of shift workers in the plants of two companies located in the eastern central part of the United States. Respondents included both male workers and their wives.

From the respondents' reports, it appeared that night workers had difficulty with sexual relations and were concerned about the safety of their wives in their absence. Afternoon workers lost touch with their children (Mott et al., 1965:111). Men who work two jobs also find that time demands cut down family participation, and this occurs despite the men's coping with the family monetary needs that lead to "moonlighting." A 1969 survey of the labor force, for example, showed that 40 percent of such workers reported they held second jobs to meet regular household expenses and another 10 percent were using their work "overload" to pay off debts (Perrella, 1970:58). Thus the man in the lower occupational range, like the man in the upper occupational range, finds the degree of his job success sets real constraints on his family participation.

The critical variable that seems to explain the curvilinear relation between occupational success and marital satisfaction (see Proposition 5.2) is the male's acceptance of family responsibilities. The success constraint propositions posit that the amount of family participation is lessened by competing job responsibilities for men at the professional and managerial levels and by lack of income for men at the laborer, service, and unemployed levels. For both extremes of the occupational hierarchy, husbands and their wives appear to be less happy when husbands' family participation goes down.

Power seems to be a mediating factor (Proposition 5.4). The successful use their power to escape family responsibilities which would encourage couple value consensus. The failures lack the power that legitimizes their family participation.

The haven of the companionship family where conjugal power is relatively equal and husbands help out with child care does appear to exist among men in jobs in the middle ranges of occupational prestige. Rainwater (1965:315) found this to be true of men in lower-level bureaucratic and quasi-professional occupations and at the craftsmen or foremen level in his midwestern interview study of 409 spouses, which included 152 couples interviewed separately. Uninterested in their jobs, these men worried about how their personal interests could threaten their family-centered existence.

An interesting test case of this curvilinear thesis is that of retired men. Whether or not the retirement is voluntary, they are unemployed. As with the unemployed, one would expect those who have been less involved in their families to be most unhappy at no longer having a job. If they conform to our curvilinear thesis, those at the top of the occupational hierarchy and those at the bottom should experience the most distress. Both groups during their work life have been relatively uninvolved in their families—professionals and managers because of occupational success, lower blue-collar workers because of occupational failure. In contrast, those in the middle ranges whose jobs have lacked intrinsic interest have had the earnings to legitimize family participation and the time for it.

Evidence suggesting a curvilinear relation between occupational prestige and attitudes toward retirement does exist. Simpson, Back, and McKinney (1966:78), in a study of 300 retired males and 160 male workers within five years of retirement in North Carolina and Virginia, found that looking forward to retirement was least widespread among high-level professionals, managers, and government officials and low-level semiskilled workers. It was most widespread among the middle-level occupations of clerks, salesmen, skilled workers, and foremen.

Values, however, can change the relation between the man's income provision and his family participation as specified in Proposition 5.8.

5.8. The relation between men's occupational success and their family power is contingent on family values. When men's family status is not dependent on their occupational performance, there will be no association between family power and their occupational success.

Komarovsky (1940) found with her sample of 59 families in which the husband had been unemployed at least a year in the depression years of 1935–36 that men maintained family power when love and esteem were present in the marital relation prior to job loss. And McLaughlin (1971:303), in a study of southern Italian families living in Buffalo from the turn of the century to 1930, noted that male authority persisted despite periodic unemployment. It was supported by "strong cultural traditions," so that occupational success was not essential. Thus any test of the success constraint theory must take into account the family values that buttress the man's power position in the family.

Propositions 5.2 to 5.8 attempt to explicate the marital interaction whereby occupational success or its lack affects marital satisfaction. The evidence relevant to the propositions is illustrative but not conclusive. The Blood and Wolfe and the Scanzoni cross-sectional surveys with representative urban samples, the Dizard longitudinal study, and the Komarovsky case history investigation supply bits and pieces of information but no systematic test. The intervening process which posits a growing apart of couples where husbands do not fulfill family responsibilities needs to be explicated. Since the propositions are contrary to those derived from exchange theory, a currently popular perspective, their test will have implications beyond the subject matter of men's occupations.

The Occupational Elevator

We have written of success constraints on males' family performance whether due to achievement or failure. Let us now examine specifically the effects of upward or downward mobility in the occupational system on men's marriages. All employed men including those in noncareer occupations can experience advancement or demotion in their status, whether intergenerationally or within their own occupational history. Such changes are indexed by occupational change across the blue-collar–white-collar occupational line, within the blue-collar or white-collar categories of occupations, or within the career line of one occupation.

Exchange theory would predict that upward occupational mobility should be associated with greater marital happiness, since the wife would have her economic needs better met by the husband and would reciprocate through affective rewards and effective house care. Downward mobility with its decreases in husband income would result in the reverse process and less marital satisfaction. Some structure functionalists focusing on the upper ranges of the occupational hierarchy might say that the occupational involvement of the upwardly mobile husband would be made possible by the family focus of the wife.

We have already cast doubt on these arguments in the case of both the successful and the unsuccessful by noting the operation of values. The Dizard study suggested that the successful man's devotion to his occupation leads to values divergent from those of his home-based wife and so to less marital satisfaction. Among downwardly mobile men whose status is evaluated on other than provider roles, loss of occupation and income does not affect the man's power (see Proposition 5.8). From this thinking we derive the following proposition:

6.1. When wives evaluate men in terms of their occupational role performance, occupational mobility is directly related to marital satisfaction.

Our proposition receives support from Pearlin's interview research (1975) using a sample of 2,300 respondents drawn from blocks chosen at random in the urbanized area of Chicago. Mobility was operationalized by Pearlin in terms of the occupational status of the respective spouses' fathers as related to the husbands' occupations. The results were first specified as to whether the respondent married up or down in terms of occupation. Spouses who married down expressed more stress concerning marital problems than did those who married up. But when it came to perceptions of value consensus on family issues and such other indicators of marital quality as the depth of communication, the satisfaction with affection received, and whether or not the exchange of marital rewards was fair, values intervened. Spouses who valued status advancement were more apt to experience marital stress when they had married down. When they had married up, however, spouses who placed great importance on moving to a higher-prestige class were satisfied and in agreement on the various marital measures (Pearlin, 1975:350–56, tables 2–7). Thus the effect of occupational success or failure on spousal relations appeared to depend not alone an actual achievement, but on how important achievement was to the individual.

In Dizard's (1968) longitudinal study of middle-class subjects, it was also possible to look at the effects on marriage relations of husbands' moving up to professional or managerial occupations, remaining in the same occupation, or moving to one of lower occupational prestige. His findings do not support our proposition. Couples in which the husbands were upwardly mobile experienced a greater likelihood of declines in marital satisfaction than did couples in which the husbands were downwardly mobile. The couples who had experienced "failure"—all the couples were relatively well off—were less likely to decline in agreement on marital issues, although they were more apt to consider divorce and vie for dominance (Dizard, 1968:49). We do not know these couples' feelings about the importance of upward mobility, but it may have been that they placed family values of companionship and participation above those of occupational success.

Emotional Maintenance Theory

One of the critical functions of the family, Parsons has postulated from his particular structure-functional perspective, is the regulation of emotional balance in the personality of the individual (Parsons, 1955). Through its provision of emotional support, the family encourages the individual to perform the various roles in the occupational system which his social placement entails. In an extension of this reasoning, we would argue that this emotional support might also provide personal gratifications that would substitute for those missing on the job. "Men can look to their homes as havens from job monotonies and as sources of the satisfactions lacking in the occupational sphere" (Aldous, 1969:712).

The evidence is clear that job satisfaction, in terms of satisfaction with the work itself or the work situation, lessens as one goes down the occupational prestige scale (Kahn, 1974). Professionals, managers, and the self-employed tend to be more satisfied than clerical, sales, and unskilled workers. Thus we have the following proposition relating the two continuous variables:

7.1. Occupational prestige is directly related to job satisfaction.

Given the Parsonian thesis, the following proposition should find empirical support:

7.2. Husbands' job satisfaction is negatively related to husbands' family participation.

Family participation and the emotional involvement such participation entails should compensate for the unpleasant job characteristics.

The evidence, however, does not support the proposition. Among men in occupations with low prestige, job satisfaction is low, but we have seen that low income and unemployment lead to the man's withdrawal from family participation. (See also Komarovsky, 1962:257.)

Even in the middle occupational levels, families, instead of supplying emotional support, can exacerbate occupational problems. When family and occupational demands peak at the same time, the man's job and family satisfaction both decline. From questionnaires on job satisfaction filled out by 6,621 employees in an electric utility company, Wilensky (1961) reports that job satisfaction among upper blue- and lower white-collar workers was related to the family life cycle. Job satisfaction was high among bachelors and young married men with no dependents. It fell off as children (with their attendant time and financial demands) arrived. The decline was deeper and longer the more children there were. When wives were not working, workers reached the low point in job morale earlier. As children left home, job satisfaction began to rise along with increased income and declining family responsibilities.

Marital satisfaction seems to show the same curvilinear relation as job satisfaction over the family life span, with less satisfaction in the middle years of marriage. (The studies' findings are weakened by their cross-sectional nature, use of questionnaires, high attrition rates, and convenience samples.) Rollins and Cannon (1974) found such a trend with a nonprobability sample of 489 married Mormons, as did Rollins and Feldman (1970) with an area probability sample of 799 middle-class married persons in Syracuse, New York. Blood and Wolfe (1960), however, did not find such a trend with their Detroit data, and Spanier, Lewis, and Cole's study (1975) with probability samples from Newark, Ohio; Ames, Iowa; and Clarke County, Georgia gave the curvilinear thesis only limited support. Research of a longitudinal character is clearly

needed to examine the relation between job satisfaction and marital satisfaction over the family life cycle. Research is also lacking that would permit us to distinguish the effects of occupational success from job satisfaction in relation to marital satisfaction.

As far as the emotional maintenance theory is concerned, present data do not support it. The following proposition states the relation that the existing data suggests:

7.3. There is a curvilinear relation between husbands' job satisfaction and their participation in the family, with least participation occurring at the high and low extremes of job satisfaction.

Males' participation in the family, as we have noted before, seems to be the critical intervening variable between various indicators of males' occupational activities and marital satisfaction. We, accordingly, state the following proposition:

7.4. There is a curvilinear relation between job satisfaction and marital satisfaction, with the least marital satisfaction occurring at the high and low extremes of job satisfaction.

This proposition reminds us again of Proposition 5.2, which summarizes the success constraint theory. There is the same curvilinear relation posited between marital satisfaction and an occupational variable, in this case job satisfaction instead of occupational success. Clearly, research is needed to determine if job satisfaction and marital satisfaction are related. Support for Proposition 7.4 would then necessitate additional investigation. It would determine if family participation was the critical intervening variable as in Proposition 7.3 and if job satisfaction had an effect independent from occupational success on marital satisfaction. With this suggestion for further research, we conclude the section on men's occupations and marital relations.

FINAL THOUGHTS

This chapter has demonstrated why sociologists have often characterized the family as a conservative institution. It is not only that families transmit the cultural heritage from one generation to the next. Religious and educational institutions also do this and in the case of the latter more systematically and in greater amplitude. Families are conservators of the status quo because they, deliberately or not, transmit their class position to their children.

The first and third sections of this chapter contain the propositions detailing how the occupationally successful, through provision of educational opportunities and occupational aspirations, provide a status floor below which their children tend not to fall. The less successful, through inability to provide the necessary opportunities and aspirations, tend to set a ceiling on their children's status. Thus the argument of some functionalists that there is only a limited association between men's family background and their ultimate occupational achievement was shown to be less consonant with the results of empirical research than a conflict theory approach.

We are not denying that occupational mobility exists. The chapter contains propositions relating occupational mobility to fertility planning and to size of family (Proposition 2.14), as well as to marital satisfaction (Proposition 7.1). Proposition 1.1 seemed best to summarize the data on family background and occupational achievement. It stated a curvilinear relation, with the association being least in the middle occupational groups and the greatest at the high and low extremes.

This proposition concluded our societal perspective on the family as a conservator of intergenerational occupational placement, but it introduced the first of what proved to be a number of curvilinear relationships. As one of our early readers noted, sociologists tend to hypothesize linear relations, but reality often insists on taking a curvilinear form. Thus, to cite a few examples, Proposition 2.8 states that the influence of fathers' education and occupations is greatest at the middle of the sons' life cycles rather than at earlier or later stages. There also appears to be a curvilinear relation between socioeconomic resources and marriage timing, with men having the lowest and highest resources delaying marriage (Proposition 2.10). Among the social psychological propositions, what we called success constraint theory posited a curvilinear relation between occupational success and marital satisfaction. And there was some indication that this theory (see Proposition 5.2) better explained existing data than the linear rationale of exchange theory (Proposition 5.1).

Perceptive readers may have noted as they moved through the previous four sections that the data became more "soft," and the propositions, accordingly, more speculative. The structural propositions in the first two sections were largely documented by data from large-scale surveys as well as U.S. Census data. The later social psychological propositions necessarily drew their support from studies in which intrafamilial dynamics were explored in detail with a limited number of cases. This was particularly true in the section on men's occupations and marital relations.

There is one central theme, however, that appears to tie the propositions in the four sections together. This is the association between the husband-father's occupation as it affects his family participation and various marital and parent-child variables. For example, men in middle-level occupations which permit such family participation through providing sufficient income to legitimate it, but not enough competing time demands to prevent it, appear to be most active in their families. And their marital satisfaction seems to be higher than that of other groups. (See the discussion concerning Propositions 5.2–5.8).

Proposition 3.4 suggests that this participation in the form of paternal encouragement can also contribute to children's having high occupational and educational aspirations. This proposition is important because it indicates how family intergenerational occupational transmission may be broken in the lower ranges of the occupational prestige hierarchy. Sons of men in the middle- and higher-level occupations according to Proposition 3.3 have the resources to encourage their sons to identify with them, to take on their occupational and educational values. This seems true even when work preoccupations prevent their family participation. Such resources are lacking to men in lower-level occupations. Whether or not they want their sons to aspire to higher educational and occupational achievements than theirs, the sons are less likely to internalize paternal values. Fathers' specific encouragement of sons' seeking the educational certification that would permit their attainment of higher-level occupations, therefore, is necessary. This encouragement is all the more critical, as Proposition 2.8 indicates, since these men do not have the occupational income that would enable them to provide such an education for their sons. Sons of men in the lower occupational range will be largely dependent on their own efforts to get the requisite education for higher-level occupations. Paternal encouragement can strengthen their achievement attempts. Yet, as the discussion concerning the success constraint theory and Proposition 3.3 showed, men in lower-level occupations tend to be less likely to participate in family matters. Figure 10.4 summarizes these proposition linkages.[26]

Throughout the chapter, our thinking has run up against the obstacle of lack of evidence. This point seems a good place to remind the reader of some of the places where research clarification is needed. We can begin with the process whereby fathers transmit occupational values to the next generation. Research suggests paternal identification and encouragement as critical, as noted above, but given their implications for social mobility among the less favored and social stability among the more favored, we need specific documentation. How, after all, do men in lower-status occupations acquire the conviction that their sons can do better? Are they in occupations where they are in contact with persons in higher-status occupations? The same is true for the relation between occupational achievement and family participation. Most of the propositions in the fourth section of the chapter are based on this relation which lacks specific investigation.

In connection with the relation between men's occupations and their family participation, one of the most timely

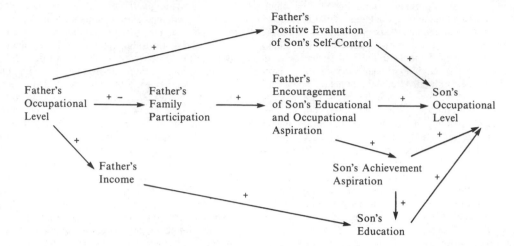

"spin-offs" has to do with the issue of divorce. Proposition 2.11 stated a positive reciprocal association between men's marital stability and their occupational achievement. The documentation for the proposition showed a negative association between marital stability and occupational achievement.[27] But marital satisfaction seems to be related to occupational achievement in a curvilinear way (Proposition 5.2). Women appear to dislike marriages in which occupations compete successfully with families for men's time. As women become more financially independent due to employment outside the home, they may be unwilling to accept less marital satisfaction even when it is coupled with the affluent way of life a husband's occupational success can buy. We would like to speculate that under these circumstances less marital satisfaction will become translated into higher divorce rates for men in demanding upper-level occupations. Our speculative proposition can be put in general terms, given our success constraint rationale for the relation of occupational achievement and marital satisfaction.

The first proposition relates the continuous variables of occupational participation, operationalized as time spent on the job, to family participations:

8.1. There will be a negative relation between men's occupational participation and their family participation.

From this proposition we move to our speculative proposition which we are willing to state as holding within all occupational groups, whatever their type—laborer, sales, skilled, etc.

8.2. There will be a positive relation within occupational groups between divorce rates and men's occupational participation.

The test of Proposition 8.2 would require a more fine-grained analysis of specific occupations and marital stability than usually occurs. The research of Rosow and Rose (1972:596) is a notable exception and provides some support for our argument. Among California doctors involved in divorce complaints during the first six months of 1968, the rank order correlation was .33 (Kendall's tau) between complaint rates and the average hours devoted to patient care, and so not to families, in eight medical specialties.

This proposition brings us to the issue of women's labor force participation and its reciprocal association with men's occupations on a number of variables we considered in this chapter. Since women's employment is not our concern, we will only note here research areas where its effect on men's work and man's families is particularly marked. The early discussion on men's occupations and their families' status alerted us to the question of the contribution of women's employment to family status. One recent study (Duncan and Perrucci, 1976), with 1970 U.S. Census data and longitudinal data from a national sample of 1961–1964 college graduates, has already shown that women's careers do not hamper their husbands' occupation-related geographic mobility.

Data concerning dual career couples married in the 1970s when the women's movement was stronger may present a different picture. The effect of conflicting geographic mobility demands for occupational advancement of husbands and wives could result in divorce (see Proposition 4.2) or couples who cohabit on weekends or holidays if women no longer are willing to move to meet their husbands' career requirement. Husbands, however, could make their residence dependent upon their wives' career needs, in effect giving wives' occupations top priority. Under such circumstances, wives would be the primary occupation holder in families, a result at odds with Parsons' (1949) thinking reviewed earlier.

Wives' employment may also modify the relation between husbands' success and marital satisfaction. As the studies cited in note 25 suggest, women's involvement outside the home can make them more accepting of their successful husbands' occupational preoccupations.

We are left, however, with a contradiction. How do we reconcile this increased marital satisfaction due to women's employment outside the home with our speculation that divorce will become more common as women become less dependent on the salaries of their occupationally preoccupied husbands? The occupational commitment of women's employment, we believe, is the critical variable among the affluent. Professional women are increasingly expecting that family responsibilities will be shared equally between husbands and wives. These women being occupationally committed themselves may better understand the commitment of their husbands. They would not, however, be satisfied in marriages in which busy husbands left them with major family responsibilities.

The situation differs when women's occupational involvement is secondary to their family roles. They may find working gives them more shared interests with busy husbands, who will necessarily engage in more participation in their families (Dizard, 1963). Employed wives will be happier in their marriages than their full-time-housewife peers, while still accepting major family responsibilities. Thus women's employment must be specified as to occupational commitment to determine its influence on their acceptance of husbands' occupational participation, their marital satisfaction, and even the stability of their marriages.

In our efforts in this as in other areas, we have occasionally thought that we were expected to make bricks without straw, since relevant data are more conspicuous by their absence than their presence. If we have been successful in our endeavors, future codifiers of research on men's occupations and their families should have an easier time of it. We have indicated where we are now and where research is lacking. We have provided propositions for testing in the context of various "minitheories," and often the operationalization of important variables. Our readers, accordingly, can better tease out the dependencies and reciprocities of these two foci of men's concerns to our mutual benefit. We wish them good fortune in their endeavors.

NOTES

1. The emphasis is on sons' rather than daughters' occupational placement because our topic focuses on the relation between males' occupations and the family.

2. Fine-grained research is called for to determine the extent of women's contribution to family status. Sampson and Rossi (1975), in a study of 267 black and white respondents, again (as in the 1974 study) found that the wife's occupation and education had some effect on the social status of the household independent of husband's characteristics. The primary weakness in previous studies is that the individual has been taken as the unit of analysis. Future research should focus on couples to ascertain the relative contribution of spouses to family status. Further, data are needed which allow analyses within selected occupational groups to determine if wives' contributions to family status are conditioned by level of occupational status and/or income. For example, Hall (1975:254) argues that a married woman's presence in the labor force has a status impact on the family simply because of the dual incomes. If the dual incomes are low, the status impact may be slight, but if they are high, the wife's contribution to the status of the family can be high.

3. The importance of "old school ties" in occupational placement, as well as earnings, is emphasized in a number of studies. West (1953) lists income figures to support the fact that graduates of the "Ivy League" colleges have the highest earnings. In an unusual study of the upper class, Blumberg and Paul (1975) analyzed characteristics of the bride and groom from marriage announcements appearing in the society pages of the Sunday *New York Times* from 1962 to 1972. Over 86 percent of the fathers were in business or professional occupations. In terms of the groom's education, over half of the sample attended "Ivy League" colleges. The grooms followed directly in their father's occupational footsteps: 47 percent were businessmen; another 43 pe cent were professionals, led by lawyers. (For similar findings from the *Philadelphia Social Register,* see Baltzell, 1958).

4. The lines and the arrows between variables indicate the direction of the "path." Thus son's education affects son's occupation and not the reverse. The curved line between X and V with an arrowhead at both ends indicates no assumption about the causal or temporal ordering of these variables. Lines with no source indicated, carrying arrows to each of the effect variables, represent residual paths. These residuals stand for all other influences on the variable in question, including variables not entered, measurement errors, departure from assumptions of additivity and linearity, etc.

5. Note that this proposition is concerned with the characteristics of individual fathers as they affect the occupational achievement of individual sons, as contrasted with proposition 1.2, in which the focus is on the macro level of analysis.

6. Rosen's (1962) research lends some support here, in that he finds larger families more likely to value responsibility as well as conformity. However, family sociologists could suggest a number of explanations (other than "responsibility") for the interaction effect stated in Proposition 2.3. Perhaps the simplest explanation is an economic one. A large family has fewer economic resources for the oldest son just when he needs them for higher education. By the time the youngest son graduates from high school, the family may be less strapped financially. An alternate explanation might apply to the small family. Here the first-born may receive the greatest attention from parents who, after they have proved their "parental competence," take their subsequent one or two children more or less for granted. These effects are also likely to vary between different occupational strata as well as by religion.

7. Utilizing aggregate data from a number of demographic studies in the United States, France, the Netherlands, and Scotland, Zajonc finds evidence that a child's rate of mental development is influenced by the amount of adult knowledge she/he "shares." A child's intelligence tends to expand more rapidly when parental knowledge is not shared by two or more closely spaced sibs. In the special case of only children, Zajonc (1976:234) explains that the benefits of a small family are apparently counteracted by the lack of opportunity to serve as "teachers" to younger children. Last children also suffer that handicap, but, as Zajonc explains, a last child born many years after the birth of the next-to-last enters an environment of intellectually more mature children, a condition that helps overcome the nonteacher handicap.

8. The Coleman et al. (1966) survey (a stratified two-state probability sample of the public schools in the United States and the District of Columbia) provides evidence by race of the probability of meeting college entrance requirements. Coleman et al., in comparing the twelfth-grade achievement test scores of six racial groups, found that the rank order of their scores (from high to low) was as follows: white; Oriental American;

Indian American; Mexican American; Puerto Rican; black (219). Only for the Orientals did test score averages approach the white group averages, and in two tests (mathematical achievement and nonverbal ability) the distribution of the Oriental students' scores was higher than that of white students in most regions. According to the Coleman et al. analysis, family background factors (including parental interest and aspiration variables as well as occupation, education, family size, etc.) accounted for a large proportion of the variance in verbal achievement scores at grades 6, 9, and 12 (298). This was especially true for Orientals, and least true for blacks.

9. Evidence that blacks assess this racial differentiation in the relative advantage of educational attainment more realistically than do whites is documented by Sampson and Rossi (1975). Investigating racial differences in the bases upon which family status is accorded, they reported that race and occupation were ranked highest by blacks whereas whites weighted education as more important than race.

10. Further research is needed on the influence of the black mother's occupation–income on the son's occupational attainment and mobility. McCord et al. (1969) emphasize that, particularly in low-income families, the black mother is a major force in the occupational achievement of her children. In a study of the employed poor in Washington, D.C., Willie (1969) found an association between the social mobility of a two-parent family and the education, occupation, and income of the wife-mother.

11. Hauser and Featherman (1974) support Duncan's earlier findings with 1970 data. They conclude that in 1972 as in 1962 the occupational disadvantages of blacks must be attributed to unfavorable patterns of occupational mobility throughout their careers, and not to their impoverished social origins.

12. Other evidence (Siegel, 1965) also indicates that parental background (particularly variables indicating socioeconomic status) exercises a weaker influence on the educational and occupational attainment for blacks than for whites. Portes and Wilson (1976), from an analysis of a nationwide sample of high school boys, report that parental status, measured ability, and school grades explain the highest proportion of variance in educational attainment for whites. For blacks, on the other hand, self-esteem and educational aspirations are the strongest predictors. Since grades and background appear less significant for black males' educational attainment, Portes and Wilson hypothesize that the educational process for blacks is more solely dependent on "personal self-reliance and ambition" (429).

13. This is especially true with regard to black males. The evidence is very carefully outlined by Sorensen (1975:468–70), who analyzed intragenerational, occupational mobility rates for 738 black and 851 white males using life history data. Looking at jobs held over time he concluded that "black males, early in their careers, obtain an occupational achievement closer to the best they can expect than do whites" (469).

14. Bell (1971) examined the life cycle squeeze as associated with husband's occupational career and extended family relationships. His evidence again supports the social placement rationale presented here. Bell concluded that the importance of the extended family in alleviating the "life-cycle crunch" depends on the father's occupational status: the higher the status, the greater the likelihood that the extended family will offer financial aid.

15. The literature that examines the association of socioeconomic status variables and mate selection is generally based on an interest in relative degrees of "homogamy" of spouses (cf. Centers, 1949; Sundal and McCormick, 1951). Since assortative mating is so pronounced in contemporary America, we would not expect the kind of marriage "match" a man makes to be a significant predictor of his occupational achievement or income. In fact, Blau and Duncan (1967:343–45) found the net effect of the wife's characteristics on husband's occupational status to be neglible, because husband's and wife's education and socioeconomic background are generally highly intercorrelated.

16. Bartz and Nye (1970) offer a much-needed systematization of the research on early marriage and social class.

17. Miao (1974), in a report on marital stability by race, discusses how fluctuations in economic conditions are more severely magnified within the black community.

18. The latter effects make it questionable that characteristics of wives, per se, advance their husbands in their occupational careers. Adding the variables of wife's intelligence, education, need achievement, and

strength of drive to get ahead and her father's occupational status to the model, Duncan, Featherman, and Duncan (1968:191) found, only increased the explained variance in husband's occupational status by 0.004. This small contribution in explanatory importance may well be the result of the analytic method, which assumes independence and lack of strong intercorrelations among the variables. These assumptions are violated by the strong correlation between husband's and wife's characteristics.

19. Duncan, Featherman, and Duncan (1968:266) explicitly state that this subsample is not representative of all men in the OCG cohort. It excludes men with unusual marriage histories. It further excludes those whose families have just begun as well as those whose families began so long ago that the oldest child has reached age 14. Altogether the analysis is limited to some 48 percent of all native non-Negro men age 25 to 34 in the civilian labor force or to some 56 percent of the ever-married men in this category.

20. We caution again, as in the above section on timing, about the danger of generalizations based on analyses where the independent variables display such high intercorrelations.

21. Scanzoni (1971:179) notes that among blacks negative identification with the father leads to higher occupational achievement.

22. In his later thinking on this division of labor, Parsons (1955) labeled the men's roles instrumental, since they were concerned with task accomplishment in relation to the external world. Women's roles were expressive, being concerned with integration within the family. We will not specifically discuss this largely discredited dichotomy (Aronoff and Crano, 1976; Oppenheimer, 1975), as it is not directly relevant to our topic.

23. Scanzoni (1971:236), with the 198 black husbands and 202 black wives he interviewed in Indianapolis, found that husbands' occupational prestige, income, and education were not positively related to the respondents' satisfaction with the companionship, physical affection, and empathy they obtained in their marriages. As occupational success did not increase emotional gratifications, so it also did not lessen expressions of marital hostility. The respondents, it should be noted, were from different households, were not in the lower lower class, and had been married at least five years (Scanzoni, 1971:23–25). He uses relative deprivation of black families in comparison with white families to explain these findings, which are contrary to exchange theory.

24. Rollins and Cannon's critique (1974) of Blood and Wolfe's scoring procedure for companionship and other measures of marital satisfaction indicates an underestimation of the degree of marital dissatisfaction. Because of this bias, the relationships we report represent conservative estimates.

25. In his sample of comparatively affluent upper white-collar husbands and their wives, Dizard (1968:58, table 4.5) found wives who had been employed showed more agreement on family issues than nonemployed wives, regardless of the amount of the salary increases their husbands had experienced over the years of the longitudinal study. Also, husbands whose wives were employed were in more agreement on basic family issues than husbands whose wives were not employed. More importantly, wives of men whose income had markedly increased over the marriage were happier in their marriages, showed more agreement with their husbands on family issues, and thought less of divorce when they increased their activities in voluntary organizations. A decline in such activities led to a lessening of consensus and marital happiness and an increase in thoughts of divorce (Dizard, 1968:65, table 4.9). We report these findings to indicate how women's extrafamilial activities as well as men's intrafamilial activities affect marital satisfaction in couples where men are in demanding career-type occupations.

26. Lest we be accused of overlooking structural constraints on mobility, the reader should note that we are specifically including "income" in our model. The extent to which parental encouragement in lower-class families, or sons' low educational achievements in higher-class families, can overcome structural variables making for intergenerational continuities in social status is difficult to quantify. The evidence concerning blacks, however, is not encouraging. As noted earlier, fathers appear to be unable to pass on status gains to sons, and upward mobility is difficult (Duncan, Featherman, and Duncan, 1968).

27. Proposition 4.1 specified the association by making stability contingent on spouses in career-type positions having different higher-level

occupations. This modification of the role differentiation Proposition 4.1 lacks the empirical testing Proposition 2.11 has received.

REFERENCES

ABERLE, D. F. & K. C. NAEGELE
1952   "Middle class fathers' occupational role and attitudes toward children." *American Journal of Orthopsychiatry* 22 (April):366–78.

ALDOUS, J.
1970   "Lower-class males' integration into community and family." *Transactions of the Sixth World Congress of Sociology* 4, International Sociological Association, 95–119.
1969   "Occupational characteristics and males' role performance in the family." *Journal of Marriage and the Family* 31:707–12.

ARONOFF, J. AND W. D. CRANO
1976   "Reply to Whyte." *American Sociological Review* 41:379–80.

BAHR, S. J., B. A. CHADWICK, AND J. H. STRAUSS
1975   "The effect of relative economic status on fertility." *Journal of Marriage and the Family* 37 (May):335–44.

BALTZELL, E.
1958   *Philadelphia Gentlemen: The Making of a National Upper Class.* New York: Free Press.

BARBER, B.
1957   *Social Stratification.* New York: Harcourt, Brace and World.

BARTZ, K. W. AND I. F. NYE
1970   "Early Marriage: A propositional formulation." *Journal of Marriage and the Family* 32:258–68.

BEAN, F. D. AND C. H. WOOD
1974   "Ethnic variations in the relationship between income and fertility." *Demography* 11 (November):629–40.

BELL, C.
1971   "Occupational career, family cycle and extended family relations." *Human Relations* 24 (December):463–75.

BELL, R. R.
1975   *Marriage and Family Interaction.* Homewood, Ill.: Dorsey Press.

BERENT, J.
1952   "Fertility and social mobility." *Population Studies* 5:244–60.

BLAU, P. M. AND O. D. DUNCAN
1967   *The American Occupational Structure.* New York: Wiley.

BLOOD, R. O., JR. AND D. M. WOLFE
1960   *Husbands and Wives: The Dynamics of Married Living.* New York: Free Press.

BLUMBERG, P. M. AND P. W. PAUL
1975   "Continuities and discontinuities in upper-class marriages." *Journal of Marriage and the Family,* 37 (February):63–78.

BORDUA, D.
1960   "Educational aspirations and parental stress on college." *Social Forces* 38 (March):262–69.

BOSS, P.
1974   "Psychological absence in the intact family: A systems approach to a study of fathering." Paper presented at Annual Meeting, National Council on Family Relations.

BOSSARD, J. H. AND E. S. BOLL
1956   "Adjustment of siblings in large families." *American Journal of Psychiatry,* 112:889–892.

BOUDON, R.
1974   *Education, Opportunity, and Social Inequality.* New York: Wiley-Interscience.

BRAITHWAITE, R. B.
1953   *Scientific Explanation.* London: Cambridge University Press.

BUCKLEY, W.
1958   "Social stratification and social differentiation." *American Sociological Review* 23 (August):370–79.

BURCHINAL, L. G.
1965   "Trends and prospects for young marriages in the United States." *Journal of Marriage and the Family* 27 (May):243–54.

BURR, W. R.
1973   *Theory Construction and the Family.* New York: Wiley.

CAPLOW, T.
1954   *The Sociology of Work.* Minneapolis: University of Minnesota Press.

CARTER, H. AND P. GLICK
1970   *Marriage and Divorce: A Social and Economic Study.* Cambridge, Mass.: Harvard University Press.

CENTERS, R.
1949   "Marital selection and occupational strata." *American Journal of Sociology* 54 (May):530–35.

CHRISTENSEN, H. T.
1963   "Child spacing analysis via record linkage." *Journal of Marriage and the Family* 25 (August):272–80.

CHRISTENSEN, H. T. AND O. T. BOWDEN
1953   "Studies in child spacing, II." *Social Forces* 31:346–51.

COLEMAN, J. S. ET AL.
1966   *Equality of Educational Opportunity,* vol. 1. Washington, D.C.: Government Printing Office.

COOMBS, L. C.
1974   "The measurement of family size preferences and subsequent fertility." *Demography* 11 (November):587–612.

CRITES, J. O.
1962   "Parental identification in relation to vocational interest development." *Journal of Educational Psychology* 53:262–70.

CUTRIGHT, P.
1973   "Timing the first birth: Does it matter?" *Journal of Marriage and the Family* 35 (November):585–96.
1971a   "Income and family events: Family income, family size and consumption." *Journal of Marriage and the Family* 33 (February):161–73.
1971b   "Income and family events: Marital stability." *Journal of Marriage and the Family* 33 (May):291–306.
1970   "Income and family events: Getting married." *Journal of Marriage and the Family* 32 (November):628–37.
1968   "Occupational inheritance: A cross-national analysis." *American Journal of Sociology* 73 (4):400–16.

DAVIS K.
1950   *Human Society.* New York: Macmillan.

DAVIS, K. AND W. MOORE
1945   "Some principles of stratification." *American Sociological Review* 10 (April):242–49.

DIZARD, J.
1968   *Social Change in the Family.* Chicago: Community and Family Study Center, University of Chicago.

DUNCAN, O. D. AND D. FEATHERMAN
1972   "Psychological and cultural factors in the process of occupational achievement." *Social Science Research* 1:121–45.

DUNCAN, O. D., D. L. FEATHERMAN, AND B. DUNCAN
1968   *Socioeconomic Background and Occupational Achievement.* U.S. Department of Health, Education and Welfare, Office of Education.

DUNCAN, R. P. AND C. C. PERRUCCI
1976   "Dual occupation families and migration." *American*

Sociological Review 41:252–61.

ELDER, G. H., JR.
1974   *Children of the Great Depression: Social Change in Life Experience.* Chicago: University of Chicago Press.

EMPEY, L.
1956   "Social class and occupational aspiration: A comparison of absolute and relative measurement." *American Sociological Review* 21 (December): 703– 09.

FARLEY, R. AND A. I. HERMALIN
1971   "Family stability: A comparison of trends between blacks and whites. *American Sociological Review* 36 (February):1–17.

FELSON, M. AND D. KNOKE
1974   "Social status and the married woman." *Journal of Marriage and the Family,* 36 (August):516–22.

FOLGER, J., H. S. ASTIN, AND A. E. BAYER
1970   *Human Resources and Higher Education.* New York: Russell Sage.

FRANKLIN, J. AND J. E. SCOTT
1970   "Parental values: An inquiry into occupational setting." *Journal of Marriage and the Family* 32 (August):406–09.

FREEDMAN, R. AND L. COOMBS
1966   "Childspacing and family economic position." *American Sociological Review* 31:631–48.

FREEDMAN, R. AND H. SHARP
1959   "Correlation of values about ideal family size in the Detroit metropolitan area." *Population Studies* 8:35–45.

GLENN, N. D. AND M. S. KEIR
1971   "Divorce among sociologists married to sociologists." *Social Problems* 19:57–67.

GLICK, P. C.
1957   *American Families.* New York: Wiley.

GOLDBERG, D.
1959   "The fertility of two generation urbanities." *Population Studies.* 12:214–22.

GOLDSCHEIDER, C. AND P. UHLENBERG
1969   "Minority group status and fertility." *American Journal of Sociology* 74 (January):361–72.

GOODE, W. J.
1959a   "The theoretical importance of love." *American Sociological Review* 24 (February):38–47.
1959b   "The sociology of the family: Horizons in family theory." In R. K. Merton, L. Broom, and L. S. Cottrell, Jr. (eds.), *Sociology Today.* New York: Basic Books.
1951   "Economic factors and marital stability." *American Sociological Review* 16 (December):802–12.

GRANDJEAN, B. D.
1974   "An economic analysis of the Davis-Moore theory of stratification." *Social Forces* 53 (June):542–52.

HALL, R. H.
1975   *Occupations and the Social Structure,* second ed. Englewood Cliffs, N.J.: Prentice-Hall.

HAUSER, R. M. AND D. L. FEATHERMAN
1974   "White-nonwhite differentials in occupational mobility among men in the United States, 1962–1972." *Demography* 11 (May):247–66.

HEBERLE, R.
1942   "Social factors in birth control." *American Sociological Review* 6 (December):794–805.

HODGE, R. W., D. J. TREIMAN, AND P. H. ROSSI
1966   "A comparative study of occupational prestige." In R. Bendix and S. M. Lipset (eds.), *Class, Status and Power.* New York: Free Press.

HOLLINGSHEAD, A. B.
1950   "Class differences and family stability." *The Annals of the*

American Academy of Political and Social Science 272:39–46.

JENCKS, C. AND D. RIESMAN
1968   *The Academic Revolution.* New York: Doubleday.

JENCKS, C. ET AL.
1972   *Inequality: A Reassessment of the Effects of Family and Schooling in America.* New York: Basic Books.

KAHL, J.
1965   "Some measurements of achievement orientation." *American Journal of Sociology* 70 (May):669–81.

KAHN, R. L.
1974   "The work module: A proposition for the humanism of work." In James O'Toole (ed.), *Work in the Inventory of Life.* Cambridge, Mass.: M.I.T. Press.

KARABEL, J. AND A. W. ASTIN
1975   "Social class, academic ability, and college 'quality'." *Social Forces* 53 (March):381–98.

KELLEY, J.
1973   "Causal chain models for the socioeconomic career." *American Sociological Review* 38 (August):481–93.

KEMPER, T. D.
1974   "On the nature and purpose of ascription." *American Sociological Review* 39 (December):844–53.

KERCKHOFF, A. C.
1974   "Parental influence on educational goals." *Sociometry* 37(3):307–27.
1972   *Socialization and Social Class.* Englewood Cliffs, N.J.: Prentice-Hall.

KOHN, M. L.
1969   *Class and Conformity: A Study in Values.* Homewood, Ill. Dorsey Press.
1963   "Social class and parent-child relationships: An interpretation." *American Journal of Sociology* 68 (January):471–480.
1959   "Social class and parental values." *American Journal of Sociology* 64:337–351.

KOHN, M. L. AND C. SCHOOLER
1969   "Class, occupation and orientation." *American Sociological Review* 34:659–78.

KOMAROVSKY, M.
1962   *Blue Collar Marriage.* New York: Random House.
1940   *The Unemployed Man and His Family.* New York: Dryden Press.

KUNZ, P. R.
1965   "The relation of income and fertility." *Journal of Marriage and the Family* 27 (November):509–13.

LEE, A. AND E. LEE
1959   "The future fertility of the American Negro." *Social Forces* 37:228–331.

LENSKI, G. E.
1966   *Power and Privilege: A Theory of Social Stratification.* New York: McGraw-Hill.

LEVY, J., JR.
1966   *Modernization and the Structure of Societies.* Princeton, N.J.: Princeton University Press.

LIPSET, S. M. AND R. BENDIX
1952   "Social mobility and occupational career patterns." *American Journal of Sociology,* 57 (March):494–504.

MARSH, R. M.
1971   "The explanation of occupational prestige hierarchies."- *Social Forces* 50 (December):214–22.

MASTERS, S. H.
1975   *Black-White Income Differentials.* New York: Academic Press.

MCALLISTER, P., C. S. STOKES, AND M. KNAPP
1974   "Size of family of orientation, birth order, and fertility

values: A reexamination.'' *Journal of Marriage and the Family*, 36 (May):337–43.

McCord, W., J. Howard, B. Frieberg, and E. Harwood
1969   *Life Styles in the Black Ghetto*. New York: Norton.

McLaughlin, V. Y.
1971   "Patterns of work and family organization: Buffalo's Italians." *Journal of Interdisciplinary History* 19:57–67.

Miao, G.
1974   "Marital instability and unemployment among whites and nonwhites." *Journal of Marriage and the Family*, 36 (February):77–86.

Miller, D. and G. Swanson
1958   *The Changing American Parent: A Study in the Detroit Area*. New York: Wiley.

Mogey, J.
1965   "Age at first marriage." In A. W. Gouldner and S. M. Miller (eds.), *Applied Sociology: Opportunities and Problems*. New York: Free Press.

Moore, W. E.
1965   *The Impact of Industry*. Englewood Cliffs, N.J.: Prentice-Hall.

Morgan, J. N. et al.
1962   *Income and Welfare in the United States*. New York: McGraw-Hill.

Mortimer, J. T.
1976   "Social class, work and family: Some implications of the father's occupation for family relationships and sons' career decisions." *Journal of Marriage and the Family* 38 (May):241–54.

1974   "Patterns of intergenerational occupational movements: A smallest-space analysis." *American Journal of Sociology* 79, 5:1278–95.

Mott, P. E. et al.
1965   *Shift Work: The Social, Psychological and Physical Consequences*. Ann Arbor: University of Michigan Press.

Nagel, E.
1961   *The Structure of Science*. New York: Harcourt, Brace and World.

Nye, F. I., J. Carlson, and G. Garrett
1970   "Family size, interaction, affect and stress." *Journal of Marriage and the Family*, 32:216–26.

Oppenheimer, V. K.
1975   "The sociology of women's economic role in the family." Unpublished paper.

1974   "The life-cycle squeeze: The interaction of men's occupational and family life cycles." *Demography* 11 (May):227–46.

Otto, L. B.
1975   "Class and status in family research." *Journal of Marriage and the Family* 37 (May):315–34.

Park, R. E. and E. W. Burgess
1969   "Personal competition, social selection, and status." In L. A. Coser and B. Rosenberg (eds.), *Sociological Theory*, third ed. New York: Macmillan.

Parsons, T.
1955   "The American family: Its relations to personality and the social structure." In T. Parsons and R. F. Bales (eds.), *Family Socialization and Interaction Process*. New York: Free Press.

1953   "A revised analytical approach to the theory of social stratification." In R. Bendix and S. M. Lipset (eds.), *Class, Status, and Power*. New York: Free Press.

1951   *The Social System*. New York: Free Press.
1949   "The social structure of the family." In Ruth N. Anshen (ed.), *The Family: Its Function and Destiny*. New York: Harper.

1943   "The kinship system of the contemporary United States" *American Anthropologist* 45 (January):22–38.

1942   "Age and sex in the social structure of the United States." *American Sociological Review* 7 (October):604–16.

1940   "An analytical approach to the theory of social stratification." *American Journal of Sociology* 45 (November):841–62.

Pearlin, L. I.
1975   "Status inequality and stress in marriage." *American Sociological Review* 40:344–57.

Pearlin, L. I. and M. L. Kohn
1966   "Social class, occupation, and parental values: A cross-cultural study." *American Sociological Review* 31 (August):466–79.

Perrella, V. C.
1970   "Moonlighters: Their motivations and characteristics." *Monthly Labor Review* 93:57–64.

Portes, A. and K. Wilson
1976   "Black-white differences in educational attainment." *American Sociological Review* 41 (June):414–31.

Rainwater, L.
1971   "Making the good life: Working class family and life style." In S. A. Levitan (ed.), *Blue Collar Workers*. New York: McGraw-Hill.

1965   *Family Design: Marital Sexuality, Family Size, and Contraception*. Chicago: Aldine.

1960   *And the Poor Get Children*. Chicago: Quadrangle Books.

Reed, F. W. and J. R. Udry
1973   "Female work, fertility, and contraceptive use in a biracial sample." *Journal of Marriage and the Family* 35 (November):597–603.

Rehberg, R. A. and D. L. Westly
1967   "Encouragement, occupation, education and family size: Artifactual or independent determinants of adolescent educational expectations?" *Social Forces* 45 (March):362–74.

Rogers, D.
1969   *110 Livingston Street: Politics and Bureaucracy in the New York City School System*. New York: Random House.

Rogoff, N.
1953   "Recent trends in urban occupational mobility" In R. Bendix and S. M. Lipset (eds.), *Class, Status and Power*. New York: Free Press.

Rollins, B. C. and K. L. Cannon
1974   "Marital satisfaction over the family life cycle: A reevaluation." *Journal of Marriage and the Family* 36:271–82.

Rollins, B. C. and H. Feldman
1970   "Marital satisfaction over the family life cycle." *Journal of Marriage and the Family* 32:20–38.

Rosen, B.
1962   "Social status and socialization patterns." *American Sociological Review* 27:89–100.

Rosow, I. and K. D. Rose
1972   "Divorce among doctors." *Journal of Marriage and the Family* 34: 587–99.

Rossi, P. et al.
1974   "Measuring household social standing." *Social Science Research* 3:169–90.

Sampson, W. A. and P. Rossi
1975   "Race and family social standing." *American Sociological Review* 40 (April):201–14.

Scanzoni, J.
1975   *Sex Roles, Life Styles, and Childbearing*. New York: Free Press.

1971   *The Black Family in Modern Society*. Boston: Allyn and Bacon.

1970   *Opportunity and the Family: A Study of the Conjugal Family in Relation to the Economic-Opportunity Structure.* New York: Free Press.

SCHECK, D. C. AND R. EMERICK
1976   "The young male adolescent's perception of early child-rearing behavior: The differential effects of socioeconomic status and family size." *Sociometry* 39 (March):39–53.

SCOTT, J. F.
1972   "Ascription and mobility." In G. W. Theilbar and S. D. Feldman (eds.), *Issues in Social Inequality.* Boston: Little, Brown.

SEWELL, W. H. AND V. P. SHAH
1968   "Social class, parental encouragement and educational aspirations." *American Journal of Sociology* 73(5):559–72.

1967   "Socioeconomic status, intelligence, and the attainment of higher education." *Sociology of Education* 40 (Winter):1–23.

SIEGEL, P. M.
1965   "On the cost of being a Negro." *Sociological Inquiry* 35:41–57.

SIMMONS, R. G. AND M. ROSENBERG
1971   "Functions of children's perceptions of the stratification system." *American Sociological Review* 36 (April):235–49.

SIMON, J. L.
1975   "Puzzles and further explorations in the interrelationships of successive births with husbands' income, spouses' education and race." *Demography* 12 (May):259–274.

SIMPSON, I. H., K. W. BACK, AND J. C. MCKINNEY
1966   "Orientation toward work and retirement, and self-evaluation in retirement." In I. H. Simpson and J. C. McKinney (eds.), *Social Aspects of Aging.* Durham, N.C.: Duke University Press.

SMELSER, N. J. AND S. M. LIPSET
1966   "Social structure, mobility and development." In N. J. Smelser and S. M. Lipset (eds.), *Social Structure and Mobility in Economic Development.* Chicago: Aldine.

SORENSEN, B.
1975   "The structure of intragenerational mobility." *American Sociological Review* 40 (August(:456–71.

SPANIER, G. B., R. A. LEWIS AND C. L. COLE
1975   "Marital adjustment over the family life cycle." *Journal of Marriage and the Family* 37:263–76.

STAPLES, R.
1976   *Introduction to Black Sociology.* New York: McGraw-Hill.

STEPHENSON, R. M.
1957   "Orientation and stratification of 1000 ninth graders." *American Sociological Review* 22:204–12.

SUNDAL, A. P. AND T. C. MCCORMICK
1951   "Age at marriage and mate selection: Madison, Wisconsin, 1937–1943." *American Sociological Review* 16 (February):37–48.

SVALASTOGA, K.
1965   "Social mobility: The western European model." *Acta Sociologica* 9:174–79.

TIETZE, C.
1955   "Age at marriage and educational attainment in the United States." *Population Studies* 4 (September):159–66.

TREIMAN, D. AND K. TERRELL
1975   "Sex and the process of status attainment: A comparison of working women and men." *American Sociological Review* 40 (April):174–200.

TULLY, J. C., E. F. JACKSON, AND R. F. CURTIS
1970   "Trends in occupational mobility in Indianapolis." *Social Forces* 49:186–99.

TURK, J. L.
1975   "Uses and abuses of family power." In R. E. Cromwell and D. H. Olson (eds.), *Power in Families.* New York: Halsted Press.

TURNER, R. H.
1962   "Some family determinants of ambition." *Sociology and Social Research* 46 (July):397–411.

UDRY, J. R.
1966   "Marital instability by race, sex, education, and occupation using 1960 census data." *American Journal of Sociology* 72 (September):203–09.

WARNER, W. L., M. MEEKER, AND K. EELS
1949   *Social Class in America.* Chicago: Science Research Associates.

WEBER, M.
1946   *Essays in Sociology.* New York: Oxford University Press.

WERTS, C. E.
1968   "A comparison of male vs. female college attendance probabilities." *Sociology of Education* 41:103–10.

1966   "Social class and initial career choice of college freshman." *Sociology of Education* 39 (Winter):74–85.

WEST, P. S.
1953   "Social mobility among college graduates." In R. Bendix and S. M. Lipset (eds.), *Class Status and Power.* New York: Free Press.

WESTOFF, C. F.
1956   "The changing focus of differential fertility research: The social mobility hypothesis." In J. J. Spengler and O. D. Duncan (eds.), *Population Theory and Policy.* New York: Free Press.

WESTOFF, C. F. ET AL.
1961   *Family Growth in Metropolitan America.* Princeton, N.J.: Princeton University Press.

WILENSKY, H.
1963   "The moonlighter: A product of relative deprivation." *Industrial Relations* 3:105–124.

1961   "Life cycle, work situation and participation in formal associations." In R. W. Kleemeier (ed.), *Aging and Leisure: Research Perspectives on Meaningful Use of Time.* New York: Oxford University Press, 213–42.

WILLIAMS, R.
1970   *American Society,* third ed. New York: Knopf.

WILLIE, C. V.
1974   "The black family and social class." *American Journal of Orthopsychiatry* 44:50–60.

1969   "Intergenerational poverty." *Poverty and Human Resources Abstracts* 4 (January-February):1–13.

WRIGHT, J. D. AND S. P. WRIGHT
1976   "Social class and parental values for children: A partial replication and extension of the Kohn thesis." *American Sociological Review* 41 (June): 527–37.

ZAJONC, R. B.
1976   "Family configuration and intelligence" *Science* 192 (April): 227–35.

ZAJONC, R. B. AND G. B. MARKUS
1975   "Birth order and intellectual development," *Psychological Review* 82:74–85.

III

FAMILY INTERACTION

11

MATE SELECTION IN THE UNITED STATES: A THEORETICAL SUMMARIZATION

Bert N. Adams

It is possible for rules against incest and endogamy to be so strict and inclusive as to leave the individual with only a single category of persons, such as cross-cousins, available for marriage. Or it is possible, as in our own society, for endogamous restrictions to cover only kin as far out from the individual as first cousins and for formalized exogamous restrictions to be virtually non-existent. In the latter case, the "field of eligibles" for mating is extremely broad [Adams, 1975:32].

Who marries whom and why? The issue of mate selection is one of the most interesting, most discussed, and most complex in all of family study. Two factors make it exceptionally complex. First, as noted above, the determinants of mate choice have differed from historical era to historical era and from society to society. Second, it concerns the realm of human emotion and choice, hardly an easy focus for scientific propositions. As Zick Rubin and George Levinger have pointed out, more explanations for mate selection have been proposed than have been adequately tested (Rubin and Levinger, 1974). This chapter is a step toward developing a propositional theory of mate selection in the achievement-based society and "participant-run" family system of the middle and working classes of the United States (Reiss, 1967:165, 176). While I will not attempt to produce propositions applicable to all times and places, the discussion will close with a brief summary of influences which would result in variations from the model.

Our concern is to deal with mate selection as a process, not merely in terms of independent and measurable variables. Following Ernest Burgess's and Paul Wallin's classic research into *Engagement and Marriage* (1953),

and Robert Winch's statement of *Mate-Selection* (1958) as based on complementary needs, there were two efforts in the early 1960s to deal with mate choice as a process. Charles Bolton (1961) discussed relationship development itself, while Alan Kerckhoff and Keith Davis (1962) described the process as a series of filters through which couples pass. Since then researchers and writers have amplified and altered these classic statements, and summaries such as Wesley Burr's (1973) have appeared. In producing a new propositional model, I find particularly useful a framework devised by George Levinger a number of years ago to summarize the factors making for marital cohesiveness or dissolution. Levinger brings together these factors under three concepts drawn from interaction theory: attractions, barriers, and alternative attractions (Levinger, 1965). By expanding "barriers" to include "barriers to getting into or staying in" as well as "barriers to getting out of" a relationship, these three concepts are appropriate to the task of theoretically codifying the mate selection process as well.

The theoretical model I will develop is meant to deal with the process of choosing a specific mate,[1] but I will begin with a few words about attraction to marriage itself. Considerable research has examined those factors which make the individual more or less prone to seriousness and marriage at any given time. Zick Rubin, for example, finds romanticizing, or a romantic outlook, related to intensity: "In the romantic subgroups, love scores were substantially related to the reported movement of relationships toward greater intensity" (1974:398). Likewise, Sindberg et al. find that a highly significant variable, "which rarely has been emphasized in the literature, is the conscious and overtly expressed desire to marry" (1972:612). A portion of this conscious impetus toward marriage may be, as I have noted elsewhere, the desire to escape an unhappy home (Adams, 1975:356). Other factors, such as having passed the typical marriage

NOTE: The author wishes to express appreciation for the extremely helpful comments of George Levinger, Joel Moss, Kenneth Cannon, F. Ivan Nye, and Pauline Boss on an earlier draft. Any inaccuracies and misinterpretations that remain are the author's responsibility.

259

age in this society, may strengthen the overt desire to marry (Adams, 1975:237). On the other hand, there are also influences which may retard or even negate those leading toward marriage. Suzanne Steinmetz has pointed out in conversation that availability of employment for women may, in combination with alternatives to the nuclear family such as cohabitation, reduce the strength of women's motivation to marry. Ivan Nye and Felix Berardo, in their family text, note that when couple members have decided that they are right for each other, marriage will probably occur. Then, in a footnote, they state the following:

> "Probably" because an occasional person places a higher value on single than married status. Such a person would remain single even though "in love" or having rationally decided that he has found the person best suited to him as a spouse [1973:123].

So some factors may speed up or intensify the mate selection process, while others may retard it; and we have mentioned but a few of these general influences. Keeping in mind the attraction or nonattraction of marriage in general, let us turn to the factors influencing the choice of a specific mate.

The first factor, propinquity or nonpropinquity, might be considered the necessary condition for or *barrier to* beginning. This factor is not unique to mate selection in the United States, but its limiting influence is particularly pervasive in a participant-run system where arranged marriage is not prevalent. As has been pointed out for many years in the literature, the pool of eligible mates is circumscribed by propinquity (Bossard, 1932; Katz and Hill, 1958; Catton, 1964; Ramsøy, 1966). Propinquity does not, however, mean nonmobility. Rather, its influence shifts as the individual moves about, so that one is increasingly more likely, as time passes, to marry someone currently close by than someone formerly propinquitous. According to Catton, the probability of marriage decreases as the distance between premarital residences increases, "the decrease being very rapid at first but diminishing as distance increases" (1964:526). Catton also notes that since people from the same social categories—racial, religious, ethnic, educational, and social class—tend to cluster together residentially, one effect of propinquity is to increase the likelihood of such categorical homogamy (1964:529). While there are exceptions, as in the case of the Rockefeller son who married the family maid, the homogenizing effect of propinquity generally holds. Thus the first three propositions are as follows:

1. Proximity facilitates contact, and this is a precondition for marriage.
2. Marriage is increasingly more likely, as time passes, to be with someone currently propinquitous than with someone formerly propinquitous.
3. One effect of propinquity is to increase the likeli-

hood that one will meet, be attracted to, and marry someone of the same social categories as himself/herself.

Once we have established nonpropinquity as a barrier to contact, as a limiting condition on the field of eligibles for marriage, we can then observe the bases for *early attraction*. Bernard Murstein (1970) calls this the stimulus phase, and Levinger et al. (1970) call it the encounter phase of the mate selection process. Early attraction between the sexes, Joel Moss comments, may be based upon the same factors as any other form of friendship. Thus the stimuli may include certain valued public behaviors, such as gregariousness and poise, or similar interests and abilities. Nevertheless, when early attraction includes a romantic element, the stimulus is likely to have been physical appearance and attractiveness (Murstein, 1970). Elaine Walster and Glen Elder have researched early attraction and found that physical attractiveness is the major determinant of early liking and interest in dating, and is especially crucial in boys' reactions to girls (Walster, 1966; Berscheid et al., 1971; Elder, 1969). Unfortunately, while such factors may explain early attraction, the literature is less clear in helping to determine precisely which characteristics cause one to be perceived as attractive or which behaviors appeal to what sorts of opposite-sex individuals.

Another factor which has been proposed as a possible contributor to early attraction is similarity to one's ideal image (Strauss, 1946). The idea is that all persons carry around within themselves an approximate blueprint of the sort of person of the opposite sex whom they find appealing. Richard Udry, however, has argued that the ideal mate is not an actual basis for mate selection, or even for early attraction, but rather this image probably changes "in response to new relationships into which the person enters" (1965:482). While the image of the mate one wants may or may not change, the evidence on the ideal mate image is hardly compelling as yet, and thus this factor will be left out of our proposition on early attraction.

4. Immediate stimuli such as physical attractiveness, valued surface behaviors, and similar interests result in early attraction.

This early attraction may be either *perpetuated or reduced* by two additional factors: early favorable or unfavorable reaction by others and disclosure-rapport. Several of the informational variables discussed by Burr (1973) would fall under these categories. Robert Lewis reports that early labeling as a couple by friends and family results in greater relationship perpetuation at a later time (1973:414). The lack of such labeling, or a negative reaction from significant others, would result in a weakening of the relationship. Levinger et al. (1970) speculate that following the first encounter further disclosure takes place. This disclosure may have a positive or negative effect on the relationship, as the couple members learn more about each other. A positive result of self-disclosure is what Lewis calls "pair rapport." This rapport is a matter of feeling comfortable in each other's presence, and is to some extent a function of perceiving similarities in each other (Lewis, 1973). Rapport, or being relaxed and easy around each other, is very likely to perpetuate a relationship beyond the early stimulus phase. Disclosure and rapport must not, however, be thought of as a variable or stage, but as a process, and this is made clear in Rubin's valuable discussion of commitment and intimacy:

> The development of intimacy and of commitment are closely linked, spiralling processes. When one person reveals himself to another, it has subtle effects on the way each of them defines the relationship. Bit by bit the partners open themselves to one another, and step by step they construct their mutual bond. The process only rarely moves ahead in great leaps. . . . And inasmuch as no one can ever disclose himself totally to another person, continuing acts of self-revelation remain an important part of the developmental process [1973:180–81].

Thus, keeping in mind that we are only talking about the early stages of disclosure and rapport in early attraction, Propositions 5 through 7 are as follows:

5. The more favorable the reactions of significant others to an early relationship, the more likely the relationship will be perpetuated beyond the early attraction stage.

6. The more positive the reaction of the couple members to further disclosure, the better will be the pair rapport.

7. The better the couple rapport, the more likely the relationship will be perpetuated beyond the early attraction stage.

If a relationship is perpetuated and intensified by rapport and by favorable labeling by others, *deeper attraction* may be the next stage. A portion of this will of course be the continuing disclosure noted by Rubin (1973). But the factor found to be most closely related to deeper attraction is value consensus or coorientation, i.e., the orientation of the couple members toward the same values, ideas, and goals. Robert Coombs states that "persons with similar orientations were more satisfied with their partners than individuals in dissimilar couples" (1966:171). Likewise, Levinger et al. note that disclosure may result in the discovery of coorientation, a value concept (Levinger et al., 1970). Much of Donn Byrne's work has led to the conclusion that similarity leads to liking because it provides an individual with independent evidence of the correctness of his interpretation of social reality, a kind of validation of his point of view, which in turn reinforces his feelings of competence (Byrne, 1971; Byrne and Clore, 1967). Perception is more important than reality in

the influence of value similarity on a deepening relationship. That is, it is more important that couple members perceive each other as similar in values and life orientation than that those orientations be totally orthogonal in fact.

Through the sorting-out process other similarities between couple members may increase attraction to each other. These other similarities may include a similar level of physical attractiveness, similar energy levels, and perhaps similar personalities as found in levels of emotional maturity, affective expressiveness, and self-esteem (Napier, 1971). Similar physical attractiveness (or physiognomic homogeneity) has been found by Murstein (1970), Shepherd and Ellis (1972), and Griffiths and Kunz (1973) to contribute to the deepening and perpetuating of a relationship, while differences in attractiveness are likely to result in its termination. Personality similarity, however, must be discussed in conjunction with another possible basis for deeper attraction: complementary personality needs. Several years ago Robert Winch (1958) reported that the way needs are gratified during the mate selection process is by finding a partner whose personality characteristics, and therefore needs, are the opposite of, but complementary to, one's own. If the individual is submissive, he will seek a dominant partner; if he is aggressive, he will be attracted to a passive member of the opposite sex. Winch and his students compiled evidence that complementarity was at work in mate selection (Winch, Ktsanes, and Ktsanes, 1954, 1955; Ktsanes, 1955), while others found little evidence for such complementarity (Bowerman and Day, 1956; Schellenberg and Bee, 1960; Murstein, 1961). Research continued through the 1960s in the attempt to verify or reject the notion that personality opposites attract. The bulk of that research has found that, if anything, people with similar, rather than complementary, personality characteristics are attracted to each other (Murstein, 1967; Trost, 1967; Hobart, 1963; Centers, 1971; Seyfried and Hendrick, 1973). Winch himself in 1967 revised his view to say that complementarity is one factor among others which operates at the deeper level of attraction (Winch, 1967). Thus, until substantial positive evidence is assembled, we shall omit complementary needs from our theoretical model of mate selection. Instead we shall include the personality similarities discussed by Napier and others, realizing that further research is still warranted in the area of complementarity.

Another factor which will deepen the attractiveness of a relationship is salient categorical *homo*geneity, meaning that the couple members are from the same social categories—racial, ethnic, religious, etc.—mentioned above, and those categorical distinctions are important or salient to them (Burr, 1973:87). Such categorical salience can to some extent be subsumed under value consensus, but it has elements of rapport, cultural insight, and being able to understand the other's motives and behaviors as well. It should be added that if the couple members are from different social categories but those categories are not salient to them, i.e., are not important parts of their cultural and value systems, then such heterogeneity will not stand in the way of deeper attraction.

Several additional variables leading to deeper attraction have been proposed by various writers and researchers such as Burgess and Wallin (1953) in their classic study. Birth order similarity is reported by Kemper and again by Ward as instrumental in the choice of a mate (Kemper, 1965; Ward, 1974). That is, in marriage the individual tries to reproduce his relation to his siblings in his family of orientation. Another possibility is that the individual is trying to perpetuate, through marriage, his or her relationship with the opposite-sex parent (Strauss, 1946; Napier, 1971). One researcher has found, however, that not only do males appear to be duplicating their relations with their mothers, the same can be said of females (Aron, 1974). In other words, in this society it is not so much relations with the opposite-sex parent, but relations with one's mother, that are part of one's negative or positive image of potential mates. While these ideas are intriguing and deserving of further testing, we shall leave them out of the model currently being developed. The following propositions have thus emerged in the discussion of deeper attraction:

8. The greater the value compatibility–consensus between couple members, the more likely it is that the relationship will move to the level of deeper attraction.

9. The greater the similarity in physical attractiveness between couple members, the more likely it is that the relationship will move to the level of deeper attraction.

10. The greater the personality similarity of the couple members, the more likely it is that the relationship will move to the level of deeper attraction.

11. The more salient the categorical *homo*geneity of the members of a couple, the more likely it is that the relationship will move to the level of deeper attraction.

Either before or after the level of deeper attraction is reached, several *barriers to continuation* may be confronted. The most notable of these is the opposite of the attraction basis referred to in Proposition 11. That is, salient categorical *hetero*geneity is very likely to terminate a budding relationship. If the couple are members of different religious groups or different races and if those differences matter to them, they will act as deterrents to greater seriousness. Much literature describes just how salient such categories continue to be in the United States (Greeley, 1970; Cavan, 1971; Eckland, 1968). Another barrier, again the obverse of an attraction basis and not altogether unrelated to categorical heterogeneity, is the negative reaction of significant others. The effect of this variable is, however, not completely clear, especially when the significant others are one's parents. Parental with the emerging relationship, may itself be due to

categorical heterogeneity on the part of the couple members, or to the parents' perceptions of their personalities, or other factors. But whatever its basis, such intrusion is likely to have a negative effect on the relationship in the long run, even in a participant-run mate selection system such as that of the United States. However, one caution is in order. Richard Driscoll et al. (1972) speak of "the Romeo and Juliet Effect," meaning that parental interference and opposition may in fact intensify romantic love feelings. This, however, is why we included the words "in the long run" above, for it is my feeling that while the short-run effect of parental opposition may be to "heat up" a budding relationship, the long-run effect is more likely to be termination. This is, of course, another example of a causal factor that might be included or omitted from the model, but in either case it requires further research attention.

Another possible barrier to continuation, noted by Steinmetz in conversation, is differential completion of a particular life stage. Such differential completion may take the form of one member of a couple completing high school and not the other, or one completing college and the other not, but in either case it may be a basis for relationship termination. This idea, however, needs empirical verification before being incorporated into a theory of mate selection in the United States. Propositions 12 and 13 summarize the barriers to continuation:

12. The more salient the categorical heterogeneity of couple members, the more likely it is that a relationship will be terminated either before or after reaching the stage of deeper attraction.

13. The greater the unfavorable parental intrusion, the more likely it is that a relationship will be terminated either before or after reaching the stage of deeper attraction.

Heterosexual relations do not necessarily occur one at a time. It is quite possible for an individual to be attracted to or interested in more than one member of the opposite sex at the same time. At any stage from early attraction to premarriage (and even after marriage), an *alternative attraction* may develop, one in which the influence of the attractions and perpetuators discussed thus far is stronger. The concept of alternative attraction is drawn from Thibaut and Kelley's *Social Psychology of Groups* (1959), and was used by Levinger (1965) in writing about marital dissolution. Though many of our concepts and propositions bespeak an exchange perspective, this is the one that is most directly adapted from that theoretical approach. The constant comparisons which occur throughout the premarital period, we are saying, result in the termination of a relationship when attraction to the alternative becomes stronger. It should be noted, as Joel Moss has pointed out, that the alternative need not necessarily be another human being. It might be going to law school, or changing jobs, or some other alternative—and here we find ourselves again in the realm of the attraction of "marriage in general," or of marriage versus nonmarriage. Proposition 14 summarizes this factor:

14. An alternative attraction may arise at any stage of a couple's relationship. The stronger that alternative attraction on the part of either couple member, the greater the likelihood that the original couple's relationship will be terminated.

We have spoken of the stimuli to early attraction, and of value consensus as a factor in deeper attraction. We come now to a perpetuator at this deeper level. The third part of Murstein's mate selection process is what he calls "role compatibility" (1967, 1970). Lewis (1973) calls this "accurate role taking," while Seyfried and Hendrick (1973) speak of "role reciprocity." All these authors are referring to the playing of heterosexual roles in ways that are satisfying to and predictable by both the partners. Predictability introduces a closely related factor, that of "empathy," or being able to put yourself in your partner's shoes (Kirkpatrick and Hobart, 1954; Adams, 1975:230). Empathy and predictability are important aspects of role compatibility (Murstein, 1972:625), but Rubin and Levinger have questioned whether the evidence is as yet compelling that such role factors necessarily follow after value consensus and the other factors which we included under "deeper attractions" (Rubin and Levinger, 1974). While it is possible that role compatibility should be included under "deeper attractions," we shall keep it separate and subsequent until further testing takes place.

15. The greater the role compatibility on the part of couple members, the more likely the relationship will be perpetuated.
16. The greater the empathy on the part of couple members, the more likely the relationship will be perpetuated.

At this point we move from attractions and barriers to continuation to *barriers to breakup,* the usage of "barriers" which most closely parallels Levinger's use in his discussion of "Marital Cohesiveness and Dissolution" (1965). Instead of falling prey to an alternative attraction, a given relationship may be moved toward marriage by the conscious or unconscious feeling that this person is "right for me." This may in fact be the surface expression of the unexpressed feeling that he or she is "the best I can get," after a more or less lengthy period of comparing alternatives. There are several possible reasons why one might conclude that a partner is "right for me." If relative physical unattractiveness is coupled with a mutual acceptance and attraction between two people, they may feel that the "bargain" is good for both. Likewise, low self-esteem was found by Richard Klemer to be related to marrying someone met prior to going to college (1971). One way to interpret this is to say that the person with low self-esteem feels that he or she cannot afford to take chances, but must hang on to a relationship which already

exists. After all, to break ties and start again does require a certain amount of risk taking, which the individual with low self-esteem may not be willing to undertake. Likewise, the individual who for whatever reason has not married at the "typical" age of 22 or so, may feel—when a reciprocated attraction comes along—that it is too chancy to be choosy, that this may in fact be his or her final opportunity (Adams, 1975:237; Elder, 1969).

A more generally prevalent barrier to breakup occurs when the relationship begins to take on a life of its own. This has been described in various ways by different authors. Murstein (1974) speaks of "the 'conveyor belt' influences which make compatibility a less salient consideration once the courtship progresses to the point where the network of friends and relations begins to regard the man and woman as a couple." Lewis (1973) calls the last stage of his mate selection process "dyad crystalization," but more directly applicable at this point are Charles Bolton's (1961) idea of pair "commitment" and the Levinger et al. (1970) notion of pair "communality." Bolton describes this as a relation-centered basis for continuation, while Levinger et al. speak of the "buildup of a joint enterprise." In other words, the relationship itself, at some point, becomes more than the sum total of the categorical influences, personalities, and values of the two people who constitute the couple. The two begin to work actively for the relationship's perpetuation, and, according to Bolton, a series of "escalators" move the relationship on toward marriage. These include finding a part of one's identity in being "Tom's girl" or "Jane's guy," and formal engagement—a very late and obvious escalator toward marriage (Bolton, 1961). Not only is there a positive interest in perpetuation, but Ivan Nye has pointed out that the obverse side of this coin is the cost of breaking a long-term relationship. Such a breakup necessitates contending with the expectations of significant others, having to create alternative relationships, and especially, if one partner continues to want the relationship, hurting, embarrassing, and disappointing the other. Such barriers to breakup, then, might be considered the final phase of the mate selection process, the next step being marriage itself (again provided an extremely attractive alternative does not appear). This brings us to our final three propositions:

17. The more two individuals define each other as "right" or "the best I can get," the less likely it is that the relationship will break up short of marriage.
18. The more a relationship moves to the level of pair communality, the less likely it is that the relationship will break up short of marriage.
19. The more a relationship moves through a series of formal and informal escalators, the less likely it is that the relationship will break up short of marriage.

Here, then, are the major factors in a theory of mate selection in the United States. They include barriers to beginning, barriers to continuation, and barriers to breakup. They involve early attractions, deeper attractions, alternative attractions, and several perpetuators. We have drawn largely on the works of Levinger, Murstein, Lewis, and Rubin in the 1960s and 1970s. The specific variables included are, for the most part, those which have received substantial empirical research confirmation, though we have pointed out in the foregoing that there is variation in the amount of confirmation even of the variables and processes we have decided to include, as well as of their timing. Other factors which have been proposed, but with insufficient empirical verification, e.g., the ideal mate image and complementary needs, have been left out of the model. We have attempted to incorporate both variables and processes in the same theoretical model, realizing that the former are much easier to test than the latter. It remains, of course, for various portions of this model to be tested out in causal, longitudinal, and correlational association to each other, and for variables and specifications to be added (or subtracted) as theory testing moves forward. The entire model is presented in Figure 11.1.

CAUTIONARY NOTES

Our model of mate selection in the United States cannot be directly applied to other times and places, nor equally to all portions of U.S. society. At this point I would like to summarize briefly four variables which would alter the functioning of the factors in Figure 11.1: achievement-ascription, age, sex, and parallel or interactional marriage.

In a society based on ascription there may be no "mate choice" by the individual at all. Achievement in society and personal choice of a mate seem to go together. The historical drift has been toward more and more emphasis upon individual achievement in society, and toward more and more individual choice in mate selection. Bernard Farber (1964) calls this movement toward "universal availability," or the availability of all members of the opposite sex to oneself for mating. Of course, society will not have arrived at such a point as long as salient endogamy continues to operate in mate selection. If Farber is correct, over time the influence of social categories on mate selection should continue to diminish.

We have spoken at several points about the effect of age on mate selection. If one is under the typical age of marriage, we have said that pregnancy or escape from family may be factors in mate selection. If one is beyond the typical age, the field of eligibles is severely reduced, and feelings that one's partner is "the best I can get" may be heightened in importance relative to other factors such as role compatibility and social categories.

Several differences between the sexes has been noted in the literature on mate selection. Berscheid et al. (1971) and Elder (1969), for example, find that physical attractiveness is a major determinant of early liking, but is especially crucial in boys' reactions to girls. Furthermore, while empathy and predictability are important to role compatibility, Murstein (1972) finds these more important in girls' reaction to boys. Rubin notes another distinction between the sexes in mate selection in the following manner:

> Since the woman rather than the man typically takes on the social and economic status of her spouse, she has more practical concerns to keep in mind in selecting a mate. In addition, the woman is often in a greater rush to get married than the man because of her years of "marriageability" tend to be more limited. Thus, she cannot as easily afford to be strongly attracted to a date who is not also a potentially eligible spouse (1973:205).

Males' choices are thus more romantic, or more directly correlated with love as a sufficient condition. That this sex distinction will reduce as a result of the women's movement toward equality seems likely, but must await the passage of time for verification.

A final variation in our model of U.S. mate selection is drawn from Jessie Bernard's (1964) distinction between parallel and interactional marriages. In a parallel marriage each partner lives his or her own life in the male or female world. An interactional marriage means togetherness and companionship; it means marital partners being each other's best friend. Alan Kerckhoff states the relation between these types of marriages and mate selection as follows:

> Value consensus, personality fit, and so on may well be important in mate selection where the expected marital pattern is interaction. But there is no reason to believe that these factors should affect the choice of a spouse in the same way when the expected marital pattern is parallel [1974:75].

We might carry this one step further and suggest that, while our model is meant to fit both the middle and working classes of U.S. society, the value-attitude-role variables which play such an important part in our model are apt to be more characteristic of the middle than the working classes.

The model presented in Figure 11.1, then, should work best for modern, industrial middle-class individuals in their early twenties, and should work less well in certain particulars for each deviation from that category. And finally, continuing societal changes should affect the model as well.

NOTE

1. When I say "choosing a specific mate," this is not intended to exclude completely either remarriages or cohabitation from the model being developed. The same factors, though perhaps varying in the intensity of their influence, may be at work in various kinds of relationships.

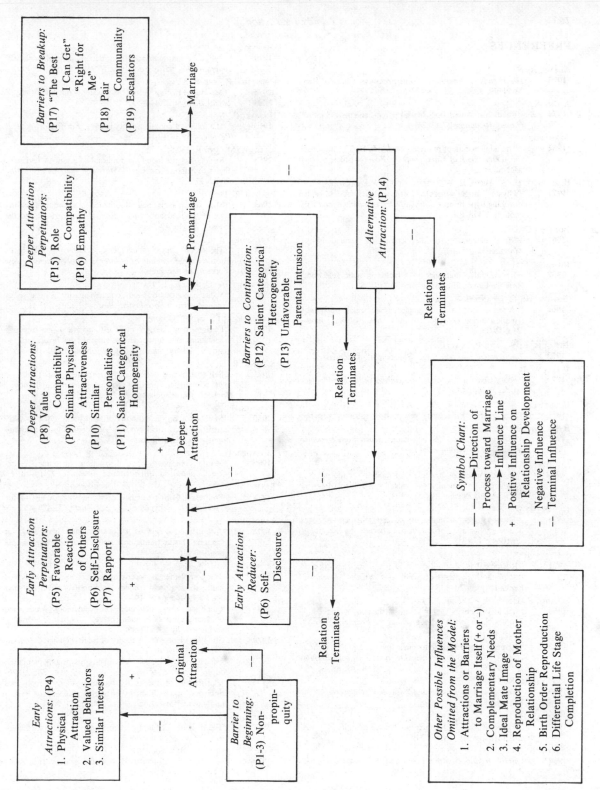

Figure 11.1. The Mate Selection Process

265

REFERENCES

ADAMS, B. N.
1975   *The Family: A Sociological Interpretation.* Chicago: Rand McNally, second ed.

ARON, A.
1974   "Relationships with opposite-sex parents and mate choice." *Human Relations* 27:17–24.

BERNARD, J.
1964   "The adjustments of married mates." In H. T. Christensen (ed.), *Handbook of Marriage & the Family.* Chicago: Rand McNally.

BERSCHEID, E., K. DION, E. WALSTER, AND G. W. WALSTER
1971   "Physical attractiveness and dating choice: A test of the matching hypothesis." *Journal of Experimental Social Psychology* 7:173–89.

BOLTON, C. D.
1961   "Mate selection as the development of a relationship." *Marriage and Family Living* 22:234–40.

BOSSARD, J. H. S.
1932   "Residential propinquity as a factor in mate selection." *American Journal of Sociology* 38:219–24.

BOWERMAN, C. E. AND B. R. DAY
1956   "A test of the theory of complementary needs as applied to couples during courtship." *American Sociological Review* 21:602–05.

BURGESS, E. W. AND P. WALLIN
1953   *Engagement and Marriage.* Philadelphia: Lippincott.

BURR, W. R.
1973   *Theory Construction and the Sociology of the Family.* New York: Wiley.

BYRNE, D.
1971   *The Attraction Paradigm.* New York: Academic Press.

BYRNE, D. AND G. L. CLORE
1967   "Effectance arousal and attraction." *Journal of Personality and Social Psychology* 6:4.

CATTON, W. R.
1964   "A comparison of mathematical models for the effect of residential propinquity on mate selection." *American Sociological Review* 29:522–29.

CAVAN, R. S.
1971   "Jewish student attitudes toward interreligious and intra-Jewish marriage." *American Journal of Sociology* 76:1064–71.

CENTERS, R.
1971   "Reciprocal need gratification in intersexual attraction: A test of the hypotheses of Schulz and Winch." *Journal of Personality* 39:26–43.

COOMBS, R. H.
1966   "Value consensus and partner satisfaction among dating couples." *Journal of Marriage and the Family* 28:166–73.

DRISCOLL, R., K. E. DAVIS, AND M. E. LIPETZ
1972   "Parental interference & romantic love: The Romeo & Juliet effect." *Journal of Personality and Social Psychology* 24:1–10.

ECKLAND, B. K.
1968   "Theories of mate selection." *Eugenics Quarterly* 15:74–88.

ELDER, G. H., JR.
1969   "Appearance and education in marriage mobility." *American Sociological Review* 34:519–33.

FARBER, B.
1964   *Family Organization and Interaction.* San Francisco: Chandler.

GREELEY, A. M.
1970   "Religious intermarriage in a denominational society." *American Journal of Sociology* 74:949–52.

GRIFFITHS, R. AND P. KUNZ
1973   "Assortative mating: A study of physiognomic homogamy." *Social Biology* 20:448–53.

HOBART, C. W.
1963   "The theory of complementary needs." *Pacific Sociological Review,* 29:73–79.

KATZ, A. M. AND R. HILL
1958   "Residential propinquity and marital selection: A review of theory, method, and fact." *Marriage and Family Living* 20:27–35.

KEMPER, T. D.
1965   "Mate selection and marital satisfaction according to sibling type of husband and wife." *Journal of Marriage and the Family* 28:346–49.

KERCKHOFF, A. C.
1974   "The social context of interpersonal attraction." In T. L. Huston (ed.), *Foundations of Interpersonal Attraction.* New York: Academic Press.

KERCKHOFF, A. C. AND K. E. DAVIS
1962   "Value consensus & need complementarity in mate selection." *American Sociological Review* 27:295–303.

KIRKPATRICK, C. AND C. HOBART
1954   "Disagreement, disagreement estimate, and non-empathic imputations for intimacy groups varying from favorite date to married." *American Sociological Review* 19:10–19.

KLEMER, R. H.
1971   "Self-esteem and college dating experiences as factors in mate selection and marital happiness: A longitudinal study." *Journal of Marriage and the Family* 33:183–87.

KTSANES, T.
1955   "Mate selection on the basis of personality type: A study utilizing an empirical typology of personality." *American Sociological Review* 20:547–51.

LEVINGER, G.
1965   "Marital cohesiveness and dissolution: An integrative review." *Journal of Marriage and the Family* 27:19–28.

LEVINGER, G., D. J. SENN, AND B. W. JORGENSEN
1970   "Progress toward permanence in courtship: A test of the Kerckhoff-Davis hypotheses." *Sociometry* 33:427–43.

LEWIS, R.
1973   "A longitudinal test of a developmental framework for premarital dyadic formation." *Journal of Marriage and the Family* 35:16–25.

MURSTEIN, B. I.
1961   "The complementary needs hypothesis in newlyweds and middle-aged married couples." *Journal of Abnormal and Social Psychology* 63:194–97.

1967   "Empirical tests of role, complementary needs and homogamy theories of mate choice." *Journal of Marriage and the Family* 29:689–96.

1970   "Stimulus-value-role: A theory of marital choice." *Journal of Marriage and the Family* 32:465–81.

1972   "Person perception and courtship progress among premarital couples." *Journal of Marriage and the Family* 34:621–26.

1974   "Clarification of obfuscation on conjugation: A reply to a criticism of the SVR theory of marital choice." *Journal of Marriage and the Family* 36, 2 (May):231–34.

NAPIER, A. Y.
1917   "The marriage of families: Cross-generational complementarity." *Family Process* 9:373–95.

NYE, F. I. AND F. M. BERARDO
1973   *The Family: Its Structure and Interaction.* New York: Macmillan.

RAMSØY, N. R.
1966 "Assortative mating and the structure of cities." *American Sociological Review* 31:773–86.

REISS, I. L.
1967 *The Social Context of Premarital Sexual Permissiveness.* New York: Holt, Rinehart & Winston.

RUBIN, Z.
1973 *Liking and Loving.* New York: Holt, Rinehart & Winston.
1974 "From liking to loving: Patterns of attraction in dating relationships." In T. L. Huston (ed.), *Foundations of Interpersonal Attraction.* New York: Academic Press.

RUBIN, Z. AND G. LEVINGER
1974 "Theory and data badly mated: A critique of Murstein's SVR and Lewis's PDF models of mate selection." *Journal of Marriage and the Family* 36:226–31.

SCHELLENBERG, J. A. AND L. S. BEE
1960 "A re-examination of the theory of complementary needs in mate selection." *Marriage and Family Living* 22:602–05.

SEYFRIED, B. A. AND C. HENDRICK
1973 "Need similarity and complementarity in interpersonal attraction." *Sociometry* 36:207–20.

SHEPHERD, J. M. AND H. D. ELLIS
1972 "Physical attractiveness and selection of marriage partners." *Psychological Reports* 30:1004–05.

SINDBERG, R. M., A. E. ROBERT, AND D. McCLAIN
1972 "Mate selection factors in computer matched marriages." *Journal of Marriage and the Family* 34:611–14.

STRAUSS, A.
1946 "The ideal and the chosen mate." *American Journal of Sociology* 42:204–10.

THIBAUT, J. W. AND H. H. KELLEY
1959 *The Social Psychology of Groups.* New York: Wiley.

TROST, J.
1967 "Some data on mate selection: Complementarity." *Journal of Marriage and the Family* 29:730–38.

UDRY, J. R.
1965 "The influence of the ideal mate image on mate selection and mate perception." *Journal of Marriage and the Family* 27:477–82.

WALSTER, E.
1966 "Importance of physical attractiveness in dating behavior." *Journal of Personality and Social Psychology* 4:508–16.

WARD, C.
1974 "Birth order effects in a survey of mate selection and parenthood." *Journal of Social Psychology* 94:57–64.

WINCH, R. F.
1958 *Mate-Selection: A Study of Complementary Needs.* New York: Harper.
1967 "Another look at the theory of complementary needs in mate selection." *Journal of Marriage and the Family* 29:756–62.

WINCH, R. F., T. KTSANES, AND V. KTSANES
1954 "The theory of complementary needs in mate selection: An analytic and descriptive study." *American Sociological Review* 19:241–49.
1955 "Empirical elaboration of the theory of complementary needs in mate selection." *Journal of Abnormal and Social Psychology* 51:508–14.

12

THEORIZING ABOUT THE QUALITY AND STABILITY OF MARRIAGE

Robert A. Lewis and Graham B. Spanier

INTRODUCTION

Understanding the forces which hold marriages together or encourage their dissolution is of great importance in this time of record high divorce rates. This chapter attempts to explain why some marriages fail and others do not. More specifically, the ultimate goal of this chapter is to build a partial theory of marital stability which identifies many of the conditions under which a marriage may remain intact or be dissolved. In order to realize this objective, we believe that we must focus our investigation primarily on marital quality, since, as we shall argue, the *quality* of most American marriages is the primary determinant of whether a marriage will remain intact.

There are two basic ways in which social scientists have viewed marital success and failure. The first approach has been to focus on "marital stability," a term which refers to whether a marriage is dissolved by death or by divorce, separation, desertion, or annulment. Using this approach, a stable marriage is defined as one which is terminated only by the natural death of one spouse. An unstable marriage thus is one which is willfully terminated by one or both spouses. A second approach has focused on the "quality" of marital relationships while they are intact. The concepts "marital adjustment," "marital satisfaction," "marital happiness," "marital integration," and others have been used to describe the quality of marriage relationships.

Objectives

The authors of this chapter have systematically examined, evaluated, codified, and reformulated virtually all of the empirical and conceptual propositions of social scientists who have attempted to investigate the quality and stability of marriage. This was an ambitious task, since we identified several hundred studies which qualified for inclusion under these general concepts. Although we cannot claim to have exhaustively reviewed every study ever conducted in this area of investigation, we are confident that our literature review has been as thorough as is practical and that this review was sufficient to give us an adequate basis for theorizing about the quality and stability of marriage.

Due to space limitations, we have decided against presenting an evaluative critique of all the empirical research in this area. This task has been attempted in a number of current reviews (e.g., Hicks and Platt, 1970; Spanier and Cole, 1976; Spanier, Lewis, and Cole, 1975). Rather, we have tentatively accepted most of the propositions as stated and have devoted our attention to the process of inductive theory building to better understand the complex interrelationship between the host of variables which are purported to be related to the quality and stability of marriage.

Plan of the Chapter

Our discussion commences with an identification, definition, and clarification of the central variables which we have used in this effort of theory building. Second, past attempts at theory building in this area are reviewed and evaluated. We then present a general classification scheme which we utilized initially to organize the mass of empirical propositions in the area, and which subsequently provided a general conceptual framework for understanding the causal processes leading to marital disenchantment and failure. Stated simply, this classifica-

NOTE: Appreciation is expressed to the members of a family theory construction seminar in 1975 at The Pennsylvania State University among whose members were Marc Baronowski, Patti Daubenspeck, Jim Hodgson, John Kennedy, Joanne Nicholson, Constance Shehan, and John Worobey. The technical assistance of Jim Brehony is gratefully acknowledged for cataloguing propositions. Wesley Burr, Ira Reiss, Stan Albrecht, and Mary Hicks provided valuable comments on an earlier version of this chapter.

tion scheme suggests that marital quality is a major determinant of marital stability, but is mediated by a number of threshold variables.

The last of our major tasks centers on a propositional inventory of all the research which has dealt with marital quality and its etymological kin. The inventory seeks to identify and induce propositions gathered from a vast amount of empirical work. The theory construction process attempts to relate these general propositions to each other but leaves to future theorists the task of deducing new sets of interrelated propositions which may guide future research. The final section suggests the utility of an exchange model for the future development of theories of marital quality and marital stability, and presents our initial attempts to evolve a theory of marital quality and marital stability.

DEFINITIONS

There has been much attention directed recently to the lack of clarity surrounding the use of many concepts used in marriage research (Lively, 1969; Hicks and Platt, 1970; Burr, 1973; Spanier and Cole, 1976). Actually, little agreement exists on the meaning and use of terms such as marital "adjustment," "satisfaction," "happiness," and "success" (Burr, 1973). This controversy is not especially relevant to our purpose here, and consequently we have attempted to avoid the problems which can develop when issues of definition are central. However, it is necessary for us to clarify the concepts which will be the major focus of our theory construction.

We have chosen to employ the general concept of "marital quality" to encompass the entire range of terms (i.e., marital "satisfaction," "happiness," "role strain and conflict," "communication," "integration," "adjustment," etc.) which have been the traditional dependent variables in marriage research. What these concepts share in common is that they represent qualitative dimensions and evaluations of the marital relationship. At the empirical level, they are highly intercorrelated. *Marital quality* thus is defined as a subjective evaluation of a married couple's relationship. The range of evaluations

constitutes a continuum reflecting numerous characteristics of marital interaction and marital functioning. High marital quality, therefore, is associated with good judgment, adequate communication, a high level of marital happiness, integration, and a high degree of satisfaction with the relationship. The definition does not convey a fixed picture of discrete categories, i.e., a high- versus low-quality marriage, but rather suggests the existence of a continuum ranging from high to low. Thus a couple's placement on the continuum would represent a composite picture which uses many criteria. These criteria, when operationalized, would be the dimensions of marital interaction and functioning which have traditionally been studied as well as some criteria which may not have yet been either proposed or studied.

"Marital stability," as we define it, is a straightforward concept indicating whether or not a marriage is intact. More specifically, *marital stability* is defined as the formal or informal status of a marriage as intact or nonintact. Strictly speaking, a stable marriage is one which is terminated only by the natural death of one spouse.[1] An unstable marriage thus is one which is willfully terminated by one or both spouses. The most common form of termination besides death is divorce. However, most couples separate before a final decree, and an informal separation before divorce would be considered an unstable marriage. Legal annulment of a marriage and desertion by one spouse are also indicators of marital instability, the former being a formal termination and the latter an informal termination.

Figure 12.1 lists the types of intact and nonintact marriages according to whether the arrangement is formal or informal. Marital stability, then, refers to the outcome of a marriage—in short, whether it is dissolved by a specific action of a spouse designed to force a termination or by the eventual death of one partner.

Theory is defined as a statement of the way in which abstract variables are related to each other and from which verifiable hypotheses are deduced (Winch and Spanier, 1974:4). Stated somewhat differently, it may be said that a theory is an interrelated set of propositions which explain or predict a given phenomenon (Hill, 1966).

Unfortunately, there is little consensus on the use of

Figure 12.1. Classification of Types of Marital Stability

	Intact (Stable)	Nonintact (Unstable)
Formal	Legally Married	Legal Separation Divorce Legal Annulment
Informal	Common-Law Marriage	Separation by Informal Agreement Desertion

such terms as "hypothesis" or "proposition." Among the great variety of definitions and uses of the term "proposition" (Braithwaite, 1953; Homans, 1964; Zetterberg, 1965; Blalock, 1969; Simon, 1969; Dubin, 1969), we are most attracted to Zetterberg's (1965) formulation. Zetterberg makes the distinction between ordinary and theoretical propositions. Ordinary propositions are related to empirical findings or testable assertions. Theoretical propositions reflect a higher level of abstraction with a greater information value.

We find this formulation most useful, since it allows us to use a single concept throughout our discussion, whereas some theorists choose to use both propositions and hypotheses as concepts in their propositional formulations of marital quality. Since we have found the use of two terms unnecessary and confusing we have used the term "proposition" throughout our discussion to refer to all relationships between variables, whether the relationship has been discovered directly through empirical research, through inference from empirical research, or by induction or deduction from other propositions at different levels of generality. Strictly speaking, we mainly report and discuss theoretical propositions in this chapter, since they were induced from empirical findings. These basic propositions we have called first-order propositions, in distinction to those of a higher order of abstraction.

THE CURRENT STATUS OF THEORY CONSTRUCTION

Conceptualizations of Marital Stability

A number of review articles have focused on marital stability and related concepts (Goode, 1961; Bernard, 1964; Bowerman, 1964; Levinger, 1965a; Nye, White, and FrieC deres, 1969; Bartz and Nye, 1970; Hicks and Platt, 1970; Burr, 1973; Spanier and Cole, 1976). Only a few of these articles, however, claim to set forth partial theories or are primarily theoretical (propositional) expositions of marital stability (e.g., Goode, 1961; Levinger, 1965a; Nye, White, and FrieHeres, 1969; Bartz and Nye, 1970; Burr, 1973).

One of the more explicit theoretical attempts has been "A Partial Theory of Family Stability" by Nye, White, and Frieeres (1969). These authors, after examining 75 empirical propositions having to do with the determinants of marital stability, formed 16 more general propositions which located three major determinants of marital stability: *positive affect* toward spouses, *constraints* against dissolution of the marriage, and *unattractive alternatives* to marriage (e.g., singleness and remarriage). The determinants of these three variables were included as well in the propositional formulation.

This work stands as one of the most parsimonious and coherent attempts at theory construction in this area. In addition, it is noteworthy in its specificity and testability,

since its level of abstraction is of a relatively low order and its concepts are easily operationalized. Since this partial theory was derived from a compilation and reformulation of empirical works, it stands as a prototype, a fine example of linking research and theory.

Another product of this theoretical enterprise by Nye and associates is Bartz and Nye (1970). Although most of this propositional formulation is concerned with the determinants of early marriage, the consequences of early marriage (conceived in terms of divorce and negative affect) were likewise reduced to propositional statements from which additional propositions were derived and set within the context of an exchange theory.

A similar attempt at theory building is that found in "Marital Cohesiveness and Dissolution: An Integrative Review" by Levinger (1965a). Although somewhat more illustrative than propositional in form, Levinger's article, relying strongly on Goode (1961), located in the existent literature a number of "bars and bonds" to marital cohesiveness (stability), which act as *barriers* against breakup of the relationship as well as *attractions* or inducements to remain in the marriage.

The attractiveness of Levinger's theory is highlighted not only by its parsimony and relative specificity but by its identification as an example of Kurt Lewin's field theory, which stresses the concept of "driving forces," those which drive a person toward an object of positive valence or away from a negative one, and "restraining forces," which restrain a person from leaving the situation or relationship. Another advantage is this theory's level of abstraction. The theory can be generalized to marital stability and dissolution in societies other than the United States, and also to conceptualizations of mate selection, courtship behavior, and even friendship phenomena. As such, this conceptual framework not only grounds the study of marital stability in the more general study of group cohesiveness and similar small-group research, but, due to its abstract nature, may well help to integrate future family research in this area into the larger body of small-group theory and research.

In spite of the popularity of some of the concepts employed, the main disappointment of Levinger's theoretical framework is its lack of extension into theory and research beyond that of its author. This lack of extension is unfortunate, since the central propositions contain very heuristic assumptions which suggest that, if one is to strengthen marital stability, one can either increase the attractions between marital partners, intensify the barriers to dissolution, decrease the attractiveness of alternative relationships, or apply various combinations of the above alternatives.

Conceptualizations of Marital Quality

In contrast to the area of marital stability there has been no systematic effort at building either a theory or even a propositional inventory in the area of marital quality, although some reconceptualization or concept clarification has been done in the area (e.g., Spanier and Cole, 1976). This neglect stems not so much from a paucity of research on the qualitative dimensions of marital relations, but from methodological problems and the onus attached to value-laden research.

Most of the early conceptualizations of variables related to marital quality which have endured have taken the form of typologies or ideal types. For example, Burgess and Locke (1945) set the pace by distinguishing institutional from companionship marriages, the latter emphasizing affection between the married partners. Gurin, Veroff, and Feld (1960) emphasized the parallel as differentiated from the interactional type of marriage, while Rainwater (1965), adopting Bott's (1957) categories for use in studying some American marriages, operationalized three types of marriage: joint conjugal, segregated conjugal, and intermediate conjugal. These types depend upon the degree of a couple's role segregation or sharing.

One of the most popular typologies of marriage quality has been that of Cuber and Harroff (1965), who categorized American marriages as either conflict-habituated, devitalized, passive congenial, vital, or total. These types were based upon the degree to which couples in their study had a utilitarian marriage as contrasted with an intrinsic marriage, suggested by the vital and total types, where the personal, intimate relationship between the husband and wife has priority over other functions such as child raising.

Research which has focused upon specific dimensions of marital quality, e.g., marital satisfaction or marital adjustment, has been abundant. It is surprising, therefore, that few attempts have been made to develop propositional inventories in this area. One notable exception is Burr's (1973) book on family theory in the chapter on "Marital Satisfaction," in which the author identifies a number of propositions relating factors that affect marital satisfaction. The 31 propositions are drawn from a variety of theoretical frameworks such as symbolic interaction, balance, and social exchange.

In the chapter on "The Effects of Premarital Factors on Marriage," Burr attempts to derive a theory from the previously atheoretical marriage prediction literature. He based the majority of his 10 propositions on independent variables such as homogamy, conventionality, significant others, skills, and motivation for marriage. Few of these variables, unfortunately, have a common theoretical base of assumptions or world view. In brief, the main limitation of this attempt at theory construction is the lack of parsimony and the sheer mass of complex interrelationships which confront the serious student of theory construction. This does not mean, however, that Burr's theoretical contributions may not be extremely useful in stimulating future research, since they contain many imaginative and creative ideas, and they integrate many previously unrelated concepts.

THE CLASSIFICATION SCHEME

All marriages have unique histories which begin long before the marriage ceremony and which follow a complex course, finally resulting in dissolution by death of one spouse, divorce, separation, annulment, or desertion. While engaged in the process of identifying and organizing hundreds of propositions related to the concepts of marital quality and stability, we found it necessary to have a general accounting scheme within which the multitude of propositions could best be organized. The scheme which we found most helpful is presented in Figure 12.2.

Figure 12.2 has considerable utility, however, beyond its classification purposes. Namely, the four general categories (premarital predispositions, marital quality during the marriage period, threshold variables, and the post-marital period) are suggestive of the processual nature of the marital interaction which determines quality and stability. In brief, marital quality is not a static but a dynamic concept. Also, marital stability not only denotes an end state but reflects an outcome of a *process* involving dyadic formation, maintenance, and dissolution over a period of time. Stated differently, our classification scheme suggests a sequential ordering of various classes of variables relevant at different times for marital stability.

Divorce itself is a process. Initially, most couples who divorce are separated for some period of time before they divorce (Goode, 1956). The separation is likely since the divorce process is often a lengthy one, spanning a period of several weeks to several months. Following a decision to divorce, the couple usually will choose, and may also be legally compelled, to separate pending a final decree. Alternatively, separation may be attempted before a decision to divorce, in order that the couple may determine whether divorce is appropriate or desired. Many couples move back and forth from married cohabitation to separation due to indecision about the future of their relationship or as a mechanism for manipulating or expressing hostility toward the spouse. Our conceptual framework, therefore, attempts to recognize that the events leading to a separation before divorce may be of greater significance to understanding marital stability than the ultimate fact of divorce.

A second observation, obvious but not trivial, is that given the same level of marital quality, one couple may separate or divorce, while another couple may not. Although there is ample evidence that indicators of marital quality are strongly correlated with marital stability (Spanier, 1976; Dean and Lucas, 1974), social scientists and family clinicians are cognizant that many poorly adjusted marriages remain intact while many marriages with average or even relatively good adjustment may be terminated by divorce. Locke's (1951) study of marital adjustment lends some support to the statement that marital quality and marital stability are highly correlated. Data collected by Spanier (1976) which compared mar-

Figure 12.2. Factors Influencing Marital Stability

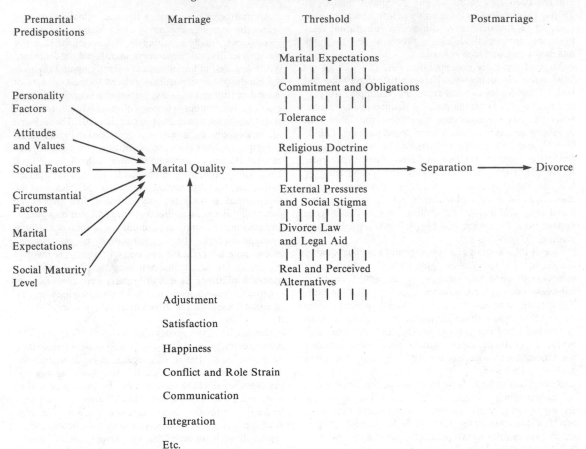

ried and divorced samples for the purposes of scale development further support this statement. But as Udry (1973) and Landis (1973) point out, marriages with high stability cannot be assumed to have high quality, and vice versa. Investigations of this phenomenon are conspicuously absent from the literature on marital stability. Our conceptual framework gives a prominent place, however, to a consideration of the relationship between marital quality and marital stability. We believe this has been a neglected area of investigation with important social implications.

Our classification scheme identifies several premarital determinants of marital quality as well as seven threshold variables which we have speculated collectively act as a "mediating barrier" between marital quality and marital stability. As such, our framework is consistent with and shares some features with Levinger's (1965a) discussion of marital cohesiveness and dissolution, Bell and Mau's

(1971) discussion of marital commitment, and Clayton's (1975) extension of the Bell and Mau work.

Levinger suggests that all relationships have some sources of attraction, some sources of barrier strength, and some sources of alternate attraction. Sources of attraction included affectional rewards such as esteem for spouse, desire for companionship, and sexual enjoyment; socioeconomic rewards such as husband's income, home ownership, husband's education, and husband's occupation; and similarity in social status such as religion, education, and age. Sources of barrier strength included feelings of obligation to dependent children and to the marital bond; moral proscriptions associated with religion and church attendance; and external pressures such as primary group affiliation, community stigma, and legal and economic bars. Sources of alternate attraction included affectional rewards from a preferred alternate sex partner, disjunctive social relations, opposing religious affiliations; and economic rewards, such as the wife's opportunity for independent income.

The seven threshold variables which we have speculated mediate most significantly between marriage and voluntary separation are:

1. Marital expectations
2. Commitment to the marriage and its associated obligations
3. Tolerance for conflict and disharmony
4. Religious doctrine and commitment
5. External pressures and amenability to social stigma
6. Divorce law and availability of legal aid
7. Real and perceived alternatives.

These threshold variables thus may be most influential in determining the circumstances under which a marriage will remain intact or terminate.

Regardless of the power of these variables in explaining marital stability, we believe that the single greatest predictor of marital stability is marital quality. Although we want to acknowledge the influence of the threshold concept, the evidence available from dozens of studies argues persuasively that indicators of marital quality will explain a great proportion of the variance in marital stability. In short, among any large sample of married couples, it is probable that those with the poorest marital adjustment, satisfaction, happiness, etc., will subsequently be most susceptible to separation and divorce. Although no single study has demonstrated or verified this statement, our review of the marital quality literature has convinced us that this is a realistic interpretation.

Accordingly, our classification system suggests that propositions salient for marital stability must focus primarily on marital quality and its associated constructs. In other words, the key to our approach to marital stability is to understand marital quality primarily and the operation of threshold mechanisms secondarily. This strategy has the advantage of not separating two closely related bodies of literature.

In defining marital quality, we have suggested that a marriage of high quality would be one which has high marital adjustment, satisfaction, and happiness and which is an adequately functioning system. Because of this definition, we realize that marital quality may be a difficult concept to operationalize. However, for our theory construction, the concept serves a useful purpose, since the greatest amount of empirical work relating to marital stability falls, according to our definition, under the rubric of marital quality. Thus qualitative evaluation of the marital relationship while it is in existence is logically the most salient focus for theory building.

Nevertheless, our organizational scheme also recognizes a vast literature on premarital determinants of marital quality. A large number of studies focusing on social, interpersonal, and circumstantial factors in the mate selection process have demonstrated the importance of including premaritally predisposing factors in the framework. Thus we have identified six general categories of variables which subsequently may have a significant impact on a given marriage.

The premarital predispositions are:

1. Personality characteristics of the future marital partners
2. Attitudes, values, and philosophy of life relating to both marital and nonmarital domains
3. Social factors
4. Circumstantial factors
5. Marital expectations of the partners
6. Social maturity level.

In summary, the classification scheme presented in Figure 12.2 not only has provided the basis for organizing the propositional inventory which follows the next section but in addition has made explicit many of our assumptions about the development of marital stability.

STRATEGY FOR THE PROPOSITIONAL INVENTORY

Since a variety of theory-building strategies were available to us, we now would like to describe the procedures and rationale behind our propositional inventory. We divided our task into six parts: (1) clarification of relevant concepts; (2) systematic identification of all published and unpublished work relating to marital stability and quality; (3) identification of all specific, relevant empirical findings located in this literature; (4) organization of these empirical findings into topical areas according to the independent variables for retroduction; (5) development of first-order propositions from each set of empirical findings by the process of induction; and (6) further development of even more general propositions induced from related first-order propositions.

First, since researchers have used a multitude of concepts to study marital quality and marital stability, we decided that a successful theory-building process must examine all relevant concepts which have been used as dependent variables in the study of marital quality or stability. Thus any research study which investigated marital adjustment, happiness, integration, stability, success, satisfaction, commitment, or other quality was included. We found that these concepts are often used interchangeably and that the choice of terms in a given study is usually related to the particular scale or index being used. The justification for labeling a scale "adjustment," "satisfaction," or otherwise, appears only rarely to have been based on careful conceptualizations (Spanier and Cole, 1976). Indeed, we consistently found that the choice of conceptual labels or scales made little difference in the substantive findings used in propositional formation. This observation further strengthened our rationale to induce all propositions which included any concept referring to marital quality.

The second stage of the inventory development involved identifying all of the published and unpublished work on marital quality and stability. Using available published work, previous reviews of the literature, *Sociological Abstracts, Psychological Abstracts, Dissertation Abstracts,* books which have attempted reviews of related literature, and the *International Bibliography of Marriage and the Family,* we began to trace all known research findings on marital quality. Additionally, we sent letters to all theorists and researchers whom we knew to have had an interest in this area. These letters requested that they identify any work completed or in progress which might be relevant to our investigation. Happily, a number of unpublished manuscripts were identified through these informal contacts. In brief, we were able to locate several hundred sources which were in some way related to the task. Approximately 300 of the sources were empirical studies which qualified for inclusion in our theory-building phase.

Each study was then reviewed and all findings relating to marital stability or quality were typed on cards, thus generating a file of empirical propositions. These references were included in the references for this chapter if we were able to use them in the construction of a first-order theoretical proposition.

The file of empirical findings was then organized according to topical areas and our classification scheme. Similar findings were collated on the basis of the independent variables used in the research. Overall we identified more than 40 separate substantive areas, many of which later defined the final organization of our propositions. In general, we found three generic areas as most meaningful: premarital factors influencing marital quality, social and economic factors, and interpersonal and dyadic factors.

First-order propositions were developed subsequently from each set of findings which had the same or very closely related independent variables and a dependent variable which qualified as an indicator of marital quality. We were impressed that in the majority of cases our propositions were based on similar, consistent findings from more than one study. Naturally, we also found real contradictions in the research literature. However, in a group of studies where the weight of evidence argued for one proposition, any contrary findings were simply considered as exceptions, i.e., as inconsistent with the wealth of other literature which was more convincing. In some cases the picture was not as clear; e.g., one or more very carefully done studies had conclusions which contradicted other studies. Occasionally this contradiction was further revealing, since an examination of the studies collectively revealed the suggestion of a curvilinear relationship, instead of a linear relationship suggested by

individual studies which had examined only part of a developmental or multifaceted phenomenon. When the empirical evidence clearly was contradictory and unresolvable, we abstained from formulating any proposition.

Due to the large body of empirical literature reviewed for this chapter, we decided against presenting in print our entire file of specific empirical findings. Clearly, such a presentation would be the most desirable approach, since it would allow the reader to see how we moved from a specific group of findings, which sometimes included as many as 20 to 40 findings for some areas, to a single proposition. However, space limitations argued against such a voluminous and tedious reporting; instead we elected to begin our presentation with the first-order, derived propositions.

Our final stage in developing the theory was to induce more general statements relating to the first-order propositions. This was possible for many, but not for all, of the first-order propositions. The opportunity to induce second- or higher-order propositions was dependent largely on the level of generality of the initial propositions and on the degree of their similarity to other propositions.

THEORY OF MARITAL QUALITY: PART I. PREMARITAL FACTORS AND MARITAL QUALITY

Burr (1973) has correctly pointed out that most of the research dealing with the relationships between premarital factors and marital variables has been concerned primarily with prediction rather than explanation. The study of prediction is a worthy endeavor, but explanation of the influence of premarital factors on marital quality is a necessary part of theory development. We know, for example, that homogamy with respect to social characteristics is positively related to subsequent marital quality. The greater the homogamy, the more accurate the prediction of high marital quality is likely to be. We can be relatively confident in such a prediction, because a wealth of data supports this notion. We are much less clear, however, about how other structural, functional, and interactional dimensions of the marital relationship are influenced by homogamy.

The present section identifies 25 first-order propositions relating premarital factors to marital quality. The reader will note that many of the propositions have parallels to those in Burr's (1973) presentation of "The Effects of Premarital Factors on Marriage." Our thorough search of the literature has corroborated almost all of his propositional formulations. In addition, we have identified several propositions which were not discussed by Burr; and most of the propositions which overlap those of Burr have been stated differently, occasionally reflecting substantive differences in interpretation.[2] The entire set of premarital propositions is presented in Table 12.1.

Table 12.1. Propositions Concerning the Relationship between Premarital Factors and Marital Quality

FIRST-ORDER PROPOSITIONS	SECOND-ORDER PROPOSITIONS	THIRD-ORDER PROPOSITIONS
Homogamy		
1. Premarital couples from different racial backgrounds will have lower marital quality than couples from the same racial backgrounds. 2. The greater the difference in socioeconomic status for premarital couples, the lower the marital quality. 3. Couples with different religious denominational affiliations will have lower marital quality than couples with the same religious denominational affiliation. 4. The greater the difference in intelligence for couples, the lower the marital quality. 5. The greater the difference in age for couples, the lower the marital quality. 6. The greater the absolute difference in status between husband and wife, the lower the marital quality.	75. The greater the premarital homogamy, the higher the marital quality.	88. The greater the social and personal resources available for adequate marital role functioning, the higher the subsequent marital quality.
Resources		
7. The greater the amount of neurotic behavior, the lower the marital quality. 8. The higher the level of education, the higher the marital quality. 9. The older the age at first marriage, the higher the marital quality. 10. The higher the social class, the higher the marital quality. 11. The better acquainted a couple is before marriage, the higher the marital quality. 12. The greater the individual's level of interpersonal skill functioning, the higher the marital quality. 13. The greater an individual's emotional health, the greater the marital quality. 14. The more positive an individual's self-concept, the greater the marital quality. 15. The greater the physical health of the marital partners, the greater the marital quality.	76. The greater the amount of premarital resources acquired for marital role functioning, the higher the marital quality.	
Parental Models		
16. The higher the marital quality in the family of orientation, the higher the marital quality in the family of procreation. 17. The higher the level of happiness in one's childhood, the higher the marital quality.	77. The greater the individual's exposure to adequate role models for marital functioning, the higher the marital quality.	

continued

Table 12.1.　Continued

FIRST-ORDER PROPOSITIONS	SECOND-ORDER PROPOSITIONS	THIRD-ORDER PROPOSITIONS
Homogamy		
18. The more positive the relationship between an individual and his or her parents, the higher the marital quality.		
Support from Significant Others		
19. The greater the parents' approval of their offspring's mate, the higher the marital quality. 20. The more an individual likes his or her future in-laws, the higher the marital quality. 21. The greater the opposition of friends to a marriage, the lower the marital quality.	78. The more support that significant others give to a couple, the higher the subsequent marital quality.	
Independent First-Order Propositions		
22. The greater the level of conventionality, the higher the marital quality. 23. Individuals who experience premarital sexual behavior which is consistent with their current value system will have higher marital quality than individuals who experience premarital sexual behavior which is not consistent with their value system. 24. Couples experiencing a premarital pregnancy will have a lower marital quality than couples not experiencing a premarital pregnancy. 25. The greater the likelihood that the motivation to marry is independent of problematic circumstantial factors, including internal or external pressures, the higher the marital quality.		

Homogamy

Sociologists have provided a great deal of evidence which suggests that homogamy operates as a norm in mate selection (e.g., Burgess and Wallin, 1953; Hollingshead, 1950; Burgess and Locke, 1953; Jacobsohn and Matheny, 1962; Kirkpatrick, 1963; Winch, 1971; Lewis, 1972, 1973a; Leslie, 1973; Clayton, 1975). It is not surprising, then, that when the norms of homogamy are violated, the possibility of negative consequences for marital quality and marital stability is increased. Propositions 1 through 6 reflect our generalizations from a wealth of data, although some of it is contradictory, that has accumulated with regard to the relationship between premarital homogamy and subsequent marital quality.

Two limitations to the credibility of these generaliza-

tions should be noted. First, the major part of the research on the consequences of homogamy versus lack of homogamy uses marital stability rather than an index of marital quality as the dependent variable. More specifically, comparisons of divorced versus nondivorced couples have been made with regard to variables such as differences in religious affiliation (Christensen and Barber, 1967), racial differences (Heer, 1974), age differences (Bumpass and Sweet, 1972), educational differences (Bumpass and Sweet, 1972), and social class differences (Scanzoni, 1968).

The research which addresses itself to the various aspects of marital quality is more scarce, more difficult to interpret, and for the most part considerably more dated. Our review has revealed a trend in which researchers appear to be moving away from studies of marital quality toward studies of marital stability. The movement from social interactional dynamics to social demographic characteristics of marriage parallels a widespread criticism of concepts such as marital adjustment, satisfaction, and happiness and the development and utilization of multivariate analytic techniques which are well suited for investigating large bodies of data (such as census data) in which variables such as marital stability, age, social class, education, race, and religion are easily obtained and controlled.

Thus we have been somewhat cautious about making inferences about marital quality from data on marital stability and from historical data which may or may not reflect the interaction patterns of contemporary marriages, although we have not ignored these data altogether.

The second limitation concerns the contradictory evidence for some of the propositions, much of which has been published during the last few years. Therefore, none of our first six propositions should be presented without qualification. Although we believe that the primary weight of evidence for each proposition suggests a positive relationship between homogamy and marital quality, there is at least one significant study for each independent variable suggesting for at least some subsample of the population studied that no relationship exists.[3] However, we found no study which suggested an inverse relationship. Therefore, we felt free to formulate by induction our first derived proposition: 75, "The greater the premarital homogamy, the higher the marital quality."

In attempting to explain marital adjustment, Burr (1973:111) has speculated that "equal status seems to be associated with the highest probability of marital adjustment, the husband having slightly higher status is next, and the husband having less status is associated with the least adequate adjustment." Apart from differences in marital quality which may result from relative status differences between husband and wife, we are confident in the sixth proposition that "the greater the absolute difference in status between husband and wife, the lower the marital quality." Burr (1973) considers a proposition similar to our Proposition 6 to be more abstract (second order), but since status is only one of many indicators of homogamy, we have presented Proposition 6 as a first-order proposition which, along with the first five propositions, is the basis for the derived proposition 75.

Resources

Nine first-order propositions (7–15) were induced to form our next second-order proposition: 76, "the greater the amount of premarital resources acquired for marital role functioning, the higher the marital quality." There is sufficient empirical evidence for this proposition, since premarital neurotic behavior seems to be negatively as-

sociated with marital quality (Pond et al., 1963; Burgess and Wallin, 1953), while social factors such as education (Cutright, 1971; Blood and Wolfe, 1960; Bumpass and Sweet, 1972; Havighurst et al., 1962; Goode, 1956), age at first marriage (Bumpass and Sweet, 1972; Landis, 1963; Inselberg, 1962; Spanier, 1971), social class (Landis, 1963; Cutright, 1971; Renne, 1970; Goode, 1956; Roth and Peck, 1951; Burgess and Wallin, 1953), and degree of acquaintance with the future spouse (Burgess and Locke, 1953; Goode, 1964; Spanier, 1971; Kirkpatrick, 1963) are all positively related to marital quality.

Furthermore, a high level of interpersonal skill functioning (Crouse et al., 1968; Burgess and Locke, 1953; Buerkle and Badgley, 1959; Levinger, 1965b), good physical health (Ballard, 1959; Renne, 1970; Burgess and Locke, 1953), a positive self-concept (Tharp, 1963; Aller, 1962; Buerkle, 1960; Gurin et al., 1960; Kotlar, 1962; Luckey, 1960a), and good emotional health (Burgess and Locke, 1953; Dean, 1966; Clark and van Sommers, 1961) can all be considered valuable skills or resources contributing to marital quality. Thus Propositions 7 through 15 lend support for our second-order proposition, 76, since there is evidence suggesting positive relationships between all of these variables and marital quality.

In sum, the independent variables suggested by these nine propositions reflect various premarital resources which undoubtedly contribute to a couple's preparation for marriage. Thus it can be suggested that the more resources acquired before marriage, the higher will be the marital quality. There are undoubtedly resources other than those mentioned above which contribute substantially to marital quality; however, those mentioned have received the greatest empirical documentation.

Parental Models

Proposition 77 is a second-order proposition derived from three first-order propositions (16, 17, 18) which deal with parent-child relationships and other childhood experiences. Proposition 77 states that "the greater the individual's exposure to adequate role models for marital functioning, the higher the marital quality." The three first-order propositions are each based on a significant number of studies from the psychiatric as well as the social psychological literature (Locke, 1947; Burgess and Wallin, 1953; Gurin et al., 1960; Stryker, 1964; Spanier, 1971; Pond et al., 1963; Dean, 1966). For instance, marital quality in the family of orientation is positively associated with marital quality in families of procreation, although it is quite likely that a number of intervening variables exist which, if controlled, would better explain such an association. Nevertheless, parents' marital quality still appears to be a good predictor of an individual's marital quality. Similarly, the more positive the individual's relationship with his or her parents and the greater the happiness the person reports having in childhood, the higher the subsequent marital quality. Thus it appears that effective role functioning by parental role models is transmitted to the offspring and subsequently contributes to the individual's own marital quality.

Support from Significant Others

Propositions 19 to 21 suggest that marital quality will be enhanced if parents, in-laws, and friends approve of the couple's relationship (Lewis, 1973b, 1975). These three propositions form the basis for the second-order Proposition 78, which states, "The more the support that significant others give to a couple, the higher the subsequent marital quality." Although substantial opposition to the marriage by nonsignificant others might influence subsequent marital quality to some degree, it is clear that opposition from significant others has a profound impact on marital quality (Mayer, 1961; Ryder et al., 1971; Driscoll et al., 1972; Lewis, 1973b, 1975). The empirical evidence also suggests that continued resistance by parents, friends, or in-laws to a marriage after it has begun may continue to adversely affect the quality of the relationship.

Independent First-Order Propositions

Four important first-order propositions (22–25) were sufficiently independent of other first-order propositions that they could not be induced further. Nevertheless, these propositions need to be stated and considered in a theory of marital quality.

Proposition 22, stating that "the greater the level of conventionality, the higher the marital quality," is based on evidence cited by Burr (1973:113) which relates 17 traits and marital adjustment.[4] These 17 traits can all be considered as indicators of conventional or nonconventional behavior, although we would add that for the majority of the traits (drinking and smoking, leisure-time activities, attitude toward premarital sex, desire for children, church membership and attendance, marriage by a religious leader, and perhaps others), standards of conventionality are perceived differently within our pluralistic society and may have changed significantly since many of the now dated studies were conducted. Thus new research must be conducted before we can state without equivocation that marital quality is always associated with conventionality, since certain types of nonconventional behavior may now or in the future enhance marital quality. New studies may give us much needed insight into this question.

The contradictory evidence relating premarital sexual behavior and subsequent marital quality has led us to speculate in Proposition 23 that individuals who experience premarital sexual behavior which is consistent with their current value system will have higher marital quality than individuals who experience premarital sexual behavior which is not consistent with their value system. This proposition, based upon our review of the literature, now may be outdated, since it undoubtedly reflects a relationship based on more traditional norms regarding the nonacceptability of premarital sexual behavior. Unfortunately, no recent evidence gives a definitive picture of what this relationship might be like now. Since it can be argued that premarital sexual intercourse per se is not as much the cause of subsequently poorer marital quality as is internal guilt, external pressures, or other intervening variables such as conventionality, traditionalism, or premarital pregnancy, we have proposed 23 as a logical and plausible alternative proposition.

Since premarital pregnancy has been found to be associated with both lower marital stability (e.g., Lowrie, 1965; Christensen and Meissner, 1953; Christensen and Rubinstein, 1956), and low marital quality (e.g., Spanier, 1971) in a number of studies, Proposition 24 notes that couples experiencing a premarital pregnancy will have lower marital quality than couples not experiencing a premarital pregnancy. This relationship has been found to exist even when educational level and age at marriage are held constant.

Proposition 25 is based on our inventory of findings and Burr's suggestion that certain types of motivation to marry are related to subsequently higher or lower marital quality. We have attempted to clarify Burr's reasoning by suggesting that there may be a powerful motivation for marriage which could have a positive or negative affect on marital quality, depending upon the source of that motivation. When, in the case of premarital pregnancy, the motivation is due to external pressures or avoidance of what the individual perceives as even greater negative consequences than marriage, then marital quality is likely to be adversely affected. When, on the other hand, the motivation to marry is due to a strong attraction which has withstood a significant test of time, the marital quality is likely to be positively affected. Proposition 25, therefore, states that "the greater the likelihood that the motivation to marry is independent of problematic circumstantial factors, including internal or external pressures, the higher the marital quality."

THEORY OF MARITAL QUALITY: PART II. SOCIAL AND ECONOMIC FACTORS

Intrapersonal factors, especially those evident prior to marriage, are not the only factors which influence the quality of marriages. Indeed, more propositions were identified in our search of the literature which linked marital quality to *inter*personal (dyadic) phenomena. Many of these were easily identified as social and economic characteristics of married couples which presumably affect the quality of their marriages (see Table 12.2).

Table 12.2.　Propositions Concerning the Relationships between Social and Economic Characteristics and Marital Quality

FIRST-ORDER PROPOSITIONS	SECOND-ORDER PROPOSITIONS	THIRD-ORDER PROPOSITIONS
Socioeconomic Factors		
26. The higher the occupational status of husbands, the higher the marital quality. 27. The more stable the spouses' economic resources and roles, the higher the marital quality. 28. The higher the family income, the higher the marital quality.	79. The greater the socioeconomic adequacy of the family, the greater the marital quality.	89. The greater the spouses' satisfaction with their life style, the greater their marital quality.
Wives' Employment		
29. The more the wife's satisfaction with her employment, the higher the marital quality. 30. The higher the husband's approval of his wife's employment, the higher the marital quality.	80. The more spouses' satisfaction with the wife's working, the more the marital quality.	
Household Composition		
31. The fewer the adults (other than husband and wife) in the household, the higher the marital quality. 32. The more the couple is able to control their fertility according to their own desires, the higher the marital quality.	81. The more the household composition is perceived as optimal, the higher the marital quality.	
Community Embeddedness		
33. The more the approval of marriage by friends and relatives, the higher the marital quality. 34. The greater the network of a couple's friends, the higher the marital quality. 35. The greater the couple's community participation, the higher the marital quality. 36. The less dense the residential population, the higher the marital quality.	82. The greater the couple's community embeddedness, the higher the marital quality.	

Socioeconomic Factors

Propositions 26–28 identify socioeconomic correlates of marital quality; i.e., the higher the occupational status of husbands, the higher the marital quality (Williamson, 1954; Kephart, 1954b; Monahan, 1955; Goode, 1956); the more stable the spouses' economic resources and roles, the higher the marital quality (Burgess and Locke, 1953; Winch, Ktsanes, and Ktsanes, 1954; Frazier, 1960); and the higher the family income, the higher the marital quality (Burgess and Cottrell, 1939; Locke, 1951; Burgess and Locke, 1953; Goode, 1962; Cutright, 1971).

A second-order proposition, Proposition 79, was induced from these three propositions; it states that "the greater the socioeconomic adequacy of the family, the greater the marital quality." This proposition also has some empirical support. Goode (1956) reports that the degree to which one's income is perceived as adequate is critical for marital adjustment, one measure of marital quality; and Green (1960) has evidence that marital satisfaction is not negatively influenced by economic failure if the husband is not expected to be a success. If the perception of *adequacy* is more important than the actual income, this would help to explain some of the apparent curvilinear relationships reported in the literature, whereby wives from very high- and very low-income families both report high marital satisfaction.

Wives' Employment

The relationships between wives' occupational characteristics and marital quality are more complex than those for husbands. Although unemployed wives generally report higher-quality marriages than do employed women (Stoltz, 1960; Nye, 1961; Axelson, 1963; Grover, 1963) and when both spouses pursue careers they report decreased marital quality, probably due to work (role) overloads (Fogarty, Rapoport, and Rapoport, 1971), other factors than employment-nonemployment appear to be equally important. For instance, social class seems to make a difference, since employment of the wife is reported to increase marital quality in lower income groups (Blood and Wolfe, 1960). Blood and Wolfe (1960:101) explain this relationship as follows: "When the husband's income is below average, the wife's earnings make a big difference in the family's ability to gain its desired standard of living. Working seems urgently desirably both to the wife and her husband who rewards her with understanding and appreciation. Thus her work strengthens the marriage bonds."

Freedom of choice, however, also appears to intervene in the relationship between wives' working and marital quality, since it has been found that the degree to which a woman is economically free to choose between home and outside labor involvement also affects marital quality (Orden and Bradburn, 1968). One might interpret this finding to mean that a wife employed because of economic necessity rather than personal choice may, because of her resentment, negatively evaluate her marriage. The same reasoning may explain why part-time employment is also associated with higher marital quality (Orden and Bradburn, 1968).

Proposition 29 was induced from a large number of findings such as those given above. This proposition states that "the more the wife's satisfaction with her employment, the higher the marital quality." This proposition seems to be supported by the work of Fogarty, Rapoport, and Rapoport (1971), who found that even when middle-class wives chose to work but experienced guilt and tensions about neglecting their families, their employment appeared to decrease their marital adjustment. This has been found to be especially true for mothers of preschool children (Orden and Bradburn, 1968). The complements of this are the findings that wherever employed wives evidenced high work commitment (Safilios-Rothschild, 1970) or wherever their working freed the couple psychologically for enjoying more sociability together (Orden and Bradburn, 1968), the wife's employment appeared to increase marital adjustment. Both of these findings suggest that job satisfactions give wives a sense of meaning and worthiness which may generalize to greater satisfactions with their marriages.

The wife's satisfaction with her employment, however, is only part of the picture. Proposition 30 was induced from a number of empirical findings which suggested that "the higher the husband's approval of his wife's employment, the higher the marital quality" (Axelson, 1963; Goode, 1964; Nye, 1961). Proposition

80 is thus an abstracted combination of 29 and 30 and is stated in terms of both spouses' satisfaction.

Household Composition

Propositions 31 and 32 were induced from a number of findings which suggest respectively that "the fewer the adults (other than husband and wife) in the household, the higher the marital quality" (Clark and van Sommers, 1961) and "the more the couple is able to control their fertility according to their own desires, the higher the marital quality" (Farber and Blackman, 1956; Christensen, 1968). Proposition 31 is consonant with our American norm of neolocal residence and our avoidance of intimate in-law relationships (Duvall, 1954). However, when the "extra" persons are children, the empirical findings are not unanimous. In general, however, marital quality has been inversely related to family size (Christensen and Philbrick, 1952).

There have been a number of notable exceptions to these findings; e.g., Farber and Blackman (1956), Luckey (1966), and Luckey and Bain (1970) have found no relationship between measures of marital satisfaction and the number of children in a household. More recent studies, however, indicate that marital quality is probably more related to child density, i.e., the ratio of children per years of marriage (Hurley and Palonen, 1967; Figley, 1973). It would appear that high child density affects both the instrumental and expressive functioning of marriage by taking many of the family's material resources and time away from the husband-wife relationship. Nevertheless, the greatest amount of empirical evidence suggests that, overall, it is a couple's ability to match their actual fertility with their desired fertility which is most related to marital quality.

Again, Proposition 81 combines 31 and 32 to make a more conclusive statement, i.e., "The more the household composition is perceived as optimal, the higher the marital quality." In sum, it would seem that although the presence of children under some conditions is positively related to marital stability, the perception of an optimal household size is more related to marital quality.

Community Embeddedness

Propositions 33 to 36 suggest that the more the approval of a couple's marriage by friends and relatives and the more the social embeddedness within their network of friends and community associates, the higher the quality of their marriage. The first empirical proposition, 33, "The more the approval of marriage by friends and relatives, the higher the marital quality," frequently has been suggested in family literature (Waller and Hill, 1951; Kirkpatrick, 1955; Bee, 1959). Evidence that familial and peer support is efficacious in mate selection and positively related to the quality of even premarital relationships has recently come to light (Ryder et al., 1971; Lewis, 1972, 1973a, 1973b).

Proposition 34, "The greater the network of a couple's friends, the higher the marital quality," is supported by a number of empirical findings (Locke and Karlsson, 1952; Burgess and Licke, 1953; Kirkpatrick, 1955; Bee, 1959). These findings suggest that it is not only the number of friends that the couple have in common and the number of friends each partner has ever had which are salient, but also the congruence of expectations between the couple and their friends. This proposition, nevertheless, must be understood in light of the qualification that wherever friends become a strong influence, they may decrease marital quality by being a competitive force. For instance, the more confidants the wife of a blue-collar worker has outside her family, the less happy is her marriage (Komarovsky, 1962). Furthermore, the more that spouses are influenced by their peers, the more unhappy their marital relationships (Whitehurst, 1968).

Proposition 35 was induced from a number of findings which indicated high correlations between a number of marital quality indices and memberships in voluntary organizations (Burgess and Locke, 1953; Kirkpatrick, 1955). This proposition, in turn, was seen as having a common denominator with the previous two propositions and Proposition 36, so as to nicely form the second-order Proposition 82, which concludes that "the greater the couple's community embeddedness, the higher the marital quality." The concept of embeddedness has received some attention recently (Goode, 1963; B. Adams, 1975) and appears to have some efficacy in explaining not only marital stability but marital quality as well. What the exact mechanisms are that may account for this relationship are not yet clear, although they probably involve personal support and reinforcement of the marital relationship.

THEORY OF MARITAL QUALITY: PART III. INTERPERSONAL AND DYADIC FACTORS

The largest number of propositions in our inventory were those which linked marital quality to dyadic factors or interpersonal characteristics in the relationship. This at first inspection may suggest circular reasoning. This criticism would only be warranted, however, if the independent variables in the propositions were also taken as indicators of marital quality, whereas the typical indicators of marital quality have been those of marital satisfaction and marital adjustment, neither of which appear as independent variables in these propositions.

Positive Regard

Propositions 37 to 42 (see Table 12.3) identify as correlates of marital quality a number of interpersonal

factors:[5] perceived similarities (Kelly, 1941; Luckey, 1960a, 1960b, 1961; Byrne and Blaylock, 1963; Tharp, 1963; Coombs, 1966; Murstein, 1967; Trost, 1967); ease of communication (Coombs, 1966; Lewis, 1966, 1967); perceived physical, mental, and sexual attractiveness (Kirkpatrick and Cotton, 1951; Burgess and Locke, 1953; Kirkpatrick, 1955; Murstein, 1970; Berscheid et al., 1971; G. Adams, 1975; Jackson and Huston, 1975; Berscheid and Walster, 1976); positive evaluations of the other (Kelly, 1941; Tharp, 1963; Luckey, 1964; Murstein and Glaudin, 1968); value consensus (Locke and Karlsson, 1952; Farber and McHale, 1959; Schellenberg, 1960; Kerckhoff and Davis, 1962; Coombs, 1966); and validation of the self by the other (Lewis, 1973a).

Since all of these propositions deal with some aspect of couples' positive regard for their partners, the induction of these six first-order propositions to a more general proposition resulted in Proposition 83, "The more positive the regard between the spouses, the greater the marital quality." Surprisingly, although Reiss (1960) posited rapport, "a felt presence of ease and relaxation," as the initial process in the development of the heterosexual love relationship, researchers of marital relationships have not reported examining evidence for or against this derived proposition.

Emotional Gratification

Propositions 43 to 53 were all found to link marital (and other heterosexual pair) quality to the expression of affection (Kelly, 1941; Locke, 1951; Kirkpatrick, 1955; Pineo, 1961; Levinger, 1965a); to esteem or respect between partners (Goode, 1956; Dittes, 1959; Walster, 1965; Holstein et al., 1971); to spousal performance in social-emotional areas rather than to instrumental (task) performance (Kotlar, 1962; Tharp, 1963; Levinger, 1964); to encouraging each other's personal growth (Dentler and Pineo, 1960; Rogers, 1972); to equalitarian power structures (Locke and Karlsson, 1952; Kirkpatrick, 1955; Christensen, 1958; Pond, Ryle and Hamilton, 1963; Stryker, 1964; Levinger, 1964); to boundary maintenance (Rapoport and Rapoport, 1965; Kemper, 1968; Lewis, 1973b); to emotional interdependence (Burgess and Locke, 1953; Pineo, 1961); to love (Winter, 1958; Reik, 1963; Knox, 1970; Orlinsky, 1972; Otto, 1972; Rubin, 1974); to sexual satisfaction (Landis, Poffenberger, and Poffenberger, 1950; Burgess and Locke, 1953; Dentler and Pineo, 1960; Kirkpatrick, 1955; Clark and Wallin, 1965; Levinger, 1965a); to greater congruence between one's ideal spousal concept and spouse as perceived (Burgess and Locke, 1953; Luckey, 1960a, 1960b, 1961; Goode, 1962; Tharp, 1963; Hawkins and Johnsen, 1969); and to the couple's identity as a couple (Waller and Hill, 1951; Lewis, 1972). Since the common denominator of all the propositions seemed to be the satisfaction of emotional gratifications, Proposition 84

Table 12.3. **Propositions Concerning Interpersonal (Dyadic) Characteristics and Marital Quality**

FIRST-ORDER PROPOSITIONS	SECOND-ORDER PROPOSITIONS	THIRD-ORDER PROPOSITIONS
Positive Regard		
37. The greater the perceived similarities between spouses, the greater the marital quality.	83. The more positive the regard between the spouses, the greater the marital quality.	90. The greater the rewards from spousal interaction, the greater the marital quality.
38. The greater the ease of communication between spouses, the greater the marital quality.		
39. The greater the perceived physical, mental, and sexual attractiveness of the other, the greater the marital quality.		
40. The more positive the evaluations of the other, the more the marital quality.		
41. The more consensus in values, the greater the marital quality.		
42. The more the validation of the self by the other, the more the marital quality.		
Emotional Gratification		
43. The greater the expression of affection, the greater the marital quality.	84. The more the emotional gratification between the spouses, the more the marital quality.	
44. The more the esteem (respect) between the spouses, the more the marital quality.		
45. The greater the spouses' social-emotional performances, the greater the marital quality.		
46. The more the spouses encourage each other's personal growth, the more the marital quality.		
47. The more equalitarian the marriage, the more the marital quality.		
48. The greater the boundary maintenance, the more the marital quality.		
49. The greater the emotional interdependence between the spouses, the greater the marital quality.		
50. The greater the love between the spouses, the greater the marital quality.		
51. The more the sexual satisfaction, the more the marital quality.		
52. The greater the congruence between one's ideal spousal concept and the actual concept of one's spouse, the greater the marital quality.		
53. The more the couple's identity as a couple, the more the marital quality.		
Communication		
54. The more the self-disclosure between the spouses, the greater the marital quality.	85. The more effective the communication between spouses, the more the marital quality.	
55. The more the sharing of violations of expectations, the more the marital quality.		

continued

Table 12.3.   Continued

FIRST-ORDER PROPOSITIONS	SECOND-ORDER PROPOSITIONS	THIRD-ORDER PROPOSITIONS
Communication		
56. The more accurate the non-verbal communication, the more the marital quality.		
57. The greater the symbolic environment (meaning) between spouses, the greater the marital quality.		
58. The greater the frequency of successful communication, the greater the marital quality.		
59. The more accurate the role-taking by spouses, the more the marital quality.		
60. The greater the congruence of role perceptions, the greater the marital quality.		
61. The more the understanding between spouses, the more the marital quality.		
62. The more the empathy, the more the marital quality.		
Role Fit		
63. The more the need complementarity, the more the marital quality.	86. The greater the role fit, the greater the marital quality.	
64. The more the role complementarity, the more the marital quality.		
65. The more congruence between the role expectations of one and the role performances of the other, the more the marital quality.		
66. The more the similarity of personality traits, the more the marital quality.		
67. The more the role sharing, the more the marital quality.		
68. The greater the sexual compatibility, the more the marital quality.		
Interaction		
69. The greater the companionship, the greater the marital quality.	87. The greater the interaction, the greater the marital quality.	
70. The more the shared activities, the more the marital quality.		
71. The more the dyadic interpenetration, the more the marital quality.		
72. The less the degree of physical separation, the more the marital quality.		
73. The more effective the problem solving, the more the marital quality.		
74. The greater the joint church attendance, the greater the marital quality.		

states that "the more the emotional gratification between the spouses, the more the marital quality."

Communication

A number of first-order propositions, 54–62, relate marital quality to the communication skills of spouses, i.e., to self-disclosure (Levinger and Senn, 1967; Taylor, 1967), including the disclosure of violations of expectations (Cutler and Dyer, 1965); to the accuracy of nonverbal communication (Navran, 1967; Kahn, 1970); to a common symbolic environment between spouses (Trost, 1964) and greater agreement on connotative meanings (Katz, 1965); to the frequency of successful communication (Hobart and Klausner, 1959; Navran, 1967; Bienvenu, 1970); and to more accurate role taking (Tharp, 1963; Stryker, 1964; Clements, 1967; Lewis, 1973a). There are a few negative findings (e.g., Stryker, 1964) in reference to the last proposition. Nevertheless, the majority of the findings appear to be consistent with Proposition 59.

Finally, in terms of communication, marital quality also appears to be related to the congruence of role perceptions (Tharp, 1963; Kotlar, 1965); to understanding between spouses (Kirkpatrick, 1955); and to empathy, the intellectual understanding of another (Burgess and Wallin, 1953; Dymond, 1954; Foote and Cottrell, 1955; Buerkle and Badgley, 1959; Lewis, 1966). A number of qualifications have been raised in regard to this particular proposition (Corsini, 1956; Hobart and Klausner, 1959; Luckey, 1961; Stuckert, 1963). However, they in no way influence the general induction of these propositions, which resulted in Proposition 85, "The more effective the communication between spouses, the more the marital quality."

Role Fit

A number of propositions in our inventory revolve around the concept of role fit, which may be partly defined as the absence of role conflict. There are a few studies which support Proposition 63, "The more the need complementarity, the more the marital quality," which is strikingly similar to the hypothesis of complementary needs developed by Winch et al. (1954). This proposition has limited empirical support (Strauss, 1947; Martinson, 1955; Huntington, 1958; Kerckhoff and Davis, 1962; Bermann, 1966). However, as a number of reviews have indicated, there is also a sizable number of studies which have found no support for this proposition, leading us to to the tentative conclusion that the evidence is not yet complete in regard to this proposition (Lewis, 1972).

Empirical evidence, however, is not as controversial for Proposition 64, "The more the role complementarity, the more the marital quality," since it is supported by studies conducted by Ort (1950), Couch (1958), Spiegel (1960), and Murstein (1967, 1970). In a generic sense, marital quality seems to be related more to the congruence between the role expectations of one spouse and the role performances of the other spouse (Ort, 1950; Mangus, 1957; Burr, 1967, 1973), and thus as Tharp (1963) interpreted these findings, it may be more a matter of the spouses' consensus on roles than any specific pattern of roles that is conducive to satisfying marital relationships.

Finally, marital quality has been found to relate to similarities in spousal personalities (Dymond, 1954; Christensen, 1958; Pickford et al., 1966), although there are other studies which do not support this proposition (Burgess and Wallin, 1953; Trost, 1967); to role sharing (Vogel, 1960); and to sexual compatibility (Locke, 1951; Burgess and Locke, 1953; Kephart, 1954a; Dentler and Pineo, 1960; Clark and Wallin, 1965). A more general statement of Propositions 63 to 68 is the derived Proposition 86, "The greater the role fit, the greater the marital quality." This proposition not only makes theoretical sense but seems to be supported at a fairly abstract level in the family conflict literature, which not surprisingly has focused on conflict rather than fit.

Interaction

Propositions 69 to 74 all refer to either the quantity or quality of marital interaction. Proposition 69 states a positive relationship between marital quality and companionship (Kirkpatrick, 1955; Blood and Wolfe, 1960; Levinger, 1965a; Hawkins, 1968), while Proposition 70 links marital quality and shared activities (Bee, 1959; Farber and McHale, 1959; Blood and Wolfe, 1960; Pond, Ryle, and Hamilton, 1963), and Proposition 71 relates marital quality to dyadic interpenetration (Waller and Hill, 1951; Altman, 1974).

Similarly, Proposition 72 reflects an inverse relationship between the degree of physical separation, such as the occupancy of separate bedrooms, and marital quality (Terman, 1938; Hill, 1949; Vogel, 1960). The quality of spousal interaction is reflected in Proposition 73, which ties effective problem solving to marital quality (Bee, 1959; Mathews and Milanovich, 1963), while the quantity of spousal interaction is indirectly reflected in Proposition 74, "The greater the joint church attendance, the greater the marital quality" (Chesser, 1957; Locke, 1951). It should be noted, however, that the findings which support the last proposition were geared more to marital stability than to marital quality. In sum, all of the propositions concerning interaction were judged to be subsets of a more general proposition, derived Proposition 87, "The greater the interaction, the greater the marital quality."

SOME THIRD-ORDER PROPOSITIONS

The process of induction was finally carried out to a third level of proposition formation. For instance, from the second-order propositions in Table 12.1 we were able to further generalize Proposition 88, "The greater the social and personal resources available for adequate marital role functioning, the higher the subsequent marital quality." From the second-order propositions in Table 12.2 we derived Proposition 89, "The greater the spouses' satisfaction with their life style, the greater their marital quality," while similarly from the propositions in Table 12.3 we induced third-order Proposition 90, "The greater the rewards from spousal interaction, the greater the marital quality."

THE PROMISE OF A SOCIAL EXCHANGE THEORY

The third-order propositions derived from our inventory, especially the last proposition, sound as if they were part and parcel of a social exchange theory of marital quality. This is due to the emphasis upon rewards and satisfactions. As we noted in an earlier portion of this chapter, the few partial theories of marital stability and marital quality that exist have also been inclined toward a social exchange approach. Burr (1973) stated a number of his propositions on marital satisfaction from an exchange viewpoint, while Nye, White, and Friederes (1969) stated their most general propositions on family stability in terms of the *positive affect* between spouses and the *constraints* against dissolution, imagery which is not far removed from notions of rewards and costs. Similarly, Levinger's (1965a) key concepts of *attractions* to remain in a marriage and *barriers* against breakup, although explicitly defined within a field theory framework, are also compatible with exchange theory assumptions and propositions.

The social exchange view of human interaction, following especially Thibaut and Kelley (1959), Homans (1950, 1958, 1961), and Blau (1964), presupposes that if the personal profit from interaction is rewarding, there is a building up of positive sentiments, i.e., a relationship continues to grow, whereas if the costs of interaction are less than the profits, the relationship probably will terminate, or at least will slow in its growth or development.

A great amount of premarital and attraction research concurs with the primary assumptions of a social exchange model of marital quality and stability. For example, Newcomb, in his study of developing relationships (1956, 1961), views liking, respect, and trust as interpersonal rewards which are essential for the growth of relationships, that is, for their movement from superficial to more intimate bases. Levinger and Snoek (1972), in

their proposal of relationship levels, assume that the development of relationships is continually contingent upon felt satisfactions. The satisfactions are based not only upon reward and cost experiences in the past but also upon anticipation of rewards and costs in future interaction.

This framework has not been utilized as thoroughly in the study of marital relationships as it has been used in the study of the acquaintance process and short-term groups. One of the reasons for this is that not only is marital study a more complex task, but, in spite of the principle of reciprocity, marriages often evidence asymmetrical exchanges and contain many different levels of exchange resources, rewards, and costs (Edwards, 1969). Although this framework has been used less to study marriages, it is most reasonable to assume that the forecast of future rewards, as balanced against future costs, as well as the memory of cumulative rewards and costs throughout the history of the marital relationship, do greatly affect both the quality and the continuance of marital relationships. In spite of the great complexity of marital relationships, the continued development of a social exchange theory of marital quality and stability appears to be one of the most fruitful tasks that could be undertaken by family theorists. In other words, the potential for a social exchange theory in this area is very promising indeed, as viewed from our inventory of propositions.

THEORETICAL INTEGRATION

A Typology of Marital Quality and Marital Stability

This chapter began with the objective of attempting to explain why some marriages fail and others do not. In the preceding sections we have presented, induced, and integrated a large number of research findings which provide some explanatory propositions about marital quality. It is clear to us, however, that an integration of these propositions alone will not be sufficient for developing a comprehensive theory of marital quality and marital stability. Indeed, the dependent variable is far too complex to allow concise and heuristic theoretical statements. Instead, we wish to take a step back from our inventory and the many studies, propositions, and previous attempts at theorizing to present what we believe to be a useful theoretical typology.

We have already made the observation that given any level of marital quality, some couples will divorce and others will not. Although marital quality and marital stability are highly correlated (Spanier, 1976), it is likely that the threshold variables discussed earlier operate as forces which allow some couples to pass over the threshold and separate (and subsequently divorce) while not allowing others to pass. Thus it is probable that there are some marriages of high quality which terminate in separation or divorce and some marriages of low quality which remain intact in spite of what may be an intolerable relationship.

Our typology makes use of assumptions from the social exchange framework and examines the relationships between four components, i.e., marital quality, marital stability, intradyadic factors which influence marital quality, and extradyadic factors which influence marital stability. Marital quality is dichotomized in Figure 12.3 as high to low (although conceptually a continuum is represented) while marital stability must be viewed in terms of the dichotomous status of intact or not intact.

Figure 12.3 diagrammatically depicts a typology of marital quality and marital stability on which all marital relationships may be represented on both a quality dimension and a stability dimension. Furthermore, the quality and stability of a relationship may vary over the life cycle, and consequently there is value in assessing a relationship at more than one point in time. For example, a marriage that is of high quality early in the relationship may be of low quality at some later point in the relationship. There may also be differences from one couple to the next, and between marriage cohorts, since the factors relevant to marital quality also vary with social and cultural changes. At a given point in time, then, we can assess a marital partnership and judge it to be of either:

   I. High quality and high stability
  II. High quality and low stability
 III. Low quality and low stability
 IV. Low quality and high stability.

Figure 12.3.   An Exchange Typology of Marital Quality and Marital Stability

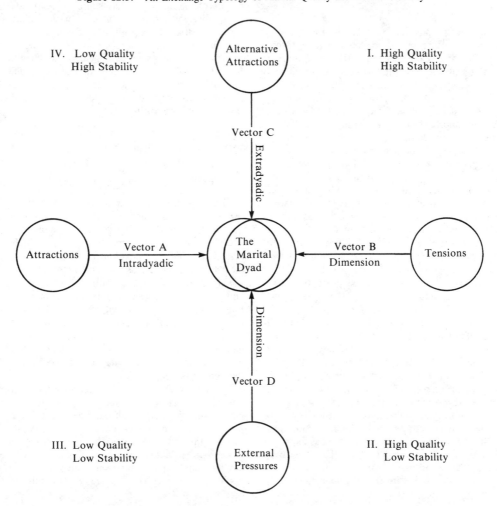

These four combinations correspond to the four quadrants in Figure 12.3. Since stability is an outcome variable, the quality components of a marriage with low stability are considered to be the qualities at the time the relationship terminated.

Our taxonomy suggests that a marital dyad will, at a given point in time, be found somewhere in one of the four quadrants illustrated in Figure 12.3. The couple may move, over time, within a given quadrant or from one quadrant to another. The dimensions presented on the axes in the figure represent the two primary dimensions which will determine the quality and stability of the relationship—or, stated differently, in which quadrant and at what location within the quadrant the couple will be found.

The horizontal axis represents intradyadic factors— namely, those factors which affect the *quality* of the marriage. As noted previously, intradyadic factors may be influenced by several premarital predispositional factors as well as a number of factors which become prominent after the wedding. Marital adjustment, satisfaction, happiness, conflict and role strain, communication, and integration are examples of the concepts relevant to marital quality. Within any dyad there are to be found a host of costs and rewards which operate in this particular relationship to move the dyad along the continuum from high to low marital quality. The rewards associated with marital quality can be defined in terms of sources of attraction to the dyadic relationship, which move a couple in the direction of high marital quality. The costs can be defined in terms of tensions, conflict, disillusionment, disagreements, lack of cohesion, and problems in communication, which move a couple in the direction of low marital quality.

The vertical axis represents extradyadic factors— namely, those factors which affect the *stability* of the marriage. The extradyadic factors are those influences which will determine whether a couple will cross the threshold described earlier. As with the intradyadic factors, there are undoubtedly both costs and rewards associated with terminating an unsuccessful marriage. Since the transition to separation and divorce is rarely an entirely positive experience (Goode, 1956), it is likely that an individual will see some attraction to as well as some avoidance of the separation on the other side of the threshold. The extradyadic factors associated with high marital stability are those external pressures and social and psychological forces which prevent an individual from crossing the threshold to separation. Strict divorce laws, strong social stigma, strict adherence to or influence from restrictive religious doctrine, low evaluation of nonmarital alternatives, high degree of commitment to marriage, and high tolerance for marital conflict and tension are factors which are likely to influence the dyad in the direction of high marital stability. Conversely, liberal divorce laws, little social stigma, little or no

adherence to or influence from religious doctrine, high evaluation of nonmarital alternatives, low degree of commitment to marriage, and low tolerance for marital conflict and tension will influence the dyad in the direction of lower marital stability. Stated differently, the strength of the alternate attractions for the individual outside the marriage are balanced against the external pressures to determine whether or not the marital dyad will have high or low marital stability.

It should be reemphasized that a couple may move from one quadrant of Figure 12.3 to another or to different points within a given quadrant over time, depending on the balance between the positive and negative intradyadic factors and the balance of extradyadic factors. For any given dyad, four factors may be plotted to give an assessment of the couple's current marriage. The vectors may be combined or summated to produce one net vector which will place the dyad at one point on the visual map presented in Figure 12.3. For example, a couple for whom the attraction vector (vector A) of intradyadic factors is considerably more intense than the tension vector (vector B) and for whom the external pressures vector (vector D) is more intense than the alternative attractions vector (vector C) will be located somewhere in quadrant I.

Intradyadic and extradyadic factors must be jointly considered, and thus dyads can be located at any point within a given quadrant. Our model is necessarily oversimplified in that we assume an arbitrary dichotomy between high and low marital quality, but this is of consequence only insofar as it is important to know the precise point where a couple might have moved from one quadrant to another. A more complex model would provide for a nonstationary vertical axis, or multiple vertical axes to allow for more gradations of marital quality.

The model attempts to demonstrate that an exchange framework is useful for understanding the balance between marital quality and marital stability. Furthermore, it illustrates a fact often overlooked in marriage research—namely, that marriages of all four types exist in any given society. The magnitude of each of the four vectors may vary from one couple to the next, from time to time for a given couple, and from one culture to the next. Thus, for example, a society with very restrictive marital dissolution laws would increase the magnitude of the external pressures extradyadic factor vector (D), and consequently we might expect to see a greater number of couples falling into either quadrant I or quadrant IV. Since it can be argued that only a small number of couples in any culture fall into quadrant II, the society with strict divorce laws would be expected to have a disproportionately high number of couples in quadrant IV.

The typology allows for the possibility of a couple being found directly on one of the borderlines. For instance, a marriage of very low quality may be balancing precariously on the border between quadrants III and IV if the extradyadic factor vectors (C and D) are equal in strength. This couple has unsatisfactory marriage but is unable to resolve whether there should be a separation or not.

Couples found in quadrant I represent the ideal. Indeed, an intact marriage of high quality is what virtually all married couples aspire to. A good deal of North American research indicates that the majority of couples can be found in this quadrant at some time during their marriage (most likely in the early years), but that only a minority of couples can be found in this quadrant at any single point in time (Spanier, 1976; Spanier, Lewis, and Cole, 1975; Hicks and Platt, 1970; Spanier, 1971; Rollins and Feldman, 1970).

Quadrant II marriages are rare. There have been no studies specifically investigating couples who have marriages of high quality which terminate in separation or divorce, but we are aware that such marriages do exist. It is plausible that the relative proportion of married couples who will fall into this category will increase in the future. As divorce laws and social response to divorce become more liberal, it is possible that greater numbers of married persons who have relatively well-adjusted and conflict-free marriages may opt for termination of the relationship due to even more attractive alternatives. We can speculate that changes in personal preferences, life styles, and redefinitions of the necessity for permanence of marital and family relationships may allow more couples who have good marriages to divorce. We must await future trends and research on these interesting trends to learn more about quadrant II marriages.

Quadrant III dyads represent an increasingly greater number of marriages. These are the relationships with low marital quality that eventually terminate. In the United States, for example, Glick and Norton (1976) conservatively estimate that more than one in three recent first marriages and 45 to 50 percent of all recent marriages are likely to terminate in divorce. The continuing increase in United States divorce rates in recent years suggests to us that Glick and Norton's estimate may again need to be revised upward. A couple found in quadrant III has a marriage which can be characterized by conflict, tension, disenchantment, unhappiness, and poor adjustment. Unlike quadrant IV couples, whom we shall discuss shortly, these couples find marriage to be sufficiently intolerable, unrewarding, or troublesome that they finally divorce. Clearly, for these couples, the extradyadic factors are weighted such that the alternate attractions anticipated after separation or divorce are more influential than the external pressures which would encourage the couple to remain married.

The couples in quadrant IV undoubtedly comprise a significant portion of married persons. The couples found in quadrant IV have marriages of low quality, but have been unable or unwilling to cross the threshold to separation or divorce. This quadrant might include the de-

vitalized or conflict-habituated relationships discussed by Cuber and Harroff (1965). As divorce becomes a more realistic alternative to a marriage of low quality, we would expect the proportion of couples in quadrant IV to decrease. In societies with minimal divorce, there are often a number of social, cultural, and legal reasons which influence the low divorce rates. Although there are certainly real differences from one culture to the next, and variable rates within cultures depending on social class, religiosity, and other social factors, it can be hypothesized that much of the variation between and within cultures can be influenced by changes in divorce laws. Thus divorce rates are an indicator of marital stability, but not necessarily marital quality. The high correlation between marital quality and marital stability is most likely to be demonstrated in countries like the United States, where the laws easily permit divorce and where other sociocultural pressures which might limit divorce are not profound. Indeed, it can be suggested that such pressures are becoming increasingly relaxed in America.

A Theory of Marital Quality and Marital Stability

To summarize, our early theorizing about the quality and stability of marriage led us to locate in the empirical literature 74 first-order propositions. We then induced 13 second-order propositions, which relate four marital variables, four social and economic variables, and five interpersonal variables to the dependent variable of marital quality. Finally, we induced three third-order propositions from these second-order propositions, which related social and personal resources, spousal satisfaction with one's life style, and rewards from spousal interaction to marital quality. Our theory of marital quality and marital stability is in Figure 12.4.

The typology described above contains three implicit assumptions which are among the major propositions of our theory. The central proposition of the theory, assumed throughout the entire chapter, can be stated in propositional form as follows: "The greater the marital quality, the greater the marital stability" (Proposition 91). We also noted in the typology the strong, negative influence of alternative attractions and the positive, external pressures upon couples to remain married. Thus our final conceptualization, as described in Figure 12.4, also presents these two sets of external forces as contingent (or control) variables which influence the central *relationship* between marital quality and marital stability.

In other words, alternative attractions negatively influence the level of *marital quality* and subsequently *marital stability,* whereas normative constraints to remain married, e.g., pressures from families, friends, religious institutions, etc., positively influence the level of *marital quality* needed for the continuance of the relationship, or *marital stability.* Proposition 92 thus states, "Alternative attractions to a marriage negatively influence the strength

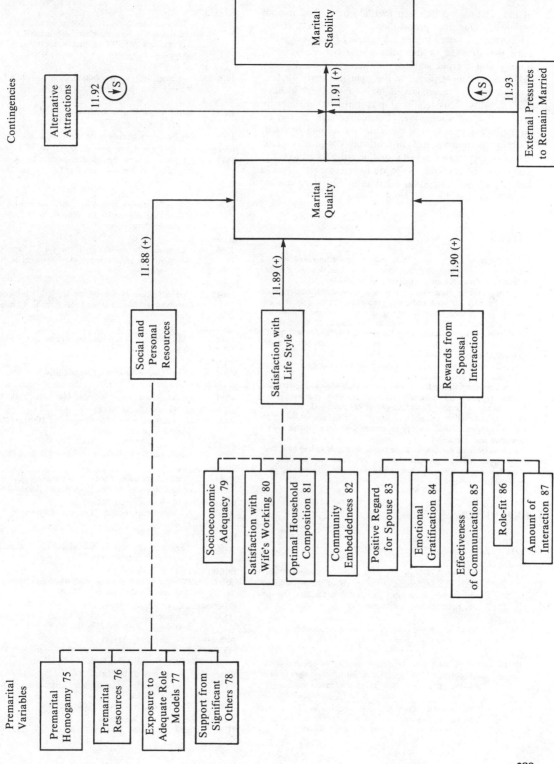

Figure 12.4. A Theory of Marital Quality and Marital Stability

of the relationship between marital quality and marital stability.'' Our final proposition, 93, conversely states, ''External pressures to remain married positively influence the strength of the relationship between marital quality and marital stability.'' These two contingency relationships are depicted at the right in Figure 12.4.

In summary, marriages of high quality tend to have high stability. This relationship is mitigated at times by more attractive alternatives, but, conversely, it may be strengthened by external pressures to remain married, such as normative and institutional constraints. This rather simple model, when tested, may be found to better integrate past research, to guide future research, and to help understand important relationships between marital quality and stability.

NOTES

1. ''Unnatural death'' refers here only to the circumstance where a married person murders his or her spouse. Any other death of a spouse is defined as natural, even if premature or by accident.

2. For example, Burr often states a curvilinear relationship when the curvilinearity has been artificially produced by plotting the relationship and putting both positive and negative scales on the positive side of the abscissa. See Burr (1973:106) as an example. In this example, the alleged curvilinear relationship between age difference and marital adjustment exists only because Burr changes his independent variable from age difference to husband's age relative to wife's.

3. Udry (1973) has illustrated this conclusion through a review of social factors involved in marital success.

4. Adaptability, desire for children, church attendance, church membership, conventional behavior, drinking and smoking, emotional stability, regularity of employment, happiness of childhood, leisure-time activities, place of marriage, marriage by a religious leader, membership in organizations, absence of neuroses, savings, attitude toward premarital sex, sociability.

5. A number of the empirical propositions which follow have been based on the study of premarital pairs. They have been included due to the fact that they too involve heterosexual love relationships at an earlier point in time.

REFERENCES

ADAMS, B. N.
1975   *The Family.* Chicago: Rand McNally.

ADAMS, G.
1975   ''Psychological attraction, personal characteristics and social behavior: Investigation of the effects of the psychological attractiveness stereotype.'' Unpublished Doctoral Dissertation, Pennsylvania State University.

ALLER, A.
1962   ''Role of the self-concept in student marital adjustment.'' *Family Life Coordinator* 11 (April):43–45.

ALTMAN, I.
1974   ''The communication of interpersonal attitudes: An ecological approach.'' In T. L. Huston (ed.), *Foundations of Interpersonal Attraction.* New York: Academic Press.

AXELSON, L. J.
1963   ''The marital adjustment and marital role definitions of husbands of working and non-working wives.'' *Journal of Marriage and Family Living* 25 (May):189–96.

BALLARD, R. G.
1959   ''The interrelatedness of alcoholism and marital conflict: 3. The interaction between marital conflict and alcoholism as seen through MMPI's of marriage partners.'' *American Journal of Orthopsychiatry* 29 (July):528–46.

BARTZ, K. W., AND F. I. NYE
1970   ''Early marriage: A propositional formulation.'' *Journal of Marriage and the Family* 32:258–68.

BEE, L. S.
1959   *Marriage and Family Relations.* New York: Harper.

BELL, W., AND J. A. MAU (EDS.)
1971   *The Sociology of the Future.* New York: Russell Sage.

BERSCHEID, E., K. DION, E. WALSTER, AND G. W. WALSTER
1971   ''Physical attractiveness and dating choice: A test of the matching hypothesis.'' *Journal of Experimental Social Psychology* 7:173–89.

BERSCHEID, E. AND E. WALSTER
1976   ''Physical attractiveness.'' In L. Berkowitz (ed.), *Advances in Experimental Social Psychology,* vol. 7. New York: Academic Press.

BERMANN, E. A.
1966   ''Compatability and stability in the dyad.'' Paper presented before the American Psychological Association, New York City, September.

BERNARD, J.
1964   ''The adjustment of married mates.'' In T. Christensen (ed.), *Handbook of Marriage and the Family.* Chicago: Rand McNally.

BIENVENU, J., SR.
1970   ''Measurement of marital communication.'' *Family Coordinator* 19:26–31.

BLALOCK, M., JR.
1969   *Theory Construction.* Englewood Cliffs, N.J.: Prentice-Hall.

BLAU, P. M.
1964   *Exchange and Power in Social Life.* New York: Wiley.

BLOOD, R. O., JR. AND D. M. WOLFE
1960   *Husbands and Wives: The Dynamics of Married Living.* New York: Free Press.

BOTT, E.
1957   *Family and Social Network.* London: Tavistock Publications.

BOWERMAN, C. E.
1964   ''Prediction studies.'' In H. T. Christensen (ed.), *Handbook of Marriage and the Family.* Chicago: Rand McNally.

BRAITHWAITE, R. B.
1953   *Scientific Explanation.* London: Cambridge University Press.

BUERKLE, J.
1960   ''Self attitudes and marital adjustment.'' *Merrill-Palmer Quarterly* 6 (January):114–23.

BUERKLE, J. AND R. F. BADGLEY
1959   ''Couple role-taking: Yale marital interaction battery.'' *Marriage and Family Living* 21:53–58.

BUMPASS, L. L. AND J. A. SWEET
1972   ''Differentials in marital instability: 1970.'' *American Sociological Review* 37:754–66.

BURGESS, E. W. AND L. COTTRELL, JR.
1939   *Predicting Success or Failure in Marriage.* Englewood Cliffs, N.J.: Prentice-Hall.

BURGESS, E. W. AND H. J. LOCKE
1945   *The Family: From Institution to Companionship.* New York: American Book.
1953   *The Family.* New York: American Book.

BURGESS, E. W. AND P. WALLIN
1953   *Engagement and Marriage.* Chicago: J.B. Lippincott.

BURR, R.
1967   "Marital satisfaction: A conceptual reformulation; theory and partial test of the theory." Unpublished Ph.D. Dissertation, University of Minnesota.
1973   *Theory Construction and the Sociology of the Family*. New York: Wiley.

BYRNE, D. AND B. BLAYLOCK
1963   "Similarity and assumed similarity in marriage." *Journal of Abnormal and Social Psychology* 67:636–40.

CHESSER, E.
1957   *The Sexual, Marital and Family Relationships of the English Woman*. New York: Roy.

CHRISTENSEN, H.
1958   *Marriage Analysis*. New York: Ronald Press.
1969   "Children in the family: Relationship of number and spacing to marital success." *Journal of Marriage and the Family* 30:283–89.

CHRISTENSEN, H. AND K. BARBER
1967   "Interfaith versus intrafaith marriage in Indiana." *Journal of Marriage and the Family* 29 (June):461–69.

CHRISTENSEN, H. AND H. H. MEISSNER
1953   "Premarital pregnancy as a factor in divorce." *American Sociological Review* 18:641–44.

CHRISTENSEN, H. AND R. E. PHILBRICK
1952   "Family size as a factor in the marital adjustments of college couples." *American Sociological Review* 17:306–12.

CHRISTENSEN, H. AND B. RUBINSTEIN
1956   "Premarital pregnancy and divorce: A follow-up study by the interview method." *Marriage and Family Living* 18(2):114–23.

CLARK, A. AND P. VAN SOMMERS
1961   "Contradictory demands in family relations and adjustment to school and home." *Human Relations* 14:97–111.

CLARK, A. AND P. WALLIN
1965   "Women's sexual responsiveness and the duration and quality of their marriages." *American Journal of Sociology* 71:187–96.

CLAYTON, R. R.
1975   *The Family, Marriage, and Social Change*. Lexington, Mass.: Heath.

CLEMENTS, W. H.
1967   "Marital interaction and marital stability." *Journal of Marriage and the Family* 29:697–702.

COOMBS, R. H.
1966   "Value consensus and partner satisfaction among dating couples." *Journal of Marriage and the Family* 28:166–73.

CORSINI, R.
1956   "Multiple predictors of marital happiness." *Marriage and Family Living* 18:240–42.

COUCH, C. J.
1958   "The use of the concept 'role' and its derivatives in a study of marriage." *Marriage and Family Living* 20:353–57.

CROUSE, B., M. KARLINS, AND H. SCHRODER
1968   "Conceptual complexity and marital happiness." *Journal of Marriage and the Family* 30 (November):643–46.

CUBER, J. F. AND P. B. HARROFF
1965   *The Significant Americans: A Study of Sexual Behavior among the Affluent*. New York: Appleton-Century.

CUTLER, B. R. AND W. G. DYER
1965   "Initial adjustment processes in young married couples." *Social Forces* 44:195–201.

CUTRIGHT, P.
1971   "Income and family events: Marital stability." *Journal of Marriage and the Family* 33 (April):291–306.

DEAN, D.
1966   "Emotional maturity and marital adjustment." *Journal of Marriage and the Family* 28:454–57.

DEAN, D. AND W. LUCAS
1974   "Improving marital prediction: a model and a pilot study." Paper presented at the annual meeting of the National Council on Family Relations, St. Louis, Missouri.

DENTLER, R. A. AND P. PINEO
1960   "Sexual adjustment, marital adjustment, and personal growth of husbands: A panel analysis." *Marriage and Family Living* 22:45–48.

DITTES, J.
1959   "Attractiveness of group as a function of self-esteem and acceptance by group." *Journal of Abnormal and Social Psychology* 59:77–82.

DRISCOLL, R., K. DAVIS, AND M. LIPETZ
1972   "Parental interference and romantic love: The Romeo and Juliet effect." *Journal of Personality and Social Psychology* 24:1–10.

DUBIN, R.
1969   *Theory Building*. New York: Free Press.

DUVALL, E. M.
1954   *In-laws: Pro and Con*. New York: Association Press.

DYMOND, R.
1954   "Interpersonal perception and marital happiness." *Canadian Journal of Psychology* 8:164–71.

EDWARDS, J. N.
1969   "Familial behavior as social exchange." *Journal of Marriage and the Family* 31:518–26.

FARBER, B. AND L. S. BLACKMAN
1956   "Marital role tensions and number and sex of children." *American Sociological Review* 21:596–601.

FARBER, B. AND J. MCHALE
1959   "Marital integration and parents' agreement on satisfaction with their child's behavior." *Marriage and Family Living* 21:65–69.

FIGLEY, C. R.
1973   "Child density and the marital relationship." *Journal of Marriage and the Family* 35:272–82

FOGARTY, M., R. RAPOPORT, AND R. RAPOPORT
1971   *Sex, Career and Family*. London: George Allen & Unwin.

FOOTE, N. N. AND L. S. COTTRELL
1955   *Identity and Interpersonal Competence: A New Direction in Family Research*. Chicago: University of Chicago Press.

FRAZIER, E. F.
1960   "The impact of urban civilization upon Negro family life." In N. W. Bell and E. F. Vogel (eds.), *Modern Introduction to the Family*. New York: Free Press.

GLICK, P. AND A. NORTON
1976   "Number, timing, and duration of marriages and divorces in the United States: June, 1975," U.S. Bureau of the Census, *Current Population Reports*, Series P-20, No. 297, U.S. Government Printing Office, Washington, D.C.

GOODE, W. J.
1956   *After Divorce*. New York: Free Press.
1961   "Family disorganization." In R. K. Merton and R. A. Nisbet (eds.), *Contemporary Social Problems*. New York: Harcourt, Brace.
1962   "Marital satisfaction and instability: A cross-cultural analysis of divorce rates." *International Social Science Journal* 14:507–26.
1963   *World Revolution and Family Patterns*. New York: Free Press.
1964   *The Family*. Englewood Cliffs, N.J.: Prentice-Hall.

GOVER, D.
1963   "Socio-economic differentials in relationship between marital adjustment and wife's employment status." *Marriage and Family Living* 25 (November):452–58.

GREEN, A. W.
1960   "The 'cult of personality' and sexual relations." In N. W. Bell and E. F. Vogel (eds.), *Modern Introduction to the Family*. New York: Free Press.

GURIN, G., J. VEROFF, AND S. FELD
1960   *Americans View Their Mental Health*. New York: Basic Books.

HAVIGHURST, R. ET AL.
1962   *Growing Up in River City*. New York: Wiley.

HAWKINS, J. L.
1968   "Association between companionship, hostility and marital satisfaction." *Journal of Marriage and the Family* 30:647–50.

HAWKINS, J. L. AND K. JOHNSEN
1969   "Perception of behavioral conformity, imputation of consensus, and marital satisfaction." *Journal of Marriage and the Family* 31:507–11.

HEER, D.
1974   "The prevalence of black-white marriage in the United States." *Journal of Marriage and the Family* 36 (May):246–58.

HICKS, M. AND M. PLATT
1970   "Marital happiness and stability: A review of the research in the sixties." *Journal of Marriage and the Family* 32:553–74.

HILL, R.
1949   *Families under Stress*. New York: Harper.
1966   "Contemporary developments in family theory." *Journal of Marriage and the Family* 28:10–25.

HOBART, C. W. AND W. J. KLAUSNER
1959   "Some social interaction correlates of marital role disagreements and marital adjustment." *Marriage and Family Living* 21:256–63.

HOLLINGSHEAD, A. B.
1950   "Cultural factors in the selection of marriage mates." *American Sociological Review* 15:619–27.

HOLSTEIN, C. M., J. GOLDSTEIN, AND D. BEM
1971   "The importance of expressive behaviors, sex, and need-approval in inducing liking." *Journal of Experimental Social Psychology* 7:534–44.

HOMANS, G. C.
1950   *The Human Group*. New York: Harcourt, Brace.
1958   "Social behavior as exchange." *American Journal of Sociology* 63:597–606.
1961   *Social Behavior: Its Elementary Forms*. New York: Harcourt, Brace & World.
1964   "Contemporary theory in sociology." In R. E. L. Faris (ed.), *Handbook of Modern Sociology*. Chicago: Rand McNally.

HUNTINGTON, R. M.
1958   "The personality-interaction approach to the study of the marital relationship." *Marriage and Family Living* 20:43–46.

HURLEY, J. R. AND D. P. PALONEN
1967   "Marital satisfaction and child density among university student parents." *Journal of Marriage and the Family* 29 (August):483–84.

INSELBERG, R.
1962   "Marital problems and satisfaction in high school marriages." *Marriage and Family Living* 24 (February):71–77.

JACKSON, D. J. AND T. L. HUSTON
1975   "Psychological attraction and assertiveness." *Journal of Social Psychology* 47:79–85.

JACOBSOHN, P. AND A. MATHENY
1962   "Mate selection in open marriage systems." *International Journal of Comparative Sociology* 3:98–124.

KAHN, M.
1970   "Non-verbal communication and marital satisfaction." *Family Process* 99:449–56.

KATZ, M.
1965   "Agreement on connotative meaning in marriage." *Family Process* 4:64–74.

KELLY, E. L.
1941   "Marital compatability as related to personality traits of husbands and wives as related by self and spouse." *Journal of Social Psychology* 13:193–98.

KEMPER, T. D.
1968   "Third party penetration of local social systems." *Sociometry* 31:1–29.

KEPHART, W. M.
1954a   "Some variables in cases of reported sexual maladjustment." *Marriage and Family Living* 16:241–43.
1954b   "Occupational level and marital disruption." *American Sociological Review* 20:456–65.

KERCKHOFF, A. AND K. DAVIS
1962   "Value consensus and need complementarity in mate selection." *American Sociological Review* 27:295–303.

KIRKPATRICK, C.
1955   *The Family as Process and Institution*. New York: Ronald Press.
1963   *The Family as Process and Institution*, second ed. New York: Ronald Press.

KIRKPATRICK, C. AND J. COTTON
1951   "Physical attractiveness, age and marital adjustment." *American Sociological Review* 16:81–86.

KNOX, D. H.
1970   "Conceptions of love at three developmental levels." *Family Coordinator* 19:151–57.

KOMAROVSKY, M.
1962   *Blue-Collar Marriage*. New York: Vintage Books.

KOTLAR, S. L.
1962   "Instrumental and expressive marital roles." *Sociology and Social Research* 46:186–94.
1965   "Middle-class marital role expectation and marital adjustment." *Sociology and Social Research* 49 (April):183–93.

LANDIS, J. T.
1963   "Social correlates of divorce or nondivorce among the unhappily married." *Marriage and Family Living* 25 (May):178–180.

LANDIS, J. T., T. POFFENBERGER, AND S. POFFENBERGER
1950   "The effects of first pregnancy upon the sexual adjustment of 212 couples." *American Sociological Review* 15:766–72.

LESLIE, G.
1973   *The Family in Social Context*, second ed. New York: Oxford University Press.

LEVINGER, G.
1964   "Task and social behavior in marriage." *Sociometry* 27:433–48.
1965a   "Marital cohesiveness and dissolution: An integrative review." *Journal of Marriage and the Family* 27:19–28.
1965b   "Altruism in marriage: A test of the Buerkle-Badgley battery." *Journal of Marriage and the Family* 27 (February):32–33.

LEVINGER, G. AND D. J. SENN
1967   "Disclosure of feelings in marriage." *Merrill-Palmer Quarterly* 13:237–49.

LEVINGER, G. AND J. D. SNOEK
1972   *Attraction in Relationship: A New Look at Interpersonal*

Attraction. New York: General Learning Press.

LEWIS, R. A.
1966 "Empathy and interpersonal perception in dating-pair relationships." Unpublished Master's Thesis, University of Minnesota.
1967 "Empathy in the dating dyad: A retesting of earlier theory." Paper delivered at the Annual Meetings of the National Council on Family Relations, San Francisco, August.
1972 "A developmental framework for the analysis of premarital dyadic formation." *Family Process* 11:17–48.
1973a "A longitudinal test of a developmental framework for premarital dyadic formation." *Journal of Marriage and the Family* 35:16–25.
1973b "Social reaction and the formation of dyads: An interactionist approach to mate selection." *Sociometry* 36:409–18.
1975 "Social influences on marital choice." In S. Dragastin and G. H. Elder, Jr. (eds.), *Adolescence in the Life Cycle*. New York: Wiley.

LIVELY, E.
1969 "Toward conceptual clarification: Case of marital interaction." *Journal of Marriage and the Family* 31:108–14.

LOCKE, H. J.
1947 "Predicting marital adjustment by comparing a divorced and happily married group." *American Sociological Review* 12 (April):187–91.
1951 *Predicting Adjustment in Marriage: A Comparison of a Divorced and a Happily Married Group*. New York: Holt.

LOCKE, H. J. AND G. KARLSSON
1952 "Marital adjustment and prediction in Sweden and the U.S.A." *American Sociological Review* 17:10–17.

LOWRIE, S. H.
1965 "Early marriage: Premarital pregnancy and associated factors." *Journal of Marriage and the Family* 27:48–56.

LUCKEY, E.
1960a "Marital satisfaction and congruent self-spouse concepts." *Social Forces* 39:153–57.
1960b "Marital satisfaction and its association with congruency of perception." *Marriage and Family Living* 22:49–54.
1961 "Perceptual congruence of self and family concepts as related to marital interaction." *Sociometry* 24:234–50.
1964 "Marital satisfaction and personality correlates of spouse." *Journal of Marriage and the Family* 26:217–20.
1966 "Number of years married as related to personality perception and marital satisfaction." *Journal of Marriage and the Family* 28:44–48.

LUCKEY, E. B. AND J. K. BAIN
1970 "Children: A factor in marital satisfaction." *Journal of Marriage and the Family* 32: (January):43–44.

MANGUS, A. R.
1957 "Role theory and marriage counseling." *Social Forces* 35:202–09.

MARTINSON, F. M.
1955 "Ego deficiency as a factor in marriage." *American Sociological Review* 20:161–64.

MATHEWS, V. AND C. MILANOVICH
1963 "New orientations on marital adjustment." *Marriage and Family Living* 25:300–04.

MAYER, J. E.
1961 *Jewish-Gentile Courtships*. New York: Free Press.

MONAHAN, T. P.
1955 "Divorce by occupational level." *Marriage and Family Living* 17:322–24

MURSTEIN, B. I.
1967 "Empirical tests of role, complementary needs, and homogamy theories of marital choice." *Journal of Marriage and the Family* 29:689–96.

1970 "Stimulus-value role: A theory of marital choice." *Journal of Marriage and the Family* 32:465–81.

MURSTEIN, B. I. AND V. GLAUDIN
1968 "The relationship of marital adjustment to personality: A factor analysis of the Interpersonal Check List." *Journal of Marriage and the Family* 30:651–55.

NAVRAN, L.
1967 "Communication and adjustment in marriage." *Family Process* 6:173–84.

NEWCOMB, T. M.
1956 "The prediction of interpersonal attraction." *American Psychologist* 11:575–86.
1961 *The Acquaintance Process*. New York: Holt, Rinehart and Winston.

NYE, F. I.
1961 "Maternal employment and marital interaction: Some contingent conditions." *Social Forces* 40 (December):113–19.

NYE, F. I., L. WHITE, AND J. FRIEDERES
1969 "A partial theory of family stability." Paper given at the Annual Meeting of the National Council on Family Relations, Washington, D.C.

ORDEN, S. R. AND N. M. BRADBURN
1968 "Dimensions of marriage happiness." *American Journal of Sociology* 73:715–31.

ORLINSKY, D. E.
1972 "Love relationships in the life cycle: A developmental interpersonal perspective." In H. A. Otto (ed.), *Love Today: A New Exploration*. New York: Dell.

ORT, R. S.
1950 "A study of role conflict as related to happiness in marriage." *Journal of Abnormal and Social Psychology* 45:691–99.

OTTO, H. A. (ED.)
1972 *Love Today: A New Exploration*. New York: Dell.

PICKFORD, J., E. I. SIGNORI, AND H. REMPEL
1966 "Similar or related personality traits as a factor in marital happiness." *Journal of Marriage and the Family* 28:190–92.

PINEO, P. C.
1961 "Disenchantment in the later years of marriage." *Marriage and Family Living* 23:3–11.

POND, D. A., A. RYLE, AND M. HAMILTON
1963 "Marriage and neurosis in a working-class population." *British Journal of Psychiatry* 109:592–98.

RAPOPORT, R. AND R. RAPOPORT
1965 "Work and family in contemporary society." *American Sociological Review* 30:381–94.

RAINWATER, L.
1965 *Family Design: Marital Sexuality, Family Size, and Contraception*. Chicago: Aldine.

REIK, T.
1963 *The Need to Be Loved*. New York: Bantam Books.

REISS, I. L.
1960 "Toward a sociology of the heterosexual love relationship." *Marriage and Family Living* 22:139–45.

RENNE, K. S.
1970 "Correlates of dissatisfaction in marriage." *Journal of Marriage and the Family* 32: (January):54–66.

ROGERS, C. R.
1972 *Becoming Partners: Marriage and Its Alternatives*. New York: Delacorte Press.

ROLLINS, B. AND H. FELDMAN
1970 "Marital satisfaction over the family life cycle." *Journal of Marriage and the Family* 32:20–27.

ROTH, J. AND R. F. PECK
1951   "Social class mobility and factors related to marital adjustment." *American Sociological Review* 16:478–87.

RUBIN, Z.
1974   "Lovers and other strangers: The development of intimacy in encounters and relationships." *American Scientist* 62:182–90.

RYDER, R. G., J. S. KAFKA, AND D. H. OLSON
1971   "Separating and joining influences in courtship and early marriage." *American Journal of Orthopsychiatry* 41 (April):450–64.

SAFILIOS-ROTHSCHILD, C.
1970   "The study of family power structure: A review 1960–1969." *Journal of Marriage and the Family* 32(4):539–49.

SCANZONI, J.
1968   "A social system analysis of dissolved and existing marriages." *Journal of Marriage and the Family* 30 (August):452–61.

SCHELLENBERG, J. A.
1960   "Homogamy in personal values and the field of eligibles." *Social Forces* 39:157–62.

SIMON, J. L.
1969   *Basic Research Methods in Social Science.* New York: Random House.

SPANIER, G. B.
1971   "A study of the relationship between and social correlates of romanticism and marital adjustment." Unpublished Master's Thesis, Iowa State University.

1976   "Measuring dyadic adjustment: New scales for assessing the quality of marriage and similar dyads." *Journal of Marriage and the Family* 38 (February):15–28.

SPANIER, G. B. AND C. L. COLE
1976   "Toward clarification and investigation of marital adjustment." *International Journal of the Sociology of the Family* 6:121–46.

SPANIER, G. B., R. A. LEWIS, AND C. L. COLE
1975   "Marital adjustment over the family life cycle: The issue of curvilinearity." *Journal of Marriage and the Family* 37 (May):263–75.

SPIEGEL, J.
1960   "The resolution of role-conflict within the family." In N. W. Bell and E. F. Vogel (eds.), *Modern Introduction to the Family.* New York: Free Press.

STOLTZ, L.
1960   "Effects of maternal employment on children." *Child Development* 31:749–82.

STRAUSS, A.
1947   "Personality needs and marital choice." *Social Forces* 25:332–35.

STUCKERT, R. P.
1963   "Role perception and marital satisfaction: A configurational approach." *Marriage and Family Living* 25:415–19.

STRYKER, S.
1964   "The interactional and situational approaches." In H. T. Christensen (ed.), *Handbook of Marriage and the Family.* Chicago: Rand McNally.

TAYLOR, A. B.
1967   "Role perception, empathy, and marriage adjustment." *Sociological and Social Research* 52:22–34.

TERMAN, L. M.
1938   *Psychological Factors in Marital Happiness.* New York: McGraw-Hill.

THARP, R. G.
1963   "Psychological patterning in marriage." *Psychological Bulletin* 60:97–117.

THIBAUT, J. W. AND H. H. KELLEY
1959   *The Social Psychology of Groups.* New York: Wiley.

TROST, J.
1964   "Mate selection, marital adjustment, and symbolic environment." *Acta Sociologica* 8:27–35.

1967   "Some data on mate-selection: Homogamy and perceived homogamy." *Journal of Marriage and the Family* 29:739–55.

UDRY, J. R.
1973   *The Social Context of Marriage,* third ed. Philadelphia: Lippincott.

VOGEL, E. F.
1960   "The marital relationship of parents of emotionally disturbed children: Polarization and isolation." *Psychiatry* 23:1–12.

WALLER, W. AND R. HILL
1951   *The Family: A Dynamic Interpretation.* New York: Dryden Press.

WALSTER, E.
1965   "The effect of self-esteem on romantic liking." *Journal of Experimental Social Psychology* 1:184–97.

WHITEHURST, R.
1968   "Premarital reference group orientations and marital adjustment." *Journal of Marriage and the Family* 30:397–401.

WILLIAMSON, R. C.
1954   "Socio-economic factors and marital adjustment in an urban setting." *American Sociological Review* 19:213–16.

WINCH, R. F.
1971   *The Modern Family,* third ed. New York: Holt, Rinehart and Winston.

WINCH, R. F., T. KTSANES, AND V. KTSANES
1954   "The theory of complementary needs in mate selection: An analytic and descriptive study." *American Sociological Review* 19:241–49.

WINCH, R. F. AND G. B. SPANIER
1974   "Scientific method and the study of the family." In R. F. Winch and G. B. Spanier (eds.), *Selected Studies in Marriage and the Family.* New York: Holt, Rinehart and Winston.

WINTER, G.
1958   *Love and Conflict.* Garden City, N.Y.: Dolphin Books.

ZETTERBERG, H.
1965   *On Theory and Verification in Sociology.* Totowa, N.J.: Bedminster Press.

13

SOCIAL PROCESSES AND POWER IN FAMILIES

John Scanzoni

We now know enough to realize that the contemporary American family does have a power structure, and furthermore, one which is not necessarily equalitarian [Heer, 1963:133].

To contemporary social scientists, it may seem incomprehensible or even ludicrous that such assertions ever needed to be made. But in the context of the early sixties such assertions were eminently plausible, as the fact is that up to that point in time power was not often investigated within the context of the family. This oversight was not due to any conspiracy, but instead may be traced to both the ideology and the theory of the times. Moreover, even beyond familial investigation, power has proven to be extraordinarily difficult for social scientists to conceptualize and measure to their collective satisfaction. Dahl makes the point that

there is little consensus about this widely employed concept other than that it is a useful one in the analysis of behavior [Deutsch, 1973:84].

EARLY APPROACHES TO POWER AND FAMILY

Theoretically, until the sixties the dominant perspective throughout sociology was functionalism; and consequently issues pertaining to power and authority within any aspect of social structure—including the family—were seldom raised. The kinds of theoretical questions asked by the functionalists tended to mute the problematic nature of power. Nonetheless, in all fairness, it must be said that prior to the sixties functionalism had little impact on the actual research literature on the family. In their 1960 essay on functionalism and family, Bell and Vogel discuss what they call "family leadership." Here they do refer to notions of authority and power and argue that

NOTE: Grateful acknowledgment is made to Wesley R. Burr, Gary LaFree, David H. Olson, and Constantina Safilios-Rothschild for helpful critiques of earlier versions of this chapter.

family power is generally diffuse rather than being concentrated in one actor; that authority must be deemed legitimate to be effective; and that family authority develops out of a series of exceedingly complex processes some of which are conscious, others unconscious (1960:22–24). While such theoretical conclusions were evocative for that time, unfortunately they were not updated, refined, or elaborated in the authors' 1968 essay. This lack of refinement occurred at the same time that within the "mainstream" of general social theory, issues of authority, power, influence, conflict, etc., were becoming increasingly prominent and significant. The rigidities of the functionalist approach to "leadership" were being discarded for the more dynamic perspectives inherent in exchange theory and in conflict theory (Dahrendorf, 1959; Homans, 1961; Blau, 1964). Unfortunately, such theoretical shifts were not filtering in any significant measure into theory and research regarding the family.

During the mid-sixties the influential *Handbook of Marriage and the Family* (Christensen, 1964) was published, but if one turns to its index one searches in vain for any reference to the term "power." Yet that volume was representative of scholars from a wide variety of theoretical perspectives, including interactionism and functionalism. The label "authority patterns" does appear in the index, but the pages devoted to it are brief. More significantly, the essayists treating authority were heavily influenced by Parsons' functionalist thought, as we shall see below. "Decision-making" also appears in the *Handbook* index, but the reader is merely referred to "authority patterns." A 1966 volume edited by Nye and Berardo sought to expand an earlier effort to identify "emerging conceptual frameworks in family analysis." Once more, however, we search the index in vain for even the slightest reference to "authority" or "power," while "decision-making" is discussed briefly in connection with consumer behaviors.

However, theoretical efforts to get at notions of power,

295

though veiled, were not totally absent even in the *Hand-book*. Expanding an essay she had written in 1959, Bernard (1964) employed "game and decision theory" to discuss what she called the "adjustments" or "conflicts" of "married mates." Game theorists (Tedeschi et al., 1973) make it clear that a game theory approach intrinsically carries with it notions of power, as well as ideas of bargaining and conflict. And while Bernard did not explicitly use either of the terms "power" and "authority" in her essay, such concepts are *implicitly* present throughout her discussion (especially 692 ff.). Significantly, in 1961 even Homans did not explicitly use the term "power," an oversight which he purposely and self-consciously corrected in his 1974 revision.

Marital Adjustment and Functionalism

The reason why notions of power and authority were not explicitly built into Bernard's theoretical models is not totally clear. In part, this omission may reflect the ideology of the times. For example, in response to what they acknowledge to be Bernard's "groundbreaking efforts," Kimmel and Havens (1966) are nonetheless severely critical of her for those efforts. Their complaint is aimed at her fundamental assumption that such an application of game and decision theory *could* be made in the first place. They claim that game theory is based on "mutual opposition," whereas "young, middle-class American couples" define marriage as based on "mutual identification." They claim to "know" that such couples define marriage as an "*equalitarian* [italics supplied], affectionate, diffuse primary relationship" (461). The sources of this knowledge are not indicated; and that oversight is serious given Heer's opposite conclusion cited at this chapter's outset.

Kimmel and Havens (1966) represent a perspective that assumes egalitarianism as a given and that strives to *promote* an ideal of mutuality which is never clearly defined. Whether it is consciously done or not, such a perspective at best minimizes the significance of marital power, or at worst suggests that the use of power is an undesirable phenomenon which should be eliminated. Above all, it seems to reject the assumption that power is an inevitable element in any social structure—including marriage—and that as such it ought to be systematically investigated for theoretical reasons and also for policy reasons—in order to develop sounder value prescriptions for marriage.

The foregoing is not to say that the issue of power had been totally ignored among pioneering sociological analyses of the family. Herbst (1952) developed a typology of marital power that had considerable impact on Wolfe's (1959) thinking. Cromwell and Olson (1975b:23) note that Herbst's approach was subsequently partially carried forth in the very influential Blood and Wolfe (1960) report. The name of Willard Waller is attached to some significant theoretical insights that have been revived by more recent theorists such as Blau (1964:78). Waller observed traditional premarital courtship processes and conceptualized a phenomenon he called "the principle of least interest" (Waller and Hill, 1951:190–92). He noted that "emotional involvement" does not usually develop at an "even tempo." One party tends to be more "involved," or "in love," or "dependent" on the other party than vice versa. The one who is less dependent therefore has greater control or power over the relationship. "That person is able to dictate the conditions of the association whose interest in the continuation of the affair is least" (191). Waller went on to indicate that power can evolve into *exploitation*, which he defines as "unfair or unjust utilization of another" (163). He also points out that courtship itself is a series of *bargains* leading to what he calls the "ultimate bargain," or marriage (160–61). Unfortunately, his subsequent analyses of the marriage relationship itself lack explicit reference to the concepts of bargaining, power, and exploitation. Perhaps at that point in the evolution of his thinking, by conceptualizing marriage as an *ultimate* bargain, he did not perceive bargaining's existence subsequent to official union (McCall, 1966). His untimely death cut short his seminal contributions, for had he lived, it seems certain that he would have been able to influence substantially the course of theory development pertaining to social power in general, as well as to the sociology of family.

What did permeate the thinking of many sociologists was functionalist-type theorizing about family authority. While there may have been little conscious or actual connection between proponents of the "marital adjustment" school and functionalists themselves, the two orientations have much in common. When Locke (1968:45), for example, defines marital adjustment as "the process of adaptation of the husband and wife in such a way as to avoid or resolve conflicts," or when Burgess et al. (1963:295) call a "well-adjusted marriage" a union in which the husband and wife are in agreement on the chief issues of marriage . . . they are in harmony," the authors are in effect emphasizing stability, consensus, and equilibrium—issues which are of prime concern to functionalists. And as with the functionalists, the "marital adjustment" perspective makes certain assumptions regarding familial power which are essentially static and theoretically sterile. As Collins (1975:225) puts it,

> The sociology of family, kinship, and socialization has been the bastion of functionalism, framing its analysis against an ideal system in which men, women, and children all fit nicely in their places.

That charge can be borne out by examining Pitts's

exposition (1964) of the functionalist approach to the family. Pitts argues that in the nuclear family a "functional requirement is that final authority be assigned without ambiguity" (1964:103). "Functional" or "beneficial" for what is implicit in the surrounding context, which discusses the effect of wife's employment on family "power-structure." Earlier in his essay Pitts had referred to the "requirement" that the family must solve the power issue "like any *enduring* [italics supplied] small group" (63). Thus his argument is that stability or group maintenance is negatively affected or threatened if the power issue is not resolved. And how is the power issue resolved? Pitts cites Zelditch and Parsons' statement that "in all but a very few societies, instrumental roles, which involve political and economic leadership, are played by the husband-father" (74).[1] He argues that "a generalized male superiority is a basic theme of the structure of the nuclear family in all known societies" (75). This includes matrilineal societies where the mother's brother "participates" in "community roles related to wars, markets, ceremonials" (76). In all instances it is the family roles which "stretch . . . to maximize the capacity of the husband [male] to participate in community roles."

While a Marxist would concur with the assertion of historic male dominance (Gillespie, 1971), the functionalist seeks for the functions of (or justifications for) male superiority. Pitts argues that it "furthers the incest-taboo training of the boy," and also of the girl (76). That is, male superiority teaches the boy that it is more valuable to seek masculine identification than to preserve a nurturant relationship with the mother. Likewise, the girl learns that it is more valuable to "win a man" than to preserve a nurturant relationship with her mother. A second "function" of male superiority, says Pitts, is that it protects the mother during pregnancy. His reasoning seems to be that in fact, since she must bear children, it would be difficult for her to be unhindered in playing community roles. Thus the husband plays those roles, gains superiority; and this is "functional" for the protection of the pregnancy-prone woman.

These absurd tautologies and *false* teleologies (Turner, 1974) illustrate why functionalism has fallen into such disrepute. Parsons and Pitts are correct in identifying the souce of the male's power in his participation in the "community" or larger society, particularly the economic system. Their fatal flaw was to freeze that arrangement—to assume that because it is there it is "functional", it does something to preserve stability, it contributes to system maintenance. And because it is "functional," it must continue to be there.

When Pitts attempts to explain effects of wife's employment on family power structure, he continues his circular reasoning. Men are instrumental, therefore involved in the community, therefore superior and instru-

mental in the family. Women are expressive in the family, and should they go to work "there can be some debate as to whether women's personality systems permit as thorough a socialization into professional patterns. The greater interest of women is in expressive relationships, which are dysfunctional . . . especially in the higher executive range . . ." (103). Therefore, says Pitts, when women work, they tend, because of their expressive orientations, to be in occupations relatively lower in prestige, power, and income than those of their husbands. Consequently, reasons Pitts, the excess amounts of these three external elements that the husband possesses carry over into the family, giving him greater internal authority (104). (Interestingly, Pitts adds that the lower-class male "reverts to superiority in strength" to maintain "male authority.") Thus the functionalist approach toward analyzing familial power is grossly circular and is combined with a view of social order that is essentially static. The younger male learns to be task-oriented, the younger female to be person-oriented. Through pursuing significant tasks, the male gains legitimate authority. Since the female is effectively barred from the most significant tasks, she must necessarily be subordinate. In short, because she is female she is person-oriented; because she is person-oriented she is subordinate; because she is subordinate there is order; because there is order younger females learn to be person-oriented and males learn to be task-oriented, and so the cycle continues.

The functionalist approach to familial power can be best described by what Brickman (1974) labels a "fully structured" relationship: "the behavior of each party is completely specified or prescribed by social norms. . . . The orientation of parties . . . is a moral orientation. . . . The reactions of the parties are often the result of their concerns to guide, respect, or obey the other party. . ." (11–12). When the authority of one party is challenged, the appropriate reaction is to *persuade* the other to conform to what is "right or wrong." And what is "right or wrong" is ascertained by norms governing the particular issue or situation.

During the nineteenth century it is likely that the great majority of marriages were "normative" or "fully structured relationships," for as Brickman notes, such a relationship is one in which there are few "resources, options, or alternatives available" and there are considerable "constraints" placed on the use of those that exist (7). Historically and cross-culturally most women were clearly subordinate owing to normative prescriptions and also to the fact they had few alternatives with which to struggle for power (Rosaldo and Lamphere, 1974). Those few alternatives that might have existed were ringed with weighty constraints. The history of the twentieth century reflects a downward trend in the proportion of marriages that can be described as "fully structured" or adequately captured by a functionalist perspective. For reasons described elsewhere (Scanzoni, 1972) the change has been toward what Brickman calls the partially structured relationship, in which "rules constrain certain behaviors but leave others to the free choice of the parties" (7). Such relationships are

> established bargaining relationships... because they regularly involve a contest between actors with a rational orientation toward maximizing their respective share of the common resources [8-9].

> Parties in partially structured relationships are likely to use inducements or reinforcements to influence one another.... Intentional or selfish aggression, activated by calculation that this aggression will be rewarded by more favorable outcomes, is an important part of partially structured [relationships] [11].[2]

Blood and Wolfe's assertion (1960:12) that marital power was no longer based on patriarchal notions, but rather on "comparative resources" was a specific way of describing the long-term movement from fully to partially structured relationships. Subsequent to their declaration that power had become problematic, the years since 1960 witnessed scores of studies to apprehend that phenomenon. The most consistent and devastating flaw in those investigations was that they tended neither to be theoretically informed nor, therefore, theoretically significant. Hence it is little wonder that they have been open to so many methodological criticisms.

REVIEW OF SUBSTANTIVE LITERATURE[3]

Besides analyses of the distribution of conjugal power within the American family (Safilios-Rothschild, 1970) similar research has been undertaken in France (Michel, 1967), Western Germany (Lamouse, 1969; Lupri, 1969), Yugoslavia (Buric and Zecevic, 1967), Turkey (Fox, 1973), Greece (Safilios-Rothschild, 1967), Ghana (Oppong, 1970), Puerto Rico (Weller, 1968), and Japan (Blood, 1967). With few exceptions (Clignet, 1970), data on conjugal power have been obtained mostly from urban samples within industrialized or industrializing countries.

Although not always designed specifically to test Blood and Wolfe's conclusions (1960), most American and European research is consistent with it. The power of the husband varies positively with his socio-economic resources (income, education, occupational prestige, or a composite of these variables). This result was obtained in the United States (Blood and Wolfe, 1960; Kandel and Lesser, 1972), Germany (Lamouse, 1969; Lupri, 1969), and apparently France (Michel, 1967).[4] Conceptualizing race as a resource, Blood and Wolfe (1960) and Centers et al. (1971) found that black males tend to have less power than their white counterparts. However, it is not so much race per se that is the explanation for that relationship. Rather, it is the systematic discrimination and deprivation

experienced by black males within the white-controlled marketplace (Scanzoni, 1977). Moreover, while traditional gender role norms tend to prescribe lesser amounts of authority to women than to men, there is some evidence that black persons tend to hold gender role norms that are less traditional than those of white persons (Steinmann et al., 1968; Scanzoni, 1975a). Available literature on Spanish-speaking Americans suggests continued persistence of the patriarchal ideology (Spiegel, 1971:171-72). Nevertheless, although patterns predominate in which "men order women," or "the husband and father is the autocratic head of the household" (Murillo, 1971:103), "there are fewer and fewer women who are willing to accept the traditional role assigned to them according to traditional values" (106).

Because of the increase in socioeconomic resources it entails, the employment of the wife increases her power, and concomitantly seems to limit the power of her husband. Again, this result has cross-cultural validity (Heer, 1958; Hoffman, 1958; Blood and Wolfe, 1960; Buric and Zecevic, 1967; Michel, 1967; Safilios-Rothschild, 1967; Weller, 1968; Lamouse, 1969; Lupri, 1969; Scanzoni, 1970; Oppong, 1970; Kandel and Lesser, 1972; Bahr, 1974).

Women with children have more limited access to externally based resources and as a result tend to be less powerful than childless wives (Heer, 1958; Blood and Wolfe, 1960; Michel, 1967; Centers et al., 1971). When the wife's socioeconomic resources are compared with those of her husband, the larger the discrepancy between them, the greater the power differential (Blood and Wolfe, 1960; Michel, 1967; Buric and Zecevic, 1967; Safilios-Rothschild, 1967; Lupri, 1969; Oppong, 1970). Furthermore, the wife's power tends to increase over the course of the family life cycle (Hill, 1965).

Critiques of "Resource Theory"

There are exceptions to the above results, however, and they have often been interpreted as indicators of the inadequacy of what has come to be known as "resource theory." The socioeconomic resources of the husband in some American (Komarovsky, 1962; Scanzoni, 1970) and in Danish (Kandel and Lesser, 1972), Greek (Safilios-Rothschild, 1967), Yugoslavian (Buric and Zecevic, 1967) and Turkish (Fox, 1973) samples do *not* enhance his power. On the contrary, increments in such resources either decrease his power or do not affect it. Middleton and Putney (1960) and Centers et al. (1971) in the United States and Safilios-Rothschild (1969) in Greece found that the articulation of the wife into the economic system had no effect on her power. Finally, in contrast to research indicating the greater powerlessness of women with children, Safilios-Rothschild's Greek data (1967) indicate that children decrease, rather than increase, the power of the husband.

The apparent deficiencies of "resource theory" have stimulated attempts to (1) clarify the relationship between resources and the distribution of power, and (2) refine that relationship via the inclusion of additional variables. (See Blood, 1963; Wilkening, 1968; Wilkening and Lupri, 1965.)

The Rodman Synthesis

The most systematic attempts at resolving the question of connections between resources and power have been made by Rodman (1967, 1972) and by Burr (1973) in his extension of Rodman's earlier piece. Rodman initially addressed himself to the "exceptions" cited above—why certain tangible resources were sometimes positively and sometimes negatively related to husband's power. His explanation is that in certain "modernizing" societies it is the middle- and and upper-status groups that first accept norms of marital egalitarianism. Thus norms may "operate as a 'contingency variable' influencing the effect that *resources* have on . . . power" (Cromwell and Olson, 1975b:26). Therefore, even though husbands in modernizing societies possess more resources than do men of lesser status, they actually "grant" their wives more power. Consequently, higher-status men may actually possess less power than lower-status men. However, as Burr (1973:194) warns, such a situation "would only be expected when a society is in the process of changing from a patriarchal normative system." After some years of modernization and a greater pervasiveness of egalitarian norms, we would expect that formerly negative associations between resources and power would turn into positive ones. Rodman himself also recognized this kind of issue when he described four stages of societies which would influence the nature of the relationship between resources and power of husbands (1972:63-65): (1) patriarchy—no variation in male authority by status (India); (2) modified patriarchy—male authority inverse to status (Greece, Yugoslavia); (3) transitional equalitarianism—authority varies positively with status (Germany, U.S.A.); (4) equalitarianism—no necessary correlation of male power with authority since women also possess high levels of resources (Denmark, Sweden).

The Burr Synthesis

Partly because of space limitations, but primarily because it has been done elsewhere (Rodman, 1972; Safilios-Rothschild, 1970; Cromwell and Olson, 1975a), we have not critiqued in detail the numerous conceptual and methodological problems of the substantive literature cited above. Below, however, as we seek to extend our thinking about familial power, we shall identify what seem to be some of the more serious of these shortcomings. A good deal of the seeming disparity and incongruity among those many studies can be overcome by

Burr's general model of marital power (1973). He has developed a set of systematic theoretical propositions which subsume important earlier findings and which integrate those findings with Rodman's 1967 paper on power and resources. That synthesis of the literature is reproduced here as Figure 13.1. What this general model does is try to begin to spell out systematically the complex interconnections between amount of power and several normative variables, several issues attached to resources, and several specific types of (tangible) resources. (Numbers in the figure refer to propositions in Burr, 1973.) Burr's synthesis is therefore an important "signboard" along the road to analysis of familial power because it tells us where we have been and forces us to consider what new paths we might now explore. Subsequent exploration of some of these paths in this chapter owes a direct debt to Burr's work.

Cromwell-Olson Benchmark

If Burr's work is a "signboard", the volume edited by Cromwell and Olson (1975a) is by their own statement (xvi) a "benchmark." They and their colleagues have not only reviewed, critiqued, and synthesized past literature—they have also provided numerous explicit guidelines and suggestions as to how further theory and research into power should proceed. To begin with, they define power as a "system property . . . the ability (potential or actual) of an individual(s) to change the behavior of other members in a social system" (Olson & Cromwell, 1975:5). "Family power," which incorporates the behaviors of household members other than the marital dyad, is to be distinguished from "marital power," which subsumes only behaviors between spouses.

While the above definition of power is evocative, it contains a serious shortcoming—namely, the assertion that power implies *change* without making explicit the converse that power may also support constancy, the capability to maintain the status quo. (However, at several places in that volume the latter notion is at least implicit: Turk, 1975; Cromwell and Olson, 1975b; Sprey, 1975; Olson et al., 1975.) Certainly in Marxist and Weberian thought the quest for power is a constant struggle between those who seek change versus those who seek constancy (Collins, 1975; Duke, 1976).

For that reason, Winter's approach (1973) to defining power may contain greater validity. He argues that it is the "ability or capacity" to produce "intended effects" on the behavior of others. We can still retain the notion that power is a "system property," and suggest that these effects exist on a continuum. Sometimes the effects may be change, sometimes no change, and oftentimes a mixture of the two leaning closer to either one pole of the continuum or the other. Emphasis on struggle for change versus constancy also highlights the issue of historic male dominance over females and the interests of the former in

Figure 13.1.   A Propositional Model of Marital Power

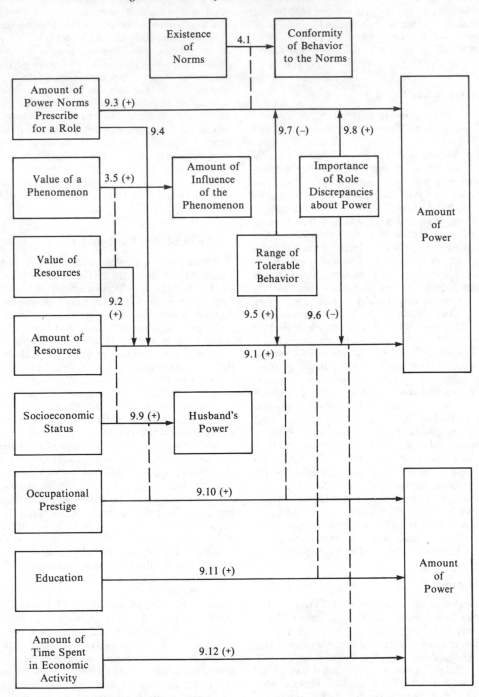

Source: Burr, 1973: 198.

preserving the status quo and of the latter in changing it (Gillespie, 1971). Indeed any discussion of familial power that overlooks this struggle and its implications is in jeopardy of being irrelevant.

Furthermore, Winter's use of the term "intended" is extremely important because it suggests that power cannot be divorced from the notion of goal orientation (Buckley, 1967), or reward seeking (Homans, 1974), or the pursuit of interests (Collins, 1975). Simultaneously, focus on rewards, interests, etc., helps tie analysis of familial power into mainstream sociological theory. Unfortunately, as the above literature review suggests, past theory and research into familial power have tended to exist outside that mainstream. Instead, as Collins (1975) argues, sociologists should be working toward a "generalizing science" in which we develop, for instance, broad "theories of power" which are able to subsume its existence in a wide variety of substantive areas including family, education, political, economic, and religious systems, etc. Collins (1975) has taken a major step in this direction, and we shall return to him later in the course of arguing that theoretically there is nothing unique about familial power and that failure to explain family power in terms of general principles will continue to contribute to relatively low level of theoretical sophistication in this substantive area (Sprey, 1972:237).

Besides defining power, Olson and Cromwell (1975) also identify three "domains" of family power: bases, processes, and outcomes. First, *bases* of family power consist "primarily of the resources an individual possesses which may increase their ability to exercise control in a given situation" (5–6). They draw upon Raven et al. (1975) to suggest six such bases or *resources*: "legitimate power" or authority, based on normatively prescribed rights; "referent power," derived from Other's identification with Person or his attractiveness to Person; "expert power," due to Other's awareness that Person has more knowledge or skills in a particular area; "informational power," from Person's superior capabilities of persuasiveness; "reward power," gratifications that Person controls; and "coercive power," Person's capabilities of inflicting punishments. (See also Safilios-Rothschild, 1970, 1976.)

Bertrand Russell is quoted as stating that "the fundamental concept in social science is Power in the same sense that Energy is the fundamental concept in physics" (Bannester, 1969:391). Bannester (1969), then, argues that if Russell's "be the First Law of Sociodynamics, then the Second surely is that . . . power is a . . . function of resources in supply and demand . . ." (p. 391). Emerson (1976) defines resource as "an ability, possession or other attribute of an actor giving him the capacity to reward (or punish) another actor." Resources clearly are often tangible, but they may just as often be intangible. Emerson's parsimonious definition subsumes the six bases suggested above and also identifies the critical issue

regarding resources, namely, that they are used to *reward* or to *punish*. And it is these *sanctions* that put teeth into a definition of power. Recall that power is defined in terms of achieving intended effects. Presumably these effects are achieved through the manipulation (actual or threatened or potential) of resources, or rewards and punishments. Even those who hold legitimate authority based on normative regulation must eventually shore up that authority in terms of positive or negative sanctions, or else it will begin to erode (Blau, 1964).

A second "domain" of family power identified by Olson and Cromwell (1975) is that of the *processes* or interaction among family members during various stages of "discussions, decision-making, problem-solving, conflict-resolution, and crisis-management" (6). Given that resources are possessed in varying degrees by the actors involved, what are the dynamics which describe how the actors utilize those resources vis-à-vis one another? Literature surveys show that this second domain is the weakest and least substantiated of the three, both conceptually and operationally (Olson and Cromwell, 1975:6). Not just in studies of family but also in all other substantive areas of sociology, the identification of processes of power utilization has been exceedingly difficult (Olson, 1969). Olson and Cromwell (1975) suggest two important dimensions within these processes. One is "assertiveness" or "the number of attempts which an individual makes to change the behavior of others. "Control" sometimes referred to as influence, is the number of effective attempts which an individual makes that actually change the behavior of others" (6). Since these concepts "take into account . . . the responses of . . . other persons," they seem to speak to the matter raised earlier regarding efforts to resist change and maintain constancy.

Sprey contributes to our understanding of power in process by criticizing studies that assume that power is based on the use of "a purely static inventory of resources." Instead, he opts for "a concept of structure that reflects a balancing of the mutual power inputs in marriages and families" (1975:65). He suggests that we should be examining "orderly process," or process that is "rule-governed" or "structured" or "structuring" (67). Evidently those terms are analogous to his description of "powering . . . the ongoing confrontation in which the power inputs of all participants are *reciprocally* put to the test" (Sprey, 1972:236). He suggests that while family members may have difficulty in reporting on the abstract concept of "power," they can, and we should ask them to "tell us what happens in terms of moves and countermoves, threats and promises, aggression and appeasement . . ." (237). Both he and Wieting and McLaren (1975) draw on *structuralism* as a possible source of insights into ways to investigate "orderly processes" within families. Later, we return to these and to additional insights in order to develop further the matter of power and processes.

The third and final "domain" identified by Olson and Cromwell is power *outcomes* (1975:6). More work has been done in this realm "than on the other two domains combined" (1975:6). It is also known as "decision-making," but that is an inaccurate label. By definition, decision making implies study of dynamics or process, but instead what is usually measured is "wives' retrospective reporting [solely] on the *outcomes*" of who decided to do what (7). While such information has been useful, the technique has numerous theoretical and methodological shortcomings, which are detailed throughout the Cromwell-Olson volume. However, the greatest flaw of that methodological approach in terms of inhibiting theory development is the static images of power, resources, and decision making it creates. Emphasis on outcomes implies a kind of finality, and also a simplistic view of the realities and the number of variables actually involved. Investigators, for instance, will cross-tabulate husband's education with the frequency of reported outcome-decisions in certain household areas. (Incidentally, there is rarely any theoretical justification for choice of these "areas": Scanzoni, 1970:143ff.) The conclusion conveyed is that this association is the end of the matter. It has been "settled" that education and decision-outcomes relate positively. Aside from perhaps one additional control variable at a time, the relationship is not systematically "elaborated" even in the Lazarsfeld et al. (1972) sense. Multivariate analysis is even more rare. More importantly, there is no effort to develop complex models which might specify the causes and consequences, e.g., "costs" of power (Sprey, 1972), of an outcome in terms of the larger familial and social context in which it exists. For these and other reasons the conclusion is inescapable that a simple bivariate association cannot possibly be the end of the matter. Instead, it seems more likely that what is labeled "outcome" is simply one stage of an ongoing process which includes important links with a variety of antecedent and consequential variables. Hence, in our critique of "outcomes", we are forced back to the primacy of "process" in seeking to grasp the elusive notion of power.

Recall that the definition of power is the capability to achieve intended effects. "Effects" could be thought of as outcomes, but the fact that effects were arrived at is not in and of itself anywhere nearly as important as knowing *how* the actor got there (resources, processes). Therefore, what has been identified as "domain 3" should in the future be relegated to a much less central position. Instead, from a more dynamic perspective (see below), that juncture is simply one stage in the *process* aspect of power, and should thus be identified.

Additional Issues

Figure 13.1 synthesized the literature to date as to how "amount of power" is influenced by the complex interplay of normative definitions and tangible and intangible resources. Several issues must be added to that complex interplay, the first of which is the *legitimacy* of power. A second is that power as a process cannot be analyzed validly apart from "adjoining" and intrinsically related processes such as attraction, exchange, negotiation, conflict, change, and so forth. This is part of what Sprey means by asserting that "the explanatory potential of the power concept is limited. . . . I see it as an intervening variable" (1975:76). A third matter pertains to the *saliency* of any particular issue, or goal, or desired reward, or interest. How vital, important, significant, crucial, or trivial is it to an actor that the "intended effect" be fully, partially, or minimally attained? A fourth and related issue is the *locus* of power. Is it more fruitful to approach it as the property of a person ("wife power," "husband power") or as the property of a situation, or system?

Looking first at legitimacy, recall that Blau argues that in any social situation norms are an intrinsic and ubiquitous element in defining the meanings of exchanges, as well as the fairness or legitimacy of the power that emerges from them (1964:22, 154, 199ff.). He suggests, (150) that his notion of power based on "fair exchange" is akin to Homan's rule of "distributive justice." Homans (1974:262–68) contends that when that rule is violated, prevailing power arrangements tend to be challenged (bargaining is generated and conflict may erupt). In short, by definition, even in what Brickman (1974) labels as partially structured relationships, norms are important structural elements which influence power and its adjoining processes.

Identification of norms as the means whereby power is legitimized, or is deemed as "fair" or "just," refines the Raven et al. (1975) notion cited earlier. Authority is not merely a resource *for* power, as they suggest. Instead it *is* power based on the normatively defined exercise of particular resources. Specifically, Buckley (1967:186) defines authority as "the direction or control of the behavior of others for the promotion of collective goals, based on some ascertainable form of their knowledgeable consent. Authority thus implies informed voluntary compliance. . . ." To produce intended effects or outcomes power can be legitimate (or authority) or it can be nonlegitimate power: "control or influence over the actions of others to promote one's goals without their consent, against their 'will', or without their knowledge or understanding" (Buckley, 1967:186). Thus the exercise of power (obtaining intended effects) is on a continuum of legitimacy such as in Figure 13.2. The nonlegitimate end of the power-legitimacy continuum may be characterized as "domination" (or exploitation), which subsumes the notion of lording it over others against their will. At the legitimate end is found authority or *institutionalized* power (Blau, 1964:211).

Under what conditions will actor B assign what degree of legitimacy (on the continuum of Figure 13.2) to actor

Figure 13.2. A Continuum of Power-Legitimacy

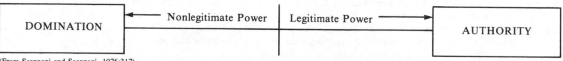

(From Scanzoni and Scanzoni, 1976:317)

A's power? Let us assume that the issue before A and B is the husband's (actor A) career advancement, clearly an interest sphere of great significance to him. To illuminate the interplay of resources and norms that might affect degree and legitimacy, we can list a series of statements derived from Blau (1964:228):

1. If the demands (or intended effects) of A exceed what prevailing norms in that context define as fair and just relative to *resource provision*, then B will feel exploited and may oppose A's demands.

   a. When A offers B no or few rewards or advantages for conformity or submission but nonetheless requires or forces B to submit, we have the polar extreme of statement 1, i.e., coercion, or coercive domination.

2. If the resources provided by A "barely" meet B's normative expectations for what is fair relative to A's demands, then B is not likely to feel exploited, but the degree of legitimacy ascribed to A's demands will be minimal as well.

3. If the benefits or rewards obtained by B from A are greater than the currently prevailing norms of "fairness" lead B to expect, then B will consider its position advantageous and will ascribe considerable legitimacy to A's demands.

Let us assume A wishes to move geographically to accept a promotion offered by his firm. The husband may intend the effect (power) of having his wife (actor B) and children go with him. But B may feel that the potential material and nonmaterial rewards A offers via his firm do not outweigh the costs of such a move. Therefore B ascribes nonlegitimacy to A's attempts to exercise power, and may indeed resist his demands (see 1 above). (The issue can be placed somewhere to the left of the bar in Figure 13.2.) Nevertheless, through various means A forces or coerces B to accompany him; and now the issue can be scaled at the left polar extreme of Figure 13.2—exercise of nonlegitimate power in this interest sphere (1a above). However in terms of 2,B may perceive some slight "profit" in the move, and the issue can now be scaled immediately to the right of the bar in Figure 13.2. The more the condition in 3 holds, i.e., the more the rewards offered exceed B's expectations of fair return, the further to the right on Figure 13.2 do we move this issue. Thus legitimate power (authority), even in such a traditionally male-centered sphere as own career interests, does not rest solely on any "inherent" normative pre-scriptions (though perhaps several decades ago it did). Instead norms, benefits, and costs interact within this sphere to establish a husband's authority or lack of it.

The second of these four additional issues pertains to the inherent linking of power to several other processes—exchange and conflict in particular as in the earlier derivations from Blau (Cromwell and Olson, 1975b: 19–21, 24–26). It would appear that a good deal of the theoretical sterility that has accompanied earlier discussions of power is owing to the failure to place it in its larger structural context (Sprey 1971). This failure appears traceable to ignoring developments in mainstream sociological theory (Duke, 1976). We shall therefore explore this matter in considerable detail below.

The third additional issue is the *saliency* of the interest-sphere, or the goal in view (Deutsch, 1973:371–73). Most earlier research failed to identify how significant or trivial the matter being decided is to the actors involved. (Two exceptions are Wilkening, 1968, and Wilkening and Lupri, 1965.) Traditionally the interests or spheres of the male have been centered more in occupation, and next in disposal of income, than in routine household maintenance (task performance) or child care. We would hypothesize that power in the two former areas is comparatively much more significant to him than power in the latter two. However, the interests of the "traditional wife" center more in the latter two areas, and for her, power there is quite significant. It is in the realm of income disposal that husband-wife interests or spheres overlap and potential for conflict have been greatest. It is not by chance that virtually every study that has probed finds the issue of income disposal is by far the one over which most couples have reported most frequent disagreements in the past (Scanzoni and Scanzoni, 1976:337). It is where interests overlap that the exercise of power has been contested most vigorously, and future "power research" will gain significance to the degree that it identifies areas of overlapping or intersecting interests where power becomes a live issue.

Analogies at the global level between the U.S. and U.S.S.R. are their earlier struggles over Berlin and, more recently, those in the Middle East and Africa. Both sides have legitimate claims to power in the Middle East and Africa, and both see their vital interests at stake; yet there are no definable boundaries as to where the power of one side ends and the other begins. Such ambiguities, whether at macro or micro levels, tend to stimulate "struggles for power." Simultaneously, the U.S. and U.S.S.R. each claim certain geographic areas as their *particular* spheres of interest or influence, in which they maintain considerable involvement, and over which they claim legitimate authority: West versus East Europe, South versus North Korea, and so forth. The U.S. does little to oppose Soviet coercion in Hungary and Czechoslovakia, and the U.S.S.R. sent none of its own troops to South Vietnam in the sixties. But Soviet troops dare not invade West Berlin, nor may the Americans invade Poland for purposes of "liberation." Similarly, within marriage, husbands and wives may possess "spheres of authority" or "provinces" over which they feel they should have maximum control. They may likewise recognize that their spouse possesses similar provinces. Challenges to the spouse's spheres of authority represent something very different from the exercise of power within one's own spheres.

Accordingly, the answer to the fourth issue regarding where to look for the most valid description of the locus of power must be the situation, or system, or particular issue (Cromwell and Olson, 1975b:20). To ask whether husband or wife has more *total* or *global* power is the wrong question, or at least it is premature. In terms of logical theory development a prior and more significant question is, does each spouse have power *where* each one wants it, and does each have as much as he/she wants? In most marriages, we may safely assume that both spouses have a certain degree of power within their own particular spheres of interest, in the same way that the U.S. and the U.S.S.R. both possess power in their own spheres of interest. Therefore the research task becomes one of identifying the spheres of interest, assessing power in those spheres and ultimately most important of all, constructing models which account for power where spouse interests overlap.

POWER AMONG PROCESSES

Sprey writes that marriage-family should be examined "within a context of conflict, which in my view, implies a framework of exchange" (1972:237). *Power becomes merely one of the important processes* to explain in order fully to analyze structure and interaction within family. This holistic view of a social system is compatible with contemporary views of social organization (Turner, 1974). Moreover it is compatible with what is known as systems "theory" (or better, "strategy") which Bertalanffy defines in modest terms as a "guiding idea" (1968:24). The "guiding idea" that Buckley (1967) develops more fully is that all social patterns are in *constant movement* and should be analyzed as being that way. As part of this analysis, Buckley draws on exchange and conflict theories and implies that the systems strategy or idea is the kind of metaframework within which the process elements of exchange, conflict, and power can all be subsumed.

Collins (1975:225) moves one critical step beyond Sprey's characterization of family as a conflict arena in general by positing that power relations within family are gender-linked, just as they are (and indeed because they are) gender-linked in the larger society.

> The family is a structure of dominance like anything else, and we are beginning to see that it enforces a great deal of inequity. In sex roles, there has been considerable male dominance in areas ranging from who gets the best occupational and political positions and who does most of the menial household labor, to who controls the scheduling of sexual intercourse and who gets most of the orgasms.

Collins does not, however, ignore the realities that women do have certain amounts of power within "women's spheres," that they do engage in conflict, and that they do "command ritual deference of their own" (225). Nevertheless, the major thrust of much literature in recent years has been to demonstrate differences in possession of power between men and women *qua* interest groups. We see this first at the societal level (e.g., see Mitchell, 1969) and second in studies at micro levels which identify means whereby these inequities are perpetuated—e.g., learning of gender roles in family and school which orient men toward instrumentality or leadership, assertiveness, autonomy, and independence (Holter, 1970). In a recent study, for example, it was found that while men perceive themselves to be more instrumental than women perceive themselves to be, there were no differences by sex in self-perceptions of expressiveness (supportiveness, warmth, nurturance, gentleness, etc.) (Scanzoni, 1975b). There are also laboratory and small-sample, in-depth studies which suggest that "women may feel considerably more uneasy than men about power relationships and competitive interactions. . . . Husbands were more comfortable with power; they seemed freer to assert independence . . ." (Raush et al., 1974:206). Johnson (1975) excoriates (mostly) male researchers of family power because, theoretically, they have ignored and failed to ask questions pertaining to the realities of pervasive male dominance. She also alleges that, methodologically, their particular measuring instruments have been far too simplistic to apprehend the complexities of gender differentiation.

Gender differentiation has of course been intimately related to the matter of interests discussed earlier. Also recall our allusion to Brickman's (1974) notion of the "fully structured" or "functionalist"-type relationship in which, in the past, relatively clear norms prescribed which sex pursued what kinds of interests. Fox uses the term "spontaneous consensus" to describe the situation in which

> participants acquiesce in the current definition of roles, with their differing degrees of discretion [power], and make no attempt, covert or overt, individual or collective, to redefine those roles, either their own or those of other participants. . . .

All members legitimize the existing distribution of discretion [power] in the sense of accepting it and being prepared to work with and through it [1974:85].

Persons "who share common goals are capable of allocating roles among themselves in the light of what they perceive as 'functional necessities' " (86).

Power and Gender Norms

Therefore, a key variable which must be introduced into a discussion of marital power is that of gender role norms. Elsewhere we have identified dimensions of gender norms that may be measured on a continuum ranging from "traditional" to "modern" (Scanzoni, 1975b:19–62). The polar end of the traditional side of the continuum is analogous to "fully structured" or "spontaneous consensus" situations. "Traditional" was defined in terms of the interests of the woman being subordinate to the interests of the husband in particular, and oftentimes to those of any children as well. "Familism" is synonymous with traditionalism. In such situations there is no denial that women have certain interests and they may indeed exert considerable power to achieve them. The critical point is that there is consensus as to a hierarchy of shared goals aimed at achieving the common good of the marriage or family group as a whole entity. At the top of the "spontaneously arrived at" hierarchy is the *husband's* occupation. If role allocation is such that he is the unique or even chief breadwinner, then the primacy of that sphere tends to permeate and affect the pursuit of all other interests within the system—his, the wife's, those of any children. Some of these affected interests include his and her leisure objectives, his and her income disposal preferences, wife's occupational aspirations, children's consumption desires, and so forth. Since there is consensus among system members that they will depend on his income provision in order to survive, there is also consensus that any competing interests which might threaten or undercut that interest must be subordinated to it. (The child wants to make noise, but father works the night shift and sleeps during the afternoon, so the child must keep still—his "interest" is subordinated. The child becomes ill and must stay home from school, and the wife takes off time from her part-time job at the store because the husband "cannot" take off from the factory "just" to stay home with kids. Even though she might prefer to go to her job, her interest is subordinated.) The list of such interest priorities is virtually endless, including, of course, the classic issue of the business or military man being continually transferred and wife and children having to forego any interests they might have in one community in order to follow him since they assume it is for the "common good" of the group to do so.

But the more we move (on a continuum of traditional-modern) away from the extreme traditional or fully struc-tured, or familistic, or spontaneous consensus situations, the more the *legitimacy* of that sort of husband power becomes more problematic. Fox (1974) himself characterizes the extreme form of his own "spontaneous consensus model" as "implausible" (88), except where persons "are moved by a common cause or by some sustaining religious, political, or ethical conviction. Such frustrations and deprivations as they are aware of in their low-discretion [power] role are pushed to the periphery of consciousness by the strength of their commitment" (86). Among contemporary (especially younger) marriages there is very likely much less spontaneous consensus over gender roles than there was some decades ago (Mason et al., 1976). The exceptions would be where strong ethical and religious convictions regarding ultimate male authority still prevail, as among conservative Catholics, Jews, Protestants, and Mormons (Westoff and Potvin, 1967).

Therefore, let us move to the opposite polar end of the gender role continuum (introduced above) to what has been labeled modernity or "individualism" (Scanzoni, 1975b). "Modernity" characterizes situations in which the interests of the woman are equal in significance to those of husband and any children. Moreover, these interests generally include serious occupational involvement. Consequently, the husband is no longer unique or even chief breadwinner; instead women and men are coproviders (Fogarty et al, 1971; Scanzoni, 1972, Rosaldo and Lamphere, 1974). This parity of occupational interests subsequently pervades all other household interests in the same fashion as did the husband's unique-provider interest. Moreover, in these coprovider situations, all remaining interests of all household members revolve around these equally predominant interests or objectives. Incidentally, the pursuit of individualistic interests by women is not inherently antithetical to household or group interests, any more than is so for male pursuit of individualistic interests. This is a topic to which we shall return later when we consider *maximum joint profit*.

It seems apparent that the more we move along the gender role continuum from traditional to modern, the more that power and its "adjoining" processes—exchange, negotiation, conflict, change—become salient issues. That is essentially Fox's argument (1974:88ff.), and it seems a valid one when we consider that by definition little or no negotiation or exercise of power is required for men and women to assume spontaneously their traditional roles as breadwinner and expressive hub, respectively. But we may assume that any woman who wishes to be coprovider with her spouse (or spouse-to-be) will have to make that interest known and be prepared to negotiate the practical behavioral implications of it for both partners and for any children. Moreover, there is no guarantee that a bargain struck at time 1 (an "outcome") regarding these interests will be defined as satisfactory and just by either or both partners six months later. In short, it is utopian sentiment to assume, as some persons evidently do, that movement toward egalitarian role structures somehow signals the "end of power" as a viable theoretical and research interest. Quite the contrary—as power becomes more problematic, it shall become more significant and require more rigorous investigation.

Power and Delineation of Interests

Use of terms such as "spontaneous consensus" and "interest spheres" is akin to the emphasis suggested by Wieting and McLaren (1975). They argue that we ought to examine power as it appears in various structural arrangements; and also that we ought to pay close attention to the *rules* that govern power within these varied forms. That emphasis on rules has been present a long time among students of conflict processes (Coser, 1956, Dahrendorf, 1959). Consequently, we need to distinguish the analysis of power exercised upon clearly delineated spheres of interest from power exercised with respect to overlapping interest spheres.

For instance, let us assume we are dealing with marriages that are structured in terms of traditional gender norms—the woman is something other than equal partner, she is junior partner or complement (Scanzoni, 1972). Let us further assume that there are at least two spheres of interest that have been totally hers since marriage by virtue of "spontaneous consensus" between her and her spouse: these interests are cooking and household decorating. To the degree husbands have few "vital interests" in these areas wives have virtually total power; i.e., they are able to achieve whatever intended effects they please. Similarly, the husband might also hold "total power" within his own occupational sphere. Presumably there had never been any bargaining over these three matters. Rather there have been prevailing norms or rules that structured them since marriage. Therefore, within interest spheres that are the province of one party, and over which there has been "emergent" consensus since the onset of the relationship, power is *relatively* straightforward to identify. It is party A or B effecting whatever results he or she wants. Moreover the power is legitimate to the degree that Other perceives considerable benefits flowing from its exercise.

However, where interest spheres overlap (e.g., consumption), or where one partner wishes to renegotiate power within a sphere over which previously there had been spontaneous consensus (e.g., wife employment), the identification of power is much less straightforward. At that point it must be examined in the context of several related processes such as the one just mentioned, i.e., negotiation. To move into this examination, let us suggest the following series of propositions:

1. The greater the education of the woman (man), the more modern, individualistic, egalitarian are the gender role norms (Holter, 1970; Scanzoni, 1975b).
2. The greater the gender role modernity, the more

likely the woman is consistently to challenge marital rules, roles, and arrangements based on previous spontaneous consensus (Collins; 1975:252ff.) In other words, she is more likely to seek to increase overlap between the partners regarding spheres of interest, thus to seek to decrease role specialization and to press for greater role interchangeability.

2a. Among overlapping interest spheres, the less the power (authority) of the husband is based on what she defines as "sufficient and necessary" resource possession and provision, the more likely she is to challenge the exercise of his power and to seek to exercise power of her own (see earlier discussion of Blau, 1964:228; Komarovsky, 1962; Scanzoni, 1970).

3. The greater the gender role modernity, the more likely she is to be employed full time (U.S. Department of Labor, 1973; Scanzoni, 1975b).

3a. The greater her modernity, the more likely she is to hold a job that provides higher levels of prestige and income, i.e., intangible and tangible resources (Scanzoni, 1975b).

4. The greater her modernity and education, the more skillful she tends to be in processes of negotiation and exchange (Emerson, 1976), which skills may be construed as intangible resources.

5. The greater her modernity and her own resources, the greater her capability to achieve within and among overlapping interest spheres the levels of intended effects (power) with which she is relatively satisfied—she considers the effects, the bargain, the outcome, to be fair and just.

Statement 2 suggests the theme discussed earlier—role modernity increases the likelihood of contested power. And 2a suggests that in a joint sphere, such as consumption, the husband who provides fewer economic resources has less "right" in the eyes of his wife to dispose of it in a way that does not first "satisfactorily" meet the interests of wife, children, and household (e.g., the working-class husband who purchases objects such as boats, motorcycles, and fishing or bowling equipment without telling the wife, who afterwards insists that "we can't afford it"). Statement 3 allows that sometimes role modernity may move women into the labor force; at other times working (for whatever reason) may increase gender egalitarianism. Statement 5 is a hypothesis which predicts that a woman's definition of distributive justice varies with her own modernity *and* resources. (Those definitions, of course, also vary by husband's resource provision, as in 2a.) She feels that the bargain or steady state regarding a particular joint sphere has satisfactorily taken her objectives into account. Her husband may feel the same way. Thus they may *both* have exercised power in negotiating a deal or a bargain. The question of who had *more* power, i.e., who was able to utilize available resources to "shape" the exchange *closest* to his/her original objectives prior to negotiation, may be second in importance to knowing *how* the "steady state" was achieved. What were the specifics of the bargains or deals that were made? How satisfied were the partners with the steady state? What reciprocities and concessions must each make to the other in subsequent negotiations?

For instance, the wife may begin to negotiate with her husband so that she can take a full-time job. She says she will pay for child care out of her earnings. Though he did not prefer her to work at all, her husband counters that if she takes a half-time job, he will pay for the child care, and moreover he will conform to her long-standing demand that he spend Saturdays with her instead of playing golf with his friends. She considers that exchange so satisfactory that she drops her original intended effect of full-time employment. She is quite satisfied because she has gotten another effect that she also wanted very much—his Saturday company. Note that both partners made concessions—they gave up "effects" they wanted to attain. Who can be said to have had *more* power in this exchange? Is that as theoretically significant as knowing some of the details of these processes, and knowing that both partners perceive that justice has been done? Incidentally, it is quite important to observe that, in empirical reality, interest spheres are seldom mutually exclusive of one another. Power, exchange, and conflict within one sphere (e.g., her occupational interests) may influence and be influenced by similar processes in another sphere (e.g., expressive and leisure interests).

Decision-Making Processes

The prior discussion triggers the question of whether we can spell out in greater detail and with some degree of validity the ongoing relationships that occur between and among power, exchange, etc. To attack this question we employ the term "decision making" advisedly and with considerable caution because of the myriad of unfortunate connotations associated with it. As observed earlier, the most glaring and misleading of these problems has been to confound relatively fixed *outcomes* with the complex, dynamic *processes* that result in outcomes. To ask "who decides what" *in no way* taps the intricacies of decision-making *processes*.

That approach is far too narrow for such a rich appellation. In fact, "decision making" is too rich and broad to be treated as a single concept, or as one variable measured by a sole indicator. Instead, let us understand it as an abstract *construct* which subsumes a variety of more concrete and measurable concepts. Following that strategy, the notion of "decision making" becomes exceedingly more theoretically significant than it was before. One of the ways in which it becomes newly important is to provide a shorthand way to describe relations among the complex processes that we have in view. Coleman's (1975) "purposive action" is synonymous with this view of decision making.

Attraction, as described by Blau (1964:38–41) is the process that brings two (or more) actors together because each perceives that Other has valued rewards, benefits, resources that Actor wants. (In the case of a married pair, this process obviously begins prior to legal sanctions.)

Exchange is the pattern whereby each provides the other with valued benefits or gratifications. *Social* exchange can be contrasted with *economic* exchange on a variety of grounds including the commodities involved but more importantly by the nature of the obligations and reciprocities engendered (Gouldner, 1960; Blau, 1964; Fox, 1974; Ekeh, 1974). A fixed point of complete repayment is almost never reached in social exchange. Ambiguities and uncertainties as to the nature of mutual obligations engender continuing inputs by all parties involved. The ongoing inputs stimulate increased feelings of mutual gratitude and *rectitude,* thus contributing to maintenance and stability of social systems (Gouldner, 1960).

The rules of exchange are concerned with who gives how much of what benefits in return for how much of what other benefits. Rules or norms may emerge out of *spontaneous consensus* with little or no conscious thought being given to them (Ekeh, 1975). (The male buys the tickets and dinner, the female provides and also receives certain physical gratifications.)

Distributive justice is the perception by one or both actors that the exchanges in which they are engaging are fair, equitable, and just. Specifically, are the outputs they receive "equitable" relative to the inputs that they make? If they are not, the result is a sense of *distributive injustice* which is akin to our earlier discussion of nonlegitimate power including domination, coercion, exploitation.

Negotiation (used in this chapter as synonymous with *bargaining*, Rubin and Brown, 1975) occurs when either partner considers prior rules of exchange regarding a particular interest sphere to be unfair and wishes to *change* them. It may also occur because either partner wishes to alter exchange elements—the relative amounts of rewards that each receives and the obligations that each assumes—within the association itself.

Maximum joint profit (MJP) or group interests (Kelley and Schenitzki, 1972) rather than individual advantage may be presumed to be the goal of both actors in such negotiations. This, however, may fluctuate according to certain variables. For example, less educated men hold more traditional gender norms (Scanzoni, 1975b). A formerly traditional wife of one of those men may have grown more egalitarian and, as a consequence, may desire to become a full-time student. In the resulting negotiations, his goal is solely his own advantage—*not* to have her return to school. He is not willing to *compromise* at all, or to seek any sort of *joint profit*. On the other hand, men who are more gender role modern are more willing to compromise so that both parties can get something to satisfy them (Scanzoni, 1978b).

Another variable that might influence MJP is whether the pair is legally bound or not. If they are bound, then one could predict that there is more likelihood of one partner (or perhaps both) more frequently seeking advantage instead of MJP.

Power is the capability to achieve "intended effects" *during bargaining and negotiations*. Thus it is most validly described, as Heath (1976) argues, as *bargaining-power*. At this point it is essential for the reader to refer back to and insert our earlier conclusions regarding, first of all, legitimate power (authority); second, interest spheres, including overlap among them; and third, the five propositions describing the conditions under which attempts would be made to exercise power (see page 306). From this perspective, *power as process* is inseparable from *negotiations as process*. Bargaining-power is inseparable from the utilization of rewards and costs designed to arrive at new (or changed) patterns of exchanges over which both can sense distributive justice. The exercise of power in these negotiations can produce *changes* in the redistribution of rewards and costs and/or in the rules of exchange themselves. The results of such changes can lead one or both partners to feel that justice has been done and that Other intends MJP, as in above illustration of Saturday golfing and wife's part-time employment. Clearly, to insert "power" at this point within this sequence of "decision-making" processes speaks to Sprey's notion (1975) of power as an "intervening" factor. It cannot be fully analyzed or explained apart from its antecedents, its consequences, its correlates. In terms of research strategy the focus is on the whole set of relevant processes in order to discover how they might impinge on one another. Power cannot be isolated and examined as a discrete entity apart from this holistic perspective. Treating power in an isolated fashion has been a particularly potent hindrance to development of theory and measurements.

In an empirical test of these notions, wives were asked to state some behavior that they wished their husbands would *stop doing* or *start doing* (reported fully in Scanzoni, 1978b). That change in their husbands' behavior is their goal but they are not able to achieve it. Thus by definition husbands are exercising more power than wives over this *particular* dispute. In Sprey's terms, husbands are *regulating* ongoing conflict. Wives are next asked what kinds of bargaining strategies they utilize to try to get their husbands to change in the way they want them to change. What means of persuasion (Straus, 1976) did they employ to try to achieve their goal, which by definition is to try to exercise power. As they reported *how* they were trying to exercise power, the next question put to them was how *successful* they were in actually tipping the *balance of power* more in their favor. Did their husbands respond to their bargaining by: "(1) compromise and change; (2) explaining why he doesn't do what you want; (3) listening but doing nothing; (4) refusing even to listen to you?"

Response 1 represents maximum wife power *in this situation*. She has gotten him to make *some* changes with which they *both* can live, i.e., MJP. She did not get all she wanted, but she has succeeded in gaining certain concessions from him. And now he has less control (power) in setting and achieving his own goals than he had prior to the negotiations. Response 2 indicates that wives have at least *enough power* to keep their husbands justifying and defending their positions. In short (and this shows how bargaining and power are inextricably "bargaining-power") he has to keep on "talking." And the more he does that, the greater the likelihood that they will eventually evolve a compromise—that the *regulated conflict* will be replaced by a *fair exchange*. Thus response 2 indicates relatively *less* power than number 1, but also *more* power than number 3. In 3 he "allows" her to keep on talking, but he does not respond in any meaningful fashion, i.e., willingness to compromise or even talk. Therefore, compared to 2 the likelihood of change on his part is less, and by definition her power is less. Response 4 represents *minimal* wife capability to achieve her intended goals. In fact she has virtually no power at all since if he will not even listen, there is hardly any way she can negotiate him into any sort of compromise. These women would be least successful in tipping the *balance of power* (over this dispute) more in their favor and less in his. Number 3 women are relatively more successful, number 2 women still more effective, and number 1 women most successful of all.

Note that analytically it has been possible to conceptualize and measure separately conflict, husband power, wife bargaining strategies, wife-power, husband change, and so forth. But in the "real world" they are as "bonded" or as intrinsically interlocked as chemical or biological elements that make up some larger whole, e.g., circulatory system, plant, compound. In this case the larger whole within which these several elements are continually exercising feedback on one another is *ongoing decision-making processes*.

Trust is an additional element intrinsic to the larger whole called decision-making. Trust is defined by Deutsch (1973:148) as "confidence" that one "will find what is desired" (rewards) from Other "rather than what is feared" (costs, punishments). *Mistrust*, therefore, is precisely the opposite—expectations of costs from Other rather than rewards. Trust is linked with power via negotiation processes, and it is linked very closely with MJP. If Actor has confidence that Other wants to provide rewards, then Actor will negotiate and bargain very differently than where mistrust is present. (Obviously, trust and mistrust exist on a continuum.) Specifically, the greater the trust, the more willing Actor will be to defer or modify certain objectives or interests, i.e., the modification of *power* or of achieving intended effects. Actor "modifies" because she/he believes that Other will, in exchange, come forward (now or later) with other important gratifications, including perhaps modifications of his/her own. To have that confidence means simultaneous confidence that Other is concerned for the profit or interests of the relationship or system as a whole (MJP). As illustrative of this process, recall once more the Saturday golfing–part-time-employment exchange.

Conversely, if Actor perceives that Other is merely modestly oriented (either now or later) toward rewarding her/him (mistrust), then negotiating positions can become extremely rigid and inflexible. This is, Actor can insist that her/his intended effects (attempts to exercise power) be attained with little or no deviation therefrom (or as Sprey (1972) observes, the exercise of "power at any cost"). Subsequently, as Fox (1974:67) notes from Zand's small-group research, "trust tends to evoke trust, distrust to evoke distrust." The more Actor mistrusts Other and becomes firmly insistent on her/his intended effects, the more Other responds in kind (though, in fact, Other may have initially "caused" Actor to mistrust her/him because of failure to be "rewarding").

As both parties make their negotiating positions more inflexible, it becomes more likely that nonlegitimate power will emerge. In exasperation Actor may simply try to coerce or force Other to conform to her/his demands, even though Other may consider that grossly unfair (distributive injustice). Therefore, the trust variable becomes important in influencing the emergence of nonlegitimate power and distributive injustice. According to Fox (1974:67–68), "institutionalized trust" is trust that is "embodied in the rules, roles, and relations which [persons] impose on, or seek to get accepted by, others." If there is high trust, it is more possible to be more flexible in allowing oneself (or one's group) to be "imposed on" (to be affected by legitimate power), because Actor perceives two things following in return. First, rewards will eventually accrue—Other has Actor's best interests in view; second, Other is now obligated to reciprocate by allowing Actor to make certain demands, to exercise legitimate power over her/him (Fox, 1974:98; Gouldner, 1960).

The Cold War was a classic example of mistrust between the U.S. and the U.S.S.R. which resulted in inflexible aims in their attempts to exercise power. The "thawing" of that "war" was accompanied by less mistrust and greater willingness by each side to modify its power demands. This is particularly evident over nuclear arms control and fits Zand's definition of trust as "the conscious regulation of one's dependence on another" (Fox, 1974:69). For the U.S. and the U.S.S.R. to *trust* each other regarding nuclear weapons, they must at the very least *depend* more and more on each other not to launch a preemptory strike. With regard to marriage-family, trust involves regulation of Actor's behavior according to Other's good will, or orientation to provide gratifications. Actor is willing to take risks and to defer or modify certain intended effects, to the extent that she/he is convinced Other will do the same. On the other side, mistrust is unwillingness to regulate one's behavior so as

to depend on Other, because of the high-risk probability of severe cost or punishment. In short, trust appears to be enormously important in understanding negotiating power, but the juxtaposition of the two processes has been noticeably lacking in past sociological endeavor.

Communication is defined by Deutsch as the process by which Actor informs (misinforms) Other of, or relays to Other, her/his interests, objectives, activities, plans, perceptions of MJP, distributive injustice, trust, and so forth (1973:165–67). In contrast to semipopular literature which in naive and sentimental fashion asserts that "failure to communicate" is at the heart of "marital breakdown," communication, like power, should be viewed as merely one element subsumed under the broad construct "decision making." It overlaps with bargaining and bargaining power because large portions of those processes are taken up with relays between Actor and Other. Each seeks to convey what her/his intended effects (power aspirations) are. Simultaneously, each conveys what modifications or deferrals (deals or bargains) in these effects he/she will settle for in exchange for particular modifications from Other.

But perhaps the most significant overlap of communication lies with what Deutsch calls "the development of trust" (1973:166). We have just seen how critical trust is in the emergence of legitimate versus nonlegitimate power. Actor's trust of Other is developed mostly by Other's *behavior* in providing rewards and punishments. But trust-mistrust is also fostered by Other's verbal statements—what Other promises or refuses to promise during their negotiations; how Other justifies behaviors that Actor considers unjust; the ways in which Other justifies why she/he "broke deals" by doing what they had promised not to do or else by failing to do what they had promised they would do. My recent research indicates that women perceive that men will agree to a compromise (response 1 above) and then over time gradually begin to ignore or even renege on it.

If we assume that a highly problematic element in communication is its accuracy (Deutsch, 1973:353–56; Brickman, 1974:228), then Actor and Other may vary in the degree to which they provide and receive accurate relays of each other's intentions. To the degree that accuracy increases *and* each perceives that increased rewards are forthcoming (along with MJP), we may conclude that we have both the necessary and sufficient conditions for optimum trust. If communications are accurate but the relays lead Actor to conclude that Other is not "rewarding," trust will diminish. Trust may also be diminished where "inaccurate" communications lead Actor to conclude that Other will not reward or is not interested in MJP, even if certain rewards actually are being received. Trust and its implications for legitimate power and fair exchanges would seem to flourish most where Other is not merely "read" accurately, but is read as being reward-intentioned.

Conflict is inseparable from and requires the exercise of power (Duke, 1976). If we slightly modify Coser (1956), conflict may be defined as *struggle against resistance* to achieve intended effects. It is one thing to seek to exercise power in negotiations wherein the objective is to arrive at a settlement that both consider fair and just, where both aim at "reasonable" intended effects. In that situation, power is exercised, probably by both parties, apart from actual conflict (but never the opposite). But at any point in the ongoingness of a social system (whether during actual negotiations or afterwards), Other may *resist* Actor's efforts to achieve justice by presenting inflexible, non-negotiable demands, by seeking to exercise *nonlegitimate power*. If in turn Actor resists or struggles, then we may say that *conflict* has been generated. (If Actor acquiesces, no actual conflict may be said to exist.)[5] Struggle may take several forms, including refusal to submit, submitting while constantly communicating dissatisfaction (perhaps hostility, as discussed below), and continually seeking to renegotiate so as to remove the injustice. The longer the conflict continues (whatever strategies are employed, including coercion and violence, as below) the more it may, in Sprey's terms (1971), be said to become *institutionalized,* i.e., an integral component within the ongoing family system. So long as conflict continues, we may conceive of it as being *regulated* (not *resolved*) by nonlegitimate power (Dahrendorf, 1959; Coser, 1956; Deutsch, 1973; Sprey, 1971). It remains an empirical issue how many and what sorts of regulated conflicts a marriage can encompass and yet remain stable, a point to which we shall return below.

We may say that a conflict has been *resolved* if through a renegotiation of costs and rewards the injustice and the nonlegitimate power are removed and a new "fair exchange" is established. Actor has, in essence, exerted power in such a way as to end Other's resistance (break the conflict situation or stalemate) and to achieve "intended effects" in this interest sphere, yet has done so in such a way that Other feels it is fair—a case of MJP. Thus while the literature concurs that conflicts are inevitable in any social system, the suggestion is also made that the process of resolution has the consequence of increasing solidarity or cohesion within that system (Coser, 1956; Blau, 1964; Deutsch, 1973). The reasons for increased solidarity owing to resolution are several. One is the removal of the injustice; another may be the increase of trust relations accomplished through negotiation of the struggle. Finally, it would appear that a new set of exchanges or patterns may have the consequence of making system members more interdependent subsequent to the struggle than they were prior to it (Scanzoni, 1977a). For instance, there may be more sets of rewards and costs present than before; and their distribution may occur within a more complex set of reciprocities in which more enduring sets of obligations are generated to a greater degree than was the case previously.

Hostility may be defined as feelings of anger and/or resentment that are *expressed* to a greater or lesser degree and in varying ways (Homans, 1974:257). Hostility is triggered by combinations of the array of processes discussed above—distributive injustice (inadequate reward provision), nonlegitimate power, regulated conflict, mistrust, inadequate frequency of or garbled communications, and so forth (Homans, 1974:178-79, 257-61; Coser, 1956). For instance, frequency of marital hostility has been shown to be related inversely to levels of tangible and intangible socioeconomic resources supplied by husbands (Scanzoni, 1970; 135-42). Theoretically, the key feature about hostility is the degree to which it is actually expressed or suppressed. Coser (1956) argues that the more and the more often hostilities are suppressed, the greater the likelihood that a social system will experience a sudden (and often violent) upheaval or "explosion" (i.e., termination). This holds whether the system be marital or nation-state. The same type of unexpected upheaval could occur where there is a series of regulated conflicts, or else where there is a series of situations in which Actor perceives injustice by Other but does not resist or struggle, hence in which by definition conflict has not occurred.

To the degree that hostility is expressed it may become "an instrumental act by which [Actor] tries to raise to a higher and more just level the amount of reward [Actor] gets" (Homans, 1974:257). Presumably conflict could be generated apart from hostility (as described above), especially where high-trust relations are present. However, a viable hypothesis would be that a certain degree of hostility tends to accompany conflict, especially when it is regulated, and that, as Homans indicates, it may indeed become an "instrumental act" or tool or strategy used by persons to try to resolve the conflict. If Actor expresses anger or resentment toward Other, this may help to convince him/her that Actor is very serious about removing the injustice and thus provide support to Actor's efforts to exercise power in that direction.

By way of contrast to hostility and conflict that are specifically goal-oriented (or what Coser, 1956, calls "realistic"), a social system such as marriage may experience conflict and especially hostility that is not apparently directed toward any particular perceived injustice ("nonrealistic"). It may be that future research could identify such behaviors as indirect offshoots or "displacements" from interest spheres where actual injustice occurs, nonlegitimate power is being exercised, relative deprivation is perceived, and so forth.

Violence, or the use of physical force against another, may also be "nonrealistic" or "realistic." In the former instance it would not have any immediately observable connection with nonlegitimate power, conflict, and injustice (Steinmetz and Straus, 1974:4; Scanzoni and Scanzoni, 1976:344). Our major focus here, however, is on the emergence of violence in connection with distributive injustice and nonlegitimate power. All such power is by our earlier definition equivalent to coercion, exploitation, and domination. A good deal of that coercion may be nonviolent—as noted earlier Actor is often "forced" into compliance because she/he possesses insufficient resources or alternatives to do otherwise. The intriguing question becomes, at what point on a continuum of coercion does nonviolence cease and physical force occur?

Evidence is accumulating which shows that attempts to regulate conflict through domination (nonlegitimate power) may easily "escalate to the point of violence" (Goode, 1971; Steinmetz and Straus, 1974). The rapidly growing literature on family violence suggests that violence is inversely related to husband's status or possession of resources (Komarovsky, 1962; O'Brien, 1971; Gelles, 1976). Men who are unable to effect their intentions through negotiations based on legitimate power and who find that nonphysical coercion may be insufficient in their attempts to achieve their own intentions may simply resort to their "ultimate weapon"—pushing, slapping, beating, even murder. Nonetheless, in spite of generally greater male strength, recent data indicate that the proportion of wives who murder husbands is as great as the converse (Federal Bureau of Investigation, 1973).

It seems safe to assume that where there is violence, it has been preceded by hostility. Violence, like hostility, may be used as a tool in conflict processes. We could hypothesize that violence is much more likely to emerge in conjunction with the *regulation* than the resolution of conflict within a particular interest sphere. The introduction of violence into processes of nonlegitimate power and conflict could be subsumed by Deutsch's notion of "destructive conflict." By "destructive" he means "a tendency to expand and escalate" (1973:351). Apart from the value-laden connotations of the term "destructive," it is useful to think of violence as a significant expansion and escalation of the struggle for marital power within a particular interest sphere. Concomitantly, having erupted within one interest sphere, violence may expand into several related interest spheres as well, thus representing a quantum escalation of the struggle for power. Future investigations will need to consider conditions under which once having expanded into violence, conflict processes deescalate into nonviolence rather than continue to escalate in violence level until one or both partners consider the total marital situation too costly for them to maintain any longer.

Decision-Making Processes and the Comparison Level for Alternatives (Cl Alt)

The exercise of these processes, including power, contribute heavily to assessments regarding whether one should maintain or dissolve an association such as marriage. That is because their exercise constitutes sets of costs and rewards that go into the calculation of *Comparison Level* (Cl) and *Cl Alt* (Thibaut and Kelley, 1959). Much past literature has conceived of power as some sort

of end point, as dependent variable. Instead, as one process among others, it has consequences for other processes as well as for the system within which it is located. For example, having to submit to nonlegitimate power may be thought of as cost or punishment even where one does not struggle. And it is obviously costly if Actor chooses to resist but is forced to submit to regulated conflict or violence. If, over a wide range of significant interest spheres, Actor perceives that both she/he and Other are exercising power legitimately to achieve distributive justice and MJP, they will label these evaluations as gratifications and add them to the positive side of the ledger. Conversely, if over this same range of interests Actor perceives that Other seeks to or actually does *dominate* via nonlegitimate power and/or regulated conflicts, or violence, they will label these evaluations as costs or punishments to be assigned to the negative side of that same ledger. The subsequent cost-reward ratio along with other costs and rewards contributes to the "decision" to terminate or to the ongoing acceptance of system maintenance.

Decision-making has been chosen as the construct under which to subsume these several overlapping processes. The construct has no immediate formal definition or empirical indicator. Instead it is defined in terms of, and is a shorthand way to describe, the intrinsic ongoing interrelatedness of these several processes. Borrowing modestly from "systems strategies," we may suggest that among and between these processes there is continual feedback and motion. Throughout the preceding discussion the impression might sometimes have been conveyed that there is a simple chronological sequence going from attraction to maintenance-dissolution. In the "real world" there is considerably more conceptual complexity than that for several important reasons. One of these is the perpetual feedback phenomenon just described. Moreover, the concepts themselves may represent processes that are occurring simultaneously (e.g., power, conflict, trust, negotiations), and it is difficult to keep them mutually exclusive vis-à-vis one another. Another related reason for complexity is that inevitably there are interconnections among several interest spheres, if for no other cause than that negotiations very often result in bargains across interest spheres, as illustrated earlier with regard to occupation and leisure interests. In any case, regardless of what label one chooses to employ as an umbrella under which to subsume these processes, power is embedded among and within them and cannot validly be explained in isolation from them. (Coleman's "purposive-action" is another label.)

Measurement of Decision Processes

Space limitations permitted only the barest discussion of how the foregoing conceptualization of power and related processes were measured in a coherent and systematic fashion. Suffice it to note that empirical efforts designed to operationalize such a ''process schema'' were carried out (Scanzoni, 1978b). While much more work is called for, the early results are promising in that they support the validity of the idea of approaching power within a network of adjoining social processes. In brief, the logic of dealing with the several decision-making processes in conjunction with one another is amenable to the rigors of empirical verification. Though it is difficult to quantify social processes and though sociologists are not in the habit of doing it, it is not an impossible task; and it is one that demands our attention if the theoretical issues involved are ever to be adequately explored.[6]

CHILDREN AND FAMILY POWER

Earlier, allusion was made to the distinction between power involving only spouses and power processes that involve children as well. However, in this chapter, owing to space limitations, our prime focus has been on the marital dyad. And while most of the literature takes that same focus, the Cromwell and Olson volume (1975a) contains several articles that deal with children's power. Some researchers seem to have assumed that children have little or no power, without much investigation of the question. For example, even economically dependent adolescents would seem to possess significant power in certain of their own interest spheres. Equally intriguing is the issue of power between parents and offspring who dwell in separate households but who engage in economic and social exchanges such as provision of college money, or financial assistance by the middle-aged couple to their newly married offspring and/or their elderly parents. We would assume that children's power could be explained by the same kinds of theoretical notions (power as process attached to adjoining processes such as exchange, negotiation, conflict, etc.) as are applied to marital power.

Nonetheless, there are at least four important hypotheses that need to be investigated when our theoretical models expand to consider children's as well as parent's power. First, as the child ages, her/his resources (tangible, intangible, external alternatives, and so forth) increase. Therefore we expect his/her power will inevitably increase as well. Second, it is likely that system rules or norms of most families currently prescribe that the interests of dependent children are ultimately subordinate to the central interests of parents—especially father's occupational interests. Third, but based on the first two hypotheses, how is the potential clash between the young person's growing power and his/her continued subordination reconciled (Davis, 1940)? What substantive differences, if any, are there between spouse-spouse negotiation, power, and conflict and the same sorts of processes between parent and child? Are negotiation, distributive justice, trust, conflict, etc., tempered by an awareness on the part of both superordinates and subordinates that

ultimately the latter will gain economic independence and thus autonomy? How do parents train their children to exercise power within and outside the family while at the same time maintaining ultimate power? What variations exist by education of parents and by gender of child and the degree to which children are taught to exercise power effectively and to be autonomous (Kohn, 1969)? Fourth, and finally, under what conditions does spouse A (and a child or children) form *coalitions* against spouse B in order to achieve effects intended by A or by any allied children?

The issue of gender raises a question which is fundamentally related to these matters. Most often in the past, newly married persons considered a child (children) to be in their best interests, or at least not prohibitively detrimental to those interests. It was assumed that the change from marriage to family was *pro forma*. Intrinsic to this ''fully structured spontaneous consensus'' was the institutionalization of female responsibility for child care. Thus there was little or no negotiation about *whether* to have children, and whose *prime* responsibility they were. However, with the revival of feminism, these patterns are apparently shifting from fully to *partially* structured relationships. Veevers (1974) has documented the emergence of preference for the ''child-free'' life style among certain well-educated, younger couples. Recent census data suggest this preference has indeed increased over the past 10 years (U.S. Bureau of the Census, 1976). And although the vast majority of women still want children, recent evidence suggests that the more gender role–modern or individualistic they are, the fewer children they intend to have and therefore the more effectively they contracept (Scanzoni, 1975b, 1976). The younger, well-educated, role-modern woman is more likely to regard the whether, when, and care of children as interests to be negotiated than as long-standing patterns to which she merely conforms. Thus processes of bargaining and power become increasingly built into husband-wife exchanges regarding fertility matters that were in the past taken for granted. Concomitantly, should a child be born, decisions regarding child care and its implications for the occupational pursuits of both spouses are more likely than before to become live issues into which power inputs are made and from which outcomes emerge which affect the interest spheres of both.

To the degree that these changes are coming about, they are in part owing to the fact that offspring do indeed have power. From infancy onward they make certain care demands on adults to which they must conform. In the past this conformity has been carried out mostly by women. The role-modern woman may see a large amount of this type of conformity as not in her best interests. Since the possibility of reduction in the actual quantity of a child's demands tends to be minimal, she can do at least two things to enhance her interests. She can reduce significantly the number of children she bears (compared to earlier cohorts of women with similar education), and she can negotiate her husband into what she considers more equitable care responsibilities. This could involve his actually taking on parenting duties and/or his sharing responsibility to see that adequate extrafamilial care is provided. In these circumstances the power of the child remains constant, but conformity to it is borne more by men, less by women than in the past. Concomitantly, within this sphere the woman has assumed more power (achieving intended effects vis-à-vis men's behaviors) than comparable women held in the past, and men have relinquished some degree of power.

SUMMARY

We began by showing how functionalism and "marital adjustment" contributed to authority patterns based on female subordination. Next we moved to a discussion of earlier research to assess "family power." The efforts of Rodman and of Burr in trying to systematize past research and to make it theoretically meaningful were also examined. Considerable space was given to reports in the Cromwell-Olson anthology (1975a) which identify theoretical and methodological issues central to our concern. Building on these several systematic efforts, we attempted to analyze power between spouses (children's power was dealt with only very briefly) in terms of general social theory. Our aim was to incorporate marital-familial power within the same theoretical frameworks that might account for power within any other social organization. In part our goal is to contribute toward development of theoretical links between micro and macro levels of analysis (Coleman, 1975). This matter becomes especially important once we accept the premise that micro male-female power relations are both consequence and cause of macro male-female authority patterns (Collins, 1975).

It was argued that power cannot be analyzed in isolation—apart from intrinsically related social processes. Though it is risky to use the much maligned term "decision making," that label was nonetheless chosen as shorthand *construct* to subsume these ongoing inherently linked processes, which include attraction, exchange, exchange rules, distributive justice, negotiation, maximum joint profit, power (nonlegitimate power versus authority), trust, communication, conflict, hostility, and violence. Efforts were made to show how these several processes blend into, overlap with, sometimes "cause," and sometimes are "caused by" adjoining processes. Power and related "decision" processes are viewed as basic elements of social systems formed and maintained by persons primarily because of the benefits they perceive may accrue to them as a result of the association. Power, or more validly, "bargaining-power," is the relative capability to maximize those goals at minimum cost. In order to do that, system actors must *deal* with one another. We conceptualize these "dealings" as the processes described above. Thus researchers interested in analyzing any one of these processes should inevitably find themselves examining the rest of them as well.

It was acknowledged that empirical investigation into highly interrelated "decision" processes is not a simple matter. However, the research task is not insurmountable, and it is hoped that through the constant interplay of theory, measurement, and analytic techniques, social scientists will be able to arrive at increasingly valid understandings of the nature of social power and social processes.

NOTES

1. See Aronoff and Crano (1975), and Whyte (1976) for debate on the Parsons and Zelditch notions.
2. Brickman labels them "conflict" relationships, but that additional terminology is not requisite for our purposes.
3. I am indebted to Martha Myers for preparing this literature review.
4. See Safilios-Rothschild (1970) and Bahr (1974) for divergence over Michel's data.
5. The operational definition of conflict is open to debate and requires much more empirical work. See Brickman (1974).
6. See section II, "Methodological and Substantive Research," in Cromwell and Olson (1975a) for further discussion of methodological issues in regard to power in families.

REFERENCES

ARONOFF, J. AND W. D. CRANO
1975 "A re-examination of the cross-cultural principles of task segregation and sex role differentiation in the family." *American Sociological Review* 40:12–20.

BAHR, J.
1974 "Effects on power and division of labor in the family." In L. W. Hoffman and F. I. Nye (eds.), *Working Mothers*. San Francisco: Jossey-Bass.

BANNESTER, E. M.
1969 "Sociodynamics: An integrative theorem of power, authority, interfluence and love." *American Sociological Review* 34:374–93.

BELL, N. W. AND E. F. VOGEL
1960 "Toward a framework for functional analysis of family behavior." In N. W. Bell and E. F. Vogel (eds.), *A Modern Introduction to the Family*. New York: Free Press.

BERNARD, J.
1964 "The adjustments of married mates." In H. T. Christensen, *Handbook of Marriage and Family*. Chicago: Rand McNally.
1972 *The Future of Marriage*. New York: World Publishing.

BERTALANFFY, L. VON
1968 *General Systems Theory*. New York: Braziller.

BLAU, P. M.
1964 *Exchange and Power in Social Life*. New York: Wiley.

BLOOD, O.
1963 "Rejoinder to 'measurement and bases of family power.'" *Journal of Marriage and the Family* 25:475–78.
1967 *Love Match and Arranged Marriage*. New York: Free Press.

BLOOD, R. O. AND D. M. WOLFE
1960   *Husbands and Wives*. New York: Free Press.

BRICKMAN, P.
1974   *Social Conflict*. Lexington, Mass.: Heath.

BUCKLEY, W.
1967   *Sociology and Modern Systems Theory*. Englewood Cliffs, N.J.: Prentice-Hall.

BURGESS, E. W., H. J. LOCKE, AND M. M. THOMES
1963   *The Family: From Institution to Companionship*. New York: American Book.

BURIC, O. AND A. ZECEVIC
1967   "Family authority, marital satisfaction, and the social network in Yugoslavia." *Journal of Marriage and the Family* 29:325–36.

BURR, W. R.
1973   *Theory Construction and the Sociology of the Family*. New York: Wiley.

CENTERS, R., B. RAVEN, AND A. RODRIGUES
1971   "Conjugal power structure: A re-examination." *American Sociological Review* 36:264–78.

CHRISTENSEN, H. T. (ed.)
1964   *Handbook of Marriage and the Family*. Chicago: Rand McNally.

CLIGNET, R.
1970   *Many Wives: Many Powers*. Evanston, Ill,: Northwestern University Press.

COLEMAN, J. S.
1975   "Social structure and a theory of action." In P. M. Blau (ed.), *Approaches to the Study of Social Structure*. New York: Free Press.

COLLINS, R.
1975   *Conflict Sociology*. New York: Academic Press.

COSER, L. A.
1956   *The Functions of Social Conflict*. New York: Free Press.

CROMWELL, R. E. AND D. H. OLSON (eds.)
1975a   *Power in Families*. New York: Wiley.
1975b   "Multidisciplinary perspectives of power." In R. E. Cromwell and D. H. Olson (eds.), *Power in Families*. New York: Wiley.

DAHRENDORF, R.
1959   *Class and Class Conflict in Industrial Society*. Stanford, Calif.: Stanford University Press.

DAVIS, K.
1940   "The sociology of parent-youth conflict." *American Sociological Review* 5:523–35.

DEUTSCH, M.
1973   *The Resolution of Conflict*. New Haven, Conn.: Yale University Press.

DUKE, J. T.
1976   *Conflict and Power in Social Life*. Provo, Utah: Brigham Young University Press.

EKEH, P. P.
1974   *Social Exchange: The Two Traditions*. Cambridge, Mass.: Harvard University Press.

EMERSON, R. M.
1976   "Social exchange Theory" In A. Inkeles, J. Coleman, N. Smelser (eds.) *Annual Review of Sociology*, Palo Alto, CA.: Annual Reviews, Inc.

FEDERAL BUREAU OF INVESTIGATION
1973   *Uniform Crime Reports 1972*. Washington, D.C.,: Government Printing Office.

FOGARTY, M. P., R. RAPOPORT, AND R. N. RAPOPORT
1971   *Sex, Career and Family*. London: George Allen & Unwin.

FOX, A.
1974   *Beyond Contract: Work, Power and Trust Relations*. London: Faber & Faber.

FOX, G. L.
1973   "Another look at the comparative resource model: Assessing the balance of power in Turkish marriages." *Journal of Marriage and the Family* 35:718–30.

GELLES, R. J.
1976   "Abused wives: Why do they stay?" *Journal of Marriage and The Family* 38:659–668.

GILLESPIE, D. L.
1971   "Who has the power? The marital struggle." *Journal of Marriage and the Family* 33:445–58.

GOODE, W. J.
1971   "Force and violence in the family." *Journal of Marriage and the Family* 33:624–36.

GOULDNER, A. W.
1960   "The norm of reciprocity: A preliminary statement." *American Sociological Review* 25:161–78.

HALLENBECK, P.
1966   "An analysis of power dynamics in marriage." *Journal of Marriage and the Family* 28:200–05.

HEATH, A.
1976   *Rational Choice Theory and Social Exchange*. New York: Cambridge.

HEER, D.
1958   "Dominance and the working wife." *Social Forces* 36:341–47.
1963   "The measurement and bases of family power: An overview." *Journal of Marriage and the Family* 25:133–39.

HERBST, P. G.
1952   "The measurement of family relationships." *Human Relations* 5:3–35.

HILL, R.
1965   "Decision-making and the family life cycle." In E. Shanas and G. F. Streib (eds.), *Social Structure and the Family: Generational Relations*. Englewood Cliffs, N.J.: Prentice-Hall.

HOFFMAN, L. W.
1958   "Some effects of the employment of mothers on family structure." Unpublished Dissertation, University of Michigan.

HOLTER, H.
1970   *Sex Roles and Social Structure*. Oslo: Universitetsforlaget.

HOMANS, G. C.
1961   *Social Behavior: Its Elementary Forms*. New York: Harcourt, Brace & World.
1974   *Social Behavior: Its Elementary Forms*, Revised. New York: Harcourt, Brace & World.

JOHNSON, C. L.
1975   "Authority and power in Japanese-American marriage." In R. E. Cromwell and D. H. Olson (eds.), *Power in Families*. New York: John Wiley.

KANDEL, D. AND G. LESSER
1972   "Marital decision-making in American and Danish urban families: A research note." *Journal of Marriage and the Family* 34:134–38.

KELLEY, H. H. AND D. P. SCHENITZKI
1972   "Bargaining." In C. G. McClintock (ed.), *Experimental Social Psychology*. New York: Holt, Rinehart and Winston.

KIMMEL, P. R. AND J. W. HAVENS
1966   "Game theory vs. mutual identification: Two criteria for assessing marital relationships." *Journal of Marriage and the Family* 28:460–65.

KOHN, M. L.
1969   *Class and Conformity*. Homewood, Ill.: Dorsey Press.

KOMAROVSKY, M.
1962   *Blue-Collar Marriage*. New York: Random House.

LAMOUSE, A.
1969   "Family roles of women: A German example." *Journal of Marriage and the Family* 31:145–52.

LAZARSFELD, P. F., A. K. PASANELLA, AND M. ROSENBERG (eds.)
1972   *Continuities in the Language of Social Research*. New York: Free Press.

LIU, W. T., I. W. HUTCHISON, AND L. K. HONG
1973   "Conjugal power and decision-making: A methodological note on cross-cultural study of the family." *American Journal of Sociology* 79:84–98.

LOCKE, H. J.
1968   *Predicting Adjustment in Marriage: A Comparison of a Divorced and a Happily Married Group*. New York: Greenwood Press.

LUPRI, E.
1969   "Contemporary authority patterns in the West German family: A study in cross-national validation." *Journal of Marriage and the Family* 31:134–44.

MASON, K. O., J. CZAJKA, AND S. ARBER
1976   "Change in U.S. women's sex-role attitudes, 1964–1975." *American Sociological Review* 41:573–596.

MCCALL, M.
1966   "Courtship as social exchange." In B. Farber (ed.), *Kinship and Family Organization*. New York: Wiley.

MERTON, R. K.
1959   "Notes on problem-finding in sociology." In R. K. Merton, L. Broom, and L. S. Cottrell, Jr. (eds.), *Sociology Today*. New York: Basic Books.

MICHEL, A.
1967   "Comparative data concerning the interaction in French and American families." *Journal of Marriage and the Family* 29:337–44.

MIDDLETON, R. AND S. PUTNEY
1960   "Dominance in decisions in the family: Race and class differences." *American Journal of Sociology* 65:605–09.

MITCHELL, J.
1969   "The longest revolution." In B. Roszak and T. Roszak (eds.), *Masculine-Feminine: Readings in Sexual Mythology and the Liberation of Women*. New York: Harper & Row.

MURILLO, N.
1971   "The Mexican-American family." In N. N. Wagner and M. J. Haug (eds.), *Chicanos: Social and Psychological Perspectives*. St. Louis: C. V. Mosby.

NYE, F. I. AND F. BERARDO
1966   *Emerging Conceptual Frameworks in Family Analysis*. New York: Macmillan.

O'BRIEN, J. E.
1971   "Violence in divorce-prone families." *Journal of Marriage and the Family* 33:692–98.

OLSON, D. H.
1969   "Measurement of Family power by self-report and behavioral methods." *Journal of Marriage and the Family* 31:545–50.

OLSON, D. H. AND R. E. CROMWELL
1975   "Power in families." In R. E. Cromwell and D. H. Olson (eds.), *Power in Families*. New York: Wiley.

OLSON, D. H., R. E. CROMWELL, AND D. M. KLEIN
1975   "Beyond family power." In R. E. Cromwell and D. H. Olson (eds.), *Power in Families*. New York: Wiley.

OLSON, D. H. AND C. RABUNSKY
1972   "Validity of four measures of family power." *Journal of Marriage and the Family* 34:224–234.

OPPONG, C.
1970   "Conjugal power and resources: An urban African example." *Journal of Marriage and the Family* 32:676–91.

PITTS, J. R.
1964   "The structural-functional approach." In H. T. Christensen (ed.), *Handbook of Marriage and the Family*. Chicago: Rand McNally.

RAUSH, H. L., W. A. BARRY, R. K. HERTEL, AND M. A. SWAIN
1974   *Communication Conflict and Marriage*. San Francisco: Jossey-Bass.

RAVEN, B. H., R. CENTERS, AND A. RODRIGUES
1975   "The bases of conjugal power." In R. E. Cromwell and D. H. Olson (eds.), *Power in Families*. New York: Wiley.

RODMAN, H.
1967   "Marital power in France, Greece, Yugoslavia and U.S.: A cross-national discussion." *Journal of Marriage and the Family* 29:320–24.

1972   "Marital power and the theory of resources in cultural context." *Journal of Comparative Family Studies* 3:50–67.

ROSALDO, M. Z. AND L. LAMPHERE
1974   *Woman, Culture and Society*. Stanford Calif.: Stanford University Press.

RUBIN, J. AND B. R. BROWN
1975   *The Social Psychology of Bargaining and Negotiation*. New York: Academic Press.

SAFILIOS-ROTHSCHILD, C.
1967   "A comparison of power structure and marital satisfaction in urban Greek and French families." *Journal of Marriage and the Family* 29:345–52.

1969   "Family sociology or wives' family sociology? A cross-cultural examination of decision-making." *Journal of Marriage and the Family* 31:290–301.

1970   "Study of family power structure: 1960–69." *Journal of Marriage and the Family* 32:539–552.

1976   "The dimensions of power distribution in the family." In H. Gruenbaum and J. Christ (eds.), *Contemporary Marriage: Bond and Bondage*. Boston: Little, Brown.

SCANZONI, J.
1970   *Opportunity and the Family*. New York: Free Press.
1972   *Sexual Bargaining: Power Politics in American Marriage*. Englewood Cliffs, N.J..: Prentice-Hall.
1975a   "Sex roles, economic factors, and marital solidarity in black and white marriages." *Journal of Marriage and the Family* 37:130–44.
1975b   *Sex Roles, Life-Styles and Childbearing: Changing Patterns in Marriage and Family*. New York: Free Press.
1976   "Sex role change and influences on birth intentions." *Journal of Marriage and Family* 38:43–60.
1977   *The Black Family in Modern Society*. Chicago: University of Chicago Press.
1978   "Social exchange and behavioral interdependence." In T. L. Huston and R. L. Burgess (eds.), *Social Exchange in Developing Relationships*. New York: Academic Press.
1979   *Sex Roles, Women's Work, and Marital Conflict*. Lexington, Mass.: D. C. Heath.

SCANZONI, L. AND J. SCANZONI
1976   *Men, Women, and Change: A Sociology of Marriage and Family*. New York: McGraw-Hill.

SPIEGEL, J.
1971   *Transactions*. New York: Science House.

SPREY, J.
1969   "The family as a system in conflict." *Journal of Marriage and the Family* 31:699–706.

1971   "On the management of conflict in families." *Journal of Marriage and the Family* 33:722–33.

1972   "Family power structure: A critical comment." *Journal of Marriage and the Family* 34:235–38.

1975   "Family power and process: Toward a conceptual integration." In R. E. Cromwell and D. H. Olson (eds.), *Power in Families*. New York: Wiley.

STEINMANN, A., D. J. FOX, AND R. FARKAS
1968   "Male and female perceptions of male sex roles." *Proceedings of the American Psychological Association*, 43:421–22.

STEINMETZ, S. AND M. STRAUS (eds.)
1974   *Violence in the Family*. New York: Dodd, Mead.

STRAUS, M. A.
1976.   "Measuring Intrafamily Conflict and Violence." Unpublished paper, University of New Hampshire, Durham.

TEDESCHI, J. T., B. R. SCHLENKER, AND T. V. BONOMA
1973   *Conflict Power and Games*. Chicago: Aldine.

THIBAUT, J. W. AND H. H. KELLEY
1959   *The Social Psychology of Groups*. New York: Wiley.

TURK, J. A.
1975   "Uses and abuses of family power." In R. E. Cromwell and D. H. Olson (eds.), *Power in Families*. New York: Wiley.

TURK, J. L. AND N. W. BELL
1972   "Measuring power in families." *Journal of Marriage and the Family* 34:215–23.

TURNER, J. H.
1974   *The Structure of Sociological Theory*. Homewood, Ill.: Dorsey Press.

U.S. BUREAU OF THE CENSUS
1976   *Current Population Reports*, series P–20, no. 288.

U.S. DEPARTMENT OF LABOR
1973   *Dual Careers: A Longitudinal Study of Labor Market Experience of Women*, vol. 2 Manpower Research Monograph no. 21.

VEEVERS, J. E.
1974   "The moral careers of voluntarily childless wives." In S. Wakil (ed.), *Marriage and the Family in Canada: A Reader*. Toronto: Copp-Clark.

WALLER, W. AND R. HILL
1951   *The Family: A Dynamic Interpretation*. New York: Holt, Rinehart and Winston.

WELLER, R.
1968   "The employment of wives, dominance and fertility." *Journal of Marriage and the Family* 30:437–42.

WESTOFF, C. R. AND R. H. POTVIN
1967   *College Women and Fertility Values*. Princeton, N.J.: Princeton University Press.

WHYTE, M. K.
1976   "Comment on Aronoff and Crano." *American Sociological Review* 41:376–80.

WIETING, S. G. AND A. T. McLAREN
1975   "Power in various family structures." In R. E. Cromwell and D. H. Olson (eds.), *Power in Families*. New York: Wiley.

WILKENING, E. A.
1968   "Toward a further refinement of the resource theory of family power." *Sociological Focus* 2:1–19.

WILKENING, E. A. AND E. LUPRI
1965   "Decision-making in German and American farm families: A cross-cultural comparison." *Sociologia Ruralis* 4:366–84.

WINTER, D. G.
1973   *The power Motive*. New York: Free Press.

WOLFE, D. M.
1959   "Power and authority in the family." In D. Cartwright (ed.), *Studies in Social Power*. Ann Arbor: University of Michigan, Institute for Social Research.

14

PARENTAL SUPPORT, POWER, AND CONTROL TECHNIQUES IN THE SOCIALIZATION OF CHILDREN

Boyd C. Rollins and Darwin L. Thomas

INTRODUCTION

Our purpose in this review is twofold: first, to present empirical generalizations and theoretical propositions about relationships between characteristics of children and parental variables of support, control attempts, and power; second, to evaluate the fit between the generalizations and propositions and two research and theory traditions in social psychology. We look to the theoretical orientations of symbolic interaction and social learning in which to place the generalizations in an effort to give meaning to the generalizations as well as to play back the empirical findings upon these two theoretical positions. For us the intrigue in the scientific enterprise emerges in the interplay between the empirical and theoretical moments. Several explicit assumptions form the basis for our work:

  1. A theory should be grounded in a substantial body of empirical generalizations (Glaser and Strauss, 1967).
  2. A theory should be verifiable; i.e., some constructs must have empirical referents and some propositions must produce empirically testable hypotheses (Homans, 1964; Thomas and Weigert, 1973; Zetterberg, 1954).
  3. A theory should be as complex as needed to match the real world. It may need to be so complex that it will have multiple independent variables, linear and nonlinear relationships, multiplicative as well as additive joint effects (Blaylock, 1969; Underwood and Shaughnessy, 1975) and dynamic characteristics such as time paths, feedback, and cycles (Blaylock, 1969).

NOTE: Appreciation is expressed to Diana Baumrind, Thomas Smith, and James Walters for their reactions to earlier drafts of this chapter. Preparation of this chapter was supported in part by the Family Research Institute at Brigham Young University and by NIMH Grant 2475-SP.

Or, it may be as simple and as elegant as $E = MC^2$. When a choice exists between the simple and the complex, the principle of parsimony suggests that the scientific establishment prefers the simple.

Assumption 3 requires further discussion. There have been several reviews of the literature in the area of parent-child relations published within the past two decades (Becker, 1964; Hoffman, 1963a; Straus, 1964; Baumrind, 1966; Goldin, 1969; Walters and Stinnett, 1971; Baumrind, 1972b; Schaefer, 1972; Streissguth and Bee, 1972; Martin, 1975). In terms of the complexity issue in parent-child relationships, only two reviews pay attention to the dynamic interactive process point of view (Streissguth and Bee, 1972; Martin, 1975). However, Martin (1975) discussed the empirical findings at a theoretically loose speculative level and failed to specify a theoretical model or set of propositions. Streissguth and Bee (1972) bemoaned the fact that they could find very few interactive process studies. The other eight reviews considered the empirical research from the standpoint of a static parent causation model, even when using evidence from longitudinal research (Schaefer, 1972).

We suspect that a static unidirectional model of parent causation is unrealistic (Cottrell, 1969; Gewirtz, 1969; Martin, 1975), even though the direction of causality in most published research is difficult to assess (Bell, 1969). Gewirtz (1969) takes issue not only with the static causation model but with "one-sided summary variables" as well. His argument is twofold. First, he maintains that extant explanatory theories of child socialization are process-oriented and assume sequential interchanges between the child and his caretaking environment. This being the case, a static model ignores the prior history of interaction as well as specific immediate antecedent responses of the child that influence both the caretaking environment and consequent responses to that environment. Therefore, Gewirtz concludes that static models fail to represent either reality or extant socialization theory. Second, he considers one-sided summary variables such as parental "nurturance," child "achievement," or child "aggression" that are typically used in static models to have measurement problems because of the emphasis on averaged responses of the environment (parent) or of the child across a number of specific indicators, across situations, and across time. Measurement is often based on self-report from the long-term memory of a respondent to questionnaire or interview questions. Such reliance on memory and cognitive summarizing processes leaves much to be desired in terms of measurement.

Gewirtz (1969) and Cottrell (1969) both present a very compelling argument against the utility of static parent causation models of child socialization and for the weakness of one-sided summary variables. Nevertheless, the vast body of research literature to date on parent-child relationships operationalizes such a static model and one-sided summary variables. Therefore, we judge that at this point in time the best summary of extant empirical research in terms of empirical generalizations must be primarily of a static nature. Hopefully such will provide a basis for indirect inference for a dynamic theory. At least, generalizations from one-sided summary variables used in static parent causation models can provide an estimate of prior history of parent-child interaction to be included in a dynamic model. Since the large majority of the empirical studies are correlations between parental attitudes or behaviors and child attitudes or behaviors, causal inference is hazardous (Bell, 1969). However, in line with the assumptions involved when the data were collected and analyzed, we judge that "being forced to choose," there would be less error in assuming that parents influence their children than the reverse in reviewing extant research. This decision was made with an awareness that much of the infant research in the past decade has documented the effect of the infant on mother-infant interaction (Lewis and Rosenblum, 1974). In the latter part of our review where we confront the empirical generalizations with our theoretical formulations, we will not feel compelled to retain either the static model or dynamic model of causality. We suspect that social reality requires something more than empirical research has thus far provided.

Other aspects of assumption 3, such as the possible use of multiple independent variables and considering some joint interaction as well as additive effects among these variables, are not so problematic for us. Five of the reviews (Becker, 1964; Straus, 1964; Baumrind, 1966, 1971; Martin, 1975) stressed the utility of studying the combined effects of parental supportive behaviors and parental control techniques in accounting for empirical regularities between parent behavior and child behavior. In an earlier review Symonds (1939) set the stage for a complex theory of parental influence in the socialization of children by suggesting the importance of the multiplicative (interaction) rather than additive joint effects of two orthogonal independent parent behavior variables; namely, acceptance-rejection and dominance-submission.[1]

Becker (1964) extended Symond's two-dimensional model to a three-dimensional model of three molar parent behaviors—warmth-hostility (acceptance-rejection), restrictive-permissive (dominance-submission), and anxious involvement–calm detachment—that jointly influence in a multiplicative manner behavioral outcomes in children. These three variables have counterparts in Schaefer's (1965) acceptance-rejection, firm control–lax control, and psychological autonomy–psychological control, and Seigelman's (1965) loving, demanding, and punishment variables. However, later reviews (Walters and Stinnett, 1971; Schaefer, 1972; Martin 1975) assessed the influence of these or similar parent behavior variables one at a time and failed to assess their combined additive effects let alone their multiplicative effects. Martin (1975) did stress the importance of future studies conducting analysis in such a manner as to "detect configurations of variables that might be related to child behaviors" (523).

Though failing to treat parental behaviors in multiplicative manner, Baumrind (1966, 1967) did use several parent behavior variables in nonorthogonal combinations to create the three typologies of authoritarian, authoritative, and permissive and has since made further distinctions among these three basic types (1971, 1972a). Also, through cluster analysis, Baumrind and Black (1967) studied multiple parent and child variables. Such use of typologies is discussed in the empirical review section later in this chapter.

The complexity of the joint effects of parent behavior variables as they relate to child behavior variables was stressed in the major review articles of Becker (1964), Straus (1964), Baumrind (1966, 1972b), and Martin (1975). In one review article Baumrind (1966) indicated the importance of the joint effects of parent support and parental control attempts. After reviewing empirical literature on parental restrictions, she cautioned that "it would appear that no conclusion can be drawn concerning the effects on the child of the variables called 'autonomy' or 'restrictiveness' until correlates with other parent variables, especially hostility, are known" (901). Also, alluding to the importance of multiplicative effects of different types of control attempts she said, "it is of interest to evaluate empirically the effects on children of various combinations of extreme scores on these two dimensions, 'firm control' and 'restricts child's autonomy,' rather than assume that they form a single dimension" (901). In a later review, Baumrind (1972b:213) assumed "that it is more meaningful to talk about the effects of *patterns* of parental authority than to talk about the effects of single parental variables.'' The variables used most extensively by Baumrind (1966, 1967) to create patterns of ''parental authority'' have included parental warmth, firm control, maturity demands, and communication (listening to child and explaining reasons for enforcement of rules).

Though interaction effects were not directly assessed in the studies by Baumrind, her typologies and their child behavior correlates provide some basis for speculation about the combined effects of parent behavior variables. However, Martin (1975) has pointed out that the ordering of multiple parent behavior variables and multiple child behavior variables by cluster analysis into circumplexes for comparative purposes as was done by Schaefer (1959) and Baumrind and Black (1967) still fails to provide a basis for concluding the relative impact of specific parent behaviors on children. Also, the typologies of Baumrind, because they do not systematically represent all of the combinations of her four basic parent behavior variables, do not allow for a definite determination of the separate and combined effects of the parent behaviors on children. Since methodologically the Baumrind research departs markedly from the bivariate research which is most frequently done, we will also analyze this separately in our review.

Besides the review articles cited above, some researchers have mapped out the domain of parental behaviors using two or more variables in terms of their joint interactive effects (Baldwin, 1955; Roe, 1957; Schaefer, 1959, 1965; Slater, 1962; Becker, 1964; Seigelman, 1965; Heilbrun and Orr, 1965; Peterson and Migliorino, 1967; Rollins, 1967; Thomas et al., 1974; Rollins and Thomas, 1975). While these researchers have expected interaction, the empirical evidence is not convincing and thus literature reviews lag considerably behind conceptualization in terms of multiplicative joint effects of parent behavior variables. Heilbrun and Waters (1968) lament, ''despite the availability of theoretical models of child rearing which stress the interactive nature of the control and nurturance child-rearing variables there still appears to be an overriding tendency to investigate these variables independently'' (914). Fortunately, the work of Heilbrun and associates from 1965 through 1971 is an exception, though they frequently failed to test directly for interaction effects, even though the data would have permitted such tests. The work of Thomas et al. (1974) has been somewhat singular in systematic tests of multiplicative combined effects of parent behaviors. It, along with the work of Baumrind (1966, 1967, 1971, 1972a, 1972b), Heilbrun and associates and recent studies to be reviewed below, provides an empirical grounding for theory formulations on the basis of the assumptions stated above. In the remainder of this chapter we will assess the domain of parental behaviors in the literature, develop a set of empirical generalizations from literature reviews and empirical studies published between 1960 and 1974, and evaluate the empirical generalizations from the symbolic interaction and social-learning theoretical orientations.

PARENTAL VARIABLES

Overview

For approximately four decades the parent-child literature has identified at least two variables of parental behavior as critical in accounting for parental influence in the socialization of children. These variables are parental control techniques and parental support (see Table 14.1). These two variables with different labels but similar connotations and denotations were identified early by Symonds (1939) as a dominance-submission continuum of behavior and an acceptance-rejection continuum of behavior. We prefer the labels of ''control attempts'' and ''support.''

The label ''control'' has been used extensively in the literature (see Table 14.1), but a careful checking of both conceptual and operational meanings of this variable indicates that it typically refers to the type or degree of intensity of influence attempts (discipline) by parents rather than the actual attainment of control. Therefore, we think ''control attempts'' is the more informative label.

Table 14.1. Labels Frequently Used for Two Dimensions of Parental Behavior[a]

CONTROL ATTEMPTS		SUPPORT	
Authoritative[b]	(5)	Acceptance	(20)
Authoritarian[b]	(35)	Affection	(15)
Autonomy	(6)	Hostile	(29)
Coercion	(5)	Love	(15)
Control[c]	(84)	Neglect	(5)
Demanding	(14)	Nurturance	(37)
Democratic[b]	(15)	Rejection	(36)
Discipline	(23)	Support	(11)
Dominance	(25)	Warmth	(31)
Induction	(8)		
Permissive	(8)		
Power[d]	(8)		
Power Assertion	(7)		
Pressure	(5)		
Protective[b]	(16)		
Punishment	(47)		
Restrictive	(24)		
Strictness	(7)		

[a]Data from 106 published studies and 129 unpublished dissertations from 1960–1974 reporting either control techniques or both control techniques and support child-rearing behavior or attitude correlates of child behaviors (all labels used in five or more studies are listed by frequency in parentheses).
[b]Compound variables implying something about both control and support techniques.
[c]Sometimes accompanied by an adjective, e.g., ''hostile'' control.
[d]Sometimes used as ''potential'' power and sometimes as ''active'' power or control.

The label "support" has been used much less than nurturance, warmth, or acceptance-rejection. Still we prefer it. Nurturance is defined in the Merriam-Webster Dictionary of 1964 as "the act or process of raising or promoting the development of: training; rearing; upbringing." This meaning is as broad as socialization itself. To use concepts in the formulation of a theory of socialization requires that the concepts have reasonable limits. We intend to use control attempts and power as well as support as elements of socialization; thus we prefer a more limited term than nurturance. The label "warmth" like "support" is a more limited concept. The difficulty with the label "warmth" stems from conceptualizing variation along its continuum. If a given relationship is classified as "warm," what is one which is higher on the scale? Is it hot? For us the "support" variable ranging from low to high poses no such problems. Many of the other labels that have been used in the literature are emotionally loaded, limiting their utility (Straus, 1964).

Since the pioneering work of Symonds (1939) the variables of control attempt and support in combination have been emphasized by Baldwin (1955), Roe (1957), Maccoby (1961), Becker (1964), Schaefer (1965), Straus (1964), Rollins (1967), Heilbrun (1968), Thomas et. al (1974), and Rollins and Thomas (1975). A variety of techniques have been used to operationalize these two variables (Baumrind, 1967; Coopersmith, 1967; Elder, 1963; Heilbrun, 1965; Hoffman and Saltzstein, 1967; Peck and Havinghurst, 1960; Peterson and Migliorino, 1967; Roe and Seigelman, 1963; Schaefer, 1965; Sears et al., 1957; Smith, 1970; Straus and Tallman, 1971; Waxler and Mishler, 1971; and Thomas et al., 1974).

The variable of parental support has been given a large number of labels in the literature (e.g., "acceptance," "nurturance," "love"), but the connotations and denotations attached to the different labels have been relatively similar. The literature concerning the consequences in children of supportive behavior from parents is quite consistent. However, the variables of parental control attempts and parental power are much more problematic. Some writers have used "power" to mean the latent potential of parents to induce compliance from their children (Hoffman, 1960; Elder, 1963; Heilbrun and Waters, 1968; and Thomas and Weigert, 1971). Others, using "power" to mean the actual process of attempting to control children, have made conceptual distinctions between types of control attempts (Hoffman, 1960; Becker, 1964; Schaefer, 1965; Hoffman and Saltzstein, 1967; Baumrind, 1966, 1967, 1971, 1972a; Aronfreed, 1969). We prefer to make conceptual distinctions between different aspects of parental control attempts and use them along with parental support as basic dimensions of parental behavior. These variables along with parental power will be used in our attempt to account for socially competent or incompetent behaviors in children.

Conceptual Clarification

Support

This construct is defined as behavior manifest by a parent toward a child that makes the child feel comfortable in the presence of the parent and confirms in the child's mind that he is basically accepted and approved as a person by the parent (Thomas et al., 1974). This definition is consistent with the connotations and denotations attached to a wider number of symbols referring to such phenomena (Rollins and Thomas, 1975). Parental support is a continuous quantitative variable. Operationally this variable is a summation of the frequencies of such parental behaviors toward a child as praising, approving, encouraging, helping, cooperating, expressing terms of endearment, and physical affection (Straus and Tallman, 1971:393). The behaviors we have called indicators of parental support are viewed as diffuse positive social sanctions by sociologists and social anthropologists (Radcliffe-Brown, 1934:531, Parsons and Bales, 1955: 371–373) and as positive social reinforcing stimuli by behavioristic psychologists (Ferster and Skinner, 1957; Stevenson, 1961).

We do not at this point in our theorizing conceptualize support as a multidimensional construct. True, there have been a variety of operationalizations, but at present both the conceptualization and the empirical results appear to us to be sufficiently consistent that further differentiation of the construct does not seem warranted. Hopefully, future research and theorizing will critically assess the need for a multidimensional construct by measuring different dimensions to see if they produce varying effects on child behavior (Ellis et al., 1976). If it could be shown for example that physical affection from one parent might have a different relationship with self-esteem in the children than does verbal expression of affection, then the need for a multidimensional construct would be apparent. At present we can find no such evidence.

Power

Power is not seen as a parental behavior such as support of control attempts. Neither is it a construct pointing to personality characteristics of parents, but rather we see power as a social relations construct of a very special nature. Social power is defined as "the potential an individual has for compelling another person to act in ways contrary to their own desires" (Hoffman, 1960:129). This is a definition by a social psychologist and is consistent with the Weberian idea of power (Weber, 1947:151), which implies a contest of wills in social interaction. In the power literature the potential ability to influence others has often been confused with the actual exercise of that ability, yet these two phenomena are distinct entities. One might have great power over others but not attempt to control their behavior

(Cartwright, 1959; Rogers, 1974; Rollins and Bahr, 1976).

French and Raven (1959) have identified five bases of potential influence or power in social relationships: reward power, coercive power, referent power,[2] legitimate power, and expert power, any one of which can vary from a small to a large amount. It is assumed that these bases of power function in an additive manner in increasing or decreasing social power. Operationally, this variable is the summation of the magnitude of each of the power bases (French and Raven, 1959). Power is a continuous quantitative variable. In application to the parent-child relationships, Smith (1970) combined reward and coercive power into one variable identified as outcome control power. We will do the same. *Outcome control power* refers to the ability of a parent to mediate rewards and punishments based upon the child's compliance or noncompliance to the desires of the parents. *Expert power* refers to the parent's special knowledge or expert ability that will assist the child to a desired goal. *Legitimate power* refers to the parent's right or authority to request compliance from the child. It reciprocally implies that the child has an acknowledged obligation to comply.

Legitimate power is based upon norms and respect rather than resources. Outcome control power and expert power are both based on the resources that the parent might utilize in child rearing. Smith (1970) found in an empirical study that each of the above power bases correlated positively with compliance of teenage children to the desires of their parents. It seems logical that with parental power defined as potential rather than actual influence, other things being equal, when parents attempt to control their children, the greater the parental power (outcome control, legitimate, or expert) the more likely the child will comply (French and Raven, 1959).

Control Attempts

Parental power might exist as potential influence but is most likely to have an effect on the child if associated with direct attempts by parents to control their children (Cartwright, 1959:195; French and Raven 1959:158; Goode, 1972:510). Control attempts are defined as behavior of the parent toward the child with the intent of directing the behavior of the child in a manner desirable to the parents. Most studies of parental discipline, dominance, restriction, or coercion have used connotations and denotations congruent with this definition. Parental control attempt is a continuous quantitative variable. Operationally, this variable is a summation of the frequencies of such indicators of parental behaviors as giving directions, instructions, commands, suggestions, punishments, and threats of punishment to a child as well as making requests, imposing rules and restrictions, and providing explanations for rules and restrictions.

In contrast to parental support, we judge that the

research evidence argues for a multidimensional view of the control attempts construct (Thomas et al., 1974). Baumrind (1971) made qualitative distinctions between "authoritarian" and "authoritative" control attempts similar to those of Hoffman (1970; Hoffman and Saltzstein, 1967) referred to as power assertion and induction. Baumrind (1966) differentiated control attempts into seven types: punitiveness, love withdrawal, explanations and flexibility, maturity demands, autonomy granting, unqualified power assertion, and firmness. However, her literature review failed to differentiate the effects of punitiveness, autonomy granting, and unqualified power assertion. Punitiveness and unqualified power assertion imply coercion. "Coercion" is the label we prefer to use for such behavior. Baumrind (1966) found similar child correlates for several types of control attempts such as firmness, maturity demands, explanations, and flexibility (communication). These latter constructs suggest some tupe of qualification in the control attempts which induce within the child internalized motivation for his behavior based on reasoning provided by the parents. We prefer to label such control attempts "induction." A remaining single variable used by Baumrind (1966), love withdrawal, also suggests some type of qualified control attempt.

The foregoing discussion leads us to conclude that coercion, induction, and love withdrawal adequately differentiate types of control attempts. Aronfreed (1969) considered love withdrawal to be a type of induction in that it "induces" in the child an internal orientation in the management of anxiety that becomes attached to potential or committed transgressions. However, following a lead from social power theorists (Cartwright, 1959) that control attempts induce a psychological force in the recipient to both comply and resist, we think "induction" and "love withdrawal" should be kept separate. Love withdrawal control attempts do not necessarily rely on reason as a basis for internalization and most likely put the child under a much stronger psychological force than induction control attempts. Therefore, we judge that it is important to differentiate between induction and love withdrawal in reviewing the empirical research.

Coercion is defined as behavior of the parent in a contest of wills, which results in considerable external pressure on the child to behave according to the parents' desires. Such a control attempt might be either an initiating control technique or a reaction to noncompliance. It is a continuous quantitative variable. Operationally, it is a summation of the frequencies of such parental behaviors as "physical punishment, deprivation of material objects or privileges, the direct application of force, or the threat of any of these" in situations where parents are attempting to influence their child's behavior (Hoffman, 1970:286).

Rather than apply external force, some parents attempt

to get the child to behave as the parent desires by inducing internal forces in the child to voluntarily comply. *Induction* is defined as behavior by a parent with the intent of obtaining voluntary compliance to parental desires by avoiding a direct conflict of wills with the child. This type of control attempt is imbedded in an informational matrix. It is a continuous quantitative variable. Operationally it is a summation of the frequencies of parental behaviors "in which the parent gives explanation or reasons" for desired behavior, often in the form of pointing out to the child consequences of the behavior for self and for others (Hoffman, 1970:286). *Love withdrawal* is defined as behavior manifested by the parent indicating disapproval of the child's behavior with the implication that love will not be restored until the child changes his behavior. It includes such parental behaviors as ignoring or isolating the child as well as explicit indications of rejection, disappointment, or coldness in response to something the child has done that displeases the parent (Aronfreed, 1969). In reviewing the empirical literature on parental behavior correlates of child behaviors, we systematically included studies using any type of control attempt—coercion, induction, or love withdrawal.

EMPIRICAL REVIEW

Method and Procedures

Our strategy for reviewing the empirical literature and developing empirical generalizations and theoretical propositions[3] about parental influence in the socialization of children has been influenced by our previous efforts at theory formulation (Rollins, 1967; Thomas, 1968; Thomas et al., 1974; Rollins and Thomas, 1975). Studies of a bivariate relationship between parental support and child behaviors have been extensively reviewed elsewhere (Walters and Stinnett, 1971). In general, the empirical studies have been in agreement with the generalization that, especially for boys *the greater the supportive behavior of parents toward children, the greater such culturally valued child behaviors as self-esteem, academic achievement, creativity, and conformity* (Rollins and Thomas, 1975:42). Therefore, we decided further search for evidence of a bivariate relationship between parental support and child behavior was not necessary for theory formulation. However, for parental control attempts, the empirical literature has repeatedly produced inconsistent results in terms of correlations of this variable with child behaviors (Rollins, 1967; Thomas et al., 1974; and Rollins and Thomas, 1975).

An example of inconsistent results is in the area of academic achievement in children. Several studies (Conklin, 1940; Kimball, 1953; Jones, 1955; Walsh, 1956; Morrow and Wilson, 1961; Kagan and Moss, 1962; Shaw and Dutton, 1962) found a negative relationship

between academic achievement in children and parental control attempts, while others (Watson, 1934; McClelland et al., 1953; Drews and Teahan, 1957; Hoffman et al., 1960; and Maccoby, 1961) found a positive relationship. According to Underwood and Shaughnessy (1975), discrepancies in empirical results and plausible explanations of these discrepancies provide grist for the mill in theory formulation. They suggest that "static variables" that are at different levels from one study to another might systematically account for discrepant findings. Because the discrepancies in terms of parental control attempts might be generalizable across a number of child behaviors, our hunches on possible explanations for discrepancies in the area of academic achievement guided our analysis in all of our literature review. We searched for such static variables and in some cases found clues in terms of sex of children and sex of parents. Our eight hunches were as follows:

1. Parental control attempts might influence boys differently than girls (Bronfenbrenner, 1961a).
2. Parental control attempts from fathers might influence children differently than control attempts from mothers (Bronfenbrenner, 1961).
3. Parental control attempts might influence younger children differently than older children (Bronfenbrenner, 1961).
4. Instruments to measure parental control attempts might operationalize qualitatively different variables from one study to another.
5. Parental control attempts might influence children from one cultural background differently than children from another cultural background.
6. The relationship between parental control attempts and child behaviors might be curvilinear rather than linear (Thomas, 1968).
7. The relationship between parental control attempts and child behaviors (academic achievement) might be contingent on the level of parental support (Heilbrun and Waters, 1968).
8. Qualitatively different types of control attempts might differentially relate to behaviors in children.

The first five hunches are somewhat self-evident. As we reviewed empirical studies, we tabulated as best we could the age, sex, and cultural background of the subjects as well as sex of parents and type of measuring instrument to determine if these variables systematically accounted for discrepant results. Age, cultural background, and type of measuring instrument failed to do so, whereas sex of child and sex of parent systematically accounted for differences in some aspects of children's behaviors.

The last three of the above hunches are not self-evident and require further discussion. Thomas (1968) has suggested that a curvilinear relationship might account for the apparent discrepancies concerning parental control attempts and child behaviors. Suppose an inverted U-shaped curvilinear relationship actually existed. If some studies measured only the lower part of the range of parental control attempts, a positive relationship would be found. On the other hand, studies measuring only the higher part of the range would find a negative relationship. Studies using the whole range but failing to test for nonlinearity would find no relationship.

The use of support as a contingent variable to account for discrepant results in the relationship between parental control attempts and academic achievement in children is a fairly complex idea. In a study by Heilbrun and Waters (1968) it was found that when parental support was low, a negative relationship existed between control attempts and achievement, but when support was high, the relationship was reversed and was positive. This is one of the reasons we judged it crucial to search for studies where control attempts and support were studied simultaneously in relation to child behavior and to observe any possible multiplicative or interaction effects of these variables.

The last hunch was concerned with qualitatively different types of control attempts. It seems reasonable that studies finding a negative relationship between control attempts and achievement operationalized parental control attempts as coercion, while those finding a positive relationship operationalized it as induction. As studies were reviewed, we interpreted control attempts as either coercion, induction, or love withdrawal when the operational indicators were unambiguous. When they were ambiguous, we classified them as undifferentiated control attempts.[4] In general, the differentiation between coercion and induction did systematically account for discrepancies in the results. However, the correlations of child behaviors with love withdrawal produced very inconsistent results and could not be interpreted. Therefore, we have omitted correlations with love withdrawal as a parental control attempt from further discussion.

The literature published from 1960 to 1974 was systematically searched for empirical studies in which parental behaviors of either control attempts or control attempts and support were correlated with child behaviors. Also, studies of parental power were reviewed. Studies using parental support only were ignored inasmuch as they have been extensively reviewed elsewhere (Walters and Stinnett, 1971). Of the 235 studies identified, 176 (75 percent) measured both parental control attempts and parental support. The others measured control attempts only. Though the majority of the studies reviewed measured both control attempts and support, 141 analyzed only the separate rather than the combined effects of these variables and only 15 (6 percent) analyzed the multiplicative joint (interaction) effects of these variables (see Table 14.2). Thus empirical generalizations focusing on the joint effects of parental control attempts and parental support are necessarily limited by the nature of the extant empirical work, which has ignored the admonition repeated each decade since Symonds (1939) that the interactive or multiplicative joint effects of these variables should be investigated. Also, except for the area of sex role orientation, very few studies utilized the construct power, and in these few cases it was usually the power of the father and mother relative to each other rather than the power of parent with reference to the child.

The child behavior correlate most frequently studied in relation to parental behavior was achievement, usually academic achievement (see Table 14.3). Other child behaviors most frequently studied included aggression, moral development, behavior problems, schizophrenia, sex role orientation, cognitive development, locus of control of reinforcement, and compliance (or conformity). In attempting to present empirical generalizations about parental and child behavior correlates, we analyzed all child behaviors included in five or more studies as well as attempting a synthesis across child behaviors. Also, we utilized the relevant conclusions from the major review articles cited above.

In each of 14 areas of child behavior, five or more empirical studies were found (see Table 14.3). Within each area the results across studies were compared and empirical generalizations developed. Most of the studies were done in the United States, and all were published between 1960 and 1974. In our review of the literature, empirical generalizations within each area were developed in the following manner: In each study the nature of the relationship between child behaviors and the parental behaviors of support and control attempts were de-

Table 14.2. Frequencies of Investigating Separate and Joint Effects of Parental Behaviors in Relation to Child Behaviors

TYPE OF INVESTIGATION	PUBLISHED STUDIES	UNPUBLISHED DISSERTATIONS	TOTAL*
Control attempts only	31	28	59
Control attempts and support:			
No joint effects	51	90	141
Compound or additive joint effects	15	5	20
Multiplicative joint effects	9	6	15
Total	106	129	235

*Studies published from 1960–1974.

Table 14.3.   Child Behaviors Correlated with Parental Behaviors or Attitudes of Support, Control Attempts, and Power

CHILD BEHAVIORS	PUBLISHED STUDIES	UNPUBLISHED DISSERTATIONS	TOTAL*
Cognitive Development	4	8	12
Conformity	5	2	7
Creativity	5	3	8
Locus of Control of Reinforcement	5	6	11
Moral Behavior	11	8	19
Self-Esteem	2	6	8
Social Competence	3	2	5
Aggression	10	5	15
Behavior Problems	4	7	11
Drug Abuse	1	4	5
Learning Disabilities	0	5	5
Schizophrenia	7	4	11
Achievement	7	15	22
Sex Role Orientation	6	8	14
Total	106	129	235

*Studies published from 1960–1974.

scribed as fully as the data allowed. Where possible, control attempts were categorized as coercion, induction, or love withdrawal. Where no such categorization was possible, they were categorized as undifferentiated control attempts. After relationships were described within each study in an area, comparisons were made across studies and generalizations induced from common patterns found.

Initially tabulations were made of parent-child correlations in terms of age and sex of child, sex of parent, source of data (self-report or observation), and measurement instruments used because these variables might systematically account for different outcomes (Bronfenbrenner, 1961a; Yarrow et al., 1968; Martin, 1975). However, because of the inability to detect any systematic differences in results based on source of information or measurement instruments, no distinction was made with reference to them except in a few unusual cases. Results were reported in terms of age and sex of children and sex of parent even though in most cases these variables did not appear to systematically account for differences in parent-child correlations.

In order to evaluate this review, the reader needs to keep in mind that no weighting attempt was made across research reports. We essentially equated all findings whether they came from a study of 50 or 500 respondents. A systematic methodological critique of each research report was impossible given the time constraint. In the future, a stiff methodological critique of such research reports would be highly desirable.

In reporting relationships between parental support or control attempts and child behaviors, relationships were described as positive (+), negative (−), or no (0) relationship with conventional symbols. Where evidence of nonlinear relationships existed, a novel system was developed by combining conventional symbols separated by

a slash mark. For example, a U-shaped relationship was represented by −/+, indicating that the relationship was negative over the lower part of the range of one of the variables but changed to a positive relationship at the upper end of the range. When evidence of interaction effects of parent behavior variables existed in some studies, such information was used to qualify the reported relationships between a single parent behavior and a child behavior in other studies. When none of our hunches systematically accounted for discrepancies across studies, in the absence of evidence for a curvilinear relationship, we used decision rules as follows: (1) a linear relationship was selected over no relationship when the evidence for each was equal; (2) positive and negative relationships were given equal weight.

In some cases we found an interaction effect between parental support and control attempts that provided a possible explanation for apparent discrepancies. For example, if an interaction between support and control attempts exists as suggested by Heilbrun and Waters (1968), order might be brought out of chaos. Suppose an interaction exists such that when control attempts are relatively high, a positive relationship exists between parental support and some child variable, but when control attempts are relatively low, the relationship is negative. This being the case, one study might have the whole range of variation on parental control attempts and find no relationship between parental support and child behavior because of the masking effect of a positive relationship when control attempts are high and a negative relationship when control attempts are low. Another study might have the "static variable" (control attempts) at only the low or high end of the range and find a negative or positive relationship, respectively.

Another possible explanation of apparent discrepant results across studies is a curvilinear relationship between parent and child variables. Following Thomas (1968), we note that none of the studies on relationships between parent and child behaviors used "zero-based" measurement. Also, the measurements lacked other criterion-based reference points and provide only relative scores in that some scores are higher than others. To dichotomize such measurement into higher and lower scores does not allow meaningful comparability from study to study. It is impossible to determine how high a "high" score is or how low a "low" score. If one assumes a curvilinear relationship existing between any two variables (e.g., child compliance and the level of parental control attempts), then the plotted curve might look something like that in Figure 14.1.

Since the measurement of parental control attempts lacks an absolute zero, and measurement values are usually interpreted relative to within-sample variation, one study might measure only the "A" range of control attempts while another study measured the "B" range. If, in such a hypothetical case, each study dichotomized parental control attempts as "high" or "low," the high scores on the "A" range would be comparable to the low scores on the "B" range and the results might indicate a positive relationship in one study and a negative relationship in the other. Also, if a third study used the whole "A" plus "B" range to dichotomize the variable and a curvilinear relationship actually existed, then the finding would be "no relationship" because of the masking effect from combining contradictory trends.

We systematically searched for evidence of both curvilinear relationships and interaction effects to try to account for discrepant findings across empirical studies. For example, the findings of curvilinear relationships between parental control attempts and child compliance in some studies point to possible resolution of some apparent discrepancies. Also, discrepant findings in the

area of academic achievement are partly accounted for by a found interaction effect of parental support and control attempts. Where the data so dictated, generalizations were qualified by sex-of-child—sex-of-parent subsets of dyads. This was particularly the case in the areas of academic achievement and gender role orientation.

For ease of presentation we divided the 12 areas of child behavior into two groups. The first consists of seven areas judged to represent competent social behavior in American society during this period of time. These areas are cognitive development, conformity, creativity, internal locus of control of reinforcement, moral development, self-esteem, and instrumental competence. The five areas of aggression, behavior problems, drug abuse, learning disabilities, and schizophrenia are judged to represent incompetent social behaviors. Two areas, gender sex role orientation and academic achievement, are atypical compared to the other areas and are treated separately.

Generalizations: Socially Competent Behavior

Cognitive Development

Our literature search included four studies that measured some aspect of parental control attempts and eight studies that measured both control attempts and parental support in relation to cognitive development in children (see Table 14.4). The studies ranged from preschool through college students in terms of ages of children. Children of both sexes were studied, but typically in relation to mothers' rather than fathers' behaviors. Of 14 tests of the relationship between parental support and cognitive development in the child, eight indicate a positive relationship, four no relationship, and two a negative relationship. The two negative relationships were both unique. One was for black preschool sons and their mothers). This was the only study that specifically analyzed data on the basis of race (the relationship was positive for black daughters and mothers). The other study with a negative relationship had a sample of upper-middle-class college daughters and their fathers. However, the fathers were also high on coercion (interaction effect of control attempts and support). When fathers were low on coercion, there was no relationship between these variables. Interaction was also found between maternal support and maternal coercion in relation to cognitive development of college daughters. However, in this case, when coercion was high, a positive relationship existed, but when it was low, there was no relationship. In two other tests there was no relationship between parents' support and cognitive development in sons. In summary, in most instances a positive relationship was found between parental support and cognitive development in children. No one explanation adequately accounts for all the exceptions. The interaction between coercion and

Figure 14.1. Plotted Curve of the Relationship between Child Compliance and Parental Control Attempts

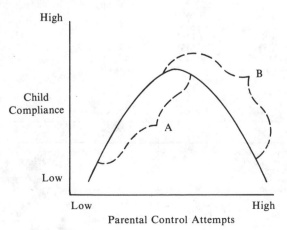

support might account for three of the four no-relationship findings if high coercion is necessary before the positive relationship between support and cognitive development occurs. However, such an explanation does not account for the two negative relationships. The generalization that best fits the reviewed data is:

Generalization 1: The greater the parental support, the higher the cognitive development in children.

We judge that the empirical data provide strong support for this generalization. However, as will be shown in generalization 40, for girls, academic achievement seems to be negatively related to parental support. Perhaps academic achievement is fairly independent of the development of cognitive skills.

Ten tests were made of the relationship between parental undifferentiated control attempts and cognitive development in children. The results indicate that four are negative, four are zero, and two are positive relationships. The four negative relationships represent all four parent-child dyads (father-son, father-daughter, mother-son, mother-daughter). One of the two positive relationships comes from the only study identifying race and is for

black sons and their mothers. Perhaps parental control attempts have different effect on black sons than on white sons. The four no-relationship tests include mothers but not fathers and children. If mothers, in general, make weaker control attempts than do fathers, then a plausible explanation of the discrepant results might be a curvilinear relationship. In this curvilinear relationship, the variation from low to moderate control attempts would be unrelated to cognitive development, but variation from moderate to high would have a negative relationship. On the other hand, if mothers of black sons in general have a greater range of variation on control attempts than fathers, a plausible explanation of the findings would be a curvilinear relationship in which the relationship is positive as control attempts vary from a small to moderate amount but changes to a negative relationship with increases from a moderate to large amount. If the control attempts in the low range are more frequently of the induction type and those in the high range are of the coercion type, then this would also account for the positive and then negative relationship.

In summary, the data equally support a negative relationship and no relationship with the possibility of a

Table 14.4. Relationships of Parental Behavior and Cognitive Development in Children

STUDY	CHILDREN			PARENT VARIABLES			
	Age[1]	N	Sex[2]	Support	Control Attempts (Unspecified)	Coercion	Induction
Altman '73	5	10	M	+ MC[3]	+ MC		
Cross '65	16	54	S	+ FS		− FS	
				0 MS		− MS	
Hauk '67	11	131	M			0 MC	
Heilbrun '65*	19	58	D	+ MD		0 MD	
Heilbrun et al., '66*	19	137	S	+ MS		− MS	
Heilbrun et al., 67a*	19	123	D	0 FD[4]		− FD[6]	
				− FD[5]		+ FD[7]	
				0 MD[4]		+ MD[6]	
				+ FD[5]		− MD[7]	
Hess & Shipman '65	4	163	M			− MC	+ MC
Leler '70	3	53	M	+ MC	0 MC		
Mannino '73	10	30	M		− MS	+ MS	
Radin '69	4	24	S	+ MS[8]	0 MS[8]		
		28	D	− MS[9]	+ MS[9]		
				+ MD	0 MD		
Sheldon '68	11	101	S	0 PS		0 PS	
Swan '70	5	264	M		− FS		
					0 MS		
					− FD		
					− MD		
Generalization				+	−	−	?

*Interaction effects of parent variables explored.
[1]Modal age of children in years old.
[2]S=son, D=daughter, M=mixed.
[3]M=mother, F=father, P=parent, D=daughter, S=son, C=child.
[4]With low coercion.
[5]With high coercion.
[6]With low support.
[7]With high support.
[8]White child.
[9]Black child.

curvilinear relationship. However, since no direct evidence was found for a curvilinear relationship, the generalization that we judge best fits the data is:

Generalization 2: The greater the parental control attempts (undifferentiated), the lower the cognitive development in children.

We judge that the empirical data provide moderate direct support for this generalization.

Thirteen tests were made of relationships between specific types of control attempts and cognitive development. One test found a positive relationship between induction and cognitive development. Of the other 12 tests between coercion and cognitive development, six were negative, three zero, and three positive relationships. Two of the three positive relationships were under conditions of a specific level of parental support, high support in the father-daughter dyad and low support in the mother-daughter dyad. The six negative relationships include all four parent-child subsets of dyads. The generalization that best fits the data is:

Generalization 3: The greater the parental coercion, the lower the cognitive development in children.

We judge that the empirical data provide moderate direct support for this generalization.

The above generalizations are congruent with those of Streissguth and Bee (1972) in their review article on mother-child interaction and cognitive development in children. They concluded that middle-class children had superior cognitive development in terms of persistence, ability to generalize, and cognitive reflexivity than lower-class children. Also, they concluded that middle-class mothers were more supportive and used less coercion than lower-class mothers.

Though our review indicates some discrepancies in terms of the relationships of parental support and control attempts with cognitive development in children, the findings in general affirm an interpretation that cognitive development is greatest when induction and support are relatively high and coercion is relatively low.

Conformity

Of seven studies reviewed, four focused on parental control attempts and support, two on control attempts only, and one on parental power (see Table 14.5). The one study on parental power indicated a positive relationship between parental power and child conformity. This result was consistent irrespective of sex of child or sex of parent. In terms of parental support (eight tests), coercion (three tests), and induction (two tests), the results were very consistent. The relationships with conformity were positive for support and induction and negative for coercion. In terms of number, the studies were focused primarily on mother-child dyads. However, the relationship between support and conformity was found for all four parent-child dyads. Though combined multiplicative (interaction) effects of support and control attempts were tested, none were found. Generalizations that best fit the reviewed data are:

Generalization 4: The greater the parental support, the greater the child conformity.

Generalization 5: The greater the parental coercion, the less the child conformity.

Generalization 6: The greater the parental induction, the greater the child conformity.

Generalization 7: The greater the parental power, the greater the child conformity.

We judge that the empirical data provide moderate direct support for these generalizations.

In terms of undifferentiated control attempts, seven tests indicate no relationship and two a curvilinear relationship. In summary, it might be concluded that no relationship exists. However, the two curvilinear relationships indicate that as control attempts increase from a relatively small to a relatively moderate amount, the relationship is positive, but as control attempts increase further to a relatively large amount, the relationship is negative. The studies finding no relationship might mask any existing relationship by testing only a linear model. We generalized above that coercion was negatively related to conformity, while induction was positively related. If inductive-type control attempts range from only a relatively low to a relatively moderate amount of control attempt force on the child, while coercive-type control attempts range from a relatively moderate to a relatively high amount of control attempt force, then a curvilinear relationship between undifferentiated control attempt and conformity would be expected.

Such results are consistent with the conclusions of Hoffman (1960) and Baumrind (1966) in review articles on consequences of parental control attempts. A theoretical rationale for the curvilinear relationship proposed above has been presented by Rollins and Thomas (1975) on the basis that control attempts by parents stimulate in the child a force to comply and a force to resist (Cartwright, 1959), and that qualification of the control attempt or induction tends to create a "resultant force" to comply, while an unqualified control attempt or coercion tends to create a resultant force to resist. We judge that the generalization that best fits the reviewed studies, review articles, and theory is:

Generalization 8: As parental control attempts (undifferentiated) increase from low to moderate amounts, conformity of the child increases; but as parental control attempts (undifferentiated) increase from moderate to high amounts, conformity of the child decreases.

Table 14.5. Relationships of Parental Behavior and Conformity in Children

STUDY	CHILDREN			PARENTAL VARIABLES				
	Age	*N*	*Sex*	*Support*	*Control Attempts (Unspecified)*	*Coercion*	*Induction*	*Power*
Brody '69	4	50	M	+ MC		− MC		
Cancian '71	6	110	M	− MC		− MC		
Chaplan '67	?	?	?		0 MC	0 MC		
Elder '63	15	9,000	M	+/− PS			+ PS	
				+/− PD			+ PD	
Smith '70	15	?	M					+ FS
								+ FD
								+ MS
								+ MD
Thomas '68*	17	?	S	+ FS	0 FS			
				+ MS	0 MS			
Thomas et al., '74*	17	740	S	+ FS	0 FS			
		718	D	+ FD	0 FD			
				+ MS	0 MS			
				+ MD	0 MD			
Generalization				+	+/−	−	+	+

*Interaction effects of parent variables tested but none found. These two studies partially overlap in that some of the same findings are reported in both sources.

We judge that the empirical data provide moderate indirect support for this generalization.

Creativity

From the decade review of the 1960s, Walters and Stinnett (1971) concluded that "consensus existed among the studies reviewed that academic achievement, leadership, and creative thinking of children was positively related to warm, accepting, understanding, and autonomy-granting parent-child relationships" (91). We found only five studies that simultaneously studied parental control attempts and parental support in relation to creativity (see Table 14.6). Also, we found three studies that measured control attempts only. In 10 tests of relationships between support and creativity in specific parent-child dyads, two were positive, two were negative, and six indicated no relationship. This is surprising in light of the conclusion of Walters and Stinnett. Even more confusing is the interaction effect found by Heilbrun (1971). When coercion was high, there was a positive relationship between support and creativity, but when coercion was low, no relationship existed. The finding of an interaction effect in the one study by Heilbrun (1971) doesn't help account for the negative relationships found by Orinstein (1961) or Siegelman (1973). Another possible explanation of the discrepancies is a curvilinear relationship between parental support and child creativity. Indirectly, evidence for such a relationship comes from an experiment by Rollins and Calder (1975). They found that a moderate amount of stress was associated with highest creativity in a problem-solving task. Creativity was less

when stress was either relatively high or relatively low. If we assume that parental support has a high negative correlation with stress in the child, then a conclusion of a curvilinear relationship between parental support and child creativity is justified. We judge that the generalization that best fits the reviewed studies is:

Generalization 9: As parental support increases from low to moderate amounts, the creativity of the child increases, but as parental support increases from moderate to large amounts, the creativity of the child decreases.

We judge that the empirical data provide only moderate indirect support for this generalization.

In eight tests of a relationship between undifferentiated control attempts and creativity, six indicated no relationship and two a negative relationship. With no evidence of a curvilinear relationship, these data support best a generalization that:

Generalization 10: There is no relationship between parental control attempts (undifferentiated) and creativity in the child.

In terms of coercion, three tests indicated a negative relationship and two a positive relationship. One of the tests indicating a positive relationship also found an interaction effect between coercion and support on creativity. It was only when support was high that a positive relationship existed between coercion and creativity. When support was low, the relationship was negative. Hoffman (1970) found that generally when coercion is high, support is low. Perhaps when high parental support occurs along with high coercion, the support mediates the generally negative impact of coercion. In terms of the above logic about stress and creativity, high coercion probably results in relatively high stress, while high support probably results in relatively low stress. If this is so, the combination of the two variables, both at high levels, would result in moderate stress and high creativity. These data provide a basis for our generalization that:

Generalization 11: The greater the parental coercion, the less the creativity of the child.

We judge that the empirical data provide strong direct support and moderate indirect support for this generalization.

The failure to find a relationship between undifferentiated control attempts and creativity might have resulted in a different interpretation if evidence had been found that induction was related to creativity. However, we found no tests of such. On the basis of the cue arousal postulate of Hebb (1955), it was proposed by Rollins and Calder (1975) that a curvilinear relationship exists between stress and creativity, with greatest creativity associated with a moderate amount of stress. If this is so, control attempts probably influence stress in terms of the degree of psychological force it exerts on the child; the greater the force, the greater the stress. As stated above, induction is assumed to be less forceful than coercion. If

this is the case, then parental support, induction, and coercion might influence creativity in the child through their single and combined effects on stress in the child. Therefore, we propose as a postulate the following:

Postulate 1: A curvilinear relationship exists between personal stress experienced by the child and the child's creativity such that as stress increases from low to moderate amounts, creativity increases; but as stress increases further from moderate to large amounts, creativity decreases.

A corollary of the above postulate is:

Corollary 1: The greater the parental induction, the greater the creativity in the child.

The logic for this corollary is that parental control attempts result in a force on the child, and thus the greater the control attempt, the greater the stress. However, induction results in less stress than coercion, so that high induction would result in moderate stress, thus high creativity.

Internal Locus of Control

The empirical research of parental correlates of internal locus of control of reinforcement in the child is of recent origin. However, we found 11 studies since 1966 that measured both parental support and some type of parental control attempts as correlates of locus of control (see

Table 14.6. Relationships of Parental Behaviors and Creativity in Children

STUDY	CHILDREN			PARENT VARIABLES		
	Age	Number	Sex	Support	Control Attempts (Unspecified)	Coercion
Busse '69	11	48	S			− FS
Dreyer & Wells '66	4	13	S		0 PC	
		12	D			
Heilbrun '71*	19	96	S	0 MS[1]		− MS[3]
				+ MS[2]		+ MS[4]
Juffer '69	8	60	M	0 PS	− PS	
				0 PD	− PD	
Nichols '64	17	796	S			− MC
		450	D			
Orinstein '61	7	45	M	− MC		+ MC
Siegleman '73	19	144	S	− PC	0 PC	
		274	D			
Silverberg '70	10	88	S	+ FS	0 FS	
		117	D	0 FD	0 FD	
				0 MS	0 MS	
				0 MD	0 MD	
Generalization				+/−	0	−

*Interaction effects of parent variables explored.
[1]With low coercion.
[2]With high coercion.
[3]With low support.
[4]With high support.

Family Interaction

Table 14.7). None of them tested for combined effects of these variables.

In 25 tests of the relationship between support and "internal control beliefs," 18 indicated a positive, one a negative, and six no relationship. All four subsets of parent-child dyads had evidence of a positive relationship. The one negative relationship was from a study with atypical methodology. The child's internal locus of control orientation (which is a subjective attribute) was inferred from behavioral observation in this one case. All of the other studies obtained a direct self-report from the child. On the sum of the evidence, the generalization that best fits the data is:

Generalization 12: The greater the parental support, the greater the internal locus of control of reinforcement in the child.

We judge that the empirical data give strong direct support for this generalization.

In terms of undifferentiate control attempts, 19 tests were made of relationships with locus of control. Of these, 12 indicated no relationship, one a positive relationship, six a negative relationship, and one a curvilinear relationship. The curvilinear relationship was such that as control attempts increased from relatively small to moderate amounts, a positive relationship existed, but with further increases in control attempts the relationship be-

came negative. We judge that the generalization that best fits the empirical data reported is:

Generalization 13: As parental control attempts (undifferentiated) increase from low to moderate amounts, internal locus of control of reinforcement in the child increases; but as control attempts (undifferentiated) increase from moderate to high amounts, the internal locus of control of reinforcement in the child decreases.

We judge that the data provide weak support for this generalization.

The results of studies of the relationship between coercion and locus of control are contradictory. Of 13 tests, one indicates a positive relationship, four a negative relationship, and eight no relationship. There is no age of child or parent-child subset of dyads that accounts for the discrepant results. Though the no-relationship applies to all dyads except mother and daughter, this dyad has a positive relationship in one test and a negative relationship in another. On the sum of the evidence, we generalize that:

Generalization 14: The greater the parental coercion, the less the internal locus of control of reinforcement in the child.

We judge that the data provide weak direct support for this generalization. A more intensive methodological review

Table 14.7.   Relationships of Parental Behavior and Internal Locus of Control of Reinforcement in Children

STUDY	CHILDREN			PARENT VARIABLES			
	Age	Number	Sex	Support	Control Attempts (Unspecified)	Coercion	Induction
Armentrout '71	11	108	S	− PC	0 PC		
		142	D				
Davis '69	11	30	S	0 PC	− PC		
Graff '67	15	120	S	+ FS		− FS	
				0 MS		0 MS	
Katkovsky et al., '67	9	23	S	+ FS	0 FS		
		18	D	+ FD	0 FD		
				+ MS	0 MS		
				+ MD	0 MD		
Katkovsky et al., '67	9	20	S	0 FS	0 FS		
		20	D	0 FD	0 FD		
				0 MS	0 MS		
				+ MD	0 MD		
Loeb '73	11	45	S	+ PS		− PS	
MacDonald '71	19	192	S	+ FS	0 FS	0 FS	
		235	D	+ FD	0 FD	0 FD	
				+ MD	+ MD	+ MD	
Pruitt '71	16	64	M	0 MS	0 MS	0 MS	+ MS
				+ MD		− MS	0 MS
Scheck et al., '73	15	589	S	+ PS	+/− PS		
Shore '67	14	279	S	+ PS		0 PS	
Sprehn '73	?	?	S	0 PS	0 PS		
Summary				+	+/−	−	+

of the studies might indicate that coercion ranged from only low to moderate amounts in the studies finding no relationship.

There was very little evidence in the studies reviewed concerning induction and locus of control of reinforcement in the child. One study found a positive relationship existed for the mother-son dyad. In a recent study (Allen, 1974) a positive relationship was found for each of the parent-child subsets of dyads. Therefore, we judge that the generalization that best fits the data is:

Generalization 15: The greater the parental induction, the greater the internal locus of control of reinforcement in the child.

We judge that the empirical data provide only weak direct support of this generalization.

Whereas Levenson (1973) concluded that it was impor-

tant to consider parent-child dyadic pairs as having different socialization outcomes, such awareness failed to help resolve discrepancies from study to study as reviewed herein.

Moral Behavior

In terms of conscience, resistance to temptation, and moral judgment our survey included 18 studies of parental behavior correlates of moral behavior in children (see Table 14.8). The results were fairly consistent irrespective of type of moral behavior, age of child, or parent-child subsets of dyads. Of 18 tests of parental support and moral behavior in the child, 11 indicated a positive relationship and seven no relationship. The generalization that best fits the data is:

Generalization 16: The greater the parental support, the greater the moral behavior of children.

Table 14.8.   Relationships of Parental Behaviors and Moral Behavior in Children

| STUDY | CHILDREN | | | PARENT VARIABLES | | | |
	Age	Number	Sex	Support	Control Attempts (Unspecified)	Coercion	Induction
Allinsmith and Greenling '55	13	?	S				+ MS
Aronfreed '61	11	?	S			− MS	+ MS
			D			− MD	+ MD
Burton et al., '61	4	?	S	+ MS		0 MS	− MS
			D	+ MD		− MD	− MD
Draper '66	12	325	M		0 PC	0 PC	
Fodor '73	15	70	S	+ FS	0 FS		0 FS
				0 MS	0 MS		0 MS
Grinder '62	11	70	S	0 MS	+ MS	− MS	0 MS
		70	D	0 MD	0 MD	− MD	+ MD
Hoffman '63b	4	22	M	0 PC			+ PC[1]
							− PC[2]
Hoffman & Saltzstein '67	13	103	S	+ MC		− MC	+ MC
		101	D	0 FC		0 FC	0 FC
LaVoie '70	15	80	S			0 FS	+ FS[1]
							− FS[2]
						0 MS	+ MS[1]
							− MS[2]
Lifshin '70	13	17	S			0 PS	0 PS
Nevius '72	10	40	S			0 MS	0 MS
Pearlin et al., '67	?	?	?			− PC	
Peck & Havighurst '60	15	17	S	+ PC		− PC	+ PC
		17	D				
Santrock '73	10	120	S	+ MS		− MS	+ MS
Sears et al., '65	4	21	S	0 FS	+ FS		+ FS
				+ FD	+ FD		+ FD
		19	D	+ MS	+ MS		+ MS
				0 MD	+ MD		+ MD
Seashore '61	15	167	S	+ FS			+ FS
				+ MS			+ MS
Shoffeitt '71	15	60	S			− MS	+ MS
Washington '63	5	40	M	+ MC			
		43	S				
Generalization				+	+	−	+

[1] With low coercion.
[2] With high coercion.

This conclusion is in agreement with the general review of moral development by Hoffman (1970). We judge that the empirical data give strong direct support to this generalization.

Undifferentiated types of parental control attempts were tested nine times in relation to moral behavior. In five tests the relationship was positive, and in four there was no relationship. We judge that the generalization that best fits the data is:

Generalization 17: The greater the parental control attempts (undifferentiated), the greater the moral behavior in children.

We judge that the empirical data give moderate direct support to this generalization.

The relationships of coercion and induction to moral behavior found in our review are similar to those reported by Hoffman (1970). Coercion is negatively and induction is positively related to moral behavior. Of 17 tests, 10 were negative and seven found no relationship between coercion and moral behavior. Induction was tested 28 times. A positive relationship was found 17 times, no relationship six times, and a negative relationship five times. However, of the five negative relationships, three were under conditions of high coercion. The empirical generalizations that best fit these data are:

Generalization 18: The greater the parental coercion, the less the moral behavior of children.

Generalization 19: The greater the parental induction, the greater the moral behavior of children.

We judge that the empirical data give moderate support to the generalization about coercion and strong support to the generalization about induction.

Stemming from the early work of Sears et al. (1957), many tests have been made between the parental use of love withdrawal as a qualified control attempt and moral behavior in children. Hoffman (1970) concluded from his review that no meaningful relationship existed because of the discrepancies from study to study. Of 16 tests in the studies we reviewed, six found a negative relationship, six found no relationship, and four found a positive relationship. One study found a positive relationship only under the conditions when parental support was high; when support was low, there was no relationship. This finding, in support of the often expressed idea (Sears et al., 1957) that unless parents are generally supportive the use of love withdrawal as a control technique will be ineffective, does not explain the frequently found negative relationships. This area appears to be very problematic and requires greater conceptual and/or methodological sophistication to bring order out of discrepancy. Therefore, we will attempt no generalizations regarding love withdrawal and moral development.

Self-Esteem

Eight studies were reviewed that measured both parental support and parental control attempts and tested their relationship with self-esteem (see Table 14.9). The results were fairly consistent irrespective of age of child or parent-child subsets of dyads. A positive relationship was found between parental support in 13 out of 15 tests. In

Table 14.9. Relationships of Parental Behaviors and Self-Esteem in Children

STUDY	CHILDREN			PARENT VARIABLES			
	Age	*Number*	*Sex*	*Support*	*Control Attempts (Unspecified)*	*Coercion*	*Induction*
Comstock '73	14	72	D	+ FD + MD	+ FD + MD		
Coopersmith '67	11	85	M	+ PC	+ PC	− PC	+ PC
Gecas '69, '71*	16	620	M	+ FS + FD + MS + MD	0 FS 0 FD 0 MS 0 MD		
Mote '66	11	79 78	S D	0 MC	0 MC	0 MC	
Samuels '69	5	93	M	+ MC	+ MC	− MC	
Thomas et al., '74*	16	740 718	S D	+ FS + FD + MS + MD	+ FS 0 FD 0 MS 0 MD		
Toto '73	14	?	?	0 PC	0 PC		
Turberg '66	11	30 30	D S	+ MC	− MC		
Generalization				+	+	−	+

*Interaction effects of parent variables tested but none found. These two studies partially overlap in that some of the same findings are reported in articles and books.

two no relationship was found. These data strongly support the generalization that:

Generalization 20: The greater the parental support, the greater the self-esteem in children.

In terms of control attempts it was difficult to determine which studies were using undifferentiated control attempts and which ones were using coercion. Only studies where the evidence was clear were classified as coercion. Other studies were classified as undifferentiated control attempts. Of those classified as undifferentiated, nine had no relationship with self-esteem, five a positive, and one a negative relationship. Since the studies finding a positive relationship covered a wide age range as well as most parent-child subsets of dyads, we judge the appropriate generalization to be:

Generalization 21: The greater the parental control attempts (undifferentiated), the greater the self-esteem of children.

However, a curvilinear relationship might account for the results, though none was found. We judge that the empirical data provide only weak support for this generalization.

In terms of coercion and induction the data support the following generalizations between type of control attempts by parents and self-esteem in children:

Generalization 22: The greater the parental coercion, the less the self-esteem of children.

Generalization 23: The greater the parental induction, the greater the self-esteem of children.

However, because of the limited number of studies in these areas, we judge that the empirical data provide only weak support for these generalizations.

Instrumental Competence

Five studies focused on instrumental competence in children. All except one study dealt with very young children (see Table 14.10). Though the number of studies is small, the results have a very high consistency. The following generalizations best fit the data:

Generalization 24: The greater the parental support, the greater the instrumental competence of children.

Generalization 25: The greater the parental coercion, the less the instrumental competence of children.

Generalization 26: The greater the parental induction, the greater the instrumental competence of children.

These conclusions are congruent with the review of parental behavior and social competence in children by Baumrind (1972a). We judge that the empirical data give strong support for these generalizations.

Summary

The seven aspects of child behavior covered thus far in our literature review all seem to be highly valued in contemporary American society and might all be judged as positive indicators of social competence, either instrumental or emotional competence (Baumrind, 1972b). The similarity of results of parental correlates across these seven areas is quite striking (see Table 14.11).

Parental support is consistently found to have a positive relationship with all aspects of social competence in children. The only exception is in terms of creativity, where a curvilinear relationship might exist. While evidence of the relationship between undifferentiated parental control attempts and aspects of social competence is not consistent across areas, an explanation is offered. It is probably not the overall amount of control attempts, but the amount within each type that is important. Since we were unable to determine from many studies a specific type of control attempt, we used undifferentiated control attempts as a residual category to place test results involving control techniques that could not be clearly identified as coercion, induction, or love withdrawal. Perhaps this resulted in a mixed bag. Nevertheless, we arrived at the generalization of a curvilinear relationship in two areas, a positive relationship in two, and a negative relationship in one. If actually a curvilinear relationship exists, then the positive or negative relationships might be instances of a limited range of variation at either the high or low end of the control attempts variable. Coercion and induction were consistently correlated across the areas of compe-

Table 14.10. Relationships of Parental Behaviors and Instrumental Competence in Children

STUDY	CHILDREN			PARENT VARIABLES		
	Age	*Number*	*Sex*	*Support*	*Coercion*	*Induction*
Baumrind & Black '67	4	85	M	0 PC	− PC	+ PC
Baumrind '67	4	32	M	+ PC	− PC	+ PC
Clapp '66	4	34	S	+ MS	− MS	
Deschner '72	2	29	M	+ MS	− MS	
Rowland '68	9	32	S	+ MS	− MS	
Generalization				+	−	+

tence with negative and positive relationships, respectively, while the relationships of love withdrawal and social competence was inconclusive in all areas.

In terms of social competence in children, in general, we propose the following theoretical propositions (see Table 14.11):

Proposition 1: The greater the parental support, the greater the social competence in children.

Proposition 2: The greater the inductive control attempts of parents, the greater the social competence in children.

Proposition 3: The greater the coercive control attempts of parents, the less the social competence in children.

The general propositions are congruent with the conclusions of Baumrind (1972b) and Martin (1975) in their reviews of parental correlates of child behaviors. The evidence provides no basis for determining if these parental behaviors combine in an additive or in a multiplicative manner in their relationships with child behavior.

Generalizations: Social Incompetent Behaviors

Whereas the foregoing seven areas represent child behaviors generally valued in Western society, the five areas covered in this section represent general problem areas. These areas become problematic if the child exhibits such behaviors not only for the parents but in other social settings as well, such as the school environment.

Antisocial Aggression

Fifteen studies were reviewed in terms of relationships between parental behaviors and aggression in children

(see Table 14.12). From eight of the studies the relationship between support and aggression was tested 15 times. Twelve indicated a negative relationship, two no relationship, and one a positive relationship. These results seem to hold across a wide range of ages for children and for all four subsets of parent-child dyads. The generalization that best fits the data is:

Generalization 27: The greater the parental support, the less the antisocial aggression in children.

We judge that the empirical data give strong direct support to this generalization.

In terms of induction there was only one test, and it indicated no relationship with aggression. However, of seven tests of undifferentiated control attempts, two tests indicated a positive relationship with aggression, three no relationship, one a negative relationship, and one a curvilinear relationship. The curvilinear relationship is such that as control attempts increase from a small to a moderate amount, a negative relationship exists, but as control attempts increase further, a positive relationship exists. With both positive and negative relationships along with a curvilinear relationship, we judge the best generalization to be:

Generalization 28: As parental control attempts (undifferentiated) increase from low to moderate amounts, aggression of children decreases; but as parental control attempts (undifferentiated) increase from moderate to high amounts, aggression of children increases.

We judge that the empirical data provide only weak indirect support for this generalization.

Coercion was studied in relation to aggression in 19 tests. Of these, 14 found a positive relationship, and five

Table 14.11. Generalizations of the Relationships of Parental Behaviors and Social Competence in Children

CHILD BEHAVIORS	PARENTAL SUPPORT	CONTROL ATTEMPTS (UNSPECIFIED)	COERCION	INDUCTION
Cognitive Development	+ (S)*	− (M)	− (M)	?
Conformity	+ (M)	+/− (M)	− (M)	+ (M)
Creativity	+/− (M)	0 (W)	− (S)	?
Instrumental Social Competence	+ (S)	?	− (S)	+ (S)
Internal Locus of Control	+ (S)	+/− (W)	− (W)	+ (W)
Moral Behavior	+ (S)	+ (M)	− (M)	+ (S)
Self-Esteem	+ (S)	+ (W)	− (W)	+ (W)
Theoretical Proposition	+	?	−	+

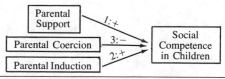

*S, M, and W indicate respectively strong, moderate, and weak empirical support for the generalization.

Table 14.12. Relationships of Parental Behaviors and Antisocial Aggression in Children

STUDY	CHILDREN			PARENT VARIABLES			
	Age	*Number*	*Sex*	*Support*	*Control Attempts (Unspecified)*	*Coercion*	*Induction*
Becker et al., '62	5	?	S	− FS	+ FS	+ FS	
				− MS	0 MS	+ MS	
Chorost '62	16	79	S	− FS		+ FS	
				− MS		+ MS	
Delaney '65	.3	33	S			+ PC	
		29	D				
English '69	11	33	S	0 MC	+ MC		
		30	D				
Eron et al., '63	9	245	S			+ PC	
		206	D				
Gordon & Smith '65	5	24	S		− MS		
Hoffman '60	11	211	S			+ PC	
Kagan & Moss '62	10	89	M	− MS		+ MS	
				− MD		+ MD	
Kausch '62	13	74	S			0 MS	
Lefkowitz et al., '63	8	875	M			+ PC	0 PC
McCord & McCord '61	13	174	S	− PS	−/+ PS	+ PS	
McCord & McCord '63	13	255	S			+ FS	
Toews '66*	15	70	S	0 PS	0 PS		
		92	D	− PD	0 PD		
Volenski '72	4	15	S	− FS		+ FS	
				− FD		0 FD	
		15	D	− MS		0 MS	
				− MD		0 MD	
Winder & Rau '62	11	108	S	+ MS		+ MS	
Generalizations				−	−/+	+	?

*Interaction effects of parent variables tested but none found.

found no relationship. The generalization that best fits is strongly supported by these data, especially for boys:

Generalization 29: The greater the parental coercion, the greater the antisocial aggression of children.

Since coercion of parents is itself often an aggressive act, this generalization is congruent with the conclusion of Bandura (1969) that agressive parents model aggressive behavior for children to imitate. It is also in agreement with an earlier review by Baumrind (1966).

Behavior Problems

Several types of socially maladaptive behaviors such as juvenile delinquency and neuroses were lumped together under a general category of behavior problems in our review because of the small number of studies in any one area. Eleven studies were reviewed that measured some aspect of parental control techniques (see Table 14.13). Of nine tests of relationships between parental support and behavior problems in children, six indicated a negative relationship and three no relationship. In summary, these studies suggest the generalization that:

Generalization 30: The greater the parental support, the less the behavior problems of children.

We judge that the empirical data give strong direct support to this generalization.

In terms of control techniques, there were no tests of the relationship between induction and behavior problems in children. In the 14 tests in terms of undifferentiated control attempts, nine positive relationships were found, one negative relationship, and four tests found no relationship. In summary, the evidence strongly supports the generalization that:

Generalization 31: The greater the parental control attempts (undifferentiated), the greater the behavior problems in children.

Of four tests of the relationship between coercion of parents and behavior problems in children, two indicated a positive relationship and two no relationship. Therefore, we judge the data give only weak support to the generalization that:

Generalization 32: The greater the parental coercion, the greater the behavior problems in children.

Drug Abuse

Closely related to other behavior problems studied in relation to parental behaviors is the area of drug abuse. Of

Table 14.13.   Relationships of Parental Behaviors and Behavior Problems in Children

STUDY	CHILDREN			PARENT VARIABLES		
	Age	*Number*	*Sex*	*Support*	*Control Attempts (Unspecified)*	*Coercion*
Apperson '61	17	?	S	− FS	+ FS	
				0 MS	0 MS	
Armentrout '71	11	260	M	− PC	+ PC	
Dielman & Cattell '72	7	156	M	− MC	+ MC	
Kent '65	7	60	M	0 MC		0 MC
Krug '65	9	796	M	− PC	+ PC	+ PC
Maloney '74	5	60	M		+ MS	
					− MD	
Peterson et al., '61	5	41	S			
		36	D		0 FC	0 FC
Russell '66	18	224	F	− PD	0 PD	
Stern '63	9	100	M		+ MC	+ MC
Townsend '68	35	131	D	− FD	+ FD	
				. 0 MD	+ MD	
Weiss '65	9	84	S		+ FC	
		16	D		0 MC	
Generalizations				−	+	+

seven tests made of the relationship between parental support and drug abuse, three found a negative relationship, and four found no relationship (see Table 14.14). Giving greater weight to evidence of a found relationship than to no finding of a relationship and with results from other social behavior disorders, we judge that the best generalization is:

Generalization 33: The greater the parental support, the less the drug abuse in children.

The data provide only weak support for this generalization.

In terms of undifferentiated control attempts the studies collectively indicate two relationships were positive, one curvilinear, and in four tests no relationships were found. Giving priority to the curvilinear relationship because most of the studies dichotomized variables preventing detection of such relationships, we judge that the generalization most warranted by the data is:

Generalization 34: As parental control attempts (undifferentiated) increase from low to moderate amounts, drug abuse in children decreases; but as parental control attempts (undifferentiated) increase from moderate to high amounts, drug abuse in children increases.

The data provide only weak support for this generalization also. The limited number of tests concerning relationships of coercion and induction with drug abuse prompted us to refrain from generalizations in these areas.

Learning Disabilities

Only five studies were found that included both parental support and control techniques and learning dis-

abilities in children (see Table 14.15). Parental support was found to correlate negatively with learning disabilities in five out of six tests. In terms of coercion all six tests found a positive relationship. In summary, the generalizations strongly supported by these data are as follows:

Generalization 35: The greater the parental support, the less the learning disabilities in children.

Generalization 36: The greater the parental coercion, the greater the learning disabilities in children.

Schizophrenia

Eleven studies were reviewed that related parental behaviors to schizophrenia in children (see Table 14.16). In terms of parental support, six out of 10 tests indicated a negative relationship. In summary, these data support the generalization:

Generalization 37: The greater the parental support, the less the incidence of schizophrenia in children.

We judge that the empirical data provide moderate support for this generalization.

Of two tests that correlated undifferentiated control attempts with schizophrenia, both tests indicated a negative relationship. The generalization this suggests is:

Generalization 38: The greater the parental control attempts (undifferentiated), the less the incidence of schizophrenia in children.

The generalization has only weak empirical support.

Coercion has been studied fairly extensively in relation to schizophrenia, and the results are fairly consistent. In

Table 14.14.   Relationships of Parental Behaviors and Drug Abuse in Children

STUDY	CHILDREN			PARENT VARIABLES			
	Age	*Number*	*Sex*	*Support*	*Control Attempts (Unspecified)*	*Coercion*	*Induction*
Baer & Corruds '74	12	136	S			+ PC	
		64	D				
Bender '74	35	70	S	0 PS		0 PS	
Berger '74	16	40	S	− FS	0 FS		
				0 MS	0 MS		
Hunt '72	19	563	M		−/+ PC		− PC
Tousignant '72	17	236	M	0 FS	+ FS		
				− FD	+ FD		
				0 MS	0 MS		
				− MD	0 MD		
Generalizations				−	−/+	+	−

Table 14.15.   Relationships of Parental Behaviors and Learning Disabilities in Children

STUDY	CHILDREN			PARENT VARIABLES		
	Age	*Number*	*Sex*	*Support*	*Control Attempts (Unspecified)*	*Coercion*
Freeman '70	?	50	M	0 MC		+ MC
Hall '63	11	40	S	+ FS		+ FS
				− MS		+ MS
Kenney '65	8	40	M			+ MC
Wetter '70	8	?	M	− MC	− MC	
Wilkins '70	8	87	M	− FC		+ FC
				− MC		+ MC
Generalization				−	−	+

Table 14.16.   Relationships of Parental Behaviors and Schizophrenia in Children

STUDY	CHILDREN			PARENT VARIABLES			
	Age	*Number*	*Sex*	*Support*	*Control Attempts (Unspecified)*	*Coercion*	*Induction*
Craig '66	19	84	D			+ MD	
Farahmand '61	30	40	M	− FC	− FC	+ FC	
Harris '65	30	60	M	− MC		+ MC	
Heilbrun '60	30	53	D	− MD		+ MD	
Heilbrun '62	19	108	D	0 MD		+ MD	
Margo & Hanson '69	20	264	S	− MS		+ MS	
McKinley '63	20	43	M			+ FC	
						+ MC	
Mischler & Waxler '68	30	100	M	− PC	− PC		− PC
Stabenau et al., '65	20	35	M	− PC		+ PC	
Vogel et al., '64	30	80	S	+ FS			
				0 MS		0 MS	
Zuckerman et al., '60	12	?	M	0 PC		0 PC	
Generalization				−	−	+	−

nine out of 11 tests a positive relationship was found. In summary, these data give strong support for the generalization that:

Generalization 39: The greater the parental coercion, the greater the incidence of schizophrenia in children.

Summary

The last five child behaviors reviewed are often identified as social problems and are negatively valued in contemporary American society. We judged them to be indicators of socially incompetent behavior. As with the socially competent behaviors, a very similar pattern of empirical generalizations were arrived at across these behaviors (see Table 14.17). All five areas indicated a negative relationship with parental support. Evidence of the relationship of undifferentiated parental control attempts and aspects of social incompetence is not consistent across areas. Nevertheless, the discrepancies are consistent with the findings in two areas of a curvilinear relationship, though the empirical support is only weak. In terms of coercion, a positive relationship is consistently found across areas. Too few tests of induction were made to warrant generalizations.

From the empirical generalizations arrived at across the aspects of social incompetence in general, we judge that the following theoretical propositions are warranted (see Table 14.17):

Proposition 4: The greater the parental support, the less the social incompetence in children.

Proposition 5: The greater the coercive control attempts of parents, the greater the social incompetence in children.

It should be noted that these propositions describe a pattern of parental behavior that is exactly opposite the pattern described in previous propositions about parental correlates of social competence in children. Therefore, Proposition 4 (social incompetence) is very similar to Proposition 1 (social competence), and likewise Proposition 5 is very similar to Proposition 3.

In neither the empirical generalizations about social competence nor the empirical generalizations about social incompetence in children did the evidence warrant an inference about the manner in which the parental behaviors combine. At the beginning of the review of empirical studies an attempt was made to search out interaction effects of parental support behaviors and parental control techniques. Though 176 studies were found that simultaneously measured both types of variables, only 15 tested or explored for interaction effects, and of these only eight found any evidence of support for multiplicative combined effects. Current theory about the multiplicative combined effects of parental support and parental control techniques such as that presented by Rollins and Thomas (1975) seems to lack grounding in the extant empirical research.

Sex-of-Child–Sex-of-Parent Dyads

Bronfenbrenner (1961) has suggested that sex of child and sex of parent be differentiated in research on socialization of children in the family. This has been echoed in reviews by Baumrind (1972b) and Martin (1975). Only two areas in our review of empirical research indicate the wisdom of this advice. They are academic achievement and sex role orientation in children. The latter has long been recognized and researched as a special case. However, we assumed that the decade of the 1960s and 1970s in the U.S. would represent an era of decline in the differential socialization of male and female children toward academic achievement. However, the published research suggests differential socialization still occurs in terms of this aspect of instrumental competence.

Table 14.17. Relationships of Parental Behaviors and Socially Incompetent Behaviors in Children

CHILD BEHAVIOR	PARENTAL SUPPORT	CONTROL ATTEMPTS (UNSPECIFIED)	COERCION
Aggression	−(S)	−/+(W)	+(S)
Behavior Problems	−(S)	+(S)	+(W)
Drug Abuse	−(W)	−/+(W)	+(W)
Learning Disabilities	−(S)	−(W)	+(S)
Schizophrenia	−(M)	−(W)	+(S)
Propositions	−	?	+

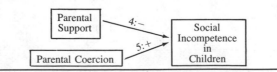

Academic Achievement

In a major review article on parent-child relations, Becker (1964) concluded that high achievement is associated with high parental support and high parental control attempts without differentiating between sex of child and sex of parent. In a subsequent review by Walters and Stinnett (1971) high support and low control attempts were alleged to be associated with high achievement. In partial agreement with Becker (1964), Baumrind (1972b) concluded that the parental behaviors associated with high achievement were high support and high control if of the inductive type and if accompanied by high power. However, she cautioned that this might not apply to girls or "disadvantaged" families. Finally, the latest published review (Martin, 1975) is in basic agreement with Becker and Baumrind except that for daughters, Martin concluded that a negative relationship exists between parental support and academic achievement.

Our review included 21 empirical studies of parental support, parental control attempts, and academic achievement (see Table 14.18). Most of them were studies of mothers and children. Of 28 tests of a relationship between parental support and academic achievement, 12 indicated a positive relationship, three a negative relationship, and 13 no relationship. Only one of the positive relationships was a study of daughters. The other 11 focused on sons or sons and daughters combined. All three negative relationships were between parents and daughters. In two studies an interaction effect was found between parental support and undifferentiated control attempts on achievement of sons such that when control was low, no relationship existed, but when control was high, a positive relationship existed. This, in part, can account for the failure in many tests to find a relationship between support and achievement for sons. If, in some studies, control was at a relatively low level while simultaneously the relationship between support and achieve-

Table 14.18.   Relationships of Parental Behaviors and Academic Achievement in Children

STUDY	CHILDREN			PARENT VARIABLES			
	Age	Number	Sex	Support	Control Attempts (Unspecified)	Coercion	Induction
Aaronson '66	7	100	S	0 MS		− MS	
Barton et al., '74	13	311	M	+ PC		− PC	
Becker '70	12	89	S	0 FS		− FS	
Berg '63	12	?	M	+ MC		− MC	
Biglin '64	10	254	M	+ MC		− MC	
Brodis '69	15	120	M	+ MS	+ MS	0 MS	
				0 MD	0 MD	0 MD	
Davids & Hainsworth '67	15	77	S	0 MS		− MS	
Elder '65	18	1,000	M			− PC	
Fazel '68	18	298	M	+ PC		+ PC	
Gill & Spila '62	17	30	S	0 MS		− MS	
		30	D	0 MD		0 MD	
Haider '70	10	57	M	+ MS	+ MS		+ MS
Healey '74*	13	176	S	0 FS[1]	− FS[3]		
		145	D	+ FS[2]	0 FS[4]		
				0 FD	0 FD		
				0 MS	0 MS		
				0 MD	0 MD		
Heilbrun '68*	19	102	S	0 MS[1]	− MS[3]		
				0 MS[2]	+ MS[4]		
Johnson '74	23+	46	D	− FD	+ FD		
				− MD	+ MD		
Kagan & Moss '62	?	44	S	+ MS	+ MS		
		45	D	− MD	+ MD		
Miller '67	5	55	M	0 MC			
Morrow & Wilson '61	17	96	M	+ MC		− MC	
Mullikan '66	19	109	M			− MC	
Pruitt '71	16	64	M	0 PC		0 PC	0 PC
Rich '65	12	300	M	0 PC	0 PC		
Generalizations			S	0[1] + [2]	− [3] + [4]	−	?
			D	−	+	0	?

*Interaction effects of parent variables explored.
[1]With low control attempts.
[2]With high control attempts.
[3]With low support.
[4]With high support.

ment was being studied, the failure to find a relationship could be expected. A theoretical explanation given by Heilbrun (1968) for this phenomenon is that the value of parental support as a reinforcement for academic achievement is a function of the sensitization effects of parental control attempts.

In summary, the above data support the generalizations that:

Generalization 40: For girls, the less the parental support, the greater the academic achievement.

Generalization 41: For boys, the relationship between parental support and academic achievement is contingent on the level of parental control attempts such that when control is low, there is no relationship, but when control is high, the greater the parental support, the greater the academic achievement.

These generalizations are congruent with the conclusions of Baumrind (1971) and Martin (1975) but not those of Walters and Stinnett (1971). The latter asserted that high support and low control facilitated achievement. On the contrary, we suggest that for girls it is low support and for boys it is high support coupled with high rather than low control attempts that facilitates academic achievement. In our judgment, these generalizations have moderate support from empirical data.

Of 18 tests of a relationship between undifferentiated control attempts by parents and academic achievement in children, seven were positive, two negative and nine indicated no relationship. The two negative relationships were both under conditions of low parental support (either father or mother) toward sons. The generalizations that best fit the data are that:

Generalization 42: For girls, the greater the parental control attempts, the greater the academic achievement.

Generalization 43: For boys, the greater the parental control attempts, the greater the academic achievement when parental support is high, but when parental support is low, the greater the control attempts, the less the academic achievement.

We judge that the empirical data give moderate support for these generalizations.

Coercion by parents is negatively related to academic achievement in 10 out of 16 tests. In five tests there was no relationship, and of these, three involved daughters and two involved children undifferentiated by sex. The negative relationships appear to be a parent-son phenomenon. The generalizations that best fit and are moderately supported by the data are that:

Generalization 44: There is no relationship between parental coercion and academic achievement for girls.

Generalization 45: For boys, the greater the coercion of parents, the less the academic achievement.

Whereas Bronfenbrenner (1961a) suggested that in general boys are undersocialized and girls are oversocialized by the combined parental behaviors of support and control, this doesn't seem to be the case in terms of academic achievement. The same pattern of parental behaviors that are associated with general social competence in both boys and girls seems to apply to only boys as far as academic achievement is concerned. To the extent that academic achievement is part of the general syndrome of instrumental competent behaviors as suggested by Baumrind (1972b) it appears that a different socialization process exists for boys than for girls. Whereas about the same parental behaviors that are associated with high conformity, high self-esteem, and high internal locus of control orientation in boys are also associated with high academic achievement, not so for girls. For girls, the pattern of parental behaviors associated with high conformity, high self-esteem, and high internal locus of control orientation is also associated with low academic achievement. This suggests that academic achievement is perhaps negatively valued for girls in contemporary American society and those girls with high academic achievement are the products of malsocialization. Perhaps the effort toward sexual equality in the 1970s in the U.S. will change the differential socialization of boys and girls, but the studies reviewed, reflecting on socialization practices of parents during the 1950s and 1960s, suggest that in practice sexual inequality exists as far as socialization for "instrumental" competence is concerned.

While the foregoing explanation of sex differences in socialization is at base a sociological explanation resting on differential values for girls and boys placed on academic achievement by society, another more biological explanation can also be offered. If one assumes, as considerable evidence seems to suggest, that males are biologically more predisposed toward aggressiveness than females, then one might conclude from a biological and social components model that support from parents best equips males who are aggressive by nature to succeed by reducing their "natural tendencies," whereas a nonsupportive environment best prepares females to succeed by making them "tough" and "hard," therefore increasing their aggressive tendencies. Such a biological-social explanation would not be popular in our contemporary world of "equality," but, nevertheless, it ought to be investigated.[5]

Sex Role Orientation

Reviews in the area of sex role orientation in children have generally emphasized the importance of the differential effects of same-sexed and opposite-sexed parents on sex role orientation in children (Walters and Stinnett, 1971). The dominance of parents relative to each other has also been considered as a contingent variable mediating the parent-child relationship. The results of our review are congruent with these ideas. We found 14 studies dealing with parental support, control techniques, and power in relation to sex role orientation (see Table 14.19). In 20 tests of the relationship between parental support and own-gender sex role orientation in children, seven were positive, one was negative, and 12 indicated no relationship. The one negative relationship was obtained for the opposite-sexed parent-child dyad of mother and son. In this case, the relationship existed only under the condition of high control attempts by the mother. All seven of the positive relationships existed in same-sexed parent-child dyads. Of the 12 no-relationship findings, nine (67 percent) represented opposite-sexed parent-child

dyads. These data in general, suggest that in terms of parental support, the behavior of the same-sexed parent is more important than that of the opposite-sexed parent in terms of the child's own-gender sex role orientation. The empirical generalizations that best fit the data are that:

Generalization 46: For boys, the greater the father's support, the greater the masculine sex role orientation.

Generalization 47: For girls, the greater the mother's support, the greater the feminine sex role orientation.

We judge that the empirical data give moderate support for these generalizations.

Only seven tests of the relationship between undif-

Table 14.19.   Relationships of Parental Behaviors and Own-Gender Sex Role Orientation in Children

STUDY	CHILDREN			PARENT VARIABLES				
	Age	*Number*	*Sex*	*Support*	*Control Attempts (Unspecified)*	*Coercion*	*Dominance of Father Relative to Mother*	*Power*
Auerbach '67	4	38	M	0 FS 0 MD				+ FS + MD
Biller '69	5	184	S				+ PS	+ FS
Boxley '73*	23+	60	S			0 FS 0 MS[1] 0 MS[2]		
Edwards '63	23+	32	S	+ FS 0 MS		+ FS − MS		
Egan '64	17	46	D			− FD		
Greenstein '66	5	?	M			0 FS 0 FD		
Kagan & Moss '62*	?	89	M	0 MS[3] − MS[4] + MD				
Kaplar '70	11	70	S	+ FS 0 MS	0 FS 0 MS			
Keller '61	5	60	S	0 FS 0 MS	0 FS 0 MS		+ PS	
Mitchell '65	14	98	S	0 FS 0 FD 0 MS + MD		+ FS 0 FD 0 MS 0 MD		
Moulton et al., '66*	19	176	S				0 PS[1] + PS[2]	
Mussen '60	5	38	S	+ FS	0 FS	0 FS		+ FS
Mussen & Rutherford '63	4	46	S	+ FS 0 FD		+ FS 0 FD		+ FS 0 FD
		17	D	0 MS + MD		0 MS 0 MD		0 MS + MD
Sebald '63	16	578	S		0 FS 0 MS			
Generalizations			S	+ FS 0 MS	0 FS 0 MS	+ FS − MS	+ PS	+ FS 0 MS
			D	0 FD + MD		− FD 0 MD		0 FD + MD

*Interaction effects of parent variables explored.   [3]With low control attempts.
[1]With low support.   [4]With high control attempts.
[2]With high support.

ferentiated control attempts and sex role orientation were made. All pertained to sons and indicated no relationship. However, when coercion was tested, three tests indicated a positive relationship, three a negative, and 11 no relationship. The three positive relationships were all in father-son (same-sex) dyads, and the three negative relationships were all in opposite-sex dyads. The generalizations that best fit the data are that:

Generalization 48: For boys, the greater the father's coercion, the greater the son's masculine sex role orientation.

Generalization 49: For both boys and girls, the greater the coercion of the opposite-sexed parent, the less the own-gender sex role orientation of children.

In terms of the dominance of father relative to mother, the studies reviewed tested only the own-gender sex role orientation of boys. Of four tests, three indicated a positive relationship and one no relationship. However, the one no-relationship case was a special case in which the dominant parent was simultaneously low on support. The generalization that best fits the data is that:

Generalization 50: The greater the relative dominance of the father over the mother, the greater the masculine sex role orientation for boys.

In terms of parental power and sex role orientation of children, the studies indicate a pattern of relationships similar to that found for parental support. Of eight tests, six indicated a positive relationship and two indicated no relationship. All six positive relationships involved same-sex parent-child dyads while both no-relationships involved opposite-sex parent-child dyads. The generalizations of these data seem fairly clear. They are:

Generalization 51: For boys, the greater the father's power, the greater the masculine sex role orientation.

Generalization 52: For girls, the greater the mother's power, the greater the feminine sex role orientation.

Summary

From 12 of the 14 areas reviewed, the evidence supported a common pattern of parental behaviors associated with social competence or incompetence in children irrespective of the sex of the child or the sex of the parent involved. As general theoretical propositions, we concluded that the greater the parental support, the greater the parental induction, and the less the parental coercion, the greater the social competence (lack of social incompetence) in children. These generalizations are very compatible with the results reported in major research monographs on parent-child relations such as Peck and Havighurst (1960) on character development, Coopersmith (1967) on self-esteem, and Baumrind (1967a) on instrumental social competence.

However, for two areas, sex-of-child and sex-of-parent differentiation was crucial in accounting for the results. These areas are academic achievement and own-gender sex role orientation. For sons, academic achievement seems to be facilitated by the same patterns of parental behaviors as other aspects of social competence. For daughters, it seems to be facilitated by parental behaviors leading to social incompetence in other areas. This suggests the awkward idea that academic achievement is not part of social competence for girls. If in fact parents value academic achievement for boys but not for girls and they also value the other aspects of social competence reviewed, then perhaps social competence in children cannot be accounted for independent of the values parents place on such characteristics in their children. Assuming this to be true, we suggest an even more general proposition (see Figure 14.2):

Proposition 6: Social competence in children is facilitated by parental support and control attempts of an inductive type if at the same time the parent values such competence in the child.

These parental behaviors without valuing the social competence or valuing the social competence without these parental behaviors would probably not result in social competence in the child.

One area of child behavior cannot be accomodated by our general proposition. This is the area of own-gender

Figure 14.2. Propositions about Parental Power, Values, and Behavioral Correlates of Social Competence in Children

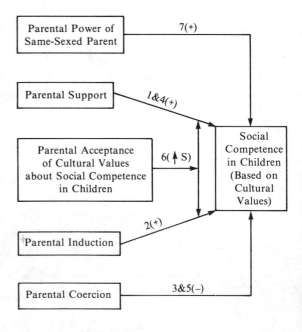

sex role orientation. Even if we assume that parents value children being relatively high on own-gender sex role orientation, the support and power of the same-sexed parent seems to be more crucial than such behaviors of the opposite-sexed parent. Also, for boys, unless they have a parental model of relative male dominance in their parents'marriage and high coercion from the father, their gender sex role orientation is not facilitated. From this information on parental power of the same-sexed parent in relation to sex role orientation in children we suggest another proposition (see Figure 14.2):

Proposition 7: The greater the parental power of the same-sexed parent, the greater the social competence in children.

The foregoing review systematically looked for research where multiple parent behavior variables were used and searched for any indication of interaction among those parental variables. In general, this search turned up very few studies and very little evidence for interaction among the parental variables. This was because most of the research used data-analytic techniques based on bivariate analysis or failed to test for interaction. At this point we ask, is there any research tradition which has systematically treated the combined or joined effects of multiple parental behaviors on the child's characteristics? The answer is, yes, that of Diana Baumrind and associates in the Institute of Human Development at the University of California, Berkeley. We now turn to a review of that research tradition to ask what can it add to our understanding of parental influence on children.

Typologies and Variables

The one ongoing research thrust which deserves separate analysis from those many research publications used in the foregoing synthesis is the above-mentioned Baumrind research. The reason we choose to analyze this research separately is simple enough. Our review summarizes the research in terms of social competence as a cluster of child behaviors. This is the focal point of Baumrind's work (1967, 1971a, 1971b). Also, in all of the research used in the foregoing synthesis, measures of parental behavior were created by the researchers, and these various parental behaviors were then related in some data-analytic procedure to various child characteristics. Usually the parental behaviors were related to the child characteristics through the use of nonparametric, analysis-of-variance, or basic correlational procedures using a bivariate procedure. Occasionally, combined effects of parental variables were tested. However, these sporadic attempts at combined effects failed to add much clarity in our synthesis and generalizations. Bivariate analytic procedures pose serious problems, since rarely in social reality is it expected that two variables co-vary while simultaneously being fee of influence from other

important variables. This is especially true of the main dimensions of parental behavior under review in this report, namely, parental support and control attempts. Aware of this problem, Baumrind (1971b) makes the case that "it is more meaningful to talk about the effects of *patterns* of parental authority than about the effects of single parental variables. Without certain other conditions being present . . . the strength or direction of an expected parent-child relationship might well be altered" (95).

Baumrind attempts to handle the problem of bivariate analysis versus the combined effects of multiple parental variables by creating a typology of parents using a multidimensional category system. Once the typology is created conceptually, the relevant defining dimensions of parental behavior are measured and the families placed in one of the categories of the typology. Once groups of families are created according to the categories, an attempt is made to compare groups on the child characteristics. Differences between parental groups on child characteristics are then discussed in terms of the consequences of differential patterns of parental behavior.

Our purpose in reviewing Baumrind's research is not to present a thorough evaluation, but (1) to ask how it relates to the central question of what the relationship is between the parental dimensions of control attempts, support, and power, and (2) to identify the major findings from her research which may be related to other research covered in this review and reformulation. To do this, we use as our main source of information the most recent and detailed account of her findings (Baumrind, 1971).

The Typology

One of the prime requisites of any category system is to have clearly defined categories so that assignment to a category can be done unambiguously. Baumrind presented eight types of parents. The four main types are the authoritarian, authoritative, permissive, and rejecting-neglecting parents. The other four are slight variants of the main four (see Table 14.20). Our central concern is to ask, how do these types of parents correspond to variations of the variables under consideration in this report, namely power, support, and control attempts? To answer this question requires a more detailed consideration of the operational indicators of each of the main dimensions used to categorize parents in the Baumrind research.

As seen in Table 14.20, four out of five clusters of behaviors of mothers and six clusters of behaviors of fathers were selectively used by Baumrind in creating the typology. As few as six and as many as nine clusters were used in combination to classify any one type. The operational meaning of the eight parental types is inherent in the descriptors for each of the clusters of parental behaviors. From a large number of specific behaviors obtained from the Parent Behavior Rating Scales, cluster analysis was used to obtain separate summary variable

Table 14.20. Empirical Descriptors* for Baumrind's Child Rearing Typologies

PARENTAL BEHAVIOR DESCRIPTORS	PARENT	CHILD REARING TYPOLOGIES							
		I**	II	III	IV	V	VI	VII	VIII
Firm Enforcement (Coercion)	Fa	H	H	H	L	L	L	?	H
	Mo	H	H	H	L	L	L	?	H
Encourages Independence (Induction and Power)	Fa	L	H	H	H	H	?	L	L
Encourages Independence (Induction)	Mo	L	H	H	H	H	?	L	L
Passive Acceptance	Fa	L	L	L	?	H	H	?	L
	Mo	L	L	L	?	H	H	?	L
Rejecting	Fa	?	?	L	L	L	L	H	H
	Mo	?	?	?	?	L	L	H	H
Self-confident, potent (Power)	Mo	?	?	?	?	?	?	?	?
Promotes Nonconformity	Fa	L	?	H	H	H	?	?	L
Authoritarianism (Coercion)	Fa	H	?	L	L	L	?	H	H

*Operational definition requirements:
H = score above mean
L = score below mean
**Child rearing typologies:
  I = authoritarian
  II = authoritative

III = authoritative nonconforming
IV = nonconforming
V = nonconforming permissive
VI = permissive
VII = rejecting-neglecting
VIII = authoritarian-rejecting-neglecting

scores for fathers and mothers on each cluster of parental behaviors.

A brief discussion of the clusters of parental behaviors and their descriptors is necessary in order to identify which clusters are similar to the main dimensions of parental behavior under review in this report, namely: support, coercion, induction, and parental power. Eleven such clusters are found in Table 14.21.

Cluster 1, "firm enforcement," includes similar items for fathers and mothers. The indicators strongly suggest that this cluster indexes a "coercive" type of parental control attempt. This is one of the dominant clusters used by Baumrind to classify parents. However, another dominant classification cluster, cluster 2, "encourages independence and individuality," is more problematic. Of the 14 items which cluster for mother's behavior, only four

Table 14.21. Interitem Correlations for Baumrind's Parent Behavior Rating Clusters

ITEMS	AVERAGE r	
	Mother	*Father*
1. Firm Enforcement (reliability = .94)		
1. Cannot be coerced by child	.66	.62
2. Enforcement after initial noncompliance	.66	.56
3. Firm enforcement	.65	.61
4. Forces confrontation when child disobeys	.61	.63
5. Willingly exercises power to obtain obedience	.58	.49
6. Disapproves of defiant stance	.52	
7. Requires child to pay attention	.50	.44
8. Promotes own code of behavior	.46	.48
9. Child must defer to parental expertise	.44	.42
10. Uses negative sanctions when defied		.52
11. Stable firm view (M-5)		.33
2. Encourages Independence and Individuality (reliability = .95)		
1. Gives reasons with directives	.58	
2. Offers child alternatives	.56	
3. Solicits child's opinions	.53	
4. Defines child's individuality clearly	.53	.52
5. Encourages intimate verbal contact	.50	.54
6. Lacks empathic understanding	−.49	−.53
7. Listens to critical comments	.49	
8. Encourages verbal give-and-take	.49	

continued

Table 14.21. Interitem Correlations for Baumrind's Parent Behavior Rating Clusters Continued

ITEMS	AVERAGE r	
	Mother	Father
9. Meaningful verbal interaction	.49	.50
10. Promotes individuality in child	.47	
11. Does not share decision making with child	−.46	
12. Expresses own individuality	.41	
13. Encourages oppositional behavior	.38	
14. Child must conform to establishment	−.38	
15. Clear ideals for child (M-5)		.58
16. Clear about parental role (M-5)		.52
17. Regards self as competent person (M-5)		.48
18. Flexible views (M-5)		.48
19. Can specify aims and methods of discipline (M-5)		.47
20. Regards self as potent and knowledgable (M-5)		.46
21. Secure during home visit (M-5)		.42
3. Passive-Acceptant (reliability = .90)		
1. Inhibits annoyance or impatience when child disobeys	.61	.47
2. Inhibits annoyance or impatience when child dawdles or is annoying	.47	.47
3. Avoids open confrontation	.54	.38
4. Gentle manner	.53	.44
5. Uses negative sanctions when defied (F-1)	−.53	
6. Disciplines harshly (F-4)	−.49	
7. Shame about expressing anger	.38	
8. Disapproves of defiant stance (M-1)		−.46
9. Becomes inaccessible when displeased (M-4)		−.41
4. Rejecting (reliability = .88)		
1. Becomes inaccessible when displeased (F-7)	.58	
2. Disciplines harshly (M-30)	.55	.55
3. Unresponsive	.53	.61
4. Assumes stance of personal infallibility (F-7)	.51	
5. Parent's needs take precedence (F-7)	.48	
6. Cool	.47	.63
5. Self-confident, Secure, Potent Parental Behavior (reliability = .92)		
1. Clear about parental role (F-2)	.58	
2. Flexible views (F-2)	.54	
3. Regards self as potent and knowledgable (F-2)	.52	
4. Secure during home visit (F-2)	.51	
5. Stable, firm views (F-1)	.50	
6. Regards self as competent parent (F-2)	.49	
7. Clear ideals for child (F-2)	.49	
8. Can specify aims and methods of discipline (F-2)	.48	
9. Retains self-control when child challenges	.47	
6. Promotes Nonconformity (reliability = .83)		
1. Child must conform to establishment (M-2)		−.53
2. Promotes individuality in child (M-2)		.51
3. Expresses own individuality (M-2)		.51
4. Sees child-rearing practices as atypical		.42
5. Values expressive traits more than instrumental traits		.42
7. Authoritarianism (reliability = .93)		
1. Listens to critical comments (M-2)		−.59
2. Solicits child's opinions (M-2)		−.57
3. Assumes stance of personal infallibility (M-4)		.54
4. Does not share decision-making power with child (M-2)		.51
5. Disobedience elicits further explanations		−.49
6. Offers child alternatives (M-2)		−.48
7. Becomes inaccessible when displeased (M-4)		.47
8. Obedience as a salient construct		.46
9. Encourages oppositional behavior (M-2)		−.43
10. Encourages verbal give-and-take (M-2)		−.43
11. Parent's needs take precedence (M-4)		.43
12. Encourages independent actions		−.40
13. Gives reasons with directives (M-2)		−.38

NOTE: Average r = the average correlation of the item with the other cluster definers; reliability = the reliability of the composite of the cluster definers (Spearman-Brown). M-5 = the location of this item in another cluster where M = Mother's cluster, F = Father's cluster, and 5 = the number of that particular cluster. This table is adapted from table 6 in Baumrind (1971:15–17).

also appear on the father's cluster with the same name. The remaining seven items which appear only in the father's cluster 2 are all found in cluster 5, "self-confident, secure, potent," for mothers. As one carefully looks at the empirical indicators, it seems that, for mothers, items in cluster 2 suggest "inductive" type control attempts while cluster 5 suggests the type of person that would be perceived by children as "powerful." For fathers cluster 2 seems to index both "induction" and "power."

Support

Of the various indices created by Baumrind (see Table 14.21) there are really none which appear to us to measure the supportive dimension in the 1971 report being analyzed here. In some of the earlier work, measures of parental warmth were evidently used. The label for cluster 3, "passive-acceptance," sounds similar but upon inspection of the empirical indicators appears to be radically different from items commonly used to measure support (see Ellis et al., 1976, for a comparison of three widely used measures of support). The "passive-acceptance" factors appears to us to be indexing something akin to an *inhibited* or *anxious* parent. The items appear to describe the type of parent who avoids open confrontation. In the nine items there are none which indicate that this parent also expresses love and acceptance toward the child. The label for cluster 3, "rejection," might be considered similar to the low end of the support continuum. However, inspection of the six empirical indicators suggest only two, "unresponsive," and "cool," which might index a lack of support. The others suggest punitiveness and love withdrawal as types of control attempts.

Control Attempts and Power

Cluster 1, "firm enforcement," in Table 14.21 appears to be the closest index to what we have defined as *coercive* control attempts. The descriptor items seem to describe a parent who is not coerced by the child, confronts the child when disobedience occurs, and willingly takes advantage of power to obtain obedience. There is considerable similarity between fathers and mothers on this factor, and we suspect this particular measure would correlate quite highly with other measures of coercion. Cluster 6 "authoritarianism" for fathers also has empirical indicators of coercion.

Cluster 2 in the Baumrind data is problematic. By considering only those items which cluster for mothers, we judge that this factor is very close to what we have defined as *induction*. The items appear to describe a mother who gives reasons along with directives to the child, offers the child alternatives, solicits child's opinions, and encourages considerable verbal give-and-take. We judge that this factor would correlate highly with other measures of induction. However, the father's cluster appears to describe a father who talks a great deal with

his children and who at the same time is also a self-confident, secure, and potent parent. We judge that this measure would correlate moderately with measures of both *power* and *induction* as we have defined them in this work. We thus prefer to label this cluster for fathers as *induction/power*. We expect this parent as descriptively portrayed would use reason based discipline as well as having considerable resources at his disposal. He would see himself and would be perceived by the child as knowledgeable and an expert. Cluster 5 "self-confident, secure, potent" for mothers appears to be the closest index to what we have defined as *power*. The items appear to us to measure the parent who knows she is competent, powerful, knowledgeable, and secure and would probably be perceived by her children as such. We prefer to label this as power.

Cluster 1, "firm enforcement," for both parents and Cluster 7, "authoritarianism," for fathers are, in combination, one of the primary defining characteristics of the eight types of parents created by Baumrind. Our interpretation that these variables index coercive control attempts is reaffirmed by a second order factor analysis of the Baumrind data (Table 14.22). Two similar factors emerged from six clusters of fathers and five clusters of mothers responses. One factor labeled "coercive" had high positive loadings on "firm enforcement" and high negative loadings on "passive-acceptant" clusters for both parents and a high positive loading on "authoritarianism" for fathers. For Baumrind, another primary defining characteristic of the eight types of parents is cluster 2, "encourages independence and individuality." As was discussed above, this cluster appears to us to be a measure of induction for mothers but seems to be confounded with power for fathers. This interpretation is generally confirmed in the second order factor analysis. As can be seen in Table 14.22 the second general factor which we label "induction/power" had a high negative loading on "rejecting" for both father and mother data as well as a high positive loading on the "self-confident, secure, and potent" cluster for mothers. Thus taken together, the second order factor analysis along with our previous discussion of the specific empirical indicators of the various dimensions of parental behavior lead us to conclude that the primary defining characteristics of Baumrind's typology of parents are *coercion* and *induction/power*.

Reinterpreted Finding

If we are correct in our assumptions that the variables of support, coercion, induction, and power are the most important in accounting for parental influence upon child behavior, then these variables as redefined above ought to account for most of the child characteristics which the Baumrind research indicated are associated with various types of parents. Baumrind compared the eight types of parents on six characteristics of children. Three of the child characteristics, hostile-friendly (antisocial aggres-

Table 14.22. Factor Analysis of Baumrind's Parent Behavior Cluster Scores*

CLUSTERS	VARIMAX ROTATED FACTOR LOADINGS	
	Coercion	*Induction/Power***
Fathers		
Firm Enforcement	.892	.165
Encourages Independence	−.020	.933
Passive Acceptance	−.775	.331
Rejecting	.291	−.807
Promotes Nonconformity	−.593	.235
Authoritarianism	.714	−.549
Mothers		
Firm Enforcement	.911	.128
Encourages Independence	−.184	.827
Passive Acceptance	−.862	.299
Rejecting	.469	−.759
Self-confident, Potent	.346	.857

*This table is adapted from a second order factor analysis completed by Dr. Diana Baumrind and staff from data in the socialization project at the Institute of Human Development, Berkeley, California. Information was obtained by personal correspondence.

**Baumrind labeled this factor "Responsive."

sion), resistive-cooperative (conformity), and achievement orientation (academic achievement) are similar to child variables in our empirical generalizations presented above in this chapter. Table 14.23 presents a summary of the reported findings on these three child variables as analyzed in terms of extreme variations of coercion while holding induction/power constant and on extreme variations of induction/power while holding coercion constant. This provides for a better test of the correlates of coercion and induction/power than the simple bivariate analyses presented in our empirical generalizations above.

In twenty-four tests, eleven supported the theoretical propositions developed in our above review. Of the thirteen tests that failed to support our propositions, nine were for girls. Thus, most of the instances where expected findings did not emerge occurred with girls rather than

boys. This is congruent with our integration of research in the preceding section. Thus Baumrind's findings tend to hold for boys better than girls. This appears to be a reoccurring trend in socialization research (Baumrind, 1972; Thomas et al, 1974; and Martin, 1975).

Though Baumrind's work failed to provide a clear-cut test of either support or combined effects of support and control attempts, the results are generally consistent with our review across many studies. Thus our reinterpretation of the Baumrind research leads us to conclude that future research should (1) focus on variables we have identified, (2) develop adequate measures for the variables, and (3) utilize multivariate analytic procedures in the study of parental influence upon child characteristics. This procedure would allow the researcher-theorist not only to develop multivariate models but to test to see which parental variables combined together account for most of

Table 14.23. Summary of Baumrind's Research Findings in Relation to Coercion and Induction

COMPARISON TYPES*	PARENTAL BEHAVIORS		CHILD BEHAVIORS					
	Coercion	*Induction/ Power*	*Aggression*		*Conformity*		*Achievement*	
			Boy	*Girl*	*Boy*	*Girl*	*Boy*	*Girl*
Type II	H	H						
with Type I	H	L	more**		more			
with Type VII	H	L	more	equal	more	equal	equal	equal
with Type VIII	H	L	more	equal	more	equal	less	equal
Type II	H	H						
with Type IV	L	H	more	equal	equal	equal	equal	equal
with Type V	L	H		equal		equal		equal
Comparisons supporting theoretical propositions	4		0	3		0	2	1

*Type III had too small a sample size for comparisons. Type VI was too ambiguous in terms of coercion and induction/power for comparisons. Type I had too few girls and Type V too few boys for comparisons. The comparisons made included all comparisons that had unambiguous and clear cut variation on coercion or on induction/power.

**Reported differences were significant at the .05 level of confidence. For example, boys of Type I parents were *more* aggressive than boys of Type II parents.

the variance in the dependent variables. With enough research of this type the relative influence singly and in conjunction with other variables could be assessed for any parent variable upon any child variable.

THEORIES OF SOCIALIZATION

In previous sections of this chapter, we formulated empirical generalizations and theoretical propositions for evidence to be used in evaluating the empirical grounding of theories of child socialization in the context of parent-child interaction. Our efforts to uncover evidence for the combined interactive effects of parental support and parental control attempts were not successful. The few studies directly testing for interaction failed to find such. The studies that did suggest interaction effects, in nearly every case, provide very indirect evidence. Either they compared typologies that were unsystematically constructed from the basic variables (i.e., Baumrind, 1967, 1971) or, if the typologies were systematically constructed (i.e., numerous studies of Heilbrun and associates), they failed to compare in one test all of the typologies necessary to determine if interaction existed between parental support and control attempts.

The empirical generalizations do provide a basis for evaluating the empirical grounding of theory in terms of the correlations of single parental variables with child variables. At the most general level, from the empirical studies reviewed and the recent review articles of Baumrind (1972b) and Martin (1975), our theoretical propositions can be summarized as follows: Socially competent behavior of children, that is, behavior that is valued in a society as desirable and has instrumental utility, is positively correlated with parental support, power of same-sexed parent, inductive control attempts, and the importance of such socially competent behavior in parents; it is negatively correlated with coercive control attempts of parents (see Figure 14.2).

The researcher-theorist welcomes systematic reviews of empirical findings. He is then in a position to think about the body of findings and ask how a given theoretical perspective may account for them, elucidate them along with related information from other sources, and suggest new research questions. It is our purpose to address the theoretical propositions from the perspective of two traditions of socialization theory, symbolic interaction and social learning.

Symbolic Interactionist View

The symbolic interactionist perspective presented is a particular brand which draws upon some of the early seminal social psychologists such as James, Mead, Cooley, and Thomas, but in addition is influenced by two related thrusts in contemporary social psychology: (1) the cognitive work represented by Zimbardo and associates, and (2) the child psychologists' work from a cognitive development perspective such as that of Piaget, Kohlberg, Flavell, etc. These three research and theory thrusts repeatedly inform our theorizing in this section. We do not go into great detail on the symbolic interactionist, the cognitive control-of-motivation, or the cognitive developmental approaches, but rather assume the reader is sufficiently informed, or can so become, to follow our reasoning. We begin by presenting some basic assumptions about the nature of man and his social world which are central to the theoretical formulations generated in this section; next we present the basic symbolic interaction model of socialization of the child in terms of parent-child interaction, and lastly we give our impressionistic evaluation of it and the type of research it would likely generate.

Assumptive Underpinnings

One of the oft-repeated but seldom studied assertions of symbolic interactionism is that *man*[6] *is actor as well as reactor*. This assumption is related to central concepts utilized to explain some basic socialization processes. Through social interaction, the newborn gradually creates a social self, usually within the context of the family (see Weigert and Thomas, 1971, for discussion of requisite universal characteristics of these initial relations). The self, once formed, is seen as having both dimensions of the known and the knower. James highlights this: "Whatever I may be thinking of, I am always at the same time more or less aware of myself, of my *personal existence*. At the same time it is I who am aware; so that the total self of me ... must have two aspects discriminated in it, of which for shortness we may call one the Me and the other the I." (Italics in the original. Cited in Deutsch and Krauss, 1965:182.) While questions about the relationship between the knower and known have intrigued philosophers for millenia, social psychologists either in their research or theorizing have done little to clarify the nature of the relationship. Most of the research focusing on the self or various derivatives invariably describes the self as object (the me). With Cooley's "looking glass self" concept the concern has largely been even more restricted to the social self—"how *I* see me because of how *others* see me." Thus, even though the symbolic interactionist's perspective has generated research on the self and a basic assumption says that part of what is experienced as self is the dimension of actor, there has, for all practical purposes been very little theorizing of research-generating questions about the action dimension of human behavior.

If the symbolic interactionist orientation has failed to generate research on the dimension of man as actor, one cannot find it in the more traditional social psychological perspective of behaviorism either. Behaviorism seems especially plagued with an emphasis on the passive nature of man. The basic passive bias inherent in the American behavioristic approach is persuasively discussed by Zimbardo (1969:3):

> A corollary to this economical system of behavior is the implicitly passive role it assigns to the individual organism being studied. An individual (rat or human being) is *subjected* to the stimulus; thus, he becomes a "subject" who was "run" under given conditions. The very semantics of the experiment betray the passive, purely instrumental view that the experimenter develops toward the organism under investigation. In fact, the subject is not only viewed as but is treated like an object. What is studied is never human action but *reaction*. Here we see a kind of self-fulfilling prophecy in which humans are given the rules of the experiment, which deprive them of any initiative, creative responding, or freedom of action. The subject is really asked to suspend his disbelief and pretend that the experimental task has meaning—to role play at being an experimental human subject who asks no questions and behaves in the predetermined simple fashion desired by the experimenter. When human beings are treated in this way, they will react according to the same functional laws of behavior as do lower animals. Under these standardized conditions the experimenter is able to posit a behavioral continuity—which in large part he has artificially created.

A corollary of the man-as-actor postulate is that questions of motivation in the sense of primary drives are largely rendered residual. If man by nature is in action, then one does not have to ask what set him into motion, but one would very likely want to ask why man chooses one course of action over some alternative. The very semantics of the above sentence point toward higher cortical processes of choice, anticipation, volition, or intentional behavior, terms which are generally rejected by hard-nosed social psychologists having cut their teeth on behaviorism, a behaviorism which not only underscores the passive nature of man but also implies a cognitionless state. Whereas behaviorism emphasized the behavioral continuity between man and beast, the interactionist would point toward interplay between cognitive processes and behavior. For the interactionist, man can best be understood by being studied on his own level because these higher cortical processes are precisely those which differentiate man from the animals. Thus emergence is not something to be rejected, but rather to be written into the basic assumptional structure of the theoretical orientation (Stryker, 1964:135). While the early writers emphasized a number of concepts which differentiate man compared to animals, such as language, self, and the central process of role taking (which simultaneously pointed toward knowledge of self as subject and object as well as to knowledge of others), they had little insight into these social processes in the human infant. For some leads we turn to the child psychology literature.

From the bulk of research and writing on the infant in the child development literature we construct the following view of the human infant which allows us to identify a second major assumption about man. Taken as a whole, we see in the child development literature considerable evidence which underscores the active dimension of human behavior. This is so even though much of the research has been generated from an experimental setting which emphasizes the *stimulus presented* to the child and then careful recording of the child's *response*. Those studies dealing specifically with the infant (first year of life) reveal a very active organism even within the first weeks and months of life. Even as early as four days and continuing as long as six months, when given a choice the infant will prefer to look at a figure resembling a human face rather than scrambled arrangements of facial components (Fantz, 1958). As the infant increases in age, when given a choice he will prefer to interact visually with a patterned stimulus rather than a nonpatterned one, and with more complex stimuli rather than with simple ones (Appleton et al., 1975).

While the visual mode is the easiest to study in terms of intentional behavior of the infant and hence what in the environment the infant chooses to pay attention to, it is reasonable to assume that similar intentional choices between alternative stimuli are occurring with other sensory inputs such as auditory and tactile inputs. It is apparent now that the infant is equipped to make rather complicated differentiations in sound. For example, it is now clear that very young infants auditorially engage in "selective attention, discrimination of voices, and early phoneme perception" such that they are able to "process speech sounds in their appropriate mode" (Appleton et al., 1975:115). These authors conclude that the research now indicates the "infants of one to five months . . . make some of the same discriminations as adults" (p. 116). In addition, research findings coming out of Russia (Fradkina, 1971, cited in Appleton et al., 1975) indicate that once the child has begun to create his own meaning system, e.g., has begun to comprehend simple commands, the child can be conditioned four times faster to words than to other sounds. We suspect that intentional cognitive processes of the child are related to the differential learning, since before this time (before seven or eight months) the conditioning time for words compared to other sounds is no different.

We are influenced not only by much of the child developmental research but by some writers who have underscored the choosing, action-producing human organism. Here we follow the seminal work of Piaget in observing his own children, the persuasive position articulated by White (1959) on the effectance- and competency-based view of motivation, and the more recent writing of Smith (1974) and Appleton et al. (1975) on infant competency, and Shantz (1975) on social cognition. We assume, based on this body of literature, that there is not only substantial evidence for the view of man as actor, but that when faced with a choice, man, from infant to functioning adult, will make many of his choices according to which one will allow him the greatest amount of control over his environment. Thus we see the question of motivation becoming problematic only when we ask why man chooses one course of action over another. Our assumption is that he does so many times on the basis of effectance motivation or choosing the course that gives the greatest potential for personal control, which results in the development of a sense of competence in the organism as an agent of change in his environment.

Admittedly, when one is working at the assumptive level, one uses more than research results for his theorizing fare. We are no different. We were impressed with Piaget's account of his son's encounter with rattles at three-plus months:

> Laurent by chance strikes the chain while sucking his fingers . . . he grasps it and slowly displaces it while looking at the rattles. He then begins to swing it very gently which produces a slight movement of the hanging rattles and an as yet faint sound inside them. Laurent then definitely increases by degree his own movements: he shakes the chair more and more vigorously, and laughs uproariously at the results obtained [cited in White, 1963:31].

An anecdotal account with children of one of the authors, Darwin L. Thomas, revealed a very similar process of active cause, but this was social in nature as contrasted with the physical object orientation in the preceding Piagetian example. Sara, three months and three weeks old, was lying on the infant seat on the couch in the living room; a three-year-old sister, Kristi, was playing nearby in the living room. In her course of play, Kristi started toward the couch. Sara was watching her, but Kristi was not looking at Sara. As Kristi approached the couch Sara started to laugh. Upon hearing the laugh, Kristi turned and ran directly to the infant seat and started to talk to Sara, who then laughed more. Kristi in return started laughing, which was in turn followed by louder laughter from Sara. This process of each making the other laugh even harder continued for over five minutes. At times Kristi would back away from the couch and then quickly approach it, coming directly to the infant seat, whereupon Sara would laugh raucously. Over the ensuing months similar encounters occurred. Kristi learned that she could make Sara laugh by just moving toward her or talking and laughing at her. In addition, it appeared as though Sara learned that her smiling and laughing had tremendous effect upon Kristi and would bring Kristi toward her from anywhere in the room. Kristi became much more successful than any other member of the family including parents and older siblings in making Sara laugh. One morning the father was playing with Sara, who was smiling and quietly laughing at him. Kristi asked, "Dad, can't you make Sara laugh like this?" whereupon she caught Sara's eye and before long both were engaged in raucous laughter. The father replied, "No, I can't do it like you." In the above social example, which child ought to be described as the stimulus? The

traditional behavioristic approach might say that the older child stimulated the infant; however, we suspect that Sara is as effective at producing the desired response from Kristi as vice versa.

Thus our second assumption is that *self-initiated behavior which produces the intended effect upon the environment (intrinsic motivation) will more likely be repeated in the future than behavior which the organism experiences as a response to some external stimuli (extrinsic motivation).* If monkeys and man show a decreased interest in working on puzzles when the solving of them is tied to an extrinsic reward (receiving food) rather than the intrinsic task-related satisfaction (Zimbardo, 1969:4), then we think it is past time for social psychologists to start looking at self-initiated action as a significant area for research and theorizing. In fact, if we could more fully know what is being experienced at the very early stages in socialization, we would not be surprised to learn that all of the infant's sensory inputs are experienced as results of his own intentional behavior. We take our cues from the early cognitive developmental psychologists. Commenting on Piaget's thoughts about early sensor impressions, Appleton et al. (1975:137) note:

> According to the Piagetian view, the first conceptions of the physical world are inseparable from the actions by which the infant knows the world. Each type of sensorimotor act is a unique way of organizing experiences which Piaget calls an "action schema." There is a sucking schema, a looking schema, and a grasping schema (among others), and objects are things to be sucked, grasped, or looked at. . . . (The infant does not) conceive of events having causes, for events are not distinguished from activities (Piaget, 1954).

Another way of saying this is to say that if the child only conceives of activities, then he may also only conceive of causes. Once the child differentiates self as object, then he or she may begin to differentiate and place causal consequences on own behavior as opposed to things that just happen to him/her. This differentiation, as in the Piagetian view (1954), would occur after the infant becomes capable of reaching and grasping behavior and repeatedly engages in intentional behavior of that type.

Not surprisingly, this competency-based view of man has developmental overtones. From the above grasping behavior, we suspect the next quantum leap in the sense of self as cause occurs with the acquisition of locomotion. As Appleton et al. (1975:144) noted, "The achievement of locomotion . . . increases the child's control of the environment and places new demands on caretakers." The next significant stage we assume emerges with the acquisition of language. Once equipped with a system of symbols, the child experiences simultaneous control over his own responses as well as control over the responses of others. Mead (1934) underscored this dimension of language in his definition of a significant symbol as a word which calls out an identical response in both the producer and the hearer.

Theorized Relationships

Given the foregoing minimal assumptions that man is actor and that many of his choices will be made on the basis of which course of action will result in the greatest competency, be it with physical or social objects, we now move into an explication of a model of socialization which we feel can account for the observed empirical generalizations in this review and other information used to inform this work. While the model is general in nature it is not construed to be all-encompassing. At the outset we assert that while the assumptions underscore the active and competency-based notion of man, it is not assumed that this will explain all human behavior. We see considerable behavior which is clearly biologically based, and we have sufficient respect for Freudian insights into unconscious dimensions of human behavior to realize that unconscious states influence rational processes. The continuing accumulations of findings in dream and hypnosis clearly underscore the phenomena of the effects of unconscious states. In addition, we do not assert that this socialization model will necessarily explain abnormal or deviant cases. We see it very much as a statement about normal development underscoring simultaneously the social and the cognitive dimensions of human behavior.

As will be remembered from the empirical review, the child behavior characteristics which are taken as consequences of supportive behavior of parents directed to children were both numerous and consistent. Indeed, one cannot spend much time in a review of child socialization research without being struck with the ubiquitous nature of the effects of this variable. Perhaps the second most striking impression is the rather remarkable consistency of results not only across the time dimension but across different developmental stages, cultural contexts, methodological variations, and sex-of-parent–sex-of-child variations (see our discussion of sex role orientation and achievement for some sex-specific results). The evidence is, we judge, incontrovertible. The presence of supportive behavior from one person to another appears to have a facilitative effect upon the recipient whether it is the terry-cloth mother supporting Harlow's monkeys, Spitz's children growing and developing normally with the supportive care of mothers in the nursery school, or dying in the foundling homes (30 deaths out of 90 some infants), or whether it is the children increasing in IQ in the Rosenthall research as well as the Brookover study, or the mentally retarded children becoming occupationally self-sufficient in the Skeels research or facilitative behavior discussed in the attachment research reviewed by Ainsworth (1973). When these are coupled with the specific dependent variables under review in this research, e.g., cognitive development, creativity, conformity, internal locus of control, moral behavior, self-esteem, and instrumental social competence, one is forced to recognize the very important effect of variations along the support dimension. Man appears to grow physically, emotionally, and socially in the presence of supportive relationships, while he encounters considerable problems in its absence. Why should this be so?

Our attempt at generalization across all the above varied research results is a simple one in that we merely ask what they could possibly all have in common. Our answer is, a responsive environment. With the emphasis upon action initiated by an individual, we ask what differs significantly between the responses to that action by a supportive and nonsupportive parent. From this perspective it is the responsiveness of the parent to the child's own initiated behavior which becomes ever so critical. The mother who loves her child becomes very responsive to the first signs of intentional behavior of the child. The first smiles, intentional or not, are responded to as if they were intentional. The first sounds, be they intentional or not, are repeated by the mother to the child. There are even now some research results in language development which indicate that the mother may change her manner of speaking to the child once the child begins to speak and she makes the change on the basis of the verbal feedback from the child (Phillips, 1973).

From the perspective of symbolic interaction we postulate that the nonsupportive parent tends to create an environment which is not responsive to the child's initial and continuing efforts at producing an effect upon the environment. In such environments, a sense of competency does not develop adequately. Pushed to an extreme, the nonsupportive and hence nonresponsive environment would be typified by the foundling home descriptions offered in the Spitz research with a ratio of 1 nurse to 10 children, with the nurse unable to respond to intentional behavior, with resulting physical and emotional problems. The extreme case being the one in which the human organism just gives up and dies, commits suicide, or goes insane in such a hostile environment—hostile in the sense that action does not produce consistent intended effects.

While the results for inductive control attempts are not as consistent as for support, nevertheless the generalization is similar at least for those behaviors which we have labeled as social competence. The negative side of behavioral disorders, or socially incompetent behavior, remains unanswered as yet. This is due to the relative lack of a sufficient number of studies from which to generalize. Thus we confine our emphasis to the socially competent types of behaviors. Our reasoning about the consequences of induction is similar to that about support. We assume that a parent who through induction tries to control the behavior of the child in an information-giving context, by pointing out possible consequences of different types of behavior, facilitates the sense of efficacy on the part of the child. In effect, this additional information about causes and consequences to the child and others should help the child to more fully understand the nature of the world and to thus be able to cope more successfully with it.

The general review shows coercive control attempts to have essentially the opposite effect from both support and induction. We posit that the basic reason is that as arbitrary control attempts increase by significant others in the child's environment, the responsiveness of that environment to that child's intentional behavior decreases. In such an unresponsive environment the child develops a view of himself as unable to deal effectively with his environment. This becomes the mirror-image opposite of the self-fulfilling prophecy in the above-described positive relationships. The unresponsive environment generates fewer attempts at intentional behavior, which further reinforces the child's view of himself as incapable.

Possible Weaknesses and Strengths

The interactionist view as outlined above does not necessarily point toward any significant interaction of multiplicative effects among the three independent variables. This does not strike us as a necessary problem, since even though interaction has been implied by countless writers for decades (Symonds, 1939; Becker, 1964; Straus, 1964; Heilbrun and Waters, 1968; Thomas et al., 1974), the empirical evidence which we were able to find in this review is very meager at best. Even so, in one line of reasoning, a case could be made for possible interaction between control attempts and support. It could be argued that under high support, which is characterized by parents highly responsive to the child's casual endeavors, an increase in control attempts by the parents ought to lead to an increase in the child's sense of competency as long as the control attempts became information cues to the child as to how his world operates. This increased information about his world, whether the control attempts came in the form of inductive or coercive control attempts, ought to provide the child with a greater information base from which to make his decisions and from which to initiate his intentional behavior. However, under a condition of low support it may be theorized that an increase in control attempts would lead to lessened social competence.

Since the symbolic interactionist view implies the dialectical process of knowledge of self as subject and object as well as knowledge of others in any social encounter, it can logically be argued that for an individual who sees self as socially incompetent, an increase in control attempts by significant others might confirm the validity of the basic definition of self and decrease the frequency of intentional behavior within that given social setting. The above holds if one views the control attempts as not related in any significant way to inducing motivational states (see Thomas et al, 1974, for discussion). This particular view of the self and its relationship to competence is consistent with the definition of Smith (1974), who asserts that "the motivational core of competence is a cluster of attitudes toward the self as potent, efficacious and worthy of being taken seriously by self

and other" (250). Since a nonsupportive, unresponsive environment would not generate that type of self-perception along the competency dimension, increased control attempts in such a situation would likely reduce the amount of intentional behavior.

A problem related to the above is that there is no hint as to what the expected relationship would or would not be among the parental behavior variables; i.e., are they positively or negatively related? Here we turn to empirical results and suggest that in the world of measurement and research these variables of support and inductive control attempts will be moderately related in a positive direction (Hoffman, 1970; and Thomas et al., 1974). In addition, we further assume that these two variables are both negatively related to coercive control attempts.

While much of the foregoing can be thought of as self-initiated action, self-determination, self-fulfillment, or self-actualization, it should not be interpreted as just another statement of Maslow's position, which appears to us to suffer from biological bias (Smith, 1974). In self-actualization writing, the ethics that emerge reduce to the position that the nature of the organism (biology) leads to an inevitable view that with self-actualization comes behavior which by its nature is more suited to the common good (rather than the common bad?). We along with Smith (1974:172) agree that vice and evil "are as much in the range of human potentiality as virtue, specialization as much as well-rounded development. Our biology cannot be made to carry out ethics, as Maslow would have it." While we do not see this as a major problem with the formulation, we do see a problem in our formulation of socialization for social competence which has been treated in some of the competency literature: the problems of male bias in much of the research and theorizing.

We noted earlier in this review, citing similar reviewers' conclusions, that the various socialization models appear to work better for boys than for girls. We suspect that the same may well be true with our competency formulations. We suspect that this may be partially a result of so many males studying and formulating explanatory schemes of socialization processes. Indeed, the very terms of "competency," "coping," and "intending behavior" strike us as decidedly instrumental (and therefore masculine in nature?). It may well be that future endeavors will take a critical look at alternative formulations which might hint at basic differences in socialization models for girls and boys. Future socialization research ought to attempt to identify subsets of males and females for which the model appears to work equally well for each. It may be that some males have very similar sex role orientations to some females and vice versa. Researchers working in this area might profitably pay particular attention to parental behaviors which have a differential effect upon the child (such as support relating to achievement for boys but not for girls). We suspect that these anomalous findings will become central in developing explanatory theoretical models for socialization of males and females.

We see the strengths of the proposed interactional formulation largely coming from the type of research that the theoretical formulations would tend to generate. It seems obvious to us that socialization research must move away from monadic formulation and unidirectional causal analysis. As numerous writers have noted (see Cottrell, 1969; and Martin, 1975, for examples) social reality can hardly be described in terminology short of concepts which refer to dyads and interaction as well as reciprocal causation (Rhiengold, 1969; Gewirtz, 1969). As Martin (1975) argued, a stimulus is simultaneously a response when one is studying social encounters. Thus we ought to develop concepts and systems of concepts which would at least have the possibility of conveying interactional and process analysis. The concepts which have grown up from behaviorism often lead to almost contradictory explanatory statements. For example, consider the following generalization made after summarizing considerable research on the infant: "In summary, the infant *responds actively* to the visual world from birth, scanning and *seeking* stimulation" (Italics added; Appleton et al., 1975:124). The particular sequencing of words betrays the belief in the basic passive nature of man which pervades much of this literature. Why does the writer feel compelled to modify "responds" with the word "active"? When our discourse is forced to become this fuzzy because of the particular concepts and theoretical formulations we choose to use, it is time to question our guiding theoretical formulations.

While Gewirtz (1969) argues that the basic S-R paradigm is dyadic by nature, the interactionist would not see this as sufficient to resolve the short-coming. Without concepts referring to the self and the other, the formulation is only partially adequate even if new concepts are derived to identify simultaneously both the stimulus and response characteristics of any social encounter, and even if the time dimension were included so that stimulus and response became points on a time line. If the interactionist position developed here were completed and research traditions generated, we predict that it would fill a current void in contemporary child psychology literature. This void is seen in a recent search of the 59 chapter titles in the two-volume third edition of the *Manual of Child Psychology* and the third, fourth, and fifth volumes of the *Review of Child Development Research,* which shows that the word "self" does not appear in any form, either by itself or in a hyphenated form. An examination of the subject index in those publications (4,039 pages) reveals that it does not appear once as a single word. Its only presence is in hyphenated form, as in "self-reward." This hyphenated approach to the self is symbolic of the ambivalence of the child psychologists toward the concept.

Of course, the relative absence of such a concept is no accident, but is a result of the overriding theoretical

formulations currently accepted as legitimate. The ambivalence just mentioned can be seen in an excellent review of the current state of knowledge in the area of social cognition (Shantz, 1975). The purpose of this review is to review how "children conceptualize other people and how they come to understand the thoughts, emotions, intentions, and viewpoints of others" (248). The author is quick to note, however, that:

> The focus is here on the child's conception of *other* people and not the child's *self*-concept and, as such, constitutes a major limitation. There are theoretical and empirical bases for asserting that there are important relations between self- and other-concepts in both children and adults (e.g., Mead, 1934; Sullivan, 1953), but this literature will not be reviewed [Shantz, 1975:259].

If the reviewer had chosen to include the child's self concept in the review, there would for all practical purposes have been little to include from the child development literature. However, we are of the opinion that the relationship between self and other in social encounters is one of the most fundamental questions child psychologists could address. Thus we propose that the self be measured along with knowledge of others.

Lastly, we see the possibility of a significant payoff for social psychology in general if a theory of self-other relationships were formed. Following Smith (1974), we sense that the social sciences in general and social psychology in particular suffer from the particular model of man that is exported to the buying public through the research, writing, and teaching of the social psychology practitioners. We believe that the model of man that comes through most repeatedly is essentially that of the behavioristic model, which implies a passive and cognitionless state of the organism. This view of man strongly contradicts the experiential base and thus creates a sizable credibility gap between the social psychologists and naive laymen. No matter how sophisticated the research designs, how compelling the findings, the man on the street, we believe, is not about to be convinced that he is not free to choose among various alternatives and that he is not the initiator of such action. Indeed, our view of man leads us to applaud the resistance of the layman to the social psychologists' view of the *vacuum self* (Smith, 1974:180). We along with the layman know that we as selves are both subject and object. Why else would we be creating this theory? Perhaps for the same reason that Skinner wrote *Beyond Freedom and Dignity,* the intrinsic satisfaction of seeing the results of our own intentional behavior. A theory of self-other relations might help generate a model of man more consonant with both the layman's and the social scientist's experiential view of man and society.

Social Learning View

There are many varieties of social learning theory. The two we will utilize both tie into instrumental learning theory with the basic assumptions that the acquisition and maintenance of behavior in children are primarily a function of extrinsic reinforcement (Bijou and Baer, 1961), yet they both allow for cognition as stressed above. They are modeling-identification theory (Bandura, 1969) and social power-exchange theory (Rollins and Thomas, 1975).

Modeling-Identification Theory

In the modeling-identification theory of Bandura, the primary mechanism for the acquisition of behavior is the imitation of a model under conditions of "vicarious reinforcement" (Bandura and Walters, 1963), while the maintenance of the behavior is by direct reinforcement. Instead of behavioral acquisition being a function of extrinsic reinforcement contingencies, the initial tendency for a new behavioral response comes from the observation of such behavior in a model and the cognition that the model is reinforced; i.e., the model's response is followed by some kind of reward. Such a cognition is called "vicarious reinforcement." Assuming such a cognitive process, the theory then must account for the conditions under which the model will be perceived as being rewarded. Hypothetically, two persons could observe the same model and one receive vicarious reinforcement and the other not. The conditions identified in the theory as most conducive of imitation exist when (1) the model is prestigious or powerful, and (2) the observer perceives a positive affective relationship between self and the model. The variables of parental power and parental support in the empirical generalizations and theoretical propositions presented in this chapter qualify as conditions that influence children's imitation of parents. If both power and support of parents toward children are high, then children more likely imitate the parents than if one or both of these parental characteristics are low. From the theory it is assumed that parents high on power and control attempts are more likely perceived by their children as being reinforced for behaving as they do than is true of parents who are low on power and control attempts. Also, parents high on support, power, and inductive control attempts are more likely to facilitate the maintenance of behavior through direct reinforcement after it has been imitated. Heilbrun (1968) refers to parental control attempts and support as perceived by children as producing a sensitized reinforcement anticipation. It seems reasonable that, in general, parents who are perceived as manifesting a lot of control attempts will also be perceived as powerful.

Though parental power and support might facilitate child imitation of parents in general, the only specific content for imitation they suggest are supportive behavior of the child toward others and a sense of power or potency in the child in his relationships with others. Though both of these qualities might be aspects of social competence, what about other aspects of social competence? We suggest that the utility of parental power and support in facilitating imitation is that in American society they represent culturally valued response patterns and produce sensitized reinforcement expectation. If imitation is a function of vicarious reinforcement as suggested above, we propose that parental power and support, as well as other parental behaviors the child might imitate, depend on being positively sanctioned by cultural values and the child's internalization of the same before the child's cognition of vicarious reinforcement is likely to occur. This suggests that social competence in children (based on cultural values) will be facilitated not only by high parental support and power but by parental acceptance of cultural values about such aspects of competence (i.e., self-esteem, achievement, internal locus of control of reinforcement), children's awareness of the parent's values, and parental modeling of the competent behaviors.

Our interpretation of modeling-imitation theory fits fairly well with the empirical generalizations developed in this review. The theory does not explicitly account for the differential relationships of inductive and coercive control attempts with social competence. However, going back to the basic assumption of the theory that imitation is a function of vicarious reinforcement, this differentiation seems meaningful. Inductive control attempts of parents constitute a model of behavior in which alternatives and their consequences are discussed, while coercive control attempts model arbitrary decisions. If children have a model and imitate inductive control attempts of parents, they obtain a rational cognitive strategy for searching among alternatives and are more likely to identify the relationships between values and outcomes in their behaviors, thus facilitating the ability to be cognizant of whether or not a model receives reinforcement for behavior.

There seems to be no basic incompatibility between modeling-identification theory and our empirical generalizations and theoretical propositions. However, our attempt to assess the fit suggests several new questions that empirical tests could answer, but, to our knowledge, have not answered yet. Some of the more salient ones are:

1. Are culturally valued behaviors of parents more likely imitated by children of high-support–high-power parents than culturally devalued behaviors?

2. Are parental behaviors more likely imitated by children when parents use inductive control attempts than when they use coercive control attempts?

3. Does the acceptance of cultural values by children influence whether or not culturally valued behaviors of parents are imitated by children?

4. Are the facilitative effects of parental power and support on child imitation of parent models contingent on the values of the parents, the values of the child, and the type of control attempts employed by the parents?

5. Are the facilitative effects of either parental power or support on child imitation of parental models contingent on each other?

A positive response to the above questions would provide additional support for the basic assumption of modeling-identification theory that imitation of a model is a function of vicarious reinforcement.

Social Power-Exchange Theory

The social power-exchange theory of Rollins and Thomas (1975) drew upon the work of Cartwright (1959), Thibaut and Kelley (1959), and Homans (1974). The basic assumption of the theory is that in social interactions, participants attempt to maximize profits (rewards minus costs) and avoid losses (punishment) and that all social interactions involve social-psychological costs and alternatives. The basic exchange is between parental support and child compliance (Richer, 1965). The basic questions posed by the theory are the conditions under which both parent and child receive profits above their comparison level for alternative exchanges. Child compliance is viewed as behavior of the child that is valued by the parent and assumed to be culturally valued (social competence).

The social power-exchange theory deals explicitly with all of the parent variables in empirical generalizations and theoretical propositions in our review. However, only support and control attempts are directly related to compliance (social competence). Parental values and parental power were considered to be contingent variables influencing the relationships between support and compliance. Also, parental power and the ratio of inductive to coercive control attempts were seen as contingent variables influencing the relationships between amount of parental control attempts and child compliance.

Whereas modeling-identification theory assumes the child to primarily be a respondent rather than initiator of action, social power exchange theory is a dynamic model of reciprocal action and reaction. The reinforcing effects of parental support on child compliance (social competence) are contingent upon the importance to the child of receiving support, alternative sources of support for the child, and the power of the parents. At the same time, the reinforcing potential of the child's compliance on parental nurturance depends on how much the parent values the behavioral compliance. If the child could obtain support from someone else at less cost than the costs involved in compliance to behavior the parents valued, and if the child's profit were less than their comparison level, the child would either fail to comply or renegotiate the terms of social exchange so that they obtained more profit. In line with the empirical generalizations and propositions presented above, the social power-exchange theory predicts that the more the parent accepts a culturally valued child behavior, the more supportive the parent. Also, the more powerful the parent, the more likely the child will manifest the culturally valued behavior (social competence).

The social power-exchange theory assumes that a parental control attempt induces two forces in a child, a force to comply and a force to resist. Compliance to the control attempt is a function of the resultant force to either comply or resist. The theory postulates that the greater the power of parents and the greater the use of inductive techniques, the less likely a parental control attempt induces resistance in the child. However, the more parents use coercive techniques, the more likely a parental control attempt induces resistance in the child.

The social power-exchange theory is congruent with the empirical generalizations and theoretical propositions presented in this chapter. The more salient empirical tests this theory suggests for moving beyond our present empirical base are:

1. Is the relationship between parental support and social competence in children contingent on parental acceptance of cultural values about social competence in children?

2. Is the relationship between parental support and social competence in children contingent on parental power?

3. Is the relationship between inductive control attempts of parents and social competence in children contingent on parental power?

4. Is the relationship between coercive control attempts of parents and social competence in children contingent on parental power?

IN CONCLUSION

Our purpose in this section is not to present a didactic restatement of the preceding material. We have done that repeatedly at section ends throughout our formulations. Rather, our intent here is to place our work in the larger intellectual enterprise of socialization research and theorizing. We take the socialization enterprise to be the systematic study of those processes of social interaction resulting in an individual becoming an adequately functioning member of a social order. Socialization, unlike some areas in the social sciences, with each new set of findings generates a recurring intrigue about the most basic socialization processes which give rise to the socialized products of attitudes, values, and behaviors. This is so because nearly all socialization research findings have implications for some very basic questions asked by succeeding generations about man and his social order. Indeed, students of socialization are forced to repeatedly rethink their basic formulations about the nature of the organism being socialized and the social process.

Is the human infant *asocial, prosocial,* or *antisocial?* It is clear from a careful between-the-lines reading of the foregoing that we are proceeding from a view of the human infant as *asocial*. This appears true whether one analyzes the research findings from the symbolic-cognitive or the social learning perspective. However, there are some hints at an emerging bias to conceptualize the infant as prosocial. The early infant research on visual patterning and selection rejects the old view of the nonseeing infant of the first few weeks. In its place appears an infant of four days to a week who chooses to visually interact with one set of stimuli over another. Thus we postulate a tendency to interact with the most responsive elements of the environment—the most responsive of which is another perceiving, thinking, choosing, action-generating object, namely, a socialized being. We are, however, uneasy at postulating a prosocial being whose biology is forced to carry human ethics, as the self-actualization thrust of Maslow postulates.

The resultant ambivalence is sidestepped rather than resolved. We opt to equip the human infant with enough innate tendencies to seek out the responsive elements of his environment and then simply note that out of interaction with responsive and reflective others, self and the social order are simultaneously created.

If we at present are a bit ambivalent about the *asocial* or *prosocial* question, likewise we are ambivalent about the question, who or what is responsible in general for the socialized outcome? We reject the oversocialized view of the nature of man implicit in much of the socialization literature, which implies that what man becomes is largely due to his environment. The rejection of that view is most clearly seen in our assumption about the human infant and the discussion of the outcomes under the heading of social competence. In short, we assume that out of interaction of a normally endowed infant with a responsive environment (physical, but most importantly a socially responsive environment) will emerge attitudes and behavior which are valued as good in our societies. Implicit in our discussion is the view that the thinking, perceiving, choosing human being is responsible, at least in major part, for the outcomes.

We suspect, however, that analyzing the socially incompetent outcomes of behavior presents us with considerably more problems. We find it difficult to assume that these outcomes of low self-esteem, aggression, drug abuse, and learning disabilities are largely the responsibility of the thinking, perceiving, choosing human being who initiated the social interaction which gave rise to these products of socialization. We find it uncomfortable to assume that these outcomes are due to innately inferior beings. Similarly, we are loath to imply that these outcomes are the sole responsibility of the social order which "produced" them. We feel an urging to insist that through it all, man is at least partly responsible for his own outcomes. We suspect that here we are merely representing a prevalent bias in much of the extant socialization

literature; namely, if the socialized outcome is "good," we tend to identify the individual as responsible in greater measure, whereas if the outcome is "bad," we tend to look to the social order for major responsibility.

While the two foregoing questions reveal some of our ambivalence toward basic socialization questions, our answer to the final question reveals no such ambivalence. The question: are there some social processes which appear to be universal so that any group could profitably be analyzed along these interactional dimensions? Our answer to this query is an unequivocal "yes."

While the foregoing socialization treatise has been purposefully limited to the family, and more specifically to parent-child interaction, we believe that any social order can be analyzed along the support, control, and power axes. At present we see no evidence to cause us to expect that variation along these dimensions would result in different socialization outcome variables in different groups or in different cultures.

We suspect that groups within a society could be placed along these continua and that outcomes would corroborate the above general trends. For example, if schools were measured on the degree of supportive behavior of teachers, control attempts (coercion or induction), and the power dimension, we predict that variations in those socially competent and incompetent behaviors identified above would appear. Indeed we predict that if research could be carried out in educational settings, where the relative influence of these independent variables could be systematically compared with the influence of curriculum changes, for example, the influence of the social interactional variables would far exceed the influence attributable to curriculum change. Indeed we suspect that research which shows a curriculum change to significantly influence outcomes (self-esteem, cognitive development, creativity, social competence) may unwittingly confound curriculum change with the social interactional variables. New programs are often introduced from a power base. Teachers are very supportive of students participating in them, and more inclined to use inductive control attempts.

At the more global societal level, we can see possible comparisons which could be made. It strikes us as possible to order societies along these dimensions as to the degree to which these different interactional styles are typical of them. Indeed the technological and democratic forms of social organization characteristic of Western societies appear to give emphasis to control attempts embedded in informational matrices from a power base relying on expertise rather than universalistic status differences. While we see some possibilities for meaningful comparisons at the societal level, we acknowledge them with considerable caution. We are more than minimally aware of the unfortunate results of social scientists suggesting cross-societal analysis from a theoretical perspective generated in and fitting nicely with their own societies' social order. Sociocentric viewpoints need to be analyzed with considerable care and accepted only after careful analyses.

Lastly, we are impressed once again with the challenges that yet face those researchers and theorists who attempt to better explicate socialization processes. At the end we feel we can better visualize the relevant research and theory questions than we did at the beginning. In this field of endeavor, to be able to better formulate the central questions is sufficient payoff. We can then move toward the next research and theory project in our quest to understand man and the social order.

NOTES

1. This is a rather complex idea. When the joint or combined effect of two (or more) variables is *multiplicative* in its relationship to a third variable, it is easy to draw incorrect conclusions unless the interaction effect has been directly tested (Blaylock, 1969:155). Incorrect conclusions can easily be drawn when two variables (X and Z) are related to a third variable (Y) either in two separate bivariate analyses or in one multiple regression analysis in which only the additive effect of X and Z is tested. For example, Y might be separately correlated with both X and Z while at the same time X and Z interact in their relationship with Y as shown in the following diagram:

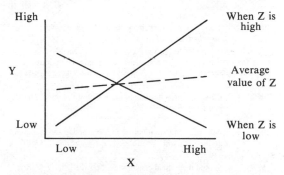

In this example, if the two lines are averaged, X has a slight positive relationship with Y. If the diagram of the same interactive effect of X and Z on Y were redrawn, putting Z on the horizontal axis, the average of the two lines for each value of X would indicate a slight positive relationship between Z and Y. Suppose X and Z were both found to have such a positive relationship with Y, but interaction had not been tested. One might be tempted to conclude that the highest value of Y would exist when both X and Z are high and the lowest value of Y would exist when both X and Z are low. However, if X and Z actually had a multiplicative effect on Y as diagrammed above, then part of the conclusion would be incorrect. Y would be highest when both X and Z are high, but Y would not be lowest when both X and Z are low. On the contrary, Y would be lowest when either X or Z was low and the other high. Such combined multiplicative effects of parental support and parental control techniques on child behaviors are repeatedly referred to in this chapter.

2. We have omitted "referent power" in our definition and discussion because it is used as a synonym of identification and identification is not independent of our constructs of parental support and general parental power.

3. The metatheoretical terms we employ in our theory construction are "empirical generalization," "theoretical proposition," "postulate," and "corollary." Empirical generalizations are empirical regularities that are found between variables across a number of studies using different measurement techniques. Our theoretical propositions are arrived at inductively by combining empirical generalizations that are judged to be special cases of more general relationships between variables. These are our main theoretical constructions. However, in a few cases we have specified postulates and corollaries of postulates. A postulate is a working assumption, while a corollary is deductively related to a postulate.

4. Because of the ambiguity in our construct of undifferentiated control attempts this variable does not have a constant constitutive meaning from section to section in our report of empirical findings. In some cases it might operationalize induction and in others coercion, but we had no way of differentiating between them.

5. We are indebted to Professor Thomas E. Smith for this insight from an earlier review of this paper.

6. In this chapter we use the term "man" in its generic definitional sense rather than as a sex-linked term.

REFERENCES

AARONSON, A. J.
1966   "An investigation into the relationship between maternal attitudes toward childrearing and the success of boys in beginning reading." Unpublished Ph.D. Dissertation, New York University.

AINSWORTH, M. D. S.
1973   "The development of infant-mother attachment." In B. M. Caldwell and H. N. Riccinti (eds.), *Review of Child Development Research*, vol. 3, Chicago: University of Chicago Press.

ALLEN, C.
1974   "Parental nurturance, induction and power assertion control attempts and internal locus of control orientation in children." Unpublished Master's Thesis, Brigham Young University.

ALLINSMITH, W. AND T. C. GREENLING
1955   "Guilt over anger as predicted from parental discipline: A study of superego development." *American Psychologist* 10:320.

ALTMAN, E. D.
1973   "Some variables in mother and child interaction related to linguistic competence in severely hearing-impaired children." Unpublished Ph.D. Dissertation, University of Denver.

APPERSON, O. L. B.
1961   "A comparison of parental behaviors with certain characteristics of their children considered relevant for adjustment." Unpublished Ph.D. Dissertation, University of Denver.

APPLETON, T., R. CLIFTON, AND S. GOLDBERG
1975   "The development of behavioral competence in infancy." In F. D. Horowitz (ed.), *Review of Child Development Research*, vol. 4, Chicago: University of Chicago Press.

ARMENTROUT, J. A.
1971   "Parental child-rearing attitudes and preadolescents' problem behaviors." *Journal of Consulting and Clinical Psychology* 37(2):278–825.

ARONFREED, J.
1961   "The nature, variety, and social patterning of moral responses to transgression." *Journal of Abnormal and Social Psychology* 63:223–41.
1969   "The concept of internalization." In D. A. Goslin (ed.), *Handbook of Socialization Theory and Research*. Chicago: Rand McNally.

AUERBACH, A. G.
1967   "Antecedents of masculinity and femininity in young children." Unpublished Ph.D. Dissertation, Purdue University.

BAER, D. J. AND J. J. CORRUDS
1974   "Heroin addict relationships with parents during childhood and early adolescent years." *Journal of Genetic Psychology* 124:99–103.

BALDWIN, A.
1955   *Behavior and Development in Childhood*. New York: Dryden Press.

BANDURA, A.
1969   "Social-learning theory of identification processes." In D. A. Goslin (ed.), *Handbook of Socialization Theory and Research*. Chicago: Rand McNally.

BANDURA, A. AND R. H. WALTERS
1963   *Social Learning and Personality Development*. New York: Holt, Rinehart and Winston.

BARTON, K., T. E. DIELMAN, AND R. B. CATTELL
1974   "Child rearing practices and achievement in school." *Journal of Genetic Psychology* 124:155–65.

BAUMRIND, D.
1966   "Effects of authoritative control on child behavior." *Child Development* 37:887–907.
1967   "Child care practices anteceding three patterns of preschool behavior." *Genetic Psychology Monographs* 75:43–88.
1971   "Current patterns of parental authority." *Developmental Psychology Monographs* 4(1):1–102.
1972a   "An exploratory study of socialization effects on black children: Some black-white comparisons." *Child Development* 43:261–67.
1972b   "Socialization and instrumental competence." In W. Hartup (ed.), *Research on Young Children*. Washington, D.C.: National Association for the Education of Young Children.

BAUMRIND, D. AND A. E. BLACK
1967   "Socialization practices associated with dimensions of social competence in preschool boys and girls." *Child Development* 38:291–327.

BECKER, A. J.
1970   "Reading achievement of boys as influenced by the child rearing attitudes of their fathers." Unpublished Ph.D. Dissertation, Case Western Reserve University.

BECKER, W. C.
1964   "Consequences of different kinds of parental discipline." In M. L. Hoffman and L. Hoffman (eds.), *Review of Child Development Research*, vol. 1. Chicago: University of Chicago Press.

BECKER, W. C., D. R. PETERSON, S. LURIA, D. J. SHOEMAKER, AND L. A. HELLMER
1962   "Relations of factors derived from parent-interview ratings to behavior problems of five-year olds." *Child Development* 33:509–35.

BELL, R. Q.
1968   "A reinterpretation of the direction of effects in studies of socialization." *Psychological Review* 75:81–95.

BENDER, R. B.
1974   "Perceived parental attitudes and their relationship to chronic alcoholism in Veterans Administration Hospital patient population: An empirical test of McCord and McCord's theory of the origins of alcoholism." Unpublished Ph.D. Dissertation, University of Arizona.

BERG, R. H.
1963   "Mothers' attitudes on child rearing and family life compared for achieving and underachieving elementary school children." Unpublished Ph.D. Dissertation, University of Southern California.

BERGER, J. A.
1974   "Adolescent drug abusers' perceptions of parental attitudes and behavior." Unpublished Ph.D. Dissertation, Long Island University.

BIGLIN
1964   "The relationship of parental attitudes and children's academic and social performance." Unpublished Ph.D. Dissertation, University of Nebraska Teachers College.

BIJOU, S. W. AND D. M. BAER
1961   *Child Development: A Systematic and Empirical Theory*, vol. 1. New York: Appleton-Century-Crofts.

BILLER, H. B.
1969   "Father dominance and sex-role development in kindergarten-age boys." *Developmental Psychology* 1:87–94.

BLAYLOCK, H. M.
1969   *Theory Construction*. Englewood Cliffs, N.J.: Prentice-Hall.

BOXLEY, R. L.
1973   "Sex-object choice in adult black males: Perception of parental relationships and early sexual behavior." Unpublished Ph.D. Dissertation, University of Washington.

BRODIS, N. F. T. A.
1969   "Parent-child relationship and self-concept as related to differential academic achievement of adolescent siblings in father absent families." Unpublished Ph.D. Dissertation, Cornell University.

BRODY, G. F.
1969   "Maternal child-rearing studies and child behavior." *Developmental Psychology* 1:66–76.

BRONFENBRENNER, U.
1961a   "Toward a theoretical model for the analysis of parent-child relationships in a social context." In J. C. Glidewell (ed.), *Parental Attitudes and Child Behavior*. Springfield, Ill.: Charles C Thomas.
1961b   "The changing American child: A speculative analysis." *Journal of Social Issues* 17:6–18.

BURTON, R. V., R. R. MACCOBY, AND W. ALLINSMITH
1961   "Antecedents of resistance to temptation in four-year-old children." *Child Development* 32:689–710.

BUSSE, T. V.
1969   "Child-rearing antecedents of flexible thinking." *Developmental Psychology* 1:585–91.

CANCIAN, M.
1971   "Affection and dominance in Zinacantan and Cambridge families." *Journal of Marriage and the Family* 33:207–13.

CARTWRIGHT, D.
1959   "A field theoretical conception of power." In D. Cartwright (ed.), *Studies in Social Power*. Ann Arbor: University of Michigan Press.

CHAPLAN, A. A.
1967   "Mothers' practices and persuasibility in pre-school children." Unpublished Ph.D. Dissertation, Columbia University.

CHOROST, S. B.
1962   "Parental child-rearing attitudes and their correlates in adolescent hostility." *Genetic Psychology Monographs* 66(1):49–90.

CLAPP, W. F.
1966   "Dependence and competence in children: Parental treatment of four-year old boys." Unpublished Ph.D. Dissertation, University of Colorado.

COMSTOCK, M. L. C.
1973   "Effects of perceived parental behavior on self-esteem and adjustment." Unpublished Ph.D. Dissertation, University of North Carolina at Chapel Hill.

CONKLIN, A. M.
1940   *Failures of Highly Intelligent Pupils*. New York: Teachers College, Columbia University.

COOPERSMITH, S.
1967   *The Antecedents of Self-Esteem*. San Francisco: Freeman.

COTTRELL, L. S.
1969   "Interpersonal interaction and the development of the self."
        In D. A. Goslin (ed.), *Handbook of Socialization Theory and
        Research*. Chicago: Rand McNally.

CRAIG, J. E.
1966   "Perceived parental attitudes and the effects of maternal
        versus paternal censure and approval in good and poor
        premorbid hospitalized female schizophrenics." Unpub-
        lished Ph.D. Dissertation, University of Wisconsin.

CROSS, H. J.
1965   "The relation of parental training conditions to conceptual
        level on adolescent boys." Unpublished Ph.D. Dissertation,
        Syracuse University.

DAVIDS, A. AND P. K. HAINSWORTH
1967   "Maternal attitudes about family life and child rearing as
        avowed by mothers and perceived by their underachieving
        and over-achieving sons." *Journal of Consulting Psychology*
        31:29–37.

DAVIS, W. L.
1969   "Parental antecedents of childrens' locus of control." Un-
        published Ph.D. Dissertation, Kansas State University.

DELANEY, D. J.
1965   "Parental antecedents of social aggression in young chil-
        dren." Unpublished Ph.D. Dissertation, Purdue University.

DESCHNER, J. G. P.
1972   "The influence of mother-child interactions on early man-
        ifestations of competence." Unpublished Ph.D. Disserta-
        tion, University of Houston.

DEUTSCH, M. AND R. M. KRAUSS
1965   *Theories in Social Psychology*. New York: Basic Books.

DIELMAN, T. E. AND R. B. CATTELL
1972   "The prediction of behavior problems in 6 to 8 year-old
        children from mothers' report of child-rearing practice."
        Journal of Clinical Psychology 28(1):13–17.

DRAPER, H. E.
1966   "Conscience orientation in children and parental attitudes
        toward independence granting and achievement induce-
        ment." Unpublished Ph.D. Dissertation, Oregon State Uni-
        versity.

DREWS, E. M. AND J. E. TEAHAN
1957   "Parental attitudes and academic achievement." *Journal of
        Clinical Psychology* 13:328–32.

DREYER, A. AND M. B. WELLS
1966   "Parental values, parental control, and creativity in young
        children." *Journal of Marriage and the Family* 28:83–88.

EDWARDS, H. E.
1963   "The relationship between reported early life experiences
        with parents and adult male homosexuality." Unpublished
        Ph.D. Dissertation, University of Tennessee.

EGAN, G. V.
1964   "Antecedents and consequences of cross-identification in
        adolescent females." Unpublished Ph.D. Dissertation, St.
        Louis University.

ELDER, G. H.
1963   "Parental power legitimation and its effect on the adoles-
        cent." *Sociometry* 26 (March):50–65.
1965   "Life opportunity and personality: Some consequences of
        stratified secondary education in Great Britain." *Sociology of
        Education* 38:173–202.

ELLIS, G. J., D. L. THOMAS, AND B. C. ROLLINS
1976   "Measuring parental support: The interrelationship of three
        measures." *Journal of Marriage and the Family* 38:713–22.

ENGLISH, G. E., JR.
1969   "Children's perception of parents in normal families contain-
        ing an aggressive, withdrawn, or nondeviant child." Unpub-
        lished Ph.D. Dissertation, University of Wisconsin.

ERON, L. D., L. D. WALDER, R. TOIGO, AND M. LEFKOWITZ
1963   "Social class, parental punishment for aggression, and child
        aggression." *Child Development* 34:849–67.

FANTZ, R. L.
1958   "Pattern vision in infants." *Psychological Record* 8:43–47.

FARAHMAND, S. S.
1961   "Personality characteristics and child-rearing attitudes of
        fathers of schizophrenic patients." Unpublished Ph.D. Dis-
        sertation, Washington State University.

FAZEL, M. K.
1968   "Child's perception of parental attitude to academic
        achievement and problem awareness." Unpublished Ph.D.
        Dissertation, Utah State University.

FERSTER, C. B. AND B. F. SKINNER
1957   *Schedules of Reinforcement*. New York: Appleton-
        Century-Crofts.

FODOR, E. M.
1973   "Moral development and parent behavior antecedents in
        adolescent psychopaths." *Journal of Genetic Psychology*
        122:37–43.

FRADKINA, F. T.
1971   "Vozniknovenie rechi u nebeuka [The beginning of speech
        in the child]." Cited in A. V. Zaporozhets and D. B.
        El'Konin (eds.), *The Psychology of Preschool Children*.
        Translated by J. Shybut and S. Simon. Cambridge, Mass.:
        M.I.T. Press.

FREEMAN, M. A. R.
1970   "A comparative analysis of patterns of attitudes among
        mothers of children with learning disabilities, and mothers of
        children who are achieving normally." Unpublished Ph.D.
        Dissertation, Northwestern University.

FRENCH, J. R. P. AND B. H. RAVEN
1959   "The bases of social power." In D. Cartwright (ed.), *Studies
        in Social Power*. Ann Arbor: University of Michigan Press.

GECAS, V.
1969   "Parent-child interaction and adolescent self-evaluation."
        Unpublished Ph.D. Dissertation, University of Minnesota.
1971   "Parental behavior and dimensions of adolescent self-
        evaluation." *Sociometry* 34:466–82.

GEWIRTZ, J. L.
1969   "Mechanisms of social learning." In D. A. Goslin (ed.),
        Handbook of Socialization Theory and Research. Chicago:
        Rand McNally.

GILL, L. J. AND B. SPILA
1962   "Some nonintellectual correlates of academic achievement
        among Mexican-American secondary school students."
        Journal of Educational Psychology 53(3):144–49.

GLASER, B. G. AND A. L. STRAUSS
1967   *The Discovery of Grounded Theory*. Chicago: Aldine.

GOLDIN, P. C.
1969   "A review of children's reports of parent behaviors."
        Psychological Bulletin 71:222–36.

GOODE, W. J.
1972   "Force in human society." *American Sociological Review*
        37:507–19.

GORDON, J. AND E. SMITH
1965   "Children's aggression, parental attitudes, and the effects of
        an affiliation-arousing story." *Journal of Personality and
        Social Psychology* 1:654–59.

GRAFF, R. L.
1967   "Identification as related to perceived parental attitudes and

powerlessness in delinquents and normals.'' Unpublished Ph.D. Dissertation, Claremont Graduate School and University Center.

GREENSTEIN, J. M.
1966   ''Father characteristics and sex typing.'' *Journal of Personality and Social Psychology* 3(3):271–77.

GRINDER, R. E.
1962   ''Parental childrearing practices, conscience and resistance to temptation of sixth-grade children.'' *Child Development* 33:808–20.

HAIDER, S. J.
1970   ''Parental attitudes and child-rearing practices as related to academic underachievement.'' Unpublished Ph.D. Dissertation, University of Illinois at Urbana-Champaign.

HALL, M. D.
1963   ''Parent-child interactions in latency-age boys with learning inhibitions.'' Unpublished Ph.D. Dissertation, University of Minnesota.

HARRIS, N.
1965   ''Controlling maternal attitudes: Clincal and socio-cultural implications.'' Unpublished Ph.D. Dissertation, Yeshiva University.

HAUK, M. W.
1967   ''Effects of maternal attitudes, field-dependence and curiosity on weight and volume conservation in children.'' Unpublished Ph.D. Dissertation, Catholic University of America.

HEALEY, R. E.
1974   ''Parental behavior as related to children's academic achievement.'' Unpublished Ph.D. Dissertation, Catholic University of America.

HEBB, D. O.
1955   ''Drives and C.N.S. (conceptual nervous system).'' *Psychological Review* 62:243–53.

HEILBRUN, A. B.
1960   ''Perception of maternal child rearing attitudes in schizophrenics.'' *Journal of Consulting Psychology* 24(2):169–73.
1969   ''Perceived maternal child-rearing and effects of delayed reinforcement upon concept acquisition.'' *Developmental Psychology* 1(5):605–12.
1970   ''Perceived maternal child-rearing experience and the effects of vicarious and direct reinforcements on males.'' *Child Development* 41:253–62.
1971   ''Maternal child rearing and creativity in sons.'' *Journal of Genetic Psychology* 119:175–79.

HEILBRUN, A. B. AND H. K. ORR
1962   ''Perception of maternal childrearing attitudes, personality of the perceiver, and incipient psychopathology.'' *Child Development* 33:73–83.
1965   ''Maternal childrearing control history and subsequent cognitive and personality functioning of the offspring.'' *Psychological Reports* 17:259–72.
1966   ''Perceived maternal childrearing history and subsequent motivational effects of failure.'' *Journal of Genetic Psychology* 109:75–89.

HEILBRUN, A. B., H. ORR, AND S. N. HARRELL
1966   ''Patterns of parental childrearing and subsequent vulnerability of cognitive disturbance.'' *Journal of Consulting Psychology* 30(1):51–59.

HEILBRUN, A. B. AND B. J. GILLARD
1966   ''Perceived maternal childrearing behavior and motivational effects of social reinforcement in females.'' *Perceptual and Motor Skills* 23:439–46.

HEILBRUN, A. B., S. N. HARRELL, AND B. J. GILLARD
1967a   ''Perceived childrearing attitudes of fathers and cognitive control in daughters.'' *Journal of Genetic Psychology* 111:29–40.

1967b   ''Perceived maternal childrearing patterns and the effects of social nonreaction upon achievement motivation.'' *Child Development* 38:267–81.

HEILBRUN, A. B. AND D. B. WATERS
1968   ''Underachievement as related to perceived maternal child-rearing and academic conditions of reinforcement.'' *Child Development* 39:913–21.

HEILBRUN, A. B. AND N. A. NORBERT
1970   ''Maternal child-rearing experience and self-reinforcement effectiveness.'' *Developmental Psychology* 3(1):81–87.

HESS, R. D. AND V. C. SHIPMAN
1965   ''Early experience and the socialization of cognitive modes in children.'' *Child Development* 36:869–86.

HOFFMAN, L. W., S. ROSEN, AND R. LIPPITT
1960   ''Parental coerciveness, child autonomy, and child's role at school.'' *Sociometry* 23:15–22.

HOFFMAN, M. L.
1960   ''Power assertion by the parent and its impact on the child.'' *Child Development* 31:129–43.
1963a   ''Childrearing practices and moral development.'' *Child Development* 34:295–318.
1963b   ''Parent discipline and the child's consideration for others.'' *Child Development* 34:573–85.
1970   ''Moral development.'' In P. H. Mussen (ed.), *Carmichael's Manual of Child Psychology*, third ed., vol. 2. New York: Wiley.

HOFFMAN, M. L. AND H. D. SALTZSTEIN
1967   ''Parent discipline and the child's moral development.'' *Journal of Personality and Social Psychology* 5:45–57.

HOMANS, G. C.
1964   ''Contemporary theory in sociology.'' In R. E. L. Faris (ed.), *Handbook of Modern Sociology*. Chicago: Rand McNally.
1974   *Social Behavior: Its Elementary Forms*, revised ed. New York: Harcourt Brace Jovanovich.

HUNT, D. G.
1972   ''A study of perceived parental permissiveness and the degree of marijuana usage among offspring.'' Unpublished Ph.D. Dissertation, University of Pittsburgh.

JOHNSON, Z. C.
1974   ''Parental childrearing attitudes and the development of achievement motivation in daughters.'' Unpublished PhD. Dissertation, Boston University.

JONES, E.
1955   ''The probation student: What he is like and what can be done about it.'' *Journal of Educational Research* 49:93–102.

JUFFER, M. M.
1969   ''Socialization of children with varying levels of originality: An analysis of parent-child interaction.'' Unpublished Ph.D. Dissertation, Iowa State University.

KAGAN, J. AND H. A. MOSS
1962   *Birth to Maturity.* New York: Wiley.

KAPLAR, J. E.
1970   ''Creativity, sex-role preference, and perception of parents in fifth-grade boys.'' Unpublished Ph.D. Dissertation, University of Massachusetts.

KATKOVSKY, W., V. C. CRANDALL, AND S. GOOD
1967   ''Parental antecedents of children's beliefs in internal-external control of reinforcements in intellectual achievement situations.'' *Child Development* 38:765–76.

KAUSCH, D. F.
1962   ''Manifestations of aggression in children as a function of parental behavior.'' Unpublished Ph.D. Dissertation, University of Nebraska.

KELLER, E. D.
1961   ''Parents' self-reports, children's representations of parent

behavior, and masculinity in young boys." Unpublished Ph.D. Dissertation, State University of Iowa.

KENNEY, E. T.
1965   "Level of ego development and authoritarianism of mothers with children who differ in IQ and school adjustment." Unpublished Ph.D. Dissertation, Washington University.

KENT, R.
1965   "Children of mothers with authoritarian ideology." Unpublished Ph.D. Dissertation, Yeshiva University.

KIMBALL, B.
1953   "Case studies in educational failure during adolescence." *American Journal of Orthopsychiatry* 23:406–15.

KRUG, R. S.
1965   "Attitudinal and behavior differences in child-rearing practices between parents of clinic and nonclinic children: A questionnaire assessment." Unpublished Ph.D. Dissertation, University of Illinois.

LaVOIE, J. C.
1970   "Punishment and adolescent self control: A study of the effects of aversive stimulation, reasoning, and sex of parent." Unpublished Ph.D. Dissertation, University of Wisconsin.

LEFKOWITZ, M. M., L. O. WALDER, AND L. D. ERON
1963   "Punishment, identification and aggression." *Merrill-Palmer Quarterly of Behavior and Development* 9:159–74.

LELER, H. O.
1970   "Mother-child interaction and language performance in young disadvantaged Negro children." Unpublished Ph.D. Dissertation, Stanford University.

LEVENSON, H.
1973   "Perceived parental antecedents of internal, powerful others, and chance locus of control orientations." *Developmental Psychology* 9:268–74.

LEWIS, M. AND L. A. ROSENBLUM
1974   *The Effect of the Infant on Its Caregiver.* New York: Wiley.

LIFSHIN, J. H.
1970   "Conscience orientation and family interaction in early adolescent boys." Unpublished Ph.D. Dissertation, Michigan State University.

LOEB, R. C.
1973   "Concomitants of boys' locus of control examined in parent-child interactions." Unpublished Ph.D. Dissertation, Cornell University.

MACCOBY, E. R.
1961   "The choice of variables in the study of socialization." *Sociometry* 24:257–371.

MACDONALD, A. P., JR.
1971   "Internal-external locus of control: parental antecedents." *Journal of Consulting and Clinical Psychology* 37:141–47.

MALONEY, T. R.
1974   "A study of the relationship between behavior disorders in four and five year old children and the temperament of their mothers." Unpublished Ph.D. Dissertation, St. Louis University.

MANNINO, J. B.
1973   "The relationship of three maternal-social conditions to boys' level of abstract concept formation." Unpublished Ph.D. Dissertation, Washington University.

MARGO, P. A. AND B. A. HANSON
1969   "Perceived maternal nurturance and control of process schizophrenics, reactive schizophrenics, and normals." *Journal of Consulting and Clinical Psychology* 33:507.

MARTIN, B.
1975   "Parent-child relations." In F. D. Horowitz (ed.), *Review of*

Child Development Research, vol. 4. Chicago: University of Chicago Press.

McCLELLAND, D. C., J. W. ATKINSON, R. A. CLARK, AND E. L. LOWELL
1953   *The Achievement Motive.* New York: Appleton-Century-Crofts.

McCORD, W., J. McCORD, AND A. HOWARD
1961   "Familial correlates of aggression in nondelinquent male children." *Journal of Abnormal and bsocial Psychology* 62:79–93.

1963   "Family interaction as antecedent to the direction of male aggressiveness." *Journal of Abnormal and Social Psychology* 66:239–42.

McKINLEY, R. A.
1963   "Perceived parental attributes of schizophrenics as a function of premorbid social adjustment." Unpublished Ph.D. Dissertation, State University of Iowa.

MEAD, G. H.
1934   *Mind, Self, and Society.* Chicago: University of Chicago Press.

MILLER, W. H.
1967   "Relationship between mother's style of communication and her control system to the child's reading readiness and subsequent reading achievement in first grade." Unpublished Ph.D. Dissertation, University of Arizona.

MISCHLER, E. G. AND N. E. WAXLER
1968   *Interaction in Families: An Experimental Study of Family Processes and Schizophrenia Processes.* New York: Wiley.

MITCHELL, L. H.
1965   "Dominance and femininity as factors in the sex role adjustment of parents and children." Unpublished Ph.D. Dissertation, University of California, Berkeley.

MORROW, W. R. AND R. C. WILSON
1961   "Family relations of bright high-achieving and underachieving high school boys." *Child Development* 32:501–10.

MOTE, F. B.
1966   "The relationship between child self concept in school and parental attitudes and behaviors in child rearing." Unpublished Ph.D. Dissertation, Stanford University.

MOULTON, R. W., P. G. LIBERTY, JR., E. BURNSTEIN, AND N. ALTUCHER
1966   "Patterning of parental affection and disciplinary dominance as a determinant of guilt and sex typing." *Journal of Personality and Social Psychology* 4:356–63.

MULLIKAN, R. K.
1966   "A study of parental attitudes: self concepts and personality characteristics of deviant achievers of average ability." Unpublished Ph.D. Dissertation, University of Utah.

MUSSEN, P. AND L. DISTLER
1960   "Child-rearing antecedents of masculine identification in kindergarten boys." *Child Development* 31:89–100.

MUSSEN, P. AND E. RUTHERFORD
1963   "Parent-child relations and parental personality in relation to young children's sex-role preferences." *Child Development* 34:598–607.

NEVIUS, J. R.
1972   "The relationship of child-rearing practices to the acquisition of moral judgments in ten-year-old boys." Unpublished Ph.D. Dissertation, University of Southern California.

NICHOLS, R. C.
1964   "Parental attitudes of mothers of intelligent adolescents and creativity of their children." *Child Development* 35:1041–50.

ORINSTEIN, A. S.
1961   "An investigation of parental child-rearing attitudes and

creativity in children." Unpublished Ph.D. Dissertation, University of Denver.

PARSONS, T. AND R. F. BALES
1955   *Family, Socialization and Interaction Process.* New York: Free Press.

PEARLIN, L. I., M. R. YARROW, AND H. A. SCARR
1967   "Unintended effects of parental aspirations: The case of children's cheating." *American Journal of Sociology* 73(1) (July):73–83.

PECK, R. F. AND R. HAVIGHURST
1960   *The Psychology of Character Development.* New byork: Wiley.

PETERSON, D., W. C. BECKER, D. J. SHOEMAKER, Z. LURIA, AND L. A. HELLMER
1961   "Child behavior problems and parental attitudes." *Child Development* 32:151–62.

PETERSON, D. R. AND G. MIGLIORINO
1967   "Pancultural factors of parental behavior in Sicily and the United States." *Child Development* 38:967–91.

PHILLIPS, T. R.
1973   "Syntax and vocabulary of mother's speech to young children: Age and sex comparisons." *Child Development* 44:182–85.

PIAGET, J.
1954   *The Construction of Reality in the Child.* New York: Basic Books.

PRUITT, J. H.
1971   "Maternal attitudes, internal-external expectancy and academic achievement of inner-city adolescents." Unpublished Ph.D. Dissertation, Case Western Reserve University.

RADCLIFFE-BROWN, A. R.
1934   "Social sanction." In E. R. A. Seligman (ed.), *Encyclopedia of the Social Sciences,* vol. 13. London: Macmillan.

RADIN, N. L.
1969   "Childrearing antecedents of cognitive development in lower-class preschool children." Unpublished Ph.D. Dissertation, University of Michigan.

RANKIN, P. T., JR.
1946   "The relationship between parent behavior and achievement of inner city elementary school children." Unpublished Ph.D. Dissertation, University of Michigan.

RHEINGOLD, H. L.
1969   "The social and socializing infant." In D. A. Goslin (ed.), *Handbook of Socialization Theory and Research.* Chicago: Rand McNally.

RICH, J. E.
1965   "Relationship between parents' expressed attitudes on child rearing and their children's school achievement." Unpublished Ph.D. Dissertation, University of Oregon.

RICHER, S.
1965   "The economics of child-rearing." *Journal of Marriage and the Family* 30:462–66.

ROE, A.
1957   "Early determinants of vocational choice." *Journal of Counseling Psychology* 4:212–17.

ROE, A. AND M. SIEGELMAN
1963   "A parent-child relations questionnaire." *Child Development* 34:355–69.

ROGERS, M. F.
1974   "Instrumental and infra-resources: The bases of power." *American Journal of Sociology* 79:1418–33.

ROLLINS, B. C.
1967   "A working paper on a theory of parental influence in the socialization of children." Unpublished paper presented at the Annual Symposium on Family Theory, National Council on Family Relations, San Francisco.

ROLLINS, B. C. AND S. J. BAHR
1976   "A theory of power relationships in marriage." *Journal of Marriage and the Family* 38:619–27.

ROLLINS, B. C. AND C. CALDER
1975   "Academic achievement, situational stress, and problem solving flexibility." *Journal of Genetic Psychology* 126:93–105.

ROLLINS, B. C. AND D. L. THOMAS
1975   "A theory of parental power and child compliance." In R. Cromwell and D. Olson (eds.), *Power in Families.* Beverly Hills, Calif.: Sage Publications.

ROWLAND, T. S.
1968   "Mother-son interaction and the coping behavior of young boys." Unpublished Ph.D. Dissertation, Michigan State University.

RUSSELL, H. L.
1966   "Perceptions of mothers and fathers by normal, school problem, and illegitimately pregnant adolescent white females." Unpublished Ph.D. Dissertation, University of Houston.

SAMUELS, S. C.
1969   "An investigation into some factors related to the self concepts in early childhood of children from middle and lower class homes." Unpublished Ph.D. Dissertation, Columbia University.

SANTROCK, J. W.
1973   "Family structure, maternal behavior and moral development in boys." Unpublished Ph.D. Dissertation, University of Minnesota.

SCHAEFER, E. S.
1959   "A circumplex model for maternal behavior." *Journal of Abnormal and Social Psychology* 59:226–35.
1965   "Children's reports of parental behavior." *Child Development* 36:552–57.
1972   "Parents and educators." In W. Hartup (ed.), *Research in Young Children.* Washington, D.C.: National Association for the Education of Young Children.

SCHAEFER, E. S. AND N. BAYLEY
1963   "Maternal behavior, child behavior and their intercorrelations from infancy through adolescence." *Monographs of the Society for Research in Child Development* 28(3).

SCHECK, D. C., R. EMERICK, AND M. M. EL-ASSAL
1973   "Adolescent's perceptions of parent-child relations and the development of internal-external control orientation." *Journal of Marriage and the Family* 35:643–54.

SEARS, R., E. MACCOBY, AND H. LEVIN
1957   *Patterns of Child Rearing.* Evanston, Ill.: Row, Peterson.

SEARS, R. R., L. RAU, AND R. ALPERT
1965   *Identification and Childrearing.* Stanford, Calif.: Stanford University Press.

SEASHORE, C. N. H.
1961   "Family dynamics in relation to conscience and deviant behavior among adolescent boys." Unpublished Ph.D. Dissertation, University of Michigan.

SEBALD, H.
1963   "Parent-peer control and masculine-marital role perceptions of adolescent boys." Unpublished Ph.D. Dissertation, Ohio State University.

SHANTZ, C. U.
1975   "The development of social cognition." In E. M. Hetherington (ed.), *Review of Child Development Research,* vol. 5. Chicago: University of Chicago Press.

SHAW, M. C. AND B. E. DUTTON
1962   "The use of the parent attitude research inventory with the parents of bright academic underachievers." *Journal of Educational Psychology* 53:203–08.

SHELDON, E.
1968   "Parental child-rearing attitudes and their relationship to cognitive functioning of their pre-adolescent sons." Unpublished Ph.D. Dissertation, Syracuse University.

SHOFFEITT, P. G.
1971   "The moral development of children as a function of parental moral judgments and child-rearing practices." Unpublished Ph.D. Dissertation, George Peabody College for Teachers.

SHORE, R. E.
1967   "Parental determinates of boys' internal-external control." Unpublished Ph.D. Dissertation, Syracuse University.

SIEGELMAN, M.
1965   "College student personality correlates of early parent-child relationships." *Journal of Consulting Psychology* 29:558–64.
1973   "Parent behavior correlates of personality traits related to creativity in sons and daughters." *Journal of Consulting Psychology* 40:43–47.

SILVERBERG, R. A.
1970   "The relationship of children's perceptions of parental behavior to the creativity of their children." Unpublished Ph.D. Dissertation, New York University.

SLATER, P. E.
1962   "Parental behavior and the personality of the child." *Journal of Genetic Psychology* 101:53–68.

SMITH, M. B.
1974   *Humanizing Social Psychology*. San Francisco: Jossey-Bass.

SMITH, T. E.
1970   "Foundations of parental influence upon adolescents: An application of social power theory." *American Sociological Review* 35:860–73.

SPREHN, G. C.
1973   "Correlates of parent behavior and locus of control in nine to twelve year old males." Unpublished Ph.D. Dissertation, Emory University.

STABENAU, J. R., J. TUPIN, M. WERNER, AND W. POLLIN
1965   "A comparative study of families of schizophrenics, delinquents, and normals." *Psychiatry* 28:45–59.

STERN, N. W.
1963   "Maternal personality, attitudes, and child-rearing practices, and their relation to child adjustment." Unpublished Ph.D. Dissertation, Northwestern University.

STEVENSON, H. W.
1961   "Social reinforcements in children as a function of CA, sex of E, and sex of S." *Journal of Abnormal and Social Psychology* 63:147–54.

STRAUS, M. A.
1964   "Power and support and structure of the family in relation to socialization." *Journal of Marriage and the Family* 26:318–26.

STRAUS, M. A. AND I. TALLMAN
1971   "SIMFAM: A technique for observational measurement and experimental study of families." In J. Adous, T. Condon, R. Hill, M. Straus, and I. Tallman (eds.), *Family Problem Solving*. Hinsdale, Ill.: Dryden Press.

STREISSGUTH, A. P. AND H. L. BEE
1972   "Mother-child interactions and cognitive development in children." In W. Hartup (ed.), *Research on Young Children*. Washington, D.C.: National Association for the Education of Young Children.

STRYKER, S.
1964   "The interactional and situations approaches." In H. T. Christensen (ed.), *Handbook of Marriage and the Family*. Chicago: Rand McNally.

SULLIVAN, H. S.
1953   *The Interpersonal Theory of Psychiatry*. New York: Norton.

SWAN, R. W.
1970   "Parental styles associated with conceptual development of preschool children." Unpublished Ph.D. Dissertation, University of Southern California.

SYMONDS, P.
1939   *The Psychology of Parent-Child Relationships*. New York: Appleton-Century-Crofts.

THIBAUT, J. W. AND H. H. KELLEY
1959   *The Social Psychology of Groups*. New York: Wiley.

THOMAS, D. L.
1968   "Parental control and support in socialization and adolescent conformity: A cross national study." Unpublished Ph.D. Dissertation, University of Minnesota.

THOMAS, D. L., V. GECAS, A. WEIGERT, AND E. ROONEY
1974   *Family Socialization and the Adolescent*. Lexington, Mass.: Health.

THOMAS, D. L. AND A. J. WEIGERT
1971   "Socialization and adolescent conformity to significant others: A cross-national analysis." *American Sociological Review* 36:835–47.
1973   "Socialization theory and the family: The problem of fit between form and context." *Social Science Information* 12:139–55.

TOEWS, W. F.
1966   "Self-esteem, perception of parental control and hostility of adolescents." Unpublished Ph.D. Dissertation, Brigham Young University.

TOTO, S. E.
1973   "Altering parental attitudes toward child-rearing practices and its effect on adolescent self-esteem." Unpublished Ph.D. Dissertation, Boston University, School of Education.

TOUSIGNANT, N. P.
1972   "Perceived parental environment and reported drug use among participants of drug rehabilitation programs." Unpublished Ph.D. Dissertation, Catholic University of America.

TOWNSEND, J. K.
1968   "Reports of parent behavior (RPBI) related to current behavior and MMPI scores in female psychiatric patients." Unpublished Ph.D. Dissertation, University of North Carolina at Chapel Hill.

TURBERG, J.
1966   "An investigation of the association of maternal attitudes and childhood obesity and the self-concept of the obese child." Unpublished Ph.D. Dissertation, New York University.

UNDERWOOD, B. J. AND J. J. SHAUGHNESSY
1975   *Experimentation in Psychology*. New York: Wiley.

VOGEL, W., C. G. LAUTERBACK, M. LIVINGSTON, AND H. HALLOWAY
1964   "Relationships between memories of their patient's behavior and psychodiagnosis in psychiatrically disturbed soldiers." *Journal of Consulting Psychology* 28:126–32.

VOLENSKI, L. T.
1972   "Parental attitudes and children's social behavior." Unpublished Ph.D. Dissertation, Oregon State University.

WALSH, A.
1956   *Self Concepts of Bright Boys with Hearing Difficulties*. New York: Teachers College, Columbia University.

WALTERS, J. AND N. STINNETT
1971   "Parental-child relationships: A decade review of research." *Journal of Marriage and the Family* 33:70–111.

WASHINGTON, D. V.
1963   "Discipline and conscience development." Unpublished Ph.D. Dissertation, Northwestern University.

WATSON, G.
1934   "A comparison of the effects of lax versus strict home training." *Journal of Social Psychology* 5:102–105.

WAXLER, N. E. AND E. G. MISHLER
1971   "Parental interaction with schizophrenic children and well siblings." *Archives of General Psychiatry* 25:223–31.

WEBER, M.
1947   *The Theory of Social and Economic Organization.* New York: Free Press.

WEIGERT, A. J. AND D. L. THOMAS
1971   "Family as a conditional universal." *Journal of Marriage and the Family* 33:188–94.

WEISS, A.
1965   "Parental discipline as perceived by behavior problem and non-behavior problem children." Unpublished Ph.D. Dissertation, New York University.

WETTER, J.
1970   "The relation of parent attitude to learning disorder." Unpublished Ph.D. Dissertation, University of California, Los Angeles.

WHITE, R. W.
1959   "Motivation reconsidered: The concept of competence." *Psychological Review* 66:297–333.

1963   "Ego and reality in psychoanalytic theory." *Psychological Issues, Monograph II,* vol. 3, no. 3. New York: International Universities Press.

WILKINS, M. A.
1970   "Comparisons of attitudes toward childrearing of parents of certain exceptional and normal children." Unpublished Ph.D. Dissertation, University of Texas at Austin.

WINDER, C. L. AND L. RAU
1962   "Parental attitudes, associated with social deviance in preadolescent boys." *Journal of Abnormal and Social Psychology* 64:418–24.

YARROW, M. R., J. D. CAMPBELL, AND R. V. BURTON
1968   *Child Rearing.* San Francisco: Jossey-Bass.

ZETTERBERG, H. L.
1954   *On Theory and Verification in Sociology.* Totowa, N.J.: Bedminster Press.

ZIMBARDO, P. G.
1969   *The Cognitive Control of Motivation.* Glenview, Ill.: Scott, Foresman.

ZUCKERMAN, M., B. H. BARRETT, AND R. M. BRAGIEL
1960   "The parental attitudes of parents of child guidance cases: I. Comparisons with normals, investigations of socioeconomic and family constellation factors, and relations to parents; reactions to the clinics." *Child Development* 31:401–17.

15

THE INFLUENCE OF SOCIAL CLASS ON SOCIALIZATION

Viktor Gecas

Interest in social class influences on child rearing and socialization in general has been increasing over the past 40 years and has produced a substantial, at times lively, often messy and chaotic literature, reflecting the influence of several disciplines and numerous perspectives. The early work, in the thirties and forties, was strongly influenced by Freudian theory of human development and focused primarily on such patterns of parental behavior as feeding practices, toilet training, and handling of sexual matters. The assumption was that these dimensions of parent-child interaction have a profound effect on later personality development. With the decline of psychoanalytic theory in this area, helped along by research such as Sewell's (1952) which found basically no relationship between these patterns of infant care and later personality development of the child, the emphasis shifted to a much broader range of variables dealing with parental behavior and to the quality of the parent-child relationship. At the same time, greater attention became directed toward the effects of social structure, especially social class, on patterns of socialization, reflecting largely the increasing influence of sociological perspectives.[1] Other disciplines have also left their mark—psychology, anthropology, education, sociolinguistics. This multidisciplinary fertilization has produced a literature characterized by numerous theoretical skirmishes and several major battles. Socialization is one of the more volatile topics in family sociology, especially when the focus is on social class, race, or ethnic comparisons.[2]

At this point we need to clarify our two major concepts, socialization and social class, and specify the parameters of our analysis. The concept of socialization usually refers to the process of development or change that a person undergoes as a result of social interaction and the learning of social roles. It encompasses such phenomena as a child learning language, a convict "learning the ropes" in prison, a student preparing to become a lawyer (for a discussion of various definitions of socialization, see Clausen et al., 1968). Although most of the research has dealt with *child* socialization, the process obviously continues throughout a person's life (cf. Brim, 1966, for a development of this view).

The process of socialization can be studied with regard to at least two different aspects: (1) the products of development and change in the person being socialized, such as the development of various competencies, cognitions, motivations, and feelings in the child; and, (2) with regard to the agents of socialization and factors in the social environment which influence them. This chapter deals with the latter aspect of socialization. Specifically, the focus is on parents as agents of socialization (their behavior, attitudes, and quality of the relationship with the child), and an inquiry into how their position in the stratification system affects their role as agents of socialization. It should be stressed, then, that socialization in this chapter does *not* refer to the development of the child, but rather to the behavior of the *parent* as it is directed toward the child (either consciously or unconsciously, explicitly or implicitly, intentionally or unintentionally). Undoubtedly this parental behavior has some effect on the child—if it did not, there wouldn't be much point in studying it. But the examination of that effect is left to other chapters in this volume. Throughout this chapter we will use the terms "socialization," "child rearing," "parental behavior," and "parent-child interaction" interchangeably.

The concept of social class is even more problematic than socialization. That there is social stratification in our society can hardly be disputed—people differ considerably in terms of power, prestige, and resources, and the material consequences of these differences are readily

NOTE: This project was supported by a postdoctoral fellowship (NIMH Grant 08268) at the University of California, Berkeley, and by Project 0295, Department of Rural Sociology, Agricultural Research Center, Washington State University, Appreciation is extended to Alan C. Kerckhoff, Jeylan T. Mortimer, and Ira L. Reiss for their helpful comments and criticisms of an earlier draft, and to Sally Gecas for her technical assistance.

apparent. However, there is considerable disagreement among scholars as to the nature of this social differentiation and the criteria to be used to designate different social strata.

At the heart of the conceptual difficulty is the difference between the Marxian concept of "class" and the Weberian concept of "status": " 'classes' are stratified according to their relation to the *production* and acquisition of goods; whereas 'status groups' are stratified according to the principles of their *consumption* of goods as represented by special 'styles of life' " (Weber, 1946:193). The American stratification system seems to reflect status groups more than class groups, yet, as Otto (1975) has argued in his excellent critique of family stratification research, social class is the predominant conceptual designation. We agree with Otto that the concept of status or socioeconomic status (SES) is a more appropriate stratification concept than social class when applied to American society. However, an inventory of the literature in an area dealing with stratification cannot afford the luxury of very precise and narrow definitions of major concepts, or it will wind up inventorying very little. We will use the concepts of social class and socioeconomic status (SES) as synonymous and interchangeable.

Essentially there are two questions that this chapter deals with: (1) *How* does social class affect parental behavior? (2) *Why* does social class affect parental behavior? The first question will be addressed through an inventory of findings on social class and socialization, to assess the degree to which social class makes a difference. The second question requires a consideration and a formulation of theories to explain class differences in socialization (if differences exist). Since this is a book on theory construction, most of our effort will be directed toward the second task.

METHODOLOGICAL PROBLEMS IN COMPARING FINDINGS ON SOCIAL CLASS AND SOCIALIZATION

Before we engage in this attempt to cumulative knowledge, it is important to consider some of the obstacles and pitfalls we face. It might help us understand why there is so much variability in findings which appear to be dealing with the same relationships.

Problems of comparability exist at every stage of the research process: research design, sampling, measurement, and data analysis. Table 15.1 shows the range in

Table 15.1. Description of Key Studies

REFERENCE	DESCRIPTION OF SAMPLE	MEASURE OF SOCIAL CLASS
Anderson (1936)	A representative, but nonprobability, national sample, including various sections of the country, SES levels, and types of community: 2,758 white families, 202 Negro families, with a total of 4,000 children between 1 and 12 years old.	Seven classes based on the Minnesota Scale for Occupational Classification: (1) professional, (2) semiprofessional and managerial, (3) clerical and skilled craftsmen, (4) farmers, (5) semiskilled, (6) slightly skilled, (7) day laborers.
Bayley and Schaefer (1960)	Part of the Berkeley Growth Study: 31 mothers interviewed and observed in 1928–1929 (children ages 1 to 3), and interviewed again in 1939–42 (children ages 12 to 14).	SES indicators include education, occupation, and income, and a composite scale.
Duvall (1946)	Purposive sample of 433 Negro and white (Jewish and non-Jewish) mothers of 5-year olds, interviewed in 1943–44. Data collected at "regular meetings of mothers' groups."	Four levels based on Warner's classification, combining occupation and education: (1) professionals and managers, (2) lower-order professionals, (3) skilled blue collar, (4) semi- and unskilled.
Davis and Havighurst (1946)	Interview study of 100 mothers of 5-year-old children, middle-class sample drawn from mothers of nursery school children; lower class from "areas of poor housing."	Two-level classification of SES following Warner, based on occupation, education, residential area, type of home, etc.
Sears et al. (1957); Maccoby and Gibbs (1954)	Interviews with 372 mothers of kindergarten children in two residential areas in Boston, parents American-born and living together.	Two-level SES classification following Warner: middle class, working class.
Miller and Swanson (1958)	112 boys in grades 7–8, all at least third-generation Americans, Christian, from unbroken homes, living in Detroit, Michigan.	Four SES levels assigned on the basis of occupation and education: upper middle, lower middle, upper working, lower working.
Miller and Swanson (1960)	Random sample of 479 white mothers with child under 19 and living with husband, in Detroit.	Four SES levels (same as above) based on U.S. Census occupation categories.

continued

Table 15.1.   Description of Key Studies Continued

REFERENCE	DESCRIPTION OF SAMPLE	MEASURE OF SOCIAL CLASS
Littman et al. (1957)	Random sample of 206 husband-wife pairs whose children's names appeared in the pre-school census and school roll lists for Eugene, Oregon.	Distinction between middle class and lower class based on same procedure as Sears et al. (1957).
Elder and Bowerman (1963)	A 40 percent random sample of seventh-grade white Protestant students from unbroken homes, who were in school in April and May of 1960 (in central Ohio and North Carolina) when a structured questionnaire was administered by teachers.	Two social classes based on U.S. Census occupation categories: middle and lower.
Rosen (1956)	The entire male population of sophomores in two public high schools in New Haven, Connecticut: 120 subjects, white, model age of 15.	Hollingshead Index of Social Position, based on education and occupation of father. Results in five social class levels.
Rosen (1961)	(A) A purposive sample of 427 mothers and sons (ages 8–14) from four states. (B) the entire population of boys (9–11) in elementary schools of three small Connecticut towns.	Same as above.
McKinley (1964)	Questionnaire data obtained from 260 eleventh- and twelfth-grade boys from three high schools around Boston.	Hollingshead Index of Social Position—five SES levels.
Waters and Crandall (1964)	Drawn from the Fels Research Institute longitudinal data. Direct observation (in the home) of mother-child interaction (N=107). Children of nursery school age. Observations conducted in the 1940s, 1950s, and 1960s.	Hollingshead Index of Social Position—five SES levels.
Hess and Shipman (1965)	163 Negro mothers and their 4-year old children. Mothers interviewed in the home and observed in the lab in interaction with their children in a structured game situation.	Four SES levels based on occupation and education: (1) upper middle: professional and managerial, (2) upper lower: skilled blue collar, (3) lower lower: semiskilled and unskilled, (4) ADC families, father absent.
Kohn (1969)	Washington Study (1956–57): Interviews with 339 mothers "from families broadly representative of the white middle and working classes"— but not representative of Washington, D.C. All mothers had fifth-grade children. In a random subsample of 82 families, the father and child were also interviewed.	Hollingshead Index of Social Position. SES levels 1, 2, and 3 combined to constitute "middle class"; levels 4 and 5 constitute "lower class."
	National Study (1964): representative national sample of 3,101 men. All SES levels except "unemployed" included.	Same as above.
Cook-Gumperz (1973)	Interviews with all of the 5-year-old children, and their mothers, who were enrolled in nine selected elementary schools in a "working class" area, and five schools in a "middle class" area, around London, England, in 1964. N=236 mother-child pairs.	SES based on education and occupation of both parents. Three SES categories: middle, working, and "mixed."
Bernstein and Henderson (1973)	Subsample of 50 middle-class and 50 lower-class mothers drawn from the sample described above (Cook-Gumperz).	Same as above.
Erlanger (1974)	A secondary analysis of retrospective data from a national survey for the Violence Commission; 1136 adults (white and black), in 100 clusters in all parts of the U.S.	SES indicator: "What [class] would you say your family was when you were growing up— middle class or working class?"
Thomas et al. (1974)	Questionnaire surveys of high school adolescents in Minneapolis (N=620), St. Paul (N=447), New York (N=365), and 480 freshmen at San Francisco State University during 1967–68.	Two levels of SES based on father's occupation: "blue collar" (lower class) and "white collar" (middle class).
Scheck and Emerick (1976)	All available ninth-grade males in eight midwestern public high schools (N=552).	Hollingshead Index of Social Position, with education and occupation of father used separately and in combination.

sample size from several dozen to several thousand cases, from procedures based on random selection and purposive quota samples; and they cover a wide range of populations—children, adolescents, mothers, fathers, couples, families. Most of the research designs are based on interview surveys, but others are also represented, such as questionnaire surveys and laboratory-observational studies. With regard to data analysis, most of the studies reviewed reported percentage differences between social class categories, along with tests of significance. A small proportion also had measures of association. The specificity of relationships and range of controls utilized varied considerably—some controlled or specified variables which would be expected to affect the relationships studied, such as sex of parent and of child, age of child, religion. A problem which Bronfenbrenner's (1958) survey was especially sensitive to was the specification of the time during which the parental behavior in the analysis occurred. Often the difference between the date at which the information was obtained and the actual period to which the information refers was difficult to determine from the research reports. This problem is especially serious in studies which depended on retrospective accounts given by subjects about earlier periods of their socialization.

But probably the biggest problems in comparing and synthesizing research stem from differences in measurement and categorization. Social class seems to be especially plagued by these problems, stemming from lack of consensus on several key issues: (1) whether social class is a discrete or a continuous variable; (2) whether it is unidimensional or multidimensional; (3) whether social differentiation is a function of the local community or society at large; (4) whether it is a subjective phenomenon scaled by self-report or an objective phenomenon to be measured by observable indicators (cf. Hess, 1970a, and Otto, 1975, for more extensive discussions of these issues).

Table 15.1 describes the indicators and class categories used in studies of social class and socialization. They range from simple dichotomies, i.e., middle class versus lower class, to multilevel scales such as the five-category Hollingshead Index of Social Position, to continuous scales such as Duncan's (1961) SEI scale. One of the serious problems of categorization is the variation in the use of cutoff points for separating, for example, middle-class from lower-class subjects. If the social class indicator is occupational prestige, some establish the cutoff point at the mean of the distribution, others make categorical distinctions between types of occupation, such as "white collar" versus "blue collar." The problem of categorization and comparison becomes more difficult when multiple indicators are used, i.e., occupation, education, income, residence. The most frequently used measure found in our review was the Hollingshead Index of Social Position, based on a combination of father's

education and occupation. Otto (1975) argues strongly against the use of composite measures of social status:

> The construction of composite indicators is warranted only if it has first been shown that the composite is a unidimensional construct with respect to the variables of interest.... Otherwise, one runs the risk of concealing rather than revealing relationships [325].

He condemns their frequent use in family research because "such ensembles tend to be atheoretical and ad hoc; they mask rather than expose relationships; they promote conceptual invalidity; they contribute to a confusion of findings rather than to a cumulative family theory" (1975:325).

Similar criticisms can be directed to the range and combinations of indicators used in measuring the various dependent variables (cf. Tables 15.2 to 15.5). These problems raise the serious questions of validity and comparability. For example, to what extent do these items drawn from different studies measure parental use of physical punishment? "Was the child spanked in the last month?" (Anderson, 1936); "What is the most successful way to get a child to obey?" (Davis and Havighurst, 1946): "How often does your (mother/father) discipline or punish you by spanking, slapping, or striking you?" (Elder and Bowerman, 1963). These items all appear to get at *some* aspect of physical punishment, but they are clearly not identical.

In view of these methodological differences, we should not be surprised at the considerable variation in findings dealing with the same concepts and, as a result, at average correlations that are low. But we push on in spite of these obstacles, deriving some comfort from Bronfenbrenner's (1958) observation:

> The possibility of obtaining interpretable findings . . . rests on the long chance that major trends, if they exist, will be sufficiently marked to override the effects of bias arising from variations in sampling and methods [406].

INVENTORY OF EMPIRICAL GENERALIZATIONS

We have adopted several guidelines in the formulation of empirical generalizations which should mitigate against the feeling of hopelessness at trying to make sense out of this empirical diversity, on the one hand, and guard against the tendency to make facile generalizations, largely on the basis of investigators' generous interpretations of their own findings, on the other. (1) We are more interested in the *strength* of relationships than in their statistical significance, and so will be especially concerned with measures of association or (if these are not reported) with the extent of percentage differences. (2) The degree to which there is consensus on a particular relationship from a number of studies will be used as a second criterion for assessing generalizations. (3) Greater weight in interpreting the relationships will be given to the findings of major studies in the area. In summary, our confidence in an empirical generalization about social class and child rearing will be based on the strength of reported associations and on the degree of consensus between various studies, with an emphasis on the results of the most representative and competent studies.

The dependent variables in this inventory are rather diverse but can be grouped into five main categories of parental behavior and parent-child interaction: (1) modes of parental control, (2) affective relationship between parent and child, (3) power relationship, (4) emphasis on independence and achievement, and (5) nature of parent-child communication. Fortunately we do not have to start from scratch in reviewing findings on social class and child rearing, but can rely to some extent on several past reviews. Bronfenbrenner's (1958) assessment of research on several of the categories of variables mentioned and Erlanger's (1974) review and critique of research on class differences in use of physical punishment are especially relevant. Also Hess (1970a) and Kerckhoff (1972) are good overviews of the literature on social class and socialization. We have relied on these previous reviews when appropriate and modified and expanded them when necessary in conducting our own assessment of the literature.

Social Class and Modes of Control

"Modes of parental control" has been the most popular focus of research of social class and socialization. It refers to the manner in which the parent disciplines the child, constrains him, or channels his behavior. The strategies of control examined have ranged from reliance on reasoning with the child to use of physical punishment, with the latter receiving the greatest attention.

One of the most consistent claims in the literature is that there is a greater reliance on the use of physical punishment as a means of disciplining and controlling the child in lower-class families than in middle-class families, and our own assessment of the research is generally consistent with this view (see Table 15.2). But the relationship is rather weak and highly variable. In comparing the findings of the 14 studies reported in Table 15.2, we find that the percentage point difference between middle-class (MC) and lower-class (LC) parents ranges from +6 (i.e., MC more frequently using physical punishment) to −41 (LC more), with an average difference of −9 percentage points. Correlations, when available, are found to be usually in the low .20s, and they tend to be lower for girls than boys. Of the 18 relationships for which significance levels are reported, only eight are statistically significant at the p<.05 level. In general, more recent studies appear to show less of a class difference than earlier studies. This corresponds with Bronfenbrenner's (1958) observation

that class differences in discipline techniques have been decreasing.

Our overall assessment is that there is a weak but generally consistent negative relationship between social class and parental use of physical punishment:

Generalization 1(G1): SES is negatively related to use of physical punishment.

Erlanger (1974) concluded that social class accounts for about 2 percent of the variance in parental reliance on physical punishment. Our assessment of the strength of the relationship (based on the consideration of additional studies) is somewhat more generous—about 4 percent of explained variance.

The weak relationship between social class and use of physical punishment is also evident in other methods of control. Middle-class parents are more likely to use techniques other than physical punishment to discipline or control the child, but there is considerable variation in findings reported by the various studies, and, overall, the relationships are not very strong (see Table 15.3). Use of reasoning and "psychological techniques" (i.e., shame and guilt) have the strongest positive relationships to SES, with average percentage point differences of +20 and +18 respectively. "Deprivation of privileges" and "isolation of the child" have somewhat weaker associations with SES, with average percentage differences of +9 and +13 respectively. "Scolding" and "ignoring behavior" have the weakest class associations, are the most variable, and are slightly negative in average class association (−6 and −1 respectively). Of these other discipline techniques, then, there is sufficient basis for stating as empirical generalizations only the first two mentioned:

G2: SES is positively related to use of reasoning.

G3: SES is positively related to use of shame and guilt.

For each of these relationships the estimate of explained variance is between 3 percent and 4 percent.

But this is only part of the story regarding class differences in methods of control. Melvin Kohn (1969) suggests that it may be less important to know *what* parents do in disciplining their children than to determine *when* parents do it. Accordingly, he has focused on social class differences in the *circumstances* or conditions under which parents discipline children. Eight situations were specified by Kohn: when the child (1) plays wildly, (2) fights with brothers or sisters, (3) fights with other children, (4) loses his temper, (5) refuses to do what you tell him, (6) steals something, (7) smokes cigarettes, and (8) uses language parent disapproves of. Kohn found that middle-class parents (especially mothers) were quite discriminate in their use of physical punishment depending on whether the child's behavior was defined as "wild play" or as "loss of temper." They were much more likely to use physical punishment in the latter situation (40

Table 15.2. Findings of Major Studies on Use of Physical Punishment[a]

REFERENCE	PERCENT FAVORING PHYSICAL PUNISHMENT	SIGNIFICANCE LEVEL P	PERCENTAGE POINT DIFFERENCE
Anderson (1936)	Indicator: "Was child spanked in the last month?" Upper upper 61% (283)[b] Lower lower 78% (165)	<.001	−.17
Davis and Havighurst (1946)	Indicator: "What is the most successful way to get a child to obey?" Middle 53% (45) lower 51% (47)	N.S.	+2
Littman et al. (1957)	Indicator: Primary punishment for rule infraction Father-child: Middle 19% (85) lower 15% (121)	N.S.	+4
	Mother-child: Middle 12% (85) Lower 15% (121)	N.S.	−1
Sears et al. (1957)	Indicator: Frequency of spanking or slapping. Middle 17% (34) working 33% (57)	<.001	−16 r=−.26
Maccoby and Gibbs (1954)	Indicator: Scale on frequency of spanking ranging from 1 (never used) to 9 (very often used). Middle 3.9% (198) working 4.8% (174)	<.01	(.9 point on scale of 9)
Miller and Swanson (1958)	Indicator: "Suppose your child of 10 were to do something you feel is very wrong, something you warned him against doing...." Upper middle 15% (33) Lower lower 31% (65)	N.S.	−16
Miller and Swanson (1960)	Indicator: "What ways have you found most useful with your boy to get him to do right and keep him from doing wrong?" *Sample I:* Middle 11% (38) working 52% (77)	<.001	−41
	Sample II: Middle 18% (57) working 35% (48)	<.05	−18
Bayley and Schaefer (1960)	Indicator: Degree of punitiveness—item not specified. 1929 sample: Boys (SES × punishment) Girls 1938 sample: Boys Girls		r=−.31 r=−.12 r=−.23 4=−.08
Elder and Bowerman (1963)	Indicator: "How often does your (mother/father) discipline or punish you by spanking, slapping, or striking you?" Use of physical punishment at least "once in a while." Father-son: Middle 37% (110) lower 44% (147)		−7
	Father-daughter: Middle 18% (53) lower 28% (96)		−10
	Mother-son: Middle 39% (114) lower 42% (138)		−3
	Mother-daughter: Middle 23% (65) lower 34% (119)		−11
Heinstein (1964) (cited in Erlanger, 1974)	Indicator: Physical punishment as usual method of punishment. *Sample I* Mother-son: College ed. 58% (80) No college 52% (352)	N.S.	+6
	Mother-daughter: College ed. 44% (72) No college 51% (304)	N.S.	−7
	Sample II Mother-son: College ed. 49% (88) No college 53% (321)	N.S.	−4

continued

Table 15.2. Findings of Major Studies on Use of Physical Punishment[a] Continued

REFERENCE	PERCENT FAVORING PHYSICAL PUNISHMENT	SIGNIFICANCE LEVEL P	PERCENTAGE POINT DIFFERENCE
	Mother-daughter: College ed. 38% (96) No college 55% (288)	<.01	−17
McKinley (1964)	Indicators: Use of "relatively severe techniques of discipline." Mother-child: Upper class 40% (62) Lower class 47% (92)	N.S.	−7
	Father-child: Upper class 33% (72) Lower class 49% (92)	<.05	−16
Waters and Crandall (1964)	Indicator: Scale ranging from "mild reprimands to severe punishment." SES and maternal behavior (sex of child did not make a difference).	<.01	r=−.25
Kohn (1963, 1969)	Indicator: Report that physical punishment is used occasionally or frequently versus infrequently or never. Mother-son: Middle 14% (79) working 16% (82)	N.S.	−2
	Mother-daughter: Middle 9% (75) working 16% (77)	N.S.	−7
Erlanger (1974)	Indicator 1: "As a child, were you spanked frequently, sometimes, or never?" Percent responding "frequently." Men: Middle 20% (25) working 35% (112) Women: Middle 25% (41) working 34% (90)		−15 −9
	Indicator 2: Approval of spanking in everyday situations. Percent who scored "high" on approval (white sample). College ed. 38% (59) h.s. or less 42% (137)		−4

[a]This builds on Erlanger's summary of the research on social class differences in use of physical punishment (1974:70–72). It is both a modification and an extension of his review.
[b]Number in parentheses indicates frequency.

percent versus 4 percent) because, Kohn argues, this represents to the parent the child's loss of self-control, a valued characteristic. Lower-class mothers, on the other hand, reported the use of physical punishment with essentially equal frequency in both situations (40 percent versus 43 percent). It is the consequences of the child's behavior, i.e., disruptive behavior in this case, which are most likely to elicit parental response. Gecas and Nye (1974) provide corroborative evidence for this suggestion that middle-class parents are more likely to respond to the child on the basis of their interpretation of the child's *intent* or motive for acting as he does, while lower-class parents are more likely to respond on the basis of the overt act. They found a greater difference in the way middle-class parents acted toward the child when he "accidentally breaks something" versus when he "intentionally disobeys" than there was in the responses of lower-class parents, especially for mothers. With regard to use of physical punishment, there was a 50 percentage point difference between the two situations for MC mothers compaired to a 34 percentage point difference for LC mothers. We can state these relationships as our fourth and fifth empirical generalizations:

G4: SES is positively related to discipline on the basis of child's motives and intentions.

G5: SES is negatively related to discipline on the basis of child's overt acts.

Kohn (1969) also reported an interesting sex difference in parental discipline: lower-class mothers were found to be more severe on daughters than sons when they "defiantly refuse to do what they are told"; there was no such marked difference for middle-class mothers. The finding is suggestive of greater sex role stereotyping in the lower class (i.e., greater expectations of obedience for girls than boys), but since there is no other research corroborating the finding, we are reluctant to state it as an empirical generalization.

Power Relationship between Parent and Child

"The nature of the power relationship between parent and child" refers essentially to the distinction between an authoritarian or autocratic relationship and an equalitarian or democratic relationship. Findings dealing with social class differences in the power relationship parallel to

Table 15.3. Other Modes of Control

REFERENCE	METHOD OF CONTROL OR DISCIPLINE			SIGNIFICANCE LEVEL	PERCENTAGE POINT DIFFERENCE OR CORRELATION COEFFICIENT
Anderson (1936)	Indicator: "Which of the following methods of controlling the child are used?"				
	Ages 1–5:	*Upper Class*	*Lower Class*		
	Reasoning	73% (200)	43% (68)	<.01	+30
	Deprivation of privileges	44% (121)	19% (30)	<.01	+25
	Scolding	42% (115)	63% (99)	<.01	−21
	Ignoring	41% (112)	12% (19)	<.01	+29
		Ages 6–12:			
	Reasoning	89% (82)	33% (15)	<.01	+56
	Deprivation of privileges	74% (68)	37% (17)	<.01	+37
	Scolding	53% (49)	67% (31)	N.S.	−14
	Ignoring	30% (28)	4% (2)	<.01	+26
	Isolation	38% (35)	9% (4)	<.01	+29
Davis and Havighurst	Indicator: Percentage of mothers mentioning various procedures as "most successful ways of getting children to obey."				
		Middle	*Lower*		
	Reasoning	53% (24)	57% (27)	N.S.	− 4
	Deprivation of privileges	0% (0)	6% (3)	N.S.	− 6
	Scolding	53% (24)	55% (26)	N.S.	− 2
	Isolation	13% (6)	17% (8)	N.S.	− 4
Sears et al. (1957)	Indicator: The extent to which each of these techniques is used to control child, on a scale ranging from 1 (never used) to 9 (frequently used). Correlations between SES and use of —				
	Reasoning			N.S.	r= .11
	Withdrawal of love			<.05	r=−.20
	Deprivation of privileges			<.05	r=−.11
	Isolation			N.S.	r= .06
	Ridicule			<.01	r=−.24

REFERENCE	METHOD OF CONTROL OR DISCIPLINE	*Father*		*Mother*		*Father*	*Mother*
Littman et al. (1957)	Indicator: Type of punishment for rule infraction.						
		Middle	*Lower*	*Middle*	*Lower*		
	Reasoning	19%	22%	20%	20%	− 3	0
	Scolding	34%	44%	39%	32%	−10	+7
	Isolation	12%	15%	33%	27%	− 3	+6
	Deprivation of privileges	12%	6%	4%	6%	+ 6	−2
	Ignoring	2%	6%	12%	13%	− 4	−1

REFERENCE	METHOD OF CONTROL OR DISCIPLINE			SIGNIFICANCE LEVEL	PERCENTAGE POINT DIFFERENCE OR CORRELATION COEFFICIENT
Miller and Swanson (1960)	Indicator: "What ways have you found most useful with your boy to get him to do right and keep him from doing wrong?" "Psychological techniques"—use of shame and guilt.				
	Sample I:				
	Middle 29% (33) working 9% (10)			<.01	+20
	Sample II:				
	Middle 38% (40) working 21% (22)			<.05	+17
Elder and Bowerman (1963)	Indicator: "How often does your (mother/father) discipline or punish you by nagging, yelling, scolding, criticizing, or making fun of you?" Percent using these negative verbal methods at least "once in a while."				
		Middle	*Lower*		
	Father-son	29%	36%		− 7
	Father-daughter	22%	30%		− 8
	Mother-son	33%	36%		− 3

continued

Table 15.3.   Other Modes of Control Continued

REFERENCE	METHOD OF CONTROL OR DISCIPLINE			SIGNIFICANCE LEVEL	PERCENTAGE POINT DIFFERENCE OR CORRELATION COEFFICIENT
	Mother-daughter	28%	32%		− 4
Kohn (1969)	Conditions under which mother disciplines child. Use of physical punishment when son—				
	Condition I: Plays wildly—"described as willful aggression or destruction":				
	Middle 4% working 43%			<.05	−39
	Condition II: Loses his temper—"described as violent or aggressive outburst":				
	Middle 40% working 40%			N.S.	0
	Mother's responses when their children defiantly refuse to do as they are told.				
		Middle	*Working*		
	Mother-son:				
	Physical punishment	13% (6)	0% (0)	<.05	+13
	Scold, admonish, threaten	59% (27)	66% (21)	N.S.	− 7
	Do nothing	9% (4)	34% (11)	<.05	−25
	Mother-daughter:				
	Physical Punishment	9% (3)	25% (7)	N.S.	−16
	Scold, admonish, threaten	63% (21)	57% (16)	N.S.	+ 6
	Do nothing	12% (4)	4% (1)	N.S.	+ 8

some extent those on modes of control (the two variables are not unrelated). However, they appear to be more consistent and the relationships stronger for the power variable.

Duvall's (1946) distinction between "traditional" and "developmental" conceptions of the "good mother" and the "good child" was an early attempt to focus on the power dimension (among other things) between parent and child. "Traditional" conceptions of parent and child emphasize discipline and control of the child; "developmental" conceptions stress a democratic, evolving relationship. Duvall found that 39 percent of the responses of upper-class mothers were "traditional" and 61 percent "developmental," compared to 60 percent and 40 percent respectively for lower-class mothers. The percentage differences were even greater in maternal conceptions of the "good child," averaging 36 percentage points between the two social classes. Elder and Bowerman (1963), in assessing the degree to which the parent is perceived as autocratic or authoritarian by adolescents about decisions concerning the child, found smaller SES differences (average difference = 9 percent) but in the same direction. Waters and Crandall (1964) reported a correlation between SES and maternal restrictiveness of the child of r = − .43. Bayley and Schaefer (1960) found correlations between SES and degree of equalitarianism in parent-child relationships almost as strong for boys (r = .35 and .41 for the 1929 and 1938 samples respec-

tively) but weaker for girls (r = .20 and .03). In summary, the evidence is relatively firm for the following two generalizations:

G6: SES is positively related to equalitarian relationship between parent and child.

G7: SES is negatively related to autocratic relationship between parent and child.

Parental Support, Affection, and Involvement

This category refers to the affective dimension of the parent-child relationship—the degree of support, affection, and involvement the parent expresses in dealing with the child. It is sometimes considered as the complementary dimension to parental control, and the two have been combined as orthogonal dimensions of social relations in general (cf. Parsons and Bales, 1955, distinction between instrumental and expressive processes in small groups), and parent-child interaction in particular (cf. Becker, 1964, and Thomas et al., 1974).

Our inventory of findings shows a rather consistent, positive relationship between social class and parental affection and involvement. Along with the evidence on support and affection in Table 15.4, Zunich (1962), McKinley (1964), Rosen (1964), and Hess and Shipman (1968) found a positive relationship between SES and parental involvement with the child, i.e., parents being

Table 15.4. Parental Support and Affection

REFERENCE	VARIABLES, INDICATORS, AND FINDINGS	SIGNIFICANCE LEVEL	PERCENTAGE POINT DIFFERENCE OR CORRELATION
Bayley and Schaefer (1960)	Variable (items not specified).		
	Expresses affection: *1929*		
	Boys (18)		r= .24
	Girls (16)		r= .04
	Cooperative: Boys (18)		r= .32
	Girls (16)		r= .15
	1938		
	Expresses affection: Boys (18)		r= .21
	Girls (16)		r=−.12
	Cooperative: Boys (18)		r= .22
	Girls (16)		r= .18
Sears et al. (1957)	Variable: Parental warmth toward child, based on analysis of open-ended questions.		
	Mother-child:		
	Middle 51% (101) working 37% (64)	<.01	+14
	Father-child:		
	Middle 60% (119) working 56% (97)	N.S.	+ 4
Elder and Bowerman (1963)	Variable: Use of "symbolic rewards." "How often does your (mother/father) ever give you praise, encouragement, or approval for what you do?" Percent responding "frequently" or "very often."		

	Middle	*Lower*		
Mother-son	39% (115)	34% (113)		+ 5
Mother-daughter	58% (166)	41% (143)		+17
Father-son	35% (103)	28% (93)		+ 7
Father-daughter	53% (152)	36% (125)		+17

REFERENCE	VARIABLES, INDICATORS, AND FINDINGS	SIGNIFICANCE LEVEL	PERCENTAGE POINT DIFFERENCE OR CORRELATION
Waters and Crandall (1964)	Variables based on Fels Parent Behavior Scales (N=107). SES correlated with—		
	Maternal affectionateness	N.S.	r= .08
	Maternal approval of child's actions	<.01	r= .26
	Maternal protectiveness	N.S.	r= .16
Kohn (1969)	Variable: Father's supportiveness, based on four-item index dealing with encouragement, praise, and advice father gives child.		

	Middle	*Working*		
Father-son, reported by:				
Mothers	51% (43)	29% (21)	<.05	+22
Fathers	64% (16)	36% (9)	<.05	+28
Children	68% (17)	24% (6)	<.05	+44
Father-daughter, reported by:				
Mothers	37% (30)	28% (20)	N.S.	+ 9
Fathers	19% (4)	9% (1)	N.S.	+10
Children	15% (3)	18% (2)	N.S.	− 3

REFERENCE	VARIABLES, INDICATORS, AND FINDINGS
Thomas et al. (1974)	Variable: Parental support, measured by a four-item index dealing with parental praise, comfort, and help, ranging from 4 (low) to 20 (high).

Samples		*Middle*	*Lower*	*Scale Point Difference*
San Francisco:	Mother	15.2 (317)	15.0 (163)	+ .2
	Father	14.1 (317)	13.4 (163)	+ .7
Minneapolis:	Mother	14.7 (322)	14.5 (298)	+ .2
	Father	14.6 (322)	13.5 (298)	+1.1
St. Paul:	Mother	14.8 (340)	14.8 (107)	0
	Father	14.4 (340)	13.6 (107)	+ .8
New York:	Mother	15.1 (252)	15.6 (113)	− .5
	Father	14.9 (252)	13.9 (113)	+1.0

continued

Table 15.4. Parental Support and Affection Continued

REFERENCE	VARIABLES, INDICATORS, AND FINDINGS	SIGNIFICANCE LEVEL	PERCENTAGE POINT DIFFERENCE OR CORRELATION
Scheck and Emerick (1976)	Variable: Loving, measured on a 5-point Likert-type scale. Father's education × loving:		
	Mother-son	p<.01	r= .12
	Father-son	p<.01	r= .13
	Father's occupation × loving:		
	Mother-son	N.S.	r= .06
	Father-son	p<.01	r= .11

supportive, attentive, helping, talking, and playing with the child.

G8: SES is positively related to parental affection and involvement.

But here, again, the findings are not uniform. Percentage point differences range from −3 to +44, with an average difference of +15. Correlations appear in the mid-.20s for boys, and in the mid-.10s for girls. Sex of parent appears to be important, but it is difficult to tell in which direction. Findings from Bowerman and Elder (1964), Kohn (1969), Rosen (1964), Rosenberg (1965), and Thomas et al. (1974) indicate that there is a greater class difference in fathers' support and involvement; Sears et al. (1957) found a greater class difference in mothers' support; and Elder and Bowerman (1963) found essentially no difference. There are some other strains in the research literature which bear on this issue but are not consistent enough to be much more than suggestive. Brim (1957) observes that there is a tendency for each parent to be relatively more affectionate and lenient with a child of the opposite sex, while more strict with a child of the same sex (cf. Maccoby and Jacklin, 1974, ch. 9, for a summary of studies supportive of this cross-sex relationship). But Bronfenbrenner's (1961a) analysis indicates that this relationship is pronounced only in lower-class families. Kohn's (1969) finding that lower-class wives have a strong preference for their husbands to perform the disiplinarian role with regard to sons, and middle-class wives' strong preference for husbands to be supportive of sons, is related to Bronfenbrenner's observation. Also, Mortimer (1976) found a positive relationship between family income and son's feeling of closeness to his father. These are suggestive findings which still need greater specification and consistency to be theoretically useful.

Independence and Achievement Emphasis

The relationship between social class and parents' emphasis on independence and achievement for their children appears positive, consistent, and fairly strong. Bronfenbrenner's review (1958, especially his tables 8 and 9) shows this to be one of the strongest class-related child-rearing variables. In assessing these findings he states:

> By and large, the middle-class mother expects more of her child than her working-class counterpart. All five of the statistically significant differences support this tendency and most of the remaining results point in the same direction. The conclusion is further underscored by the findings on class differences in parental aspirations for the child's academic progress [415].

Bronfenbrenner found nine of the 11 reported relationships to be statistically significant and in the direction of middle-class parents having higher academic aspirations for the child than lower-class parents. What is even more important is that the levels of association range from moderate to strong. Bayley and Schaefer (1960) reported correlation coefficients (between SES and degree of autonomy granted to child) of r = .40 and .13 in their samples of boys, and r = .22 and .23 for the girls' samples. Waters and Crandall (1964) reported a correlation of r = .34 between SES and parents' "acceleration attempts" (i.e., emphasis on independent problem-solving techniques and achievement skills). Rosen (1956, 1961) found substantial class differences in achievement motivation scores (n Ach): 83 percent of the upper classes scored high compared to 23 percent of the lower class. The following empirical generalization seems to be fairly well grounded:

G9: SES is positively related to emphasis on independence and achievement.

Communication and Linguistic Behavior

To some extent, the nature of communication and linguistic behavior between parent and child is evident in all of the previous variables considered, so there will be some overlap between these findings and those previously examined, especially for parental modes of control. But there is also a distinctive slant to the communication variables which justifies their separate consideration.

Table 15.5 is a sample of studies dealing with social class and communication between parent and child, showing the types of variables considered and the strength

Table 15.5. Communication and Linguistic Behavior

REFERENCE	VARIABLES, INDICATORS, AND FINDINGS	SIGNIFICANCE LEVEL	PERCENTAGE DIFFERENCE OR CORRELATION
Elder and Bowerman (1963)	Variable: Parental explanations for rules. Percent of children indicating parents *infrequently* explain rules.		
	Middle *Lower*		
	Father-son 33% 40%		− 7
	Mother-son 30% 38%		− 8
	Father-daughter 22% 39%		−17
	Mother-daughter 17% 25%		− 8
Waters and Crandall (1964)	Variable: Coerciveness of maternal suggestions. Degree to which suggestions to child require optional (low) or mandatory (high) compliance (N=107).	<.01	r=−.43
Miller and Swanson (1960)	Variable: Obedience requests—degree to which they are arbitrary or explained. Percent explained. Middle 64% (27) working 26% (10)	<.01	+38
Hess and Shipman (1965)	Variable: Mode of communication between mother and child: person- versus status-oriented.		
	Middle *Lower*		
	Person-oriented 37% (15) 21% (7)		+16
	Status-oriented 28% (11) 51% (17)		−23
	Information mothers would give to child on first day of school.		
	Middle *Lower*		
	Imperative 49% (19) 87% (32)		−38
	Instructive 39% (15) 16% (6)		+23
	Supportive 77% (30) 43% (16)		+34
	Preparatory 33% (13) 8% (3)		+25
Cook-Gumperz (1973)	Variables: Imperative control, positional control, and personal control. *Imperative* control—of the four indicators two were statistically significant (p<.05) with regard to mean differences between middle class and working class: MC<WC. *Positional* control—of the five indicators, one was significant (p<.01): MC<WC. *Personal* control—of the 12 indicators, seven were significant (p<.05): MC>WC.		
Bernstein and Henderson (1973)	Variable: Use of language in teaching child. (1) Middle-class parents found to place greater emphasis on use of language in dealing with interpersonal relations; working-class parents place greater emphasis on use of language in the transmission of skills. (2) Within the skill area, MC parents place greater emphasis on the transmission of principles of "how things work." (No significance levels reported).		

of their relationships to SES. The first three studies (Elder and Bowerman, 1963; Waters and Crandall, 1964; and Miller and Swanson, 1960) deal with the relationship between social class and parental use of commands and imperatives in speaking to the child. Hoffman (1960) refers to this as parental use of "unqualified power assertions," which take the form of threats and direct commands and the refusal to discuss alternatives, explain the request, or reason with the child. The verbal communication in this relationship is typically one way, from parent to child. Hoffman found a negative relationship between SES and parental use of "unqualified power assertions." Elder and Bowerman (1963) and Miller and Swanson (1960) use the extent to which parent explains

rules and requests for obedience as the indicator of this variable. For Waters and Crandall (1964) and Hess and Shipman (1964) the indicator is use of imperatives and coerciveness of suggestions. Each of these studies shows lower-class parents to rely more on the use of commands and imperatives, and middle-class parents to more likely explain the reasons for a rule or request. The percentage point differences between the two class categories range from 7 to 38, and the one reported correlation coefficient is substantial, r = .43. The empirical generalization can be stated as:

G10: SES is negatively related to parental use of commands and imperatives.

A second aspect of the communication dimension deals with the nature or referent for parental explanations to the child. Bernstein (1970) distinguished between "positional appeals" and "personal appeals." The former relate the child's behavior to the norms associated with a particular status or position in a social system; i.e., "Girls don't act that way" reflects a sex status rule, or "You're too young to cross the street" calls forth an age status rule. In "personal appeals," on the other hand, the focus is upon the child as an individual rather than upon his formal status; i.e., "If you eat any more cookies, you will get sick" or "Your brother will be unhappy if you take his toy." Personal appeals take into account the individual and interpersonal components of a social relationship, and stress the child's individuality; positional appeals emphasize the child's commonality with others in his status. The evidence, though somewhat skimpy (Cook-Gumperz, 1973: Hess and Shipman, 1965), is consistent in indicating that middle-class parents rely more on person-oriented communications, while lower-class parents rely more on position-oriented appeals in dealing with the child:

G11: SES is positively related to use of personal appeals.

G12: SES is negatively related to use of postional appeals.

A third aspect of communication deals with styles of teaching the child. Bernstein makes a distinction between parental conceptions of the child's learning as either "self-regulating" or "didactic" (Bernstein and Henderson, 1973). Parents who have a "self-regulating" conception of learning teach the child by giving him autonomy to explore, but also emphasize the principles behind why things work the way they do. In "didactic" learning, parents are more likely to simply show the child how a thing works; that is, they focus more on the operations than the principles. The idea is interesting, but evidence for a class difference in these two styles of teaching and conceptions of learning is rather thin (although the notion is congruent with some of the previous relationships between SES and communication). The expectation is that middle-class parents emphasize the teaching of principles (and have a self-regulating conception of learning), whereas lower-class parents emphasize the teaching of operations (and have a didactic conception of learning). Bernstein and Henderson's (1973) research is reported as supporting this relationship (although percentage differences and significance levels were not reported). Baldwin and Baldwin (1973), in a laboratory-observational study of mother-child interaction, found black lower-class mothers were significantly more likely than white middle-class mothers to adopt a "*didactic* teaching role in free play." In support of their interpretation, Bernstein and Henderson (1973) cite other research which indicates similar results: Bernstein and Young (1967) asked mothers to rank in order of importance six possible uses of toys, and found middle-class mothers

ranked "to find out about things" more highly than did working-class mothers; Jones (1966) reported that middle-class mothers saw the role of the nursery school child as an active role; whereas working-class mothers were more likely to consider "play" in the nursery school to have less educational significance. In general, while the strength of these relationships is unknown, there seems to be some convergence of evidence for the following generalizations:

G13: SES is positively related to emphasis on self-regulating teaching-learning.

G14: SES is negatively related to emphasis on didactic teaching-learning.

Overview of Empirical Generalizations

Our brief journey through the empirical literature on social class and socialization has produced 14 generalizations. They vary in strength and extent of empirical support, but none of them are particularly strong relationships. The best we can say for most of them is that the findings upon which they are based are generally consistent. The explained variance in most cases is less than 10 percent. This is hardly an empirical bedrock upon which to build theory. If this is all that were involved (the explanation of such weak relationships), the enterprise of theory construction on this topic would not be worth the effort. We would be building castles on quicksand. But the process of explaining a consistent, if small, relationship between a major molar variable like social class and important dependent variables may lead us to new concepts and variables which not only sharpen for us what it is about SES that has an effect on socialization but increase the amount of the dependent variable which we are able to explain. It is primarily with this latter possibility in mind that we consider theories of social class and socialization.

INVENTORY OF THEORIES AND ANALYTIC PERSPECTIVES ON SOCIAL CLASS AND SOCIALIZATION

The topic of socialization has historically been a battleground for numerous theories. Most of the major theoretical paradigms (in Kuhn's sense, 1970) in the social and behavioral sciences have had something to say about how the infant becomes a person and how the person changes over his life course. But the number of theories decreases considerably when we limit our topic to the influence of social class on parent-child interaction. To be sure, some of the general theories still have something to say on this relationship. But generally their usefullness in accounting for the findings in this area has yet to be established.

Most of our attention will focus on theories "indige-

nous'' to the area. These are typically theories of the
''middle range,'' i.e., are concerned with explaining a
more limited range of social phenomena, are less abstract
than general theories, and are closer to the empirical data.
Since we are interested in explaining social class differences in socialization, theories about this relationship
will differ mainly in terms of the *intervening* concepts and
variables that they utilize to link social class to parent-
child interaction. A distinction can be made between
those indigenous theories which focus on *ideational* concepts, such as values, beliefs, and ideologies; those which
emphasize the *structure* or form of social relations and
group processes; and those that posit *psychological* concepts as the mechanisms which relate social class to
parental behavior. We will call these three types of
theories ideational, structural, and psychological respectively.

Ideational Theories

Both historically and in terms of the development of
ideas on the relationship between social class and socialization, it is appropriate to start with Bronfenbrenner's classic synthesis and interpretation of studies conducted up to the late 1950s. By carefully arranging studies
in chronological order Bronfenbrenner was able to show
orderly change in parental practices where before there
appeared contradictory findings. Comparing the results of
15 studies conducted from 1932 to 1957, Bronfenbrenner
showed that American mothers had become more ''permissive'' with regard to such infant care patterns as
feeding, weaning, and bowel and bladder training, but
that these changes had been greater for middle-class
mothers than for lower-class mothers. In fact, from 1930
until about 1945, lower-class mothers were consistently
reported to be more permissive than middle-class
mothers. They were more likely to breast-feed, to follow
a self-demand schedule, to wean the child later, and to
begin toilet training at a later age. After World War II,
middle-class mothers have been reported as more permissive in each of these areas (1958:424).

What is of special interest to us here is Bronfenbrenner's explanation of *why* these changes have occurred and
why the class differences may be expected to continue.
He observed that changes in the pattern of infant care
employed by middle-class mothers closely corresponded
to the changes in practice advocated by presumed experts.
He cites Wolfenstein's (1953) content analysis of the
United States Children's Bureau bulletins on infant care,
for the time period roughly comparable to his study. She
describes the advice given to mothers during the period
1929–38 as emphasizing regularity, rigid scheduling, and
strictness in dealing with the infant. But in the succeeding
period a shift had taken place, and the experts were
advocating leniency, indulgence, and permissiveness in
dealing with the infant. The prevailing academic conceptions of human nature and child development had shifted

during this time from Watsonian psychology to various
neo-Freudian-based psychologies, and this was reflected
in the advocation of more relaxed relations between
parent and child. Bronfenbrenner argued that middle-
class mothers were more likely than lower-class mothers
to be exposed to current information on child care. He
concluded that middle-class parents changed their practices because they were influenced by what the experts
told them. For lower class-parents, who are less educated
and less exposed to professional advice, changes in
child-rearing patterns came slower.

Bronfenbrenner offers this general proposition to explain changes in child rearing:

> Child-rearing practices are likely to change most quickly in
> those segments of society which have closest access and are
> most receptive to the agencies or agents of change, e.g.,
> public media, clinics, physicians, and counselors [1958:411].

This proposition suggests that the mechanism by which
social class affects parental behavior is the parents' *differential exposure* to mass media and professional advice.
And since middle-class parents have closer access and are
more receptive to these agents of change than are lower-
class parents, they are more likely to change. The logical
sequence can be restated as:

$$\text{SES} \xrightarrow{(+)} \begin{array}{l} \text{degree of} \\ \text{exposure to} \\ \text{agents of} \\ \text{change regarding} \\ \text{ideas about} \\ \text{child rearing.} \end{array} \xrightarrow{(+)} \begin{array}{l} \text{change in child-} \\ \text{rearing practices} \end{array}$$

This model, of course, locates the *content* of the ideas
about child rearing and their source of change in the
''agents or agencies of change,'' i.e., the mass media and
various categories of professionals who write on matters
of child rearing. It says nothing about differences in
conditions of life associated with social class per se which
could be a source of values, ideas, and beliefs about
child-rearing. In other words, Bronfenbrenner's analysis
looks outside the class and family systems to explain
changes in ideas about child-rearing. In fact, since these
ideas and beliefs reflect changes and developments in
academic spheres, which are difficult to predict, they are
left unexamined.

Most of the other ''ideational theories'' of class and
socialization assume a functional link between the class
structure in society and child-rearing practices. They
focus on differences in conditions of life associated with
social class position (especially conditions dealing with
the occupational and economic spheres) which give rise to
values and orientations which parents hold, which in turn
affect their patterns of child-rearing. In that sense, they
are part of the broader intellectual tradition in sociology
which has been concerned with the social structural bases
of knowledge and belief—the tradition of Marx, Durkheim, Weber, and Mannheim.

By far the most comprehensive and carefully grounded theory in this group is that of Melvin Kohn (1959, 1963, 1969). Kohn concentrates on occupation as the most salient aspect of social class and distinguishes between "white collar" occupations and "blue collar" occupations. He argues that the occupational conditions characteristic of these two groups give rise to certain *adaptive* values and perspectives which are transmitted by the parents in the socialization of their children—both directly as conscious attempts to inculcate values in their offspring and indirectly through different styles of parent-child interaction.

This provides a somewhat different interpretation of Bronfenbrenner's findings. Whereas Bronfenbrenner interpreted the differences in socialization practices between middle-class and lower-class parents as primarily a historical phenomenon, Kohn sees these changes as reflecting the influence of deep-seated and relatively enduring value differences between the two social classes. These values are as enduring as the occupational conditions from which they emerge, and they do not seem to have changed appreciably over the past half century. That is why, Kohn maintains, there was almost no change reported by Bronfenbrenner in the *quality* of the parent-child relationship characteristic of middle-class and lower-class families: (1) parent-child relationships in the middle class were consistently reported as more accepting, equalitarian, and supportive, while those in the lower class were reported as more concerned with maintaining order and obedience; (2) middle-class parents had higher expectations for the child with regard to responsibility, competence, and progress in school; (3) lower-class parents were consistently more likely to employ physical punishment in disciplining the child, while middle-class parents relied more on reasoning, guilt, and other "psychological" methods. These characteristics of parent-child relationships are more closely connected to the *values* that parents hold. The specific infant care techniques which were found to have changed, such as weaning and toilet training, do not indicate a change in basic values. On the contrary, Kohn maintains that the values middle-class parents hold predispose them to be receptive to and to seek out advice on child-rearing techniques from experts and other sources which will help them achieve their goals more effectively (1969:7).

What, then, are the relevant conditions of life associated with middle-class and lower-class occupations and the values that they give rise to, and how are these values expressed in parent-child interaction? To answer these questions, we will have to take a closer look at Kohn's theory and evaluate it in terms of its degree of empirical support.

Overview of Kohn's Theoretical Rationale

Kohn's starting point is the assumption that the beliefs, values, and ideologies that people hold and their behavioral expressions can be traced to their position in social structure (1969:8). And the most important aspect of social structure at the societal level is social class, because social class so pervasively affects conditions of life:

> Members of different social classes, by virtue of enjoying or suffering different conditions of life, come to see the world differently—to develop different conceptions of social reality, different aspirations and hopes and fears, different conceptions of the desirable [1963:471].

This statement from Kohn provides the logic and the link for his analysis of the effect of social class on parental behavior. The concept of *values*— which Kohn defines as "conceptions of the desirable," which serve as criteria for choice and guides to action (1969:7, 18), becomes the key analytic concept for bridging the gap between position in the stratification system and child socialization. Values in general, but parental values in particular, i.e., "parents' conceptions of what characteristics would be most desirable for boys or girls the age of their own children" (1963:473), are a function of the *conditions of life* associated with class position. The conditions of life which Kohn is most interested in are found primarily in the occupational sphere and are conditions which are conducive to or restrictive of the expression of self-direction in work. By occupational self-direction Kohn means "the use of initiative, thought and independent judgment in work" (1969:140).

In discussing the conditions of life distinctive of different classes, Kohn (1969) identifies three ways in which middle-class occupations (white collar) differ from lower-class occupations (blue collar). First, white-collar occupations typically require the individual to deal more with the manipulation of ideas, symbols, and interpersonal relations, whereas blue-collar occupations deal more with the manipulation of physical objects and require less interpersonal skill. Second, white-collar occupations involve work that is more complex, requires greater flexibility, thought, and judgment, while in blue-collar occupations the individual is more subject to the standardization of work. Third, the degree and closeness of supervision is less in white-collar than in blue-collar occupations. As a result of these differences between the conditions of white-collar and blue-collar occupational circumstances, two basic value orientations emerge. White-collar workers are more likely to enunciate values dealing with *self-direction,* such as freedom, individualism, initiative, creativity, and self-actualization; while blue collar workers are more likely to stress values of *conformity* to external standards such as orderliness, neatness, and obedience. The essential difference between these two sets of values is that self-direction focuses on *internal* standards of behavior, whereas conformity focuses on *externally* imposed rules.

The last link in this theoretical scheme is between parental values and parental behavior. Kohn maintains that these value orientations are reflected in the style or circumstances of parental discipline. Because of the greater emphasis white-collar parents place on self-direction and internal standards of conduct, they are more likely to discipline the child on the basis of their interpretation of the child's intent or motive for acting as he does. Blue-collar parents, on the other hand, placing greater stress on conformity, are more likely to react on the bases

of the consequences of the child's behavior. Parental values, then, tend to be extensions of the modes of behavior that are functional for parents in their occupational structures, and they become apparent in the context of socialization.

Kohn's explanatory system can be diagrammed as follows with each of the relationships identified by a number to facilitate subsequent discussion:

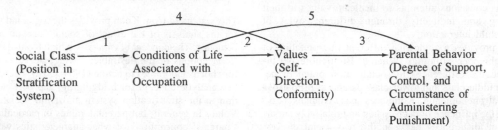

Much of the necessary empirical information to test the various relationships in the model has been provided by Kohn. Our strategy will be to state each of the key relationships in propositional form and assess the degree of empirical support that can be brought to bear on it.

Empirical Assessment of Kohn's Theory

Since values are the key variable in Kohn's theory, it is important to first establish whether values are in fact related to social class. If it is found they are not, then there is no need to proceed further. The general proposition can be stated as follows:

Kohn's Proposition 4: Social class is positively related to parental values of self-direction and negatively related to values of conformity.

Put another way, in terms of a class comparison, the proposition states that middle-class parents are more likely to value self-direction in their children, whereas lower-class parents are more likely to value conformity.

The empirical evidence for the relationship is provided in the form of percentages and correlation coefficients. In all three studies that Kohn uses to test his theory (Washington, Turin, and the National Study) the percentage differences between middle-class and lower-class parents on the major indicators of self-direction–conformity values are consistently significant at the .05 level. But it is the correlation coefficients which are most useful to us in assessing the strength of the relationship. The canonical correlations (Eta) of class to values range from .38 to .50. This means that from 14 percent to 25 percent of the variation in parental values (of self-direction–conformity) can be explained by the parents' social class membership. This indicates a moderately strong association, and it was found to be very consistent, i.e., across studies, samples, and ages and sexes of children and parents.

What is even more impressive, however, is that the relationship between social class and parental values is relatively unaffected by various demographic and family variables. Controlling on race, region, community size, religion, and national background reduced the correlation between social class and parental values by approximately 10 percent (1969:70–71). On the other hand, these other variables by themselves have little effect on parental values when class is controlled. The most powerful of these is national background, with a partial correlation of r=.13.[3] This does not give much support to the view which stresses that parental values are primarily transmitted through groups having distinct subcultures, i.e., ethnic or religious groups (Strodtbeck, 1958; Rosen, 1959), at least not with regard to values of self-direction or conformity.

On the basis of this analysis of the relationship between social class and parental values Kohn concludes, ''In this exceptionally diverse society . . . social class stands out as more important for men's values than does any other line of social demarcation, unaffected by all the rest of them, and apparently more important than all of them together'' [1969:72].

This assessment may be essentially correct if a bit exaggerated. In a careful attempt to replicate and extend Kohn's thesis, using data from the 1973 NORC General Social Survey, Wright and Wright (1976) found that social class accounts for between 41 percent and 63 percent of the total variance in self-direction explained by the model. The other variables in the explanatory model included place of residence, family variables (number of children, wife's employment status, marital happiness), race, religion, and ethnicity. While social class was clearly the most important variable, Wright and Wright caution that Kohn's emphasis on social class ''overlooks at least two-fifths and perhaps as much as three-fifths of the explainable variance in the depended variable.'' But in defense of Kohn's position, some of the variables in Wright and Wright's regression model are hardly ''major lines of social demarcation.'' Kohn (1976), in turn, criticizes Wright and Wright (1976) for comparing the effect of social class against that of an ''ill-defined collection of variables . . . [having] no theoretical meaning'' (1976:542). This procedure may increase the amount of explained variance in parental values, as Kohn points out, but it does not contribute to our understanding of the processes involved in the formation of values.

The next logical question is, what is it about social class that affects parental values? Kohn's answer directs us toward the occupational sphere and particularly toward those conditions of work which allow or inhibit self-direction. Three conditions were examined: (1) closeness of supervision on the job, (2) substance of work involving dealing with people or data versus dealing with things, and (3) degree of complexity of work. Together, these conditions form an index of occupational self-direction. The proposition for this segment of the model can be stated as follows:

Kohn's Propositions 1 and 2: Occupational self-direction is a major *intervening* variable between social class and parental values.

Stated another way, the question is, To what degree is the relationship between social class and parental values attributable to the occupational conditions affecting self-direction in work?

First, controlling on social class, Kohn found that each of the three work conditions conducive to occupational self-direction is significantly related to parents' valuation of self-direction in their children. The correlation coefficients were all rather small, ranging from .06 to .12, but they were all statistically significant and large enough to show that these work conditions have an effect on parental values independent of the effect of social class. Next, to see how much of the relationship between social class and parental values is attributable to these occupational conditions, Kohn controlled on occupational self-direction. He found that this reduced the correlation between class and parental values by 65 percent. That implies that two-thirds of the relationship between class and parental values is due to the occupational self-direction.

This supports Kohn's idea that the degree to which men's work situation allows for self-direction is a major reason for the relationship between social class and parental values. But Kohn pursued the matter one step further by considering other conditions of work which might also account for the relationship between class and parental values. Other aspects of occupation examined were (1) extent of bureaucratic structure in the work setting, (2) ownership status of the job, (3) time pressure, (4) amount of overtime, (5) amount of competition, (6) job security, (7) job satisfaction, and (8) occupational commitment. Kohn found that these other occupational conditions also

have an effect on parental values, but much less so than occupational self-direction. Controlling for all these other occupational conditions reduced the class correlations by about 33 percent. Some of this correlation, however, appears to be due to the overlapping effect of occupational self-direction. Kohn found the correlation of class and parental values to be reduced no more when *both* sets of occupational conditions are statistically controlled than when only those that are determinative of occupational self-direction are controlled. Kohn concludes that ''only those aspects of occupation involved in occupational self-direction prove to be of any great importance for explaining the relationship of class to values . . .'' (1969:187).

However, a nonoccupational condition which did have a strong independent effect on values, even when occupational self-direction was controlled, was *education*. In fact, its effect was as strong as that of occupational self-direction. Kohn interpreted these findings as showing that class relationships are built on the cumulative effects of education and occupational experience. ''The former is pertinent insofar as it provides or fails to provide the *capability* for self-direction, the latter insofar as it provides or fails to provide the experience of *exercising* self-direction in so consequential a realm of life as work'' (1969:188).

There is some doubt, however, about the extent to which the effect of education and occupation are independent and cumulative. Wright and Wright (1976) clearly found education to be more important than occupation in explaining the value of self-direction. i.e., when education was controlled, the relationship between occupation and self-direction almost disappeared, whereas when occupation was controlled, the relationship between education and self-direction was still statistically significant. Scheck and Emerick (1976) also found education to be more important than occupation in their study of child-rearing practices. However, both of these studies dealt only with occupational *status* and not with occupational *conditions* of work and, as Kohn (1976) emphatically stresses, it is the latter variable that is the more relevant to the emergence of these values. In his more recent analysis of these data, Kohn (Kohn, 1971; Kohn and Schooler, 1973) has shown that occupational conditions have a strong effect on values independent of the effect of education (there is a spirited exchange of commentaries on this issue between Kohn and the Wrights in the *American Sociological Review* 41 [1976]:538–548).

The importance of education, however, is not inconsistent with Kohn's basic model. One explanation which Wright and Wright (1976) offer for their findings is that education may be a determinant of the opportunity to exercise self-direction in work. Similarly, Kohn argues that education is consequential for parental values mainly because it facilitates intellectual flexibility and breadth of perspective, which are essential ingredients for self-directed values. It is a reasonable interpretation, but it casts some doubt on the importance of work characteristics per se as an explanation of parental values.

It also suggests a reconstruction of the basic model presented in the diagram on page 380 to include education (see Figure 15.1). (This reformulation was provided by Kohn in a communication with Ira Reiss in 1973. Kohn attempts to integrate education more fully into his theoretical model in his new introduction to *Class and Conformity*, 1977).

So far the evidence supports the first three segments of Kohn's model, i.e., social class–conditions of life–parental values. Unfortunately, Kohn provides no direct evidence on the link between parental values and parental behavior. Rather, he uses the evidence from the first two sets of relationships as an explanation for the relationship between social class and parental behavior. That is, social class should be related to parental behavior *because* of its relationship to parental values via their link to occupational conditions of life.

The behavioral variable considered in relationship to social class and explained in terms of values stemming from conditions of occupational self-direction is parental punishment of the child. In considering social class differences in parental punishment of the child, Kohn is less interested in explaining *what* kinds of techniques parents use than he is in accounting for *when and why* parents punish their children. Actually, his theory is able to explain both questions. Most of the reported research which considers class differences in parental punishment has addressed the first question and, as reported in the previous section, has generally found that lower-class parents are more likely to use physical punishment, whereas middle-class parents rely more on "psychological techniques," such as threat of love withdrawal, appeals to guilt, and reasoning with the child. Since Kohn has shown that middle-class parents place a higher value on the development of self-direction and internal standards of conduct in their children, it follows that they would be more likely to use punishment techniques which take into account the child's internal dynamics. Lower-class parents, on the other hand, with their greater emphasis on conformity and obedience, would be expected to rely on the most direct means of punishment of the child.

Kohn's theory, however, is even more suited to explaining the question of class differences in the *conditions* under which parents are likely to punish their children. His theory predicts that middle-class parents are more likely to punish their children on the basis of their *interpretation* of the child's *motives* for acting as he does, especially when they interpret the child's behavior to be inimical to the value of self-direction. Lower-class parents are more likely to punish the child on the basis of the *external* consequences of the child's actions. In support of this prediction Kohn found middle-class parents were quite discriminate in the use of physical punishment depending on whether the child's behavior was defined as "wild play" or "loss of temper." They were much more likely to use physical punishment in the latter situation because, according to the theory, this represents to the parent the child's loss of self-control, a valued characteristic. Lower-class parents, on the other hand, were found to use physical punishment with equal frequency in both situations—for them it is the consequences of the child's behavior, i.e., disruptive behavior in this case, which are most likely to elicit a parent's response. In short, the conditions under which middle-class and lower-class parents punish their children were found to be congruent with their respective values of self-direction and conformity.

We have gone into considerable detail describing Kohn's value theory and examining the evidence for it. Now we must step back and give it an overall assessment. Referring back to the analytic model presented earlier (see p. 380) we can summarize the degree of empirical support for the various relationships as follows:

There is strong empirical support for relationships 1, 2, and 4 either from Kohn's own data or from the research of

Figure 15.1.

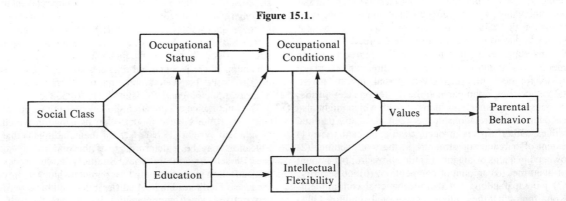

others. Kohn's case for the link between social class and parental values, and the reason for that link, e.g., occupational conditions of life, is convincing. Kohn presents no direct evidence for relationships 3 and 5; however, there is considerable indirect evidence. The associations established in Propositions 1, 2, and 4 are the basis for explaining the relationship between social class and parental behavior, and by implication the relationships between values and behavior, and conditions of life and behavior.

Furthermore, in light of these relationships, other explanations of the relationship between class and child socialization can be reconsidered and reinterpreted. Kohn's reinterpretation of Bronfenbrenner's theory of changes in parental practices has already been discussed. Miller and Swanson's (1958) theory perhaps comes closest to Kohn's in terms of its logic. They too considered conditions in the occupational sphere as the key to understanding the relationship between social class and parental values and behavior. Unfortunately, Miller and Swanson apparently focused on the wrong aspect of occupation. Their distinction between "bureaucratic" and "entrepreneurial" occupations did not prove very useful. And their prediction that fathers in bureaucratic occupations would be more likely to stress values of conformity in child-rearing, while those in entrepreneurial occupations would emphasize individualism, was not supported empirically. Kohn, in testing the effect of this condition of work on parental values, found about the same low level of association as did Miller and Swanson.

In general, then, Kohn's theory is impressive and appears to be the strongest explanation of the concepts and variables *considered*. Its limitations are with regard to concepts and variables which were *not considered* or were treated as peripheral. That is, our criticism of Kohn's value theory is less with regard to what he has done than in terms of what he hasn't done. (This is obviously an unfair criticism, since one can't do everything. But here we are less interested in fairness than in completeness.)

What does Kohn's theory leave out that should be included in a more complete explanation of social class and child socialization? There are two major directions in which the model of socialization can be elaborated: (1) by elaborating the range of variables encompassed by Kohn's concepts, and (2) by adding family structure and process variables to the model. The first direction would lead us to consider other parental behaviors besides circumstances of disciplining children, other parental values besides self-direction–conformity, and other class-linked conditions of life besides those dealing with the work situation.[4] The last point is especially important, since Kohn mentioned that his studies excluded the poverty segment of the population (as well as the elites). As we shall see, the literature on poverty points to a number of

other "conditions of life" characteristic of the poor which affect their patterns of child-rearing.

The second direction of elaboration is through the addition of group structure and process variables as intervening between social class and socialization, such as family size, division of labor, conjugal power structure, family composition. It is true that Kohn does consider some of these, but in a rather limited way, i.e., primarily as they affect parental values. These will constitute a major focus of attention when we consider the "structural" theories of class and socialization.

Structural Theories

Whereas the emphasis in the ideational theories is on values, beliefs, or ideologies as mediating between social class and socialization, structural theories stress family structure and process as intervening variables, such as family size, division of labor in the home, patterns of authority and decision making, etc. To be sure, these structural elements may in turn give rise to values, attitudes, or beliefs, and vice versa. But typically these outcomes are given no more than peripheral attention. If other intervening concepts are posited in the analytic sequence from family structure to parent-child interaction, they are likely to be other family patterns or styles of interaction. We should emphasize, however, that structural and ideational theories of social class and socialization are not incompatible. In fact, they are quite complementary in some respects, as we shall see later in the chapter.

In the structural theories, conditions of life associated with social class are viewed as affecting the structure and functioning of families, which in turn affect the way in which parents raise their children. This explanatory model essentially bypasses any specific cultural contents of socialization (i.e., values, etc.), which are the major concern of the ideational theories.

A key aspect of family structure is family size. While there is no integrated theory of social class and socialization based on family size as a mediating factor, there is substantial suggestive evidence of its importance. For example, Bossard and Boll (1956) have noted the effects of family size on many aspects of family and personality functioning. They observed that role specialization increases with family size. As the size of the family increases, better internal organization and a higher degree of discipline are required for the sake of efficiency and order. A greater number of persons in the group creates greater interdependence between members for cooperation and consensus. Order becomes more problematic. It is perhaps for this reason that parental (especially father) authoritarianism is often associated with the large family system.

The theoretical and speculative literature on family size

suggests several outcome variables which are relevant to our concerns (see Figure 15.2). These theoretical relationships are not very well developed or tested, but they have some empirical support. Nye et al. (1970) provide some evidence for the relationship between family size and parental control. They found that parents of large families were more likely to employ corporal punishment in controlling children, whereas smaller families were more likely to employ discussion and reasoning strategies. Elder and Bowerman (1963) and Scheck and Emerick (1976), in studies of adolescents, found that as family size increases, parents are reported as less communicative and more controlling, more likely to use physical punishment, less likely to explain rules of conduct to the child, less likely to give praise and support, and the father is more likely to be perceived as the authority in the family. These relationships generally held within social class categories (middle class and lower class) and for boys and girls, with some variation.

Rosen (1961) offers a careful, if limited, examination of three of these variables in the model. His theory focuses on the explanation of achievement training and achievement motivation and considers family size and socioeconomic status as antecedents. Rosen defines achievement training as [socialization practices in which] "parents set high goals for their child to attain, when they indicate a high evaluation of his competence to do a task well, and impose standards of excellence upon problem solving tasks, even in situations where such standards are not explicit" (1961:574). Rosen argues that children from small families will experience greater achievement training than children from larger families. In the small family the parents can devote more time and effort to each child and give attention to his progress. By contrast, "the large family is more likely to value responsibility above individual achievement, conformity above self-expression, cooperation and obedience above individualism" (1961:577). Parenthetically, this description of the large family is very similar to the *social class* differences in parental values that Kohn found. It is, therefore, not

surprising that there is a relationship (inverse) between social class and family size (cf. Hollingshead and Redlich, 1958, for empirical support). Rosen's explanatory model can be diagrammed as in Figure 15.3.

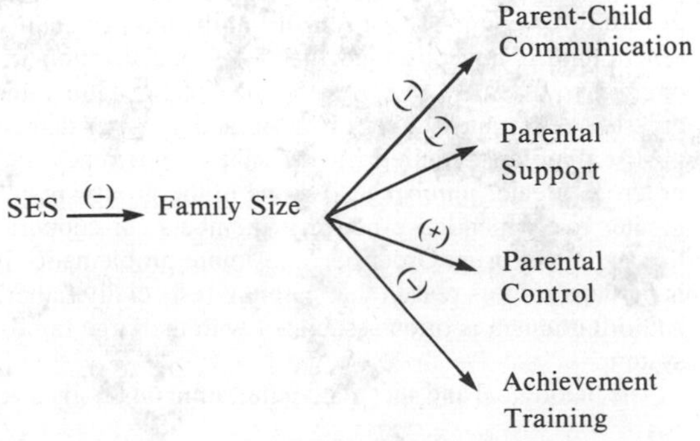

His findings show a statistically significant positive relationship between social class and son's achievement motivation, and a significant negative relationship with family size. The effect of social class on achievement motivation was found to be mediated by family size to some extent, but social class also had a substantial effect independent of family size. The effect of family size was also independent of social class. Unfortunately, there were no measures of association reported to enable us to assess the degree of association between these variables. In summary, the work of Bossard and Boll (1956), Elder and Bowerman (1963), Nye et al. (1970), Scheck and Emerick (1976), and Rosen (1961) gives us some basis for a structural explanation of the effect of social class on parental behavior.

The most prominent and elaborate structural theory, however, is that of Basil Bernstein (1964, 1970, 1971, 1973) and his associates. The theory centers on linguistic styles or codes. Bernstein defines the concept of linguistic code as "the principle which regulates the selection and organization of speech events" (1970:31), and distinguishes between two types on the basis of degree of complexity, concreteness, and explicitness: *restricted code* and *elaborated code*. In the restricted code, the range of meanings and syntactical alternatives is more limited. Meanings are usually implicit and context-specific; that is, a great deal is taken for granted by the speaker about the degree to which meanings and assumptions are shared. In describing the restricted code, Bernstein states, "Such a communication code will emphasize verbally the communal rather than the individual, the concrete rather than the abstract, the substance rather than the elaboration of process, the here-and-now rather than explorations of motives and intentions . . ." (1970:29). By contrast, the elaborated code is characterized by language which is more complex (i.e., larger vocabulary, greater frequency of modifiers, greater use of subordinate clauses, greater grammatical accuracy and sentence complexity); meanings are elaborated and explicit rather than assumed, and they are relatively context-free. The speaker using an elaborated code is more aware of and

Figure 15.2.

Figure 15.3.

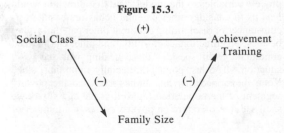

more likely to take into account the perspective of the listener. An elaborated code is better able to deal with temporal, spatial, and logical relationships. It is a more analytic mode, compared to the restricted code, which is more subjective.

Bernstein's theory attempts to explain, among other things, social class differences in communication patterns between parent and child, modes of social control exercised by the parent, and parental approaches to teaching the child. His explanation depends on showing how social class is linked to linguistic codes. He does this by arguing that the two codes are realized in two different types of social relations characteristic of groups. Bernstein states:

> A restricted code will arise where the form of social relations is based upon closely shared identifications, upon an extensive range of shared expectations, upon a range of common assumptions. Thus a restricted code emerges where the culture or subculture raises the "we" above "I." . . . The use of a restricted code creates social solidarity at the cost of the verbal elaboration of individual experience [1970:32].

By contrast, the social relations giving rise to an elaborated code emphasize individualism over communality, where the "I" prevails over the "we." Bernstein describes this social milieu as follows:

> [An elaborated code] will arise wherever the intent of the other person cannot be taken for granted. Insofar as [this is true], then speakers are forced to elaborate their meanings and make them both explicit and specific. . . . This pressure forces the speaker to select among syntactic alternatives and encourages differentiation of vocabulary [1970:33].

Referring to Durkheim's distinction between mechanical and organic solidarity, Bernstein suggests that restricted codes emerge from social relations based on mechanical solidarity, whereas elaborated codes emerge from organic solidarity. In order to link these types of social relations to the stratification system, Bernstein makes an important (and problematic) assumption: mechanical solidarity is more typical of social relations in the lower class, whereas organic solidarity is characteristic of social relations in the middle class. As a result, lower-class persons are more likely to have developed a restricted code and middle-class persons an elaborated code.

But there is also another, and perhaps more defensible, link between social class and liguistic codes via the organization and flexibility of social roles in the society and in the family. The important distinction is between open and closed role systems, i.e., those which permit a range of alternatives for the expression of meanings versus those which reduce the range of alternatives:

> The greater the range of alternatives permitted by the role system, the more individualized the verbal meanings, the higher the order and the more flexible the syntactic and vocabulary selection, and so the more elaborated the code. . . . The greater the reduction in the range of alternatives (i.e., closed role system), the more communal or collective the verbal meanings and the lower the order of complexity and more rigid the syntactic and vocabulary selections—thus the more restricted the code [1970:34].

Where the role system is closed, meanings are likely to be assigned to the role incumbent. In an open role system, the incumbent has greater latitude in creating new meanings by exploring and extending his roles. The conditions of life of lower-class persons are considered to be more compatible with a closed role system, especially in the occupational sphere, whereas those of middle-class persons are more conducive to an open role system (Kohn's model would predict this relationship as well).

Another key assumption is made at this point: that the role structure of the family reflects what the parents take to be the ascriptive ordering of the larger society (Cook-Gumperz, 1973:14). Put another way, the person's experience and perception of the role systems in which he is involved outside the family will be reflected (and in a sense reproduced) in the organization of family roles. In this view, the social structure of the family is a microcosm of the social structure of the larger society which the individual most directly experiences. As a result, middle-class families would be expected to exhibit an open role system to a greater degree than lower-class families, while the latter would be expected to more frequently show a closed role system.

A less strained rationale for the link between social class and family role structure is provided by Bott (1957). She argued that in "tight-knit" social networks, i.e., where friends, neighbors, and relatives know one another well, marital roles are more likely to be segregated and, in general, a lower value is placed on the marital relationship. The spouses in this type of social setting are less dependent on each other for emotional and psychological support, since they satisfy many of these needs through extrafamily relations. Bott, as well as Bernstein, suggests that "tight-knit" social networks and consequently segregated, position-oriented family roles are more characteristic of lower-class than of middle-class families.

For Bernstein, the role system of the family is, in fact, the key mechanism for linking social class and linguistic codes. On the basis of the degree of role flexibility and role discretion, as well as the related criteria of strength of boundary maintenance, he distinquishes between *position-oriented* families and *person-oriented* families (1971:184–85). In the position-oriented family, there is a segregation of roles and a formal divison of areas of responsibility according to the status of the family member. i.e., age and sex. Family roles are relatively clear-cut and inflexible, and they tend to be ascribed.

In person-oriented families, by contrast, the distribution of family power and influence is a function of the psychological qualities of the person rather than his formal status. Achieved status, under these circumstances, becomes more important. The role system is more flexible and continuously changing as a result of the different interests and attributes of its members. It would also follow that the authority structure in such families would be more democratic, while in the position-oriented families it would be more authoritarian.

Bernstein's distinction between "position-oriented" and "person-oriented" family role systems is reminiscent of Duvall's (1946) earlier distinction between "traditional" and "developmental" family types, as well as Bott's (1957) distinction between "segregated" and "joint" marital roles. In these typologies, one type is marked by rigidity, conventionalism, and an emphasis on the past, and the other type is characterized as flexible, open to change, and willing to experiment on the basis of present and perceived future contingencies. In some respects this is a useful distinction, and for Bernstein it is crucial since it describes the contexts within which his linguistic codes develop.

Position-oriented family systems are associated with closed communication styles (restricted linguistic code); person-oriented family systems are associated with open communication styles (elaborated linguistic code). Since the degree of role discretion is relatively limited in position-oriented families, the communication style is less likely to encourage the verbal elaboration of individual differences and is less likely to lead to the verbal elaboration of judgments and their bases and consequences and the verbal exploration of individual intentions and motives (1970:40). But in person-oriented families, where there is less role segregation and role discretion is relatively broad, there is a greater need for communication which clarifies and makes explicit meanings, intentions, and motives. In the open communication patterns characteristic or person-oriented families, children would be socializing parents as much as parents would be socializing children.

The last segment of Bernstein's sociolinguistic theory connects these family role systems and their communication styles with parental behavior, especially parental modes of social control. Bernstein distinguishes between three modes of control on the basis of the degree of latitude or range of alternatives accorded the child: imperative, positional, personal. The *imperative* mode allows the most limited range of alternatives, allowing the

child only the possibilities of compliance, rebellion, or withdrawal. It is expressed through a restricted linguistic style, with such statements as "Don't do that!," "Shut up!," or "Go to your room!" In both of the other two modes the child is allowed a greater range of response, but they differ in the basis used for requesting the child's compliance. The *positional* mode of control refers the behavior of the child to the norms which inhere in a social status; i.e., "Boys don't cry" (sex status norm). The basis of positional appeals is that the child is explicity linked to a social category, and the rule applicable to the social category becomes applicable to him. Bernstein maintains that positional appeals can be given in restricted or elaborated codes, but the implication is that they are more closely associated with restricted codes. And certainly the parallel between positional modes of control and the position-oriented family type is obvious. Similarly the connection between *personal* modes of control and person-oriented family systems is also apparent. In personal appeals the parent focuses on the uniquely individual characteristics of the child and his specific circumstances rather than on the child's status attributes. Bernstein states that the personal mode can be found within both restricted and elaborated codes. But here again it is clear that it is typically associated with elaborated codes.

There are other child-rearing variables as well which Bernstein posits as associated with these explanatory variables in his theory. Social class differences in parental styles of teaching and conceptions of the way in which children learn are explained with reference to differences in family structure and linguistic styles. Here again the important analytic distinction is between open family role systems with elaborated linguistic styles and closed role systems with restricted styles of communication.

In summary, the "flow" of Bernstein's theory and the interrelationships between the major concepts can be diagrammed as shown at the bottom of this page.

We will evaluate Bernstein's theory by the same procedure that we used with Kohn's theory—an assessment of the empirical evidence available for each of the relationships in the analytic model. Much of the evidence for the theory comes from Bernstein's own research and that of his colleagues at the University of London's Institute of Education.

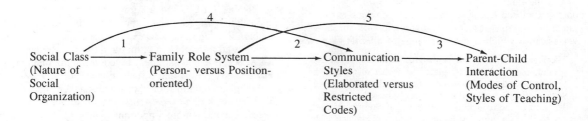

Evaluation of Bernstein's Sociolinguistic Theory

Since Bernstein's theory is primarily keyed to linguistic or communication styles, it is appropriate to begin with an evaluation of the relationship between social class and linguistic codes. This relationship can be stated in propositional form as follows:

Bernstein's Proposition 4: Social class is positively related to the use of an elaborated linguistic code, and negatively related to the use of a restricted code.

Stated in categorical terms the proposition asserts that middle-class parents are more likely to use an elaborated linguistic code, while lower-class parents are more likely to express a restricted code. Primary evidence for this relationship comes from the work of Cook-Gumperz (1973), one of Bernstein's students. The biggest problem in testing this relationship was in the development of a measure of language usage which would enable a distinction between elaborated and restricted codes. It is evident that Cook-Gumperz expended considerable effort on this task. Her coding scheme (applied on open-ended interviews) is quite complex, involving multiple indicators of grammatical categories, such as pronouns and modifiers, and assessments of sentence complexity. The use of cluster analysis to assess the adequacy of the indicators in measuring the two linguistic codes gave some evidence of validity. But the results were not unambiguous. Her findings showed a weak relationship, but in the predicted direction, between social class and linguistic codes. This corresponds with the evidence from Bernstein's early research (1960), which also found modest class differences.

Several other studies, however, indicate a class difference in language style or usage generally along the lines suggested by Bernstein. Schatzman and Strauss (1955) found middle-class speakers more likely to consider the perspective of the listener and more likely to elaborate their statements than were lower-class residents, in describing a tornado which hit their community. Hess and Shipman (1965) similarly found less egocentricity in the speech of middle-class mothers, compared to lower-class mothers, and referred to this greater role-taking characteristic of the language used as "person oriented." Lawton (1968) found greater use of adjectives and other modifiers in the language of middle-class subjects. Baldwin and Baldwin (1973), in a laboratory-observational study of mother-child interaction, found lower-class mothers to use less complex syntax than middle-class mothers in communicating with their children. But Baldwin and Baldwin were more impressed with the overall *similarity* in communication patterns between mothers and children of different social classes. Since the class difference they found was rather small, they seriously questioned whether it had any social significance.

An even stronger reservation about class differences in language style and complexity is raised by Labov (1970). Based on his studies of language of blacks in Harlem, Labov attacked the concept of "linguistic deprivation" implied in such class-related concepts as Bernstein's "restricted code." In his more recent writings Bernstein (cf. 1970) has been quite sensitive to this issue and has insisted that his claim that lower-class parents have a restricted code does not imply a devaluation of their language style. He states, "The use, or abuse, of this distinction [between elaborated and restricted codes] has sometimes lead to the *erroneous* conception that a restricted code can be directly equated with linguistic deprivation, linguistic deficiency, or being nonverbal" (1970:26). However, on the basis of Bernstein's description of these codes it is easy to see how this accusation could be made. Labov does acknowledge and report a number of differences between the "nonstandard English" of Negro ghetto children and the language characteristic of middle-class persons, but at the same time he vigorously argues against *any* implications of these differences for the competence or cognitive capacity of the language users. Since this issue is less relevant to our present considerations, we won't pursue it here. However, it will be resurrected in the section on poverty and socialization, where it will be an important issue.

In general, the evidence, though neither extensive nor very impressive, does support the relationship between social class and language usage along the lines suggested by Bernstein. Middle-class parents are more likely to use an elaborated language style, while the language of lower-class parents is more likely to be restricted.

The question of *why* is there a relationship between social class and these two linguistic styles leads us to a consideration of family structure and its relationship to social class and linguistic codes. Bernstein argues that the kinds of social relations that nurture or encourage the development of elaborated codes are those in which the roles and role systems are open, flexible, and egalitarian, e.g., "person-oriented." Restricted codes are more congruent with a social milieu in which the roles are more rigid, status-specific, and relatively clear-cut, e.g., "position-oriented." These relationships can be stated in propositional form as follows:

Bernstein's Proposition 2: Person-oriented family role systems are associated with the use of an elaborated code. Position-oriented family role systems are associated with the use of a restricted code.

There is no empirical evidence for this relationship offered either by Bernstein or any other sources that we have investigated. Yet it sounds logical and makes intuitive sense. It seems reasonable that the degree of role flexibility and openness would be related to styles of communication differentiated on the basis of degree of complexity and egocentricity. But these are speculations untested by empirical evidence.

The second aspect of the question of why is social class related to linguistic styles is the relationship between social class and family role systems. Bernstein assumes that the family role structure is a reflection of the social structure and social relations experienced by individuals in the society at large. He further assumes that the experience of social reality by middle-class persons is different from the social reality experienced by lower-class persons, especially with regard to the degree of autonomy and role flexibility. This idea can be expressed in the following proposition:

Bernstein's Proposition 1: Social class is positively related to the openness and flexibility of family roles.

Stated categorically the proposition asserts that middle-class families are more likely to have an open role system (person-oriented) while lower-class families are more likely to have a closed role system (position-oriented).

Bernstein provides no direct empirical evidence for this relationship, but there is some indirect evidence from other sources. A distinction which has become almost standard fare in family sociology was introduced by Burgess and Locke (1945) between "institutional" and "companionship" families. The former referred to families which had a relatively rigid and inflexible role system, a clear-cut division of labor, and hierarchical authority structure. "Companionship" families, on the other hand, were described as more open, flexible, adaptive, and democratic. Duvall (1946) expanded on this distinction in her typology of "traditional" versus "developmental" families and, in her interview study of 300 mothers, linked these types to social class. Lower-class mothers were found to be more "traditional" in their conceptions of parenthood, whereas middle-class mothers were more "developmental." Subsequent studies by Elder (1949) and Connors et al. (1954) have corroborated the social class association of "traditional" and "developmental" family types. It is evident that these typologies are very similar to Bernstein's conception of "position-oriented" and "person-oriented" families.

There is still one question that remains to be answered regarding family role system: how important is it as an intervening variable between social class and linguistic codes? Unfortunately, there is no empirical basis for answering this question. Since Bernstein provides no data (and other sources do not address the issue), we are unable to assess whether the relationship between social class and communication styles depends upon the nature of family roles. Therefore, at this point the importance of the family role system as an intervening variable is hypothetical.

The crux of Bernstein's theory, however, as it applies to social class and socialization, is the strength of the relationship between *linguistic codes* and parental behavior. First, let us consider again the kinds of parental behaviors the theory purports to explain. There are two main outcome variables dealing with parent-child interaction to which the theory is addressed: modes of parental control and styles of teaching. The findings dealing with modes of control refer primarily to the positive association between social class and use of *personal* modes of control and the negative association between social class and use of *positional* and *imperative* modes of control. The relationship stated this way comes from Cook-Gumperz (1973) research which was directly derived from Bernstein's theory. But other research findings which have (in general) indicated a class difference in the use of physical punishment or psychological techniques of disciplining the child would also be relevant.

Class differences in styles and modes of teaching the child refer to the finding that middle-class parents are more concerned with teaching the child *principles* of how things work, whereas lower-class parents place more emphasis on teaching the child the *operations* needed to make things work. This relationship can be expressed in other ways, such as the positive association between social class and parents, likelihood of *explaining* to the child why a request is made, why a command is given, or why something happens. Bernstein considers this empirical relationship quite important because it implies, for him, the operation of two different theories of learning which parents of different social classes possess. The middle-class parents' implicit theory of learning is described as *self-regulating,* emphasizing the child's active role and his capacities or reflexiveness and autonomy. The lower-class parents' implicit theory of learning is *didactic,* where the child learns by being told or shown what to do (cf. Bernstein and Henderson, 1973).

The findings, then, to which the theory is addressed are significant and important. But how important is linguistic style in explaining them? The empirical evidence for the link between linguistic codes and parental behavior is very scanty. The only direct evidence that we have come across is offered by Cook-Gumperz (1973). She found the elaborated code indicators had a substantially wider pattern of association with *personal* control strategies, than did the restricted code indicators. But the restricted code indicators had only a slightly greater association with *positional* control strategies. And imperative control was unrelated to either linguistic code. There is, then, some support for the relationship between language style and modes of parental control. But no evidence is available for the effect of linguistic styles on modes of teaching. As a result, we must conclude that the status of linguistic code as an intervening (and explanatory) variable between social class and parental behavior is doubtful.

In summary, the empirical support for Bernstein's sociolinguistic theory is not very impressive. Referring back to the explanatory model in the diagram on page

386, relationships 1 and 4 had moderately strong support; relationship 3 had weak support; and there was no evidence to assess relationships 2 and 5. Our impression is that the theory is coherent and intellectually provocative, but that it needs to be tested more extensively before a verdict is rendered on its utility in explaining social class differences in parental behavior.

We have devoted considerable space to examining Bernstein's theory for the same reasons we went into such detail with Kohn's theory: (1) they are both prominent and elaborate theories of social class and child-rearing; but also (2) they each serve as prototypes of structural and ideational explanations respectively. Unfortunately, no comparable prototypes exist for the remaining theories to be considered. Presentation of these will be organized around theoretical issues, as in the previous sections, but they won't be as closely connected with *a* particular theorist.

Theories of Psychological States and Orientation

The theories in this group consider the most important mediating variables between social class and parent-child interaction to be the psychological states, orientations, and personality characteristics of parents which are affected by their position in the stratification system. Typically, the psychological characteristics examined have strong positive and negative valuations associated with them, and it is also typical to find the negative attributes associated with membership in the lower classes and the positive attributes associated with the higher class levels. As a result the focus of the studies operating from these perspectives is on lower-class populations, with middle-class subjects used more as a control or comparison group. The general explanatory model of the psychological orientations theories can be stated as follows: conditions of life associated with lower-class position negatively affect the parent's psychological adjustment, competencies, and sense of well-being which are reflected in styles of parent-child interaction and the general child-rearing environment.

It is evident that some of this theorizing has been influenced by Freudian psychodynamics. The clearest expression of the neo-Freudian tradition in this area, aside from the early works on patterns of socialization and stages of psychosexual development (such as Whiting and Child, 1953, and Davis and Havighurst, 1948), is found, surprisingly, in a sociological work (McKinley, 1964). In this theory, McKinley (1964) combines a Parsonian view of society with a neo-Freudian conception of personality, via the frustration-aggression hypothesis, in order to account for class differences in degree of parental supportiveness, aggression, and severity toward the child. His model can be stated as follows:

SES is related to the degree of frustration experienced in the occupational sphere, which in turn affects the

degree of severity, agression, and authoritarianism in parent-child interation.

McKinley's theoretical rationale is based on the Parsonian conception of the interdependence of systems at various levels of abstraction: cultural, social structural, and personality. This is reflected in a sequence of theoretical statements and propositions as they relate to social class and socialization: (1) The most basic assumption, at the level of the cultural system, is that there is an achievement ethos in American society (the legacy of the ''Protestant ethic'') which is the major basis for evaluating individuals (McKinley, 1964:29–46). This ethos is the basis for determining who will get how much of the desired goods in society, i.e., wealth, power, and esteem. (2) The achievement ethos places major emphasis on work and occupation in determining one's position in the stratification system. (3) Success, or the lack of it, in the occupation sphere has certain psychological consequences for the individual (personality system), e.g., frustration or gratification and satisfaction. According to McKinley, low socioeconomic status results in a state of frustration for several reasons: (a) it denies the individual a sense of worth and approval; (b) it denies him certain nonpsychic rewards (such as material wealth) that are consequences of approval by society; and (c) it means others have greater control over him, thus limiting his alternate routes to satisfaction (1964:7). (4) This frustration leads to aggression and other kinds of destructive behavior. (5) Aggression generated by frustration stemming from occupational and social class circumstances is often displaced to the family, since there are fewer constraints on the expression of aggression here than in the work situation. This is especially evident in the conception and performance of parental roles. (6) On the basis of this reasoning, we would expect that the socialization techniques used by lower-class parents would be ''more severe and aggressively tinged'' than those of middle-class parents. It would also follow that the degree of power the parent exercises over the child would vary inversely with social class; and the level of warmth and emotional support in the parent-child relationship would vary directly with social class.

There is ample empirical support for the prediction of social class differences in degree of parental constraint, supportiveness, and severity of discipline of the child. The important question here is the extent to which this relationship is a function of class-related frustration experienced by the parent.

Evaluation of Frustration-Aggression Theory

McKinley provides no direct evidence for the importance of frustration as an intervening variable between class and socialization, but he offers several types of indirect evidence, both from his own research and from that of others. Evidence from various sources was used to argue the case that the lower classes are more frustrated with their lot, i.e., class differences in degree of work satisfaction (Beers, 1953; Kornhauser, 1938), rates of mental illness (Hollingshead and Redlich, 1958), frequency of sexual intercourse (Kinsey et al., 1948) and emphasis on traditional male role (Stycos, 1955)—all cited in McKinley (1964:74–82). Even though it is puzzling how some of these factors can be interpreted as indicators of frustration, there appears to be some empirical basis for the claim that "frustration with one's lot" is inversely related to socioeconomic status.

In considering the effect of frustration on parental behavior, McKinley relies on his own research, which is based primarily on questionnaire data from high school boys. He considers two variables as indicators of father's frustration: degree of work satisfaction and degree of work autonomy. He found work satisfaction to be inversely related to father's "severity of socialization" of the child. This relationship was evident in each of the three social classes considered (upper, middle, and lower). In fact, the influence of work satisfaction on paternal behavior appeared to be greater than that of social class, as indicated by the size of percentage differences between categories (no tests of significance or measures of association were given).

Within-class comparisons were also reported for the relationship between father's work autonomy and severity of socialization. Using several indicators of severity of socialization (i.e., use of physical punishment, strictness, and demands for obedience), McKinley found a general tendency for work autonomy to be negatively related to severity of socialization, but the relationship (again in terms of percentages) was weak and somewhat erratic; i.e., there were occasional reversals of direction for some social class categories on some indicators of severity of socialization (1964:132–33). Some of this could have been due to the rather crude measure of work autonomy, measured in terms of the father's being either "self-employed" or "other employed" (this latter category further divided on the basis of a subjective assessment of occupations as characterized by "high" or "low autonomy").

This evidence on the effect of work autonomy, though hardly impressive, is congruent with Kohn's (1969) findings relating conditions of occupation to parental behavior via parental values discussed above. We also think Kohn's explanation of the basis for this relationship more convincing.

There are a number of other psychological concepts embedded in different theories and analytic perspectives which are posited as intervening between social class and socialization. In examining these, we will need to shift the class comparison downward to give greater focus to the bottom of the stratification scale. The reason for this is that the literature on poverty provides the basis for much of this theorizing. We should emphasize at the outset that even though this body of literature emphasizes psycholog-

ical and personality variables in its explanatory paradigms, it is not limited to psychological variables as intervening between social class and parental behavior. The literature on poverty manifests ideational and family structural variables as well. But the major thrust is clearly on psychological variables.

Poverty and Socialization

Perhaps no issue in socialization is more controversial, with as little consensus on theory and findings, as the nature of poverty socialization. The main point of confrontation is between those who believe that the poor possess certain social and psychological "deficits," developed as a result of the conditions of poverty but taking on an autonomy, a way of life, of their own, and those social scientists who argue against either the "deficit" position or the "way of life" position, and rather stress the *situational* adaptations of the poor (where differences are perceived) to the physical deprivation and social structural circumstances of their existence. The debate is quite heated between these two groups, not only because the issues posed have important theoretical implications involving several different disciplines but also because of the political implications of each position. In general, the policy implication of the "deficit" perspective is that in order to eliminate poverty, we need to change the *poor*—their values, attitudes, psychological orientations, aspirations, or language—so that they would be better able to compete in mainstream American society. This implication derives mainly from the work of Oscar Lewis (1959, 1966a and b), who introduced the very influential concept of "culture of poverty." Lewis stated that "it is more difficult to eliminate the culture of poverty, than to eliminate poverty *per se*," and that "the elimination of physical poverty per se may not be enough to eliminate the culture of poverty" (1966a:li,lii). This means, as Valentine (1968, 1971) and others have argued, that since the most significant and intractable problem associated with poverty exists within the poor people themselves, it is more urgent for our society to abolish the special lifeways of the poor than to try to eliminate the physical condition of poverty. There is little doubt that Valentine and other "anti-deficit" theorists (for example Labov, 1970; Cole and Bruner, 1972; Vaca, 1972; Hylan Lewis, 1971) see the "deficit" perspective, especially the "culture of poverty" version, as not only incorrect but dangerous:

> The complex of conceptions, attitudes, and activities that has grown up around the "culture of poverty" has had a predominantly pernicious effect on American society. This complex has been a keystone in the crumbling arch of official policy toward the poor [Valentine, 1971:194].

One of the instances of "official policy" that Valentine is referring to is the War on Poverty initiated during Lyndon Johnson's administration, which was heavily influenced by the "culture of poverty" perspective (cf. Gladwin, 1967) and most visibly directed toward perceived incompetencies and deficits of the poor in such programs as Head Start and Job Corps.

In general, the policy implications of the "anti-deficit" theorists are that the structures within society (i.e., economic system, education system, political system) should be changed in order to eliminate the condition of poverty. Their position is that if the physical and social conditions which give rise to poverty are eliminated, the various adaptive lifeways and psychological orientations of the poor (which are considered deficiencies or incompetencies) will also be eliminated. These policy implications are politically more revolutionary, and generally less popular with those in political power.

We are neither prepared nor inclined to explore in detail the literature and the issues on the political implications of the perspectives on poverty and socialization. Our intent is to simply draw the reader's attention to this aspect of the problem, since it has affected both theory and research on poverty, and is the major reason why the poverty literature is so important. It is also the main reason the poverty literature is such an empirical and theoretical morass. Our strategy in assessing these theories will be the same as we have used for the previous theories, i.e., to examine the empirical evidence available in support of theoretical statements. Our task is made somewhat easier in that we are dealing only with the effects of poverty on parent-child interaction, and not on the *consequences* of this interaction for child development. This latter topic has received most of the heat.

Deficit Theories of Poverty and Socialization

Since the "culture of poverty" formulation is the most prominent aspect of the deficit perspective, we will focus on it in organizing the poverty literature. Oscar Lewis (1959, 1966a and b, 1968) introduced the concept and developed its rationale in several of his better works, and we will rely on these for an overview of his basic position. In describing the "culture of poverty" Lewis states:

it is the label for a specific conceptual model that describes . . . . a subculture of Western society with its own structure and rationale, a way of life handed on from generation to generation along family lines. . . . It is a culture in the traditional anthropological sense in that it provides human beings with a design for living . . . and so serves a significant adaptive function. . . . Wherever it occurs, its practitioners exhibit remarkable similarity in the structure of their families, in interpersonal relations . . . in their value systems, and in their [psychological] orientations [1966a:3].

The physical, and to some extent social, conditions under which the poor live give rise to adaptive responses (both psychological and behavioral) which become a way of life into which children are socialized, making the way of life self-perpetuating. Lewis stated that in his studies he had identified approximately 70 traits that characterize the culture of poverty. These he grouped under four categories: (1) the relationship between the subculture

and the larger society; (2) the organization of the slum community; (3) the nature of the family; and (4) the attitudes, values, and character structure (psychological orientations) of the individual (1966a:5). By far the greatest attention has been directed to the fourth category, which is usually considered (by both advocates and antagonists) as the core feature of the culture of poverty. Lewis describes it this way:

The individual who grows up in this culture has a strong feeling of fatalism, helplessness, dependence, and inferiority . . . a strong present-time orientation with relatively little disposition to defer gratification and plan for the future . . . [1966a:7].

Other psychological characteristics of the poor frequently mentioned by Lewis and others are authoritarianism in interpersonal relations (Lipset, 1960; Cohen and Hodges, 1963), fatalism (Lewis, 1966; Rainwater, 1960; Chilman, 1966; Irelan and Besner, 1967), rejection of intellectuality, emphasis on concreteness, and various cognitive deficiencies (Deutsch et al., 1968; Lewis, 1966b; Cohen and Hodges, 1963), negative self-concept (Sarbin, 1970; Chilman, 1966), and higher frequencies of mental disorders in general (Hollingshead and Redlich, 1958; Srole et al,. 1962).

These psychological characteristics are thought to be consequences of the life conditions of the poor. The most conspicuous condition, of course, is the material or physical *deprivation* associated with poverty: poor and crowded living conditions, chronic unemployment, low wages, job insecurity, welfare, lack of savings, and constant shortage of cash (Lewis, 1966a:5; Irelan and Besner, 1967). Other conditions frequently mentioned all seem to be related, in one way or another, to economic deprivation. The poor are relatively *powerless* in dealing with various social institutions, such as schools, courts, hospitals, political organizations, etc. They are less able to exercise power through status, prestige, or institutional affiliation. As a result, they are also more *vulnerable* to misfortune—more vulnerable to economic disaster because of low financial reserves, more vulnerable to loss of work, loss of health, loss of spouse, and loss of personal freedom. They have more *limited alternatives* available to them. Lack of power, money, education, and prestige limits mobility and opportunities for the poor. And a final condition frequently associated with poverty is that the poor are more *isolated* from the rest of society. It wasn't too long ago that they were referred to as the "invisible poor" (cf. Harrington, 1962). These conditions, as well as others less frequently mentioned, are discussed in greater detail by Lewis (1966a, 1966b), Hess (1970a, 1970b), and Irelan and Besner (1967).

These conditions of poverty are viewed as the context within which the "culture of poverty" develops. The most prominent outcome is the psychological orientations and adaptations mentioned. But two other domains are also considered affected: the values of the poor and their family relations. With regard to values, Lewis stated there is an awareness of middle-class values, and that the poor may even claim some of them as their own, but that they generally do not live by them. "They will declare that marriage by law, by the church or by both is the ideal form of marriage, but few will marry . . . [engaging in consensual unions instead]" (1966a:7). Rodman (1963) talks about this pragmatic accommodation of the poor to circumstances which make the enactment of certain values difficult, a "value stretch." The overall treatment of values, however, by the deficit theorists is very sketchy and tends to merge with (and be overshadowed by) the conceptualizations of psychological orientations and personality characteristics of the poor.

On the other hand, it is quite clear that poverty is perceived to have a detrimental effect on family relations. The general picture that emerges from these descriptions is of unstable, disorganized, and authoritarian families characteristic of the culture of poverty.[5]

The basic model for the "deficit" theories can be stated as in Figure 15.4.

How the various elements described as characteristics of the "culture of poverty" affect (or are reflected in) parental behavior toward the child is not very well articulated. Some of the statements are quite general, such as that the child is socialized into the culture of poverty, or that the child adopts as his own the attitudes and orientations of his parents. Much of this socialization process is at the level of implication; i.e., the parents' personalities and psychological orientations will affect the way they raise their children. From these kinds of statements we would infer that poverty-level parents would manifest some of the same characteristics in child rearing as described for lower-class parents, but perhaps in more exaggerated form, i.e., they are likely to be authoritarian, to use imperative and positional forms of control, to be low on expressions of affection, and to use restricted linguistic codes.

Assessment of the "Deficit Theories" of Poverty and Socialization

Since the group of variables falling under the label of "psychological orientations and personality characteris-

tics" is the heart of the deficit perspective, we will focus on this group, and even so only on those concepts which have received the most research attention. We will not lose much by ignoring the other two intervening concepts in the model—values and family structure. Both have been considered in discussion of the previously examined theories.

Seven concepts will be examined in assessing the deficit theory: fatalism or locus of control, time orientation, ability to defer gratification, achievement motivation, authoritarianism, emphasis on concreteness in thinking, and self-esteem. These are the core psychological orientation variables associated with the "culture of poverty," and they have received enough research attention to allow us at least a preliminary assessment of their utility. In our assessment of the empirical evidence for the relationships between social class and these psychological factors, we will rely heavily on Allen's (1970) review of personality correlates of poverty.

One of the main ideas regarding the psychology of the poor is that their *time orientation* is focused on the present. It is argued that the present has a greater immediacy for the poor than it has for persons higher in the stratification system, and often life must be dealt with on a day-to-day basis. Thinking in future terms is a luxury which can be indulged only if immediate needs are satisfied. The relationship can be stated as a proposition:

P1: Social class is negatively related to present-time orientation.

Not many studies have systematically investigated this relationship, and those that have done so used children as subjects. The piece of research frequently cited as support for this proposition was done by LeShan (1952). On the basis of his study of lower-class and middle-class children (they were asked to tell a story which was then analyzed for temporal orientation), he concluded that lower-class children are less future-oriented. However, apparently there were errors in the statistical treatment of the data. Subsequent recalculations (Green and Roberts, 1961) indicate the results were not statistically significant. A number of other studies examined by Allen (1970) either found no class differences in time orientation or had equivocal results. On the basis of this empirical research

Figure 15.4.

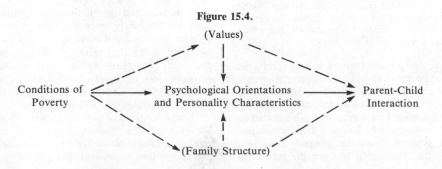

Allen concludes that the assumption that the poor have a shorter time perspective is untenable (1970:247).

Related to the idea that the poor have a present time orientation is the belief that they are less able (or inclined) to *defer gratification*. That is, they are believed to be more inclined to indulge themselves in immediate pleasures rather than postpone these for possibly greater rewards in the future. The proposition is:

P2: Social class is positively related to ability to defer gratification.

In a sense, this idea is the psychological expression of the "Protestant ethic," which has at its core a strong emphasis on hard work and self-denial and has been considered a part of the middle-class ethos.

Support for this proposition is based largely on inferences drawn from indirect sources interpreted as suggesting the lower class's inclination toward immediate gratification, i.e., Kinsey et al. (1948) on premarital sexual experiences (although more recent studies by Reiss, 1967, found no class differences in sexual permissiveness); Straus (1962) on lower educational attainment; Schneider and Lysgaard (1953) on patterns of consumption. But Allen found very little direct research support for a class difference in deferring gratification. Seagull (1964) and Shybut (1963) reported no class difference; and Mischel (1958) found a suggestive relationship between father's absence from home and child's preference for immediate rewards, but all of the children in his study were from the lower class. On the basis of this empirical review, Allen's conclusion is quite an understatement: "the prediction of a difference between lower and middle classes on willingness to delay gratification does not receive unanimous empirical support" (1970:248). We conclude the prediction is not supported.

Another central idea about the psychological orientation of the poor is that they are *fatalistic*, that is, they believe in fate or chance or luck or something *outside themselves* as responsible for their lives. In the research literature fatalism is usually conceptualized as "locus of control," with the destinction made between "internal control" and "external control" (fatalism). The poor are believed to attribute control of their lives to external sources. A behavioral consequence of fatalism or external control is resignation and apathy.

P3: Social class is positively related to internal control and is negatively related to external control.

Allen's assessment of the empirical literature suggests that this proposition is supported. Franklin (1963, cited in Allen, 1970), using a national stratified sample of adolescents, found a significant negative relationship between social class and feelings of external control. Battle and Rotter (1963) also found a class difference in the predicted direction. Less direct, but consistent and supportive evidence is also available on social class differences in feelings of alienation and anomie (Bell, 1963; Langner

and Michaels, 1963; Lefcourt and Ladwig, 1965). One contrary piece of research is provided by Titus (1966), who found no social class differences in internal-external control. But the bulk of the evidence seems to be in support of the proposition. This does not necessarily mean, however, that the character or psychology of the poor is any different from persons of higher class levels. Perception of external control by the poor may actually be an *accurate* assessment of their life circumstances.

Those who are fatalistic or high on external control are also likely to be low on *achievement motivation* (n Ach). McClelland (1961) and Atkinson (1958) are responsible for much of the theoretical and methodological development of n Ach. High achievement motivation indicates a strong impetus to excel, to set high standards for oneself, and to take moderate risks to accomplish one's goals. We would not expect people who believe that the direction of their lives is outside of their control to be very high on achievement motivation. The proposed social class relationship is:

P4: Social class is positively related to achievement motivation.

There is substantial empirical support for a positive relationship between social class and achievement motivation. In several carefully done studies Rosen (1956, 1959, 1961) consistently found lower-class subjects (adolescent boys) to score lower on n Ach than middle-class adolescents. Veroff et al. (1960) found a significant class difference based on the nationwide study of adolescents. Littig and Yeracaris (1965), testing the relationship on adults, found n Ach was related to the individual's present SES but not to that of his father. Also, Kohn's data (1969:ch. 8) indicate that where the respondent's class position differs from that of his parents, his values are likely to be much closer to those of his *achieved* class position than to those of the class position in which he was raised. This suggests that n Ach is less an aspect of personality developed early in the process of socialization than it is an adaptation to *present* social conditions. A cautionary note on interpreting these n Ach results is raised by Veroff et al. (1960), who suggest a possible class bias of the TAT measure.

The poor are thought to be more *authoritarian* in interpersonal relations. Belief in the validity of strength as the source of authority arises from the simplification of life experiences and from constant subordination (Irelan and Besner, 1967). Christie and Jáhoda (1954) discuss this tendency in terms of an authoritarian personality characteristic of the lower classes. Lipset (1960) considers it a reflection of the tendency for lower-class persons to select the least complex alternative. In family relations, this tendency would be evidenced in the greater reliance on formal authority, rather than reason, as the proper source of decisions. Therefore, the proposition is:

P5: Social class is negatively related to authoritarianism.

Empirical evidence for this proposition is diffuse, frequently indirect, but generally supportive. Much of it comes from an interpretation of class differences in parental behavior (such as the research of Hess and Shipman, 1965, and Cook-Gumperz, 1973, discussed above). Cohen and Hodges (1963) found that lower-class fathers tend to equate respect from children with their compliance and obedience. Bronfenbrenner's (1958) studies of class differences in parental punishment could be interpreted as giving indirect support for this proposition. The problem, however, in using these studies as evidence of class differences in authoritarianism is that this concept is being considered as an *intervening* variable between social class and these same parental behaviors which are being used to explain it! But there is some direct evidence of a social class relationship to authoritarian attitudes. Kohn (1969) found a correlation of $r = -.39$ between SES and parental attitudes labeled "authoritarian conservatism," which provides moderate support for the proposition. It should be noted, however, that Kohn does not view these attitudes as reflective of deep-rooted personality structures (as does Lipset, for example, in his conception of an authoritarian personality), but rather as reflective of values associated with occupational conditions of life (also see Gabennesch, 1972, for an elaboration of this view).

There is a cluster of personality traits attributed to the poor which generally refers to the tendency toward simplification of experience—anti-intellectual, pragmatic, concrete, having a preference for the familar. Riessman (1962), in describing this aspect of "the culture of the underprivileged," states that "the anti-intellectualism of the underprivileged individual is one of his most significant handicaps. . . . His practical orientation does not encourage abstract ideas. Education, for what it does for one in terms of opportunities, may be desirable, but abstract intellectual speculation, ideas that are not rooted in the realities of the present, are not useful and indeed may be harmful" (1962:56). This psychological orientation which limits thought and experience is viewed as psychologically dysfunctional, leading to cognitive deficiences (i.e., lower IQs, less competence in reasoning and problem solving). And as such it is perceived as a major element in the self-perpetuation of the "culture of poverty":

P6: Social class is negatively related to simplification of experience.

Most of the research cited in support of this proposition deals with social class differences in linguistic styles, e.g., the research of Bernstein (1971, 1973), Hess and Shipman (1965), Schatzman and Strauss (1955). From these reports, inferences are made regarding class differences in cognitive styles and competencies (cf. Sarbin, 1970; Deutsch, 1963; Bereiter and Engelmann, 1966). The inference does not seem unreasonable considering the intimate relationship between language and thinking in most of the literature on these topics. Despite Bernstein's (1970) disclaimer of any *evaluative* implications of his work concerning the cognitive competencies of lower-class persons, his work has perhaps the clearest implication for the "cognitive deficit" referred to in this proposition. By being limited to a "restricted linguistic code," characterized by speech patterns that are relatively concrete, simple, undifferentiated, egocentric, and ambiguous, lower-class persons would be expected to be psychologically more oriented toward the simple and concrete (anti-intellectual and pragmatic) and to have lower cognitive abilities at abstract reasoning and analytic thinking. The basis for many of the programs dealing with "early stimulation" was this association between the perception of an intellectually impoverished environment and intellectual impoverishment.

The evidence and its interpretations on this topic are hardly a closed issue. In fact they constitute one of the most hotly contested subjects in the poverty literature. Our own examination of the empirical basis for Bernstein's theory indicates that the empirical associations between social class and linguistic style are consistent but rather weak, and hardly a firm base from which to infer class differences in cognitive orientation.

Labov (1970), a linguist, provides the most direct attack on the linguistic deficit hypothesis. in his analysis of the language of ghetto blacks in Harlem, Labov shows that the language is as complex, differentiated, and "logical" as standard English. And that these ghetto children are as verbal and linguistically adept as middle-class kids. In fact, he maintains that they may even be more verbally adept, since survival in the street and status in the peer group depend largely on one's verbal skills. Labov's data are based largely on participant observation and the analysis of recorded interviews with his ghetto subjects. He is quite critical of the conclusions about linguistic and cognitive competence of lower-class people based on data obtained in university or laboratory settings (especially such research as that of Bereiter and Englemann, 1966, and Deutsch, 1967). The basis of his critique is that the relevant linguistic and communicative variables are not controlled in these settings, such as interpretation of the stimulus, perception of behavioral exceptions, motivation to respond, etc. In fact, Labov states that the experimenter is typically not even aware that these factors are problematic, especially for lower-class and minority subjects to whom these settings may be unfamiliar and threatening. He maintains that those groups ordinarily diagnosed as culturally deprived have the same underlying competencies as those of the middle class, any differences in cognitive performance being due largely to the circumstances of the testing situation (a view shared by others; cf. Cole and Bruner, 1972).

Labov is also critical of data based on survey research, such as that of Bernstein and associates. Here again he argues that inferences about linguistic capability are being made on the basis of linguistic data gathered outside the various *natural* situations in which the language is normally expressed. Since the interview situation is probably more threatening to lower-class than to middle-class subjects, their linguistic behavior is more likely inhibited and distorted in these settings, and consequently their cognitive capacities are underrated. Inferences about psychological capacities based on such data are highly questionable.[6]

How, then, are we to assess the empirical validity of the proposition that social class is related to cognitive capacity? That there are language differences (in dialect, phraseology, even linguistic style to some extent) is apparent—even Labov shows this in his work on "nonstandard English." It is also apparent that these differences are reflected in behavior ("Pygmalion" is a classic example). What is *not* apparent is that there are social class differences in cognitive capacity, based either on these language differences or on heredity. There is not enough empirical support to accept this proposition.

Given the perception that the poor possess some of the psychological characteristics discussed above, and that they are viewed as failures in significant aspects of life (occupation, family), they would be expected to have a low opinion of themselves (see Lewis, 1966, and Sarbin, 1970). The prediction is:

P7: Social class is positively related to self-esteem.

The empirical research on class differences, with remarkable consistency, does *not* support this proposition. Six of the studies reviewed by Allen (1970) found no difference in self-evaluation between lower- and middle-class groups (Hill, 1957; Silverman, 1964; Klausner, 1953; McDonald and Gynther, 1963, 1965; and Soares and Soares, 1969—cited in Allen, 1970), and others were either confounded or uninterpretable (Keller, 1963; Havighurst and Toba, 1949; and Mason, 1954). One well-designed study of grade school children (Soares and Soares, 1969) even found a reverse relationship: the lower-class children had more positive self-perceptions than the middle-class children. Even those studies which have found a positive relationship between social class and self-esteem reported it to be quite weak. Rosenberg and Simmons (1971) found a moderate relationship between social class and self-esteem for whites but no relationship for blacks, and the difference between black and white self-esteem was insignficant. Rosenberg concluded from his earlier findings that "there is no indication that the distribution of self-acceptance in a group is related to the social prestige of that group in American society..." (1965:56). Coopersmith (1967), who also found a slightly positive relationship, also concludes, "Poverty... may have deleterious consequences upon other personality traits, but [it has] little, if any, effect upon self-esteem" (151). On the basis of these findings the proposition that lower-class persons have generally lower conceptions of themselves than middle-class persons is untenable.

In retrospect, how much empirical support can be claimed for the position that poverty (or lower-class status) gives rise to psychological deficits? Not much. Of the seven psychological orientations and personality variables examined, three received some empirical support (locus of control, achievement motivation, and authoritarianism), and the remaining four were either refuted (present time orientation, deferring of gratification, and negative self-concept) or the evidence was too conflicting and equivocal to make an assessment (simplistic thinking–cognitive incompetence). Even for those relationships that received support the associations are quite weak. The average percentage differences on items between middle-class and lower-class groups was about 10 percent, and the correlations when given were in the .20s and low-.30s range. Furthermore, there is serious question about the methodological adequacy of much of this research. It seems to be in an even worse state than the other areas of investigation on social class and socialization. Allen (1970) puts it this way after assessing the evidence for six of the psychological variables:

> The quality of much of the research in the personality-poverty area is seriously deficient even when examined with charity. Failure to provide controls for obvious confounding effects (such as influence of social class of the investigator, and intelligence), small and nonrepresentative samples, and measuring instruments of dubious validity... are all too common. In many studies sweeping generalizations have been made about poverty and personality on the basis of unsystematic observation and unwarranted inferences [259].

The deficit perspective has had an inordinate influence among social scientists and policy makers, considering its weak empirical base. One reason for this is suggested by Valentine: "the notion of a 'culture of poverty' has become a dogma, an orthodoxy which is simply purveyed and repeated, rather than being subjected to critical examination" (1971:204). It has been relatively immune to research. The Federal government has also played a role in legitimizing and popularizing some of these ideas. For example, in an important summary monograph published by HEW (*Growing Up Poor*), Chilman (1966) reviewed the various family and personality characteristics associated with poverty by Oscar Lewis and other deficit theorists and suggested policy-oriented solutions on the basis of the perceived existence of these detrimental characteristics. Most of these dealt with various kinds of "enrichment" programs, directed at children and adults in various contexts (home, school, community), for the purpose of changing those *psychological barriers* to social mobility and integration of the poor into mainstream American society. These policies may have been well-meaning but, as the evidence suggests, misguided.

There is one more issue which needs to be considered with regard to the deficit paradigm: what effect do these psychological variables have on parent-child interaction? With a few exceptions, the consequences of psychological orientations on parent-child interaction have been unexamined. Of the variables which were found to be related to social class (locus of control, achievement motivation, authoritarianism), only parental authoritarianism has received any attention concerning its consequences for parental behavior. There is some basis for expecting parental authoritarianism to make a difference in the way in which parents act toward their children, i.e., greater rigidity, formality, inflexibility, greater reliance on physical punishment, less open affection and support. The problem is that it is hard to separate these behavioral outcomes from psychological orientation and authoritarianism—they are often used as *indicators* of authoritarianism.

On the whole, the psychological theories have not contributed much to an understanding of the relationship between social class and parent-child interaction. This might be due in part to the polemics and politics concerning the "cultural and cognitive deficit" theories, in which the psychological concepts we have examined have been largely embedded. Or we may simply have considered the wrong variables. At any rate, at this point the structural and ideational theories examined appear more solvent explanations of social class and socialization.

THEORETICAL INTEGRATION

It is apparent from this assessment of theories dealing with social class and socialization that they vary considerably in complexity, abstractness, and especially their degree of empirical support. But it is also apparent that in spite of this variation, each of the three theoretical positions has some degree of validity. Unfortunately, we cannot determine at this point how much of the explanatory power of each of these theories is due to the *interaction* effects of their major concepts with the explanatory concepts of the other theories.

A major objective of this volume is the development of theory for the various substantive areas of family sociology. But the task of producing a synthesis of the various theories considered into a theory of social class and socialization is formidable. Variations in assumptions, rationales, and levels of support for key relationships are major obstacles. Our explanatory concepts are all too often neither necessary nor sufficient conditions to account for variations in the dependent variables—if levels of association are any indication. At best we hope for consistency and convergence of findings to mitigate to some extent the low levels of association.

But the situation is not hopeless. We can at least move in the right direction. Our modest step toward theoretical integration and synthesis will be to develop propositional bridges where possible between the theories which have

had some empirical support. In the process we may move closer toward the development of a common paradigm, which is a prerequisite for the development of cumulative knowledge in an area (cf. Freese, 1972).

At this point it might be helpful to review what it is that is being explained. The phenomena in the form of empirical generalizations all deal with social class differences in parental behavior. Briefly, the most consistent findings have shown a positive relationship between social class and degree of parental support, affection, tolerance, and involvement with the child; use of reasoning, guilt, and other psychological and person-oriented methods of discipline; disciplining the child on the basis of the child's motives and feelings; emphasis on two-way communication between parent and child, reliance on reasoning, and discussion in verbal communication with child; emphasis on independence and achievement; involvement of father in child socialization; emphasis on reasons for rules; and democratic relationship between parent and child. On the other hand, the evidence points to a negative relationship between social class and use of physical punishment; disciplining the child on the basis of overt acts and behavioral consequences; use of commands and imperatives in communication with the child; emphasis on conformity to rules and obedience; and an authoritarian parent-child relationship. These relationships indicate that the first cluster of characteristics is more strongly associated with socialization in middle-class families, whereas the second cluster is more typical of lower-class families. These, essentially, constitute the phenomena to be explained.

The overall model of the explanatory concepts and their interrelationships is presented in Figure 15.5. Each of the boxes in the model represents groups of variables which if specified and interconnected would make the model immensely more complicated.

On the basis of our empirical assessment we can identify the strongest causal chain in the model as social class→self-direction in work and education→values→parent-child interaction. It can be stated as a set of sequential, interrelated propositions:

1. As SES increases, degree of occupational self-direction and education increases.
2. As degree of self-direction increases, parental values of self-direction increase and values of conformity decrease.
3a. As values of self-direction increase, parental concern with internal states of the child increases.
3b. As values of conformity increase, parental concern with external aspects of the child's behavior increases.
4a. As parental concern with internal states of the child increases, parental reliance on personal modes of control, reason, explanation, and psychological techniques of discipline increases.

Figure 15.5. Theoretical Model of Social Class and Socialization

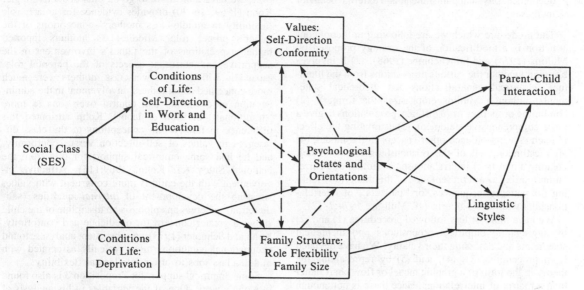

KEY: Solid lines indicate theoretically based propositions.
Hash lines indicate bridging propositions.

4b. As parental concern with external behavior of child increases, parental reliance on physical punishment and imperative and positional controls increases.

The content of this theoretical sequence derives from Kohn's particular conceptualizations. But the content of these concepts in the model need not be limited to these particular "conditions of life" or of occupation, or these particular values, or these parental behaviors. The concepts in the model are quite abstract and subsume a wide range of variables. The basic premise of this theoretical orientation is that values, beliefs, and ideology derive from our positions in the social structure. The task is to demonstrate how specific values are related to specific elements of social structure. With each new set of values, the social structural antecedents and the parent-child consequents must be demonstrated.

The family structure sequence is probably the second most credible explanatory chain. For the sake of simplicity, we will only consider one element of family structure—the degree to which the family role system is open and flexible. Other elements may also be important in the model, such as family size and power structure. The sequence of interrelationships can be stated as a propositional chain:

1. As SES increases, flexibility in family roles increases.

2. As flexibility in family roles increases, reliance

on elaborated codes increases, and reliance on restricted codes decreases.

3a. As reliance on elaborated codes increases, use of reason, explanation, personal modes of control, emphasis on principles in teaching, and two-way parent-child communication increases.

3b. As reliance on restricted codes increases, parental reliance on physical punishment, use of imperatives and positional controls, and one-way communication from parent to child increases.

Since there is a direct line in the model from family structure to parent-child interaction, the same propositional sequence could be posited minus the intervening concept of linguistic codes. It was not clear from the empirical literature how important "linguistic codes" is as an intervening concept. It appears to us that its main contribution is to the explanation of the dependent variables dealing with verbal interaction between parent and child.

Of the psychological states and orientations put forth by the several psychological theories considered, the most promising explanatory concept (empirically and with an eye to theory building) is fatalism or locus of control.[7] The propositional sequence for this concept is:

1. As SES decreases, conditions of life reflect more deprivation and powerlessness.

2. As deprivation and powerlessness increase, fatalism (external control) increases.

3. As fatalism increases, parental emphasis on obedience, physical punishment, and external behavior increases.

The prodedure which we are following in theory construction is a modification of the strategy proposed by Mullins (1974) and Stinchcombe (1968). (1) It involves bringing together the various propositions from the literature (empirical generalizations and theoretical statements, although Mullins emphasizes the former); (2) combining properties from different propositions to give a more comprehensive statement; (3) estimating the effect of each concept on each other concept in the model; (4) after estimating all of the relationships in the model, creating a matrix of interrelationships (similar to a correlation matrix) as a representation of the theory; (5) looking for patterns, sequences, or "clusters" of interrelationships within this matrix (cf. Mullins, 1974:7–12).

We have more or less followed procedures (1) and (2) by aggregating empirical propositions and theoretical statements and assessing their validity. We have deviated from procedures (3), (4), and (5) by representing the theory in the form of a graphic model or flow chart rather than a matrix of interrelations, since there is not enough basis for estimating intercorrelations for many of the relationships. But not much has been lost by our reliance on the flow chart. This form of theory representation makes more sense in areas of theory building which already have several theories available. This provides a basis for the conceptual and theoretical clustering and patterning without depending on a conceptual matrix for this to emerge. The rationale behind the two procedures is the same. But while the matrix automatically provides interconnections between the various propositions, clusters, or theoretical positions, these must be more directly spelled out in our approach.

There are five key propositions which interconnect the three theoretical positions included in the overall model:

1. As values of self-direction increase, degree of family role flexibility increases.

2. As family role flexibility increases, fatalism (external control) decreases.

3. As values of self-direction increase, fatalism decreases.

4. As fatalism decreases, use of elaborated linguistic code increases, and use of restricted code decreases.

5. As use of elaborated linquistic code increases, values of self-direction increase. As use of restricted linguistic code increases, values of conformity increase.

The directionality of these propositions is uncertain. Most of them appear to be symmetrical. The logic of the interrelationship of these intervening concepts in the propositional form stated above is based on inference from the nature of their relationships to social class and parental behavior. For some of the propositions, however, we have a bit more to go on than deductive logic. Kohn (1969:116–20) provides evidence for greater role flexibility in middle-class mothers' conceptions of the father's proper role. Middle-class mothers reported higher expectations of the father's involvement in the supportive and nurturant aspects of the parental role, especially with sons. Lower-class mothers were much more concerned about fathers' involvement in the administration of discipline and control over sons (a more "traditional" division of labor). Kohn attributed this difference in family role conceptions to the class differences in values of self-direction versus conformity, and he had some empirical support for this from the National Study (cf. Kohn, 1969:115). Affective involvement with the child is more congruent with values stressing the development of *internal* qualities (self-direction), whereas an emphasis on discipline of the child shows a greater concern for obedience and conformity. Kohn and Schooler (1973), in subsequent analyses, found occupational conditions more typically associated with middle-class jobs to affect intellectual flexibility.

Some empirical support for Proposition 3 is also found in Kohn's work. One of the variables in his analysis of general values and orientations, which he related to the specific parental values of self-direction–conformity, was "attribution of responsibility"-essentially the same as locus of control. The evidence, however, was more suggestive than direct.

Proposition 5 is quite consistent with Bernstein's association of linguistic codes with parental conceptions of the child and the nature of learning (Bernstein and Henderson, 1973). Emphasis on language in teaching the child principles of how things work, Bernstein argued, suggests that the parents have a "self-regulating" theory of learning, whereas lack of such emphasis reflects a "didactic" theory of learning. The distinction between these parental theories of learning is parallel to the values of self-direction and conformity respectively. But the major argument for these derived propositions depends on deductive inference and therefore is based on the soundness of the original propositions, and these, as we have seen, vary considerably in degree of empirical support.

RESIDUAL AND UNDERDEVELOPED THEORETICAL CONCERNS

The integrated theoretical model which we have presented is fairly parsimonious and accounts for much of the empirical ground between social class and socialization. At the risk of now being unparsimonious we will consider several directions of theoretical elaboration and expansion.

None of the theories in the overall model deals directly with social class differences in sex role socialization. A few oblique references have been made to the relevance of sex of parent and sex of child in considering some of the propositions. One of the problems of expanding theory in this direction is that findings of social class differences in the relevance of sex of parent and child in the socialization process are not very firm (no empirical generalizations were stated dealing with sex differences). However, two suggestive observations are worth pursuing. One deals with the greater involvement of middle-class fathers in nurturant and supportive parenting (Kohn, 1969; Thomas et al., 1974). The other refers to the observation that there is more sex role differentiation in the socialization of children by lower-class parents than by middle-class parents (Bronfenbrenner, 1961). Neither is a very strong relationship, but together they point to the greater relevance of gender (an ascribed status) in the parent-child interaction of lower-class than of middle-class families.

This proposition could be deduced from each of the four major explanatory concepts in our model, which probably have a cumulative effect in this case. It could be predicted that families with a relatively inflexible role system organized around ascribed statuses, in which parents value conformity and obedience in their children, attribute responsibility for their circumstances to external sources, and use a restricted linguistic style, would be more likely to emphasize conformity to traditional sex role conceptions in socializing their children. Conversely, to the extent that parents value individual achievement, stress self-direction and control over one's lot and express this individualistic orientation in their role relationships and linguistic patterns, we would expect to find relatively little sex role differentiation in child socialization. The theoretical model, then, is quite appropriate to these empirical observations.

A very basic consideration which has been part of the residual background of every proposition consideration in this chapter, but has not been directly addressed, is the nature of parenthood in America. To a large extent, addressing this issue focuses attention on the sociohistorical context for the empirical generalizations which the theory of social class and socialization was developed to explain.

The nature of parenthood can be considered in terms of each of the three major analytic concepts in the model: family structure, values, and psychological orientations. But we get at the heart of the matter most directly by conceptualizing it as an examination of the parent *role*. Conceptually, role is defined as a set of behavioral expectations associated with a status or position in a social system. It has a value dimension; i.e., how much value do people place on parenthood compared to other roles? And it has a psychological dimension reflected in the *identity* of parent that individuals hold as a substantive part of their self-conceptions (cf. Brim, 1960, for a conception of personality as an aggregate of the various roles people play; Stryker, 1968, and Gecas, 1973, for discussions of

identity hierarchies based on roles; and Sarbin, 1970, for the importance of the evaluative aspects of identity in lower-class socialization).

In considering the nature of parental roles, two directions of specification have appeared in the literature. The first (and predominant) direction has been the application of Parsons and Bales's (1955) expressive-instrumental formulation to the area of the family in general (cf. Zelditch, 1955) and parental roles in particular (Brim, 1957; Kohn, 1969; Sewell, 1963). The influence of this formulation seems to have run its course in family sociology, without adding much to our understanding either of group processes or of parenthood.

The second direction has been a concern with the meanings, values, and stresses and strains of the parental role. The literatue is more diffuse here, but it has a greater theoretical potential for our topic. Probably the core of this material is the parenthood-as-crisis literature. The transition to parenthood has been described as a crisis for the individual and the marriage, since it involves a realignment of old roles, the adoption of new ones, and the redefinition of previous family relationships. (See Rossi, 1968, and LeMasters, 1970, for extensive discussions of the reasons why transition to parenthood would be expected to be problematic in American society.)

But the research of parenthood as crisis has produced highly inconsistent results. For example, LeMasters (1957), in a study based on a nonprobability sample of 46 middle-class couples, reported that 83 percent of the parents indicated that the birth of the first child precipitated an ''extensive'' or ''severe'' crisis. Dyer (1963), using a similar sample, also concluded that the transition to parenthood is a crisis for most people, even though his findings were not as pronounced as those of LeMasters. Hobbs (1965, 1968) and Russell (1974), on the other hand, using probability samples which included couples from a much broader SES range, found little or no evidence of crisis in the transition to parenthood.

Jacoby (1969) suggests an interesting possibility for reconciling these very diverse results, which fits well with this chapter's focus. Noting that the studies which found a greater degree of crisis and disruption in transition to parenthood were based on middle-class samples (LeMasters and Dyer) and those that found less disruption were based on random samples (Hobbs and Russell), Jacoby suggests that the transition to parenthood is more difficult for middle-class than for lower-class parents. He goes on to discuss a number of reasons in support of this interpretation: (1) middle-class standards and expectations in child rearing are higher; (2) lower-class women are more strongly oriented toward home and family and place greater value in having children; (3) parenthood is more likely to interfere with career aspirations for middle-class women; (4) the middle-class husband-wife relationship is more strongly established at the time of birth. Swinehart's

(1962) finding that middle-class mothers express greater concern about the adequacy of their maternal role behavior is congruent with this interpretation.

Along with the nature of parenthood and conceptions people have of parental roles, there are undoubtedly other sociohistorical phenomena and processes which could be expected to have an effect on parental behavior, and which are probably differentially related to social class, such as redefinition of sex roles, increasing employment of wives outside the home, experimentation with "alternate family forms," and changing conceptions of childhood. As a line from a popular song chimes, "The times they are a-changing." Sociological theories cannot be too closely tied to historical phenomena if they are to be very useful. But neither can we altogether ignore the historical context within which social class influences on socialization occur. History provides us a vantage point for examining the assumptions upon which our theoretical formulations rest.

One final limitation needs to be emphasized. This essay has dealt only with the effects of social class on *parental* behavior, and for this reason alone it is incomplete. Our main interest in trying to explain parental behavior is that we perceive it as consequential for the child's development. We were strongly tempted to pursue our inquiry this next logical step. But the task would have been unmanageable for one chapter. This limitation would have been more serious except for the fact that several other chapters in this volume focus on the consequences of parental behavior for the child.

NOTES

1. Bronfenbrenner's (1958) work is especially strategic since it offered a historical and sociological explanation of changes in social class patterns in child rearing.

2. A good example is the current battle between the cultural–cognitive deficit theorists and the egalitarian theorists concerning social class differences in values, language, and socialization patterns and their effect on cognitive capacities (more will be said on this issue in the theory section of the chapter).

3. Of the family structure and process variables considered (such as family size, spouse's age, marital happiness), the only variable found to correlate with father's values, independent of class, was wife's employment.

4. Kohn has moved in that direction to some extent by including education in the reformulated model.

5. A good deal of the attention directed toward family structure is the result of Daniel Patrick Moynihan's controversial report *The Negro Family: The Case for National Action* (1965), in Rainwater and Yancey (1967).

6. But even more controversial is the argument proposed by Jensen (1968, 1970) of *innate* class differences in intellectual ability (also cf. Shockley, 1969). Jensen's argument is essentially the reverse of the other deficit theories: instead of arguing that environmental conditions (poverty), via linguistic deprivation or inadequacy, affect cognitive capability (intelligence), Jensen maintains that cognitive ability (biologically determined) affects language and life circumstances. Jensen interprets the consistent finding of a significant positive relationship between social class and IQ scores to mean that those in the upper classes are generally more intelligent than those in the lower classes, and furthermore that this difference is largely genetic. His explanation can be summarized as follows (Jensen, 1970): In a society in which social stratification is based to a large extent on *achieved* status through the application of one's skill and competence (i.e., a "meritocracy"), individuals in the higher social class levels should reflect higher levels of intellectual competence than those in the lower levels. This occupational selectivity on intelligence plus the tendency for people to marry within their social class position results in class differences in intelligence and their hereditary transmission.

Criticism of Jensen's position has come from many directions. Challenges range from the difficulty of separating environmental and genetic effects, to the question, what do IQ tests really measure? We are not prepared to go into the IQ controversy here, other than to state that there is still no agreement on the extent to which various standard IQ tests are free of cultural bias.

7. A case could also be made for authoritarianism, since it was found to have a moderately strong association with social class.

REFERENCES

ALLEN, V. L.
1970　　"Personalty correlates of poverty." In V. Allen (ed.), *Psychological Factors in Poverty*. Chicago: Markham Publishing Company.

ANDERSON, J. E.
1936　　*The Young Child in the Home*. White House Conference on Child Health and Protection. New York: Appleton-Century.

ATKINSON, J. W.
1958　　*Motives in Fantasy, Action and Society*. Princeton, N.J.: Van Nostrand.

BALDWIN, A. L. AND C. P. BALDWIN
1973　　"The study of mother-child interaction." *American Scientist* 61:714-21.

BATTLE, E. S. AND J. B. ROTTER
1963　　"Children's feeling of personal control as related to social class and ethnic group." *Journal of Personality* 31:82-490.

BAYLEY, N. AND E. S. SCHAEFER
1960　　"Relationships between socioeconomic variables and the behavior of mothers toward young children." *Journal of Genetic Psychology* 96:61-77.

BECKER, W. C.
1964　　"Consequences of different kinds of parental discipline." In J. L. Hoffman and L. W. Hoffman (eds.), *Review of Child Development Research*, vol. 1. New York: Russell Sage.

BELL, C. D.
1963　　"Processes in the formation of adolescent's aspirations." *Social Forces* 42:179-86.

BEREITER, C. AND S. ENGELMANN
1966　　*Teaching Disadvantaged Children in the Preschool*. Englewood Cliffs, N.J.: Prentice-Hall.

BERNSTEIN, B.
1960　　"Language and social class." *British Journal of Sociology* 11:271-76.
1964　　"Elaborated and restricted codes: Their social origins and some consequences." In J. J. Gumpery and D. Hymes (eds.), *The Ethnography of Communication*, special publication of *American Anthropologist* 66.
1970　　"A sociolinguistic approach to socialization, with some reference to educability." In F. Williams (ed.), *Language and Poverty*. Chicago: Markham Publishing Company.
1971　　Class, Codes and Control, vol. 1: *Theoretical Studies toward Sociology of Language*. London: Routledge & Kegan Paul.
1973　　*Class, Codes, and Control*, vol. 2: *Applied Studies toward a Sociology of Language*. London: Routledge & Kegan Paul.

BERNSTEIN, B. AND D. HENDERSON
1973   "Social class differences in the relevance of language to socialization." In B. Bernstein (ed.), *Class, Codes, and Control,* vol. 2. London: Routledge & Kegan Paul.

BERNSTEIN, B. AND D. YOUNG
1967   "Social class differences in conceptions of the use of toys," *Sociology,* 1, 2.

BOSSARD, J. H. AND E. BOLL
1956   *The Large Family System.* Philadelphia: University of Pennsylvania Press.

BOTT, E.
1957   *Family and Social Network.* London: Tavistock Publications.

BOWERMAN, C. E. AND G. H. ELDER, JR.
1964   "Variations in adolescent perception of family power structure." *American Sociological Review* 29:551–67.

BRIM, O. G., JR.
1957   "The parent-child relation as a social system: Parent and child roles." *Child Development* 28:343–64.
1960   "Personality development as role learning." In I. Iscoe and H. W. Stevenson (eds.), *Personility Development in Children.* Austin: University of Texas Press.
1966   "Socialization through the life cycle." In O. G. Brim, Jr. and S. Wheeler (eds.), *Socialization after Childhood.* New York: Wiley.

BRONFENBRENNER, U.
1958   "Socialization and social class through time and space." In E. E. Maccoby, T. M. Newcomb, and E. L. Hartley (eds), *Readings in Social Psychology.* New York: Holt, Rinehart and Winston.
1961a   "Toward a theoretical model for the analysis of parent-child relationships in a social context." In J. Glidewell (ed.), *Parent Attitudes and Child Behavior.* Springfield, Ill.: Charles C Thomas.
1961b   "The changing American child: A speculative analysis." *Journal of Social Issues* 17:6–18.

BURGESS, E. W. AND H. J. LOCKE
1945   *The Family: From Institution to Companionship.* New York: American Book.

CHILMAN, C. S.
1966   *Growing Up Poor.* Washington, D.C.: U.S. Department of Health, Education and Welfare.

CHRISTIE, R. AND M. JAHODA (EDS.)
1954   *Studies in the Scope and Method of "The Authoritarian Personality."* New York: Free Press.

CLAUSEN, J. A.
1968   *Socialization and Society.* Boston: Little, Brown.

COHEN, A. AND H. HODGES
1963   "Characteristics of the lower blue-collar class." *Social Problems* 10:303–34.

COLE, M. AND J. S. BRUNER
1972   "Cultural differences and inferences about psychological processes." *American Psychologist* 36 (November): 867–76.

CONNERS, R., T. JOHANNIS, AND J. WALTERS
1954   "Intrafamilial conceptions of the good father, good mother, and good child." *Journal of Home Economics* 46:187–91.

COOK-GUMPERZ, J.
1973   *Social Control and Socialization: A Study of Class Differences in the Language of Maternal Control.* London: Routledge & Kegan Paul.

COOPERSMITH, S.
1967   *Antecedents of Self-Esteem.* San Francisco: Freeman.

COWARD, B. E., J. R. FEAGIN, AND J. A. WILLIAMS, JR.
1974   "The culture of poverty debate: Some additional data. *Social Problems* 21(5):621–33.

DAVIS, A. AND R. J. HAVIGHURST
1946   "Social Class and color differences in childrearing." *American Sociological Review* 11:698–710.

DEUTSCH, M.
1963   "The disadvantaged child and the learning process." In A. H. Passow (ed.), *Education in Depressed Areas.* New York: Bureau of Publications, Teachers College, Columbia University.
1967   *The Disadvantaged Child.* New York: Basic Books.

DEUTSCH, M., I. KATZ, AND A. R. JENSEN (EDS.)
1968   *Social Class, Race, and Psychological Development.* New York: Holt, Rinehart and Winston.

DUNCAN, O. D.
1961   "A socioeconomic index for all occupations." In A. J. Reiss, Jr. et al., *Occupations and Social Status.* New York: Free Press.

DUVALL, E.
1946   "Conceptions of parenthood." *American Journal of Sociology* 52:193–203.

DYER, E.
1963   "Parenthood as crisis: A re-study." *Marriage and Family Living* 25:196–201.

ELDER, G. H., JR. AND C. E. BOWERMAN
1963   "Family structure and childrearing patterns: The effect of family size and sex composition." *American Sociological Review* 28:891–905.

ELDER, R.
1949   "Traditional and developmental conceptions of fatherhood." *Marriage and Family Living* 11:98–100.

ERLANGER, H. S.
1974   "Social Class and corporal punishment in child rearing: A reassessment." *American Sociological Review* 39:68–85.

FREESE, L.
1972   "Cumulative sociological knowledge." *American Sociological Review* 37:472–82.

GABENNESCH, H.
1972   "Authoritarianism as world view," *American Journal of Sociology* 77 (March): 857–75.

GECAS, V.
1973   "Self-conceptions in migrant and settled Mexican Americans." *Social Science Quarterly* 54:579–95.

GECAS, V. AND F. I. NYE
1974   "'Sex and class differences in parent-child interaction: A test of Kohn's hypothesis." *Journal of Marriage and the Family* 36:742–49.

GLADWIN, T.
1967   *Poverty U.S.A.* Boston: Little, Brown.

GREEN, J. E. AND A. H. Roberts
1961   "Time orientation and social class: A correlation." *Journal of Abnormal and Social Psychology* 62:141.

HARRINGTON, M.
1962   *The Other America: Poverty in the United States.* New York Macmillan.

HESS, R. D.
1970a   "Social class and ethnic influences upon socialization." In P. H. Mussen (ed.), *Carmichael's Manual of Child Psychology,* vol. 2. New York: Wiley.
1970b   "The transmission of cognitive strategies in poor families: The socialization of apathy and underachievement." In V. L. Allen (ed), *Psychological Factors in Poberty.* Chicago: Markham Publishing Company.

HESS, R. D. AND V. SHIPMAN
1965   "Early experience and the socialization of cognitive modes in children." *Child Development* 36:867–86.
1968   "Maternal attitudes toward the school and the role of the

pupil: Some social class comparisons.'' In A. H. Passow (ed.), *Developing Programs for the Educationally Disadvantaged*. New York: Columbia University Press.

HILL, T. J.
1957   ''Attitudes toward self: An experimental study,'' *Journal of Educational Psychology* 30:395–97.

HOBBS, D. F.
1965   ''Parenthood as crisis: A third study.'' *Journal of Marriage and the Family* 27:367–72.
1968   ''Transition to parenthood: A replication and an extension.'' *Journal of Marriage and the Family* 30:413–17.

HOFFMAN, M. L.
1960   ''Power assertion by the parent and its impact on the child.'' *Child Development* 31:129–43.

HOLLINGSHEAD, A. AND F. REDLICH
1958   *Social Class and Mental Illness*. New York: Wiley.

IRELAN, L. M. AND A. BESNER
1967   ''Low income outlook on life.'' In L. Irelan (ed.), *Low Income Life Styles*. Washington, D.C.: U.S. Department of Health, Education and Welfare.

JACOBY, A. P.
1969   ''Transition to parenthood: A reassessment.'' *Journal of Marriage and the Family* 32 (November):720–27.

JENSEN A.
1968   ''Social class, race, and genetics: Implications for education.'' *American educational Research Journal* 5:1–42.
1970   ''Learning ability, intelligence, and educability.'' In V. L. Allen (ed.), *Psychological Factors in Poverty*. Chicago: Markham Publishing Company.

JONES, J.
1966   ''Social class and the under-fives,'' *New Society* 22 (December):935–36.

KERCKHOFF, A. C.
1972   *Socialization and Social Class*. Englewood Cliffs, N.J.: Prentice-Hall.

KINSEY, A., W. POMEROY, AND C. MARTIN
1948   *Sexual Behavior in the Human Male*. Philadelphia: W. B Saunders.

KLAUSNER, S. Z.
1953   ''Social class and self-concept.'' *Journal of Social Psychology* 38:201–05.

KOHN, M. L.
1959   ''Social Class and parental values.'' *American Journal of Sociology* 64:337–51.
1963   ''Social class and parent-child relationships: An interpretation.'' *American Journal of Sociology* 68:471–80.
1969   *Class and Conformity: A Study in Values*. Homewood, Ill.: Dorsey Press.
1971   ''Bureaucratic man: A portrait and an interpretation.'' *American Sociological Review* 36:461–74.
1976   ''Comment on Wright and Wright: Social Class and Parental Values (ASR, 1976),'' *American Sociological Review* 41 (June): 538–45.
1977   *Class and Conformity: A Study in Values* (2nd edition). Chicago: University of Chicago Press.

KOHN, M. L. AND C. SCHOOLER
1973   ''Occupational experience and psychological functioning: An assessment of reciprocal effects.'' *American Sociological Review* 38:97–118.

KUHN, T.
1970   *The Structure of Scientific Revolutions*. Chicago: University of Chicago Press.

LABOV, W.
1970   ''The logic of non-standard English.'' In F. Williams (ed.), *Language and Poverty*. Chicago: Markham Publishing Company.

LANGNER, T. M. AND S. T. MICHAELS
1963   *Life Stress and Mental Health*. Glencoe, Ill.: The Free Press.

LAWTON, D.
1968   *Social Class, Language, and Education*. London: Routledge & Kegan Paul.

LEFCOURT, H. M. AND G. W. LADWIG
1965   ''The American Negro: A problem in expectancies.'' *Journal of Personality and Social Psychology* 1:377–80.

LEMASTERS, E. E.
1957   ''Parenthood as crisis.'' *Marriage and Family Living* 19:352–55.
1970   *Parents in Modern America*. Homewood, Ill.: Dorsey Press.

LESHAN, L. L.
1952   ''Time orientation and social class.'' *Journal of Abnormal and Social Psychology* 47:539–92.

LEWIS, H.
1971   ''Culture of poverty? What does it matter?'' In E. B. Leacock (ed.), *The Culture of Poverty: A Critique*. New York: Simon & Schuster.

LEWIS, O.
1959   *Five Families: Mexican Case Studies in the Culture of Poverty*. New York: Basic Books.
1966a   ''The culture of poverty.'' *Scientific American* 215(4):19–25.
1966b   *La Vida: A Puerto Rican Family in the Culture of Poverty—San Juan and New York*. New York: Random House.
1968   *A Study of Slum Culture: Backgrounds for La Vida*. New York: Random House.

LIPSET, S. M.
1960   ''Working class authoritarianism.'' Chap. 3 in *Political Man*. New York: Doubleday.

LITTIG, L. W. AND C. A. YERACARIS
1965   ''Achievement motivation and inter-generational occupational mobility.'' *Journal of Personality and Social Psychology* 1:386–89.

LITTMAN, R. A., R. C. MOORE, AND J. PIERCE-JONES
1957   ''Social class differences in childrearing: A third community for comparison with Chicago and Newton.'' *American Sociological Review* 22:694–704.

MACCOBY, E. E. AND P. K. GIBBS
1954   ''Methods of childrearing in two social classes.'' In W. E. Martin and C. B. Standler (eds.), *Readings in Child Development*. New York: Harcourt, Brace & World.

MACCOBY, E. E. AND C. N. JACKLIN
1974   *The Psychology of Sex Differences*. Stanford, Calif.: Stanford University Press.

MCCLELLAND, D. C.
1961   *The Achieving Society*. Princeton, N.J.: Van Nostrand.

MCKINLEY, D. G.
1964   *Social Class and Family Life*. New York: Collier-Macmillan.

MILLER, D. R. AND G. E. SWANSON
1958   *The Changing American Parent*. New York: Wiley.
1960   *Inner Conflict and Defense*. New York: Holt.

MILLER, S. M. AND M. REIN
1965   ''The war on poverty: Perspectives and problems.'' In B. B. Seligman (ed.), *Poverty and a Public Issue*. New York: Free Press.

MISCHEL, W.
1958   ''Preference for delayed reinforcement: An experimental study of a cultural observation.'' *Journal of Abnormal and Social Psychology* 56:57–61.

MORTIMER, J. T.
1976   ''Social class, work and the family: Some implications of the father's occupation for familial relationships and son's career decisions.'' *Journal of Marriage and the Family* 38(May):241–56.

MULLINS, N. C.
1974   "Theory construction from available materials: A system for organizing and presenting propositions." *American Journal of Sociology* 80(1):-15.

NYE, F. I., J. CARLSON, AND G. GARRETT
1970   "Family size, interaction, affect, and stress." *Journal of Marriage and the Family* 32:216-26.

OTTO, L.
1975   "Class and status in family research." *Journal of Marriage and the Family* 37:315-332.

PARSONS, T. AND F. BALES
1955   *Family, Socialization, and Interaction Process.* New York: Free Press.

RAINWATER, L.
1960   *And the Poor Get Children.* Chicago: Quadrangle Books.
1964   "Marital sexuality in four cultures of poverty." *Journal of Marriage and the Family* 26:457-66.

RAINWATER, L. AND W. L. YANCEY
1967   *The Moynihan Report and the Politics of Controversy.* Cambridge, Mass.: M.I.T. Press.

REISS, I.
1967   *The Social Context of Premarital Sexual Permissiveness.* New York: Holt, Rinehart and Winston.

REISSMAN, F.
1962   *The Culturally Deprived Child.* New York: Harper.

ROACH, J. L. AND O. R. GURSELIN
1967   "An evaluation of the 'culture of poverty' thesis." *Social Forces* 45:383-92.

RODMAN, H.
1963   "The lower class value stretch." *Social Forces* 42:205-15.

ROSEN, B. C.
1956   "The achievement syndrome: A psychocultural dimension of social stratification." *American Sociological Review* 21:203-11.
1959   "Race, ethnicity, and the achievement syndrome." *American Sociological Review* 24:47-60.
1961   "Family structure and achievement motivation." *American Sociological Review* 26:574-85.
1964   "Social class and the child's perception of the parent." *Child Development* 35:1147-54.

ROSENBERG, M.
1965   *Society and the Adolescent Self-Image.* Princeton, N.J.: Princeton University Press.

ROSENBERG, M. AND R. G. SIMMONS
1971   *Black and White Self-Esteem: The Urban School Child.* Washington, D.C.: American Sociological Association, Rose Monograph Series.

ROSSI, A. S.
1968   "Transition to parenthood." *Journal of Marriage and the Family* 30:26-39.

RUSSELL, C. S.
1974   "Transition to parenthood: Problems and gratifications." *Journal of Marriage and the Family* 36(2):294-301.

SARBIN, T. R.
1970   "The culture of poverty, social identity, and cognitive outcomes." In V. L. Allen (ed.), *Psychological Factors in Poverty.* Chicago: Markham Publishing Company.

SCHATZMAN, L. AND A. STRAUSS
1955   "Social class and modes of communication." American Journal of Sociology 60:329-38.

SCHECK, D. C. AND R. EMERICK
1976   "The young male adolescents's perception of early childrearing behavior: The differential effects of socioeconomic status and family size." *Sociometry* 39(1):39-52.

SCHNEIDER, L. S. AND S. LYSGAARD
1953   "The deferred gratification pattern: A preliminary study." *American Sociological Review* 18:142-49.

SEAGULL, A. A.
1964   "The ability to delay gratification." Doctoral Dissertation, Syracuse University.

SEARS, R. R., E. E. MACCOBY, AND H. LEVIN
1957   *Patterns of Child Rearing.* Evanston, Ill.: Row, Peterson.

SEWELL, W. H.
1952   "Infant training and the personality of the child." *American Journal of Sociology* 58:150-59.
1963   "Some recent developments in socialization theory and research." *Annals of the American Academy of Political and Social Science* 349:163-73.

SHOCKLEY, W.
1969   *Human Quality Problems and Research Taboos: New Concepts and Directions.* Greenwich, Conn.: Educational Records Bureau.

SHYBUT, J.
1963   "Delayed gratification: A study of its measurement and its relationship to certain behavioral, psychological, and demographical variables." Master's Thesis, University of Colorado.

SILVERMAN, M. I.
1964   "The relationship between self-esteem and aggression in two classes," *Dissertation Abstracts* 25:2616.

SOARES, A. T. AND L. M. SOARES
1969   "Self conceptions of culturally disadvantaged children." *American Educational Research Journal* 6:31-45.

SROLE, L., T. S. LANGNER, S. T. MICHAEL, S. T. OPLER AND T. A. C. RENNIE
1962   *Mental Health in the Metropolis.* New York: McGraw-Hill.

STINCHCOMBE, A.
1968   *Constructing Social Theories.* New York: Harcourt, Brace & World.

STRAUS, M.
1962   "Deferred gratification, social class, and the achievement syndrome." *American Sociological Review.* 27:326-35.

STRODTBECK, F. L.
1958   "Family interaction, values, and achievement." In D. C. McClelland, A. L. Baldwin, U. Bronfenbrenner, and F. L. Strodtbeck (eds.), *Talent and Society.* New York: Van Nostrand.

STRYKER, S.
1968   "Identity salience and role performance." *Journal of Marriage and the Family* 30:558-65.

SWINEHART, J. W.
1962   "Socio-economic level, status aspiration, and maternal role." *American Sociological Review* 28:391-99.

THOMAS, D. L., V. GECAS, A. WEIGERT, AND E. ROONEY
1974   *Family Socialization and the Adolescent.* Lexington, Mass.: Heath.

TITUS, W. R.
1966   "Relationship of need for achievement, dependency, and locus of control in boys of middle and low socio-economic status." Doctoral Dissertation, Indiana University.

VACA, N.
1970   "The Mexican-American in the social sciences." *El Grito* 4:17-51.

VALENTINE, C. A.
1968   *Culture and Poverty: Critique and Counter-Proposals.* Chicago: University of Chicago Press.
1971   "The 'culture of poverty': Its scientific significance and its implications for action." In E. B. Leacock (ed.), *The Culture of Poverty: A Critique.* New York: Simon & Schuster.

VEROFF, J., J. W. ATKINSON, S. FELD, AND G. GURIN
1960   "Apperception to assess motivation in a nation-wide interview study." *Psychological Monographs* 74:12.

WATERS, E. AND V. CRANDALL
1964   "Social class and observed maternal behavior from 1940–1960." *Child Development* 35:1021–32.

WEBER, M.
1946   *From Max Weber: Essays in Sociology.* Translated and edited by Hans Gerth and C. Wright Mills. New York: Oxford University Press.

WHITING, J. W. AND I. L. CHILD
1953   *Child Training and Personality.* New Haven, Conn.: Yale University Press.

WOLFENSTEIN, M.
1953   "Trends in infant care." *American Journal of Orthopsychiatry* 23:120–130.

WRIGHT, J. D. AND S. R. WRIGHT
1976   "Social class and parental values for children: A partial replication and extension of Kohn's thesis." *American Sociological Review* 41.

ZELDITCH, M.
1955   "Role differentiation in the nuclear family: A comparative study." In T. Parsons and F. Bales (eds.), *Family, Socialization, and Interaction Process.* New York: Free Press.

ZUNICH, M.
1962   "Relationship between maternal behavior and attitudes toward children." *Journal of Genetic Psychology* 100:155–65.

16

DISCIPLINARY TECHNIQUES AND THEIR RELATIONSHIP TO AGGRESSIVENESS, DEPENDENCY, AND CONSCIENCE

Suzanne K. Steinmetz

INTRODUCTION

So important are the child-rearing techniques which are utilized for cultural transmission, learning of roles, and the development of self that it has been suggested that "the central force for change in history is neither technology nor economics, but the 'psychogenic' changes in personality occurring because of successive generations of parent-child interaction" (deMause, 1974:3). An abundance of evidence suggests that the methods parents select for socializing their children reflect their perception of the attributes children need in order to successfully fulfill adult roles (e.g., Kohn, 1969; Miller and Swanson, 1958). The sheer volume of research on child rearing over the last four decades further attests to the importance placed on this topic.

Since so much concern has been shown regarding the effectiveness of specific socialization techniques, it is desirable to critically evaluate these data and derive a set of propositions describing these relationships. This chapter will examine the effectiveness of disciplinary techniques utilized during goal-oriented parent-child interaction on three behavior systems: aggression, dependency, and conscience development. "Goal-oriented" in this paper will be used in a manner similar to the Sigel et al. (1957:357) use of "influence":

The essential condition for the appearance of an influence technique is the occurrence of a divergence between the

behavior of the child and the wish of the parent regarding the behavior.

The use of "goal-oriented" is also similar to Baumrind's use of the term "parental control":

those parental acts that are intended to shape the child's goal-oriented activity, modify his expression of dependent, aggressive and playful behavior and promote internalization of parent standards [1967:54].

Recognizing that parent-child interaction is a two-way process (Yarrow et al., 1971; Thomas, et al., 1968; Gewirtz, 1969; Scarr, 1969), goal-oriented interaction in this chapter is expanded to include *purposeful interaction, with the intention of attempting to change, modify, reward or punish behavior, attitudes, or goals between parent and child.* Goal-oriented interaction is differentiated from other forms of interpersonal interaction such as parent and child sharing leisure-time activities— e.g., sports events, movies, or eating together when no conscious effort to effect a change takes place. It is, of course, recognized that all interaction between parent and child is an integral part of the family environment which influences effective child rearing. This chapter, however, will primarily be concerned with the active attempts to effect a change.

Limitations in Child-rearing Studies

A major limitation one faces when using existing child-rearing research to investigate disciplinary techniques and their effectiveness is the lack of clear definitions of concepts and variables used in the studies. Personality characteristics of the parents, attitudes toward child rearing, and behaviors are frequently used interchangeably. For example, Chamberlin (1974) compares authoritarian with accommodative styles. He defines authoritarian approaches as frequent use of orders, com-

NOTE: I wish to express my sincere thanks to Margaret Barker, Judith Vaughn, and Barbara Sandin for library assistance and Dorothy Windish for typing. Criticisms and suggestions valuable in revising this chapter were provided by Viktor Gecas, Deborah S. Kliman, Mary Jane Strattner-Gregory, Barbara H. Settles, and Darwin Thomas. This chapter could not have been completed without the generous support of the College of Human Resources and Dean Alexander R. Doberenz. Part of the work was carried out under NIMH grant #27557. Finally, I wish to acknowledge the editors of this volume, Wesley R. Burr, Reuben Hill, F. Ivan Nye, and Ira L. Reiss for continued support, encouragement, and valuable suggestions throughout the preparation of this chapter.

mands, threats and punishment. i.e., disciplinary techniques. Hoffman (1960) suggests that the authoritarian parent shows less empathy for the child, little consideration for his feelings, less awareness of the child's needs, less explaining of reasons to the child—a combination of personality characteristics, disciplinary techniques, and parental attitudes. While Harris et al. (1950) define authoritarian and permissive parents in terms of childrearing environments, the definitions used by Symonds (1939) and Kagan and Moss (1962) combine childrearing environments e.g., warm, hostile, restrictive, with disciplinary techniques. In fact, almost all studies reviewed used different definitions for similarly labeled constructs of child rearing. While this presents few problems for any one study, comparisons across studies become problematic.

Disciplinary Techniques

The relationship between parents' use of specific disciplinary techniques and children's aggressiveness, dependency, and conscience development are presented in Tables 16.4, 16.5, and 16.6 at the end of this chapter. Disciplinary techniques are defined as the specific objective responses which a parent utilizes in order to change, modify, or prevent undesirable behavior in the child. They have been generally categorized as psychological or love-oriented, and power-assertive techniques. Love-oriented techniques are further divided into two categories, positive and negative. The techniques subsumed under these categories are presented below:

> *Love-oriented positive* techniques, also referred to as induction, include praise, reasoning, compromise, mediation.
> *Love-oriented negative* techniques include isolation, showing disappointment, shaming, ridicule, and withdrawing love or attention.
> *Power-assertive* techniques include physical punishment, deprivation of privileges, yelling, shouting, tangible rewards, forceful commands, and verbal threats.

Delineating Parameters

There are several factors which have been used to define the parameters of this chapter. First, the independent variables being examined are disciplinary techniques. Thus the chapter will not examine, as independent or antecedent variables, personality variables, attitudes, or environmental setting, e.g., warmth or hostility. A second parameter, which is derived from the first, is the limiting of antecedent-consequent investigation to parental use of the three groups of disciplinary techniques and their effect on aggression, dependency, and conscience in

children. Thus an examination of the interrelationships between two or more of the above behavioral systems will not be undertaken. Since the literature linking these behavior systems involves other aspects of the child-rearing process such as autonomy, warmth, and hostility, which are outside the parameters of this chapter, the effect of these variables on the three behavior systems will not be considered.[1]

Another factor deals with level of confidence in the data. Many child-rearing studies involve small samples, e.g., Lefkowitz et al. (1963), 58 children; Sears et al. (1965), 40 children; Baumrind (1967), 32 children; and Hoffman (1963a, 1963b), 22 children. Even a sizable correlation may fail to reach significance. Other studies with larger samples—Sears et al. (1957), 379 children; Hoffman and Saltzstein (1967), 444 children—could report significant findings with a weak correlation. Although statistical significance provides confidence that the relationship is not due to chance, the amount of variance explained by extremely low (but significant) correlation (r^2) is so small that its contribution to an understanding of the child-rearing processes becomes questionable. For this reason, correlations which were .05 or less were reported as zero, and the strength and direction of a relationship *as well as* the statistical significance obtained are all taken into consideration in the interpretation of findings and deriving of propositions.

DEVELOPMENT OF AGGRESSION

Aggression can be defined as "a goal response to instigation to insure an organism" (Sears et al., 1953:179). According to Sears et al. (1957:221), aggression can be divided into two types: an instinctual emotional response to restraint or discomfort expressed as rage or anger; and a response with the goal to hurt or inflict injury, which is the product of social learning.

Feshbach (1970) labels this second type motivational aggression, and further subdivides it into instrumental and expressive aggression. Instrumental aggression is directed toward the achievement of a goal, while in expressive aggression it is the aggressive act itself which is the goal (Steinmetz and Straus, 1974).

Theoretical Perspective of Aggression

Based on the frustration-aggression research of Dollard et al. (1939), which utilizes psychoanalytic and learning theories, the child learns to respond aggressively to many frustrations in an automatic way. Since many of the child's previous frustrations and discomforts had been removed by his parents when he behaved aggressively, he responds aggressively in hopes of similar attention. As the child matures, the aggressive acts themselves are a source of gratification (expressive aggression) as well as a mechanism for obtaining gratification of other needs (instrumental aggression). Parental control of the child's aggression, however, becomes a source of conflict for the child, i.e., the desire to behave aggressively versus fear of the consequences. The anxiety produced in the child from this fear of parental punishment coupled with his desire to act aggressively is reflected by guilt, avoidance, dislike, and worry. This suggests two possible processes. First, a frustration-aggression model postulates that severe punishment results in an increase in frustration and higher levels of aggressive behavior in the child. Second, a displacement model suggests that severe punishment inhibits the child's aggressiveness in the parents' presence but increases his aggressiveness in another setting. Modeling theory provides an explanation applicable to both processes. According to modeling theory, parental use of high levels of physical punishment provides a model of aggressive behavior which the child "imitates," resulting in a highly aggressive child. This aggression may be directed toward the punishing agent or displaced toward another target.

Yarrow et al. (1968:57), in summarizing theories of aggression, notes that:

> The frequency and intensity with which aggression appears in child behavior are viewed then as determined by both excitatory and inhibitory factors, and by conflict-produced drive arising from the combined presence of these factors.

The approach-avoidance conflict decreases aggression toward the punitive agent, but may increase aggression toward other persons or objects when not in the punitive agent's presence.

Physical Punishment

One of the most frequently studied relationships in child rearing is that between parental use of physical punishment and aggressiveness in the child. These studies, summarized in the Supplementary Table 16.2, at the end of this chapter, were selected for comparison

Table 16.1. Summary of Relationships between Physical Punishment and Measures of Aggression in Children Controlling for Sex and Age

	2 YEARS			NURSERY SCHOOL			KINDER-GARTEN			3RD GRADE			3RD–6TH GRADE			4TH–6TH GRADE			6TH GRADE		
	B[1]	G	X	B	G	X	B	G	X	B	G	X	B	G	X	B	G	X	B	G	X
At Home																					
Mother			+	+	+	+	+/0	+				+	+				+		−	−	
Father							+/u[2]	+			+			+		+					
When Punished for Aggression																					
Mother				+	+	+			+										−	−	
Father				+	+																
Aggression in School																					
Mother				−	−[3]	+			+	+/n[4]											
Mother				+	n[5]																
Mother				+	+[6]																
Father				−	+	+	+/u			+											
Prosocial Aggression																					
Mother				+	+	+													0	+	
Father				−/0	+														0	+	
Aggression to Mother																					
Mother				+	+																
Father				0	+																
Aggression to Father																					
Mother				+	−																
Father				+	−																
Self-Aggression																					
Mother				−	−														+	+	
Father				−	−																

[1] B = boys; G = girls; X = combined boys and girls.

[2] The symbol u represents a positive relationship between low and high amounts of physical punishment and aggression, and a negative relationship between moderate amounts of physical punishment and aggression.

[3] Youngest child was 2–11 years; oldest was 6–0 (Yarrow et al., 1968).

[4] The symbol n represents a negative relationship between high and low amounts of physical punishment and aggression, and a positive relationship between moderate amounts of physical punishment and aggression.

[5] Youngest child was 3–4 years; oldest was 5–5 (Sears et al., 1953).

[6] Youngest child was 4–1 years; age of oldest was not given (Sears et al., 1965).

because they considered the disciplinary techniques; e.g., use of physical punishment or praise, as separate from personality measures or attitudes; or physical punishment was the major variable in the factor. The reader should be aware that this table, as well as other tables summarizing studies, various dimensions of a disciplinary technique such as frequency and intensity are combined into a single measure. The relationships between parental use of physical punishment and aggressiveness in children are summarized for ease of comparison in Table 16.1.

These data provide a strong basis for a general proposition relating physical punishment and aggression. Lefkowitz et al. (1963), Eron et al. (1961), and Winder and Rau (1962) found high, positive, significant relationship for both mothers' and fathers' use of physical punishment and child's aggressiveness, and Becker et al. (1962) and Sears (1961) found similar relationships for mothers' use. Chamberlin (1974), Hoffman (1960, 1963a, 1963b), and Hoffman et al. (1960) found high, positive, and significant relationships between power-assertive techniques— i.e., use of physical punishment, deprivation of privileges, and tangible rewards—and measures of aggression in children. These data provide considerable support for the proposition stated below:

1. A positive relationship exists between parents' use of physical punishment and aggressiveness in children.

The Act Being Punished

However, this relationship in part is contingent upon whether the physical punishment was administered for acts of aggression or for other disobedient acts. For example, Sears et al. (1957) found a significant (.23) relationship between physical punishment for aggression and child's aggression, yet no relationship was found when the physical punishment was for nonaggressive behavior. Sears et al. (1965) also supported this relationship. They found that physical punishment and aggression toward mother had correlations of .06 for boys and .18 for girls, but when the relationship between punishment for aggression and aggression was examined, the correlations were .23 and .17. A similar pattern was observed for fathers' use of physical punishment and aggressiveness (.14, −.16) and punishment for aggression and aggressiveness (.25, .11) in boys and girls, respectively.

Although Yarrow et al. (1968) question the relationship evidenced in these studies, their data substantiate many findings. For example, while a negative correlation (−.17) between general use of physical punishment for boys' aggressiveness was found, the relationship between physical punishment for aggression and boys' aggressiveness was .15. The low correlations between physical punishment to control aggression and girls' aggressiveness (.10), when compared with the high correlations

obtained between general use of physical punishment and aggression (.24, .17), and the correlations between severity of physical punishment for aggression and girls' aggressiveness (.25,.37) suggest several relationships congruent with other findings.[2]

First, it appears that, consistent with Sears et al. (1957) and Becker et al. (1962), the relationship between physical punishment for aggression and the child's aggressiveness is a different phenomenon than that between general use of physical punishment and aggressiveness. Second, the suspiciously low correlation for girls (compared with other correlations for girls) suggests that the relationships might be curvilinear. Finally, although physical punishment for aggression is not highly or consistently related to aggressiveness in girls, severity of physical punishment for aggression is positively and significantly related.

A similar relationship is found for boys. Although moderate (but not significant) negative relationships exist between use of physical punishment and aggression for boys, strong (and in one measure highly significant) relationships (.42, .20)[3] existed between severity of punishment for aggression toward parent and aggressiveness in boys.

Although a positive (but not significant) relationship between use of physical aggression and aggressiveness in boys was found, the nonlinearity of the relationship may be suppressing correlations which are based on the assumption of linearity. These findings suggest a fair degree of confidence can be placed in the proposition stated below:

2. A positive relationship exists between mothers' use of physical punishment and the child's aggressiveness. This relationship is contingent upon child's "aggressiveness" being the act punished. If the act being punished is not "aggression," the relationship is inconsistent.

Curvilinear Patterns

Becker et al. (1962) found that a curvilinear pattern existed between fathers' use of punishment and aggression in boys. Fathers who used moderate amounts of punishment had sons who were rated as less aggressive, both at home and in school, than did fathers who used either low or high amounts. Reversed patterns of curvilinearity were found for girls; Sears et al. (1953) and Becker et al. (1962) found that moderate amounts of physical punishment (as compared with either low or high amounts) were related to high levels of aggressiveness in both school and home, for girls.

Patterns of curvilinearity, which have appeared in several studies, and the suspiciously low correlations in studies where analysis has been based on the assumptions of linearity, suggest the following propositions:

3. A curvilinear relationship exists between mothers' use of physical punishment and aggressive-

ness in girls: low and high amounts of punishment exhibit a negative relationship; moderate amounts of punishment exhibit a positive relationship.

4. A curvilinear relationship exists between fathers' use of physical punishment and aggressiveness in boys: low and high amounts of punishment exhibit a positive relationship; moderate amounts of punishment exhibit a negative relationship.

Crossed-Sex Relationships

Crossed-sex relationships were found between physical punishment and aggression in young children. Of the 16 measures of this relationship between mothers and sons (Sears et al., 1965; Sears, 1961; Becker et al., 1962; and Sears et al., 1953) five were positive and significant, nine were positive, and only two measures were not in the predicted direction.

A similar crossed-sex relationship exists between father and daughter (Becker et al., 1962; Sears et al., 1965). Of the 11 measures of fathers' use of physical aggression and aggressiveness in girls, six were positive and highly significant. Four were positive (two did not report significance), and one relationship was negative. Only one study, Yarrow et al. (1968), failed to support the above relationship. Out of six measures, only one was in the predicted direction, and this relationship was not significant. Therefore, considerable confidence can be placed in the propositions presented below:

5. A positive relationship exists between fathers' use of physical punishment and aggressiveness in girls.

6. A positive relationship exists between mothers' use of physical punishment and aggressiveness in boys.

Age-Related Effects

Although these studies cover a wide age range, the cross-sectional design makes discerning age-related effects problematic. One study (Sears, 1961) obtained two different measurements (age five and 12), which enables some comparisons. First, correlations between aggressiveness at ages five and 12 were $-.03$ for boys and $-.08$ for girls. Although physical punishment to control aggressiveness was positively correlated with aggressiveness at age five (.18, girls; .22, boys), it was negatively related to aggression in 12-year-old children ($-.13$, girls; $-.20$, boys).

Additional comparisons can be made, using the Sears et al. (1965) study of nursery school children. While physical punishment inhibits self-aggression (injury or punishment to oneself) among five-year-olds (Sears et al., 1965), it appears to foster self-aggression among 12-year-olds (Sears,1961).

Finally, although physical punishment was strongly and significantly related to prosocial aggression (using aggression in socially acceptable ways such as punishment for rule breaking) among five-year-old girls (.49),

this relationship decreased among adolescent girls (.22). A similar but weaker relationship was found for boys.

Therefore, while both physical punishment and punishment for aggression tend to be positively related to aggressive behavior in preschool children, the use of punishment for aggressiveness tends to be negatively related to antisocial aggression among 12-year-olds, a finding which does not hold for general use of physical punishment. It appears that physical punishment for aggression has a long-term effect on extinguishing the aggressive drive, instead of instigating frustration and increasing aggression. The use of physical punishment as a disciplinary technique tends to decrease prosocial aggression (.49 to .22) for girls and (.09 to 0) for boys, and to increase self-aggression ($-.13$ to .12) for girls and ($-.18$ to .11) for boys, with an increase in age.

Because only one study examined age-related relationships and only one relationship, prosocial aggression for girls, reached significance, these propositions must be considered as suggestive and require further verification:

7. A negative relationship exists between mothers' use of punishment for aggressiveness and antisocial aggression in adolescents.

8. A positive relationship exists between mothers' use of physical punishment and prosocial aggression in girls. The strength of this relationship decreases with age.

9. A relationship exists between mothers' use of physical punishment and self-aggression in children. This relationship, which is contingent upon the age of the child, is negative for nursery school children and positive for 12-year-old children.

The propositions describing the relationships between physical punishment and aggression are diagrammed in Figure 16.1.

Nonphysical Punishment and Aggressiveness

In addition to physical punishment, other disciplinary techniques appear to be related to aggressiveness in children.

Power-Assertive Techniques

The data (see Table 16.4) suggest that for both girls and boys the use of tangible rewards, deprivation of privileges, and withdrawal of love, all negative love-oriented and power-assertive measures, is related to aggression in the home.

Winder and Rau (1962) found positive significant correlations between mothers' and fathers' use of deprivation of privileges and aggressiveness in fourth- to fifth-grade boys. Sears (1961) found a similar relationship among sixth-grade boys and self-aggression and a positive relationship among preschool girls and aggression toward parents. Yarrow et al. (1968) found negative

Figure 16.1. Physical Punishment and Aggression

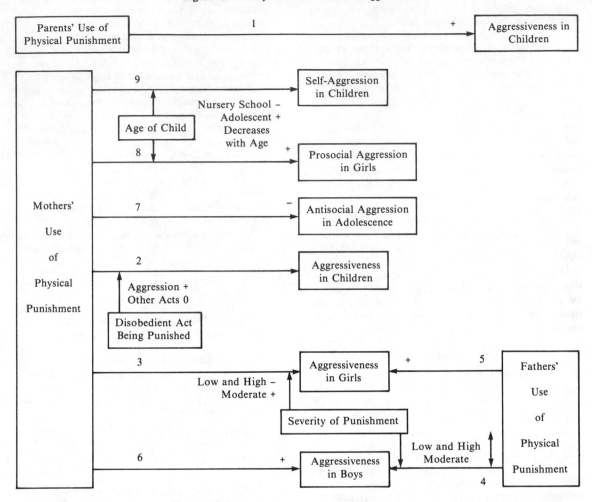

correlations between deprivation of privileges and aggression in boys. It appears that while deprivation of privileges inhibits aggressiveness in preschool boys, it fosters aggressiveness in grade school boys.

Sears (1961) and Yarrow et al. (1968) found a positive relationship between mothers' use of tangible rewards as a disciplinary technique and aggressive behavior in their children.

The generally strong, significant correlations found in the above studies suggest the following propositions:

10. A relationship exists between parents' use of deprivation of privileges and aggressiveness in boys. This relationship is positive for older boys and negative for preschool boys.

11. A positive relationship exists between mothers'

use of tangible rewards and aggressive behavior in children.

Negative Love-Oriented Techniques

Negative love-oriented techniques, e. g., withdrawal of love, avoidance, ridicule, rejection, and use of isolation, tend to show a positive relationship to aggressiveness in girls and a negative relationship to aggressiveness in boys. However, observation of the child's behavior resulted in significant and positive correlations (.47) between isolation and aggressiveness in boys (Sears et al., 1965).

Mothers' use of love withdrawal techniques appears to be negatively related to aggression in preschool boys; and positively related to aggressiveness, in school, for preschool girls (Yarrow et al., 1968). Among sixth graders, the use of love withdrawal discipline was highly correlated for boys (.48) and girls (−.40), suggesting a trend toward a reversal of effects with increasing age (Sears, 1961). While love withdrawal techniques inhibited aggression for preschool boys, they fostered self-aggression in sixth-grade boys. Love withdrawal fostered aggressiveness in school for preschool girls and inhibited self-aggression among sixth-grade girls.

Ridicule appears to be a sex-linked technique. When aggression toward mother was being measured, cross-sex negative relationships were found. Mothers' use tended to inhibit aggressiveness in boys, while fathers' use inhibited aggressiveness in girls. Cross-sex positive relationships were found when the measure was aggressiveness toward father. One final negative love-oriented technique, rejection, was significantly and positively related to aggressiveness in boys (Winder and Rau, 1962).

These findings are presented as propositions below:

12. Among preschool children the relationship between parents' use of withdrawal of love and aggressiveness is positive for girls and negative for boys. Among adolescent-age children, the relationship is negative for girls and positive for boys.

13. A positive relationship exists between mothers' use of rejection and aggressiveness in boys.

14. The relationship between mothers' use of ridicule and aggressiveness toward parents by boys is positive for aggressiveness toward fathers and negative for aggressiveness toward mothers.

15. The relationship between fathers' use of ridicule and aggressiveness toward parents by girls is positive for aggressiveness toward fathers and negative for aggressiveness toward mothers.

Positive Love-Oriented Techniques

Parental use of positive love-oriented disciplinary techniques, e.g., reasoning and praise, and their effect on aggressiveness in children were also investigated. Reasoning with preschool children appears to foster aggressiveness at home for boys (Yarrow et al., 1968, and Hatfield et al., 1967) but inhibit the use of aggression in school among girls. The effect of praise on childrens' aggressiveness, however, was weak and inconsistent. These data suggest the following proposition.

16. The relationship between mothers' use of reason and aggressiveness in girls is positive for aggression at home and negative for aggression in school.

The propositions describing the relationship between noncorporal methods and discipline and aggressiveness in children are diagrammed in Figure 16.2.

Inconsistencies

There are numerous examples of inconsistencies in these data. Yarrow et al. (1968) had perhaps a larger share of contradictory findings between different measures of the child's behavior than Becker et al. (1962) or Sears et al. (1965). For example, among girls isolation and aggression had a correlation of .42 based on the interview but only .13 based on the questionnaire. Reasoning was correlated with aggression in boys .42 based on the interview, and −.11 based on the questionnaire. Withdrawal of love had a weak positive correlation of .14 using questionnaire data, and a weak negative correlation of −.15 using interview data.

There are two possible explanations for the inconsistencies between the three measures (mothers' interview, mothers' questionnaire, and teachers' rating) in Yarrow et al. (1968), as well as the discrepancies between their data and those of other studies: range of ages in the sample and length of time between measures.

In commenting on the inconsistencies found in their data, Sears et al. (1965:37) noted that the age range for their sample (20 months for boys, 15 for girls) was "sufficient in preschool years to permit substantial variation in experiences and level of maturation." In Yarrow et al. (1968), the range of ages for the nursery school sample was 2–11 to 6–0 years, a total of 37 months, considerably greater than that noted by Sears.

When a group of children being measured range in age from under three to six years old, critical years in the child's development, it is necessary to consider the effect of age in the analysis. For example, a study may report a lack of a relationship between two variables. However, if age were controlled, a strong negative correlation for one age group and a strong positive correlation for the other might be discovered. Unfortunately, it is not possible to test this hypothesis with the Yarrow et al. (1968) data. One can, however, find some support for this position by examining other sources of data.

Kagan and Moss (1962:88) compared child's aggressiveness to mother for four time periods. These correlations, presented below, suggest that while the stability of the child's aggression scores is weak and nonsignificant for measures between younger age groups, the stability is considerably stronger between measures at later periods for the same children. Furthermore, Sears (1961) found only nonsignificant correlations of −.03 for boys and −.08 for girls between measures of aggression in nursery school and sixth grade.

A second source of support is provided by examining

Table 16.2. Age Periods and Child's Aggression toward Mother

	0–3 TO 3–6 YEARS		3–6 TO 6–10 YEARS		6–10 TO 10–14 YEARS	
Boys	.24	NS	.61	.001	.56	.01
Girls	.26	NS	.59	.001	.49	.01

Figure 16.2. Nonphysical Punishment and Aggression

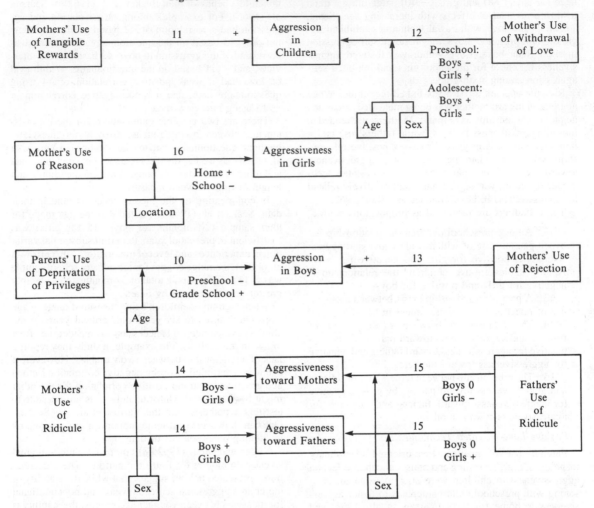

the data in Becker et al. (1962) provided in Table 16.4. This sample, which consisted of kindergarten children five to six years, shows considerably more stability between measure of aggression than does, for example, Sears et al. (1965) or Yarrow et al. (1968).

A final source of support is provided by comparing aggression scores obtained from children in preschool and later when they were in the sixth grade (Sears, 1961). The relationship between physical punishment and aggression when measured during the preschool years was .22 for boys and .23 for girls. Measures obtained during sixth grade, however, were weak and nonsignificant (.08, .06). When punishment for aggression and child's aggressiveness for the two age groups are compared, the differences are intensified .14, .18 for preschoolers, −.20, −.13 for

sixth-grade boys and girls, respectively. These data suggest that age has an important effect on the relationship between parental use of physical punishment as a disciplinary technique and amount of aggressiveness exhibited by the child. Furthermore, this effect appears to be intensified with younger (pre-school-aged) children. Unfortunately, the limitations of the data do not allow for an investigation into the specific direction or degree of this relationship.

A second factor contributing to the inconsistencies exhibited between measures involves the length of time between subsequent measurements. Yarrow et al. (1968: 17–18) note that the mother completed the questionnaire at the time the child entered nursery school; about one-half year later, she responded to the interview, and two months after this, the teachers rated the child. Therefore, the measures which they obtained have been influenced by different maturation levels and the effect of schooling on the child's behavior, as well as different situations (school versus home) and different relations (parent versus teacher).

Another major problem encountered when attempting to compare the finding of various studies is the lack of similarity in the variable comprising the punishment factor. The measures selected to detect the use of physical punishment usually confound the frequency and intensity of the technique with the disciplinary technique itself. Furthermore, the punishment factor often contains general attitudes toward punitiveness.

Several additional factors appear to contribute to the inconsistent relationships noted between discipline and aggression. First, many relationships appear to be sex-linked. Thus studies which fail to control for the sex of the child may fail to find important relationships. Second, some relationships exhibit curvilinearity. Therefore, correlations which assume linearity may be suppressing the true relationship. Another consideration is that the target toward which the child's aggression is directed, e. g., parents, teachers, siblings, may produce relationships of a different degree and direction. Thus comparing data from studies which are based on measurement of aggression toward different targets is likely to result in inconsistent findings.

A final factor contributing to inadequacies in the data revolves around inconsistent measurement of the concept "intent to injure," a basis aspect of the definition of aggression. Measures designed to tap this aspect in studies of aggression have varied considerably from direct physical acts such as hitting or slapping or threats to less direct forms of aggression such as tattling and verbal disapproval (Sears et al. 1953; Sears et al. 1965; Sears, 1961).

DEVELOPMENT OF DEPENDENT BEHAVIOR

This section of the chapter will investigate the relationship between the disciplinary techniques used by parents and measures of the child's dependent behavior. This section will not investigate attachment, which is centered around the mother-child bond at birth and in early infancy, and is often measured as the infant's reaction to separation, e.g., Schaffer and Emerson (1964). Attachment also differs from dependency in that it is dependency on a specific target, the mother.

Dependency according to Murray (1938) is behavior which has as its goal the obtaining of nurturance from other people, or which clearly indicates the reliance upon the help of others is the individual's dominant method of striving to meet his goals. Bandura and Walters (1963) define dependency as "a class of responses that are capable of eliciting positive attending and ministering responses from others."

Dependency is considered a drive system which consists of "persistent behavior which is maintained or increased in intensity in the presence of obstacles to goal attainment... [and] becomes to some degree autonomous from the original motivating conditions under which it was established" (Maccoby and Masters, 1970:86). It is derived conceptually from association of parental behavior with drive reduction. The child, when not responded to by the parent, becomes frustrated and produces a secondary drive for physical contact. This drive is considered developed when the child demonstrates his abilities to perform a task but insists that the caretaker do so.

Dependency is thought to contain five components: seeking help, seeking physical contact, seeking proximity, seeking recognition, and seeking attention. Beller (1955, 1959) and Sears et al. (1953) found that children differed consistently on these five measures from one another in their composite score, providing support for a general dependency drive. Maccoby and Masters (1970) suggest that a higher degree of trait consistency exists when ratings rather than behavior observations are used.

Since punishment and frustration cannot be avoided by the young child, the strength of the drives will depend on the amount of reinforcement as well as the amount of punishment. Thus a curvilinear relationship would be expected. The child's effort to obtain his goals are increased in number and strength by interference or frustration until a certain point when a lack of reward or reinforcement occurs. At this point the child would seek other sources of dependency gratification. Thus an increase in punitiveness increases dependency, but extreme punitiveness extinguishes the dependency-seeking drive and results in withdrawal. Unfortunately, linear correlation, the most usual method of analysis, will not expose these relationships.

Antecedents of Dependency in Children

Studies of antecedent childhood socialization practices and dependency have focuses almost exculsively on maternal warmth versus hostility-rejection and dependency. Although maternal warmth was not found to be significantly related to dependency (Baumrind and Black, 1967; Sears et al., 1965; Kagan and Moss, 1962; Yarrow et al., 1968), rejection and hostility did appear to be associated with dependency (Winder and Rau, 1962; Sears et al., 1957; McCord et al., 1962; Smith, 1958). Except for withdrawal of love, specific disciplinary techniques and their influence on the development of dependency have not been extensively studied. The findings presented in Supplementary Table 16.5, from which the propositions on dependency were derived, might be considered serendipitous data resulting from "shotgun" computer analysis which correlates all variables with each other. Thus tables which report only those findings that attain statistical significance limit the researcher's ability to discern consistent (but not significant) trends. Because of this limitation many of the propositions presented in this section must be considered as suggestive, not definitive.

Physical Punishment

Based on the data available, the use of physical punishment shows no systematic relationship to dependency in children. As shown in Table 16.3 three studies found no relationship for girls; four studies found no relationship for boys. Four studies produced positive relationships between physical punishment and dependency in boys (three of which were strong) and two studies found positive relationships for girls. A negative relationship existed in two studies for boys, and three studies for girls. Multiple measures within single study also produced conflicting results. Sears et al. (1957), reporting on four measures, found consistent, strong, positive relationships for boys and strong, negative relationships for girls. Yarrow et al. (1968), however, reporting on three measures, found inconsistent contradictory relationships for boys and girls. Becker and Krug (1964) utilized data reported by mothers, fathers, and the child's teacher. Their data suggest that when father rated the child's behavior, a positive relationship was found between fathers' use of physical punishment and dependency in boys (.23). When mother rated the child's behavior, a significant negative relationship (−.34) between her use of physical punishment and dependency in boys was found. Other findings were not consistent, although a trend for teachers to report a negative relationship for boys and no relationship for girls was found in Yarrow et al. (1968).

Sears et al. (1957:171) suggest that "use of physical punishment . . . was not related to the child's being dependent. It was only when punishment was focused upon . . . aggressive acts directed toward the parent that a relationship between punishment and dependency emerged." Thus it is not possible to predict the relationship between parental use of physical punishment and dependency in children with any degree of confidence based on available data.

Deprivation of Privileges

The use of deprivation of privileges shows a somewhat greater degree of consistency, but the level of confidence provided by the data must be considered moderate.

The three measures provided by Yarrow et al. (1968) are positive but weak for boys, and negative and somewhat stronger for girls. Winder and Rau (1962) found a significant relationship for mothers' use of deprivation of privileges for boys. Sears (1961) found weak negative correlations for both boys and girls. These findings suggest a tentative proposition:

17. A relationship exists between mothers' use of deprivation of privileges and dependent behavior exhibited by children. This relationship is positive for boys and negative for girls.

Tangible Rewards

Sex-linked differences appear between the use of tangible rewards and the child's dependent behavior. Sears et al., (1965) found that fathers' use of tangible rewards produced a strong, significant, negative relationship to dependency in boys for both the summed dependency score and proximity (−.48, −.58). Mothers' use of tangible rewards, however, exhibited a positive relationship to boys' dependency (Smith, 1958; Yarrow et al., 1968; Sears, 1961). The relationships for girls were weak, nonsignificant, and contradictory in direction. Based on the above data a proposition is suggested:

18. The relationship between the use of tangible rewards and the amount of dependent behavior exhibited by boys is negative for fathers' and positive for mothers' use of tangible rewards.

Praise

Three studies reported data on parents' use of praise and dependency in children. The only finding to reach statistical significance was that between fathers' use of praise and both the summed dependency and subscale proximity measures (.24, .58) for boys (Sears et al., 1965). Sears (1961) found moderate nonsignificant correlations between mothers' use of praise and dependency in boys (.19) and a weaker negative correlation for girls (−.11). Baumrind (1967) found negative, nonsignificant correlations between parental use of praise and dependent behavior in children. Since the sex of the child has produced consistent differences in both the direction and strength of correlations between disciplinary techniques and child's behavior, a measure which does not control for sex of the child reduces the confidence one can place in the data, especially when the findings are nonsignificant. Therefore, only one relationship can be stated with confidence:

19. A positive relationship exists between parents' use of praise and dependent behavior exhibited by boys.

Withdrawal of Love

Social learning theory has been used to explain the relationship between parental use of love withdrawal and dependent behavior in children. According to this theory the parent, if viewed as an attractive model, provides a meaningful relationship which fills the child's dependency needs. When this model withdraws love, threatening the relationship, the child discontinues the undesired behavior in an attempt to reinstate the relationship. The model then becomes a powerful social reinforcer and increases the child's dependency on this model.

Hoffman (1963a) provided data which suggest that among parents who are categorized as low in power-assertive techniques, love withdrawal is positively related to nurturance seeking from adults (.56). Among high users of power-assertive techniques, no relationship was found. This provides some support for the thesis that children whose parents are low users of power-assertive techniques might find the relationship with their parents more attractive and important and therefore perceive withdrawal of love as more threatening than children whose parents use power-assertive discipline.

Experimental studies (e.g., Hartup, 1958; Gewirtz and Baer, 1958) equate nurturance withdrawal or social deprivation (i.e., the adult experimenter refuses to interact with the child for a short period of time prior to the experimental task) with love withdrawal. Although these studies confirm the relationship between love withdrawal and dependency (defined as the effectiveness of the social reinforcer), it is questionable that this can be considered equivalent to parental disciplinary techniques used on a day-to-day basis.

Studies based on parents' ratings and behavioral observation of children do provide some support for findings from experimental research. Sears et al. (1957) found a correlations of .19 (p=.01) between mothers' use of love withdrawal and child's dependent behavior. Baumrind (1967) found a positive (approaching significance) relationship for fathers' use of this technique and a positive, significant relationship for mothers' use of this technique and child's dependency. These data suggest the following proposition when the sex of the child is not controlled:

20. A positive relationship exists between parents' use of withdrawal of love and the amount of dependent behavior exhibited by children.

However, Chamberlin (1974), in an observational study of two-year-olds, divided the parents into accommodative (love-oriented) and authoritarian (power-assertive) groups. Using a measure of combined love-oriented techniques, he failed to find differences between the two groups on measures of dependency.

When the sex of the child is considered, the relationship between love withdrawal and dependency tends to become less stable. Sears (1961) found nonsignificant negative correlations for boys, while Yarrow et al. (1968), using three different sources of data, found correlations of .20, −.06, and −.41. Only one of the measures from Yarrow et al. (1968) reached significance for boys (−.41), and this was teachers' rating of dependency in school. The correlations for girls based on Yarrow's data produced contradictory results; and only one correlation (.33) was significant in the Sears (1961) study.

Therefore, when sex of the child is considered, only limited support is found, and the following proposition must be considered as suggestive:

21. The relationship between mothers' use of with-drawal of love and the amount of dependent behavior exhibited at home is positive for boys and girls; in school, it is negative for boys.

Rejection

The relationship between parental use of rejection and child's dependency was investigated by Sears et al. (1957) and Winder and Rau (1962). Sears found a positive significant relationship between mothers' use of rejection and dependency in children. Unfortunately sex differences were not reported. Winder and Rau (1962), in a study of fourth-, fifth-, and sixth-grade boys, also reported positive significant relationships between mothers' and fathers' use of rejection and dependent behavior in boys. Although only two studies reported these relationships, the levels of significance obtained increase the confidence one can have in the following proposition:

22. A positive relationship exists between parental use of rejection and dependent behavior exhibited by children.

It should be noted that it is possible that other studies examined, but did not report or did not find a significant relationship between, rejection and children's dependent behavior.

Ridicule

Only one study reported a relationship between use of ridicule and measures of a child's dependent behavior. Baumrind (1967) reported a significant positive relationship between mothers' use of ridicule and dependency. A similar relationship, although weaker, was found for fathers. Separate analysis examining the effects of sex of the child was not reported. Since only one study reported this finding, although significant, the proposition presented below must be considered as somewhat tentative:

23. A positive relationship exists between mothers' use of ridicule and dependent behavior exhibited by children.

Reason

Baumrind (1967) reported a negative relationship between parents' use of reason and children's dependent behavior (p=.01). However, when sex of the child and parent was controlled, a significant positive relationship (.52) between mothers' use of reason and the reassurance-seeking component of dependency in girls was found (Sears et al., 1965). Yarrow et al. (1968) also reported positive correlation between mothers' use of reasoning and dependency in girls (.15) and boys (.15, .33). Only one correlation (.33) was significant. It also should be recognized that in Baumrind's study the measure was the child's self-reliance in completing a task, while in the Yarrow et al. and Sears studies the measures of summed dependency were attention wanted, closeness wanted, and separation anxiety. It may be that the parent who uses reason as a method of interaction fosters a desire for continued interaction because it is perceived as a positive experience—a different phenomena than the child who clings to a parent because of insecurity or fear of loss of a parent.

Some support for this position is provided by examining the components of the summed dependency score (Yarrow et al., 1968). Mothers' use of reason had a correlation of .39 with attention wanted, .29 with closeness wanted, and .16 with separation anxiety. This suggests that while the use of reason fosters self-reliance, it concomitantly fosters a desire for increased interaction, as noted in the propositions below:

24. A negative relationship exists between parents' use of reason and dependent behavior in children.

25. A positive relationship exists between mothers' use of reason and the attention-seeking component of dependency.

The above propositions between disciplinary techniques and the amount of dependent behavior exhibited by the child are diagrammed in Figure 16.3.

Lack of Replicability

There are several factors which contribute to the inconsistent finding and the low level of replicability across studies. First, the effect of maturation must be considered. Differences which appear between measures may be a result of the child's continual cognitive and physical growth. Thus differences between a measure obtained from parental interviews and subsequent measurement of the child's behavior may be reflecting maturation processes rather than inconsistency between two respondents or instability of the measure. A second factor is lack of specificity both relation-specific and situation-specific. Lack of relation specificity occurs when the instrument does not specify the same recipient of the dependent behavior across measures. While evidence (Heathers, 1955) suggests that dependency is generalized across adults (mother, father, teacher), it is not generalized for all measures to children. Lack of situation specificity results from attempts to compare behavior in an experimental setting, or in the classroom, with the child's behavior in the home. A third factor is the problem of systematic bias when respondent provides the data for both antecedent and consequent behavior. A fourth factor

Figure 16.3.   Relationship between Disciplinary Techniques and Child's Dependent Behavior

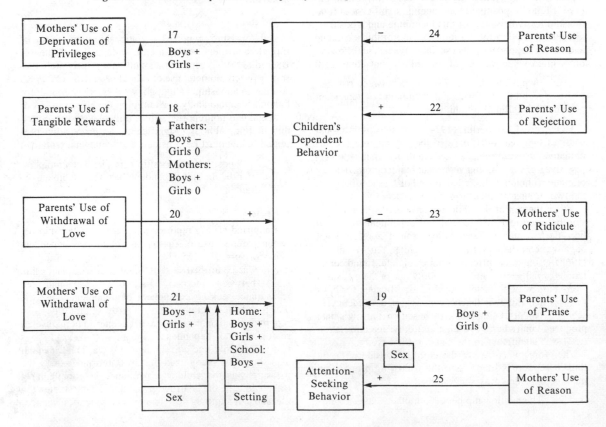

is related to sex-linked dependency behavior. Since dependent behavior is more acceptable for girls, it is possible that a greater degree of dependent behavior would have to be exhibited before their behavior is perceived as dependent by parent. A final factor considered by Maccoby and Masters (1970:146) suggests that the developmental level of the child is differentially related to the components of dependency measures. They note that:

1. Proximity seeking declines with age. Attention seeking does not.
2. Proximity seeking is increased under fear arousal. Attention seeking is not.
3. Attention seeking generalizes from adult targets to child targets. Proximity seeking does not.
4. Preschool-age attention seeking involves asking for and giving help, attention, nurturance. Proximity seeking does not.

DEVELOPMENT OF CONSCIENCE

Conscience, according to Aronfreed (1963), consists of the cognitive and affective processes which act as an internalized governor over an individual's behavior. The conscience influences the individual's ability to resist temptation, to express shame (if the transgression is witnessed by others), or to feel guilt (painful feeling of self-blame and self-criticism or remorse which are produced by deviation from proper behavior, Whiting and Child, 1953:219); when transgressions of moral standards occur (Miller and Swanson, 1960).

Most studies of conscience develop follow the theoretical model set forth by Sears et al. (1957). This model suggests that warm, loving parents who use love-oriented techniques foster parental identification and an acceptance of parental values and standards as the child's own. The child learns to take on the rewarding and punishing function formerly performed by the parents, thus replacing externalized control resulting from fear of punishment and fear of loss of loved parent with internal controls of guilt and remorse. According to Yarrow et al. (1968:95), "conscience is generally defined as an internalized control in which the child comes to punish or reward himself as though he has made the parents' standard his own." In psychoanalytic terms the individual, through the identification process, had developed an adequate superego.

The child develops this ability to internalize the parents' standards through identification which, according to Sears et al. (1957), is the process of role practice. This role practice "is more complex than simple trial and error because it requires the child to perceive and imagine himself in the place of a model" (370). The child will strive for identification if he sees the model as rewarding. A rejecting parent, one who uses power-assertive–materialistic techniques, will inhibit the process of identification, since the child will seek to avoid the parent,

resulting in a low level of conscience development. However, some studies have identified two forms of identification: positional, identification with the power and control aspects of the parental role; and personal, identification in which the child seeks to emulate the personal attributes of the parent (Slater, 1961; Hoffman, 1970a).

There are three criteria for recognizing the operation of conscience in young children: the ability to resist temptation, parental role playing, and evidence of guilt after transgressions. This suggests that the conscience is composed of at least two major components. The first is the degree to which an individual resists temptation. The second component involves the degree to which the individual expresses guilt or shame. This latter component has usually been labeled "conscience" in most studies (Sears et al., 1957; Sears, 1961; Sears et al., 1965; Yarrow et al., 1968; Burton et al., 1961). The data from which the discussion and propositions in this chapter are derived can be found in Table 16.6 at the end of this chapter.

Resistance to Temptation

Resistance to temptation has been studied in relation to disciplinary techniques as frequently as conscience. The greatest number of these studies are carried out in an experimental setting where the experimenter manipulates the nurturance withdrawal. The similarity between the child's performance under these circumstances and the effect of parents' use of discipline on resistance to temptation in nonlab settings has not been shown. The results of these studies are inconclusive for most relationships between discipline and resistance to temptation.

Withdrawal of Love

Allinsmith and Greening (1955) suggest that love withdrawal might foster the child's turning of anger inward, producing guilt. Maccoby (1959) hypothesized that the use of love withdrawal might result in the child later responding to deviation by withdrawing love from himself, resulting in lower self-esteem and increased self-criticism. Since guilt and self-criticism are used as measures in conscience, then, love withdrawal would appear to be efficient disciplinary technique for fostering the development of conscience in children. Two studies, Burton et al. (1961) and Grinder (1962), examined data on the effects of withdrawal of love on resistance to temptation. The findings, which must be considered as tentative, are a reversal of the relationship found between withdrawal of love and confession, and are contingent upon both the age and sex of the child. For preschool children the relationship was positive for boys and negative for girls. For 12-year-olds a positive relationship was found for girls, and a curvilinear relationship in which high and low use of withdrawal of love produced a negative relationship and moderate use a positive relationship was found for boys. Other relationships were weak and contradictory.

Reason

Sears et al. (1965) found a high, statistically significant relationship (.51) between mothers' use of reason and resistance to temptation in girls. While Grinder (1962) provides support for this finding, Burton et al. (1961) found a negative relationship. Experimental studies provided additional support for the efficiency of providing a rationale and the child's subsequent resistance to temptation. LaVoie (1974a) found that the use of a rationale increased the efficiency of an aversive stimulus. When no aversive stimulus was used, the use of a rationale significantly increased the child's resistance to temptation. In another study, LaVoie (1974b) found that aversive stimulus was most effective in instilling resistance to temptation with first and second graders, (500 seconds), followed by reasoning and tangible rewards (225 seconds each), withdrawal of love, (200 seconds), and praise (210 seconds). Over time (three segments four minutes long) the use of aversive stimulus decreased in the ability to foster resistance to temptation among respondents, while all other techniques became more efficient. Sex-linked

relationships were also found. Mothers' use of a rationale was found to be effective in increasing resistance to temptation in girls, while fathers' use increased resistance to temptation in boys (Parke, 1967; LaVoie, 1974a, 1974b; Fodor, 1973).

Ridicule

Only one study, Sears et al. (1965), reported a correlation between ridicule and resistance to temptation. They reported a high, positive, and statistically significant relationship (.51) between fathers' use of ridicule and dependent behavior in girls.

Because of the somewhat limited support provided in these data, the following propositions, which are diagrammed in Figure 16.4, must be offered with reservation:

26. A positive relationship exists between mothers' use of reasoning and resistance to temptation by girls.

27. A positive relationship exists between fathers' use of reasoning and resistance to temptation by boys.

28. A positive relationship exists between fathers' use of ridicule and resistance to temptation by girls.

29. The relationship between mothers' use of love

Figure 16.4.   Disciplinary Techniques and Resistance to Temptation

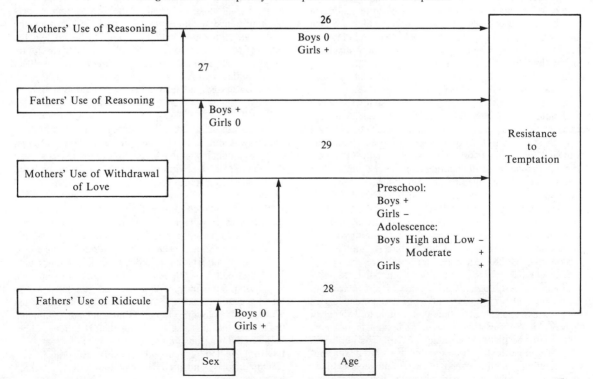

withdrawal techniques and resistance to temptation is contingent upon the age and sex of the child. For preschool children a positive relationship is found for boys, a negative one for girls. For adolescents there is a positive relationship for girls; there is a curvilinear relationship, with high and low use of love withdrawal producing a negative and moderate use producing a positive relationship, for boys.

Conscience

The most general relationship between discipline and conscience is the tendency for power-assertive techniques (physical punishment, deprivation of privileges, and tangible rewards) to be negatively related, and for positive love-oriented techniques (reasoning and praise) to be positively related, to conscience development. Unger (1962) found that love-oriented techniques compared with power-assertive techniques were positively correlated with conscience development. Hoffman (1970b) hypothesizes that power-assertive techniques result in external moral orientation based on fear of detection and punishment, while parental use of induction as a disciplinary technique fosters an internal moral orientation characterized by high guilt independence of external sanctions.

Comparing the findings of four major studies (Sears et al., 1957; Sears, 1961; Sears et al., 1965; Burton, 1968) with their data, Yarrow et al. (1968:112) conclude that:

the disciplinary techniques have shown neither strong nor consistent association across studies. The theoretical prediction for the class of love-oriented techniques to be positively related is not well supported, for both negative and positive association appear.

It should be noted, however, that based on factor analysis, love-oriented techniques are found to have both a positive and negative component (Roberts and Cooper, 1967). Therefore, combining these components into one generalized technique obliterates relationships which become apparent when these techniques are analyzed separately.

Positive Love-Oriented Techniques

Burton et al. (1961) and Hoffman and Saltzstein (1967) found consistent differences between reasoning (positive love-oriented) and withdrawal of love (negative love-oriented) and their effect on conscience development. Positive love-oriented techniques, praise and reasoning, are positively correlated with a strong conscience (Sears et al., 1957; Sears, 1961; Sears et al., 1965; Burton, 1968; Yarrow et al., 1968; Burton et al., 1961; Grinder, 1962; Hoffman and Saltzstein, 1967; Shoffeitt, 1971; Nevius, 1972). Although not all correlations reached statistical significance, they are in the predicted direction. Shoffeitt (1971), Hoffman and Saltzstein (1967), and

Sears et al. (1965) reported relationships between fathers' use of love-oriented techniques and conscience. Unfortunately, only Shoffeitt reported both significant and nonsignificant relationships, so it is not possible to assess other trends. However, the findings suggest that fathers' use of reasoning is positively correlated with a high level of conscience development in both girls and boys. Sears et al. (1965) found a strong, significant correlation (.58) between fathers' use of psychological rewards (e.g., praise and encouragement), versus tangible rewards, and high conscience development in girls. A correlation of .52 between fathers' use of praise and high conscience development in girls was also found. The consistency and levels of significance of these data provide a high degree of confidence in the propositions presented below:

30. A positive relationship exists between parents' use of positive love-oriented discipline and levels of conscience in children.
31. A positive relationship exists between mothers' use of praise and level of conscience in children.
32. A positive relationship exists between mothers' use of reason and level of conscience in children.
33. A positive relationship exists between fathers' use of praise and level of conscience in girls.
34. A positive relationship exists between fathers' use of reason and level of conscience in girls.

Negative Love-Oriented Techniques

Negative love-oriented discipline (e.g.) isolation, withdrawal of love) also appears to exhibit a relationship to conscience development. Shoffeitt (1971) and Nevius (1972) found a significant negative relationship between parents' use of love withdrawal and teenaged boys' level of moral development. Hoffman and Saltzstein (1967) in a sample of seventh graders found a positive correlation between fathers' use of love withdrawal and moral judgment in girls. They also found a significant positive relationship between mothers' and fathers' use of love withdrawal and indicators of guilt in girls, and mothers' use of love withdrawal and guilt in boys. Using nursery school samples, Yarrow et al. (1968), Burton (1968), and Sears (1961) found relationships between love withdrawal and conscience which were negative for boys and positive for girls.

These findings appear to be sex- and age-linked. While mothers' use of love withdrawal discipline exhibits a positive relationship to conscience in nursery school girls, it is negatively related to conscience among seventh-grade girls. However, the relationship between mothers' use of love withdrawal and conscience is negative for nursery school boys and positive for seventh-grade boys. Furthermore, fathers' use of love withdrawal showed a positive relationship to level of moral development for girls (Hoffman and Saltzstein, 1967) and a negative relationship for boys (Shoffeitt, 1971; Nevius, 1972), while mothers' use of love withdrawal was negatively related to adolescent boys' level of moral development (Shoffeitt, 1971).

Because of girls' earlier maturity, it is possible that mothers' use of love withdrawal is effective in fostering conscience in preschool girls but not in preschool boys. However, with increased maturity, withdrawal of love fosters conscience in boys. As girls mature, withdrawal of love apparently inhibits identification with mother and conscience development but fosters identification with father.

Isolation is positively correlated with level of conscience (Burton et al., 1961; Sears et al., 1957). When this relationship is examined by sex of the child, however, the findings are not so stable. Although Sears et al., (1965) found a positive, but not significant, relationship between isolation and level of conscience in girls (r=.24), Burton (1968) and Yarrow et al. (1968) found negative relationships (−.12, −.10, −.31). Yarrow's study also found negative correlations between isolation and level of conscience in boys (−.23).

Significant cross-sex relationships were found between mothers' use or ridicule and level of conscience in boys (−.43) and fathers' use of ridicule and resistance to temptation in girls (.51).

The consistency provided by these data, especially when they are analyzed separately for boys and girls, is not as impressive as that found for positive love-oriented techniques. Therefore, the propositions listed below must be viewed as having somewhat limited support:

35. A positive relationship exists between mothers' use of isolation and level of conscience in children.

36. The relationship between mothers' use of withdrawal of love and level of conscience in pre-school boys is negative while for adolescent boys it is positive. For girls a positive relationship is found for pre-school and a negative relationship for adolescent girls.

37. The relationship between fathers' use of love withdrawal and conscience is positive for girls and negative for boys.

38. A negative relationship exists between mothers' use of ridicule and conscience development in boys.

Power-Assertive Techniques

One of the more consistent relationships is that between use of object oriented or power assertive techniques and level of conscience. Parents' use of these techniques, consisting of physical punishment, deprivation of privileges and tangible rewards, is negatively and significantly related to level of conscience in children (Hoffman and Saltzstein, 1967; Burton et al., 1961; and Shoffeitt, 1971). Of the three disciplinary techniques which comprise the composite measure of power assertion, physical punishment appears to be most stable. Only two studies (Nevius, 1972, and Yarrow et al., 1968) out of eleven which reported this specific relationship failed to support the negative relationship between parents' use of physical punishment and level of conscience in children.

Deprivation of privileges is positively correlated with conscience development in girls, but the relationship for boys is contradictory and weak. The data on the use of tangible rewards is also contradictory. The only statistically significant finding was reported in Yarrow et al. (1968), in which use of tangible rewards was negatively correlated with conscience development in boys. This trend was also found in two other studies. However, a positive, but nonsignificant, relationship was found between tangible rewards and level of conscience in Sears et al. (1965) and Burton (1968). For girls, no significant or consistent relationship were found. These data suggest the following propositions:

39. A negative relationship exists between parents' use of power-assertive discipline and conscience development in children.

40. A negative relationship exists between mothers' use of physical punishment and conscience development in children.

41. A positive relationship exists between mothers' use of deprivation of privileges and conscience development in girls.

The data from which the first two propositions were drawn were consistent and highly significant, providing considerable confidence in them. The third proposition must be considered as tentative. The propositions which describe the relationships between disciplinary techniques and conscience are diagrammed in Figure 16.5.

Confession and Admission

Confession of the transgression, although a component of many measures of conscience, has been analyzed separately in several studies.

Power-Assertive Techniques

Parents' use of power-assertive techniques was found to be negatively correlated with confession for boys in Hoffman and Saltzstein's (1967) study. Mothers' use of physical punishment was negatively correlated with confession for girls in the Yarrow et al. (1968) study, and exhibited a negative correlation for children in Lefkowitz et al. (1963). This last study produced a curvilinear relationship between fathers' use of physical punishment and confession. Parents who used moderate amounts of physical punishment (two choices of physical punishment) had children who obtained higher confession scores than did children whose parents used either low (one choice) or high (three or four choices) of physical punishment. Furthermore, Sears et al. (1965) found a high, positive, significant relationship (.48) between fathers' use of deprivation of privileges (a component of power assertiveness) and confession by boys.

Figure 16.5. Disciplinary Techniques and Conscience

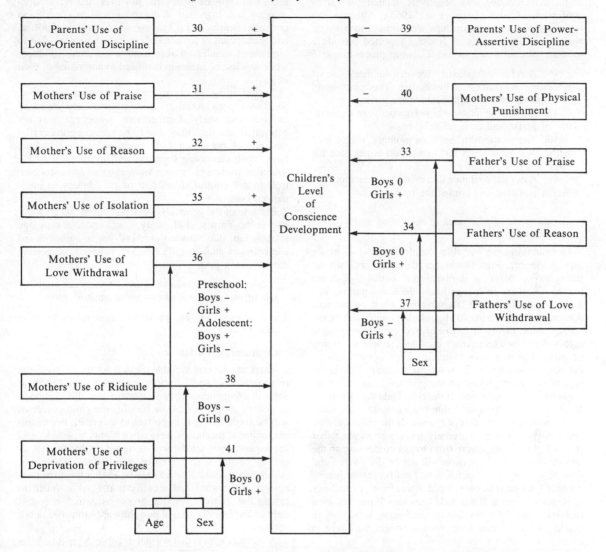

The following propositions are suggested by these findings:

42. A negative relationship exists between parents' use of power-assertive techniques and confession scores for boys.

43. A negative relationship exists between mothers' use of physical punishment and children's confession scores.

44. A curvilinear relationship exists between fathers' use of physical punishment and childrens' confession scores. Moderate amounts of physical punishment have a positive relationship; low and high amounts of physical punishment have a negative relationship.

45. A positive relationship exists between fathers' use of deprivation of privileges and confession scores of boys.

Positive Love-Oriented Techniques

Positive love-oriented techniques were also found to be related to measures of confession. Mothers' use of reason was positively and significantly correlated (.25) with confession for girls (Yarrow et al., 1968), and negatively and significantly correlated (−.56) for boys (Sears et al.,

1965). Mothers' use of praise, also a positive love-oriented technique, was negatively related ($-.43$) to confession in boys (Sears et al., 1965). Although the reporting of these relationships was limited to a single study, the high significant findings reported provide a measure of confidence in the following propositions:

46. A relationship exists between mothers' use of reasoning and confession by children. This relationship is negative for boys and positive for girls.

47. A negative relationship exists between mothers' use of praise and confession by boys.

48. The relationship between mothers' use of love withdrawal techniques and confession is negative for boys and positive for girls.

49. A negative relationship exists between mothers' use of isolation and confession by boys.

Comparisons of Measures of Admission and Confession

In examining the variable "confession," two major aspects emerge. First is whether the child confesses the transgression before it is discovered, because of either fear of discovery or fear of losing the loved parent. The second is admission of transgression when confronted. Although it is tempting to suggest that confession of the transgression *before it is discovered* evidences a more highly developed conscience than does simple admission of guilt *when discovered,* several other factors must be considered which revolve around risk taking. First is the fear of discovery, based on the probability of the transgression being discovered. If the child feels the likelihood is small, he may be more inclined to withhold confession. A second factor is the fear of reprisal. If the child feels the punishment might be extremely severe, he might rather risk a slightly more severe form by not confessing on the chance that his transgression will not be discovered and thus he will avoid all punishment. Finally, fear of loss of parents' love must be considered. Aside from any feelings of remorse or guilt, if the child fears loss of parents' love or respect and believes that by confessing he will more quickly reinstate this love, then he might be likely to choose confession over admission.

Although numerous studies collected data by which to test the difference between confession and admission, the practice of using several variables to form a composite measure plus the exclusion of correlation matrices from the appendices results in only one study, Yarrow et al. (1968), on which to examine these differences.

Some interesting sex-linked differences appear which are blurred in summary measures of confession and conscience. Generally it appears that certain disciplinary techniques lead to confession for girls while similar techniques lead to admission of guilt for boys. For example, the low use of power-assertive techniques and high use of reasoning are related to admission of guilt in boys.

High use of reasoning and power-assertive techniques is related to confession in girls; however, the relationship consists of a high use of deprivation of privileges and tangible rewards and a low use of physical punishment and withdrawal of love. Confession in boys is related to high use of withdrawal of love and a low use of isolation, while low use of isolation is related to admission of guilt in girls.

These findings must only be considered as suggestive, since most correlations are nonsignificant and are based on only one study. Furthermore, since age was not controlled, the data may simply be reflecting the earlier maturity of preschool girls compared with preschool boys. With increasing cognitive and social maturity the source of conscience moves from external (parental control) to self-control, from fear of punishment to internalized control.

Because of the generally weak nonsignificant relationship in the Yarrow et al. study, confidence for only one relationship, that between mothers' use of isolation and admission of guilt by girls ($r=.31$), is found, suggesting the following proposition:

50. A negative relationship exists between mothers' use of isolation and admission of guilt by girls.

These propositions are presented in diagram form in Figure 16.6.

Confounding Variables

There are several variables which act to confound the relationship between disciplinary techniques and measures of components of conscience. First, the likelihood of getting caught versus the benefits the child perceives will be forthcoming is important to ascertain. For example, material incentives were often highly desirable, and the experimental setting was designed so that the risk of getting caught was perceived as minimal. Therefore, comparisons across studies may be testing the attractiveness of the reward and security portrayed as much as testing the control over transgressions, which may rest only on the fear of external punishment (Aronfreed et al., 1963).

A second factor is that normal day-to-day parental rules may not be congruent with the rules expressed in the experimental setting. For example, children are usually told to remove the needle when the record is over in order to prevent damage to the record and needle. Yet Sears et al. (1965) in one measure to test resistance to temptation had a situation which required the child to choose between a scratching record or watching a hamster who might get out of his cage. Rather than measure resistance to temptation, one must ask if these experimental settings are not, perhaps, measuring obedience to authority (see Milgram, 1973).

A third point is that parents who express high aspiration for their children may produce in their children a strong

Figure 16.6. Disciplinary Techniques and Confession

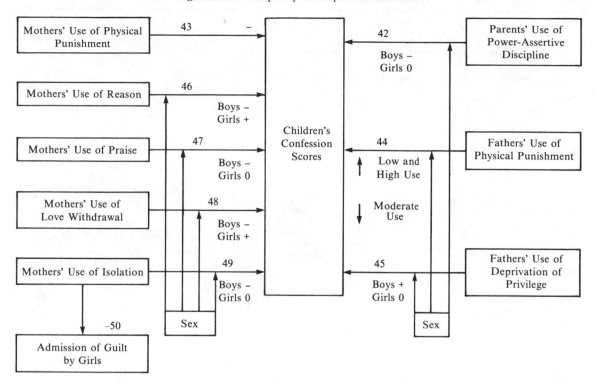

desire for success (Pearlin et al., 1967). In these instances cheating in order to win and be successful in their parents' eyes is more salient for children than fear of loss of love by deviating.

A fourth source confounding the data results from research being conducted primarily with young children and utilizing a social learning model which presumes that self-control results from avoidance learning during childhood (LaVoie, 1974a). Research findings suggest that moral development and impulse control continue until the late teens and early 20s (Bloom, 1964; Kohlberg, 1964; Kramer, 1968). Saadatmand et al. (1970) found different age-related motivation. While avoidance learning was the motivation for three-year-olds, instrumental behavior used to secure positive reinforcement, e.g., love or attention, was the motivation for six-year-olds; and previously learned behaviors, which are relatively unaffected by the experimental treatment, accounted for eight-year-olds' behavior; LaVoie and Looft (1973) found no significant relationships between type of discipline and six measures of resistance to temptation among adolescent boys.

A final variable, the effectiveness of the rationale, requires that sufficient information and legitimization must be provided. LaVoie (1974a) found that respondents who resisted deviation found the rationale a sufficient and legitimate reason for not handling the prohibited objects.

CONCLUSION AND IMPLICATIONS FOR FUTURE RESEARCH

This chapter has examined the specific relationships between disciplinary techniques and three behavior systems: aggression, dependency, and conscience. This summary section will evaluate each disciplinary technique and its effect on the combined three systems. These data, which have been arranged by sex of parent administering the discipline and sex of the child, are presented in the typology below (see Table 16.3). In general, mothers' use of power-assertive techniques (physical punishment, deprivation of privileges, and tangible rewards) produces aggressive dependent boys who are low in conscience development, and aggressive but nondependent girls who are low in conscience development.

Negative love-oriented methods (withdrawal of love, ridicule, isolation) when administered by mothers produce aggressive, dependent children with moderate levels of conscience development. Mothers' use of positive

Table 16.3. Typology of Discipline and Behavior

	MOTHERS' USE			FATHERS' USE		
	Aggression	*Dependency*	*Conscience*	*Aggression*	*Dependency*	*Conscience*
Boys						
Physical punishment	+	0	−	+	0	− n confession
Deprivation of privileges	− nursery + adolescent	+	−	− nursery + adolescent	0	− + confession
Tangible rewards	+	+	−	0	−	−
Reason	0	+	+ − confession	0	+	+
Praise	0	+	+ − confession	0	+	+
Withdrawal of love	− nursery + adolescent	− school + home	− nursery + adolescent − confession resist temptation: + nursery n adolescent	0	+	−
Ridicule	+ to mother − to father	+	−	0	0	+
Isolation (rejection)	+	+	− confession	0	+	0
Girls						
Physical punishment	+	0	−	+	0	− confession
Deprivation of privileges	+	−	−	+	0	−
Tangible rewards	+	0	−	0	0	−
Reason	+ home − school	+	+	0	+	+
Praise	0	0	+	0	0	+
Withdrawal of love	+ nursery − adolescent	+	+ nursery − adolescent + confession resist temptation: − nursery + adolescent	0	+	+
Ridicule	0	+	0	+ to mother − to father	0	0
Isolation (rejection)	+	+	− admit guilt	0	+	0

love-oriented techniques (praise and reason) produces boys who are dependent and have strong conscience development (but who resist confessing transgressions), and dependent girls with strong conscience development who are aggressive at home (but not in school).

The trends for fathers' use of disciplinary techniques are similar to those found for mothers, but the limited number of studies which examined fathers' child-rearing techniques does not provide the level of confidence provided by the studies investigating mothers' child-rearing practices.

In order to explain the processes involved in these relationships, it is helpful to first examine the theoretical framework which provided the foundation for much of this research.

General Theory

In most of the major studies examined, attempts to explain the mechanisms involved in the development of aggression, conscience, and dependency come from psychoanalytic and social learning theory and share a common theoretical thread. The key to this theoretical approach is identification, the mechanism by which the child's behaving like the parents or perceiving the similarity between self and parents becomes intrinsically rewarding (Sears et al., 1957:3). Through identification with the parent, the child develops dependency needs which, when not fulfilled, produce frustration and aggression. Identification also fosters the development of conscience. i.e., the child's adoption of parental standards as his own.

Identification is found to be an integral part of the three behavior systems under investigation in this chapter. First, a dependency need for the parent is developed in the child as a result of the parent providing nurturance and responding to his needs. A second step involves the parents' inability to respond to each and every demand of the child, resulting in the child feeling deprived of maternal stimulation. A third step, according to Bandura and Walters (1963), involves observational learning. The child models the behavior of the parents and by this means can reward himself, thus providing a substitute for the parent when affectionate interaction and nurturance are withdrawn.

Both rewards (the parent has overlooked the aggression or responded to the aggression by rewarding the child with attention) and punishment (which increases frustration) are hypothesized to increase aggressive responses. The outlet for this aggression, however, changes as the child matures. While the infant displays a generalized instantaneous response to frustration, the older child's behavior becomes more directed toward hurting the person frustrating him. With increasing maturity, most children learn to redirect these aggressive feelings and to express them in a culturally accepted way such as the use of verbal expression of disapproval of antisocial actions, or advocating the use of corporal punishment for infractions of rules. These socially acceptable means of expressing aggression have been labeled prosocial aggression by Sears (1961). The identification process is also an integral part of the development of conscience. Parental control of the young child involves direct, external control. Through role practice (Sears et al., 1957:369) the child discovers and learns new actions by observing what the other does and then practicing this new role by pretending to be the other person. The child's behavior is controlled first through direct means by the parent; next through fear of punishment or fear of the loss of a loved parent; and finally, when the child has learned to take on the rewarding and punishing functions of the parent, through identification and conscience.

This identification process requires that the child have strong dependency needs for the parent, needs which are fostered in early childhood when the child learns to expect nurturance. These same dependency needs, when frustrated, result in the development of aggression. Thus the three behavior systems are theoretically intertwined.

In order that the data provided in Table 16.3 be more congruent with the theory, modifications, based on the sex of the child, are required. For boys, the use of power-assertive techniques appears to result in increased frustration, which produces further aggressiveness but also reinforces the child's dependency needs—possibly because the increased frustration is related to increased feeling of insecurity. For girls, power assertive techniques appear to produce a different effect: although they increase girl's aggressiveness, they simultaneously produce nondependent behavior. If power-assertive techniques inhibit identification with the mother, the boy's reaction to these techniques appears to be one of frustration and insecurity while the girl's response is anger and a decrease in the attractiveness of the mother as a source for fulfilling dependency needs. If, as has been suggested (Bronfenbrenner, 1961; Minton et al., 1971), girls receive more nurturance than do boys, this may provide the basis for girls' self-assurance as well as provide a desirable model which the child imitates and thus acts aggressively. Boys, who receive less external manifestations of love, respond to the mother's power-assertive techniques with a fear of losing a valued and scarce resource. As a result, boys become frustrated and exhibit increased aggression, but also become insecure and exhibit increased dependency.

Positive love-oriented techniques foster role practice and result in a well-developed conscience. These techniques also foster dependency, but an analysis of the components of measures of dependency suggests that it is the "attention wanted" component, not the "anxiety separation" component, which is involved. Thus positive love-oriented techniques foster not only identification with the parent and emulation of parental qualities but also the desire for continued interaction with this parent. Since these techniques foster higher amounts of verbal and cognitive interaction between parent and child, they may also foster a higher degree of self-assurance and ability to stand up for one's position—which may be defined as inappropiate behavior for girls, i.e., aggressiveness.

Negative love-oriented methods inhibit identification for boys and girls. Thus frustration produced results in increased aggression and dependency and fosters only moderate levels of conscience development. Unlike power-assertive techniques, in which the parent controls the child through direct means, or positive love-oriented methods, in which the child's desire to emulate the parental role controls behavior, negative love-oriented techniques operate on the basis of fear of punishment or loss of parental love.

Implications for Future Research

Although the focus of this chapter was on examining the effect of parental use of specific disciplinary techniques on the development of aggression, conscience,

Supplementary Table 16.4. Discipline and Aggression

STUDY	AGE	CHILD'S BEHAVIOR		PHYSICAL PUNISHMENT	DEPRIVATION OF PRIVILEGES	TANGIBLE REWARDS	USE OF PRAISE	WITHDRAWAL OF LOVE	REASON	ISOLATION	RIDICULE
Sears (1961)[1]	Nursery school							*General Use*			
			Boy	.22	0	0	0	.14			
			Girl	.23	.28	.13	.18	-.07			
								Punishment for Aggression to Parents			
			Boy	.14							
			Girl	.18							
	6th grade							*General Use*			
		Self-agg.	Boy	.11	.24	.39	-.14	.48			
			Girl	.12	.06	.19	0	-.40			
		Prosoc. agg.	Boy	0	.06	-.09	0	.10			
			Girl	.22	-.08	0	0	-.14			
		Antisoc. agg.	Boy	-.08	.10	0	-.14	0			
			Girl	-.06	0	0	-.09	-.10			
								Punishment for Aggression to Parents			
		Self-agg.	Boy	0							
			Girl	.11							
		Prosoc. agg.	Boy	0							
			Girl	.18							
		Antisoc. agg.	Boy	-.20							
			Girl	-.13							
Yarrow et al. (1968)[2]	Nursery school	Agg. at home: Quest.	Boy	-.17	-.15	.25	—	-.24	.11	-.07	
			Girl	.24	0	.07	—	.14	0	.13	
		Inter.	Boy	-.07	-.17	.29	—	-.12	-.42	0	
			Girl	.17	.07	.25	—	-.15	-.08	.42	
		Agg. in school: Observe	Boy	-.16	-.24	0	—	0	-.11	.08	
			Girl	-.20	-.07	.16	—	.31	.42	.12	
								Physical Punishment for Aggression to Parents			
		Agg. at home: Quest.	Boy	.15							
			Girl	.10							
		Inter.	Boy	0							
			Girl	0							
		Agg. in school: Observe	Boy	0							
			Girl	0							

Study	Age/Grade	Measure			
Winder and Rau (1962)[3]	4th–6th grade	Aggression:	Mother	.03	
			Father	.001	(Rejection) .05
Lefkowitz et al. (1963)	3rd grade		Mother: 0[4]	11.08	
			1	13.71	
			2	16.19	(p = .01)
			3 & 4	18.39	
			Father: 0	9.79	
			1	14.96	
			2	15.16	(p = .01)
			3 & 4	14.89	

Nonphysical punishment and aggression $r = .03$

Study	Age/Grade	Measure		
Hatfield et al. (1967)	4–5 years	Self-agg.	Boys	.38
			Girls	.55
Eron et al. (1961)[5]	3rd grade	Agg. in home:	Mother	.47
			Father	.46
Sears et al. (1957)	5 years	Aggressive acts:		.23
		Other misdeeds:		0

(Only measured general use of physical punishment, not physical punishment for aggression).

Becker et al. (1962)[6], 5–6 years

Agg. in home:

		Mothers	Fathers
MI:	Boys	.29	.16
	Girls	.61	.48
MR:	Boys	0	.22
	Girls	.45	.36
FI:	Boys	.09	.30
	Girls	.30	.47
FR:	Boys	0	.23
	Boys	.32	.55

Agg. in school:

		Mothers	Fathers
TR:	Boys	.35	.15
	Girls	.12	.35

Agg. in child:

		Mothers			Fathers		
		Low	Med	High	Low	Med	High
PR:	Boys	30	42	57	45	35	53
	Girls	25	45	50	29	43	60
TR:	Boys	27	42	62	47	38	55
	Girls	15	48	24	28	34	40

continued

Supplementary Table 16.4 Discipline and Aggression Continued

STUDY	AGE	CHILD'S BEHAVIOR		PHYSICAL PUNISHMENT		DEPRIVATION OF PRIVILEGES	TANGIBLE REWARDS	USE OF PRAISE	WITHDRAWAL OF LOVE	REASON	ISOLATION		RIDICULE	
Sears (1961)[7]	5 years	Boys		47	47	53 (NS)								
		Girls		35	45	54 (.01)								
	12 years	Boys		69	59	51 (.08)								
		Girls		47	45	46 (NS)								
Sears et al. (1958)[8]	Nursery school	Agg. in school:	Boys	4	8	14								
			Girls	5	9	1								
Sears et al. (1965)	Nursery school			Mo.	Fa.				*General Use*		Mo.	Fa.	Mo.	Fa.
		Total anti-soc. agg.	B	-.09	-.37*						.47*	0	-.49*	0
			G	.14	0								0	-.10
		Total pro-soc. agg.	B	.09	-.17						.45*	-.19	-.18	.31
			G	.49*	.34								.25	0
		Agg. to mother	B	.06	0						-.16	.09	-.17	.26
			G	.18	.10								.06	-.37*
		Agg. to father	B	.14	.49*						-.39*	.13	.40	0
			G	-.16	-.30								-.06	.36*
		Agg. in school	B	.62*	.10									
			G	-.13	.36*									
		Self-agg.	B	-.18	-.09									
			G	-.13	-.34									
									Punishment for Aggression to Parents					
		Total anti-soc. agg.	B	.15	-.13									
			G	0	.40*									
		Agg. to mother	B	.23	-.10									
			G	.17	.30									
		Agg. to father	B	.25	.32									
			G	.11	.39*									
		Agg. in school	B	.22	-.10									
			G	.23	.44*									
		Total prosoc.	B	.35*	0									
			G	.32	.44									
		Self-agg.	B	0	-.40*									
			B	0	-.15									

Chamberlin (1974) — 2 years

	Accommodative[9]	Authoritarian[10]	
Mother's rating	4.7	5.7	p = .05
Mother's interview	9.76	10.25	p = .02
Home observation	2.80	4.60	p = .02

Hoffman (1963a) — Nursery school   (hostile acts/30 min.)

	Low power-assertive	High power-assertive
Hostility to children (C)	0	0
Hostility to teacher (T)	0	.56
Withholding love:		
Hostility to children	−.50	−.31
Hostility to teacher	−.68*	−.73*

Hoffman (1960) — Nursery school

	Hostility toward		Power-assertive toward		Resistance to influenced by	
	C	T	C	T	C	T
Unqualified power-assertion						
Mothers						
Middle	.42	.28	.33	0	.90***	.62*
working class	.76**	.11	.70*	0	.67*	.26
Combined classes	.60**	.51*	.48*	0	.68***	.42*
Fathers						
Middle class	.15	.23	0	0	0	.12
working class	−.28	.20	−.56	0	.25	−.14

Hoffman et al. (1960) — 3rd–6th grade

Parental coerciveness

	High hostility percent	High self-assertive percent
High quartile[11]	52	57
Remainder of sample	32	43

*P = .05   **P = .01   ***P = .005

[1] The .05 level of significance is reached by an r of .21 for girls; and an r of .23 for boys.
[2] The .05 level of significance is reached by an r of .25.
[3] Levels of significance reported.
[4] Number of physical punishment responses chosen.
[5] Although significance levels for correlations were not reported, with N=60 for mother and N=50 for father, both correlations are significant at .01.
[6] Statistical significance at .05 for girls requires an r of .34 for boys and an r of .33 for girls.
[7] Estimated ratings derived from graph. Values inverted for ease of comparison. A low conduct score = low conduct problem.
[8] Median number of aggressive acts.
[9] Spanking once a week or less, and use of positive love-oriented methods.
[10] Spanking once a day or more, and use of power-assertive discipline.
[11] Difference between propositions is significant at .05 (one-tailed test).

MR = mothers' rating; MI = mothers' interview; FI = fathers' interview; FR = fathers' rating; PR = parents rating; TR = teachers' rating.

Supplementary Table 16.5. Disciplinary Techniques and Child's Dependent Behavior

STUDY	AGE	PHYSICAL PUNISHMENT	DEPRIVATION OF PRIVILEGES	TANGIBLE REWARDS	USE OF PRAISE	WITHDRAWAL OF LOVE	ISOLATION	REJECTION	REASON	RIDICULE
Sears et al. (1953)	Nursery school	Boys: High 28 Moderate 25 Low 30 Girls: High 17 Moderate 35 Low 37 (Punitiveness power-assertive) Boys: .20 to teacher .47 other children .38 total rating .29 total observed Girls: −.10 to teacher −.07 other children −.10 total rating −.48 total observed	Median dependency scores							
Sears et al. (1957)[1]	Kindergarten					.19**		.12*		
Sears (1961)[2]	Nursery school	Boys .06 Girls 0	−.08 −.06	.15 .09	.19 −.11	−.10 .33				
Winder and Rau (1962)[3]	4th–6th grade	Mother .01 Father .01	.01							
Becker et al. (1962)[4]	5–6 years	*Mothers' use* Boys .11 Girls .23 *Fathers' use* Boys 0 Girls .06								
Becker and Krug (1964)	5–6 years	MR: Boys −.34 .08 Girls −.19 .10 FR: Boys .07 .23 Girls −.15 0 TR: Boys −.20 −.16 Girls 0 0						.01 .05		

Smith (1958), 3–4 years

			(Leave field)
Boys	− 39*	.07	−.20
Girls	10	−.36*	.29

Yarrow et al. (1968)[5], Nursery school

			Mothers' Rating	(Leave field)
Boys	− 17	.09	.22	.15	−.09
Girls	− 14	−.21	−.13	.15	.06
Boys	0	.16	−.18	.33*	0
Girls	0	0	.06	0	.21
Boys	42	0	.33*	−.20	−.08
Girls	07	−.14	−.09	.12	.20

Mothers' Rating −.06 / .20 *Mothers' Interview* .20 / 0 *Teachers' Rating* −.41* / −.12 *Mothers' Use*

Sears et al. (1965), Nursery school

Mothers' Use / *Fathers' Use*

	Mothers' Use	*Fathers' Use*	Mo.		Fa.
Reassurance-seeking: Girls	.52*				
Summed-dependency: Boys	.24*	−.48*	4.4	NS	4.0
Touching: Boys	.58*	−.58*	3.6		3.4

Baumrind (1967), 3–4 years

	Mo.		Fa.	Mo.		Fa.	Mo.		Fa.	Mo.		Fa.	Parents		
Pattern I (self-reliant)	2.6	NS	2.2	4.4	NS	4.0	1.2	NS	1.4	1.3	NS	1.6	23.6	NS	4.3
Pattern III (dependent)	2.1		1.9	3.6		3.4	2.0		2.1	2.4		1.9			

Chamberlin (1974), 2 years

	Authoritarian	Accommodative	
Mothers' rating: Dependent/inhibited	5.3	5.0	NS
Interview: Withdraw from strangers	9.55	10.00	NS
Approach to mother	9.73	10.21	.05

*Significant at 0.5 level.   **Significant at .01 level.
[1]For significance at .05 level, r = .35 for boys, r = .37 for girls.
[2]For significance at .05 level, r = .23 for boys, r = .21 for girls.
[3]Levels of significance are reported.
[4]For significance at .05 level, r = .33 for boys, r = .34 for girls.
[5]For level of significance of .05, r = .25 is needed.

Supplementary Table 16.6. Disciplinary Techniques and Conscience

STUDY	AGE	CHILD'S BEHAVIOR		PHYSICAL PUNISHMENT	DEPRIVATION OF PRIVILEGES	TANGIBLE REWARDS	REASON	WITHDRAWAL OF LOVE	USE OF PRAISE	ISOLATION	RIDICULE
Sears (1961)[1]	Nursery school	Conscience	B	-.25*	-.14	-.17		0	.19		
			G	-.25	.11	0		.11	.19		
Sears et al. (1957)[2]	Kindergarten	Conscience	B	-.23*	-.07	-.06	.18*	.09	.19*	0	
			G	-.18*	-.08	0			.16*		
Sears et al. (1965)[2]	Nursery school	Conscience *(Mother's Use)*	B	-.14	.16	.21	.32	.08	.50	0	-.43
			G	-.51*	0	.25	.11	0	.23	.24	0
		Conscience *(Father's Use)*	B						0		
			G						.52*		
		(Psy. rewards vs. tang. rewards = .58)*									
Burton (unpub.) (1968)[2]	Nursery school	Conscience	B	-.24	.14	.11	.10	-.18	.13	.11	
			G	-.17	.18	-.15	.28	.10	.16	-.12	
			B	-.26		-.09	.24	-.34*	.12	0	
			G	0		.07	.22	0	.27	0	
Yarrow et al. (1968)[3]	Nursery school	Conscience	B	.07	0	-.27*	.16	-.06		-.23	
			G	-.07	.24*	-.11	.08	0		-.10	
		Confession	B	-.18	-.06	0	0	-.10		-.22	
			G	0	.10	0	.25*	.22		0	
		Admission of deviance	B	-.14	-.08	-.09	.10	0		0	
			G	0	.16	.10	.07	.07		-.31*	
Sears et al. (1957)	Kindergarten	Percent high conscience	H	15	18	20	30	27	32	29	
			L	32	33	28	16	24	17	17	

Object-oriented (Deprivation of Privileges, Tangible Rewards)
Love-oriented (Withdrawal of Love, Use of Praise, Isolation)
Love-oriented .10

When dichotomized into above and below
median, t-test significant at .05.

| Whiting and Child (1963) | Cross-cultural | Guilt |

Nonphysical punishment and Confession
r = -.01.

| Lefkowitz et al. (1963) | 3rd grade | |

Mean confession scores
Mother:
0^4 = 6.30 (P=<.01)
1 = 5.82
2 = 5.52
3 & 4 = 5.46
Father:
0 = 5.96 (P=<.01)
1 = 5.19
2 = 5.78
3 & 4 = 5.16

| Unger (1962)[5] | 6th grade | Conscience |

(Induction: withdrawal of love, praise, ridicule)
.20

Table (continued) — study results for parental discipline and conscience/moral measures

continued

Study	Age	Category	Power-assertive — Mother's report	Son's report	Mothers' Use / Fathers' Use — Mother's report	Son's report	Mother's report	Son's report
Shoffeitt (1971)	11–16 years		−.37***		.29** (Mothers' Use)		−.23*	
			−.21		.49*** (Fathers' Use)		−.35**	.15*
Nevius (1972)	10 years	*Middle class:*						
		Stage I	−.23	0	−.13	−.27	.70**	.10
		Stage II	.07	.06	0	0	0	−.42
		Stage III	−.12	.15	0	.27	−.22	0
		Lower class:						
		Stage I	−.07	0	.20	.10	−.11	−.21
		Stage II	0	−.20	.22	.66**	−.10	.55*
		Stage III	.11	.11	0	.17	.11	−.13
Hoffman (1970)	7th grade	*Girls:*						
		Humanistic	7.00	7.20				
		Conventional	9.00	6.83	E > H*		C*, H* > E	
		External	10.00	5.25				
		Boys:						
		Humanistic	8.75	8.00				
		Conventional	6.75	7.67	E > H*, C**		C*, H* > E	
		External	11.00	4.50				
Burton et al. (1961)	4–5 years	Conscience	−.30*	−.16*	.18*		.25*	

Burton et al. (1961) — Resistance to temptation (Percent Resisted)

	High	Low	High	Low	High	Low
Boy[6]:						
High	8	10	8	14	12	10
Low	10	10	12	6	3	15
Girl[6]:						
High	8	12	5	15	5	15
Low	13	3	9	8	6	11

(also: 30[8], 25[9])

Grinder (1962), 6th grade — Resistance to temptation (Percent Resisted)

	H	M	L	H	M	L	H	M	L	H	M	L
Boy[7]	16	24	30	30	20	30	23	20	19	32	18	10
Girl	31	33	57	33	35	35	35	35	27	42	58	27

(also: Boy 29 19 12 / Girl 63 27 32; 31 27 32)

Sears et al. (1965)[10], Nursery school

	Mothers' use	Fathers' use
Resistance to temptation:	.48 boys	.51 girls
Confession:	−.56 boys	−.43 boys / .51 girls

Supplementary Table 16.6 Disciplinary Techniques and Conscience Continued

STUDY	AGE	CHILD'S BEHAVIOR	PHYSICAL PUNISHMENT	DEPRIVATION OF PRIVILEGES	TANGIBLE REWARDS	REASON	WITHDRAWAL OF LOVE	USE OF PRAISE	ISOLATION	RIDICULE
LaVoie (1974a)	15–16 years		_Latency in seconds_			_Frequency in seconds_		_Duration in seconds_		
			Mother	_Father_		_Mother_	_Father_	_Mother_	_Father_	
		Aversive, stimulus								
		Rationale absent	1,338.7	667.1		2.0	4.6	41.6	366.0	
		Rationale present	1,601.3	1,090.8		.7	2.7	9.2	35.3	
		Non-aversive, stimulus								
		Rationale absent	245.6	141.8		7.1	9.3	848.9	643.5	
		Rationale present	1,476.8	1,062.3		2.2	3.7	100.1	147.5	
LaVoie (1974b)	1st & 2nd grade	Resistance to temptation Latency	500 seconds	225 seconds	225 seconds	225 seconds	200 seconds	210 seconds		
		Frequency of deviation:								
		1st time		.85	2.75	3.10	3.00			
		2nd time		1.00	1.75	1.75	2.40			
		3rd time		1.25	1.50	2.00	2.00			
Parke (1967)	1st & 2nd grade		CONTINUED NURTURANCE		WITHDRAWAL OF NURTURANCE					
			Girls	_Boys_	_Girls_	_Boys_				
		Female experimenter								
		Latency	183.2	408.0	446.6	194.9				
		No. of deviations	6.5	5.2	1.7	6.5				
		Duration of deviation	96.7	63.0	10.2	52.3				
		Male experimenter								
		Latency	469.9	353.5	424.8	409.8				
		No. of deviations	3.0	6.7	2.7	4.3				
		Duration of deviations	24.7	76.6	16.6	68.5				
Hoffman and Saltzstein (1967)[11]	7th grade		Power-assertive							
			Boys	_Girls_	_Boys_	_Girls_	_Boys_	_Girls_		
		Mother's Use								
	Middle class	Guilt	0	–P	+C	+P	0	–C		
		Inter. moral jud.	0	–N	0	+C	0	0		
	Lower class	Confession	–P	0	0	0	+N	0		
		Inter. moral jud.	0	0	0	+C	+C	0		
		Father's Use								
	Middle class	Guilt	0	–C	+C	0	0	0		
		Inter. moral jud.	0	0	0	0	0	+C		
		Confession	–P	0	–P	0	0	0		
	Lower class	Guilt	–C	0	0	0	0	+C		

Study	Grade		CAUCASIAN GUILT-INTERNAL CONTROL	SAMOAN SHAME-EXTERNAL CONTROL	
Grinder and McMichael (1963)	6th & 7th grade	Remorse	13.65	11.58	p = .05
		Confess	13.53	11.21	p = .05
		Resist temptation	8.53	6.79	p = .05

			DISCIPLINE		OBEDIENCE REQUESTED	
Miller and Swanson (1960)[12]	7th & 8th grade	*Severity of guilt*	*Psychological %*	*Physical Punishment %*	*Arbitrary %*	*Explained %*
	Death wish	high	38[12]	38	39	30
		med	38	13 p=.30	27	32 NS
		low	24	45	34	38
	Theft	high	29	26	30	27
		med	59	63 p=.19	56	64 NS
		low	12	11	14	9
	Disobedience	high	58	52	50	61
		low	42	48 NS	50	39 NS
	Resistance to temptation concerning:					
	Theft	Yield	55	59	66	41
		Resisted	45	41 NS	34	59 p=.04
	Disobedience	Yield	81	76	86	65
		Resisted	19	24 p=.30	14	35 p=.05
	Externalization after:					
	Theft	Present	47	38	48	41
		Absent	53	62 p=.02	52	59 NS
	Disobedience	Present	61	45	59	51
		Absent	39	55 p=.06	41	49 NS

*Significant at .05 level.   **Significant at .01 level.   ***Significant at .005 level.
[1]Significance at .05 level; r = .21 for girls; r = .23 for boys.
[2]Reported in Yarrow et al. (1968:110-11).
[3]Significance at .05 level; r = .24.
[4]The number of physical punishment responses chosen.
[5]Dichotomized into psychological VS. physical disciplinary techniques.
[6]The higher the score, the greater the resistance.
[7]Originally reported as number of children who resisted, or yielded; converted to percentage for ease of comparisons.
[8]High and low = greater resistance; moderate = low resistance.
[9]High and low = low resistance; moderate = greatest resistance.
[10]Only correlations significant at <.05 are reported in the study.
[11]C = child's report; N = mother's current practice; P = mother's report 10 years earlier; all relationships significant at <.05.
[12]Originally reported as frequencies. Converted to percentage for ease of comparisons.

and dependency in children, it is obvious that many variables interact to influence development in these three behavior systems. For example, to increase prediction it would appear to be necessary to consider not only the disciplinary techniques used but also the general family environment, i.e., acceptance or rejection of the child, or the general warmth or hostility exhibited by the parents. The day-to-day patterns of interaction within the family also need to be considered. Screaming or yelling at a disobedient child in an active, boisterous family may not have the same effect as screaming or yelling at a child by parents in a family where members generally interact in a controlled, quiet manner. Furthermore, since physical punishment for aggression produces a different outcome than general use of physical punishment, it is suspected that the misbehavior for which the discipline was administered may affect the outcome. The timing of the discipline and the consistency with which this discipline is applied should be considered in a fully developed theory.

One final aspect encountered when attempting to develop an empirically derived theory of socialization is the lack of consensus regarding definition and measurement of components of the constructs: aggression, dependency, and conscience. The most consistent findings across studies tended to be those examining the effects of physical punishment on the three behavior systems. It may be that instead of reflecting the strength of the impact of this technique on children, the consistency across studies merely reflects the conceptual clarity and consensus among parents and investigators in their defining and measuring of physical punishment.

This suggests that although limited in scope, the more fruitful initial attempts to develop an empirically derived theory of socialization will be those which are limited to clearly defined and operationalized variables which are the building blocks of the socialization process. This also suggests that a major concern of future research should be on careful definition and conceptualization of socialization variables so that the observed differences in research on parental use of disciplinary techniques and their effectiveness are not confounded with differences in definition and measurement.

NOTES

1. For reviews of studies on aggression, dependency, and conscience, see Zigler and Child (1968–69); Maccoby and Masters (1970); Hoffman (1970b); Feshbach (1970); Becker (1964); and Martin (1975).

2. This was found in Yarrow et al. (1968), Appendix B, correlating variable 14 (severity of punishment for aggression toward parent) with variables 32 and 42 for girls (interview and questionnaire data on aggression toward parent).

3. This was found in Yarrow et al., (1968), Appendix B, correlating variable 14 (severity of punishment for aggression toward parent) with variables 32 and 42 for boys (interview and questionnaire data on aggression toward parent).

REFERENCES

ALLINSMITH, W. AND T. C. GREENING
1955   "Guilt over anger as predicted from parental discipline: A study of superego development." *American Psychology* 10:320.

ARONFREED, J.
1963   "The effects of experimental socialization paradigms upon two moral responses to transgression." *Journal of Abnormal and Social Psychology* 66:437–48.

ARONFREED, J., R. A. CUTICK, AND S. A. FAGEN
1963   "Cognitive structure, punishment, and nurturance in the experimental induction of self-criticism." *Child Development* 34:281–94.

BANDURA, A. AND R. H. WALTERS
1963   *Social Learning and Personality Development*. New York: Holt, Rinehart and Winston.

BAUMRIND, D.
1967   "Child care practices anteceding three patterns of preschool behavior." *Genetic Psychology Monographs* 75:43–88.

BAUMRIND, D. AND A. E. BLACK
1967   "Socialization practices associated with dimensions of competence in preschool boys and girls." *Child Development* 38:291–328.

BECKER, W. C.
1964   "Consequences of different kinds of parental discipline." In M. L. Hoffman and L. W. Hoffman (eds.), *Review of Child Development Research* vol. 1. New York: Russell Sage.

BECKER, W. C. AND R. S. KRUG
1964   "A circumplex model for social behavior in children." *Child Development* 35:371–96.

BECKER, W. C., D. R. PETERSON, Z. LURIA, D. J. SHOEMAKER, AND L. A. HELLMER
1962   "Relations of factors derived from parent-interview ratings to behavior problems of five-year olds." *Child Development* 33:509–35.

BELLER, E. K.
1955   "Dependency and independence in young children." *Journal of Genetic Psychology* 87:25–35.
1959   "Exploratory studies of dependency." *Transactions*. New York: Academy of Science Series 2, 21(5):414–26.

BLOOM, B. S.
1964   *Stability and Change in Human Characteristics*. New York: Wiley.

BRONFENBRENNER, U.
1961   "Some familial antecedents of responsibility and leadership in adolescents." In L. Petrullo and B. M. Bass (eds.), *Leadership and Interpersonal Behavior*. New York: Holt, Rinehart and Winston.

BURTON, R. V.
1968   Unpublished data cited in Yarrow et al., *Child Rearing*. San Francisco: Jossey-Bass.

BURTON, R. V., E. E. MACCOBY, AND W. ALLINSMITH
1961   "Antecedents of resistance to temptation in four-year-old children." *Child Development* 32:689–710.

CHAMBERLIN, R. W.
1974   "Authoritarian and accommodative child-rearing styles: Their relationships with the behavior patterns of two-year-old children and with other variables." *Journal of Pediatrics* 84(2):287–93.

deMAUSE, L.
1974   *The History of Childhood*. New York: Psychohistory Press.

DOLLARD, J., L. W. DOOB, N. E. MILLER, O. H. MOWRER, AND R. R. SEARS
1939   *Frustration and Aggression*. New Haven, Conn.: Yale University Press.

ERON, L. D., T. J. BANTA, L. O. WALDER, AND J. H. LAULICHT
1961   "Comparison of data obtained from mothers and fathers on child-rearing practices and their relation to child aggression." *Child Development* 32:457–72.

FESHBACH, S.
1970   "Aggression." In Paul H. Mussen (ed.), *Carmichael's Manual of Child Psychology,* vol. 2.

FESTINGER, L.
1957   *A Theory of Cognitive Dissonance.* Evanston, Ill.: Row, Peterson.

FODOR, E. M.
1973   "Moral development and parent behavior antecedents in adolescent psychopaths." *Journal of Genetic Psychology* 122:37–43.

GEWIRTZ, J. L.
1969   "Levels of conceptual analysis in environment-infant interaction research." *Merrill-Palmer Quarterly* 15:7–47.

GEWIRTZ, J. L. AND D. M. BAER
1958b   "The effects of brief social deprivation on behaviors for a social reinforcer." *Journal of Abnormal and Social Psychology* 56:46–56.

GRINDER, R. E.
1962   "Parental child-rearing practices, conscience, and resistance to temptation of sixth-grade children." *Child Development* 33:803–20.

GRINDER, R. E., AND R. MCMICHAEL
1963   "Cultural influences on conscience development: Resistance to temptation and guilt among Samoans and American Caucasians." *Journal of Abnormal and Social Psychology* 66(5):503–07.

HARRIS, D. B., H. G. GOUGH, AND W. E. MARTIN
1950   "Children's ethnic attitudes: II. Relationship to parental beliefs concerning child training." *Child Development* 21(3):169–81.

HARTUP, W. W.
1958   "Nurturance and nurturance-withdrawal in relation to the dependency behavior of preschool children." *Child Development* 29:191–201.

HATFIELD, J. S., L. R. FERGUSON, AND R. ALPERT
1967   "Mother-child interaction and the socialization process." *Child Development* 38:365–414.

HEATHERS, G.
1955   "Emotional dependence and independence in nursery school play." *Journal of Genetic Psychology* 87:37–57.

HOFFMAN, L. W., S. ROSEN, AND R. LIPPITT
1960   "Parental coerciveness, child autonomy and child's role at school." *Sociometry* 23:15–22.

HOFFMAN, M. L.
1960   "Power assertion by the parent and its impact on the child." *Child Development* 31:129–43.

1963a   "Parent discipline and the child's consideration for others." *Child Development* 34:573–88.

1963b   "Personality, family structure, and social class as antecedents of parental power assertion." *Child Development* 34:869–84.

1970a   "Conscience, personality, and socialization techniques." *Human Development* 13:90–126.

1970b   "Moral development." In Paul H. Mussen (ed.), *Carmichael's Manual of Child Psychology,* vol. 2.

HOFFMAN, M. L. AND H. D. SALTZSTEIN
1967   "Parent discipline and the child's moral development." *Journal of Personality and Social Psychology* 5:45–57.

KAGAN, J. AND H. A. MOSS
1962   *Birth to Maturity: A Study in Psychological Development.* New York: Wiley.

KOHLBERG, L.
1964   "Development of moral character and moral ideology." In M. L. Hoffman and L. W. Hoffman (eds.), *Review of Child Development Research,* vol. 1. New York: Russell Sage.

KOHN, M. L.
1969   *Class and Conformity: A Study in Values.* Homewood, Ill.: Dorsey Press.

KRAMER, R.
1968   "Moral development in young adulthood." Unpublished Doctoral Dissertation, University of Chicago.

LAVOIE, J. C.
1974a   "Punishment and adolescent self-control." *Developmental Psychology* 8(1):16–24.

1974b   "Type of punishment as a determinant of resistance to deviation." *Developmental Psychology* 10(2):181–89.

LAVOIE, J. C. AND W. R. LOOFT
1973   "Parental antecedents of resistance-to-temptation behavior in adolescent males." *Merrill-Palmer Quarterly* 19(2):107–16.

LEFKOWITZ, M. M., L. O. WALDER, AND L. D. ERON
1963   "Punishment, identification and aggression." *Merrill-Palmer Quarterly* 9:159–74.

MACCOBY, E. E.
1959   "Role-taking in childhood and its consequences for social learning." *Child Development* 30:239–52.

MACCOBY, E. E. AND J. C. MASTERS
1970   "Attachment and dependency." In Paul H. Mussen (ed.), *Carmichael's Manual of Child Psychology,* vol. 2.

MARTIN, B.
1975   "Parent-child relations." In E. M. Hetherton (ed.), *Review of Child Development Research,* vol. 5. Chicago: University of Chicago Press.

MCCORD, W., J. MCCORD, AND P. VERDEN
1962   "Familial and behavioral correlates of dependency in male children." *Child Development* 33:313–26.

MILGRAM, S.
1973   *Obedience to Authority: An Experimental View.* New York: Harper & Row.

MILLER, D. R. AND G. E. SWANSON
1958   *The Changing American Parent: A Study in the Detroit Area.* New York: Wiley.

1960   *Inner Conflict and Defense.* New York: Holt, Rinehart and Winston.

MINTON, C., J. KAGAN, AND J. A. LEVINE
1971   "Maternal control and obedience in the two-year-old." *Child Development* 42:1873–94.

MISCHEL, W. AND J. GRUSEC
1966   "Determinants of the rehearsal and transmission of neutral and aversive behaviors." *Journal of Personality and Social Psychology* 3:197–205.

MURRAY, H. A.
1938   *Explorations in Personality.* New York: Oxford University Press.

NEVIUS, J. R.
1972   "The relationship of child-rearing practices to the acquisition of moral judgements in 10-year-old boys." Unpublished Dissertation, University of Southern California.

PARKE, R. D.
1967   "Nurturance, nurturance withdral, and resistance to deviation." *Child Development* 38:1101–10.

PEARLIN, L. I., M. R. YARROW, AND H. A. SCARR
1967   "Unintended effects of parental aspirations: The case of children's cheating." *American Journal of Sociology* 73(1):73–83.

ROBERTS, M. R. AND L. M. COOPER
1967   "Patterns of parental discipline." *Journal of Social Psychology* 71:257–66.

SAADATMAND, B., L. JENSEN, AND A. PRICE
1970   "Nurturance, nurturance withdrawal, and resistance to temptation among three age groups." *Developmental Psychology Manual of Child Psychology,* Vol.2.

SCARR, S.
1969   "Social introversion-extroversion as a heritable response." *Child Development* 40:823–32.

SCHAFFER, H. R. AND P. E. EMERSON
1964   'Patterns of response to physical contact in early human development" *Journal of Child Psychology and Psychiatry and Allied Disciplines* 5:1–13.

SEARS, R. R.
1961   "The relation of early socialization experiences to aggression in middle childhood." *Journal of Abnormal and Social Psychology.* 63:466–92.

SEARS, R. R., E. E. MACCOBY, AND H. LEVIN
1957   *Patterns of Child-rearing.* Evanston, Ill.:Row, Peterson.

SEARS, R. R., L. RAU, AND R. ALPERT
1965   *Identification and Child-rearing.* Stanford, Calif.: Stanford University Press.

SEARS, R. R., J. W. M. WHITING, V. NOWLIS, AND P. S. SEARS
1953   "Some child-rearing antecedents of aggression and dependency in young children." *Genetic Psychology Monographs* 47:135–203.

SHOFFEITT, P. G.
1971   "The moral development of children as a function of parental moral judgements and child-rearing practices." Unpublished Dissertation, George Peabody College for Teachers.

SIGEL, I. E., M. L. HOFFMAN, A. S. DREYER, AND I. TORGOFF
1957   "Influence techniques used by parents to modify the behavior of children: A case presentation." *American Journal of Orthopsychiatry* 27:356–64.

SLATER, P.
1961   "Toward a dualistic theory of identification." *Merrill-Palmer Quarterly* 7:113–26.

SMITH, H. T.
1958   "A comparison of interview and observation measures of mother behavior." *Journal of Abnormal and Social Psychology* 57:278–82. ·

STEINMETZ S. K. AND M. A. STRAUS
1974   *Violence in the Family.* New York: Harper & Row.

SYMONDS, P. M.
1937   *The Psychology of Parent-Child Relationships.* New York: Appleton-Century.

THOMAS, A., S. CHESS, AND H. G. BIRCH
1968   *Temperament and Behavior Disorders in Children.* New York: New York University Press.

UNGER, S. M.
1962   "Antecedents of personality differences in guilt responsivity." *Psychological Reports* 10:357–58.

WHITING, J. W. M. AND I. L. CHILD
1953   *Child-Training and Personality: A Cross-cultural Study.* New Haven, Conn.: Yale University Press.

WINDER, C. L. AND L. RAU
1962   "Parental attitudes associated with social deviance in preadolescent boys." *Journal of Abnormal and Social Psychology* 64:418–24.

YARROW, M. R., J. D. CAMPBELL, AND R. V. BURTON
1968   *Child-Rearing: An Inquiry into Research and Methods.* San Francisco: Jossey-Bass.

YARROW, M. R., C. Z. WAXLER, AND P. M. SCOTT
1971   "Child effects on adult behavior." *Developmental Psychology* 5(2):300–11.

ZIGLER, E. AND I. W. CHILD
1968-9 "Socialization," in G. Lindzey and E. Aronson (eds.) Handbook of Social Psychology vol. 3. Reading, Mass.: Addison-Wesley.

17

THE FAMILY AND RECREATION: TOWARD A THEORETICAL DEVELOPMENT

John E. Carlson

INTRODUCTION

The principal objective of this chapter is to incorporate several theoretical and empirical developments relevant to recreation into a framework useful for understanding this increasingly important aspect of family and individual behavior. Several factors suggest the importance of such an effort at this time.

Leisure time has increased rapidly during the past several decades in American society. Longer paid vacations, shorter work weeks, and more three-day weekends have been the primary forms this increase in time has taken. Along with this has been an increase in discretionary income available for recreational use. Planning problems associated with this increase have caused researchers to focus on the factors affecting an individual's choice of recreational activities. The most ambitious study of this type has been the National Recreation Survey by the U.S. Outdoor Recreation Resources Review Commission (1962). Background factors tested in that survey explained less than 50 percent of the variation in recreational choices. Less ambitious studies also have failed to increase the ability to predict recreational activities. A lack of adequate theory is a possible explanation for this inability to accurately predict recreational choices.

Much recreational activity is engaged in by family units. This is especially characteristic of outdoor activities (Burch 1964; King 1968). However, much research focuses on the individual as the primary unit in recreational behavior and essentially ignores the group aspects of recreation. As Cunningham and Johannis (1960:25) have indicated,

most of the empirical research which has been reported treats the impact of non-work time on *individual* behavior. Research concerned with the influence of non-work time on family member's roles or the family as a unity of interacting participant role behavior is at a premium.

Even though this statement was written over 15 years ago, it still seems to be true; little research or theory focuses on the interaction patterns associated with family recreation. Blood and Wolfe (1960) found in their sample of Detroit families that recreation was one of the three major sources of disagreement between spouses. They suggested the need for additional research in family recreation. Other studies related to family recreation have usually focused on background factors associated with recreational choice by individuals or centered around the effects of recreation on marital satisfaction (West and Merriam, 1969; Benson, 1952; Gerson, 1960; Scheuch, 1960; Stone, 1963).

Most of the studies on recreation can be criticized on several grounds. Primarily, few if any have any theoretical framework. They are essentially descriptive studies which have tended to ignore theoretical issues. Many studies focus on a particular recreational area, thereby placing additional limitations on the value of the results. Finally, although these studies have shown that the family is the most frequent group engaging in recreational activities, few have focused specifically on the interrelationships between recreational activities and family behavior.

Because of inadequate theory and research, increasing demand for recreation, and more time and money available for recreation, development of a theoretical framework for integrating these studies into a more useful analytic tool seems justified. Such a framework would also indicate the most relevant areas for future research. Through this chapter I will attempt to integrate the societal, individual, and family determinants of recreational choice into a general theory of recreational behavior.

NOTE: This work was supported, in part, by the Agricultural Experiment Station, University of Idaho, Moscow, Idaho. I wish to thank Wesley Burr, Reuben Hill, Margaret Rae Jensen, and F. Ivan Nye for their many helpful suggestions. Inadequacies and errors in the chapter as published are entirely the responsibility of the author.

439

PROBLEMS OF DEFINITION

This chapter is not intended to focus on problems of definition; yet to minimize confusion, some terms must be defined. In this analysis the family will mean the husband, wife, and any children interacting with them in a given situation. That is, what is thought of by most Americans as being a family will serve as minimum criterion for a family in this analysis.

Numerous writers have attempted to define recreation and leisure (DeGrazia, 1962; Clawson, 1964; Burch and Taves, 1961; Arendt, 1959). The definition of recreation used here is similar to the conceptualization of leisure presented by Dumazedier (1967). When he asked French workers to indicate the types of activities which contrast with leisure, this list resulted:

1. the job
2. supplementary work or occasional odd jobs
3. domestic tasks (housework and the strictly utilitarian aspects of animal care, miscellaneous chores, gardening)
4. care of the person (meals, bathing, and dressing, sleep)
5. family ritual and ceremonies, social and religious
6. obligations (visits, anniversaries, political meetings, church duties)
7. necessary study (for study circles, school or professional examination).

Furthermore, when French workers were asked to list the functions of leisure, the responses grouped into three categories: relaxation, entertainment, and personal development. On the basis of these responses, recreation was defined as:

> activity—apart from the obligations of work, family and society—to which the individual turns at will, either for relaxation, diversion or broadening his knowledge and his spontaneous social participation, the free exercise of his creative capacity [Dumazedier, 1967:16–17].

This definition still seems to present conflicting elements. For example, "the free exercise of his creative capacity" seemingly could be part of one's paid occupation as well as an aspect of recreation or leisure. Kelly (1972) attempted to alleviate this problem when he developed a multidimensional approach to defining recreation and leisure. He developed a two-by-two table utilizing two dimensions of work and leisure. One relates to the relationship of the activity to work—whether it is dependent or independent of work. The other dimension identifies how much the activity is chosen by the individual or determined by work constraints or pervasive norms of society.

Certain activities may not fall clearly within the domain of either work or recreation. Sewing, knitting, puttering around, and gardening may be semiobligatory and semi-pleasurable activities, which might be characterized as semi-recreational activities. Also, activities which may be recreational or semirecreational for one person may be work for another person.

THEORETICAL APPROACHES RELEVANT TO RECREATION

Discussions on recreation and leisure have utilized many theoretical approaches in attempting to construct explanatory frameworks. While no approach seems sufficient by itself, each contains certain aspects relevant for a theory of recreation. In addition several theoretical concepts not presently utilized (at least not explicitly) in recreation theory appear relevant for theory development in recreation.

The Compensatory Hypothesis

This hypothesis has the premise that when an individual is given the freedom to choose his activities, he will engage in activities sharply different from his occupational commitment. Such a hypothesis posits a safety-valve effect; when a person becomes bored or when monotony sets in, the person seeks a sharply different activity to avoid a mental breakdown. Several sociologists have pointed out that this hypothesis still holds the attention of many involved in the planning of playgrounds, campgrounds, and wilderness areas (Wilensky, 1960; Green, 1964). Several studies lend at least partial support to this hypothesis (Burch, 1969; U.S. Outdoor Recreation Resources Review Commission, 1962). For example, these studies showed that urbanites tend to flock to the country for their recreational activities. Yet when viewing more specific activities, this hypothesis receives less support. Hendee and Campbell (1969) suggested that some campers may not be seeking isolation and solitude when they go into the forest; their observations suggested that the social aspects of camping are not given due consideration in the development of recreational areas. Dumazedier (1967:72–73), in his study of French workers, indicates that

> systematic observations . . . lead us to believe that leisure is far from being a factor compensating for fragmentized and repetitive work.
>
> Let us not deceive ourselves into thinking that spontaneous activities compensate for the dullness of daily work. Awareness of a style of life and a general education are required; otherwise, dull work is most often accompanied by dull leisure.

In summary, the compensatory hypothesis is apparently supported by research which explains some general variation in recreational activities, but that it is not satisfactory for precise explanations.

The Similarity Hypothesis

This hypothesis is essentially the opposite of the compensatory idea. It is based on the premise that individuals desire consistency in their life styles. This idea is often found in social psychological literature about "force of habit" which keeps individuals on a steady and familiar behavior pattern. Furthermore, this hypothesis posits that individuals avoid situations which may produce tension and seek situations which provide consistency in behavior.

Aspects of cognitive dissonance theories (Bhrem and Cohen, 1962) closely relate to the similarity hypothesis presented here. This hypothesis suggests that when given a choice, an individual will choose those recreational activities which continue his familiar routine. The "busman's holiday," in which he takes a ride on a bus on his day off, illustrates the principle. Charlesworth (1964:32) suggested that "another arresting fact is the more monotonous a worker's job the more monotonous the recreation he seeks in his free time." Yet studies have indicated that this is not the clear-cut "fact" that Charlesworth would like to believe. For example, although foresters tend to seek active recreation, therefore being in line with the similarity hypothesis, doctors and other middle-class workers seemingly desire more active and diverse forms of recreational activity (U.S. Outdoor Recreation Resources Review Commission, 1962; Burch, 1969).

Burch suggested that these two hypotheses—compensatory and similarity—though seemingly opposite may converge at the level of group membership. Therefore, recreational activities may be shaped by pressures within groups rather than within individuals. As a result of his findings, Burch suggested reference group theory as a more profitable theoretical framework for studying recreation.

Reference Group Theory

Burch relied on Shibutani's definition of a reference group as the basis for his theoretical framework. For Shibutani, a reference group is

> an audience consisting of real or imaginary personifications, to whom certain values are imparted. It is an audience before whom a person tries to maintain or enhance his standing.... People are selectively responsive only to the reactions of those who are included in their reference group, for it is primarily in their eyes that they attempt to maintain their standing. Each person seeks recognition primarily in his social world [1962:132, 143].

This theory suggests that a person's social behavior is largely a function of his reference groups; that is, "gross social issues and psychological drives are significantly filtered and re-directed by the social circles of workmates, family and friends" (Burch, 1969:138). Since a reference group can include both "real and imaginary personifications," the norms and values of the society may also be discussed within this particular framework. This is a necessary criterion for a theoretical framework of recrea-

tion. Burch's study of campers indicated that one's workmates, friends, and family did indeed exert a strong influence on particular styles of recreational behavior (Burch, 1969).

Opportunity Theory

This approach is commonly used in discussing rural-urban distinctions in recreation. The opportunity hypothesis implies that participation in different forms of recreation depends on their availability (Hendee, 1969). Since city residents have less opportunity to engage in rural activities, they will be underrepresented in them. On the other hand, city dwellers will be overrepresented in urban-oriented activities. This theory was tested in a national survey and received substantial support (U.S. Outdoor Recreation Resources Review Commission, 1962).

Exchange Theory

Exchange theory (Homans, 1961; Thibaut and Kelley, 1959) seems appropriate in discussing recreational behavior for several reasons. For one, it reaches beyond person-person interaction to include person-task interaction. Some of the more important variables affecting recreational choice seem to be of a person-task nature. For example, availability of recreational opportunities, the size of one's family, and the level of income of the family are some of the variables not considered directly within a reference group framework, yet they must be considered in any theory of recreational behavior. Furthermore, since most recreational activities are voluntary, engaging in a particular activity or group of activities is likely to be strongly related to the perceived net rewards resulting from such activities.[1] Driver and Tocher (1970) utilize this notion of exchange in their behavioral approach to recreation. Also, exchange theory may offer the best theoretical basis for the generation of family theory (Edwards, 1969).

One idea in exchange theory is that individuals or groups tend to engage in those types of activities which they find most satisfying or, in exchange terms, most profitable. If a person should find that a particular activity is not rewarding (or costs are higher than rewards), he may try various activities until he finds one which is profitable to him. This seems relevant for recreation and provides a basis for deducing that:

> 1. The greater the net reward realized from a recreational activity or set of activities in the past, the more frequently that activity or set of activities will be chosen from among alternatives in the future.

Exchange theory also suggests that the frequency of engaging in a particular recreational activity or set of activities by a person or group is influenced by the frequency with which the activity is rewarded and the ratio of expectations (CL) to the alternatives available to a person should he be dissatisfied with a particular activity (CL_{alt}). If the activity always results in a high net profit, it will be engaged in more often than if a high net reward is obtained only periodically. The other idea is that the more the reward that is expected (CL) exceeds the rewards that would be expected from alternatives (CL_{alt}), the more frequently an activity is undertaken. The following propositions make these relationships more specific:

2. The more often a recreational activity or set of activities results in a high net reward, the more frequently the activity or set of activities will be engaged in.

3. The greater the expectations (CL) exceed the (CL_{alt}) for a particular recreational activity, the more frequently the activity will be engaged in.

Another relevant idea from exchange theory is that the frequency of engaging in recreational activities and the net reward are related in another way. Thibaut and Kelley (1959) refer to this in terms of satiation and fatigue. This is, as in economics when a point of diminishing returns is reached, where the rewards of a particular unit of recreational activity reach a maximum, then begin to decline. The activity may continue until the reward of each additional unit drops below the cost of each unit (marginal utility); at this point voluntary activity will cease. This phenomenon could partially explain the more varied recreational activities of the higher social class levels. They may more frequently have the time and money to repetitively engage in particular activities which they find more rewarding. By engaging in a variety of rewarding activities, individuals are not likely to reach a satiation point in any particular activity. Thus,

4. Given voluntary behavior, the more frequently a recreational activity is engaged in, the more likely a point of diminishing returns (marginal utility) will be met and net reward will decrease.

Another aspect of recreational activities is the relationship between a person's rewards from his behavior and his expectations (CL) concerning that particular activity. If his net rewards exceed his expectations (CL), he is likely to be satisfied. Conversely, if his net rewards fall below his expectations (CL), he is likely to be dissatisfied with the activity. If he is dissatisfied with the activity, several alternatives are open to him. If his net rewards are close to his CL_{alt}, he may terminate the activity and choose from the alternatives open to him (likely the one with the highest reward expectation). If his activity is not entirely voluntary, he may be forced to continue the activity even though he is not being rewarded by it.

Another idea deals with the realtionship between investments and the range of alternatives open to a person. Some evidence suggests that campers who have been camping for many years have changed their camping style

as a result of increased pressure on their favorite camping areas. They have moved from an easy-access style of camping to a more remote style of camping (Burch, 1969). Perhaps this can be explained by the relationship between a person's net rewards and his expectations, along with the availability of acceptable alternatives in the form of more remote areas of camping. Also the investments in equipment and reference group supports may limit available alternatives. In other words, campers' costs will be less if they change their style of camping instead of changing their whole style of recreation. This leads to the proposition that:

5. The greater the investments in a particular style of recreational activities, the narrower the range of alternatives available to an individual or group.

These propositions relate primarily to one aspect of recreation, the interaction of the person and the activity. While this appears to be the most visible application of exchange to recreation and leisure, it is not the only one. These five relationships are diagrammed in Figure 17.1.

SOCIETAL ASPECTS OF RECREATION

Some of the more important variables affected by industrialization will now be discussed as they relate to changing recreational patterns. The typology of Burch and Taves (1961) is presented in Figure 17.2 to help clarify certain societal changes that have affected recreational patterns.

Rhythm and Time Conceptions

Man orients himself in his work, play, religious worship, and other aspects of his social life according to a certain rhythm.

The closer man's activities are bound to nature, the more he is conscious of the rhythm of the seasons in determining activities within his structure. Some suggest that man's patterns of leisure along with its meanings will be influenced by his culture's rhythm and time orientations (Burch and Taves, 1961).

Thus subsistence man has his leisure activities and time as well as his other activities shaped by the shift of seasons rather than the minutes on a clock or his own whims. In the least industrialized societies time is measured by seasons rather than minutes; speed and efficiency are cyclical rather than ever present. A person's orientation toward life appears to differ if one has the conception of minutes passing away or if one sees life as divided into planting, harvesting, fallow, and their attendant problems. The former is concerned with time remaining after work, the latter with tasks to be done (Burch and Taves, 1961).

As shown in Figure 17.2, the relationship between

Figure 17.1. Exchange Theory Propositions Concerning Person-Activity Interaction in Recreation

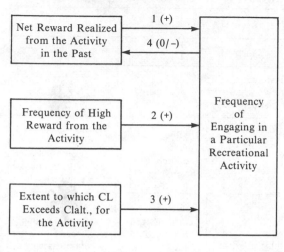

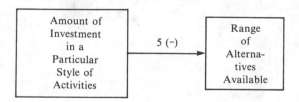

industrialization and the amount of time available for recreation is curvilinear. Primitive societies have the most nonwork time; with increasing industrialization the amount of nonwork time declined, but it has recently increased among certain segments of the more highly industrialized societies. Recent studies have indicated that the lower classes seem to have as much or more time for recreation as the upper classes. Veblen's *Theory of the Leisure Class* (1934) has much less relevance today than when he criticized the upper classes for their use of leisure time. "Conspicuous consumption" is no longer class-specific but can be viewed in the recreational activities of a majority of Americans. The general consensus is that the future will bring increases in discretionary time for all social classes, especially the blue-collar classes. Many agencies and industries are moving toward a four-day week to increase the size of the blocks of free time, and some have reduced the total hours worked per week.

Shifts in Values of Work and Leisure

The values societies attach to work and leisure largely determine the emphasis placed on each. Yet values change, and this is especially evident with the advent of industrialization. For example, Dubin found that less than one-fourth of his sample of industrial workers indicated that their job was their central life interest (Dubin, 1956). Several factors seem to have affected attitudes toward work in our society. The increase of mass production using the assembly-line process has resulted in many jobs being repetitive, thus potentially boring. As a result, a trend toward viewing work as something that has to be done but not something to be desired seems to be developing. Davis summarizes the effects of new technology and computerized production lines:

> in the past most jobs required a certain amount of mental ability, though obviously there was great variation from one job to another. Many occupations offered some degree of personal challenge, of skills, coordination, strength or judgment and even aesthetic choice. As these qualities of work are lost, perhaps the individual turns to some form of recreation to seek his fulfillment [1970:117].

While the effect of early Calvinistic attitudes toward work cannot be accurately measured, such attitudes have no doubt had some effect on the values held toward work and leisure in our society. The Protestant ethic placed a high value on work and success; recreation was to be used only to contribute to further work success. Davis (1970) cited evidence that there is a trend toward a higher value being placed on recreation for its own sake.

Burch and Taves (1961:12) have suggested that along with changing attitudes toward work, attitudes toward leisure have

> shifted from celebration of labor completed, to refreshment so that a labor may continue more effectively, to what seems to be the development of property rights in set amounts of non-work time.

This combination of changing attitudes toward both work and leisure provides numerous problems for man in industrialized societies.

While modern man does not necessarily have more free time, he has more regimentation of his time and more choices available for use of free time. He also may be affected by holdovers of earlier values such as religious norms which uphold the virtues of work and the frivolity of idleness. Since most individuals are faced with more leisure time than necessary merely to recuperate from labor, they are faced with the problem of deciding how to use this additional time. In short, man today finds himself making decisions under the regimentation of time and changing values, and without the clear directions of subsistence man, in his selection of leisure activities (Burch and Taves, 1961).

Socioeconomic Influences

The socioeconomic environment of a society is important as a determinant of leisure patterns in several ways. To begin with, in complex societies recreational activities

Figure 17.2. Typology of Leisure Patterns

Economy	Preindustrial		Transitional		Production	Consumption
Society	Tikopia	Maori	Suye Mura	Gosforth		U.S.A.
Leisure Values	Celebration of work done		Refreshment to do more work: "work ethic"			New synthesis developing
	Leisure intermixed with work; labor viewed negatively		Distinctions develop between work and play		Leisure and work sharply delineated; labor viewed positively	Work has aspects of play; play takes on aspects of work; leisure big business
Time Orientations	No calendar; lunar calendar		Shift from lunar to Gregorian calendar; seasons diminishing in importance; market values introduced		Gregorian calendar, tied to market fluctuations more than seasonal variations	Time ration-segmented; time has price; rhythms set by technological and social inventions
	Life tied to cycles of the seasons					
	Activity governed by intrinsic requirements					
Exchange	Reciprocal barter		Money introduced		Money	
Amount of Time Available	4- to 6-hour work days, 150-175 holidays	8-hour work days, 150 holidays	Increasing amount of time devoted to work, fewer and fewer holidays, 60- to 80-hour work weeks		40- to 60-hour work weeks, 60-70 holidays or vacation days per year	Average 3,700 hours free time per year

and facilities cost money. Thus different activities would be expected to be associated with variations in income level; several studies have borne this out (Clarke, 1956; White, 1955; Burdge, 1969). Greater amounts of discretionary income in higher-income families allow them to obtain more leisure goods and participate in more varied recreational activities (U.S. Outdoor Recreation Resources Review, 1962).

Mass production in industrial societies has meant lower prices per unit of merchandise. This increased efficiency of production makes various recreational items available to more income levels. Another factor resulting in a wider availability of recreational products is the credit structure of the society. Through the use of credit, families with moderate incomes can purchase items such as campers, snowmobiles, etc., which would be impossible to buy if cash were required at the time of purchase.

The increased use of mass media for advertising has also influenced acceptance of recreational products. A whole segment of the economy is geared toward the production of recreational equipment and advertisement

is an important aspect of its business. The recent emphasis on snowmobiling is an example of the influences of advertising in opening up a new area of recreation. The existence of such products seems to have some effect on the rates of participation and the composition of the participating groups in recreational activities. For example, women may not be willing to go camping or hunting if they must live in a tent and cook outdoors; on the other hand, if they can have the comforts of home in a trailer or camper, they may even enjoy going on a hunting trip with their husbands.

Class differences result in qualitative as well as quantitative differences in leisure patterns. The life styles of various classes strongly influence their forms of recreation. Dumazedier (1967) gives an example of this by citing a factory in France which provided several tennis courts for its employees free of charge. The managers came, while the workers who did show up promptly departed. Evidently they felt ill at ease. The qualitative aspects of recreation are likely to be as important as the quantitative aspects.

Summary

Rhythm and time conceptions, shifts in attitudes and values toward work and leisure, and changing socioeconomic environments seem to be influential cultural variables affecting recreation patterns (Burch and Taves, 1961; Dumazedier, 1967). The effects of these variables can be summarized in the following tentative propositions:

6. The more industrialized the society, the more regimented the time dimension of an individual's life.

7. The greater the rate of social change in other sectors of the society, the greater the likelihood of changes in attitudes and values toward work and leisure.

8. The greater the amounts of discretionary time and income in a society, the greater the portion of the economy likely to be oriented toward the production of recreational goods and services.

The propositions indicate the general societal impact on recreational activities of a society and the pursuits of its members. The effects are cyclical in nature in that the feedback from the members of the society regarding recreation modifies the cultural factors.

SOCIAL BACKGROUND FACTORS

Primary reference groups for most individuals include both the family of orientation, where one spends most of his childhood, and the family of procreation, where the addition of spouse and children provides an arena where group decision making becomes an important ingredient in behavioral choices.

The transition from family of orientation to family of procreation may have important implications in explaining recreational choices, implications which have received little emphasis in recreational research and theory. While some of the same factors are at work in both the family of procreation and the family of orientation, sufficient differences exist to warrant a separate discussion of each. The following discussion will look at an individual as a child in the family of orientation and then as an adult in the family of procreation. Thus we will be focusing first on the importance of childhood socialization within the family of orientation, then on factors affecting parental activities related to recreation in the family of procreation.

Family of Orientation

Several of the theoretical notions discussed earlier focus on the importance of the family of orientation in developing particular orientation toward recreation. Potentially there are four basic forms of recreational activity:

1. An individual can participate in activities by himself.

2. He can participate with family members.

3. He can engage in recreational activities with others who are not family members.

4. His recreation may combine family and others.

The opportunity for participation in all of these forms is most likely to occur as a member of a family of orientation. One's basic orientation toward recreation also will be formed during this time. Three general aspects of the family of orientation affect this development:

1. Opportunity variables that tend to determine the range of recreational activities available to the family and, therefore, the individual family member

2. Socialization within the family, which affects both the kinds of activities and the form in which the activities will take place

3. The reward-cost process emerging from the actual engagement in a given recreational activity

Opportunity Variables

Variables which seem to have potential restraining influence on the range of recreational activities available to a given family are the family's socioeconomic level and the opportunity structure of the family.

SOCIOECONOMIC LEVEL. The family's socioeconomic level forms a basis for establishing one's style of life. Income has consistently been shown to be associated with variations in recreational activities (U.S. Outdoor Recreation Resources Review Commission, 1962; Sessoms, 1963; Burch, 1964). Similar patterns emerge when looking at the effect of occupation and education. In Sessoms' (1963) review of recreational research he found eight studies supporting the observation that the number of recreational pursuits was positively correlated with income—the higher the income, the more numerous the pursuits. He found similar support for occupation and occupational prestige. To summarize:

> the higher the occupational prestige level, the more numerous and varied are the pursuits. Participation in crafts, spectator, commercial and home-centered activities are inversely related to occupational level. This observation was reported in 6 regional surveys, the largest of which was Clarke's study of 574 males in Columbus, Ohio (1956). Camping and canoeing appeared to be upper occupational activities. Boating, on the other hand, is an activity of the middle and upper-lower occupational groups. Hunting, gardening and picnicking were found not to be significantly related to occupational prestige [Sessoms, 1963:113].

The National Recreation Survey (U.S. Outdoor Recreation Resources Review Commission, 1962) also found socioeconomic variables to be associated with different types of recreation. Using factor analysis, four general types of activities emerged from the data. These were active recreational activities, backwoods recreation (i.e., backpacking), water-related activities and passive activities such as relaxing or card playing. On the basis of a multiple regression model, several variables were found to be closely associated with each of the activity types.

Active recreation was found to be most directly affected by age level, with the younger more likely to participate. Also related were the presence of children and nonfarm residence, both being positively correlated. Backwoods recreation was found to be positively correlated with income level, and passive recreational activities were positively related to educational level and age. Water-related activities are positively correlated with occupational status (U.S. Outdoor Recreation Resources Review Commission, 1962).

Socioeconomic factors affect recreational choice in several ways. High-income families have more discretionary income available for recreational purchases. For example, the average income of individuals floating the Middle Fork of the Salmon River during the summer of 1971 was about $20,000 a year.[2] Also, education provides one with different interests and desires in spending discretionary time. The exact importance of education and occupation in affecting recreational choice has not been determined. Burch (1969) demonstrated that the compensatory and similarity hypotheses are in some ways related to these variables. Also, the amount of discretionary time and its distribution are associated with socioeconomic level, although the exact relationships are more complex than would at first appear (Wilensky, 1961).

The family's socioeconomic level governs to a large extent the kind and number of recreational activities family members are exposed to. The conclusion is:

9. The higher the socioeconomic level of the family of orientation, the wider the range of recreational alternatives available to the members of the family.

OPPORTUNITY STRUCTURE. As would be expected, a family's socioeconomic level affects the opportunity structure of an individual's recreational choices. As previously discussed, various alternatives or opportunities are associated with socioeconomic level. For example, a lower class family will not be as likely to engage in yachting as a middle- or upper-class family. Because of this, a lower-class child is not likely to have the opportunity to engage in yachting as a type of recreation. One's residence also limits the recreational opportunities of families (Hendee, 1969). For example, given equal incomes, a family living several thousand miles from a skiing facility is not as likely to ski as a family living a hundred miles from such a facility. Thus,

10. The greater the opportunity to engage in a recreational activity or set of activities, the more likely that activity or set of activities will become a part of the individual's recreational choices.

Socialization Factors

An individual's initial recreational patterns are developed early in life within the family of orientation. During the preschool years, one's recreation is likely to be totally a function of the family of orientation. A distinction between two aspects of socialization will be made here even though in actuality they are very closely related. The first is the general process of childhood socialization, the second is a group of phenomena referred to by recreational theorists as "pleasant childhood memories." Because recreation is an activity associated with pleasant rewards, the datum of "pleasant child memories" as a factor in the process of socialization seems particularly important in recreational choice.

Socialization includes all aspects which tend to influence an individual's development and adaptation to the various roles he is to play in society. Included in this are the ways an individual learns to use his discretionary time. Kohn (1969) shows that one's socialization varies according to his family's social class level. For this reason the hypothesis is that families at various social class levels socialize their children into different styles of recreation (Kelly, 1974). Strong relationships have been shown to exist between childhood recreational activities and adult activities (Green, 1964; Burch and Wenger, 1967; Sofranko and Nolan, 1970). The findings of Sofranko and Nolan's study of hunters and fishermen in Pennsylvania indicated the importance of childhood participation in establishing adult patterns.

An individual's recreational activities may be individual-oriented or family-oriented, depending on his childhood socialization. Kohn (1969) demonstrated that socialization toward individualism versus familialism varies among families of different social classes. Burch and Wenger (1967) have suggested that the most enjoyable childhood recreational experiences are those most likely to be continued into adulthood.

Another important factor in the socialization process is the influence of non-family-oriented reference groups. As a child moves outside the family of orientation, he establishes reference groups which modify existing patterns of behavior as well as create new ones. For example, belonging to a Boy Scout group may create an interest in outdoor activities which may have been nonexistent within the family of orientation. Burch felt that reference groups provided a point of convergence for both the compensatory and similarity hypotheses (Burch, 1969). That is, reference groups modify individual-oriented tendencies of recreational choice that may exist.

Age is a factor related to socialization in that some activities that are engaged in at one age level are not likely to be engaged in at a different level. For example, Boy Scout membership occurs during a particular age span, then ceases. Also, age is related to the dating system in our society. Dating as a form of recreation is primarily an activity of the young people in America. One would expect that as dating becomes a common form of recreation, that frequency of activities with the family would decline. Stone (1963) found support for this notion. Older teenagers were found to participate less often with family members than younger teenagers. At the same time Stone found little difference among age groups in *desire* to have recreation with family. Over half indicated that they would like more family activities, while only 6 percent would like fewer activities.

Age also relates to the establishment of one's family of procreation, thus introducing a whole set of variables into the recreational decision-making process. These aspects of socialization can be summarized in the following propositions:

11. The wider the range of recreational alternatives for parents, the more likely children will be socialized into a wide range of recreational activities.
12. The greater the number of nonfamily reference groups, the greater the possibility of socialization into a wide range of recreational activities.

Reward-Cost-Profit Factors

The final factors in recreational choice are related to the actual outcomes of the various recreational experiences of the individual. In other words, an individual will select from the range of alternatives available to him those activities which provide the greatest profit. Some of these activities may be the result of continual experimentation with new activities or those most enjoyable during childhood. Burch and Wenger's (1967) research led them to posit the concept of "pleasant childhood memories" as important in adult recreational choice. Other than Burch and Wenger's indirect support of this notion, little research has been done relevant to this aspect of recreational choice.

Summary

This section has analyzed the social background variables most directly relevant to an individual's recreational patterns. The relationships among these variables are presented in Figure 17.3. Now we will look at factors that potentially modify recreational choice when the family of procreation is established.

Family of Procreation

This section is concerned with the modifying effects of the family of procreation on an adult's recreational behavior. This aspect of recreation has received little emphasis in research and theory. As Cunningham and Johannis (1960) indicated over 15 years ago, little research focuses on the interaction patterns and decision-making processes associated with family recreation. Possibly the inability to explain more than about 30 percent of

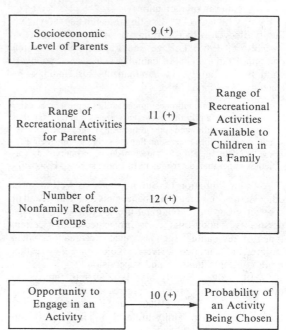

Figure 17.3. Factors Affecting the Early Development of an Individual's Range of Recreational Preferences

the variation in recreational activities on the basis of an individual's background characteristics (U.S. Outdoor Recreation Resources Review Commission, 1962) is because of the failure to consider the group processes within the family of procreation as well as other situational factors, including interaction processes in other social systems, especially work organizations. The theoretical perspective presented in this analysis views the family of procreation as an intervening variable affecting recreational patterns of family members. Here four sets of variables seem to be important:

1. A set affecting the range of opportunities by either restricting or enhancing probability of engaging in certain activities
2. A set related to family integration
3. A set relating to decision making
4. A set relating to the reward-cost factors involved in specific recreational activities

Opportunity Variables

The socioeconomic level and opportunity structure of an individual's recreational activities in the family of orientation are also limiting factors in the family of procreation. The effects of these variables are very similar regardless of whether one is a spouse in the family of procreation or a child in the family of orientation. The additional variables of family life cycle and family size emerging within the family of procreation tend to modify existing patterns of recreation.

FAMILY LIFE CYCLE. Existing research has shown that family lifecycle affects certain types of recreational activity (Burch, 1966; LePage and Ragain, 1974). Burch compared three styles of camping with age of youngest child in the family. In summarizing his findings, he stated:

> I argue that combination camping families represent the early stages of the family life-cycle, easy access-camping families represent middle and post-retirement stages and remote-camping families represent those just beginning their life-cycle. ''Biological factors are limitations or intervening variables rather than determinants of leisure style.'' [1966:610].

A major limitation of Burch's study as well as most other studies of recreational behavior is that it consisted of a select group of recreational users. From an exchange perspective, additional costs are expected for certain types of recreation, such as outdoor recreation, when children are from two to five years old, since they require more constant attention and supervision.

FAMILY SIZE. Family size is related to family life cycle, although its effects on recreation and choice may be independent. Burch (1966) found that family size was less important than family life cycle in affecting style of camping. King (1968) found campers more likely to have children than the general population was. Thus, while camping activity is associated with families with children, the number of children per se does not seem to influence recreational activities. The findings from my own data provide some support for the notion that family size has a limiting effect. Small families are more likely to engage in active outdoor activities, whereas larger families are more likely to engage in passive outdoor and group indoor activities.

As Burch suggested, these factors are ''limitations or intervening variables rather than determinants of leisure style.'' They tend to filter out activities that are beyond the possibility of a given family at a given time.

Family Integration

While it is recognized that family integration is a multidimensional concept (Nye and Rushing, 1966), it seems to be a useful concept to describe a set of family characteristics which emphasize a family life style as being family-centered on one end of the continuum and individual-centered on the other end. The notion of family integration seems to be a value held by spouses that is transferred to the rest of the family in terms of the activities they engage in. It can be hypothesized that such a value would also affect the way family members approach recreational activities. This can be stated as follows:

13. The greater the family integration, the more

likely a family will engage in recreational activities as a group.

Family Decision Making and Recreational Patterns

One of the least understood and most important aspects of family behavior is related to the decision-making process in each family. When an individual marries and subsequently establishes a family, he may no longer be able to carry out as many of his own desires and wishes as before. The background factors which before may have accurately predicted his behavior are now altered through a decision-making process which includes his spouse and other members of the family as well as kinship reference groups on both sides of the family. He may now modify his own recreational activities in light of the desires and wishes of other family members. Very little research has dealt with this aspect of recreation. At the same time, many have found that when small children are present, most recreational activities are engaged in by family units. Burch indirectly alerted us to the importance of considering husband-wife interaction in recreation by presenting findings which suggested that different styles of camping emerge, depending on the background experiences of the husband and wife (1969:141):

1. Easy access [camping] husband-wife pairs are more likely to have never camped with their parents than pairs in the other 2 styles [combination and remote camping].
2. When compared with the other camping styles, more easy access [camping] wives have greater camping experience than their husbands.
3. When compared to the other styles of camping, remote [camping] husbands are more likely to have had greater experience than their wives.
4. When compared to the other 2 styles of camping, remote camping husband-wife pairs are more likely to have had experience with their parents.
5. When husbands and wives have had variations or differences in camping experience, husbands have more likely had remote experience.

These findings imply that decisions made within the family modify or reinforce the behavioral patterns established at an earlier time. Burch summarizes his findings by indicating that the

> family of orientation is a significant reference for some adult male leisure decisions while [the] family of procreation is a significant referent for married females [1969:141].

The agreement or lack of agreement on common recreational activities provides a basis for the kind of decision to be made. According to Turner (1970) a basic continuum exists from consensual to accommodative decisions within the family. Turner (1970:97) defines group decision making as ''a process directed toward unambivalent group assent and commitment to a course of action or inaction.'' Decision making is looked upon as a continuous process, subject to constant reevaluation. Participants in decision making are expected to be more committed to decisions than are others. But "when an individual makes a decision, he is committed to it by his action or inaction, regardless of how he may regret the decision later" (1970:98).

According to Turner, kinds of decisions range from consensual to accommodative. A decision where all involved feel equally committed and give equal assent is a consensual decision; a decision where agreement is reached by compromise, bargaining, or coercion is accommodative. "An accommodation is always an agreement to disagree, to adopt a common decision in the face of recognized and unreconciled private desires" (1970:98). Commitment is unconditional in the case of consensual decisions but is conditional when an accommodation is made. Thus the ground rules of the exchange, as well as the outcome of the exchange, differ according to whether the decision is consensual or accommodative.

No one short of a masochist desires to be on the short end (the loser) in all decisions. No one wants to do most or all of the giving for very long. Eventually, a high proportion of accommodative decisions which favor one participant over the other (or at the expense of the other) is likely to lead to a modification or termination of interaction in the relationship. This conclusion is supported by Gouldner (1960), where he discusses the "norm of reciprocity" as a universal expectation in continuing interpersonal interaction. The norm of reciprocity is "a generalized moral norm which defines certain actions and obligations as repayments for benefits received" (1960:170). Thus consensual and accommodative decisions are based on a universal normative expectation of reciprocity as well as specific status obligations associated with particular roles.[3]

Another type of decision discussed by Turner is *de facto*. *De facto* decisions often occur because of failure to arrive at a satisfactory decision in time to carry out the desired behavior; decisions are made after the fact. For example, a family member may wish to go to a special sports event but other members have different plans. If they are unable to arrive at a decision, the event may pass with no one attending. In such a case the decision is made by the fact that the event passed with no one attending.

These different types of decisions are closely related to two important aspects of the group: the degree of value consensus and the communication among group members. Consensual decisions usually require the highest degree of value consensus and the greatest ability of group members to communicate with each other. Also, consensus could be conceptualized as providing *maximum profit* for all members of the family. Accommodative decisions are usually the result of divergent value orientations among group members and/or the inability to arrive at consensus through communication. *De facto* decisions are likely to be the result of an inability to communicate with group members, causing the decisions to be made after the fact.

In that recreational responsibilities within families are not highly structured, disagreements over recreational decisions are highly probable (Carlson, 1972). As indicated before, recreational activities can range from those involving only one member of the family to those involving one or more total family units. This wide range of potential choices with few normative restrictions as to how these choices are made suggests an area of potentially high disagreements among family members. In fact Blood and Wolfe (1960) found that recreational activities elicited the third highest frequency of disagreements between spouses. Several factors will affect the kinds of decisions made regarding recreational choices, such as family size, stage in the family life cycle, socioeconomic status, etc. Based on minimal research findings, several propositions related to recreational decison making can be stated:

14. The wider the range of common recreational activities engaged in by members of the family, the more frequent the consensual decisions about recreation.

15. The greater the communication in the family, the less the likelihood of accommodative and *de facto* decisions about recreation.

16. The larger the family and the older the children, the less the likelihood of consensual decisions about recreation.

17. The more similar the social class backgrounds of the spouses, the more likely their recreational patterns will be family-oriented.

These propositions suggest that family configurations have an influence on the kinds of decisions made regarding recreational choices. Also, the degree of satisfaction in recreational activities, both individual and family, will be partially a function of the kind of decision resulting in the activity choice. For example, a consensual decision will result in the greatest amount of satisfaction for all involved. This is likely a factor in the studies that have shown a positive correlation between family recreation and marital satisfaction (West and Merriam, 1969; Benson, 1952; Gerson, 1960; Scheuch, 1960; Stone, 1963). The major problem with this relationship has been determining the cause-effect relationship. Possibly the type of decision is affecting both marital satisfaction and engagement in joint recreational activities.

On the other hand, when accommodative or *de facto* decisions are made, some members of the group will not receive maximum satisfaction from the experience. Take as an example the family that goes on a weekend camping trip with one member who had other plans for the weekend. The probability is high that the family will have less satisfaction because the one member is unhappy at having to do something he didn't want to do in the first place. In all accommodative decisions, some members of the group will be engaging in the activity at less than total commitment. Several propositions related to these notions can be stated:

18. The more frequent the consensual decisions regarding recreational choices, the greater the total family satisfaction from recreational activities.

19. A positive correlation exists between family recreation and marital satisfaction, but the cause-effect relationship is unclear.

20. The more frequent the consensus in decisions regarding recreational choices, the more likely recreational activities will be engaged in as a family unit.

Figure 17.4 presents the interrelationships among the

propositions related to the characteristics of the family of procreation as related to recreational activities.

THEORETICAL INTEGRATION

Ideally theoretical models should follow the approach to theory construction suggested by Blalock (1969), who proposed a mathematical approach because

the kinds of verbal theories that serve as first approximation to deductive theories are often far too simple and unclear to stand as adequate formulations; mathematical models should eventually replace or supplement such verbal theories [1969:3].

Figure 17.4. Factors Affecting Recreational Behavior within the Family of Procreation

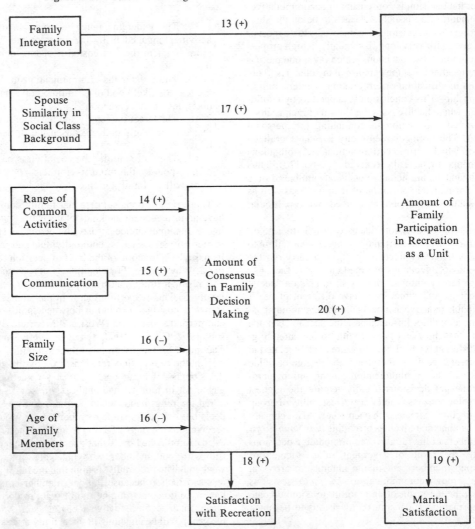

On the other hand, such precise models require more detailed data than exist in most recreational research. Where data have been available, attempts at constructing mathematical models of campsite use and fishing behavior have been relatively successful (Dyer and Whaley, 1968; Wennergren and Nielson, 1968). It seems useful, however, to speculate briefly about a more general model that may be able to integrate the propositions developed throughout the chapter. At the most general level the societal characteristics regarding recreation and leisure such as rhythm and time dimensions, values placed on work and recreation, and socioeconomic influences seem of central importance. As one moves toward a micro level of analysis, the background factors strongly influencing individuals in the family of orientation seem at an early age to mold one's recreational tastes. Variations in socialization, the opportunity structure, family size, family life cycle, and age are the primary background factors. In the family of procreation an additional set of factors emerge, centered on the decision-making process. This process combines the value system brought into the group by individuals with the perceived individual versus group profits. The resulting decision will range from total consensus to some degree of accommodation on the part of one or more group members. This in turn will influence the expected group reward from the activity. The actual behavioral outcome will be a result in this initial expectation and the actual behavior-person interaction as in the exchange model presented earlier in Figure 17.1.

Most research in the past has at least implicitly been based on a model utilizing primarily social background factors as determinants of recreational choice. The model presented here suggests that group decision making might be an important intervening variable that should be considered more fully in future recreational research. In addition, the inclusion of an exchange framework seems beneficial in explaining and predicting recreational behavior. In any event, the model presents a framework for integrating future research. And theoretical development has been sparse in the study of recreation and leisure in the past.

NOTES

1. Two sets of variables determine rewards and costs; those which are external to the relationship are exogenous, while those intrinsic to the relationship are endogenous. The exogenous variables include values, needs, skills, tools, etc., brought into a relationship by the individual. They may be an internal part of a person, but they are external to a relationship in that they do not develop as a result of the relationship. Also included in this category would be any effects culture might have on the particular behavior. Endogenous variables, on the other hand, are those which develop from the relationship itself, such as satisfaction or dissatisfaction (Thibaut and Kelley, 1959).

Two other concepts are needed to develop an exchange theory of recreational behavior. Thibaut and Kelley (1959) refer to them as comparison level (CL) and comparison level for alternatives (CL$\alpha\lambda\tau$). Comparison level refers to the *expectations* an individual has and feels he has a

right to have regarding a particular activity. In short, CL relates to a person's expectations concerning rewards and costs of a particular activity, while CLalt. is concerned with the *alternatives* available to a person should he become dissatisfied with a particular activity. In recreational activities these two standards are important in terms of the outcomes from a particular activity or set of activities.

2. Unpublished data gathered for a study funded by the University of Idaho Water Resources Institute. Based on interview sample of floaters during the summer 1971.

3. This discussion of consensual and accommodative decisions is adapted from Libby and Carlson (1973:370-71).

REFERENCES

ARENDT, H.
1959   *The Human Condition.* New York: Doubleday.

BENSON, P.
1952   "The interests of happily married couples." *Marriage and Family Living* 14:276-80.

BHREM, J. AND A. COHEN
1962   *Explorations in Cognitive Dissonances.* New York: Wiley.

BLALOCK, H.
1969   *Theory Construction.* Englewood Cliffs, N.J.: Prentice Hall.

BLOOD, R. AND D. WOLFE
1960   *Husbands and Wifes.* New York: Free Press.

BURCH, W.
1964   "Nature as symbol and expression in American social life." Unpublished Ph.D. Thesis, University of Minnesota.
1966   "Wilderness: The life-cycle and forest recreational choice." *Journal of Forestry* 64:606-10.
1969   "The social circles of leisure: Competing explanations." *Journal of Leisure Research* 1:125-45.

BURCH, W. AND M. TAVES
1961   "Changing functions of recreation in human society: Outdoor recreation in the Upper Great Lakes area." Lake States Forest Experiment Station Paper 89:8-16.

BURCH, W. AND W. WENGER
1967   "Social characteristics of participants in three styles of family camping." PNW Forest and Range Experiment Station Research Paper PNW-48.

BURDGE, R.
1969   "Levels of occupational prestige and leisure activity." *Journal of Leisure Research* 1:363-73.

CARLSON, J.
1972   "A sociological analysis of factors affecting recreational behavior." Unpublished Ph.D. Dissertation, Washington State University.

CHARLESWORTH, J.
1964   "A comprehensive plan for the wise use of leisure." In James Charlesworth (ed.), *Leisure in America: Blessing or Curse?* Philadelphia: American Academy of Political and Social Science Monograph 4.

CLARKE, A.
1956   "The use of leisure and its relation to levels of occupational prestige." *American Sociological Review* 21:301-07.

CLAWSON, M.
1964   "How much leisure, now and in the future?" In James Charlesworth (ed.), *Leisure in America: Blessing or Curse?* Philadelphia: American Academy of Political and Social Science Monograph 4.

CUNNINGHAM, K. R. AND T. B. JOHANNIS, JR.
1960   "Research on family and leisure: A review and critique of selected studies." *Family Life Coordinator* 9:25-32.

DAVIS, H.
1970   "Technological change and recreation planning." In B. L.

Driver (ed.), *Elements of Outdoor Recreation Planning*. Ann Arbor, Mich.: University Microfilms.

DEGRAZIA, S.
1962   *Of Time, Work and Leisure.* New York: Twentieth Century Fund.

DRIVER, B. L. AND S. R. TOCHER
1970   "Toward a behavioral interpretation of recreational engagements, with implication for planning." In B. L. Driver (ed.), *Elements of Outdoor Recreation Planning.* Ann Arbor, Mich.: University Microfilms.

DUBIN, R.
1956   "Industrial workers' worlds: A study of the central life interests of industrial workers." *Social Problems* 3:131–42.

DUMAZEDIER, J.
1967   *Toward a Society of Leisure.* Translated from French. New York: Free Press.

DYER, A. A. AND R. S. WHALEY
1968   "Predicting use of recreation sites." Utah Agricultural Experiment Station Bulletin 477.

EDWARDS, J.
1969   "Family behavior as social exchange." *Journal of Marriage and the Family* 31:518–26.

GERSON, W. M.
1960   "Leisure and marital satisfaction of college married couples." *Marriage and Family Living* 22:360–61.

GOULDNER, A. W.
1960   "The norm of reciprocity: A preliminary statement." *American Sociological Review* 25:161–78.

GREEN, A.
1964   *Recreation, Leisure and Politics.* New York: McGraw-Hill.

HENDEE, J.
1969   "Rural-urban differences reflected in outdoor recreation participation." *Journal of Leisure Research* 1:333–41.

HENDEE, J. AND F. CAMPBELL
1969   "Social aspects of outdoor recreation. The developed campground." *Trends* 10:12–16.

HOMANS, G.
1961   *Social Behavior: Its Elementary Forms.* New York: Harcourt, Brace & World.

KELLY, J.
1972   "Work and leisure: A simplified paradigm." *Journal of Leisure Research* 4:45–54.
1974   "Socialization toward leisure; A developmental approach." *Journal of Leisure Research* 6:181–93.

KING, D.
1968   "Socioeconomic variables related to campsite use." *Forest Science* 14:45–54.

KOHN, M.
1969   *Class and Conformity: A Study in Values.* Homewood, Ill.: Dorsey Press.

LAPAGE, W. F. AND D. RAGAIN
1974   "Family camping trends: An eight year panel study." *Journal of Leisure Research* 6:101–12.

LIBBY, R. AND J. CARLSON
1973   "A theoretical framework for premarital sexual decisions in dyad." *Archives of Sexual Behavior* 2:365–78.

NYE, F. I. AND W. RUSHING
1966   "Toward family measurement research." In Catherine S. Chilman (ed.), *Approaches to the Measurement of Family Change.* Washington, D.C.: U.S. Department of Health, Education and Welfare.

SCHEUCH, E. K.
1960   "Family cohesion in leisure time." *Sociological Review* 8:37–51.

SESSOMS, H. D.
1963   "An analysis of selected variables affecting outdoor recreation patterns." *Social Forces* 42:112–15.

SHIBUTANI, T.
1962   "Reference groups and social control." In Arnold Rose (ed.), *Human Behavior and Social Processes.* Boston: Houghton Mifflin.

SOFRANKO, A. AND M. NOLAN
1970   "Selected characteristics, participation patterns and attitudes of hunters and fishermen in Pennsylvania." Pennsylvania State University Agricultural Experiment Station Bulletin 770.

STONE, C. L.
1963   "Family recreation: A parental dilemma." *Family Life Coordinator* 12:85–87.

THIBAUT, J. AND H. KELLEY
1959   *The Social Psychology of Groups.* New York: Wiley.

TURNER, R.
1970   *Family Interaction.* New York: Wiley.

U.S. OUTDOOR RECREATION RESOURCES REVIEW COMMISSION
1962   Study Reports 1–24. Washington, D.C.: Government Printing Office.

VEBLEN, T.
1934   *The Theory of the Leisure Class.* New York: Modern Library.

WENNERGREN, E. B. AND D. NIELSON
1968   "A probabilistic approach to estimating demand for outdoor recreation." Utah State Univeristy Agricultural Experiment Station Bulletin 478.

WEST, P. AND L C. MERRIAM, JR.
1969   "Camping and cohesiveness: A sociological study of the effect of outdoor recreation on family solidarity." Minnesota Forestry Research Notes, no. 201.

WHITE, C.
1955   "Social class differences in the uses of leisure." *American Journal of Sociology* 61:145–50.

WILENSKY, H.
1960   "Work, careers and social integration." *International Social Science Journal* 12:543–60.
1961   "The uneven distribution of leisure: The impact of economic growth on 'free time'. *Social Problems* 9:32–56.

18

SIBLING RELATIONSHIPS IN THE FAMILY

Jay D. Schvaneveldt and Marilyn Ihinger

INTRODUCTION

Growing up in a family context which includes brothers and sisters is an experience which 80 percent of American children share (Mussen et al, 1974). It is reasonable to assume that the experiences children share with siblings have a profound influence on their socialization and personality development processes. It is surprising that so central and fundamental an experience has received so little conceptual, empirical, and theoretical attention.

Emphasis on the socialization process by family researchers and theorists has traditionally centered on the recursive parent-child relationship. Only recently has the nonrecursive aspect of parent-child-sib socialization been emphasized. Richard Bell (1968) and Harriet Rheingold (1969) emphasize the socialization effects of children, especially infants, on parents. Sutton-Smith and Rosenberg (1970) demonstrate the multifaceted nature of influence within families; not only do parents have impact upon sibling development, but siblings have significant influence on each other.

This chapter is intended to pull together some empirical and theoretical propositions from this primitively researched area, and to sensitize other researchers to the importance of this area of socialization. It diverges from others in this volume insofar as the data base from which we pull empirical propositions is limited. To the extent that sibling interaction and socialization have been investigated in the research literature, one can assume the propositions we have posited have some level of support. Other propositions are emergent in nature, and the reader

is cautioned to keep in mind their speculative nature. The reader will find this chapter lacks the precision and conciseness found in other chapters. The area of sibling socialization has far to go to meet the requirements of Hage (1972) regarding "precise continuous" propositional statements, and our efforts represent only an initial step in this direction. Our work should be regarded as an invitation to others to join us in this task, rather than any conclusive statement on sibling interaction.

The seminal article of Irish (1964) emphasized a paucity of interest and research in the area of sibling interaction. He pointed out the fixation of birth order researchers on assessing particular personality traits and their failure to examine interaction among sibling roles. Irish provided insights into the importance siblings have upon each other and then delineated several factors that impede sib research. With few exceptions, however, research and theory have not been expanded beyond Irish's early formulation. The theory presented below extends the work of Irish in addressing the issue of sibling interaction. His suggestion to focus on interaction coupled with our positive experience of employing exchange theory in our analysis has been most helpful. We begin by critically discussing the research on birth position and demonstrate its inadequate contribution to the knowledge of sibling interaction.

BIRTH ORDER–SIBLING RESEARCH

This chapter will not attempt to give a comprehensive review of all previous work on birth order–sibling relationships. Several excellent reviews of this research are available to the reader (Kammeyer, 1967; Adams, 1972). We do, however, address the issue of birth order because of its continued interest as a topic for research related to sib behavior. What we attempt to show is that this body of research is an inadequate beginning point in the search for determinants and effects of sib interaction.

As a number of reviews and critiques have shown, birth

NOTE: The authors acknowledge research support from the College of Family Life Project 295 2208 3901 06052 at Utah State University and research assistance of Mary Gay Taylor. Grateful acknowledgment is made of the contribution of Kenneth Kammeyer and D. Eugene Mead, who served as reviewers for this chapter. Reuben Hill and Irving Tallman also provided valuable evaluation and suggestions for the chapter. Many, although not all, of their suggestions have been incorporated into the final manuscript.

order–sibling interaction studies are not known for innovative methodology or carefully formulated research designs. For the most part this research has been *ex post facto,* disjointed, tangential, and motivated by curiosity rather than theory. The most common independent variables have been ordinal position, sex of siblings, number of siblings, and the spacing interval between birth of children. Dependent variables have been voluminous and include educational attainment, eminence, aspirations and motivation, deviant behavior (including juvenile delinquency), mental illness, alcoholism, anxiety, dependence, conformity, affiliation, personality characteristics, orientations toward parents, competition, love, respect, protectiveness, jealousy, domination, and leadership.

A number of theoretical orientations have been employed to explain the importance of birth order, sibling position in the family, and consequences of these relationships. These include family resources (Bayer, 1967; Blood, 1972; Blau and Duncan, 1967), dethronement (Adler, 1928; Bossard and Boll, 1960), anxious or relaxed parent (Adams, 1972), physiological status of mother (Bayer, 1967), only-child uniqueness (Adams, 1972), and sibling interaction theory (Bossard and Boll, 1960; Sutton-Smith and Rosenberg, 1970). No systematic theory has emerged, however, that has been integrating or successful in linking these variables together.

Both Adams (1972) and Kammeyer (1967) refer to the ease with which one can collect data related to birth order and sibling position within the family group. This ease has led to a potpourri of dependent variables as noted above. Both of these authors note the weaknesses of such explanations when they appear after the fact to explain a relationship which became apparent while the researchers were attempting to study other variables. It is almost routine to gather data on number, age, and sex of children ''just in case'' one wishes to see how such variables may be related to dependent variables under study. Many studies show a direct relationship between birth order position and some dependent variable, while others attempt to explain why birth order seems to make a difference. A number of scholars have recognized that birth order is at best a proxy or indicator for something that is going on in the family. ''Sibling status is a locus for specific learning contingencies, and once these contingencies have been formulated the study of sibling status itself becomes irrelevant'' (Sutton-Smith and Rosenberg, 1970:13). Outside of some physical theories which argue in terms of uterine fatigue with later-born children, there seems to be no defensible reason to argue that numerical position by itself can be an explanatory variable.

In a pioneering work, Adler (1928) argued for the importance of birth order as a crucial variable in determining personality. Stager and Katzoff (1936), on the other hand, early questioned the importance of birth order in determining personality formation. Critical reviews have

regularly been published in the last several decades (Chen and Cobb, 1960; Schachter, 1969, 1963; Clausen, 1965; Warren, 1966; Altus, 1966; Bayer and Folger, 1967; Kammeyer, 1967; Miley, 1969; Adams, 1972; and Schooler, 1972) with varying positions taken as to the array of findings and recommended directions for future work. The cautious assessment of McCandless (1969) is typical of appraisals rendered in behalf of ordinal position research:

> Most studies provide results that would be expected from observation, common sense, and application of a reasonably sophisticated learning theory to the social situation of ''first childness.'' But, from a practical point of view, little help is given in understanding or guiding children by knowing their status within the family. ''First childness'' is a demographic variable that is mildly helpful in predicting group behavior, but of little value in predicting the individual. It may be of crucial importance for a given child, of none for another [807].

Researchers have varied from a position of recommending quick and painless burial for a dead area to a stance which calls for further research on a number of variables. In between these two positions we have Kammeyer (1967), who calls for conceptual clarity, adequate definitions, explanation, and theoretical guidance in ordinal position research. Schooler's (1972) work is a plea to be sensitive to methodological artifacts in a host of studies done on the impact of ordinal position on several dependent variables. In short, Schooler asserts that sampling errors, failure to control for social-economic status, and the demographic makeup of populations tend to neutralize or even dismiss most of the reputed relationships between birth order status and dependent variables such as success of the first-born children. Schooler (1972) and Adams (1972) have noted the attractiveness of birth order as a potentially useful variable in the study of family dynamics. The clean-cut nature of the variable is quickly tarnished when one employs the necessary controls on social class, sex of sibling, family density, and population cohort. In addition, critical methodological weaknesses accompany most of these ordinal position studies. These include the following:

Sample Problems

Sample size has tended to be small, nonrandom, and a student-type audience (notable exceptions are the studies by Bayer, 1967; Schooler, 1972; and Zajonc and Markus, 1975).

A detailed and critical review of the literature of birth order effects by Schooler (1972) clearly illustrates the problem in failing to adequately sample and define the cohort from a demographic point of view. Schooler concludes that where there has been a long-term trend toward a great number of new families being started each year (greater than in the previous year), there will naturally be more first-born than last-born children. Also, in a population where the average family size is decreasing and this trend continues year after year, there will be more last-born than first-born children as fewer couples begin child rearing than find themselves ending the period of child rearing. It is not difficult to explain why first-borns are overrepresented in a number of populations given that we have a dual process of decreasing family size and an increase of new families being started in the United States. Currently the birth rate per thousand is very low, but we have a very large cohort of post-World War II babies who are in the marriage and childbearing market.

Adams (1972) illustrates the problem of mixing cohort conceptualization and overgeneralization of ensuing findings. One can collect data on a cohort in terms of "same event" such as going to a university or obtaining inoculations for swine flue in certain clinics. This only assesses the place and time and does not adequately deal with potential variance in the makeup of such persons. This problem is compounded when data from such studies are then generalized to a different population. The child-rearing philosophy and fad can also influence the experience of any age or ordinal-positioned child. Being reared in the permissive-quiet 1950s may have a very different impact upon children than being reared in the angry-disillusioned environment of the 1960s and early 1970s.

In addition to the cohort problem there is the problem of dealing with developmental time and stage of the family life cycle. A study comparing oldest children in a group of families with a group of last-born children runs the risk of compounding historical events, comparing parents of different ages, and violating earlier comments about family size and socioeconomic status. Some families are complete, while others are not. It is a simple matter to identify first-born children, but middle-born and last-born children are subject to change over time. Adams (1972) calls for research which samples whole or completed families, and some research has attempted this (Taylor and Schvaneveldt, 1977).

Adams (1972) calls for better control in regard to total sibship size in research; it is not enough to identify the sex of the child or define ordinal position. Adequate methodology is needed which deals with sex, sibship size, age spacing, sex ratio, and multiple sibling units.

Adams (1972), Schooler (1972), and others have illustrated the problem of not using completed families in the study of sibling status variables. This weakness is compounded by what can be labeled an overemphasis on the early years of development as they affect personality formation. Several authors (Orlansky, 1949; Sewell, 1952; Sears et al., 1957) have been frustrated in their attempt to show the impact of early child-rearing systems on later personality composition or general functioning. We may have overbought and hence overgeneralized data for families based on the alleged impact of the early years. In fact, it may be in the teenage period or launching period that parental impact and sibling interaction effects are greatest (Irish, 1964). Empirical evidence is necessary before any conclusion can be drawn. In any case, one can legitimately argue that development and socialization within the family are not static, but ever changing, and emphasis on socialization and interaction at all stages of the family life cycle might fruitfully contribute to our knowledge.

Lack of Theory Underpinning or Theoretical Interpretations

A number of authors have noted the common fact that researchers will obtain data on birth order and/or sibling status while pursuing some other area of research. Often birth order and sibling status are then related to some dependent variable to determine any broad connections. Lacking theoretical focus, this methodological approach backs the researchers into a corner regardless of the outcome of the comparison. This invariably leads to *ex post facto* explanations that add little to theory.

Measurement Problems

A number of issues exist here that are problematic. Validity, reliability, and adequate control factors have not dominated this area of research.

Social class and educational level of parents have not been adequately controlled in most research. It is thus almost impossible to determine whether reputed findings are due to sibling and/or birth order status or due to differences in resources of their respective families.

Sex of siblings has not been adequately controlled. Often researchers merely talk about a sample of males or females and do not deal with numbers of other brothers or sisters. Brim (1958) is an example of research where this issue has been addressed, and he shows how sex role content can be influenced by an older sister or a brother. Researchers have been expedient in studying this area as ordinal position is "easy" to measure (Adams, 1972). Not only can this "ease" be questioned, but the measurement problems associated with alleged effects of ordinality abound.

Another major problem in a number of studies has been the failure to differentiate between first-born and only-born children. Quite often, researchers have merely used the dichotomy of first-born and later-born, or the trichotomy of first-born, middle-born, and last-born.

To summarize, the authors believe it is appropriate to raise the question of commitment to an empirical base which has apparently trapped behavioral scientists in a number of ways in the ordinal position–sibling behavior area. We feel that the critical impact of placement of birth in the early socialization years has been overbought. We do not question the importance of the early years in determining much about personality formation and later behavior, but we feel that developmentally this is a process that continues up through adulthood and is not arrested at an artificial age of five or six. We further believe that the developmental process is also influenced by the behavior of sibling members, not alone by the order in which children are born into the family. It is too simplistic to hope that a structural variable such as ordinal position could possibly have effects on such a diverse set of child and adult behaviors.

A THEORY OF SIBLING BEHAVIOR

Insofar as birth order data are associated with personality characteristics (dependency, responsibility, creativity, conformity, etc.) this data base can be fruitfully recast into the arena of sibling interaction if these personality attributes studied as dependent variables in this research are translated as "incipient roles." The concept of incipient role is useful for this purpose, since it points to the attribute of personality as a propensity to play a specific role (for example, helpfulness as a propensity to play the helping hand). Role making within the family is undertaken when role scripts are lacking or no longer fit the incumbents. Children may be role-cast in line with their ascribed personality attributes as responsible, ambitious, or conforming if eldest child, or dependent, or lovable if youngest child.

The definition of role in this analysis follows Bates's (1956) definition: "a part of a social position consisting of a more or less integrated or related sub-set of social norms which is distinguishable from other sets of norms forming the same position" (314). An incipient role is a role associated with a newly acquired position, or one that is newly expanded. Incipient role reflects the notion of role making (Turner, 1962; Aldous, 1972). Aldous posits that role making occurs when "interaction patterns are improvised on the spot by the actors with whatever patterning that occurs developing out of habituation rather than initial normative prescriptions. The actors are, in a sense, creating normative explications within the family group itself" (1972:156). Turner's (1962) original notion was that few roles in our society are rigidly prescribed by norms and that we "make" rather than "play" role performances. We conceptualize that role making within the family is more ambiguous and difficult for children than for parents. The idea of personality attribute translated into incipient role suggests that if an oldest child is a responsible (dependent, ambitious, conforming, or what have you) child, s/he will be more likely to perform specified roles, or role-make differently than a child who does not share this attribute. Bossard and Boll (1950) allude to the incipient role notion: "Children . . . are distinctive individuals . . . and their conditioning experiences only accentuate the difference. Once this individual characteristic of every child in the family is kept in mind, it follows as a matter of course that each sibling will have his own distinctive relation to, and effect upon, every other sibling" (1950, p. 97).

The question of recasting personality attributes into roles and role making is one of focus. When focus is on the nature of the group, rather than the personalities of those in the group, the study leads to generating knowledge about the characteristics of the group, and to patterns of group interaction. Our analysis assumes that sibling groups share the same characteristics as other small face-to-face groups; that is, the sibling group has a communication network, shares power and affective relations with clique alignments, operates in accord with norms, roles, and functions, and generates cooperation and conflict.

In this refocusing of sibling interaction in the family we employ five assumptions:

1. The family can be viewed as having three separate subsystems—spousal, parental-child, and sibling-sibling. All of these subsystems function as semiclosed systems within the family group.
2. Siblings are both recipients and instigators of socialization. Family interaction is a dynamic arena in which spouses affect each other, parents affect children, children affect parents, and siblings affect each other.
3. Sibling interaction is a continuous developmental process not limited to the early "critical" years.
4. The nature of family composition and interaction are determining factors in personality development and social behaviors of members.
5. Sibling groups have distinctive group properties and characteristics as do other small groups.

The obvious nature and apparent simplicity of ordinal position and sibling status as categories have seduced researchers into bypassing the essential steps of definition and concept clarification. We shall point to some of the problems as we attempt to clarify the concepts.

Sibling Status

A sibling is a brother or sister and this implies a blood relationship. Two or more children in a family are necessary to have a sibling relationship. A number of studies incorrectly discuss sibling relationships in families of only children. Sibling relationships in a family can take the form of brother(s)-sister(s), brother(s)-brother(s), and sister(s)-sister(s). Siblings may be classified also by ordinal location as eldest brother, eldest sister, youngest brother, youngest sister, and so on, categories which overlap but are not identical with the more general categories of ordinal position of first-born, middle-born, and last-born.

Ordinal Position

This concept expresses order or succession in a series and in our case the birth order position of children in a family. It differs from sibling status in not having gender specified and in having a place for the only child. Ordinal position in a family can range from only child to . . . N.

1. *Only child.* This indicates one child in a family. Only-child status cannot be assumed unless family size is complete.

2. *Middle-born children.* This refers to child number 2 out of a sibling group of three, any child other than first- or last-born, or the grouping of all children in a family between first-born and last-born status.

3. *Last-born child.* This refers to the last child born in the family. It is apparent that only children are both first-born and last-born.

Sibling Relationship

This refers to the nature of the interaction between brothers and sisters. Sibling relationships can be influenced by gender, age, number, spacing interval, the ratio of male to female sibs, age of parents at time of birth, and the age of children at the time they are launched from the family setting, Other factors such as travel of family members, health, isolation, absence, and mobility of sibs can also influence the nature of sibling relationships. Family guests, strangers in the family, extended kin, and roomers may all influence the complexity and nature of sibling relationships (Bossard and Boll, 1960; Schvaneveldt, 1973; Blood, 1972; Modell and Hareven, 1973).

Interaction

Interaction refers to "the social behaviors involved when two or more persons interstimulate each other by any means of communication, and hence modify each other's behavior" (Schvaneveldt, 1966:103). Bossard and Boll (1960) use the concept to cover the range of contacts between persons and the ways in which they influence one another. They see family interaction as the "reciprocal relationships between the members of a family in their continuing life with each other" (1960:69). Siblings are key family members and often central to the quantity and quality of family interaction. Further, sibling interaction is important in its own right.

Position

A position is a location in a social structure which is associated with a set of social norms (Bates, 1956:314).

Role

A role is a part of a social position consisting of a more or less integrated or related subset of social norms which is distinguishable from other sets of norms forming the same position (Bates, 1956:314).

Norm

A norm is a pattern of commonly held behavior expectation. It is a learned response held in common by members of a group (Bates, 1956:314).

Family as a System

Burgess (1926) viewed the family as an arena of interacting personalities. Dollard (1935) later added that each family had its own history and catalogue of ritualistic events as studied by Bossard and Boll (1950). A newly married couple is faced with the task of integrating the different roles and habits carried over from two parental families into a mutually acceptable script for a working dyad. What typically happens when a child enters this dyad? We must borrow two concepts from Farber (1964) and assess such a family in terms of "closed" and "opened" systems. Closed systems tend to duplicate themselves, and a closed system is maintained by fostering isolation, preservation, slow turnover, and sentimental factors which include the emotional ties between parents and children. In contrast to the family viewed as a closed system, the family as an open system has a more permeable boundary between the family and forces outside the family, and is much more fluid in operation. Change, reform, and deviance would be more common in open systems.

This conceptualization of closed and open systems is a useful concept to explain what happens when a child enters a family. The family changes from a dyad to a triad with the entry of the child, and immediately the channels are set for reducing the closed nature of the family dyad. Hill and Aldous (1969) state that children serve as socializing agents for parents insofar as children lead their parents to a number of activities outside of the family context. School, church, peer groups, and community organizations compete with or supplement how parents socialize their children. Hill and Aldous indicate that "because the formal education organization has received societal sanction to place the child in the role of learner and to teach him a certain minimum of skills and values, all parents have to take the school efforts into account in their interaction with the child" (926).

Beginning with the first, and increasing with subsequent children, the family becomes more open. In this process sibling(s) have an impact on the socialization and interaction processes that occur within the family by opening up the family interaction process. Thus the first-born is socialized in a more closed system than is child number 2, 3, 4, and on to other ordinal positions.

Bank and Kahn (1975) assert that sibs perform a pioneering function for one another, usually the older sibs blazing and marking trails for younger sibs. Sibs have powerful impact upon one another through these pioneering activities and also contribute to degree of openness of its family system. For example, we may gain insight as to why first-born sibs are more sexually conservative than later-born sibs by applying the concepts of pioneering and open-closed systems (Reiss, 1967). As the family becomes more open, parents become more experienced and permissive, and last-born children have more open routines than do first-born children. Thus we formulate the proposition:

1. The entry of a child into the family fosters openness in the system, and this openness increases with each subsequent child who joins the family unit.

This total family system, whether open or closed, can be conceptualized as comprising two subparts: the child-sibling and parental-spousal subsystems. Each of these is viewed as semiclosed; that is, children have access to some parts of the parental subsystem (involving time, attention, affection, etc.) but are barred from participation in some spousal activities (budgeting activities, sexual behavior, etc.). Similarly, linkages exist between parent and child, but parents may not have access to certain behaviors that sibs share with each other (exchanging confidences, smoking pot, etc.). Our special interest here is on interaction and influences within the sibling subsystem, but we feel we cannot ignore intersystem connections in discussing intrasystem behavior. Consequently we will include in our analysis a discussion of the impact of sibs on parents as well as the impact of parents on sibs, whenever it is appropriate to our analysis.

Characteristics of the Sib Subsystem: Coalition Formation

Blood (1972) indicates that coalitions develop in the family for the purpose of engaging in conflict. Coalitions may also form for the purpose of solidarity or to maximize rewards for participating members. Parental behavior may cause children to bond together into a solidary cabal. Older children can bond with younger siblings, or the older sibs may array against the younger sibs. Caplow (1959) found that sibling coalitions of same-sex siblings were most common. He also found that age differences in sibling coalitions was small. The sibling coalitions he studied typically persisted after sibs left the parental home.

Coalitions between sibs may be fostered due to the large age range that exists in the family system. Parents are much older than their children and have the experience, resources, and power to dominate the group. It is not surprising that sibs band together to wield authority against other sib coalitions as well as to counteract the impact of parents. Caplow (1968) outlines the various possibilities for the formation of coalitions in the sib subsystem of the family. Borrowing from him, we present in proposition format:

2. "When the parental coalition is so solidary that no child is ever allowed to form a winning coalition with one parent against the other, we may expect to see strong coalitions among the children, and even a condition of general solidarity uniting all the children of a large family" (Caplow, 1968:99; from Bank and Kahn, 1975:315).

3. "When one parent is clearly dominant, a . . . coalition is likely to form between the weaker parent and a child, which may lead in turn to the formation of sibling coalitions against the favored child or to other very complicated patterns in a sizeable family" (Caplow, 1968:99, from Bank and Kahn, 1975:315).

4. "When father and mother are nearly equal in power, but do not have a strong parental coalition, sibling rivalry will be intense and bitter as the children compete among themselves for the shifting coalition opportunities offered by their parents" (Caplow, 1968:99, from Bank and Kahn, 1975:315).

Siblings in a family are captives, especially when brothers and sisters are young. They are forced to resolve their problems among themselves and/or with the help of parents. Propositions as presented by Caplow (1968) help to clarify potentiality for rivalry in the nature of the interaction that occurs in a family. The eldest may serve as the leader for a coalition against mother and father, not because of the magic of being first-born, but because of power ascribed by his siblings and closer access to the parental dyad. Tattling and squealing become legitimate behavior in sibling coalitions. Parents often arbitrate between sibling factions, but sibling coalitions also can arbitrate for each other. It can be costly as well as rewarding to have a big sis or a kid brother in the family.

Sibling coalitions in the family perform policing functions for parents and for their own emotional-physical well-being. Sibs can play their parents off against each other with cunning accuracy and reap rewards for the sibship system. Blood (1972) asserts that sibs are most successful in doing this when they remain "aloof from an alliance with either parent" (559). Family isolates, "black sheep," scapegoats, winners, losers, and "pets" may all be fostered by the degree and intensity with which sibling coalitions function within the family system.

Coalitions among and between siblings in the family can have both an integrative and a disruptive effect. Blood (1972) suggests that families are forced to resolve tension between coalitions and often do this by creating a stalemate between members of vying coalitions. If a sib's family cannot handle the friction, Blood states that they may divert their hostilities toward an enemy outside the family unit, or they may pretend the conflict is nonexistent.

Positional Shift in the Sib Subsystem

Displacement or dethronement is the process of losing the position or status one once held alone. Bossard and Boll (1960) state that "until other children arrive, the first-born is alone, in the center of the stage. His adjustments are only to adults. He learns to accomodate only to older persons. These older persons are apt to be pliant and tolerant. Usually it is their first experience with parenthood. Their behavior is prone to be tentative. They proceed experimentally. The first is the practice child" (101). With the arrival of a second child in this setting, the potential for crisis of displacement for the first child is high, especially if parents do not adequately prepare a child for the forthcoming sib. The space interval between births is important in assessing dethronement. "It is particularly important in the case of the oldest child, because it determines the severity of the crisis" (Bossard and Boll, 1960:101).

Dethronement is important in the sibship system because it fosters attention seeking—which takes the form of dwelling on past performance (e.g., reverting to baby talk) or developing new behavior techniques. Disruption in food intake and bathroom behavior are two common areas of stress and attention seeking for the young dethroned child.

These ideas can be summed in the proposition:

5. The age of a child and the efforts of parents in preparing the child for a new sib affect the outcome of the dethronement process for a young child.

The surrogate parental role coupled with admonitions to follow the example set by older brothers and sisters places the oldest child in a contemptuous role at times. Blood (1972) even suggests that "in a close parallel to the leadership differential between parents, the eldest child tends to become the instrumental leader of the sibling group and the beloved last child becomes the expressive leader or at least the expressive focus of the group" (476).

It is believed that the trauma of dethronement causes the oldest child to be more achievement-oriented (Adler, 1928; Blood, 1972; Adams, 1972). Psychologically, the oldest sibling is motivated to achieve, succeed, and defer to parental wishes in an attempt to win back status, position, and affirmation which at one time was shared with no one else. The foundation for developing leadership is tied to dethronement and ordinal position. The first-born is older, stronger, more experienced, and usually gets to do things first. "He is the pioneer, the pathfinder, the trail blazer" (Bossard and Boll, 1960:102). Bossard and Boll (1960) indicate that "he regards his superiority over his brothers and sisters often as his natural right. It is this situation which explains, possibly, his higher rate of achievement and success . . ." (102).

Enthronement or retention is the process of holding on to and perhaps even smothering from a parental point of view. It is most likely to occur with the last child and probably because parents know this is the end of child care and they want to maintain parental roles. During the last few years before he/she leaves home, the youngest child is likely to have the parents to her/himself. Enthronement is the process of parental forces seeking to savor the last child as she/he passes through the family harbor. It is the process of experiencing with the poet, "I shall not pass this way again" and one must savor that time.

The phenomenon of dethronement should be examined in developmental terms. Becoming a big brother or big sister is made possible by the arrival of the second child, activating a cluster of nurturing, protective, and helping roles which being an "only" child on a throne did not

offer. We do not have clear data on what is the optimal interval for this to occur, but five years has been suggested (Adams, 1972). Enthronement is not expected to influence the sib relation except as it contributes to the perception that the youngest is "spoiled" (Latts, 1966).

Processes within the Sibling System

Insight regarding the important contributions of siblings to one another may be gained by assessing the functions performed on a day-to-day basis. Specific examples and propositions showing how siblings function in the sibship complex are evident in the research literature.

From observations derived from clinical settings, Bank and Kahn (1975) outline and illustrate a number of functions which sibs perform for each other. Two such functions performed are identification and differentiation. These authors view these processes as the "'glue' of the sibling relationship" (319). While these processes are known to occur between parent and child, Bank and Kahn posit they also occur between sib and sib. Identification in the sibling complex is "the process by which a sib sees himself in the other, experiences life vicariously through the behavior of the other, and begins to expand on possibilities for himself by learning through a brother's or sister's experience . . ." (319).

Differentiation, the opposite side of identification, is the process for defining identity and your "space" in the family rather than fusion with other siblings. "Differentiating serves, then, as a way of externalizing or projecting deeply felt needs or anxieties" (320). Casting this function into proposition form, we may state that:

6. "Selfhood" as a sibling is fostered by the dual processes of identifying with siblings in certain areas and rejecting or differentiating from them in other areas.

A third function suggested by Bank and Kahn (1975) is that of mutual regulation—the process by which sibs serve as mirrors, sounding boards, and testing grounds for one another. "Siblings provide an 'observing ego' for one another that can exert an effective and corrective impact upon, and for, each other. The mutual regulatory process among brothers and sisters proceeds on the basis of fairness and honest relationship among relative equals" (321). They can be more open with each other and fear less about reprisal. Thus we can say that:

7. Sibling interaction in terms of mutual regulation serves to guide and sanction behavior so as to maximize rewards and reduce cost in the sibling complex, and this serves to increase sibling solidarity.

Direct services constitute a fourth function performed by siblings for each other.

In everyday sibling ecology, brothers and sisters can make life easy or difficult for one another; they can be quiet, facilitative, sloppy and obstructive, or neat and cooperative. They teach each other skills, lend each other money, manipulate powerful friendship rewards for one another, and serve as controllers of resources; introduction to a new friendship group often depends on the kind auspices of one sibling to another. Brothers and sisters can act as buffers for each other, interposing themselves between their sibs and the outside world [321–22].

These direct services are the powerful day-to-day business of living with one's sibs. In propositional form we have:

8. The exchange of goods and services in the sibling complex facilitates interaction in the group and this increases sibling solidarity.

Negotiating with parents for one another is a fifth major function of siblings. Bank and Kahn (1975) assess this function in terms of coalitions. One type of coalition is termed balancing by Bank and Kahn. A sibling can collude with a parent or other sibling(s) to equalize forces or neutralize conflict.

Another way of dealing with parents is to form a coalition of siblings to offset the tremendous power of the parental dyad. "Siblings together can negotiate with more strength against the parents than one of them acting alone. At the same time, if both sibs are misbehaving, neither sibling can be seen as the only offending party" (322). Thus we see in action the old adage "Together we stand, divided we fall."

Yet another way of dealing with parents is with the use of secrets and tattling. If we assume that siblings have a partially closed system from parents, then they may know much more about each other's behavior than either parent. "Siblings are the guardians of each other's private worlds. Willingness to make and maintain each other's privacy often serves as a powerful bond of loyalty among the children" (323).

Siblings also deal with parents as "translators." Translation is a process of mediation between siblings, between the sib and parental relationship, and mediation of issues outside the family to parents. Children can often function as expert translators in helping parents to understand the "baby talk" of a younger sibling. Translating is a process by which siblings increase the degree of family openness as they filter and channel issues from the broader culture into the family complex. In proposition form we have:

9. To the degree that siblings serve as a bridge for one another between their world and that of adults, sibling solidarity is enhanced.

A final function in dealing directly with parents is labeled pioneering by Bank and Kahn (1975). "Pioneering seems to occur when one sibling initiates a process thereby giving permission to the others to follow accordingly" (324). The leader or pioneer sib in a given situation blazes the trail and gains reward in so doing, while the follower profits by modeling and may be excused

from any responsibility in the process of following. "These pioneering patterns include breaking explicit family rules, staying out late, smoking dope, driving the family car, spending allowance on the 'wrong things,' or taking new development pathways—e.g., leaving the family (or) adopting different morals/political codes, and lifestyles unimaginable to parents" (324). Older siblings are more likely to function as pioneers in the family and enjoy more status-power because of this performance. This notion is stated in propositional form:

10. To the degree that sibling pioneering activities are seen as positive by parents they will be reinforced for such behavior in the family complex and will serve to generate harmony within the family.

Conversely:

11. To the degree that sibling pioneering activities are negatively viewed by parents, conflict between parents and the pioneering child will be generated within the family complex.

Some functions performed by sibs for each other may be so important that severe feelings of mourning and loss result when the sib leaves home (Bank and Kahn, 1975). Brother-sister relations can be altered in a variety of ways: through hospitalization, leaving home for school, marrying, or moving away. From their clinical perspective, Bank and Kahn stipulate that this separation may be an important precipitant of psychological disturbance in another sibling. This notion not only suggests the impact of siblings on one another in the family system but posits the longevity of the impact. If the departed sibling performed intercession or important translating functions for other sibs, his/her absence may be the source of great distress. In propositional form we offer:

12. To the degree that sibs provide essential mediating services between parents and other sibs, sibling departures provide clues for assessing the emotional well-being of siblings in the family.

Sibling Roles

In postindustrial America, urban and suburban children no longer serve the same useful function for the operation of the common household as they have in the past. In rural areas, chores essential to household functioning may be performed by children, while doing the dishes, keeping their bedroom clean, and walking the dog or caring for pets, are the types of responsibilities assigned to middle-class suburban or urban siblings. The sharing of responsibility for household operation is not always necessary or mandatory. We do know from personal experience as well as empirical data, however, that children are usually included in the household division of labor. Evidence from Johannis (1957) indicates the degree to which teenage siblings participate in child care and control activites. Bossard and Boll (1960) claim that discipline of younger children by older children seems more prevalent in larger families. Hoffman (1963) and Douvan (1963) state that children are more likely to share in household task performance when the mother is employed, although data from Nye and Hoffman (1963) indicate that the husbands of middle-class working mothers were more likely to share in household tasks, but children were not. Latts (1966) found that there was clear evidence of task allocation on the basis of ordinal position: middle children do more task performance, and the youngest child does the least of all. Latts also found that girls spend more time doing tasks around the house than boys. Thus sibling division of labor follows a somewhat predictable pattern, at least regarding age and sex—older children care for younger sibs and females do more household tasks than males. We formulate that:

13. "The larger the number of younger siblings in the family, the more a child is expected to do chores around the house" (Blood, 1972:474, based on data from Minturn and Lambert, 1964).

This lack of prescribed roles for children means that children must become somewhat creative in making their position in the family a meaningful one. Bossard and Boll (1960) contend that "whenever the number of persons are in continuing association with each other, specialization of function of the individual members tends to occur" (1960:107). They identify eight personality roles that children in large families develop to help create a meaningful position. These include (1) the responsible sib, (2) the popular, well-liked, sociable sib, (3) the socially ambitious sib, (4) the studious sib, (5) the self-centered, isolated sib, (6) the irresponsible sib, (7) the sick sib, and (8) the spoiled sib.

From Bossard and Boll we assert that:

14. The larger the family size, the greater the number and specialization of roles.

Bossard and Boll (1960) also suggest that as the more positive roles are chosen by early-born children, later-born sibs will adopt a negative role rather than remain undifferentiated. This personality role typing reflects our earlier idea of incipient role. That is, individual characteristics of a child are utilized by that child to create an "identity" or reputation that is unique within the family circle. Bank and Kahn (1975) cite Zuk (1972) and add to the list of roles that children in the family define for themselves. One of these is a "go-between" role. In this process a sibling tries to mediate the quarrels in the family and assumes the role of peacemaker. Brim's (1958) early work on sex role learning by siblings shows evidence that siblings have a key effect on a sib's sex role attributes (expressive or feminine and instrumental or masculine). These available data indicate that task roles are as-

signed to siblings by parents and these assignments vary with age and sex. More subtle personality roles, or "reputations" of siblings, are also developed within the family by children in order to establish a personal uniqueness within the family system. Bossard and Boll (1960) assert that these reputations are perpetuated by family members and are peculiarly long-lasting. This idea can be stated in the following propositional form:

15. As personality attributes or status (age, sex) attributes vary, children will utilize such attributes to establish a unique "identity" with the family.

According to Bossard and Boll (1960) family size affects the number and variety of roles that are adopted within the family. They also note that as the size of the family increases, the importance of the sibling substructure seems to increase. This idea couched in proposition style reads:

16. There is an inverse relationship between the number of siblings in the family system and the impact of parents on siblings—as the number of siblings increases, the impact of parents on siblings decreases.

Sex Role Development in the Sibling System

Lynn (1974) and Kagan (1964) are illustrative works showing the impact of parents on children in terms of sex role learning and sex role identification. We wish to show the impact of sibs on each other in terms of sex role learning and identification. The longevity and intensity of sibling interaction are two important factors which influence modeling, one type of sex role learning. George Bernard Shaw (1914) vividly describes the social complex in which children are forced to carve out their identity and sex role orientation:

The old observation that members of large families get on in the world holds good because in large families it is impossible for each child to receive what schoolmasters call "individual attention." The children may receive a good deal of individual attention from one another in the shape of outspoken reproach, ruthless ridicule, and violent resistance to their attempts at aggression; but the parental despots are compelled by the multitude of their subjects to resort to political rather than to personal rule, and to spread their attempts at moral monster-making over so many children, that each child has enough freedom, and enough sport in the prophylactic process of laughing at its elders behind their backs, to escape with much less damage than the single child [xix–xx].

If we detour from the sheer number of sibs in a family to the sex composition of sibs in a family, we are able to assess the impact of complex sex roles upon male-female orientation. Brim (1958) attempted to understand this complex by assuming that one learns how to perform one's own role by role taking with fellow sibs in the family. The powerful sib in the family will be most influential in the process of role taking. Two hypotheses tested by Brim are that (1) children with sibs of the opposite sex will display more traits of the opposite-sex sibling than sibs without opposite-sex sibs, and (2) children with sibs of the opposite sex who are older will display a greater impact of the influence of the opposite sex. The power notion in Brim's work comes from the age differential and the sex role identification model and is based on an expressive orientation for females and instrumental orientation for males (Parsons and Bales, 1955).

In this rather clean-cut hypotheses testing, Brim found support for both assertions. Boys with sisters were higher on the expressive dimension, girls with brothers evidenced a somewhat higher level of instrumentality, but the pattern of impact with girls was less clear, perhaps due to the neutralizing influence of the close contact between girls and the mother in the family. Brim was also able to demonstrate the power of the older sib on a younger sib and show how this power is mediated via opposite sex role confrontations. Reiss (1976) argues this same model can be used to explain why older siblings are lower on sexual permissiveness and the younger sibling is hence more permissive as a result of learning from the older sib.

A major contribution of the Brim (1958) hypothesis is the convergence between one's own role and that of others which may impinge upon the actor. Brim refers to this process as "a spill-over of elements belonging to another's role into one's own performance when it is not necessarily appropriate" (2). Thus in a sibling complex, one can expect interaction between siblings of the opposite sex to create a base where sex role orientation characteristics would transfer across sex roles: ". . . interaction between two persons leads to assimilation of roles . . ." (2), in this case, sex roles. We may therefore posit that:

> 17. Assimilation of sex roles in the sibling complex is facilitated by the presence of opposite-sex members, and the impact is greatest from elder to younger siblings.

Norms and Issues of Distributive Justice

Normative expectations for behavior exist within the sibling subsystem just as within the total family system. Bossard and Boll (1960) report that grown children saw each other as more fair to one another in childhood than the parents had been to them, explaining that children understand the persistence of misbehavior more accurately than adults (315). Bank and Kahn (1975) assert that siblings live in their subsystem according to specific "rules," just as actors in other systems do. They know how far each other may go, and in what direction each may go. Bonds of loyalty and competitiveness dictate the extent to which sibs engage in "tattling" or secretive behavior. Siblings also learn how to negotiate and bargain effectively with one another; normative bounds define the

limits within which a brother or sister can con or manipulate another sib.

What generates this set of normative regulations within the sib subsystem? Piaget (1932) asserts that rule learning and "justice" originate within the peer group. In a theory of sibling conflict and the parental referee role Ihinger (1975) postulates that rules and notions of "justice" are first gained from the imposition of parental rules of "fair" treatment within the family system. That is, children learn the norm of sharing and the notions of equality and equity very early from parental behaviors; and these are learned best if they are clearly and unambiguously communicated verbally to children. This set of justice norms is adopted and implemented by sibs within their own interactions, and is further influenced by parental consistency and congruity between parents, as parents "follow through" (or fail to do so) with consequences. This theory assumes that conflict between sibs is directly related to the foregoing consistency and congruence factor. When parents allocate resources and arbitrate and referee in inconsistent and incongruent ways, sibs determine that it is more rewarding to engage in conflict over valued resources than to abide by stipulated rules. Sib conflict is generated in testing parental limits and boundaries. These ideas may be stated as the following theoretical proposition:

> 18. When parents approach an arbitration situation with consistency and congruence according to justice norms which have been clearly articulated, there will be less conflict interaction between siblings.

This proposition positing that parental consistency and congruity result in less sibling conflict is reflected in Caplow's (1968) proposition 2 (19), wherein a parental coalition of solidarity may lead to solidarity and the formation of a united front among siblings.

The open-closed notion of family boundaries is also relevant. Ihinger's (1975) theory additionally states that as children mature and are exposed to justice elements outside the family, they will challenge the family justice norms if they are comparatively perceived as unfair or unsatisfactory. This links proposition 1 (which states the openness of the family system increases with each additional child) with a comparative process as children mature and are exposed to norms and behaviors external to the family.

Conflict and disagreements arise between sibs, who, as "captive audience" to each other, are forced to spend long hours with each other, usually with definite limitations of space, objects, and interests (Bossard and Boll, 1960:91). This high level of intimacy offers the opportunity for close scrutiny or observation of other family members' behavior. This scrutiny reveals any experience of inequity and may lead to coalition formation or physical aggressiveness among sibs.

The art of self-defense is first learned in these conflict situations; not only defense against physical harassment but psychological manipulations are acquired which avoid and deflect physical harassment. These may have long-term learning effects. Toman's (1959) work hypothesizes that behaviors acquired through sib interaction affect the way actors make marital adjustments to spouses. Unfortunately, as with much of the previous work in this area, Toman's hypotheses have not had adequate empirical testing, and they remain speculative propositions. Latts (1966) found in his sample of four-sib equisex families that brothers fight most with each other and the younger brothers also fight most with the younger sisters. There was some fighting among sisters, but not as much as among brothers. The general principle that emerged from his data was that a sib fought most frequently with the sib with whom s/he spent the most time.

The other side of the coin of conflict interaction in the sib relation is reflected in bonds of loyalty, affection, and cooperation that develop and strengthen the sib relation. In deriving propositions about the existence and degree of this affect as it is expressed in the sib complex, exchange principles become a theoretical resource. Homans's (1961) propositions (as stated by Burr, 1973) directly address the situations of sentiment and interaction:

> The amount of interaction influences the amount of sentiment and this is a positive, monotonic relationship [53].
>
> The amount of sentiment influences the amount of interaction [53].
>
> If the profit from interaction is rewarding, the sentiment produced by interaction tends to be positive, whereas if the profit is costly the sentiment tends to be negative [56].

There is some research evidence on the relation between sentiment and interaction. Latts (1966) found that more conflict (but not necessarily less liking) was associated with the sibling one interacted with the most. There did not appear to be any definite pattern of relationship between spending time together and liking one another. His research also reports that sisters were considered more affectionate and friendly. Both Latts's and Bossard and Boll's (1960) research on siblings in large families found that the second sib was the best liked, the family "socio-emotional star." Bossard and Boll explain this phenomenon: "It seems in many cases as if, finding the post of responsibility preempted, he or she (and most often it is a he) proceeds to gain recognition and self-esteem through personal charm rather than personal power" (1960:108).

Bowerman and Dobash tested directly the structural effects of age, sex, and birth order on sib affection for one another. Their findings report that "females are more likely to have favorable feelings (toward their sibs) than are males, the same sex sibling is the preferred sib, on the average subjects feel closer to an older than to a younger sibling, affect toward sibs generally declines somewhat as adolescents get older, and there is a little more sibling closeness in two-child than in larger families" (1974:53).

Bossard and Boll (1960) report that in their sample of 64 sibs "sib rivalry and conflict appeared to have been minimal, and secondary to the primary bond of loyalty in the sib subset" (315). In the large families they studied, the emphasis was on sacrifice, on the group rather than on the self. This research suggests that to derive a theoretical proposition relating degree of affect to sib interaction, one must take into account structural aspects of the sib complex: age is a variable, for the expression of affect changes over time; sex is a variable, for females are socialized as more expressive; size is a variable, for siblings tend to interact with those sibs closest in age and sex to their own position; a parental coalition and solid front constitute a variable, for the degree of parental unity is hypothesized to affect sibling conflict which may or may not be related to degree of sib affection. A theoretical proposition generalizes:

> 19. The degree of sibling affect that emerges from sibling interaction is influenced by variables of age, sex, spacing of siblings, and degree of parental cohesiveness.

Power within the Sibling Subsystem

We have described some of the behavior manifestations that evolve within the sibling subgroup—the affective relationships, coalition formation, development of norms and roles, etc. A final important group characteristic is the leadership dimension, or power and authority relations that develop to influence the interpersonal relationships between sibs. Power is defined as the ability to exert one's will on others. Legitimization of power entails the recognition of another's right to exercise power; this legitimized power is authority.

Studies of power relations between members of the parental-spousal subsystem are numerous (Safilios-Rothschild, 197). Power (control) as a variable in the parent-child relation is also frequently studied (Smith, 1970; Thomas et al., 1974; Bowerman and Elder, 1964). The power and influence relation between siblings has been relatively ignored (see Sutton-Smith and Rosenberg, 1970, for an exception).

Data from Ferreira and Winter (1968) examining family interaction in 36 normal families and 49 abnormal families in treatment demonstrate that the power differences "between mothers and fathers were barely detectable, but the differences between the generations and between successive children were clearcut" (Blood, 1972:480). Thus some evidence supports a differentiation between sibs with regard to power and influence.

When considering power and influence among sibs, age and sex factors are critical variables. We need to ask, however, if there are other factors operating independent of age and sex to explain the power relations that develop between children in a family.

French and Raven (1960) have distinguished five bases of power which may enlighten an analysis of sib power:

a. Reward power, based on P's perception that O has the ability to mediate rewards for him

b. Coercive power, based on P's perception that O has the ability to mediate punishment for him

c. Legitimate power, based on the perception by P that O has a legitimate right to prescribe behavior for him

d. Referent power, based on P's identification with O

e. Expert power, based on the perception that O has some special knowledge or expertness.

At least one researcher (Smith, 1970, 1971) has applied this typology to the parent-child relation. It may also be a useful classification to increase understanding of the power relation that exists between sibs. Probably the most important factor influencing power in the sib system is the legitimacy given it by parents. Authority may be bestowed when parents designate or allocate responsibility to a child based on age or sex. Older children, given the responsibility to care for younger sibs, may be vested with the authority to "make sure they behave." Likewise, authority may be invested due to parental assignments of special responsibilities to a child (such as grocery shopping, chauffering duties, etc.) that other children in the family do not have. This authority and responsibility are observed by younger sibs and accepted as legitimate. This follows directly from French and Raven's assertion, "Designation by a legitimizing agent is a third basis for legitimate power. An influencer O may be seen as legitimate in prescribing behavior for P because he has been granted such power by a legitimizing agent whom P accepts" (1960:617).

Related to this parental designation as a source of power we find acceptance of the social structure as another basis for legitimate power: "If P accepts as right the social structure of his group, organization, or society, especially the social structure involving a hierarchy of authority, P will accept the legitimate authority of O who occupies a superior office in the hierarchy" (1960:617). This type of power is especially likely to prevail in the sib system. Children are born into an environment where obvious superiority in strength and knowledge exists in members already comprising the family group. This initial "inferior" status fosters the early acceptance of the group structure. However, maturity and an alternative comparison level that a child may develop with exposure to an environment outside the family may result in a rejection of the legitimate status hierarchy of the family. The internal dynamics within the family influence this later assessment.

Cultural values are another source of legitimate power, according to French and Raven, and these values are often based on specific characteristics of an actor (age, sex, intelligence, beauty, wealth, etc.). These cultural values may indicate that certain "characteristics are specified by the culture as giving the holder the right to prescribe behavior for P, who may not have these characteristics" (1960:616). Thus a child may be ceded deference and power because of recognized mental or physical skills the sib holds. Blau (1964) has described how status (power) differentials arise through exchange transactions when one actor has abilities or resources another actor needs. The same principle applies to siblings. The ability and willingness to assist with homework, to repair a bicycle tire, etc., are valuable commodities exchangeable for deference and power. This type of power coexists with expert power, which is invested in an actor on the basis of a perception that s/he has special knowledge.

The identification function discussed earlier (page 459) facilitates the existence of referent power as a basis of sibling influence. According to French and Raven, "the stronger the identification of P with O, the greater the referent power of O/P" (1960:618).

Coercive power exists in the sib relation to the degree that one sib can evoke punishment (physical-mental abuse, parental interference, etc.) upon another sib. Consistent behavior based on coercive power on the part of one sib may result in coalition formation within the sib group against the offender. This can isolate a sib from further interaction and make it precarious to tattle to parents. These behaviors can foster alienation between sibs in the sib system.

Reward power may be utilized within the sib group to the degree that sibs have differential resources which are viewed as valuable or desirable to other siblings. Such resources might include toys, games, equipment, money, etc. These material goods are useful for bartering, loaning, or negotiating exchanges between sibs. The possession of such goods increases reward power to the extent that other sibs desire them. These notions produce the following theoretical propositions:

20. When parents designate authority and responsibility to a sibling, other sibs will perceive this designation as legitimate and grant power and authority to that sib.

21. To the degree that a sib holds resources that are perceived as desirable by other sibs, the power and authority of that sib will increase.

22. To the degree that a sib utilizes coercive power to intimidate another sib, alienation in the sib system will increase.

SUMMARY

We have attempted to glean and mold propositions in an area of family socialization where, beyond the immediate family, only a few select friends and kinsmen have access to the socialization of the child. Hence the treatment rendered by a mother, father, and other siblings in this pivotal system holds the potential for much impact. Children are dependent on parents and other adults for life sustenance. Parents typically feel responsibility to nurture, socialize, and mold the children into their valued society images. Our focus has stressed the importance of the sib subsystem in the greater family system, and the importance of siblings in the socialization process. We have noted that siblings not only come in two sexes but come at different times in the family setting. The eldest child comes into a different family climate from child number 10.

While parents have superiority over their children in both age and experience, we have noted that older siblings hold some of the same advantage over their younger brothers and sisters. Coalitions of siblings and of siblings with parents emerge and often continue throughout adulthood. We thus have argued that sibling relationships and interaction are important not only in the early years of socialization, but that this influential interaction continues throughout the family life cycle.

First-born children enjoy the longest history with their parents, and this cumulative base creates an interactive potential for greater sharing and problem solving. The oldest child is most likely to be called on for help and advice as well as criticism for failing to set examples for other sibs. Sibling position is obviously related to size of the family group. The size of the group influences the type and patterning of behavior that go on in a group. Role taking and role making among siblings are influenced not only by the size of the group but by the history of the members and the nature of the interaction together. The literature indicates more specialization of roles and task definition in large families. Bossard and Boll (1960) report that members rely more on each other in a large family and specifically that older ones engage in care and control of their younger siblings. Blau and Duncan (1967) note that resources in large families are more likely to be scarce and time and attention to any single child are attenuated. Sibship influence and coalition formation are most operative in this type of setting.

There is less interaction and less intensity of confrontation between parents and children in larger families. This creates a group situation for a child in which a deficit socialization experience is most likely to occur. Time to monitor school work, work on a one-to-one basis, meeting emotional needs, and just time to enjoy the uniqueness of each child are not as likely to happen. Our overall conclusion is that the structural variable of family size does make a difference in terms of sibling status and the opportunity structure available to children.

We have noted several methodological problems in the area as well as the lack of useful theoretical orientations to guide such work. We have suggested ways to forward concept clarification and have identified several areas for the extraction of useful propositions. We suggested a lessened commitment to early childhood socialization

theory and advocated the study of sibling interaction over much longer periods of time. In addition, we argue that the sib subsystem is important in its own right and that children in a family are much more than captive pawns. Siblings are both the recipients and the instigators of much of the interaction that occurs in the family system.

We have attempted an integration of previously disparate ideas and have employed various portions of the interactional and exchange frameworks in our analysis. While there has not been a systematic employment of these principles and concepts, we have found them most useful in attempting to render focus and clarity. We believe that further work in the area of sibling relationships can be enriched by using these two approaches.

Our analysis of this area indicates that number of children, spacing interval, sex composition, and ordinal position are all important factors in explaining the nature of family interaction. Children are instrumental in opening up the typical closed nature of the nuclear family. We believe that children also interact in a relatively closed sibling system in the family, suggesting there are boundaries that differentiate the spousal subsystem of the parents and the parent-child subsystem. Communication patterns, power structures, socialization techniques, and life style are profoundly influenced by what goes on in the sibling world and the degree to which this world negotiates and engages in diplomacy.

While we have engaged in a considerable amount of refocus, reassessment, and recasting of data into a different framework, it is obvious that much needs to be done if this area is to be developed into a richer theoretical bank for understanding family behavior. We hope that the propositions as formulated serve as useful models for the teasing out of others. Charting and explaining the determinants and consequences of sibling relations are in much need of further work, and perhaps the theoretical analysis presented here will be helpful in forwarding that goal.

REFERENCES

ADAMS, B. N.
1972   "Birth order: A critical review." *Sociometry* 34(3) (September):411–39.

ADLER, A.
1928   "Characteristics of the 1st, 2nd and 3rd child." *Children* 3(5):14.

ALDOUS, J.
1972   *The Developmental Approach to Family Analysis*, vol. 1 (mimeographed). Minneapolis.

ALTUS, W. D.
1966   "Birth order and its sequelae." *Science* 151 (January):44–48.

BANK, S. AND M. D. KAHN
1975   "Sisterhood-brotherhood is powerful: Sibling sub-systems and family therapy." *Family Process* 14(3):311–37.

BATES, F. L.
1956   "Position, role, and status: A reformulation of concepts." *Social Forces* 34(4) (May):313–21.

BAYER, A. E.
1967   "Birth order and attainment of the doctorate: A test of economic hypotheses." *American Journal of Sociology* 72 (March):540–50.

BAYER, A. E. AND J. K. FOLGER
1967   "The current state of birth order research." *International Journal of Psychiatry* 3 (January):37–39.

BELL, R. Q.
1968   "A reinterpretation of the direction of effects in studies of socialization."*Psychological Review* 75(2):81–95.

BLAU, P.
1964   "Justice in social exchange." *Sociological Inquiry* 34 (Spring):193–206.

BLAU, P. M. AND O. D. DUNCAN
1967   *The American Occupational Structure*. New York: Wiley.

BLOOD, R. O.
1972   *The Family*. New York: Free Press.

BOSSARD, J. H. S. AND E. S. BOLL
1950   *Ritual in Family Living*. Philadelphia: University of Pennsylvania Press.
1960   *The Sociology of Child Development*. New York: Harper.

BOWERMAN, C. AND R. M. DOBASH
1974   "Structural variations in inter-sibling affect." *Journal of Marriage and the Family* 36 (February):48–54.

BOWERMAN, C. E. AND G. H. ELDER, JR.
1964   "Variations in adolescent perception of family power structure." *American Sociological Review* 29 (August):551–67.

BRIM, O. G.
1958   "Family structure and sex role learning by children: A further analysis of Helen Koch's data." *Sociometry* 21(1):1–16.

BURGESS, E. W.
1926   "The family as a unity of interacting personalities." *The Family* 7:3–9.

BURR, W. R.
1973   *Theory Construction and the Sociology of the Family*. New York: Wiley.

CAPLOW, T.
1959   "Further development of a theory of coalitions in the triad." *American Journal of Sociology* 64 (March):488–93.
1968   *Two against One: Coalition in Triads*. Englewood Cliffs, N.J.: Prentice-Hall.

CHEN, E. AND S. COBB
1960   "Family structure in relation to health and disease." *Journal of Chronic Diseases* 12:544–67.

CLAUSEN, J. A.
1965   "Family size and birth order as influences upon socialization and personality." Bibliography and abstracts. New York: Social Science Research Council.

DOLLARD, J.
1935   "The family: Needed viewpoints in family research." *Social Forces* 35 (October):109–13.

DOUVAN, E.
1963   "Employment and the adolescent." In F. I. Nye and L. W. Hoffman (eds.), *The Employed Mother in America*. Chicago: Rand McNally.

FARBER, B.
1964   *Family: Organization and Interaction*. San Francisco: Chandler.

FERREIRA, A. J. AND W. D. WINTER
1968   "Decision-making in normal and abnormal two-child families." *Family Process* 7:17–36.

FRENCH, J. R. P. AND B. RAVEN
1960   "The bases of social power." In D. Cartwright and A. Zander (eds.), *Group Dynamics: Research and Theory*. Elmsford, N.Y.: Peterson.

HAGE, J.
1972   *Techniques and Problems of Theory Construction in Sociology*. New York: Wiley.

HILL, R. AND J. ALDOUS
1969   "Socialization for marriage and parenthood." In D. A. Goslin (ed.), *Handbook of Socialization Theory and Research*. Chicago: Rand McNally.

HOFFMAN, L. W.
1963   "Effects on children: Summary and discussion." In F. I. Nye and L. W. Hoffman (eds.), *The Employed Mother in America*. Chicago: Rand McNally.

IHINGER, M.
1975   "The referee role and norms of equity: A contribution toward a theory of sibling conflict." *Journal of Marriage and the Family* 37(3):515–24.

IRISH, D. P.
1964   "Sibling interaction: A neglected aspect in family life research." *Social Forces* 42:269–88.

JOHANNIS, T. B.
1957   "Participation by fathers, mothers and teenage sons and daughters in selected child care and control activity." *The Coordinator* 6 (December 2):31–32.

KAGAN, J.
1964   "Acquisition and significance of sex typing and sex role identity." In M. L. Hoffman and L. W. Hoffman (eds.), *Review of Child Development Research*. New York: Russell Sage.

KAMMEYER, K.
1967   "Birth order as a research variable." *Social Forces* 46(1):71–80.

LATTS, S. M.
1966   "The four-child, equi-sexed, intact family: Its organization and interactional patterns." Ph.D. Dissertation, University of Minnesota.

LYNN, D. B.
1974   *The Father: His Role in Child Development*. Monterey, Calif.: Brooks/Cole.

MCCANDLESS, B. R.
1969   "Childhood socialization." In D. A. Goslin (ed.),*Handbook of Socialization Theory and Research*. Chicago: Rand McNally.

MILEY, C. S.
1969   "Birth order research 1963–67: Bibliography and index." *Journal of Individual Psychology* 25:64–70.

MODELL, J. AND T. K. HAREVEN
1973   "Urbanization and the malleable household: An examination of boarding and lodging in American families." *Journal of Marriage and the Family* 35(3):467–79.

MUSSEN, P. H., J. J. CONGER, AND J. KAGAN
1974   *Child Development and Personality*. New York: Harper & Row, 439.

NYE, F. I. AND L. W. HOFFMAN, EDS.
1963   *The Employed Mother in America*. Chicago: Rand McNally.

ORLANSKY, H.
1949   "Infant care and personality." *Psychological Bulletin* 46:1–48.

PARSONS, T. AND R. F. BALES
1955   *Family, Socialization and Interaction Process*. New York: Free Press.

PIAGET, J.
1932   *The Moral Judgment of the Child*. New York: Free Press.

REISS, I. L.
1967   *The Social Context of Premarital Sexual Permissiveness*. New York: Holt, Rinehart and Winston.
1976   *Family Systems in America*. Hinsdale, Ill.: Dryden Press.

RHEINGOLD, H. L.
1969 "The social and socializing infant." In D. A. Goslin (ed.), *Handbook of Socialization Theory and Research*. Chicago: Rand McNally.

SAFILIOS-ROTHSCHILD, C.
1970 "The study of family power structure: A review 1960–1969." *Journal of Marriage and the Family* 32(4):539–52.

SCHACHTER, S.
1959 *The Psychology of Affiliation*. Stanford, Calif.: Stanford University Press.

SCHOOLER, C.
1972 "Birth order effects: Not here, not now!" *Psychological Bulletin* 78(3):161–75.

SCHVANEVELDT, J. D.
1966 "The interactional framework in the study of the family." In F. I. Nye and F. Berardo (eds.), *Emerging Conceptual Frameworks in Family Analysis*. New York: Macmillan.
1973 "The shuttle child as stranger in the family." Research paper presented at National Council on Family Relations, Toronto.

SEARS, R. R., E. E. MACCOBY, AND H. LEVIN
1957 *Patterns of Child Rearing*. New York: Harper & Row.

SEWELL, W. H.
1952 "Infant training and personality of the child." *American Journal of Sociology* 58:150–59.

SHAW, G. B.
1914 *Misalliance*. New York: Brentano's.

SMITH, T.
1970 "Foundations of parental influence upon adolescents: An application of social power theory." *American Sociological Review* 35(5) (October):860–73.
1971 "Birth order, sibship size, and social class as antecedents of adolescents acceptance of parent's authority." *Social Forces* 50(2) (December):223–31.

STAGER, R. AND E. T. KATZOFF
1936 "Personality as related to birth order and family size." *Journal of Applied Psychology* 20:340–46.

SUTTON-SMITH, B. AND B. G. ROSENBERG
1970 *The Sibling*. New York: Holt, Rinehart and Winston.

TAYLOR, M. G. AND J. D. SCHVANEVELDT
1977 "Birth order as related to missionary service in the Mormon Church." Unpublished Research Paper, Utah State University.

THOMAS, D. ET AL.
1974 *Family Socialization and the Adolescent*. Lexington, Mass.: Heath.

TOMAN, W.
1959 "Family constellation as a characteristic and marriage determinant." *International Journal of Psychoanalysis* 40 (September):316–19.

TURNER, R. H.
1962 "Role-taking: Process versus conformity." In A. M. Rose (ed.), *Human Behavior and Social Processes*. Boston: Houghton Mifflin.

WARREN, J. R.
1966 "Birth order and social behavior." *Psychological Bulletin* 65 (January):38–49.

ZAJONC, R. B. AND G. B. MARKUS
1975 "Birth order and intellectual development." *Psychological Review* 82(1):74–88.

ZUK, G.
1972 *Family Therapy: A Triadic-based Approach*. New York: Behavioral Publications.

19

COMMUNICATION IN COUPLES AND FAMILIES

Harold L. Raush, Ann C. Greif, and Jane Nugent

BACKGROUND

Introduction

This review is concerned with the interpersonal transactions of couples and families. It examines such transactions from a particular point of view, that of communication. In one sense communication is an extremely broad concept. It is quite accurate to speak of communication whenever an event in one system affects, influences, or alters an event in another system. Within a family, each member—whether through words, actions, gestures, silences, or even presence or absence—affects other family members. Our effort here shall be to organize and conceptualize such "communications" theoretically and in terms of research findings.

Yet given so broad a conception of communication, even the limitation to family transactions yields a seemingly infinite range of material for analysis. For example, there can be no doubt that such factors as social class, age, sex differences, ethnic background, cultural practices, etc., affect the communications among family members.[1] Further, personality and situational variables influence the content and style of communications. From a systems point of view one can argue that whatever influences one member (or element) of a family system to communicate will have repercussions throughout the system.

Faced with an almost limitless scope and literature for analysis, our conscious choice for examination and review is guided by an approach specific to communication theory. Communication in its formal theory has to do with the *flow* of information between systems. Our review limits itself to attempting to characterize the flow between family members. It omits consideration of the multivari-

ous factors that may compose a particular system or system element, though clearly that composition will affect its relations with other systems. That is, the focus is on what goes on between A and B, rather than on what causes A and B to act as they do. The restriction of focus enables a coherent theoretical and research framework. Within such a framework the variables we have noted such as social class, etc., become primarily factors for research control. That they remain unexamined as causal influences or as independent-dependent variables may limit the scope of a communicational approach to the family. However, as we hope to indicate, that very limitation does provide an unparalleled analytic power.

The Formal Background

In a formal sense communication theory has its roots in problems of transmission of telephonic signals across space. From attempts to solve telecommunication problems in World War II a conceptual and mathematical framework evolved. The mathematical approach developed by Shannon (Shannon and Weaver, 1949) became known as "information theory," and it proved to have wide applicability. The precision it offered in indexing the relationships between signal input and output could be expanded from the engineering of telecommunication systems to the study of biological (cf. Quastler, 1953) and psychological systems (Miller and Frick, 1949; Garner and Hake, 1951; Garner, 1962).[2] The extension of this approach to the study of interpersonal processes came relatively late.

The development of telephonic communication theory coalesced in time with the development of cybernetics, a multidiscipline defined by Wiener (1948) as "the study of control and communication in the animal and the machine." Like formal communication theory, cybernetics is concerned with input-output relations. The term itself is from the Greek for "helmsman" or "governor," and the theory and its application delineate the use of

---

NOTE: Appreciation is expressed to Sherod Miller, Kay Troost, Ira Reiss, and Wesley Burr for their suggestions after reading an earlier version of this chapter.

signal systems whereby output is governed or corrected by return "loops" communicating with input-producing mechanisms.

Both formal communication theory and cybernetics can be seen as part of the broader framework called systems theory. The word "system" has had various definitions. Miller (1965) defines a system simply as "a set of units with relationships among them" (200). Systems theory emphasizes not the units but the relationships. The focus is on the organization of elements and on their arrangement either spatially or temporally. It is the interdependence rather than the attributes of the elements which is of primary concern. A further distinction is made between closed systems, in which structures can be treated as self-contained, and open systems, which are in continuous interchange with an external environment (cf. Ashby, 1968; Bertalanffy, 1968). Closed system theory can apply to the laws of the physical sciences; biological and social sciences require the more recent developments of a theory of open systems (cf. Buckley, 1967, 1968).

The three formal branches—communication theory, cybernetics, and systems theory—overlap in their concepts, foundations, and methodological approaches. They are concerned with relations between (or among) systems; they emphasize signal rather than energy transformations; they tend to reject notions of simple linear causality and experimental variable independence. It is in this latter aspect that the three directions coalesce toward a radical departure from earlier traditions of scientific method.

The overlap, important as it is for the development of a unified theory, leads to confusion when, as is true at present, the relations among concepts across the three theories are unclear. This is particularly so when the formal theories, developed to describe machine and biological systems, are transposed to the field of human interrelationships. In that transposition there is a borrowing and intermingling of terms from different levels of analysis. Communication theory as applied to couples and families presents inevitably a greater hodge-podge of terms and levels than is in its origins of telecommunication. Moreover, with movement to human interactions, formerly precise meanings become transformed to analogic or heuristic usages; and it is not always clear when this is happening. Indeed, there are those who object to what they consider a misusage of concepts and methods (cf. Cherry, 1966). Nonetheless—however confounded, adulterated, and imprecise the transformations—they have had major impact on our conceptions of family relations. Given the heightened contemporary interest in all forms of human interactions, the impact of these concepts and methods will, we expect, increase. The two problems, that of borrowing and intermingling of terms and that of precise versus analogic usage, will not be solved in the review to follow. Although our focus will be communication, concepts from cybernetics

and, to a lesser extent, from systems theory will appear. Moreover, in the study of family communications new concepts emerge and old concepts expand their meanings.

Family Process and Clinical Background

Unlike the application of principles from physics to solve problems of engineering, communication theory as an approach to the understanding of close human relationships cannot be said to be an application of formal communication theory to human affairs. What is shared by telephonic and human communication theories is a concern with relations between and within systems and the attempt to explicate an approach to the study of such relations. It is perhaps more than anything else the *zeitgeist* which has led to commonalities in language and modes of thinking.

The increased complexity of machine system relations and man-machine relations, as in problems of automation and computer design, and the increased complexity of organizational relations seem more than matched by increasing complexity in human face-to-face relationships. Guidelines to relationships formerly prescribed by culture and tradition have become more diffuse. Industrialization and mobility have led to isolation of the nuclear family from traditional and community supports. Modes of relation in marriage and family have become matters to be worked out by each individual unit rather than prescribed givens. Hess and Handel (1959) describe five processes as shaping family life: (a) establishing a pattern of separateness and connectedness; (b) establishing a congruence of images; (c) evolving modes of interaction into central family themes; (d) establishing the boundaries of the family's world of experience; and (e) dealing with significant biosocial issues of family life, that is, defining such things as what it means to be male or female and younger or older. A social system in which such processes are matters to be worked out by each family unit—rather than cultural givens—requires communication among family members. When each family must evolve its own destiny, it faces tasks not only of developing its own rules but also of defining how and by whom these rules are made and the conditions for change. A massive burden is thus placed on communication. That burden increases as definitions of marriage and of family become increasingly blurred (cf. Constantine and Constantine, 1971).

Clinical work with families evolved within this context. Problems of living within a family structure came to be seen less as a matter of adjustment of individual internal needs to fixed circumstances and more as a matter of relationships—how they evolve, how they stabilize, how they change. In this reorientation toward how people work things out with each other, families rather than individuals come to be viewed as the significant unit for analysis and for therapeutic intervention. From the study of disturbed families, clinicians working independently (Ackerman, 1958, Bowen, 1961; Jackson, 1957) observed that the behavior of individual family members was directly related to the structure of the family as a unit and to the maintenance of the family as a system. The texture of the structure and its maintenance were in the communications of members to one another. Change in individual behavior patterns required change in patterns of interpersonal communication.

Communication Theory in Close Relationships

A communications approach to the understanding of close relationships developed in the 1950s and 1960s through the remarkable conjunction of researchers and clinicians brought together in Palo Alto, California. Gregory Bateson (who has had perhaps the major single sustained influence), in attempting to synthesize his anthropological work with developing ideas in cybernetics, was brought ever more deeply into the study of psychopathological communication. His association with Jurgen Ruesch, a psychiatrist studying disturbed communication and communications in psychotherapy, led to publication of a volume entitled *Communication: The Social Matrix of Psychiatry* (Ruesch and Bateson, 1951). The development in 1958 of the Mental Research Institute in Palo Alto led to a wider network of interdisciplinary investigators who studied couple and family communication processes. Publications by Haley, Jackson, Satir, Watzlawick, Weakland, and others as well as by Bateson derived from this conjunction. In 1967 a major summarization of the theoretical viewpoint was presented by Watzlawick, Beavin, and Jackson. Their *Pragmatics of Human Communication* is perhaps the single, basic theoretical text.

The fundamentally dramatic departure from traditional clinical theory and practice was the shift from emphasis on the individual and from a view of the family in terms of its individual component members to the notion of the family as a system. The behavior of individual members is to be understood only within the context of the current system. Psychiatric classification of individuals thus loses its relevance; psychiatric symptoms and "abnormality" are behaviors that are appropriate to a particular ongoing communicational context.

Since the system can be understood only in its entirety, a focus on an individual member is apt to be misleading, conducing the investigator or clinician to false attributions of causality. The system is its own cause. It operates in the present; deviant individual behavior is seen as a necessary part in the functioning of a particular family system; and change, if it is to occur, must involve the major components of the system. Shared theoretically with the behavior modification approaches are an emphasis on current behavior as opposed to historical influ-

ences and a rejection of references to internal motives. A major difference is in the attention given to the systemic nature of the family. Clinical evidence is often adduced to demonstrate that improvement in a symptomatic family member—the so-called "identified patient"—in individual treatment is followed by the appearance of pathology in one or more formerly "healthy" members (Haley, 1963; Jackson, 1957). This point has been illustrated in F. Scott Fitzgerald's novel *Tender Is the Night* and in John Cassavetes' film *A Woman under the Influence*. Even in this bare outline the theoretical stance and the practical implications can be seen as a radical shift from traditional psychiatric thinking.

The rejection of past and of motivational references parallels formal communication theory. From the point of view of that theory an unknown structure (the so-called "black box") need not be examined internally in order to understand its function within a system. Sufficient understanding can be achieved with minimal inference by examining observable input-output relations, i.e., communications as they are modified by the structure. In actuality, theoretical writings, clinical practice, and research studies fail to maintain a consistent parallelism with formal communication theory; and inferences abound.

The reasons for the seeming inconsistency lie in the greater complexity of human communication. A simple telephonic network aims at exact reproduction of messages from sender to receiver, and independent components can be developed toward this goal. It is doubtful, though, that the aim of exact reproducibility characterizes most messages between people. Moreover, in human communication, unlike the telecommunication system, the system components are not independent. As Dittmann (1973) notes, source, source encoder, and channel encoder are all in the sending person, and channel decoder, user decoder, and user are all in the receiving person. The problem of random "noise" between independent components of a telecommunication system is replaced by the problem of systematic distortion in the linked components of human communicators.

Furthermore, human communication seldom consists of single messages from a defined sender to a defined receiver. In any continuous interchange a particular message, as Bateson (1972b:288) notes, may serve as stimulus to the other's following message, response to the other's prior message, or reinforcement to the other's prior response. It is the *pattern* of interchange which interests the student of human relationships, and it is the repetitions and changes in these patterns which are of interest in continuing relationships as in marriage or family life. Identification and understanding of such patterns inevitably involve more inferences and time-oriented references than the rigorous black box approach of telecommunication theory would suggest.

THE CONCEPTS

Redundancy

Formal Communication Theory

If a mechanical signal transmission system were perfect, every unit entered at the source would be exactly reproduced at the other end of the line. The most efficient system would be one in which each message element at the source was equally probable and independent of any preceding message element. In that case we would have zero redundancy.

Mechanical transmission systems are, however, subject to noise. Channels between sending and receiving poles are imperfect, and errors can be made. In a zero-redundant system errors in transmission or reception would be undetectable and uncorrectable. Similarly, if every letter or every word in the English language occurred with equal probability and each letter or word was independent of that which preceded it—i.e., zero redundancy—the language would be wholly efficient. Except, as Attneave (1959) notes,

> every typographical error would result in a sentence which made sense, but a sense different from that intended by the author [35].

In mechanical transmission, redundancy may be added to overcome noise. For example, each message symbol may be repeated one or more times, or more subtle techniques for employing redundancy may be devised (cf. Shannon and Weaver, 1949). In language neither words nor letters appear with equal probability, and some combinations of words and letters are more probable than other combinations (the letter t is more likely to be followed by an h than by a f). We can often guess missing letters in a word or missing words from a sentence. In fact, printed English has been estimated by Shannon to show a redundancy of 75 percent, that is, loosely speaking, everything is repeated about three times (Attneave, 1959).

Redundancy is thus "a powerful safeguard against error and misunderstanding in communication" (Attneave, 1959:35). It is based upon events being unequally probable and sequentially dependent. That is to say, it represents a *patterning* whereby events constrain one another. If the patterning or constraint were complete—100 percent redundancy—then one could predict from any event (or message element) what the next event (or message element) would be. Clearly, human behavior is neither zero nor 100 percent redundant.

Relationship Patterns

The above discussion deals with single and simple messages. When we turn to communications involving continuing reciprocal interchange in close relationships, redundancy takes on an expanded but related meaning. Even in presumably single messages redundancy becomes more complex in emotionally significant relationships. For example, nonverbal channels of communication (tone, facial expression, gesture) may be redundant with the verbal channel (words and sentences) making for clarity (cf. Mehrabian and Weiner, 1967), or the two channels may serve to convey different messages, even canceling one another.

Of greater interest to those concerned with relationships extended over time, as with couples and families, are the redundancies of the repeated patterns of communication. When expanded by family theorists, redundancy becomes perhaps the most central construct by which the family is described and in the pragmatic sense known. A basic tenet of communication research with couples and families is that it is the redundancy of certain interactive styles that gives a family system its own individualized structures (cf. Watzlawick et al., 1967).

Both researchers and clinicians attempt to recognize and define the redundancies represented in repeated communication patterns. Thus considerable clinical appraisal and considerable formal research have been devoted to identifying and characterizing the communicational redundancies of disturbed families. Such efforts involve inference (as to patterns) and time orientation (as to repetitions) beyond telecommunication theory.

RELATIONSHIP RULES. In a simple telecommunication system optimal redundancy is that form and amount of repetition needed to transmit a message over extraneous noise in the system. In the family system optimal redundancy is more difficult to define, especially since there are different "levels" of redundancy. Redundancy can represent a pattern of interaction. Certainly, every family must develop a set of rules and transformations which characterize messages between people. Like linguistic rules and transformations, these can be applied to different messages. The relationship rules of families—whether overtly or covertly defined—represent statements of redundancies (Jackson, 1965a, 1965b).

But redundancies can extend to other levels, defining who says and does what to whom, and they can come to include rules by which specific members are rigidly positioned into fixed roles—the pattern coming to include fixed assignments. The difference is between the family, for example, in which any one member can raise a conflictual issue, any other member may argue this, and any third member may mediate and the family in which, for example, it is always father who raises the issue, always mother who argues it, and always the child who mediates. In this sense the family with a consistent "scapegoat" (Vogel and Bell, 1960) represents a "heavier" redundancy than does the family in which each member can play different parts as these are required. In couples and families too little redundancy would seem to make for message confusion and chaos—rules nonexistent or defined and redefined momentarily; excessive redundancy would make for boredom and inefficiency and perhaps inhibit the transmission of new information into the system (cf. Kantor and Lehr, 1975).

SYMMETRICAL AND COMPLEMENTARY PATTERNS. In 1936 Bateson described two interaction patterns representing two systems of relationship rules. The descriptions have been adopted by family communication theorists for characterizing couple and family relations (cf. Watzlawick et al., 1967). In the *symmetrical* interaction pattern partners mirror one another's behavior; the rule is that of equality and minimization of status differences. In the *complementary* interaction pattern one partner's behavior is the complement of the other's—for example, an assertive act by one is followed by a submissive act by the other; the rule is inequality and maximization of difference. Both styles of relationship are interlocking. That is:

> One partner does not impose a complementary (or symmetrical) relationship on the other, but rather each behaves in a manner which presupposes, while at the same time providing reasons for, the behavior of the other: their definitions of the relationship fit [Watzlawick et al., 1967:69].

Watzlawick et al. (1967) suggest that in healthy relationships both patterns are present, with symmetry expressed in some areas and complementarity in others. Either interactional style carried to extreme within a relationship can evolve to a pathology. The rule of symmetry can escalate to intense competition over "equality" as in an arms race; the rule of complementarity can lead to inappropriate fixed rigid positions as in the case of a parent and now grown-up child continuing in complementary caretaking and dependent roles. In healthy relationships a phase of symmetry seems to signal a switch to complementarity and vice versa.

The limitation to two classes of rule systems, *mutual* symmetry and *mutual* complementarity, seems unnecessarily simple. As an orienting frame, the scheme is perhaps most useful in pointing to rule discrepancies and nonmutuality. Such is the case when one partner defines the relationship as complementary whereas the other partner defines it as symmetrical. Conflicts between parents and adolescent children seem often related to such discrepancies and can sometimes be fairly readily resolved by overt recognition of the differences among participants in their definition of relationship rules. International conflicts also at times suggest differences in the relationship as it is defined by the participants.

Multiple Communication Channels

Observers of interpersonal communication have noted that messages between participants in an interchange most often involve more than one communication channel and often present simultaneous facets requiring differential coding. Usually the matter is put dichotomously: a message conveys a *content,* given by its wording; but it is also a statement of *relationship*. That is, a message serves in part to transmit what we usually think of as information about something, but it also transmits something about the nature of the ties between participants. Communication theorists often label the informational part of a message as its *report* aspect and the relational part as its *command* aspect (Watzlawick et al., 1967).[3]

Digital and Analog Communication

A similar differentiation was made by Ruesch (1954, 1955). Ruesch called one category "digital" and the other category "analogic," roughly equating these with verbal and nonverbal modes of expression, respectively. The terms have been adopted by family communication theorists.

Digital communication occurs when words, signs, or symbols are used to convey information and when those words, signs, or symbols carry meaning only arbitrarily. The word "cat"—to use an example from Watzlawick et al. (1967)—does not carry any information about the object to which it refers apart from the usage given to its three letters in the English language. Digital communication is primarily verbal. However, the defining characteristic of digital communication is the *arbitrary denotation* of an object or idea. Analog communication, on the other hand, must in some way represent or mirror that which is being expressed. Drawing a picture of a cat or imitating the movement of a cat is an example; something analogous to the object is the vehicle to convey meaning. Watzlawick et al. compare analogic communication to the nonverbal dimension of human behavior:

> What then is analog communication? The answer is relatively simple: it is virtually all nonverbal communication. This term, however, is deceptive, because it is often restricted to body movement only, to the behavior known as kinesics. We hold that the term must comprise posture, gesture, facial expression, voice inflection, the sequence, rhythm, and cadence of words themselves, and any other non-verbal manifestation of which the organism is capable, as well as the communicational clues unfailingly present in any *context* [their italics] in which an interaction takes place [1967:62].

Bateson (1972b:411–25) considers analog or nonverbal communication to be "precisely concerned with matters of relationship—love, hate, respect, fear, dependency, etc." (412), and he argues against the notion that the analog system is more primitive in an evolutionary sense than is digital language. Analog communication is difficult, though not impossible, to translate into digital form. In a sense, much of the task of psychotherapy involves such translation.

Apparent in the above quotation are the implicit equations by communication theorists between digital and report and between analog and command aspects of messages. Whether or not one equates, however, the report and command aspects of human communications with digital and analogic forms, respectively, the special interest to the student of interpersonal relationships lies in the simultaneous presentation of either analogic and digital or report and command. That is, a single message— and this contrasts with other theories which have made similar conceptual differentiations—contains both elements. A message between family members not only conveys certain obvious information on a *content* level, i.e., "Close the door," but also serves to define the *relationship* itself, i.e., "I am the mother and you are my child and you will close the door." This command aspect of any message contains not only a definition of the relationship between family members but also a definition of who the speaker is and who the recipient of the message is. The family becomes, therefore, an important source of self-delineation and identity for each of its members. At each moment, from each communication, the family or the couple is defined by these implicit demands or assertions from a family member as to what the relationship is like.

Formal communication theory is concerned with transmission of informational *content;* communication theory as an approach to couples and families is primarily concerned with *relationships* among participants. It is this difference in interest that directs family researchers and clinicians toward command rather than report aspects of communications. Theoretical and clinical discussions and research coding schemes reflect the difference in interest. Thus there is an emphasis on what partners A and B (or family members A, B, C, and D) are "doing" to one another (or how they are relating to one another) rather than on the content of their communications. Inferences as to relationships are often drawn from who interrupts whom and how much, from who talks most, who talks first, who talks last, and from discrepancies in content of communications.

The Double Bind

The multiplicity of communication channels is seen perhaps most clearly in different performances of the same play: the words are the same, but differences in tone, gesture, physical position, costume, etc., convey different interpretations. And the simultaneous flow of (at least) two types of information, one dealing with content, the other with relation, has powerful implications. As noted earlier, information from different channels may be redundant, serving to reduce ambiguity. Formal expression, voice tone, position, posture, and gesture may, for example, be consistent with words in conveying an affectionate or angry interchange. But the messages from different channels may serve to create paradox through the simultaneous assertion of two mutually exclusive messages. A typical example is that of the mother who,

having asked her child for a hug, stiffens and withdraws as he approaches and then to the child's subsequent withdrawal responds, "Don't you love your mother?" What was labeled the "double bind" (Bateson et al., 1956)[4] consists of such mutually exclusive injunctions, presented at different levels of abstraction or through different channels, along with a tertiary injunction that forbids both comment on the paradox and escape from the field. Further criteria for the double bind are the involvement of the participants in an intense relationship and repeated experiences of this nature. Double binds thus can only occur in the context of close and long-lasting relationships as in families.

Under conditions of recurrent double binds the kinds of communications that are labeled as schizophrenic can be seen as appropriate responses to a logically absurd, impossible situation. The theorists take pains to note that they do not view the double bind as the *cause* of schizophrenia. They point to humor and creativity as potential resolutions to double binds (Bateson et al., 1956; cf. Watzlawick et al., 1967); moreover, they conceive of growth and change within psychotherapy as derived from the induction of double binds which call for the client's reframing of his experiences (Haley, 1963; Watzlawick et al., 1967:230-56; Watzlawick et al, 1974; see also Olson, 1972:85-86). Yet it is clear that these investigators conceive of schizophrenic modes of behavior as induced from family communication patterns. Similar conclusions have been reached in independent clinical investigations by Wynne et al. (1958) and by Laing (1971).

Among the concepts of family communication theory the double bind would seem the one most amenable to formal empirical examination. It has, however, proved to be curiously elusive, and in its relation to schizophrenia the double bind, although logically compelling, remains unproven.

Communication and Metacommunication

The relations between report and command aspects of communication remain obscure not only empirically but also theoretically. It is unclear whether report and command are different aspects or different channels or different "levels" of communication. As to the latter, the command aspect is said to represent metacommunication, i.e., communication about communicating:

> the former [report] conveys the "data" of the communication, the latter [command] how this communication is to be taken. "This is an order" or "I am only joking" are verbal examples of such communications about communication. The relationship can also be expressed by shouting or smiling or in a number of other ways. And the relationship may be clearly understood from the context in which the communication takes place ... *Every communication has a content and a relationship aspect such that the latter classifies the former and is therefore a metacommunication* [Watzlawick et al., 1967:53-54; their italics].

The equation between the command (or relational) aspect and metacommunication is confusing. Consider, for example, the statement

> The ability to metacommunicate properly is not only the *conditio sine qua non* of successful communication, but is intimately linked with the enormous problem of awareness of self and other [Watzlawick et al., 1967:53].

following the statement

> the more spontaneous and "healthy" a relationship, the more the relationship aspect of communication recedes into the background [52].

Both hypotheses derive from a communications approach, and both are open to investigation. They each say important things about human relationships. They are not contradictory, and both could be true. However, equating metacommunicative and relationship aspects obfuscates matters. The further equation of "relationship" with "nonverbal" or with "analog" adds confusion, as a reading of the last quote, substituting these latter words for the adjectival "relationship," would suggest.

If we consider metacommunication as commentary on an ongoing communicative process, we are on safer ground. Metacommunications are then simply expressions about communication. Such expressions may be verbal ("I am only joking") or nonverbal (expressed in tone, gesture, etc). In either case they are at an abstractive level which provides a context within which specific communications are framed.

Metacommunication is not specifically human. Other mammals signal contexts for interaction—for example, "This is play, not attack." It is essential, of course, that such metacommunicative signals be conjointly understood by the participants. In this latter respect the greater diversity and lesser fixity of *human* signal patterns create opportunities for misunderstanding.[5] The *unexpressed* inferences that humans form about their own and others' communications further increase the likelihood for misunderstanding.

We have, in summary, noted four classes of information: (a) Messages convey content. Content messages are predominantly verbal, but can be nonverbal; for example, A points a direction in response to B's request. (b) Messages convey relationship. These can be verbal ("I love you") or nonverbal (an embrace). (c) Messages can be about messages or about the ongoing communication process. Such messages may concern content or relationship, and the signals may be verbal or nonverbal. Since they are messages which label (a) or (b) and are at a higher level of abstraction, they are called metacommunications. The fourth class (d) is inferences about communications. Participants may or may not be aware of their inferences about their own and others' communications, but patterns of communication may provide information to the observer about the inferences of participants. When inferences are made overt, they become (c) metacommuni-

cations. The complexity and richness of communications within the family and marital couple spring from the relations among these classes; confusion, discrepancy, and conflict may also spring from these relations. The same statements may be made about human communication theory.

Disjunctiveness

A fundamental hypothesis of family communication theorists is that it is disjunctiveness in information between these classes which can give rise to misunderstanding, conflict, and symptomatic behavior. The clearest case is in disjunctiveness between report and command aspects. For example, a husband noting that his wife is acting coolly toward him asks, "What's wrong?" The wife replies, "Nothing at all," but conveys by her tone of voice that she is seriously upset. A simple disjunction between report and command can be resolved through further communication among participants and specifically by metacommunication. That is, the husband may say, "You say nothing is wrong, but you act as though something is bothering you." If, however, (a) a *rule* of the relationship forbids metacommunication, (b) the disjunction is recurrent, and (c) the relationship is intense and inescapable, then the situation is that of double bind.

Other forms of disjunctiveness have been noted:

DISQUALIFICATION. The sender of a message who is unable or unwilling to communicate may defend himself by communicating in a way that invalidates his own communications. Implied is the notion that communication is required and that the relationship between participants would be threatened by an unequivocal statement.

> Disqualifications cover a wide range of communicational phenomena, such as self-contradictions, inconsistencies, subject switches, tangentializations, incomplete sentences, misunderstandings, obscure style or mannerisms of speech, the literal interpretations of metaphor and the metaphorical interpretations of literal remarks, etc. [Watzlawick et al., 1967:76].

At one level disqualification is a form of confused (and confusing) communication; at another level it is an indication of a pathological relationship in which one or both participants seem obliged to obscure their feelings and thoughts as to their own identities, the identity of the other, and the nature of the relationship. Disturbed families should hypothetically exhibit a greater degree of this type of communicational confusion, given the pain and anxiety surrounding the relationships within the family. Communication theory is unclear as to the impact of disqualification upon other family members. If we assume that other family members do in some way recognize disqualifications, disqualification should lead to feelings of confusion and anxiety regarding the relationships among family members. However, this train of analysis has not been fully pursued.

DISCONFIRMATION. One may accept, reject, or disconfirm another's communications. Disqualification focuses on the *sender* of the message and on the disjunctiveness in the message as it is encoded. Disconfirmation represents a parallel focus on the *receiver* who acts in such a way to deny not only the other's message but also the legitimacy of the other's (or sender's) message. That is,

> while rejection amounts to the message "You are wrong," disconfirmation says in effect "You do not exist" [Watzlawick et al., 1967:86].

Specifically, disconfirmations often take the form of a "mind reading" which denies the other's experience. An example might be "You think you're worried but you're really not." Such disconfirmations are said to be prominent in families with a schizophrenic member. Laing and Esterson (1964) refer to the phenomenon as "imperviousness" and note cases in which children who openly describe themselves as depressed are described by parents as "always happy." The concept of disconfirmation is probably best reserved as a referent to specific communications. When such communications become generalized and enduring in a relationship, it may be hypothesized that a pathological family structure has evolved. Generalized terms for such structures, derived from relatively independent clinical investigations, include Laing's "collusion" (1969) and "mystification" (1965), Wynne et al.'s "pseudo-mutuality" (1958), Bowen's "undifferentiated family ego mass and fused family system" (Anonymous, 1972), Minuchin's "enmeshment" (1974), and Boszormenyi-Nagy's "intersubjective fusion" (1965). In all such structures there are unverbalized commitments to deny experiential differences among family members. It would seem reasonable that these structures and the individual and family pathologies arising from them would reflect a history of recurrent disconfirmations, but the evidence cannot be said to be conclusive.

PUNCTUATIONAL DISJUNCTIONS. Communication is a sequential process. In close relationships (as compared to some casual encounters and most psychological experiments) it involves a chain of events temporally organized. As noted, in a long-term relationship sequences are likely to be recurrent. Inferences as to relationships are drawn from these sequences not only by investigators but also by the participants themselves. A major contribution of family communication theorists has been to note that a chain of events may be "punctuated" in different ways (Bateson and Jackson, 1964). Watzlawick et al. (1967:56–59) give an example of the husband who passively withdraws in response to his wife's nagging, whereas the wife nags in response to her husband's withdrawal. Each partner punctuates the sequence differently: The husband, "I withdraw because you nag"; the wife, "I nag because you withdraw." Thus the husband punctuates his behavior as a response to his wife, and the wife punctuates her behavior as a response to her husband. Disjunctiveness in inferences about communicational patterns, based on differences in punctuation, is said to be "at the root of countless relationship struggles" (Watzlawick et al., 1967:56).

Participants not only may punctuate sequences differently but will often engage in spurious causal arguments as to who started the chain. The causality is, however, fundamentally circular. Research investigators, too, may punctuate chains of events differently depending on their point of entry into a process and the steps they observe (cf. Raush, 1972:283). Moreover, more complex punctuational differences can arise from changes over the course of a sequence of interactive events. Thus, even with stable interaction contingencies between partners, a husband, for example, may move in a sequence of interchange from an initial position of dominance to a final position of submission, concurrent with his wife's shift from initial submission to final dominance (cf. Raush, 1972:285–87; Raush et al., 1974:157–70). How the partners (or observers) label each other will depend upon whether they focus on early or late phases of the sequence.

At still higher abstractive levels, punctuation involves the attribution of fixed roles to participants in a relationship. An example would be the labeling of family members as the dependent one, the dominant one, the scapegoat, the victim, etc. Within the postulated circular causal structure of a system such "personal" labels are seen as spurious and misleading. The terms, as Bateson (1972) puts it bluntly, "refer to something artificially chopped out of interactive sequences" (304). The more adequate causal view, from the communicational orientation, is indicated by the Judge in Genet's *The Balcony,* who insists that the thief must remain a thief if he himself is to remain a judge. Though causal labeling may represent a false or limited punctuation of relational events, it can lead to self-fulfilling prophecies.

> For instance, a person who acts on the premise that "nobody likes me" will behave in a distrustful, defensive, or aggressive manner to which others are likely to react unsympathetically thus bearing out his original premise [Watzlawick et al., 1967:99].

THE RESOLUTION OF DISJUNCTIONS. It has been suggested that the resolution to problems of disjunctive communications lies in metacommunication. A first metacommunicative step is recognition of the disjunction; following steps would move toward unambiguous, clearer communications. At times, family communication theorists seem to imply that adequate metacommunication is all that is needed for solving family and couple relationship problems; and indeed, some family therapists seem to focus primarily on promoting greater communicational clarity (Satir, 1964).

Certainly, all therapists metacommunicate in their attempts to clarify problems, and certainly metacommunication is one problem-solving approach used by most couples and families. Yet metacommunication is neither as easy as it sounds—a communication about communication—nor does it per se resolve relationship issues. Even "normal" couples are rarely able to metacommunicate about disjunctions when interpersonal conflict escalates (Raush et al., 1974). It would seem that anxiety (or perhaps any intense affect) inhibits the capacity that metacommunication requires, that of abstracting oneself from the immediacy of the ongoing process.

Covert rules which forbid certain communications may exist in a relationship. Relationships characterized by pervasive disqualifications, disconfirmations, double binds, or punctuational disjunction seem to contain hidden rules against metacommunication. Bateson (1972:271-308) suggests that there is an economy in the "habit" of not seeing rules. An examination of premises for each action—as with the centipede asked to describe his walking movements—would be inefficient and inhibitory. The argument may be true; but it is unconvincing as an explanation of the power of covert rules in inhibiting examination of and metacommunication about the relationship when it is often obvious to participants that something is very wrong.

Within the framework of the theory, communication theorists are hard put to account for the fixity of those rule systems which state that metacommunications may neither be presented nor be heard, or to account for the effect of stress in inhibiting metacommunication, or to account for cases in which metacommunication is ineffective in inducing change. There is a recognition that in pathological communication participants cannot metacommunicate until they are able to step *outside* the circle of immediate contingencies (Watzlawick et al., 1967:95-96; see also Watzlawick et al., 1974). A parallel leap had to be made by communication theorists, *outside* the confines of a strict communications approach, in order to account for stability and change in relationships and communicational patterns.

Homeostasis and Feedback

In a now classic paper Jackson (1957) introduced the notion of "family homeostasis." On the basis of many psychiatric observations in which individual improvement on the part of the treated patient was followed by drastic repercussions for the marital partner or other family members, Jackson postulated a dynamic interplay of forces toward maintaining equilibrium in the family system. Among some of the families he observed it seemed necessary for one member to be "ill" or "crazy" or "bad" in order to maintain that system in its mode of functioning. Thus the patient's "illness" or symptomatic behavior could be seen as part of a governing process by which the system as a whole was kept in balance (see also Fry, 1962).

When the balance was threatened by confrontation with internal or external demands and/or changes, relational rules were drawn upon to reestablish the balance. Such conditions of threat enabled the outside observer, such as the therapist, to see more clearly the rules of the system as reflected in communication patterns (Jackson, 1965a). The concept of homeostasis in human interaction was put bluntly and unequivocally by Haley (1962) in a "First Law of Relationships": "When an organism indicates a change in relation to another, the other will act upon the first so as to diminish and modify that change" (277: see also Haley, 1963:189).

Homeostasis requires a mechanism, and that mechanism is in the cybernetic concept of *feedback*. As noted earlier, feedback refers to an informational loop whereby output data become a source affecting input. As contrasted with a linear chain in which *a* influences *b,* which in turn influences *c,* etc., the feedback process represents a circular chain—*c,* for example, leading back to influence *a,* which then in turn affects *b, c,* etc. (Watzlawick et al., 1967:28–32).

Negative Feedback: Deviation-Countering Processes

The stability-maintaining homeostatic process is generally considered to represent *negative feedback*. That is, the output signal modifies the input so as to minimize deviations. A commonly used example is that of a furnace thermostat which signals deviations so that heat will be produced or turned off when temperature deviates too low or too high, respectively, from the thermostat setting. As Miller (1965) notes, "Negative feedback maintains steady states in systems. It cancels an initial deviation or error in performances" (227); he suggests that all living systems are controlled by negative feedback mechanisms, and he notes different types of feedback loops.

One need not depend on dramatic instances, such as the family symptom fluctuations described by Jackson, in order to see homeostatic and corrective feedback operations in group and family life. Communications of groups of "healthy" children, in contrast to those of hyperaggressive children, are characterized by actions which attenuate potentials for group disruption (Raush, 1965; Raush and Sweet, 1961). Similarly, observations of relatively healthy couples yield multiple indications of participants aiding each other in maintaining an even keel (Raush et al., 1974; Rosmann and Alexander, 1975).

Although it might be tempting to hypothesize a relation between homeostatic (or negative feedback) operations and "healthy" family functioning, clearly family communication theorists intend no such implications. Watzlawick et al. (1967:139–46) provide an extended description (from Laing and Esterson, 1964) of homeostatic and negative feedback mechanisms in a family with a schizophrenic child. "All families that stay together," they suggest, "must be characterized by some degree of negative feedback, in order to withstand the stresses imposed by the environment and the individual members'' (146).

Indeed, Jackson (1965b) and Watzlawick et al. (1967) believe disturbed families to be particularly refractory to change and excessively preoccupied with maintaining a status quo by means of negative feedback, but there is no firm evidence that more disturbed families are characterized by tighter homeostatic balance and greater negative feedback. The concepts themselves are sufficiently vague so that, for example, negative feedback seems to mean one thing when applied to a disturbed family and another when applied to a "healthy" family.

Positive Feedback: Deviation-Amplifying Processes

Far less described and investigated and far more confused is the concept of positive feedback.[6] Miller (1965) defines the term: "When the signals are fed back over the feedback channel in such a manner that they increase the deviation from a steady state, *positive feedback* exists" (227). Positive feedback networks are therefore often called deviation-amplifying processes in contrast with the deviation-counteracting processes of negative feedback.[7] Both processes represent mutual causal systems in that output events influence input. In the positive feedback loop, however, an initial process is amplified rather than diminished. A seemingly insignificant starting kick can evolve to massive consequences.

The usual conception of positive feedback has been that of a chain reaction leading to a destructive outcome. Maruyama (1963), however, illustrates positive feedback processes in such areas as economic change, the growth of a city from the chance settlement of an ambitious farmer, evolutionary changes in species, and embryonic development. Learning, in the sense that it facilitates rather than inhibits new learning, exemplifies positive feedback; sexual excitation is another example. The importance of positive feedback is recognized by Maruyama in terming the study of deviation-amplifying mutual causal processes "the second cybernetics" (deviation-counteracting, negative feedback studies representing the "first"). As negative feedback may account for stability in a family system, positive feedback may account for change (Watzlawick et al., 1967:146–47). Indeed, if Haley's "First Law" completely characterized relationships, relationships—including marital and familial ones—would never develop.

Speer (1970) applies the notion of positive feedback to the family. He points to the inadequacy of a family systems approach based on change-resistant or change-minimizing concepts. Following Buckley (1967), he suggests that positive feedback operations are vital for coping with environmental change and that the sources of growth, innovation, and creativity in social systems lie in positive feedback processes. Speer believes that it is the

troubled family which functions homeostatically in contrast to the positive feedback operations in families with an orientation toward growth. Speer underlines the need for studying healthy, fulfilled families in order to understand the functioning and importance of positive feedback.

Unfortunately, it is not always clear whether a communicative exchange represents negative or positive feedback. For example, complementarity is said to exemplify negative and symmetry to exemplify positive feedback (Watzlawick et al., 1967:58). From one focus, the amplification of a symmetrical vying for who is more equal can be described as a positive feedback runaway, but by the same token the increasing amplification of complementary communications can take on runaway proportions (cf. Hoffman, 1971). Both can eventuate in destructive blowups. From another focus both symmetry and complementarity can serve to correct deviations from a steady state. Discussions of well-functioning families imply a balance in these functions, such that symmetrical communications serve to correct roles from becoming too fixed, and complementary communications serve to correct roles from becoming too competitive. Hoffman (1971), who presents the major analysis of deviation-amplifying processes in netural groups, points to the importance of system levels:

> any feedback loop may have deviation-amplifying *and* [her italics] counteracting effects at the same time, depending on which system one is looking at [294].

Thus from a point of view within a family a process may be deviation-amplifying, whereas from the point of view of the family's relations with the environment the process may be deviation-correcting.

Although family communication theorists speak of deviation-correcting and -amplifying, of governors and calibrations, the terms are analogies rather than specific referents. Deviation from *what* is unanswered except in the vague sense of family rules, the potency of which are unaccounted for; *what* the governor is and *what* calibrates the system are unstated, except in the vague sense of a conjoint process among participants; *what* signals process and its changes is unclear. Communication theorists are loath to enter into what they consider the "black box" of internal processes. But clearer explication of the concepts of homeostasis and of negative and positive feedback may demand a turning to the individual subsystems that intermesh in human relationships and to an understanding of the communicative effects in relationships of individual goals, anxieties, and schemata based on past experiences.

That is not to say that the concepts, even in their analogic use, fail to have major implications. Given that the family is an open system in relation to its environment and that even the most simple course of family life involves developmental changes, problems of stability and change can be thought of in terms of homeostatic and negative and positive feedback processes. As Hoffman (1971) notes, some recent psychotherapeutic approaches to work with families (see Minuchin, 1974) consciously seek, for example, to induce crises and equilibrium disturbances through which mutual causal processes may be recalibrated.

FORMAL RESEARCH

Quantitative studies of couple and family communication are relatively new. With some notable exceptions (Strodtbeck, 1951, 1954) direct quantifiable observations of couples or families did not begin to be reported until the early sixties. A review of family interaction in disturbed and normal families (Jacob, 1975) states that nearly 50 percent of direct family-observational studies appeared since 1968.

Moreover, the influence of family communication theory as discussed in the previous pages, in any direct sense, is even more recent in relation to formal research. The Bateson, Jackson, Haley, and Weakland introduction to the double bind did not appear until 1956; Jackson's discussion of family homeostasis appeared in 1957; Haley's advocacy of family experiments as "a new type of experimentation" was published in 1962. And not until 1967, with the appearance of the Watzlawick, Beavin, and Jackson volume, was there a consistent, integrated summary statement of family communication process as a whole. Given the lag between theoretical conception, the execution of research, and publication, it is perhaps too early to see a full reflection of the theory in the research literature. The primary impact has been on clinical work, since it has been in clinical observations that the theory has its sources.

With a few exceptions, research studies relating to communication in couples and families reflect particularized interests in family processes rather than the major conceptualizations of family communication theory. A combination of social need and Federal support led studies in the direction of the unsolved etiological problems of schizophrenia. As the first formal statement of the family communications approach and as a specific theory of schizophrenia, the double-bind theory was a natural candidate for study, and research studies began to appear in published form in 1965 (cf. Olson, 1972). Other studies of family communication seem to relate to the general *zeitgeist,* rather than to the theoretical formulations discussed above.

A detailed review of research relating to communication in couples and families would be beyond the scope of this chapter. Fortunately, the need is obviated by several excellent summary analyses. Riskin and Faunce (1972) evaluate quantitative studies of couple and family interactions from the 1960s through June 1971. Jacob (1975)

presents a critical review of family interaction studies (to June 1973) which compare disturbed and control families and which include both parents and at least one child as participants. The Riskin and Faunce paper contains a 26-page glossary of key terms, variables, and techniques employed in studies. The Jacob paper tabulates and analyzes methodologically 57 direct-observational studies. Both papers present extensive lists of references. Although differing in orientation, with Riskin and Faunce more theoretically and Jacob more empirically oriented, both papers comment intensively on methodological problems; and they overlap considerably in conclusions and recommendations. A review of research by Olson (1972) on the double bind, although more restricted in scope, has general relevance to problems of research in human communication. All three papers are essential reading for those who would engage in quantitative research in the area.

Methodological Issues

It is far easier to give questionnaires to or conduct laboratory experiments with captive populations of college students than to study families in interaction. In every respect—sampling, time and personnel considerations, instrumentation, data-coding, and analysis problems—the investigator of family interaction is faced with uncertainties and with necessities for compromise. For example, it is easier to match a "schizophrenic" with a "normal" subject in age than it is to match, let us say, the four members of one family with four members of another; experimental control problems expand geometrically as one moves from individuals to a family group. Methodological adequacy must be evaluated in part with cognizance of the difficulties.

For such reasons the sample sizes in family-observational studies tend to be small (see table 2, Jacob, 1975:38–42). A more serious matter is that—understandably in view of massive time commitments—the same sample is used as a source for multiple reports. The 57 studies cited by Jacob derive, as he notes, from a substantially lower number of samples, with concomitant danger that biasing errors become proliferated. Jacob describes six sources of methodological inadequacy in observational studies of disturbed and normal families: (1) lack of comparability on demographic variables, (2) bias due to lack of "blind" analysis by judges, (3) unreliability of observer judgments, (4) failure to analyze data separately for male and female children, (5) failure to observe and assess experimental and control families in the same settings, and (6) lack of comparability of control and experimental families in terms of hospital or treatment status. The six criteria serve Jacob as a basis for reviewing the 57 cited reports.

Riskin and Faunce (1972) focus on the problems which make it difficult to compare different studies. Their critique, in pointing to demographic issues, investigator and judge biases, problems of reliability, setting differences, and treatment status differences, overlaps Jacob's analysis. In addition, they point to such salient factors as differences in investigators' purposes and interests, in specific tasks assigned to families, in the continuum from "naturalistic" to "experimental" orientation, in labeling and diagnostic classification schemes, in units of observation and analysis, and in focus on verbal and/or nonverbal modes of communication. They identify 21 such areas, and they comment on the conspicuous lack of replication of studies and the conspicuous terminological confusions in the field.

Substantive Findings

Jacob (1975) presents straightforwardly the findings of studies comparing disturbed and normal families. He classifies the findings under four domains: (1) conflict, (2) dominance, (3) affect, and (4) communication clarity and accuracy. One may note that the outcome measures employed for each of these domains are heavily weighted toward terms having communication connotations. Thus conflict variables consist of such measures as speech interruptions, intrusions, simultaneous speech, and rated disagreements; measures of dominance consist of who wins a game or decision, successful interruptions, number and duration of speeches, who talks first and/or last, and ratings of dominance; affect is measured by rating or codings of expressiveness, amount of positive or negative affect, tension release, laughter, hostility, defensiveness, and affective intensity; communication clarity and accuracy involve direct ratings of the variables themselves or of such variables as confusion, vagueness, type of instruction by parent to child, and acknowledgment of others' communications.[8]

At the risk of some, though not great oversimplification, the overall findings are, briefly, equivocal and inconclusive. In perhaps only one area, that of communication clarity and accuracy, are the results of different studies consistent:

Schizophrenic families communicate with less clarity and accuracy than do normal families [Jacob, 1975:55].

Jacob notes, however:

The major exception . . . is that the more objective and less inferential measures of disruptions in communications reveal few reliable differences between groups [55].

Jacob concludes:

In summary . . . family interaction studies . . . have not yet isolated family patterns that reliably differentiate disturbed from normal groups [56].

Riskin and Faunce (1972), though less systematic in their review of findings and though not limited to disturbed-normal family comparison studies, come to substantially similar conclusions. To this we may add the further note of generally negative results in formal research approaches to the double bind (Olson, 1972). All three reviews place major emphasis for the ambiguous findings on methodological limitations and weaknesses. The articles by Jacob and by Riskin and Faunce see recent hopeful trends toward methodological improvement.

Studies Directly Related to Family Communication Theory

As suggested above, studies directly related to the concepts of family communication theorists are relatively recent in origin. These may be reviewed briefly using the headings of the previous section. It should be noted that the review to follow ignores major methodological and substantive issues. Its primary purpose is that of indexing some recent directions; for detail, the works themselves should be consulted.

Redundancy

As noted, redundancy as used by family communication theorists has many meanings. Given the theoretical emphasis on multiple communication channels, a natural focus for investigation would seem to lie in the study of redundancies in messages conveyed through different channels. There has, however, been little work in this area with respect to couples or families. Some relevant studies are indicated below under the heading "Multiple communication channels."

The major research emphasis has been on redundancy as *patterning*. One direction of research has been in comparison of the predictability of patterns of interaction between groups labeled as normal or abnormal. Thus, for example, there have been suggestive findings that families with a psychiatrically hospitalized member tend to be more rigid—i.e., more predictable or more redundant—than control families in their intrafamilial interactions (cf. Haley, 1964, 1967; Lennard and Bernstein, 1969). Such findings have been questioned (Waxler and Mishler, 1970) as resulting from scoring artifacts; when the latter are taken into account, the data suggest less predictability in interactions of families with a schizophrenic member. To date, no conclusions can be drawn about the relative redundancies of patient and nonpatient families in patterns of interaction. Most such analyses have derived from the sums of frequencies of designated behaviors. Mishler and Waxler (1975) note that these data yield no information about sequences of interaction and are consequently inadequate for examining redundant patterns within families. They develop a method, based on multivariate informational analysis, for describing and analyzing sequences of interactions. Their preliminary comparisons between normal and schizophrenic families with good or poor premorbid histories indicate more trends than significant differences. Their method does, however, appear to offer an approach closer to conceptualizations of redundancy as discussed by family communication theorists.

A second and perhaps more fruitful direction of research is less concerned with psychopathology and more with the examination of redundancies within the family unit. Thus Jacob and Davis (1973) report consistency among normal families in individual family patterns of talking and interrupting across three fairly different experimental tasks. It should be noted, however, that all tasks were undertaken in a laboratory setting and that an earlier study by O'Rourke (1963) found significant differences between performance on the same family task when administered in the family's home and when administered in the laboratory. Although family communication theorists refer to redundancies as a function of individual family rules, redundancies created by situations need to be also recognized. Lennard and Bernstein (1969) pointed to the effects of different social contexts on the interaction of schizophrenic patients. Raush et al. (1974), in studies based on multivariate informational analyses including couples and situations, found not only couple consistencies in interactions across situations but also situational consistencies across couples. Like different couples, different situations produced different responses. Moreover, again as with different couples, response contingencies differed in different situations; that is, the response by partners to a given message was a function, in part, of the situation. Situations, like families, have communicational rules.[9] Studies of couple and familial redundancies might well direct themselves toward both components and toward the interaction of familial and situational rules.

Several studies suggest that redundancy, as patterning, increases in close and/or continuing relationships. Winter et al. (1973) found that as compared to "synthetic" couples, married couples showed greater "spontaneous agreement"—the latter defined as agreements on questionnaire responses prior to consulting with one another. Furthermore, the married couples required less explicit informational exchange and reached conjoint decisions in a shorter time than did "synthetic" couples in a problem-solving task. Unfortunately, selective factors leading to choice of marital partners, as readily as any increased redundancy due to the relationship, could lead to these results. More recently, Ferreira and Winter (1974) have examined the connection between "spontaneous agreement," defined as above, and both marital duration and satisfaction. They report a significant positive relation between "spontaneous agreement" and duration of marriage; the positive correlation did not hold, however, for couples who were in marital counseling. Both sets of couples, those in counseling and those not, showed more "spontaneous agreement" than did "synthetic" couples. Again, the results are open to alternative interpretations. The simplest of these is perhaps that

couples who agree on things are more apt to remain married longer and are less apt to seek outside help for their marriages. In the studies by Raush et al. (1974) 46 young couples were seen in the fourth month of marriage; the 13 of these couples who became parents during the course of the studies were seen twice additionally. By the fourth month of marriage couples seemed to have established distinctive patterns of communication differentiating them from other couples in their approach to interpersonal conflicts. Some of these patterns could be modeled by a Markov chain (cf. Hertel, 1971; Raush, 1972), suggesting redundancy in partners' responses to one another over a sequence of interchanges. Moreover, patterns appeared to be maintained over the approximately two years between marriage and the final phases of the study. Wackman and Miller (1975) in a recent unpublished report also find a high degree of stability in the communication patterns of couples (married approximately five years) when compared over a two-year interval. Interestingly, their data suggest that far greater consistency over time is found in the *couple* pattern rather than in the *individual* husband or wife communications. The data are consistent with conceptions of the couple as a relatively stable communicational system. Some evidence for increasing redundancy with duration of marriage is suggested by more rapid resolutions at the later phases of the study by Raush et al., but such results might easily be accounted for by other factors.

One aspect of redundancy is the patterns of symmetry or complementarity which characterize communications. These relational concepts would seem clearly amenable to formal research operations. But whereas there have been many studies of individually oriented variables relating to dominant or submissive behaviors of family members (cf. Jacob, 1975), the conjoint dimension reflected in symmetry and complementarity has received little formal study. A major recent attempt is that of Ericson and Rogers (1973) who developed a coding system directly related to family communication concepts. In their procedure symmetry and complementarity are coded from the sequential exchanges between partners rather than from individual messages. Although the data reported are insufficient for evaluation, the approach appears promising.

Multiple Communication Channels

Although there has been research examining the relations between verbal and nonverbal behaviors (cf. Dittmann, 1973), we were unable to find direct studies of these relations in couple and family communications. The lack of studies cannot be said to be due to a lack of interest in nonverbal behavior or—with the increasing use of audio- and videotape recording—to difficulties of measurement. Indeed, we have noted the frequent employment of such variables as interruptions, intrusions, simultaneous speech, laughter, etc. Moreover, voice tone and gesture are often used in coding procedures for aid in identifying and labeling specific acts. But in the former case of interruptions, intrusions, etc., nonverbal behavior is studied by summing frequencies without reference to verbal content. However, where tone and gesture influence coding, verbal and nonverbal aspects are confounded. An area for investigation suggested by communication theory is in the conditions and effects of redundancy or discrepancy between the different channels.

Among studies having implications for such investigation are Mehrabian and Wiener's (1967) findings that conflicting verbal and nonverbal message components, when presented to normal subjects, did not result in confusing or conflicting interpretations by the recipients. Rather, nonverbal aspects carried the major weight, and conflicting verbal material was often ignored in the interpretations. Their study does not, however, deal with partners in close or continuing relationship or with messages which can have powerful effects on the participants. A study by Kahn (1970) compared the accuracy of satisfied and dissatisfied couples in interpreting nonverbal communications under conditions in which standard verbal content could have several different meanings. The data suggest that dissatisfied couples were less accurate than satisfied couples in their nonverbal communications, but whether the source of inaccuracy was in sender, receiver, or both could not be determined. Neither command and report nor analogic and digital comparisons (if distinguished from nonverbal and verbal aspects, respectively) have, so far as we know, been part of formal studies.

The double-bind theory derives from the notion of multiple communication channels. Mishler and Waxler (1968) in their intensive studies of family interaction in schizophrenia, however, found themselves unable to establish clear, operational criteria for the double bind. The stated criteria—three forms of injunction (often further distinguished as digital, analogic, and contextually metacommunicative), resulting in paradox, chronically repeated in an intense, long-lasting relationship—seem impossible to meet in an experimental examination. Olson (1972) in his encompassing review notes the difficulties and the failure of empirical research studies in adequately testing the substantive issues of the double-bind hypothesis as a theory of schizophrenia. Furthermore, as a theory of the *etiology* of schizophrenia—which some communication theorists reject in somewhat ambiguous fashion—investigation demands longitudinal studies which, with the kind of data the theory calls for, seem impossible to achieve.

To what extent metacommunication, as communication about the communication process, serves to resolve potential double binds and other communicative problems for couples and families is unknown. Raush et al. (1974), who report messages among their normal couples which "edge" on double binds (though the examples they give are more of the nature of disqualifications and disconfirmations), fail to find instances of metacommunicative resolutory responses under conditions of interpersonal conflict. If we consider metacommunication as commentary on the relationship, the findings of Murphy and Mendelson (1973) support the notion that with the "healthy" relationship "the relationship aspect of communication recedes into the background" (Watzlawick et al., 1967:52). Couples with low marital adjustment, they found, communicated more about their relationship and less about the context of the task—a conjoint TAT story construction—than couples in their high-adjustment group.[10] As we noted, the usage of the term "metacommunication" is overly broad and confusing. Commentary on either a relationship or on another's message can take many forms. Distinction among these forms should logically precede study of the conditions for and effects of metacommunication.

Disqualifications of one's own messages and disconfirmations of partners' messages would seem to preclude what one tends to think of as "good" relationships. Yet Raush et al. (1974) find no evidence that such presumably pathological communications necessarily make for "unhappy" marriages as defined by the partners themselves or by other criteria which evaluate the quality of their lives together. Lennard and Bernstein (1969) also found minimal differences between schizophrenic and control families in disconfirming messages. Raush et al. (1974) suggest, however, that these communicative aspects inhibit growth and development in the relationship and adaptation to changing circumstances.

A major area awaiting fuller investigation is the matter of punctuation. Researchers have yet to deal adequately with the sequential aspects of exchange which characterize human interaction. Raush (1972) and Mishler and Waxler (1975) suggest some approaches to analysis, but data relating to couples and families are almost negligible. A further step, which does not necessarily wait upon refined methodological analysis of sequences, is in the examination of how participants interpret sequences of interaction. We have yet to learn how causal attributions relate to chains of successive events, and even the simplest phenomenological descriptions by participants in communicative interchange could tell us much about relationships.

Homeostasis and Feedback

Jackson's (1957) suggestion that psychiatric symptoms in a family member serve to keep the family system as a whole in balance has become an established dictum of family therapy. It is also the basic hypothesis (or sometimes assumption) of the above-noted formal studies of links between psychopathology and family communications (cf. Lennard and Bernstein, 1969; Mishler and Waxler, 1968). A recent study by Hadley et al. (1974)

provides some indirect support for the notion of symptomatic behavior as a homeostatic effort to maintain family balance. Hadley et al. find positive correlations between symptom onset and the developmental crises created by the addition or loss of a family member. Studies having a more direct bearing on homeostasis per se are reported by Hubbell et al. (1974) and by Rosmann and Alexander (1975). The former compared parental behavior when interacting with younger and older children in an instructional task. Of particular interest is the finding that although parents alternated in taking the "dominant" position (such alternations being related to age and sex of the child), the total number of "dominant" behavioral units for the parental pairs remained constant. Rosmann and Alexander (1975) studied verbal communications in three "well-adjusted" families. They find that an experimental interdiction of communication in an intrafamilial dyad results in compensatory shifts in other dyads so that total frequency and duration of family communications remain stable. Moreover, their data yield evidence of an initial overcompensatory response to the restriction of communication, prior to the system's reestablishment of former levels. Although their number of subjects is small, the methodology they present could greatly facilitate research in this area.

The few formal studies that do exist relating to homeostasis all concern negative feedback, that is, stability-maintaining mechanisms. Much less understood (and unstudied) are positive feedback processes. To date, we can find no data relevant to the notion of deviation-amplifying mechanisms. Yet a family communications theory requires understanding of the processes that enable change from one steady state to another and that can result in system transformations. Methods for studying positive feedback, and subsequent data, would shed light on the balance between stability and change hypothesized to be indicative of healthy family (and system) functioning.

SOME TENTATIVE PROPOSITIONS

Introduction

The foregoing sections of this chapter have considered theory and research in relation to couple and family communications. In the course of presentation a number of statements which come close to formal propositions have been offered. As a guide to directions for future research, it may be useful to reiterate these propositional statements.

We should note, however, that even those statements which seem most clearly to take specific propositional form are limited by lack of clear definitional terms. This lack is not to be resolved by arbitrary and premature operationalization. The research literature is already confounded by operationalizations which neither derive from

nor test the theories they presumably refer to. A basic requisite for future work is the *empirical* development of definitions consistent with parallel theoretical concepts, and the establishment of formal definitions is itself a major research endeavor.

Consequently, the following propositions are offered for empirical exploration rather than as firm derivations from theory or research. We shall note where they appear in the body of this report (by page reference) and whether they are supported by formal research (FR) or by clinical inference (CI). We shall also indicate our own very subjective confidence (high, medium, low) in the statements.

The Propositions

1. The System

The system is its own cause. It operates in the present. Deviant individual behavior is seen as a necessary part in the functioning of a particular family system, and change if it is to occur must involve the major components of the system (page 470; CI; medium).

1a. The behavior of individual family members can be understood only within the context of the current system (page 470; CI; high).

1b. Consistency in the communicational system will be greater than the consistency in individual elements. For example, the family as a whole will show a more consistent communicational pattern than will individual members (pages 470, 480; CI, FR; high).

1c. Change in individual behavior patterns is accompanied by change in patterns of interpersonal communication (among family members) (pages 470, 476; CI; medium). A stronger form of the statement is that change in individual behavior patterns *requires* change in patterns of interpersonal communication among family members.

Redundancy

Different family interactive styles are characterized by different patterns of redundancy. The relationship rules of families represent one form of redundancy (page 471; CI; medium). These statements are more tautological than propositional. They do, however, suggest some interesting corollaries.

2a. The communicational patterns of overly enmeshed families will be characterized by excessive redundancy, whereas the communicational patterns of overly disengaged families will be characterized by too little redundancy (page 472; CI; high).

2b. Too little redundancy will lead to message confusion and chaos in family communications—rules nonexistent or defined and redefined momentarily; excessive redundancy will lead to inefficiency and will inhibit the transmission of new information into the family (page 472; CI, FR; high).

2c. Message redundancy increases with duration of marriage (page 480; FR; medium).

2d. Disturbed families will be characterized by higher levels of redundancy (i.e., greater rigidity and predictability in communicational patterns) than will control families (pages 471, 479–80; CI, FR; low).

2e. Situations, as well as families, have communicational redundancies (page 480; CI, FR; high).

3. Symmetry and Complementarity

Healthy relationships will demonstrate a balance in patterns of similarity and complementarity. Rigid symmetry or complementarity will be associated with family disturbance (page 472; CI; medium).

3a. In healthy relationships a phase of symmetry will signal a switch to complementarity and vice versa; symmetrical communications will serve to correct roles from becoming too fixed, and complementary relationships will serve to correct roles from becoming too competitive (pages 472, 477, 480; CI, FR; low).

3b. Discrepancies among participants, whether their relationship is to be defined as symmetrical or complementary, will induce relationship conflicts. Such conflicts (as between parents and children) can sometimes be readily resolved by overt recognition of differences of participants in their definition of relationship rules (page 472; CI; medium).

4. Channel Disjunctiveness

Disjunctiveness in information between verbal and nonverbal (digital and analogic, content and command) channels gives rise to misunderstandings, conflict, and symptomatic behavior (page 474; CI; low). Preliminary research findings suggest, however, that conflicting verbal and nonverbal message components do not result in confusing or conflicting interpretations for normal subjects (see page 481).

4a. A source of disjunctiveness may be inaccuracy in the interpretation of nonverbal messages. Data suggest that dissatisfied couples are less accurate than satisfied couples in interpreting nonverbal messages (page 481; FR; low).

5. Disqualification

Disqualifying messages (self-contradictions, inconsistencies, tangentializations, etc.) will be characteristic of (causally related to) families with pathology. The obverse of the proposition is that relationship difficulties within the family will lead to disqualifying communications (page 474; CI; low).

5a. Disqualifying communications by one family member will lead to feelings of confusion and anxiety about family relationships by recipients (page 474; CI; medium).

6. Disconfirmation

Disconfirming messages (messages which deny the *legitimacy* of the other's communication or the other's experiential differences) will be characteristic of (causally related to) disturbed families (page 475; CI; low).

6a. Pathological structures will reflect a history of recurrent disconfirmations among family members (page 475; CI; low).

7. Punctuation

Discrepancies among participants in the punctuation of communicational sequences will result in (reflect) relationship conflicts (page 475; CI; medium).

7a. Recurrent punctuations, leading to fixed causal labels, may result in conjointly accepted fixed roles (e.g., scapegoat, victim) for individual family members (page 475; CI; medium).

8. Metacommunication

Disjunctions in communications can be resolved by metacommunication (page 475; CI; medium).

8a. The solution to a relational conflict requires metacommunication at a level higher than the conflict itself (note: such a metacommunicational step may be even as simple as a resolution to avoid the conflict issue) (page 475; CI; medium).

8b. Anxiety (or perhaps any intense affect) will inhibit the capacity for metacommunication (pages 476, 481; CI, FR; medium). One might consequently expect less metacommunication in pathological as compared to control families. Data, however, suggest that in "healthy" relationships metacommunicative comments about the relationship recede into the background and that dissatisfied marriages are characterized by one partner's attempt to metacommunicate against the wishes of the other (pages 481, 487).

8c. Metacommunication will be rare when interpersonal conflict escalates (pages 476, 481; CI, FR; high).

9. Homeostasis

"When an organism indicates a change in relation to another, the other will act upon the first so as to diminish and modify that change" (Haley) (page 476; CI, FR; medium). The obverse of this proposition is that although negative feedback operations are required for maintaining stability in all family systems, positive feedback is essential for coping with change (page 477; CI; medium).

9a. All families will exhibit negative feedback (particularly under conditions of stress) (pages 476–77, 482; CI, FR; high).

9b. Disturbed families will be more preoccupied

with maintaining a status quo through negative feedback than will normal families (pages 477, 479; CI, FR; low).

9c. Positive feedback operations serve as a source of growth, innovation, and creativity in "healthy" families (page 477; CI; medium).

CONCLUSIONS

Theory

From the conjunction of systems theory, cybernetics, and communication theory there seems to be emerging a unified discipline. Analogic to psychoanalytic metapsychology, the three approaches can be said to represent different levels of analysis. Systems theory, at the broadest abstractive level, offers a structural approach in its concern with boundaries and permeability or rigidity of systems; cybernetics, at an intermediate abstractive level, represents an economic point of view in its concern with signal (rather than, as in psychoanalytic theory, energy) transformations and quantitative control; communication theory, at the most concrete level, suggests a dynamic orientation in its concern with the specific forces which maintain or change relationships.

In its approach to human relations what we have here called family communication theory has made a significant leap. It has shifted the focus of understanding from the intraindividual to the interpersonal. Although that shift in emphasis is not in itself entirely new—having been long foreshadowed in traditions dating from Cooley, G. H. Mead, and H. S. Sullivan—what are new are the conceptual tools and the approach to analysis. The implications of the concepts and of the analytic approach have yet to be fully realized. Even at the methodological level, the rejection of notions of variable independence and of linear causality has profound significance for the human sciences. Moreover, the concepts themselves have at least a potential concreteness that is often absent in metaphorical calls for new approaches.

Yet what we have called a theory is not quite a theory. It is a conglomeration of more or less related concepts, with the relations among them obscure. The seeming rigor, the black box approach, the attempt at a unified, comprehensive statement are more pretense than real. Take, for example, the first basic "axiom" stated by Watzlawick et al. (1967): "One cannot not communicate" (51). The statement may be true, but it is nonetheless empty. It says no more than would the equivalent "axioms" of the behaviorist—"One cannot not behave"—or of the psychoanalyst—"One cannot not associate." The statement is, however, not altogether empty rhetoric. It has a function and that function is to *point* to a neglected area of importance. In this sense, the statement is, to use communicational terms, more analogic than digital. So too with the concepts and theoretical statements. The notions

we have discussed—redundancy, patterns and rules of relationship, punctuation, digital and analog channels, metacommunication, homeostasis and feedback—are less theory, less hypotheses, and more *orientational* pointings which say, in effect, "Look here."

As we have suggested previously, the concepts, as explicated, can be readily criticized. Redundancy, as noted, has been used so broadly that it becomes each and every form of consistency, and at times seems all but interchangeable with the family system itself. The relations between digital-analog, report-command, and verbal-nonverbal channels of communication are not only confounded empirically but are conceptually inconsistent and at times contradictory. Metacommunication loses any specific meaning when it comes to represent both concrete messages and the entire contextual frame of communication. Homeostasis, feedback, and governors and calibrating processes lack sufficient specificity to be of much more than metaphorical use. Moreover, at this stage the separate concepts remain just that. In a loose way they are all related to the family conceived of as a system, but they do not form the coherent integrated network that one may expect of a developed theory.

Beyond the weaknesses in what is dealt with, we may note what is left out. Family communication theory addresses itself to the dimension of *power* in intimate enduring relationships. In that address it broaches and tackles issues too long ignored (one might even say repressed) in close relationships. The balances it speaks of in family rules, in symmetry and complementarity, in report and command, in homeostasis, all concern distributions of power. The theory may well be credited in pointing to the dilemmas of power, its use (and misuse) in couple, family, and psychotherapy relations. It is, however, somewhat paradoxical that a theory concerned with intimate relationships leaves out affection. Nowhere is *love* mentioned. If *power* was once the "dirty word" of intimacy, so now it is with *love*.

One may attribute the exclusion of love and indeed the banishment of any affect dimension or passion from the theory to two positions. The first is that of the black box: the attempt to look at only input and output observables and to avoid inferences as to internal mechanisms. Yet inferences are made. From communications of the participants inferences are drawn as to family rules, their rigidity or flexibility, their openness or closedness to recognition, their bindingness on family members. Indeed, diagnoses of and attempts to modify family structures depend on such inferences. The second position, a modification of the first, is in the attempt to keep concepts and inferences at the relational level and to reject individual-motivational terms. The scarcity of relational concepts in the literature and in common parlance is often decried by family communications theorists. Yet perhaps here theorists have too readily bought the premise that affective terms represent *individual* motivations, rather than argue that these too are fundamentally *relational*. The notion of contextual levels in communication is a basic significant contribution of the theory. It is unnecessary and inconsistent that the affective dimensions of close relationships fail to be considered—as one of the major contextual frames influencing communicative processes.

It is also surprising that a *family* communication theory makes so little mention of developmental issues.[11] Communicational processes have a developmental course in general maturation and learning about interpersonal behavior, in the initiation, growth, and termination of specific relationships, and in the stages of the family life cycle. Both specific and general developmental aspects of communication would seem fruitful areas for theory and research.

A third theoretical gap lies in the limited consideration given to the interface between the family and its environment. If individuals cannot be understood apart from the family system in which they function, so too the family cannot be understood without examining its interconnectedness with its environment. Certainly, it would be impossible to organize the universe in order to talk about the family. Yet the structure of boundaries between the family and its immediate environment and the characteristics of communications across these boundaries need explication if communications within a family are to be comprehended. Again here, the notion of contextual levels may be of service.

Our criticisms of the "theory" must also be put in context. To note the immaturities of the adolescent is not to condemn him for not being fully adult. The family communications approach is young. It is ambitious in its attempt to develop a truly interpersonal psychology. And if it is at times pretentious, it is also exceptionally promising. It tackles important problems, and it points to new directions for conceptual analysis and research.

Research

We noted earlier the methodological critiques by Jacob (1975) and by Riskin and Faunce (1972), and we noted their hopefulness about trends toward methodological improvements.

Yet what is particularly discouraging is not so much methodologically inadequate studies, but rather the fact that even such carefully planned, executed, and analyzed studies as that by Mishler and Waxler (1968) have yielded so little in the way of clear findings. Even those differences which have been found between normal families and families with a schizophrenic child, although statistically significant, seem incommensurately small and minor in relation to the dramatic pathology. Moreover, despite investigators' sometimes heroic efforts at establishing controls, the relevance of differences between disturbed and control families for questions of etiology

remains speculative (cf. Rabkin, 1965) in the absence of longitudinal studies.

Unfortunately, but assuredly, to this date formal observational studies of family communications have contributed little or nothing to our understanding of either etiology or family relationships in schizophrenia. It is perhaps ironic that family communication concepts derive so largely from observations of disturbed families yet are of so little use in formal studies which attempt to distinguish patterns of disturbed and normal families.

The problems of research seem to demand more than methodological refinements. On one hand the conceptual statements of family communication theory set high requirements for research. Haley in his advocacy of family experiments in 1962 states:

> The problem is to measure how members of a "group with a history" *typically* [his italics] respond to each other, while attempting to eliminate as much as possible the effect of that particular setting on their performance [269].

To what extent laboratory tasks of "planning something together," agreeing on a questionnaire or Rorschach response, or engaging in a competitive game evoke *typical* family interaction is open to question. As Riskin and Faunce note:

> Highly reliable, tightly controlled laboratory conditions may be achieved, but the price may be the loss of the complex aspects of the family interaction [1972:377].

Difficulties in matching research operations to conceptual requirements have perhaps served to foster spurious equations. Thus "interruptions" are equated with power, simultaneous speech with conflict, "who talks first" with dominance. The search for reliable operational measures seems at times to degenerate to the expectation that a simple, single index will somehow magically capture the complexities of human interchange.

The other side of the problem is, as noted above, in the slipperiness of the concepts themselves. The tendency of some family communication theorists (cf. Watzlawick et al., 1967) to put statements in the form of axioms and propositions provides only the illusion of scientific precision. Such statements seem to suggest hypotheses which on closer examination are of uncertain relevance to the theoretical position. A case in point is the double bind. It can account for schizophrenic communications, but it is not the "cause" of schizophrenia. The double bind also accounts for humor, poetry, creativity, and even therapeutic change. But what accounts for whether one will become a humorist, poet, schizophrenic, or therapist is unclear. Even its progenitor, Bateson, recognizes the slipperiness of the double-bind conception and is doubtful of its openness to systematic testing (cf. Olson, 1972). Other concepts are at a level of abstraction which makes them difficult to pin down. Riskin and Faunce express the problem clearly:

It seems that the family research field is seriously handicapped by a lack of intermediate level concepts. There is, if anything, an overabundance of abstract concepts and theories, e.g., ''power,'' ''dominance,'' ''self-esteem,'' ''homeostasis,'' ''conflict,'' ''family rules,'' ''double-bind,'' ''pseudo-mutuality'' . . . etc. And there are many factors requiring minimal inference which can be measured with high reliability, e.g., ''who talks,'' ''interruptions,'' ''who follows whom,'' amount of ''silence,'' amount of ''talking'' . . . etc. Noticeably lacking, however, are the intermediate concepts and steps through which to relate the low-order observational data and variables to high-order abstractions [1972:399–400].

Some further suggestions for research directions may be offered:

(a) The boundedness of family communications research to issues of psychopathology and to schizophrenia in particular seems at this stage misguided. Inadequacies in diagnostic classifications and almost insoluble problems in establishing traditional control samples and procedures ensure ambiguity of findings. It is not that psychopathology cannot serve to help explore diverse patterns of communication. It has so served in the development of the theoretical concepts. The error is in the reverse extrapolation—in the extension of communication concepts as solutions to *the cause* of schizophrenia. Such extensions are, at the least, premature. They lead to pseudo-hypotheses and to the illusion of the simple magical index which will unravel the phenomena of psychopathology and its development.

Furthermore, the search for unitary causes is untrue to the fundamental premises of the approach: its rejection of linear causal notions and its emphasis on circular feedback processes within systems. From the latter point of view outcomes can provide no information about initial ''causes'' (see Maruyama, 1963); and initial ''causes'' need not have implications for changing the system. Within its own premises, communications ''theory'' can have little more than speculations to offer about the origins of schizophrenia, but it potentially has something to say about modifying schizophrenic communications.

The boundedness of research to psychopathology is related to the economics of research and the sociology of research grant support. It is not intrinsic to the concepts themselves. Greater progress in clarification would, we suggest, result from the study of communication processes in the development and life cycle of the range of close relationships.

(b) Quantitative research, as we have noted, has been based on individually oriented counts and measures— who interrupts, who speaks, who wins, etc., and how often. The search for constancies at these elemental levels has not been successful. Communication ''theory'' is concerned not with constancies of communicational elements (that A does x to B), but with constancies of relations over sequences of events (that A does x to B when B does y to A, and that when A does x, B is likely to follow with z). We would suggest that quantitative research be directed either toward relational variables (e.g., symmetry) or to the *contingencies* of messages as they occur over time.

Qualitative research on communication has not yet been fully exploited. We need to know how people themselves punctuate their communication sequences, how they perceive the rules of their relationships, what they see as redundancies and disjunctions, how they conceive of feedback control processes. Qualitative approaches enabling such explorations have yet to be adequately explicated.

(c) Finally, it would be most unfortunate if research on communications ''theory'' emulated the studies of psychoanalytic ''theory'' in the late forties and early fifties. All too often such studies were directed at ''proving'' or ''disproving'' whether repression, projection, reaction formation, the Oedipus complex, or castration anxiety, etc., existed. One can similarly foresee studies directed toward ''proving'' or ''disproving'' the existence of redundancy in family patterns, of family rules, of punctuation, of homeostasis in families, etc.

The concepts we have discussed in this chapter do not demand verification or disproof. They demand rather an examination of their scientific and practical utility. For example, with regard to redundancy, legitimate questions concern the conditions under which family patterns fail to achieve consistency and the conditions under which they become so rigidly established that they fail to be amenable to change when circumstances require change. With regard to punctuation we may ask about the conditions which influence whether interacting participants punctuate their communications similarly or differently, and what the implications of the punctuations are for future interactions. With regard to homeostasis we need to know about the conditions under which it is signaled, the implications of too finely or too loosely calibrated systems, and the conditions which enable the system to evolve new levels of balance. The research (and pragmatic) utility of communication ''theory'' will not stand or fall on any evaluation of its concepts as absolutes. It will stand or fall on whether the phenomena to which the concepts point can be explored and elaborated and can be shown to have further implications for a deeper understanding of how people in continuing close relationships affect one another.

NOTES

1. A classic example of such analysis is Komarovsky's (1967) *Blue Collar Marriage.*

2. Dittmann (1973) presents an excellent brief nonmathematical explication of communication theory and its extensions. Cherry's book (1966) offers a thorough review of the theory and its research applications. Attneave (1959) imparts the mathematical aspects in a highly readable form.

3. Various other labels have been applied to these different aspects—rational versus emotional, informational versus integrational, symbolic versus emotive (cf. Dittmann, 1973:9–15). Most recently, Kuhn (1974) makes a sharp distinction between *communications* characterizing informational exchange and *transactions* characterizing transfers of value.

4. See also Bateson et al., 1963; Bateson, 1972a; Watzlawick, 1963; Watzlawick et al., 1967.

5. The other side of this, suggested by Raush et al. (1974:8–17), is that greater diversity and lesser fixity enable adaptation to changing circumstances.

6. In popular literature and discourse there is sometimes also the wholly erroneous equation of negative and positive feedback with negative and positive reinforcement.

7. The biological terms "morphostasis" and "morphogenesis" have also been used for negative and positive feedback processes, respectively (Maruyama, 1963; Speer, 1970).

8. For analysis of the concepts of "acknowledgment" and "clarity of communication" and the diverse terms and measures employed see Riskin and Faunce (1972:397–99).

9. As Lennard and Bernstein (1969) note, the family setting is itself a particular social context producing interactions different from other social contexts.

10. On the other hand, Wackman and Miller (1975) suggest on the basis of their data that marital dissatisfaction is associated with repeated impasses in which one partner attempts to communicate about the relationship against the resistance of the other to such discussion.

11. In contrast, Minuchin's (1974) structural family theory has a clearly developmental orientation.

REFERENCES

ACKERMAN, N. W.
1958   *The Psychodynamics of Family Life*. New York: Basic Books.

ANONYMOUS
1972   "Toward the differentiation of a self in one's own family." In J. L. Framo (ed.), *Family Interaction*. New York: Springer.

ASHBY, W. R.
1968   "Principles of the self-organizing system." In W. Buckley (ed.), *Modern Systems Research for the Behavioral Scientist*. Chicago: Aldine.

ATTNEAVE, F.
1959   *Applications of Information Theory to Psychology: A Summary of Basic Concepts, Methods, and Results*. New York: Holt.

BATESON, G.
1936   *Naven*. London: Cambridge University Press.
1972a   "Double bind, 1969." In G. Bateson, *Steps to an Ecology of Mind*. New York: Ballantine Books.
1972b   *Steps to an Ecology of Mind*. New York: Ballantine Books.

BATESON, G. AND D. D. JACKSON
1964   "Some varieties of pathogenic organization." *Journal for Research in Nervous and Mental Disease* 42:270–83.

BATESON, G., D. D. JACKSON, J. HALEY, AND J. H. WEAKLAND
1956   "Toward a theory of schizophrenia." *Behavioral Science* 1:251–64.
1963   "A note on the double bind: 1962." *Family Process* 2:154–61.

BERTALANFFY, L. VON
1968   "General system theory: A critical review." In W. Buckley (ed.), *Modern Systems Research for the Behavioral Scientist*. Chicago: Aldine.

BOSZORMENYI-NAGY, I.
1965   "A theory of relationships: Experience and transaction." In I. Boszormenyi-Nagy and J. L. Framo (eds.), *Intensive Family Therapy: Theoretical and Practical Aspects*. New York: Harper & Row.

BOWEN, M.
1961   "Family psychotherapy." *American Journal of Orthopsychiatry* 31:40–60.

BUCKLEY, W.
1967   *Sociology and Modern Systems Theory*. Englewood Cliffs, N.J.: Prentice-Hall.

BUCKLEY, W. (ED.)
1968   *Modern Systems Research for the Behavioral Scientist*. Chicago: Aldine.

CHERRY, C.
1966   *On Human Communication: A Review, a Survey, and a Criticism*, second ed. Cambridge, Mass.: M.I.T. Press.

CONSTANTINE, L. L. AND J. M. CONSTANTINE
1971   "Group and multilateral marriage." *Family Process* 10:157–77.

DITTMANN, A. T.
1973   *Interpersonal Messages of Emotion*. New York: Springer.

ERICSON, P. M. AND L. E. ROGERS
1973   "New procedures for analyzing relational communication." *Family Process* 12:245–67.

FERREIRA, A. J. AND W. D. WINTER
1974   "On the nature of marital relationships: Measurable differences in spontaneous agreement." *Family Process* 13:355–69.

FRY, W. F., JR.
1962   "The marital context of the anxiety syndrome." *Family Process* 1:245–52.

GARNER, W. R.
1962   *Uncertainty and Structure as Psychological Concepts*. New York: Wiley.

GARNER, W. R. AND H. W. HAKE
1951   "The amount of information in absolute judgments." *Psychological Review* 58:446–59.

HADLEY, T. R., T. JACOB, J. MILLIONES, J. CAPLAN, AND D. SPITZ
1974   "The relationship between family developmental crisis and the appearance of symptoms in a family member." *Family Process* 13:207–14.

HALEY, J.
1962   "Family experiments: A new type of experimentation." *Family Process* 1:265–93.
1963   *Strategies of Psychotherapy*. New York: Grune & Stratton.
1964   "Research in family patterns: An instrument measurement." *Family Process* 3:41–65.
1967   "Experiment with abnormal families." *Archives of General Psychiatry* 17:53–63.

HERTEL, R. K.
1971   "The application of stochastic process analyses to the study of psychotherapeutic processes." *Psychological Bulletin* 77:421–30.

HESS, R. D. AND G. HANDEL
1959   *Family Worlds: A Psychosocial Approach to Family Life*. Chicago: University of Chicago Press.

HOFFMAN, L.
1971   "Deviation-amplifying processes in natural groups." In J. Haley (ed.), *Changing Families: A Family Therapy Reader*. New York: Grune & Stratton.

HUBBELL, R. D., M. C. BYRNE, AND J. STACHOWIAK
1974   "Aspects of communication in families with young children." *Family Process* 13:215–24.

JACKSON, D. D.
1957   "The question of family homeostasis." *Psychiatric Quarterly* Supplement 31:79–90. Reprinted in D. D. Jackson

(ed.), *Communication, Family, and Marriage,* vol. 1. Palo Alto, Calif.: Science and Behavior Books, 1968.

1965a   "Family rules: The marital *quid pro quo.*" *Archives of General Psychiatry* 12:589–94.

1965b   "The study of the family." *Family Process* 4:1–20.

JACOB, T.
1975   "Family interaction in disturbed and normal families: A methodological and substantive review." *Psychological Bulletin* 82:33–65.

JACOB, T. AND J. DAVIS
1973   "Family interaction as a function of experimental task." *Family Process* 12:415–27.

KAHN, M.
1970   "Non-verbal communication and marital satisfaction." *Family Process* 9:449–56.

KANTOR, D. AND W. LEHR
1975   *Inside the Family.* San Francisco: Jossey-Bass.

KOMAROVSKY, M.
1967   *Blue-Collar Marriage.* New York: Vintage Books.

KUHN, A.
1974   *The Logic of Social Systems.* San Francisco: Jossey-Bass.

LAING, R. D.
1965   "Mystification, confusion and conflict." In I. Boszormenyi-Nagy and J. L. Framo (eds.), *Intensive Family Therapy: Theoretical and Practical Aspects.* New York: Harper & Row.

1969   *Self and Others.* New York: Pantheon.

1971   *The Politics of the Family and Other Essays.* New York: Pantheon.

LAING, R. D. AND A. ESTERSON
1964   *Sanity, Madness and the Family.* London: Tavistock.

LENNARD, H. L. AND A. BERNSTEIN
1969   *Patterns in Human Interaction.* San Francisco: Jossey-Bass.

MARUYAMA, M.
1963   "The second cybernetics: Deviation-amplifying mutual causal processes." *American Scientist* 51:164–79.

MEHRABIAN, A. AND M. WIENER
1967   "Decoding of inconsistent communications." *Journal of Personality and Social Psychology* 6:109–14.

MILLER, G. A. AND F. C. FRICK
1949   "Statistical behavioristics and sequences of responses." *Psychological Review* 56:311–24.

MILLER, J. G.
1965   "Living systems: Basic concepts." *Behavioral Science* 10:193–237.

MINUCHIN, S.
1974   *Families and Family Therapy.* Cambridge, Mass.: Harvard University Press.

MISHLER, E. G. AND N. E. WAXLER
1968   *Interaction in Families: An Experimental Study of Family Processes and Schizophrenia.* New York: Wiley.

1975   "The sequential patterning of interaction in normal and schizophrenic families." *Family Process* 14:17–50.

MURPHY, D. C. AND L. A. MENDELSON
1973   "Use of the observational method in the study of live marital communication." *Journal of Marriage and the Family* 35:256–63.

OLSON, D. H.
1972   "Empirically unbinding the double bind: Review of research and conceptual reformulations." *Family Process* 11:69–94.

O'ROURKE, V.
1963   "Field and laboratory: The decision making behavior of family groups in two experimental conditions." *Sociometry* 26:422–35.

QUASTLER, H. (ED.)
1953   *Essays on the Use of Information Theory in Biology.* Urbana: University of Illinois Press.

RABKIN, L. Y.
1965   "The patient's family: Research methods." *Family Process* 4:105–32.

RAUSH, H. L.
1965   "Interaction sequences." *Journal of Personality and Social Psychology* 2:487–99.

1972   "Process and change: A Markov model for interaction." *Family Process* 11:275–98.

RAUSH, H. L., W. A. BARRY, R. K. HERTEL, AND M. A. SWAIN
1974   *Communication, Conflict and Marriage.* San Francisco: Jossey-Bass.

RAUSH, H. L. AND B. SWEET
1961   "The preadolescent ego: Some observations of normal children." *Psychiatry* 24:368–80.

RISKIN, J. AND E. E. FAUNCE
1972   "An evaluative review of family interaction research." *Family Process* 11:365–455.

ROSMANN, M. R. AND J. F. ALEXANDER
1975   "A direct test of family homeostasis." Unpublished paper, University of Virginia.

RUESCH, J.
1954   "Psychiatry and the challenge of communication." *Psychiatry* 17:1–18.

1955   "Nonverbal language and therapy." *Psychiatry* 18:323–30.

RUESCH, J. AND G. BATESON
1951   *Communication: The Social Matrix of Psychiatry.* New York: Norton.

SATIR, V.
1964   *Conjoint Family Therapy: A Guide to Theory and Technique.* Palo Alto, Calif.: Science and Behavior Books.

SHANNON, C. E.
1951   "Prediction and entropy of printed English." *Bell Systems Technology Journal* 30:50–64.

SHANNON, C. E. AND W. WEAVER
1949   *The Mathematical Theory of Communication.* Urbana: University of Illinois Press.

SPEER, D. C.
1970   "Family systems: Morphostasis and morphogenesis, or 'Is homeostasis enough?'" *Family Process* 9:259–78.

STRODTBECK, F. L.
1951   "Husband-wife interaction over revealed differences." *American Sociological Review* 16:468–73.

1954   "The family as a three-person group." *American Sociological Review* 19:23–29.

VOGEL, E. F. AND N. W. BELL
1960   "The emotionally disturbed child as the family scapegoat." In N. W. Bell and E. F. Vogel (eds.), *A Modern Introduction to the Family.* New York: Free Press.

WACKMAN, D. B. AND S. MILLER
1975   "Analyzing sequential interactional data: Two empirical studies." Unpublished paper, University of Minnesota Family Study Center.

WATZLAWICK, P.
1963   "A review of the double bind theory." *Family Process* 2:132–53.

WATZLAWICK, P., J. H. BEAVIN, AND D. D. JACKSON
1967   *Pragmatics of Human Communication: A Study of Interactional Patterns, Pathologies and Paradoxes.* New York: Norton.

WATZLAWICK, P., J. WEAKLAND, AND R. FISCH
1974   *Change: Principles of Problem Formation and Problem Resolution.* New York: Norton.

WAXLER, N. E. AND E. G. MISHLER
  1970   "Sequential patterning in family interaction: A methodological note." *Family Process* 9:211–20.

WIENER, N.
  1948   *Cybernetics*. New York: Wiley.

WINTER, W. D., A. J. FERREIRA, AND N. BOWERS
  1973   "Decision-making in married and unrelated couples." *Family Process* 12:83–94.

WYNNE, L. C., I. M. RYCKOFF, J. DAY, AND S. I. HIRSCH
  1958   "Pseudomutuality in the family relations of schizophrenics." *Psychiatry* 21:205–20.

IV

THE FAMILY AND PROBLEMS

20

DETERMINANTS OF FAMILY PROBLEM-SOLVING EFFECTIVENESS

David M. Klein and Reuben Hill

The study of family problem solving differs from the study of other substantive domains in at least two important respects. First, problems have no natural boundaries. Virtually anything can become problematic in families as well as other social groups. Thus family problems and problem-solving behaviors cut across most of the other substantive interests represented in this volume. For example, mate selection becomes problematic when there is variation in the goals and opportunities of candidates for mutual pairing (Chapter 11). Some substantive domains suggest causal mechanisms relevant to the family problem-solving process. For example, social class differences in socialization practices may influence the problem-solving skills that children develop to employ later in their own families of procreation (Chapter 15). Still other domains point both to areas where problems might arise and to operating causal mechanisms. For example, dyadic commitment might be problematic in one marriage and might facilitate effective problem solving in another (Chapter 12).

Because family problem solving cuts across other substantive interests of family scholars, it seems appropriate to view family problem solving as a broad perspective from which to analyze many facets of family life. Following this approach, a theory of family problem solving ought to be a fairly general theory with a wide range of application. The scholars who have contributed to this field tend to share the optimism that the problem-solving perspective has the potential of becoming a general theory of family processes.

That this goal has not yet been achieved points to the second major difference between the study of family

problem solving and the study of other phenomena covered in this volume. The problem-solving perspective is a relatively new one among family scholars. Unlike many other substantive domains where empirical studies, findings, and generalizations outstrip the body of explanatory theory, the opposite condition exists with respect to family problem solving. Most of the creative work in the latter area has been theoretical and speculative. Verificational research programs with this focus are less than a decade old, and many more such programs are required before the empirical status of alternative theories of family problem solving can be adequately evaluated.

The fact that family problem-solving research tends now and promises in the future to be relatively well grounded in theory puts it at an advantage in comparison to those substantive domains with masses of underinterpreted and unintegrated data. The quality of research work is almost always enhanced if it has a well-organized theoretical underpinning.

This positive judgment needs to be tempered, however. While there is no shortage of scholarly theorizing about family problem solving, this body of theory has two major shortcomings: it tends to be unintegrated and it tends to be unsystematic. Extant theories about family problem solving lack integration in that they focus on different factors operating in the problem-solving process. Even when the process is approached in a closely comparable fashion, the ultimate phenomenon to be explained varies widely. That is, students of family problem solving have not yet agreed upon the nature of the dependent variable. Furthermore and somewhat surprisingly, there is little cross-referencing among the works of family problem-solving theorists. Without the benefit of a critical dialogue, family problem-solving theory has not yet demonstrated a cumulative effect.

Regarding the systematization problem, the situation here is not unique. As in most other substantive areas of family theory, lists of more or less explicit and testable

NOTE: The work on which this chapter is based was made possible by a research program grant on family problem solving (NIMH Grant 1 RO1 MH15521) and a training grant in family research (NIMH Grant 5 TO1 MH08357). We wish to thank Wesley Burr, Robert Leik, Barbara Settles, and Irving Tallman for their helpful comments on earlier drafts of this manuscript.

493

propositions have been developed, but the way they interrelate to form a theoretical system has been underexplored. The promise of pursuing verification research programs in the area of family problem solving depends heavily upon the prior integration and systematization of theoretical ideas. The major purpose of this chapter is to provide the groundwork for rectifying these deficits.

The plan of the balance of the chapter is as follows. First, the heritage of family problem-solving analysis will be outlined. This examination locates the historical precedents for the emergence of family problem solving as an area of scientific concern. Second, an attempt will be made to conceptualize family problem solving in a rigorous way and to point toward a key dependent variable around which the study of family problem solving might profitably be organized. Third, several existing partial theories about family problem solving will be reviewed. They represent both the range of approaches and the recurring themes that characterize the field to date. Fourth, a formal theory will be presented. This theory will attempt to integrate the insights of the existing theories and to provide a more comprehensive framework. The theory will be confronted with the available, if sparse, research findings in order to give a preliminary assessment of its confirmatory status. Fifth and finally, the integrated theory will be evaluated by conventional criteria. Theoretical and methodological issues which remain to be explored as well as suggestions for future research will be highlighted throughout.

HISTORICAL BACKGROUND

The heritage of family problem-solving analysis can be traced through the development and convergence of five streams of scientific work: (1) the family and social problems, (2) family crises and adjustment, (3) normal family development, (4) small-group problem solving, and (5) organizational decision making. Each of these foci is briefly treated below.

The family has often been viewed as the source or the setting in which certain large-scale social problems arise. For example, Goode describes a number of familiar problems including divorce, physical and mental pathology, and illegitimacy (Goode, 1961). Later work in this stream makes a careful distinction between problems of family disorganization and problems of family deviance (Sprey, 1966).

Work with this emphasis has been productive in a number of ways. It has paid attention to the social structural origins of problems that have a direct bearing on family life. It has spawned interest in articulating comprehensive lists of problems facing families, addressed the question of whether or not problems accumulate in particular families to yield the so-called ''problem-proneness'' syndrome, and provided useful classification

schemes for family assistance programs (Brim et al., 1961; Geismar and LaSorte, 1964; Beck and Jones, 1974).

At the same time, the social problems approach has had a number of limitations. It has tended to be descriptive rather than explanatory in emphasis. When an explanatory effort is made, it is usually directed at the causes of family problems rather than their solution. When solutions do receive attention, the approach is normally ameliorative or treatment-oriented. That is, families are seen as more or less helpless groups that must turn outward for assistance. They are not active agents in their own problem-solving efforts. This bias seems to be a by-product of the kinds of problems addressed. Focusing on ''major'' problems with societal relevance and with implications for social policy and programs, the social programs approach necessarily leaves residual the routine coping that families manage to muster with their own strengths and resources.

The work on family crises and adjustment parallels the social problems approach in at least two ways (Hill, 1949; Hansen and Hill, 1964; Farber, 1964). First, by focusing on problems of more or less catastrophic proportions, the crisis approach lends itself to the analysis of family disorganization and thus retains a close tie to social policy and program application. Second, the crisis approach has produced further refinements in the classification of problem types.

On the other hand, this stream has departed from the social problems orientation in at least two important ways. First, it has generally viewed families as active agents in their own problem-solving efforts. This is reflected in a concern with the definition of problematic situations by families as crucial in the emergence of family problems. It is also reflected in the emphasis on the response to crisis or the attempts by family members to regain order after a period of disruption. Second, the crisis approach has specified phases in the pattern of response to crisis. Some primitive notions of interaction process are introduced, and families are seen as working through a number of steps toward recovery.

The theory of family crisis solving has never been articulated in a systematic way by today's standards, and even if it were, there remains a question about whether or not such a theory would generalize from severe problems to the full range of problems that families encounter. The reader is alerted to Chapter 22 by Hansen and Johnson for a more detailed treatment of these issues.

The study of normal family development has provided a framework somewhat distinct from the two approaches thus far discussed (Rapoport, 1963; Hill and Rodgers, 1964; Duvall, 1971; Aldous, 1974). Under the influence of this framework, the family is seen as routinely passing through a number of stages of development, each of which presents problematic role transitions. Thus, for example, adjustment during the early months of marriage and adjustments to parenthood, launching, and retirement are all brought under the purview of the family problem-solving perspective. While a sensitivity to developmental phenomena adds to the range of relevant problem types and increases awareness of the possible interactional dynamics involved in problem solving, developmentalists have not yet provided a comprehensive theory of family problem-solving processes.

The streams of research on small-group problem solving and organizational decision making have a long and parallel history. They may be considered in tandem because of their shared emphasis on discussion procedures and rational information processing. Also, small task groups studied in the laboratory or in field settings have often been used as the basis for inferences about decision-making practices in large-scale organizations. Sophisticated research programs like those conducted by Bales and associates (Bales and Strodtbeck, 1951) and Maier and associates (Maier, 1970) have produced a wealth of data and propositions about the structure and interaction processes of small groups as they affect group problem solving.

Since families are small groups, it is only natural that the concepts and principles developed in these other settings be borrowed and applied to family problem solving. Unfortunately, this strategy presents a number of difficulties which, combined, have probably resulted in the underutilization of materials available from these sources. First, the composition, history, and bonds of attachment in a family are quite different from those in an ad hoc group or a bureaucratic task group. Thus the principles developed in these nonfamily settings may have to be greatly modified when they are applied to families. Second, the kinds of tasks which are designed to be problematic in small-group and organizational research may be unlike the kinds of problems which families encounter. Thus the comparability of situations across types of collectivities remains to be established. Finally, despite the large amount of information available about group problem solving, as with the other streams of work considered this knowledge has not been systematized into a comprehensive theory. Although several excellent reviews of this research tradition are available (Hoffman, 1965; Maier, 1967; Kelley and Thibaut, 1969), all of them are discursive treatments of central ideas. Thus until this material is integrated and formalized, it will have to be borrowed in a piecemeal fashion.

Nevertheless, the small-group and organizational perspectives open up distinctive avenues not available in other approaches. They provide rich detail about structural and interactional factors likely to be of some importance for family problem solving. They highlight the role of decision making and add further insight about the phasing of problem-solving processes.

These several streams of work, both within and outside

the study of the family, have developed strong traditions. Within the last decade there has been an attempt to blend the merits of each stream into a more comprehensive approach to family problem solving. In part, this convergence is the result of scholars with backgrounds and interests in several of the established lines of work becoming strategically located within a common professional network at selected institutions so that ideas could cross-fertilize (Aldous et al., 1971). The extent to which each of the ancestral approaches has left its mark will become apparent in subsequent chapter sections.

CONCEPTUALIZING FAMILY PROBLEM SOLVING

In order to move beyond commonsense notions about problem solving and to provide some degree of specificity, the following definitions of key concepts are offered.

Problems and Problem Solving

A *problem* is viewed here as *any situation involving an unachieved but potentially attainable goal in which the means for overcoming barriers to achieving the goal, though not immediately apparent, are considered feasible*. Certain elements of this definition deserve further clarification. A *goal* may be viewed as any desired state of affairs whose attainment requires some sort of activity. Underlying this definition is the assumption that behavior is purposive or goal-directed. To assert that a goal is *unachieved but potentially attainable* means that a discrepancy between the current state of affairs and the desired state is perceived to exist and that it is viewed as reducible. Thus situations are not considered to be problems if they are viewed by actors as entirely impossible to resolve. Furthermore, goal attainment is expressed in relative terms; that is, the goal-state discrepancy as well as progress toward reducing the discrepancy may vary in magnitude. *Barriers* are conditions impeding goal attainment. Such barriers include resources which must be acquired and obstacles or resistance which must be overcome in order to progress toward goal attainment. *Means* are actions taken to obtain or use available resources for goal attainment. Finally, *feasible though not immediately apparent* means that there is some degree of uncertainty associated with goal-striving activity, but not so much uncertainty that the situation is viewed as hopeless.[1]

The above description of a problem coincides roughly with conventional scientific models of means-end systems. It includes both a cognitive or perceptual component and a behavioral component, and it posits at least a minimal level of motivation toward goal attainment. This view is more limited, however, than a general means-end scheme in that the notions of barrier and uncertainty are explicitly included. Thus goals which can be achieved through habitual response patterns and with virtually no effort or reflection are not viewed here as problematic.

The next key term to distinguish is "problem *solving*." In accord with the view of problems just presented, problem solving is defined as goal-striving behavior. Faced with problems actors are seen as behaving with the intent of solving their problems. This perspective sees human behavior as an active, coping, achievement-oriented phenomenon rather than as passive or fatalistic. This is not to say that problem solvers never become overwhelmed and resigned in the face of problematic situations, but only that our focus is on behavior elicited with the intent of meeting and overcoming such situations. It is assumed that actors attempt to solve their problems, that some are more or less successful, and that successful behavior can be learned. When we move to consider problem-solving behavior in groups, and families in particular, we will be focusing on this positive aspect of goal striving. Problem solving in groups is viewed from an interactional perspective. The behavior of family members is at least to some degree coordinated as they interact to solve a problem of mutual concern.

This accent on behavior designed to solve problems should not be confused with reaching a solution. All problem-solving activity may be viewed as resulting in some outcome, which is simply to say that such behavior has consequences. Among these consequences may be some modification of the goal-attainment discrepancy. But a solution need not completely irradicate the discrepancy. Rather, we will mean by solution any outcome of problem-solving activity that is evaluated in terms of its approximation to the operating goal. Thus problem-solving behavior does not imply successfully solving a problem, but rather attempting to do so and evaluating the effort in terms of its relative success or failure.

Since our concern in this chapter is with family problem solving, it is necessary to introduce some preliminary notions about group problem solving and the nature of the family group.

Problem Solving in Groups

When we move from problem solving by individuals to problem solving by groups, two considerations are of the utmost importance: the nature of the goal structure and the organization of the behaviors of the group members.

While groups are sometimes defined in terms of goals which their members share, it should be obvious that group members do not necessarily view the objectives of the group in precisely the same way at all times. Even for families, where the goal structure is sometimes thought to be more homogeneous or integrated than for most other groups, it is probably unrealistic to assume that the goals of members are consistently shared. This presents an analytical problem for the study of problem solving in families as well as other groups. How can groups problem-solve if the problem is defined differently by various group members?

One way out of this difficulty is to assume from the start that problem-solving goals in groups are shared by members. Thus, although the goals for the group may at times be viewed differently by participants, problem solving does not begin until some common goal is agreed upon. Behavior associated with the clarification of goals and the establishment of goal consensus may occur in groups, but it is not considered to be problem-solving behavior.

Alternatively, the concession might be made that negotiating for a common goal constitutes problem solving, but problem solving of a special kind, that is, a sort of meta-problem solving. The goal in such negotiations is the establishment of goal consensus, and the meta-goal (goal consensus) is assumed to be shared.

As an example, consider a family that begins a discussion about where to go for a vacation. The husband-father and wife-mother may have different preferences; one wants to go east and the other west. However, the son suddenly interjects that he doesn't want to go anywhere at all, but wants to stay home to be with his friends. In this situation we might decide to focus on the "where to go" issue and assume for analytic purposes that the desirability of some sort of traveling vacation is shared by all family members. At least we would be willing to treat the establishment of the traveling vacation goal as a preliminary problem that need not concern us.

Recognizing that such an analytic decision may not seem fair to all group members (in this case, to the son), we might argue that two problems are really involved: whether or not to take a traveling vacation and, if so, where to go. Many problems are likely to be embedded in just this way, and the advantage of separating them is that each can be given separate treatment. It is not farfetched to suppose that the analytic advantage is accompanied by a pragmatic advantage for groups themselves. By treating the problem in terms of its hierarchical goal structure, groups are likely to do a better job of dealing with the situation.

A disadvantage of this perspective is that the goal structure may contain an infinite regress. An apparent goal may imply meta-goal consensus which is unwarranted, the meta-goal may imply an even more basic goal which is itself assumed to be shared and perhaps incorrectly, and so forth. It is to be hoped that this regress is not infinite, that somewhere there is at least a goal shared by all group members to the effect that the group itself is worth preserving and that its purpose is to work together for the mutual benefit of all. However, even this fundamental goal might be challenged, as can be witnessed by the frequency with which groups, and even families, dissolve for lack of any common purpose. Of course, some groups may also continue to function for long periods of time under the shroud of an assumed, but false, consensus.

The point of this extended discussion of group goal structures is to emphasize their precarious nature. While goals can be profitably distinguished for analytic purposes, it is hazardous to assume that goals are shared before problem solving begins. Therefore, another way of dealing with this issue is to treat the clarification and establishment of goals as an explicit part of the problem-solving process. Rather than a residual preliminary to problem solving or a separate problem in its own right, goal setting may be viewed as a necessary element in the solving of any particular problem. In our family vacation example, the satisfactory resolution of where to go depends on clarification of a mutual concern and examination of the goal structure to see if a consensus exists, and then dealing with any discovered goal dissensus. During this process, the nature of the problem itself may change, and a comprehensive theory of group problem solving should account for this phenomenon.

This latter approach will be adopted here. As a consequence, the mutual sharing of a goal by family members will not be built into the definition of a problem itself, but will be treated as an antecedent variable which influences the rest of the problem-solving process. In this way it will be possible to incorporate situations in which problem-solving behavior occurs and some outcome is reached, but without the benefit of goal consensus. That such events often occur seems intuitively reasonable. Furthermore, such a perspective preserves the integrity of each family member and avoids the so-called "group fallacy," an assumption that characterizes a group as "single-minded" and always performing in a well-integrated, organically pure fashion. It is not expected that this analytic decision will resolve the eternal dispute about the emergent reality of groups, but it seems to be the most realistic alternative when problem solving is assessed from an interactional point of view.

The second important consideration in group (as opposed to individual) problem solving relates to the way in which the behaviors of individual members are organized. When individuals problem-solve, much of their effort may be viewed in terms of perception and of cognition. Apart from trial-and-error learning by way of overt performance attempts which take place, much of the relevant analysis at the level of individual problem solving will involve reflective thinking. While individual perception and cognition are undoubtedly important for group problem solving, a peculiarity of problem solving at the group level is that it entails overt interaction among group members. Often this interaction will take the form of a discussion of the problem, the search for a mutually agreed-upon decision to act in certain ways, the division of responsibilities for taking action, and some method for evaluating performances and outcomes. Sometimes this interaction process will not be so elaborate, as when one member of a family makes certain assumptions about the problem and the action required and unilaterally attempts to solve it on the presumed behalf of all members.

Nevertheless, the distinctive aspect of group problem solving is that it normally involves some sort of participation by two or more persons. As participation patterns take shape, the way in which the actions of various group members become coordinated takes on theoretical significance. The interaction structure for problem solving by families eventually becomes stylized in many cases, so that problem-solving roles may be identifiable. For example, one member may be designated "the arbiter of disputes," another "the collector of information about financial resources," still another "the nonparticipant," and so on.

That groups develop relatively stable role structures for coping with problems contrasts with the emphasis placed on uncertainty when we defined a problem earlier. The apparent contradiction can be resolved if we remember that any group effort, no matter how novel the situation, occurs within the context of a preexisting role structure, at least in groups with a history. Many problems may require role reorganization or even a minimum of role structure in order to be dealt with adequately. However, in the face of uncertainty, the best predictor of how a group initially organizes to attempt to solve a problem may be its past role structure. The failure of the traditional structure to lead to a solution may then provide an impetus to reorganize.

The essential point is that group problem solving involves multiple actors who are addressing the problem in a nonrandom way. Later, we will be concerned with identifying more or less functional systems of interaction in families, as this matter plays an important part in the theory we will be presenting. Here it is sufficient to point to the centrality of interdependent actions in a group of individual problem solvers. While the perceptual and cognitive components of interaction process are recognized as important, relatively more emphasis will be placed on directly observable patterns of interaction in families.

The Family as a Problem-Solving Group

To this point we have been operating as if the definition of the family is unproblematic and as if a family is a problem-solving unit resembling other groups. Both of these notions now deserve examination.

While it is recognized that family structure is cross-culturally variable, we will define the family here as the nuclear family unit consisting of one male, one female, and their children. Whether or not we accept Murdock's (1949) claim to its universality, the nuclear family is unquestionably the most common form of family structure extant.

Earlier we referred to the compositional, historical, and attractional peculiarities that exist in families. These features warrant further clarification.

The nuclear family differs from other cooperative small groups in that it is "kinship structured" (I. Reiss, 1971). A family is organized on the basis of strong normative bonds which foster emotional ties among its members. These bonds may be biological, cultural, or affinal (in most societies they are usually all three), but whatever their bases, they imply the strongest type of socially sanctioned mutual commitment possible in a society. Still, we must remember that not all families exhibit such idealistically high degrees of cohesiveness. A family's problem-solving performance will likely reflect, in part, the strength of the bonds holding its members together in a group.

The family also differs from other social groups and organizations in that its life cycle is generally coterminous with the life course of at least one of the original parents; that is, a particular nuclear family ceases to exist when the last of the original parents dies. Moreover, unlike other organizations, the incumbents in the various family positions are not entirely replaceable. Although incumbents in the positions of husband and wife can be replaced, those who hold the biological roles of parents or children or siblings are not replaceable (except perhaps in the cases of adoption and quasi-kin in communal families). This fact gives the family biologically linked maturational characteristics which are not inherent in other social groups. Thus a family can be considered as having a life cycle in a manner similar to a living organism (Duvall and Hill, 1948).

Practically speaking, a family may cease to operate as a group when some of its members take on separate residences. Thus when the children leave home to establish their own nuclear units or when marital dissolution effectively removes one of the parents from the system of interaction, the membership status of one or more members may be in doubt. Such considerations suggest that the boundaries of the family must be judged on a case-by-case basis, with the criterion being whether or not the group of adults and their children interacts as if they were a family. We have not built common residence into our definition of the nuclear family for this reason, but it is the two-generation family sharing a residence that we usually have in mind.

The family shares in common with other natural groups a history and a future. Both conditions influence the nature of its organization and the decisions that it makes at any one time. It also shares with many natural groups a multipurpose character; that is, its functions are varied and dependent upon changing contingencies in the environment and in its own composition. Thus, although a family generally develops a relatively complex division of labor, the various rights, duties, and skills required in particular roles are likely to change with given situations over time. This is seen most clearly in the roles which children play as they grow and mature. An important consequence of the time-linked variability in member traits found in families is that structural change and flexibility are likely to be important factors in family problem-solving performance.

A final distinction can be made between problem solving *by* families and problem solving *in* families. The former implies that the whole group is involved, whereas the latter implies that only certain members are involved, even though consequences may still accrue to the entire group. As is the case with many other groups and organizations, family systems contain primary subsystems. The marital, parent-child, and sibling subsystems are often separated for analysis. In a problem centering on the resolution of marital conflict, for example, we might not expect the children to be as involved as they would presumably be when a family vacation is at issue. Although the boundary between them is not always clear-cut, we are concerned here as much with problems that occur in families as with the problems of families. While it is important to keep in mind the idea of system relevance, we will for the most part use a vocabulary that addresses the family in its entirety. At the same time, we will attempt, as mentioned earlier, to be sensitive to the "group fallacy."

Problem-Solving Effectiveness

Having clarified our general orientation to problems and problem solving and their operation in groups and especially in families, we move now to conceptualize the dependent variable in the theory of family problem solving. As was mentioned in the introduction, there exists a lack of scientific consensus about the most appropriate dependent variable. We cannot hope to settle the issue or to impose a consensus by fiat, but we will discuss alternatives and make a reasoned decision on that basis.

One way of dealing with this issue is to circumvent it by asserting that problem solving has no identifiable outcome. Instead, problem solving is viewed as a continuous ebb and flow of social interaction, with feedback mechanisms resulting in temporary halts and eventual reinstigation of the process. Each solution gives rise to new problems, so that the situation is undergoing endless modification. Associated with this view are claims to the effect that "everything is related to everything else, sooner or later."

However appealing these are as descriptions of naturally occurring events, they fail to provide an anchor point for theoretical and empirical assessment. We opt instead for a causal model with specifiable parameters. We recognize that in its most sophisticated development, such a model will have to be nonrecursive. While certain feedback processes will be mentioned as we proceed, for the most part they will be relegated to a class of topics deserving further exploration.

Another option is to select family problem-solving *behavior* as the dependent variable. There is little doubt that in order to understand how families attempt to solve their problems, we must be able to predict and explain the interaction strategies employed. A number of existing social psychological theories might be readily adaptable for this purpose.

On the other hand, choosing behavior or interaction patterns as the dependent variable presents certain difficulties. For example, how is a general concept like behavior to be translated into relevant quantitative terms? Some system of classification is called for which orders behaviors along theoretically meaningful continua. One direction along this line might be to identify interaction styles used by families as they cope with problematic situations. Another, more frequently encountered approach is to reconstruct interaction sequences. The work on phasing has this emphasis. Its objectives are to identify the steps through which families might work to solve problems, determine the chronological arrangement of those steps, and discover the extent to which actual families deviate from the idealized sequence.

Further classificatory work along these lines has undeniable merit, but there is reason to believe that it would be insufficient for a full understanding of family problem-solving processes. The purposive character of problem solving, its goal-seeking orientation, suggests that outcomes or products of family interaction can be evaluated not only by family members but by outside observers as well. How well goals are achieved and problems solved then becomes the focus of attention.

The effectiveness of problem solving is an end-point product against which to assess the entire process. It has advantages over the "behavior as dependent variable" approach because behavior can be viewed as an intervening mechanism. It is important not only to explain interaction patterns but also to explain interaction patterns as outcomes. For this reason, family problem-solving effectiveness will be selected and defined as the dependent variable of interest.

Research in the small-group and organization traditions suggests two fundamental evaluative dimensions: solution quality and solution acceptance (Maier, 1952; Kretch et al., 1962; Maier, 1970; Patton and Giffin, 1973). The terms used to designate these dimensions vary widely, and a sample of such terms is provided above.

These dimensions differ in a number of respects. Quality focuses on an extrinsic task, while acceptance focuses on intrinsic member gratification. Quality is assessable by some objective standards, while acceptance is largely subjective. Quality is normally associated with work group performance, while acceptance is normally associated with human relations or interpersonal skills de-

Descriptors for Two Dimensions of Problem-Solving Effectiveness

SOLUTION QUALITY	SOLUTION ACCEPTANCE
Goal achievement	Satisfaction with solution
Efficiency	Satisfaction with process
Productivity	Morale
Task accomplishment	Relationship maintenance
Originality	Self-actualization

velopment. Such distinctions are not entirely pure, however, and the overlaps should be noted.

First, solution quality is amenable to subjective as well as objective assessment (e.g., how successful group members think they have been), and morale can often be inferred from interactions patterns. Second, the various indicators of acceptance may themselves suggest goals. Some groups may have as their objective the enhancement of member relationships. Thus it has been suggested that the selection of one or more indicators of group effectiveness should depend on the specific goals involved (Kretch et al., 1962:454–55). Third, acceptance often implies a willingness to act on the basis of decisions reached, so that it includes the postdecisional quality of problem-solving efforts. Finally, there is an increasing recognition that even task-oriented groups depend on maximizing at least some features of the acceptance dimension in order to fulfill their extrinsic purposes over the long run. However, the relationship between the two primary dimensions appears to be rather complex. While at times it may be possible or even necessary to maximize both dimensions together, at other times quality may be increased only at the expense of acceptance, and vice versa (Maier, 1970).

While the two-dimensional model of problem-solving evaluation does not remove all ambiguities, it provides a useful starting point for a formal definition of family problem-solving effectiveness. The importance of the quality dimension derives from our definition of a problem, and the importance of the acceptance dimension seems intuitively reasonable given the emotional intensity of most family relationships.

Accordingly, *family problem-solving effectiveness* is defined as *the degree to which family problems are solved* (quality) *to the mutual satisfaction of family members* (acceptance). High-quality solutions that are enthusiastically received will be more effective than low-quality solutions that receive no support or only mixed support. Problem solving that results in intermediate levels of effectiveness will be characterized by moderate quality and moderate acceptance, by high-quality solutions that are poorly received, or by low-quality solutions that are enthusiastically received.

The precise functional relationship between quality and

acceptance is subject to further investigation. Maier (1970:277) suggests that the two combine in a multiplicative way, so that if either is low, net effectiveness is low. We will take up this issue later when we discuss the operationalization of problem-solving effectiveness. To date the issue has been largely avoided because family researchers have devoted most of their attention to the quality of performance. Sometimes "problem-solving ability" and "problem-solving success" are used interchangeably with other terms to denote the qualitative aspect of effectiveness. This emphasis is somewhat surprising, but it probably reflects the relative ease with which objective measures are obtainable as well as confidence in their reliability. The consequence of this emphasis, however, is that most of the available data leave questions about acceptance unexplored, so that much of the theory remains untested.

PARTIAL THEORIES ABOUT FAMILY PROBLEM SOLVING

We now turn to analyze a series of existing partial theories about family problem solving. These theories are "partial" for three reasons. First, none of them attempts to explain everything about family problem solving. Some focus on effectiveness as a dependent variable, and some do not. All have been chosen for examination here, however, because we feel that they have direct implications for problem-solving effectiveness. Second, none of them claims to provide a complete explanation of whatever they attempt to explain. That is, each theory suggests some important factors which are asserted to be related to some aspect of family problem-solving performance, but none claims to provide the only, the best, or the most detailed explanation. Finally, these theories are partial because the structure of their explanations is not fully integrated. That is, the deductive or causal mapping of relationships among key variables is not spelled out so that the network can easily be judged to be optimally connected or in need of revision. Working from theories which are partial in the above ways has several implications for an integrative theory-building effort.

First, whenever a phenomenon to be explained is very abstract (e.g., family problem solving), it is unlikely that a single dependent variable will be sufficient to cover the entire range of the domain of interest. Thus in selecting effectiveness as our dependent variable of interest, our theory will necessarily only be partial in the scope of the phenomena to be explained. Moreover, it will not be any more comprehensive than the source theories from which it is drawn.

Second, it is always presumptuous to claim a complete explanation of any phenomenon. Thus our own theory of family problem-solving effectiveness may not be the only, the best, or the most detailed explanation possible. However, it seems reasonable to argue that theories vary in the degree to which their explanations are complete in this sense. For example, single-factor theories are likely to be less adequate than multifactor theories, and theories which posit no interactive or contingent relationships are likely to be less adequate than those which do. By drawing from the insights of several existing partial theories, we hope to develop a theory which can provide a more complete explanation than any of the original ones can provide separately. This does not mean that even more complete explanations are not possible or desirable.

Finally, structural incompleteness has implications for the language of theorizing. The source theories which we will examine vary in the extent to which their assertions are formalized and explicit. All of them tend to adopt a discursive or narrative mode of presentation, although clear expressions of propositions are often identifiable. At the same time, the assertions which are advanced tend to yield lists of propositions in a "set-of-laws" format (Reynolds, 1971) rather than integrated networks of propositions. In many cases, embedded propositions can be formalized and recast into a network after the fact. We have attempted this exercise at several points, but space limitations prevent a demonstration of the procedure here (see Klein and Hill, 1972; Klein et al., 1973). Such recasting often reveals dangling propositions, redundancies, and other uncertainties about the relationships among variables or among propositions. One set of procedures we have employed to deal with these issues is provided in Exhibit 20.1.

It is tempting to conclude that a discursive format encourages structural incompleteness, and that the adoption of a formal language from the outset would alleviate many of these structural problems. Still, structural specificity does not guarantee structural completeness, since some theorists prefer a "set-of-laws" structure no matter what language they adopt. We do not want to leave the impression that we are critical of the theorists we will discuss for doing badly something they did not intend to do. Few of the partial theories we treat were designed to be explicit propositional networks. Instead, they were theoretical discussions introducing potentially important ideas. However, in many cases it is possible to transform these discussions into formulations with a higher level of precision. We surmise that the theorists under view here would be sympathetic toward this transformation, but they need not be faulted for failing to do it themselves.

Our intent is to express as much of our theory as possible in a formal language with a network structure. In this way we hope that the mechanisms of explanation are more explicit than in the source theories from which we draw, and that our theory is thereby less partial than earlier ones in the structural sense.

The partial theories to be examined below have been selected for several reasons. We wish to demonstrate that:

1. Family scholars have attempted to construct theories of family problem-solving effectiveness or

Exhibit 20.1.   Procedures for Inventorying, Formalizing, and Integrating a Dense Discursive Treatment of a Suspectedly Coherent Theory

Often one is perplexed as to how to make sense of rich discursive materials with potential theoretical significance. Here we offer the outline of a step-by-step strategy for dealing with this problem that has proved useful in our work. Its chief merits are that it organizes materials systematically and achieves some ''data reduction'' according to explicit criteria. Many steps involve assumptions and judgments, so that the process is not entirely mechanical. However, symbolic notation is substituted for substantive variables and relationships wherever possible in order to facilitate manipulation and to help remove the substantive biases of the analyst when making technical judgments. Since these procedures are explicit, they afford replication, reliability checks, and reasonable debate among members of a team of analysts working with common materials.

1. The manuscript is divided into manageable sections around identifiable themes. Each section is formalized and integrated separately via steps 2 through 6.
2. Key concepts are identified, translated into variables where necessary, and listed.
3. Bivariate propositions linking the variables are abstracted and placed on index cards using symbolic notation compatible with a causal imagery.
4. Cards are manipulated and arranged to produce a maximally connected network.
5. Ambiguities, redundancies, and dead ends are resolved.
6. A revised model is constructed that is as simple as possible but as complex as necessary to convey the mechanisms implicit in the text.
7. A master variable list is constructed and each variable assigned a suffix that identifies the section(s) in which it appears.
8. Variables are eliminated from consideration which do not meet one of these criteria: appearance in two or more sections, emphasis in the text (importance assigned by the original author, or the number of times used in a section), appearance as an intervening linkage or contingency that makes the effects of other variables vary, and appearance in other known theories.
9. The reduced set of variables is cross-classified in a matrix of direct effects, with antecedents along one axis and consequences along the other. The following tabulations are calculated: number of times appearing as a direct antecedent, number of times appearing as a direct consequence, number of times appearing as a contingency, and number of times appearing in a relationship affected by a contingency. These tabulations are then summed to form a connectedness score for each variable.
10. The variables are stratified according to their connectedness. The most connected variables are then selected for further analysis, based on an intuitive assessment of the distribution of connectedness.
11. Types of linkage are identified for each variable based on the following categories: has multiple antecedents and multiple consequences, has multiple antecedents and a single consequence, has a single antecedent and a single consequence, has multiple antecedents and no consequences, has no antecedents and multiple consequences, has no antecedents and a single consequence. (This classification scheme has proved to be effective in dividing variables into roughly equal-sized groups. Other schemes may be required with other theories to achieve the same results.)
12. Separate causal models are constructed for variables in each linkage category. These models are successively appended to the previous ones, working from the most connected to the least connected category. This iterative procedure yields a master causal model that is consistent, clear, well organized, yet still complex.
13. The master model is examined to locate transitive relationships that can reasonably be eliminated under the assumption that they add no information and can be derived from the sign rule.
14. The final reduced version of the master model is prepared and subjected to whatever further assessment is desired.

theories that bear on family problem-solving effectiveness; that is, we need not and must not begin from ''scratch'' without the benefit of prior insights.

2. Some of this theorizing has continuity; that is, some of it deals with a shared range of ideas, and some of it builds upon previous work in the list of source theories treated here.

3. There is variety in the approaches taken; that is, the emphases in the various source theories cover a broad enough range to make their integration problematic and to provide a justification for taking stock of this domain at this time.

These selection criteria make it likely that some potentially relevant work has been rendered residual. For example, there are a large number of appealing partial theories in the small-group literature which could profitably be translated, one by one, into a family context with varying degrees of modification required. There is a vast

literature on family problems that certainly has implications for a comprehensive theory of family problem-solving effectiveness. Also, the current emphasis on the family as a decision-making system by home management researchers and educators adds relevant material (Gross et al., 1973; Deacon and Firebaugh, 1975). While the range of work already existing in the social sciences and even in the family field is quite large, we hope to provide a theoretical focus and organization for this material that so far has been lacking.

Straus's Communication Block and Cognitive Style Theories

Murray Straus (1968) was concerned with explaining the empirical relationship between social class and problem-solving effectiveness, especially to problems of adaptation to rapid social change. His data from a cross-national study of family triads exhibited a positive relationship between social class and problem-solving performance; i.e., working-class family groups had less success at solving a laboratory problem than did middle-class families. A better understanding of the causal mechanism linking social class to problem-solving effectiveness may some day provide the basis for a class-specified theory of family problem-solving effectiveness.

Straus explored several possible explanations with his data, many of which were methodological rather than theoretical in focus, and he concluded that two were most adequate: a "communication block" theory and a "cognitive style" theory. The basic proposition of the communication block theory is "that group problem solving is impeded if members of the group lack the communication skills to share items of information needed for the solution, or if the organization of the group inhibits such communication" (418). Straus cited 17 social psychology and family references which presumably provide plausible arguments or research evidence consistent with this proposition. The basic proposition of the cognitive-style theory is "that the solution of novel problems demands a flow of ideas to be tried as possible solutions . . . and working-class persons have had less opportunity to develop the mental flexibility needed for this type of creativity" (419). No prior work is cited in support of this proposition, but it appears to be reasonable.[2]

Several reservations need to be kept in mind regarding Straus's theories and research, most of which he has acknowledged. First, the class differences in problem-solving effectiveness were all in the expected direction, but were of small magnitude and not statistically significant in the U.S. sample, except in later trials. This may mean that middle-class families learn through experience to play the game successfully faster than working-class families, but it may also mean that the task does not discriminate very well between classes in industrialized societies vis-à-vis overall performance. Straus claimed that the task was not sufficiently difficult to produce the expected gap between classes in the U.S. (423).

Second, although the class differences in communication and creativity were large for all samples, the relationships between communication and problem-solving effectiveness and between creativity and problem-solving effectiveness were quite modest, especially in the U.S. sample. More importantly, communication and creativity each explained little of the variation in problem-solving effectiveness; i.e., the partial correlations between social class and effectiveness first holding communication constant and then holding creativity constant were only slightly less (between 11 and 20 percent less) than the zero-order correlations in both cases. Thus additional factors are likely to be crucial for an adequate explanation of family problem-solving effectiveness.

Third, only part of the multivariate structure of the proposed explanation was tested. Social class was not introduced as a statistical control, the relationship between communication and creativity was not explored, and the independent effects of these three variables on effectiveness were not assessed. Thus, it is difficult to recast Straus's explanation in terms of a fully specified and integrated causal model.

Fourth, communication was not experimentally controlled to enable a systematic assessment of its effect on problem-solving effectiveness.

Fifth, operationalizations of the key variables raise further issues. Would measures of social class based on ordinal scaling or other status characteristics show more complex relationships than that revealed by a dichotomized class variable based on a single component? The measure of effectiveness used does not require that family members coordinate their activity. Thus, does the way participation is distributed among family members affect group performance? Likewise, does it matter how creativity is distributed among family members? Finally, does the relative emphasis placed on verbal versus nonverbal communication affect performance differently for different social classes? Straus warned, for example, that high levels of verbal interaction may be counterproductive in large working-class families where the scarcity of privacy leads to a "norm of civil inattention" (426).

The major contribution of Straus's theorizing has been to focus on family organization, interaction, and cognitive abilities as potentially important factors in the family problem-solving process. As a result, further theorizing and research have been stimulated.

Tallman's Structural-Cultural Theory

Irving Tallman has built upon Straus's work in several ways. He has incorporated Straus's ideas in a more complex theory (Tallman, 1970), he has tested a portion of this expanded theory (Tallman and Miller, 1974), and he has used a research procedure that has much continuity with Straus's game simulation (Straus and Tallman, 1971).

Tallman's theory of family problem-solving effectiveness, which can be considered a "structural-cultural" theory, focuses on the following types of explanatory concepts: existing structural arrangements, cultural beliefs, interaction variables, and personality traits. Exhibit 20.2 presents a nearly exhaustive list of these variables and indicates their ultimate impact on family problem-solving effectiveness.

Tallman's theory includes Straus's key variables, amount of communication and creativity, but these ideas are treated in a somewhat different fashion. Instead of viewing communication and creativity as independent factors associated with separate explanations of family problem-solving effectiveness as Straus apparently did,

Exhibit 20.2   Ultimate Impact of Antecedents on Family Problem-Solving Effectiveness (Tallman, 1970)

Exogenous Variables

Opportunity to manipulate the environment (+)
Prior family problem-solving effectiveness (+)

Personality Variables

Self-esteem (+)
Esteem for other family members (+)
Individual responsibility for seeking solutions (+)
Probability of defining a situation as problematic (+)
Parental willingness to relinquish prerogatives (+)

Interaction Variables

Number and diversity of contributions (+)
Solution orientation (a)
Amount of critical evaluation (+)
Degree of error correction (+)
Extent to which a personal contribution is felt (+)
Degree of communication centralization in the organizing
  phase (+)
Objectivity of evaluation (+)
Extent to which leader encourages contributions (+)
Extent to which efforts are coordinated (+)
Amount of problem seeking (+)

Structural Variables

Freedom from conformity pressure (+)
Openness of communication channels to competent members (+)
Degree of goal and role consensus (+)
Centralization of authority (+)
Developmental flexibility (+)
Extent of division of labor (+)
Amount of affection and support (+)
Elaborateness of language codes (b)
Adequacy of role performance (+)
Legitimacy of authority (+)
Congruence between affect and power distributions (+)
Likelihood of coalition and clique development (−)

Cultural Belief Variables

Degree of belief in mastery over nature (+)
Extent to which distributive justice beliefs are merit-based (+)
Legitimacy of distributive justice beliefs (+)
Impersonality of relational belief (i.e., universalism) (+)

a = indeterminant because opposing effects operate through different mechanisms or intervening paths.
b = indeterminant because the variable operates only as a contingency or conditioning factor upon a particular process.

Tallman links these ideas in a common causal process, represented by the following diagram which is excerpted from our interpretation of his larger model:

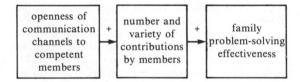

"Openness" incorporates the organizational feature which Straus argued was an important aspect of family communication patterns. Notice that "openness" does not guarantee that the amount of intrafamily communication will be high, but it provides a setting which should encourage high rates of communication. "Openness," as represented here, is also specified according to the distribution of competencies in the family group. Tallman discusses the developmental implications of this idea, and we will take this up at a later point. Here we wish to focus on the location of communication and creativity in the model.

"Contributions" appears to be conceptually related to both communication and creativity. Indeed, it can be argued that creativity, operationalized as the number of different solutions suggested, is one indicator of "contributions." But creative suggestions about solutions are only one possible kind of task-relevant contribution. Discussions of the nature of the problem, procedural matters, and so on, might also provide indicators of

"contributions." Furthermore, not all interaction that takes place in a problem-solving setting will necessarily be task-relevant. Therefore, global measures of the amount of communication may contain extraneous or at least conceptually distinct elements.

These considerations suggest a hierarchy of progressively limited types of communication that might occur during problem solving: (1) all communication, irrespective of whether or not it is task-relevant, (2) task-relevant contributions, and (3) novel or creative solution ideas expressed. It appears, therefore, that Tallman adopts a middle ground in his attempt to interrelate communication and creativity. He views creativity as one of several types of communication and takes a subset of all communications that includes creativity, namely task-relevant contributions, as the crucial theoretical factor directly affecting family problem-solving effectiveness. Straus appears sympathetic to these distinctions, since he refers to creativity at one point as an indicator of communication content (Straus, 1968:419).

The complexity of Tallman's theory can be appreciated. Since it was originally expressed in a mostly discursive format, we attempted to identify its implicit structure by inventorying, formalizing, and integrating the key ideas therein. In the space of less than nine journal pages, we were able to locate 39 distinct variables and 61 distinct propositions interrelating those variables (Klein et al., 1973). Each of these ideas could be expressed at about the same level of abstraction without redundancy. That is, the theory could not be folded into a more compact version except by an arbitrary criterion that eliminated ideas appearing to be less "central" (which reduced the minimum number of elements to 20 variables and 33 propositions). The reliability of our effort is not known, although several members of our team attempted this exercise on two or more occasions, with somewhat different results each time.

We belabor the point about the complexity of Tallman's theory for an important reason. Its mode of expression in combination with its density of theoretically relevant ideas makes this work subject to varying substantive interpretations. Therefore, it should be discussed, and, more fundamentally, it should be used by others as a guide to further research with a high degree of care and caution.

Nevertheless, Tallman's structural-cultural theory has several valuable features which permit us to make use of it in formulating our own theory. First, it adds the complexity which seemed to be deficient in Straus's earlier theorizing. It suggests a range of phenomena that need to be taken into account in an adequate theory of family problem-solving effectiveness. Second, it builds on theory and research in the social psychology of small groups, making important modifications in order to apply more accurately to a family context. Third, it gives clues about possible relationships among key variables so that a causal model may be constructed. Finally, it can stimulate research, as our brief discussion of one attempt will now demonstrate.

Tallman and Miller (1974) sought to discover the effects of two primary factors on family problem-solving effectiveness, and to see if either helped explain a social class difference in effectiveness which they observed in their data. This difference was similar to the one Straus had observed earlier, except that it was statistically significant in the Tallman-Miller U.S. sample. The two factors of interest to Tallman and Miller were "verbal capacity" and family power structure.

In his previously developed theory, Tallman (1970) had argued that openness of communication structures and elaborateness of language codes should facilitate family problem-solving effectiveness. Open communication permits the sharing and evaluation of ideas through group discussion. Elaborate language codes had previously been shown to be characteristic of middle-class persons and to facilitate a person orientation rather than a position orientation during family interaction (Bernstein, 1962; Hess and Shipman, 1965). A person orientation was now theorized to encourage the flexibility required to organize for problem solving according to situational exigencies. For Tallman and Miller, therefore, verbal capacity was conceptualized as consisting of a quantitative dimension (openness and amount of communication) and a qualitative dimension (elaborateness of speech style). The greater verbal capacity of white-collar families was predicted to account for their greater problem-solving effectiveness.

In the earlier version of the theory, Tallman also had asserted that a centralized family power structure would facilitate problem-solving effectiveness by providing the required coordination of efforts. Here, however, Tallman and Miller argued that congruence between the normatively prescribed family power structure and the actual power structure (i.e., conformity to power structure norms) would be the important mechanism by which family power would influence problem-solving effectiveness. In white-collar families, egalitarian actual power was predicted to increase family problem-solving effectiveness, whereas in blue-collar families, husband-father dominated actual power was predicted to increase effectiveness.

In effect, Tallman and Miller took a segment of Tallman's earlier theory, modified it, and tested it. Straus's amount of communication variable was reassessed in terms of verbal capacity, but his creativity variable was not, and additional variables were introduced.[3]

The results obtained by Tallman and Miller (see also Miller, 1976) suggest that none of the aspects of verbal capacity are related to family problem-solving effectiveness, nor do they account for social class differences in effectiveness. Most surprising is the failure to replicate Straus's positive relationship between amount of communication and family problem-solving effectiveness. Tallman and Miller actually found a modest inverse relationship between these two variables.

With regard to the effects of power structure on effectiveness, the predicted patterns were obtained and the results were reasonably consistent whether the expenditure decision-making or game leadership measures were used. Tallman and Miller interpret an observed negative relationship between the self-esteem of the white-collar husband-father and his game leadership as support for the idea that these men are able to defer to other family members out of a position of strength, whereas blue-collar husband-fathers are more rigid in their concern over maintaining their authority. Still, blue-collar families appear to maximize their problem-solving effectiveness when a husband-dominant power structure is maintained, while white-collar families are more effective when their power structure is decentralized. Elsewhere, Tallman and Miller have offered a *post factum* explanation of the relatively poor performance of blue-collar families which are not led by the husband-father. They suggest that he either is "discredited and preempted from playing the expected role of leader and decision maker" or else is simply incompetent in that role (1970:43).

It is tempting to conclude that all propositions regarding verbal capacity or communication have little or no merit in a theory of family problem-solving effectiveness, and that power and especially conformity to norms about family power play a more important role. However, the first part of the conclusion faces the somewhat contradictory findings by Straus, and this contradiction has not yet been reconciled.[4] Furthermore, there are other reservations to keep in mind about the Tallman-Miller effort.

First, the social class differences in effectiveness did increase slightly in the later (silent) trials, suggesting the learning effect which Straus had previously observed. What would happen if the sequence of this manipulation was randomized? Even though the importance of verbal communication may not be as great as previously asserted, what about the role played by nonverbal communication?

Second, only a small portion of Tallman's original theory has been systematically tested, so that the effects of additional variables on the family problem-solving process are unknown. For example, although the distribution of successful influence attempts has been investigated, the distribution of communication (especially creativity and other task-relevant behaviors) among family members has not been assessed.[5]

Third, crucial aspects of the explanatory mechanisms to which Tallman and Miller restrict themselves were not directly studied. For example, norms about power and person versus position orientation were inferred to be operating in expected ways but were not measured.

Fourth, certain measures may be problematic, as was suggested to be the case in Straus's research. For example, Tallman and Miller examined power in a limited number of ways, and elaborateness of speech style was measured for only one family member and not during problem-solving interaction.

Fifth, design differences may account for the new findings reported by Tallman and Miller as well as the different results obtained by Straus. For example, the efficacy of an egalitarian power structure in white-collar families might be reduced if parent-daughter triads were studied.

Finally, and perhaps most importantly, one or two studies do not provide a firm basis for either accepting or rejecting a theory, and additional research with efforts to replicate design parameters is clearly needed. It is also likely that the generalizability of these findings may be limited to certain types of family problems, as Tallman and Miller acknowledge (1974:24). For example, the SIMFAM game places time constraints on problem-solving behavior. Four minutes were permitted for solving each of the game rules, and families solved about half of these rules on the average. Tallman and Miller (1970) have acknowledged that white-collar families may not be better problem solvers, just faster (Riessman, 1962). If so, it is possible that the class differences in effectiveness would disappear for problems with little or no time pressures involved. This observation also has implications for appropriate measures of effectiveness (i.e., quality of solution versus time taken to reach one).

In spite of these reservations, we would argue that major gains have been made as a result of the work by Tallman and his associates. Theoretical and methodological issues have been both broadened and sharpened, providing the basis for shaping a more integrated theory.

Cohen's Communication-Style Theory

Rosalyn Cohen (1974) investigated an idea which Straus had earlier suggested in passing and which Tallman and Miller had studied in terms of speech patterns, namely, that social classes differ in the communication style which is most effective for each during family problem solving. Cohen carried this idea further by proposing that white-collar families rely on high levels of verbal communication, whereas blue-collar families rely on high levels of nonverbal communication to facilitate effectiveness. In addition, Cohen was interested in the role which communication style plays in family problem solving independent of social class considerations, as well as in replicating the Tallman and Miller findings with respect to leadership patterns.[6]

Among Cohen's findings, two important ones were that visual interaction did account for some of the variation in family problem-solving effectiveness, but that it did not differentiate between classes in the expected way. Even though blue-collar families engaged in visual interaction slightly more often than did white-collar families, moderate amounts of visual interaction were more conducive than high amounts to family problem-solving effectiveness for both classes. Visual interaction seemed to facilitate problem solving for the white-collar families, especially when combined with verbal communication. In contrast, high rates of visual interaction reduced effectiveness of problem solving for blue-collar families. Also, white-collar families performed slightly better overall when they started with a talking trial, while blue-collar families performed slightly better overall when they started with a silent trial. Cohen suggested that these last results point to the possibility that early game experience establishes performance patterns that are hard to break.

Several of Cohen's findings are of interest because they either corroborate or contradict earlier findings. First, no overall class difference in family problem-solving effectiveness was found: This contrasts both with Straus and with Tallman and Miller, discussed above. Second, for both classes, the rate of verbal communication was positively and significantly related to family problem-solving effectiveness as measured by game performance, but verbal communication and effectiveness were unrelated when the latter was measured in terms of the ability to verbalize the game rules. This is consistent with Straus's findings but contradicts those of Tallman and Miller. Third and finally, both classes performed best when two (unspecified) members shared task leadership. This contradicts the interaction effect between class and leadership pattern reported by Tallman and Miller.

The fact that many of Cohen's findings were not statistically significant, and her sample relatively small, means that they should be viewed cautiously. Still, the lack of consistency in findings across studies is striking. With regard to the class differences in family problem-solving effectiveness, Cohen suggested that the sequence of talking and silent trials may help explain the difference between her results and those of Tallman and Miller. By having all families engage in talking trials first, Tallman and Miller may have given white-collar families an initial advantage which carried over to the silent trials. However, this explanation does not account for the positive relationship between social class and family problem-solving effectiveness found by Straus.

Furthermore, satisfactory explanations for the discrepant results regarding verbal communication and leadership pattern as factors in family problem solving remain to be advanced. It may be that overall rates of communication are less stable predictors of family problem-solving effectiveness than is the distribution among members or the content of communication. Furthermore, neither Tallman and Miller nor Cohen had very many families that exhibited egalitarian leadership (9 percent to 18 percent depending on sample and social class), so that the findings here may be judged cautiously. In any case, most of the support for the class leadership interaction effect was based on the pregame decision-making task which only Tallman and Miller used. Finally, neither study directly measured norms about family power, so the negative effect of deviance from power structure norms upon effectiveness is still a moot assertion.

The theorizing and research by Straus, Tallman and Miller, and Cohen can best be summarized as attempts to uncover organizational, interactional, and cognitive factors which affect family problem-solving effectiveness and which do so differently according to the social placement of families. Tallman's theory is the most comprehensive, and only a few of its features have yet been subject to empirical investigation. Still, there is at least some support for the following variables as effectiveness facilitators: amount or rate of verbal communication, amount or rate of visual interaction, creativity, and a legitimate power structure (i.e., one which is compliant with attendant norms). No support yet exists for speech style as a factor in family problem-solving effectiveness, but this phenomenon has so far been examined only superficially. Finally, other forms of nonverbal behavior have yet to be studied for their effects on family problem-solving effectiveness.

We now turn to theories that have been formulated independently of the series already considered, and which become progressively dissimilar from that series.

Turner's Decision-Making Theory

Ralph Turner's approach to family problem solving, which appears in a small segment of his family textbook

(1970:111–16), is similar to Tallman's (1970) in several respects. Both were independently developed at about the same time and were responsive to the same body of social psychological literature. It is not surprising, then, that similar variables and mechanisms are asserted to be important in the problem-solving process by these two scholars. Furthermore, both theories are presented in a discursive and densely packed format. However, as far as we know, Turner's theory has not yet directly stimulated any research with family groups. We will highlight the major elements in Turner's theory, paying special attention to its convergence with and divergence from other theories and to crucial issues which it raises.

Turner places family problem solving within the context of a more general decision-making process. All decision making is said to begin with a problem, and the outcome sought is a solution to the problem (101–11). It is for this reason that we have labeled his theory a "decision making" theory. Alternatively, it is possible to view problem solving as the more general process within which decision making plays a major role, perhaps as one of several phases (Aldous, 1971). Propositions abstracted from Turner's discussion and their implications are treated below.

1. The role of creativity in family problem solving:
   1a. The amount of information acquired about a problem positively influences the number of alternative solutions considered, and the number of alternative solutions considered positively influences the effectiveness of family problem solving.
   1b. The complexity of the problem positively influences the strength of the relationship in Proposition 1a.

As was the case in Straus's and Tallman's theories, Turner asserts that it is important for families to consider a wide range of solution alternatives in order to maximize family problem-solving effectiveness. He notes that research comparing the relative effectiveness of individuals and groups demonstrazes that groups are better able than individuals to generate large amounts of information about a problem and, thereby, to produce more alternative solutions from among which the best solution can be selected. However, this idea must be specified according to the nature of the problem. Individuals are better able than groups to solve simple problems. This suggests that the complexity of a problem determines the amount of information exchange required to solve it. The introduction of "amount of information acquired" as a variable in this sequence points to the role of information searching in problem solving. This phenomenon is beginning to be systematically explored in family research (Straus, 1971).

2. Factors stimulating creativity:
   2a. The diversity of member background and orientation positively influences the degree of

conflict among members, and the degree of conflict among members positively influences the number of alternative solutions presented.

2b. The openness of family members (and especially of the more powerful members) to alternative solutions positively influences the number of alternative solutions presented.

2c. The extent to which a solution alternative is important to a family member positively influences the number of alternative solutions presented.

Given that the creative examination of a problem is necessary in order to solve it, the question arises as to how best to stimulate such creativity. Turner notes that groups, including families, often draw on a limited range of solution alternatives, preferring to adhere to familiar solutions used for familiar problems. The implication is that new problems may require novel solutions. Furthermore, Turner calls attention to research which demonstrates that a dominant power figure tends to impose his or her own preferred solution unless steps are taken to increase the resistance of subordinates and to generate some initial conflict. The implication here is that power figures tend to be conservative and less open to novel solutions than subordinates. Turner suggests that if a novel solution is especially important to a subordinate, that person will try harder to overcome the resistance of a stubborn authority. Finally, Turner observes that since families combine two kinship lines and diverse age and sex subcultures, they are in a good position via this heterogeneous experience and orientation to offer a wide range of solution alternatives.

By way of caution, it should be pointed out that conflict or dissensus may lead to an interminable struggle that prevents the selection of one solution for implementation. Thus conflict may need to be combined with openness in order to increase the range of suggested solutions which receive serious consideration. Although Turner does not clarify the factors which might encourage openness, Tallman (1970) has suggested that self-esteem and a sense of mastery over nature are two possibilities. Beyond this, Turner suggests that openness and commitment to solution alternatives may be compensatory mechanisms for getting ideas aired. That is, even if some family members are not open to alternatives, these may still be voiced if they are important enough to the members who hold them.

The change in focus from the discussion of creativity to its antecedents needs to be appreciated. In the former case the reference is to alternatives *considered,* while in the latter case the reference is to alternatives *presented.* There is no guarantee that an alternative presented will be given consideration by the family group. Turner's next series of propositions is designed to bridge this gap.

3. The role of evaluating contributions during family problem solving:

3a. The number of alternative solutions presented positively influences the number of alternative solutions considered.

3b. The extent to which relevant competencies are equally distributed positively influences the strength of the relationship in Proposition 3a.

3c. The extent to which areas of competency are segregated by position in the family inversely influences the strength of the relationship in Proposition 3a.

Turner suggests that the factor which determines whether or not ideas presented receive a serious hearing and fair appraisal is a cognitive "censoring effect" with two manifestations: a conception of differential competency and a conception of mutually exclusive areas of competency. Although Turner does not emphasize this point, the age and gender composition of families is likely to influence both the distribution of a single competency and the distribution of several competencies. Hence it may become important in future refinements of his theory to take into account such variables as the degree of role segregation and the degree to which the family power structure is centralized, as well as the developmental changes in these variables as families move through the life cycle. For example, as children become older, the distribution of competencies in families may tend to homogenize in certain respects. This would suggest that the alternative solutions offered by families with older children are more likely to be given consideration than the alternative solutions offered by families with younger children. Therefore, we would expect families with older children to consider a wider range of alternative solutions and ultimately achieve qualitatively better solutions than families with younger children. However, other factors may be operating as well. For example, if there is consensus in the family that certain members are incompetent to contribute to the discussion of solution alternatives, more may be gained by excluding these incompetent members than is lost by having a restricted range of ideas available. Considerations such as these were taken up by Tallman (1970), so that Turner and Tallman may be considered to complement one another on this issue.

Special care is required in interpreting Proposition 3a. While it should be understood that this proposition probably does not operate apart from the contingencies specified in Propositions 3b and 3c, it can be considered from other perspectives as well. First, Proposition 3a is likely to operate within natural limits. It is especially difficult to give a fair consideration to very many solution alternatives when time pressures exist. Also, the possibility of information overload comes into play when a large number of ideas are expressed. Thus time constraints and upper limits on the capacity for information processing are likely to influence the extent to which presented ideas are evaluated. Second, a simple correlation between the number of ideas presented and the number considered may mask a learning process whereby a member's participation is extinguished over time as his or her ideas fail to be given consideration. This possibility points to the value of considering the historical context in which family problem solving occurs and not just a single episode of problem solving.

Another critical issue may be the extent to which objective competencies correspond to subjectively conceived competencies. Turner emphasizes the cognitive or perceptual aspect of competency assessment, but we have rephrased his assertions to leave open the way in which competencies might be measured. It should be clear that if family members fail to appreciate competencies which actually exist, valuable information will be lost. Furthermore, if members disagree about the distribution of competencies, the attitudes of the more powerful members are likely to prevail and the effectiveness of the solution finally selected may suffer in the sense that all members will not be equally satisfied with the outcome. For example, children may begin to feel that they are competent before parents are willing to acknowledge and accept such developments. If this occurs in the context of preemptive decision making on the part of the parents, children may resent the fact that they were not allowed to fully participate in the problem-solving process. As a consequence, children may engage in strategic behaviors to undermine the effectiveness of the adopted solution.

Because of these considerations, the assertion that the age of children positively influences the effectiveness of family problem solving must be viewed cautiously. An important determinant of family problem-solving effectiveness may be the degree to which family members are flexible or adaptable to developmental changes in perceived and actual competencies. Training children to be competent, autonomous, and responsible problem solvers may be one way of maximizing the range of alternative solutions considered when group problems are encountered. Again, these ideas have been explored by Tallman (1970) and others (Hess and Shipman, 1965; Kohn, 1969; Bee, 1971).

A deficiency in Turner's theory is that it does not carry out the full implications of the evaluative process. This is perhaps most evident in the following observation. Even though getting many ideas thoroughly evaluated may be important for effective problem solving, this does not guarantee that one solution alternative, let alone the best one, will be selected. Thus the heart of decision making, supposedly Turner's special concern, is not examined in any detail.

4. The role of risk taking in family problem solving:
    4a. The degree of risk taking influences the effectiveness of family problem solving; this relationship is curvilinear such that extreme levels of risk taking (high or low) are associated with low effectiveness and moderate levels of risk taking are associated with high effectiveness.

    4b. The extent to which the responsibility for problem-solving outcomes is diffuse positively influences the degree of risk taking.

    4c. The extent to which family relationships are well defined (positions secure) and harmonious (i.e., the degree of mutual support) positively influences the degree of risk taking.

Elsewhere, Tallman has considered the role of risk taking in family problem solving (Tallman et al., 1974), so that once again we find continuity between these two theories. Here Turner argues that moderate amounts of risk taking facilitate family problem-solving effectiveness. While the consideration of novel solutions would appear to involve some risk (e.g., the risk of ridicule for bringing up unconventional ideas or the risk of uncertainty and possible failure associated with novel solutions), it is not clear that novel solutions would always be the most effective ones. Also, it is not clear whether risk taking operates directly on family problem-solving effectiveness as we have stated, or whether it also operates indirectly via its effect on the number of alternative solutions presented or considered.

In any case, Turner argues that when the responsibility for the outcome rests with the member who suggests a risky decision, the risk is less likely to be taken than when the responsibility is diffused within the group. Also, "the willingness to take risks is undoubtedly greater when the individual is assured of social support and when his social position is secure. The latter condition should apply to a strongly bonded family unit, when relationships within the family are well defined and harmonious" (1970:114). Turner seems to have in mind here the idea of family integration as an antecedent of risk-taking behavior. The question of how to combine a high degree of integration with high degrees of heterogeneity and conflict is not explored, but it would seem to be crucial for Turner's theory. Perhaps integration permits conflicting points of view to be aired within a constructive climate.

The way we have expressed these propositions involving risk taking, very high levels of responsibility diffusion and family integration would produce high enough degrees of risk taking that solution effectiveness would be retarded. Instead, it may be more accurate to assert that at least Proposition 4c is curvilinear in a way similar to Proposition 4a. Thus moderately low *or* moderately high levels of integration would lead to moderate levels of risk taking and, thereby, maximize family problem-solving effectiveness, whereas extremely low *or* high levels of integration would make risk taking unlikely. This modification seems intuitively appealing because it suggests the imagery of an "overadjusted" family immobilized in the face of new demands.

Despite its ambiguities and omissions, Turner's theory accomplishes two important objectives which assist in developing a comprehensive theory of family problem-solving effectiveness. It not only shares some common ties with the other work already reviewed, but it also opens up new avenues of exploration. One interesting difference between Turner's theory and the ones considered earlier is that it is the only one which is not organized around an attempt to explain social class differences in family problem solving. This may be viewed either as a shortcoming or an advantage. It is a shortcoming in that a potentially important variable is omitted and some of the continuity with other theories lost. This deficiency can be partly overcome, however, by specifying the values of Turner's antecedent variables which families of different classes attain. The failure to date to find clear-cut and consistent relationships between social class and family problem-solving effectiveness implies either that social class has been overemphasized as a factor in the past or that different problem-solving processes apply to the various classes. Although the second of these implications seems more appealing at the present time, if the first is correct then it becomes a productive strategy to focus on other mechanisms at the expense of social class.

Aldous's Group Comparison Theory

Of all the theories treated here, the one developed by Joan Aldous (1971) is the most intricate. It is ambitious enough in the range of ideas covered to perhaps warrant the label "the omnibus theory of family problem solving." This theory shares all the assets and liabilities of Tallman's and Turner's theories associated with format of presentation, breadth of coverage, sources, internal organization, and heuristic value. As proclaimed by the title of Aldous's work, "A Framework for the Analysis of Family Problem Solving," this contribution might best be considered a conceptual perspective rather than a theory. We will highlight the primary foci of the framework, emphasizing its distinctive features.

First, one of Aldous's main purposes is to compare families and ad hoc groups on characteristics relevant to problem solving. The value of doing this has been stressed before. The volume of research on problem solving in contrived groups is quite large in comparison to research on family problem solving, and if a theorist wishes to translate propositions and hypotheses from the former domain to the latter, he or she should be cognizant of required modifications. This stylistic feature of Aldous's framework has led us to use "group comparisons" to label her theory.

Aldous uses the results of these comparisons to identify places in the problem-solving process where families should have strengths and weaknesses relative to ad hoc groups. This emphasis on comparisons leads Aldous to concentrate on descriptive rather than predictive statements. Thus, for example, she advances the "hypothesis . . . that the pressure to work for a quality solution to a problem is generally less among families than among more self-conscious problem solving groups such as committees or task forces" (267). While such

statements might be exactly what is desired in order to do careful comparative research, they must be recast to draw out their implications for family problem-solving effectiveness. From the above example, for instance, one might want to assert that self-conscious analysis facilitates effectiveness (measured qualitatively). We have attempted to perform this recasting where necessary, the results of which are discussed later.

A second distinctive feature of Aldous's framework is its emphasis on phases in the problem-solving process and its critique of pure rationality. Systematic theorizing and research on phasing during family problem solving are only in the embryonic stage (e.g., Hill, 1970; Straus, 1971; Aldous et al., 1974; Tallman et al., 1974). Since the analysis of these phases is more compatible with a cybernetic than a causal imagery of theory, we leave this analysis for the most part residual. A bridge between these strategies might be found if it could be argued and demonstrated that adequacy of performance in one phase of problem solving influences adequacy of performance in subsequent phases (as Hill has demonstrated for several economic domains, including residential changes, durable goods acquisitions and job changes, among others, 1970).

With respect to rationality, Aldous asserts that families are at a disadvantage compared to other groups or to some ideal. Thus families operate with less than complete knowledge of possible alternatives, pursue solutions in order to "get by" rather than to maximize effectiveness, seldom define problems explicitly or plan their attack against them, act out of expediency, thrive on excitement and surprise rather than plodding analytically through a situation, and operate with less than complete control over outcomes (267–69). While such characteristics may indeed be valid for most families, they do not change the direction one would take in formulating a theory of family problem-solving effectiveness. Thus from Aldous's insights we extract the idea of "phasing rationality" and view it as a facilitator of effective problem solving.

A third distinctive feature of Aldous's framework is her careful differentiation between problems of coordination and problems of creativity. From her discussion it is possible to pull out many propositions which argue that the mechanisms for maximizing effectiveness under these two conditions are different or even opposed. At the risk of oversimplifying, these two mechanisms involve a well-defined and expediently organized group structure and process for problems of coordination and an open, flexible and methodical group structure and process for problems of creativity. Family research that fully explores and tests the implications of these two problem-solving strategies has yet to be designed and carried out. It might be that all family problems require some degree of coordination *and* creativity so that the distinction is not as simple as it first appears.

Finally, Aldous's framework is unique in its balanced focus on three primary structural characteristics of family groups: affect, communication, and power. While earlier work had acknowledged these dimensions and even researched one or two of them at a time, Aldous's theory provides the first attempt to explore the richness of each of these aspects of group life and their implications for family problem solving. It might even be accurate to say that she constructs three partial theories, one out of each dimension and begins to show how they overlap.

In Exhibit 20.3, we present a nearly exhaustive list of variables that we have identified in Aldous's theory and summarize the direction of their ultimate or net effect on family problem-solving effectiveness where it is possible to do so. This array masks the mechanisms asserted to be operating, but those can also be determined via careful linguistic analysis and integrating procedures (see Exhibit

20.1). The eight groups in the table have been provided as an expedient device for organizing the total set of variables. Although the classification might be challenged at some points, the fairly good fit of variables in separate categories suggests that there are a limited number of basic dimensions or global factors that are important for a theory of family problem-solving effectiveness.

We wish to call attention to a few of the more interesting variables in Exhibit 20.3 which suggest ideas not yet discussed with respect to Aldous's theory or other theories.

"Playfulness" is an orientation which Aldous stresses as a problem-solving facilitator. By not taking a problem too seriously and by striving to make problem solving a pleasurable experience, families can not only reduce

---

Exhibit 20.3. Ultimate Impact of Antecedents on Family Problem-Solving Effectiveness (Aldous, 1971)

Task Variables

Ability to manipulate the situation (+)
Problem complexity (b)
Extent to which problem is voluntarily defined (+)
Cooperation requirements (b)
Creativity requirements (b)

Structural Input Variables

Prior group organization (a)
Focus on group maintenance (a)
Group cohesiveness (a)
Focus on socialization (−)
Life cycle stage (+)
Resource adequacy (+)
Social and legal responsibility for the group (−)
Diffusion of responsibility for group performance (+)

Power Structure Variables

Degree of power structure organization (+)
Centralization of power structure (−)
Sense of autonomy among group members (a)
Legitimacy of power (+)
Ascriptiveness of power structure (a)
Arbitrariness of power exercise (−)
Discrepancy between power and ability distributions (−)
Threats and promises by weak members (+)
Fear of power exercise (−)
Coalition formation (+)
Consideration of the views of weaker members (+)

Affect Structure Variables

Supportiveness of affect structure (+)
Amount of social reward exchange during problem solving (+)

Attitudes, Motivations, and Personality Variables

Boredom (−)
Anxiety (−)
Playfulness (+)
Tolerance for uncertainty (+)
Problem-solving persistence (a)
Self-esteem (+)
Threat to self-esteem (−)

Consensus Conflict Variables

Cultural homogeneity (−)
Intragroup conflict (+)
Ratio of issue-oriented to personality-oriented conflict (+)
Fear of competition (−)
Acceptance of individual differences (+)
Disagreement permissiveness (+)
Freedom from conformity pressures (+)
Agreement on solution (+)

Communication Structure Variables

Degree of communication structure organization (+)
Encouragement of all members to contribute (+)
Information sharing (+)
Proportion of information volunteered (+)
Development of a shorthand communication code (+)
Inability to communicate (a)
Refusal to understand (a)
Role-taking accuracy (+)
Directiveness of communication (a)

Process Variables

Phasing rationality (+)
Solution orientation (a)
Time to solution (a)
Risk taking (a)
Normative basis for evaluation (−)
Activity coordination (+)
Number and variety of alternative solutions considered (+)
Cooperation in solution implementation (+)

---

a = indeterminant because opposing effects operate through different mechanisms or intervening paths.
b = indeterminant because the variable operates only as a contingency or conditioning factor upon a particular process.

hostilities and stimulate creativity but also help make future encounters with problems attractive rather than demonic. Unfortunately, as Aldous warns, this orientation is probably not realistic for families with severely limited economic and other resources.

The notion of the "ratio of issue-oriented to personality-oriented conflict" suggests that it is not the amount or degree of differences of opinion within a family that alters the course of problem solving, but rather *how* these differences are expressed and managed that counts. Among other things, this idea can be used to qualify Turner's treatment of conflict in order to remove some of the ambiguity in his theory.

"Development of a shorthand communication code" adds a new wrinkle to the treatment of communication variables involving verbal capacity and visual interaction. In particular, Aldous's argument that this shorthand facilitates family problem-solving effectiveness runs against Tallman's unconfirmed expectation that an elaborate speech style promotes effectiveness. Verbal as well as nonverbal shorthand cues may play a larger role in the problem solving of well-established groups than most other aspects of communication.

Finally, Aldous's introduction of "cooperativeness in solution implementation" provides a needed safeguard against the temptation to view problem solving as ending when an alternative solution is chosen. Selecting a course of action is problematic enough for many families, but goal attainment is not assured by such decisions. Thus for many naturalistic problems the outcome cannot be determined in one "sitting" or one discussion session. The design of most problem-solving research in the social sciences probably blinds researchers and theorists alike to the time dimension involved here. It remains a challenge to cope with this shortcoming and with the methodological problems which make advances in this area difficult to achieve.

Like Tallman's theory, Aldous's framework recast as a theory can stimulate a great deal of needed verificational research on the antecedents of family problem-solving effectiveness. Like Turner's incipient theory, Aldous's has not yet provided that stimulation. Of all the theories discussed so far, Aldous's is the most difficult to translate into a system with theoretically grounded research implications, but it may also be the one with the most potential payoffs once this is accomplished.

Weick's Organized Confusion Theory

Karl Weick's contribution (1971) may be the most radical and provocative of all problem-solving theories advanced to date—in the sense of introducing overlooked factors affecting family problem-solving effectiveness but especially in suggesting alternative frameworks for viewing the entire process. His stated purpose is to "enrich the pool of conceptual mutations available to scholars" (31), and in so doing he departs from conventional thinking on the matter in significant ways.

Weick's analysis can be separated into three parts: a discussion of special properties of families as problem-solving units, the search for an appropriate family problem-solving metaphor, and a compendium of suggestions about the problem-solving process. Once again, the treatment is primarily discursive, so that we are forced to cull out the key assertions at a risk of leaving behind the essential context. We have coined the label "organized confusion" to reflect twin themes in Weick's essay. On the one hand, the principles governing the family problem-solving process are ultimately knowable and upon occasion may be articulated by family members, even if only after the fact and in a rationalized manner. In this sense, family problem solving is organized. On the other hand, the surface manifestation of family problem solving in operation is highly disorganized and difficult to grasp and conceptualize. In this sense, family problem solving is confusing.

Weick treats in detail 11 properties that he believes help distinguish families from other problem-solving groups:

1. Families work at solving problems when the energy levels of members are relatively low (i.e., at the beginning or end of the day).

2. Family members "mask" expert power and allocate responsibility for problem solving on the basis of legitimate power *unless* legitimacy is firmly established and sufficiently reaffirmed and roles are well defined and accepted.

3. Requisite knowledge for family problem solving is distributed unevenly among family members as is investment in the outcome; the most informed member values acceptance more than the quality of outcome and is, therefore, able to selectively control the flow of information to maximize acceptance at the expense of quality.

4. Since affection in families tends to be "noncontingent" (i.e., constant at a high, positive level), family problem solving is relatively independent of learning through reinforcement.

5. The discussion of family problems often occurs in "cascading" fashion (one problem "hitchhikes" along with another), indicating that family members can be more interested in releasing emotional tension than in bringing up concerns that they want attacked instrumentally or rationally.

6. Families have both a voluntary (psychic) and involuntary (biological, legal) membership component; psychic withdrawal is a potential threat and, thus, an instrument of power.

7. Family problem solving is "embedded" in ongoing activity rather than readily isolatable in the fashion of a council meeting; as a result it is difficult to know (as an insider *or* as an outsider) when problem solving is occurring; members may recognize that they have been prob-

lem solving only retrospectively (after the solution has already been reached).

8. Family problem solving occurs in relative isolation from outside influences (it is "encapsulated") and thus is likely to become stylistically rigid within a given family group.

9. Many family problems contain a "developmental confound"; that is, they are best left untreated and relegated to "normal, natural trouble" that will pass with time. Family members also vary in their developmental sensitivities, some assuming constancy of each other's traits and behaviors and others anticipating developmental change.

10. Families carry over large amounts of "unfinished business," and members lack consensus on criteria of satisfactory problem resolution; thus presumed solutions to one problem evoke new problems.

11. The ecology of families is relatively disorderly and gestural, and body cues are cryptic at best.

What can be made of this provocative caricaturing of family properties and problem-solving contexts? On the one hand, we are alerted to the possibility that unique aspects of family life make family problem solving different from problem solving in virtually any other group. Of course, this remains only a possibility, since we do not have sufficient research to know whether or under what conditions the above characterization is accurate, nor do we have sufficient research carried out under such conditions to know whether the presumed differences affect problem solving in significant ways. Weick emphasizes the need for this kind of research, and we endorse his recommendations.

On the other hand, the above characterization does seem to have clear implications for problem-solving *effectiveness*. Family problem solving, in Weick's view, is a messy business. It is relatively unstructured and full of distractions and roadblocks. It should be possible to convert each of his 11 descriptions into one or more variables which inversely affect problem-solving effectiveness. If it can be assumed and eventually demonstrated that families vary sufficiently from one another on these characteristics, then the same variables can be expected to play a role in an adequate theory of *family* problem-solving effectiveness.[7]

Thus the following variables might be treated as antecedents of family problem-solving effectiveness (with facilitating values in parentheses): energy level of members (high and uniform), basis of power (expertise), information distribution (evenly dispersed, information shared), consensus among members on criteria of effectiveness (high), affection (contingent upon prior problem-solving effectiveness), number of problems considered in a given session (one, or else clearly separated on the agenda), problem embeddedness (low), boundary maintenancy for information search (low), developmental flexibility of members (high and evenly distributed), process termination (when a mutually satis-

factory solution is reached), ecological setting (structured to facilitate communication).

Taken in this vein, most of Weick's variables do not appear so novel as they might otherwise. The important question is whether or not such variables are really variable and manipulable. From an ameliorative viewpoint, one would expect problem-solving effectiveness to be maximized in cases where families set aside special times when members are fresh, alert, and motivated, and when the setting promotes open and effective communication. It is not farfetched, under these circumstances, to view the family problem-solving session as a sort of council meeting (Dreikurs and Grey, 1970).

One final observation about Weick's caricature of unique family properties is in order. If it could be argued that families are as effective on the average as any other group in producing solutions to their problems *despite* the handicaps which Weick addresses, then the problem for theory and research becomes one of locating those compensating features of families which permit them to perform as well as they do. While Weick's discussion at points seems to follow this line of reasoning, he gives no clues as to what might be involved in these compensating mechanisms beyond post hoc dissonance reduction through rationalization. Since Aldous (1971) *has* considered some of these mechanisms, an attempt to integrate the ideas of these two theorists has promise.

The second major part of Weick's theory-building attempt is his search for an appropriate family problem-solving metaphor. Several of these metaphors are discussed:

A. Metaphors about cognition and behavior
    1. "The detective": scientific puzzle solving; rational, planned, goal-oriented, deliberate; the more dominant metaphor, according to Weick
    2. "The creator": scientific ingenuity; active, exploratory, goalless, unsystematic, quasi-random, retrospective

B. Metaphors about group boundaries
    1. "Same old faces": closed system, stable membership, high familiarity and frequent interaction, stable history of interaction; the more dominant metaphor, according to Weick
    2. Multiple generations: fluid membership by the addition of strangers and departure of veterans, varying composition and interaction network by situation, attempted socialization by veterans and resistance by the less experienced

C. Metaphors about environmental perspectives in groups
    1. "The malevolent environment": competition against a threatening world, internal cohesion, assertiveness, vigilance and suspicion, group solidarity rigidly enforced
    2. "The capriciousness environment": absurdity,

socioemotional expressiveness, lack of control, passivity toward or minimization of problems
D. Metaphors about groupness
   1. The family as a group: feelings of togetherness, coordinated activity, shared meanings and values; the more dominant metaphor, according to Weick
   2. The family as a nongroup: retrospective construction of group characteristics (especially when problem solving is embedded), ambivalence in commitment to group, search for individual identity, asymmetrical social influence or coercion rather than mutual accord

Weick argues that the metaphor which the scientist adopts as well as that which his subjects adopt greatly influences the image of family problem solving which emerges. This is undeniably an important issue, especially when the image held by a scientist fails to match that in the families being studied. Also Weick's assertion that the detective, same-old-faces, and group metaphors predominate in the literature seems reasonable, since these metaphors are emphasized in most of the other theories surveyed in this chapter.

There are at least two lessons for a theory of family problem solving in this discussion of metaphors. First, we need to know how each metaphor or combination of metaphors is distributed among the families we study. To date we remain almost entirely ignorant on this point, having relied on assumptions about such metaphors without checking them out empirically. For example, if the metaphors can be shown to vary by social class, ethnicity, or religious affiliation, their predictive utility will be enhanced. Second, family scholars need to be more careful and explicit about the metaphor or combination of metaphors they adopt to characterize family problem solving.

Any theory-building attempt involves some selection among metaphors. The reader will already have noticed that we've adopted more of a detective than a creator metaphor in our own theory (family problem solving as goal-oriented activity, and so on). In part, this reflects our attempt to mirror what is already known or assumed about family problem solving. Also, the creator metaphor, at its extreme, verges on indeterminism to such a degree that it would be impossible to make it the basis for a systematic theory. With respect to the other metaphors we hope to be more open and inclusive.

The third and final portion of Weick's treatment provides a compendium of ideas about problem-solving processes in families about which, Weick laments, we know very little. These ideas can be summarized as follows:

Attention Span

Problem-solving skills in families are heterogeneous (due to the typically peculiar age composition of families). In particular, the attention spans of members are unevenly distributed. Attention span is inversely related to solution orientation (pressing for a quick solution). A group's attention span is a function of the shortest individual span in the group. Attention span is positively related to retrospective construction of meaning. Uncertainty in a situation inversely influences attention span. Attention span (length of and homogeneity of) positively influences family problem-solving effectiveness.

A number of other derived propositions and hypotheses can be developed out of the foregoing list. The thrust of the discussion, however, clearly points to factors that ought to affect family problem-solving effectiveness.

Problem-Solving Templates

Groups develop increasingly complex ways of knowing.[8] These ways of knowing, or templates, are successively accumulated as groups develop and are successively discarded as groups dissolve (the evolutionary process is reversible). The amount of ambiguity in a problematic situation positively influences the extent to which regression to more primitive templates occurs. The degree to which "groupness" is stressed in a family is positively related to template complexity (groups with weak social ties use more primitive information-gathering processes, and so on). The number and complexity of templates utilized positively influence group (and therefore) family problem-solving effectiveness.

If we can put aside the formidable problem of conceptualizing and measuring knowledge templates, Weick's assertions have interesting implications. They suggest that families become "better" problem-solving units over time as long as group cohesiveness is maintained. They suggest that the information-processing rules which families apply depend on the nature of the problem (the ambiguity in the situation). If it could be established that the development of knowledge templates is related to social class, an explanation for class differences in family problem-solving effectiveness could be formulated.

Certain difficulties remain in this imagery, however, difficulties that go beyond operationalization. If the minimum level required to solve a problem is controlled, the number of templates used should be directly related to the level of the highest one available. Thus Weick's assertions about the effects of the number and complexity of knowledge templates on problem-solving effectiveness are partly redundant. This difficulty can be overcome if number and complexity eventually become weighted differentially in importance, or if the requirement of stepwise regression toward more primitive templates can be relaxed so that some groups can be observed to leapfrog backward toward more primitive ways of knowing. Furthermore, it is hard to appreciate that failure to solve a problem at several decreasing levels of complexity is indicative of effective problem solving. Perhaps the number of templates used should be defined in terms of their range *across* problematic situations, so that a family that uses a wide range of knowledge systems in a wide variety of settings would be viewed as having the requisite flexibility to solve many kinds of problems. Finally, if Weick's insights about individual differences are applied to this context, the possibility that family members will have different levels of template development must be taken into account (perhaps in the same way that heterogeneity in attention span is asserted to affect problem-solving performance). For example, the evolution of more complex knowledge templates as the family moves along its life span may be in part attributed to the increasing maturity of its younger members in their levels of cognitive development. At some point in the life cycle of the family (when the pressures for independence by children reach their peak, roles become ambiguous and ties between parents and children weaken), one might expect a regression toward more primitive knowledge templates.

Severity

Family members are likely to differ in the degree of severity they attribute to a given problem. Consensus on severity is developed in one of three ways: regression toward mean severity as members mutually influence their definitions of the situation, drift toward low severity when families tend to avoid problems and/or if perception of severity is positively related to attention span, and drift toward high severity when the member perceiving the problem as most severe has the most investment in and power over the outcome.

It seems obvious that the severity (importance?) attached to a problem (individually and collectively) will affect the way in which a family will deal with it, although Weick does not speculate as to what these effects might be (probability of defining the situation as "normal, natural trouble"?). However, an implicit assumption here is that consensus on perception of severity positively influences family problem-solving effectiveness.

Means Interdependence

Groups form around diverse ends (goals) which require common means (coordination). As a result of coordinating their activities, groups develop common ends (mostly related to group maintenance) which, in turn, give rise to diverse means (division of labor). As members individuate once more and sense new ambiguities in their environments, ends diversify gain. This spiraling process continues among repeated events in an ongoing group and also characterizes the history of a group from its formation to dissolution.

Here we have presented only a capsule summary of a complex process described by Weick. While it has heuristic value, it raises as many questions as it suggests answers. Weick's main intent seems to be to impress upon us the cyclical interplay between individuation and collectivization in group life as well as to reassert the impor-

tance of the social construction and reconstruction of reality. How this model's methodological vagaries can be overcome and turned into problems for research is not addressed. The model's relevance for family problem solving is left to the reader to infer. While the model does suggest how goal consensus arises and thus warns that problem-solving groups are not merely and always oriented to solving collectively defined problems, the inverted means-ends sequence loses much of its force once a group has accumulated a history. One doesn't need to assert that families form around common ends or begin to solve a problem with a shared goal in mind in order to assert that goal consensus is an important facilitator of problem-solving effectiveness. Finally, Weick's assertion that the model is consistent with the retrospective construction of meaning is specious. The model is just as consistent with the view that group members are aware of the process described and define problems "realistically" according to where they are located in the process.

Throughout, Weick has attempted to challenge provincial thinking about problem solving in families. This attempt must be judged successful, although the net effect, we believe, has been to expand the content rather than to alter the form of the arguments in the theory. Above all, Weick draws attention to the distinction between problem solving as viewed by family scholars and problem solving as viewed by family members themselves, and presses us to take both conceptions into account and to close the gap between them where possible.

Reiss's Consensual Experience Theory

The final theory to be discussed in this section has been generated in conjunction with an extensive laboratory research program conducted by David Reiss and his associates over the last 10 years. Along with the work of Tallman and his colleagues, this program is currently the most active of those we have covered.

The distinctive feature of Reiss's theory is that it is built primarily upon a psychiatrically oriented social psychology. In contrast, all the other theories considered here are more sociological or small-group social psychological in origin and emphasis. Although this distinction is a matter of degree, one consequence has been a virtual absence of cross-fertilization of ideas and strategies between Reiss and the other theory-building teams or individual scholars.[9] As we shall see, however, many of the ideas which Reiss and his associates have advanced can be readily incorporated into the mainstream of theorizing about family problem solving.

Since Reiss's work is undergoing continual evolution (Reiss, 1973; Reiss and Costell, 1974), it is difficult to present a definitive summary of his ideas. We have chosen to focus on the version that appeared in 1971 (Reiss, 1971a, 1971b, 1971c). Fortunately, in spite of subtleties and embellishments, the key ideas in Reiss's theory can be simply stated.

The theory of consensual experience (Reiss's own label) begins with the notion that "each family develops its own shared and distinctive view or explanation of its environment and the patterns or principles that govern its people and events" (Reiss, 1971a:2). The fundamental proposition is that a family's orientation toward its environment affects its problem-solving performance.

Three modes of experiencing the environment are proposed. In the first, the environment is viewed as masterable. It is predictable, knowable, and controllable. At the same time, family members assist one another in interpreting the environment. Thus cues from the environment as well as from other members are fully explored. In the second mode, the orientation indicates a sense of mastery and trust as in the first mode, but family members approach the environment individualistically; they do not utilize the information about the environment which other members possess. In the third mode, the environment is viewed as threatening, chaotic, and unknowable. Family members utilize cues from each other but are ineffective in interpreting environmental cues.

Next, Reiss proposes a typology of families. The scheme incorporates the environmental orientations just discussed and adds distinguishing features of family interaction, perception, and cognition during problem solving. The characteristics of each type of family are summarized in Exhibit 20.4.

Reiss judges this classification scheme to be consistent with studies from at least 14 clinical and five nonclinical sources. These sources, along with Reiss's preliminary research, suggest that certain populations may differentially exhibit the three family types. Environment-sensitive families are most often to be found in the middle class where there is no serious psychopathology and in a Jewish culture with an Eastern European origin. Interpersonal distance–sensitive families are most often to be found where a member is an overt delinquent or has other character disorders. Consensus-sensitive families are most often to be found in the working class where a member is diagnosed as schizophrenic and in a culture with southern Italian origin. The psychiatric properties of these populations (normal, delinquent, and schizophrenic) are later used to assess the theory and the viability of the family classification scheme.

Next, Reiss discusses three dimensions of family problem-Solving performance: "effectiveness," elsewhere called "configuration" (Reiss, 1973), "coordination," and "closure." The nominal and operational definitions of these dimensions are summarized below.

Problem-Solving Effectiveness

"[The] contribution that the family, working as a group, makes to the problem's solution" (1971a:11); the extent to which a solution is subtle, detailed, and highly structured as opposed to being coarse, simple, and chaotic. Operationalization: complexity of solution during the family trial of a pattern recognition, card-sorting task; increase in complexity from an individual trial to a family

---

Exhibit 20.4. Characteristics of Three Types of Families (adapted from Reiss, 1971a)

Environment-Sensitive

1. Joint perception of environment as masterable and trustworthy
2. Sensitivity to cues from environment and from each other member; cue intake maximized
3. Consensus on the nature of the problem; problem viewed as externally given and impersonal
4. Logical search for solution
5. Open exchange of information among members; information objectively evaluated
6. Delayed closure on solution until as much evidence as possible is examined
7. Agreement on solution

Interpersonal Distance–Sensitive

1. Joint perception that problem analysis and solution are means for individual to demonstrate independence and individual decisiveness and mastery
2. Cue intake from environment maximized but not exchanged among members
3. Joint perception of information sharing as weakness and that actions cannot be evaluated by other members
4. Solution selected quickly on the basis of little information, or indefinite accumulation of information without closure on a solution

Consensus-Sensitive

1. Joint perception of environment as threatening, chaotic, and unknowable
2. Cue intake from other members maximized, but little cue intake from environment
3. Joint perception that problem analysis and solution are means to maintain uninterrupted agreement; no dissent tolerated
4. Consensus on solution reached early without consideration of environmental information unless that information is distorted or oversimplified
5. Sense of order derived from predictability of the responses of other members

trial; increase in complexity from the initial individual trial to a final individual trial, with an intervening family trial.

Coordination

"[M]embers' ability and willingness to develop problem solutions similar to each other" (1971a:13), with agreement based on a shared universe of experience. Operationalization: standard deviation of members' trial times; similarity of solutions among members.

Closure

"[The] family's proclivity for suspending or applying ordered and coherent concepts to raw sensory experience" (1971a:13); speed with which a solution is adopted and maintained despite additional information. Operationalization: stability of solution across trials; ratio of time spent in the first half of a trial to the total time spent during the trial.

The theory of consensual experience culminates in a cross-classification of family types and dimensions of problem-solving performance. This matrix is reproduced in Table 20.1. In clarifying the matrix, Reiss speculates that interpersonal distance–sensitive families might score a bit higher, on the average, than consensus-sensitive families do on problem-solving effectiveness (1971a:13). Also, interpersonal distance–sensitive families are expected to be variable on closure, either because some of them rush to a solution while others never reach one (see Exhibit 20.4) or because members within such a family use differential pacing of closure to demonstrate their individuality or independence from other members (1971a:15). Reiss emphasizes that the measure of problem-solving effectiveness reflects quality of performance only from the researcher's point of view. Interpersonal distance–sensitive and consensus-sensitive families might be just as effective in problem solving if the definition of the problem were taken from their perspective. Thus interpersonal distance–sensitive families will judge the problem as one of demonstrating personal competence, while consensus-sensitive families will judge the problem as one of joining forces against a hostile (research) environment.

The empirical assessment of Reiss's theory to date (1971b, 1971c) has yielded two important findings. First, the three dimensions of problem-solving performance appear to be independent components and to be factorially loaded by the expected sets of variables (1971b). Second, the three types of families drawn from psychiatrically diagnosed populations match up reasonably well with the expected patterns of problem-solving performance scores (1971b, 1971c).

Despite these generally positive results, a number of issues remain. Some of the problems signaled by these issues can be treated as deficiencies in the theory itself, while others are questions which Reiss acknowledges need further analysis within the framework of the theory.

1. Are problem-solving effectiveness and closure independent dimensions? While Reiss argues that his theory demands and his results support an affirmative answer (1971b), inspection of Table 20.1 raises doubts about this. Indeed, both within and across types of families, the theory seems to argue that effectiveness and closure will be *inversely* related. The failure to demonstrate this inverse relationship with his samples might be viewed as a weakness of the theory. The larger issue is whether effectiveness, coordination, and closure *should* be expected to be independent of one another. If they are in fact empirically independent, then it will be difficult to argue that they are causally related. So far, Reiss appears to expect that, within type of family, these dimensions will be functionally or causally interdependent.

2. Has the independent variable (orientation toward the environment) been adequately measured? So far, Reiss has used a sampling design based on psychiatric diagnosis criteria to identify types of families. He has not, however, demonstrated directly that these samples vary in their orientations toward the environment or that family members share their orientations. Part of the problem here is that the description of family types (see Table 20.1) contains elements of both independent variables (orientations, cognitions, perceptions) and dependent variables (problem-solving interaction patterns). At points Reiss refers to the problem-solving dimensions as "dimensions of family orientation to the environment" (1971a:4) and as "dimensions of family consensual experience"

Table 20.1. Cross-Classification of Family Types and Dimensions of Problem-Solving Performance (adapted from Reiss, 1971a)

TYPE OF FAMILY	DIMENSIONS OF PROBLEM-SOLVING PERFORMANCE		
	Effectiveness	*Coordination*	*Closure*
Environment-sensitive (Normal)	High	High	Low
Interpersonal Distance–sensitive (Delinquent)	Moderate to low	Low	Variable
Consensus-sensitive (Schizophrenic)	Moderate to low	High	High

(1971a:11). The result of this conceptual confusion is that it is difficult to determine the theorized causal ordering among variables. It appears, then, that Reiss has constructed a model that is closer to a conceptual typology than to a theory. But while he suspends the question of causality with the available data, he does acknowledge that the question is important to his efforts (1971a:3).

3. Would the observed relationships hold using a different sampling design or different task situations? This is a question for future research rather than a criticism of Reiss's work to date. However, its implications are crucial for family problem-solving theory. Within a sample of "normal" families, can the three types of families be identified, perhaps along social class lines? More generally, how do class and psychiatric diagnosis interact to affect environmental orientations, and by what mechanism? What about tasks that are less obtrusive from the research standpoint? That orientation to the environment may affect problem solving seems especially reasonable when problems are externally imposed, as is typically the case in family research. Thus the research context becomes part of the relevant environment. Would these orientations be expected to play such an important role when problems are defined as residing within the family and not requiring surveillance or information provided by outside agents?

Setting aside these conceptual and methodological issues, Reiss's work has several important implications for a comprehensive theory of family problem-solving effectiveness. First, it alerts the theorist and researcher to the potential effects of environmental orientations on problem-solving performance. Second, it points to the potentially pervasive influence of shared attitudes and perspectives within a family on problem-solving effectiveness. Third, it reminds us that the evaluation of family problem-solving performance may depend on whether the insiders' or outsiders' perspective is taken. Finally, it cautions against an uncritical classification of problem-solving performance concepts. Do coordination and closure, for example, influence problem-solving effectiveness, or are these really three independent aspects of the same underlying construct?

By now the parallels between Reiss's theory and the theories discussed previously should be apparent. We close this section by highlighting some of these convergent themes.

The environment-sensitive type of family resembles the ideal portrayed in most other theories, especially with respect to openness of communication and information acquisition as well as delayed closure on solutions. For example, we might expect interpersonal distance-sensitive and consensus-sensitive families to be characterized respectively by the communication blocks and inhibited creativity which Straus (1968) isolates. Tallman (1970) goes further by explicitly including the belief in environmental mastery as an independent variable in his theory.

An explanation for the frequently postulated class differences in problem-solving effectiveness is suggested by Reiss's speculation that families will sort themselves into types around socioeconomic characteristics.

Consensus and conflict, which figure most prominently in theories by Tallman (1970), Turner (1970), and Aldous (1971), take on added importance in Reiss's theory. Instead of emphasizing the functional consequences of consensus and conflict at various points in the problem-solving process, Reiss argues that shared organization and interpretation of experience are universal, although they take on different forms in different families. Thus we might expect consensus to affect family problem-solving effectiveness in different ways depending on the level at which it is conceptualized.

Weick's focus on the personal criteria which family members use to analyze problems is mirrored by Reiss's distinction between the insider's and the outsider's perspective.

There is a noticeable overlap between the content of some of Weick's metaphors and Reiss's family types. In particular, the "malevolent environment" and "capricious environment" metaphors seem to characterize consensus-sensitive families equally well. To the extent that these metaphors are distinct alternatives, the consensus-sensitive family type may be broken down into subtypes. Weick's failure to identify an environmentally masterful and trusting metaphor may reflect his attempt to go beyond the predominant ways of stereotyping families. However, Reiss's environment-sensitive families appear to approach problems from the perspective of Weick's "detective" metaphor. Finally, Reiss's interpersonal distance–sensitive families might distinguish themselves from environment-sensitive families on Weick's metaphors about groupness with the former operating as nongroups and the latter as groups in the more traditional sense.

TOWARD AN INTEGRATED FORMAL THEORY

To this point we have traveled through much of the terrain of family problem-solving theory. Along the way we have encountered theories ranging from the relatively simple (Straus, Reiss) to the relatively complex (Aldous, Tallman). We have noticed sequential and inspirational linkages among some of the efforts (especially Straus, Tallman, Cohen) as well as somewhat novel approaches (Weick, Reiss). We have been alerted to verification attempts in some cases (Straus, Tallman, Cohen, Reiss) but not in others. We have pointed to fortuitous overlaps in perspective (e.g., Turner with Tallman) as well as the idiosyncracies of each theory.

Since we are primarily engaged in theory building rather than in evaluating existing ideas, this chapter might start rather than culminate here. However, our specific aim is to integrate what is known or assumed about the factors affecting problem-solving effectiveness. Thus it is important to reflect existing ideas as accurately as possible in our theory, to organize them in a parsimonious yet inclusive way, and to make judgments about controversial claims and issues. There may be several ways to accomplish this juggling act (Klein, 1974), but it would not be possible at all unless the existing body of theory was carefully examined first. An additional advantage of preserving the integrity of existing theories at the outset is that each may spawn continuing refinements and modifications through additional research and/or guesswork. One way to make future theorizing about family problem solving manageable is to focus on a single perspective and to fully explore its potential. While the task before us is to integrate the full range of materials that have been indexed, a less ambitious but more selective

strategy is likely to have payoffs as well, eventually creating the need for other attempts at integration.

In order to present our theory in a coherent format, the following procedures are adopted. First, the variables from all examined source theories are identified and each is placed under one of several umbrella concepts judged to best capture the nature of the variable. Second, each block of variables is internally examined, definitions are proposed, and the relationships among variables within a block explored. Third, causal relationships among entire blocks of variables are proposed, primarily in terms of their existence and direction. Finally, relationships among particular variables located in different blocks are identified and their parameters specified. While these steps reflect the process used to organize our theory, the presentation begins by examining interblock relationships

Figure 20.1.   Block Diagram of Factors Affecting Family Problem-Solving Effectiveness

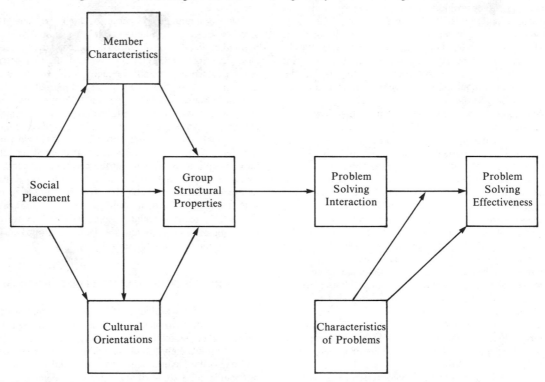

Problem-solving effectiveness—the degree to which family problems are solved, to the mutual satisfaction of family
      members
Problem-solving interaction—the behaviors of family members as they attempt to solve a problem of mutual concern
Characteristics of problems—aspects of the task situation which identify the type of problem occurring
Group structural properties—organizational features of a family which exist prior to the onset of problem-solving
      interaction
Cultural orientations—systems of shared beliefs, values, and meanings in a family regarding the relationships among
      members and the relationship of the family to its environment

at the general level, next explores intrablock definitions and relationships, moving in the direction from consequent to antecedent block, and successively introduces interblock relationships among particular variables as each additional block is appended. Available empirical support for relationships will be examined along the way.

Certain precautions should be borne in mind regarding these procedures. The number and titles of blocks have been developed inductively and intuitively, so that they have no finality about them. Assignment of variables to a single block has hazards which we will identify shortly, after the basic block structure is indicated. The number of variables in a block is based on collapsing redundant ideas from two or more sources or redundancies within a source. We have no evidence that this application of the procedure has been reliable, but our earlier work suggests that high intercoder reliability can be achieved with sufficient training. Finally, interblock relationships are presented recursively (unidirectional causality), but we appreciate that feedback processes are likely to occur. Some of the more likely ones will be briefly discussed as we proceed.

The primary categories of factors asserted to affect family problem-solving effectiveness and their causal mechanisms are indicated in Figure 20.1.

It should be clear that the model in Figure 20.1 is not a theory, but its purpose is to orient the reader to the basic structure of a proposed theory. Predominantly sociological concerns are represented by the inclusion of social placement, cultural orientations, and group structural properties and their effects on a group-level outcome, family problem-solving effectiveness. Predominantly psychological concerns are represented by the inclusion of member characteristics and their effects. The mix of these concerns is accentuated by incorporating family interaction as an intervening link between more remote antecedents and problem-solving effectiveness, and by allowing for variation in outcome and in the process of reaching the outcome according to situational factors (characteristics of problems). It might be equally important to justify why linkages between certain blocks have not been included. At this point we argue only that additional linkages are not ruled out in principle, but the ones drawn are expected to be the strongest and most consistent.

Before examining the missing details of the block diagram, certain classification problems require comment. Ideally, variables derived from the source theories could be unambiguously allocated to one and only one of the identified blocks. The following issues are relevant, however, and we have no clear-cut means of dealing with them.

Often, the only evidence for the existence of group structural properties comes from inferences made on the basis of observed or reported problem-solving interaction.[10] The preexisting structure is, thus, assumed to be mirrored in the structure which emerges via such interaction. While it is relatively easy to separate these two blocks conceptually, greater effort is required to obtain independent measures of corresponding variables in them.

The treatment of social placement and cultural orientations as distinct from group structural properties may be strained. This separation is a matter of convenience and, while the distinction between social placement and cultural orientation isn't especially problematic, group structural properties can be viewed as the remaining sociological variables.

The distinction between member characteristics and the group-level variables is difficult to maintain. This is because the characteristics of each member are often aggregated for analytic purposes and their distribution is treated as a group property. This problem is pervasive in the social sciences, and we have attempted to be sensitive to it throughout.

Having noted these caveats, we now begin to examine the structure of intrablock and interblock elements.

Problem-Solving Effectiveness

Earlier in this chapter we dealt with conceptual issues involving our dependent variable. Here we emphasize operational considerations.

We have found it useful to distinguish between two evaluative dimensions of effectiveness. The quality of a solution refers to the degree to which it meets some determinate standards. In family problem-solving research to date, solution quality has most often been measured in terms of the ability to solve game rules by trial-and-error activity (Straus, Tallman, Cohen), and in terms of the complexity or elegance of a solution where no solution is either right or wrong (Reiss). Occasionally, the ability to verbalize game rules (Cohen) and the time taken to reach a solution (Tallman) have been used to measure solution quality. Additional measures can be constructed which are tailored to the nature of the task, but all of them would address the degree of goal attainment in one way or another.

By calling for the assessment of solution quality according to determinate standards, we do not mean to downgrade the perceptual and personal nature of goals. Thus cognitive or perceptual measures of goal attainment are appropriate as well as more objective measures. So long as the goals of family members are identifiable and identical, and coincide with the goal structure perceived by the researcher, the measurement of solution quality at the group level is fairly straightforward. That these conditions may not always hold serves as a warning to the researcher who is concerned with the nuances of measurement involved here.

The other evaluative dimension of effectiveness refers to the degree to which solutions are jointly accepted by family members. While acceptance might be measured by subjective ratings on satisfaction with outcomes and satisfaction with the process by which an outcome has been reached, this procedure has not yet been employed in family research. Reiss (1971c) has measured the extent to which individual members working alone agree on a solution, but he views this as an indicator of tacit "coordination" rather than of effectiveness.[11]

In general, we suggest that quality and acceptance are both necessary for an effective solution to a family problem. Thus effectiveness will be a multiplicative function of scores on its two dimensions. However, it is likely that quality and acceptance will be differentially important, depending on the nature of the problem and the dispositions of family members. For example, if the problem is "deciding where to go on a vacation," it may not be possible to assign different qualitative values to the alternative vacation sites, even though members may be able to rank their preferences in a rigorous way. In such cases, the arrival at a solution which is maximally satisfying to all members may be the best indicator of problem-solving effectiveness. If, however, the problem is "how to pay for Johnny's college education," both dimensions are likely to be important. On the one hand, the dollar value of family resources can be compared with expected or actual costs and a goal discrepancy figure reasonably calculated. On the other hand, in order to maximize the family's ability to subsidize Johnny, he may have to work part time, and this might be a relatively unsatisfactory solution to him even if it was the solution adopted. In cases where there is only one correct solution (e.g., solving game rules), quality may be the overriding consideration, in part because no member will accept anything but the correct solution and all will be greatly dissatisfied if that solution is not reached.

When it can be safely assumed that quality and acceptance are perfectly correlated, a measure of both dimensions is not required. However, our purpose in introducing two *conceptually* independent dimensions to effectiveness is to caution against uncritically assuming their *empirical* equivalence. Even families that fail to solve a given problem by either objective or subjective standards may, nevertheless, be relatively satisfied with their performance, members mutually accepting their failure and even deriving some intrinsic rewards from the experience.

A final consideration involves the measurement of acceptance in its own right. While the degree of agreement on the choice of a solution can be handled by familiar measures of dispersion, the degree of satisfaction with a solution calls for more subtle analysis. The mean level of satisfaction in a group is an immediately apparent possibility, but it might also be argued that the degree of satisfaction expressed by the least satisfied member will be of critical importance. This latter option rests on the assumption that the effectiveness of a problem solution depends on its consequences for family functioning, and that one sufficiently disenchanted family member is enough to upset the effective implementation of a solution.

Since little is yet known about the way quality, acceptance, and their various indicators actually operate during family problem solving, more research is called for which incorporates a wide range of possible measures of effectiveness.

Problem-Solving Interaction

The ways in which the behavior of family members is organized for problem solving constitute the factors theorized to have the greatest immediate impact on family problem-solving effectiveness. The importance of interaction for problem solving is indicated by the strong emphasis it is given in virtually every problem-solving theory formulated to date. We propose four principal axes along which problem-solving interaction can be analyzed: its amount, its distribution, its sequencing, and its normativity.

The *amount of interaction* which occurs can be classified in several ways. The following variables emerge from the theoretical and research work to date:

1. Amount of verbal communication—the amount of talking among family members that occurs during problem solving (possible operationalizations: total acts, total acts per standardized time unit, etc.)

2. Creativity—the number of alternative solutions suggested (possible operationalizations: the number of distinct suggestions, each weighted by their originality); the originality of the solution adopted (possible operationalizations: the extent to which a solution is different from solutions previously adopted by a family)[12]

3. Elaborateness of language codes—the variety of linguistic expressions employed during problem solving (possible operationalizations: mean word length, mean phrase length; total time pausing, mean pause length; frequency of subordinate clauses, adjectives, conjunctions, etc.)[13]

4. Amount of support—the extent to which positive affect is transmitted among family members during problem solving (possible operationalizations: number of statements of encouragement, praise, endearment, etc.; ratio of positive to negative affect statements)

5. Amount of nonverbal communication—number of gestural cues transmitted among family members during problem solving (possible operationalizations: frequency and duration of looking at another family member; intonation and stress in speech; bodily expressions conveyed by posture and movement)

6. Amount of conflict—number of disagreements expressed during problem solving (possible oper-

ationalizations: number of different points of view regarding the issue under discussion; number of disparaging remarks or acts of rejection directed at other family members; ratio of issue-oriented to personality-oriented conflict).[14]

Distribution of interaction refers to the relative concentration of the values of variables like those just discussed in particular subunits of the family, including individual members. For example, support may be mutually exchanged within the marital dyad quite frequently but may occur infrequently among other family members or between either parent and other members. Likewise, one member may be the recipient of the vast majority of supportive statements, may dominate verbal communication, may contribute the most solution alternatives, and the like. Established sociometric methods and dispersion measures can be used to identify clique structures, stars, and diffusion with respect to any of the basic interaction variables already discussed. Whether or not family interaction is prone to be unevenly distributed among members is subject to debate. If families provide a learning environment stressing modeling mechanisms, interaction patterns are likely to homogenize across family members. Thus, for example, if one member begins to exhibit an elaborated language style, the probability that others will increases as well. We will see later that the distribution of interaction is influenced in large part by family structural properties.

While the distribution of interaction can provide evidence of leadership, at least three additional considerations are important in determining the family power structure during problem solving. The first deals directly with the ability to control the course of problem solving. Family members may differ in the extent to which their ideas are considered, agreed to, and eventually incorporated in the solution. Applying the distributive notion to this phenomenon, the following variable can be identified:

7. Centralization of power—the degree to which influence over the outcome is concentrated in a family member or subgroup during problem solving (possible operationalizations: mean difference between members in number of suggested solutions which receive consideration, in number of contributions agreed to as valid or acceptable; the reciprocal of the proportion of members whose original contributions are incorporated in the solution).

It should be noticed that power here refers to more than whose solution is adopted (i.e., who wins the decision-making battle), although in some cases this may be the best or only available datum upon which to describe the power structure. Usually, it should be possible to observe members differentially contributing to the definition of the situation, to the elaboration of factors and contingen-

cies which presumably need to be taken into account, and to the pacing of the process itself.

The second consideration with respect to power during family problem solving concerns its style. Some leaders may make their mark by being actively involved in the substance of the discussion, contributing many novel ideas, reflecting on and exploring the positive and negative ramifications of the ideas of others, making suggestions or demands and having them adopted and so on. Other leaders, however, may take on a facilitative role whereby they coordinate the activity of others without becoming embroiled in the substantive issues themselves. While this distinction has up to now been ignored in theories of family problem solving,[15] it is central in other work on group problem solving (see especially Maier, 1970). Assuming that at least one leader can be identified during family problem solving (or applying leadership style to behaviors irrespective of their distribution across members), the following variable is adduced:

8. Coordinative leadership—the extent to which leadership is facilitative during problem solving (possible operationalizations: number of questions asked, degree to which exploration of ideas and criticisms are encouraged, absence of evaluative statements, number of attempts to understand strange ideas, extent to which minority opinions and members are protected, number of attempts to transform disagreements into situational problems, absence of attempts to sell a solution, degree to which others are encouraged to reach a solution, degree to which ideas of others are summarized, frequency with which the nature of the problem is reiterated).

The third and, here, final consideration with respect to power during family problem solving concerns the basis upon which it is allocated (French and Raven, 1959; Smith, 1970; Raven et al., 1975). Although power in groups may have a number of bases, one important dimension is the extent to which power is either achieved or ascribed. Among the family problem-solving theorists treated in this chapter, both Aldous (1971) and Weick (1971) draw attention to power based on expertise, which is one way that achievement may be manifested. Perhaps more frequently power is ascribed to members in families according to age, gender, generational status, or some combination of these relatively immutable traits. Expert power needs to be differentiated from such ascriptions.

9. Expert power—the extent to which leadership during family problem solving is concordant with situationally relevant skills, knowledges, or experiences as opposed to achieved traits such as age, gender, or generational status.

Several precautions are in order regarding the interpretation of expert power. First, as the definition suggests, it is viewed as situationally variable. Thus an expert in one area such as the financial budget is not necessarily an expert in another area such as school curriculum options. Although impressions of expertise may generalize so that one family member tends to lead during all problem solving because of expertise in only a few past problem-solving contexts, this is not a requirement of our definition of expert power.

The second precaution concerns the chance cooccurrence of expert and ascribed power. It may be, for example, that the father is the expert in a number of areas so that the basis of power in those areas appears ascriptive according to gender and generational status. In order to determine the actual basis of power, therefore, it is necessary to accurately measure relative expertise and to apply it to the full range of problem contexts which families face. Only if leadership is more associated with expertise than it is with ascriptive traits can it be concluded that expert power is relatively high. Furthermore, if expertise itself tends to vary with ascriptive variables, as is quite likely to be the case in families with respect to age, then the extent to which power is based on expertise could be determined only by examining the relationship between expertise and leadership controlling for ascriptive variables.

The third precaution directly concerns the measurement of expertise. While it is reasonable to expect that objective and valid indicators of problem-solving skills, knowledges, and experience can be developed, the prevailing view of power bases stresses their subjective character (cf. Raven et al., 1975:219). Family members must all agree in their belief, whether accurate or not, that one member possesses superior ability in a particular problem-solving task in order for expert power to exist. We point to this issue only to once again call attention to the wider issue of objective versus subjective measures of variables in our model. The optimum strategy, of course, is to build both kinds of measures into a test of the theory.

The *sequencing of interaction* refers to the steps, if any, which families can be discerned to follow as they move from identifying a problem to implementing a solution and evaluating the outcome. The various steps or phases suggest a number of variables which we believe can be captured economically in one central idea, namely, phasing rationality.[16]

10. Phasing rationality—the orderliness with which a family progresses through the problem-solving process (possible operationalizations: time spent on problem identification relative to time spent seeking and selecting a solution; extent to which potential problems are labeled and allocated to separate treatments; time spent searching for information relative to total time problem-solving; extent to which evaluating potential solutions is delayed; objectivity of evaluation of alternative solutions; time to solution; extent to which commitment to a solution is provisional; degree to which members cooperate in implementing a solution; extent to which phases occur in sequence without skips; extent to which earlier phases are reinitiated when a later phase either stagnates or receives insufficient attention).

It is apparent that phasing rationality is a complex idea incorporating many possible indicators, few of which suggest measurement procedures. This situation reflects the curious fact that the components of this global variable have received much rhetorical endorsement but have resisted incorporation into research problems. We deem this to be a most fruitful area for future empirical inquiry. While the analysis of phasing rationality depends heavily on one's specification of phases, sufficient groundwork in classification schemes has already been provided to warrant more theoretically oriented efforts (Bales and Strodtbeck, 1951; Aldous, 1971; Patton and Giffin, 1973).

Even though others have argued that families tend, on the average, to be irrational or at least nonrational (Weick) or are rational within the limits of their resources (Aldous), these arguments do not eliminate the possibility that families vary in their rationality or can learn to change the degree to which they are rational. The value of phasing rationality as a variable in our theory depends, of course, on this possibility.

Normativity of interaction refers to the degree to which problem solving conforms to established norms about behavior in a family. In its broadest application, this idea encompasses the conformity to norms about the amount, distribution, and sequencing of interaction during problem solving. In practice to date, emphasis has been placed on the degree to which the distribution of power conforms to norms about power (Tallman and Miller, 1974). Having acknowledged the potentially wider application, we focus on the following variable:

11. Legitimacy of power—the extent to which power during family problem solving conforms to the normative expectations about power (possible operationalizations: mean satisfaction of family members with the behavior of the leader; similarity between survey responses to questions about power structure norms and observed power structure during problem solving).

The conception of norms we have in mind refers to personal beliefs about obligations to behave in particular ways. While these norms are undoubtedly influenced by the norms held by other family members, there is no assumption that family members share normative beliefs, i.e., that normative consensus is to be taken for granted. Likewise, this conception of norms does not include the structure of normative beliefs outside the family or the perception of these generalized beliefs by family members, although here again we would expect that personally felt obligations would be partially dependent on the broader cultural context of normative beliefs.

Finally, it should be noted that illegitimate power is indicated if a family member abdicates his or her position of authority as well as if he or she exceeds the prescribed level. So long as power is viewed in relative terms, this dual direction of deviance is likely to be appreciated. One consequence of this perspective is that a centralized power structure can be illegitimate in more than one basic way. Not only would such a power structure be illegitimate if the norms were equalitarian, but it also would be illegitimate if the norms called for centralization in a position other than that observed during problem solving. Norms about the amount, sequencing, and style of power are, of course, potentially as relevant as norms about its distribution. Thus the legitimacy of power can be empirically assessed in a number of fairly distinct ways.

Interrelationships among Interaction Variables

Because of their potential number, the relationships among interaction variables are likely to be complex. The proposed patterns of relationships are shown in Exhibit 20.5 and Figure 20.2, recognizing that indirect effects not specified are also likely to exist in some cases:

1. Leaving aside for a moment the distributive variables as well as the amount of nonverbal communication and conflict, which pose special analytic problems, the remaining interaction variables are asserted to be positively related in a manner similar to that in Figure 20.2 and Exhibit 20.5. Notice that the dependent variables in this set, creativity and verbal communication, are the primary independent variables in Straus's theory (1968) and that they are expected here to be positively but not necessarily causally interrelated. In effect, we expect verbal communication and creativity to be partially explained by other interaction variables and to be explained by similar causal processes. Support and phasing rational-

ity are not expected to be related because of the critical importance of the timing of support. Especially if mutual support occurs very early in the problem-solving process, a family may "rush to judgment" before having adequately considered alternative solutions. In general, however, a supportive atmosphere is expected to encourage the exchange of a variety of ideas. Also, expert power is expected to have its primary effect on phasing rationality. Power based on ascription is likely to make families solution-oriented and to restrict the generation of ideas in a way which underutilizes the talents of all family members (Aldous, 1971).[17] While the exact number and causal ordering of relationships among interaction variables may be crucial for some family theories, here our principal objective is to indicate that the variables in this set should be positively interrelated.

2. The distributive variables (centralization or concentration of . . .) are in general asserted to be positively related; that is, the extent to which interaction is evenly or unevenly distributed is expected to be characteristic of most of the ways of assessing interaction in a given family. Figure 20.3 and Exhibit 20.6 present one way of causally ordering the distributive variables. An exception to the general pattern involves the concentration of nonverbal communication. If, for example, one family member is doing most of the talking, the other members will be largely confined to communication by nonverbal means. However, evenly distributed verbal communication is also likely to be accompanied by evenly distributed nonverbal communication. In the absence of any firmly established or reasonable conditions in which concentrated nonverbal communication is likely to arise, this variable might be tentatively eliminated from consideration.

Additional sets of assertions are required in order to link the distribution variables in Figure 20.3 with the nondistributive variables in Figure 20.2.

3. Coordinative leadership and phasing rationality are

Exhibit 20.5. Propositions Involving Relationships among Selected Nondistributive Interaction Variables

1. The legitimacy of power exercised during family problem solving positively influences the extent to which leadership is coordinative.
2. The extent to which leadership is coordinative positively influences the amount of support exhibited during family problem solving.
3. The extent to which leadership is coordinative during family problem solving positively influences the elaborateness of language codes.
4. The amount of support exhibited during family problem solving positively influences creativity.
5. The amount of support exhibited during family problem solving positively influences the amount of verbal communication.
6. The elaborateness of language codes positively influences the degree of phasing rationality during family problem solving.
7. The extent to which family power during problem solving is based on expertise positively influences the degree of phasing rationality.
8. The degree of phasing rationality positively influences creativity during family problem solving.
9. The degree of phasing rationality positively influences the amount of verbal communication during family problem solving.
10. Creativity during family problem solving is positively related to the amount of verbal communication during family problem solving.

Figure 20.2. Proposed Relationships among Selected Nondistributive Interaction Variables

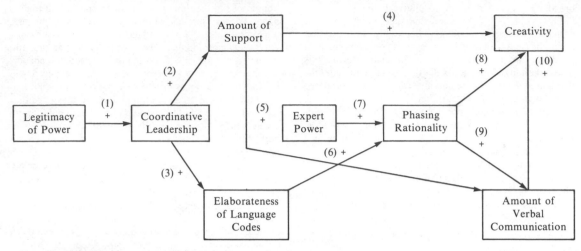

NOTE: Numbers in parentheses are provided to assist in cross-referencing with propositions in Exhibit 20.5.

asserted to inversely influence the distributive variables. Indeed, it might be argued that the primary purpose of coordinative leadership and phasing rationality is the democratization of problem-solving interaction. Again, however, an exception seems warranted. Coordinative leadership is expected to be positively related to centralization of power because a family in which every member is highly coordinative is unlikely to address any substantive issues at all. On the other hand, organizing for problem solving by centralizing power does not guarantee that power will be exercised in a coordinative fashion. Thus the empirical relationship between coordinative leadership and centralization of power should be weak and positive, but not causally determined.

Expert power is also likely to inversely affect the distributive variables, especially centralization of power. However, this relationship should hold only if expertise itself is evenly distributed. In any case, expert power should democratize problem-solving interaction only in the long run, that is, over a number of episodes. In any given problem-solving situation, interaction (and especially power) is likely to be concentrated if either an ascribed leader or an expert dominates.

4. At an abstract level, the normative dimension of

Figure 20.3. Proposed Relationships among Distributive Interaction Variables

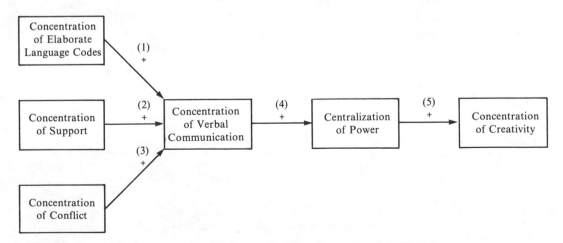

NOTE: Numbers in parentheses are provided to assist in cross-referencing with propositions in Exhibit 20.6.

Exhibit 20.6. Propositions Involving Relationships among Distributive Interaction Variables

1. The concentration of elaborate language codes in a family positively influences the concentration of verbal communication during family problem solving.
2. The concentration of support among family members during problem solving positively influences the concentration of verbal communication during family problem solving.
3. The concentration of conflict among family members during problem solving positively influences the concentration of verbal communication during family problem solving.
4. The concentration of verbal communication during family problem solving positively influences the centralization of family power during problem solving.
5. The centralization of family power during problem solving positively influences the concentration of creativity during family problem solving.

interaction is asserted to be unrelated to the distributive dimension. For example, the legitimacy of power is expected to be unrelated to the centralization of power, since it is possible for either a centralized or equalitarian power distribution to be legitimate. However, once the legitimate form of power is identified via other variables, it should be possible to predict whether power will be centralized or not in particular families.

5. It is asserted that the distributive variables will influence the interaction variables about which they are distributed. The nature of these relationships depends on the particular variables under consideration.

 a. The concentration of X_1 inversely influences the amount of X_1. For example, the concentration of creativity is expected to inversely influence the amount of creativity during problem solving. The rationale here is that more of something can be obtained by spreading it around the group. In the case of creativity, a snowballing or reciprocal reinforcement effect is expected. Creative suggestions from several sources stimulate even more creative suggestions. This kind of process is not expected to occur for verbal communication in general, since it is relatively easy for one family member to dominate a conversation without pauses and for some members to feel as if they have little to say even if given the opportunity. Furthermore, if every member talks a little bit, a family may foreclose further discussion under the assumption that it has achieved a democratic ideal, while if every member talks profusely and perhaps even simultaneously, relatively little information will be exchanged and effective communication will be reduced.

 b. The concentration of X_1 inversely influences X_2. For example, the concentration of support is expected to inversely influence creativity. The rationale here is that at least some family members require support in order to encourage creative suggestions from them. If only one or two members are supported, they will be the only creative ones (see Figure 20.3), and this concentration of creativity will retard overall creativity in the group (see point 5a, above). Several possible exceptions to this basic pattern seem warranted. First, it is unlikely that the distributive variables will affect

the amount of verbal communication for reasons already given. Second, the amount of nonverbal communication and the amount of conflict are expected to be positively influenced by the distributive counterparts of other variables. Thus, for example, concentration of elaborate language codes should positively influence the amount of nonverbal communication, and concentration of support should positively influence the amount of conflict. In the former case, the rationale is that the "audience" (members using restricted codes) must add nonverbal content to their messages in order to react to the elaborate speaker in an effective way. In the latter case, we assume that support is universally valued and to the extent that it is not evenly distributed, unsupported members are likely to disagree with the ongoing process. The hypothesized relation between support and conflict is best summarized as follows: If support is both high and evenly distributed, conflict is either unlikely or is issue-oriented when it occurs.

6. The final set of relationships among interaction variables involves the relationship of nonverbal communication and conflict to the other nondistributive variables (i.e., those in Figure 20.2).

 a. Coordinative leadership, phasing rationality, and legitimacy of power are all asserted to positively influence the ratio of issue- to personality-oriented conflict and to be unrelated to the amount of nonverbal communication.

 b. The amount of nonverbal communication is asserted to be inversely related to both the amount of verbal communication and elaborateness of language codes, while the amount of conflict is asserted to be positively related to the amount of verbal communication.[18]

 c. The ratio of issue- to personality-oriented conflict is asserted to positively influence creativity. More generally, the amount of conflict is asserted to positively influence the amount of nonverbal communication, and to inversely influence both elaborateness of language codes and amount of support.

No definitive empirical evidence exists either for or against any of the relationships involving interaction variables in a family problem-solving context. This is due largely to the failure to differentiate dimensions or facets of interaction and to explore the implications of their simultaneous operation. The above assertions thus help map out one fruitful area of future research effort.

Effects of Interaction Variables on Family Problem-Solving Effectiveness

If all of the interaction variables were positively and strongly interrelated, their predicted effects on family problem-solving effectiveness could be easily summarized. Even though the interaction variables are likely to be interrelated in a somewhat more complex fashion, we still expect their effects to be fairly uncomplicated. The general assertion is this: *the nondistributive interaction variables positively influence effectiveness, while the distributive variables inversely influence effectiveness.* Of course, the signs of these effects reflect the manner in which the interaction variables are conceptualized. Thus, for example, increases in the distributive variables decrease family problem-solving effectiveness only because the high end of the range of variation in the distribution of interaction is treated as the concentrated end.

Several important cautions should be borne in mind regarding the interaction-effectiveness relationships.

First, they are considered to hold net of other variables not yet considered. We will later see, for example, that the nature of the problem acts as a contingency on the effects of several interaction variables.

Second, the effects of interaction variables often depend on the way those variables are operationalized. The clearest example of this is provided by the conflict variable. Specifically, the total amount of conflict should have less impact on family problem-solving effectiveness than the ratio of issue- to personality-oriented conflict. Similarly, disagreements early in the problem-solving process should have substantially different consequences for effectiveness than do disagreements later in the process. One aim of coordinative leadership in problem-solving phasing is to maximize early differences to increase the range of solutions considered and to minimize later differences once a solution has been chosen.

Third, interaction in some cases should affect solution quality and solution acceptance in different ways. For example, a high level of mutual support probably increases acceptance more than it increases quality. In general, we expect the nondistributive features of interaction to have more of their effect on solution quality and the distributive features to have more of their effect on solution acceptance.

Fourth, the anomalies in the relationships among interaction variables discussed above point to special considerations about interaction-effectiveness assertions. Most of these anomalies involve the amount or concentration of verbal and nonverbal communication. The net

result of simultaneously taking them into account seems to be that no one of these four variables is consistently and strongly related to family problem-solving effectiveness. The reason for this conclusion is that communication frequencies are rather global in nature and unspecific as to content, and thus admit the possibility of irrelevant or at least unknown factors canceling out communication effects. The other anomalies concern the centralization of power and the postulated independence of normative and distributive variables. In the former case, the answer is that centralization of power can positively influence family problem-solving effectiveness, but only under certain conditions (for example, when it is coordinative in style and legitimate). In the latter case, the answer is that while unrelated in principle, the normative and distributive dimensions have independent or perhaps statistically interactive effects on family problem-solving effectiveness. Thus, for example, legitimate power should increase effectiveness no matter how power is distributed, but a particular distribution of power should increase effectiveness only when it is legitimate (Tallman and Miller, 1974).

Two further considerations are important for assessing the interaction-effectiveness relationship: the relative strength of the relationships involving particular interaction variables and explanations as to why these relationships should hold in the first place. We have already made some distinctions about expected size or strength of relationships. Beyond these, our general expectation is that variables in the causal sequence more proximately related to family problem-solving effectiveness have more of an impact on effectiveness than those less proximately related variables. This principle should also hold for other variables captured by Figure 20.1. One implication of this expectation is that creativity appears to have the strongest predicted impact on family problem-solving effectiveness.

The primary value of creativity is that it opens up the possibility of improvements in solution quality by exposing the family to additional alternatives. Still, creative interaction by itself can guarantee the selection of neither a high-quality solution nor one which all members accept. We surmise that the way families organize themselves, especially as reflected in phasing rationality, combines with creativity to jointly affect family problem-solving effectiveness. Thus part of the explanation for the interaction-effectiveness relationship is to be found in the way the interaction variables themselves interact statistically during problem solving.

Having examined several of the implications of treating interaction variables jointly, we are led to an interesting conclusion. Some of these interaction variables appear to cluster around underlying and common dimensions of activity. For example, it might be useful to treat the amount of communication (both verbal and nonverbal), creativity, and conflict as reflecting "the number and diversity of ideas exhibited during problem solving.'' It is just such a dimension toward which Tallman (1970) seemed to be moving in his first theorizing (see page 502 above). Three other key interaction variables appear to cluster around a second dimension of activity. Elaborate language codes, coordinative leadership, and phasing rationality all suggest an information-processing system that is governed by a set of intricate rules and procedures. If we call this dimension ''the complexity of information processing,'' it is possible to notice parallel ideas espe-

cially in Weick's ''knowledge templates'' and in Tallman's more recent work (Tallman, 1972; Tallman and Miller, 1976).

The source theories we have examined plus our own reflections on the previous pages all seem compatible with the assertion that the advantage of numerous and diverse ideas during family problem solving is conditional upon the complexity of information processing. Without elaborate language codes, coordinative leadership, or phasing rationality, large amounts of communica-

---

Exhibit 20.7. Summary of Theorized Effects of Interaction Variables on Family Problem-Solving Effectiveness

1. The amount of verbal communication among family members positively influences family problem-solving effectiveness; this relationship is weak overall, but stronger for effectiveness measured in terms of solution quality.
2. The concentration of verbal communication among family members inversely influences family problem-solving effectiveness; this relationship is weak overall, but stronger for effectiveness measured in terms of solution quality.
3. The creativity of family members during problem solving positively influences family problem-solving effectiveness (especially when effectiveness is measured in terms of solution quality).
4. The concentration of creativity among family members inversely influences family problem-solving effectiveness (especially when effectiveness is measured in terms of solution acceptance).
5. The elaborateness of language codes in a family positively influences family problem-solving effectiveness (especially when effectiveness is measured in terms of solution quality).
6. The concentration of elaborate language codes in a family inversely influences family problem-solving effectiveness (especially when effectiveness is measured in terms of solution acceptance).
7. The amount of support in a family during problem solving positively influences family problem-solving effectiveness (especially when effectiveness is measured in terms of solution acceptance).
8. The concentration of support among family members during problem solving inversely influences family problem-solving effectiveness (especially when effectiveness is measured in terms of solution acceptance).
9. The amount of nonverbal communication among family members positively influences family problem-solving effectiveness; this relationship is weak overall, but stronger for effectiveness measured in terms of solution quality.
10. The concentration of nonverbal communication among family members inversely influences family problem-solving effectiveness; this relationship is weak overall, but stronger for effectiveness measured in terms of solution acceptance.
11. The amount of conflict in a family during problem solving activity positively influences family problem-solving effectiveness; this relationship is weak overall, but it is stronger (a) when conflict is measured in terms of the ratio of issue- to personality-oriented conflict and (b) when effectiveness is measured in terms of solution quality; this relationship is inverse when effectiveness is measured in terms of solution acceptance.
12. The concentration of conflict early in the problem solving process positively influences problem-solving effectiveness.
13. The concentration of conflict among family members inversely influences family problem-solving effectiveness (especially when effectiveness is measured in terms of solution quality).
14. The centralization of power in a family inversely influences family problem-solving effectiveness; this relationship is weak overall.
15. The extent to which leadership is coordinative in a family during problem solving positively influences family problem-solving effectiveness (especially when effectiveness is measured in terms of solution quality).
16. The extent to which family power during problem solving is based on expertise positively influences family problem-solving effectiveness (especially when effectiveness is measured in terms of solution quality).
17. The extent of phasing rationality during problem solving positively influences family problem-solving effectiveness (especially when effectiveness is measured in terms of solution quality).
18. The legitimacy of an interaction pattern exhibited during problem solving positively influences family problem-solving effectiveness (especially when the interaction pattern is measured in terms of power and when effectiveness is measured in terms of solution acceptance).
19. Centralization of power interacts with coordinative leadership and legitimacy of power such that when centralized power is coordinative or legitimate, but especially when it is both coordinative and legitimate, the centralization of power in a family positively influences family problem-solving effectiveness.
20. The number and diversity of ideas expressed during problem solving (measured in terms of the amount of verbal communication, the amount of nonverbal communication, creativity, and the amount of conflict) interact with the complexity of information processing during problem solving (measured in terms of the elaborateness of language codes, coordinative leadership, and phasing rationality) such that the complexity of information processing positively influences the sign of the relationship between the number and diversity of ideas and family problem-solving effectiveness; that is, when the complexity of information processing is high, the number and diversity of ideas positively influence effectiveness; on the other hand, when the complexity of information processing is low, number and diversity inversely influence effectiveness.

tion, creativity, and conflict cannot be channeled into effective—that is, high-quality and highly acceptable—solutions because this activity is unstructured and, in effect, constitutes an "overload" on the capacity of the family to deal meaningfully with the problem at hand.

The propositions generated by the considerations treated in this section are listed in Exhibit 20.7. In subsequent sections we have not taken full advantage of the insights about clusters of interaction variables just discussed. However, the value of doing so in future theorizing is apparent. This will provide one way of searching for parsimonious principles that describe the family problem-solving process.

There is some empirical support for a few of the relationships discussed in this section, and also a trace of disconfirming evidence. These findings are summarized in Table 20.2. It is readily apparent, however, that the array of data available to evaluate this crucial portion of the theory is not yet impressive.

Characteristics of Problems

It has been recognized for some time that situational factors influence the problem-solving process in groups.

Special attention has increasingly been given in the literature to those situational factors which involve the intrinsic nature of the problems that families and other groups confront.

As recently as 1965, one experienced researcher pointed to both the importance of task characteristics and the lack of attention they had received up to that time:

> Problem solving has been used with reference to tasks as varied as judging the number of dots briefly displayed on a large card, to providing answers to arithmetic reasoning problems, to solving complex problems faced by the managements of large business organizations.... [One] might expect that the factors producing effective performance should vary greatly in these different types of problems.... This rather obvious point has generally been neglected. It calls for the systematic development of a taxonomy of problems (Hoffman, 1965:122–23).

Subsequently, several attempts have been made to classify problems into types according to certain task dimensions.

The most recently developed taxonomy of problems is that by Tallman and his associates (Tallman et al., 1974). We have abstracted and synthesized 10 dimensions from this work and that of other family and small-group

Table 20.2. Empirical Evidence Relevant to the Zero-Order Effects of Interaction on Family Problem-Solving Effectiveness

INTERACTION VARIABLE	PREDICTED SIGN OF EFFECT	STUDIES	COMMENTS
Amount of verbal communication	+ (weak)	Straus (1968) Tallman-Miller (1974) Cohen (1974)	Modest support Modest inverse relationship found Supported but depends on other variables
Creativity	+	Straus (1968)	Modest support
Elaborateness of language codes	+	Tallman-Miller (1974)	No relationship found
Amount of support	+	none	
Amount of nonverbal communication	+ (weak)	Straus (1968) Cohen (1974)	Apparently modest support Supported but curvilinear
Amount of conflict	+ (weak)	none	
Concentration of verbal communication	− (weak)	Tallman-Miller (1974)	Supported but depends on other variables
Concentration of creativity	−	none	
Concentration of elaborate language codes	−	none	
Concentration of support	−	none	
Concentration of nonverbal communication	− (weak)	Cohen (1974)	Modest support
Concentration of conflict	−	none	
Centralization of power	− (weak)	Tallman-Miller (1974) Cohen (1974)	Supported but depends on other variables Supported on curvilinear
Coordinative leadership	+	none	
Phasing rationality	+	Reiss (1971a, 1971b, 1971c)	Inferentially supported but depends on other variables
Legitimacy of power	+	Tallman-Miller (1974)	Inferentially supported
Expert power	+	none	

scholars (Shaw, 1971, ch. 9; Adams, 1971, ch. 15; Aldous, 1971).

1. *Difficulty or complexity*—amount of effort required to solve a problem; number of operations, skills, or types of knowledge required to solve a problem

2. *Solution multiplicity*—number of correct solutions to a problem; number of means for attaining solutions to a problem; difficulty of verifying a solution as correct

3. *Conjunctivity*—degree of coordination, cooperation, or integrated action by family members required to solve a problem

4. *Pervasiveness*—number of families affected by a problem (ubiquity of problem)

5. *Intellectual-manipulative requirements*—ratio of mental to motor requirements for solving a problem

6. *External-internal source*—whether a problem is imposed by outside forces or self-imposed by the family or one of its members

7. *Requisite time*—maximum time required to solve a problem, ranging from an immediate response to a series of responses over an extended period of time

8. *Object barrier-interpersonal barrier*—whether a problem directly concerns material objects or their symbolic representations, on the one hand, or member relationships, on the other

9. *Rule-boundedness*—degree to which explicit and available procedures are required to solve a problem

10. *Control*—degree to which a family and its members can influence the course of events leading to the outcome of a problem[19]

It is difficult to specify operational procedures or indicators for these task dimensions because one would first have to compile an exhaustive and detailed list of family problems. In general, however, it should be possible to locate problems that cover the range of variation in these dimensions, perhaps by using established and reliable ranking methods. A supplementary procedure would involve the subjective evaluation of particular problems by family members. Not only would perceptual measures likely deviate from more objective measures (over- or underestimating control, etc.), but also differential perception within families is likely to occur in some cases and to affect the course of problem solving. For some dimensions, subjective measures would require a careful distinction between general and personal reference points. For example, a family member might believe that families in general have a good deal of control over the problem of how to allocate discretionary income, but may also believe that his or her own family lacks this control due to limited resources. At the very least, comparing the effects of objective and subjective measures of task dimensions would help determine whether it is the intrinsic nature of problems or their felt nature which is more important for effectively solving family problems.

The attention to task dimensions is recent enough to have not yet been taken into account in research on family problem solving. Most problems studied appear to have been moderate in difficulty, low on solution multiplicity, low on pervasiveness, externally imposed, low on requisite time, high on rule-boundedness and control, and to have involved object as opposed to relational barriers. While there has been some variability in conjunctivity and intellectual versus manipulative requirements, these dimensions have not been systematically varied in order to compare their effects. The upshot is that we do not yet have any empirical knowledge about characteristics of family problems and their importance for family problem solving.

Relationships among Characteristics of Problems

Ideally, the task dimensions identified above should be empirically as well as conceptually independent of one another. In a factor analysis of problems outside of the family context, Shaw (1971) has demonstrated that the first five dimensions on our list are empirically independent. Still, it is possible to question the reasonableness of some of his findings. It seems reasonable that conjunctive problems would be more complex or difficult than disjunctive ones because the former require organizational efforts that may not be readily apparent to family members. Pervasive or ubiquitous problems and those high on solution multiplicity might also be expected to be relatively complex or difficult, in the former case because prevalence could indicate an endemic failure to find solutions and in the latter case because more choices are involved. If pervasiveness and difficulty were assessed perceptually, however, it could be argued that it is only those problems which families feel they face alone which are especially difficult, since they have little recourse to successful models for problem solving in the environment. Similarly, pervasive problems seem more likely to admit to multiple solutions than would unique problems because no two families are likely to approach the problem-solving process in exactly the same way. If family members know or believe a problem is pervasive, they are also likely to know or believe that it can be handled in a variety of ways.

We also expect other relationships within the several task dimensions. These relationships, along with those just discussed, are presented in Table 20.3. Additional factor analyses should help determine whether or not the 10 dimensions we have identified can be further reduced in number.

Effects of the Characteristics of Problems

Characteristics of problems might be expected to have three kinds of effects on the other variables discussed so far: direct effects on family problem-solving effectiveness, effects on problem-solving interaction, and effects

Table 20.3. Predicted Relationships between Characteristics of Family Problems

	(A)	(B)	(C)	(D)	(E)	(F)	(G)	(H)	(I)	(J)
(a) Difficulty, complexity		+	+	+			+	−	−	−
(b) Solution multiplicity	+			+					−	+
(c) Conjunctivity	+						+	−		
(d) Pervasiveness	+	+				+	+			−
(e) Intellectual-manipulative requirements*								−		
(f) External-internal source*				+				+		
(g) Requisite time	+		+	+					−	**
(h) Object barrier-interpersonal barrier*	−		−		−	+				
(i) Rule-boundedness	−	−					−			+
(j) Control	−	+		−			*		+	

*Since they afford only a nominal level of measurement, requirements, source, and barrier are assigned arbitrary ordinal properties here, with intellectual requirements, external sources, and object barriers scored in the high direction.

**Curvilinear, with control greatest for problems with a moderate amount of requisite time.

on the relationships between interaction and effectiveness.

It is very important to distinguish the imageries associated with these three causal mechanisms. In the first case, the situational features of problems themselves are expected to affect the likelihood and degree of effective problem solving. These situational features or task dimensions set boundaries beyond which no amount of effort or skill can improve problem-solving performance. These limits are built into the nature of the situation. Where the definition of the situation is perceptually malleable, we would expect the restrictions imposed to be less rigid. Nevertheless, those definitions of the situation themselves impose restrictions on the degree of effectiveness achievable.

In the second type of effect, the characteristics of problems are expected to alter the interaction patterns displayed by families during problem solving. It might be argued that families, in response to the nature of the problem, would energize the interaction patterns necessary to maximize problem-solving effectiveness.

In the third type of effect, characteristics of problems provide conditions in which certain interaction patterns either promote, retard, or fail to affect family problem-solving effectiveness. In this case, there is clearly no assumption that in response to situational constraints families either do or fail to do what is required in order to solve their problems. Instead, the presumption is that if certain conditions prevail, the facilitative interaction patterns will be different from those operating when another set of conditions prevails. This type of effect cannot tell us whether or not or under what conditions a particular interaction pattern will in fact be adopted.

With regard to the direct effects of the characteristics of problems on family problem-solving effectiveness, the following propositions are advanced:

1. Problem difficulty, solution multiplicity, conjunctivity, and pervasiveness all inversely influence family problem-solving effectiveness.

2. Rule-boundedness and control positively influence family problem-solving effectiveness.

3. The remaining characteristics of problems (intellectual-manipulative requirements, external-internal source, requisite time, and object barrier-interpersonal barriers) are unrelated to family problem-solving effectiveness.

By their very nature, difficult or complex problems should be, on the average, less effectively solved than easy or simple problems. The assumption underlying this argument is that as the effort, knowledge, or skill required to solve a problem increases, there will be fewer families possessing these resources. More simply stated, we assume that families vary in the degree to which they possess problem-solving resources.

Problems with multiple solutions should be solved less effectively than problems with single solutions because more choices are involved and the verifiability of the solution is more tenuous in the former type of problem. However, it might also be argued that for problems with multiple solutions at least some acceptable solution is likely to be found, whereas a problem with only one correct solution has a greater chance of not being solved at all. Therefore, we expect the relationship between solution multiplicity and problem-solving effectiveness to be relatively weak.

Conjunctive problems are less likely to be solved effectively than disjunctive problems because of the additional organizational requirements than the former entail. A family which lacks cooperative skills might find a conjunctive problem to be beyond its means, while a disjunctive problem of the same sort would pose no special hardships. These possibilities add structural complexity to the theory which we have not made explicit in our orienting model (Figure 20.1), but such possibilities deserve attention.

Pervasive or ubiquitous problems should be solved less effectively on the average than problems unique to a family because their relatively high incidence suggests that they are chronic, unavoidable, or unmanageable. Part of this relationship may be due to the expected inverse relationship between pervasiveness and control (Table 20.3). If all families experience a certain problem, this suggests that it is beyond the control of any one family. However, the inverse effect of pervasiveness on family problem-solving effectiveness may be weakened by feelings of isolation associated with problems unique to a given family. Pervasive problems at least provide a plethora of models from which a family can draw to solve its version of the problem. A family which is alone in facing a problem cannot turn outward for this kind of assistance. The net effect of pervasiveness on problem-solving effectiveness, is, therefore, likely to be relatively weak and likely to depend on how family members perceive and react to their situation. Again, this suggests a structural complexity in the theory which goes beyond Figure 20.1.

The proposed positive effects of rule-boundedness and control and the absence of effects involving the remaining characteristics of problems seem less in need of special comment or justification at this time. It should be obvious, however, that here again a family's resources likely affect those relationships. For example, even though intellectual problems may not be inherently more or less solvable than manipulative problems, a family with low intellectual but high manipulative capacities is likely to have more trouble with the first kind of problem than with the second.

It is important to keep in mind that each problem has its own configuration of situational characteristics. Certain of these characteristics may, therefore, counterbalance or interact in the way they place restraints on family problem-solving effectiveness. It is the "whole" problem, not its constituent task dimensions operating independently, which makes it more or less solvable. This caution mitigates against the likelihood that a problem will have all the "wrong" characteristics going for it. In such extreme cases, the "problem" is literally unsolvable and becomes residual to our theory-building task. A discrepancy between goal and performance which offers no possibility of reduction by family activity will be defined by the family as "in Allah's hands," therefore not strictly the family's problem.

Any proposed effect of task variables (characteristics of problems) on interaction variables has two implications: either families respond to the situation in ways which facilitate effective problem solving, or else those situations place constraints on a family's ability to engage in facilitative kinds of interaction. As an example of each of these possibilities, consider the following causal sequences:

a) conjunctivity — concentration — family problem-
   $\longrightarrow$ of interaction $\longrightarrow$ solving effectiveness

b) requisite + phasing + family problem-
   time $\longrightarrow$ rationality $\longrightarrow$ solving effectiveness

In sequence a we begin, reading from center to right, by noting that concentrated interaction (in any of its manifestations) decreases problem-solving effectiveness. To this we add the notion that conjunctive problems are less likely to produce concentrated interaction than are disjunctive problems. Even though we have already argued that conjunctivity inversely influences family problem-solving effectiveness, the conclusion now seems to be that certain problems (conjunctive ones) are more likely to produce interaction patterns which facilitate effective problem solving than are other problems (disjunctive ones).

In sequence b we begin, reading from center to right, with the assertion that phasing rationality promotes problem-solving effectiveness. Then we note the time requisite effect, that problems requiring an immediate response are less likely to elicit phasing rationality than are problems requiring long-term responses. In essence, the time constraints in the former type of problem make a facilitative interaction pattern less likely to occur than if the problem possessed a different kind of time requirement.

Both of the implications illustrated above are present in any proposed relationship between the characteristics of problems and problem-solving interaction. If one end of a task dimension promotes interaction patterns which facilitate effective problem solving, the other end of that task dimension has the opposite effect. While we expect effects like those in a and b to exist, we also expect them to be weak and irregular. Hence no arrow is drawn between characteristics of problems and problem-solving interaction in Figure 20.1. While the inherent characteristics of problems pose limits on the selection of interaction patterns, they do not completely determine that selection.

The most fundamental way in which situational characteristics of problems should affect the problem-solving process is by changing the kinds of interaction patterns required to maximize family problem-solving effectiveness. For example, when a problem is complex or difficult, it is more important that coordinative leadership be employed in order to solve it than when the problem is simple. Similarly, concentrated interaction should retard problem-solving effectiveness only when the problem arises from internal sources; externally imposed problems may even require centralized power and other forms of concentrated interaction in order to be effectively solved.

The effects of interaction on family problem-solving effectiveness which are contingent upon the nature of the problem can be assessed as follows. In our discussion of effects of interaction variables we proposed that the nondistributive interaction variables positively influence family problem-solving effectiveness, while the distributive variables inversely influence effectiveness. *We now expect the size and strength of these relationships to be greatest when problems are difficult or complex, when solution multiplicity is high, when problems are conjunctive, when problems are pervasive, when problems emphasize intellectual requirements, when problems arise from internal sources, when the requisite time is long, when problems present relational barriers, when problems are non-rule-bound, and when families have a relatively low degree of control over the outcome.* As these task dimensions begin to take values toward the opposite end of their respective continua, either interaction patterns lose their influence on problem-solving effectiveness or else the opposite kind of interaction from that usually associated with effective problem solving begins to facilitate effective problem solving.

It is difficult at this time to specify which of these interaction patterns simply lose their impact and which reverse their impact. The former result is generally expected, but examples of the latter can be articulated, as we have done for internal versus external source and centralization of power. Disjunctive problems may require concentrated interaction, characterized either by one family member engaging in problem-solving activity exclusively or by each member working on his or her own. Furthermore, problems which are exceedingly simple or which require an immediate response are unlikely to be solved effectively if families "oververbalize" and "overorganize" in seemingly rational ways. It is just this sort of insensitivity to situational demands which probably accounts for the invective "You're making a mountain out of a molehill."

As always, certain exceptions to the general pattern of relationships can be noted here. The most important of these exceptions should include the following:

1. The positive effect of the legitimacy of power on family problem-solving effectiveness does not vary with the characteristics of problems.

2. The inverse effects of the concentration of interaction on family problem-solving effectiveness do not vary with pervasiveness, intellectual-manipulative requirements, requisite time, or control.

3. The positive effects of the amount of interaction on family problem-solving effectiveness do not vary with the source of the problem (external or internal).

4. The positive effects of the amount of creativity and support and phasing rationality on family problem-solving effectiveness do not vary with pervasiveness or intellectual-manipulative requirements.

5. The positive effects of elaborate language codes and amount of nonverbal communication on family problem-solving effectiveness do not vary with barriers, rule-boundedness, or control.

6. The positive effect of creativity on family problem solving effectiveness does not vary with requisite time or barriers.

7. The positive effect of expert power on family problem-solving effectiveness varies with problem complexity but does not vary with the other characteristics of problems.

These essentially null propositions mean that the characteristics of problems are expected to affect the relationships between interaction and problem solving effectiveness quite selectively. Still, each interaction pattern (except legitimacy of power) is believed to have some situational contingency operating on its relationship with effectiveness, and each task dimension is believed to have some set of effects of this sort. Of the 170 possible contingencies between 10 characteristics of problems and 17 interaction variables influencing problem-solving effectiveness, only 69 (41 percent) are eliminated via these null propositions.

The general assertion that situational contingencies affect the relationship between interaction and problem-solving effectiveness has far-reaching implications. Most importantly, it means that we should not expect particular kinds of interaction patterns to universally facilitate effective family problem solving. Before we can draw firm conclusions about which sorts of interaction are "best" for families, we need research which systematically controls the type of problem under investigation. This opens up a frontier for family problem-solving research which to date has been sorely neglected, largely because the crucial characteristics of family problems have not been well understood.

Group Structural Properties

The structural properties of a family as a group are organizational features existing prior to the onset of problem-solving interaction. Many of these features can be relatively stable, reflecting the accumulated history of a family's experience as a group. Family interaction patterns themselves, and most especially problem-solving interaction patterns, can be viewed as structural properties. It is possible, for example, to advance a general proposition that the typical way in which a family has interacted in the past influences its problem-solving interaction in the present. If a typical interaction pattern can be identified, support exists for the stability of interaction over time, and the above proposition argues for the continuation of that stability.

While reasonable arguments can be made for this "continuity proposition," it also can be questioned in several respects. A brief look at these questions can give us a clearer understanding of the nature of those group structural properties appropriate for the present analysis.

A stable family organization implies the existence of an integrated micro-cultural base. This base is characterized by shared role expectations, values, goals, and sentiments toward the family and its members, definitions of a situation, and criteria for evaluating the effectiveness of problem-solving efforts. Whether this cultural base makes stable interaction possible or, in reverse, whether the cultural base arises out of stable interaction is an interesting issue but one that need not detain us. The more crucial question is, what is gained or lost by assuming that a family's cultural base is integrated in the first place? Is it not possible that the members of a given family define situations differently, have incompatible goals, and so on? If consensus on role expectations and values, and shared sentiments are treated as variables instead of constants, we are much less likely to view structural stability in families as a given. Hence group structural properties can reflect differences as well as similarities within the group at a particular point in time.

Differences among family members go beyond the cultural factors mentioned here and extend to biologically ascribed and socially achieved traits such as age, gender, and cognitive, interpersonal, and motor skills. Indeed, if there is any remarkable difference between families and most other groups, it is with respect to or as a consequence of their differing distributions on these traits. Hence the homogeneity of family composition and competencies is an important type of group structural property.

The temporal stability of family organization is another feature which is subject to doubt. The developmental history of family groups is punctuated by changes involving size, gender composition, competencies of members, and role relations both within the family and with external social systems. The only relatively stable elements of this developmental process may be an orderly progression through life cycle stages and an adaptability or flexibility to changing circumstances. Even developmental flexibility is likely to vary from family to family and from time to time, so that it can be treated as a variable rather than as a constant.

These considerations about constancy and variability, stability and change, lead us to propose three major types of group structural property for analysis: those reflecting the degree of microcultural integration, the distribution of traits, and the developmental changes in family organization:

Family Integration

1. Consensus—the degree to which family members share in common the following: role expectations for family members, definitions of the situation, goals, and criteria for evaluating problems and problem-solving performance

2. Cohesiveness—the degree to which family members are attracted to each other and to the family as a group.

Distribution of Traits

3. Homogeneity of age composition—the extent to which the ages of family members are similar

4. Homogeneity of gender composition—the sex ratio in a family

5. Homogeneity of competencies—the extent to which particular problem-solving skills and overall problem-solving skill are evenly distributed among family members.

Developmental Variables

6. Family life cycle stage—a relatively distinct period in a family's career demarcated by significant changes in the normative content of members' roles[20]

7. Family size—the number of members in a family

8. Developmental flexibility—the ability of a family to alter its interaction patterns in response to the changing characteristics of its members over their individual life cycles.

While most of these variables are readily interpretable and their operationalizations straightforward enough that we have offered no illustrative indicators, several comments are in order about their definitions.

Consensus can be conceptualized and measured at a perceptual level as well as in terms of simple agreement (Scheff, 1967). Thus, for example, each member's understanding of each other member's role expectations can be treated as an important element of consensus. Since a number of objects (expectations, definitions, goals, and evaluation criteria) can be consensual or dissensual, a global measure would combine each of these objects in some fashion. Still, it cannot be assumed without empirical demonstration that consensus is uniform across objects. Tallman, Aldous, Weick, and Reiss all emphasize one or more of these manifestations of consensus in their theories. Only Reiss, among them, does not treat consensus as varying in degree as specified by our definition. Instead, Reiss assumes that consensus is invariably high and that what distinguishes individual families is the form or type of consensus which predominates.

The idea of cohesiveness is borrowed from Aldous (1971), although it has a long history in small-group research (Cartwright and Zander, 1968). Our definition distinguishes attraction between pairs of group members and attraction to the whole group under the assumption that a combination of the former may not be perfectly correlated with a combination of the latter.

With the exception of the distribution of competencies (Turner, 1970), variables reflecting the distribution of traits have not been emphasized in other family problem-solving theories. Since families ordinarily link members in two distinct generations, we would not expect families to be as homogeneous in age as most other natural groups. However, the age of parents at the birth of the first child, the age similarity between the parents, and the spacing of children are all potentially important structural variables. Each of these is captured by the notion of homogeneity of age composition as we have defined it. As for the homogeneity of gender composition, it tends to decrease as the sex ratio approaches 1.0. Thus, for example, the relatively extreme sex ratios of five males to one female (5.0) and five females to one male (0.2) are equally less homogeneous than a three-to-three split on gender (1.0).

One or more developmental variables are treated in each of the earlier works by Tallman, Turner, Aldous, and Weick. In order to operationalize family life cycle stage, it is essential that significant changes in a family's role complex be distinguishable from insignificant changes and that a role complex itself be empirically accessible. Fortunately, these measurement problems have been fairly well worked out over the period in which the developmental framework has been consciously employed (see especially Rodgers, 1962). While the concept of family size appears to pose no analytic problems, it is well to remember that we normally have in mind the nuclear family sharing a common residence. Thus the unit of analysis is a functioning group in the sense in which Campbell (1958) and Shaw (1971) conceive it. In this view, interdependence via interaction and a common fate are the most critical features of "groupness." Finally, the idea of developmental flexibility derives principally from Tallman's (1970) notion of the openness of communication to competent members.[21] If competence is age-related, and there is every reason to believe this is the case in families, then norms about who may participate in the

communication network during problem solving ought to shift as a family moves through its life cycle. However, since competence may have a large subjective component, it is possible and even likely that family members will disagree on occasion about which of their members are competent. Thus developmental flexibility is probably difficult to maximize. Whether or not it is achieved at all is likely to depend on whether or not the family directly addresses it as an organizational issue. One fruitful area of future family problem-solving research might concentrate on how organizational problems are themselves resolved in order to facilitate subsequent and more instrumental problem solving.

Interrelationships among Group Structural Properties

Figure 20.4 and Exhibit 20.8 summarize the relationships we expect to regularly occur among the group structural properties introduced above. The general flow of these relationships suggests that families start out with relatively high levels of integration and flexibility, but as they grow in size and develop through stages, the competencies of members become less homogeneous and, as a result, integration and flexibility decline. Later, however, both because of the maturation of members and eventually of reduced size, competencies become homogeneous again, resulting in an increase in integration and flexibility.

The relationships involving family size are largely mathematical artifacts rather than being empirically falsifiable. This can be demonstrated by examining a hypothetical case. Table 20.4 presents the data for such a case. We assume here that:

Figure 20.4. Proposed Relationships among Group Structural Properties

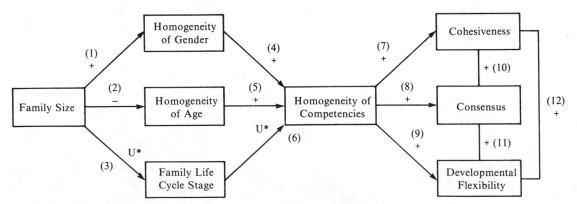

NOTE: Numbers in parentheses are provided to assist in cross-referencing with propositions in Exhibit 20.8.

*Curvilinear relationships with the left-hand variable plotted as the independent variable.

Exhibit 20.8. Propositions Involving Interrelationships among Group Structural Properties

1. Family size positively influences the homogeneity of gender composition in a family.
2. Family size inversely influences the homogeneity of age composition in a family.
3. Family size is curvilinearly related to family life cycle stage such that size is greatest during the intermediate stages of the family life cycle.
4. The homogeneity of gender composition in a family positively influences the homogeneity of competencies in a family.
5. The homogeneity of age composition in a family positively influences the homogeneity of competencies in a family.
6. Family life cycle stage influences the homogeneity of competencies in a family; this relationship is curvilinear such that the homogeneity of competencies is lowest during the intermediate stages of the family life cycle.
7. The homogeneity of competencies in a family positively influences the degree of cohesiveness in a family.
8. The homogeneity of competencies in a family positively influences the degree of consensus in a family.
9. The homogeneity of competencies in a family positively influences the degree of developmental flexibility in a family.
10. The degree of cohesiveness in a family is positively related to its degree of consensus.
11. The degree of consensus in a family is positively related to its degree of developmental flexibility.
12. The degree of cohesiveness in a family is positively related to its degree of developmental flexibility.

1. The husband is 24 years of age at marriage and the wife is 22.

2. They have three children born to them, equally spaced two years apart, with the first child born at about the second wedding anniversary.

3. There is an equal probability that each child will be of a given gender (this is taken into account in Table 20.4 by averaging across all possible combinations of gender composition up to a family size of five).

4. Each child is launched at age 18 and is no longer counted as a member of the nuclear family.

Given these assumptions and the criteria for demarcating stages in Table 20.4, several things are apparent.

First, the homogeneity of gender increases most significantly with the addition of the first child and decreases most significantly with the launching of the last child. Second, the homogeneity of age decreases most significantly with the addition of the first child and increases most significantly with the launching of the last child. Finally, family life cycle stage does not affect homogeneity of gender or age except insofar as changes in size are used as stage transition points.

Three other observations about the relationships in Figure 20.4 deserve comment:

1. Family size affects family life cycle stage primarily because the former is one of the criteria used to specify the

Table 20.4. Hypothetical Values of Selected Group Structural Properties over Time

GROUP STRUCTURAL PROPERTY	DURATION OF MARRIAGE IN YEARS								
	0			5	10	15	20		25
Family size	2	3	4	5			4	3	2
Family life cycle stage*	I	II		III		IV	V		VI
	.50	.67	.75	.80			.75	.67	.50
Proportion male or female		.33	.50	.60			.50	.33	
			.25	.40			.25		
				.20					
Homogeneity of gender**	.00	.17	.17	.20			.17	.17	.00
Ages of members	24	26	28	30	34	39	44	46	48
	22	24	26	28	32	37	42	44	46
			0	2	4	8	13	16	16
				0	2	6	11	14	
					0	4	9		
Mean age of members	23	17	14	13	17	22	29	35	47
Standard deviation of age	1	14	15	15	15	15	16	17	1
Homogeneity of age***	.71	.07	.06	.07	.07	.07	.06	.06	.71

*I: childless; II: childbearing-preschool; III: school age; IV: adolescent; V: launching; VI: empty nest.
**Homogeneity of gender = mean deviation from .50.
***Homogeneity of age = reciprocal of standard deviation of age.

latter. Since stage progression normally varies in only one direction (increasing over time), it is difficult to express stage as a function of size. Figure 20.5 reflects this by suggesting the following plot:

Figure 20.5.

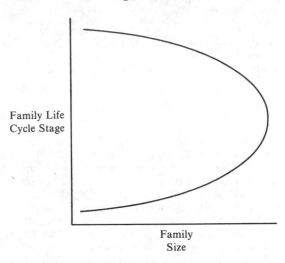

Family Life Cycle Stage

Family Size

Nevertheless, changes in family size are, with rare exceptions, logically prior to changes in family life cycle stage.

2. Homogeneity of gender and of age have counterbalancing effects on homogeneity of competencies. Thus the burden for determining the homogeneity of competencies falls largely on family life cycle stage. Of course, a number of other factors are potentially important in affecting the distribution of competencies, including the effectiveness of socialization.

3. Cohesiveness, consensus, and developmental flexibility are not treated as causally linked but simply as covariates. Most likely, these three variables share symmetrically causal relationships, so that a change in any one of them will result in a change in the others. Furthermore, developmental flexibility may be curvilinearly related to the other two. That is, if cohesiveness and consensus exceed some upper threshold, developmental flexibility may be reduced. The reasoning here is that extremely integrated families are structurally rigid and are unable to adapt to changing conditions in their environments or to changes in their own composition.

Table 20.4 provides one further insight. If it can be assumed that the overall level or fund of competencies in a family is directly proportional to the mean age of family members (at least up to the point where the physical and social concomitants of aging begin to erode those competencies), Table 20.4 shows that the addition of each newborn child reduces this fund. Once childbearing stops, however, the level of competencies begins to recover and continues to increase through the launching

stage, which ends with two adults in the postparental period.

Effects of Group Structural Properties

Our orienting model (Figure 20.1) suggests that group structural properties largely affect family problem-solving effectiveness by way of their effect on problem-solving interaction. Once again we encounter a general argument which seems eminently reasonable but which has not been investigated in relevant research.[22]

We assert that, in general, *group structural properties positively influence the nondistributive interaction variables* (i.e., amount of support, phasing rationality, and so on) *and inversely influence the distributive interaction variables* (i.e., concentration of support, centralization of power, and so on). Given the general pattern of expected relationships between the interaction variables and family problem-solving effectiveness, we also expect that the indirect effects of structural properties on family problem-solving effectiveness will be positive. Of course, the sign and strength of these relationships depend upon a number of qualifications including the direction in which variables are scaled, exceptions in the effects of interaction variables and conditioning effects of the characteristics of problems already noted, and the relatively remote causal position of structural properties.

In addition, a number of exceptions to the general pattern of effects which structural properties have on interaction need to be identified:

1. Whether or not consensus positively influences the frequency and distribution of interaction in any of its manifestations depends on the substantive nature of consensus. It seems reasonable, for example, that role expectations could sanction low levels of verbal communication, creativity, and so on, as well as high levels. To the extent that dissensus can bog down a family in disputes over how to problem-solve (that is, lead to procedural difficulties), we expect that consensus has a direct and positive effect on family problem-solving effectiveness independent of its effects on some of the interaction variables.

2. Family size should affect some interaction variables in ways exactly opposite to the general pattern. For example, although a large family should display relatively great amounts of verbal and nonverbal communication as well as creativity, it also is likely to display relatively low levels of support, language code elaboration, and legitimacy of power while exhibiting relatively concentrated verbal communication, concentrated language elaboration, and centralized power.

3. The homogeneity of gender composition is expected to have limited effects on problem-solving interaction. Families homogeneous on gender ought to display restricted creativity and conflict. Furthermore, to the extent that the relative power of individual family mem-

bers as well as the formation of coalitions is based on gender identity, then the distribution of power in a family might depend on which gender is in the majority. In a similar way, if verbosity is gender-linked, families with a very low sex ratio would be expected to display higher rates of verbal communication than families equally heterogeneous on gender but with a very high sex ratio.

4. The homogeneity of both age and competencies (which we expect to be positively related—see Figure 20.4) is likely to inversely influence some interaction variables, especially creativity and the amount of conflict. The rationale for this expectation draws from ideas advanced by Turner (1970) and Aldous (1971). Both of these theorists borrow from work on risk taking in ad hoc groups, asserting that the diffusion of responsibility positively influences risk taking in such groups. Aldous uses this insight to argue that families tend to be conservative, avoiding risks because of social constraints against responsibility diffusion (1971:273). Turner accompanies his discussion of risk taking with the argument that heterogeneity of member characteristics positively influences creativity and conflict. The challenging questions here are two: what interaction variables already identified represent risk taking, and what structural variables affect the diffusion of responsibility? To answer the first question, we will assume that conflict and creativity are indicators of risk taking because they signal the disruption of a stable and routinized system. To answer the second question, we refer to Turner's antecedents of conflict and creativity. It is at least conventional wisdom that large families with children widely spaced in age (and thus heterogeneous in competencies) employ the elder children to take on a good share of the responsibilities for child care and household chores. Hence it is precisely where these values on the aforementioned structural properties exist that conflict and creativity are most likely to be maximized.

5. Some of the effects of the homogeneity of competencies probably depend on the overall level of competency in a family. For example, a family in which every member has well-developed speech skills is as homogeneous in this respect as a family where no member has well-developed speech skills. Still, we would expect the former family to utilize more elaborate language codes than the latter.

6. The amount of problem solving interaction is likely to be related in a curvilinear way to family life cycle stage, with peaks in amount occurring during the period that the children are adolescents or young adults.

7. Cohesiveness and consensus are as likely to be affected by interaction patterns as to influence those patterns, which is to say that among the structural properties these are probably the least stable. Even though cohesiveness and consensus are likely to be modified, if only temporarily, during the course of a problem-solving effort, the initial levels of these variables are likely to

affect problem-solving interaction according to the general assertion advanced earlier (page 534). That is, cohesiveness and consensus positively influence the amount of interaction, coordinative leadership, expert power, phasing rationality, and legitimacy of power, and inversely influence the concentration of interaction and centralization of power.

However, the effects of cohesiveness and consensus on problem-solving interaction are subject to varying interpretations. While compatible in most respects, the theories of Aldous (1971) and Turner (1970) offer subtle but potentially important differences of emphasis here. Aldous stresses the negative effects of family integration variables (consensus and cohesiveness) on conflict, phasing rationality, and creativity. Her reasoning seems to be that families which enter a problem-solving situation with a stable prior organization will be more concerned with group maintenance than with effective problem solving. Thus when conflict, phasing rationality, and creativity are required for effective problem solving, such families will perform relatively poorly (except perhaps by their own standards). Turner, on the other hand, stresses the positive effects of family integration. This stability of organization presumably provides an atmosphere of mutual support which makes issue-oriented conflict and creativity possible. There are a number of ways this difference in emphasis might be resolved. For the present, we suggest that both interpretations are correct and that their apparent incompatibility is mostly a result of focusing on different ranges of variation in family integration. When family integration is moderate to very high (implying rigidity), Aldous's interpretation holds, and when family integration is moderate to very low, Turner's interpretation holds. Hence we derive the following proposition: family integration influences conflict and conformity, and this is a curvilinear relationship such that conflict and creativity are depressed at the extremes of family integration. With cohesiveness and consensus, as elsewhere in life, it is possible to have too much of a good thing.

8. The ways in which structural properties affect conflict depend on whether the sheer amount of conflict or the ratio of issue- to personality-oriented conflict is considered. For example, consensus, cohesiveness, and developmental flexibility are expected to positively influence the ratio of issue- to personality-oriented conflict. On the other hand, the gross amount of conflict is expected to be positively influenced by family size, inversely influenced by homogeneity of gender, and influenced by family life cycle stage in a curvilinear way such that conflict is greatest when children are adolescents.

Finally, we will explore a somewhat different way of looking at the relationship between group structural properties and problem-solving interaction, even though it has not yet been explicitly incorporated in our formal model.

Earlier we argued that problem-solving interaction and effectiveness covary and that the sign and strength of this covariance are influenced by various characteristics of problems. While the same type of argument might apply here,[23] it is another form of this argument which is especially intriguing. Instead of viewing covariance as a consequent variable as in a conventional contingency, it can be viewed as an antecedent variable. So, in this context we might assert that the covariance between group structural properties and problem solving interaction influences family problem solving effectiveness.

While we introduced the discussion of group structural properties with the warning that a blanket version of the continuity proposition was questionable, there are undoubtedly cases where continuity exists, that is, where a family enters a problem-solving situation with a stable prior organization and routinized pattern of interaction. Insofar as these regularities can be measured by indicators of group structural properties,[24] we might assert that the strength of the relationships already specified between structural and interactional variables positively influences problem-solving effectiveness. So, for example, problem-solving effectiveness is enhanced when high cohesiveness leads to great amounts of verbal communication. Likewise, problem-solving effectiveness is enhanced when problem-solving interaction conforms with the norms implied by our variable of consensus. While we have treated the legitimacy of power as an interaction variable, it is perhaps more properly viewed as an "interstitial" variable in the sense that it can be defined in terms of the covariance between a group structural property (consensus about how power should be distributed) and problem-solving interaction (how power actually is distributed). More generally, the revived continuity proposition would assert that the congruence between prior organization and present problem-solving interaction positively influences family problem-solving effectiveness. One difficulty with this proposition is that it does not specify those conditions under which continuity will occur. To circumvent this difficulty, it would be necessary to add propositions beyond those we have supplied.

Members, Orientations, and Social Placement

Inasmuch as we include a relatively limited number of variables within the remaining three blocks of our orienting model (Figure 20.1), we will condense their analysis into a single section.

When introducing our model, we indicated that basic orientations toward intrafamilial relationships and the environment (cultural orientations), skills or competencies which members possess (member characteristics), and the location of a family in the broader societal context (social placement) all have an impact on the process of family problem solving. Let us now examine these factors before considering their interrelationships and their effects on problem solving.

Cultural Orientations

1. Sense of mastery—the extent to which the environment is viewed as knowable, trustable, and controllable (operational definitions: future orientation, deferred gratification, internal locus of control, openness to change)

2. Autotelesis—the extent to which activity is engaged in for its intrinsic satisfactions (operational definitions: playfulness, degree of exchange of socioeconomic rewards)

3. Particularism—the extent to which social relationships preserve the integrity of members (operational definitions: acceptance of individual differences, permissiveness toward disagreements, freedom from conformity pressures, sense of autonomy, extent to which morality is based on intentions rather than overt deviance).

Member Characteristics

1. Complexity of information processing—the amount of information processed and the number of information-processing rules used (operational definitions: openness to alternatives, ambiguity tolerance, number of levels of abstraction used in cognition)

2. Problem-solving motivation—readiness to pursue collective goals (operational definitions: energy level, attention span, persistence)

3. Self-esteem—the extent to which a member feels a personal sense of worth).

Social Placement

1. Social status—the location of a family in a socioeconomic system of stratification (operational definitions: education, occupation, income, consumption style)

2. Societal complexity—the complexity of information processing and number of opportunities for choices among alternatives in a society's institutions (operational definitions: level of economic development, rate of social change, degree of occupational specialization, level of industrialization, predominance of scientific and materialistic values, degree of bureaucratization).

The first thing to notice about these variables is the unit of analysis implied in each.

Cultural orientations are assumed here to be characteristics of families. It should be apparent, however, that individuals (and perhaps other social systems) could easily be assigned scores on sense of mastery, autotelesis, and particularism. Consistent with our approach throughout this chapter, we advise caution about the possibility that family members differ among themselves on variables such as these. At this point we are willing to assume that families develop fairly consistent patterns of orientation and that they are relatively effective socializers of children in these matters. Although not explicitly incorporated into our model at this rendering, we would expect dissensus in a family about these cultural variables to adversely affect problem-solving effectiveness by way of its structural and interactional consequences.

Characteristics of members are assumed to apply to individuals. We have selected characteristics that are thought to be largely socially determined and to reflect problem-solving competencies. From our discussion of group structural properties, one might imagine that the biologically determined characteristics of gender and age are also relevant here. Certainly gender and age contribute to variation in those competencies we have included. A more salient issue here is how to construct propositions which combine individual and collective units of analysis. It is insufficient to argue that the characteristics of any given member influence group structure and/or interaction, since various members may have differing levels of the relevant characteristics and thus affect problem solving in incompatible ways. Somehow the contributing characteristics of all members (or at least certain crucial members) must be taken into account at once. For the present we make the simplifying assumption that the effects of the characteristics of different family members are additive. Thus, for example, the motivation or self-esteem of the group can be taken to be equal to the sum of the motivations or self-esteems of all members.[25]

Social placement variables imply a collective level of analysis but two distinct comparative procedures. In the case of social status, what matters is each family's rank in a hierarchy containing all families within a given society. In the case of societal complexity, what matters is the position of the society in which a family resides as compared with other societies along appropriate dimensions.

Both of our social placement variables have key measurement issues associated with them. First, neither social status nor societal complexity is necessarily unidimensional. Far from perfect correlations are often reported among the traditional measures of these variables. Second, the social status of a family is less likely to be adequately measured by the status characteristics of only one member than traditional practice suggests. Thus some way of combining individual contributions into a group measure is as important here as it is for our variables listed under member characteristics. Finally, the notion of societal complexity is subject to tenuous evolutionary assumptions.

Relationships among Variables Representing Member Characteristics, Cultural Orientations, and Social Placement

We expect all the within-block relationships involving member characteristics, cultural orientations, and social placement to be positive and to correspond to the causal patterns provided below:

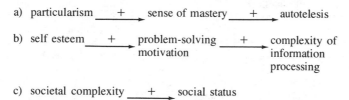

Once again, possible exceptions to the general pattern must be noted. In the case of cultural orientations, it might be argued that a low sense of mastery produces high autotelesis. That is, failing to achieve sufficient indication that a family has been instrumentally successful in dealing with its environment, one might turn to a more casual, playful approach that emphasizes intrinsic rewards. To some extent Weick (1971) and Reiss (1971a) adopt this view and Aldous (1971) appears to be sympathetic to it. However, it seems just as reasonable that a sense of mastery frees the problem solver to pursue additional socioemotional benefits from the problem-solving experience. In the case of member characteristics, there seems to be little reason to believe that they will be strongly interrelated. Whether or not they are, each is expected to influence the problem-solving process in ways described shortly. Finally, in the case of social

placement, the effect of societal complexity on social status must be viewed as operating within the bounds of minimal stratification. In general, we expect the status hierarchy to be more compressed in complex societies than in simple societies. This means that the effects of social class on family problem solving should be more pronounced in simple societies than in complex ones, as indeed Straus has reported (1968). However, we do not claim that complex societies eliminate status distinctions, nor is there any sound reason for such a claim.

Effects of Member Characteristics, Cultural Orientations, and Social Placement

The variables in this section have been inspired by a number of sources. Sense of mastery is treated by Tallman (1970) and at least alluded to by both Weick

(1971) and Reiss (1971a). Autotelesis is given its name by Moore and Anderson (1971), and similar ideas are alluded to by Weick (1971) and more explicitly treated by Aldous (1971). Aspects of particularism receive heavy emphasis by Tallman (1970) and Aldous (1971), and seem implied in the work of Turner (1970) and Reiss (1971a). Complexity of information processing is implied by Tallman (1970), Reiss (1971a), Turner (1970), and Weick (1971), the latter in his rather obscure discussion of "knowledge templates." Problem-solving motivation is given heavy emphasis by both Weick (1971) and Aldous (1971). Self-esteem figures in the work of Aldous (1971) and especially Tallman (1970; Tallman and Miller, 1974). Social status has been a central concern in most and at least mentioned in all the major research efforts (Straus, 1968; Reiss, 1971a; Tallman and Miller, 1974; Cohen, 1974).[26] Finally, societal complexity finds its way into Straus's theory and research (1968).

While all of these sources have something to say about at least one of these variables, as a set they are most systematically treated in one place (Tallman, 1972). The central idea for Tallman is "structural complexity." It is defined in much the same way as we have defined complexity of information processing for the individual family member. However, Tallman views complexity of information processing as applicable to virtually any unit of analysis, and in fact the heart of his theory is that complexity of this sort is transmitted across units of analysis. Thus, for example, the degree of complexity at the societal level, especially as reflected in occupational roles, is transmitted to families. As families attempt to solve their problems (using more or less complex information processing), individual family members are socialized to process information in either complex or simple ways.

Tallman is mostly concerned here with explaining societal development in terms of information processing, and the family is only an intervening tool in this causal chain. Still, the ways in which families go about solving their problems are likely to reflect predominant problem-solving strategies in the broader societal and especially occupational context (the social placement block in Figure 20.1), by way of the orientations families develop (the cultural orientation block) and the information-processing techniques each family member has learned (the member characteristics block).

Consistent with Tallman's argument, *we expect all the variables in the three blocks in Figure 20.1 to be positively interrelated.* The causal sequence is difficult to specify in some cases but we think the chain should run from social placement to member characteristics to cultural orientations. In addition, each block is expected to have independent effects on group structural properties. These latter effects are expected to be positive for the most part. Thus, for example, autotelesis positively influences cohesiveness, self-esteem positively influences de-

velopmental flexibility, and social class positively influences consensus. As for exceptions, until further medical or genetic advances occur or until infanticide becomes widespread, homogeneity of gender is unlikely to be affected by anything beyond chance (except in cases of adoption, communal groups, and other variant family forms). Also, the direct effects of societal complexity are likely to be limited to inverse influences on homogeneity of age and family size. In general, homogeneity of age and homogeneity of family size are expected to be inversely influenced by the antecedent variables in our theory.

One final observation is in order concerning the effects of social placement variables. Most prior theorizing has asserted or at least implied that the effects of social class and/or societal complexity are part of a causal chain (as in Figure 20.1), with social placement indirectly influencing family problem-solving effectiveness by way of mediating structural and interactional variables. A large portion of the effects of social placement variables, however, may turn out to be conditioning or contingency effects as in the model below.

The conventional chain model suggests that family problem-solving effectiveness ultimately regresses on social placement. Since social placement is relatively unmanipulable, certain categories of family are disadvantaged from the outset and appear to have little recourse except to resign themselves to poor problem-solving performance. In contrast, the contingency model above suggests that the means of organizing and interacting to solve problems is simply different (not "better" or "worse") for different categories of family. In this case there is no expectation that lower-class families, for example, are handicapped in their problem-solving efforts. Our omission of this contingency notion from Figure 20.1 is not meant to prejudge the relative empirical fit of these two mechanisms, but has been an expository convenience only. Indeed, the inconclusive results of the program of research aimed at explaining presumed class differences in family problem-solving effectiveness may reflect a misplaced theoretical emphasis. Future research and theory development will likely profit from a direct confrontation and, if necessary, combination of these

Figure 20.6.

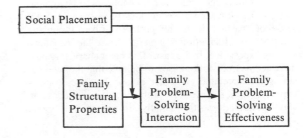

models in order to more adequately deal with factors largely outside the control of families themselves.

Tallman's work provides two additional insights about family problem solving that have not been explicitly incorporated into our orienting model.

First, the complexity of information processing is closely paralleled by the complexity of information itself or, more generally, the complexity of situations. We would not be surprised, therefore, to find that member characteristics and cultural orientations combine to influence the characteristics of problems (especially complexity, solution multiplicity, conjunctivity, rule-boundedness, and control). In order to make this linkage, it would be necessary to assume that families seek out or construct problem-solving environments in which their resources can be put to effective use. While such an argument combines overtones of both functionalism and phenomenology, there is no reason why these approaches cannot be incorporated into our theory, as we have had occasion to remark earlier.

Second, Tallman's use of feedback between levels of analysis suggests that the operation of feedback at various points in our theory ought to be fully explored. We have already indicated some places where this might occur. Furthermore, feedback on a larger scale from family problem-solving effectiveness should occur in at least two ways: (1) A family's problem-solving experiences in the present are expected to influence its problem-solving experiences in the future. This suggests that families are subject to learning principles. (2) A similar sort of feedback is expected to be transmitted across successive generations of families. Thus children are partly socialized by problem-solving experiences in their families of orientation and carry over "member characteristics" to their families of procreation. Of course, feedback on this scale requires an especially onerous research strategy, calling for long-term longitudinal designs. The game simulation approach has been developed (Straus and Tallman, 1971; Tallman et al., 1972) partly in an effort to minimize this difficulty, and it undoubtedly will remain a major tool of the family problem-solving researcher.

OVERVIEW AND IMPLICATIONS

This concluding section offers a reflection on the theory of family problem-solving effectiveness. We want to examine the theory for its underlying perspectives and we want to ask how well it has achieved its purposes.

Perspectives Underlying the Theory of Family Problem-Solving Effectiveness

The theory advanced in these pages is predominantly a prescriptive theory. As such, it should be able to advise families and family members about courses of action which will maximize the effectiveness of their problem-solving efforts. Our most basic assumptions, therefore, are that effective problem solving is desirable and is viewed as desirable by most family members.

Being prescriptive in emphasis, our theory is not so much concerned with describing what families actually do in attempting to solve their problem. Our only descriptive assumption is that families do in fact vary on the variables of interest. Among other things, this means that not all families are equally effective in solving their problems. This approach separates us from problem-solving theorists who have endeavored to show either that problem-solving theories developed in nonfamily contexts may not apply to families (Weick, 1971) or that families have distinctive assets and liabilities and therefore have different approaches to problem solving than do other groups (Aldous, 1971). We do not take issue with efforts to demonstrate that a family is in many respects a unique kind of group. However, we remain convinced that the same basic process that influences family problem-solving effectiveness also influences problem-solving effectiveness in other social contexts. Not every variable in the process need be important for every context, and the effects of some variables may vary with context, but generalizable principles of problem solving seem within grasp. If our theory helps point the way toward those principles, it will have served one of its major purposes.

Although more prescriptive than descriptive, our theory purports to be as predictive as any other family problem-solving theory. We maintain a constant vigil to advance relationships among variables that we expect to hold empirically. By striving to be more explicit about these relationships and to include a larger and more intricate set of relationships than most theories, we hope to assist in increasing predictive power over what now can be claimed.

Since the integration of existing ideas has been one of our chief objectives and since this has been attempted in an area that is today relatively underresearched, it is not surprising that our theory takes on an eclectic flavor. Thus at least a bit of each of the perspectives represented in our source theories finds its way into our theory. All of the following perspectives appear to be compatible with our approach:

1. Systems theory, with an emphasis on the interdependence among actors and actions, selective boundary maintenance, inputs and outputs, feedback, and adaptation or structural modification

2. Microfunctionalism, with an emphasis on purposive behavior geared toward its consequences and with its efficient causes rooted in structural variables, and allowing for equilibrium maintenance as well as an instrumental-expressive distinction

3. Cybernetic theory, with an emphasis on informa-

tion processing at both the level of individuals and that of groups

4. Phenomenology and especially symbolic interactionalism, with an emphasis on the intersubjective construction of meaning, and on cognition and perception

5. Developmentalism, with an emphasis on changes in member characteristics, group composition, and role relations over time

6. Conflict theory, with an emphasis on the productive consequences of conflict and change, and on group integration as problematic

7. Behaviorism, with an emphasis on overt interaction and learning.

It is also possible that, with appropriate translation, additional perspectives such as exchange theory could be applied to the basic mechanisms in our theory.

While admitting alternative perspectives, our theory does not incorporate all the nuances in the explanatory mechanisms of its sources. For example, we have intentionally underplayed the nonrationalistic approach of Weick (and to a lesser extent of Aldous). Instead, we have attempted to transform descriptions into predictions. Thus Weick's nonrational families are viewed as relatively ineffective problem solvers. They are not condemned to this fate, however, since rationality is itself viewed as problematic and variable.

The polemics of social science discourse have yet to settle the issue as to whether one perspective is "better" than another. Our solution, therefore, has been to work toward a theory that is flexible enough to admit several perspectives, at least versions of which tend not to be dogmatic or closed.

The Quest for Theoretical Integration

Our theory takes the form of "contingent causality." That is, the process is expressed in terms of influences among variables, and the nature of these influences are themselves often variable. Essentially, forces external to the family help shape internal forces, but the latter are more important because they are causally more proximate. Furthermore, the effects of the internal forces are often contingent upon the external forces.

What has our integration strategy been? How successful has it been? We began by inventorying the existing theoretical literature on family problem solving. Each concept, relationship, and theoretical argument was taken out of its embedded context and reconstructed in terms of statements about variables, propositions, and networks of propositions. A set of intricate causal models emerged. Each had been pruned of redundancies, dangling linkages, and apparent irrelevancies. This part of the task represented theory repair work.

Because our sources did not provoke one or more deductive systems of explanation, we opted to retain a predominantly causal imagery and to operate at a single level of abstraction.

While each partial theory could be formally reconstructed along these lines, the massive complexity of several of the theories we examined mitigated against a search for serial linkages and overlaps which might result in a master model. This is in principle a workable strategy, but it requires computer assistance as the number and permutation of propositions in several of the more complex theories are merged. Inspection of the various theories (especially those of Tallman and Aldous) suggested that the identified variables could be condensed and grouped into several classes and subclasses, regardless of their causal sequence in any of the partial theories themselves. The identification of these clusters, then, provided the basic integration tool for dealing with previously formalized partial theories.

Once each variable in the pool had been positioned, further redundancies were located and eliminated. Each source theory was then consulted in order to determine the most appropriate causal ordering and sign of relationship between variables. Since not all blocks of variables were implied in some source theories, we had to speculate how unspecified intervening linkages might best be interpreted. In many cases, specific variables appeared underconnected with other parts of the process because individual source theories had not taken into account the full set of variables we now had available. In other cases, we attempted to add relationships that seemed compelling when variables were juxtaposed.

Structural Complexity of the Theory

The product of our multistage effort has been a relatively complex causal network that has emerged from the application of both elaboration and simplification procedures (Klein et al., 1973; Klein, 1974). The accent has been on the side of elaboration. Thus the population density of variables in our theory is unquestionably large; but it is not nearly so large as it might have been nor as it might actually deserve to be.

Table 20.5 presents several indicators of the degree of structural complexity in the present form of our theory. Considering only unidirectional, bivariate relationships between variables and assuming that each variable has one best index or indicator (Table 20.5, panel A), our theory is only about one-half (.47) as interconnected as it is possible to be (Mullins, 1971). If bidirectional relationships are taken into account, the theory reaches only one-quarter its potential complexity. These proportions are nearly preserved when only the direct (unmediated) effects on our dependent variable are examined (.56 and .28 for unidirectional and bidirectional relationships, respectively).

Table 20.5 (panel B) also shows the density of var-

Table 20.5. Indicators of Structural Complexity in the Theory of Family Problem-Solving Effectiveness

INDICATOR *(number of variables, N = 44)*	UNIDIRECTIONAL			NOT CONTROLLING FOR DIRECTION		
	1	*2*	*3*	*4*	*5*	*6*
	number possible	*number explicitly asserted*	*connectedness (2/1)*	*number possible*	*number explicitly asserted*	*connectedness (5/4)*
A. No restrictions						
direct relationships between antecedent variables and family problem-solving effectiveness	43 (N−1)	24	.56	86 2(N−1)	24	.28
relationships among all variables	946 $\frac{N(N-1)}{2}$	445	.47	1,892 N(N−1)	474	.25
B. Given Figure 20.1:						
relationships among all variables	634	445	.70	1,268	474	.37
intrablock relationships	216	132	.61	432	161	.37
interblock relationships	418	313	.75	836	313	.37
relationships involving characteristics of problems as contingencies	170	101	.59	340	101	.30
and involving one or more:						
problem-solving interaction variables (n = 17)	459	331	.72	918	336	.37
characteristics of problems (n = 10)	225	127	.56	450	147	.37
group structural properties (n = 8)	228	177	.78	456	181	.40
member characteristic variables (n = 3)	41	37	.90	82	37	.45
cultural orientation variables (n = 3)	41	37	.90	82	37	.45
social placement variables (n = 2)	29	21	.72	58	21	.36

iables and relationships in selected portions of the theory, given the restrictions imposed by Figure 20.1. Among unidirectional possibilities, the theory is about two-thirds (.70) as interconnected as it could be, with the greatest density found among interblock relationships (.75). Again, allowing for bidirectionality substantially reduces connectedness. Furthermore, structural complexity in our theory varies according to the block of variables examined. Only in the cases of "member characteristics" and "cultural orientations" does the unidirectional measure of complexity approach its maximum, and no block reaches as much as one-half its potential density using the bidirectional measure. Finally, Table 20.5 shows that the largest (although not the densest) portion of the theory involves interaction variables (331 of 445 unidirectional relationships), reflecting the relative importance we attach to those variables. In sum, measured against the standard of maximum possible interconnectedness, our theory can be judged as moderately complex.

Beyond the device of treating many bivariate relationships as nonexistent, the major simplifying procedures we have used include (a) eliminating redundancies in variables where terms and definitions significantly overlap, and submerging dissimilar conceptualizations into alternative indicators, (b) summarizing relationships in terms of clusters of variables when they are expected to be uniform (but also noting exceptions), and (c) employing joint or interactive effects selectively (primarily in treating characteristics of problems as contingency variables). However, at points in this chapter we have resorted to assertions which would make the theory even more complex than it is. Such assertions primarily involve feedback mechanisms, additional joint or interactive effects, and relationships expected to be weak or erratic. That they have been worth mentioning indicates to us that the theory might deserve to be made even more complex than we have indicated. We also doubt that 44 variables exhaust the domain of potentially important factors in the family problem-solving process.

Two main avenues are open for simplifying our theory even further. The first involves the rigorous use of deductive explanation. Is it possible that the hundreds of propositions we have asserted could be treated as theorems which are logically derived from a relatively small set of axioms? One might move inductively from our materials in search of such axioms. Alternatively, one might identify existing sets of axiomatic principles and determine which of these best explains the multivariate model. Both strategies above will invoke analytic problems, but we do not prejudge their effectiveness.[27] The second avenue involves a program of empirical research designed to identify the relative importance of each variable and relationship in the theory. This, too, presents analytical difficulties because the effort would have to be accomplished piece-meal and with a number of perhaps untenable assumptions about invariance. Nevertheless, the empirical approach promises simplification by way of eliminating at least some variables and/or relationships. Future journeys down the deductive and empirical avenues can, and we expect will, go hand-in-hand.

A Final, but Tentative Evaluation

How does our theory stack up against criteria for evaluating theories? One must expect mixed results here. Its testability should be very great, but because of a paucity of relevant research, it can be judged neither to have much empirical fit nor to be well grounded at this time. The predictive power of the theory should be great, but this will depend on how well developed the operational procedures for measuring the variables become, among other things. The theory appears relatively clear and explicit, but it is surely not parsimonious. Moreover, we may not be the best judges of clarity, since this is an intersubjective criterion. The theory appears to be both internally and externally consistent, but not especially unique.[28] Further checks are required before consistency can be determined with assurance. The theory seems at least minimally connected, but it is too soon to decide if it is optimally connected. As for generality and abstractedness, the theory occupies middle ground, although we believe it applies to all types of family problems and potentially to nonfamily social contexts as well. Whether or not the theory has either heuristic or practical value is a matter for future assessment.

NOTES

1. While we have defined feasibility in terms of uncertainty, the relationship between the two is most likely parabolic, as portrayed above:

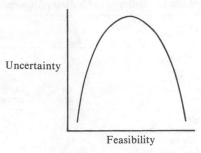

Hence when means appear to be totally feasible or infeasible, there is no uncertainty about the action to take. Only in the intermediate range of feasibility does a high level of uncertainty exist. Moreover, our definition of a problem implies that a problem exists between some ceiling and floor of uncertainty and beyond some floor of feasibility. Depending on where these thresholds operate, the boundaries of a two-dimensional "problem space" would look something like this:

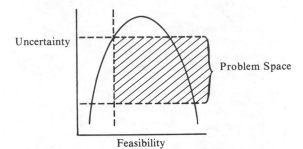

In this case, a problem can exist only when feasibility is high and uncertainty is moderate. It remains an empirical question whether or not the subjective mapping of problem space by family members fits the pattern suggested here, but we hypothesize that the fit would be reasonably good.

2. Straus employed the "ball and pusher" version of the simulation game SIMFAM (for details, see Straus and Tallman, 1971) in Minneapolis, San Juan, Puerto Rico, and Bombay, India. The problem is to figure out the rules of the game, i.e., how to hit targets with the balls on the basis of immediate feedback about right or wrong solution attempts. Repeated trials are used, varying the game rules and permitting other experimental manipulations. The game or puzzle involves sufficient motor activity that it should not be biased in favor of groups of intellectually superior persons, which might be expected to be found disproportionately in middle-class families. Straus's key variables were operationalized as follows:

a. Social class—husband-father engaged in nonmanual work (middle class) versus husband-father engaged in manual work (working class).

b. Problem-solving effectiveness—proportion of green lights (correct solution feedback) to all lights flashed.

c. Amount of communication—total number of verbal and nonverbal acts directed between family members.

d. Creativity—number of different suggestions for playing the game offered by each family member (summed across members), irrespective of either the practicality of the idea or whether it was actually tried out.

3. It is important to note the differences in research design between the Straus and Tallman-Miller studies. The following are the important changes made by Tallman and Miller:

a. The "bean bag" version of SIMFAM was used, being administered in the families' homes.

b. Twelve- to fourteen-year-old sons were included in family triads (Straus had included young adolescent children of both genders).

c. The study was conducted with one U.S. sample, in Riverside, California.

d. Verbal communication was experimentally manipulated by having two talking trials followed by two silent trials.

e. The measure of problem-solving effectiveness was clearly conjunctive, (the family was considered to have solved the problem when all three members had received green lights three times in a row); also, a "time to solution" measure was utilized.

In addition to effectiveness, just discussed, and social class, which was measured as Straus had measured it, the other key variables were operationalized by Tallman and Miller as follows: Openness of communication structure was measured by the experimental manipulation, which either permitted or eliminated the possibility of verbal communication. Also, amount of communication during talking trials was measured as Straus had measured it. Elaborateness of speech style was measured by systematically coding a segment of the wife-mother's pregame interview responses for the number of modifiers and clauses used. Two measures of actual power were employed: who made the final decision during a pregame discussion task involving the expenditure of a large sum of money (classified as husband-father-led, shared, and wife-mother-led), and leadership during the game based on the relative number of successful influence attempts by each member (dichotomized for analysis into husband-father-led and all other patterns).

4. Tallman and Miller have suggested that the contradiction may be due to the fact that Straus used a disjunctive task and an individual rather than a group measure of effectiveness (1970:27). In their own work, Tallman and Miller found with disjunctive game rules and a group effectiveness measure that class and decision-making differences were greatly attenuated (1970:37–40). However, they do not report results which would be directly comparable with Straus's findings, i.e., results based on communication rates and individual measures of problem-solving effectiveness.

5. In a preliminary report of their findings, Tallman and Miller (1970) do shed some light on this issue. They began with the proposition drawn from small-group research that a combination of centralized power and open channels of communication is most conducive to effective family problem solving. Then they constructed measures of the distribution of communication based on total acts and on influence attempts during the game. Tests for statistical interaction involving these measures, social class, and decision-making power produced interesting results. The prediction was modestly confirmed for blue-collar families, but for white-collar families the following combination of communication and power structures facilitated effectiveness: shared decision making with closed channels of communication (i.e., uneven distribution of total acts and influence attempts).

Tallman and Miller interpreted these findings as follows:

It appears likely that the necessity for the family to both filter and evaluate information and, at the same time, allow maximum group participation can be handled either by all family members contributing suggestions which are evaluated by one person or one person presenting suggestions which are evaluated by all family members [30].

Our findings indicate that optimal problem solving occurs under one of two organizational structures: for blue-collar families, the optimal structure is final decision power centralized in the father with open communication channels, but for white-collar families, the optimal structure is shared decision-making power and closed channels of communication [41–42].

While these ideas deserve notice and further investigation, caution should be used in assessing the available data. The results are based on power measures taken from the decision-making task and not from game behavior, the latter being more relevant to their prediction. This would not necessarily be debilitating except Tallman and Miller report that their measures of power distribution in the two settings have a zero correlation. Thus it is hazardous if not impossible to make inferences from their data about the way communication and power structures combine to affect family problem-solving effectiveness in the SIMFAM game. Fur-

thermore, their measures of communication channels, especially participation in influence attempts, are contaminated with indicators of power. Tallman and Miller recognized this and were, therefore, reluctant to use measures of power taken from game behavior to test the proposition at issue. It appears that further methodological refinements are in order before the fundamental idea here can be fully evaluated.

6. Cohen's research design paralleled the procedures used by Tallman and Miller, with certain exceptions. Her study was conducted with a Minneapolis sample in a research laboratory. Furthermore, the sequence of talking and silent trials was randomized through a counterbalancing technique and performance on a pregame decision-making task was eliminated from the design. The social class, verbal communication, and effectiveness variables were operationalized as Tallman and Miller had operationalized them, and another measure of effectiveness was added (the number of game rules correctly verbalized). In contrast with Tallman and Miller, Cohen classified leadership during the game into three possible patterns only: dominated by one member, shared by two members and egalitarian, or fully decentralized. Nonverbal behavior was operationalized in terms of visual interaction, specifically, the frequency with which one-way or mutual glances occurred. Game behavior was videotaped to assess this phenomenon.

7. This is the same strategy required to translate Aldous's comparisons between families and other groups into a theory of family problem-solving effectiveness.

8. The examples which Weick provides (from James, 1960, and Campbell, 1966) more or less converge at the lower end as "random movement," but take on different forms at the upper end, being "deciding 'no'" and "cultural accumulation," respectively. Perhaps a mathematical, empirical testing, logicodeductive system best represents the higher end of the continuum.

9. This isolation may have begun to erode in 1973 when members of various teams met at the annual conference of the National Council on Family Relations in Toronto. However, Reiss was still an isolate at an earlier gathering (Aldous et al., 1971). While Turner himself has been an isolate throughout this period, his ideas have not been so remote, since he shares professional ties with the other sociologists and social psychologists represented here. We make these remarks about the relative confluence or isolation of scholars and their work because we are impressed with the role played by social networks among scientists in the development of theories.

10. Inferences frequently run in the opposite direction as well. Knowing something about the predominant modes of family organization, it is tempting to assume knowledge of the ways families organize for problem solving. However, these inferences should be recognized as theoretical *predictions* and nothing more.

11. By the same token, Reiss employs time to solution as a performance measure but treats it as an indicator of "closure" rather than of effectiveness.

12. Notice that, technically, the latter definition of creativity refers to outcomes, not interaction. Because creative solutions are likely to be products of special interaction patterns and because we do not want to prejudge them as either more or less effective than other solutions, we have included them under the heading of interaction.

13. See Bernstein (1974, especially chs. 5 and 6) and Miller (1976) for a detailed examination of conceptual and measurement issues regarding language codes.

14. The conceptualization and operationalization of conflict are problematic because of noticeable overlaps with creativity and amount of support. Conflict is given separate visibility here because of the central place it occupies in several source theories. Ideally, it should be possible for families to be creative without being polemical and to evidence high rates of positive support in spite of high rates of personality-oriented conflict.

15. There is a strong impression from Tallman's (1970) theory that facilitative or coordinative leadership is important for family problem solving, but the stylistic factor is not emphasized nor has Tallman investigated leadership style in his research to date.

16. Although we have attributed this idea to Aldous (1974), it does not originate with her work, and the label "phasing rationality" is used here for the first time to our knowledge. For an earlier attempt to conceptualize

and measure a similar notion in the context of family consumption choices, see Hill (1970, ch. 9).

17. In discussing expert power, Weick (1971) continues the tendency started by French and Raven (1959) of contrasting it with legitimate power, apparently based on ascriptive attributes. It seems more in line with reason and with a Weberian tradition, at least, to view power based on expertise, coercion, rewards, and so on, as capable in principle of being either legitimate or illegitimate.

18. An important issue here involves the possible limits of information exchange. If verbal and nonverbal channels are viewed as complementary, then there is no reason to believe that they must interfere with or restrict one another. In this case, the rates or amounts of verbal and nonverbal communication might be unrelated or even positively related. However, if the use of one channel (verbal or nonverbal) limits the use of the other, then the inverse relationship between amounts of verbal and nonverbal communication is more reasonable. Since both sides of this issue have some merit, we expect that amounts of verbal and nonverbal communication will be inversely related only when one or the other exceeds some as yet unspecified threshold.

19. Where control is virtually absent, a problem resembles a game of chance. Where control is partial, a problem resembles a game of strategy. The amount and distribution of control in problematic situations has been analyzed in terms of game-theoretical constructs by Moore and Anderson (1971) and Tallman et al. (1974).

20. This definition draws from key treatments of the family development framework (Aldous, 1974: Duvall, 1971; Hill and Rodgers, 1964; Rodgers, 1962, 1973). Following Rodgers (1962:24), we recognize that "stage" implies an invariable and irreversible sequence which may not typify family careers, and that "family life cycle category" might therefore be a preferred label for this variable.

21. Weick's treatment of metaphors about group boundaries is also relevant here.

22. The empirical work which has been done has tended to control for variation in structural properties in order to examine the effects of other variables on family problem-solving effectiveness. For example, virtually all researchers to date have studied families or family subsystems with precisely three members (two parents and one child). While this strategy has the virtues of making research problems manageable and replicable, it also delays the testing of more comprehensive theories.

23. For example, the amount of control over a situation is expected to inversely influence the extent to which group structural properties positively influence family problem-solving interaction. Thus when control is low (and uncertainty high), families will tend to revert to previously established means of dealing with problems.

24. The kinds of structural variables we have identified seem at best to provide indirect measures of organizational continuity. What are really needed here are measures of structure and interaction *over time* so that an account of the accumulated history of stability and/or change can be obtained.

25. An additive approach also requires standardization for variation in group size. There are certainly other assumptions which might be more appropriate for certain purposes. Thus, for example, Weick (1971) seems to believe that the attention span of a group is equal to the attention span of its least attentive member. Alternative weighting procedures should be compared so that this issue becomes a methodological exercise that is resolved via empirical testing. It is, of course, also possible that measures of group traits will be developed independently on the basis of relational properties among group members (Lazarsfeld and Menzel, 1969). For example, we suggested earlier that "complexity of information processing" at the level of the family (as opposed to the individual member) might include such variables as elaborateness of language codes, coordinative leadership, and phasing rationality (see page 520).

26. While past work has been more prone to use "class," we prefer "status" in order to allow for finer gradations in stratification and to remove the usual requirement that class-based stratification implies clear cut identities on the part of stratum occupants.

27. An additional task before us is to more clearly indicate how our theory operates "as a whole." This might involve the formulation of structural equations to express the effects of several variables operating at once. It might also involve the development of a computer simulation to explore the dynamics of a system of variables operating through time. Still another approach would be to explore in more detail the rationales for the various assertions we have made. While this latter strategy is likely to initially call for an elaboration of implicit mechanisms, it could eventually lead to parsimonious principles.

28. Judges place varying emphasis on external consistency (compatibility with previous theories) and uniqueness (novelty) as criteria for good theory (Miller, 1973), and it is virtually impossible to satisfy both criteria.

REFERENCES

ADAMS, B. N.
1971   *The American Family: A Sociological Interpretation.* Chicago: Markham Publishing.

ALDOUS, J.
1971   "A framework for the analysis of family problem solving." In J. Aldous, T. Condon, R. Hill, M. Straus, and I. Tallman (eds.), *Family Problem Solving: A Symposium on Theoretical, Methodological, and Substantive Concerns.* Hinsdale, Ill.: Dryden Press.
1974   *The Developmental Approach to Family Analysis,* vol. 1: *The Conceptual Framework.* Minneapolis: University of Minnesota.

ALDOUS, J., T. CONDON, R. HILL, M. STRAUS, AND I. TALLMAN (EDS.),
1971   *Family Problem Solving: A Symposium on Theoretical, Methodological, and Substantive Concerns.* Hinsdale, Ill.: Dryden Press.

ALDOUS, J., L. GRAVENHORST, D. M. KLEIN, A. KOLMAN, AND P. MATTESSICH
1974   "Situational perspectives on families' definition behavior." Paper presented at the Annual Meeting of the National Council on Family Relations, St. Louis.

BALES, R. F. AND F. L. STRODTBECK
1951   "Phases in group problem solving." *Journal of Abnormal Social Psychology* 46:485–95.

BECK, D. F. AND M. A. JONES
1974   *Progress on Family Problems: A Nationwide Study of Clients' and Counselors' Views on Family Agency Services.* New York: Family Service Association of America.

BEE, H. L.
1977   "Socialization for problem solving." In J. Aldous et al. (eds.), *Family Problem Solving: A Symposium on Theoretical, Methodological, and Substantive Concerns.* Hinsdale, Ill.: Dryden Press.

BERNSTEIN, B.
1962   "Social class, linguistic codes, and grammatical elements." *Language and Speech* 5:221–40.
1974   *Class, Codes and Control.* New York: Schocken Books.

BRIM, O. G., JR., R. W. FAIRCHILD AND E. F. BORGATTA
1961   "Relations between family problems." *Marriage and Family Living* 23:219–26.

CAMPBELL, D. T.
1958   "Common fate, similarity, and the indices of the status of aggregates of persons as social entities." *Behavioral Science* 3:14–25.
1966   "Evolutionary epistemology." In P. A. Schlipp (ed.), *The Philosophy of Karl R. Popper.* La Salle, Ill.: Open Court Publishing.

CARTWRIGHT, D. AND A. ZANDER (EDS.)
1968   *Group Dynamics: Research and Theory,* third ed. New York: Harper & Row.

COHEN, R. L.
1974   "Social class differences in the problem solving process: An

integration of social organization, language and nonverbal communication.'' Unpublished Ph.D. Thesis, University of Minnesota.

DEACON, R. E. AND F. M. FIREBAUGH
1975   *Home Management: Context and Concepts.* Boston: Houghton Mifflin.

DREIKURS, R. AND L. GREY
1970   *A Parents' Guide to Child Discipline.* New York: Hawthorn Books.

DUVALL, E. M.
1971   *Family Development,* fourth ed. Philadelphia: Lippincott.

DUVALL, E. M. AND R. HILL
1948   *Report of the Committee on Dynamics of Family Interaction.* Washington, D.C.: National Conference on Family Life (mimeograph).

FARBER, B.
1964   *Family: Organization and Interaction.* San Francisco: Chandler Publishing Co.

FRENCH, J. R. P., JR., AND B. H. RAVEN
1959   ''The Bases of Social Power.'' In D. Cartwright (ed.), *Studies in Social Power.* Ann Arbor: University of Michigan Press.

GEISMAR, L. L. AND M. A. LaSORTE
1964   *Understanding the Multi-Problem Family.* New York: Association Press.

GOODE, W. J.
1961   ''Family Disorganization.'' In R. K. Merton and R. A. Nisbet (eds.), *Contemporary Family Problems.* New York: Harcourt, Brace.

GROSS, I. H., E. W. CRANDALL, AND M. M. KNOLL
1973   *Management for Modern Families.* Englewood Cliffs, N.J.: Prentice-Hall.

HANSEN, D. A. AND R. HILL
1964   ''Families under stress.'' In H. T. Christensen (ed.), *Handbook of Marriage and the Family.* Chicago: Rand McNally.

HESS, R. D. AND V. SHIPMAN
1965   ''Early experience and the socialization of cognitive modes in children.'' *Child Development* 34:869–86.

HILL, R.
1949   *Families under Stress.* New York: Harper.
1970   *Family Development in Three Generations: A Longitudinal Study of Changing Family Patterns of Planning and Achievement.* Cambridge, Mass.: Schenkman Publishing Co.

HILL, R. AND R. H. RODGERS
1964   ''The developmental approach.'' In H. T. Christensen (ed.), *Handbook of Marriage and the Family.* Chicago: Rand McNally.

HOFFMAN, L. R.
1965   ''Group problem solving.'' In Leonard Berkowitz (ed.), *Advances in Experimental Social Psychology,* vol. 2. New York: Academic Press.

JAMES, W.
1960   ''The energies of men.'' In H. Preston (ed.), *Great Essays.* New York: Washington Square Press.

KELLEY, H. H. AND J. W. THIBAUT
1969   ''Group problem solving.'' In G. Lindzey and E. Aronson (eds.), *Handbook of Social Psychology,* vol. 4, second ed. Reading, Mass.: Addison-Wesley.

KLEIN, D. M.
1974   ''Strategies of theory integration: A neglected area of theory construction methodology.'' Unpublished manuscript.

KLEIN, D. M. AND R. HILL
1972   ''Inventorying partial theories.'' Paper presented at the An-

nual Meeting of the National Council on Family Relations, Portland, Oregon.

KLEIN, D. M., R. HILL, B. C. MILLER, AND J. SCHVANEVELDT
1973   ''Toward a propositional theory of problem solving: Forging integrative linkages.'' Paper presented at the Annual Meeting of the National Council on Family Relations, Toronto, Canada.

KOHN, M. L.
1969   *Class and Conformity.* Homewood, Ill.: Dorsey Press.

KRETCH, D., R. S. CRUTCHFIELD, AND E. L. BALLACHEY
1962   *Individual in Society.* New York: McGraw-Hill.

LAZARSFELD, P. F. AND H. MENZEL
1969   ''On the relation between individual and collective properties.'' In A. Etzioni (ed.), *A Sociological Reader on Complex Organizations.* New York: Holt, Rinehart and Winston.

MAIER, N. R. F.
1952   *Principles of Human Relations.* New York: Wiley.
1967   ''Assets and liabilities in group problem solving: The need for an integrative function.'' *Psychological Review* 74:239–49.
1970   *Problem Solving and Creativity in Individuals and Groups.* Monterey, Calif.: Brooks/Cole.

MILLER, B. C.
1973   ''Assessing and reworking Ira Reiss' theory of premarital sexual permissiveness.'' Paper presented at the Annual Meeting of the National Council on Family Relations, Toronto, Canada.

MILLER, G. J.
1976   ''Family problem solving as a function of speech style, power relations, and role integration.'' Unpublished Ph.D. Thesis, University of Minnesota.

MOORE, O. K. AND A. R. ANDERSON
1971   ''Some principles for the design of clarifying educational environments.'' In J. Aldous et al. (eds.), *Family Problem Solving: A Symposium on Theoretical, Methodological, and Substantive Concerns.* Hinsdale, Ill.: Dryden Press.

MULLINS, N. C.
1971   *The Art of Theory: Construction and Use.* New York: Harper & Row.

MURDOCK, G. P.
1949   *Social Structure.* New York: Macmillan.

PATTON, B. R. AND K. GIFFIN
1973   *Problem-solving Group Interaction.* New York: Harper & Row.

RAPOPORT, R.
1963   ''Normal crises, family structure and mental health.'' *Family Process* 2:68–79.

RAVEN, B. H., R. CENTERS, AND A. RODRIGUES
1975   ''The bases of conjugal power.'' In R. E. Cromwell and D. H. Olson (eds.), *Power in Families.* New York: Wiley.

REISS, D.
1971a   ''Varieties of consensual experience: I. A theory for relating family interaction to individual thinking.'' *Family Process* 10:1–28.
1971b   ''Varieties of consensual experience: II. Dimensions of a family's experience of its environment.'' *Family Process* 10:28–35.
1971c   ''Varieties of consensual experience: III. Contrasts between families of normals, delinquents and schizophrenics.'' *Journal of Nervous and Mental Disease* 152:73–95.
1973   ''Theory as bootstrap: The concept of family consensual experience as an organizer for exploratory research on family problem solving.'' Paper presented at the Annual Meeting of the National Council on Family Relations, Toronto, Canada.

REISS, D. AND R. COSTELL
1974   ''Family and organization: Conflicting and corresponding

constructions of reality." Paper presented at the Annual Meeting of the National Council on Family Relations, St. Louis.

REISS, I.
1971   *The Family System in America*. New York: Holt, Rinehart and Winston.

REYNOLDS, P. D.
1971   *A Primer in Theory Construction*. Indianapolis: Bobbs-Merrill.

RIESSMAN, F.
1962   *The Culturally Deprived Child*. New York: Harper & Row.

RODGERS, R. H.
1962   "Improvements in the construction and analysis of family life cycle categories." Unpublished Ph.D. Thesis, University of Minnesota.

1973   *Family Interaction and Transaction: The Developmental Approach*. Englewood Cliffs, N.J.: Prentice-Hall.

SCHEFF, T. J.
1967   "Toward a sociological model of consensus." *American Sociological Review* 32:32–46.

SHAW, M. E.
1971   *Group Dynamics: The Psychology of Small Group Behavior*. New York: McGraw-Hill.

SMITH, T. E.
1970   "Foundations of parental influence upon adolescents: An application of social power theory." *American Sociological Review* 35:860–73.

SPREY, J.
1966   "Family disorganization: Toward a conceptual clarification." *Journal of Marriage and the Family* 28:398–406.

STRAUS, M. A.
1968   "Communication, creativity, and problem solving ability of middle- and working-class families in three societies." *American Journal of Sociology* 73:417–30.

1971   "Information search experiment." In R. Hill (ed.), application for continuation grant, MH15521-04, University of Minnesota.

STRAUS, M. A. AND I. TALLMAN
1971   "SIMFAM: A technique for observational measurement and experimental study of families." In J. Aldous et al. (eds.), *Family Problem Solving: A Symposium on Theoretical, Methodological, and Substantive Concerns*. Hinsdale, Ill.: Dryden Press.

TALLMAN, I.
1970   "The family as a small problem solving group." *Journal of Marriage and the Family* 32:94–104.

1972   "Social structure and socialization for change." Paper presented at the Annual Meeting of the National Council on Family Relations, Portland, Oregon.

TALLMAN, I., D: KLEIN, R. COHEN, M. IHINGER, R. MAROTZ, P. TORSIELLO, AND K. TROOST
1974   *A Taxonomy of Group Problems and Implications for a Theory of Group Problem Solving*. Minnesota Family Study Center Technical Report 3, University of Minnesota.

TALLMAN, I. AND G. MILLER
1971   "Communication, language style, and family problem solving." In R. Hill (ed.), application for continuation grant, MH15521-03, University of Minnesota.

1974   "Class differences in family problem solving: The effects of verbal ability, hierarchical structure, and role expectations." *Sociometry* 37:13–37.

1976   "Social structure and individual problem solving: A theory of social change." Paper in progress.

TALLMAN, I., L. WILSON, AND M. STRAUS
1972   "SIMCAR: A game simulation method for cross-national family research." Unpublished manuscript.

TURNER, R. H.
1970   *Family Interaction*. New York: Wiley.

WEICK, K. E.
1971   "Group processes, family processes, and problem solving." In J. Aldous et al. (eds.), *Family Problem Solving: A Symposium on Theoretical, Methodological, and Substantive Concerns*. Hinsdale, Ill.: Dryden Press.

21

DETERMINANTS OF VIOLENCE IN THE FAMILY: TOWARD A THEORETICAL INTEGRATION

Richard J. Gelles and Murray A. Straus

Prior to 1971 violent family members were among the missing persons of family research. No articles whose titles contained the word "violence" had appeared in *The Journal of Marriage and the Family* before the special issue on violence in November 1971 (O'Brien, 1971). The few references to violence between family members almost invariably dealt with pathological extremes. They tended to be either in the form of analyses of crime statistics such as homicide and assault (see for example Wolfgang, 1958; Pittman and Handy, 1964), discussions of particular cases of conjugal homicide or child abuse or filicide (see for example Kempe et al., 1962; Steele and Pollock, 1974; Schultz, 1960; and Snell et al., 1964), or presentations on possible intervention strategies in family violence (see for example Bard, 1969; Bard and Berkowitz, 1969; and Parnas, 1970).

Implicit in most of the previous work on intrafamily violence is the idea that physical violence is abnormal and/or grows out of some social or personal pathology. By contrast, the program of research in which we have been involved since 1970 tends to make the opposite assumption. While granting that some instances of intrafamily violence are an outgrowth of social or psychological pathology, we maintain that physical violence between family members is a normal part of family life in most societies (Straus, 1976b), and in American society in particular.

The term "normal" has at least three meanings: statistically frequent, culturally approved, and approved by the user of the adjective. Our research (some of which will be summarized later in this chapter) provides evidence for the normality of intrafamily violence in the first two of these three meanings. Furthermore, as suggested by conflict theorists, it is assumed that conflict in social relationships—whether in the family, in the streets, or between nations—is an inevitable and necessary part of social relationship, but physical violence is not. Dahrendorf (1959:231), for example, holds that "violent conflict may at times be desirable. . . . Generally speaking, however, it would seem to be the task of social policy to try to regulate the inevitable conflicts of social life by other means. . . ." If the structure of the society or family does not provide nonviolent means for individuals and groups to redress grievances and to engage in efforts to further their interests vis-à-vis other individuals or groups, physical violence may be the only way to correct injustices, to bring about needed social change, and to maintain the viability of the social unit. Thus, although our own value preferences are clearly opposed to violence, this cannot be an absolute preference (Straus and Steinmetz, 1974:322–23).

The empirical part of our family violence research program has emphasized the determinants of intrafamily violence. This work includes exploratory studies of college students' experience with violence at home (Straus,

NOTE: Appreciation is expressed to Melvin Wilkinson, Suzanne Steinmetz, and Ira L. Reiss for their helpful suggestions on an earlier version. This chapter has benefited from comments and insightful critiques of a number of people to whom it is a pleasure to express our appreciation. These include (1) the editors and chapter reviewers: Wesley R. Burr, F. Ivan Nye, Suzanne K. Steinmetz, and Melvin Wilkinson; (2) Howard Shapiro, our colleague at the University of New Hampshire; (3) students at the University of New Hampshire, especially those in Straus's seminar on violence: Sandra G. Atwell, Richard A. Bulcroft, Bruce W. Brown, Joseph C. Carroll, Keith M. Farrington, Joyce Foss, Gerald T. Hotaling, and Jean Giles-Simms, and at Rhode Island, Martha Mulligan. Several of these students wrote detailed critiques, and all contributed importantly to the development of our work on family violence through the exchange of ideas in this seminar and through their seminar papers (many of which will appear in Straus and Hotaling, 1978).

The Family Violence Research Program, of which this chapter forms a part, has been supported by grants from the Office of Child Development and the National Institute of Mental Health, including MH15521 and MH27557 at the University of New Hampshire and OCD/NCCAN 90-C-425 at the University of Rhode Island. A description of the Family Violence Research Program and a bibliography of publications may be obtained from Gelles or Straus. We are of course indebted to these agencies for funds which have made this research and research training program possible.

1971, 1974a; Steinmetz, 1974), in-depth interviews about the extent of violence in a sample of 80 families (Gelles, 1974, 1975a, 1976), an analysis of the National Violence Commission data (Owens and Straus, 1975), a content analysis of children's literature (Huggins and Straus, 1975), and a study of a nationally representative sample of 2,200 families carried out in 1976 and due to be published in 1978 (Straus et al., 1978).

The program of research has also included some theoretical work focused on the determinants of intrafamilial violence; for example, Straus's use of systems theory (1973), Gelles's structural model of conjugal violence (1974), Allen and Straus's work on the resource theory (1975), Straus's critique of the "catharsis" or ventilation approach to violence (1974a), and an analysis of structural and cultural theories of intrafamily violence (Straus, 1971; 1974b).

The work mentioned in the previous two paragraphs has involved seven different theories purporting to explain the occurrence of physical violence within the nuclear family. In addition we have identified and at least partly analyzed eight other theories, making a total of 15 different theories. The richness of the theoretical resources available to those concerned with family violence is to a considerable extent due to the long history of research on aggression and violence in nonfamily settings, much of which can be applied to the special case of the family. Finally, there are conceptual frameworks whose potential for explaining intrafamily violence is noted in this paper. But this theoretical richness can also be confusing. Therefore, in addition to presenting the different theories, one aim of the chapter is to begin the process of integrating these 15 theories into a more comprehensive explanatory theory of the determinants of violence between family members.

It may be helpful at this point to have an overview of the major sections of the chapter. Section 1 discusses why violence is an important aspect of family interaction and the question of whether anything is to be gained by attempting to construct a theory of *intrafamily* violence, given the fact that much theoretical work is being done on violence in other groups and settings. Section 2 takes up conceptual issues, including formal definitions of conflict, aggression, and violence, and discusses some of the problems with these definitions. Section 3 is devoted to the development and illustration of a taxonomy of family violence. Sections 4 and 5 summarize 15 theories of interpersonal violence and consider the applicability of each to the specific case of the family. Finally, in section 6 a start at a theoretical integration is made. This is done by diagramming the causal flow asserted by 13 of the theories reviewed and combining the 13 causal flow diagrams into an overall theoretical model showing some of the major ways in which these theories interrelate and complement each other.

1. IS A SPECIAL THEORY NECESSARY FOR *FAMILY* VIOLENCE?

An important preliminary question which arises as a focus for efforts at developing an integrated theory of family violence is, why is such a theory needed? That is, why focus empirical and theoretical attention on the specific case of interpersonal violence between family members? Would it not be more profitable to simply work toward a general theory of interpersonal violence rather than a specific theory of intrafamilial violence?

The question of whether one can or should develop a theory of violence which applies only to the family can be answered yes if the family has variables that are not found in other groups, or if the relationships between the variables are different for the family than for other groups. While the family does not contain variables which are absent in other groups, the family does contain a special relationship between variables which is not found elsewhere. The family is high on both intimacy and privacy. As will be noted later in this section, this relationship tends to distinguish the family from other social groups and may be a partial explanation for the high level of violence typically found in families as compared to other groups.

Aside from the unique character of the family which argues for a special theory of violence, such a theory is important for three additional reasons. First, some of the variables which the family shares with other groups are much more visible in the family. Second, an unusually high rate of violence seems to characterize familial relations. And third, attempting to answer the question of why the family is so high in violence opens the way to discovering important variables which might not otherwise be observed.

A. *The Extent of Intrafamily Violence*

No one has yet reported data which would give a precise indication of the extent of intrafamily violence in America.[1] Without this type of information one can only infer and speculate about how much intrafamily violence exists. Some of our findings together with other indicators lead us to believe that violence is a pervasive and common feature of American family relations. It may be more common to the institution of family than is love. Our reasons for suggesting this are based on the following data and indicators:

Physical Punishment

We start with this aspect of the use of physical force within the family because it is probably both the most frequent aspect and the best researched.

Various studies in the U.S.A. and England (Blumberg, 1964–65; Bronfenbrenner, 1958; Erlanger, 1974; Stark and McEvoy, 1970) show that between 84 and 97 percent of all parents use physical punishment *at some point* in the child's life. Moreover, contrary to what might be guessed, physical punishment continues for most children well into adolescence. Bachman's study of a large sample of tenth graders (1967) found that 61 percent had been slapped. Studies by Steinmetz (1971, 1974) and Straus (1971) found that this pattern also applies to high school seniors. In each of the three samples studied, about half had been hit or threatened with being hit during their senior year.

Of course, physical punishment is not the same as other violence, primarily because it is normatively approved and because of the presumed altruistic motivation. But it is violence nonetheless because it involves the intentional use of physical force to cause pain. In certain respects, it has the same consequences as other forms of violence, despite the good intentions. For example, the studies of physical punishment show that parents who use physical punishment to control the aggressiveness of their children are probably *increasing* rather than decreasing the aggressive tendencies of their children (Bandura, 1973; Eron et al., 1971; Owens and Straus, 1975; Sears et al., 1957). In short, there are grounds for believing that violence begets violence, however peaceful and altruistic the motivation. In addition to its possible effects on training children in the use of violence, parental use of physical punishment may also lay the groundwork for carrying this use of force to the point at which it can be considered child abuse.

Child Abuse

Estimates of the incidence of child abuse range from a low of 6,000 cases per year (Gil, 1970:60) to a high of 1 million (*New York Times*, 1975). These estimates are influenced by a variety of factors which make using or interpreting these data quite difficult (Gelles, 1975b), but conservative estimates of child abuse run to a figure of between 200,000 and 500,000 cases a year in the United States (see Light, 1974).

Murder

Murder is the one aspect of intrafamily violence on which there are reasonably good data. Steinmetz and Straus (1974) suggest that this is because it is a crime which leaves physical evidence that cannot be ignored in the same way that the normative bias of the society caused both laypersons and researchers to ignore other forms of intrafamily violence in the past. A graphic indication of the extent of intrafamily murder can be gleaned from our estimate that each year about as many people are murdered by their relatives in New York City in any one year as were killed in bloody disturbances in Northern Ireland from 1969 to 1978. Between 20 and 40 percent of all homicides in the United States involve domestic relationships. The high proportion of intrafamily homicide is not confined to the United States (Curtis, 1974). For example, the African societies studied by Bohannan (1960:243) range from 22 to 63 percent intrafamily homicides, and the highest rate (67 percent) is for a Danish sample.

Assault

Turning to nonlethal physical violence between husband and wife, one source of data is police reports. Just as relatives are the largest single category of murder victim, so family fights are the largest single category of police calls. One legal researcher (Parnas, 1967:914) estimates that more police calls involve family conflict than do calls for all criminal incidents, including murders, rapes, nonfamily assaults, robberies, and muggings. Twenty-two percent of all police fatalities come from investigating problems between man and wife or parent and child (Parnas, 1967). Aggravated assault between husbands and wives made up 11 percent of all aggravated assaults in St. Louis (Pittman and Handy, 1964:467), and 52 percent in Detroit (Boudouris, 1971:668). These figures probably are an underestimate of the percentage of assaults between husbands and wives due to the fact that many police officers attempt to dissuade wives from filing assault charges and many wives do not see an attack by a husband as a case of legal assault. Therefore, one cannot tell from these data on police calls and assault charges just what proportion of all husbands and wives have had physical fights, since it takes an unusual combination of events to have the police called in.

Both Levinger (1966) and O'Brien (1971) studied applicants for divorce. O'Brien found that 17 percent of his cases spontaneously mentioned overt violent behavior, and Levinger found that 23 percent of the middle-class couples and 40 percent of the working-class couples gave "physical abuse" as a major complaint. These figures may be underestimates because there were probably violent incidents which were not mentioned or which were not listed as a main cause of the divorce. Perhaps these figures should be at least doubled. However, for nondivorcing couples physical violence may be less. Or it may be, as we suspect, that the difference is not very great.

The closest thing to data on a cross section of the population is to be found in a survey conducted for the National Commission on the Causes and Prevention of Violence which deals with what violence people would approve (Stark and McEvoy, 1970). These data show that one of four men in this survey, and one out of six women, would approve of slapping a wife under certain conditions. As for a wife slapping a husband, 26 percent of the men and 19 percent of the women would approve. Of course, some people who approve of slapping will never do it, and some who disapprove *will* slap—or worse. Probably the latter group is larger. If so, we know that husband-wife violence at this minimal level occurs in at least one-quarter of American families, but we think these are sharp underestimates.

Finally, our own pilot studies give some indication of the frequency of violence in the family. The first of these studies (Gelles, 1974) is based on informal depth interviews in 80 families. This study revealed that 56 percent of the couples had used physical force on each other at some time. For 20 percent of these 80 families husband-wife violence was a regular and patterned occurrence (six or more times per year).

In another exploratory study, students at the University of New Hampshire responded to a questionnaire about conflicts which occurred in their families during their senior year in high school, including questions on whether or not the parties to the disputes had ever hit, pushed, shoved, or threw things at each other in the course of one of the disputes.

The results show that during that one year 62 percent of these high school seniors had used physical force on a brother or sister, and 16 percent of their parents had used physical force on each other. These are figures for a single year. The percentage who had *ever* used violence is probably much greater. How much greater is difficult to estimate. One cannot simply accumulate the 16 percent for one year over a total number of years married because some couples will never have used violence and others will have done so repeatedly. Nevertheless, it seems safe to assume that it will not always be the same 16 percent. So it is probably best to fall back on the 56 percent estimate from the 80 depth interviews.

As noted at the beginning of this section, with the exception of homicide, none of the data just summarized are based on samples of adequate size or representativeness. But taken together they offer a persuasive counterargument to the widespread view that violence within families is a rare phenomenon found in scattered families. On the contrary, this evidence suggests that it is a major feature of American family life (and probably in most other societies—see Straus, 1976b).

Part of the widespread misperception is due to an unconscious commitment to the myth of the family as nonviolent (Steinmetz and Straus, 1974:6–17). This creates a perceptual blindness on the part of the public and ''selective inattention'' on the part of social scientists. For example, most people do not think of the almost universally present physical fights between siblings as violence. Even fewer think of physical punishment as violence. But even if these are excluded, the fact remains that one is more likely to be murdered by a family member than by anyone else. Moreover, although some want to reverse our figures and say that 80 percent of the spouses studied by Gelles did *not* have a regular pattern of hitting each other, and that 44 percent of the spouses studied by Gelles *never* hit each other, this claim is itself evidence of the extent to which a marriage license is unconsciously accepted as a hitting license. This can be seen imagining the same statistics for a factory, a church, or a university. Would it be taken as evidence of nonviolence if the studies showed that 44 percent of the workers, faculty, or members of a congregation never hit each other, and 80 percent did not do so on a regular basis?

B. The Special Case of the Family

In one sense family violence may be looked at as not essentially different than other forms of violence. From this perspective research on family violence could be conducted so as to verify or develop one or more of the general theories of interpersonal violence. On the other hand, violence in the family may be considered, for a variety of reasons, a *special* case of violence which requires its own body of theory to explain it. We suggest that violence between family members is a special enough case to require study in its own right. This is partly because of the extraordinarily high incidence of intrafamily violence, partly because all general theories need to be specified to apply to particular manifestations of the phenomenon they seek to explain, and partly because even though the family shares certain characteristics with other small groups, as a social group and as an institution of society the family has distinctive characteristics. These are likely to be important for understanding why the family is such a violent group, social setting, and institution. Therefore, this section identifies some of the aspects of the family which are important to consider in the development of an explanation of intrafamily violence.

Time at Risk

The most elementary family characteristic accounting for the high incidence of violence is the fact that so many hours of the day are spent interacting with other family members. Although this is an important factor, the ratio of intrafamily violence to violence experienced outside the family far exceeds the ratio of time spent in the family to time spent outside the family. A moment spent comparing the family with other groups in which large amounts of time are spent, such as work groups, provides a concrete way of grasping the fact that far more is involved than just ''time at risk.''

Range of Activities and Interests

Most nonfamily social interactions are focused on a specific purpose. But the primary-group nature of the family makes family interactions cover a vast range of activities. This means that there are more ''events'' over which a dispute or a failure to meet expectations can occur.

Intensity of Involvement

Not only is there a wider range of events over which a dispute or dissatisfaction can occur, but in addition the degree of injury felt in such instances is likely to be much greater than if the same issue were to arise in relation to someone outside the family. The failure of a work colleague to spell or eat properly may be mildly annoying (or more likely just a subject for derision). But if the bad spelling or table manners are those of one's child or spouse, the pain experienced is often excruciating.

Impinging Activities

Many family activities have a "zero sum" aspect. Conflict is structured into such things as whether Bach or Mendelssohn will be played on the family stereo, whether to go to a movie or bowling, or a lineup for use of the bathroom. Less obvious but equally important is the impinging on one's personal space or self-image brought about by the life style and habits of others in the family, such as those who leave things around versus those who put everything away, or those who eat quickly versus those who like leisurely meals.

Right to Influence

Membership in a family carries with it an implicit right to influence the behavior of others. Consequently, the dissatisfactions over undesirable or impinging activities of others is further exacerbated by attempts to change the behavior of the other.

Age and Sex Discrepancies

The fact that the family is composed of people of different sexes and age (especially during the child-rearing years), coupled with the existence of generational and sex differences in culture and outlook on life, makes the family an arena of culture conflict. This is epitomized in such phrases as "battle of the sexes" and "generational conflict."

Ascribed Roles

Compounding the problem of age and sex differences is the fact that family statuses and roles are, to a very considerable extent, assigned on the basis of these biological characteristics rather than on the basis of interest and competence. An aspect of this which has traditionally been a focus of contention is socially structured sexual inequality, or, in contemporary language, the sexist organization of the family. A sexist structure has especially high conflict potential built in when such a structure exists in the context of a society with equalitarian ideology. But even without such an ideological inconsistency, the conflict potential is high because it is inevitable that not all husbands have the competence needed to fulfill the culturally prescribed leadership role (Kolb and Straus, 1974; Allen and Straus, 1975).

Family Privacy

In many societies the normative, kinship, and household structure insulates the family from both social controls and assistance in coping with intrafamily conflict. This characteristic is most typical of the conjugal family system of urban-industrial societies (Laslett, 1973).

Involuntary Membership

Birth relationships are obviously involuntary, and underage children cannot themselves terminate such relationships. In addition, Sprey (1969) shows that the conjugal relationship also has nonvoluntary aspects. There is first the social expectation of marriage as a long-term commitment, as expressed in the phrase "until death do us part." In addition, there are emotional, material, and legal rewards and constraints which frequently make membership in the family group inescapable, socially, physically, or legally. So when conflicts and dissatisfactions arise, the alternative of resolving them by leaving often does not, in practice, exist—at least in the perception of what is practical or possible.

High Level of Stress

Paradoxically, in the light of the previous paragraph, nuclear family relationships are unstable. This comes about because of a number of circumstances, starting with the general tendency for all dyadic relationships to be unstable (Simmel, 1950:118–44). In addition, the nuclear family continuously undergoes major changes in structure as a result of processes inherent in the family life cycle: events such as the birth of children, maturation of children, aging, and retirement. The crisis-like nature of these changes has long been recognized (LeMasters, 1957). All of this, combined with the huge emotional investment which is typical of family relationships, means that the family is likely to be the locus of more, and more serious, stresses than other groups.[2]

Normative Approval

Another aspect of the family which is important for understanding why so much violence occurs within that setting is the simple but important fact of *de jure* and *de facto* cultural norms legitimizing the use of violence between family members in situations which would make the use of physical force a serious moral or legal violation if it occurred between nonfamily members. This is most obvious in the rights of parents to use physical force. But there is also considerable evidence of deeply rooted, though largely unverbalized, norms which make the marriage license also a hitting license (Straus, 1976a).

Socialization into Violence and Its Generalization

An important part of the explanation for the high level of intrafamily violence is the fact that violence is first experienced in the family and is experienced in relations with those who profess love for one another. The basis for this starts with the fact that physical punishment is nearly universal. When physical punishment is used, several things can be expected to occur. First, and most obvious, is learning to do or not do whatever the punishment is intended to teach one to do or not do. Less obvious but equally or more important are two other lessons which are so deeply learned that they become an integral part of the personality and world view.

The first of these unintended consequences is the association of love with violence. The child learns that those who love him or her the most are also those who hit and have the right to hit. The second unintended consequence is the lesson that when something is really important, it justifies the use of physical force. Finally, we suggest that these indirect lessons are not confined to providing a model for later treatment of one's own children. Rather, they become such a fundamental part of the individual's personality and world view that they are generalized to other social relationships, and especially to the relationship which is closest to that of parent and child: that of husband and wife. Therefore, it is suggested that early experiences with physical punishment lay the groundwork for the normative legitimacy of all types of violence but especially intrafamily violence. Experience with physical punishment provides a role model—indeed a specific "script" (Gagnon and Simon, 1973; Huggins and Straus, 1975)—for such actions. In addition, for many children, there is not even the need to generalize this socially scripted pattern of behavior from the parent-child nexus in which it was learned to other family relationships because, if our estimates are correct, millions of children can directly observe and use as a role model physical violence between husbands and wives (see also Gelles and Straus, 1975; Owens and Straus, 1975).

2. CONCEPTUAL ISSUES

A. *Definitions of Violence and Aggression*

For purposes of this chapter, *violence* is defined as "an act carried out with the intention of, or perceived as having the intention of, physically hurting another person." The "physical hurt" can range from slight pain, as in a slap, to murder. The basis for the "intent to hurt" may range from a concern for a child's safety (as when a child is spanked for going into the street) to hostility so intense that the death of the other is desired.

Inclusion of the requirement of "intent" has long been a source of confusion and controversy in definitions of aggression and violence. In part this is because intent and motive are meanings which are attached to acts (by the actor or by those with whom the actor interacts) at the time or after the act occurs (Bandura, 1973:4). To deal with this problem, we added the phrase "or perceived as having the intention of" to the definition. In a later section on attribution theory, this will be analyzed in more detail.

In addition to problems of intent and attribution, there are a host of problems connected with the "physical hurt" (i.e., outcome) part of the definition, some of which are also discussed in later sections. For the present, however, it should be noted that many hurt-intending acts are not successful, and some acts which were not intended to cause harm do result in hurt; and that this definition does *not* require any physical hurt to actually result—only that the act be intended to hurt, or be perceived as having that intention.

Aggression is a more general concept than violence. It refers to any malevolent act, i.e., an act carried out with the intention of, or which is perceived as having the intention of, hurting another. The injury can be psychological, material deprivation, or physical pain or damage. When the injury is pain or damage, it can be called "physical aggression" and is then synonymous with "violence" as used in this chapter. This definition of aggression is consistent with the way aggression has usually been defined in the social psychological literature (Johnson, 1972; Rule, 1974), with the exception of addition of a phrase to make it consistent with the recent work on attribution processes in aggression (Tedeschi et al., 1974).

Theoretical and Ideological Confounding

One of the major sources of confusion surrounding the concepts of aggression and violence is that both are entangled with various theoretical and ideological concerns which have no necessary linkage to either concept. In relation to "aggression," for example, psychoanalytic and much ordinary language uses "aggression" to refer to deliberately noxious acts *and also* to such things as drive level, assertiveness, and exploratory behavior. These often have noxious consequences even though they are not the "goal response" of the act.

A problem of this type with the concept of violence is that it is a "label" or a political term as well as a scientific concept. It is used by members of the political left to describe almost any aspect of society of which they disapprove. Thus some critics of the Federal Aid to Dependent Children program label it as "violent" because of its negative impact on the family. Other groups refer to entire social systems—such as capitalism—as "violent." However, the most immediate source of confusion is with the use of "violence" by Laing and Cooper (1964): the molding of the behavior or personality of an individual by others—especially other family members. We recognize the phenomenon to which they refer, but it is nonetheless a separate phenomenon, as can be seen from the fact that they rarely refer to instances in which either physical or verbal aggression is used. In fact, the "violence" which Laing has in mind can be achieved more effectively without violence as that term is used here.

In contrast to these ideological uses of "violence" the definition used in this chapter is purely behavioral: it is a physical act. Of course, one cannot separate an act from its social meaning. But clarity demands that we separate the behavior from its social meanings in a way which allows for the variety of meanings which exist in a society or across societies, and which also specifies what those meanings are. It is for this reason that the variable of "legitimacy" is used as one of the dimensions to form the taxonomy presented in section 3. That is, the labeling, political, or ideological aspect of the concept of violence is treated as a *variable,* rather than assumed to always be negative as in the usage illustrated in the previous paragraphs. This reflects the fact that the same act of physical hurting is negatively valued by some or in some circumstances, and positively valued by others or in other circumstances. Furthermore, it follows from the above that any theory of violence in the family (or in any other situation, or for that matter a theory of any kind of social behavior) must consider social definitions and norms concerning the behavior in question.

A related question concerns the reason for including "moderate corporal punishment" of children within the definition of violence. There are two main reasons for this, despite the fact that it violates ordinary usage. First, as noted above, and in more detail in section 3, the main difference between "moderate corporal punishment" and what would be considered a chargeable assault if the actors were unrelated adults—for example, two workers or a foreman and a worker—is whether the act of physical force is normatively approved or disapproved. A second reason is based on the evidence summarized in the last part of section 1B, which indicates that physical punishment provides the fundamental learning situation for the normative legitimacy of other types of intrafamily violence, including husband-wife violence.

Is Violence a Separate Phenomenon?

In one sense violence is simply one mode of carrying out an aggressive act. Could we therefore eliminate the problem of political connotations by eliminating the term and just calling it "physical aggression"? One reason for singling out physical aggression by the use of the term "violence" is parallel to Etzioni's insistence on the importance of differentiating coercion in general and forceful coercion (1971): the use of physical force to carry out an aggressive act is qualitatively different from other modes of being injured. Thus, although violence shares with other types of aggressive acts the central characteristic of malevolence or harm-doing intent, the nature of the intended harm (physical injury) is unique. This is exemplified in the ancient children's taunt: "Sticks and stones may break my bones but names will never hurt me." In short, the consequences are different.

A final reason for considering physical violence separately from other aggressive acts is that grouping all aggressive acts together prevents explaining why the aggressor chooses this particular modality. Since there are many ways of being aggressive, we need to find out the particular causal sequence which underlies the use of

physical violence compared to other modes of hurting another. In short, the antecedents of physical aggression may be different from the antecedents of other modes of aggression. A general theory of aggression may be necessary, but it is not sufficient to explain physical aggression. For example, physical aggression may occur because there is an audience to a dispute that considers it "unmanly" to use insults and other forms of verbal aggression.

Force

William Goode (1971) restricts the use of the term "violence" to the illegitimate use of physical force. On the other hand, if the act is socially legitimate—such as spanking a child or tear-gassing demonstrators who will not disperse—Goode labels it "force" rather than "violence." This is roughly equivalent to ordinary English usage—which is both an advantage and disadvantage. The disadvantage comes about because of the ambiguity in identifying what is legitimate and what is not. For example, shall we use the parent's conception of when it is legitimate to spank a child? The child's conception? The middle-class conception? The working-class conception? Or the legal conception? In the case of the demonstration, the actions of the police in using tear gas are seen as illegitimate by the demonstrators and hence as "violence." But the police define such actions as necessary and as legitimate and hence as "force." Thus the problem of "whose definition?" makes an unambiguous distinction between force and violence virtually impossible. Nevertheless, the idea of legitimacy is extremely important, as will be shown in the next section, and in the section on attribution theory.

B. Conflict and Violence

The conceptual complexity and confusion associated with the idea of "conflict" rivals that surrounding "aggression" and "violence." Moreover, since there is a certain overlap between "conflict" and "violence," some of the confusion associated with conflict also overlaps and serves to further muddy the waters for those trying to get a clear picture of violence. Therefore, even though this chapter is not concerned with conflict per se, some space must be devoted to specifying and differentiating conflict from aggression and violence. For purposes of this paper, the discussion will be restricted to three central concepts used by conflict theorists (even though many more are involved): "conflict of interest," "conflict," and "hostility."

Conflict of Interest

When conflict theorists talk about the ubiquity of conflict, they are referring to what is here called "conflict of interest," that is, to the fact that members of a social group, no matter how small and intimate, are all seeking to live out their lives in accordance with personal agendas which inevitably differ. These differences range in importance. Whose TV show will be watched at eight? Should money be saved or spent on a vacation? Which is more important to control, inflation or unemployment? There is no way to avoid such conflicts without running the risks of group rigidification and ultimate disintegration, to which conflict theorists have alerted us.[3]

Conflict

The second phenomenon which must be distinguished if we are to have any hope of doing sound theoretical or empirical research on intrafamily conflict is the method used to advance one's interest, that is, the means or the behavior used to resolve conflicts. Two families can have the same level of conflict over the types of interests mentioned in the previous section. But even though the conflicts in that sense are identical, the two families may differ vastly—and with profound consequences—in respect to how they deal with these conflicts. One family might resolve the issue of which TV program by rotation, another by a "first there" strategy, and another by who is physically strongest or most willing to threaten force.

Some conflict theorists have attempted to deal with the conceptual confusion by using the term "conflict" to refer to conflict of interest, and a different term to refer to conflict in the sense of the means of advancing one's interest. Thus Dahrendorf (1959) refers to the means of engaging in conflict as "conflict management." However, the situation remains confused because other theorists follow the opposite strategy. Coser (1956:8) uses "conflict" to refer to the behavior used to pursue one's interest. So when Coser and Dahrendorf use the term "conflict," they are often referring to quite different phenomena, the one to the conflict of interest and the other to the means of pursuing that interest. There is no resolution in sight for this confusing state of affairs. The best that can be done is to make clear what usage one is following. Therefore, in the context of the present chapter Coser's usage will be followed; i.e., "conflict" will be used to refer to the overt acts which people carry out in response to a conflict of interest. These can range from attempts to advance one's interest by showing the moral, logical, or factual superiority of the desired outcome, to acts of verbal and physical aggression.

Hostility

When, for whatever reason, members of a group have a feeling or dislike or antipathy for each other, this fact is also often referred to as conflict. But paradoxically, as conflict theorists have pointed out, hostility is likely to be extremely high when conflict in the sense of conflict of interest is repressed. This is because such a situation—namely, the existence of conflicts of interest and the repression of conflict in the sense of attempts to do something about those conflicts of interest—means that the actors are prevented from achieving ends which are important for them. Hostility develops out of this frustration. Of course, hostility can arise from other sources as well. But that only highlights the need to keep distinct the phenomena of conflict of interest, conflict, and hostility. Therefore, in this chapter, "hostility" will be restricted to refer to the level of negative cathexis between members of the family group. Finally, and most directly relevant to the purposes of this chapter, there can be hostility without violence or violence without hostility.

It follows from the previous discussion that further theoretical work on conflict in the family requires as a minimum first step that we avoid the all too common confusion of "conflict of interest," "conflict," "hostility," and "violence." Similarly, clear empirical work on intrafamily conflict also depends on having separate measures of these variables. One approach to developing some of the needed measures is the Conflict Tactics Scales (Straus, 1978).

C. Other Conceptual Distinctions

There are a great many conceptual distinctions which are relevant for precise theoretical or empirical work on violence within families, some of which will be briefly delineated in this section.

Aggression and Aggressiveness

As implied by the definitions previously given for verbal and physical aggression, the concept of aggression as used in this chapter refers exclusively to *acts* of interpersonal behavior. On the other hand, the concept of aggressiveness refers to a dispositional state of an actor, which may or may not result in aggression. A dispositional state or personality variable such as aggressiveness is only one of many "instigators" or factors which can bring about a violent act. Acts of extreme violence may be committed by people with a low level of aggressiveness; conversely, highly aggressive persons may constrain or sublimate such tendencies and rarely or never carry out an act of verbal or physical aggression.

Aggression and Assertion

One of the most thorny confusions in the thicket of conceptual confusion which surrounds research on conflict, aggression, and violence is that between aggression and assertion. Assertion or assertiveness is very close to conflict. It means pursuing one's interests. And like conflict, it leaves open the question of how these interests are to be pursued. One can be assertive in the sense of standing up for one's rights and interests without being aggressive in the sense of doing so by an act intended to harm another. Nevertheless, there is a pervasive tendency to equate the two. This is most clearly manifested by psychoanalytic theory, in which aggression is almost identical with assertiveness, drive level, or the instinct for survival. It is also ingrained in the folk concepts from which Freud's theory sprang. Thus we speak of "an aggressive manager" when we mean one who strives hard.

There are a number of reasons for this conceptual confusion, including the following: (1) Assertiveness can lead to the injury of others, even though the intent to injure was not present. Thus our hard-working manager may not want to drive another company out of business but may do so because the efficiency of his firm lets it offer goods at a price which is impossible for some other firm. That is, an assertive act and an aggressive act can lead to the same outcome and therefore tend to be confused. (2) There is envy and jealousy of assertive people because of the power and material goods which tend to flow to such people. This can lead others to impute aggression as a means of explaining or disavowing the difference between their own accomplishments and those of the assertive person. (3) Despite the genuine negative feeling in our society about aggression and violence, there is often a large payoff for such acts (Buss, 1971; Feshbach, 1971). Aggression *is* one mode of being assertive and often a very successful mode. So it is easy to confuse the assertiveness with one particular way of being assertive.

The confusion between aggression and assertiveness is particularly important for the study of violence in the family because it is reflected in strategies urged by one group of marriage counselors and advice books: those in what can be called the "constructive aggression" school, as represented, for example, in Bach and Wyden's *The Intimate Enemy* (1968). Some of these authors do make a distinction between aggression and assertiveness by distinguishing between fighting and "fighting fairly." But even when that is the case, the distinction tends to be overshadowed by the general tone which lumps aggression and assertiveness together and often imbeds the description of assertive acts in a context which strongly implies the positive nature of aggression and the positive contribution to mental health and social relations of the cathartic effects of ventilating (in the sense of acting out) one's aggressive feelings. A review of the research literature and some new evidence reported by Straus (1974a) suggests exactly the opposite: that the emphasis should be on *non*-aggressive assertiveness. This is based on the repeated finding that aggressive acts tend to evoke counteraggression and an escalation of the aggressive content of the conflict (often to the point of physical violence) rather than lead to a constructive solution to the objective issue.

3. TYPES OF FAMILY VIOLENCE

There are a number of dimensions which can be used to construct a taxonomy of family violence—for example,

(1) who the initiating and recipient actors are, (2) the extent to which the violence is victim-precipitated, (3) the severity of the violence or injury, (4) whether the long-range consequences of the violence are intended to be or turn out to be beneficial to the recipient, as in the case of physical punishment, (5) the extent to which the aggressor perceives his actions as being required by social norms and obligations (as in the case of a judge sentencing a murderer) versus perception of the act as personally motivated (Rule, 1974).

Some of these dimensions overlap, and all will be important for certain purposes. However, we suggest that there are two dimensions of violence which are likely to be important in any consideration of family violence. These are the degree to which the use of violence in a given situation is legitimized by social norms and the degree to which the use of violence is for instrumental purposes. Although each of these two dimensions are continuous, for clarity of exposition we will dichotomize them.

Legitimacy

In respect to the legitimacy dimension we will call one end of the continuum "legitimate violence." This refers to the use of physical force in situations where it is approved or required by the norms of the society, such as spanking a child in most societies or flogging a prisoner in some societies, or shooting an enemy soldier in time of war. The "illegitimate violence" side of the dichotomy refers to such acts as spanking a disobedient wife in contemporary American society or shooting a soldier of a country with which there is not an official or unofficial war underway.[4]

Instrumentality

For the instrumentality dimension we distinguish "expressive violence" and "instrumental violence." By expressive violence we mean the use of physical force to cause pain or injury as an end in itself—for example, hitting someone who is the source of anger, insult, or rage. By instrumental violence we mean the use of pain or injury as a punishment to induce another person to carry out some act or refrain from an act.

A difficulty with this dichotomy as a single dimension is that expressiveness and instrumentality are not necessarily mutually exclusive. In fact, there will be many situations where an instrumentally focused violent act also contains strong expressive components. In addition, it seems likely that there can be causal linkage between expressivity and instrumentality in the use of violence. That is, a family member who is aggressive and who obtains satisfactions from the infliction of pain on others may, as a result, tend to choose the use of physical force as a frequent modality for exercising social control. Despite these problems, we feel that most violent acts can be classified as *primarily* instrumental or primarily expressive with reasonable reliability and that such a classification will be a useful analytic tool, even though, like all other analytic tools, it does not encompass the full reality of the phenomenon under consideration.

A Four-Cell Taxonomy

By dichotomizing these two dimensions and combining them in a two-dimensional property space, four types of violence are distinguished which may have wide theoretical and practical utility. These are shown in Figure 21.1.[5]

Legitimate-Expressive Violence

At first glance it may seem doubtful that this cell has an empirical reference. Is it ever legitimate in the normative sense to injure someone else just to get relief from one's own feelings or needs? The answer seems to be "yes." Support for this type of violence in the family includes the widespread beliefs that it is better to spank a child than to "hold in" one's anger and better to let siblings "fight it out" than to interfere (provided things do not get out of hand). The following is typical advice to parents:

> It seems to me we have to assume that, being human, almost every parent who ever lived hit his kid sometime or other. Being human, we get mad and lose our patience, and the swift swat is the result. Let's accept that as a basic premise of our discussion [LeShan, 1970:34].

At a more theoretical level, the idea of "catharsis" is an example of legitimate-expressive violence. This is the belief that the expression of "normal" aggression between family members should not be bottled up. The idea that allowing so-called "normal aggression" to be expressed serves as a tension-releasing mechanism, thus reducing the likelihood of severe violence, is widespread

Figure 21.1. Four Types of Violence

Instrumentality \ Legitimacy	(+)	(−)
(+)	Legitimate-Expressive	Illegitimate-Expressive
(−)	Legitimate-Instrumental	Illegitimate-Instrumental

in both popular thinking and among certain social scientists. Bettelheim (1967), for example, holds that excessive training in self-control is typical of American middle-class families. He argues that this denies children outlets for the instinct of human violence and thereby fails to teach them how to deal with violent feelings. We have elsewhere presented a detailed critique of the validity of these ideas, labeling them as "the catharsis myth" (Steinmetz and Straus, 1974; Straus, 1974a). But irrespective of the presumed cathartic consequences, it is clear that this is a widespread type of violence in the American family. It is possible that almost all brothers and sisters have carried out acts of expressive violence which would be regarded as legitimate in the sense of being provoked—"he deserved it." Just how many parents hit their child after reaching "the breaking point" (as opposed to hitting as punishment or as deterrent) we cannot even guess, and the same applies to blows between husbands and wives.

Illegitimate-Expressive

This is the most widely recognized type of violence in the family because it includes the most spectacular and extreme forms of violence: child abuse and murder. But the rates for child abuse and murder do not really tell us much about the frequency of illegitimate-expressive violence because there is an enormous number of such acts that do not reach the point of bringing a child to the attention of the authorities or producing a corpse. Included in this category are acts of angry violence between siblings which are "undeserved" or which cause "excessive" pain or injury, "excessive" physical punishment (but not so excessive as to require medical attention and hence be categorized as "child abuse" under current social norms), and the innumerable fights between husband and wife which cannot be justified under the rubric of catharsis or as something which he or she "had coming." A typical example of such violence between husband and wife is illustrated by the following excerpt from one of the families interviewed by Gelles (1974):

> He just got violently mad at me. . . . It was during a big snow storm. . . he didn't want to get up and shovel the car out. He said my son and I could do it. And my son can't even shovel. . . so I came in and asked him if he wouldn't please help. Well, he was too busy reading his papers and didn't want to be bothered and he was tired. And I guess I pushed him to the point where I bitched at him for not helping me. . . he was driven to the point where he got up, threw his papers down, and came at me. He called me very bad names and sent me from here to there with an open hand. And my right eye hemorrhaged completely.

Legitimate-Instrumental

Although we previously indicated that illegitimate-expressive violence is the most widely *recognized* type of violence between family members, this does not mean that it is the most widely *occurring* type. In fact, we suggest that the most frequent type is instrumental violence which is permitted or required by the norms of the society, i.e., legitimate-instrumental violence. Such use of physical force as a means of inducing some desired act or as a means of preventing an undesired behavior occurs in all of the role relationships of the nuclear family with greater or lesser frequency. The greatest frequency is in the parent-child relationship in the form of physical punishment.

The survey conducted for the National Commission on the Causes and Prevention of Violence, for example, found that 93 percent of those interviewed reported having experienced physical punishment as a child (Stark and McEvoy, 1970). Other studies report similar figures (for example, Blumberg, 1964–65) and two studies reveal that even among adolescents in their last year of high school, half had been hit or threatened with being hit by their parents (Straus, 1971; Steinmetz, 1974). In every state in the union it is legal for parents to strike children, that is, to use physical punishment. Indeed, most Americans see a moral obligation for parents to use physical punishment as a means of controlling children if other means fail (Stark and McEvoy, 1970), and a goodly proportion see it as the most desirable means of controlling children. "Spare the rod and spoil the child" is not a dead way of life in contemporary America even though it is no longer the dominant ideology.

Legitimate-instrumental violence is by no means confined to physical punishment by parents. Parents frequently delegate such authority to older children in relation to their siblings, and children are quick to follow the role model of their parents. Although the *legal* right of a husband to physically punish a wife (Calvert, 1974) no longer exists, the informal norms of certain social groups (and specific families in all segments of society) still legitimize the use of physical force to control an errant spouse (Straus, 1976a). For example, Parnas (1967) reports that the police come to know the customs of different groups in their areas and respond to complaints of "family disturbances" according to these presumed norms. He illustrates this with the case of a Puerto Rican woman who, when asked by the judge "should I give him 30 days" for beating her, replied "No, he is my husband, he is supposed to beat me." For black slum families, with their matricentric pattern of organization, Parnas reports that the police in some instances have come to accept (and therefore treat lightly or ignore) women "cutting" their husbands or lovers.

While it may be true that norms legitimizing husband-wife violence are to be found in certain ethnic, racial, or social class groupings of American society, such norms seem to occur also within individual families throughout the society. Gelles (1974) found repeated evidence of this in a study of eighty families in two cities in New Hampshire. Consider the following example:

I have slapped her in the face or arms to shut her up . . . it's usually when the kids get hurt. She just goes completely spastic. . . . She just goes wild so you have to hit her or something to calm her down so she'll come to her senses. . . . It's not because I'm trying to hurt her because of something she's done. I'm trying to knock her to her senses more or less. . . . I had to slap her in the face and hit her arm to calm her down.

We do not know the specific frequency of legitimate-instrumental violence of the type illustrated by this case since Gelles's study was designed to explore the internal family process which produces violence rather than to obtain statistical estimates of frequency. Clearly, such figures are an elementary but important part of our knowledge of violence in the family which needs to be supplied by future research.

Illegitimate-Instrumental

The line between legitimate and illegitimate instrumental violence is indefinite because, as noted earlier, this is really a continuum which we have dichotomized for convenience of exposition. Just as normatively approved "cathartic" slapping by a parent can reach the point of injury and thus be classified as child abuse, so can normatively approved physical punishment easily be carried to the point where, despite the benevolent intentions of the parent in punishing the child "for his own good," society will regard it as abusive rather than educative. Similarly, a wife who accepts a certain level of violence from her husband in response to her transgressions will reach the point of defining it as illegitimate if it exceeds a certain level of severity or if it occurs too often with little provocation.

Which Norms?

The preceding paragraph seems to suggest that a family group or a society accepts a certain level of instrumental use of force as legitimate and that it is only when this level is exceeded that the violence falls into the illegitimate-instrumental category. But this is misleading because it fails to take into account the fact that there exists a small proportion of families for whom *any* use of force, including any physical punishment, is abhorrent. Moreover, even for the much larger proportion of families who accept a certain level of violence, the degree and type of violence which is legitimate depends on the circumstances.

But the situation is more complicated than that. There seems to be a dual set of norms, the first consisting of the overtly recognized and accepted norms prohibiting husband-wife violence, and the second consisting of the unverbalized but operating norms of everyday life (Straus, 1976a). The actors may, in fact, deny that they could control the course of their behavior. But this does not alter the fact that such decisions follow lawful patterns in relation to cultural norms and the goals of the system.

As Garfinkel (1967) and others have shown, some of the most important decision rules for social interaction are so internalized and taken for granted that the actors automatically invoke them in appropriate situations. In relation to violence between family members this can be illustrated by an example from a marriage-counseling case (told by Carlfred Broderick). One of the problems was that the husband frequently hit the wife. The husband agreed that this was wrong but said that there was nothing he could do because he hit his wife when he "lost control." The marriage counselor asked, "Why don't you stab her?" The implication here was that if the husband really had lost control he would have stabbed or shot his wife or otherwise have injured her. That he did not stab her was proof that he had not "lost control." The implicit, unrecognized, but nonetheless operating norms for this husband enabled him to hit his wife but not stab her (and then account for the act by saying he lost control).

The dual norms just described, however, are only one of the complications and ambiguities inherent in the legitimacy dimension of this taxonomy. Leaving aside inconsistent norms within the individual, there is also the question of inconsistency or conflict in the norms as perceived by different individuals and groups. Gelles (1974:86–90), for example, examined five different normative perspectives which often disagree. These are the "offender"; the "victim"; a "joint perspective" such as intrafamily consensus on what is permissable; agents of control such as psychiatrists, social workers, and police; and the normative perspective of the investigator.[6]

It is obvious that the typing of violence will, for the most part, depend on which of the five different perspectives are used. Furthermore, it should not be surprising that each perspective is quite likely to be different from the others—what the offender sees as legitimate the victim may not; what the researcher finds appalling the family may find normal and stable. In supplying illustrative examples for each of the four types in the taxonomy, judgments of what appeared to constitute the prevailing standards of the society were used. However, illustrations of how the categorization would be different using the perspective of a given subculture or of a given family were also given. Whose definition of legitimacy to use in any specific investigation or analysis depends on the purposes of the analysis. Thus a crucial decision which must be made at the outset in any study of family violence is which perspective, or combination of perspectives, to utilize in categorizing legitimacy.

4. THEORIES OF INTERPERSONAL VIOLENCE APPLIED TO THE FAMILY

Up to this point in the chapter the concern has been largely with definitional, conceptual, and taxonomic issues. These are issues which must be clarified if there is to be any hope of making progress on the task of analyzing explanatory theories, and even more the case if one wishes to integrate theories. Adherents of each of the theories discussed below may not necessarily agree with our definitions of aggression and violence. It would be desirable if there were such a consensus. But whether they agree or not, the objective of integrating the theories requires that there be standardization within this chapter of at least some of the key concepts.

A. Conceptual Frameworks and Theories

It is also essential to indicate the way in which the terms "theory" and "conceptual framework" are used in this chapter. By theory we mean a set of interrelated concepts, and propositions relating concepts and variables, which are intended to explain the existence of or variation in a phenomenon—in this case violence. By conceptual framework we mean a set of concepts and relational propositions which are believed to be useful for the *development of* an explanatory theory.

The line between conceptual framework and theory is blurred because often what is termed a theory is really a conceptual framework, in that it is not intended to explain why some *specific* phenomenon is the way it is (e.g., functionalism), and because a conceptual framework is typically a part of an explanatory theory. When the set of concepts and propositions is sufficiently integrated and focused on a specific phenomenon so that it can be appropriately classified as a theory is also a matter of judgment.

For purposes of this chapter we will operationalize the distinction by classifying as a theory any set of concepts and propositions which has been offered *as an explanation of aggression and/or violence*. The term "conceptual framework" will be used for those sets of concepts and propositions which are reviewed here because they seem to be important tools for developing such a theory, but which, to our knowledge, have not yet been specifically applied to the explanation of aggression and violence.

B. Theories and Interpersonal Violence

Although research on *family* violence has been sparse and exploratory, there has been a great deal of research on the causes of interpersonal violence. For the purposes of this chapter we inventoried 15 theories and conceptual frameworks which seem to have some relevance for understanding violence between family members.[7] These are:

Intraindividual Theories
   1. Psychopathology
   2. Alcohol and drugs

Social Psychological Theories
   3. Frustration-aggression
   4. Social learning
   5. Self-attitude

6. "Clockwork Orange"
7. Symbolic interaction
8. Exchange theory
9. Attribution theory

Sociocultural Theories
10. Functional
11. Culture of violence
12. Structural
13. General systems
14. Conflict
15. Resource

As a preliminary attempt to organize these theories it is convenient to group them into three basic levels of analysis based on the type of causal factor which is fundamental to the theory: intraindividual, social-psychological, or sociocultural. The fundamental point of each theory will be briefly stated together with brief comments on the problems of particular theories. The "fundamental point of each theory" really expresses our judgment concerning the aspect of the theory which appears to be most crucial for understanding intrafamily violence and most different from other theories.

C. Intraindividual Theories

Intraindividual theories explain violence in terms of some quality of the individual actor. Both biologically based qualities, such as genes or chromosomes, and acquired characteristics, such as aggressive personality or personal defects or aberrations, are the foci of intraindividual-level explanations. We have omitted most of the major intraindividual theories of violence from consideration here—those based on genetic, instinctual, or biological factors—because of their limited relevance for explaining violence in the family (see note 7). However, the psychopathology and alcohol and drugs theories will be discussed because the former is the most widely used explanation of child abuse and the latter represents a widely held view concerning the causes of husband-wife violence.

Psychopathology

The psychopathology approach to violence postulates that violence is caused by an abnormality which occurs within some individuals. According to the psychopathological theory, individuals are violent because of some internal aberration, abnormality, or defective characteristic. These characteristics include inadequate self-control, sadism, psychopathic personality types, and undifferentiated types of mental illness.

The psychopathological model has been used to explain many highly publicized occurrences of mass violence (Manson killings, Richard Speck slayings, etc.) but its major application to the family has been as an explanation of child abuse (Wasserman, 1967; Steele and Pollock, 1974; Kempe et al., 1962). The problems with this

approach have been documented elsewhere (Spinetta and Rigler, 1972; Gelles, 1973). The drawbacks of this theoretical explanation can be summarized as a combination of inadequate scientific evidence to support the theory and the confusion which arises as a result of the inability of the theory to adequately explain which abnormal personality traits are associated with violence, as well as the circularity of using acts of violence as indicators of mental illness.

Alcohol and Drugs

More a "conventional wisdom" (MacAndrew and Edgerton, 1969) than a full-fledged theory, the alcohol and drugs explanation is that these substances act as disinhibitors which release the violent tendencies that exist in humans. The theory rests on the assumption that alcohol and drugs act to break down inhibitions in the superego and thus release man's inherited or acquired potential to be violent.

The alcohol and drugs approach has been a favorite "folk theory" of intrafamilial violence, since many people (victims, offenders, agents of social control, mass media) point to the fact that participants in domestic violence are often drinking or drunk prior to the attack. The Snell et al. (1964) analysis of wifebeating, for example, states that wifebeating is extremely common among alcoholic men.

There is little rigorous scientific support for the "alcohol and drugs as causes of violence" theory. MacAndrew and Edgerton (1969) devote an impressive monograph to disputing the conventional wisdom about alcohol, and one of our studies (Gelles, 1974) proposed that the association between alcohol and violence is probably *not* a function of the disinhibiting properties of alcohol. Rather, being drunk may provide individuals with a convenient excuse for their untoward behavior. Drinking becomes a means of "deviance disavowal" or a "time out" from the normal rules of behavior and being drunk is used to neutralize the deviance of violence toward family members. Thus, some men get drunk to give them an excuse to hit their spouses and children.

D. Social-Psychological Theories

Social-psychological theories examine the interaction of the individual with his social environment, i.e., with other individuals, groups, and organizations. Such theories locate the source of violence in these relationships, for example, in certain interpersonal frustrations, learning processes, or self-attitudes which reflect attitudes of others. Among the best-known theories of aggression, frustration-aggression theory, and social learning theory explain violence at the social-psychological level of analysis. In addition to these two theories, there are five other social-psychological approaches which will be evaluated in this section: self-attitude theory, what we shall call "Clockwork Orange" theory, symbolic interaction theory, exchange theory, and attribution theory.

Frustration-Aggression

This theory was first specified by Dollard et al. (1939) and modified by Miller (1941; see also Berkowitz, 1962). Frustration-aggression theory postulates that aggressive behavior results when some purposeful activity is blocked. Organisms tend to aggress toward objects which block important goals, or displace the aggression to a "safer" object. Although cultural forces can accentuate or inhibit aggression, this theory proposes that the tendency to respond aggressively is built into the human organism.

Our view of the frustration-aggression relationship accepts the ubiquity and importance of the phenomenon but differs from the usual formulation in two ways. First, following Farrington (1975), we restrict the use of this theory to the tendency to express aggression as a response to the emotion which the individual feels when some goal is blocked. Second, we regard the tendency to aggress in response to frustration as the product of learning, rather than as an innate drive.[8]

The frustration-aggression theory is particularly relevant to the family. The family is a likely setting for aggression because it is the location of many frustrating events. In fact, the family, by virtue of its structure and function, can be viewed as inherently frustrating for its members. Among some of the inherent frustrations are the burdens and uncertainty of child rearing, the confining of sexuality to a single marital partner, the difficulty of solving problems simply by leaving, the assigning of roles and responsibility on criteria other than interest or competency, and the spatial and temporal overlap and conflict of many family activities (see also section 1B).

Although the frustration-aggression theory is credible and seems intuitively valid, there are some major problems with the theory as currently stated. First, it does not explain under what conditions frustration leads to aggression (Etzioni, 1971:717). Second, in some societies frustration is followed by passive withdrawal (Mead and MacGregor, 1951:176). Lastly, the theory does not differentiate physical aggression from verbal abuse and aggression (Etzioni, 1971:717).

Social Learning Theory

Learning theory assumes a *tabula rasa,* or clean slate, conception of the individual, and accounts for violent behavior as a learned phenomenon. Violence here is viewed as a product of a successful learning situation which provides the individual with knowledge about the response (violence) and what stimuli are to be followed by the response (when is violence appropriate).

There are a number of aspects of learning theory (Bandura, 1973). One examines the process of learning violence through exposure to violence and imitation (Bandura et al, 1961). Another looks at how exposure to violence and experience with violence lead to learning norms which approve of violence (Owens and Straus, 1975). Lastly there is the role model approach, which proposes that violence can be learned through viewing violence in an appropriate role model (Singer, 1971).

The learning theory approach to violence when applied to the family would postulate that the family serves as a training ground for violence. The family provides examples for imitation and role models which can be adopted in later life as the individual draws from his childhood experiences to develop the appropriate parent or conjugal role (see "Socialization into Violence and Its Generalization" in section 1B). It also provides rewards and punishments which (often unintentionally) encourage and reinforce violence (Patterson et al., 1973).

Evidence from child abuse research (Steele and Pollock, 1974; Kempe et al., 1962; Gil, 1971; and Gelles, 1973), together with research on homicidal offenders which finds that they were the recipients of a high level of violence as children (Palmer, 1962; Guttmacher, 1960), makes this theory quite relevant to explaining violence in the family.

Self-Attitude Theory

Kaplan's self-attitude theory (1972) is a modification of social learning theory. It proposes that violence occurs when the individual struggles to cope with negative self-attitudes which arise out of devaluating psychosocial experiences. Individuals who lack self-esteem are seen as prone to adopt deviant patterns of behavior as a means of receiving attention from others and achieving a positive self-attitude. Aggression provides such a vehicle because of the individual's experience in cultural or subcultural settings which covertly or overtly permit or encourage aggression. Thus young males are seen likely to choose the path of violence in order to establish a positive identity (Kaplan, 1972:608).

Self-attitude theory seems to be a well-organized theory that in some ways is similar to the resource theory of violence presented in the next section. Its drawback, like the drawbacks of other theories, is that its propositions are not sufficient to explain the high level of violence in the family and why family members are likely victims of individuals who have experienced self-devaluing experiences.

"A Clockwork Orange" Theory

The name for this theory of violence is derived from Burgess's (1962) book of the same title.[9] "A Clockwork Orange" serves as a broad label for the variety of explanations of violent acts which locate the cause of violence in boredom, the urge to seek thrills, or excessive reciprocity (Palmer, 1972). A number of authors have suggested that some violence arises out of boredom or "thrill seeking"—for example, Cohen's discussion of delinquents (1955) and Klausner (1968) on stress seeking.

Palmer's work is most directly relevant because he

posits an optimum stress or tension level. The degree of reciprocity or fit between social roles affects the tension level. He argues that in many situations "the glove fits too smoothly" and that an excessive reciprocity in roles produces such an absence of tension that it leads to frustration because the assumed optimal stress or tension level is not being met. Thus individuals in this situation commit violent acts as an attempt to stir things up (Palmer, 1972:51).

Farrington (1975) utilized the notion of an optimum stress level to develop a theory specifically related to intrafamily violence. He defined stress as an imbalance between the demands with which an individual or family is faced and the response capabilities which are available to use in dealing with these demands. He argues that all individuals and family units come to develop personal and unique optimum stress levels at which they function most comfortably. To the extent that the discrepancy between demands and response capabilities changes significantly, either by exceeding or falling short of this customary level, the changes of intrafamily violence are increased.

Although the book used to title this theory illustrates violence toward strangers, we can visualize family situations where the glove fits too smoothly and family members try to "stir things up" just to make things interesting. Gelles (1974), in fact, did find that some women use force and violence to stir up their sexually passive husbands or to provoke their "dull" husbands.

One problem with this theory is the assumption that low tension is frustrating. If it is, this theory seems to be defining frustration differently from the definition used in frustration-aggression theory. However, one could replace the phrase "low tension leads to frustration" with "lack of stimulation increases tension and tension can lead to violence under certain conditions." One could also measure "lack of stimulation" and thus reduce the problems encountered in operationalizing "frustration" (Hunt, 1971; Wilkinson, 1974). In addition, measuring "lack of stimulation" would deal with the criticism of "Clockwork Orange" theory that it is largely a retrospective "accounting process" (e.g., "I was violent, therefore I must have been bored") by which the stigma of being violent is managed or disavowed (Scott and Lyman, 1968).

Symbolic Interaction

Although a symbolic interaction approach has not yet been used to formulate a theory of violence, it is included in this review because of the fundamental nature of the social processes on which this approach focuses. We have drawn from Plummer's symbolic interaction theory of sex (1974) as a basis for suggesting some of the elements which are likely to be central in any symbolic interaction.

A symbolic interactionist view of violence would reject a biological drive approach and concentrate instead on the subjective, symbolic side of social life. Its focus would be on the nature of meanings of violence, how these mean-

ings are built up, how they persist, how they are modified, and the consequences of these meanings in situations. A symbolic interaction theorist studying violence would be concerned with how the responses of others constrain action. Thus this perspective would concern itself with the process involved in the "construction of violence"— the dynamics of the situation, careers and life cycles of violent episodes, and the encounters between actors in violent situations.

Applied to family relations, this approach might concern itself with the evolving social meanings of violence among family members. Violence between family members might reflect the shared meanings and role expectations of the individual family members. However, as noted above, researchers committed to the symbolic interaction approach have not yet focused this approach on violence. Therefore, at this stage, the symbolic interaction theory is more a conceptual framework than a formal theory. It guides how violence may be viewed in the family, and provides concepts which are important for ultimately arriving at an integrated theory.

Exchange Theory

In the context of this chapter, exchange theory, like symbolic interaction theory, is classified as a conceptual framework because to our knowledge it has not been used as an analytic tool to investigate interpersonal violence. Nor do the general presentations of exchange theory (Blau, 1964; Homans, 1961, 1967; Thibaut and Kelley, 1959) focus on the substantive area of family. Nevertheless, some students of the family have attempted to use exchange theory (see Edwards and Brauburger, 1973; Foss, 1974; Richer, 1968; Scanzoni, 1972; Scanzoni and Scanzoni, 1976). Some indication of the potential of exchange theory for explaining intrafamilial violence is given in Goode's Burgess Award essay (1971). The major assumption of exchange theory is that interaction is guided by the pursuit of rewards and the avoidance of punishments (costs) and that an individual who supplies reward services to another obliges him to fulfill an obligation and thus the second individual must furnish benefits to the first (Blau, 1964:89). If reciprocal exchange of rewards occurs, the interaction will continue, but if reciprocity is not achieved, exchange theorists argue that the interaction will be broken off.

Intrafamilial relations are more complex than those in simply dyadic relations or in less permanent and less normatively structured groups. Thus, for at least two reasons, the lack of reciprocity does not automatically mean that family relations will be broken off. The first is highlighted by Thibaut and Kelley's work on comparison levels and suggests that satisfaction-dissatisfaction with relationships is also influenced by the alternatives which are available to the individuals. Thus although a husband or wife may receive fewer rewards than they would like, they remain in the interaction because they have few other alternatives to gain rewards from. The second reason for continued interaction in the face of a seeming imbalance of costs and rewards is highlighted by Homans's concept of "distributive justice." According to Homans, it is not maximizing rewards minus costs in the absolute which the individual seeks, but "justice" in the distribution of outcomes. This is essentially a social comparison process. It comes about when, relative to others, a person perceives that he receives rewards proportional to his individual investment. Justice prevails if those who invest more in terms of effort, skill, status, etc., receive more, and those investing less receive less. In the family there can therefore be great differences in the rewards received by different actors based on a perception of correspondingly great differences in inputs. However, when the principle of distributive justice is violated, "When a person's activity does not receive the reward he expected or receives punishment he did not expect, he will be angry, and in anger, the results of aggressive behavior are rewarding" (Homans, 1967:35).

The notions of reciprocity, alternatives, and distributive justice can be seen in the occurrence of child abuse. Certain children make excessive demands on their parents due to personal or social circumstances. In addition, a parent, due to lack of reciprocity from a spouse, may seek certain social-emotional gratifications from a child. When these rewards are not received, the costs of child rearing may be greater than the rewards. Furthermore, the alternatives available to the parent are minimal (the role relationship between parent and child is almost impossible to break, with the exception of death). Thus with few or no alternatives and high dissatisfaction with the relationship, the parent may resort to violence. However, as in the case of several other theories, the reason for adoption of a violent response (as opposed to some other action) is not explained by exchange theory. We will later suggest that the missing elements are to be found primarily in the processes dealt with by symbolic interaction, social learning, and cultural theories of violence.

A similar combination of lack of alternatives and violation of the principle of distributive justice is helpful in understanding conjugal violence. It should be noted that it is easier to explain why a spouse would remain with a violent partner (lack of alternatives) than it is to explain why the one partner adopted violence (see Gelles, 1976, for a discussion of why wives stay with battering husbands). Another facet of conjugal violence which can be seen through the exchange perspective is the use of violence to inflict "costs" on one's partner. Exchange theorists (Homans, 1967) note that to inflict costs on someone who has injured you is rewarding. The idea of "revenge being sweet" can be used to examine why wives resort to extreme forms of violence in response to being punched or hit by their husbands and why husbands resort to violence to silence a nagging wife.

As with the case of child abuse, it must again be pointed out that exchange theory only deals with the antecedent conditions of violence, not how and why violence was chosen to redress a lack of reciprocity. Consequently, it is necessary to link exchange theory with one or more other theories in order to explain why violence is chosen to redress the injustice and lack of reciprocity. We will suggest at least some of these necessary linkages in the final section of the chapter where we address the question of integrating all of the theories reviewed in the present section.

Attribution Theory

As represented in the work of Bem (1967, 1970) and Kelley (1971), "Attribution refers to the process of inferring or perceiving the dispositional properties of entities.... Attribution theory describes the process by which the individual seeks and attains conceptions of the stable dispositions or attributes" (Kelley and Thibaut, 1969:7). Attribution theory is included in this review as a conceptual framework, because, as with other perspectives which have not yet been applied to violence, it seems likely to be important for understanding violence in general, for understanding the high frequency of violence in the family, and for understanding the part played by the family in learning violent roles and self-images. Hotaling (1975) has already made a start in this direction by specifying the particular combination of family rules and family structural characteristics which produces a high probability that a family member will attribute malevolent intent to the acts of another family member.

More generally, Tedeschi et al. (1974) note there are countless difficulties with including the notion of "intent" in any definition of aggression and violence—especially the fact that intent must be imputed rather than observed. According to Tedeschi et al. it is the imputation of intent to do harm that is important, and since this is dependent on the perceptions, cognitions, and values of the observer, it is the process of imputation rather than intention which needs to be made central in research on aggression.

Although their discarding of intent seems unwise, we do agree with the importance of understanding the process by which a malevolent intent is imputed and which provides the basis for labeling an act or person as aggressive. We suggest that the concept and methodology of attribution theory will prove valuable in any such effort. Moreover, both symbolic interaction theory and social learning theory can be helpful in understanding the linkage between these two critical cognitive aspects of aggression (intent and attribution). When a child carries out an act which results in harm, a harmful intent can be attributed by others even though this was not part of the child's purpose. If this attribution is communicated to the child (as will often be the case), it provides one of the bases for the child to form an identity and self-image as "aggressive," and as the child comes to know the wider social meaning of being aggressive, he/she can act in

terms of this more general meaning of being aggressive. Or to put this in the language of social learning theory, when the attribution of malevolent intent is communicated to the child, this characteristic of the response produced by the child's act becomes paired with, and conditioned to, the other responses to his or her act.

E. Sociocultural Theories

Sociocultural theories of violence examine social structures or arrangements such as norms, values, institutional organization, or systems operations to explain individual violence. Although they focus on macrolevel variables such as social structures, functions, subcultures, or social systems, the theories at this level, of necessity, also include concepts and processes which exist at the intraindividual and socialpsychological level as well. There are six theories of violence which are reviewed at this level of analysis: (1) functional, (2) culture of violence, (3) structural, (4) general systems theory, (5) conflict theory, and (6) resource theory. Theories (4) and (6) have been specifically adapted to explain violence between family members.

Functional Theory of Violence

It has been proposed that violence, although it causes injury and sometimes death, can fulfill certain social functions—if not in the short run, at least over time (Coser, 1967:74). Coser argues that violence can serve three basic functions (1967). He proposes that violence may function for the individual as an area of achievement, for the community as a danger signal, and for nonparticipants or observers as a catalyst for action.

Applying these social functions of violence to the family we can see that violence can be used in the small system of the family to compensate for inadequate rewards in the occupational world at large (Coser, 1967:80). "Machismo," or the ideology of the sexually aggressive male in the Latin American family, and violence in the urban slums may also be seen as a means of achieving social status when other avenues of achievement are blocked (Brown, 1965:263–71; Toby, 1966).

Violence can also serve as a danger signal and as a catalyst for action:

> Within the family, . . . violence can serve as a means of communication and as a catalyst bringing about needed changes when all else fails. Take the situation of a family in which there is a serious problem between a husband and wife, but the husband just doesn't listen, or get the message, or ignores the message and the problem. Finally, in desperation, the wife throws something at him or hits him. At least in middle class families, that is such a shocking event that the husband can no longer ignore the seriousness of the problem. It is like the hoisting of a danger signal which cannot be ignored (or is very difficult to ignore).
>
> But perhaps even then the unignorable is ignored or merely superficially patched over. Months later, another and more

violent episode occurs—one which is so violent that there is an injury or the neighbors call the police. As a result of this violent episode, the family is referred to a marriage counselor or other mediating agent, with the result that a viable solution is worked out. In this sequence of events, violence has served as a catalyst to bring into action forces which would not otherwise have been present.

> In principle, there should never be a situation when all else fails. In practice, such situations do exist because alternative modes of resolving conflicts and inequalities are either unknown to the persons involved, unavailable to them, or unavailable until some violent act serves as a catalyst to bring nonviolent methods of change into the picture. Therefore, unless we are prepared to live with inequity and injustice, it is almost inevitable that violence will remain a part of the human condition because there will probably always be situations in which only violent acts can trigger needed changes [Straus and Steinmetz, 1974:323].

Other variants of functionalist theory of intrafamilial violence are illustrated by (1) Bakan's assertion (1971) that the widespread use of violence toward children may be seen as a case of population control through filicide, and (2) the view that "moderate violence" is necessary to release pent-up frustrations. This proposition holds that the release of "normal aggression" can reduce the likelihood of severe violence. This view has been challenged by Bandura and Walters (1963) in relation to child rearing and by Straus (1974a) in relation to husband-wife interaction.

There is a major difficulty with applying the central idea of the functional theory of violence to the family (i.e., that violence is a mechanism which—when all else fails—enables the social unit to overcome institutionalized rigidities and therefore to be flexible and adaptive enough to survive). In principle the underdogs of the family (wives and children) could use this mechanism, and sometimes they do (Straus and Steinmetz, 1974:323). But this is infrequent because of their less developed physical strength and because of the greater normative disapproval of a child or wife striking a husband than of a husband striking a child or wife. More often, it is the husband who uses violence in marital conflict, and this is most typically to maintain his superior position vis-à-vis the wife and the wife who uses force on a child (Steinmetz, 1975).[10]

Culture-of-Violence Theory

This theory takes as its starting proposition the fact that violence is unevenly distributed in the social structure, most notably in the higher rates of violence in the lower socioeconomic sectors of society (Coser, 1967:55; Palmer, 1962; Wolfgang and Ferracuti, 1967). This theory proposes that the differential distribution of violence is a function of differential cultural norms and values concerning violence (Wolfgang and Ferracuti, 1967). That is, culture-of-violence theory views violence as a learned response. The learning comes about as a

result of membership in a cultural or subcultural group and reflects effective socialization into that subculture's value system and norms. Thus the aggressive dispositions of violent persons are the result of participation in and learning from a subculture (Wolfgang and Ferracuti, 1967).

In applying culture-of-violence theory to the family we can again view the family as a training ground for violence, since it is a major unit in transmitting the subculture (Steinmetz and Straus, 1974, part IV). Thus, through associations, family members may learn that violence toward spouses and children is acceptable, and that to be an affiliated member of the subculture, a husband is expected to use force and violence on his family or at least condone the use.

Culture-of-violence theory is an extension of the propositions of learning theory. As postulated by Wolfgang and Ferracuti (1967) culture-of-violence theory does not seek to explain how the subcultural values originate, nor does it explain how these values can be modified or changed over time.

The failure to deal with the question of the genesis of the subculture is the most important limitation of culture-of-violence theory. Why do those at the bottom of the socioeconomic ladder (or other groups with a culture valuing violence) come to have this culture? Our view is that the subculture of violence, like any culture, reflects the structural realities faced by the group. It is essentially a codification of the forms of behavior which have become typical within that group. Over time, these typical modes of behavior become expressed and symbolized as cultural norms and values. This codification of typical behavior makes it easier for members of the group to learn and to carry out the actions which, on the average, they will find themselves engaged in. Consequently, an answer to the question of the genesis of a subculture must be sought in the physical and social environment of a group and its own social organization. In short, we see a culture of violence as emerging in response to more fundamental forces which affect members of a group (Steinmetz and Straus, 1974:8–10; Straus, 1976b). Some of these factors have already been alluded to in the discussion of functional theory, and others will be considered in our discussions of the structural and resource theories of violence.

This does not mean to deny causal efficacy to culture. Quite the contrary, once having come into existence, a culture is a structural entity with its own dynamics and influence on behavior (Straus, 1974b). This view of culture as a dynamic entity in its own right is the basis for what can be called a "cultural consistency" theory of violence. This theory asserts that norms which deal with the extent to which violence may be used reflect the operation of the culture *as a system*. Within this system cultural norms concerning violence can be deduced from the basic norms and values characteristic of a group. Thus family norms having no manifest reference to violence act to increase or hold down the actual level of family violence in a certain subculture. This is illustrated in a paper by Carroll (1975) applying cultural consistency theory to the Mexican-American and Jewish ethnic groups. Carroll concluded that such basic norms as severe male dominance and submission to the father are systematically linked to the high level of Mexican-American family violence. In Jewish culture, the emphasis on the pursuit of knowledge and the use of the mind is linked to the low levels of family violence believed to characterize this group.

Structural Theory of Violence

The structural approach to violence also begins with the assumption that deviance is unevenly distributed in the social structure (Durkheim, 1951; Merton, 1938), with violence being more common among those occupying lower socioeconomic positions. Second, it is postulated that people in certain structural positions (for example, low socioeconomic status) suffer greater frustrations. Third, a frequent response to these frustrations and deprivations is to react with violence (Coser, 1967:59). Finally, this reaction is institutionalized through differential socialization which leads those reared in different segments of society to use different modes of dealing with stress and frustration (Coser, 1967:623; Steinmetz and Straus, 1974:233). In summary, the structural theory of violence explains violence as a result of differential distribution of some of the main causes of violence (stress and frustrations) and the differential learning experiences which provide models, norms, and values that legitimize the use of violence.

This structural approach to violence has been applied to the family by Gelles (1974, ch. 7) in the form of five propositions which are used to explain the occurrence of intrafamilial violence. Since these propositions were arrived at inductively through exploratory research, they still remain to be tested with a more representative sample and using more rigorous measures and tests.

An advantage of the structural approach to violence is that it already integrates much of the current thinking about interpersonal violence. It includes in it references to frustrations, learning experience, and subcultural modes of adapting to stress. In most respects, this theory of violence is as close to an integrated theory of violence as we have. However, in its present form it does not include some of the major aspects of family and family relations which would refine our explanation and predictions about intrafamilial violence. These facets of the family will be discussed in the following section.

General Systems Theory

The crux of general systems theory goes beyond the

specification and analysis of what has been called a "causal loop" by Maruyama (1963) or a "quantitative reflexive" process by Black and Broderick (1972). A causal loop is a feedback process only in the sense of variables mutually influencing each other, as when a fat person becomes anxious over his appearance and then eats as a mode of dealing with his anxiety, gaining even more weight. Causal loops of this type are extremely important. But restricting the analysis to such loops omits consideration of the cybernetic process which is at the heart of general systems theory (Buckley, 1967). A feedback loop in the cybernetic sense involves a monitoring or information process in relation to the goals or purposes of the system. Thus a cybernetic feedback process includes gathering and interpreting information about the state of the system, comparing this information with criterion goals or states, and then taking corrective action (in this case violence) to maintain the state or goal. Here the analogy is to a thermostat, with the goal being the temperature at which it is set. As Wilkinson (1975) puts it: "The cybernetic model assumes that systems attempt to keep key variables relatively invariant. . . . The focus is on how this is done and what other variables have to change in order to do this."

Following this model, Straus's application of general systems theory (1973) seeks to account for violence between family members by viewing the family as a goal-seeking, purposive, adaptive system. Violence is treated as a system product or output rather than as a product of an individual pathology. The theory specifies some of the "positive feedback" processes which can produce an upward spiral of violence and some of the "negative feedback" processes which serve to maintain or dampen the present level of violence (or nonviolence). The theory also examines the morphogenic processes which alter the role structure of the family in the service of criterion goals.

Straus's use of general systems theory has been primarily to identify the cybernetic and morphogenic processes which account for the *continuing* presence of a given level of family violence. However, the question of the reasons for any violence at all has not been systematically analyzed by means of this theory, even though it is posed implicitly in section 1B of this chapter and in Straus's critique and empirical study of the catharsis or ventilation approach to family conflict and violence (1974).

Conflict Theory

Conflict theory may be regarded as a special case of functional theory (as in the work of Coser, 1967) or as an entirely separate theory (as in the work of Dahrendorf, 1968). We choose the latter approach because our focus here is not on the positive and negative consequences of violence, but on the basic assumption that conflict is an inevitable part of all human association.

A conflict approach to violence views individual actors, groups, and organizations as seeking to further their own "interests" rather than as a consensus-equilibrium-seeking system. Thus the conceptual framework implied is one that looks at conflict as natural, consensus as problematic, and focuses on conflict management rather than system maintenance. Dahrendorf (1968) outlines three basic stages in his conflict model: conflict, confrontation, change. Violence is a mode of carrying out conflict which is likely to occur when other modes of pursuing individual or group interests break down due to faulty conflict management at the confrontation stage.

Sprey's work has substituted a conflict model of the family for the traditional consensus-equilibrium approach (1969). The family is viewed as an arena of confrontation and conflicting interests (Sprey, 1969:702). This perspective is also present in the analysis of Steinmetz and Straus (1974:5-6). Violence is likely to occur in the family as an outcome of these conflicts because violence is a powerful mode of advancing one's interests when other modes fail (Straus and Steinmetz, 1974:302) or, in some families, a means of first choice. Whether or not the use of violence as a mode of resolving conflicts is functional or dysfunctional is an important but different issue.

Intrafamily Resource Theory

The final theory we shall review is one of the two we encountered which has been explicitly applied to violence between family members. The application to the family articulated by Goode (1971) begins with the assumption that all social systems "rest to some degree on force or its threat." Violence and threats of violence are fundamental to the organization of social systems, and thus should be found in the family. Goode argues that the greater the resources a person can command, the more force he can muster. However, the more resources a person can command, the less he will actually deploy the force in an overt manner (1971:628). Violence is used as a resource when other resources are insufficient or lacking. Thus a husband who wants to be the dominant person in his family but has little education and a job which is low in prestige and income and lacks interpersonal skills may have to resort to violence to maintain a dominant position. In addition, as noted in the discussion of functional theory, underdog family members resort to violence to redress grievances when they have few alternative resources at their disposal; for example, a wife faced with a husband who persistently ignores or devalues something of critical value to her may force his attention to the issue by throwing something.

Empirical data from O'Brien's research (1971) support the propositions offered by Goode. For example, in families where the husband's achieved status was lower than his wife's, O'Brien found a greater tendency to use force and violence on family members than when the husband had the "resource" of a higher-prestige occupation.

5. THE DISTINCTIVE CONTRIBUTIONS OF SELECTED THEORIES

Having identified general features of each of the 15 theories and aspects of these theories which seem to be salient for understanding intrafamily violence, there are several ways in which the analysis might proceed. One direction can be called an *elaborating and specifying strategy,* and another can be called an *integrating strategy*.

The *elaborating and specifying* strategy calls for steps such as (1) providing precise definitions of the key concepts of each theory, much as was done in the introductory sections of the chapter, where aggression and violence were defined and explicated; (2) providing operational definitions of these concepts by specifying the methods by which they have been or could be measured (see Straus, 1976c, for an example); (3) further identifying the variables by giving some indication or estimate of their range of variation and central tendency; (4) explanations and specifications which make clear how each of these variables is different from other variables with which it might be confused; (5) consideration of the form of association between variables in the theory, and especially the identification of non-linear relationships.

The *integrating* strategy calls for steps which will enable the identification of the complementary and interacting nature of the causal process pointed to by each theory. For this to be within the realm of comprehension of the authors and most readers, it is necessary to shift focus from the wealth of detail described under the elaborating and specifying strategy to a concern with only the most salient features of each theory.

Both the elaborating and the integrating strategies are necessary parts of the larger agenda for arriving at an integrated theory of family violence. However, each is such a major task that doing both in one chapter proved impossible. We therefore chose to concentrate on the integrating strategy, leaving to others the critical tasks outlined under the elaborating and specifying strategy.

The first step in pursuing the integrating strategy was to construct Exhibit 21.1. This is a tabular summary of each theory, designed to aid us and the reader in the task of bringing into focus the most distinctive contributions of each theory, and the part each can play in explaining family violence.

When the term "explains" is used in Exhibit 21.1, it is not meant to imply "*fully* explains." On the contrary, we view the cause of violence as being located in the complex *interrelation or interaction* of all these types of explanatory factors. In fact, the entries in this table are stated in a way which emphasizes the complementary nature of the factors. As indicated by our use of "interrelation" between factors, a comprehensive theory of violence must do more than simply identify the psychological, social psychological, and sociological causes of violence if it hopes to do better than the minimal predictive power inherent in the correlations of .20 to .30 typically found in studies of aggression and violence. Rather, the effect of each of these types of factors is contingent on each of the others.

An example of the need to consider the interactions of the causal factors specified in different theories is provided by the resource theory of intrafamily power. Empirical tests of the idea that the greater an individual's resources (i.e., occupational prestige, income, education, etc.), the greater his or her power in the family (Goode, 1971) show a number of inconsistent findings. However, Rodman (1972) has grouped these studies according to the normative prescriptions of the society or group sampled by each study. He shows that resources make a difference in societies which have cultural norms concerning family power (such as the United States) that are sufficiently flexible to permit the issue to be decided

---

Exhibit 21.1. **Summary of the Distinctive Contributions of Selected Theories of Violence**

THEORY	CONTRIBUTION
Psychopathology*	The fact that only a very small proportion of mentally ill persons are violent forces a search for the social factors which lead this minority to be violent.
Alcohol and Drugs*	Has the same theoretical status as psychopathology, i.e., little evidence of any direct link to violence. What one does under the influence of alcohol and other drugs must be explained by reference to social psychological and sociocultural factors. However, alcohol use is of great practical importance because of the frequency with which it is associated with violence in our society.
Frustration-Aggression	Also occupies a theoretical position similar to that of psychopathology because the theory, as generally conceived, does not explain the process by which frustration is linked to aggression, except by positing an innate aggressive drive in response to frustration. However, when viewed as a special case of social learning theory, it explains why the tendency to respond to frustration by aggression is so common (see note 8). It helps explain family violence because the family is the focus of high personal involvement and of high frustration.

Social Learning	Asserts that human aggression and violence are learned conduct and specifies the learning process, especially direct experience and observing the behavior of others. Explains both the variation between persons and the variation between situations in the tendency to respond aggressively by reference to prior experience, reinforcement patterns, and cognitive processes.
Self-Attitude	Asserts that in a society, culture, or group which values violence, persons of low self-esteem may seek to bolster their image in the eyes of others and themselves by carrying out violent acts. Explains the propensity to violence of those for whom society makes it difficult to achieve an adequate level of self-esteem.
"Clockwork Orange"	Asserts that there is an optimum level of stress or tension and that if the life circumstances do not provide this level, aggression and violence will occur as a means of moving toward the optimum level. Explains the "senseless" aggression and violence which can occur in highly integrated, smoothly functioning groups, such as an apparently model family.
Symbolic Interaction	Specifies the process by which a self-image and identity of a person as "violent" are formed, and the process by which violent acts acquire individual and socially shared meaning. Explains the origin and maintenance of the structure of meaning which is necessary for all human social behavior, including violence.
Exchange	Asserts that interaction in marriage is governed by partners seeking to maximize rewards and minimize costs in their exchange relations; that actors expect rewards to be proportional to investments ("distributive justice"); and that costs and rewards are judged in the light of alternatives. Explains the growth of resentment, anger, and hostility when the principle of distributive justice is violated.
Attribution	Specifies the process used by actors to impute the dispositional state (motivations) of others. Explains how the structure of family relations is such that there is high probability of malevolent intent being attributed to the actions of other family members, thereby setting in motion an escalating cycle of resentment and aggression.
Functional	Asserts that violence can be important for maintaining the adaptability of the family to changing circumstances and hence important to its survival. Explains why violence persists in human association, including the family.
Culture of Violence	Asserts that social values and norms provide meaning and direction to violent acts and thus facilitate or bring about violence in situations specified by these norms and values. Explains why some sectors of society or different societies are more violent than others; essentially that they have cultural rules which legitimize or require violence.
Structural	Asserts that social groups differ in respect to their typical level of stress, deprivation, and frustration and in the resources at their disposal to deal with these stresses. Explains why different sectors of society or different families are more violent than others: because that they combine high stress with low resources.**
General Systems	Describes the cybernetic and morphogenic processes which characterize the use of violence in family interaction. Explains the way in which violence is managed and stabilized.
Conflict	Asserts that fundamental causal factors which lead to violence are the different "interests" of family members. Explains why there is conflict and violence is one of the most integrated and solidary of human groups.
Resource	Asserts that violence is one of the resources which individuals or collectivities can use to maintain or advance their interests. By pointing to the range of other resources available to a person or group, it explains the circumstances under which violence is used: essentially when these other resources are not effective.

*The statements in this table about psychopathology and alcohol as causes of violence need further explication. In this space the best we can do is to illustrate our reasoning. In respect to alcohol use as a cause of violence, we hold that the behavior of intoxicated persons reflects social definitions of what one does when drunk or high. In American society actions of drunk or high individuals are typically viewed as behavior which the individual cannot control; thus drunk or high individuals are given a "time out" from normal social norms, and their behavior is viewed accordingly (Lang et al., 1975; Schachter and Singer, 1962; Washburn, 1961). Moreover, these definitions and normative statements vary from society to society, from sector to sector, as do also the rates of alcohol and drug use. One must therefore have resource to sociocultural factors to understand both the frequency and the nature of alcohol and drug use and the behavior associated with such use, and to social-psychological theories (especially social learning and symbolic interaction theories) to understand the aggressive and violent behavior of individuals under the influence of such drugs.

Our view of psychopathology as a cause of violence is directly parallel. Specifically, there is nothing known to be inherent in mental illness which leads the afflicted person to behave in an aggressive or violent way, except insofar as a person who is violent is labeled as mentally ill. Rather, the behavior of mentally ill persons varies from society to society, from sector of society to sector, and according to the particular life circumstances of the afflicted person (Scheff, 1963).

**Also explains the emergence and maintenance of a culture of violence: when the structural conditions lead to violence as a characteristic mode of coping with the circumstances of a group, violence becomes codified in the form of values which justify and norms which simplify carrying out the violent acts. See Owens and Straus (1975).

on an individual-characteristics basis. Under other normative circumstances analyzed by Rodman, the relationship may be absent or reversed. Rodman therefore reformulated the resource theory as a theory of "resources in cultural context."

The same principle is also illustrated in Straus's discussion of his finding that the more dissatisfied the wife with the husband's income, the greater the probability of the husband's having hit his wife in the previous 12 months (Straus, 1974b:65–67). In order to account for this relationship, it was necessary to include in the analysis such factors as (1) the fact that income and occupation are the key determinants of prestige in an industrial society, whereas in a society basing prestige on some other basis, such as kinship affiliation, the observed relationship probably would not be found, and (2) the cultural norms which favor male leadership in the family. Straus (1974b) argues that if the culture did not impose the expectation of male leadership, and if the society did not accord prestige and power on the basis of income and occupation, low income and consequent low power of a husband would not tend to be compensated for by the use of violence to exercise power.

6. TOWARD AN INTEGRATED THEORY OF FAMILY VIOLENCE

In presenting the 15 theories, we could have emphasized the way in which each of these theories offers *competing* explanations for the same phenomenon, as, for example, was done in Owens and Straus's comparison of "cultural" versus "structural" explanations of the origins of proviolence attitudes (1975). Instead, and particularly in Exhibit 21.1, we deliberately focused on those parts of the theories which represent each theory's most distinctive contribution as compared to the other theories being considered. The emphasis is on presenting the theories so that each is complementary rather than competitive with the other.

One can gain a preliminary idea of the extent to which these theories complement rather than compete with each other through the use of the distinction made earlier in this chapter between "instrumental" and "expressive" types of violence. Certain of the theories are primarily explanations of instrumental violence and others of expressive violence. The theories focused on explaining instrumental violence are the (1) intrafamily resource, (2) self-attitude, (3) exchange, (4) functional, and (5) conflict theories. The theories which seek to explain expressive violence are the (1) psychopathology, (2) alcohol and drugs, (3) "Clockwork Orange," and (4) frustration-aggression[11] theories.

Six of the 15 theories in the summary table are not included in the above listing because they seem to be explanations of processes which apply to both instrumental and expressive violence. The structural theory explains the nature of variations in the organization of society which are associated with high levels of stress and the "differential association" which produces subgroup variation in the frequency of violence. The cultural theory refers to the norms and values concerning violence that are characteristic of different societies and subgroups within societies. Social learning, symbolic interaction, and attribution theory each explain a different aspect of the social psychological processes by which the experience of participation in a violent society or sector of society is translated into individual self-images, meanings, and roles which produce specific acts of violence.

Finally, general systems theory identifies the goal-seeking cybernetic principles by which all of these parts are integrated into an ongoing but constantly changing social system.

Although the above grouping of theories helps to specify the aspect of the causal sequence leading to violence on which each theory focuses, there remains considerable unclarified overlap between the theories. It is the combination of this overlap with the complementary nature of the theories which offers the possibility of arriving at some degree of overall integration of the separate theories. We have made a step in this direction by means of Figure 21.2, which includes 13 of the 15 theories reviewed in this chapter.

There are two key areas in which the 13 theories included in Figure 21.2 (which from here on will sometimes be called "partial theories" to distinguish them from the integrated theory) draw on common explanatory principles, and which therefore provide part of the basis for the integration of the partial theories. The first of these is the set of relationships and processes embodied in the social learning and symbolic interaction theories. Although these are discussed separately and they appear separately diagrammed in Figure 21.2, to a certain extent social learning theory represents the label and language for these processes developed by psychologists, and symbolic interaction theory represents the label and language developed by sociologists to refer to many of the same processes. We decided, for purposes of this chapter, to refer to both theories under the title social learning–symbolic interaction theory. Both the theories deal with processes without which the other theories we have reviewed cannot be applied to the specific question of intrafamily violence.

The second element which occurs at many points in this integration of the theories is the frustration-aggression relationship, i.e., the tendency to respond to frustration and/or stress by aggression. In our view the relationship between frustration or stress and aggression is a learned response pattern which, in turn, can be explained by social learning–symbolic interaction theory. However, readers who are not comfortable with this interpretation need only be willing to assume the existence of a causal relation between frustration or stress and aggression, irrespective of whether the underlying process is social learning, a biologically evolved response tendency, or some combination of these.

By themselves, these two areas of overlap or common elements in the partial theories would not permit the integration shown in Figure 21.2. Two additional elements seem to be necessary: some provision for the ubiquity of change in social relationships and, most important of all, some specification of the process by which new cultural norms and values are established and old cultural elements retained as characteristics of a society or group.

Implicit in Figure 21.2 is the idea that cultural norms

and values arise out of enduring patterns of social interaction and in the long run tend to remain as part of the culture only if these cultural elements continue to reflect the actual interactional structure of the society. The process by which actual experience with violence (i.e., observation of it, or participation in it as a victim or initiator) is transformed into the behavioral repertoire of the actors as specified by social learning and symbolic interaction theory. When a sufficiently large or a sufficiently influential portion of a population has acquired these behavioral patterns, then there is a tendency to standardize and crystallize them in the form of cultural norms and values. Consequently, the intraindividual, social psychological, and sociocultural theories are inherently integrated by virtue of being mutually interdependent aspects of the same social processes (see the analysis of cultural and social organizational theories of violence in Straus, 1974b) and at the same time provide the basis for integrating the other partial theories with each other.

Interpreting Figure 21.2

Having specified what seem to be the underlying bases for the integration of the partial theories shown in Figure 21.2, we can turn to a more specific examination of that chart. Although the chart may appear to have a left-to-right causal flow, such a directional orientation is not part of the theory. The unintended appearance of directionality comes about because each of the component or partial theories was originally diagrammed with a left-to-right causal flow, thus lending an overall left-to-right impression when the 13 partial theories are combined in the one diagram.

Instead of attempting to move from left to right, Figure 21.2 is best approached by starting with any one of the 13 partial theories. The distinctive features of that theory can be examined within the section of the chart devoted to that theory. Then, by following the lines to and from the theory chosen, one can get some idea of key linkages to other theories. For example, if one is interested in examining exchange theory as an explanation for intrafamily violence, one starts with the block representing that theory located in the upper right corner of Figure 21.2. Tracing out the relational propositions indicated by the arrows within that block, one can obtain an understanding of the parts of exchange theory which we selected for purposes of explaining intrafamily violence. However, as noted in the verbal summary of this theory, the principles of exchange theory do not, by themselves, explain why violence is chosen to redress the lack of reciprocity.

The missing processes are those highlighted by social learning and symbolic interaction theory: specifically the role models for dealing with conflict and frustration by means of physical force; and the self-image, meanings, and role expectations concerning violence learned as a result of interaction with others. These contingencies are indicated in Figure 21.2 by the vertical arrow intersecting the line between box E-5 and the Violence box to its right.

Similarly at the other end of the causal sequence, exchange theory does not indicate why problems of reciprocity and distributive justice are so frequent in the family. At this point some of the special characteristics of the family, such as roles being ascribed on the basis of age and sex rather than interest and/or competence, should come into the chart. But these were omitted because the diagrammatic complexity needed to include that level of variable as well as each of the 13 theories would render the chart unreadable. However, part of the answer to the question of why problems of reciprocity and distributive justice are particularly common in the family is to be found in certain of the other theories. In particular, as Sprey (1969, 1971) and others have noted, the family, like other social groups, is characterized by both conflict and consensus as the normal state of the system. Since, as was noted in discussing the special characteristics of the family which require a special theory of intrafamily violence, the intensity of commitment and interest in the family is particularly great, conflict over furthering these interests is likely to be correspondingly intense (Coser, 1963); hence the arrow from conflict theory box C-1 to exchange theory box E-1. At the same time, this same level of commitment and mutual interdependence of the members makes it particularly likely that one member will constrain, infringe on, or injure the other, even though without malevolent intent. Irrespective of intent, these infringements and constraints increase the probability that the terms of exchange between family members will be perceived as inequitable and therefore set in motion the processes diagrammed in the exchange theory block. This linkage is indicated by the arrow from attribution theory box AT-2 to exchange theory box E-1.

General Systems Theory

Another related departure of Figure 21.2 from our conception of the processes producing intrafamily violence is that no systematic attempt was made to diagram either positive or negative feedback loops. In particular, there are 13 places in the diagram where violence is shown as an output variable. Causal feedback loops are needed at each of these 13 points because it is inherent in the nature of the theory, with its emphasis on social learning and on aggression as a learned response to frustration, that each violent occurrence is likely to enhance one or more of the causal elements, such as the level of stress and frustration and opportunities to observe and imitate violent behavior. Finally, Figure 21.2 departs from a true systems model in that it contains no provision for a cybernetic process by which behavior is monitored and controlled in relation to the goals of the actor or system.

Paradoxically, then, Figure 21.2 omits the one theory which we feel has the greatest promise for providing a true integration of all these partial theories: general systems theory, particularly as expounded by Buckley (1967). There are two reasons for this omission. First, as of this

Figure 21.2. Key Elements of Thirteen Theories of Violence and Some of Their Relationships

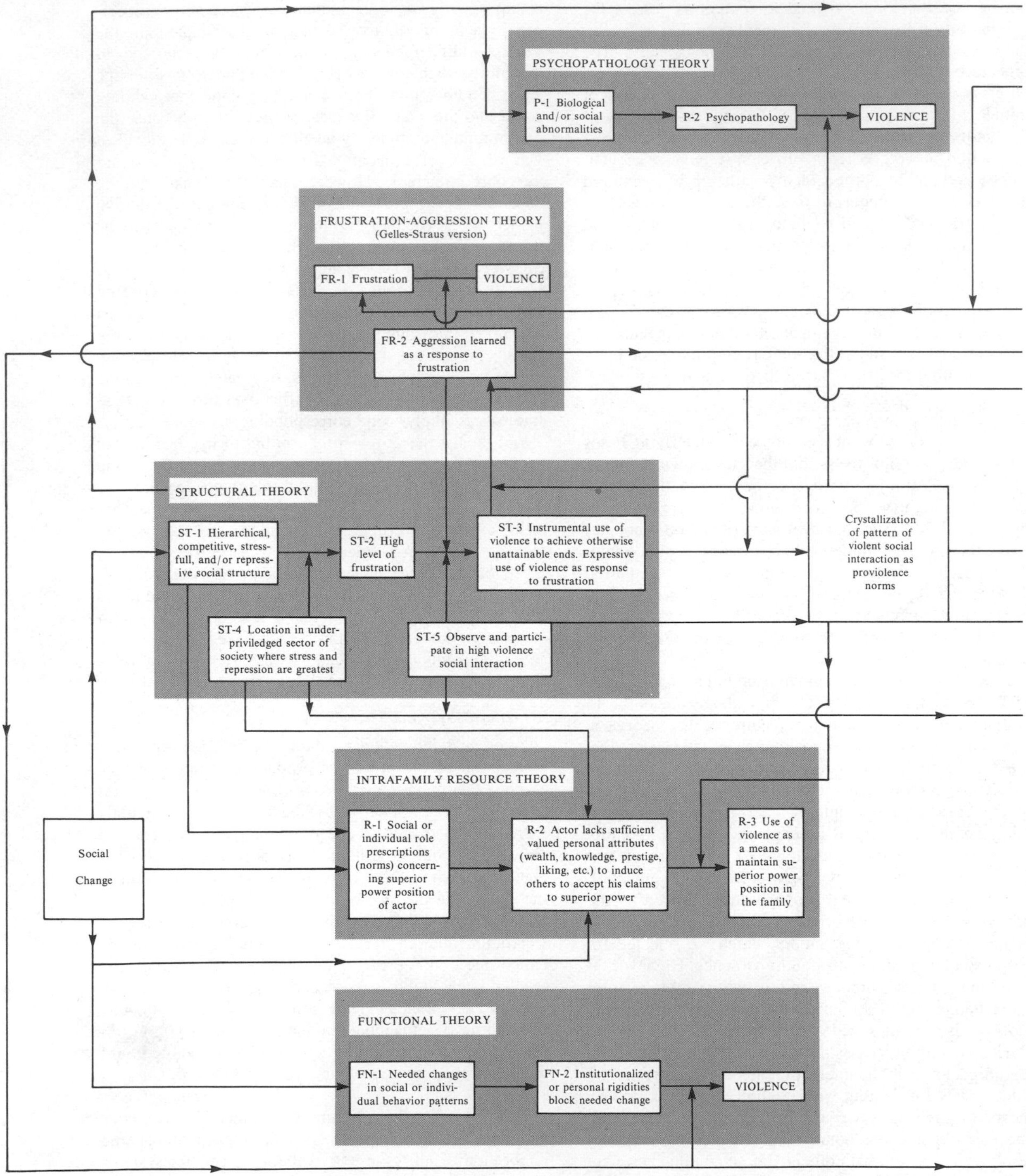

PSYCHOPATHOLOGY THEORY

P-1 Biological and/or social abnormalities → P-2 Psychopathology → VIOLENCE

FRUSTRATION-AGGRESSION THEORY
(Gelles-Straus version)

FR-1 Frustration VIOLENCE

FR-2 Aggression learned as a response to frustration

STRUCTURAL THEORY

ST-1 Hierarchical, competitive, stressfull, and/or repressive social structure

ST-2 High level of frustration

ST-3 Instrumental use of violence to achieve otherwise unattainable ends. Expressive use of violence as response to frustration

ST-4 Location in underpriviledged sector of society where stress and repression are greatest

ST-5 Observe and participate in high violence social interaction

Crystallization of pattern of violent social interaction as proviolence norms

INTRAFAMILY RESOURCE THEORY

R-1 Social or individual role prescriptions (norms) concerning superior power position of actor

R-2 Actor lacks sufficient valued personal attributes (wealth, knowledge, prestige, liking, etc.) to induce others to accept his claims to superior power

R-3 Use of violence as a means to maintain superior power position in the family

Social Change

FUNCTIONAL THEORY

FN-1 Needed changes in social or individual behavior patterns

FN-2 Institutionalized or personal rigidities block needed change

VIOLENCE

572

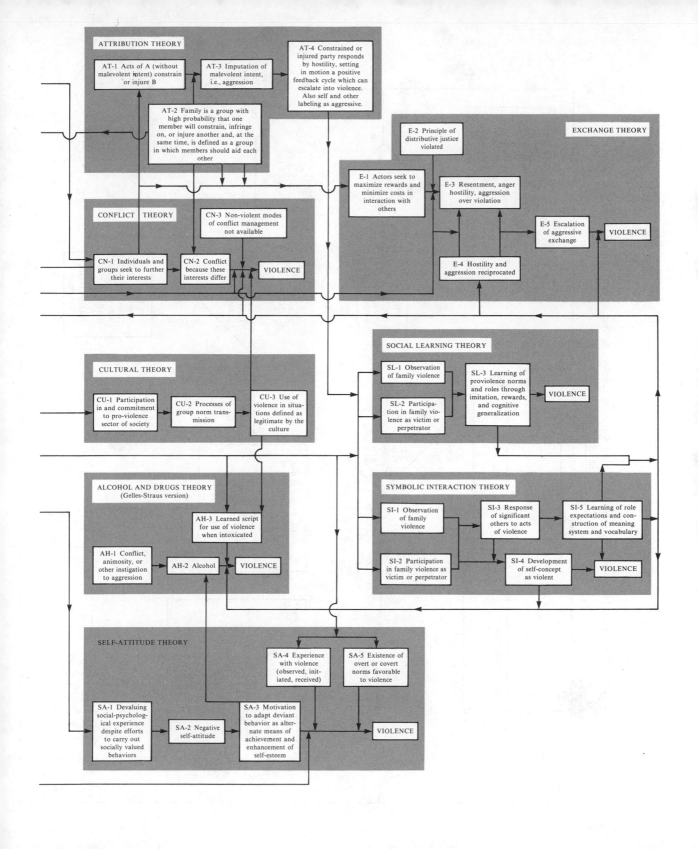

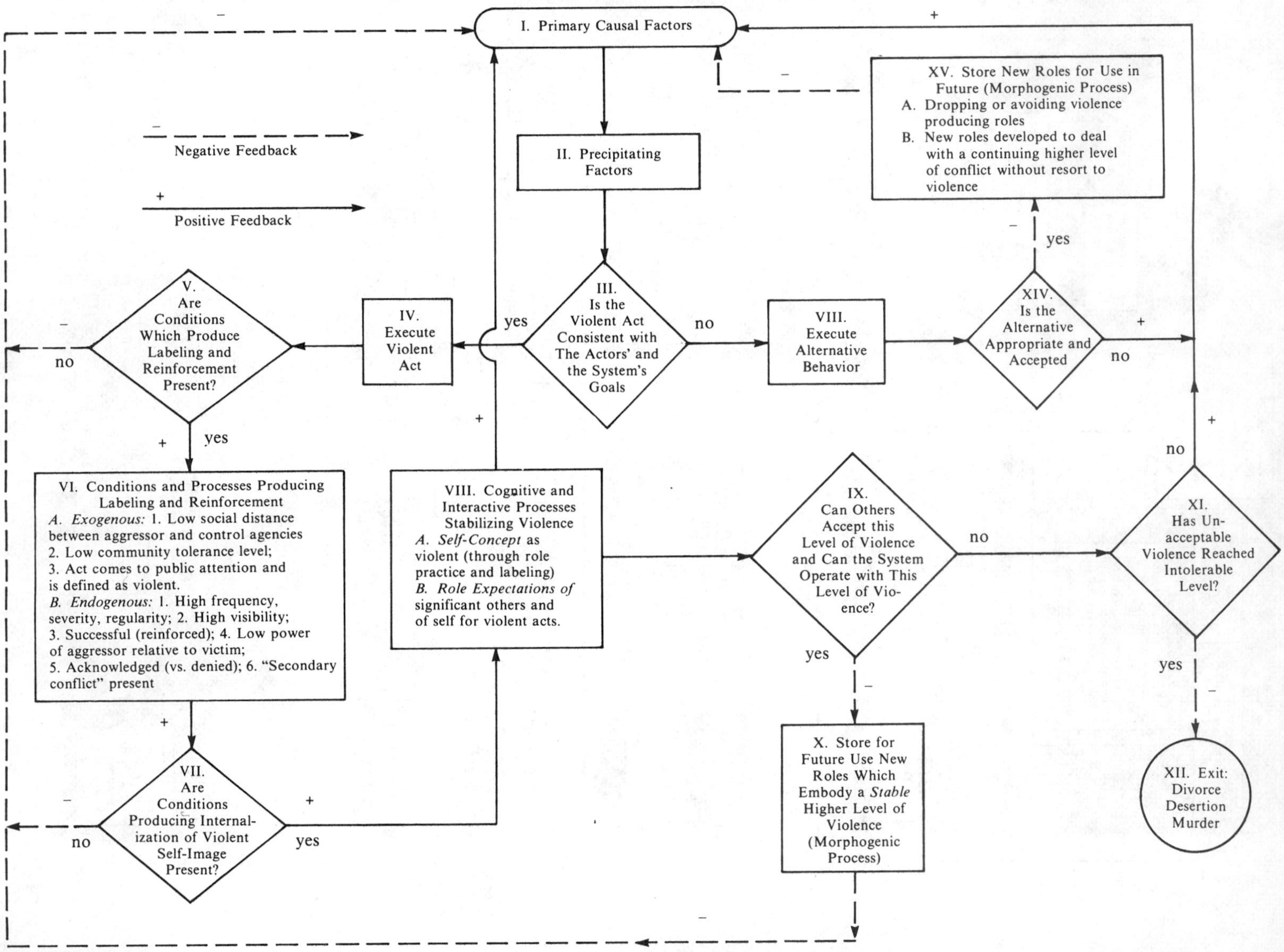

Figure 21.3. Flow Chart Illustrating Cybernetic System Aspects of Labeling, Attribution, and Learning Theories of Violence

writing, we have not made sufficient progress toward expressing each of the partial theories in the form of a cybernetic system. Second, even if we were close enough to this goal to make such a diagram possible in principle, in practice the diagram would become so complex as to be utterly useless. Some indication of the level of complexity which would be required can be gained from examining Figure 21.3. This diagram is a cybernetic representation of certain aspects of social learning and attribution theory. A detailed explanation of the diagram is given in the article by Straus (1973) from which this diagram is taken. Yet even though it is restricted to only *parts* of two *partial* theories, it already taxes one's ability to digest the contents. Moreover, the cybernetic flow charts (similar to Figure 21.3) representing each of the 13 partial theories would also have to be related to each other with at least an equal level of density of causal arrows.

One should not conclude from the above that a general systems theory integration of the partial theories is not possible. We remain convinced of the feasibility and desirability of a general systems approach. However, it is obvious that much work lies ahead before this possibilty is realized. In addition the interrelations of all the elements necessary to encompass the 13 theories diagrammed in Figure 21.2 probably cannot be presented in a single meaningful flow chart. Rather, presentation is likely to take the form of charts within charts, that is, an overall summary chart, then a series of charts (such as Figure 21.3) "unpacking" the internal processes within each of the 13 theories, and then a third series of charts unpacking the boxes within the second set of charts.

In our opinion, the only adequate unified representation of such a general systems theory integration of these partial theories is likely to be in the form of a computer simulation, because the complexity of a verbal or diagrammatic representation would be beyond human ability to comprehend. In addition, as simulation models of the economy have shown, computer simulations have a self-correcting aspect similar to that of empirical research: when the model is run, the typical first results tend to be meaningless or ridiculous. This sets in motion an iterative process whereby the model is progressively refined. Finally, computer assimilations can be used as an experimental tool. Different parameters, assumptions, and relationships are introduced, withdrawn, or modified, and the simulation is then run to examine the effects of these changes.

Micro- and Macrolevel Theories

It is useful to distinguish two types of theories of intrafamily violence. On the one hand, there are what can be called "macrolevel" theories. They attempt to explain the overall level of intrafamily violence within a given society or sector of society as compared to other societies or sectors, and especially the seeming paradox that it is more frequent within the family than within any other group. The second type of theory can be called a "microlevel" theory. This type focuses on the fact that even though violence occurs more often in the family than in other groups, it is not typical of the family or of any other group in the sense of being the modal pattern of interaction. In all groups—even the most violent, such as the family—the typical pattern of interaction does not use physical force, even though the threat of force may underly typical interactions (Goode, 1971). Thus microlevel theories are needed to explain why violence occurs more in some families than in others, and also to explain why violence occurs when it does within the history of specific families.

The variables making up *macro* theories refer to the characteristics of the family as an institution and social group compared to other institutions and groups, and also the characteristics of the society. The variables in a *micro* theory are those which differentiate families from each other. However, the distinction is by no means as sharp as the preceding two sentences suggest. First, no society is uniform even in its most central characteristics. Thus the variables defining the family as an institution and a group will also be variables on which there is family-to-family variation. Second, the meaning and consequences of the family-to-family-difference variables depends on the nature of the societally structured variables. This is illustrated by Rodman's "resources in cultural context" theory of power (1972) and its application to the specific issue of the relation between power and violence by Allen and Straus (1975). Our attempt to suggest an integrated theory of family violence in Figure 21.2, therefore, includes both societal-level and familial-level variables, as well as individual-level variables, but with the emphasis on the former two.

Limitations and Accomplishments of Figure 21.2

The previous section detailing the absence from our integrative efforts of cybernetic control processes presents what is probably the major limitation of what has been accomplished by Figure 21.2. But there are also other limitations. One of these is that the figure does not specifically include the special characteristics of the family which, as we argued early in the chapter, are at the root of a need for a distinctive theory of *family* violence. As in the case of the omission of cybernetic control processes, this omission was necessary to prevent an already complex chart from becoming completely uninterpretable. A third limitation is that Figure 21.2 by no means traces out all the likely interrelations of the partial theories making up the integrated theory. We have drawn arrows indicating those interrelations which seemed necessary and simply stopped the process when it became apparent that any further connecting arrows would pose still another threat to the readability of the chart.

Still another limitation concerns the degree of empirical support for each of the relational propositions indicated by the causal arrows in Figure 21.2. Within each of the partial theories there is generally empirical support for the relationship, but only rarely is this for the specific case of the family. However, the between-theories arrows largely reflect our deductive reasoning, and for the most part have not been empirically tested. Thus one needs to regard each of the causal arrows as representing a hypothesis to be tested.

Finally, although some of the boxes in Figure 21.2 are presented as constants in the original theories from which they are drawn, the safer assumption seems to be that all are variables, even though some may have a nonzero value as their minimum. In addition the shapes of the relationships are largely unknown. However, it should not be assumed that the relationships are linear. In fact, if one has to make an *a priori* guess, the best guess is that more will be nonlinear than linear. Both of these issues are questions for empirical investigation.

Given these and other limitations of the integration, what has been accomplished which makes the effort worthwhile? First, aside from the integration effort itself, the preparatory steps have a value of their own. The identification of the special characteristics which make the family a violence-prone group is one such contribution. Another is the conceptual clarification and specification which have been achieved by the definitions and comparisons of the concept of violence with related concepts such as aggression and force. Closely related is the potential analytic utility of the taxonomy of violence based on the conceptual specification work. Finally, the effort to identify and summarize the salient aspects of as many explanatory theories as possible is, by itself, a contribution to understanding the processes which influence family behavior. Furthermore, we have included among the 15 theories summarized in this chapter three which, prior to our work, have not previously been applied to the issue of interpersonal violence generally or to intrafamily violence specifically (exchange theory, symbolic interaction theory, and general systems theory). Although our application of these three theories to the explanation of intrafamily violence is brief and only suggestive, these may turn out to be fruitful suggestions.

Turning to the integration itself, several things seem to have been accomplished: (1) We think that our mode of relating these theories to each other shifts the emphasis from the less productive question of which theory is correct to a more accurate and more productive focus on what aspect of the total process each theory explains. (2) In addition to revealing the unique contributions of each theory, our integrative efforts suggest the underlying dependence of all the theories on the process of social learning and on the role played by stressful structural arrangements. (3) Although we did not attempt to trace out all the interrelations between the theories (and may indeed have missed some of the key relationships), a number of important relationships have been identified.

Since these relationships between theories were arrived at deductively, their empirical validity is not known. But the process has at least pointed to a series of important relationships which, without the formal effort at integration, probably would not have become a focus of attention and inquiry. (4) The integrative effort represented by Figure 21.2 is an aid to further theoretical development and refinement. It makes available a convenient means of examining any of its 13 explanatory theories and their interrelations. A family researcher or theorist interested in any one of the 13 theories included in that chart is likely to find it highly rewarding to attempt to set forth a more detailed set of linkages than was practical for purposes of this chapter.

7. SUMMARY AND CONCLUSIONS

This chapter attempts to deal with both the conceptual clarification and causal relationship aspects of constructing a theory to explain the determinants of physical violence within the family. It started with an analysis of the unique characteristics of families which call for a special theory of intrafamily violence, as compared to simply assuming that more general theories automatically apply to the family. Among the factors which require a special theory are: 1. high level of physical violence in the family; 2. the consequent need for a theory to explain why it is that family members physically attack each other more than any others; and 3. such special characteristics of the family as the intensity and commitment of family members to that group, the privacy of the family and its internal operations, and the explicit norms giving parents the right to strike children and the implicit norms making the marriage license a hitting license.

The conceptual definition and specification part of the chapter was devoted to presenting and clarifying the definition of violence as the intentional use of physical force on another person. This definition of violence was related to and distinguished from such related concepts as aggression, force, and coercion. In addition, a taxonomy of violence was constructed by crossing the variables of "instrumental versus expressive" violence with "legitimate versus illegitimate" violence. Each of the resulting four types of violence were explained and illustrated by examples from a recent study of intrafamily violence.

The second half of the chapter presents 15 theories of violence and applies these to the specific case of intrafamily violence. The presentation of these 15 theories is highly selective in the sense that only those aspects of the theory which seemed most relevant for the case of intrafamily violence are described; and even then, to lay the groundwork for the later integration of these theories, we deliberately selected the distinctive, nonoverlapping, or complementary aspects of each theory. Finally, it was possible to move toward the integration of 13 of these 15 partial theories because of the social learning and social structural elements which underly so many of the theories. The social structural elements identify the organizational conditions which produce violence, and the social learning elements provide the social psychological mechanism by which these structural conditions are transformed into individual behavior and crystallized into cultural norms and values.

The tangible manifestation of our integration of the 13 theories is in the form of an overall theoretical diagram containing a subsection for each theory. Causal arrows are used to link elements from each of these 13 partial theories with elements of one or more of the other theories.

A major limitation of the resulting theoretical integration is that for the most part it does not show the feedback loops which are likely to be present and does not contain any provision for cybernetic control of the system. In short, despite our commitment in principle to a general systems theory formulation, various practical considerations prevented acting on that commitment at this time. The resulting theoretical integration has other limitations, such as not explicitly taking into account the unique features of the family which require a theory of violence specific to the case of the family. We believe, however, that the present integration has at least brought a certain level of clarity to an aspect of family which has suffered from the confusion of what seemed like an overabundance of theories. The integration is based on the premise that these are not 13 competing theories (even though they do have overlapping and competing elements), but rather that each of these theories points to a part of the explanatory process which tends to be neglected (or secondary) in the other theories. To the extent that our integration has been successful, it serves to confirm this initial assumption and to pave the way for a more specific and detailed integration. We believe that this is most likely to occur through the application of principles of general systems theory, and that it is most likely to be given concrete embodiment in the form of a computer simulation program. The technology for such simulations is already available. What has been missing is the formulation of the theories in terms amenable to computer simulation and enough of the key parameters to at least partly base such a simulation on empirically derived data. The recent growth of theoretical and empirical research on intrafamily violence, on which this chapter is based, offers the possibility that such a compute based integration will be achieved within perhaps a decade.

NOTES

1. A national sample survey of American families addressed to this and other related issues is now being analyzed (Straus et al., 1978).

2. Another of the many paradoxes about the family is highlighted by historical and cross-cultural studies. From this perspective, which focuses on the family as an institutional or organizational structure, the family is one of the most stable and adaptable organizations known. The fact that it also has a high level of stress is not incompatible with either the role instability or the viability of the family as an organizational form. This point was clarified for us in a memo by Melvin Wilkinson, who notes:

I believe that some propositions from systems theory can help explain this. Systems that have a lot of variety or heterogeneity have a greater capacity for variety or flexibility in their responses (Buckley, 1967). In other words, the greater the variety within a system, the greater its adaptability. The family has tremendous variety by its very nature. It usually includes spouses of different sexes of different ages from different families and children of various ages and sexes. However, the great variety leads to different interests and goals and therefore to problems of cohesion. So one could say that the amount of variety in a system is positively related to difficulty in maintaining cohesion. In this sense one might argue that the family is inherently unstable. But in most societies the forces that hold the family together are very strong, i.e., approved sexual outlet, social pressures, blood-ties, laws, companionship, need for security, stability and so on. Consequently, the high variety does not necessarily lead to disintegration. But the high variety does lead to conflict and tension, both of which in moderate amounts are beneficial to the system and facilitate learning and adaptability. So one could say that as long as there are strong forces that promote family cohesion, that the family will be a very flexible and adaptable unit. In the U.S. the forces that promote family cohesion are weakening and at the same time the family is losing variety. There are fewer children, converging sex roles, and more single parent families. Systems theory would then predict that the family would become less adaptable.

3. However, there is a tendency among those writing from a conflict theory perspective to imply that the more conflict the better, or at least to not discuss the question of how much conflict is necessary or desirable.

The question of how much conflict is desirable is also beyond the scope of this chapter. But we would like to suggest that it is an important question for empirical research, and to further suggest the hypothesis that there is a curvilinear relation between the amount of conflict and group well-being. That is, the absence of conflict in the sense of conflict of interest is theoretically impossible and, even if it could be brought about, would be fatal for group well-being. But at the same time, very high levels of conflict can create such a high level of stress and/or such rapid change that group welfare is adversely affected.

4. While spanking a wife is generally regarded as illegitimate, it is necessary to point to the simultaneous presence of contrary norms which, as we said, make the marriage license a hitting license. See section 1 of this chapter and note 6 for references on the ubiquity of conflicting norms.

5. Jerome Frank (1972) has developed a similar taxonomy combining the instrumental-expressive dimension with the dimension of individual versus collective violence. He introduces the legitimacy dimension in the text accompanying the taxonomic table but, unfortunately, does so in a way which confounds collective violence with legitimacy. See also Rule (1974).

6. We are using the concept of "norm" as a property of a collective or group, such as a family, an ethnic group, or a nation. However, the neatness of this is undercut by the fact that typically there are multiple and often contradictory norms referring to the same phenomenon (Embree, 1950; Ryan and Straus, 1954; Evers, 1969). Thus different individuals can perceive and internalize different norms.

7. We have omitted from our inventory those theories which base their explanation on genetic, instinctual, or biological factors. Although these explanations do have some importance for a comprehensive consideration of violence in the family, in the interest of brevity we have omitted the more intraindividually oriented theories. A major problem with all of the theories is that they do not explain why the object of the violence is a family member. Even if we assume the correctness of the claim that aggression and violence are basic human instincts, such theories do not explain why such instinct leads to the object of violence being a family member rather than someone else. The 15 theories which are included are all in some way amenable to answering this question.

8. Bandura (1973) classifies frustration-aggression theory along with other biologically based intraindividual theories as a "drive theory." This reflects the original formulation of Dollard et al. (1939). However, our view of frustration-aggression theory is that it is a special case of social learning theory, but one which (because of historical priority and popular usage) requires separate treatment. We do not accept the idea that humans or other animals have built into their neural systems a drive toward aggression or an inherent tendency to respond to frustration with aggression. Rather, the link between frustration and aggression occurs only if the organism has been rewarded for an "aggressive" response to frustration. This is likely to occur because (1) the inherent effect of frustration is discomfort, tension, and increased motor activity; (2) even gross bodily movement by a young organism is likely to be successful in removing or overcoming many frustration conditions; (3) there is, therefore, a high probability of early reward for physical activity in response to frustration, which of course reinforces and makes more probable the use of physical force as a response to frustration; and (4) in the case of humans, harm-doing or aggressive *intent* can be imputed by others and this definition of the act can be learned by the child. See page 564 for further explication of the process by which attributions of intent can become part of the identity and response repertoire of the child.

9. Although the main theme of *A Clockwork Orange* was behavior modification, the title for our theory is drawn from the episodes in the book where Alex and the Drooges commit violent acts when there is nothing to do.

10. Of course, it can also be contended that the use of force by the husband to maintain a superior position in relation to the wife, and by the wife to maintain control of the children, is functional for the continuance of the family. This is illustrative of the type of thinking which has brought functionalist theory into bad repute.

11. Frustration-aggression theory can be used to explain expressive violence in that aggression can be viewed as a response to the affective state aroused by frustration (see Farrington, 1975).

REFERENCES

ALLEN, C. M. AND M. A. STRAUS
1975   "Resources, power, and husband-wife violence." Paper read at the 1975 Annual Meeting of the National Council on Family Relations. To appear in Straus and Hotaling, 1978.

BACH, G. R. AND P. WYDEN
1968   *The Intimate Enemy*. New York: Morrow.

BACHMAN, J. G.
1967   *Youth in Transition*. Ann Arbor: Institute for Social Research, University of Michigan.

BAKAN, D.
1971   *Slaughter of the Innocents: A Study of the Battered Child Phenomenon*. San Francisco: Jossey-Bass.

BANDURA, A.
1973   *Aggression: A Social Learning Analysis*. Englewood Cliffs, N.J.: Prentice-Hall.

BANDURA, A., D. ROSS, AND S. A. ROSS
1961   "Transmission of aggression through imitation of aggressive models." *Journal of Abnormal and Social Psychology* 63(3):575–82.

BANDURA, A. AND R. H. WALTERS
1963   *Social Learning and Personality Development*, 254–58. New York: Holt, Rinehart and Winston. Reprinted in Steinmetz and Straus, 1974.

BARD, M.
1969   "Family intervention police teams as a community mental health resource." *Journal of Criminal Law, Criminology and Police Science* 60(2):247–50.

BARD, M. AND B. BERKOWITZ
1969   "Family disturbance as a police function." In *Law Enforcement Science and Technology* 2. Chicago: I.I.T. Research Institute.

BEM, D. J.
1967   "Self-perception: An alternative interpretation of cognitive dissonance phenomenon." *Psychological Review* 74:183–200.

1970   *Beliefs, Attitudes and Human Affairs*. Belmont, Calif.: Brooks/Cole.

BERKOWITZ, L.
1962   *Aggression: A Social Psychological Analysis*. New York: McGraw-Hill.

BERNARD, J.
1972   *The Future of Marriage*. New York: Bantam Books.

BETTELHEIM, B.
1967   "Children should learn about violence." *Saturday Evening Post* 240 (March 11):10–12. Reprinted in Steinmetz and Straus, 1974.

BLACK, K. D. AND C. B. BRODERICK
1972   "Systems theory vs. reality." Paper presented at the Annual Meeting of the National Council on Family Relations.

BLAU, P. M.
1964   *Exchange and Power in Social Life*. New York: Wiley.

BLUMBERG, M.
1964–65 "When parents hit out." *20th Century* 173 (Winter):39–44. Reprinted in Steinmetz and Straus, 1974.

BOHANNAN, P.
1960   "Patterns of murder and suicide." In P. Bohannan (ed.), *African Homicide and Suicide*. New York: Antheneum.

BOUDOURIS, J.
1971   "Homicide and the family." *Journal of Marriage and the Family* 33 (November):667–76.

BRONFENBRENNER, U.
1958   "Socialization and social class through time and space." In E. E. Maccoby, T. M. Newcomb, and E. L. Hartley (eds.), *Readings in Social Psychology*. New York: Holt.

BROWN, C.
1965   *Manchild in the Promised Land*. New York: New American Library. Pp. 263–71 reprinted as "The family and the subculture of violence" in Steinmetz and Straus, 1974.

BUCKLEY, W.
1967   *Sociology and Modern Systems Theory*. Englewood Cliffs, N.J.: Prentice-Hall.

BURGESS, A.
1962   *A Clockwork Orange*. New York: Ballantine Books.

BUSS, A. H.
1971   "Aggression pays." In J. L. Singer (ed.), *The Control of Aggression and Violence*. New York: Academic Press.

CALVERT, R.
1974   "Criminal and civil liability in husband-wife assaults." In Steinmetz and Straus, 1974.

CARROLL, J. C.
1975   "A cultural consistency theory of family violence in Mexican-American and Jewish subcultures." Paper read at the 1975 Annual Meeting of the National Council on Family Relations. To appear in Straus and Hotaling, 1977.

COHEN, A. K.
1955   *Delinquent Boys: The Culture of the Gang*. New York: Free Press.

COSER, L. A.
1956   *The Functions of Social Conflict*. New York: Free Press.
1963   "Violence and the social structure." *Science and Psychoanalysis* 6:30–42. Reprinted in S. Endleman (ed.), *Violence in the Streets*. Chicago: Quadrangle Paperbacks, 1970.
1967   *Continuities in the Study of Social Conflict*. New York: Free Press.

CURTIS, L. A.
1974   *Criminal Violence: National Patterns and Behavior*.

Determinants of Violence in the Family: Toward a Theoretical Integration   **579**

Lexington, Mass.: Lexington Books.

DAHRENDORF, R.
1959   *Class and Class Conflict in Industrial Society*. London: Routledge & Kegan Paul.
1968   *Essays in the Theory of Society*. Stanford, Calif.: Stanford University Press.

DOLLARD, J., L. W. DOOB, N. E. MILLER, O. H. MOWRER, AND R. R. SEARS
1939   *Frustration and Aggression*. New Haven, Conn.: Yale University Press.

DURKHEIM, E.
1951   *Suicide: A Study in Sociology*. Translated by J. A. Spaulding and G. Simpson. New York: Free Press.

EDWARDS, J. M. AND M. B. BRAUBURGER
1973   "Exchange and parent-youth conflict." *Journal of Marriage and the Family* 35 (February):101–07.

EMBREE, J. F.
1950   "Thailand: A loosely structured social system." *American Anthropologist* 52:181–93.

ERLANGER, H. S.
1974   "Social class differences in parents' use of physical punishment." In Steinmetz and Straus, 1974.

ERON, L. D., L. O. WALDER, AND M. M. LEFKOWITZ
1971   *Learning of Aggression in Children*. Boston: Little, Brown.

ETZIONI, A.
1971   "Violence." In R. K. Merton and R. A. Nisbet (eds.), *Contemporary Social Problems,* third ed. New York: Harcourt Brace Jovanovich.

EVERS, H. D. (ED.)
1969   *Loosely Structured Social Systems: Thailand in Comparative Perspective*. New Haven, Conn.: Yale University Southeast Asia Studies.

FARRINGTON, K.
1975   "A general stress theory of intra-family violence." Paper read at the 1975 Annual Meeting of the National Council on Family Relations. To appear in Straus and Hotaling, 1978.

FESHBACH, S.
1971   "Dynamics and morality of violence and aggression: Some psychological considerations." *American Psychologist* 26:281–92.

FOSS, J. E.
1974   "Satisfaction, dependence, and marital outcomes." Mimeographed paper, University of New Hampshire Department of Sociology.

FRANK, J. D.
1972   "Some psychological determinants of violence and its control." *Australia and New Zealand Journal of Psychiatry* 6:158–64.

GAGNON, J. AND W. SIMON
1973   *Sexual Conduct: The Social Sources of Human Sexuality* Chicago: Aldine.

GARFINKEL, H.
1967   *Studies in Ethnomethodology*. Englewood Cliffs, N.J.: Prentice-Hall.

GELLES, R. J.
1973   "Child abuse as psychopathology: A sociological critique and reformulation." *American Journal of Orthopsychiatry* 43 (July):611–21. Reprinted in Steinmetz and Straus, 1974.
1974   *The Violent Home: A Study of Physical Aggression between Husbands and Wives*. Beverly Hills, Calif.: Sage Publications.
1975a   "Violence and pregnancy: A note on the extent of the problem and needed services." *Family Coordinator* 24 (January):81–86.
1975b   "The social construction of child abuse." *American Journal of Orthopsychiatry* 44 (April):363–71.

1976   "Abused wives: Why do they stay?" *Journal of Marriage and the Family* 38 (November):659–68.

GELLES, R. J. AND M. A. STRAUS
1975   "Family experience and public support of the death penalty." *American Journal of Orthopsychiatry* 44 (July):596–613. Reprinted in H. Bedau and C. M. Pierce (eds.), *Capital Punishment in the United States*. New York: AMS Press, 1976.

GIL, D. G.
1970   *Violence against Children: Physical Child Abuse in the United States*. Cambridge, Mass.: Harvard University Press.
1971   "Violence against children." *Journal of Marriage and the Family* 33 (November):637–48.

GOODE, W. J.
1971   "Force and violence in the family." *Journal of Marriage and the Family* 33 (November):624–36. Reprinted in Steinmetz and Straus, 1974.

GUTTMACHER, M.
1960   *The Mind of the Murderer*. New York: Farrar, Straus & Cudahy.

HOMANS, G. C.
1961   *Social Behavior: Its Elementary Forms*. New York: Harcourt, Brace & World.
1967   "Fundamental social processes." In N. Smelser (ed.), *Sociology*. New York: Wiley.

HOTALING, G. T.
1975   "Facilitating violence: Why intimaes attribute aggression." Paper presented at the Theory Construct n Workshop at the Annual Meeting of the National Council on Family Relations.

HUGGINS, M. D. AND M. A. STRAUS
1975   "Violence and the social structure as reflected in children's books from 1850 to 1970." Paper read at the Annual Meeting of the Eastern Sociological Society. To appear in Straus and Hotaling, 1978.

HUNT, J. M.
1971   "Intrinsic motivation: Information and circumstance." In H. M. Schroder and P. Suedfeld (eds.), *Personality Theory and Information Processing*. New York: Ronald Press.

JOHNSON, R. N.
1972   *Aggression in Man and Animals*. Philadelphia: W. B. Saunders.

KAPLAN, H. B.
1972   "Toward a general theory of psychosocial deviance: The case of aggressive behavior." *Social Science and Medicine* 6:593–617.

KELLEY, H. H.
1967   "Attribution theory in social psychology." In D. Levine (ed.), *Nebraska Symposium on Motivation,* Lincoln: University of Nebraska Press.
1971   *Attribution in Social Interaction*. Morristown, N.J.: General Learning Press.

KELLEY, H. H. AND J. W. THIBAUT
1969   "Group problem solving." In G. Lindzey and E. Aronson (eds.), *The Handbook of Social Psychology,* second ed., vol. 4. Reading, Mass.: Addison-Wesley.

KEMPE, C. H. ET AL.
1962   "The battered child syndrome." *Journal of the American Medical Association* 181 (July 7):17–24.

KLAUSNER, S. Z. (ED.)
1968   *Why Man Takes Chances: Studies in Stress-Seeking*. New York: Doubleday.

KOLB, T. M. AND M. A. STRAUS
1974   "Marital power and marital happiness in relation to problem solving ability." *Journal of Marriage and the Family* 36 (November):756–66.

LAING, R. D. AND D. G. COOPER
1964   *Reason and Violence: A Decade of Sartre's Philosophy, 1950–1960.* London: Tavistock.

LANG, A. R., D. J. GOECKNER, V. J. ADESSO, AND G. A. MARLATT
1975   "Effects of alcohol on aggression in male social drinkers." *Journal of Abnormal Psychology* 84 (October):508–18.

LASLETT, B.
1973   "The family as a public and private institution: A historical perspective." *Journal of Marriage and the Family* 35 (August):480–92.

LEMASTERS, E. E.
1957   "Parenthood as crisis." *Marriage and Family Living* 19 (November):352–55.

LESHAN, E.
1970   "The pros and cons of spanking." *Woman's Day* (July): 34ff. From *Natural Parenthood: Raising Your Child without a Script*. New York: New American Library.

LEVINGER, G.
1966   "Sources of marital dissatisfaction among applicants for divorce." *American Journal of Orthopsychiatry* 36 (October):803–07. Reprinted in Steinmetz and Straus, 1974.

LIGHT, R. J.
1974   "Abused and neglected children in America: A study of alternative policies." *Harvard Educational Review* 43 (November):556–98.

MACANDREW, C. AND R. B. EDGERTON
1969   *Drunken Comportment: A Social Explanation.* Chicago: Aldine.

MARUYAMA, M.
1963   "The second cybernetics: Deviation amplifying mutual causal processes." *American Scientist* 51:164–79.

MEAD, M. AND F. C. MACGREGOR
1951   *Growth and Culture: A Photographic Study of Balinese Children.* New York: Putnam.

MERTON, R. K.
1938   "Social structure and anomie." *American Sociological Review* 3 (October):672–82.

MILLER, N. E.
1941   "The Frustration-Aggression Hypothesis." *Psychological Review* 48:337–42. Reprinted in L. Berkowitz (ed.), *Roots of Aggression.* New York: Atherton, 1969.

NEW YORK TIMES
1975   "U.S. finds 'epidemic' child abuse rate. *New York Times*, November 30.

O'BRIEN, J. E.
1971   "Violence in divorce prone families." *Journal of Marriage and the Family* 33 (November):692–98.

OWENS, D. M., AND M. A. STRAUS
1975   "The social structure of violence in childhood and approval of violence as an adult." *Aggressive Behavior* 1(2):193–211.

PALMER, S.
1962   *The Psychology of Murder.* New York: Thomas Y. Crowell.
1972   *The Violent Society.* New Haven, Conn.: College and University Press.

PARNAS, R. I.
1967   "The police response to domestic disturbance." *Wisconsin Law Review* 914 (Fall):914–60.
1970   "Judicial response to intra-family violence." *Minnesota Law Review* 54 (January):585–644.

PATTERSON, G. R., J. A. COBB, AND R. S. RAY
1973   "A social engineering technology for retraining families of aggressive boys." In H. E. Adams and I. P. Unikel (eds.), *Issues and Trends in Behavior Therapy.* Springfield, Ill.: Charles C Thomas. Reprinted in Steinmetz and Straus, 1974.

PITTMAN, D. J. AND W. HANDY
1964   "Patterns in criminal aggravated assault." *Journal of Criminal Law, Criminology and Police Science* 55(4):462–70.

PLUMMER, K.
1974   "Some relevant directions for research in the sociology of sex: An interactionist approach." Paper presented at the Annual Meetings of the British Sociological Association.

RICHER, S.
1968   "The economics of child rearing." *Journal of Marriage and the Family* 30 (August):462–66.

RODMAN, H.
1972   "Marital power and the theory of resources in cultural context." *Journal of Comparative Family Studies* 3 (Spring):50–69.

RULE, B. G.
1974   "The hostile and instrumental functions of human aggression." In J. de Wit and W. W. Hartrup (eds.), *Determinants and Origins of Aggressive Behavior.* The Hague, Netherlands: Mouton.

RYAN, B. F. AND M. A. STRAUS
1954   "The integration of Sinhalese society." *Research Studies of the State College of Washington* 22 (December):179–227.

SCANZONI, J. H.
1972   *Sexual Bargaining.* Englewood Cliffs, N.J.: Prentice-Hall.

SCANZONI, L. AND J. SCANZONI
1976   *Men and Women and Change: A Sociology of Marriage and Family.* New York: McGraw-Hill.

SCHACHTER, S. AND J. E. SINGER
1962   "Cognitive, social, and physiological determinants of emotional state." *Psychological Review* 69(5):379–99.

SCHEFF, T. J.
1963   "The role of the mentally ill and the dynamics of mental disorder: A research framework." *Sociometry* 26 (December):436–53.

SCHULTZ, L. G.
1960   "The wife assaulter." *Journal of Social Therapy* 6(2):103–11.

SCOTT, M. B. AND S. M. LYMAN
1968   "Accounts." *American Sociological Review* 33 (February):46–62.

SEARS, R. R., E. E. MACCOBY, AND H. LEVIN
1957   *Patterns of Child Rearing.* Evanston, Ill.: Row, Peterson.

SIMMEL, G.
1950   *The Sociology of Georg Simmel.* Edited by K. Wolf. New York: Free Press.

SINGER, J. L. (ED.)
1971   *The Control of Aggression and Violence.* New York: Academic Press.

SNELL, J. E., R. J. ROSENWALD, AND A. ROBEY
1964   "The wifebeater's wife: A study of family interaction." *Archives of General Psychiatry* 11 (August):107–13.

SPINETTA, J. J. AND D. RIGLER
1972   "The child-abusing parent: A psychological review." *Psychological Bulletin* 77 (April):296–304.

SPREY, J.
1969   "The family as a system in conflict." *Journal of Marriage and the Family* 31 (November):699–706.
1971   "On the management of conflict in families." *Journal of Marriage and the Family* 33 (November, No. 4):722–31.

STARK, R. AND J. MCEVOY III
1970   "Middle class violence." *Psychology Today* 4 (November): 52–65.

STEELE, B. F. AND C. B. POLLOCK
1974   "A psychiatric study of parents who abuse infants and small

children.'' In R. E. Helfer and C. H. Kempe (eds.), *The Battered Child,* second ed. Chicago: University of Chicago Press.

STEINMETZ, S. K.
1971   ''Occupation and physical punishment: A response to Straus.'' *Journal of Marriage and the Family* 33(4) (November):664–66.
1974   ''Occupational environment in relation to physical punishment and dogmatism.'' In Steinmetz and Straus, 1974.
1975   ''Intra-familial patterns of conflict resolution: Husband/wife; parent/child; sibling/sibling. Unpublished Ph.D. Dissertation, Case Western Reserve University.

STEINMETZ, S. K. AND M. A. STRAUS (EDS.)
1974   *Violence in the Family.* New York: Harper & Row. (Originally published by Dodd, Mead, 1974.)

STRAUS, M. A.
1971   ''Some social antecedents of physical punishment: A linkage theory interpretation.'' *Journal of Marriage and the Family* 33 (November):658–63. Reprinted in Steinmetz and Straus, 1974.
1973   ''A general systems theory approach to a theory of violence between family members.'' *Social Science Information* 12 (June):105–25.
1974a   ''Leveling, civility, and violence in the family.'' *Journal of Marriage and the Family* 36 (February):13–29, plus addendum in August 1974 issue. Reprinted in *Nursing Education* (1974); and in R. W. Cantrell and D. F. Schrader, *Dynamics of Marital Interaction.* Dubuque, Iowa: Kendall/Hunt, 1974.
1974b   ''Cultural and social organizational influences on violence between family members.'' In R. Prince and D. Barrier (eds.), *Configurations: Biological and Cultural Factors in Sexuality and Family Life.* Lexington, Mass.: Lexington Books–D. C. Heath.
1976a   ''Sexual inequality, cultural norms, and wife-beating.'' *Victimology* 1(1):54–76. Also reprinted in E. Viano (ed.), *Victims and Society,* Washington, D.C.: Visage Press, 1976; and in J. R. Chapman and M. Gates (eds.), *Women into Wives: The Legal and Economic Impact of Marriage.* Sage Yearbooks in Women Policy Studies, vol. 2. Beverly Hills, Calif.: Sage Publications, 1976.
1977   ''Societal morphogenesis and intrafamily violence in cross-cultural perspective.'' *Annals of the New York Academy of Sciences* 285:719–30.

1978   ''Measuring intrafamily conflict and violence: The Conflict Tactics (CT) Scales.'' *Journal of Marriage and the Family* 40 (in press).

STRAUS, M. A., R. J. GELLES, AND S. K. STEINMETZ
1978   *Violence in the American Family.* New York: Doubleday/Anchor.

STRAUS, M. A. AND G. T. HOTALING, EDS.
1978   *Social Causes of Husband-Wife Violence* (forthcoming.)

STRAUS, M. A. AND S. K. STEINMETZ
1974   ''Violence research, violence control, and the good society.'' In Steinmetz and Straus, 1974.

TEDESCHI, J. T., R. B. SMITH, III, AND R. C. BROWN, JR.
1974   ''A reinterpretation of research on aggression.'' *Psychological Bulletin* 81(9):540–62.

THIBAUT, J. W. AND H. H. KELLEY
1959   *The Social Psychology of Groups.* New York: Wiley.

TOBY, J.
1966   ''Violence and the masculine ideal: Some qualitative data.'' In M. E. Wolfgang (ed.), *Patterns of Violence: The Annals of the American Academy of Political and Social Science,* vol. 364. Philadelphia: American Academy of Political and Social Science. Reprinted in Steinmetz and Straus, 1974.

WASHBURNE, C.
1961   *Primitive Drinking: A Study of the Uses and Functions of Alcohol in Preliterate Societies.* New Haven, Conn.: College and University Press.

WASSERMAN, S.
1967   ''The abused parent of the abused child.'' *Children* 14 (September-October):175–79.

WILKINSON, M. L.
1974   ''An information processing systems model of variety, tension, and components of creativity.'' Dissertation presented to Brigham Young University.
1975   ''System theory vs. tradition: Vive la différence?'' Mimeograph.

WOLFGANG, M.
1958   *Patterns in Criminal Homicide.* Philadelphia: University of Pennsylvania Press.

WOLFGANG, M. AND F. FERRACUTI
1967   *The Subculture of Violence.* New York: Barnes & Noble.

22

RETHINKING FAMILY STRESS THEORY: DEFINITIONAL ASPECTS

Donald A. Hansen and Vicky A. Johnson

The scope and clarity of Burr's recent (1973) inventory of propositions about families under stress places this area of theory in a different phase of development than is addressed in most of the chapters in this volume. To use the imagery of dialectics: Burr has synthesized the theories that have gained coherent form in nearly half a century of family stress research, thereby accomplishing the task that now must be approached in other areas. The next step in family stress theory, as we see it, is not to extend or elaborate Burr's synthesis, but—demonstrating a greater respect for it—to seek a productive antithesis; to challenge the established traditions, not with the intent of abandoning them, but with the hope of contributing to the emergence of a new synthesis that incorporates and transcends them.

This chapter, then, offers no overview of theories of family stress, nor does it summarize the research propositions that have gathered in the decades of family stress research. Neither does it directly grapple with the full range of variables that have been identified as relevant to the area, for example in Hill's (1949:141) classic "ABCX model": A (stressor event) interacting with B (the family's crisis-meeting resources) interacting with C (the definition the family makes of the event) produces X (the crisis). Rather, it focuses on the fulcrum variable in that model, taking "definitional aspects" as the turning point in a search for a more coherent array of central, "core" variables in family stress theory. Further, we do not hesitate to set aside or delimit other variables that, within

NOTE: This investigation was supported in part by an Academic Senate Research Grant, University of California, Berkeley. We are grateful to Eileen Kane and Bobie Figy for technical assistance and to many colleagues and graduate students for comments and suggestions, particularly to Margaret Bubolz, Wesley Burr, Kenneth Cannon, Paul Glasser, Susan Klein, Karl Knobler, Edward Noffsinger, and Jane Oyer. We regret that we could not do justice to all of their diverse suggestions. Throughout this essay our debt to the work and inspiration of Reuben Hill should be apparent.

the restrictions of a short chapter, would distract us from that search.

Given these limitations, this chapter must be read in the context of Burr's contribution, which is represented in diagrammatic form in Figure 22.1 and in propositional form in Appendix I to this chapter. (Both forms are Burr's; see Burr, 1973, for the contexts of arguments that surround the extracts.)

I. CONCEPTUAL PROBLEMS IN THE CURRENT SYNTHESIS

Burr's conceptual model displays a fundamental strength in this stream of family theory. The major theorists who laid the foundations of the field—from Burgess and Angell on through Hill—have followed the lead of G. H. Mead and Cooley in a search for structural correlates and characteristics of meaningful, reflexive interactions of individuals under stress, a search that has persistently avoided convenient assumptions of structural control and functional determination. Thus the development of this theoretical area presents an unusual continuity, in contrast to most other substantive areas, which have undulated in emphases between varieties of structural and interactional analyses.

At the heart of the perspectives on which family stress theorists have built is the concept "definition of the situation." The concept is sensitizing, but it has presented nagging difficulties in conceptualizing the complex dialectics of interactive individual definitions and structural characters. This difficulty is also reflected in Burr's synthesis, which interrelates concepts that vary markedly, from the abstract and general (e.g., "positional influence") to the more concrete and content-specific (e.g., "externalization of blame"); on another dimension, they vary from those that refer to process qualities of relationships (e.g., "personal influence") to those that

Figure 22.1.   Propositions about Families under Stress, as Identified by Burr

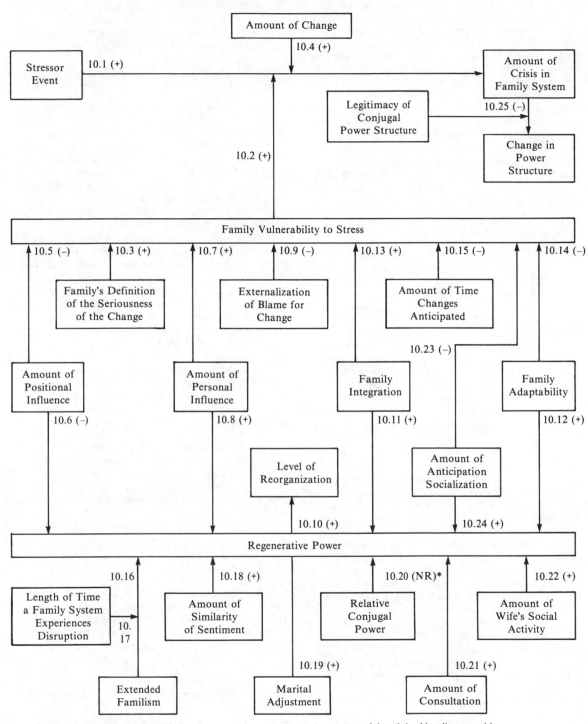

SOURCE: Burr, 1973: 216. See Appendix I to the present chapter for Burr's formulations of the relationships diagrammed here.
*No relationship thought to exist.

describe more static structural qualities or states of relationship (e.g., "legitimacy of conjugal power structure"). In itself this is no problem, for it is reasonable that abstract processes and structures inhere in content, i.e., that they have no separate existence from the concrete. Problems are likely to develop, however, when such diverse concepts are linked to one another.

In this light, Burr's synthesis can be seen as an organization of specific and concrete research propositions around a core set of abstract process relations concepts. In such a synthesis, the coherence of the abstract core concepts is of central importance; the following discussion takes that core as its primary concern. In our effort, we will be mindful of an array of problems, closely related to the difficulties presented by "definition of the situation," that continue to plague family stress theory. Three of these problems deserve special note.

The Restrictive Focus of "Crisis"

Habit and established agreements play an important part in family interaction. Indeed, disruptions of established routines have been taken to be the distinguishing characteristics of familial "crisis." This emphasis is seen in Hill's now-classic definition of crisis as "any sharp or decisive change for which old patterns are inadequate" (1949:51). Thus, Burr notes, crisis is conceived as a continuous variable, denoting variation in the "amount of disruptiveness, incapacitatedness, or disorganization" of the family (1973:200). Given this definition, it must be concluded that crisis is endemic to some families; and it can be argued that a high level of disorganization in some cases might be essential to the maintenance of family relationships and even stimulating of creative potentialities. (See, for example, Bebbington, 1973.) If this is so, the distinction between disruptive "crisis" and "creative disorganization" is difficult to identify and maintain.

It is questionable, then, whether all "sudden or decisive changes" in capacities or organization should be termed "crises." Indeed, what for some families may be a crisis (in commonly accepted usages of the term) may be more akin to a "regenesis" for other families in which members accept disruptions of habit and tradition not so much as unwelcome problems, but more as opportunities to renegotiate their relationships. This possibility is virtually ignored in the concept of "crisis," however, for it is used as a descriptive term to refer to only one kind of the various responses to stress.

To be sure, the concept of crisis may be useful if we are interested only in those families that under stress fall into processes that are "destructive" to family "unity." We argue, however, that even if we seek to understand only why some families "fall apart" under stress, still we must understand why they did not fall apart before, and that we must employ the same contexts of understanding for both conditions. In other words, in the following sections we seek conceptualizations that resist the idea of a *necessary* discontinuity of behavior or a sick state to explain family relations in conditions of unusual stress. This line of argument, however, suggests a further problem in the current synthesis of theory in our field.

The Elusive Qualities of Family Interaction and Influence

In Angell's (1936) pioneering study of the hardships of economic depression, two process variables were offered as keys to family recovery: "family integration" and "family adaptability." More recently, in Hansen's (1965) attempt to identify modes of relationships that interrelate in variable cohesion, coercion, and control in the family, "personal influence" and "positional influence" were suggested as core variables. Both Angell's and Hansen's formulations remain undeveloped and problematic. It is not surprising, then, that in Burr's synthesis their relationship to one another is not identified clearly; however, this deficiency limits the utility of these concepts. Nonetheless, for reasons that we hope will become clear in the contexts of our discussion, we concur with Burr (see Figure 22.2, abstracted from Figure 22.1) that these four concepts continue to hold considerable promise for the study of families under stress.

In the following sections, we will attempt to rework these concepts and to interlink them to one another in a conceptualization that allows us to address the ways individual family members influence one another in the maintenance and change of patterns of family interaction.

Family relations, of course, can be characterized in various ways: by regularities of behavior, by functional consequences, by types of inherent expectations or definitions. Research is most easily mounted if focus is restricted to regularities of behavior—what we have identified as "interactions." But ease is not the only criterion, nor is it necessarily the critical one, even in research.

Figure 22.2. Core Concepts in Family Stress Study, as Identified by Burr

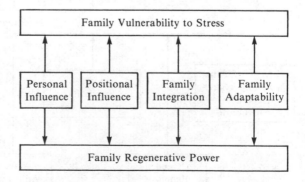

We shall argue that at this time unless we attend more closely to the meaning aspects of familial relations, seeking an interpretive perspective on the individual member's efforts to coordinate with other members, we will miss essential qualities of stress processes. We do not suggest that this strategy will lead to a complete and adequate theory of family stress behavior, but rather that at this stage of research understanding it offers a promising route for exploration.

The Distracting Influence of "Vulnerability" and "Regenesis"

At the core of Burr's synthesis, "vulnerability" and "regenerative power" serve as dependent variables. Roughly equating Hill's (1949) "crisis meeting resources" with Hansen's (1965) "vulnerability," Burr notes that "neither of these theorists defines this variable, but it apparently denotes variation in a family's ability to prevent a stressor event . . . from creating some crisis or disruptiveness in the system" (1973:201–02). Although the equation rather restricts Hill's concept of crisis meeting resources, it demonstrates the circularity that can result when descriptive concepts are related to one another: the vulnerable family is one that is unable to resist disruption; the disrupted family is one that is vulnerable.

A similar argument can be made about the limitations of the concept "regenerative power," which Hansen (1965) introduced to refer to the variable ability of a family to recover from a crisis. Unfortunately, this "outcome" variable has remained so vague it offers little other than a convenient label for qualities of relationships that are more explicitly defined with other concepts.

To put this point another way, these concepts appear to have little to offer at this time to either research or theory, for to effectively define them in terms of observable referents would require the knowledge they are intended to help identify. But this should not lead us to turn our backs on the tantalizing problem that these terms attempt to address. Why is it that some families that are "vulnerable" apparently lack "regenerative power," while other "vulnerable" families quickly recover? Why do some that are disrupted only by the most severe stresses also recover quickly, while others show little "regenerative power" once they have fallen into disarray?

It is important to recognize that a time factor is implied in the relationship of vulnerability and regeneration: as they are defined, the two concepts refer to disorganization at different stages in a family's experience with stress. This suggests that in the effort to reconceptualize the phenomena these concepts attempt to describe, we must attend more closely to their relationship to one another. In the following sections, we suggest one route to reconceptualization, through a distinction that parallels "vulnerability" and "regenerative power": a distinction between "established patterns of family interaction" and

"institutive patterns of family interaction." By established patterns we mean those familiar regularities of everyday family life (e.g., ways of playing, dining, and discussing) as well as the established emergency routines which family members may bring into play when confronting individual or collective problems (e.g., meeting as a decision-making council, adopting general helping roles when a parent is sick). In most families, under normal or endemic stresses of everyday life these established routines display a general persistence. Close observation also reveals a slow and continual disruption, however—for example, as parents age, as the character of the surrounding neighborhood changes, or as the young family moves from comparative austerity toward the more comfortable middle years of family development. In the following sections, then, we will speak of *variable disruptions of established patterns*.

By "institutive patterns of interaction" we refer to regularities that are of recent origin and not yet fully routine, familiar, or accepted. Thus we do not mean to include interaction sequences that are simply novel, random, or experimental (although experimenting itself may be either an established or institutive pattern). Institutive patterns of interaction can also be seen in most families under the normal stresses of everyday life, but the range and number are highly variable, both from family to family and, within any family, from time to time. In our discussion, then, we will speak of *variable negotiations of institutive patterns*.

Institutive patterns are often linked to disruptions of established patterns (e.g., in changing family roles as the child enters adolescence). But it is not necessarily so. When old patterns of interaction are disrupted and discarded, new patterns do not necessarily take their place; similarly, new patterns can develop even though the old ones are maintained. Thus "institutive patterns" and "established patterns" are treated in our discussion as separate variables that are independent of each other.

With these concepts attention shifts from the vague and restrictive question "What makes a family in crisis vulnerable and/or regenerative?" Now the question becomes "How do families interact in stressed situations, and what are the relative probabilities that they will maintain established patterns and/or negotiate institutive patterns?" In the following sections we attempt to identify a central array of concepts that will facilitate research into this question. But first, we consider the variable qualities of stress.

II. CHANGE, AMBIGUITY, AND RELATIVITY: DELIMITING THE CONCEPT OF "STRESS"

Continuing difficulties in specifying the nature of stressors on the family make it difficult to avoid tautological reasoning: Stressors are identified in terms of their effects, and these effects are subsequently taken as evidence of stressors. In part, this may be because, as Croog (1970:22) points out, virtually anything in family life may be potentially traced back as a "stressor". But in part it also seems due to the failure, in Burr's terms, to define the stressor as a variable, beyond the idea that it denotes "something different from the routine changes within a system that are expected as part of its regular, routine operation" (1973:201).

Classification Schemes of Stress Events

Eliot (1942), Hill (1949), and Hansen and Hill (1964) have attempted to address the elusive definition in a variety of classification systems. The latter authors (1964:794), for example, identified four themes running through sociologists' classificatory efforts: (a) the effects of presence or absence of physical features of stress; (b) the tensions or hardships that precede impact of the stressor or evidence of strain; (c) the presence or absence of factors that allow members to blame one another for the stress; (d) the probable effect on the family of community response and resources.

Theorists more committed to psychosocial models have taken a compatible but distinctly different view. Croog (1970:21), for example, first defines stress as "a condition of tension within an individual which occurs as a response to one or more stressors," then follows Howard and Scott (1965) to define a stressor as "any problem condition that is posed to the individual or organism for solution." In a later article, Scott and Howard (1970) argue that problem conditions can be categorized on the locus of their initiation: in the internal physical environment of the organism, in the external physical environment, in the organism's own psychological environment, in the social culture.

This mechanical model has the virtue of attending physical, phenomenological, and ecological contexts of the individual's tensions, a virtue we shall endorse later but one to which we do not pretend in our current discussion. However, the model runs into difficulties when we consider another essential perspective that has been neglected in stress research: the perspective on stress as a process, rather than a simple event or set of events that is imposed on an organism or family. Much of the confusion in conceptualizing stress, as Mechanic (1974) suggests, results from seeing stress as a short-term, single stimulus, rather than as a complex set of changing conditions that have a history and future: "Thus mastery of stress is not a simple repertoire, but an active process over time and relationships to demands that are themselves changing, and that are often symbolically created by the groups within which man lives and new technologies which such groups develop" (Mechanic, 1974:35; see also Dubos, 1965, and Mechanic, 1975).

Definitional Schemes of Stress

Mechanic's account emphasizes the interplay of the individual's definitions with his or her situational contexts. This parallels Lauer and Lauer's conception of "stress" as a "disoriented state," precipitated by an extreme "tension between the cognitive and contextual facets of the individual's existence" (1976:523), as well as Zollschan's "exigency theory" of change and institutionalization, which hinges on the discrepancy between what is desired or expected and what is experienced (1964:89).

This definitional line of argument is taken another important step toward clarity in Elder's pathbreaking study *Children of the Great Depression* (1974). Elder focuses the more general concern with cognitive and contextual tensions on the "problematic disparity between the *claims* of a family in a situation and its *control* of outcomes," which in his study was seen even more specifically as the "gap between socioeconomic needs and the ability to satisfy them. Crises may thus arise when claims are elevated well beyond control potential and realities, or when changes in the situation markedly diminish control of outcomes" (1974:10; italics added).

Zablocki (1976) adds another dimension to this discussion in his interlinking of the degree of "risk" present in the situation with the degree of "hope." Following this procedure, but substituting Elder's concepts of "control" and "claims" for Zablocki's terms, we see the possibility of other stress situations that may confront members of a family.

In Figure 22.3, the "crises" Elder has identified are located in the cell labeled "predicament." But other stressed conditions are also suggested, allowing this brief inventory:

1. Familial malaise: stresses of diminishing control and claims
2. Familial binds: stresses of diminishing claims and/or increasing control
3. Familial predicaments: stresses of increasing claims and/or diminishing control
4. Familial challenges: stresses of increasing claims and control.

This line of argument appears promising, and we intend to pursue it in future research. In the present chapter, however, we turn to a rather important inadequacy in the construct, which points to the possibility of an even more general quality that underlies much if not most of the tensions in the relationship of "claims" to "control."

Change and Stress: Modified Definitional Schemes

A linkage of change and stress at the broad historical and cultural levels is suggested by Lauer and Lauer

Figure 22.3. A Simple Taxonomy of Claims-Control Situations

Claims

Adapted from Zablocki (1976) and Elder (1974).

(1976), who question Smelser's (1959) proposition that psychic disturbances are an integral part of the processes of large-scale, long-term structural changes, such as those that attended the Industrial Revolution in England. This may often be the case, Lauer and Lauer argue, but psychic stress is not *always* widely experienced in times of pervasive change. They point to M. Mead's (1966) study of the Manus Islanders, to Lloyd's (1969) study of western Nigerians, and to Lerner's (1958) study of six Middle Eastern nations as examples that do not support the proposition that stress is a *necessary* part of *all* change (1976:526–29).

This suggests that not only the objective rate of change but also the perceived rate is crucial in the experience of stress. A similar suggestion has emerged in recent medical psychological literature. In their early research, for example, Holmes and Rahe (Rahe et al., 1964; Holmes and Rahe, 1967; Rahe, 1972) argued that any recent life changes, whether experienced as desirable or undesirable, bring stress to the individual and thereby induce illness. Recently, however, Rahe (1974) has shifted toward the position of critics who emphasize the importance of the individual's appraisals of the events. Similarly, Selye's (1956) pioneering work on stress took a noncognitive position, but his more recent writing (1974) suggests that some stressors are good and others bad, depending on psychological mediations. Other researchers, notably Lazarus (1974) and Haan (1977) emphasize these mediations more strongly, arguing that cognitive appraisals and coping procedures must be understood if we are to understand individual differences in response to change.

Evidences of those differences abound, not only in physiological and psychological research but in historical-cultural studies as well. Lauer and Lauer note

the indicators of stress in Jacksonian America—pervasive fears, personal pathologies, proliferation of new movements and organizations, and widespread violence—but note also evidences that at least some persons faced the future with "unbounded optimism and delicious anticipation." "As a number of historians have noted," they write, "optimism and despair were two contradictory themes that existed in precarious tension. The question is, why did these two diverse responses exist? Why do some people endure debilitating stress while others seem to revel in the swiftness of change?" (1976:541).

Lauer and Lauer turn to symbolic interactionism for the proposed answer. Shibutani argues that to understand an individual's behavior we must know "(1) his definition of the situation, (2) the kind of creature he believes himself to be, and (3) the audience before which he tries to maintain his self-respect" (1961:279). Widespread and rapid social change, Lauer and Lauer note, undercut all three of these social psychological bases for action. Thus it is not change per se but the *rate of change* that is related to stress.

Further, they argue, the effects of the rate are diminished when the change is perceived to be either "desirable" or "under control." (Note the close parallel with Elder's terms, "claims" and "control," discussed above.) Lauer and Lauer have thus specified a distinct construction, which links the Holmes and Rahe contention (see above; see also Dohrenwend, 1973) that change itself is the critical element of stress, to the emphasis of Lazarus and Haan (see above) on the mediating effects of definitional processes such as "claims" and "control."

The empirical case for or against this construction remains to be established. It is possible, for example, that the relationship of the variables is the opposite of that posited by Lauer and Lauer, i.e., that "rate of change" mediates a fundamental relationship of claims and control to stress. It is also possible that both forms of relationship might be seen in various situations for various persons. Whatever the case, this line of argument suggests the workings of a correlate of stress that is even more general and pervasive than "claims and control": the pervasive but variable qualities of uncertainty or ambiguity. We turn now to that variable.

"Ambiguity": A Further Specification of Definitional Schemes

The discussion that follows further delimits the definitional conceptualizations of stress discussed above. Thus it should be approached not as an alternative to, say, Elder's construct, but as a specification of what we believe to be one critical aspect of acting in a changed situation.

If stress is identified as dependent on a complex interplay of changing conditions and definitions, then a necessary (though far from sufficient) requirement for understanding family interactions under stress is the identification of the varied *qualities* of stressed situations that render those conditions problematic to the individual family member. The thrust of our argument is that, whatever else is involved, the definitional qualities are critical; more specifically, the uncertainties and unfamiliarities introduced by change, regardless of the character of the change, are among the most stressful qualities of a changed situation. Of necessity, we ignore many other stressful qualities, such as physical deprivations and emotional disturbances, except as they affect the ambiguities of the situation to be defined. We believe that our reasons for this choice will be made clear in the following pages.

"Ambiguity" itself is an ambiguous term. By it we refer to cognitive and/or evaluative uncertainty. At one level, then, we can follow Elder in concern with uncertainties of control and claims; similarly, we might follow Shibutani to focus on uncertainties in the situation that must be defined, uncertainties in one's own conception of self, uncertainties about one's reference groups. Thus "ambiguity," as we use the term, is closely related to the expectations and goal orientations that are involved in family interactions.

Like the related emphases on "role dilemmas" (see Rapoport and Rapoport, 1969) and on the presence or absence of established "coping rituals" for unfamiliar situations (see Roghmann et al., 1973), our conception of "ambiguity" emphasizes the definitional differences in the varied responses of apparently similar families to apparently similar stresses. This emphasis parallels a growing literature in psychology which attends the individual's cognitive appraisals of his or her situation.

In one study, for example, Davidson and Kelley (1973) found that psychiatric patients (N=20) coped with a stressful film more effectively when a nurse was present. The authors suggest that the nurse represented a "safety signal"; in our terms, her presence reduced the ambiguities of risk or control to the individual viewer. Similarly, the speech and movement of very young children at play in an unfamiliar room are disrupted when their mothers leave the room, but return to "pre-absence" levels when the mothers return (Cox and Cambell, 1968; see also the interpretations of Bowlby, 1969). "It is as if the familiar representation 'I am with my parent' absorbs, transforms, or neutralizes" unfamiliar elements, notes Kagan (1974:244–45); but if "discrepancies" mount, a child will cry even when on the mother's lap. In a related essay, discussing a series of studies on preschool children's fearful responses to novel persons, objects, and environments, Smith (1974:109–15) argues that fear responses are seldom marked when the child has control over his or her approach to the novelty, for this allows control of the salience of the novelty, or more generally,

of the degree of ambiguity experienced at any specific time. When the child has control, novelty elicits exploration as well as fear responses. Interestingly, investigation of novel objects is generally rapid, compared to investigation of novel persons and novel environments. Smith suggests that this difference is due to the greater unpredictability of persons and the greater unfamiliarity of a "new" environment. A similar interpretation might be made of propositions about the disturbing and stimulating effects on children of a family move to a new home (Coombs, 1962–63; Stubbenfield, 1955).

Clearly, however, the relationship of ambiguity and other components of stress to an individual's display of distress is highly variable; individuals not only perceive and interpret their situations differently, they also employ psychological defenses, regressions, and other coping strategies in differing ways and to differing degrees. (See, for example, Haan, 1969; Katz et al., 1970; Kent, 1958; Korner, 1970; Weinstock, 1967; Wolff et al., 1964.)

Among other things, an emphasis on the relationships of ambiguity to familial interaction allows us to consider the relationship of misperceptions to familial coordination, as well as to individual processes of coping and adapting—including the possibility that the relationships may be positive. Indeed, misperceptions may make it easier for both individual and family to cope with problems; for example, psychological or interpersonal denial through fostering illusions of competence or control (see Houston and Hodges, 1970; Lefcourt, 1973; Stein, 1970). Misperceptions may also allow negotiation of new familial myths, or what Byng-Hall (1973) terms "consensus role images," that resolve apparent ambiguities and, in effect, insulate the family from the disruptive effects of further ambiguity, perhaps at the expense of one or more individual members. (See Ferreira, 1963; Paul and Bloom, 1970.) The parallel of this process with the formation and maintenance of ideologies and scapegoats at the societal level is suggestive.

In essence, we see conditions of heightened ambiguity as occasions for the individual's and family's "reconstruction" as well as the "destruction" of social reality, in which interacting persons seek information that will help them define their individual situations and negotiate new agreements. "It is by consulting each other and comparing their experiences that they alter their ways of acting," Shibutani (1966:182–83) writes of individuals caught up in the uncertainties of a crisis situation: "Rumor is an important part of this process of transformation. As such, it is not a pathological phenomenon, but an integral part of the process whereby men develop more adequate ways of coping with new circumstances." Commenting on this argument, McLeod and Chaffee (1972:94) note that the search for information to help define ambiguous situations may operate whenever "the demands for action require some structuring of the situation."

We will further develop some of these ideas in the following sections. At this point, however, we can offer a first, gross approximation of the complex relationship of ambiguity to family interaction. We employ the two concepts introduced in section I: "established patterns of family interaction" and "institutive patterns of family interaction."

Available research suggests that the relationship of ambiguity to disruptions of established patterns of interaction is curvilinear: *moderate (or endemic) ambiguity disrupts established patterns little, but lowered ambiguity is somewhat disruptive and heightened ambiguity is highly disruptive of established patterns*. The relationship of ambiguity to institutive patterns of interaction is also expected to be curvilinear, but in a somewhat different way: *the greater the ambiguity, the greater the negotiation of institutive patterns, except at extreme levels of ambiguity, which discourage institutive patterns*. These relationships are diagrammed in Figure 22.4.

Clearly, these starkly stated relationships might be influenced by many other variables, some of which are considered in our more formal propositions that follow. As clearly, our treatments throughout this chapter of "interactive patterns" and "ambiguity" are highly restricted; and there are many other aspects of stress that we have ignored. It should be noted that in our formal propositions, we often restrict ourselves even further, using the term "heightened ambiguity" to refer to that general level of ambiguity which encourages *both* institutive patterns and disruptions of established patterns (indicated on the horizontal coordinate in Figure 22.4).

Figure 22.4. The Relationship of Ambiguity to Patterns of Family Interaction

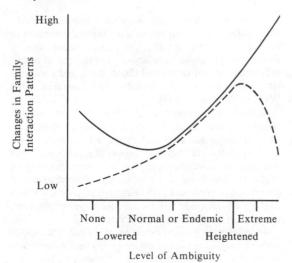

Solid line: Disruption of established interaction patterns. Broken line: Precipitation of institutive interaction patterns.

Anticipation, Ambiguity, and Interaction Patterns

So far we have not mentioned time as a factor in stress behavior. In any situation in which immediate action is not required, time and the "experience" of time clearly interplay with the variables under study. Elder's "claims" and "controls," for example, may be considered functions of time; if claims or control is increasing or decreasing with time, family members may experience a "time pressure" that adds to the intensities of the varied stresses of their situation. Indeed, Zablocki (1976:451) defines crisis as a "predicament" (e.g., a problematic disparity between claims and control) *plus* "time pressure."

Time, however, has not played a great part as a concept in family research. We do not propose to attempt to remedy this condition, but to call attention to it: temporal factors, we believe, should be given close and continuing attention in family research and theory, and particularly in areas concerned with change, such as stress study.

Although there is little direct evidence of the effects of temporal variables in stress study, their import is suggested in studies of "anticipation." Hansen and Hill (1964:794–95), for example, have argued that the "length of time a stressful impact is anticipated" is related to familial "vulnerability" or, in our terms, to the disruptions of established patterns of interaction. Their observation derived especially from disaster research, which offers examples of unanticipated and sudden impact, such as the explosion of a chemical factory, to other disasters that are anticipated and methodically prepared for, such as annual floods. The implication is readily drawn (see Figure 22.1) that there is a linear, inverse relationship between amount of time stressful events are anticipated and disruptions of interaction patterns.

Laboratory research of Lazarus and his associates suggests that the relationship is more complex. Their studies of the relation of anticipation to anxiety in the individual consider two aspects of emotional processing: (1) emerging cognitive appraisals of the significance of the event, and (2) evaluation in choosing and bringing into action coping activity. The duration of anticipation appears to be related differently to these two aspects.

In a very brief period of waiting there may not be enough time for the individual to fully assimilate or appraise the nature of what is about to happen. Thus, as Breznitz's (1967) research suggests, there may be an "incubation of threat": the heart rate of subjects, threatened with a severe electric shock at the end of three, six, and 12 minutes, increased more the longer the waiting period. The longer the anticipation, the greater the stress reaction. (See also Folkins, 1970.) Indeed, disaster research evidences similar processes in families and communities (Hill and Hansen, 1962; Drabek and Boggs, 1968).

But at the same time, the longer the individual has to

reappraise the threatening situation, the more likely is he or she to work out procedures for dealing with the stress. Thus the longer the duration of anticipation, the less the stress reaction. This is seen in the "work of worrying" which Janis (1958) identified in surgical patients; those who had gone through worry work before an operation were better able to tolerate postoperative pain. Similar interpretations can be made of familial adjustments to the stresses of a child's experiences with polio (Davis, 1963) or the implantation of a cardiac pacemaker (Galston and Gamble, 1969). Given time, an indeterminate and indefinite threat can be coped with in ways that little disrupt interaction patterns, and may even contribute to increases in satisfaction and instrumental effectiveness.

Lazarus and Averill (1972) report a series of laboratory studies oriented around anticipation of electric shocks, under three conditions of uncertainty— event uncertainty: not knowing whether the shock will occur; event certainty, temporal uncertainty: knowing the shock will occur, but not when; and event and temporal certainty: knowing that the shock will occur and exactly when. The research suggests that temporal ambiguity—not knowing when the harm will be met—initially leads to higher levels of stress, but given time stress reponse is lowered as coping processes such as denial or avoiding thought about the shock are mobilized.

Clinically oriented research suggests that individuals and their families may display similar processes, related to event and temporal ambiguity. In a study of the family interactions of 10 young females suffering anorexia nervosa, Amdur et al. (1969) found an increase in behavioral symptoms at times of "stress," such as the approach of discharge from the hospital or graduation from high school; these periods seem to correspond to changes in subjects of family communication.

A more distinct pattern is reported by Bermann (1973), who observed one family's interactions through some six months that preceded the father's open heart surgery. The data in this case study are somewhat rare, for prior to the family's discovery that the surgery was necessary, home visits had been initiated by clinic staff concerned with the son's difficulties, thus allowing "before and after" comparison of the family's behavior. In the three months immediately following the announcement of the threatening surgery, patterns of interaction were found to be little changed, regardless of the variables selected for analysis. But as the date of surgery neared, the family members appeared to awaken to the "inexorability of their future," and the patterns of their interaction were considerably reordered, leaving the family in a condition of "simulated" harmony.

Although the relationship undoubtedly is far more complex, extant research reports suggest that *in conditions of heightened ambiguity, the longer the time of anticipation, the less the disruptions of established patterns of interaction and the more the negotiations of institutive patterns.*

In the following sections, we do not directly pursue this or other variables of time. Our neglect, however, should be recognized as a necessary tactic of the moment, and not a recommended strategy for contemporary theory and research. If we could deal effectively with time variables in the following discussion, we would, for we consider them crucial to an understanding of the definitional aspects of individual and family life. At this point, however, it is necessary to restrict our focus as we further consider ambiguity, which we have identified as a fundamental and pervasive quality of stressed conditions that makes the definitional aspects of family interaction especially problematic.

III. EMERGENCE AND RELATIVITY IN COMMUNICATION: REWORKING THE CONCEPT OF ADAPTABILITY

In family stress theory, as we have noted, Burr (1973) has identified a promising core of concepts. In this and the following sections we will look more closely at these concepts, attempting to rework them in a coherent schema that links definitional and behavioral aspects of family relations. Patterns of interaction, we shall argue, are in large part a function of (1) communication and (2) "coorientations," which for the moment we may consider to be "family agreements" or "consensus." In this section we shall look more closely at communication, then move to a discussion (and a more adequate definition) of coorientation in section IV.

Ambiguity, Explicit Appeals, and Interaction Patterns

"Communication" refers to at least three distinguishable qualities of human interaction: explicit meanings or messages (semantic qualities); linguistic coding, used to arrange the particular structure of the message (syntactical qualities); and contextual clues, cues, and concomitants (behavioral, or "pragmatic" qualities; see Watzlawick et al., 1968).

Semantic and syntactical capacities have to do with the abilities of individuals to exchange explicit verbal messages in ways that both participants understand. In our discussion, it is the "appeal" aspect of explicit messages that appears most important, for such messages may be useful in identifying and establishing compatibilities in perceptions or role and goal orientations. (For a sensitizing inquiry into familial interaction patterns and communication, see Hill et al., 1959.)

In some relationships, however, it is clear that explicit appeals may have little effect on family agreements, and in some instances may diminish consensus. The idea, popular in business executive circles in recent years, that failures of coordination are due to misunderstandings and can be remedied by increased "communication" is grossly imperfect, for it is clear that information exchange may lead to an awareness of value and role incompatibilities. At times, these incompatibilities may become apparent even though the explicit messages emphasize common agreements. (See, for example, McLeod and Chaffee, 1972:90–93.)

Wackman (1973) reports consistent evidence in three studies (Newcomb, 1961; Pasdirtz, 1969; Wackman and Beatty, 1971) that interpersonal communications function not so much to persuade, but as vehicles of information exchange. These studies, however, emphasized the explicit messages of communication, which suggests the utility of inquiry into other aspects of communication in efforts to understand renegotiations of familial relationships. It is part of our common-sense knowledge, for prime example, that it is not simply what is said, but also how it is said that "makes the difference," i.e., that tells the listener what the speaker thinks of him or her, or about the subject of conversation. This bit of common sense has been given little attention in sociological research on families, although it has developed over the past quarter century among followers of Gregory Bateson.

To follow Bateson's usage, a message not only conveys a report (content); it also carries a command (a statement about the relationship of the sender to the receiver). Communications, that is, not only convey information but also serve to define relationships:

> All such relationship statements are about one or several of the following assertions: "This is how I see you . . . this is how I see you seeing me . . ." and so forth in theoretically infinite regress. Thus, for instance, the messages "It is important to release the clutch gradually and smoothly" and "Just let the clutch go, it'll ruin the transmission in no time" have approximately the same information content (report aspect), but they obviously define very different relationships [cited in Watzlawick et al., 1968:52].

In contrast to the content aspects of communication, which tend to procede via explicit concepts, relational aspects of communications procede in greatest part in ways that often can be conveyed only in "analogic" fashion. This analogic character of relational modes of communication, then, poses difficult problems for the analysis of familial agreements and interaction patterns. Yet the importance of the analogic, relational communication in familial relations is fundamental, as the works of the followers of Bateson and Laing clearly suggest. (See, for example, Jackson, 1968; Laing et al., 1966.)

We are suggesting, then, that sociological research on families under stress is highly compatible with the emphasis on communication analysis that has heavily influenced medical-psychiatric studies of family processes. It is encouraging to note that the possibilities of this compatibility have begun to be explored in family sociology and social psychology. (See Alexander, 1973; Bugental et al., 1972; O'Keefe, 1973.) It would seem promising at this point also to follow such neglected leads as those of Ferreira and Winter (1968), whose research indicates that

"abnormal" families communicate less than "normal" ones.

In our current concern with the relationship of heightened ambiguity to family interaction patterns, however, we would focus on another aspect of communication: the types of appeals that individuals make, through either explicit or relational communication, to maintain or alter their interaction patterns. Those appeals, following George Herbert Mead's (1932) arguments, can be seen in terms of "emergence" and "relativity."

Ambiguity, Emergence, and Relativity

In stable situations, characterized by orderly interaction and no more than "endemic" levels of ambiguity, the individual tends to define his or her present activity not by describing the immediate moment itself, but by describing that moment in relation to other moments past and present. This, roughly, is what G. H. Mead termed "emergence." By contrast, in what we have characterized as conditions of "heightened ambiguity," the individual's attention turns more closely to his or her immediate locale. Emergent assumptions and expectations—which would serve to define the present situation in terms of past and future orders—are questioned. If the heightened ambiguity continues, the present uncertainty invalidates the usefulness of an orderly past and, since past and future are bound together, the future is also emptied of meaning for the present condition. This, roughly, is a condition of "relativity."

To restate G. H. Mead's highly complex argument even more simply: In times of uncertainty, individuals attempt to identify order in their immediate surroundings, thereby altering their remembrance of what has been and their anticipation of things to come; the perceived present, that is, essentially rewrites past and future. By contrast, in fairly stable times, the immediate present is defined on the basis of order identified in past and/or future. Remembrances and anticipations, that is, structure the perception of the present moment.

Both emergence and relativity processes may be precipitated by ambiguities in social interaction. If patterns of family interaction are strongly established, ambiguity that is not severe may be readily handled through "emergence appeals": the interacting individuals will urge one another to maintain coherence, through continuing and subtle reconstruction of present ambiguities in relation to things past and in relation to things anticipated. Thus, unless ambiguity grows severe or interaction patterns are weak or already disrupted, ambiguity strengthens consensus, i.e., contributes to more coherent patternings of intrapersonal and interpersonal knowledge.

By contrast, if heightened ambiguities persist—to the point, for example, that family members begin to suspect that they do not indeed share meanings and values, or do not agree in their expectations of one another—the probabilities of "relativity appeals" increase: the individuals seek coherence in the clues and cues offered by their immediate surroundings and appeal to other family members to do so; thereby the meanings of events in the chronological past and future are "rewritten," not just for the individual, but for the interacting family members.

McHugh (1968), following Mead, imaginatively discussed some of the ways individuals make sense of ambiguities in social interactions. McHugh's interest was in procedural rules rather than in definitional content or technical rules, in questions of "how" rather than "what." His striking accomplishment was to carry Mead's philosophical arguments into the laboratory, requiring subjects to respond to messages of varying ambiguity. Discussing the significance of his findings, McHugh offered some suggestive propositions that might be restated in terms of our present argument.

In conditions of continuing ambiguity, McHugh argues, the individual may first experience a state of powerlessness or "the expectation that one's own behavior cannot determine the outcome he seeks." If the ambiguity persists, powerlessness gives way to either of two possible outcomes. One is meaninglessness, or "the inability to interpret environmental events, to apply norms to observations." In this condition, the individual is unable to believe that his symbolic representations are related to present events, and he withdraws, psychologically if not physically. This is a condition of anomie, the rejection of a search for coherence in either the social present or the past-future.

This response to ambiguity is also evidenced (Morris, 1970) in the experience of soldiers (N = 225) who suffered adjustment reactions, characterized by a sense of exhaustion, futility, and depression, in the fourth to sixth months of their one-year tour of duty in Vietnam. The disturbed soldiers complained of "job assignments outside of their expertise or of token duties to keep them busy, of shortages, delays, uncertainties and ambiguities found everyday on the job." Reacting against ambiguities which other men accepted as part of the temporary craziness of war, these soldiers became immobilized. Interestingly, after the six-month "hump" of their 12-month tours had passed, they tended to find a renewed sense of hope in the future, as the idea of their return home took on a sense of reality.

In short, meaninglessness, apathy, and anomie essentially involve a basic acceptance of the validity of previous knowledges about the past and future, and an inability to find satisfying coherence in the immediate; thus the individual attempts to withdraw from the immediate and is, in essence, immobilized. (In Figure 22.3, this condition is approximated as "malaise.") But powerlessness may also give way to innovation, that is, rejection of the generally accepted symbolic representations and a search for replacements. In an innovative mode, the individual denies the validity of the previously accepted past and future and attempts to create or discover meaning in the present.

Anthony (1970) notes a familial condition which is similar to McHugh's apathy and anomie in the individual. He terms it a "pseudo-narcotic" syndrome, in which family members under the stress of a parent's mental or tubercular illness lose significant contact, and individuals "spend their time daydreaming, religiously occupied, or engaged in reviewing the past or planning unrealistically for the future." In those families in which the disintegrating process is reversed, Anthony notes what we might term reflexive innovation, in which "attempts to identify with the patient's predicament and to see the situation from his perspective lead to many reversals in role play" (1970:145).

It is important to recognize that *both* emergence and relativity are crucial to both the maintenance and the change of family interaction patterns. In any interaction, individuals are likely to vacillate, intrapersonally and interpersonally, between emergence and relativity modes and appeals. "Emergence and relativity," McHugh suggests, "are two faces of a dialectic. They operate in tandem, but not concurrently" (1968:136).

Ambiguity, "Adaptability," and Appeals

This perspective offers insight into one of Burr's core concepts: "family adaptability," or the family's capacity to meet obstacles and shift courses. Angell adopted the term in his study of families in the depression, to summarize three principle variables of family rigidity: (a) a materialistic philosophy of life among members, (b) traditionalism in family mores, and (c) irresponsibility of one or both parents (Angell, 1936:17).

The first two specifications in Angell's concept suggest relationships in which emergence appeals are emphasized but relativity appeals discouraged. Perhaps not surprisingly, Angell's three emphases suggest what was a basic proposition in G. H. Mead's life work: that a social order of creative individuals requires an interplay of emergence and relativity, not only in the individuals' processing of knowledge but in their interactions with one another. The processes and appeals of emergence contribute to stable patterns of interaction; the processes and appeals in a relativity mode contribute to changes in the pattern, in response to changes in conditions and individual needs and desires.

It can be proposed, then, that in a family successfully coping with conditions of heightened ambiguity, individual members will evidence a dialectic of emergence and relativity processing, and their communication will display an in interplay of emergence and relativity appeals. Further, to the degree that emergence appeals predominate, the family is seen to be inflexible and brittle; to the degree that relativity appeals dominate, the family is seen to be unstable, confused. In either case, just as when neither type of appeal is much in evidence, institutive patterns are unlikely. The family may appear to be highly coordinated, particularly if emergence appeals predominate (i.e., established patterns may be little disturbed), but the processes whereby new patterns of interaction might be established to better meet the stresses of ambiguity are not operative.

This appears to have been the condition of the family in Bermann's previously noted study (see page 590). In the three months prior to the father's surgery, Bermann notes, "initiations are either inconsequentially noncontroversial or threatening antagonisms; reactions are either those of ready acquiescence or of withdrawal. The middle areas are diminished or gone" (1973:86). This leaves a family in a simulated harmony, in which the facade of social exchange is maintained. (See also Wynn et al., 1958, and Lerner, 1968, for discussions of the related concept of "pseudo-mutuality" in families of schizophrenics.)

Our argument in this section may be summarized, roughly, with a series of propositions:

1. The more pronounced are relativity appeals between family members, the more disrupted are established patterns of interaction.

2. The more pronounced are emergence appeals between family members, the less disrupted are established patterns of interaction.

3. The more pronounced are *both* emergence and relativity appeals between family members, the more the negotiations of institutive patterns of interaction.

4. The greater the ambiguity, the greater the exchange of relativity appeals.

These propositions are presented in Figure 22.5.

Figure 22.5. Propositions about the Relationship of Emergence and Relativity Appeals to Patterns of Family Interaction

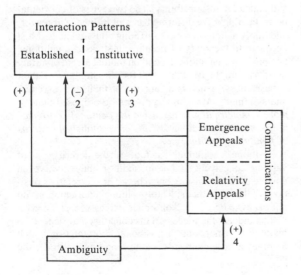

IV. COORIENTATION: REWORKING THE CONCEPTS OF INTEGRATION, LEGITIMACY, AND PERSONAL AND POSITIONAL INFLUENCE

We have suggested, in the traditions of Angell, Burgess, and Hill, that family interaction patterns require some degree of consensus among family members. By consensus, we refer to much the same interpersonal phenomena that George Herbert Mead described as "successful role taking," that John Dewey referred to as "interpenetration of perspectives," and that Alfred Schutz called "intersubjectivity." Consensus, then, contributes to the patterning of family interaction: attributing motives to other members, the individual is able to choose from his repertoire of actions those which seem most appropriate. Consensus, then, does call attention to an important aspect of family life: the *range* of agreements or shared perspectives. But "consensus" and "agreement" are somewhat inexact terms for the study of definitional aspects of families under stress.

Symmetry and Extensiveness in Coorientation

Scheff suggests that "coorientation" refers

> not merely to agreement, but to a situation in which there is agreement, awareness of agreement, awareness of awareness, and so on. These higher levels of coorientation are absolutely essential to an understanding of social coordination... [1967].

Coorientation, then, calls attention to two aspects of interpersonal understandings that are masked by more simple conceptions of agreement or consensus: variations in *extensiveness* and *symmetry*. Although the extensiveness of "reciprocating understandings" might be seen as potentially infinite (for example, "I know that you know that I know that you know that I know..." etc.), it is workable to identify three degrees of extensiveness: *agreement* (A); *understanding* of the other person's agreement (U); and *realization* that the other person understands your agreement (R). Corresponding to these are *disagreement* (D); *misunderstanding* (M); and *failure to realize* (F) (Laing et al., 1966). Thus the concept of extensiveness allows us to approach such elusive variables as empathy, "tacit knowledge," and intersubjectivity.

Symmetry refers to the mutuality of agreement, understanding and realization. Two individuals might agree with one another, both might understand they agree, and each might realize that the other understands, in a symmetrical coorientation: mother—RUAUR—child. If only one person understands and/or realizes that the two agree, the relationship is asymmetrical: mother—RUAMF—child.

Thus, as any educator knows, patterns of interaction can be maintained despite asymmetry. This line of thought is taken a step further with the classic example of the relationship of confidence man to victim (an example frequently displayed in marriages as well), which suggests that patterns of interaction can be maintained and even emerge despite disagreement *and* asymmetry: confidence man—RUDMF—victim (see Hansen, 1969).

Such relationships might be explained solely by resort to concepts such as deception, psychological denial, or indifference. But it is more difficult to deal with the possibility that patterns of interaction can be maintained despite disagreement, even when coorientation is *extensive*. This possibility is raised by the research of Chaffee and McLeod (1970; also McLeod and Chaffee, 1972, especially pp. 83–93 on family communication structure), who employ the terms "agreement," "accuracy" (similar to "understanding"), and "congruency" (similar to "realization"). O'Keefe (1973) reports on a number of unpublished studies relating communication and coorientation variables, calling into question Newcomb's (1953; 1961) notion of a "strain towards symmetry," which seems to predict that lack of perceived agreement between two individuals is likely to produce a strain toward agreement, presumably through more communication. Pasdirtz (1969; also see O'Keefe, 1973:527; and McLeod and Chaffee, 1972:90–93), studying changes in coorientations following short discussions of controversial issues, found that congruence of attitudes increased markedly between some spouses even though agreement did not. This suggests that in their communication the couple emphasized their points of recognized agreement and avoided communication that might threaten their beliefs that their coorientations were symmetrical and extensive. By contrast, other couples increased primarily in agreement, while those who showed no tendency to avoid voicing their differences increased markedly in accuracy but actually decreased in agreement. (These patterns are related to familial typologies based on communication structures, following Newcomb. See McLeod and Chaffee, 1972.)

Habit may account for the maintenance of some interaction patterns despite recognized disagreement, at least in short time spans. But if a disagreement is important to the individuals involved, it is likely that even habitual patterns of interaction that are relevant to the disagreement soon will be disrupted or, as often happens, the disagreement will be muted or altered (for example, through the creation of new myths or rationalizations). Something more than "habitual compliance" is needed to account for the maintenance of interaction patterns despite recognized disagreements.

Coorientation and Authority

Consider the relationship of a prisoner to his captor. Clearly, compliance of one or both parties is indicated. It is not simply a "habitual compliance," however; it is a compliance that relates to concepts of power and legitimacy.

Komarovsky (1940), studying the unemployed man and his family, distinguished "primary authority" from "instrumental authority." The two were taken to vary independently, such that the family could evidence a marked influence of both. Burr (1973:217) notes the relationship of these concepts to Hansen's (1965) "personal and positional influence." Further, conceptual interlinkings are evident in the relation of both Komarovsky's and Hansen's concepts to Angell's "family integration," which he defined as the "bonds of coherence and unity running through family life, of which common interests, affection and a sense of economic interdependence are perhaps the most prominent" (Angell, 1936:16).

These conceptual similarities suggest that we might profitably orient research efforts to two types of coorientation in familial relations: "personal coorientation," similar to Angell's "common interests" and "affection" and in which Komarovsky's "primary authority" inheres; and "positional coorientation," in which Angell's "sense of economic interdependence" and Komarovsky's "legitimacy" inhere.

A brief discussion of this distinction is in order. The distinction, somewhat modifying Hansen's treatment of "personal and positional influence" (1965:1969), rests on the proposition that individuals interacting over time tend to develop both "personal coorientations"—revolving around concerns of at least one person with the other's individual needs and desires—and "positional coorientations"—revolving around solutions to problems the members share because of the conflicts and demands that inhere in their common membership in families, groups, and communities.

Most generally, personal coorientations are identified with concepts such as love, neighboring, brotherhood, and friendship. Positional coorientations are identified by concepts such as authority hierarchy, division of labor, and educative responsibility. The two types of coorientations, then, involve differing bases of influence or power, and imply actions that have differing consequences. Most pertinent to the study of families in stressed conditions, personal coorientations depend on mutual assent or attraction, and might be examined for the strength of their cohesiveness, which is a function of their extensiveness and symmetry. Most simply, it can be proposed that *the more symmetrical and extensive the personal coorientations, the more mutually satisfying are established patterns of family interaction.*[1]

Positional coorientations, too, can be described as of varying cohesiveness; but in addition they involve an emphasis on the discrepancy between the relative positions of the individuals. Thus positional coorientations do not *necessarily* depend on either extensiveness or symmetry. Indeed, the success of the con artist may depend on his ability to negotiate a positional coorientation which involves a disagreement on long-range goals, under the guise of a personal coorientation which involves an agreement on immediate goals—a relationship neither symmetrical nor extensive.

Although authority inheres and emerges in both positional and personal coorientations, it is positional coorientation that most effectively contributes to an understanding of traditional concepts of "legitimacy." For authority that inheres in personal coorientations is essentially based on equality; authority is invested in an individual, and accepted by another because the two agree that they are more or less "equals" as humans and family members. To be sure, the agreement to invest authority in one person rather than another may rest on the shared recognition of differences in age, size, sex, interest, or competence; but the agreement rests on the belief that each person accepts the other as an equal in more fundamental qualities.

In conventional usage, however, "legitimacy" rests on an acceptance of hierarchical differences. Thus we speak of "legitimacy" if there is a simple agreement or consensus on positional roles: father—??A??—son. A lack of this simple agreement indicates coercion or manipulation. Nonetheless, the more extensive and symmetrical the positional coorientation, the stronger the bases of legitimacy. Thus it can be proposed that *the more symmetrical and extensive the positional coorientations, the more effective the instrumentalities of established patterns of family interaction.*

If the two types of coorientation differ in their bases of interpersonal influences and in their contributions to familial satisfactions and instrumentalities, it is reasonable to consider the possibility that they will relate to differences in interaction patterns in conditions of heightened ambiguity.

Coorientation, Ambiguity, and Interaction Patterns

Following G. H. Mead (1932), it can be argued that both personal and positional coorientations depend on processes of corrective monitoring of agreement forms between participants, especially through glances and nonverbal communication, as well as through explicit communications and other kinds of "appeals" that one individual makes in an effort to influence another's orientations, actions, and attributions. The types of appeals that family members make to one another vary considerably, of course; and we have already discussed differences in "emergence" and "relativity" appeals. At this point another distinction suggested by Bernstein (see Hansen, 1969, ch. 2; also Cooke-Gumperz, 1973) will be useful in relating "personal" and "positional" coorientations to patterns of family interaction.

"Appeals to positional coorientations" refer the "regulated" individual to specific normative prescriptions which do not depend on his or her own individual personal characteristics. Focus is generally on manifest behaviors and on the consequences of actions. By contrast, "appeals to personal orientations" refer to the feelings of the regulator or the significance of the act. Either way, the appeal is mediated through the special characteristics of the individual who is being regulated or influenced.[2] Thus personal coorientations are reflexively achieved.

In personal coorientations, then, the "rules" of interaction are individualized: they are negotiated by individuals in situations specific to them, thereby serving to differentiate each individual from others even though they may have accepted the same rules and overtly act in much the same way. In positional coorientations, by contrast, individuals are virtually assigned family roles; rules are transmitted in such a way that they are received in situations where the specific context of the relation is less relevant. Thus little differentiation is established between those regulated: each is seen to hold a "position" for which more or less typified expectations are shared.

Positional coorientations—because of potential coercion, explicitness of shared expectations, and normative sanctions received from the community and family members—tend to be stable and rigid. Personal coorientations, in comparison, enjoy little external support, and rely for their strength on attention to personal qualities and meanings of the participants. Thus positional coorientations can be characterized by instrumental efficiency and stability, personal coorientations by flexibility and responsiveness.

Of the many implications of this perspective on coorientation, one seems particularly pertinent to the present discussion: the two types of coorientation can be described by differing qualities of "endemic" ambiguity, and thus by the likelihood of differing responses to heightened ambiguity. Positional coorientations tend to be clear-cut compared to personal coorientations; that is, positional "rules" of interaction are relatively less ambiguous. Thus, somewhat paradoxically, conditions of heightened ambiguity (1) pose a more serious threat to families strong in positional coorientations; yet they (2) are more likely to induce changes in interaction patterns in families that are strong in personal coorientations. In conditions of heightened ambiguity, then, both personal and positional coorientations help resist disruptions of established patterns of interaction, but in the long run personal coorientations are more closely related to the negotiations of new patterns that are interpersonally satisfying.

These relationships are approximated in Propositions 5 and 6, which are diagrammed in Figure 22.6.

5. In conditions of heightened ambiguity, the less the range, symmetry, and/or extensiveness of either personal or positional coorientations, the greater the disruption of established patterns of interaction.

Hill's study of war separation stress suggests the viability of this proposition. (See Burr's propositions

Figure 22.6. Propositions about the Relationship of Personal and Positional Coorientations to Patterns of Family Interaction

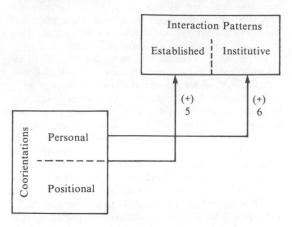

10.20 and 10.21 in Appendix I to this chapter; see also Burr's discussion, 1973:212–13.) Hill argues that in the strain of separation and reunion, *"The consultive process in the family is more important than the seat of ultimate authority"* (Hill, 1949:224). In our terms, the consultive process on instrumental decisions contributes to the extensiveness and symmetry of positional coorientations.

> 6. In conditions of heightened ambiguity, the less the range, symmetry, and/or extensiveness of personal coorientations, the less the negotiation of institutive patterns of interaction.

Hill's (1940) study also supports this proposition, suggesting that symmetry of personal coorientations *throughout* a family—which Hill defined as the absence of cliques, and Burr (1973:212) terms "similarity of sentiment"—is related to "adjustment," or in our terms to institutive patterns of interaction. (See proposition 10.18 in Burr's model, Appendix I to this chapter.) Similarly, various researchers have found a relationship between "marital adjustment" and what we would term institutive patterns. (See Burr, 1973:212, and proposition 10.19 in Burr's model, Appendix I.)

Such propositions ignore the "additive effect" of personal and positional coorientations, however. Theoretically, a family might be described as entirely "personal" or entirely "positional" in relationships. But in real-life families, such pure relationships are highly improbable; the two types of relationships are distinguishable only analytically. This is seen, perhaps most clearly, in again considering the relationship of the prisoner to his jailer. Although in some situations this relationship, at least for short spans of time, may be fairly characterized as essentially "positional," given time personal appeals and coorientations also emerge—for example, in the

phenomena that have come to be known as "brainwashing" or "coercive persuasion."

Because of this interactive influence it may be of limited utility to identify propositions that relate either "personal influence" or "positional influence," but not both, to patterns of family interaction. Somewhat more promising is the attempt to identify some sort of "ideal typical" forms of relationship, based on varying mixtures of personal and positional coorientations. This was approximated by Hansen (1965), who focused on "strength of personal and positional influence," which now appears to be more vague and less amenable to research specification that "coorientations." Burr (1973:203–05) succinctly summarized the "additive effect" of the variables in relation to disrupted interaction at various points in time. Burr's diagram, with terminology slightly modified, is presented in Figure 22.7, which can be seen to offer a specification of what has been descriptively discussed as "vulnerability" and "regenerative power."

V. COMMUNICATION, COORIENTATION, AND INTERACTION PATTERNS IN CONDITIONS OF HEIGHTENED AMBIGUITY: SUMMARY PROPOSITIONS

Interaction patterns, we have argued, may be seen as a partial function of communication and coorientation. In section III we discussed the relation of interaction patterns to emergence and relativity appeals in communication, essentially holding coorientations constant. In section IV, we reversed emphases, essentially holding communica-

Figure 22.7. Propositions about the Relationship of Coorientation Types to Patterns of Family Interaction in Conditions of Heightened Ambiguity

Symmetry and Extensiveness
of Personal Coorientations

		Low	High
Symmetry and Extensiveness of Positional Coorientations	**High**	1. Moderate 2. Low	1. Low 2. High
	Low	1. High 2. Low	1. High 2. Moderate

tion constant as we discussed the relation of interaction patterns to personal and positional coorientations. In this section, we will allow both communication and coorientation to vary.

Given the context of the preceding discussions, the relationship of emergence and relativity appeals to personal and positional coorientations may be presented in propositional form, without elaboration. To facilitate presentation of these and the following propositions, however, the core concepts in our partial theory of communication and coorientation are represented in Figure 22.8.

7. In conditions of heightened ambiguity, the greater the exchange of relativity appeals, the greater the changes in both personal and positional coorientations.

8. In conditions of heightened ambiguity, the greater the range, symmetry, and extensiveness of positional coorientations, the greater the exchange of emergence appeals, especially those relating to positional coorientations.

9. In conditions of heightened ambiguity, the greater the range, symmetry, and extensiveness of the personal coorientations, the greater the exchange of both emergence and relativity appeals, relating to both personal and positional coorientations.

Our basic argument in Propositions 1, 2, and 3 held that (a) disruption of interaction patterns is a function of increased relativity appeals and decreased emergence appeals, and (b) negotiation of institutive patterns of

family interaction is a function of the interplay of relativity and emergence appeals (see Figure 22.5).

In section IV, two related propositions were advanced (see Figure 22.7 for a more adequate expression):

5. In conditions of heightened ambiguity, the less the range, symmetry, and/or extensiveness of either personal or positional coorientations, the greater the disruption of established patterns of interaction.

6. In conditions of heightened ambiguity, the less the range, symmetry, and/or extensiveness of personal coorientations, the less the negotiation of institutive patterns of interaction.

The relationships are more deserving of research, however, if Propositions 5 and 6 are interrelated with Propositions 1, 2, and 3, i.e., if both communication and coorientation are allowed to vary. Of the many promising propositions that derive, two are represented below, and in Figure 22.9:

10. There is an additive effect between emergence appeals and coorientations in their relationship to established patterns of interaction; the greater the exchange of emergence appeals *and* the greater the range of symmetry and extensiveness of both personal and positional coorientations, the less the disruptions of established patterns of interaction.

10a. In conditions of heightened ambiguity, the relationships of Proposition 10 are weakened.

11. There is an additive effect between personal

Figure 22.8.   Patterns of Family Interaction in Conditions of Heightened Ambiguity: Core Concepts

Figure 22.9.   Propositions about the Relationship of Familial Communications, Coorientations, and Interaction Patterns in Conditions of Heightened Ambiguity

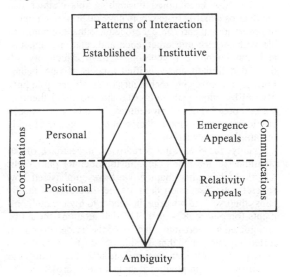

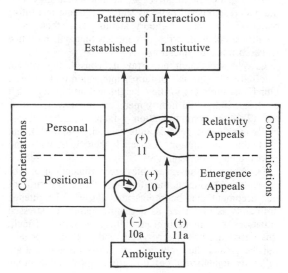

coorientations and appeals in their relationship to institutive patterns of interaction; the greater the exchange of both emergence and relativity appeals *and* the greater the range, symmetry, and extensiveness of personal coorientations, the more the negotiation of institutive patterns of interaction.

11a. In conditions of heightened ambiguity, the relationships of Proposition 11 are strengthened.

Although logically other propositions follow, our argument suggests these may be key relationships amenable to research at this time.[3]

VI. SUMMARY OF ARGUMENT

By way of summary, let us move through the basic arguments that have led to propositions 10 and 11, this time in a somewhat different sequence:

A. Time linkage is noted in the tantalizing relationship of vulnerability to regenerative power, suggesting that these descriptors refer to differences in patterns of family interaction at different points of a family's experience with stress.

B. Those differences in interaction can be conceptualized as variations in (1) the maintenance or disruptions of established patterns of family interaction, and (2) the negotiation of institutive (or new) patterns. Established and institutive patterns vary to an important degree independently; it is this independence that is expressed in observations, for example, that some highly vulnerable families are more regenerative than are less vulnerable families. The pertinent research question, however, now becomes, how do families interact in stressed situations, and what are the relative probabilities that they will maintain established patterns and/or negotiate institutive patterns? One task of theory at this point, then, is to identify a coherent array of concepts that will facilitate research into this question.

C. We seek such an array by considering certain "definitional aspects" of family interaction under stress. Our focus turns (1) to the "heightened ambiguity" that confronts individual family members under varied stresses, (2) to the communication of family members (especially their "emergence" and "relativity" appeals), and (3) to the coorientations (especially their "personal" and "positional" coorientations).

D. Although these variables are in dialectical or process relation to one another, for clarity the central thrust of our argument can be represented linearly: heightened ambiguity is identified as a generic feature of stressed situations, making definitions of those situations difficult; this encourages both emergence and relativity appeals, but the greater the ambiguity, the more pronounced are relativity appeals; increased relativity appeals encourage

changes in interpersonal coorientations; the greater the changes in coorientations, the more likely are changes in interaction patterns, seen as (1) disruptions of established patterns and/or (2) negotiations of institutive patterns.

E. To predict the likelihood of disruptions and/or negotiation, however, the other variables represented by our core concepts (Figure 22.8) must also be allowed to vary. It is then proposed that established patterns of interaction are more likely to be maintained and less likely to be disrupted (1) the greater the range, extensiveness, and symmetry of *both* personal and positional coorientations, and (2) the more prevalent the emergence appeals between family members.

F. Institutive patterns are more likely to be negotiated (1) the greater the range, extensiveness, and symmetry of personal coorientations, and (2) the more prevalent both emergence and relativity appeals between family members.

It is obvious that the definitional concepts presented in these propositions are difficult to operationalize, yet it should be noted that McHugh (1968) has effectively dealt in the laboratory setting with complex propositions of ambiguity related to definitions. Indeed, Davis (1963) has approached this perspective in his study of polio victims and their families. Further, researchers in various areas are working toward instruments to assess familial "coorientations" (see, for example, Calonico and Thomas, 1973; Goldstein et al, 1968; McLeod and Chaffee, 1972; O'Keeffe, 1973; Reiss, 1967, 1971; Reiss and Sheriff, 1970) as well as familial communications (see, for example, Alexander, 1973; Faunce and Riskin, 1970; Ferreira and Winter, 1968; Kahn, 1970; McPherson, 1970; Pollay, 1969; Rausch et al., 1974; Riskin and Faunce, 1970; Sheinkopf, 1973).

It has also been noted throughout this chapter that medical-psychiatric researchers have displayed a number of observational and clinical procedures that are compatible with inquiry into emergence and relativity appeals, and that cognitive psychologists have effectively addressed delimited and specified aspects of our theory. Further, the emerging techniques of small-group inquiry offered by ethnomethodologists and grounded theorists suggest possibilities of procedures that have not yet been employed to any marked degree in the sociological study of families under stress.

Finally, the somewhat paradoxical appearance of our "antithesis" must be noted. In the opening paragraphs and throughout this chapter, we have emphasized how severely our discussion delimits the traditions of family stress theory—and we urge the reader to review our comments (on pages 582–590). The delimitations should be recognized as short-range tactics of theory development, reflecting our belief that, at this point, it is essential to more closely consider the core variables that inform our arguments and propositions about family stress.

Yet in our effort can be seen another thrust toward a more comprehensive perspective than is represented in the traditions of our field. This thrust—or perhaps "yearning" is more descriptive—is attended less closely in this chapter, yet we endorse it as a long-range strategy for theory development in our field. The perspective we yearn toward would allow us to attend not only (1) variably stressed individuals interacting in familial situations but also (2) the transactive or community relationships of stressed individuals and families, in the contexts of (3) historically specific social and cultural structures, processes, and transformations, as well as (4) the psychological and even physiological processes of the interacting individuals, assessed (5) not simply in laboratory settings, but in their natural environments of familial and community relationships. It is encouraging to note that similar yearnings are to be seen in other areas of stress research and theory (see, for example, Haley, 1962; Haan, 1977; Lazarus and Cohen, 1976).

The paradox in our discussion, then, is seen as more apparent than real if it is recognized that our tactical delimitations are part of a long-range strategy aimed at more comprehensive theory. For no matter how a theory ranges over levels of physical and social complexity and over time and between cultures, it fails to be comprehensive if its central concepts lack clarity.

APPENDIX I.   BURR'S SYNTHESIS IN PROPOSITIONAL FORM

Proposition

10.1:   A stressor event in a family social system influences the amount of crisis in the system, and this is a positive relationship.

10.2:   When a stressor event occurs, the vulnerability to stress influences the amount of influence the stressor event has on the amount of crisis, and this is a positive relationship.

10.3:   The definition a family makes of the severity of changes in the family social system influences the family's vulnerability to stress, and this is a positive, monotonic relationship.

10.4:   The amount of change that occurs when a stressor event occurs in the family social system influences the amount of crisis that results from the event, and this is a positive relationship.

10.5:   The amount of positional influence in a social system influences the vulnerability of families to stress, and this is an inverse relationship.

10.6:   The amount of positional influence in a social system influences the regenerative power, and this is an inverse relationship.

10.7:   The amount of personal influence in a social system influences the vulnerability of families to stress, and this is a positive relationship.

10.8:   The amount of personal influence in a social system influences the regenerative power, and this is a positive relationship.

10.9:   The externalization of blame for changes in the family social system influences the vulnerability of the family to stress, and this is an inverse relationship.

10.10:   The regenerative power of families influences the level of reorganization after a period of crisis, and this is a positive relationship.

10.11:   Family integration influences regenerative power, and this is a positive relationship.

10.12:   Family adaptability influences regenerative power, and this is a positive relationship.

10.13:   The amount of family integration influences the vulnerability to stress, and this is a positive relationship.

10.14:   The amount of family adaptability influences the vulnerability to stress, and this is an inverse relationship.

10.15:   The amount of time stressful events are anticipated influences the vulnerability to stress, and this is an inverse relationship.

10.16:   The amount of extended familism influences the regenerative power of families.

10.17:   The length of time a family system experiences disruption influences the relationship in proposition 10.16, which asserts that extended familism influences the regenerative power of families, and this is a quadratic relationship in which variations in short periods of time are inversely related and variations in long periods are positively related to the regenerative power.

10.18:   The amount of similarity of sentiment in a family influences the regenerative power of families, and this is a positive relationship.

10.19:   The amount of marital adjustment influences the regenerative power of families, and this is a positive relationship.

10.20:   The amount of relative power of spouses is not related to the regenerative power of families.

10.21:   The amount of consultation in decision making influences the regenerative power of families, and this is a positive relationship.

10.22:   The amount of social activity of wives outside the home is related to the regenerative power of families, and this is a positive relationship.

10.23:   The amount of anticipatory socialization for changes in the family social system influences the vulnerability of families, and this is an inverse relationship.

10.24:   The amount of anticipatory socialization for changes in the family social system influences the regenerative power of families, and this is a positive relationship.

10.25:   The legitimacy of the power structure in a family influences the amount of change in the power structure that occurs in family crises, and this is an inverse relationship.

APPENDIX II: COMPONENTS OF BURR'S SYNTHESIS RELATED TO THE PRESENT DISCUSSION

The capacity to generate effective research is one measure of a theoretical proposition; the capacity to coherently organize extant research findings is another. In the case of the family crisis literature, we would argue, the concepts of coorientation, communication, and ambiguity offer a coherent core of concepts that link sociological traditions to streams of research and theory in related disciplines. In the context of those concepts the varied findings of the field may also take more coherent form.

Most of the propositions represented in Burr's model (see Figure 22.1 and Appendix I), for example, have been treated in our discussion. "Amount of crisis," "amount of change," "vulnerability," and "regenerative power" have been reworked, essentially in concepts of "established" and "institutive" interaction patterns; the relationships of these to "family interaction" and "family adaptability" (Burr's propositions 10.11, 10.12, 10.13, and 10.14) are represented in our propositions relating emergence and relativity appeals and personal and positional coorientations; so too are Burr's propositions 10.5, 10.6, 10.7, and 10.8, as well as the concept of "legitimacy" and "change in power structure" (see proposition 10.25). Burr's individual propositions, it should be emphasized, retain their individual viability; we here only suggest an alternative context of understanding.

In our discussion of ambiguity, we have suggested (but not pursued) interlinkings with "anticipation" (see Burr's proposition 10.24); in our discussion of personal and positional coorientations, we have dealt with "similarity of sentiment" and "marital adjustment" and "power and consultation" (propositions 10.18, 10.19, 10.20, and 10.21).

Each of these propositions, of course, requires considerably more development. Burr's propositions 10.16 and 10.17, for example, refer to Hill and Hansen's (1962:202) observation that a low degree of extended familism seems to prepare families for disaster and short-term recovery better than does a high degree of extended familism—but the relationship is reversed as the family copes with the long-term effects of disaster.

In the context of our discussion of ambiguity, it can be posited that the degree of extended familism at once (1) increases the possibilities of ambiguity that might be experienced by any familial component and (2) increases the possibilities of coping with ambiguity. The relationship of extended familism to disrupted and emergent coordinations, then, is similar to that of anticipation. (See our discussion on page 590.)

NOTES

1. It should be noted that this quality of familial relationships can lend family members an unusual power over one another, in what Esterson terms a "tyranny of love" (1970:45). In a perceptive essay reviewing Esterson, Laing (1971) and Cooper (1970), Kanter depicts this tyranny: "To the extent that one's image of oneself and the family depends on everyone else conveying the appropriate images of all members; then each family member carries a heavy burden not to violate expectations, but also not to question the premises on which these expectations rest" (1974:313). We have not yet considered this, among many other possibilities, in our developing theory.

2. A similar distinction is used by Lennard et al. (1965) in analysis of families of schizophrenics; a related but somewhat different distinction is made by McLeod and Chaffee, who speak of "socio-oriented" communication that is "designed to produce deference, and to foster harmony and pleasant social relationships in the family," and of "concept-oriented" communication, involving "positive constraints to stimulate the child to develop his own views about the world and to consider more than one side of an issue" (1972:83).

3. Most importantly, it does not seem reasonable to argue, within the theoretical perspective we have developed, that the interplay of relativity appeals with coorientations is closely related to the maintenance of established patterns of interaction, for relativity appeals disrupt patterns of interaction regardless of coorientations. Nor does the interplay of positional coorientations and appeals seem promising as a correlate of emergent patterns of interaction, for once positional coorientations become asymmetrical or restricted, emergence appeals tend to be received as irrelevant and relativity appeals tend to further reduce coorientation. Of course it is a familiar tactic of families experiencing a "crisis of legitimacy" to simply "agree to agree," as is illustrated in Bermann's (1973) report. It seems likely, however, that the strength of such agreement rests on either the strengths of personal coorientations or on external constraints. It should be recognized that the necessity of appealing to this likelihood suggests critical limitations in the above propositions, emphasizing again the "antithetical"—and hence "unfinished"—character of this chapter.

REFERENCES

ALEXANDER, J. F.
    1973   "Defensive and supportive communications in family systems." *Journal of Marriage and the Family* 35:613–17.

AMDUR, M. J., G. J. TUCKER, T. DETRE, AND K. MARKHUS
    1969   "Anorexia nervosa: An interactional study." *Journal of Nervous and Mental Diseases* 148:559–66.

ANGELL, R. C.
    1936   *The Family Encounters the Depression*. New York: Scribner.

ANTHONY, E. J.
    1970   "The impact of mental and physical illness on family life." *American Journal of Psychiatry* 127:138–46.

BEBBINGTON, A. C.
    1973   "The function of stress in the establishment of the dual-career family." *Journal of Marriage and the Family* 35:530–37.

BERMANN, E.
    1973   "Regrouping for survival: Approaching dread and three phases of family interaction." *Journal of Comparative Family Studies* 4:63–87.

BOWLBY, J.
    1969   *Attachment and Loss*, vol. 2: *Separation*. New York: Basic Books.

BREZNITZ, S.
    1967   "Incubation and threat: Duration of anticipation and false alarm as determinants of the fear reaction to an unavoidable frightening event." *Journal of Experimental Research in Personality* 2:173–79.

BUGENTAL, D. E., L. R. LOVE, AND J. W. KASWAN
    1972   "Videotaped family interaction: Differences reflecting presence and type of child disturbance." *Journal of Abnormal Psychology* 79:285–90.

BURGESS, E. W.
    1926   "The family as a unity of interacting personalities." *Family* 7:3–9.

BURR, W. R.
1973   *Theory Construction and the Sociology of the Family.* New York: Wiley.

BYNG-HALL, J.
1973   "Family myths used as defence in conjoint family therapy." *British Journal of Medical Psychology* 46:239–50.

CALONICO, J. M. AND D. L. THOMAS
1973   "Role-taking as a function of value similarity and affect in the nuclear family." *Journal of Marriage and the Family* 35:655–65.

CHAFFEE, S. H. AND J. M. MCLEOD
1970   "Coorientation and the structure of family communication." Paper presented to the International Communication Association, Minneapolis. (Reported in O'Keefe, 1973, and McLeod and Chaffee, 1972.)

COOK-GUMPERZ, J.
1973   *Social Control and Socialization: A Study of Class Differences in the Language of Maternal Control.* London: Routledge & Kegan-Paul.

COOMBS, J.
1962–63   "How the emotional problems of children are affected by family moves." Unpublished Thesis, University of London. (Reported in T. Moore, 1969, "Stress in normal childhood." *Human Relations* 22:235–50.)

COOPER, D.
1970   *The Death of the Family.* New York: Pantheon.

COX, F. N. AND D. CAMPBELL
1968   "Young children in a new situation with and without their mothers." *Child Development* 39:123–31.

CROOG, S. H.
1970   "The family as a source of stress." In S. Levine and N. A. Scotch (eds.), *Social Stress.* Chicago: Aldine.

DAVIDSON, P. O. AND W. R. KELLEY
1973   "Social facilitation and coping with stress." *British Journal of Social and Clinical Psychology* 12:130–36.

DAVIS, F.
1963   *Passage through Crisis: Polio Victims and their Families.* Indianapolis: Bobbs-Merrill.

DOHRENWEND, B. S.
1973   "Life events as stressors: A methodological inquiry." *Journal of Health and Social Behavior* 14:167–75.

DRABEK, T. E. AND K. S. BOGGS
1968   "Families in disaster: Reactions and relatives." *Journal of Marriage and the Family* 30:443–51.

DUBOS, R.
1965   *Man Adapting.* New Haven, Conn.: Yale University Press.

ELDER, G. H., JR.
1974   *Children of the Great Depression.* Chicago: University of Chicago Press.

ELIOT, T. D.
1942   "Family crises and ways of meeting them." In H. Becker and R. Hill (eds.), *Marriage and the Family.* Boston: Heath.

ESTERSON, A.
1970   *The Leaves of Spring: A Study in the Dialectics of Madness.* London: Tavistock.

FAUNCE, E. E. AND J. RISKIN
1970   "Family interaction scales: II. Data analysis and findings." *Archives of General Psychiatry* 22:513–23.

FERREIRA, A. J. AND W. D. WINTER
1968   "Information exchange and silence in normal and abnormal families." *Family Process* 7(2):251–76.

FOLKINS, C. H.
1970   "Temporal factors and the cognitive mediators of stress reaction." *Journal of Personality and Social Psychology* 14:173–84.

GALSTON, R. AND W. J. GAMBLE
1969   "On borrowed time: Observations on children with implanted cardiac pacemakers and their families." *American Journal of Psychiatry* 126:104–08.

GOLDSTEIN, M. J., L. L. JUDD, E. H. RODNICK, A. ALKIRE, AND E. GOULD
1968   "A method for studying social influence and coping patterns within families of disturbed adolescents." *Journal of Nervous and Mental Disease* 147:233–51.

HAAN, N.
1969   "A tripartite model of ego functioning." *Journal of Nervous and Mental Disease* 148:14–30.

1977   *Coping and Defending: Processes of Self-environment Organization.* New York: Academic Press.

HALEY, J.
1962   "Family experiments: A new type of experimentation." *Family Process* 1:265–93.

HANSEN, D. A.
1965   "Personal and positional influence in formal groups: Propositions and theory for research on family vulnerability to stress." *Social Forces* 44:202–10.

1969   Chapters 2, 4, and 5 in D. A. Hansen (ed.), *Explorations in Sociology and Counseling.* Boston: Houghton Mifflin.

HANSEN, D. A. AND R. HILL
1964   "Families under stress." In H. T. Christensen (ed.), *Handbook of Marriage and the Family.* Chicago: Rand McNally.

HILL, R.
1949   *Families Under Stress.* New York: Harper.

HILL, R. AND D. A. HANSEN
1962   "The family in disaster." In G. Baker and D. Chapman (eds.), *Man and Society in Disaster.* New York: Basic Books.

HILL, R., J. M. STYCOS, AND K. BACK
1959   *The Family and Population Control.* Chapel Hill: University of North Carolina Press.

HOLMES, T. S. AND R. H. RAHE
1967   "The social readjustment rating scale." *Journal of Psychosomatic Research* 11:213–18.

HOUSTON, B. K. AND W. F. HODGES
1970   "Situational denial and performance under stress." *Journal of Personality and Social Psychology* 16:726–30.

HOWARD, A. AND R. A. SCOTT
1965   "A proposed framework for the analysis of stress in the human organism." *Behavioral Science* 10:141–60.

JACKSON, D. (ED.)
1968   *Communication, Family and Marriage.* Palo Alto, Calif.: Science and Behavior Books.

JANIS, I.
1958   *Psychological Stress.* New York: Wiley.

KAGAN, J.
1974   "Discrepancy, temperament, and infant distress." In M. Lewis and L. A. Rosenblum (eds.), *The Origins of Fear.* New York: Wiley.

KAHN, M.
1970   "Non-verbal communication and marital satisfaction." *Family Process* 9:449–56.

KANTER, R. M.
1974   "Intimate oppression." *Sociological Quarterly* 15:302–14.

KAPLAN, D. M., A. SMITH, R. GROBSTEIN, AND S. E. FISCHMAN
1973   "Family mediation of stress." *Social Work* 18:60–69.

KATZ, J. L., H. WEINER, T. F. GALLAGHER, AND L. HELLMAN
1970   "Stress, distress, and ego defenses: Psychoendocrine re-

sponse to impending breast tumor biopsy." *Archives of General Psychiatry* 23:131–42.

KENT, H. B.
  1958   "Regression under stress to early learned behavior." *Proceedings of the 77th Annual Convention of the American Psychological Association* 4:459–60.

KOMAROVSKY, M.
  1940   *The Unemployed Man and His Family.* New York: Dryden Press.

KORNER, I. N.
  1970   "Hope as a method of coping." *Journal of Consulting and Clinical Psychology* 34:134–39.

LAING, R. D.
  1971   *The Politics of the Family.* New York: Pantheon.

LAING, R. D., H. PHILLIPSON, AND A. R. LEE
  1966   *Interpersonal Perception: A Theory and Method of Research.* London: Tavistock.

LAUER, R. H. AND J. C. LAUER
  1976   "The experience of change: Tempo and stress." In G. K. Zollschan and W. Hirsch (eds.), *Social Change: Explorations, Diagnoses, and Conjectures.* Cambridge, Mass.: Schenkman.

LAZARUS, R. S.
  1974   "Psychological stress and coping in adaptation and illness." *International Journal of Psychiatry in Medicine* 5:321–33.

LAZARUS, R. S. AND J. R. AVERILL
  1972   "Emotion and cognition: With special reference to anxiety." In *Anxiety: Current Trends in Theory and Research,* vol. 2. New York: Academic Press.

LAZARUS, R. S. AND J. B. COHEN
  1976   "Theory and method in the study of stress and coping in aging individuals." Stockholm: Fifth WHO Conference on Society, Stress and Disease: Aging and Old Age.

LEFCOURT, H. M.
  1973   "The function of the illusions of control and freedom." *American Psychologist* 28:417–25.

LENNARD, H. L., M. R. BEAULIEU, AND N. G. EMBREY
  1965   "Interaction in families with a schizophrenic child." *Archives of General Psychiatry* 12:166–83.

LERNER, D.
  1958   *The Passing of Traditional Society.* New York: Free Press.

LERNER, P. M.
  1968   "Resolution of intrafamilial role conflict in families of schizophrenic patients: II. Social maturity." *Journal of Nervous and Mental Disease* 145:336–41.

LLOYD, P. C.
  1969   *Africa in Social Change.* Middlesex, England: Penguin.

McHUGH, P.
  1968   *Defining the Situation: The Organization of Meaning in Social Interaction.* Indianapolis: Bobbs-Merrill.

McLEOD, J. M. AND S. H. CHAFFEE
  1972   "The construction of social reality." In J. T. Tedeschi (ed.), *The Social Influence Processes.* Chicago: Aldine.

McPHERSON, S.
  1970   "Communication of intents among parents and their disturbed adolescent child." *Journal of Abnormal Psychology* 76:98–105.

MEAD, G. H.
  1932   *Philosophy of the Present.* Chicago: University of Chicago Press.

MEAD, M.
  1966   *New Lives for Old: Cultural Transformation—Manus, 1928-1953.* New York: Morrow.

MECHANIC, D.
  1974   "Social structure and personal adaptation: Some neglected

dimensions." In G. V. Coelho, D. Hamburg, and J. E. Adams (eds.), *Coping and Adaptation.* New York: Basic Books.
  1975   "Some problems in the measurement of stress and social readjustment." *Journal of Human Stress* 1:43–48.

MORGAN, J. N.
  1968   "Some pilot studies of communication and consensus in the family." *Public Opinion Quarterly* 32:113–21.

MORRIS, L. E.
  1970   "'Over the hump' in Vietnam: Adjustment patterns." *Bulletin of the Menninger Clinic* 34:352–62.

NEWCOMB, T. M.
  1953   "An approach to the study of communicative acts." *Psychological Review* 60:393–404.
  1961   "The study of consensus." In R. K. Merton et al. (eds.), *Sociology Today.* New York: Basic Books.

NYE, F. I., J. CARLSON, AND G. GARRETT
  1970   "Family size, interaction, affect and stress." *Journal of Marriage and the Family* 32:216–26.

O'KEEFE, G. J., JR.
  1973   "Coorientation variables in family study." *American Behavioral Scientist* 16:513–36.

PASDIRTZ, G. W.
  1969   "An approach to the study of interaction processes." Paper presented to the Association for Education in Journalism, Berkeley. (Reported in McLeod and Chaffee, 1972, and O'Keefe, 1973.)

PAUL, N. AND J. D. BLOOM
  1970   "Multiple-family therapy: Secrets and scapegoating in family crisis." *International Journal of Group Psychotherapy* 20:37–47.

POLLAY, R. W.
  1969   "Intrafamily communication and consensus." *Journal of Communication* 19:181–201.

RAHE, R. H.
  1972   "Subjects' recent life changes and their near-future illness reports." *Annals of Clinical Research* 4:250–65.
  1974   "The pathway between subjects' recent life changes and their near-future illness reports: Representative results and methodological issues." In B. S. Dohrenwend and B. P. Dohrenwend (eds.), *Stressful Life Events.* New York: Wiley.

RAHE, R. H., M. MEYER, M. SMITH, G. KJAER, AND T. H. HOLMES
  1964   "Social stress and illness onset." *Journal of Psychosomatic Research* 8:35–44.

RAPOPORT, R. AND R. N. RAPOPORT
  1969   "The dual career family: A variant pattern and social change." *Human Relations* 22:3–30.

RAUSCH, H., W. A. BARRY, R. K. HERTEL, AND M. A. SWAIN
  1974   *Communication, Conflict and Marriage.* San Francisco: Jossey-Bass.

REISS, D.
  1967   "Individual thinking and family interaction. II. A study of pattern recognition and hypothesis testing in families of normals, character disorders and schizophrenics." *Journal of Psychiatric Research* 5:193–211.
  1971   "Varieties of consensual experience: I. A theory for relating family interaction to individual thinking; II. Dimensions of a family's experience of its environment." *Family Process* 10:1–35.

REISS, D. AND W. H. SHERIFF
  1970   "A computer-automated procedure for testing some experiences of family membership." *Behavioral Science* 15:431–43.

RISKIN, J. AND E. E. FAUNCE
  1970   "Family interaction scales." *Archives of General Psychiatry* 22:504–12.

1972 "An evaluative review of family interaction research." *Family Process* 11:365–455.

ROGHMANN, K. J., P. D. HECHT, AND R. J. HAGGERTY
1973 "Family coping with everyday illness: Self reports from a household survey." *Journal of Comparative Family Systems* 4:49–62.

SCHEFF, T. J.
1967 "Toward a sociological model of consensus." *American Sociological Review* 32:32–45.

SCOTT, R. AND A. HOWARD
1970 "Models of stress." In S. Levine and N. A. Scotch (eds.), *Social Stress*. Chicago: Aldine.

SELYE, H.
1956 *The Stress of Life*. New York: McGraw-Hill.
1974 *Stress without Distress*. Philadelphia: Lippincott.

SHEINKOPF, K. G.
1973 "Family communication patterns and anticipatory socialization." *Journalism Quarterly* 50:24–30, 133.

SHIBUTANI, T.
1961 *Society and Personality*. Englewood Cliffs, N.J.: Prentice-Hall.
1966 *Improvised News: A Sociological Study of Rumor*. Indianapolis: Bobbs-Merrill.

SMELSER, N. J.
1959 *Social Change in the Industrial Revolution*. Chicago: University of Chicago Press.

SMITH, P. K.
1974 "Social and situational determinants of fear in the play group." In M. Lewis and L. A. Rosenblum (eds.), *The Origins of Fear*. New York: Wiley.

STEIN, M.
1970 "The function of ambiguity in child crises." *Journal of the American Academy of Child Psychiatry* 9:462–76.

STUBBENFIELD, R. L.
1955 "Children's emotional problems aggravated by family moves." *American Journal of Orthopsychiatry* 25:120–26.

WACKMAN, D. B.
1973 "Interpersonal communication and coorientations." *American Behavioral Scientist* 16:537–50.

WACKMAN, D. B. AND D. F. J. BEATTY
1971 "A comparison of balance and consensus theories for explaining changes in ABX systems." Paper presented to the International Communication Association, Phoenix.

WATZLAWICK, P., J. H. BEAVIN, AND D. JACKSON
1968 *Pragmatics of Human Communication*. New York: Norton.

WEINSTOCK, A. R.
1967 "Family environment and the development of defense and coping mechanisms." *Journal of Personality and Social Psychology* 5:67–75.

WOLFF, C. T., M. A. MASON, AND J. W. MASON
1964 "Relationship between psychological defenses and mean urinary 17-hydroxycorticosteroid excretion rates: I. A predictive study of parents of fatally ill children." *Psychosomatic Medicine* 26:576–91.

WYNN, L. C., I. M. RYCKOFF, J. DAY, AND S. I. HIRSCH
1958 "Pseudo-mutuality in the family relations of schizophrenics." *Psychiatry* 21:205–20.

ZABLOCKI, B.
1976 "The use of crisis as a mechanism of social control." In G. K. Zollschan and W. Hirsch (eds.), *Social Change: Explorations, Diagnoses and Conjectures*. Cambridge, Mass.: Schenkman.

ZOLLSCHAN, G.
1964 "Working papers in theory of institutionalization." In G. K. Zollschan and W. Hirsch (eds.), *Explorations in Social Change*. Boston: Houghton Mifflin.

ZOLLSCHAN, G. AND D. A. HANSEN
1969 "On motivation: Toward socially pertinent foundations." In D. A. Hansen (ed.), *Explorations in Sociology and Counseling*. Boston: Houghton Mifflin.

ZOLLSCHAN, G. AND R. PERRUCCI
1964 "Social stability and social process: An initial presentation of relevant categories." In G. K. Zollschan and W. Hirsch (eds.), *Explorations in Social Change*. Boston: Houghton Mifflin.

23

FAMILY PROCESS AND CHILD OUTCOMES

Carlfred B. Broderick and Harvey Pulliam-Krager

INTRODUCTION

The development of an identifiable corpus of concepts and perspectives which might be labeled family process theory probably ought to be dated from the late fifties. By that time the more or less isolated clusters of family therapists at Palo Alto (Bateson, Jackson, Haley, Weakland et al.), NIMH (Bowen, Wynne, et al.), Yale (Lidz et al.), and the Family Mental Health Clinic in New York City (Ackerman et al.) to name only some of the most prominent groups, had begun to acknowledge that they were all working on the same basic premise, namely, that schizophrenia and other personality disorders could best be understood and treated as the product of specific patterns of family interaction. No two groups used the same vocabulary, but increasingly it became apparent that they were all discussing the same basic theoretical and methodological issues. To this time, however, there has been little standardization or consolidation of terminology across schools. The journal *Family Process,* founded in 1962 (by Don Jackson and Nathan Ackerman), has become the major publications outlet for the movement, although articles with this perspective continue to appear in many psychiatry and psychotherapy journals as well.

Despite some efforts to communicate in each direction, the family process movement remains largely out of contact with the main body of family theory and research. Partly this results from the disciplinary barriers. Most scholars in the movement came to it out of family therapy, and their background is more likely to be psychiatric than sociological (Group for the Advancement of Psychotherapy, 1970). A second, even more basic issue, however, is that they are interested in the observable, ongoing interaction patterns of individual families rather than the social characteristics of those families or the attitudes or beliefs of individual family members. As many have noted, the study of social process requires tools of measurement and analysis different from those familiar to either psychiatry or sociology. Nevertheless, the analysis of ongoing family interaction, of family communication patterns, is of great interest to students from many disciplines studying the family. In this chapter our effort will be to summarize and evaluate the body of theory on family functioning and its consequences which has emerged out of the movement.

Not all of the efforts to analyze family process have come out of the clinical perspective, however. As early as 1959 Hess and Handel were concerned with "understanding and describing in nonpathological terms the complexities of analyzing family interaction" (Hess and Handel, 1959:12). They proposed five "processes" which together constituted family process, namely:

1. Establishing a pattern of separateness and connectedness
2. Establishing a satisfactory congruence of images
3. Evolving family themes
4. Establishing the boundaries of the family's world of experience
5. Evolving defintions of male and female and of older and younger [1959:12].

Reviewing these and subsequent listings, it has seemed to us that two of the five categories are more basic than the others. Evolving family themes and establishing a congruence of images among family members seem to be only mechanisms under the general heading of establishing a pattern of separateness and connectedness. The establishment of adequate family models of male and female, older and younger seems to be derivative of the nature of the relationships among members and the relationships between them and their social environment.

More recently Kantor and Lehr (1975:41) lent some support to the centrality of this dichotomy when in their observations of the management of family space they wrote:

Basically the question on space that a family has to answer for itself is twofold. First, how does it develop, defend, and maintain its system and subsystem territories? [Elsewhere they call this "bounding."] Second, how does it regulate distance among its own members?

The first of these points seems to be related to Hess and Handel's "establishing the boundaries of the family's world of experience." The second is closely related to their "establishing a pattern of connectedness and separateness" among family members.

As we have reviewed the complex family process literature, it has seemed to us that much of it could be conceptualized as relating to one or the other of these two issues. For this reason we have chosen to organize our review of the theoretical literature and subsequently our summary model around these central concerns.

As we attempt to synthesize a unified model of family process and its outcomes, it is inevitable that we will not do justice to individual theoreticians and their idiosyncratic systems of explanation and definitions. But if some of the nuances which distinguish closely related concepts are necessarily lost in our efforts to be integrative, our hope is that the trade-off is a profitable one.

As partial compensation, Exhibit 23.1 abstracts from the original sources brief definitions of the major constructs of some of the key theorists. Table 23.1 attempts to locate some of these concepts under the headings in our analysis where they best fit. To some extent, then, Exhibit 23.1 is a glossary and Table 23.1 an index to the next section.

Exhibit 23.1. Definitions and Origins of Concepts from Family Process Theory

---

Boundaries: the rules defining who participates in family subsystems and how. (Minuchin, 1974:53)

Bounding: the mechanism by which families establish and maintain their territory within the larger community space by regulating both incoming and outgoing traffic. Traffic, in its most general sense, means people, objects, events, and ideas. (Kantor and Lehr, 1975:68)

Coalitions: alliances among family members. (Minuchin, 1974:61)

Complementary relationship: an interlocking relationship in which dissimilar but fitted behaviors evoke each other. (Watzlawick et al., 1967:69)

Demystification: the first phase of therapy, which consists largely of untangling the "knot of mystification" by raising issues that may never have been raised before. (Laing, 1965:61)

Detriangulation: the process by which a person is differentiated out of his family system so that he can relate to others by responding rather than reacting—reacting means that one's behavior is under the control of another, whereas responding means that the other person's position is taken into account but is not the cause of one's behavior. (Bowen, 1973:123)

Disengagement: one type of boundary functioning which is considered extreme and refers to a transactional style—or preference for a type of interaction—among family members. Members of disengaged families typically function autonomously but have a skewed sense of independence and lack feelings of loyalty and belonging and the capacity for interdependence and for requesting support when needed. (Minuchin, 1974:55)

Disqualification: a method of denying a relationship by denying one or more of the four elements of communication which are conceptualized as (1) I (2) am saying something (3) to you (4) in this situation. (Haley, 1963:89)

Double bind: an interactional process in which the "victim" is caught in a paradoxical relationship due to receiving simultaneous, conflicting messages at different levels of communication (verbal and nonverbal, for example) and is also prevented from leaving the relationship. (Bateson et al., 1956)

Emotional divorce: a marked emotional distance between the marital partners. (Bowen, 1960)

Enmeshment: one type of boundary functioning which is considered extreme and refers to a transactional style—or preference for a type of interaction—among family members. Members of enmeshed families typically may be handicapped in that the heightened sense of belonging requires a major yielding of autonomy. The lack of subsystem differentiation discourages autonomous exploration and mastery of problems. (Minuchin, 1974:55)

Family consensual experience: the experience (or perception) held in common by family members concerning the family's environment as well as the family's relationship to the environment. Three types are distinguished: (1) *environment-sensitive* families perceive their environment as orderly and capable of being understood and mastered; (2) *distance-sensitive* families regard the environment as split into unrelated and independent universes, one for each family member who acts to preserve the uniqueness of his own universe; and (3) *consensus-sensitive* families see the environment as confusing and chaotic, and their members emphasize joining together for mutual protection. (Reiss, 1971)

Family types: based on both structural arrangements and strategic styles three basic family types are distinguished: (1) *closed family system,* which typically relies on stable structures (fixed space, regular time, and steady energy) as reference point for order and change; (2) *open family system,* in which order and change are expected to result from the interaction of relatively stable evolving family structures (movable space, variable time, and flexible energy); (3) *random family system,* in which unstable structures are experimented with as reference points for order and change (dispersed space, irregular time, and fluctuating energy). (Kantor and Lehr, 1975:119)

Homeostasis: the relative constancy of the internal environment of the family, a constancy which is maintained by a continuous interplay of dynamic forces (Jackson, 1957); synonymous with "dynamic equilibrium" and signifying the fluid, creative adaptability to change, which at the same time assures that measure of coordinated control which prevents the family from being overwhelmed by a barrage of stimuli in excess of its capacity to accommodate. (Ackerman, 1958)

---

continued

Exhibit 23.1. Definitions and Origins of Concepts from Family Process Theory Continued

Meta: a prefix meaning changed in position or form; beyond, transcending or higher. For example, a *metaperspective* refers to a perspective about perspectives.

Metacommunication: a communication about a communication; it is the relationship-defining element of a communication and qualifies the content of the message (what is actually said). (Watzlawick et al., 1967:39)

Metamessage: synonymous with metacommunication.

Mutuality: a relationship characterized by a divergence of self-interests. (Wynne et al., 1958)

Mystification: a misdefinition of the issue of who is doing what to whom (Laing, 1967:57–77); "the one person (p) seeks to induce in the other person some change necessary for his (p's) security." (Laing, 1965:67)

Perverse triangle: a triangle in which the separation between the generations is breached in a covert way. (Haley, 1971)

Pseudohostility: alienation among family members which remains limited to a surface level and covers the need for intimacy among family members. (Wynne et al., 1958)

Pseudomutuality: a predominant absorption in fitting together at the expense of the differentiation of the persons in the relationship. (Wynne et al., 1958)

Restructuring: the alteration of transactional patterns among family members; restructuring operations, which may include tasks for family members to carry out at home away from the therapist, demand specific changes in family organization and transactional patterns. (Minuchin, 1974:131–37)

Rubber fence: a quality of flexibility in the family boundary which enables the family to expand its boundaries to encompass things that are complementary and contract its boundaries to exclude noncomplementary things. The family role structure becomes all-encompassing for its members. (Wynne et al., 1958)

Schism: marital unions characterized by a chronic failure to achieve complementarity of purpose or role reciprocity; or may be marked by an excessive attachment to the parental home. (Lidz, 1957)

Scapegoating: a mode of conflict resolution in which attention is shifted away from the parental conflict and focused on the "problem behavior" of another family member (usually a child). (Vogel and Bell, 1960)

Skew: a condition of marital unions characterized by one weak partner and one strong partner in which the strong partner dominates the weaker one. (Lidz et al., 1957)

Symmetrical relationship: a relationship characterized by equality. (Watzlawick et al., 1967:68)

Therapeutic paradox: the "cause" in the therapeutic relationship, it involves the psychotherapist (a) setting up a benevolent framework defined as one wherein change is to take place, (b) permitting or encouraging the client to continue with his unchanged behavior, and (c) providing an ordeal that will continue as long as the client continues with unchanged behavior. Typically it takes the form of "prescribing the symptom." (Haley, 1963:188)

Triangulation: the process by which a dyadic emotional system encompasses a third system member for the purpose of maintaining or reestablishing homeostatic balance. (Bowen, 1971)

Undifferentiated family ego mass: a quality of "stuck togetherness" which is a conglomerate emotional oneness that can exist at all levels of intensity. (Bowen, 1971:169)

One other task remains before proceeding to our analysis of family process. We must establish a typology of child outcomes to which various family styles of connectedness and boundary maintenance may then be related.

Among family process theorists the most commonly seen typology of child outcomes is schizophrenic-normal. A few differentiate a third category of delinquent or antisocial which they compare to the other two.

Researchers in the field have been far more varied in the types of outcomes which have interested them. Several have compared the families of children who have different degrees of disturbance. For example, Singer and Wynne (1965) compared diagnosed schizophrenics, borderline schizophrenics, and nonschizophrenics, while Lerner (1968) compared schizophrenics who had had a "good premorbid level of social competence" with schizophrenics classed as having had a "poor premorbid level of social competence." Others have compared far more diverse groupings. Cheek (1964) examined the family interaction of alcoholics, reformatory inmates, schizophrenics, and normals. Rabkin (1965) compared the families of neurotics, schizophrenics, persons with

behavioral disorders, and normals. Still others have used groups involving the families of physically ill children and of psychosomatically ill children (Minuchin et al., 1975). Unhappily, little clarity has emerged from all of these ad hoc comparisons. Some efforts to develop a systematic typology have been made. For instance, Alkire et al. (1971) categorized child outcomes on two dimensions: the content of the symptomatic behavior (aggressive or passive) and the locale in which it occurred (at home or away from home). The fourfold typology which emerged was then sensibly and logically related to the patterns of parental power.

On balance it seemed best to us to stick with the threefold typology most often discussed in the theoretical literature: schizophrenic-normal-delinquent. Only for these three groups does a large enough corpus of literature exist to make systematic links between outcome and family patterns.

Definitions in these areas are fraught with difficulties. The parameters of each of the three categories have been the subject of considerable professional debate. Probably the greatest amount of attention has been given to the question of defining schizophrenia, since the theory de-

Table 23.1. Summary of Chief Constructs by Theorist

		PARADOXICAL BONDING			
THEORIST	DOUBLE BINDING	PARENTAL POWER STRUGGLES	MISSOCIALIZATION*	BOUNDARY MAINTENANCE	THERAPEUTIC STRATEGIES
Bowen	Undifferentiated family ego mass	Emotional divorce Triangulation	Undifferentiated family ego mass		Differentiation (detriangulation)
Kantor and Lehr			Closed family type	Bounding Family types (closed, open, and random)	
Laing	Mystification				Demystification
Lidz	*Folie en famille*	Schism Skew		*Folie en famille*	
Minuchin		Cross-generational coalition	Enmeshment	Boundaries	Restructuring
Palo Alto Group (Bateson, Haley, Jackson, Watzlawick)	Double binding Disqualification	Perverse triangle Symmetrical Complementary			Metacommunication Therapeutic paradox
Reiss			Consensus-sensitive	Consensual experience	
Wynne	Pseudomutuality Pseudohostility	Pseudomutuality Pseudohostility		Rubber fence	
Miscellaneous		Scapegoating			

*We believe missocialization constitutes a special case of paradoxical bonding.

veloped initially as an effort to explain the familial roots of this elusive syndrome. Several definitions are given here from various leaders in the movement. The definitions vary from a focus on internalized mental processes, through interactional styles, to arbitrary social definition. For brevity some of these definitions are condensed and paraphrased.

Schizophrenia: a. concerns the disturbed symbolic processes without degradation of the intelligence potential. The core problem: disordered concept formation, concretistic thinking, mislabeled metaphors, impaired categorical thinking, intrusion of primary-process material, derailment of association, etc. (Lidz et al, 1957).

b. involves inadequate ego strength as manifested in poor reality testing and in the incapacity to integrate new roles into the changing self with appropriate independence and flexibility (Wynne and Singer, 1963).

c. is characterized by conspicuous and exaggerated errors and distortions regarding the nature and type of messages sent and received from others (Bateson, 1960).

d. is the avoidance of defining the relationship with others. This is achieved by negating any of all of the formal characteristics of any message, which are (a) I (b) am saying something (c) to you (d) in this situation. That is, one can deny that he is the one speaking, that he is saying anything, that you are the one he is talking to, and/or that this is the situation. It seems apparent that the list of ways to avoid defining a situation is a list of schizophrenic symptoms (Haley, 1967:89–93).

e. does not exist as a biochemical, neurophysiological, or psychological fact. We do not assume its existence, nor do we adopt it as a hypothesis, nor do we propose a model of it. It can be said to exist only as the label applied by an outsider to behavior he does not understand or approve (Laing, 1964:12).

To summarize, the various authorities seem to focus on at least four interrelated aspects of schizophrenic behavior: (1) thought disorders, (2) communication and relational disorders, (3) social inadequacy and inflexibility, and (4) conspicuously nonnormative behavior (evoking labeling and negative reactions in others).

Normal is defined residually—that is, it is the category of all those who remain after those officially labeled as deviant have been removed, or those individuals or family members who have never been brought to the attention of a community agency or received any type of psychotherapy. The concept of normality is not one of optimal functioning. It is precisely that heterogeneous group constituting the unlabeled remainder. Later in the chapter we shall return to the issue of whether further differentiation within this category may not be profitable.

Delinquents are defined as those young people who have been arrested and convicted for breaking the law but who have not been labeled as "mentally ill." Inasmuch as it is known that most lawbreakers in this age group are not apprehended, the relationship between this group and "normals" is fuzzy at best. The construct has been of value primarily in tacking down one end of several continua which feature schizophrenia on the other end. This will be developed more fully below.

ESTABLISHING APPROPRIATE FORMS OF CONNECTEDNESS AND SEPARATENESS AMONG FAMILY MEMBERS

"Appropriate" suggests social norms governing the forms of connectedness and separateness which ought to relate family members to one another. In discussing such norms, family process theorists often specify that these norms shift from stage to stage in the family life cycle and that one of the chief ways in which the behavior of disturbed children varies from the norm is that they either ignore the shift toward greater freedom and individuality which society defines as appropriate for developing children or they fail to acknowledge the need for more restrictive norms at earlier ages. The family bonds are thus liable to be too close and demanding for the child's age or too lax. The former is held to lead toward schizophrenia and related forms of mental illness, while the latter is felt to be conducive to delinquency and related forms of antisocial behavior. In effect, the former group are oversocialized and missocialized while the latter are undersocialized by their families.

Paradoxical Bonding

Among others, Bowen with his concept of *undifferentiated family ego mass* and Minuchin with his concept of *enmeshed* families have focused particularly on the failure of schizophrenegenic families to permit their children to achieve appropriate degrees of autonomy as they grow older. These two concepts have connotations which go beyond closeness, however. There is an unwholesomeness in the quality of the relationships which is captured more effectively in two additional sets of concepts. Bateson and his associates at Palo Alto introduced in 1954 the concept of the *double bind* which not only suggests that the parties are overconnected but also incorporates the element of paradoxical bonding. The paradox lies in two conflicted imperatives with a third imperative not to leave the field. Although hypothetically any two mutually exclusive commands could meet the requirements of the definition, the illustrations most frequently given involve an injunction to come close and an injunction to keep one's distance.

The same elements seem to be involved in Wynne's concepts of *pseudomutuality* and *pseudohostility,* which involve powerful injunctions to maintain amity in the face of pervasive underlying conflict or to maintain conflict in the face of pervasive underlying bonding.

One of the intuitive strengths of these theoretical constructs is that they conjure up vivid mental images of emotional jeopardy which are convincing at a precognitive level. Once having visualized in one's mind the child

victim of a double bind, caught in a web of conflicting imperatives with neither the option of escape nor the solace of understanding his own plight, who could doubt the plausibility of a flight to mental illness? Or who, having ever been exposed to science fiction, could contemplate an undifferentiated family ego mass without a chill running down his spine? Who is unmoved by the dread vision of friend revealed as foe, of alien spirit glimpsed through familiar forms evoked by the term "pseudomutuality"? Even the term "enmeshment" conjures up sensations of entangled claustrophobia not easy to dismiss.

That eerie, elusive, upsetting quality is, we believe, characteristic of paradoxical bonding and is what links it to the production of schizophrenia in children. At a later point in the chapter we will examine more closely the linkages between the familial and personality variables.

The families of delinquents are characterized as lacking this exact pattern but exhibiting another which Kantor and Lehr's framework would suggest is a temporal parallel to the spatial paradox of double binding, namely inconsistency. While the schizophrenic's family imposes conflicting injunctions at one and the same time, forbidding flight, the delinquent's family exposes the child to conflicting injunctions at different times and permits (or at least fails to prevent) flight. This last issue, of course, has to do with boundary maintenance in the two types of families and will be discussed below.

Parental Power Struggles

Another form of paradoxical bonding between a child and his family occurs when the child is caught in a parental power struggle. These come in two varieties. If the parents are more or less equally matched opponents, Watzlawick et al. (1967) label the conflict as *symmetrical.* If they are unequal, with one in a dominant (or active) situation and one in a submissive (or passive) situation, the conflict is labeled as *complementary.*

In referring to the former type of power struggle (which he calls *emotional divorce*) Bowen (1960) notes that there is some evidence that this sort of dysfunction is more damaging to the child than is actual separation. Lidz et al. (1963) believes that female children are particularly susceptible to the destructive influence of this pattern, which he called marital *schism,* while male children's symptoms are associated with the complementary configuration, which he called marital *skew.* His reasoning (however unpalatable to contemporary tastes) is that traditional familial sex roles are not effectively modeled in these families and that this lack inhibits the development of adequate identification and ego strength on the part of the child.

Minuchin adds a key element to the picture when, in discussing the disengagement of one parent (usually the father), he points out that this is almost always associated with a cross-generational *coalition* between the other parent and the symptomatic child. It is not implied, of course, that such "coalitions" are typically warm and supportive relationships. Rather, the lack of culturally approved involvement between husband and wife is compensated for by an inappropriate degree of involvement between parent and a child. The emotional tone of the involvement, as we have already seen, is likely to be paradoxical.

We believe that this is closely related to the pattern which Vogel and Bell (196) described as *scapegoating*. In this conceptualization the symptomatic child is seen as bearing the sins of his parents' split much as the "scape goat" was ordained to bear the sins of the people in ancient Israel. Ultimately the goat was abandoned as propitiation. In parallel fashion when a family feels that its basic stability is threatened by a growing rift between the parents, one alternative is to divert attention from the threatening parental split to a relatively safe scapegoat from among the children. Some have argued that the weakest and most vulnerable child is chosen (van der Veen and Novak, 1971; Novak and van der Veen, 1970). Others find it more credible to believe that the child who is most disruptive is chosen.[1] In either case, a classic vicious cycle develops in which the attacks on the child evoke worse behavior which in turn warrants further attack and so forth until the child's symptoms are fully developed.

On the face of it, it would seem that Minuchin's "*coalition*" and Bell and Vogel's *attack* are almost semantic opposites. Yet a careful reading of the clinical examples offered suggests that each is describing the same type of paradoxical relationship. In one case the connectedness and in the other the hostility is focal.

The counternormative presence of coalitions across generational lines and lack of coalition within the marital pair has been called by Haley the *perverse triangle*. As we shall see in a later section of the chapter, there is some support in the process literature for the notion that this configuration is related to personality disturbances of various kinds, including psychosomatic disturbances and phobias, as well as schizophrenia (e.g., Minuchin, 1974:102–04). Outside the process literature there is a considerable body of research linking this type of family pattern to delinquency also (for example, see Glueck and Glueck, 1960; Nye, 1959). In order to differentiate the two types of outcomes, it is necessary to invoke the different style of boundary maintenance discussed in the next section of this chapter.

Missocialization

At the beginning of this section it was noted that both the children of overclose families and of underclose families might have difficulty in articulating with the demands of the larger society as they grow older and approach adult status. This dilemma will be discussed more fully below as a special problem in boundary maintenance, but it deserves mention here as a third type

of paradoxical bond. Theorists have pointed out that the child who has been carefully and systematically socialized to remain dependent on the family when all other societal agents are pushing him to assume increasingly responsible and autonomous positions in the world at large is in a prototypical double bind. Similarly the child whose parents have been so erratic and contradictory in their socialization as to leave him without internalized commitment to basic social norms is caught in a bind when society demands conformity.

ESTABLISHING APPROPRIATE FORMS OF CONNECTEDNESS AND SEPARATENESS BETWEEN FAMILY MEMBERS AND THE OUTSIDE WORLD

Boundary maintenance, as this family function is often designated, consists of two parts: (1) keeping harmful or disruptive influences out of the family, protecting it from unwanted intrusion; and (2) keeping access to supportive and nurturant elements in the external world open and active.

Commonly, theorists describe three styles of boundary maintenance: a very *closed* style which permits little exchange between family members and others, a *selective-open* style which differentially filters out negative elements and facilitates supportive exchange, and finally a *wide-open* style which is successful neither at keeping members in nor keeping negative elements out.

Closed Style

Reiss (1971) conceptualized boundary maintenance style as a function of what he called *family consensual experience,* that is, families related to the outside world according to their beliefs about what it was like out there. What we have called the "closed" family he calls the *consensus-sensitive* family. It sees the environment as chaotic and unknowable. Members place great importance in joining with other family members in maneuvers for mutual protection, and this generally involves a rapid and collective consensus in a fixed stylized version of how the environment is patterned.

Kantor and Lehr (1975, ch. 9) focus on the mechanisms that "closed" families use to achieve stability and equilibrium. As compared to other families they structure their interactions around limited space, regular time, and steady energy, resisting any external influence which might challenge the system.

Among the clinical theorists this style of boundary maintenance is seen to be closely associated with the generation of schizophrenia in its children. The schizophrenegenic family has been widely described as having particularly comprehensive and impermeable boundaries. We have already noted in connection with the *double-binding* concept that one element in that pattern is the constraint against leaving the field despite conflict. The same element is either implicit or explicit in the other paradoxical-bonding constructs such as "undifferentiated family ego mass," "pseudomutuality-pseudohostility," and "enmeshment." Perhaps the most vivid imagery related to this specific aspect of schizophrenic families is Wynne's *rubber fence,* which stretches but never really lets anyone in or out.

One of the consequences of this social isolation is that children caught in the paradoxical bond have minimal opportunity to gain a *metaperspective* on their situation; that is, the child is underexposed to alternative vantage points which might identify and clarify the dilemma he is in. One of the qualities of the double bind, according to Bateson and his associates (Bateson et al., 1956) is that the contradictory nature of the imperatives may not be acknowledged. This leads to what Laing has called *mystification.* As we shall argue below, mystification is the proximate cause of schizophrenic behavior.

Selective-Open Style

Reiss (1971) labels the family with this style the *environment-sensitive* family. Such families perceive their environment as orderly and capable of being understood and mastered. Through his own explorations of the environment each member serves to amplify and clarify the patterning in the environment for others in the family.

Kantor and Lehr (1975, ch. 9) label this the *open* family. It maintains a moving equilibrium and shifting boundaries. Space in such families is movable; time, variable; and energy, flexible. Yet all of this motion is relatively orderly and predictable.

This is the family most likely to produce "normal" children. Relatively little work has been done on boundary maintenance in normal families by family process scholars; outside of that field, however, Zimmerman and his colleagues (Zimmerman and Broderick, 1954, 1956; Zimmerman and Cervantes, 1960; Cervantes, 1965) have demonstrated that "successful" families insulated themselves from threats to their values by surrounding themselves with close friends of similar value commitments. By contrast, families with delinquents or school dropouts were far less likely to interact with a network of friend families. When they did interact with other families, they did not choose families who reflected and reinforced their own value system. Thus one quality of the boundaries of normal families is that they are *selectively* permeable, granting access to nonthreatening elements and not to others.

Wide-Open Style

No family could function without some boundary maintenance being performed, but we are concerned here with the most nearly boundaryless end of the continuum of openness in family functioning. Reiss (1971) calls these families *distance-sensitive*. They see the environment as split into unrelated and independent segments, one for each family member. Each member acts to preserve his unique environment and regards the family members' perceptions and actions as irrelevant to his relationship with his own universe.

Kantor and Lehr (1975, ch. 9) call this the *random* family. Here the reference points for maintaining equilibrium and boundaries are themselves erratic and shifting. Family structures are unstable with space dispersed, time irregular, and energy fluctuating.

This family is competent neither to keep its children in nor to keep strangers out. It fails to prepare its children to articulate effectively with the sources of potentially legitimate rewards such as the school and the job market. And finally, it fails to deal effectively with the influences of antisocial elements, such as neighborhood gangs, on its children.

What it does provide, thus avoiding mental illness, is ample opportunity for demystification (Laing, 1965) from any familial paradoxical bonds. Adopting the outside perspective of their peers, these children have no difficulty in identifying parental inconsistencies.

AN EMERGENT MODEL LINKING FAMILY PROCESS AND CHILD OUTCOMES

As this chapter has gone through successive drafts, the summary model has become progressively simpler, In its present form it bears a certain resemblance to Bateson and his colleagues' final conceptualization of the double-bind theory of schizophrenia.

It is a multiplicative rather than an additive model, and it predicts multiple outcomes. For these reasons we have chosen to diagram it using a flow chart or process format (see Figure 23.1) rather than the accounting-model format used in most other chapters. In this format the diamonds represent choice points or, if you prefer, dichotomous variables. The rectangles represent intermediate or terminal outcomes. The arrows represent the flow of children through various familial circumstances toward one or another personality outcome.

As we have seen in the review of the theory literature, the key to everything in the model is the presence or absence of paradoxical pressures. We have suggested that these may emanate from a single parent, from a parental power struggle, or from a disparity between the demands of the family and the demands of the social environment (school, peers, etc.). Lacking such pressures, the child will proceed to develop within the normal range; and his final category might be termed *unchallenged normal.* He lacks a metaperspective in his life, but there is little motivation to gain one since he is feeling no real discomfort with the course of his life.

Figure 23.1.

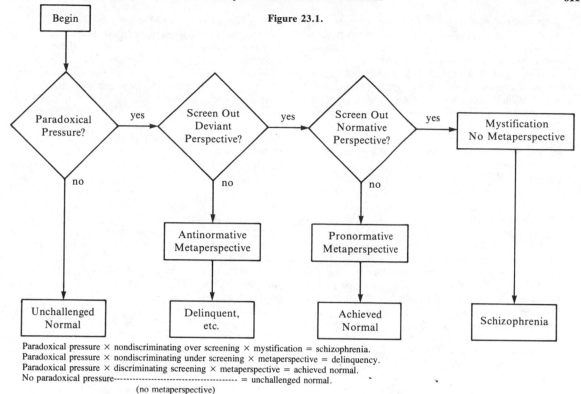

Paradoxical pressure × nondiscriminating over screening × mystification = schizophrenia.
Paradoxical pressure × nondiscriminating under screening × metaperspective = delinquency.
Paradoxical pressure × discriminating screening × metaperspective = achieved normal.
No paradoxical pressure--- = unchallenged normal.
            (no metaperspective)

In the presence of paradoxical pressures the outcome depends on the nature of the family boundary maintenance. If the family successfully screens out all external views, then the child is deprived of the opportunity to achieve a metaperspective on the dilemma he is in. Under these classic "double bind" conditions what Laing has called *mystification* (1965) takes place; that is, confusion about what is real and what is not and about what is acceptable and what is not grows until finally the child manifests the symptoms of schizophrenic withdrawal or of some related condition.

When the family has such poorly maintained boundaries that it does not effectively regulate its child's contacts with deviant—that is, antinormative—elements in the environment, mystification is avoided. The child is likely to resolve his paradoxical bond by turning against the socially responsible component and embracing the hostile, alienated stance. Such a child does not "go crazy," but often ends up in trouble for violating social norms.

Finally, if a family operates its boundaries differentially and its child is relatively shielded from deviant elements while being exposed to many pronormative elements (school, church, family friends, etc.), then a metaperspective is achieved and mystification is avoided. The result is a child in the normal range but at a very different level of understanding of himself, his family and

his world. This *achieved normality* is qualitatively quite different from the "unchallenged normality" of those who have never been exposed to paradoxical demands. Bateson has written "if the pathology can be warded off or resisted the total experience may promote creativity" (Bateson, 1969; unpublished, quoted in Olson, 1972).

EVALUATION OF THE MODEL

Research on the variables contained in this model has suffered from segmentalization. Precisely because it is a multiplicative model, it cannot be tested by taking one variable at a time. A fair number of studies, for example, have attempted to evaluate the relationship between some form of parental paradoxical injunctions and schizophrenia in the child. Not one of them has collected data also on the family's style of boundary maintenance. It is not surprising that the result has been confusing. Most often disappointing results are blamed upon problems of design and especially of measurement (see Olson's review article, 1972). Methodological criticisms are well founded. Yet it seems clear to us that even were the designs and measures otherwise fully adequate, one must expect muddy results at best if one variable in a multiplicative system is attended to without controlling on the others.

Despite this, it may be useful to cite two or three of the most interesting studies of each of the three types of paradoxical pressures, if only to further illustrate the problem. Rinquette and Kennedy's (1966) study on double binding had several sets of cliniciansc(including some who had coauthored the earlier theoretical work on the concept) evaluate 20 letters of mothers to hospitalized schizophrenic sons, 20 letters from mothers to their sons in the army, and 20 letters written by hospital staff as though they were writing to hospitalized schizophrenic sons. The most dramatic finding was that there was so little agreement among judges in identifying double-binding messages (actually less among the most expert group and most among the most naive). From our point of view it was almost equally interesting to note that none of the judges could distinguish among the three sets of letters. Double binding turned out to be common in all three sets, as might be expected if the present model is accepted as accurate.

Other studies (e.g., Beakel and Mehorabian, 1969, and Bugenthal et al., 1970) have analyzed ongoing parent-child interaction in a laboratory or clinic setting looking for contradictions between verbal and nonverbal cues. Still others looked for the denial of paradoxical meanings in evaluations of ambiguous proverbs (Sojit, 1969, 1971), or had disturbed and normal young people report on the frequency of paradoxical messages from their families (Berger, 1965).

Although there has been a scattering of positive results (e.g., Bugenthal et al., 1970), as a group these studies reinforce the observation that the questions asked are inappropriate or at least insufficient.

The second type of paradoxical pressure, that resulting from getting involved in a parental power struggle, has also received some attention, though again as an isolated variable. In one series of studies Sojit (1969, 1971) asked the parents of several sets of variously diagnosed children to explain the meaning of a proverb to their child. Parents of nondisturbed children typically explained to their child that there were two possible interpretations and pointed out the contradiction. The parents of schizophrenic children (and to a lesser extent the parents of delinquent children) by contrast tended to be contradictory and conflicting in their explanations, with each parent defending a different interpretation. Ferreira (1960) in another observational study of the parents of delinquent and nondelinquent children found that the former were more likely to undercut each other, disqualifying each other's messages to the child.

A number of studies focused on the triangulation problem, which in our analysis is just another indicator of paradoxical bonding. In these studies the issue of mixed messages was not addressed. Instead the issue of parental split, with the child being coopted into coalition with one parent, was focal. Lennard et al. (1965) in an observational study of family triads found that among families with a schizophrenic child there was significantly less communication between father and mother and more between mother and son than was found among the "normal" triads. Similarly Schuham (1972) compared families with a disturbed child to families of nondisturbed children using a "revealed difference" technique and found more parent-parent agreement in the families of nondisturbed children and more parent-child agreement in families with a disturbed child. In a particularly neat design Sharan (1966) compared the interaction of 24 sets of parents with their schizophrenic child and, separately, the interaction of these same parents with a normal sibling. He found evidence that patient children were more supportive of their opposite-sex parent than were their normal siblings. It is of interest that this level of paradoxical bonding does not appear to occur as commonly in normal families as in others but appears equally characteristically in the families of delinquents and schizophrenics.

The third type of paradoxical bonding, that involving mutually exclusive demands from the family and from the extrafamilial environment, has figured importantly among theorists especially in explaining why certain symptomatic behaviors occur when they do in the developmental process. No research literature has grown up around the issue, however, probably because it would be so difficult to measure the extrafamilial half of the paradoxical injunction.

As for the boundary maintenance part of the model, we have already referred to research by Zimmerman and his associates on the differential screening of the "successful" families as compared to families of delinquents and dropouts. McPherson et al. (1973) found that children who were withdrawn and socially isolated (as contrasted to those who were aggressive-antisocial or passive-negative) had parents who were overprotective and who excluded external stimuli.

Reiss, in a series of experiments (1967a, 1967b, 1968, 1969, 1971), found that the families of schizophrenics, when given experimental tasks which revealed several dimensions of their interaction, were less receptive to outside cues, copied each other's work rather than innovating, and in short evidenced many of the characteristics of overrestricted boundaries. The families of delinquents showed disruptive relationship problems similar to those in schizophrenics' families, but they handled them differently. Instead of maintaining a high level of attention to internal familial cues and ignoring extrafamilial sources, they tended to do the opposite.

Although these studies are consistent with the model shown in Figure 23.1, they are too fragmentary to test it. It is hoped that future studies will be broad enough in their scope to permit the testing of the system of relevant variables as a system.

It is of passing interest to note that much of family therapy can be seen as addressing the same system of variables. As the therapist approaches the family in an effort to effect changed child outcomes, he or she is liable to enter the system at one or more of the key points in the model. In families with schizophrenic or emotionally disturbed children it would be common to work toward these goals:

1. Introducing a metaperspective, thereby demystifying the paradoxical bonding.

2. Detriangulating the child so that he is not so enmeshed in a perverse coalition with one parent against the other. Often one element in this is the mending of the split between the parents so that they take a more unified (less paradoxical) stand toward the child and look to each other rather than the child as the appropriate partner in problem solution efforts.

3. Opening family boundaries for the child initially through the therapy itself (the therapist being an outsider) but eventually through getting the family to permit age-appropriate autonomy and thereby increase his or her extrafamilial contacts.

With the families of delinquents the therapeutic goals are a little different but have some of the same elements:

1. Introducing a metaperspective that is not antinormative through establishing rapport with the child on a one-to-one basis, or more commonly through a peer group counseling experience.

2. Attempting to restructure the family so that it is less chaotic (mending parental rifts, negotiating new family rules which apply to parents as well as children, etc.). Often the child's bad behavior itself may be a major motivation to "close ranks."

3. Reducing the influence of deviant peers or, if that is not possible, working with the whole peer group to change toward normative goals.

Family therapy, viewed through this lens, seems less disjunctive and complex. Various therapists have different strategies, but in our view there is, in practice, a great convergence upon these goals.

In summary, family process theory seems to converge upon a multivariate explanation of the relationships between family process and child outcomes. Figure 23.1 represents our distillation of that convergence. In order to move forward the field seems badly to need four things:

1. The work of Kantor and Lehr and others needs to be expanded in order to permit the measurement of paradoxical relationships *in situ*. From this it may become possible to abstract more economical measuring techniques which could then be validated against comprehensive family evaluations.

2. More attention needs to be given to styles of bounding and especially to differential screening as one key aspect of this process. To date this has never been studied within the movement, yet it seems to be a crucial differentiating factor.

3. The variables need to be studied as elements in a multiplicative system and not one by one.

4. The outcome variable, personality type, needs to be further specified and a richer typology developed.

It seems clear that the field is ripe for some major steps forward as the differences among therapists are gradually absorbed into a common theoretical framework.

NOTE

1. Reuben Hill, editorial comment upon early draft of this chapter.

REFERENCES

ALKIRE, A. A., M. J. GOLDSTEIN, E. H. RODNICK, AND L. L. JUDD
1971 "Social influence and counter influence within families of four types of disturbed adolescents." *Journal of Abnormal Psychology* 71:32–41.

BATESON, G.
1960 "Minimal requirements for a theory of schizophrenia." *Archives of General Psychiatry* 2:477–91.

BATESON, G., D. D. JACKSON, J. HALEY, AND J. H. WEAKLAND
1956 "Toward a theory of schizophrenia." *Behavioral Science* 1:251–64.

BEAKEL, N. G. AND A. MEHRABIAN
1969 "Inconsistent communication and psychopathology." *Journal of Abnormal Psychology* 74:126–30.

BERGER, A.
1965 "A test of the double-bind hypothesis of schizophrenia." *Family Process* 4:95–104.

BOWEN, M.
1960 "A family concept of schizophrenia." In D. D. Jackson (ed.), *Etiology of Schizophrenia*. New York: Basic Books.
1971 "The use of family theory in clinical practice." In J. Haley (ed.), *Changing Families*. New York: Grune and Stratoon.
1973 "Toward the differentiation of a self in one's own family." In J. L. Framo (ed.), *Family Interaction: A Dialogue between Family Researchers and Family Therapists*. New York: Springer.

BUGENTHAL, D. E., J. W. KASWAN, L. R. LOVE, AND M. N. FOX
1970 "Child vs adult perception of evaluative messages in verbal, vocal, and visual channels." *Developmental Psychology* 2:367–75.

BUGENTHAL, D. E., L. R. LOVE, AND M. N. FOX
1972 "Videotaped family interaction: Differences reflecting presence and type of child disturbance." *Journal of Abnormal Psychology* 79 (June):285–90.

CERVANTES, L.
1965 *The Dropout: Causes and Cures*. Ann Arbor: University of Michigan Press.

CHEEK, F. E.
1964 "The 'schizophrenic' mother in word and deed." *Family Process* 3:155–77.

FERREIRA, A. J.
1960 "The 'double-bind' and delinquent behavior." *Archives of General Psychiatry* 3:359–67.

GROUP FOR THE ADVANCEMENT OF PSYCHIATRY
1970 *Treatment of Families in Conflict: The Clinical Study of Family Process*. New York: Science House.

GLUECK, S. AND E. GLUECK
1959 *Predicting Delinquency and Crime*. Cambridge, Mass.: Harvard University Press.

HALEY, J.
1963   *Strategies of Psychotherapy*. New York: Basic Books.
1971   "Toward a theory of pathological systems." In G. Zuk and I. Boszormenyi-Nagy (eds.), *Family Theory and Disturbed Families*. Palo Alto, Calif.: Science and Behavior Books.

HESS, R. S. AND G. HANDEL
1959   *Family Worlds*. Chicago: University of Chicago Press.

JACKSON, D. D.
1957   "The question of family homeostasis." *Psychiatric Quarterly Supplement* 31:79–90 (part I).

KANTOR, D. AND W. LEHR
1975   *Inside the Family: Toward a Theory of Family Process*. San Francisco: Jossey-Bass.

LAING, R. D.
1965   "Mystification, confusion and conflict." In I. Boszormenyi-Nagy and J. L. Framo (eds.), *Intensive Family Therapy*. New York: Springer.
1967   *The Politics of Experience*. New York: Ballentine Books.

LAING, R. D. AND A. ESTERSON
1964   *Sanity, Madness and the Family: Families of Schizophrenics*. London: Tavistock Publications.

LENNARD, H., M. BEAULIEU, AND N. EMBREY
1965   "Interaction in families with a schizophrenic child." *Archives of General Psychiatry* 12:166–83.

LERNER, P. M.
1968   "Resolution of interpersonal role conflict in families of schizophrenic patients: II. Social maturity." *Journal of Nervous and Mental Disease* 145:336–41.

LIDZ, T., A. R. CORNELISON, S. FLECK, AND D. TERRY
1957   "The interfamilial environment of schizophrenic patients: II. Marital schism and marital skew." *American Journal of Psychiatry* 114:241–48.

LIDZ, T., S. FLECK, Y. O. ALENEN, AND A. CORNELISON
1963   "Schizophrenic patients and their siblings." *Marital Psychiatry* 26:1–18.

MCPHERSON, S., M. GOLDSTEIN, AND E. RODNICK
1973   "Who listens? Who communicates? How? Styles of interaction among parents and their disturbed adolescent children." *Journal of Abnormal Psychology* 28:393–403.

MINUCHIN, S.
1974   *Families and Family Therapy*. Cambridge, Mass.: Harvard University Press.

MINUCHIN, S., L. BAKER, B. L. ROSMAN, R. LIEBMAN, L. MILMAN, AND T. C. TODD
1975   "A conceptual model of psychomatic illness in children." *Archives of General Psychiatry* 32:1031–38.

NOVAK, A. L. AND F. VAN DER VEEN
1970   "Family concepts and emotional disturbance in the families of disturbed adolescents with normal siblings." *Family Process* 9:157–72.

NYE, F. I.
1959   "Maternal employment and the adjustment of adolescent children." *Marriage and Family Living* 26:240–44.

OLSON, D. H.
1972   "Empirically unbinding the double bind: A review of research and conceptual reformulation." *Family Process* 11:69–94.

RABKIN, L. Y.
1965   "The patient's family: Research methods." *Family Process* 4:105–32.

REISS, D.
1967a   "Individual thinking and family interaction: I. Introduction to an experimental study of problem solving in families of normals, character disorders, and schizophrenics." *Archives of General Psychiatry* 16:80–93.
1967b   "Individual thinking and family interaction: II. A study of pattern recognition and hypothesis testing in families of normals, character disorders, and schizophrenics." *Journal of Psychiatric Research* 5:193–211.
1968   "Individual thinking and family interaction: III. An experimental study of categorization performance in families of normals, character disorders, and schizophrenics." *Journal of Nervous and Mental Disease* 146:384–403.
1969   "Individual thinking and family interaction: IV. A study of information exchange in families of normals, character disorders, and schizophrenics." *Journal of Nervous and Mental Disease* 149:473–90.
1971   "Varieties of consensual experience: III. Contrasts between families of normals, character disorders, and schizophrenics." *Journal of Nervous and Mental Disease* 152:73–95.

RINQUETTE, E. L. AND T. KENNEDY
1966   "An experimental study of the double-bind hypothesis." *Journal of Abnormal Psychology* 71:136–41.

SCHUHAM, A. I.
1972   "Activity, talking time and spontaneous agreement in disturbed and normal families." *Journal of Abnormal Psychology* 79:68–75.

SHARAN, S.
1966   "Family interaction with schizophrenics and their siblings." *Journal of Abnormal Psychology* 73:345–53.

SINGER, M. T. AND L. C. WYNNE
1965   "Thought disorders and the family relationship of schizophrenics: IV. Results and implications." *Archives of General Psychiatry* 12:201–12.

SOJIT, C. M.
1969   "Dyadic interaction in a double-bind situation." *Family Process* 8:235–59.
1971   "The double-bind hypothesis and the parents of schizophrenics." *Family Process* 10:53–75.

VAN DER VEEN, F. AND A. L. NOVAK
1971   "Perceived parental attitudes and family concepts of disturbed adolescents, normal siblings, and normal controls." *Family Process* 10:327–44.

VOGEL, E. F. AND N. W. BELL
1960   "The emotionally disturbed child as a family scapegoat." In N. W. Bell and E. F. Vogel (eds.), *A Modern Introduction to the Family*. New York: Free Press.

WATZLAWICK, P., J. BEAVIN, AND D. D. JACKSON
1967   *The Pragmatics of Human Communication: A Study of Interactional Patterns, Pathologies and Paradoxes*. New York: Norton.

WYNNE, L. C., I. RYCKOFF, J. DAY, AND S. HIRSCH
1958   "Pseudomutuality in the family life of schizophrenics." *Psychiatry* 21:205–20.

WYNNE, L. C. AND M. T. SINGER
1963   "Thought disorders and the family relations of schizophrenics: I. A research strategy." *Archives of General Psychiatry* 9:191–98.

ZIMMERMAN, C. C. AND C. B. BRODERICK
1954   "The nature and role of informal living groups." *Marriage and Family Living* 16:107–11.
1956   "The family self protective system." In C. C. Zimmerman and L. Cervantes (eds.), *Marriage and the Family*. Chicago: Henry Regnery.

ZIMMERMAN, C. C. AND L. F. CERVANTES
1960   *Successful American Families*. New York: Pageant Press.

24

FAMILY DETERMINANTS AND EFFECTS OF DEVIANCE

Stephen J. Bahr

INTRODUCTION

A large number of research studies have found different aspects of family structure and interaction to be related to various types of deviant behavior, particularly to crime and delinquency. A number of theories have been constructed which attempt to account for these empirical findings and explain why deviance occurs. The purpose of this chapter is to identify, evaluate, and refine existing theories of deviant behavior and determine the role of the family in each theory.

Deviance refers to behavior that violates normative rules (Cohen, 1966). It is "any kind of conduct that in some way fails to meet shared behavioral expectations" (DeFleur et al., 1971:376), and elicits corrective or punitive reactions form social control agents. Conformity and deviation are matters of degree, and a certain amount of rule violation is usually tolerated. No behavior is intrinsically deviant, but deviance is what a collective defines as deviant. Therefore, a given act may violate the expectations of one group but be perceived as perfectly normal in another.

It would be impossible to focus on all the many different types of behavior and rules under the general heading of deviance. Two criteria have been used to narrow the scope of this chapter to a manageable size. First, the focus will be primarily on the acts that have been defined as serious crime in the United States. The terms "crime" and "delinquency" will be used synonymously in this chapter, the latter referring to criminal acts committed by minors. Second, previous theorizing will be used as a guide in directing the chapter.

Limiting this chapter to serious crime has several advantages. First, this narrows somewhat the almost endless number of acts that may be considered to be deviant. Thus scapegoating, underachievement, mental illness, premarital sex, extramarital sex, and a large variety of other acts that may be considered deviant are not discussed. Second, focusing on serious crime makes this chapter more useful to policy makers. A perennial social problem in the United States is the rising crime rate, and large sums of money are directed toward the problem of crime in America. Policy makers, politicians, and citizens are continually seeking to understand serious crime and find ways to reduce it. Third, in the area of serious crime a theoretical evaluation is needed, since considerable theorizing and research has already taken place. In many other types of deviant behavior the theory and research are not as advanced, and thus a theoretical evaluation would prove much less fruitful at this time. Fourth, behavior that is defined as serious crime in the U.S. is generally proscribed in other societies as well. Serious crime involves elements of injury, theft, or damage and includes murder, forcible rape, aggravated assault, robbery, burglary, larceny, and auto theft. These acts have been consistently proscribed cross-culturally and historically (Wellford, 1975; Lemert, 1972:22; Linton, 1952:660; Hoebel, 1954:286–87). Although major cross-cultural differences exist regarding how violations are punished, there is evidence that all societies have found it functional to control the kinds of behavior defined as serious crime in America (Wellford, 1975:335).

This chapter is divided into nine sections. After this introduction, six major theoretical orientations are identified, discussed, and evaluated in the second through seventh sections. The major elements in each theory are explicated and the results of empirical tests reported. In the eighth section the effects of deviance on the family are explored, while the ninth section is a summary and conclusion.

The theoretical orientations examined are (1) differential association, (2) social control, (3) anomie, (4) psychoanalytic, (5) deterrence, and (6) labeling. Although other theories could have been included, these six

NOTE: The author expresses appreciation to F. Ivan Nye, J. Ross Eshleman, and Melvin Wilinson for their helpful suggestions and to Marilyn Balderas for typing the manuscript. This research was supported in part by the College of Family Living, Brigham Young University, Provo, Utah 84602.

615

seem to stand out among the many existing theoretical formulations of deviant behavior. Each has been the focus of a considerable amount of critical discussion and empirical research over a number of years. Although these six theories are distinct entities, they are not necessarily mutually exclusive.

DIFFERENTIAL ASSOCIATION

Certainly one of the most influential theories of deviance is Sutherland's differential association (Sutherland, 1939; Sutherland and Cressey, 1966). A number of studies have attempted to empirically test the theory of differential association (Jensen, 1972; Krohn, 1974; Reiss and Rhodes, 1964; Short, 1957, 1958; Stanfield, 1966; Voss, 1964), and it has attracted a large amount of critical discussion (Cressey, 1960; Sutherland and Cressey, 1966:83–98).

The major assumptions underlying differential association theory can be summarized as follows: (1) Criminal behavior is learned within intimate personal groups and involves all the mechanisms involved in any other learning. (2) In the process of interpersonal communication one becomes associated with definitions favorable and unfavorable to law violation. (3) A person becomes a criminal "because of an excess of definitions favorable to violation of law over definitions unfavorable to violation of law" (Sutherland and Cressey, 1966:81). Thus, learning criminal behavior depends on the degree to which one is associated with procriminal definitions, i.e., differential association. (4) Definitions favorable and unfavorable to law violation are acquired primarily through the peer group and the family.

Building on these assumptions, Sutherland and Cressey (1966:225–28) identified a number of important variables in their discussion of the etiology of crime. They did not define the variables precisely, but from their discussion four variables appeared to be paramount: (1) association with criminal patterns, (2) attachment to family of orientation, (3) values of family of orientation, (4) social class. Sutherland and Cressey maintained that association with criminal patterns is the critical causal variable in the etiology of crime. They suggested that the family has little direct effect on delinquency and that unless delinquent patterns exist outside the home, the family will have little effect on delinquency, no matter what the attachment to one's family:

> If the family is in a community in which there is no pattern of theft, the children do not steal, no matter how much neglected or how unhappy they may be at home. . . . A child does not necessarily become delinquent because he is unhappy. Children in unhappy homes may take on delinquency patterns if there are any around for them to acquire [1966:227–28].

Attachment was seen as a variable that may insulate one from criminal associations:

> The important element is that isolation from the family is likely to increase the child's associations with delinquency behavior patterns and decrease his associations with antidelinquency patterns [1966:226].

It was not clear in their discussion how "attachment to family of orientation" is related to "values of family of orientation." Sutherland and Cressey seemed to suggest that the two are distinct variables and that values and ways of "seeing" things are acquired from one's family and influence the type of associations one has. Social class was also seen as a variable antecedent to criminal associations.

The major elements of differential association as set forth by Sutherland and Cressey (1966) may be stated in propositional form as follows:

1. The number of criminal patterns one becomes associated with has a positive relationship to the probability of criminal behavior.

2. The amount of attachment to the family of orientation has a negative relationship with the number of criminal patterns one becomes associated with.

3. The more the values of the family of orientation are law-abiding, the less the probability that one will have associations with criminal patterns.

4. The higher the social class, the lower the probability that one will have associations with criminal patterns.

A fifth proposition may be inferred from their discussions of the theory. They indicated that in the home one learns to pay close attention to certain persons and behavior patterns and to pay little attention to others (Sutherland and Cressey, 1966:226). This suggests that the values of the family of orientation may inhibit the effect that associations with criminal patterns may have on criminal behavior. This may be stated in propositional form as follows:

5. The more law-abiding the values of the family of orientation, the less the probability that associations with criminal patterns will result in criminal behavior.

Sutherland and Cressey did not explicitly define their variables or state the theory in propositional form, but these five propositions appear to capture the essence of their thinking. Proposition 5 was not viewed by Sutherland and Cressey as a major element in the etiology of criminal behavior, however. A causal diagram of these propositions is presented in Figure 24.1.

Two basic procedures appear necessary to empirically test the above propositions. First, the correlations between the antecedent variables and criminal behavior need to be computed while controlling for criminal associations. If Sutherland and Cressey are correct, these partial correlations should be negligible, while the comparable zero-order correlations should be significantly different from zero. Second, the correlation between

Figure 24.1. A Causal Model of Differential Association

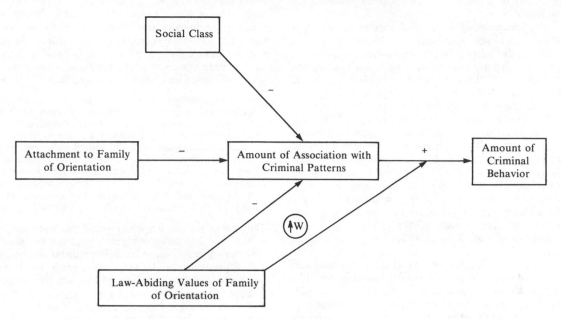

criminal associations and criminal behavior should be computed while controlling for type of orientations portrayed in the family. The data would be consistent with the theory if the correlation between delinquent associations and delinquent behavior decreases as the orientation of the family becomes more law-abiding.

Four studies were located which reported data relevant to the differential association model. Stanfield (1966), using data from the Cambridge-Somerville Youth Study, examined the relationships among (1) type of discipline by the father (lax or erratic versus consistent), (2) the extent of peer activity (frequent or occasional), (3) the father's occupational status (high or low), and (4) juvenile delinquency. A youth was considered to be delinquent if he had appeared in court for one or more juvenile offenses. Stanfield appeared to assume that when discipline is consistent rather than lax or erratic, the values of the family are more law-abiding and attachment to the family is greater. The zero-order correlations showed that delinquency was associated with lax-erratic discipline, frequent gang activity, and low occupational status, although the later correlation was not statistically significant at the .05 level. This is consistent with a number of other data sets that have found social class to be unrelated to or only weakly associated with delinquency (Akers, 1964; Dentler and Monroe, 1961; Hirschi, 1969; Nye et al., 1958; Stinchcombe, 1964) and indicates that perhaps Sutherland and Cressey overemphasized the effect of social class on delinquent behavior.

When level of peer activity was controlled, the rela-

tionship between the father's discipline and delinquency was the same as the zero-order correlation between discipline and delinquency (Gdd = .47; Gdd.p = .48).[1] Thus type of discipline was associated with delinquency irrespective of level of peer activity. The correlation between frequency of peer activity and delinquency was smaller when discipline was consistent rather than lax or permissive. When discipline was consistent, delinquency was infrequent whether or not the boy was actively involved in a gang. When discipline was lax, delinquency tended to be more frequent among those with frequent peer activity (Stanfield, 1966:415). These data are not consistent with the hypothesis that the effect of the family operates primarily through peer associations. Type of discipline was more highly correlated with delinquency than level of peer activity, and the association between discipline and delinquency was not affected when level of peer activity was controlled. However, the data appear to be consistent with Proposition 5, that the effect of criminal associations on criminal behavior is less if the family values favor obeying the law.

Stanfield also found that when peer activity was occasional, the association between discipline and delinquency was relatively small (G = .28), while when peer activity was frequent, the comparable association was moderately large (G = .60). Although this relationship does not appear to operate in precisely the way Sutherland and Cressey hypothesized, it is consistent with much of their thinking. The effect of the family appears strongest when peer activity is high, while if adolescents are not heavily involved in a peer group where delinquent patterns may be learned, the family appears somewhat less important.

The second study directly relevant to the model in Figure 24.1 was conducted by Jensen (1972). He analyzed the relationships among paternal supervision, paternal support, association with delinquent friends, perception of "trouble" in the neighborhood, delinquency rate of the area, and delinquent behavior. The sample consisted of 17,500 junior and senior high students from western Contra Costa County in California. Jensen found that the correlations of paternal supervision and support with delinquency were not affected by association with delinquent friends. In addition, the correlations were not affected by perception of trouble in the neighborhood or whether one was living in a high-delinquency area. These findings are clearly contrary to the arguments of Sutherland and Cressey. Parental supervision and support were related to delinquency even among those with definitions that favored obeying the law.

Linden and Hackler (1973) used questionnaire data collected from 200 teenage boys in Seattle to determine how attachments to parents, to conventional peers, and to deviant peers were related to self-reported delinquency. They found that attachments to parents and conventional peers were negatively related to delinquency, while attachments to deviant peers were not associated with delinquent involvement. However, attachment to deviant peers did interact with conventional attachments to affect delinquent involvement. In the absence of ties to conventional peers and adults, ties to deviant peers appeared to be conducive to delinquent involvement.

The fourth study examined the effects of parental and peer associations on marijuana use (Krohn, 1974). The sample consisted of 515 freshmen at the University of Maryland who participated in a summer orientation program. Krohn found that willingness to associate with parents was negatively correlated with amount of association with drug users and with amount of marijuana use, while the latter two variables had a strong positive correlation with each other. When the extent to which one associates with drug users was controlled, the correlation between willingness to associate with parents and marijuana use became negligible. Thus it appears that poor parent-adolescent relationships increase the probability that the adolescent will interact with drug-using peers, which, in turn, increases the likelihood that the adolescent will use marijuana (Krohn, 1974:83). This is consistent with the Sutherland-Cressey model.

Perhaps the best-documented proposition of differential association theory is that association with delinquent peers is positively correlated with delinquent behavior (Jensen, 1972; Krohn, 1974; Reiss and Rhodes, 1964; Short, 1957, 1958; Stanfield, 1966; Voss, 1964). However, Glueck and Glueck (1950:164) maintained that

delinquent behavior determines delinquent associations rather than the reverse as hypothesized by Sutherland. Since existing data are cross-sectional, it is difficult to determine empirically which causal sequence is the more valid. Liska (1969) has used research on attitude formation and attitude change, particularly the work of Newcomb (1943; Newcomb et al., 1967), to evaluate these two conflicting formulations. He found that:

> In social conditions where attitudes have not yet formed, social interaction (particularly with attractive others) results in the formation of similar attitudes. In social conditions where attitudes have formed and interaction is sharply restricted, social interaction (particularly with attractive others) results in attitude change toward similarity. However, in social conditions where attitudes have formed but interaction is not unduly restricted, attitudes also function to direct interaction and attraction towards interaction with and becoming attracted to those who hold similar attitudes [Liska, 1969:492].

Thus Sutherland may be correct when attitudes are not yet formed or social interaction is restricted, while the Glueck hypothesis that delinquent behavior produces association with delinquents may be valid when interaction is not unduly restricted *and* attitudes are formed. The importance of Liska's analysis is that it specifies the conditions under which each process may operate.

Existing research indicates that socialization in slum neighborhoods may restrict interaction (Short and Strodtbeck, 1965). Liska (1969:492) noted that in slum neighborhoods the opportunity for selection of interactive partners may be limited, and therefore it is "plausible to interpret the relationship between delinquent associations and delinquent involvement in terms of the Sutherland causal theory." Krohn's research provides some empirical support for the Sutherland rather than Glueck position:

> The results indicate that 65 percent of those who have used marijuana were introduced to drugs by a good friend and that 14 percent were turned on by a close relative. These data suggest that associations with drug users influenced the respondent's behavior regarding drug use rather than the respondent's drug-taking behavior influencing his choice of friends. This result provides evidence refuting the criticism of differential association theory which was based on the contention that it was behavior which led to association rather than association leading to behavior [Krohn, 1974:82].

On the other hand, Hirschi (1969:159) interpreted his delinquency data in favor of the Glueck position.

The following conclusions may be inferred from the above studies:

1. The type of family interaction appears to have a direct relationship with delinquent behavior rather than operating indirectly through peer associates as suggested by Sutherland and Cressey. However, the family appears to affect drug use indirectly through peer associates as suggested by differential association theory. Apparently supply and learning of proper tech-

niques make drug use more directly dependent on peer associations than other types of delinquent behavior.

2. The level of peer activity conditions the effect of the family on deviant behavior. As the amount of association with peers increases, the effects of the family on delinquency tend to increase.

3. Attachment to the family and values of the family appear to condition the effect of peer group associations on delinquency. The more one is attached to his family, the less the effect of peer group associations on delinquent conduct.

4. Association with delinquent patterns tends to produce delinquent behavior and attitudes, particularly if attitudes and behavior patterns are still in the formation process or interaction is restricted.

5. One tends to choose friends with behavior patterns and attitudes similar to his own if interaction is not unduly restricted and attitudes are already formed.

These findings suggest a number of modifications of differential association theory as set forth by Sutherland and Cressey. Although a simple causal diagram cannot capture the complete essence of these ideas, a revised model is presented in Figure 24.2. The major modifications included in this model are that (1) family variables have a direct influence on criminal behavior, (2) association with criminal patterns interacts with family variables to affect amount of criminal behavior, (3) crim-

inal behavior affects associations as well as the reverse, and (4) the effects of criminal behavior on criminal associations depend upon the extent to which interaction is restricted and the extent to which values and attitudes are definite.

Existing data indicate that attachment to family of orientation and association with criminal patterns are perhaps the two most important antecedent variables in the revised model. It is important to recognize the nature of the interaction between attachment and association: the more one associates with criminal patterns, the more attachment to the family will reduce the probability of criminal involvement; conversely, the greater the attachment to the family, the less the effect of criminal associations on criminal behavior.

A number of criticisms have been leveled against differential association. One of the major criticisms is that it is not precise enough to allow for empirical testing. Differential association theory has also been criticized for not specifying the process by which certain individuals are recruited into the criminal world. Furthermore, the theory does not specify how experiences at different age periods may affect behavior at later times. Finally, the theory ignores the pressures of situational inducements.

In this section an attempt has been made to clarify the theory by identifying and revising several propositions implicit in the formulations of Sutherland and Cressey. The revised formulation requires further clarification,

Figure 24.2. Revised Model of Differential Association

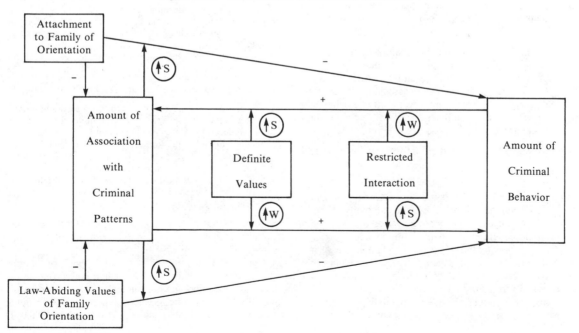

however. For example, the independent variables need more precise definitions, the model needs to be tested with more refined measures, and the dependent variable requires clarification. In this chapter the scope is limited to serious crime, yet the differential association model may be applicable to other types of deviance. On the other hand, some have argued that criminal behavior is sufficiently heterogeneous that theories of specific types of crime are needed (Gibbons, 1973).

In concluding this section the revised version of differential association theory is stated in propositional form. The first three propositions remain as previously stated:

1. The number of criminal patterns one becomes associated with has a positive relationship to the probability of criminal behavior.
2. The amount of attachment to the family of orientation has a negative relationship with the number of criminal patterns one becomes associated with.
3. The more the values of the family of orientation are law-abiding, the less the probability that one will have associations with criminal patterns.

Since it was not confirmed by empirical data that social class was related to association with criminal patterns, this proposition was omitted. The following proposition replaces it:

4. The more the values of the family of orientation are law-abiding, the less the probability of criminal behavior.

Proposition 5 is as stated earlier, while Proposition 6 is a logical derivation of Proposition 5 and is consistent with empirical data:

5. The more law-abiding the values of the family of orientation, the less the probability that associations with criminal patterns will result in criminal behavior.
6. The greater the number of associations with criminal patterns, the stronger the negative relationship between extent to which values of family of orientation are law-abiding and probability of criminal behavior.

Propositions 7 to 10 were inferred from existing empirical data:

7. The greater the attachment to the family of orientation, the less the probability of criminal behavior.
8. The greater the attachment to the family of orientation, the less the probability that associations with criminal patterns will result in criminal behavior.
9. The greater the number of associations with criminal patterns, the stronger the negative relationship between amount of attachment to the family of orientation and probability of criminal behavior.
10. The greater the involvement in criminal behavior patterns, the greater the probability that one will associate with others who exhibit criminal behavior patterns.

The final four propositions specify the relationship between associations with criminal patterns and criminal behavior:

11. The more definite one's values and attitudes, the less the effect of association with criminal patterns on probability of criminal behavior.
12. The more restricted the social interaction, the greater the effect of associations with criminal patterns on criminal behavior.
13. The more definite one's values and attitudes, the greater the probability that criminal involvement will result in association with others who exhibit criminal behavior patterns.
14. The more restricted the social interaction, the less the probability that criminal involvement will result in association with others who exhibit criminal behavior patterns.

SOCIAL CONTROL THEORY

The basic question underlying social control theory is, why do individuals not commit deviant acts? Deviance is taken for granted and it is assumed that conformity must be explained:

> The human infant has no concept of "right" dress, safe driving speeds, moral sex behavior, private property, or any of the other norms of the society, whether custom or law. Conformity, not deviation, must be learned. . . . It is our position, therefore, that in general behavior prescribed as delinquent or criminal need not be explained in any positive sense, since it usually results in quicker and easier achievement of goals than the normative behavior [Nye, 1958:5].

A basic assumption of control theorists is that deviant impulses are experienced by all, not just by the deviant:

> Clinical study reveals that the impulses to steal and murder and rape are universal. Apparently, the difference between the law-abiding adolescent and the hoodlum is not that one has impulses to violate the rules of society while the other does not. Both are tempted to break laws at some time or other—because laws prohibit what circumstance may make attractive: driving an automobile at 80 miles an hour, beating up an enemy, taking what one wants without paying for it [Toby, 1957a:17].

Some of the major proponents of social control theory are Toby (1957a, 1957b), Nye (1958), Matza (1964), Reckless (1973), Hirschi (1969).

Nye (1958) identified four major types of control mechanisms: (1) direct control, which is imposed externally by restriction and punishment; (2) indirect control, which is based on affectional identification with parents and other noncriminal persons; (3) internalized control, which is exercised from within through conscience; and (4) availability of alternative means to goals and values. The family was seen as an important element in all four types of control, and the quality of the parent-child relationship was viewed as critical in the development of both indirect and internalized control. Nye maintained that affectional relationships with parents and others constrain individuals because they want to please those they are attached to and "do not want to embarrass their parents by 'getting into trouble,' and even more often they do not want parents to be hurt by and disappointed in their failure" (1958:6).

Toby also saw the family as a major source of both indirect and direct control. He maintained that the more integrated the family is, the more it will be able to exercise control and insulate its children from antisocial influences. The work of Toby (1957b) illustrates the value of social control theory in understanding the relationship between the family and deviance. Since girls and young children generally receive closer supervision than boys and older children, he maintained that lack of family control will affect girls more than boys and young children more than older children. This differential family control by age and sex of the child helps account for (1) the stronger relationship between broken homes and delinquency among girls and preadolescents, and (2) the disproportionate representation of girls and preadolescents among black and urban delinquents (1957b:512).

Attachment, commitment, involvement, and belief were identified by Hirschi (1969) as four elements that bind a person to society. He maintained that delinquent acts occur because an individual's bond to society is weak or broken. Attachment appears to be the most important element of the bond and refers to affectional ties one has with other individuals. Lack of attachment was seen as a major cause of deviance, while attachment to others, particularly conventional persons, was hypothesized to be a major deterrent to crime.

Reckless (1963) set forth what he called "containment theory" and hypothesized that deviance is a function of an inner control system and an outer control system:

> Inner containment consists mainly of self components, such as self-control, good self-concept, ego strength, well-developed superego, high frustration tolerance, high resistance to diversions, high sense of responsibility, goal orientation, ability to find substitute satisfactions, tension-reducing rationalizations, and so on [1973:55].

Existing empirical data appear generally consistent with the basic tenets of social control theory. Nye (1958) examined a large number of variables regarding parent-adolescent relationships and delinquent behavior and found that almost all were related to delinquent behavior in a manner consistent with social control theory. One particularly important finding was that acceptance of parent and child by each other was related to delinquency.

Mutual acceptance would appear to be an important source of indirect control and may increase the effectiveness of direct control. Discipline that involved partiality, unfairness, or child rejection was ineffective as a direct control and also reduced the effectiveness of indirect and internal controls.

It was reported by Hirschi (1969) that the more a child was attached to and identified with his parents, the lower were his chances of delinquency. He argued that this attachment tends to bind the child to parental expectations and therefore to the norms of the larger system. The data presented by Hirschi on attachment to peers, attachment to school, commitment, involvement, and belief were also generally consistent with social control theory.

A replication of Hirschi's study was conducted by Hindelang (1973) among male and female adolescents in rural upstate New York. His findings were consistent with Hirschi's except that attachment to peers was found to be positively rather than inversely related to delinquency. Hindelang (1973:487) suggested that Hirschi's control theory needs to be reconceptualized to differentiate between attachment to conventional and unconventional peers. This suggestion is consistent with the earlier-cited finding of Linden and Hackler (1973) that delinquency was lowest among those attached to conformist and unattached to deviant peers, while the proportion of delinquents was highest among those who had ties with deviant peers and lacked ties to conventional peers.

Reckless and his associates (Reckless et al., 1956; Reckless et al., 1957; Scarpitti et al., 1960; Scarpitti et al., 1962; Reckless and Dinitz, 1967) conducted a study of boys in high-delinquency areas to test the extent to which inner containment can predict delinquency. Sixth-grade teachers identified two groups of boys, those they felt would never experience police contact (insulated) and those they felt were headed for trouble with the law (vulnerable). After a four-year period the insulated boys, compared to the vulnerable boys, were substantially lower on official and self-reported delinquency and had more positive self-concepts. Reckless and his associates concluded that a favorable self-concept acts "as an inner buffer or inner containment against deviancy, distraction, lure, and pressures," while a poor self-concept is "indicative of weak inner direction (self or ego), which in turn does not deflect the boy from bad companions and street corner society" (Scarpitti et al., 1962:517). In addition, they found that the insulated boys were remarkably high on social responsibility and perceived their family interaction as very favorable:

> There appeared to be close supervision of the boys' activities and associates, an intense parental interest in the welfare of the children, and a desire to indoctrinate them with nondeviant attitudes and patterns. This parental supervision and interest seemed to be the outstanding characteristic of the family profiles [Reckless et al., 1956:745].

One of the problems with the research by Reckless and associates is that their use of "self-concept" was broad and somewhat ambiguous (Schwartz and Tangri, 1965). It appears that many of the items used by Reckless and his associates to measure self-concept might more appropriately be considered measures of attachment to parents and stake in conformity. There is also some question as to why a person with a poor self-concept should be more vulnerable to delinquency (Tangri and Schwartz, 1967). But while their use of self-concept has ambiguities, their findings are consistent with the work of Nye (1958), Hirschi (1969), and others and suggest that attachment to parents may have a direct effect on delinquency.

There have been a number of other studies which have reported data consistent with the social control perspective. Reiss (1951) found that the strength of an individual's inner controls was significantly related to delinquent recidivism. It was reported by Deitz (1969) that delinquents compared to nondelinquents were less self-accepting and identified less with their parents, particularly the father. In a comparison of delinquent and non-delinquent girls Riege (1972) reported that nondelinquents were more satisfied with the affective roles of both parents. The delinquent girls reported a greater need to share time with their parents and to have more strictness in the home. Their home situations were also perceived as less positive, and they felt that they did not resemble their parents. Giannell (1970) found that offenders tended to have fewer internal inhibitions than nonoffenders.

Delinquents were found by Zucker (1943) to have a faulty superego. He compared 25 delinquents with 25 nondelinquents who were matched on socioeconomic status and IQ. The delinquents had much poorer affectional relationships with their parents and reported a greater need for closer association with their parents. Those with weak attachment to parents tended to exercise less restraint, and the lower the affection, the greater the tendency for the adolescent to retaliate.

Several social psychological studies complement the delinquency research on social control. A positive relationship was found between the attraction an individual had for a group and the control the group exercised over the individual (Back, 1951; Cartwright, 1951; Festinger et al., 1950; Newcomb, 1953).

Four concepts have been central to the various formulations of social control theory: (1) indirect control, (2) stake in conformity, (3) direct control, (4) internal control. Indirect control is based primarily on affectional attachment to parents and other noncriminal persons (Nye, 1958:5; Hirschi, 1969). Stake in conformity (Toby, 1957a; Hirschi, 1969) is similar to indirect control in that it is based on investment in and attachment to conventional persons and groups. "Indirect control" appears to be the more common term and will be used subsequently in this chapter.

Direct controls are explicit, external restrictions that are placed on an individual. These may be formal laws which proscribe certain kinds of behavior, such as homicide laws, or informal rules such as those parents place upon their children regarding fighting, staying out late, or stealing. Direct controls may be enforced by punishments for violations and/or rewards for conformity.

It appears that the effectiveness of direct controls may depend upon one's attachment to parents and others. Rules may be imposed but may be violated freely if there is no attachment between the individual and his parents. On the other hand, a child that is strongly attached to his parents will, up to a point, obey their rules as well as societal rules because of the attachment. The research by Nye (1958) indicated that as direct control becomes excessive or harsh, the probability of delinquency increases.

Internal control is the conscience an individual has which directs his behavior. If rules are internalized, they become part of an individual so that they are obeyed not because violation is illegal, but because it is right. For example, an individual will not steal if he feels honesty is morally right, regardless of the legal or parental rules regarding theft. Thus if a rule is internalized, external control is unnecessary. In this case one's conscience guides his behavior, and the existence of law prohibiting a behavior is secondary. However, it would appear that internal control is partly a function of direct controls. Over time certain external rules may gradually become a part of oneself, and therefore the external rules may no longer be necessary for that individual. Thus internal control may weaken the relationship between direct control and criminal behavior; the greater an individual's internal control, the less effect external controls will have on the probability of his becoming involved in criminal behavior.

These concepts have been placed in the causal diagram shown in Figure 24.3. This diagram appears generally consistent with the research reviewed earlier and integrates several major concepts of social control theory. An attempt is now made to further clarify these concepts and apply them to the family.

As noted earlier, indirect control is based primarily on attachment to parents and other conventional persons. It has been found that attachment to parents is particularly important and may be viewed as separate from attachment to other conventional persons (Nye, 1958; Hirschi, 1969). Therefore it seemed fruitful to conceptualize indirect control as two distinct elements, attachment to parents and attachment to other conventional persons. It would appear that attachment to parents influences the amount of attachment to other conventional persons.

The variable "amount of direct control" is conceived as a continuous variable that ranges from a very small to an extremely large amount. It also includes elements of fairness, harshness, and consistency. In the middle range

Figure 24.3. A Causal Diagram of Social Control Theory

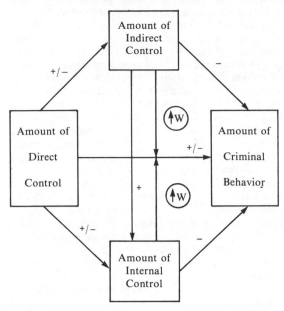

these two elements are sufficiently correlated to be included as one variable. Parental control appears to be a major aspect of external control (Nye, 1958; Reckless et al., 1956) and is identified here as à distinct variable. Parental control that is consistent, fair, and moderate appears to increase the internalization of law-abiding values.

From existing literature it seems useful to divide internalized control into ''self-concept'' and ''law-abiding values.'' Reckless and his colleagues (Reckless et al., 1956; Reckless et al., 1957) have found that a positive self-concept is important in constraining criminal inclinations. It may be inferred from the research of Nye (1958), Hirschi (1969), and Reckless et al. (1956) that the probability of acquiring law-abiding values is greater when attachment to parents is considerable, and when parents are interested in their children's activities and supervise them rather closely. A causal model integrating these concepts is presented in Figure 24.4. This model identifies specific familial variables that have been found to affect the probability of criminal involvement. This model may be stated in propositional form as follows:

15. As parental control increases from a small to a moderately strong level, the amount of attachment to parents will tend to increase; as parental control increases beyond a moderately strong level, the amount of attachment to parents will tend to decrease.

16. As parental control increases from a small to a moderately strong level, the amount of attachment to other conventional persons will tend to increase; as

of this variable it is assumed that respondents will perceive direct control to be less harsh, more consistent, and more just than if control is extremely lax or excessive. Although some might argue that amount and type of control should be differentiated, it is assumed here that

Figure 24.4. Empirical Model of Social Control Theory

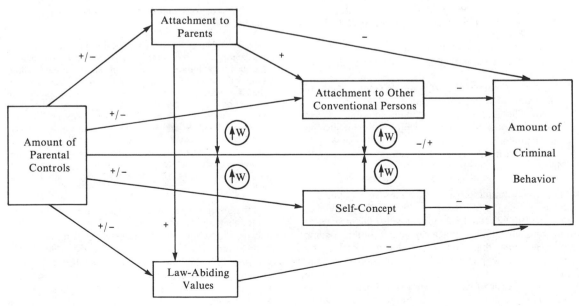

parental control increases beyond a moderately strong level, the amount of attachment to other conventional persons will tend to decrease.

17. As parental control increases from a small to a moderately strong level, criminal involvement will tend to decrease; as parental control increases beyond a moderately strong level, the probability of criminal involvement will tend to increase.

18. The greater the attachment to parents, the weaker the relationship between amount of parental control and criminal behavior.

19. The greater the attachment to other conventional persons, the weaker the relationship between amount of parental control and criminal behavior.

20. The more law-abiding one's values, the weaker the relationship between amount of parental control and criminal behavior.

21. The higher one's self-concept, the weaker the relationship between amount of parental control and criminal behavior.

22. As parental control increases from a small to a moderately strong level, the self-concept will tend to become more positive; as parental control increases beyond a moderately strong level, self-concept will tend to become less positive.

23. As the parental control increases from a small to a moderately strong level, the extent to which one internalizes law-abiding values will tend to increase; as parental control increases beyond a moderately strong level, the extent to which one internalizes law-abiding values will tend to decrease.

24. The greater the attachment to parents, the lower the probability of involvement in criminal behavior.

25. The greater the attachment to parents, the greater the probability that one will become attached to other conventional persons.

26. The greater the attachment to parents, the greater the probability that one will internalize law-abiding values.

27. The more law-abiding one's values, the lower the probability of criminal involvement.

28. The greater the attachment to other conventional persons, the lower the probability of criminal involvement.

29. The higher one's self-concept, the lower the probability of criminal involvement.

The major limitation of social control theory appears to be the assumption of "natural motivation" for deviance. Hirschi (1969:230) noted in his study that the miscalculations of control theory appear to stem from this assumption. He found that, contrary to a pure social control theory, group support did affect the likelihood of delinquency. He suggested two solutions to this problem. First, some ideas of group processes and their effects on individuals must be included in the theory. Second, he

indicated that delinquency may do something for an individual such as contribute to his self-esteem. The ideas of Reckless and his associates (Reckless and Dinitz, 1967) appear useful in this context. Individuals with adequate self-concepts may not need to join deviant groups or break rules to gain attention and esteem, while this is one possible motivation for criminal involvement among individuals with poor self-concepts. The model in Figure 24.4 incorporates self-concept as a variable and thus overcomes this limitation to some extent.

The work of Gold (1963) is one attempt to integrate group process and social control ideas. He maintained that delinquency results from two forces, lack of control and provocation. His data are consistent with other research in showing that delinquency is higher among those less attached to their parents and schools. Gold emphasized that weakened controls do not necessarily increase violation of legal norms. He proposed that the motivation comes from status deprivation, which provokes unattached boys to commit deviant acts. A low self-concept may be considered one type of status deprivation.

To date the work of Briar and Piliavin (1965) is perhaps the most defensible integration of group process ideas with social control theory. They hypothesized that delinquency is the product of commitments to conformity and situationally induced motives to deviate (45). Like Toby (1957a) and Hirschi (1969), Briar and Piliavin indicated that the stake one has in conformity restrains deviant impulses. Attachment to parents was hypothesized to be the most important element in the development of conformity commitments. They stated further that often delinquency appears to be the result of inducements in particular situations rather than any inherent motivation or pathology.

> Because delinquent behavior is typically episodic, purposive, and confined to certain situations, we assume that the motives for such behavior are frequently episodic, oriented to short-term ends, and confined to certain situations. That is, rather than considering delinquent acts as solely the product of long-term motives deriving from conflicts or frustrations whose genesis is far removed from the arenas in which the illegal behavior occurs, we assume these acts are promoted by short-term situationally induced desires experienced by all boys to obtain valued goods, to portray courage in the presence of, or be loyal to peers, to strike out at someone who is disliked, or simply to "get kicks" [Briar and Piliavin, 1965:36].

Thus the group is seen as an inducer toward delinquency in certain situations but is not assumed to be an intimate or cohesive unit within which extensive learning of deviant attitudes and skills takes place.

In summary, the basic position of social control theory has received consistent, empirical support. The stronger one's attachment to conventional persons and groups, particuarly the family, the less likely one will commit deviant acts. The absence of attachment increases the probability of crime regardless of the presence of group support for deviance. However, contrary to a pure social control theory, group support and inducement appear to affect the likelihood of delinquency. Nevertheless, the view of differential association theory that crime must be taught in intimate, personal groups greatly overstates the case (Hirschi, 1969:229). A propositional model was developed which integrated and clarified the major concepts of social control theory and applied them to the family. There are some similarities between the social control model developed here and the revised model of differential association presented in the previous section. An attempt to integrate these two models will be made later in this chapter.

ANOMIE THEORY

Anomie theory is based on the idea that a strain resulting from the inability to reach legitimate desires produces deviance. When one is not able to obtain what he feels he deserves, he becomes frustrated and turns to illegitimate means to achieve the desired end. It is assumed that individuals are reasonably well socialized, and an explanation for their deviant acts is sought.

One of the first to develop the concept of anomie was Emile Durkheim (1951). He maintained that suicide rates would increase during a period of depression or increased prosperity because in both situations the normative order would be disrupted, leaving a state of normlessness or anomie. During a period of increased prosperity social norms which restrain aspirations were hypothesized to be weakened, resulting in unrealistically high aspirations. The disappointment resulting from these unattainable goals was assumed to produce increases in suicide. Similarly, a sudden depression makes existing expectations unattainable and the resulting strain will be manifested in rising suicide rates, according to Durkheim.

Undoubtedly the most prominent anomie theorist is Robert Merton, who developed a general explanation of deviant behavior using the concept of anomie (Merton, 1938, 1968). Crucial to his formulation was a distinction between culturally defined goals, and norms which define and regulate the acceptable means for achieving these goals. Anomie was defined as a disjuncture between goals and means, a strain which exerted pressure toward deviant behavior. Merton identified four possible ways of adapting to the strain of anomie: (1) innovation, (2) ritualism, (3) retreatism, and (4) rebellion. Innovation occurs when cultural goals are accepted but illegitimate means are used to achieve the goals. In ritualism the legitimate means are accepted but the cultural goals are rejected; i.e., the means become the end. A rejection of both means and goals is termed retreatism. Finally, rebellion is the rejection of existing goals and means and the substitution of a new set of goals and means. Rebellion involves attempts to *change* the existing social order rather than to perform accommodative actions *within* this structure (Merton, 1938:675). Innovation appears to be the most common response to the strain of anomie.

According to Merton, American society has two basic conditions which create anomie. First, certain success goals are given much more emphasis than the means for achieving the goals. Merton acknowledged that wealth does not stand alone as a symbol of success but asserted that it does occupy a high place in our value system. The second condition which induces anomie is the restriction among certain groups of the legitimate means of attaining success.

In summary, Merton hypothesized that deviance is caused by a gap between cultural goals and means institutionalized for achievement of the goals. In this perspective the force toward deviance is strain which results from the place one occupies in the social structure. This perspective assumes that there is nothing peculiar or pathological about an individual deviant and that he does not necessarily need to be treated or changed. The deviant is assumed to be a normal individual who responded normally to the strain of the particular position he occupies. It is the social structure that may be pathological, and it is this toward which programs and treatments should be directed. Underlying the entire anomie perspective is the hypothesis that deviance is directly related to class. Anomie is assumed to be greater in the lower class, since it is there that legitimate opportunities appear to be restricted. It is also assumed that socialization is relatively effective, that individuals will conform unless strain induces them to violate rules.

Although anomie theorists have said relatively little about the family, they acknowledge that it plays a crucial role in the development of anomie:

> It is the family, of course, which is a major transmission belt for the diffusion of cultural standards to the oncoming generation. But what has until lately been overlooked is that the family largely transmits that portion of the culture accessible to the social stratum and groups in which the parents find themselves [Merton, 1957:158].

Anomie is a class-based theory, and "it is the *family,* not merely the individual, that is ranked in the class structure. The family is the keystone of the stratification system, the social mechanism by which it is maintained" (Goode, 1964:80).

Merton has noted that the projection of parental ambitions onto the child is one specific way in which family interaction may create anomie:

> In a recent research on the social organization of public housing developments, we found among both Negroes and Whites on lower occupational levels, a substantial proportion having aspirations for a professional career for their children. Should this finding be confirmed by further research it will

have large bearing upon the problems in hand. For if compensatory projection of parental ambition onto children is widespread, then it is precisely those parents least able to provide free access to opportunity for their children—the ''failures'' and ''frustrates''—who exert great pressure upon their children for high achievement. And this syndrome of lofty aspirations and limited realistic opportunities, as we have seen, is precisely the pattern which invites deviant behavior [1957:159].

Perhaps the major limitation of anomie theory is that it does not explain why one type of adaptation to the strain occurs rather than another. Given that a disjuncture between goals and means exists, why does one adapt to that strain by innovation rather than ritualism? A related criticism is, why do some individuals who are under a strain conform while others deviate? In fact, one might argue that the most frequent adaptation to the strain of anomie is conformity. The process by which adaptation to anomie strain occurs has not been clearly spelled out. A third limitation of anomie is that deviance is conceived too much as an outcome rather than a process that occurs as a result of interaction with others (Cohen, 1965; Short, 1964). Finally, anomie theory has been criticized for being too general. The assumption that there is a general success value in American society appears untenable (Clinard, 1964:55).

Empirical data have generally not been consistent with hypotheses derived from anomie theory. A major piece of disconfirming evidence is that social class has not been found to be associated with criminal behavior (Akers, 1964; Clinard, 1952; Dentler and Monroe, 1961; Geis, 1974a, 1974b; Hirschi, 1969; Nye, 1958; Nye et al., 1958; Sutherland, 1949; Stinchcombe, 1964; Winslow, 1968). In addition, aspirations do not appear to be related to deviance as anomie theory implies. For example, Short (1964:115) noted that high educational and occupational aspirations do not pressure boys toward deviance. Similarly, Hirschi (1969:227) found that ambition reduces the chance of crime. In general, source of strain has not been found to be related to criminal or deviant behavior, and this indicates that the concept of strain is unnecessary.

Cloward and Ohlin (1960) extended Merton's anomie theory in an attempt to explain why strain results in one form of deviance rather than another. They maintained that the particular adaptation to strain will depend on the availability of illegitimate means. Opportunities for learning deviant roles may vary according to type of area and group. Their work was an attempt to integrate anomie theory and differential association theory. In essence, they stated that anomie produces the strain toward deviance while the particular way one adapts to this strain depends upon differential opportunity. Assuming that opportunity was provided by existing social organization, Cloward and Ohlin (1960) hypothesized that there would be three major types of delinquent subcultures: criminal, conflict, and retreatist.

The formulation of Cloward and Ohlin is an interesting, creative extension of anomie theory. Particularly valuable is the integration of anomie theory with differential association and the specification of why deviance takes one form rather than another. Nevertheless, many of the limitations of anomie theory remain in Cloward and Ohlin's opportunity theory. It is still a class-based theory, and the pressures toward deviance need greater specification. Empirical studies have failed to identify subcultures of the type hypothesized by Cloward and Ohlin and suggest that greater attention be given to ongoing group processes and to competence in interpersonal relations (Short, 1964).

Winslow (1968) examined anomie theory within the context of the adolescent social system rather than within the society as a whole. He attempted to apply anomie to a situation more immediate to adolescents as Short (1964:116) suggested. Winslow predicted that juvenile delinquency would vary inversely with position in the adolescent system: the lower one's position within the youth system, the greater the inclination to select illegitimate means. He also expected that on the broader societal level anomie theory would not be supported by his data. The data were generally consistent with Winslow's expectations. Those in the lowest level of the adolescent system had higher delinquency rates than members of the middle and upper levels of the adolescent system. It appeared that individuals in the lowest status attempted to obtain interpersonal and status rewards through illegitimate means. The data were not consistent with general anomie theory as applied to the society as a whole. Parental success pressures were less when the parents were in the lower class, indicating that success aspirations were not similar across social strata as hypothesized in traditional anomie theory. Perceived opportunities did not vary by parental socioeconomic status. Finally, no relationship was found between parental socioeconomic status and delinquency, indicating that serious delinquency in the middle class was more prevalent than predicted by Merton (1938).

An attempt to apply anomie to the family system was made by Jaffe (1963). Lack of value consensus was conceived as the primary component of family anomie. It was hypothesized that a state of confusion and normlessness, i.e., anomie, existed within a family when a consensus on values did not exist. Jaffe maintained (1963: 147) that ''family anomie helps explain the malfunctioning of individual controls and delinquency proneness. Where there is evidence of family value confusion and ambiguity, the youngster is often forced to find his way by a process of trial and error. . . .''

Jaffe (1963) found that a lack of value consensus within the family had a significant, positive correlation with delinquency proneness. In addition, several objective factors (a poor marriage, crowding, low income, employment change, and illness) were correlated with high value confusion. Ambivalent parental identification and powerlessness appeared to result from lack of value consensus. Jaffe concluded that family anomie was a fruitful concept for predicting delinquency proneness.

It may be useful to identify and clarify the major concepts in Jaffe's application of anomie theory to the family. The central independent variable was value consensus within the family. This is a continuous variable in which low scores indicate dissensus and high scores consensus. Value consensus appeared to be the degree to which family members, particularly the parents, were unified on important attitudes and standards.

Jaffe hypothesized that parental identification and feelings of powerlessness were both affected by the degree of value consensus. Parental identification was the degree to which children were attached to their parents and desired to be like them. The concept of powerlessness apparently referred to feelings of competence and the perceived ability to control one's life situation. At one extreme (high powerlessness) are individuals who feel that they have little or no control over situations that confront them. At the other extreme (low powerlessness) are individuals who feel that they have the ability to control their life. Jaffe used delinquency proneness as his dependent variable. In the present context this has been changed to amount of criminal behavior. A causal diagram of Jaffe's theory of family anomie is presented in Figure 24.5. The five propositions in this model are as follows:

30. The greater the amount of value consensus within the family, the greater the amount of parental identification.
31. The greater the amount of value consensus within the family, the fewer the feelings of powerlessness.

Figure 24.5. A Diagram of Jaffe's Theory of Family Anomie

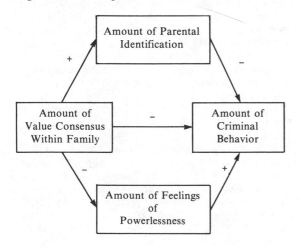

32. The greater the amount of parental identification, the lower the probability of criminal involvement.
33. The greater the amount of value consensus within the family, the lower the probability of criminal behavior.
34. The greater the feelings of powerlessness, the greater the probability of criminal involvement.

In summary, according to anomie theory a strain is produced by a disjuncture between goals and means. Crime and deviance are the results of attempts to adapt to the strain. Anomie theory has sensitized us to the importance of social structure as a cause of crime and deviance since it does not assume that individual deviants are pathological. However, empirical data have consistently not supported a number of basic propositions of Merton's theory of anomie. Perhaps one of the most useful criticisms of anomie theory is Short's (1964) suggestion that the concept of social structure be broadened to include situations more immediate to individuals. The works of Winslow (1968) and Jaffe (1963) are two attempts to apply anomie theory to more specific contexts. Although both of these studies have limitations, the data are generally consistent with expectations and suggest a direction for future theorizing and research within the anomie perspective. The work of Jaffe appeared particularly useful because it applied anomie theory to the family. A comparison of Jaffe's theory to the other theories will be made later in this chapter.

PSYCHOANALYTIC THEORY

There is no question that psychoanalytic theory has been a very influential perspective in the field of deviant behavior. Although psychoanalytic theory has taken a variety of forms, a few basic assumptions characterize most of the writings within this perspective. It is a control theory in which all individuals are assumed to be born with primitive urges or drives that are aggressive, destructive, and antisocial. Children are assumed to be "criminal" and unadjusted at birth, and thus no other motivation for deviance is required. The basic task of socialization is to develop a superego, which is a shell of inhibition, a set of internalized controls. Deviance is hypothesized to be the result of defects in the superego. Psychoanalytic theory clearly assumes that deviance is the result of individual pathology. One commits deviant acts because there is something wrong with him, and treatment of the individual is called for.

Family life is central to psychoanalytic theory, for it is believed that the superego develops during the early socialization within the family. Although there is no reasonably complete list of reasons for inadequate superego development, two factors stand out in the psychoanalytic literature: (1) lack of parental affection and support; (2) lax and inconsistent discipline (Bandura and Walters, 1959; Cohen, 1966:56; Schoenfeld, 1971). According to psychoanalytic writers, affection and support provide the basis for identification with parents, which includes the internalization of the moral standards of the parents (Cohen, 1966:56). It is said that the child internalizes (introjects) the image he has formed of his parents and that this image becomes his superego (Schoenfeld, 1971). Discipline that is lax and inconsistent is considered to be a cause of an erratic and inconsistent superego which cannot prevent primitive impulses from finding their expression in criminal conduct (Schoenfeld, 1971:476). Early childhood is assumed to be the critical time period in personality development, and criminal behavior in later life is linked to events during this period.

These ideas have been placed in a simple causal diagram in Figure 24.6. Although this diagram does not capture many elements of psychoanalytic theory, it explicates a theme that pervades the psychoanalytic literature. Personality dysfunction (i.e., a faulty superego of some type) is seen as the cause of deviance. Early childhood experiences are viewed as the cause of the personality dysfunction, and lack of parental affection and/or inconsistent discipline are two specific things that may occur in early childhood to produce the personality dysfunction.

In evaluating psychoanalytic theory generally, and the model in Figure 24.6 specifically, four limitations appear particularly important. First, a basic assumption of psychoanalytic theory is that deviants are pathological, that they have faulty personalities. Empirical data do not appear to be consistent with this assumption (Schuessler and Cressey, 1950; Waldo and Dinitz, 1967). When one considers that (a) the extent of crime among respectable "nonoffenders" is large (Geis, 1974a, 1974b; Leonard and Weber, 1970; Magnuson and Carper, 1968), (b) professional criminals generally have little contact with law enforcement and correctional agencies (Gibbons, 1973:264), and (c) personality measures often have a middle-class conventional bias; therefore, the validity of the assumption that crime and other deviance is the result of personality pathology is questionable.

Second, many of the specific hypotheses derivable from psychoanalytic theory are not unique to the theory. For example, a negative association between parental affection and delinquency is also derivable from social control theory.

Third, in psychoanalytic theory personality differences are assumed to be temporally antecedent to deviant behavior, and consequently psychoanalytic theorists have not even considered the possible influence of deviant behavior on personality. If negative personality characteristics result from commission of deviant acts and/or from apprehension and labeling of the deviant, psychoanalytic theory does not address the question it is designed to answer.

Finally, there is often a problem of tautology between the antisocial impulses and the deviant behavior they supposedly explain:

> For example, aggressive or acquisitive acts are often explained by underlying aggressive or acquisitive impulses. The evidence for these impulses, the grounds upon which they are imputed, turns out to be the aggressive or acquisitive act to be explained. This is akin to explaining fatigue by "exhaustion" [Cohen, 1966:61].

Numerous empirical studies have found various aspects of the family environment to be related to deviance, particularly to delinquency (Rodman and Grams, 1967). Many of these findings, which were reviewed earlier, are consistent with the psychoanalytic perspective, particularly those that have found parental affection and type of discipline to be related to deviance (Deitz, 1969; Fodor, 1972; Giannell, 1970; Hirschi, 1969; Nye, 1958; Reckless et al., 1956; Riege, 1972; Tec, 1970; Zucker, 1943). However, these findings are also consistent with other theoretical perspectives, particularly with social control theory. Furthermore, these data do not provide support for basic assumptions of psychoanalytic theory such as the assumption that man is born antisocial or that superego development is linked to Freud's psychosexual stages (Schoenfeld, 1971). Unless a closer correspondence between these assumptions and empirical findings is demonstrated, the principle of parsimony suggests that social control theory be accepted rather than psychoanalytic theory.

The model in Figure 24.6 is similar in some respects to the social control model presented earlier. A major difference between the two is the concept of superego. Perhaps the assumption of personality pathology in the psychoanalytic model can be overcome by replacing the concept of "superego" with "internalization of law-abiding values." The latter concept performs a similar function but does not assume personality malfunction. Although this modification may do violence to basic psychoanalytic assumptions, it appears necessary to make the psychoanalytic model consistent with existing re-

Figure 24.6. A Model Derived from Psychoanalytic Theory

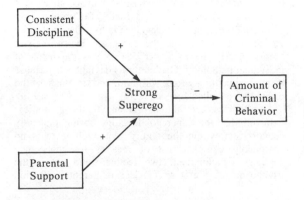

search. This revised model includes concepts similar to those included in the social control model. It is diagrammed in Figure 24.7 and may be stated in propositional form as follows:

35. The more consistent the discipline of parents, the greater the internalization of law-abiding values.
36. The greater the level of parental support, the greater the internalization of law-abiding values.
37. The greater the internalization of law-abiding values, the lower the amount of criminal behavior.

DETERRENCE THEORY

The basic postulate of deterrence theory is that negative sanctions produce conformity to norms. Until recently the prevailing thought in criminological writing was that punishment does not deter crime (Morris and Hawkins, 1969; Reckless and Dinitz, 1967; Tannenbaum, 1951). This position was supported by research which found that homicide rates were not lower in areas that had the death penalty compared to areas without the death penality (Schuessler, 1952; Sellin, 1967; Walker, 1965; Mattick, 1963). Studies of corporal punishment (Caldwell, 1944) and recidivism rates also appeared inconsistent with the deterrence position (Morris, 1951; Tittle and Logan, 1973:372). However, more recent research suggests that deterrence theory was dismissed prematurely. In a review of existing literature Tittle and Logan (1973) noted that (1) the research on capital punishment had a number of logical and methodological deficiencies, (2) data to adequately test the deterrence question are not available, (3) the available data are less contrary to deterrence theory than is usually assumed, and (4) deterrence theory has often been viewed in a simplistic way. They concluded:

Almost all research since 1960 supports the view that negative sanctions are significant variables in the explanation of con-

formity and deviance. Therefore social scientists would appear to be on firm ground in at least treating the issue of deterrence as an open question. . . . It is clear, however, that the evidence is not conclusive. At this point we can safely say only that sanctions have some deterrent effect under some circumstances. It is now necessary to undertake careful research in an attempt to specify the conditions under which sanctions are likely to be important influences on behavior [1973:384].

In a recent book Gibbs (1975) illustrated the complexity of the deterrence issue. First, he distinguished between marginal and absolute deterrence. Absolute deterrence is determined by a comparision of a situation in which the behavior under question is not punished and a situation in which it is punished. There have been no studies of this type of deterrence, although studies of this type could be conducted in families and other small groups. Marginal deterrence is a comparison of the effects of two penalties of differing strength on behavior. Second, Gibbs (1975) noted that deterrence may be specific or general. Specific deterrence is the effect of punishment on those who have broken a rule: does punishment decrease the probability that one will commit an offense a second time? General deterrence is the impact the punishment of an offender has on nonoffenders. Recent work on vicarious reinforcement suggests that general deterrence may have a significant impact on conformity and deviance (Bandura, 1969: 118–216). The different types of deterrence do not necessarily operate in the same direction. For example, it is logically possible that punishment increases deviance for those punished while decreasing deviance for those not punished (Tittle, 1969; Tittle and Logan, 1973).

Deterrence theory is complicated further by the variety of ways punishment may be applied. Various combinations of severity and certainty of punishment exist. In addition, there is the question of perceived and objective severity and certainty of punishment. Finally, there are a variety of ways in which deviance may be reduced or increased that have nothing to do with deterrence (Gibbs, 1975). These factors need to be controlled in studies of deterrence to ensure that the results are due to the negative sanctions and not other uncontrolled variables.

The basic proposition of deterrence theory is that crime is negatively associated with certainty and severity of punishment. In recent research it was found that certainty of punishment was related to crime independent of severity of punishment (Tittle, 1969; Erickson and Gibbs, 1973). The relation between severity of punishment and crime was the more certain the punishment, the greater the association between severity of punishment and criminal involvement (Erickson and Gibbs, 1973).

Recently economists have brought their version of deterrence theory into the field of crime and deviance. This recent thrust began with Becker's (1968) article "Crime and Punishment: An Economic Approach." Becker maintained that criminals are not sick, abnormal,

Figure 24.7.   Revised Psychoanalytic Model

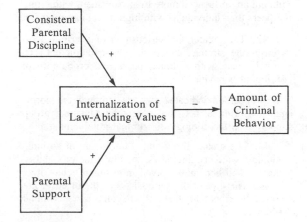

or deprived and that theories of anomie or psychological inadequacies are not necessary. Criminals are seen as relatively simple, normal people like the rest of us, and it is hypothesized that their behavior can be explained by simply extending the economist's usual analysis of choice. Sullivan's comments (1973:139–40) are representative of this school of thought:

> Traditional explanations of criminality have applied the concepts of depravity, insanity, deviance, abnormality, and deprivation. Economists maintain that criminals are rational and normally calculating people maximizing their preferences subject to given constraints.... Since criminals calculate costs and benefits, the economist concludes that we must increase the cost to them by increasing the probability that they will be caught or by increasing the punishment if they are caught.

A recent economic analysis by Votey and Phillips (1974) supported the position that crime can be deterred by making it more costly. They maintained that law enforcement has a strong deterrent effect even for offenses like homicide where emotion and irrationality appear high (Gibbs, 1968; Phillips et al., 1971).

Despite its potential, the economic model of crime has a number of limitations. First, many of its adherents' insights and conclusions are not new but simply restatements of existing knowledge. For example, Becker (1968) claimed that we do not need anomie, but the one major conclusion of recent economic analyses is that crime is related to economic opportunities, a conclusion anomie theorists made years ago (Merton, 1938; Cloward and Ohlin, 1960). Second, the economic analyses are based on global statistics. Ignored are crimes not included in the statistics, the biases of official statistics, and the general complexity and diversity of crime and criminal statistics. Third, the economic model has a class bias similar to anomie theory, since it focuses on the explanation of official rates. Fourth, although it could be extended to the micro level, analyses have been primarily at a broad macro level only. Fifth, the recent economic theories of crime appear to be historically naive. Their models are based on relatively small time periods and ignore the facts that (1) during the 1930s crime rates decreased contrary to their model and (2) delinquency and crime appear to be increasing among the affluent. Finally, the recent economic models of crime have not taken into account crucial social variables such as one's reference group. For example, it may be relative economic status (Easterlin, 1973) or relative deprivation that is important in explaining crime, yet this type of analysis has not been conducted in the criminal area.

The task now for deterrence theorists is to develop and test models that take into account the complexities of the deterrence question. One recent attempt to develop a general theory of deterrence was made by Silberman (1976). He examined the relationships among certainty of punishment, severity of punishment, involvement with criminal peers, moral commitment, and criminal involvement. An integrated set of propositions were developed from his empirical findings. His propositions have been revised slightly, integrated with other deterrence research (Erickson and Gibbs, 1973), and placed in the causal model shown in Figure 24.8. This model includes two major additions to the propositions set forth by Silberman (1976). First, research by Erickson and Gibbs (1973) suggested that the effects of severity of punishment depend on the level of certainty of punishment. Second, the normative variable "seriousness of offense" was included because it appears to affect individual decisions regarding criminal involvement. Silberman did not include this variable in his analysis at the individual level. The value of this model is that it integrates the basic deterrence hypothesis with other relevant variables and specifies the conditions under which certainty and severity of punishment affect criminal involvement.

This model may be stated in propositional form:

38. The greater the association with peers who have committed a criminal offense, the greater the perceived severity of punishment for criminal offenses.
39. The greater the moral commitment of an individual toward criminal laws, the less likely he will associate with peers who have committed criminal offenses.

This proposition asserts that "individuals who believe that commiting certain offenses is morally wrong are relatively unlikely to associate with those who commit these offenses" (Silberman, 1976:458).

40. The greater the degree of involvement with peers who have committed criminal offenses, the greater the probability of criminal involvement.
41. The lower the moral commitment of an individual toward criminal laws, the stronger the positive relationship between involvement with criminal peers and probability of criminal involvement.

This proposition asserts that those with low moral commitment are influenced more by involvement with criminal peers than individuals with high moral commitment.

42. The greater the seriousness of a criminal offense, the stronger the postive association between involvement with criminal peers and probability of criminal behavior.

This proposition indicates that the stronger the norms against a criminal act, the more important peer group support is in the etiology of criminal involvement.

43. The greater the moral commitment of an individual toward criminal laws, the lower the probability that he will become involved in criminal behavior.
44. The greater the seriousness of the offense, the lower the probability that one will commit that criminal offense.

Figure 24.8. A Deterrence Model of Crime

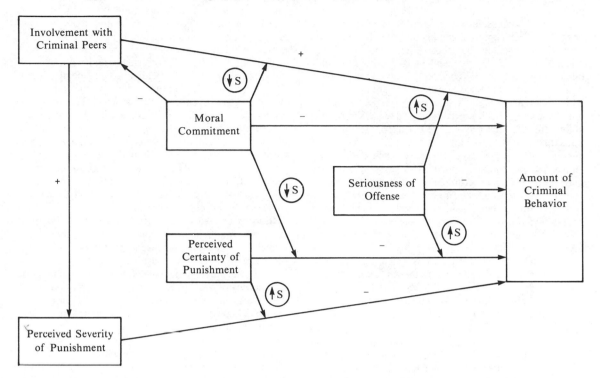

45. The greater the perceived certainty of punishment, the lower the probability of criminal involvement.

46. The lower the moral commitment of an individual toward criminal laws, the stronger the negative relationship between perceived certainty of punishment and probability of criminal involvement.

47. The greater the seriousness of a criminal offense, the stronger the negative relationship between perceived certainty of punishment and probability of criminal involvement.

48. The greater the perceived severity of punishment, the lower the probability of criminal involvement.

49. The greater the perceived certainty of punishment, the stronger the negative relationship between perceived severity of punishment and probability of criminal involvement.

LABELING THEORY

The final theoretical framework considered here is labeling theory. Tannenbaum (1951) was one of the first to present the basic ideas of labeling theory, while other important labeling theorists are Lemert (1951), Erikson (1962), Kitsuse (1962), Becker (1963), and Schur (1971). This framework focuses upon the process and effects of defining individuals as deviants, i.e., how individuals become labeled deviants and how this affects their self-concept and the probability that they will commit deviant acts in the future. Labeling theory is an interactionist theory of deviance (Becker, 1974) that builds upon the social psychology of George Herbert Mead (1934) and Charles Horton Cooley (1902). The basic postulate is that one's definition of himself depends upon the reactions of others, that one's self-concept and behavior are influenced significantly by the way one is characterized and labeled by others. This key idea has been applied to rule formation and violation, particularly within the context of a formal system of criminal justice, and developed into what is known today as labeling theory. The major assertions of this framework may be summarized as follows (Schrag, 1974:707–11; Wellford, 1975):

1. No act is intrinsically deviant, but deviance is defined and sanctioned by the powerful.

2. A person does not become a deviant or criminal by violating the law, but by reactions of authorities and significant others who confer the status of deviant. Many violate laws and norms, but only a few are apprehended and processed as deviants. Thus the act of "getting

caught," not rule violation itself, begins the labeling process.

3. The deviant label makes it difficult to maintain a positive self-concept. In resolving this, the offender often attempts to discount the label by rejecting those who reject him, thus developing antagonistic attitudes toward others, especially social control officials. This provides motivation for continued conflict and further offenses, which elicit more negative reactions by society and crystallize the antagonistic attitudes of the deviant and reactor alike. Through this process the offender "acquires the traits first imputed to him and becomes the antisocial person he was labeled to be. In some cases beginning with an isolated and perhaps innocuous violation, an offender may be propelled by criminalization procedures into a career of crime as a way of life" (Schrag, 1974:709).

4. "Getting caught" and processed by social control agents is often a function of the characteristics of the offender rather than the characteristics of the offense (Wellford, 1975:333).

5. Social control systems based on labeling rituals and the dramatization of evil (such as the American criminal justice system) do not deter law violation, but actually promote it by placing persons labeled as criminals into subordinate statuses:

> The treatment of law violators accordingly serves as a self-fulfilling prophecy. It forecloses noncriminal options and coerces offenders into a criminal role. Hence, criminal justice may be seen as a system for defining, detecting, identifying, labeling, segregating, and emphasizing the things officially regarded as evil, finding a scapegoat, and making people sensitive to crime and the consequences thereof. It tends to produce criminals by the very kinds of activities it is allegedly designed to alleviate [Schrag, 1974:709].

A number of empirical studies have reported data relevant to labeling theory. Marshall and Purdy (1972) attempted to explain the overrepresentation of certain social categories (blacks, males, and lower-class individuals) in conviction statistics of drinking and driving. Their data were generally consistent with labeling theory, since race, sex, and socioeconomic status were related to conviction when frequency and seriousness of drinking were controlled. Social status had much less impact when drinking-driving was highly frequent or serious, indicating that status factors have a greater input on conviction when the situation is more ambiguous (low frequency or low seriousness).

Klein (1974) examined the extent to which recidivism rates of juvenile offenders differed between high-diversion (low labelers) and low-diversion (high labelers) police departments. According to labeling theory the departments which are prone to officially process offenders (low diversion) will stigmatize offenders and induce them into further deviance, and therefore will produce higher recidivism rates than departments which tend to divert delinquents. Diversion was the proportion of ar-

rested juveniles who were released rather than inserted further into the juvenile justice system. Klein (1974:297) found that first offenders recidivated more in low-diversion departments than in high-diversion departments, while the opposite was true among multiple offenders. This suggests, consistent with labeling theory, that first offenders will recidivate significantly less if diverted (released) rather than officially labeled and processed by the juvenile justice system. The data also suggested, however, that multiple offenders recidivate significantly *less* if processed by the juvenile justice system than if released (diverted). This is not consistent with the spiraling effect hypothesized by labeling theorists. Thus it would appear that multiple offenders are deterred from future offenses by official processing, while first offenders are induced to commit further deviant acts by official processing.

In another recent study Ageton and Elliott (1974) found that over a four-year period youth with police contact had a small but significant increase in delinquent orientations compared to peers who had no such contact (r = .10). Neither actual involvement in delinquent behavior nor the delinquency of one's peers appeared to be as important as police contact in explaining the increased orientation toward delinquency. In addition, white males appeared to be more susceptible than others to official labeling (Ageton and Elliott, 1974:97). The authors concluded that the data tend to support labeling theory. However, because of the low correlation between police contact and delinquent orientations and because of the ethnic differences, they maintained that "the impact of interaction with the Juvenile Justice System on the development of delinquent orientation is not as comprehensive as many labeling theorists would have us believe" (Ageton and Elliott, 1974:97).

Two other observations of Ageton and Elliott appear noteworthy. First, individuals who lack commitment to basic societal values may be less susceptible to labeling than individuals with greater commitment. Second, they suggested that the nature of the home environment needs to be examined if a more definitive statement about the effects of labeling on subsequent delinquency is to be obtained.

Harris (1975) examined the effects of imprisonment on the perceived value of "going straight" and of "going crooked." His purpose was to determine if official intervention increased the chances that one would view criminal activities as rewarding and become more committed to deviance. The data were consistent with labeling theory in that the expected value of "going straight" decreased and the expected value of "going crooked" increased as length of imprisonment increased. The expected value of criminal choice became relatively strong with extended imprisonment and was also associated with the inmates' perceived probability of future criminal behavior. Harris (1975:85) concluded that the data "support the fundamental labeling viewpoint that being deviant is (or becomes) a relatively rational state of affairs from the subjective standpoint of actors so defined.''

The data also showed a curvilinear relationship between imprisonment and the expected value of criminal choice. During the initial incarceration the expected value of criminal choice decreased with length of imprisonment, while with extended imprisonment the value of criminal choice increased as length of imprisonment increased. These data indicate, contrary to labeling theory, that initial, limited incarceration may have a deterrent effect.

In another study Harris (1976) reported that a spoiled identity does not necessarily result from deviant commitment and self-definition. Among whites criminal commitment and self-typing were negatively related to spoiled identity, as expected. However, among blacks criminal self-typing was not related to identity spoilation, and criminal commitment was associated with less spoilation, i.e., higher self-esteem and stability of self. Ascriptive status was used to account for these findings. Harris reasoned that since whites were ascriptive members in our society, when they were caught violating ''their own'' membership codes, it would spoil their identity. On the other hand, blacks were viewed as ascriptive nonmembers. Being caught violating ''someone else's'' codes would not be expected to spoil their identity and might even enhance it. This interpretation is consistent with the observation of Ageton and Elliott (1974), noted above, that individuals who lack commitment to basic societal values may be less susceptible to labeling than individuals with greater commitment.

In summary, existing research suggests, consistent with labeling theory, that (1) official processing tends to label individuals and increase the probability of future deviance, (2) diversion of offenders by social agents tends to decrease the overall recidivism rate, and (3) the perceived rewards of criminal activities are greater for those with extended incarceration than those with limited incarceration experience. However, research also indicates that the effects of labeling (1) are not as strong, pervasive, or simple as often assumed, (2) do not spiral as hypothesized, (3) appear curvilinear, and (4) vary by factors such as ethnic group and sex. Official sanctions appear to have both labeling and deterrent effects.

Labeling theory has made a number of significant contributions to our understanding of deviant behavior. First, it has emphasized that deviant involvement is a process of interaction. Too often deviance theories have taken a static position based on certain structural or personality characteristics. Thus the interaction between offender and community, deviant and labeler, is emphasized. Second, it has focused attention on the unanticipated consequences of criminal justice. Third, the relativity of perceptions, judgments, and rules is highlighted. This has focused attention on the arbitrariness of

law and the question of how and why a given behavior is defined as illegal while another behavior is not.

Despite its popularity, labeling theory has several limitations. Some of the assumptions underlying the theory are questionable (Wellford, 1975). Labeling theory is also limited in scope, since it does not answer the question of the etiology of initial acts of deviance. In addition, to date labeling theorists have focused primarily on the formal sanctions and the definitions imposed by formal agents of social control. Labeling theory needs to be broadened to include other types of stigmatization, particularly informal labeling within families and peer groups. This should include a specification of the relationship between informal and formal labeling.

One other glaring omission of labeling theorists is their overly passive view of the deviant (Rogers and Buffalo, 1974). The fact that an individual has some input into the labeling process has generally not been considered. This point was made forcefully by Levitin (1975), who noted that ''deviants in encounters with normals may be even more active than normals encountering normals in trying to legitimate preferred definitions'' (556). A typology of nine adaptations to the deviant label has been developed by Rogers and Buffalo (1974) and hopefully will stimulate work on this neglected aspect of labeling theory.

It has been relatively rare for labeling theorists to state their ideas as explicit propositions. Such statements can be extremely valuable in clarifying theoretical ideas so that they may be evaluated and refined. Therefore an attempt is now made to state as explicit propositions some key ideas from labeling theory. No claim is made that labeling theorists would agree with the model presented or that it is a complete presentation of labeling theory. Nevertheless, the model captures some major propositions of labeling theory and integrates them in a way that is generally consistent with empirical research.

The propositional model is presented in Figure 24.9. The starting point is some type of rule-violating behavior. Labeling theorists assume that the beginning of the labeling process is often the result of random violations or trial violations as one attempts to meet the stresses of life. These may be but are not necessarily criminal violations. Labeling which finally results in criminal involvement may begin with relatively minor infractions, including the violation of informal group norms. Although labeling theorists do not focus on initial rule violations, most would agree that there is a positive relationship between amount of rule violation and probability of being identified as a rule violator.

A crucial aspect of the labeling process is ''getting caught'' and being identifed as a rule violator. In the model developed here a distinction has been made between the ''identification of rule violator'' and receiving an ''explicit negative sanction.'' Some individuals are identified as rule violators but receive only minor or no negative sanctions from informal and formal social con-

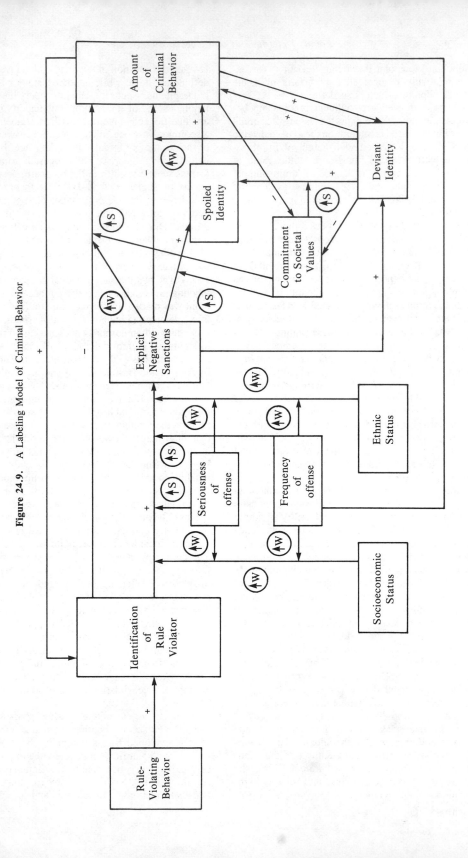

Figure 24.9. A Labeling Model of Criminal Behavior

634

trol agents. For example, many arrestees are released, and conviction and sentencing depend on a variety of factors. This distinction has sometimes been left implicit in existing formulations of the labeling process.

Existing research indicates that ethnic group, socioeconomic status, frequency of the offense, and seriousness of the offense affect the probability that an identified rule violator will receive explicit negative sanctions (Marshall and Purdy, 1972). The higher one's socioeconomic status, the less likely negative sanctions will be applied after "getting caught." Similarly, minority-group status is likely to increase the probability and severity of negative sanctions. The effect of socioeconomic and ethnic status on the probability of negative sanctions appears to be less when the seriousness and frequency of offenses are high.

When identified violators are not sanctioned or given only a mild sanction, the probability of future rule violation appears to decrease. For example, Klein (1974) found that among first offenders recidivism was less if they were released rather than processed by the juvenile justice system. This suggests that identification of the rule violator may have a negative effect on future criminal behavior. Perhaps the threat of punishment involved in "getting caught" acts as a deterrent to future deviance.

Two propositions appear central to the labeling process. First, it is hypothesized that negative sanctions tend to spoil one's identity and reduce self-esteem. Second, it is maintained that negative sanctions tend to increase the probability that one's self-typing (identity) is deviant. It is also proposed that a deviant identity may tend to spoil one's identity, although this may not be the case in some circumstances. The research cited above is generally consistent with these propositions. It is further hypothesized that both a deviant and a spoiled identity are positively associated with criminal behavior.

The findings of Ageton and Elliott (1974) and Harris (1976) indicate that commitment to basic societal values conditions the labeling effects of negative sanctions. Among those with low commitment, criminal self-typing does not appear to be related to identity spoilation. However, among those with a high commitment, criminal self-typing and a spoiled identity appear to have a positive relationship. Those with less commitment have less to lose, for they have little status in the dominant system. Therefore, low commitment may also depress the positive relationship between negative sanctions and a spoiled identity.

First offenders are likely to have greater commitment to basic societal values than recidivists. Therefore the deterrent effect of "getting caught" may be greater among first offenders than multiple offenders (Klein, 1974). When a negative sanction is actually applied, the deterrent effect of threat of punishment may be weakened. This reasoning is consistent with the findings of Klein (1974) as well as those of Goode (1972).

Existing research does not support the spiraling effect hypothesized by labeling theorists. Two feedback effects operate to depress labeling effects. First, as one's identity incorporates deviant elements, his or her commitment to basic societal values probably decreases. This, in turn, would weaken the effects of sanctions on identity spoilation. It is also likely that participation in criminal behavior increases deviant self-conceptions and decreases commitment to societal values.

Two other feedback loops appear to be self-evident. First, as amount of criminal behavior increases (i.e., frequency of offense is increasing), the effects of status factors on labeling will tend to decrease. Second, amount of criminal behavior will increase the probability that the offender is caught and identified as a rule violator.

This model may be stated in propositional form as follows:

50. The greater the amount of rule-violating behavior, the greater the probability that one will be identified as a rule violator.

51. There is a positive relationship between being identified as a rule violator and the probability that one will receive explicit negative sanctions.

52. The higher one's socioeconomic status, the weaker the relationship between identification as a rule violator and probability of negative sanctions.

53. The higher one's ethnic status, the weaker the relationship between identification as a rule violator and probability of explicit negative sanctions. In other words, minority-group members are more likely than others to be sanctioned if they are caught violating the rules.

54. The more serious the offense, the less the effect of socioeconomic status on the positive relationship between identification as a rule violator and probability of explicit negative sanctions.

55. The more serious the offense, the less the effect of ethnic status on the positive relationship between identification as a rule violator and probability of explicit negative sanctions.

56. The more frequent the offense, the less the effect of socioeconomic status on the positive relationship between identification as a rule violator and probability of explicit negative sanctions.

· 57. The more frequent the offense, the less the effect of ethnic status on the positive relationship between identification as a rule violator and probability of explicit negative sanctions.

58. The greater the seriousness of the offense, the stronger the positive relationship between identification as a rule violator and probability of negative sanctions.

59. The greater the frequency of the offense, the stronger the positive relationship between identification as a rule violator and probability of negative sanctions.

60. There is a negative relationship between iden-

tification as a rule violator and amount of criminal behavior.

61. The greater the amount of negative sanctions, the weaker the negative relationship between identification as a rule violator and amount of criminal behavior.

62. The greater one's commitment to societal values, the stronger the negative relationship between identification as a rule violator and amount of criminal behavior.

63. The greater the amount of negative sanctions, the lower the amount of criminal behavior.

64. The more deviant one's identity, the weaker the negative relationship between amount of negative sanctions and amount of criminal behavior.

65. The greater the amount of negative sanctions, the greater the identity spoilation.

66. The greater one's commitment to societal values, the stronger the positive relationship between amount of negative sanctions and amount of identity spoilation.

67. The greater the amount of identity spoilation, the greater the probability of criminal behavior.

68. The greater the amount of negative sanctions, the greater the probability that one's identity will become deviant.

69. The more deviant one's identity, the lower one's commitment to societal values.

70. The more deviant one's identity, the greater the amount of identity spoilation.

71. The greater one's commitment to societal values, the stronger the positive relationship between amount of deviant identity and amount of identity spoilation.

72. The more deviant one's identity, the greater the probability of criminal behavior.

73. The greater the amount of criminal behavior, the lower the commitment to societal values.

74. The greater the amount of criminal behavior, the more deviant one's identity.

75. The greater the amount of criminal behavior, the greater the probability that one will be identified as a rule violator.

This is a fairly general model that may be applied to different types of groups including the family. Labeling that occurs within families may operate according to this model except that initially the dependent variable may be informal violations rather than criminal behavior. However, the informal labeling process within families may lead to more serious violations as the labeling process unfolds.

Although the model is based on existing research, further research is needed to validate and refine it. Since the model is a fairly complex model, a high priority is to attempt to simplify the model by eliminating propositions that are found to be relatively unimportant. Research which tests this model on families and other types of informal groups would also be valuable. Particularly important would be an examination of how informal labeling affects the more formal labeling process.

EFFECTS OF DEVIANCE

The theories considered to this point have attempted to explain why deviance and conformity occur. This has been the dominant focus in the area of deviance. A related and neglected question is how does an individual's deviance affect other group members. Although labeling theory seems particularly suited to examining the effects of deviant acts, labeling theorists have ignored the initial reaction to deviant acts, particularly the informal reactions. They have focused primarily on the reactions of official social control agents and the effects these reactions have on recidivism.

Research suggests that the initial response to deviance tends to be inclusive. However, continued resistance by the deviant to group pressure toward conformity results in a shift to the exclusive response by the group. Inclusive responses tend to occur if deviation is perceived as limited in scope, subject to change, and limited to areas which the group does not highly value. When deviant acts are perceived by the group to be pervasive, unchangeable, and in highly valued areas, an exclusive response is likely to occur (Orcutt, 1973:264).

Small-group research suggests that the tones of inclusive and exclusive responses are very different. Inclusive responses are characterized by very intense interaction, low to moderate attitudinal (covert) hostility, and high overt hostility. On the other hand, the exclusive responses consist of a low level of interaction, a low level of overt hostility, and a high level of covert, attitudinal hostility.

Reactions of families to the deviance of individual family members appear similar to the patterns described by Orcutt. For example, Jackson (1954, 1956) reported that prolonged and intensive efforts to modify the drinking behavior of the alcoholic husband occurred before the exclusive act of separation was taken. Studies of the reaction to a family member's mental illness follow a similar pattern (Yarrow et al., 1955). Thus, in general, deviant acts by a family member appear to intensify interaction and increase verbal hostility. If attempts to control the deviant behavior fail, an exclusive reaction is likely. It is at this point that formal agents of control are likely to be called upon by the family. Intense interaction and verbal hostility are apt to decrease at this time while attitudinal hostility increases.

These ideas are diagrammed in Figures 24.10 and 24.11 and may be stated propositionally as follows:

76. Deviant acts by a family member tend to in-

Figure 24.10. Diagram of Effects of Deviance on Family Interaction

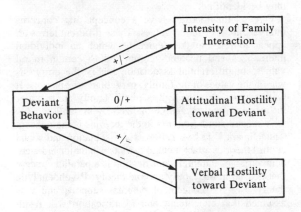

crease the intensity of family interaction. If the deviant behavior increases or does not decrease, the intensity of family interaction tends to decrease.

77. Deviant acts by a family member tend to increase the amount of verbal hostility expressed toward the deviant member. If the deviant behavior increases or does not decrease, the amount of verbal hostility expressed toward the deviant member will tend to decrease.

78. No relationship exists between the initial deviant acts by a family member and attitudinal hostility toward him. If the deviant behavior increases or does not decrease, attitudinal hostility toward the deviant will increase.

79. As the intensity of interaction within the family increases following deviant acts of a member, amount of deviant behavior by that member will tend to decrease.

80. As the amount of verbal hostility toward the deviant increases, the amount of deviant behavior by the deviant member will tend to decrease.

The specific impact of a given type of deviance on the family is likely to vary greatly. For example, Capel et al. (1973) found wide variation in the reactions of wives to the discovery that their husbands were drug users, although almost all of the reactions were of the inclusive type and followed the general pattern identified by Orcutt (1973). The specific impact of deviance undoubtedly depends upon the characteristics of the family prior to the deviance. Gibbs (1971), for example, found that the imprisonment of mothers had little effect on their children. In her study, lack of housing, a broken marriage, and separation from the children usually occurred before the criminal offense, and thus the offense and imprisonment had little additional impact on the children. Friedman and Esselstyn (1965), on the other hand, found that committing a father to jail was followed by a decrease in the school performance of his children, and that girls seemed to be affected more adversely than boys. Cottle (1976) reported that the incarceration of the mother may be very detrimental to her children. Even rather "poor" parents may be meeting some basic needs of their children that cannot be met when the home is broken by incarceration of a parent. Cottle (1976) noted that the incarceration of a parent may decrease the self-esteem of children and increase their feelings of abandonment and loneliness.

The findings from this line of research have been placed in the diagram in Figure 24.11. The propositions for this model are as follows:

81. There is a positive relationship between amount of criminal behavior by parents and probability of separation from their children.

82. Separation from parents tends to decrease the self-esteem of the child.

83. Separation from parents tends to increase feelings of loneliness in children.

Figure 24.11. Preliminary Model of Effects of Parents' Criminal Behavior on Their Children

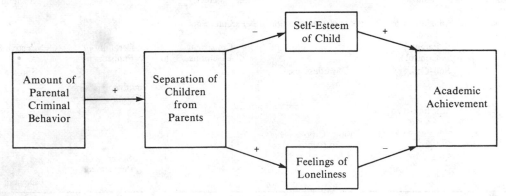

84. The higher the self-esteem of the child, the greater his level of academic achievement.

85. The higher the feelings of loneliness in the child, the lower his level of academic achievement.

Empirical research which examines the specific ways in which the various types of deviant acts of family members affect other family members has just begun. The models presented in Figures 24.10 and 24.11 are attempts to further integrate existing data but need empirical testing and refinement. There are two areas in which future research and theorizing would appear to be particularly fruitful. First, the effects on children of the deviance of siblings and/or parents need to be examined thoroughly. Second, the processes which precede and follow deviance require specification. Currently the magnitudes of the effects of various criminal and deviant behaviors on family life are largely unknown. In addition, the conditions which may suppress or amplify those effects have not been determined.

SUMMARY AND CONCLUSION

In this chapter six major theoretical frameworks have been identified and evaluated. After reviewing relevant empirical data, each theory was revised and placed in propositional form. The purpose was to refine each framework so that it was more consistent with empirical data. Each theory was reviewed separately, and little attempt was made to compare the theories. A comparison of the revised theories is needed and is now presented. Although the six theories are distinct entities and have different emphases and assumptions, a number of their major concepts have similarities. Table 24.1 presents the major concepts of each theory so that their similarities may be identified.

Five of the theories have a concept that concerns internalization of moral values. These different terms all appear to refer to the degree to which an individual internalizes and becomes committed to certain moral values. In differential association theory the emphasis was on the values of the family, particularly the parents. It was assumed that the values of the family are a major influence on the values internalized by the children.

A second similarity among the theories is the concept "attachment." In both differential association and social control theories attachment to parents is a major independent variable. Parental identification is a parallel concept that is used in the family anomie theory. Psychoanalytic theory uses the concept of parental support, and it is assumed that attachment and identification will result when parental support is high.

Punishment and other controls are key variables in four of the theoretical frameworks. The concept "parental control" from social control theory is similar to "consistent discipline" in the psychoanalytic model. The concept of consistent discipline implies that parental controls are moderately strong but not excessive, while amount of parental control includes elements of fairness and consistency. Deterrence theory and labeling theory use more general concepts, but their meanings have some similarities to "consistent discipline" and "parental control." Certainty of punishment would be expected to be highly correlated with consistency of discipline while discipline may be considered a sanction.

The theories of social control, family anomie, and labeling all use some form of self-concept. Labeling

Table 24.1.   A Comparison of the Major Concepts in Six Theories of Deviance

DIFFERENTIAL ASSOCIATION	SOCIAL CONTROL	FAMILY ANOMIE	PSYCHOANALYTIC	DETERRENCE	LABELING
Law-abiding Values of Family	Law-abiding Values		Law-abiding Values	Moral Commitment	Commitment to Societal Values
Attachment to Family	Attachment to Parents	Parental Identification	Parental Support		
	Parental Control		Consistent Discipline	Certainty of Punishment	Negative Sanctions
	Self-Concept	Powerlessness			Spoiled Identity
Association with Criminal Patterns				Involvement with Criminal Peers	
	Attachment to Others				
		Value Consensus in Family			
				Severity of Punishment	
					Deviant Identity

theory refers to spoiled identity and lowered self-esteem which results from sanctions, while family anomie theory uses the concept "feelings of powerlessness." Self-concept as used by social control theorists refers to feelings of self-worth and -esteem.

In two theories, differential association and deterrence, association with criminal elements is an important variable. The deterrence concept "involvement with criminal peers" is more specific than the "association with criminal patterns" used in differential association theory, but both concepts refer to the same basic phenomenon.

These commonalities among the various frameworks suggest that it may be useful to attempt an integration. Therefore, a final theoretical model is presented which integrates major elements of the six theories. Only those elements that were in more than one theory were included in this final model.

The integrated model is presented in Figure 24.12. This model includes variables that have been found consistently in research to be related to crime and deviant behavior. It also includes elements, albeit selectively, from each of the six models reviewed in this chapter. There is no claim that this is an all-inclusive model, as some types of things cannot be captured in this type of model. In an effort to keep the model simple, a number of possible variables and relationships were excluded. Nevertheless, it integrates a large amount of research and theoretical thinking into a relatively simple model. This model may be used to explain not only criminal behavior but also a number of other types of deviant behavior. In addition, the model has a number of practical implications that could be used for educational and policy purposes.

The final model may be placed in propositional form as follows:

86. There is a positive relationship between parental support and amount of attachment to parents.

87. There is a positive relationship between parental support and amount of moral commitment.

88. There is a positive relationship between parental support and self-esteem.

89. There is a positive relationship between value consensus and attachment to parents.

90. There is a positive relationship between value consensus and moral commitment.

91. There is a positive relationship between value consensus and self-esteem.

Figure 24.12. Integrated Model of Deviant Behavior

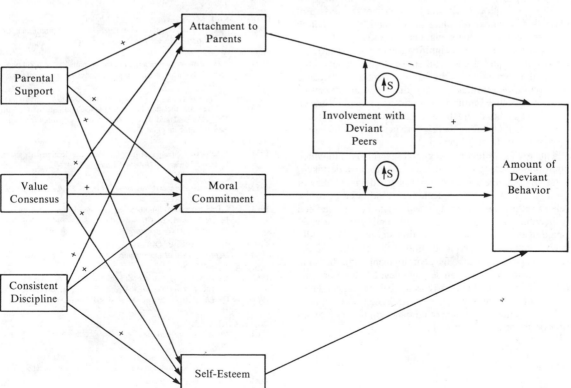

92. There is a positive relationship between consistent discipline and attachment to parents.

93. There is a positive relationship between consistent discipline and moral commitment.

94. There is a positive relationship between consistent discipline and self-esteem.

95. There is a negative relationship between attachment to parents and amount of deviant behavior.

96. The greater the involvement with deviant peers, the stronger the negative relationship between attachment to parents and amount of deviant behavior.

97. There is a positive relationship between involvement with deviant peers and amount of deviant behavior.

98. There is a negative relationship between moral commitment and amount of deviant behavior.

99. The greater the involvement with deviant peers, the stronger the negative relationship between moral commitment and amount of deviant behavior.

100. There is a negative relationship between self-esteem and amount of deviant behavior.

In each of the six theories discussed in this chapter the family played an important role. Early family socialization is the core of the psychiatric approach, while parent-child attachment is central to social control theory. The family appears to play a significant role in informal labeling. In both anomie and labeling theory the family plays a crucial social placement function, since it is through the family that social class is transmitted. One's social status is seen as a significant factor in the production of strain and the attachment of official labels. Differential association sees the family as important because its location determines the type of peers one associates with and because family values and attachment influence the extent of involvement with delinquent patterns. The deterrence and labeling theories are general, but they may be applied to family interaction.

This review of theories suggests several areas in which additional research and theorizing need to be undertaken. First, the possible effects of a member's deviant behavior on a group have been neglected. Second, studies of the relationship between family variables and deviance need to become more sophisticated and applied to a broader range of deviant behavior. Existing studies have usually been limited to a few structural characteristics of the family (divorce, social class, employment of mother) and have focused primarily on delinquency. Furthermore, the dynamic nature of the family as a labeler and/or a deterrent in all types of deviance needs consideration. Finally, it is crucial that the effects of deviance on family interaction be more fully explored.

NOTE

1. Gdd is the zero-order correlation between discipline and delinquency, while Gdd.p is the partial correlation between these two variables while controlling for level of peer activity. G is Goodman and Kruskal's (1954) gamma (see also Davis, 1971:82–106). Stanfield did not report correlation coefficients, but I have computed these from his data.

REFERENCES

AGETON, S. AND D. S. ELLIOTT
1974   "The effects of legal processing on self-concept." *Social Problems* 22:87–100.

AKERS, R. L.
1964   "Socio-economic status and delinquent behavior: A retest." *Journal of Research in Crime and Delinquency* 1:38–46.

BACK, K. W.
1951   "Influence through social communication." *Journal of Abnormal and Social Psychology* 46:9–23.

BANDURA, A.
1969   *Principles of Behavior Modification.* New York: Holt, Rinehart and Winston.

BANDURA, A. AND R. H. WALTERS
1959   *Adolescent Aggression.* New York: Ronald Press.

BECKER, G. S.
1968   "Crime and punishment: An economic approach." *Journal of Political Economy* 76:169–217.

BECKER, H. S.
1963   *Outsiders: Studies in the Sociology of Deviance.* New York: Free Press.
1974   "Labeling theory reconsidered." In S. L. Messinger, S. Halleck, P. Lerman, N. Morris, P. V. Murphy, and M. E. Wolfgang (eds.), *The Aldine Crime and Justice Annual: 1973.* Chicago: Aldine.

BRIAR, S. AND I. M. PILIAVIN
1965   "Delinquency, situational inducements, and commitment to conformity." *Social Problems* 13:35–45.

CALDWELL, R. G.
1944   "The deterrent influence of corporal punishment upon prisoners who have been whipped." *American Sociological Review* 9:171–77.

CAPEL, W. C., J. S. CLARK, B. M. GOLDSMITH, AND G. T. STEWART
1973   "Wives, families and junk: Drug abuse and family life." In C. L. Bryand and J. G. Wells (eds.), *Deviancy and the Family.* Philadelphia: F. A. Davis.

CARTWRIGHT, D.
1951   "Achieving changes in people: Some applications of group dynamics theory." *Human Relations* 4:381–92.

CLINARD, M. B.
1952   *The Black Market: A New Study of White Collar Crime.* New York: Holt, Rinehart and Winston.
1964   "The theoretical implications of anomie and deviant behavior." In M. B. Clinard (ed.), *Anomie and Deviant Behavior.* New York: Free Press.

CLOWARD, R. A. AND L. E. OHLIN
1960   *Delinquency and Opportunity.* New York: Free Press.

COHEN, A. K.
1965   "The sociology of the deviant act: Anomie theory and beyond." *American Sociological Review* 30:5–14.
1966   *Deviance and Control.* Englewood Cliffs, N.J.: Prentice-Hall.

COOLEY, C. H.
1902   *Human Nature and the Social Order.* New York: Scribner's Sons.

COTTLE, T. J.
1976   "Angela: A child-woman." *Social Problems* 24:516–23.

CRESSEY, D. R.
1960   "Epidemiology and individual conduct: A case for criminology." *Pacific Sociological Review* 3:47–58.

DAVIS, J. A.
1971   *Elementary Survey Analysis.* Englewood Cliffs, N.J.: Prentice-Hall.

DeFLEUR, M., W. V. D'ANTONIO, AND L. B. DeFLEUR
1971   *Sociology: Man in Society.* Glenview, Ill.: Scott, Foresman.

DEITZ, G. E.
1969   "A comparison of delinquents with nondelinquents on self-concept, self-acceptance, and parental identification." *Journal of Genetic Psychology* 115:285-95.

DENTLER, R. A. AND L. J. MONROE
1961   "Social correlates of early adolescent theft." *American Sociological Review* 26:733-43.

DURKHEIM, E.
1951   *Suicide.* Translated by J. A. Spaulding and G. Simpson. New York: Free Press.

EASTERLIN, R. A.
1973   "Relative economic status and the American fertility swing." In E. B. Sheldon (ed.), *Family Economic Behavior.* Philadelphia: J. B. Lippincott.

ERICKSON, M. L. AND J. P. GIBBS
1973   "The deterrence question: Some alternative methods of analysis." *Social Science Quarterly* 54:534-51.

ERIKSON, K. T.
1962   "Notes on the sociology of deviance." *Social Problems* 9:307-14.

FESTINGER, L., S. SCHACHTER, AND K. BACK
1950   *Social Pressure in Informal Groups.* New York: Harper.

FODOR, E. M.
1972   "Delinquency and susceptibility to social influence among adolescents as a function of level of moral development." *Journal of Social Psychology* 86:257-60.

FRIEDMAN, S. AND T. C. ESSELSTYN
1965   "The adjustment of children of jail inmates." *Federal Probation* 29:55-59.

GEIS, G.
1974a   "Advocational crime." In D. Glaser (ed.), *Handbook of Criminology.* Chicago: Rand McNally.
1974b   "Upperworld crime." In A. S. Blumberg (ed.), *Current Perspectives on Criminal Behavior.* New York: Knopf.

GIANNELL, A. S.
1970   "The role of internal inhibition in crime causation." *Journal of Social Psychology* 81:31-36.

GIBBONS, D. C.
1973   *Society, Crime and Criminal Careers,* second ed. Englewood Cliffs, N.J.: Prentice-Hall.

GIBBS, C.
1971   "The effect of the imprisonment of women upon their children." *British Journal of Criminology* 11:113-30.

GIBBS, J. P.
1968   "Crime, punishment, and deterrence." *Southwestern Social Science Quarterly* 48:515-30.
1975   *Crime, Punishment and Deterrence.* New York: Elsevier.

GLUECK, S. AND E. GLUECK
1950   *Unraveling Juvenile Delinquency.* New York: Commonwealth Fund.

GOLD, M.
1963   *Status Forces in Delinquent Boys.* Ann Arbor: Institute for Social Research, University of Michigan.

GOODE, W. J.
1964   *The Family.* Englewood Cliffs, N.J.: Prentice-Hall.
1972   "The place of force in human society." *American Sociological Review* 37:507-19.

GOODMAN, L. A. AND W. H. KRUSKAL
1954   "Measures of association for cross classifications." *Journal of the American Statistical Association* 49:732-64.

HARRIS, A. R.
1975   "Imprisonment and the expected value of criminal choice: A specification and test of aspects of the labeling perspective." *American Sociological Review* 40:71-87.
1976   "Race, commitment to deviance and spoiled identity." *American Sociological Review* 11:432-42.

HINDELANG, M. J.
1973   "Causes of delinquency: A partial replication and extension." *Social Problems* 20:471-87.

HIRSCHI, T.
1969   *Causes of Delinquency.* Berkeley, Calif.: University of California Press.

HOEBEL, E. A.
1954   *The Law of Primitive Man.* Cambridge, Mass.: Harvard University Press.

JACKSON, J. K.
1954   "The adjustment of the family to the crisis of alcoholism." *Quarterly Journal of Studies on Alcohol* 15:564-86.
1956   "The adjustment of the family to alcoholism." *Marriage and Family Living* 18:361-69.

JAFFE, L. D.
1963   "Delinquency proneness and family anomie." *Journal of Criminal Law, Criminology and Police Science* 54:146-54.

JENSEN, G. F.
1972   "Parents, peers and delinquent action: A test of the differential association perspective." *American Journal of Sociology* 78:562-75.

KITSUSE, J. I.
1962   "Societal reactions to deviant behavior: Problems of theory and method." *Social Problems* 9:247-56.

KLEIN, M. W.
1974   "Labeling, deterrence and recidivism: A study of police dispositions of juvenile offenders." *Social Problems* 22:292-303.

KROHN, M. D.
1974   "An investigation of the effect of parental and peer associations on marijuana use: An empirical test of differential association theory." In M. Riedel and R. P. Thornberry (eds.), *Crime and Delinquency: Dimensions of Deviance.* New York: Praeger.

LEMERT, E. M.
1951   *Social Pathology.* New York: McGraw-Hill.
1972   *Human Deviance, Social Problems, and Social Control,* second ed. Englewood Cliffs, N.J.: Prentice-Hall.

LEONARD, W. N. AND M. G. WEBER
1970   "Automakers and dealers: A study in criminogenic market factors." *Law and Society Review* 4:407-24.

LEVITIN, T. E.
1975   "Deviants as active participants in the labeling process: The visibly handicapped." *Social Problems* 22:548-57.

LINDEN, E. AND J. C. HACKLER
1973   "Affective ties and delinquency." *Pacific Sociological Review* 16:27-46.

LINTON, R.
1952   "Universal ethical principles: An anthropological view." In R. Anshen (ed.), *Moral Principles of Action.* New York: Harper.

LISKA, A. E.
1969   "Interpreting the causal structure of differential association theory." *Social Problems* 16:485-92.

MAGNUSON, W. G. AND J. CARPER
1968   *The Dark Side of the Market Place.* Englewood Cliffs, N.J.: Prentice-Hall.

MARSHALL, H. AND R. PURDY
1972   "Hidden deviance and the labelling approach: The case for drinking and driving." *Social Problems* 19:541-53.

MATTICK, H.
1963   *The Unexamined Death*. Chicago: John Howard Association.

MATZA, D.
1964   *Delinquency and Drift*. New York: Wiley.

MEAD, G. H.
1934   *Mind, Self, and Society*. Chicago: University of Chicago Press.

MERTON, R. K.
1938   "Social structure and anomie." *American Sociological Review* 3:672–82.
1957   *Social Theory and Social Structure*, revised ed. London: Collier-Macmillan.
1968   *Social Theory and Social Structure*, enlarged ed. New York: Free Press.

MORRIS, N.
1951   *The Habitual Offender*. Cambridge, Mass.: Harvard University Press.

MORRIS, N. AND G. HAWKINS
1969   "From murder and from violence, good Lord deliver us." *Midway* 10:63–95.

NEWCOMB, T. M.
1943   *Personality and Social Change*. New York: Holt, Rinehart and Winston.
1953   "An approach to the study of communicative acts." *Psychological Review* 60:393–404.

NEWCOMB, T. M., K. E. KOENIG, R. FLACKS, AND D. P. WARWICK
1967   *Persistence and Change: Bennington College and Its Students after Twenty-five Years*. New York: Wiley.

NYE, F. I.
1958   *Family Relationships and Delinquent Behavior*. New York: Wiley.

NYE, F. I., J. F. SHORT, JR., AND V. J. OLSON
1958   "Socioeconomic status and delinquent behavior." *American Journal of Sociology* 63:381–89.

ORCUTT, J. D.
1973   "Societal reaction and the response to deviation in small groups." *Social Forces* 52:259–67.

PHILLIPS, E. L., E. A. PHILLIPS, D. L. FIXSEN, AND M. M. WOLF
1971   "Achievement Place: Modification of the behaviors of pre-delinquent boys within a token economy." *Journal of Applied Behavior Analysis* 4:45–59.

RECKLESS, W.
1973   *The Crime Problem*, fifth ed. New York: Appleton-Century-Crofts.

RECKLESS, W. C. AND S. DINITZ
1967   "Pioneering with self-concept as a vulnerability factor in delinquency." *Journal of Criminal Law, Criminology and Police Science* 58:18–25.

RECKLESS, W. C., S. DINITZ, AND B. KAY
1957   "The self component in potential delinquency and non-delinquency." *American Sociological Review* 22:566–70.

RECKLESS, W. C., S. DINITZ, AND E. MURRAY
1956   "Self concept as an insulator against delinquency." *American Sociological Review* 21:744–46.

REISS, A. J., JR.
1951   "Delinquency as the failure of personal and social controls." *American Sociological Review* 16:196–207.

REISS, A. J., JR. AND A. L. RHODES
1964   "An empirical test of differential association theory." *Journal of Research in Crime and Delinquency* 1:5–18.

RIEGE, M. G.
1972   "Parental affection and juvenile delinquency in girls." *British Journal of Criminology* 12:55–73.

RODMAN, H. AND P. GRAMS
1967   "Juvenile delinquency and the family: A review and discus-

sion." In The President's Commission on Law Enforcement and Administration of Justice, *Task Force Report: Juvenile Delinquency and Youth Crime*. Washington, D.C.: Government Printing Office.

ROGERS, J. W. AND M. D. BUFFALO
1974   "Fighting back: Nine modes of adaptation to a deviant label." *Social Problems* 22:101–18.

SCARPITTI, F. R., S. DINITZ, AND W. C. RECKLESS
1962   "Delinquency vulnerability: A cross group and longitudinal analysis." *American Sociological Review* 27:515–17.

SCARPITTI, F. R., E. MURRAY, S. DINITZ, AND W. C. RECKLESS
1960   "The 'good' boy in a high delinquency area: Four years later." *American Sociological Review* 25:555–58.

SCHOENFELD, C. G.
1971   "A psychoanalytic theory of juvenile delinquency." *Crime and Delinquency* 17:479–80.

SCHRAG, C.
1974   "Theoretical foundations for a social science of corrections." In D. Glaser (ed.), *Handbook of Criminology*. Chicago: Rand McNally.

SCHUESSLER, K.
1952   "The deterrent influence of the death penalty." *Annals* 284:54–62.

SCHUESSLER, K. F. AND D. R. CRESSEY
1950   "Personality characteristics of criminals." *American Journal of Sociology* 55:476–84.

SCHUR, E.
1971   *Labeling Deviant Behavior*. New York: Harper & Row.

SCHWARTZ, M. AND S. S. TANGRI
1965   "A note on self-concept as an insulator against delinquency." *American Sociological Review* 30:922–26.

SELLIN, J. T.
1967   *Capital Punishment*. New York: Harper & Row.

SHORT, J. F., JR.
1957   "Differential association and delinquency." *Social Problems* 4:233–39.
1958   "Differential association with delinquent friends and delinquent behavior." *Pacific Sociological Review* 1:20–25.
1964   "Gang delinquency and anomie." In M. B. Clinard (ed.), *Anomie and Deviant Behavior*. New York: Free Press.

SHORT, J. F., JR., AND F. L. STRODTBECK
1965   *Group Processes and Gang Delinquency*. Chicago: University of Chicago Press.

SILBERMAN, M.
1976   "Toward a theory of deterrence." *American Sociological Review* 41:442–61.

STANFIELD, R. E.
1966   "The interaction of family and gang variables in the aetiology of delinquency." *Social Problems* 13:411–17.

STINCHCOMBE, A. L.
1964   *Rebellion in a High School*. Chicago: Quadrangle Books.

SULLIVAN, R. F.
1973   "The economics of crime: An introduction to the literature." *Crime and Delinquency* 19:138–50.

SUTHERLAND, E. H.
1939   *Principles of Criminology*. Philadelphia: J. B. Lippincott.
1949   *White Collar Crime*. New York: Holt, Rinehart and Winston.

SUTHERLAND, E. H. AND D. R. CRESSEY
1966   *Principles of Criminology*, seventh ed. Philadelphia: J. B. Lippincott.

TANGRI, S. S. AND M. SCHWARTZ
1967   "Delinquency research and the self-concept variable." *Journal of Criminal Law, Criminology and Police Science* 58:182–90.

TANNENBAUM, F.
1951 *Crime and the Community*. New York: Columbia University Press (originally published in 1938 by Ginn and Co.).

TEC, N.
1970 "Family and differential involvement with marijuana: A study of suburban teenagers." *Journal of Marriage and the Family* 32:656-64.

TITTLE, C. R.
1969 "Crime rates and legal actions." *Social Problems* 16:409-23.

TITTLE, C. R. AND C. H. LOGAN
1973 "Sanctions and deviance: Evidence and remaining questions." *Law and Society Review* 7:371-92.

TOBY, J.
1957a "Social disorganization and stake in conformity: Complementary factors in the predatory behavior of hoodlums." *Journal of Criminal Law, Criminology and Police Science* 48:12-17.
1957b "The differential impact of family disorganization." *American Sociological Review* 22:505-12.

VOSS, H. L.
1964 "Differential association and reported delinquent behavior: A replication." *Social Problems* 12:78-85.

VOTEY, H. L., JR. AND L. PHILLIPS
1974 "The control of criminal activity: An economic analysis." In D. Glaser (ed.), *Handbook of Criminology*. Chicago: Rand McNally.

WALDO, G. P. AND S. DINITZ
1967 "Personality attributes of the criminal: An analysis of research studies, 1950-65." *Journal of Research in Crime and Delinquency* 4:185-202.

WALKER, N.
1965 *Crime and Punishment in Britain*. Edinburgh: University of Edinburgh Press.

WELLFORD, C.
1975 "Labelling theory and criminology: An assessment." *Social Problems* 22:332-345.

WINSLOW, R. W.
1968 "Status management in the adolescent social system: A reformulation of Merton's anomie theory." *British Journal of Sociology* 19:143-59.

YARROW, M. R., C. G. SCHWARTZ, H. S. MURPHY, AND L. C. DEASY
1955 "The psychological meaning of mental illness in the family." *Journal of Social Issues* 11:12-24.

ZUCKER, H. J.
1943 "Affectional identification and delinquency." *Archives of Psychology* 40:1-60.

NAME INDEX

SUBJECT INDEX